WESTERN CIVILIZATIONS

W · W · NORTON & COMPANY · NEW YORK · LONDON

ROBERT E. LERNER

STANDISH MEACHAM

EDWARD MCNALL BURNS

WESTERN

CIVILIZATIONS

Their History and Their Culture

TWELFTH EDITION

For Dietlind and Olivia;
Edith, Louisa, and Samuel

Printed in the United States of America

The text of this book is composed in Bembo
with the display set in Sabon.
Composition by Arcata/Kingsport.
Manufacturing by Arcata/Hawkins.
Book design by Antonina Krass.
Layout by Ben Gamit.

Acknowledgments and copyrights appear on pp. 1081–1092,
which constitute a continuation of the copyright page.

ISBN 0-393-96206-7

W. W. Norton & Company, Inc., 500 Fifth Avenue, New York, N.Y. 10110
W. W. Norton & Company Ltd., 10 Coptic Street, London WC1A 1PU

2 3 4 5 6 7 8 9 0

CONTENTS

MAPS

Maps in Color

(Maps appear facing or following the pages indicated)

Maps in Black and White

PREFACE

George Orwell once remarked that "keeping the past up to date is a full-time job." This insight seems particularly telling as a result of the startling rush of events during the last few years. "Trends" that seemed so clear only yesterday have turned out to be no trends at all. In addition, dramatic advances in historical scholarship have cast new light on old problems and have placed into prominence subject matters that historians previously had all but ignored. Accordingly we have worked hard to keep the past up to date for this twelfth edition of *Western Civilizations*. Yet we have always worked within the framework of authorial principles bequeathed to us by E. M. Burns—principles that may have served to make this book a "textbook classic." We offer a history of civilizations—an evolving account of the ways in which human beings have organized their lives in response to changing environments and persistent needs. Thus we complement narrative passages with discussions of ideas and societal institutions, and we draw heavily on pictorial material to give our readers the best impression possible of how our civilizations really looked. We try as well to avoid a tone of disembodied truth, both because we do not believe there is such a thing and because we want to engage and maintain our readers' attention. Our urgent desire is to demonstrate without resorting to cheapness that "first-year history" need not be viewed as a chore but might be welcomed as a source of intellectual excitement, even delight.

Although we have gone over *Western Civilizations* line by line in our effort to keep the past up to date, teachers will wish to know where the most significant changes occur. Chapter 5, on Greek civilization, is almost entirely new. Among its new features are a completely reconceived section on women and men in the daily life of ancient Athens, a consideration of the role of the Greek alphabet and the transformation of military techniques in the rise of the *polis,* and an emphasis on the differences as well as similarities between Athenian and modern democracies. About half of the Roman chapter (Chapter 7) is also new. Major innovations here include an altered treatment of the nature of family life (we have greatly changed our estimation of the role of women), a greater emphasis on the significance of slavery within the Roman economic and social system, and a reorganized discussion of Roman golden-age and silver-age literature. Other noteworthy changes in Parts One and Two are: a revised discussion of the stages of Hebrew religious development; an account of the volcanic eruption on the island of Thera; a reorganized presentation of Minoan social and cultural history; streamlined treatment of Epicureanism and Hellenistic religion; a new discussion of the conversion of Constantine. Finally, we have replaced the abbreviation "A.D." with "C.E.": students no longer know the meaning of *anno domini,* and C.E. (standing for "Common Era") assumes no particular religious commitment.

In the medieval chapters certain terms that would not be readily understandable to beginners, such as *see* and *benefice,* have been eliminated. The treatment of the formation of the Russian Empire in Chapter 12 now distinguishes carefully between Russia proper and the other Slavic-speaking territories. In Chapter 13 the treatment of the Greek studies of the humanists has been rewritten; corrections have also been made in discussions of the work of Raphael and Michelangelo. Chapter 15 contains a rewritten paragraph on Pascal (students are reminded that a computer language was named after him!). Chapter 16 has been reorganized to place greater emphasis on the conflicts produced by changes occurring throughout the society and economy of early-modern Europe and particularly by the effects of proto-industrialization. Treatment of Rousseau has been moved from Chapter 19 (the French Revolution) to Chapter 18 (the Enlightenment) and has been completely rewritten with the aim of presenting Rousseau's ideas on education as well as government.

Chapter 19, which deals with the French Revolution, has been reshaped; a rewritten section on the origins of the Revolution attends to recent scholarship on the relationship between social structure and politics. Material in Chapter 25, on the challenge of science, has been expanded, as have sections on Russia before the First World War (Chapter 26) and during the war (Chapter 27). In Chapter 28, the treatment of the Soviet Union, Italy, and Germany has been modified in the light of scholarly analysis that distinguishes between authoritarian dictatorships in those three countries. Finally, material in the last two chapters has been thoroughly updated and includes a discussion of the collapse of the Soviet Union, the reordering of politics in Eastern Europe, the reunification of Germany, the economic integration of Western Europe, as well as events in other parts of the fast-changing world of the 1990s.

Robert Lerner has been responsible for Chapters 1 through 15, as well as Chapter 18; Standish Meacham for the rest. To borrow a phrase from the tenth century savant, Gerbert of Rheims: "we write what we know, and what we do not know we learn." In seeking guidance, we always learn much from colleagues and reviewers. For this edition we are enormously indebted to reviews provided by Clifford Backman (Boston University), David Graf (University of Miami), Carolyn Lougee (Stanford University),

Daniel Orlovsky (Southern Methodist University), Peter Sahlins (University of California, Berkeley), Richard Saller (University of Chicago), Arlene Wolinsky (San Diego Mesa College), and Stephen Wessley (York College of Pennsylvania), and the anonymous reviewers commissioned by our publisher. Robert Lerner is also grateful to Stephen Harris, Alauddin Samarrai (St. Cloud State University), Nancy Spatz (University of Northern Colorado), Heide Stier, Steven Williams (University of Northern Iowa), and Rachel Wolford for alerting him to numerous errors, dubieties, and infelicities. Standish Meacham acknowledges the thoughtful advice and suggestions received from Nancy Barker and David Crew (University of Texas). To Simon Cordery and Ann Rodrick he owes special and heartfelt thanks. Without their timely, patient, and professional assistance, he could not have completed this assignment. At W. W. Norton and Company the supervisors of this edition have been Robert Kehoe and Steven Forman. A. Deborah Malmud has gathered illustrations with resourcefulness and awesome perseverance. Our editor, Sandy Lifland, has been unfailingly patient and helpful, teaching us gracefully about a range of matters from Kepler's Laws to Lifland's Laws of "that and which."

Robert Lerner
Standish Meacham

WESTERN
CIVILIZATIONS

Part One

THE DAWN OF HISTORY

Our story—the human story—begins about two million years ago in Africa. Very recent field research has demonstrated that the earliest "humanlike" species was that of an upright, large-brained primate who foraged for food on the African savannahs some twenty thousand centuries before today. Four hundred thousand years later humanlike creatures began migrating out of Africa, and during the next million and a quarter years such creatures—spread throughout the Eastern Hemisphere— learned how to use fire and to communicate with each other by means of speech. "Neanderthal" peoples followed on the evolutionary chain, and then, around 40,000 years ago, peoples who were fully modern humans from the anatomical point of view. These earliest humans colonized America and Australia and also painted beautiful murals on the walls of western European caves. With the invention of agriculture in western Asia about 10,000 years ago came a dramatic change in the entire nature of human existence, for humans engaged in agriculture stopped being wanderers and settled instead in villages. Sedentary life led "rapidly" (over the course of about 5,000 years) to civilization—government, writing, arts, and sciences on the one hand; war, social inequalities, and oppression on the other. The earliest Western civilizations emerged in Mesopotamia around 3200 B.C. Thereafter, until about 600 B.C., the most prominent civilizations outside of eastern Asia and America were those of the Mesopotamians, Egyptians, Hebrews, Minoans, and Mycenaeans.

Chapter 1

THE EARLIEST BEGINNINGS

What is particularly interesting about our species? For a start, we walk upright on our hindlegs at all times, which is an extremely unusual way of getting around for a mammal. There are also several unusual features about our head, not least of which is the very large brain it contains. . . . Our forelimbs, being freed from helping us to get about, possess a very high degree of manipulative skill. Part of this skill lies in the anatomical structure of the hands, but the crucial element is, of course, the power of the brain. . . . The most obvious product of our hands and brains is technology. No other animal manipulates the world in the extensive and arbitrary way that humans do. The termites are capable of constructing intricately structured mounds which create their own "air-conditioned" environment inside. But the termites cannot choose to build a cathedral instead. Humans are unique because they have the capacity to choose what they do.

—Richard E. Leakey, *The Making of Mankind*

1. THE NATURE OF HISTORY

Catherine Morland, the heroine of Jane Austen's novel *Northanger Abbey,* complained that history "tells me nothing that does not either vex or weary me. The quarrels of popes and kings, with wars or pestilences in every page; the men all so good for nothing, and hardly any women at all, it is very tiresome." Although Jane Austen's heroine said this around 1800, she might have lodged the same complaint until quite recently, for until deep into the twentieth century most historians considered history to be little more than "past politics"—and a dry chronicle of past politics at that. The content of history was restricted primarily to battles and treaties, the personalities and politics of statesmen, the laws and decrees of rulers. But important as such data are, they by no means constitute the whole substance of history. Especially within the last few decades historians have come to recognize that history comprises a record of past human activities in every sphere—not just political developments, but also social, economic, and intellectual ones. Women as well as men, the ruled as well

History more than battles and treaties

3

as the rulers, the poor as well as the rich, are part of history. So too are the social and economic institutions that men and women have created and that in turn have shaped their lives: family and social class; manorialism and city life; capitalism and industrialism. Ideas and attitudes too, not just of intellectuals, but also of people whose lives may have been virtually untouched by "great books," are all part of the historian's concern. And most important, history includes an inquiry into the causes of events and patterns of human organization and ideas—a search for the forces that impelled humanity toward its great undertakings, and the reasons for its successes and failures.

As historians have extended the scope of their work, they have also equipped themselves with new methods and tools, the better to practice *New historical methods* their craft. No longer do historians merely pore over the same old chronicles and documents to ask whether Charles the Fat was at Ingelheim or Lustnau on July 1, 887. To introduce the evidence of statistics, they learn the methods of the computer scientist. To interpret the effect of a rise in the cost of living, they study economics. To deduce marriage patterns or evaluate the effect upon an entire population of wars and plagues, they master the skills of the demographer. To explore the phenomena of cave-dwelling or modern urbanization, they become archeologists, studying fossil remains, fragments of pots, or modern city landscapes. To understand the motives of the men and women who have acted in the past, they draw on the insights of social psychologists and cultural anthropologists. To illuminate the lives and thoughts of those who have left few or no written records, they look for other cultural remains such as folk songs, folk tales, and funerary monuments.

Of course with all their ingenuity historians cannot create evidence. An almost infinite number of past events are not retrievable because they transpired without leaving any traces; many others are at best known imperfectly. Thus some of the most fundamental questions about "how things *quest for valid reconstructions* were" in the past can either never be answered or answered only on the grounds of highly qualified inferences. Questions regarding motives and causes may not have definite answers for other reasons. Since individual humans often hardly understand their own motives, it is presumptuous to think that anyone can ever be entirely certain about establishing the motives of others. As for the causes of collective developments such as wars, economic growth trends, or changes in artistic styles, these are surely too complex to be reduced to a science. Nonetheless, the more evidence we have, the closer we come to providing valid reconstructions and explanations about what happened in the past. Moreover, the difficulties inherent in assembling and interpreting all sorts of data for the purposes of historical analysis should not be regarded with despair but looked upon as stimulating intellectual challenges.

Approaches to history Should we go to the past to celebrate one or another lost age or seek to learn how we got to be the way we are now? Obviously neither one of these extremes is satisfactory, for nostalgia almost invariably leads to distortion, and at any rate is useless, whereas extreme "present-mindedness" also

Limited evidence and the

leads to distortion, and at any rate is foolish in its assumption that everything we do now is better than whatever people did before. It seems best, then, to avoid either revering the past or condescending to it. Instead, many historians seek to understand how people of a given era strove to solve their problems and live their lives fruitfully in terms appropriate to their particular environments and stages of development. Other historians alternatively look for change over time without postulating a march of progress to a current best of all possible worlds. Such historians believe (and let us hope they may be right) that identifying patterns and mechanisms of change will allow a better understanding of the present and a greater possibility of plotting prudent strategies for coping with the future.

2. OUT OF AFRICA

The study of the earliest phases of human history, known as paleoanthropology, or human paleontology, has been revolutionized in the second half of the twentieth century by a series of momentous fossil discoveries made in East Africa. Before these finds paleoanthropologists assumed that humankind originated in Southeast Asia, whereas now they know the site of human origins was in Africa; and before then they thought that the earliest humanlike creatures originated about one million years ago, but now they double that figure.

Paleoanthropology transformed by fossil discoveries in East Africa

Many of the most sensational East African fossil discoveries were made by a remarkable family of British paleoanthropologists, the Leakeys, and the other finds probably would have not been achieved without the Leakeys' initial impetus. Louis Leakey (1903–1972), the son of a British missionary in Kenya, decided early in life to search for fossil traces of early humanity in East Africa, a pursuit then considered by most experts to be foolhardy. (An individualist, Leakey continued to amaze many observers until shortly

The work of the Leakey family

Mary, Louis, and Richard Leakey Hunting for Fossils. This photograph, taken in 1966, shows the three Leakeys (first, fourth, and fifth from the left) searching for fossil treasures in Kenya.

before his death by stalking African animals without any weapons in order to gain insights into how primeval human ancestors managed to survive.) In 1931 Leakey satisfied himself that he was on the right track in his fossil hunting by his discovery in Tanzania (then Tanganyika) of primitive hand axes fashioned by a species of early man approximately one million years ago. Impeded by other professional responsibilities and a lack of funds, he made little progress in his fossil research for more than a quarter-century thereafter. Then, in 1959, an enormous breakthrough was made, not by Louis Leakey himself, but by his wife and co-investigator, Mary Leakey. Searching through a Tanzanian site in that year, Mary discovered some seemingly humanlike teeth and cranial bone fragments; when she put all her fragments in place and confirmed their dating, it turned out that she had a nearly complete skull of a creature vaguely like a human who lived 1.8 million years ago. Because of the skull's huge jaw and large teeth, the press quickly dubbed Mary's find "Nutcracker Man."

In fact Nutcracker Man was not a man but an advanced species of ape that walked erect. Recognizing this themselves, Louis and Mary Leakey wondered whether anything more human might be found in the vicinity, and sure enough, a mere two years later their eldest son, Jonathan, provided an answer by discovering the 1.8 million-year-old cranial remains of an erect primate with a much larger brain than Nutcracker Man's. Louis Leakey recognized that these fossils belonged to a different species that clearly was a direct ancestor of modern humans; therefore he placed it in the "manlike" rather than "apelike" genus and named it *Homo habilis,* or "man having ability."

Once it became clear that East African sites were the best places to look for evidence of human origins, other breathtaking finds occurred with bewildering rapidity. In 1972 a team led by the Leakeys' second son, Richard (currently the leading paleoanthropologist of the dynasty), discovered in Kenya pieces of a skull of *Homo habilis* that were more complete than those found by his brother, and that were about 200,000 years older. In 1974 a team headed by the American Donald Johanson discovered in Ethiopia 40 percent of the entire skeleton of an erect ape that lived about three and a quarter million years ago. (Johanson named this creature "Lucy" because as her bones were being assembled in the field camp someone was playing on a tape recorder the Beatles' song "Lucy in the Sky with Diamonds.") A year later Johanson and his team turned up numerous bones of at least thirteen of Lucy's contemporaries, and a year later Mary Leakey found in Tanzania footprints of an erect ape who walked there 3.75 million years ago. As of this writing, amazing discoveries continue: in 1984 Richard Leakey's team in Kenya found a skeleton of a 1.6 million-year-old human ancestor so complete that had it been a *Homo sapiens* it could almost have been used for an anatomy-class lecture in a medical school.

Of course discovering skulls and skeletons is one thing, and interpreting the evidence another. Not surprisingly, there is still much uncertainty and controversy concerning human origins, and theories are overhauled con-

Fossil Footprints Discovered by Mary Leakey. By studying these footprints she discovered in 1976, Mary Leakey could determine that the creatures who left them behind some three and three-quarters million years ago walked upright.

Bipedality

tinually as better alternatives are proposed and new evidence adduced. Nonetheless, two fundamental propositions advanced within the last twenty years are now beyond the range of dispute. One is that the first "split off" between the chain of evolution that led to modern humans and the chain that includes all surviving apes did not relate to larger brain size, as was once thought, but rather concerned "bipedality," or upright walking. The proof for this is found in Lucy and the other erect apes like her whose fossils were found by the Johanson team, for the arm and leg bones of these creatures show that they walked upright, but the skulls show that their brains were small, indeed little more than the size of a chimp's. Since substantially larger brains are first present in fossils dating to a million and a quarter years after Lucy, there is no doubt that bipedality came before larger brain size.

The Lucy evidence also shows that the advantage of moving on two feet did not immediately lie in freeing the hands for the fashioning and employment of tools and weapons because such could only come about with larger brain size. Instead, it now seems likely that upright apes gained an advantage in the struggle for survival over other apes because they could grab their food, run with it, and then eat it in hiding. Since they did this in daytime they also needed to sweat more, which is why those who had less fur survived best. In fact some paleoanthropologists now think that larger brains first became a biological advantage because larger brain size could better regulate the body heat of upright apes. The genetic shift to bipedality because of advantageous feeding is a nice illustration of the fact that "Mother Nature" does not plan evolution with great foresight: free hands could have led to toolmaking, but for one or two million years they did not.

"Mother Nature," as the recent fossil discoveries in Africa have shown, is also sloppy since she created many apelike species such as Lucy that no longer survive. This is another way of saying that the second fundamental proposition about human evolution now beyond the range of dispute is that the second genetic "split off" leading to humans did indeed relate to brain size. *Homo habilis,* the first known species leading to modern man, existed at least as long ago as two million years and had a brain about 50 percent larger than its contemporary erect apes such as Nutcracker Man. Unquestionably it was this brain that allowed *Homo habilis* to replace the erect apes within 100,000 to 200,000 years, for it enabled him to employ tools. Self-evidently *Homo habilis*'s tools were extremely crude—bones of animals, limbs from trees, and, most sophisticated, pieces of stone chipped to create sharp edges. It seems that, rather than being used for hunting, such tools helped the earliest humans increase their food supply by digging for tubers, cutting plants, cracking open nuts, and slicing scavenged meat. But gathering food with tools not only gave the earliest humans a greater and more varied food supply, it was also the first step toward civilization because it called for a degree of group cooperation hitherto unknown among the primates.

"Lucy"

Bipedality and advantageous feeding

Homo habilis *and larger brain size*

3. FROM *HOMO HABILIS* TO *HOMO SAPIENS*

Homo erectus

Aside from his toolmaking abilities, we know very little about the activities of *Homo habilis,* who appears to have merged into his successor on the evolutionary chain, *Homo erectus* ("erect man"), in Africa around 1.6 million years ago. But we know a great deal more about this successor, who lived from about 1.6 million years ago to about 300,000 years ago. *Homo erectus* was the species that first migrated out of Africa and started peopling the earth; it was also this species that first engaged in collective hunting and learned how to use fire. So well was *Homo erectus* able to adapt himself to the extremely disparate environments in which he lived, that he survived for more than five times as long as our own species, *Homo sapiens,* has existed so far.

Homo erectus; greater size and intelligence

From the physical point of view the differences between *Homo erectus* and his predecessor, *Homo habilis,* were dramatic. Whereas *Homo habilis* was probably about the size of a pygmy, *Homo erectus* was about as tall as most modern humans. The nearly complete skeleton that Richard Leakey's team discovered in 1984 was that of a *Homo erectus* boy of about twelve years old. Since this boy was already about five and a half feet tall, he probably would have been a six-footer had he reached maturity; indeed, the boy was also so stocky that as Leakey observed, he "might have made a fine football player" on a prehistoric varsity team. Chances are the *Homo erectus* boy could also have executed a fairly complicated offensive play because of his intelligence. *Homo erectus* had on the average a cranial capacity more than 40 percent greater than that of *Homo habilis,* and there is some fossil evidence to show that the shape of his brain had changed in the direction of our own.

Language and cooperation

Homo erectus's intelligence enabled him to migrate from Africa to Europe and Far Eastern Asia, and to adjust in the process to a wide variety of climates. Apparently the most important single invention of the species was the use of language: reconstructions of the *Homo erectus* larynx show that the species was able to make most of the sounds we do; moreover, although speech leaves no direct fossil remains, it is all but certain that *Homo erectus*'s tools were fashioned in adherence to complex rule systems that could only have been communicated by means of spoken languages. *Homo erectus* certainly knew how to cooperate in big-game hunting and in processing and distributing the food obtained from these activities. Prominent in such cooperation would have been the establishment of mutually beneficial male and female roles in food-gathering and food-processing. Finally, by at least 400,000 years ago *Homo erectus* learned how to use fire. Whether he knew how to start a fire is impossible to say, but he certainly could control fire for the purposes of keeping warm, protecting himself against marauding animals, and perhaps using fire to cook food.

Homo Erectus Skull. This skull dates from "only" about half a million years ago.

About 300,000 years ago *Homo erectus* gradually began to evolve into *Homo sapiens*—indeed, so gradually that it is very difficult to tell from surviving remains where the one species left off and the other began. What is

An Artist's Reconstruction of Homo Erectus Hunters Returning from the Hunt

certain is that anatomically the physical changes that took place over the course of several hundred centuries would have been most obvious above the neck, for although *Homo erectus* had something very roughly like a football player's physique, he still had an "ape-like" sloping forehead and a brain case on average about 70 percent the size of our own. Paleoanthropologists tend to agree that between *Homo erectus* and the fully modern human species there were two transitional stages of *Homo sapiens*—archaic *Homo sapiens,* living from about 300,000 to about 125,000 years ago, and "Neanderthal Man," living from then until about 40,000 years ago.

Transition from Homo erectus to Homo sapiens

Owing to numerous archeological discoveries in Europe and the Near East (the first "Neanderthal" bones were found in the Neanderthal valley of the Neander River in Germany in 1856—hence the name), we are vastly better informed about the transitional phase of *Homo sapiens* known as Neanderthals than we are about any variety of early humans that came before them. Perhaps most in need of emphasis is the fact that although "Neanderthal" is often used as a synonym for primitive and dim-witted and although a Hollywood film about Neanderthal people makes them communicate in "uggah-muggah" talk, they were genetically as little different from one of the modern human races as any one of the modern races is different from another. Put another way, although Neanderthals were more barrel-chested than we are and had a somewhat differently shaped cranium, if a Neanderthal male were dressed in Western business clothes and placed on Wall Street or Madison Avenue he would fit right in.

The Neanderthal phase

The Neanderthal people were skilled toolmakers and crafty hunters. Whereas earlier humanlike species usually relied on one or two all-purpose tool/weapons, the Neanderthals created about sixty different specialized tools, including knives, scrapers, borers, and spearheads. Most of these they fashioned from stone, but they also employed bone for making more delicate tools in processes that called for very careful handling. Neanderthals

Tool making and hunting

Neanderthal Man

also built shelters out of tree branches or bones, or, when caves were at hand, dwelled in them when shelter was needed and equipped them with great stone hearths. So successful were they in hunting that some Neanderthal bands limited themselves to hunting just one game species, such as bear or deer, rather than any animal they could kill. Some anthropologists have speculated that ritualistic reasons may have lain behind such hunting behavior—possibly the Neanderthals thought they were honoring the spirits of the game species they favored. Whether or not any Neanderthal people were ritualistic hunters, some were surely the earliest known humans to devote their time collectively to anything more than the quest for material survival. Some Neanderthals definitely buried their dead in distinctly reverential ways and provided them with food and goods apparently meant to aid them in their voyages to an afterlife.

How the Neanderthal variety of humanity evolved into the fully modern variety is a source of puzzlement to the experts since the process transpired within a more or less narrow range of time throughout the Eastern Hemisphere. (People like the Neanderthals inhabited Africa and eastern Asia around the time the Neanderthals lived in Europe and western Asia.) Suffice it to say that between 40,000 and 30,000 years ago the Neanderthals were gone, and the Eastern Hemisphere was populated by human beings anatomically just like us. Concurrently the newly evolved human species migrated into the Western Hemisphere, needing no boats for this because there was then a land connection between Siberia and Alaska. Since Australia was colonized (in still mysterious ways) before 30,000 years ago, the entire globe then knew human habitation more or less as it does today.

4. EARLY HUMAN ART AND EARLY HUMAN SURVIVAL

Early human art: Cave murals

One of the first things modern humans accomplished was the creation of some of the most stunning paintings known in the entire history of human art—the famous cave murals of southern France and northern Spain executed between 30,000 and 12,000 years ago. In over 200 caves so far discovered (the most famous of which are the cave of Lascaux in southern France and that of Altamira in Spain), the earliest known artists painted breathtaking murals of prancing animals—bison, bulls, horses, ponies, and stags. The emphasis in this cave art was unquestionably on movement. Almost all of the murals depict proud game species running, leaping, chewing their cud, or facing the hunter at bay. An ingenious device for giving the impression of motion was the drawing of additional outlines to indicate the areas in which the leg or the head of the animal had moved. The cave painters sometimes succeeded in achieving startling three-dimensional effects by profiting from the natural bumps and indentations of their cave surfaces. All in all, visitors today who are lucky enough to see the cave murals usually find them as evocative as any paintings hanging in the world's foremost art museums.

See color plates facing page 44

What was the purpose of these prehistoric wonders? Aesthetic delight in being surrounded by beauty must be ruled out as an explanation because the peoples who painted in caves generally lived out of doors and when they did use caves for seasonal shelters they inhabited different parts of them (usually the entrances) rather than the areas where murals are found (usually the darkest and most inaccessible parts of the caves). Abandoning one extreme of interpretation—pure aesthetic delight—some scholars have proposed another by maintaining that the cave paintings were symbolic representations of human relationships. According to this theory, cave painters were early social philosophers who tried to interpret and thereby cope with the demands of their social structures by depicting them symbolically. On this understanding the cave bison were not really meant to be bison but rather the "female element," horses the "male element," and pictures of small animals gathered around larger ones were meant to show the gathering of less important people around leaders. Needless to say, such hypotheses can never be proven or disproven without written records, but they do appear to be farfetched. For example, there is nothing very obviously feminine about bison (indeed, some symbolic interpreters have seen bison as "male" and horses as "female"), and it is hard above all to understand why artists intent upon representing human reality would portray animals and not humans.

Leaving aside the interpretative extremes of simplicity and sophistication, the view that cave art was an attempt at working sympathetic magic appears to be the most convincing explanation available. Sympathetic magic is founded on the belief that imitating a desired result will bring about that result. Regarding cave art, it seems reasonably clear that when prehistoric painters depicted bison with arrows piercing their flanks, the very act of representing such scenes was meant to ensure that arrows would pierce bison in reality. An objection lodged against the sympathetic magic theory is

Cave Artist's Lamp. Found in a French cave site in 1960, this prehistoric receptacle was used for burning wood saturated with animal fat by underground artists as they went about their work.

Cave Painting of Two Reindeer. From a cave in southern France, a painting executed by an extraordinarily gifted artist "of the French School," who worked about 15,000 years ago.

Cave Bison. Although not all the experts agree, it seems reasonably clear that this bison has been wounded with arrows or spears. If so, the representation from a cave wall in southern France supports the theory that cave artists were attempting to employ sympathetic magic.

Bison Carved from a Reindeer Horn. Perhaps the most graceful of all known European prehistoric carvings, this bison was carved from a piece of antler between 15,000 and 12,000 years ago. Whatever its use might have been no one quite knows.

that only about 10 percent of all known cave murals show killing scenes. But since almost all cave paintings do depict game, it may be answered that the portrayal of plentiful, cavorting game was meant to ensure that hunters would really find game in plenty. Moreover, further support for the view that cave artists worked as sympathetic magicians is found in the fact that archeologists have discovered traces of ritualistic practices in some of the cave areas where murals are located. From this it may be concluded that incantations and rites probably accompanied the acts of painting, and it may also be that all the magical practices were worked while the hunt itself was in progress.

The last inference assumes that the cave painters were not hunters. Although that is by no means an established fact, it is certain that the early human hunting society that produced the cave paintings was one that had arrived at extensive specialization and differentiation of labor. For example, strictly from the technical point of view, cave painting could only have been accomplished by specialists since it entailed not only the use of charcoal sticks for drawing black outlines and lumps of clay-like ores (ochres) for coloring in tones of yellows, reds, and browns, but it also drew on the mixing of earthen pigments with fat (as in the later production of tempera paints) and the employment of feathers or bracken for "brushes." Handicraft workers in the same societies concurrently developed extraordinary facility in fashioning tools, not just from stones and bones but also from antlers and ivory. Examples of the implements they added to the ancient human tool kit include fishhooks, harpoons, bows and arrows, and needles for sewing together animal skins.

Hunting in the period between 30,000 and 12,000 years ago would also have called for specialized training since artful new techniques were being added to the hunting repertory. Specifically, with darts and arrows hunters of that time learned how to bring down birds, with harpoons and fishhooks they learned how to catch fish, and by studying the instinctive movements of game animals they learned how to stampede and trap herds. Since they relied on game most of all, they migrated with game herds and there is some evidence that they followed preservation rules by not killing everything that they could. Nonetheless, masses of charred bones found regularly at archeological sites dating from this period indicate that huge quantities of game were killed and then roasted in community feasts, proving that the peoples in question not only knew how to paint and how to hunt, but also how to share.

5. THE ORIGINS OF FOOD PRODUCTION

The "Ice Age" and its impact on hunting societies

Around 12,000 years ago (i.e., 10,000 B.C.), hunting feasts occurred ever more rarely or not at all for a simple reason—the herds were vanishing. The era between 35,000 and 12,000 years ago had been an "Ice Age": daytime temperatures in the Mediterranean regions of Europe and western

Asia averaged about 60°F (16°C) in the summer and about 30°F (−1°C) in the winter. Accordingly, herds of cold-loving game species such as reindeer, elk, wild boar, European bison, and various kinds of mountain goats roamed the hills and valleys. But as the last glaciers receded northwards such species retreated with them. Some humans may have moved north with the game, but others stayed behind, creating an extremely different sort of world in comparatively short order.

Specifically, within about 3,000 to 4,000 years after the end of the Ice Age humans in western Asia had accomplished one of the most momentous revolutions ever accomplished by any humans: a switch from subsistence by means of food-gathering to subsistence by means of food-producing.* For roughly two million years humanlike species and humans had gained their sustenance by foraging, or by combined foraging and hunting. These modes of existence meant that such peoples could never stay very long in one place because they continually ate their way through local supplies of plant food, and, if they were hunters, they were forced to follow the movements of herds. But "suddenly" (that is, in terms of the comparative time spans involved) substantial numbers of humans began to domesticate animals and raise crops, thereby settling down. As soon as this shift was accomplished villages were founded, trade developed, and populations in areas of sedentary habitation started increasing by leaps and bounds. Then, when villages began evolving into cities, civilization was born. "The rest is history" in a very literal sense, for human history—as opposed to prehistory—really began with the birth of civilization and written records.

Transition from food-gathering to food-producing economies

To say that some humans became food producers all of a sudden is of course justifiable only in terms of the broadest chronological picture. Seen from the perspective of modern historical change, wherein technological revolutions transpire in a few decades or years, the change in western Asia from food-gathering to food production was an extremely gradual one. Not only did the transition take place over the course of some 3,000 to 4,000 years (c. 10,000 to c. 7000/6000 B.C.), but it was so gradual that the peoples involved hardly knew themselves what was happening. It is essential to add that had they known what was happening they almost certainly would not have approved of the basic switch from gathering to raising food because Ice-Age hunting and gathering allowed its practitioners to live in health and comparative leisure (it has been estimated that hunter-gatherers worked for only about three hours a day), whereas early food-producing yielded poorer average diets (much less variety) and entailed much harder work. Yet the progression toward food production had its step-by-step logic which did not allow individual humans much choice.

Gradual change from food-gathering to food production

The story of how humans became food producers is roughly as follows. (Details of this story are certain to be revised as research continues.) Around 10,000 B.C. most of the larger game herds had left western Asia.

---

* In earlier editions of this book this was called the "Neolithic Revolution." The term has been replaced because it suggests misleadingly that the innovation of food production was caused primarily by technological advances in stone tool-making.

*How humans became
food producers*

Yet people in coastal areas were not starving; on the contrary, they were surrounded by plenty because the melting glaciers had raised water levels and thereby had introduced huge quantities of fish, shellfish, and water fowl in newly created bays and swamps. Excavations near Mount Carmel and at the site of Jericho in modern-day Israel—locations not far from the Mediterranean Sea—prove that wildlife and vegetation in that area between about 10,000 and 9000 B.C. were so lush that people could sustain themselves in permanent settlements in an unprecedented fashion, easily catching fish and fowl, and picking fruits off trees as if they were in the Garden of Eden. But the plenty of Mount Carmel and Jericho had its costs in terms of population trends. Modern nomadic hunting peoples have low birthrates, and the same is presumed to have been true of prehistoric peoples. The given in this regard is that a woman can trek with one baby in her arms but hardly with two; hence nature finds ways to limit nomadic births for each woman to one every three or four years. (The actual biological mechanisms may differ: frequent miscarriages might come from frequent trekking, or else longer periods of suckling—induced by the mother carrying an infant in her arms longer—might delay fertility.) Once people became sedentary in Eden-like environments, however, their reproductive rates began to increase, until, over the course of centuries, there were too many people for the lush coastal terrains.

Domestication of animals

Accordingly, paleoanthropologists posit that around 9000 B.C. excess populations in western Asia started migrating inland to territories where wildlife and plant foods were less plentiful, and where they were forced to return to the nomadic ways of hunter-gatherers. What is certain is that between 9000 and 8000 B.C. some humans in Iran had taken the first known step toward food production by domesticating animals—in this case, sheep and goats. This would have been no more than the equivalent of taking out a small insurance policy. People seeking to avoid overreliance on one particular food source, and starvation if that source failed, captured live animals and gradually bred them so that they had meat on the hoof, available whenever the need arose. Owning a few sheep or goats did not inhibit the people who first domesticated them from continuing in their nomadic way of life (it is easier to travel with trained goats than with babies). But it did make them accustomed to the notion of actively manipulating their environments.

*Plant food and human
manipulation of the
environment*

Producing plant food came next. After the glaciers had receded, wild wheat and wild barley had begun to grow in scattered hilly parts of inland western Asia. Accustomed to gathering all sorts of seeds, hunter-gatherers between about 9000 and 8000 B.C. gladly drew on the wheat and barley because when these plants were ripe, gatherers could reap large amounts of seeds from them within as little as three weeks and then move on to other pursuits. Archeological discoveries reveal that the peoples in question developed flint sickles to accelerate their harvesting, mortars for grinding their harvested grain into flour, and—most significantly for future developments—lined storage pits for preserving their grain or flour. In other words, these peoples had not only begun to pay special attention to har-

An Artist's Conception of Nomadic Hunter-Gatherers Reaping Grain with Flint Sickles. In 1966 an intrepid paleoanthropologist used a 9,000-year-old sickle to see how well it could deal with wild wheat in the hills of eastern Turkey. Within an hour he had harvested six pounds of grain.

vesting wild grain, but they were saving their harvests for use over time. Again, people were manipulating their environments instead of merely adjusting to them.

Still nomads, the same people most likely would have been content to gather their grain and other foods forever. But since grain could be stored particularly well, some groups of grain gatherers may have come gradually to rely on it more and more. In such cases they would have been adversely affected by a poor growing year or by gradual depletion caused by excessive harvesting. Then, paying more attention to keeping their wild grain growing profusely, they would have noticed that the grain would grow better if rival plants (weeds) were removed, still better if the soil were scratched so that falling seeds could take root more easily, and still better if they themselves sprinkled some seeds into sparser patches of soil. The people who did these things were more influential discoverers and explorers in terms of the origins of our own modern existence than Columbus or Copernicus, yet from their point of view they were merely adjusting some of the details of their ongoing hunting and gathering way of life.

Increasing reliance on grain among nomadic hunter-gatherers

Imperceptibly, however, they became "hooked" and surrendered their nomadic ways for sedentary ones. Already having small herds as "insurance policies," they must have decided at some point that it would be equally sensible to be able to count on having patches of planted grain awaiting them when they reached a given area on seasonal nomadic rounds. And then they would have learned that planting could be done better at a different time of year than harvesting, and then that their livestock might graze well on harvested stubble, and then that they might grow more than one crop a year in the same place. Meanwhile they would have become

Sedentary plant-food production, or agriculture

more and more accustomed to storing and would have seen less and less reason to move away from their fields and their stores. And so sedentary plant-food production, or agriculture, was invented.

The earliest archeological evidence for fully sedentary agriculture comes from eastern Anatolia (modern-day Turkey), Syria, Iraq, and Iran, and dates from roughly 7500 to roughly 7000 B.C. By 6000 B.C. the entire western Asian region had adopted agriculture as the central mode of human survival. To be sure, agriculture was not the only means of survival. Livestock-raising supplemented it, and by 6000 B.C. the livestock raised included cattle and pigs as well as sheep and goats. Moreover, farming peoples continued to engage in some hunting and some gathering on the side. (Even today most farmers look forward to using their rifles from time to time, and most farmers' wives to gathering wild berries or mushrooms.) Yet settled agriculture had not only become the dominant form of human existence in western Asia by 6000 B.C., but soon after it conquered the world. Agriculture arose independently in at least three areas in China and one or two sites in America around 5000 B.C. and fanned out in Far Eastern Asia and the Western Hemisphere from there. From western Asia it reached southeastern Europe (the Balkans) by about 5000 B.C. and spread from there over the entire European continent until by about 3500 B.C. it had reached its natural European limits in Scandinavia. "Amber waves of grain" have played a central role in European—and by extension, North American—history ever since.

6. THE EMERGENCE OF VILLAGES, TRADE, AND WARFARE

Focusing here on developments in western Asia after the switch from food-gathering to food production, the next steps in the region's accelerating evolution toward civilization were the emergence of villages, the rise of long-distance trade, and the onset of bitter warfare. Villages constituted the most advanced form of human organization in western Asia from about 6500 to about 3500/3000 B.C., when some villages gradually became cities. Village organization inevitably brought about long-distance trade, and it just as inevitably provoked the growth of war. No doubt warfare has been the bane of human existence, with famine and disease, at least since the appearance of agricultural villages, but since the growth of warfare in ancient times stimulated the growth of economic and social complexity it nonetheless must be counted as a step toward the emergence of civilization.

The progression in social organization that transpired in western Asia from wandering band to village to city was essentially a progression in function from gathering food to raising food to engaging in a variety of functions that presupposed the steady supply of food. At each stage the size of the organization typically became larger, but it must not be thought that villages were always larger than bands and smaller than cities. Rather, although the typical village numbered about 1,000, during the earliest part of what might be called the "age of villages" in western Asia some villages

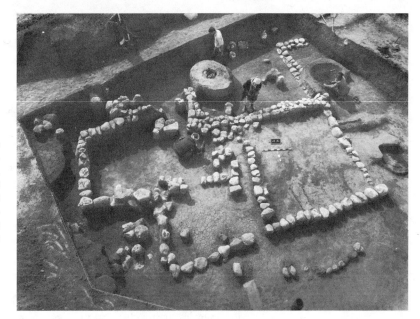

Stone Foundation of a Sedentary Dwelling. Once people in western Asia became agriculturalists, they began to build homes for year-round habitation. This stone foundation for a prehistoric house was found at the site of the village of Jarmo (in Iraq) and dates from about 6000 B.C.

numbered as few as 200 inhabitants, making them smaller than the average bands, and at the height of the period some villages housed populations of more than 5,000, making them larger than the typical subsequent city. Therefore it is wiser to put aside size and insist that a settlement cannot be considered a village if most of its inhabitants were not sedentary or if more than a very small percentage of its able-bodied inhabitants did not engage in fieldwork. To be sure, over the course of time handicrafts began to take an ever-more-prominent role in village activities after agriculture because village farmers were always seeking greater efficiencies and comforts. At first all the villagers would have engaged in a given new craft, but as the techniques of some crafts became more complicated, specialists would arise who gradually would be allowed to become full-time artisans instead of going into the fields. Nonetheless, even toward the end of the western Asian age of villages, such full-time artisans were very rare, probably comprising at most no more than one percent of the adult population.

The most important village handicrafts were pottery, weaving, and tool- and weapon-making. Of these, the emergence of the first two were immediate results of the shift to sedentary existence. Once humans became settled they obviously became particularly interested in storing, and just as obviously they no longer needed to worry about how well any storage receptacle might be suited for travel. Thus humans may have known how to make clay pots in much earlier periods, yet they did not bother to make them because such pots were too fragile to carry on treks. But when humans built villages they immediately built pots because they found them ideal for storing grain and other foods. Moreover, clay pots could also be used to haul and store water. With pottery people could thus keep drinking water in their homes, a step toward luxury perhaps comparable to the modern invention of indoor plumbing.

Handicrafts in village society: (1) pottery

Early Village Pottery. A shallow bowl from a western Asian village site dating from about 5000 B.C.

(2) weaving

Weaving also probably first arose because of the search for appropriate receptacles inasmuch as knowledge of basket-weaving seems to have preceded knowledge of clothweaving. Certainly twig baskets, which appear in the archeological record soon after settlement, were too bulky and fragile for incessant travel but more suitable than pots for certain kinds of storing and preferable to pots for bringing in harvests from the field because of their lightness. Once the weaving principle became widely known it could easily be put to use for manufacturing cloth, given that domesticated sheep were available to produce wool. And with woolen fabrics villagers had a more dependable and adaptable source of clothing than animals skins. (The weaving of cloth from plant fibers only arose with the domestication of a suitable plant, flax, the raw material for making linen, in Egypt around 3000 B.C.)

(3) tools and weapons

In contrast to pottery and weaving, the fashioning of tools and weapons was not new to humanity in the age of villages, but villagers did learn how to make tools and weapons out of new materials. The need for sharper and more durable tools became ever greater with the growth of agriculture: for example, early villagers sought the sharpest sickles and the most durable plows. And while weapons may have been used less for hunting, we will see that they were used more and more for war. At first Asian villagers seeking sharp edges recognized that some rocks could produce sharper cutting edges than others and used these whenever they could. Then they noticed that some "rocks" were particularly malleable and thus could be fashioned into pointed tips and resharpened when blunted. Such malleable "rocks" of course were not rocks at all but small pieces of copper standing free in nature, and because these were comparatively rare, between about 6500 and 4500 B.C. they were employed only for making tips and very small implements such as pins. But then someone, perhaps as the result of accidentally dropping a metallic rock into a pottery kiln, discovered that certain "rocks" (ore stones) would ooze forth copper under high heats. Whoever this person was, he or she discovered smelting, and thereafter, for roughly the next millennium, smelted copper was used in western Asia for manufacturing all sorts of containers, tools, and weapons.

Reference to the growing use of different rocks and copper inevitably introduces the subject of trade, for the sharp rocks and the copper early villagers desired were not found all over western Asia but had to be transported over long distances. Hunter-gatherers seldom, if ever, engaged in long-distance trade because they could not afford it—in other words, they produced no surpluses. Wandering from place to place such people kept their luggage to a minimum and hence were not at all oriented toward surplus production. Villagers, on the other hand, were natural storers, and not long after they started storing grain they came to realize that producing and storing more than they needed could serve as a hedge against famine and could provide goods for barter.

Long-distance trade born of surplus production

Although we will never know for certain how step followed step, it seems most likely that short-distance gift-offering and exchange based on kin-group relations preceded long-distance trade in more recognizably mercantile forms. For example, a family group in a prosperous village might have sent some grain to hungry kin in a nearby village simply as a gift or in return for an implement or two; conceivably regular offerings of gifts or regular exchanges between kin in different villages may have arisen as ceremonial means of acknowledging family ties. As exchange and accumulation of goods continued, however, certain parties inevitably became richer than others until they had the wherewithal to send an emissary over a long distance to trade for, say, a good sharp cutting stone in a location where such stones were plentiful. At any rate, there is no doubt that as early as about 6500 B.C. trade in western Asia already extended over remarkably long distances. In particular, all the villages known to have existed in Iran and Iraq had found the means of acquiring steady supplies of obsidian (a volcanic glass particularly suited for making sharp cutting edges) from sources in what is now Armenia, 400 to 500 miles away, and the same villages were also acquiring small pieces of copper from central Anatolia, about twice as far. Thereafter trade in rocks, metals, foodstuffs, fabrics, hides, and trinkets became ever more brisk, and by the end of the age of villages, goods were being transported by boats as well as moving over land.

Development of long-distance trade

But trade was not the only means of acquiring goods, for successful pillaging could serve the acquisitive even better. No one knows exactly when human warfare began, but more and more experts are coming to doubt that aggressiveness is biologically "programmed" into us. Rather, it seems that humans have no strictly biological propensity for either peace or war and that before the switch to sedentary agriculture bands of roving humans were peaceable. At the very least it is certain that there are no depictions of humans fighting humans in the Ice-Age cave paintings and that the earliest known representations of warfare appear together with settled village life. Even more dramatic is the fact that many of the earliest known villages in western Asia were fortified villages. Evidently, whatever humanity's past had been, its future was to fight and kill.

Flint Dagger. Discovered in Anatolia and dating from about 7000 B.C., this dagger made from flint-stone with an elaborately carved bone handle was a weapon worthy of a commander-in-chief.

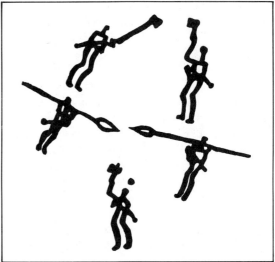

Early Representations of Warfare. On the left is a cave painting from Spain; on the right is a rock carving from Sweden. Although both representations are very difficult to date, it is almost certain that neither predated the establishment of settled agriculture in their respective regions.

Links between village life and warfare

Settled life would have inspired ongoing warfare for obvious reasons. Members of roving bands needed to cooperate with each other in hunting and gathering, and they seldom even saw members of other bands. Assuming that one band did occasionally run into another, there would have been little reason to fight since there was little or no loot to be gained. In contrast, there was loot in a village, and villagers under attack would have tended to stand and fight rather than cut and run, not only to protect their belongings, but to preserve their fields, which invariably had cost them great effort to clear and cultivate. Endemic fighting probably began during the period of transition between wandering and settlement when some bands of wanderers became bands of pillagers. Then, by the time there were many villages, one settlement definitely started fighting another to attain more property and wealth.

Warfare as a stimulus to technology and trade

Ironically, the onset of warfare stimulated the progress of technology and trade. Whether for defensive or offensive reasons, early villagers in western Asia achieved great technological advances in weaponry, experimenting in the manufacture of daggers, battle-axes, spears, slings, and maces. Moreover, an area-wide village "arms race" was probably what most stimulated the advance of metallurgy, since copper made better spear points and daggers than stone or bone, and bronze, an alloy of copper and tin, whose manufacture was perfected between 3500 and 3000 B.C., made vastly better weapons of all sorts than copper. Since metals had to be acquired by trade, villagers caught in an arms race were forced to enhance their efficiency in producing surpluses of village products so that they could acquire metals. And so the search for the best weapons stimulated economic life even while causing death and destruction.

7. THE BIRTH OF CIVILIZATIONS IN WESTERN ASIA

The last major development in western Asian prehistory was the emergence of cities, a phenomenon datable to the period between about 3500 and 3200 B.C. Since some villages imperceptibly turned into cities over the course of about five hundred years, it is easier to describe the difference between a city and a village on the basis of how the city appeared at the end of its development. Unlike the village, the city housed people from a wide variety of occupations. All early cities housed farmers, for the fields around a city needed to be tilled just like any others; cities additionally housed small numbers of artisans and merchants, since cities began to take shape at a time when some handicraft skills had become very specialized and when trading was also becoming a specialty. But the predominant personalities in cities, whose presence really determined the difference between the city and the village, were full-time warriors, administrators, and priests.

*Distinctions between city and
village*

In a nutshell, cities existed to exploit villages. The foremost city dwellers themselves of course would not have put things that way. Since they were professional warriors, administrators, and priests, they would have said that their callings were to protect their regions by military means, to enhance regional productivity by good management, and to conciliate the gods with prayers. But since none of these people worked in the fields, they surely could not have existed without the surpluses produced by those who did. Put another way, the leading city dwellers were rulers in their society, and the inhabitants of subordinated villages, as well as other city dwellers, were the ruled.

*City versus village; ruler
versus ruled*

There is no doubt that the earliest western Asian cities arose in Mesopotamia, a region in modern-day Iraq lying between the Tigris and Euphrates rivers, and it is virtually certain that the ultimate cause for this lay in population pressure. We have already seen that settled peoples tend to reproduce more quickly than wanderers. Certainly, once people in western Asia became adept at settled agriculture food yields began to increase spectacularly, and so did human numbers. By a conservative estimate the population in the hilly area of western Iran, where settled agriculture had found one of its earliest homes, increased fiftyfold between 8000 and 4000 B.C. At a certain point excess populations needed to move on to new terrains in order to survive, and this was particularly true among early agriculturalists, who tended gradually to exhaust the fertility of their lands since they knew nothing of crop rotation or fertilizing techniques. In western Asia this point was reached around 4000 B.C. when excess peoples in Iran and Iraq began to move in considerable numbers into the previously uninhabited valley between the Tigris and the Euphrates.

*The cities of Mesopotamia:
The product of population
pressure*

Two requirements are necessary for successful agriculture: fertility and moisture. The earliest western Asian agricultural settlements were located in hilly regions where grain originally grew wild. These terrains were not particularly fertile, but at least they were fertile enough to support the be-

Mesopotamian Archeological Mound. Several thousand years' worth of successive human building activities will often result in a mound of debris looking like this. Many decades of hard labor and intensive study by a team of archeologists would be necessary to recover all the historical information hidden in this mound, dating from about 5000 B.C. at the base and 500 C.E. at the top.

Irrigation and division into ruler and ruled

ginnings of crop-growing, and they did have abundant moisture from rainfall. The Mesopotamian valley, on the other hand, was extremely fertile but so lacking in moisture for long parts of the year that farming there was impossible without the introduction of artificial irrigation systems. Building and maintaining irrigation systems, however, called for a degree of planning and of intense, coordinated labor that was unprecedented in human societies until that time. The irrigation in question, initiated in the millennium between 4000 and 3000 B.C., had to be accomplished by means of leading canals and channels from the two big rivers in crisscrossing patterns over the dry lands, and the work was never completed because the canals and channels had constantly to be cleared when they began silting up. Such labors required that people be organized in force, that provisions be assembled to support them, that pots be mass-produced to serve as their food receptacles, and so forth. Obviously, therefore, planners were needed to determine how, when, and where to work, overseers were needed to direct and coerce laborers, and governors were needed to plan and oversee the overseers. Accordingly under such circumstances society became divided into the rulers and the ruled.

Militarism reinforces governmental power

As population pressure entailing the necessity for irrigation systems created a trend toward government and coercion in Mesopotamia between 4000 and 3200 B.C., the trend was reinforced by the advance of militarism. How did some people manage to emerge as rulers? Surely the main explanation lay in brute force, the strongest in society being those who were the most skilled in fighting. During the millennium in question military power would have led to governmental power and ever more military power by a continual spiraling process: metal weapons were superior to stone ones but much more expensive, thus those who had acquired wealth from subduing and exploiting others were the only ones who could have afforded to acquire metal weapons with which to subdue and exploit still more people. It is particularly noteworthy that Mesopotamia has no natural supply of any metals or metallic ores, yet relatively large quantities of metal weaponry have been found there dating from between 3500 and 3000 B.C.; obviously the warrior-rulers of Mesopotamia were becoming ever more dominant.

Given that dominant warriors needed trained administrators to help them govern and supervise the local irrigation works, the grouping together of these two classes in central locations might alone have created cities. But in fact there also emerged a full-time priesthood, which united with the first two groups in forming cities. Needless to say, religion was not invented in Mesopotamia. Belief in supernatural forces must have existed millennia earlier among the Neanderthals, who buried their dead with provisions, and among Ice-Age cave peoples, whose art apparently was meant to work magic. What was new in Mesopotamia was the emergence of a full-time priesthood—people attached to centers of ritual practice, temples—whose performance of incantations and rites was supported by the agricultural labors of others.

Priests as members of the ruling elite

Why a priestly caste first arose in Mesopotamia is a speculative question, but it seems likely that by about 3500 B.C. economic demands and social complexity there were becoming so great that people in effect needed priests. Wandering bands had no difficulty in maintaining social cohesiveness because there was little or no private property to fight over, because occupational functions were more or less equal, and because the bands were small enough in size—customarily numbering no more than 500 persons—for band members to feel united by mutual familiarity. But such conditions started changing in villages. There, communal labor and distribution were still the rule, but inequalities in possessions would have become more pronounced over time, especially with the development of trade, and the growth of village populations from the hundreds to the thousands would have made it harder for people to recognize each other on, so to speak, a first-name basis. Attacks from the outside probably provided the basis for sufficient social cohesiveness among villagers to keep them from fighting each other intensively, but during the stressful beginnings of irrigation in Mesopotamia still more cohesiveness would have been needed. On this admittedly speculative reconstruction, religion inspired people in large groups to feel loyal to a common cause and to work hard in the belief that their labors were serving the local gods. And religious dedication on this scale called for priests to propagate the faith and to preside over elaborate rituals in impressive temples.

Explanations for the emergence of a priestly caste

Discussing the origins of cities is really the same as discussing the origins of civilization, which may be defined as the stage in human organization when governmental, social, and economic institutions have developed sufficiently to manage (however imperfectly) the problems of order, security, and efficiency in a complex society. Around 3200 B.C. Mesopotamia was "civilized." That is, at least five cities existed, which all included among their inhabitants warrior-rulers, administrators, and priests, which all encompassed several monumental temples, and which all boasted in addition

Cities as the manifestation of civilization

elaborate private residences, communal workshops, public storage facilities, and large marketplaces. Rudimentary forms of record-keeping were being mastered, and writing was on its way. Herewith the story of civilizations in the West begins, and herewith we may begin following a story that is based on interpreting written evidence as well as archeological artifacts.

SELECTED READINGS

• *Items so designated are available in paperback editions.*

• Binford, Lewis, *In Pursuit of the Past: Decoding the Archaeological Record,* London, 1983. One of the world's most influential archeologists offers this highly readable and personalized description of how archeologists analyze artifacts scientifically in order to describe past social behavior and processes of change.
• De Waal Malefijt, Annemarie, *Religion and Culture: An Introduction to Anthropology of Religion,* New York, 1968. A straightforward account that reviews the ideas of leading modern social theorists in order to understand prehistoric and early religions and to locate common factors in religious practices and beliefs.
• Fagan, Brian, *Archaeology: A Brief Introduction,* 2nd ed., Boston, 1983. Defines the terminology and describes some of the basic methods of archeology. Clear and concise.
• ———, *People of the Earth,* 6th ed., Boston, 1989. The most accessible survey of all cultures without written records, ranging from the earliest humans to the Incas.
• Lamberg-Karlovsky, C. C., and J. Sabloff, *Ancient Civilizations: The Near East and Mesoamerica,* Menlo Park, Calif., 1979. A lucid discussion of how the earliest states were formed and of how the earliest civilizations became increasingly complex over time.
  Leakey, Richard E., *The Making of Mankind,* New York, 1981. The companion volume to a splendid BBC television series, lavishly illustrated. Leakey describes discoveries (including his own) concerning the earliest evolution of humanity and argues forcefully in favor of his belief that humans are not innately aggressive.
  Leroi-Gourhan, André, *The Art of Prehistoric Man in Western Europe,* London, 1968. Controversial in its symbolic interpretations of cave art, but rich in detailed information and abundantly illustrated with exquisite color photographs.
• Mauss, Marcel, *The Gift: Forms and Functions of Exchange in Archaic Societies,* New York, 1967. Originally written in 1927, this book offers enduring insights into the nature of social interaction between individuals and among groups.
• Pfeiffer, John, *The Emergence of Humankind,* 4th ed., New York, 1985. An up-to-date review of where the entire field of paleoanthropology stands, including dispassionate analyses of some of the field's thorniest problems and debates.
  Phillips, Patricia, *The Prehistory of Europe,* Bloomington, Ind., 1980. More addressed to presenting data than theories, yet crucial for understanding the evolution from Neanderthals to anatomically modern humans.
• Sandars, Nancy K., *Prehistoric Art in Europe,* rev. ed., Baltimore, 1985. A short survey contrasting with Leroi-Gourhan in its emphasis on the techniques of early art rather than on its allegedly symbolic meanings.
  Trump, D. H., *The Prehistory of the Mediterranean,* New Haven, Conn., 1980. Extends to the origins of classical civilization in Greece. Clear and concise.

Ancient Civilizations of Western Asia, Egypt, and the Aegean World

POLITICAL	ECONOMIC	
Supremacy of Sumerian cities in Mesopotamia, c. 3200–c. 2340	Development of wheeled transport in Mesopotamia, c. 3200	*3200 B.C*
Unification of Egypt; Archaic period, c. 3100–c. 2770		
Old Kingdom in Egypt, c. 2770–c. 2200		
Dominance of Akkadian Empire in Mesopotamia, 2334–c. 2200		
Sumerian revival, c. 2200–c. 2000		
Middle Kingdom in Egypt, c. 2050–1786		
Old Babylonian Empire in Mesopotamia, c. 2000–c. 1600	Extended commerce in Egypt and Crete, c. 2000	*2000 B.C.*
Height of Minoan civilization under leadership of Knossos, c. 2000–c. 1500	Horses introduced into western Asia, c. 2000	
Mycenaean civilization on mainland Greece, c. 1600–c. 1200		
Hittite Empire in Asia Minor, c. 1600–c. 1200		
New Kingdom in Egypt, c. 1560–1087		
Kassites overthrow Babylonians, c. 1550		
Mycenaean dominance on Crete, c. 1500–c. 1400		*1500 B.C.*
Destruction of Knossos and end of Minoan civilization, c. 1400	Increasing use of iron throughout western Asia, c. 1300–c. 1100	
Trojan War, c. 1250		
Hebrew occupation of Canaan, c. 1200–c. 1025		
Collapse of Mycenaean civilization in Greece, c. 1200–c. 1100		
Unified Hebrew monarchy under Saul, David, and Solomon, c. 1025–933		*1000 B.C.*
Kingdom of Israel, 933–722		
Kingdom of Judah, 933–586		
Height of Assyrian Empire, c. 750–612		
New Babylonian Empire, 612–539		
Nebuchadnezzar conquers Jerusalem, 586		*500 B.C.*
Conquest of Babylon by Persians, 539		
Conquest of Egypt by Persians, 525		

	RELIGIOUS	CULTURAL
3200 B.C.	Growth of anthropomorphic religion in Mesopotamia, c. 3000–c. 2000	Lunar calendar in Mesopotamia, c. 3200 Sumerian cuneiform writing, c. 3200 Sumerian temple architecture, c. 3200–c. 2000 Egyptian hieroglyphic writing, c. 3100 Construction of first pyramid in Egypt, c. 2770
2000 B.C.	Minoan worship of mother goddess, c. 2000 Growth of personal religion in Mesopotamia, c. 2000–c. 1600 Egyptian belief in personal immortality, c. 1800	Solar calendar in Egypt, c. 2000 Mathematical advances in Old Babylonia, c. 2000–c. 1800 Minoan art on Crete, c. 2000–c. 1500 *Gilgamesh* epic, c. 1900 Code of Hammurabi, c. 1790 Egyptian temple architecture, c. 1580–c. 1090
1500 B.C.	Religious revolution of Akhenaton, c. 1375 Moses unites Hebrews in worship of Yahweh, c. 1250	Development of alphabet by Phoenicians, c. 1400 Naturalistic art in Egypt under Akhenaton, c. 1375
1000 B.C.	Hebrew prophetic revolution, c. 750–c. 550	Astronomical observation and record-keeping by New Babylonians, c. 750–c. 400 Deuteronomic code, c. 600
500 B.C.	Eschatological phase of Hebrew religious development, c. 400 B.C.–70 C.E.	Hebrew Song of Songs, c. 450 Book of Job, c. 400

Chapter 2

MESOPOTAMIAN CIVILIZATION

In my school-days I learned the hidden treasure of writing. I solved complex mathematical reciprocals and products with no apparent solution. I read tables whose Sumerian is obscure and whose Akkadian is hard to construe. Then I advanced to the skills of archery and chariot-driving and mastered royal decorum.

—A tablet of Assurbanipal, King of Assyria, c. 650 B.C.

H istory begins in Sumer. Modern knowledge of the first 35,000 years of human life is based entirely on the archeological record, for until only a little more than 5,000 years ago humans left behind many things but no words. Around 3200 B.C., however, in a region of Mesopotamia known as Sumer, the earliest forms of writing were invented and "history began" in the sense that words were recorded that help current scholars understand what men and women were doing.

"First chapter of history"

Obviously the invention of writing alone would earn the ancient Mesopotamians a prominent place among the most inventive and influential peoples who ever contributed to the forward movement of humankind. But amazingly the peoples who inhabited Mesopotamia in the centuries between roughly 3200 and roughly 500 B.C. contributed much more. We sometimes forget that somebody had to have invented the wheel, but somebody did, and he or she was a Mesopotamian who lived around 3000 B.C. Somebody had to invent the calendar too, and somebody had to invent the mathematical functions of multiplication and division, and those persons also were ancient Mesopotamians. Aside from arriving at such inventions, the Mesopotamians were profound thinkers who pioneered in the life of the mind to such an extent that their innovations in theology, jurisprudence, astronomy, and narrative literature all became fundamental for subsequent developments in these areas of thought and expression. Assuredly the ancient Mesopotamians had their unattractive qualities; for example, their rulers were usually ruthless militarists, and their art often seems frigid or fierce. Nevertheless, the "first chapter of history," which the Mesopotamians wrote by their exploits and their documents,

A rich and diverse record of achievement

was surely one of the most important chapters in the entire book of human events.

1. ANCIENT SUMER: THE WORLD OF THE FIRST CITIES

The Sumerian era

Between 3500 and 3200 B.C., Mesopotamia, the land between the Tigris and Euphrates rivers, became the first civilized territory on the globe in the sense that its society and culture rested on the existence of cities. We may call the historical period that ensued, lasting from about 3200 B.C. to about 2000 B.C., the "Sumerian era" because the most advanced part of Mesopotamia was then its southernmost territory, Sumer, a region of mud flats, which was roughly the size of Massachusetts. During the first nine centuries of the Sumerian era no unified government existed in Sumer; instead, the region was dotted with numerous independent city-states, the most important of which were Uruk, Ur, and Lagash. Then, around 2320 B.C., all Sumer was conquered by a mighty warrior from Akkad, the part of Mesopotamia lying directly to the north. This warrior's birth name does

See color map facing page 45

ANCIENT MESOPOTAMIA

not survive, but we know that he took the title of "Sargon," which means "true king," and that contemporaries called him "Sargon the Great." Mesopotamian chronicles record that Sargon gained control of Sumer by winning thirty-four battles; when his victories finally brought him to "the lower sea" (the Persian Gulf), he washed his weapons in its waters to signify the end of struggle. For almost two centuries thereafter Sargon the Great's dynasty ruled an empire consisting of Akkad and Sumer. But around 2130 B.C. Sumer regained its independence and enjoyed a "revival" that lasted until roughly 2000 B.C., during which time most of the region was ruled by kings who resided in Ur.

Sumer's accomplishments were preponderantly influenced by its climate and geography. Although the soil between the southern Tigris and southern Euphrates was extremely fertile, irrigation was essential because there was almost no rainfall for eight months of each year and torrential spring showers came too late to water the main crops that had to be harvested in April. (The summer months were not productive in Sumer because temperatures then rose to a soil-parching 125°F.) As we have seen, collective work on irrigation projects demanded careful planning and assertive leadership, which in turn led to social stratification, professional specialization, and the emergence of cities. The situation in Sumer was further determined by the fact that southern Mesopotamia was entirely lacking in natural resources such as stone, minerals, and even trees. This meant that Sumer's inhabitants were forced to rely heavily on trade and to be very alert to any possible means of redressing economic imbalances to their advantage. In other words, the Sumerians had to subdue nature rather than live off its plenty.

One of the Sumerians' most remarkable inventions, which they perfected about the time the Sumerian era was opening (around 3200 B.C.), was wheeled transport. To appreciate how advanced this invention was from a comparative perspective, it should be noted that wheeled transport was unknown in Egypt until about 1700 B.C. and that wheels were unknown in the Western Hemisphere (except for Peruvian children's toys) until they were introduced by Europeans. Probably the first Sumerian to think of employing a circular device turning on an axis for purposes of conveyance had seen a potter's wheel, for as early as about 4000 B.C., wheels were used in pottery-making in Iran, from whence they entered Sumer about 500 years later. The process of extending the principle of the wheel from pottery-making to transport was by no means obvious: the Egyptians knew the potter's wheel by at least 2700 B.C., but they did not use the wheel for transport until a millennium later, and even then they probably did not "reinvent the wheel" but learned of it from contacts with Mesopotamia. Thus the unknown Sumerian who first attached wheels to a sledge to make a better transportation vehicle really does have to be counted among the greatest technological geniuses of all time.

The earliest Sumerian wheeled vehicles were two-wheeled chariots and four-wheeled carts. Both were drawn by oxen (horses were unknown in western Asia until they were introduced by Eastern invaders sometime be-

Sargon the Great. A bronze head thought to depict the mighty warrior who united Akkad and Sumer.

An Akkadian Soldier Leads Away Sumerian Captives. A fragment of a victory monument probably dating from the time of Sargon.

Sumerian War Chariots. The earliest known representation of the wheel, dating from about 2600 B.C., shows how wheels were carpentered together from slabs of wood. (For a later Mesopotamian wheel with spokes, see the illustration on p. 44.) One can also observe that at the dawn of recorded history, military aims stimulated technological innovation as they have ever since.

tween 2000 and 1700 B.C.), and both were mounted on wheels that were solid, not spoked: two or three slabs of wood were shaped into a circle and *Wheeled transport* fastened together with studs or braces. Ox-drawn chariots obviously did not move very quickly, yet they appear to have contributed to an advance in phalanx warfare, for surviving illustrations dating from about 2600 B.C. depict them trampling the enemy. Carts meant for hauling freight had less need for speed and must have aided the Sumerians immeasurably in their numerous irrigation and urban building projects.

Along with the wheel, the Sumerians devised another of humanity's most crucial early inventions, the lunar (moon) calendar. In a perilous climate *Lunar calendar* such as that of Mesopotamia it was absolutely essential to begin planting or harvesting at exactly the proper time; thus it was necessary to find some reliable way of marking the passage of days until the proper times for agricultural work came around. The simplest way of doing this was to utilize the cycles of the moon. Since the moon moves from the thinnest crescent back to the thinnest crescent over the course of twenty-nine and a half days, one could consider the completion of such a cycle to be a basic timekeeping unit (we would call it a month), and then count those units until the seasons themselves had made a complete revolution. Hence the Sumerians concluded that when the moon had passed through twelve such units (half assigned twenty-nine days and half thirty), a "year" had passed and it was time to start planting again. Unfortunately they did not know that a "year" is really determined by the completion of the earth's rotation around the sun and that twelve lunar cycles or months fall eleven days short of the solar year. Over the centuries they learned that they had to add a month to their calendars every few years in order to predict the recurrence of the seasons with sufficient accuracy. The Sumerian lunar reckonings were the first known human steps in the direction of what we now understand to be exact, predictive science (the measuring of nature toward the goal of fathoming its "rules of operation"). The fact that the lunar calendar itself is indeed usable if days are added from time to time is confirmed by the modern Jewish and Islamic calendars, both of which are based on lunar cycles that the Jews and Muslims inherited from ancient Mesopotamia.

Ranking together with the wheel and the calendar as one of Sumer's three most precious gifts to succeeding Western civilizations was the invention of writing. To say that writing was "invented" is slightly misleading inasmuch as the emergence of writing in Sumer was gradual, evolving over the course of a millennium (c. 3500 to c. 2500 B.C.) from the representation of ideas by means of pictorial conventions to writing (albeit not alphabetic writing) as we currently know it. Around 3500 B.C. Sumerians had begun to carve pictures in stone or to stamp them on clay as ownership marks: a picture might have stood for a person's nickname (perhaps a rock for "Rocky") or dwelling (a house by a tree). Some five centuries later the evolution toward writing had advanced vastly farther. By then Sumerian temple administrators were using many standardized schematic pictures in combination with each other to preserve records of temple property and business transactions. Although the script of this period was still pictographic, it had advanced beyond pictures standing for people and tangible things to pictures standing for abstractions: a bowl meant any kind of food and a head with a bowl conveyed the concept of eating. After five more centuries full–fledged writing had taken over, for by then the original pictures had become so schematized that they were no longer recognizable as pictures but had to be learned purely as signs, and many of these signs no longer represented specific words but had become symbols of syllables that turned into words when combined with other such signs.

Development of writing

The writing system that reached its fully developed form in Sumer around 2500 B.C. is known as *cuneiform* because it was based on wedge-shaped characters (*cuneus* is Latin for wedge) impressed on wet clay by a reed stylus with a triangular point. In total there were about 500 cuneiform characters, and many of these had multiple meanings (the "right one"

Cuneiform

Early Pictorial Writing. On the left, Mesopotamian carvings on a piece of shale, dating from about 3400 B.C., depict two men engaged in a business deal, with pictographs around them specifying what they were trading. On the right a carving from about 3200 B.C. recording a commercial transaction. The signs above stand for "fifty-four" and those below for cow: thus "fifty-four cows."

Cuneiform Writing. On the left, a Sumerian clay tablet from about 3000 B.C. Here standardized pictures were beginning to represent abstractions. On the right, carvings on limestone from about 2600 B.C. The evolution of standardized cuneiform writing is now complete: the inscription proclaims that a king of Ur has built a temple.

could only be identified in context), making the system much more difficult to learn than subsequent writing systems based on alphabets. Nonetheless, cuneiform served well enough to be used as the sole writing system of Mesopotamia for two millennia and even to become the standard medium of commercial transactions throughout most of western Asia until about 500 B.C.

Sumerian literature

All the cuneiform texts surviving from the Sumerian era were copied on clay tablets that have been excavated in modern times. Of these about 90 percent are business or administrative records, but the other 10 percent fall roughly into the category of literature—specifically, dialogues, proverbs, hymns, and fragments of mythic tales. The Sumerian dialogue was a genre in which two characters would argue opposing sides in debates—summer vs. winter, axe vs. plow, or farmer vs. shepherd. Since both sides had much to recommend them, there was usually no winner; rather, the genre seems to have been devised for teaching purposes, to help students in temple schools learn as much about a given subject as there was to know. The surviving proverbs, on the other hand, advanced firm opinions. A charming example of a worldly Sumerian proverb is "where servants are, there is quarrel; where cosmeticians are, there is slander"; from this we see that the gossipy hairdresser has been known to human civilization since the dawn of history.

Evolution of Sumerian religion

Hymns and mythic tales surviving on Sumerian clay tablets (supplemented by Sumerian texts copied by later Mesopotamians) show that assumptions concerning the gods underwent a process of steady evolution during the Sumerian era. For purposes of simplicity we may note two main phases: a shift from viewing the gods as being part of nature to imagining them acting like humans, and then a shift from assigning to the gods the attributes of humans to imagining them acting like omnipotent rulers. The oldest evidence reveals that the Sumerians originally worshiped disembodied natural forces. One "god" was the force that grew the grain, another the force of the rising sap, another the power that preserved food in storehouses. During the course of the third millennium (the time from 3000 to 2000 B.C.), however, it became easier for the Sumerians to interpret natural occurrences on the basis of anthropomorphic (human) analogies. Thus the torrid summer came to be understood as the annual "death" of the fertility god and the bringing of the harvest to the storehouse the "marriage" of the fertility god to the goddess of storage. Whether the gods were forces in nature or anthropomorphic entities, the purpose of worshiping them was to bring plenty and ward off natural disasters. But toward the end of the third millennium, after Sargon the Great's conquest of Sumer had introduced a period of national rivalries, some of Sumer's anthropomorphic gods inevitably began to assume political characteristics. Some gods were thought of as patron gods of cities, others as rulers of various spheres (such as the sky, the earth, or the underworld), and one, Enlil, was understood to be the ruler of all these rulers. These developments led ever more to notions of divine unity and divine omnipotence.

However the gods were conceived, Sumerian temples loomed mightily over Sumerian society throughout the period from 3200 to 2000 B.C. The temples literally dominated both the cities and the entire flat Sumerian skyline because they were built on huge platforms intended solely to lend them height. All were constructed out of slabs and bricks made from sundried clay because stone and wood were unavailable, and most were built in the form known as the *ziggurat,* a terraced (stepped) tower topped by a shrine. So massive was the typical Sumerian temple and so arduous the work necessary for building it, that according to modern estimates 1,500

Dominating presence of the ziggurat

Sumerian Praying Figures. The statues dating from about 2700 B.C. show Sumerians praying for the gods to bring them prosperity.

Sumerian Ziggurat. This edifice, built in Ur around 2100 B.C., is the best-preserved surviving ziggurat. As can be seen from the diagram of its original form, a shrine, reached by climbing four stories and passing through a massive portal, was the goal of the worshiper's ascent and the most sacred part of the temple.

laborers would have had to work on one for ten hours a day uninterruptedly for five years before it was finished. (Moreover, mud-brick edifices, once built, required constant large-scale repair, so building must have been nearly continuous.) Yet apparently such work was accomplished primarily in shifts by volunteers, as acts of devotion to the gods on whom all life was thought to depend.

Temple schools

Sumerian priests did not live in the temples themselves but rather in adjacent structures that were part of the temple precincts. Also dwelling within the precincts were temple administrators, craftsmen, and slaves. Since priests and administrators (the two terms may often have been synonymous) needed to learn cuneiform, temple precincts included schools for teaching it and other knowledge necessary for the priestly caste. These Sumerian schools were the earliest known schools in the history of human civilization.

The wide-ranging role of the temple

Invariably the temple complexes owned huge stretches of land outside the cities, for without the income provided by such agricultural holdings they could not have supported their vast enterprises. Usually the temple complexes also engaged in trade, selling the goods that were manufactured or stored within their precincts to buyers within their respective cities or shipping them for sale over long distances. Thus the temples were virtually "states within the state." Furthermore, before the time of Sargon they frequently were "the state" insofar as the priests of the Sumerian cities were often their cities' rulers. After the liberation from Sargon's dynasty secular kings customarily took over the rulership of Sumerian cities, but even then the king and his family would have intermarried with the families of the foremost priests.

Sumerian social structure

Aside from priests, kings, and prominent warriors (who would have been members of the families of priests and/or kings), Sumerian society knew three ranks: the "specialists" in the temple complexes, the free farmers, and the slaves. The specialists were administrators, merchants, and artisans, all of whom were reasonably well off but completely dependent on the priests. The free farmers seem to have been left with the worst land and often found it necessary to place themselves in financial debt to the temples in order to survive. As for the slaves, we know very little about them because their very existence was hardly noticed in the records, but it is virtually certain that their lives were supremely miserable.

2. OLD BABYLONIAN DEVELOPMENTS

Although the Sumerians achieved marvels in mastering their physical environment, an ecological problem that escaped their attention was the steady deterioration of their soil caused by mounting salt content, a process technically known as salinization. The irrigation of the dry soil of Sumer from the nearby rivers brought moisture, but it also brought salt, and the salt remained when the river water evaporated. On a year-by-year basis the quantities of salt thus introduced into Sumer's soil were insignificant, but on a century-by-century basis they became deleterious to its fertility. Study of surviving cuneiform tablets has shown that arable lands were becoming less productive in parts of Sumer by as early as 2350 B.C., a fact that may help to account for Sargon of Akkad's ability to conquer the whole region. Sumer was not yet so weak that it could not rise up to overthrow the Akkadians two centuries later, but by around 2000 B.C. the region was sinking into permanent economic eclipse. Unable to produce agricultural surpluses, Sumer's cities could no longer support their priests, administrators, and armies, and the area gradually yielded primacy in Mesopotamia to territories lying farther north.

Sumer's economic eclipse: Salinization

The Sumerian era of Mesopotamian history was followed by the Old Babylonian era, which lasted from about 2000 to about 1600 B.C. It must be emphasized that the first date is chosen arbitrarily, for nothing dramatic happened in the year 2000 to mark a break from one era to another. Indeed, not only was the transition from Sumerian to Old Babylonian dominance in Mesopotamia gradual, but even when the Old Babylonian era had come to its fullest flowering around 1770 B.C., its culture was not dramatically different from the Sumerian culture that had preceded it. Two criteria alone allow for drawing any sharp distinctions between Sumerians and Old Babylonians: geography and language. We have seen that the most prosperous and culturally advanced cities in Mesopotamia during the Sumerian era were those that lay farthest to the south; during the succeeding 400 years, on the other hand, the weight of civilization shifted northwards to Akkad, where for much of the time it became centered on the newly founded city of Babylon. In addition, unlike the Sumerians who had spoken a language unrelated to any other, the peoples who held sway in Mesopotamia during the Old Babylonian era spoke languages that belonged to the Semitic language group.

Gradual transition to Old Babylonian dominance

Semitic language peoples (today including Arabs, Israelis, and Ethiopians) trace their descent to a point of origin in the Arabian peninsula. Exactly why or when Semitic tribes headed toward Mesopotamia remains un-

Influx of Semitic language peoples

Hammurabi: King of Babylon and Lawgiver

Hammurabi—greatest Ammorite ruler

"Code of Hammurabi"

known. What is known is that Sargon the Great and his armies were Semites and that consequently Sumer had already undergone a period of Semitic dominance toward the end of the third millennium. The Sumerian revival occurring between 2130 and about 2000 B.C. had only been an interlude in this regard because even during that time other Semitic tribes were infiltrating Mesopotamia and taking over pockets of territory in Akkad and Sumer. Ultimately the most successful of these proved to be the Amorites, who advanced into Mesopotamia around 2000 B.C. and settled in parts of Akkad. Two and a half centuries later the Amorites conquered all of Sumer, at which point the Semitic dialect they spoke replaced Sumerian as the spoken and written language of Mesopotamia. Yet the very same Amorites adopted all other aspects of the Sumerian cultural inheritance.

Because the Amorites made the city of Babylon in Akkad the capital of their empire, they are commonly called the Babylonians, or, more often, the Old Babylonians, to distinguish them from the Chaldeans, who ruled Mesopotamia more than a millennium later. The founder of the Old Babylonian empire and unquestionably the greatest Amorite ruler was Hammurabi (1792–1750 B.C.)* At the time of his accession the Amorites were still no more than one of several warring powers in southern Mesopotamia, but in 1763 B.C. Hammurabi conquered all of Sumer, and by 1755 B.C. he had subdued all the rest of Mesopotamia to its northern extremes at the borders of Syria. As his victories mounted, Hammurabi called himself "King of Akkad and Sumer," and then "King of the Four Quarters of the World." Despite this magniloquence his empire was short-lived (political events in Mesopotamia after the reign of Hammurabi will be treated in the next section), but another of his chosen titles, "King of Justice," refers to the source of his lasting fame, for Hammurabi was the promulgator of the earliest well-preserved collection of laws surviving in the human record.

Scholars agree that the "Code of Hammurabi," a stone document containing 282 laws, was based on Sumerian legal principles with an admixture of Semitic innovations, but since they seldom agree as to which principles were Sumerian and which Semitic it is wisest to consider the entire text as being simply the fullest-known document recording "Mesopotamian jurisprudence." Before considering some of the code's main premises it must be said that it was devoid of the modern notion of "equality before the law." In the Code of Hammurabi slaves have no rights whatsoever and are subject to frightful mutilations for trivial offenses. Otherwise, two legal classes appear: "men," clearly understood to be aristocrats; and all others neither "men" nor slaves, whom the law treated poorly but to whom it offered some rights. Crimes of "men" against their nonslave inferiors were punished less severely than crimes of "men" against "men," and crimes of "men" against slaves were punished only to the extent that they resulted in "property damage" to a slave owner.

The two most famous principles underlying Hammurabi's code are "an eye for an eye" and "let the buyer beware." At first both seem dreadfully

---

* Here, and throughout, dates following a ruler's name refer to dates of reign.

primitive. In offering the recompense of exact retaliation ("if a man destroy the eye of another, his eye shall be destroyed"; "if a man breaks another's bone, his bone will be broken"), the code never considers whether the initial injury may have been accidental and is chillingly insistent on inflicting pain and humiliation. The "buyer beware" principle is less chilling but hardly seems like law. Why should the state announce in a legal code that the seller is free to get away with trickeries? Hammurabi's code becomes more intelligible only if we recognize that it aimed at different ends than modern jurisprudence. The Mesopotamians promulgated laws primarily to stop fights. Thus they thought—and by no means without reason—that a person tempted to act violently might refrain from such behavior if he remembered that whatever wound he inflicted on another would probably be inflicted upon himself. They clearly also thought that punishments would exercise a deterrent effect only if they were executed swiftly and without hope of mercy, a point of view that made it necessary for them to dismiss motive as irrelevant because investigating circumstances and motives would have taken time and opened the possibility that truly willful crimes might have gone unpunished if the criminal knew how to defend himself. As for the "buyer beware" principle, that too was meant to stop fights because a buyer knew that he had no rights and would be swiftly punished if he tried to assert any.

Having considered these practical dimensions of Mesopotamian jurisprudence, it must be added that Hammurabi's code was not entirely indifferent to the notion of justice. Although the insistence on exact retaliation is surely cruel, it is not entirely lacking in a concept of fairness inasmuch as "an eye for an eye" is surely fairer than a head for an eye or an eye for a fingernail. Secondly, abstract ethical principles are embedded in Hammurabi's code in certain instances. For example, since the Mesopotamians believed that children should be deferential to their parents, law 195 of the code stated: "if a son has struck his father, his hand shall be cut off." Finally, the state is called upon occasionally to provide social well-being rather than merely to judge and punish. The most elevated aspect of this "welfare state" dimension to the code appears in law 23, wherein it is announced that if a man is robbed and the robber cannot be found, "the city . . . in whose territory the robbery was committed shall make good to the victim his lost property." We have seen that Hammurabi did wish to be known as "King of Justice," and by the measures of his time he was entirely that; moreover, although Western concepts of justice were to develop greatly thereafter, most of the principles inherent in the Code of Hammurabi were to become points of departure for much of that future development.

Equal in fame to Hammurabi's code as a monument of Old Babylonian civilization is the poem known as the epic of *Gilgamesh*. Like the code, this work was also a Sumerian-Babylonian hybrid. Its hero, Gilgamesh, was a real historical figure—a Sumerian king who ruled around 2600 B.C.— whose exploits so excited the imagination of contemporaries that they began to tell fanciful stories about him. Retold over the centuries in the

Code of Hammurabi. The entire code of Hammurabi survives on an eight-foot column made of basalt. The top quarter of the column depicts the Babylonian king paying homage to the seated god of justice. Directly below one can make out the cuneiform inscriptions that comprise the law code's text.

Concepts of justice and social welfare

Old Babylonian literature: Epic of Gilgamesh

Sumerian tongue, the stories grew ever more fanciful until they became almost pure fiction. So entertaining were these stories that late in the third millennium the various Semitic conquerors of Sumer began to translate them into their own dialects. The surviving epic of *Gilgamesh* represents a late stage in this evolutionary process. Sometime around 1900 B.C. a Semitic speaker wove four or five of the Gilgamesh stories into a loosely structured "epic," and this version is the marvelous poem we know today.

The most remarkable qualities of the epic of *Gilgamesh* are its sheer poetic forcefulness and its startling secularity, for it recounts nothing but the adventures and aspirations of a human hero in a world governed by the inevitability of death. After engaging in mighty battles and amorous encounters Gilgamesh seeks the secret of immortality from an old man and his wife who had been saved by taking refuge in an ark when the gods had decided to destroy the world by a flood. The aged couple assure him that immortality is unobtainable, but they do disclose the location of a plant that at least will restore his lost youth. Unfortunately, after gaining this plant by heroic effort from the floor of the sea, Gilgamesh leaves it unguarded while asleep and a snake eats it. (According to the poem, this is why snakes gain new life every year when they shed their skins.) Thus the aspirant to immortality is finally forced to acknowledge that he should enjoy each day as it comes without worrying about the morrow: "Gilgamesh, whither art thou wandering?/ Life, which thou seekest, thou wilt never find,/ For when the gods created man, they let death be his share./ . . . . Gilgamesh, put on clean clothes, and wash thine head and bathe./ Gaze at the child that holdeth thine hand, /and let thy wife delight in thine embrace./ These things alone are men's concerns."

Despite these secular teachings, it would be a mistake to think that Old Babylonian culture was at all irreligious, for all Old Babylonians (the *Gilgamesh* poet included) assumed that the gods held omnipotent sway over humans. In fact since temples were just as dominant in Old Babylonian cities as they had been in Sumerian ones it is clear that religion was just as dominant as well. Moreover, surviving prayers show that the Old Babylonians had arrived at a hitherto unprecedented variety of religious commitment: personal religion. Although the gods of Sumer had "arisen out of nature" to act ever more like supremely powerful rulers, they remained gods of cities or nations rather than gods whom individual humans could address personally. Then, during the Old Babylonian period, it came to be assumed that in addition to the "political gods" who looked over human collectivities, there existed other deities who looked over the daily affairs of individual people, and that it was necessary to pray to these personal deities for personal success and forgiveness of misdeeds. For example, an Old Babylonian would plead to a goddess: "I have cried to thee as a suffering, distressed servant./ See me, O my lady; accept my prayers." The appearance of personal religion among the Old Babylonians is of particular interest to students of subsequent religious history because personal invocation to God and religious introspectiveness are basic features of the Judeo-Christian tradition. Additionally, the fact that individual Old Babylonians

Sumerian Bronze Figure. The inscription, which refers to the name of a king of Ur, allows a precise dating of 2112–2004 B.C.

were praying fervently to personal gods is noteworthy in its own terms because it shows that Old Babylonian culture was tolerating a certain degree of individualism within a society that was otherwise intent on conformism.

A final remarkable aspect of Old Babylonian culture lies in a very different area: mathematics. It is difficult to ascertain how far Old Babylonian accomplishments were indebted to Sumerian ones because the earliest records pertaining to the knowledge of mathematics in Mesopotamia are all Old Babylonian. Yet these display arithmetical and algebraic concepts that are so advanced that they must have been based on Sumerian foundations. As that may be, Old Babylonian temple scribes around 1800 B.C. were employing tables for multiplication and division, and also for calculating square roots, cube roots, reciprocals, and exponential functions. So impressive were these achievements that if only a single Old Babylonian mathematical tablet had survived it would still allow the conclusion that the Old Babylonians were the most accomplished arithmeticians in antiquity. (The Greeks were adept at geometry but not in mathematics of number.) A basic aspect of modern daily life that derives from Old Babylonian mathematical precedents is our division of the day into two sets of twelve hours, the hour into sixty minutes, and the minute into sixty seconds. When one stops to think of it, working with multiples of ten would be easier, but the Old Babylonians based their arithmetic on multiples of twelve (apparently because their most fundamental reckoning was that of twelve lunar cycles to a year), and all Western civilizations have adhered to Old Babylonian "duodecimal" time reckonings (those based on units of twelve) ever since.

Mathematics

3. THE KASSITE AND HITTITE INTERLUDE

Hammurabi's empire lasted only a century and a half after his death in 1750 B.C., and throughout that time the Old Babylonians continually faced local uprisings and foreign incursions until the rise of a second Mesopotamian-wide empire around 1300 B.C. One cause of Old Babylonian decline may have been the same process of salinization that earlier had ruined Sumer. This, however, was probably not a major influence because even though salinization might have injured the Old Babylonian economy to some degree, its effects would have been less pronounced than they had been earlier for three reasons: (1) the Old Babylonians had learned how to combat salt buildup by drainage techniques; (2) they had shifted to growing barley as their main crop rather than wheat, and barley was better able to grow in saline soil; and (3) they had learned how to conserve the fertility of their lands by leaving portions of them fallow in an annual rotation system. Thus it appears that lack of governing skills on the part of several of Hammurabi's successors, combined with some poor military judgments and inability to adjust to new fighting techniques, were the primary reasons for Old Babylon's rapid decline.

*Decline of the
Old Babylonian Empire*

The major new means of warfare employed by the enemies of the Old Babylonian Empire in the sixteenth century B.C. was swift chariot attack

Impact of light-chariot warfare

Mesopotamia's "dark age" under the Kassites

The Hittite Empire

made possible by the use of horses rather than oxen and by spoked wheels rather than wheels made from attached slabs. The peoples who first put light-chariot warfare to its best effect were the Kassites and the Hittites, both non-Semitic peoples who arrived in western Asia from the steppe lands east of the Caspian Sea toward the end of the third millennium. By the time of Hammurabi the Kassites had settled peacefully within parts of Mesopotamia, but soon after they began to war with the Old Babylonians and to take ever-greater portions of Mesopotamian territory by force. This process was nearly complete by 1600 B.C., but the last nail on the Old Babylonian coffin was not driven in by the Kassites, for descendants of Hammurabi still ruled in Babylon itself. Instead it was the Hittites, who, by a lightning raid from the north in 1595 B.C., demolished Babylon and thereby destroyed the last remnants of the Old Babylonian Empire.

Retiring northward as quickly as they came, the Hittites left the Mesopotamian field clear for Kassite domination, but the Kassites were unable to take full advantage of this opportunity, apparently because they lacked dynamic leadership as well as a binding sense of political or cultural identity. Consequently, Mesopotamia fell into a "dark age," lasting about three centuries, during which most of the south (Akkad and Sumer) was ruled by the Kassites, while the north was divided among warring Semitic and non-Semitic peoples. The period seems "dark" because if offered neither united rule nor cultural or intellectual advances. The Kassites were content to adopt the use of cuneiform and Sumerian/Babylonian administrative techniques, and even to worship the Sumerian/Babylonian gods, without introducing any noteworthy innovations, nor did their disunited neighbors in Mesopotamia's north make any noteworthy contributions to the history of civilization.

Consequently, historians' interest centers on the Hittites. Originating from the steppes of central Asia and speaking an Indo-European tongue (the Indo-European linguistic family includes Hindu, Persian, Greek, Latin, and all the Romance, Slavic, and Germanic languages of today), the Hittites had occupied most of Anatolia (modern-day Turkey) by 1600 B.C. and within the next two centuries extended their empire southward along the eastern Mediterranean to include Syria and Lebanon. Having destroyed Babylon in 1595 B.C., they immediately decided not to overextend their lines of communication by attempting to rule directly in Mesopotamia. (The Bible states accurately that Hittite rule extended "even unto the great river, the river Euphrates" [Joshua 1:4].) The Hittite Empire reached its geographical and economic peak between about 1450 and 1300 B.C., but in the thirteenth century B.C. the Hittites were placed on the defensive by invasions arising separately out of Egypt and northern Mesopotamia. In 1286 B.C. they staved off a mighty Egyptian onslaught into Syria, and later in the century they still were able to defend themselves against incursions from northern Mesopotamia launched by Semitic Assyrians. But exhaustion finally overcame them. In the years around 1185 B.C. successive waves of maritime attacks from the west (the exact origin of the "Sea Peoples" who

Hittite Sculpture. Perhaps the most highly conventionalized sculpture of the ancient world is found in Hittite reliefs.

briefly appeared in western Asia has not yet been securely identified) resulted in the utter destruction of the Hittites' power.

Although the Bible refers to the Hittites frequently, it does so always in passing (for example, Bathsheba's husband was "Uriah the Hittite"). Otherwise, virtually nothing was known about them until their Anatolian capital, Hattusas (meaning Hittite City), was excavated in 1907, bringing to light an archive of 20,000 clay tablets. In 1915 a Czech scholar, Bedrich Hrozny, deciphered the language of these tablets, announcing that it was Indo-European, and thereupon a rush of scholarly interest in the Hittites ensued. Unfortunately some of this scholarship was racially biased or ill informed and hence introduced some misconceptions about the Hittites, including the notion that they were great because they were Indo-Europeans. This is a mistake on two counts, first because it assumes that all the Hittites belonged to an Indo-European race, and second because it assumes that all members of the Indo-European race possess superior intelligence. While a homogeneous tribe of Indo-European-speaking Hittites may once have migrated from central Asia into Anatolia, as soon as its members settled down they intermingled with native peoples so thoroughly that whatever "racial purity" they once may have had became completely lost. (The same would have been true of the Semitic tribes that settled in Mesopotamia.) In any case, biology demonstrates that there is no correspondence between intelligence and race. Another myth about the Hittites is that they owed their long-term success to monopolizing a secret weapon, the manufacture of iron, which they zealously kept beyond the ken of foreigners for centuries. Strange as it may seem, this belief rests on the misreading of a single Hittite document. The truth of the matter is that the Hittites did start making and using iron in the fourteenth century B.C., but so did all their contemporaries; so far as is known, the use of iron weaponry did not give any western Asian nation an advantage over any other.

Misconceptions concerning the Hittites

If the Hittites were not supremely smart or supremely well armed, how can one explain their might? Part of the answer lies in the resources that lay at their disposal, for Anatolia, in contrast to Mesopotamia, was rich in metallic ores, especially those of copper, iron, and silver. Dwelling at the source of such metals, the Hittites could trade some of them advantageously in their raw state, and they also were well positioned to experiment in metallurgy, hence excelling first in bronze and then in iron manufacture. Although the manufacture of iron did not give the Hittites any exclusive military advantage, it did bring them wealth because iron was as useful in peace as in war (it was particularly useful for making or reinforcing agricultural implements), and because in the earliest years of iron production (from roughly 1400 to roughly 1200 B.C.) anything made from iron had great prestige value. Accordingly, the Hittites grew rich from trade in a way that would have been impossible had they inhabited another region. To this must be added the fact that they devised an efficient governmental system, whereby a "Great King" theoretically ruled supreme but actually delegated much authority to regional representatives. Aside from their metallurgy and their law, the Hittites were not particularly given to experimentation; they adopted cuneiform from the Mesopotamians, their art was conventional, and they seem to have had no independent literature. Nonetheless, endowed with sufficient wealth and governmental skill, the Hittites were able to preserve their empire and their national identity longer than was typical in the ebb and flow of western Asian peoples and kingdoms.

4. THE MIGHT OF THE ASSYRIANS

Returning to the narrative of events in Mesopotamia, we find that the Kassite "dark age" was succeeded by the period of the Assyrian Empire, which lasted from roughly 1300 B.C. until exactly 612 B.C. The Assyrians were a people of the Semitic language group, who around 3000 B.C. had settled on the Tigris in northernmost Mesopotamia, where they established a small state centered on their city of Assur. This state was never threatened by salinization problems because the northern Tigris region, being hilly and of a more temperate climate than southern Mesopotamia, needed no irrigation. Yet the Assyrians made no mark on history until the opening of the thirteenth century B.C. when they came to acquire skills in chariot warfare and began to conquer neighboring cities. By around 1250 B.C. they had become masters of the entire Mesopotamian north, and soon after they dedicated themselves to subduing the Kassites in Akkad and Sumer. Since the Kassite kingdom was moribund, they had no trouble making such conquests either. In 1225 B.C. the Assyrian monarch Tukulti-Ninurta took Babylon and ordered his scribes to record: "I captured Babylon's king and trod his proud neck as if it were a footstool. . . . Thus I became lord of all Sumer and Akkad and fixed the boundary of my realm at the Lower Sea."

Assyrian Winged Human-Headed Bull. This relief was found in the palace of King Sargon II (722–705 B.C.). It measures 16 feet wide by 16 feet high and weighs approximately 40 tons.

Direct Assyrian rule over Sumer and Akkad lasted for only eight years because the Assyrians did not have the resources to maintain a costly occupation of a region whose inhabitants resented their rule. Yet they did succeed in maintaining indirect overlordship over southern Mesopotamia for six centuries after Tukulti-Ninurta trod over his enemy, preserving their trading interests in the region and making sure that no political counterweights would rise to challenge them. Shortly after 900 B.C., moreover, the Assyrians began to expand in other directions, apparently seeking control over natural resources and access to trade routes. In the first half of the ninth century they conquered Syria and reached the Mediterranean, and around 840 B.C. they annexed southeastern Anatolia. Temporary internal political divisions kept them from advancing immediately any farther, but one hundred years later they were on the march again until conquests culminating in the reign of Sennacherib (705–681 B.C.) made them masters of almost all the inhabitable territory of western Asia.

Masters of western Asia under Sennacherib

Sennacherib's reign displays the Assyrians at their most magnificent and their most frightful. To seal his military victories Sennacherib built a splendid new capital, Nineveh, on the banks of the upper Tigris. No city remotely so splendid had ever been seen in Mesopotamia before. Within walls whose circumference was seven and a half miles lay magnificent temples and a royal palace with at least seventy-one chambers. Outside the walls were orchards and zoos with rare trees and exotic animals that Sennacherib ordered to be brought from great distances. Dissatisfied with the quality of the local water supply, the mighty king supervised an extraordi-

The splendor of Nineveh

nary engineering project whereby water was led to Nineveh by channels and aqueducts from fresh mountain springs fifty miles distant. To commemorate the successful completion of the project, rock carvings at the source depicted the gods flanked by inscriptions listing all of Sennacherib's military victories.

Derivative nature of Assyrian culture

Among the chambers in Sennacherib's palace at Nineveh was a library of clay tablets amounting to a vast repository of practical knowledge and religious lore. This knowledge came from southern Mesopotamia, for the Assyrians were entirely in the debt of ancient Sumer and Old Babylonia when it came to the life of the mind. Intent on gaining whatever practical knowledge they could for the sake of administration and commerce, and willing to worship all of Old Babylonia's gods (along with "Assur" the Assyrians' own local deity), the Assyrians began carrying off cuneiform tablets from Babylon as early as their sack of that city in 1225 B.C. Hence when Sennacherib's learned successor Assurbanipal (668–627 B.C.) rounded out the holdings of the library at Nineveh, it contained virtually the entire available store of Sumerian and Old Babylonian learning and literature.

Assyrian frightfulness

A traveler through Nineveh in the seventh century B.C. would thus have concluded that the Assyrian Empire's ruling class was not only mighty but technologically proficient and very cultivated in certain respects. On the other hand, he would have seen ample evidence of what history has taken to be the Assyrians' most distinctive trait, their "frightfulness." To be fair to the Assyrians, frightfulness was no more characteristic of their culture than it was of any other until the time of Sennacherib. Although frightfulness implies a culture's unrelenting emphasis on the virtues of brutal masculinity ("machismo"), it was the Assyrians, rather than any other Mesopotamian people, who once accepted the rule of a queen, Sammuramat (known to the Greeks and later Europeans as Semiramis). Indeed, her reign from 810

Assyrian Relief Sculptures. These panels, representative of Assyrian "frightfulness," depict the Emperor Assurbanipal on the hunt.

Cave Paintings from Lascaux. Made with charcoal outlines and rich earth colors, these paintings have maintained their haunting vividness for some 15,000 years. (Ralph Morse/Life Picture Service)

Bronze Stag. A statuette combining naturalistic and stylized qualities, dating from about 2300 B.C. Found in Asia Minor.

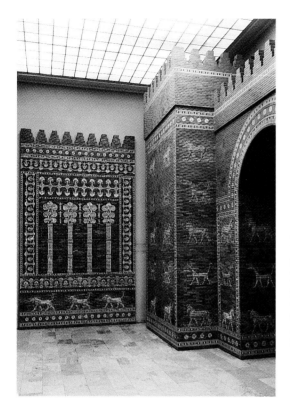

Reconstruction of the Ishtar Gate. Visitors to the Near Eastern Museum in Berlin can see this impressive reconstruction of the gate built in Babylon by King Nebuchadnezzar around 575 B.C. rising to a height of fifty feet. About half of the reconstruction is original.

Lion from Ishtar Gate. One of the many fierce animals striding Nebuchadnezzar's "wonder of the world."

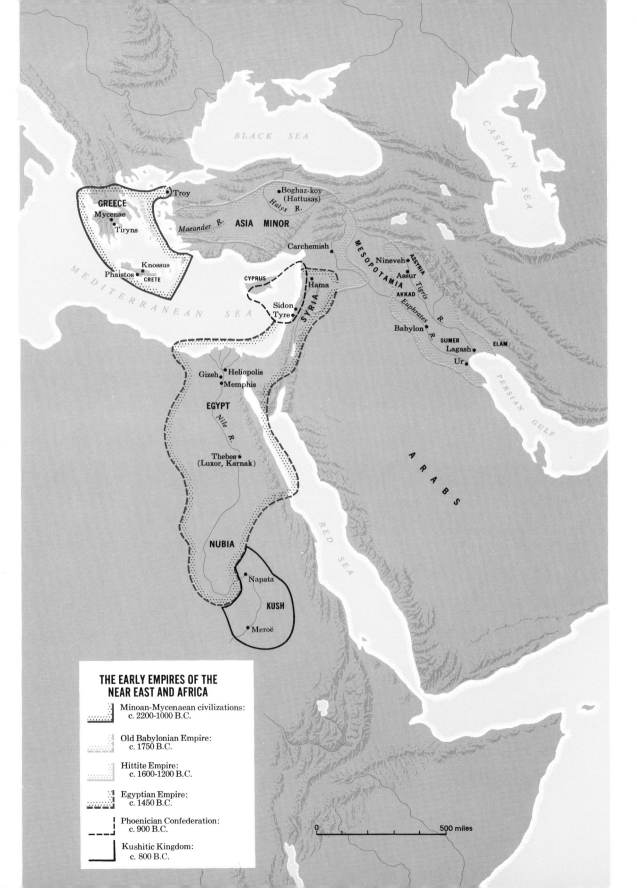

BLACK SEA

CASPIAN SEA

Troy
•Boghaz-koy
(Hattusas)
Halys R.

GREECE
•Mycenae
Tiryns

ASIA MINOR
Maeander R.

Carchemish

Nineveh
ASSYRIA
Assur
Tigris R.
MESOPOTAMIA

•Knossus
Phaistos
CRETE

CYPRUS

Hama
Sidon
Tyre
SYRIA

AKKAD

Euphrates R.

Babylon

SUMER
Lagash
Ur

ELAM

MEDITERRANEAN SEA

PERSIAN GULF

•Gizeh •Heliopolis
•Memphis

EGYPT

Nile R.

ARABS

Thebes •
(Luxor, Karnak)

RED SEA

NUBIA

•Napata

KUSH

•Meroë

THE EARLY EMPIRES OF THE NEAR EAST AND AFRICA

Minoan-Mycenaean civilizations:
c. 2200-1000 B.C.

Old Babylonian Empire:
c. 1750 B.C.

Hittite Empire:
c. 1600-1200 B.C.

Egyptian Empire:
c. 1450 B.C.

Phoenician Confederation:
c. 900 B.C.

Kushitic Kingdom:
c. 800 B.C.

0   500 miles

to 805 B.C. seemed so extraordinary to other peoples that it became the subject of legend.

Beginning with the reign of Sennacherib, however, the Assyrians began to display traits of extraordinary brutality in both their artwork and their actual policies. In the sculptured reliefs that adorned Nineveh, they cele- *Brutality in art and policy* brated war and slaughter. Scenes of lion hunting were their favorites: men with the coolest bravery yet also the coolest cruelty are shown hunting leaping lions, with special attention being paid to the death agonies of wounded beasts. Meanwhile the Assyrians were slaughtering humans just as pitilessly. One of Sennacherib's military exploits was the quelling in 689 B.C. of a revolt against Assyrian hegemony in Babylon. Once he accom- plished this he commanded his troops to pillage and destroy with the ut- most thoroughness, thereupon boasting in an inscription: "I made Baby- lon's destruction more complete than that by a flood. . . . I demolished it with torrents of water and made it like a meadow."

The Assyrian policy of frightfulness in military campaigns was meant above all to strike abject terror into the hearts of the nation's enemies. No doubt it did this, but it also succeeded in making the Assyrians more in- *Uprisings against Assyrian* tensely hated than any western Asian conquerors had been until their time. *domination* Since the conquered peoples' hatred for the Assyrians often overcame their fear of them, uprisings against Assyrian domination flickered on and off throughout the seventh century B.C., with the most frequent center of re- sistance being the area around Babylon. Although Sennacherib had presided over Babylon's destruction in 689 B.C., his son undertook the city's rebuilding for motives of prestige, and by 605 B.C. the city had once more become the focal point of southern Mesopotamian revolt. In order to quell the unrest, Sennacherib's grandson Assurbanipal laid siege to Babylon in that year and forced its surrender in 648 B.C., once more unleashing As- syrian frightfulness. As he proclaimed in one of the most inhumane ac- counts of methodical carnage ever recorded, "I tore out the tongues of many who plotted against me and then had them murdered. The others I smashed to death with the statues of their local gods. . . . Then I fed their corpses, cut into small pieces, to the dogs, to the pigs, to the vultures, and to all the birds of the sky."

One might have thought that the southern Mesopotamians would have remained submissive for a long time after that, but in fact they continued to seek any possible opportunity to throw off the Assyrian yoke. In 614 *The Babylonian-Median* B.C. this opportunity finally came in the form of an alliance with an Indo- *vengeance* European tribe, the Medes, who had recently consolidated their power in Iran, directly to the east. Two years of warfare then were all it took to de- stroy the Assyrian Empire: in 612 B.C. Nineveh fell to a united Babylo- nian-Median force, was leveled, and unlike Babylon never rose again. The rejoicing of all the conquered nations is well reflected in the Old Testa- ment Book of Nahum: "Woe to the bloody city! . . . There is no end of their corpses, they stumble upon their corpses. . . . Nineveh is laid waste, and who will bemoan her?"

5. THE NEW BABYLONIAN REVIVAL

Throughout the century of southern Mesopotamian resistance to Assyrian domination, the peoples most prominently engaged in that resistance were Semitic speakers called Chaldeans (pronounced Kaldeeans), who, with the Medes, laid waste to Nineveh. Since the Medes used their victory of 612 B.C. as a springboard for invading Anatolia, the Chaldeans were left as masters of all Mesopotamia, and since they located their capital in Babylon, they are usually referred to by historians as the New Babylonians. The most famous New Babylonian ruler was Nebuchadnezzar (604–562 B.C.), who conquered Jerusalem, transported large numbers of Judeans to Babylon, and made his empire the foremost power in western Asia. Soon after his death New Babylonian might was challenged by an Indo-European people from Iran, the Persians (closely allied and ultimately intermingled with the Medes, giving rise to the historians' joke that "one man's Mede is another man's Persian"). In 539 B.C. one of Nebuchadnezzar's successors, Belshazzar, failed to understand "the handwriting on the wall" (Daniel 5), and before he knew it the Persians had rushed into Mesopotamia so quickly that Babylon fell to them without a fight.

The city of Babylon during the era of the New Babylonians is the Babylon best known to us today, partly because of familiarity brought by early twentieth-century excavations and partly because of surviving eyewitness Greek travelers' descriptions. Babylon's size alone during this period was astounding, for it extended to 2100 acres, in comparison to the 1850 acres of Sennacherib's Nineveh and the 135 acres of the typical Sumerian city. (One of Western Europe's largest cities, Paris, had only about twice Babylon's acreage until the early twentieth century, when it began to succumb to modern "urban sprawl.") More astounding still was Babylon's color, for the New Babylonians had learned to build their major monuments in brightly colored glazed brick. The most famous example, so splendid that it was counted by the ancient Greeks as one of the "seven wonders of the world," was the city wall built by Nebuchadnezzar. Against a background of brilliant blue, lions, bulls, and dragons in shades of white and yellow promenaded the entire length of the wall and strutted in tiers along the entire height of the "Ishtar Gate" (so called because the gate was dedicated to the goddess Ishtar). German archeologists digging in the ruins of Babylon in 1902 were the first since ancient times to see this marvel, and they must have felt as thrilled as if they had discovered the Pacific. Had Nebuchadnezzar built no more than this, his fame as one of history's most magnificent builders would have been secure, but he also constructed another of the "seven ancient wonders": Babylon's "Hanging Gardens." This feat was so extraordinary that truth about it merges into legend. Apparently Nebuchadnezzar really did build ascending terraces of gardens from the Eu-

Unearthing of the Ishtar Gate. The photograph, dating from 1902, records one of the most exciting moments in the history of archeology. For the reconstruction of the gate in the Near Eastern Museum in Berlin, see color plates following p. 44.

phrates outward, each with splendid plants and trees, but it may be legendary that he did this to gratify his wife, a Median princess from Iran, who loathed southern Mesopotamia's flatness and longed for her homeland's rolling hills.

Aside from construction feats, New Babylonia's cultural accomplishments were greatest in the realm of astronomy. We have seen that in the earliest Sumerian times Mesopotamian peoples had observed the phases of the moon in order to make predictions about the recurrence of the seasons. Two thousand years later Mesopotamians were still carefully studying the night skies, but now they were concentrating on the movements of the planets and the stars because they had come to believe that some of their gods resided in the heavens and that by plotting and predicting the motions of the planets and stars they could predict which divinity was gaining power and how that might affect the course of human affairs. Such study of the heavens was brought to its perfection by the New Babylonians, who identified five "wandering stars" (we would say planets) and linked them with the powers of five different gods. (If this sounds strange, we should remember that we still call the first five planets by the names of five Roman gods—Mercury, Venus, Mars, Jupiter, and Saturn—because the Greeks and Romans inherited this system.) Going further, the New Babylonians concluded that when a given planet appeared in a particular part of the night sky or in close proximity to another planet its movement would portend war or famine, or the victory of one nation over another. Fully developed, these systems amounted to what we would call astrology, although New Babylonian astrology concerned itself exclusively with predictions about cosmic events such as floods and famines and the fortunes of nations rather than the fortunes of individual people. (The Greeks and Romans took the next step of casting personal horoscopes dependent on the configuration of the skies at the time of a person's birth.)

Today it is recognized that all astrology is superstition, but the New Babylonians' search for correspondences between heavenly events and earthly ones was scientific in terms of their time. In other words, for humans to believe that they can measure and interpret their universe and thereby learn how to benefit from it is more scientific than cowering in ceaseless fear of inexplicable mysteries. Moreover, dedicated to this belief, the New Babylonians observed celestial phenomena more closely than any other ancient peoples before them, and recorded their observations so meticulously that they later could be used and supplemented by astronomers of other civilizations. Most notably, starting in 747 B.C. Chaldean court astronomers kept "diaries" on a monthly basis in which they recorded all planetary movements and eclipses, together with reports of earthly affairs such as price changes, shifting river levels, storms, and temperatures. Continued without interruption until Greek scientists gained knowledge of them, these records became a direct point of departure for astronomical science in the Greco-Roman world.

6. THE MESOPOTAMIAN LEGACY

Babylon fades into obscurity

The Hanging Gardens of Babylon are no more. Although the city of Babylon was not damaged when it was taken by the Persians in 539 B.C., the Persian conquest marked the end of Mesopotamian civilization insofar as native peoples and dynasties would never rule in Mesopotamia again. Gradually, as Greeks replaced Persians, Romans replaced Greeks, and Arabs replaced Romans, cuneiform ceased to be used, foreign artistic and building styles were introduced, and the old cities fell into ruins, to be supplanted by new ones. (The most magnificent city to arise in the Tigris-Euphrates region after the decay of Babylon was Baghdad, founded by the Arabs.) Entirely abandoned two centuries after the birth of Christ, Babylon became so covered up by the nearby shifting waters and sands that nobody knew for sure where it was until excavations accomplished shortly after 1900.

Influence on the Hebrews

Yet the Mesopotamian legacy endures in different ways. One is by means of the Hebrew Bible. Since the earliest Hebrew peoples dwelled somewhere in Mesopotamia before they migrated to Palestine and since they spoke a language closely related to that of the Old Babylonians, it is not surprising that the earliest chapters of the Bible often allude to Mesopotamia. According to the book of Genesis King Nimrod ruled "Babel (Babylon), Erech (Uruk), and Akkad," and Abraham came to Palestine from "Ur of the Chaldees"; the "Tower of Babel," built out of "brick for stone and slime for mortar" (Genesis 11:1–9), is surely a reference to an Old Babylonian ziggurat. Ancient Hebrew and Mesopotamian points of contact are further displayed by the appearance in the *Gilgamesh* epic of a flood story very similar to the ark narrative in Genesis: not only is a human couple saved in both by floating in an ark, but they learn in both of the waters' ebbing when a bird they send forth no longer returns. More noteworthy still is the fact that fundamental Hebrew religious concepts bear relationships to ancient Mesopotamian ones. This is to not say that the Hebrews were unoriginal in their theology. Quite to the contrary, the Hebrews were the most original religious thinkers in the ancient world. Yet Old Testament theological formulations emerged from an ancient Mesopotamian matrix, and specific Hebrew religious innovations may well have been adaptations of Mesopotamian precedents. By the time of Sennacherib and Nebuchadnezzar, the Hebrews came to hate the Assyrians and Babylonians because those peoples were constantly attacking them, and thereafter the invectives of the Hebrew prophets were passed on so effectively to Christians that the name Babylon even today remains a term for the essence of sinfulness. But the insults should not be allowed to obscure the kinships and the debts.

There is also the technological and intellectual legacy of Mesopotamia. We have seen that the wheel was first used for transportation in ancient Sumer, that the earliest known writing appeared there, and that the Old

Babylonians pioneered in mathematical functions such as square and cube roots. Scholars find it difficult to determine whether all of these early Mesopotamian inventions were transmitted to other peoples by diffusion or whether some (writing above all) were invented independently elsewhere. In either case, however, the Mesopotamian inventions led step by step to modern practices taken for granted in Europe and America today. Mesopotamian jurisprudence and natural science similarly stand behind much that we today customarily take for granted. The visual world around us looks entirely different from that of ancient Mesopotamia because we have borrowed next to nothing from ancient Mesopotamian art and architecture, yet in fundamental aspects of technology and thought we owe a great debt to the ingenious people of five thousand years ago who resolved to wrest power and glory from a land of mud flats.

Technological and intellectual legacy

SELECTED READINGS

• *Items so designated are available in paperback editions.*

Cambridge Ancient History (3rd ed., vols. I–II), Cambridge, 1971–1975.
• Frankfort, H., *The Art and Architecture of the Ancient Orient,* rev. ed., Baltimore, 1970.
• Gurney, O. R., *The Hittites,* rev. ed., Baltimore, 1980. The standard survey in English.
• Jacobsen, T., *The Treasures of Darkness: A History of Mesopotamian Religion,* New Haven, 1976.
• Kramer, S. N., *Sumerian Mythology,* New York, 1961. Develops different point of view than that advanced by T. Jacobsen.
• ———, *The Sumerians: Their History, Culture and Character,* Chicago, 1963. The best general treatment of Sumerian civilization.
• Lloyd, Seton, *The Archaeology of Mesopotamia,* rev. ed., London, 1984. Technical, but clear and well illustrated.
   ———, *Foundations in the Dust,* rev. ed., London, 1980. Describes the development and accomplishments of Mesopotamian archeology.
   Macqueen, J. G., *The Hittites and Their Contemporaries in Asia Minor,* rev. ed., London, 1986. Topical coverage.
• Neugebauer, Otto, *The Exact Sciences in Antiquity,* 2nd ed., New York, 1969. Includes the basic account of Mesopotamian mathematical accomplishments.
• Oates, Joan, *Babylon,* rev. ed., London, 1986. A well-illustrated narrative that concentrates on Akkad from Sargon to the Persians and Greeks.
• Oppenheim, A. Leo, *Ancient Mesopotamia,* 2nd ed., Chicago, 1977. Concentrates on Babylonian and Assyrian culture.
   Saggs, H. W. F., *The Encounter with the Divine in Mesopotamia and Israel,* London, 1978.
   Woolley, Sir Leonard, and P. R. S. Moorey, *Ur "of the Chaldees,"* London, 1982. A revised account of Woolley's excavations at Ur which took place between 1922 and 1934.

SOURCE MATERIALS

- Epic of Gilgamesh, tr. N. K. Sandars, Baltimore, 1960.

  Grayson, A. K., and D. B. Redford, *Papyrus and Tablet,* Englewood Cliffs, N.J., 1973.

- Kramer, S. N., *History Begins at Sumer,* 3rd ed., Philadelphia, 1981.
- Pritchard, James B., *Ancient Near Eastern Texts Relating to the Old Testament,* 3rd ed., Princeton, 1969.

Chapter 3

EGYPTIAN CIVILIZATION

Thou makest the Nile in the Nether World,
Thou bringest it as thou desirest,
To preserve alive the people of Egypt.
For thou hast made them for thyself,
Thou lord of them all. . . .

—Hymn to Aton, from reign of the Pharaoh Akhenaton

Modern crowds that flood museums to view fabled treasures of Egyptian art are still captivated by the spell of one of the oldest and most alluring civilizations in history. Almost as old as the civilization founded in Mesopotamia during the fourth millennium B.C., Egyptian civilization provides a fascinating comparison to that of Mesopotamia because it was characterized by stability and serenity in contrast to the turmoil and tension of Mesopotamia. Not only were the Egyptians very peaceful for long periods of their ancient history, but surviving Egyptian statuary and painted human figures often seem to smile and bask in the sun as if they were on summer vacation.

Egypt compared to Mesopotamia

Environmental factors best explain the striking differences. Since the Mesopotamian climate was harsh, and since the Tigris and Euphrates flooded irregularly, the Mesopotamians could not view nature as dependably life-enhancing. Furthermore, since Mesopotamia, located on an open plain, was not geographically protected from foreign incursions, its inhabitants were necessarily on continual military alert. Egyptian civilization, on the other hand, was centered on the dependably life-enhancing Nile. Not only did the richly fertile soil of the Nile valley provide great agricultural wealth, but the Nile flooded regularly year after year during the summer months and always receded in time for a bountiful growing season, offering Egyptians the feeling that nature was predictable and benign. In addition, since the Nile valley was surrounded by deserts and the Red Sea, Egypt was comparatively free from threats of foreign invasion. The centrality of the Nile in ancient Egyptian life is well illustrated by the fact that the Egyptians had two words for travel: either *khed,* which meant "to go

Environmental basis of differences between Egypt and Mesopotamia

downstream," or *khent,* which meant "to go upstream." All in all, the Greek historian Herodotus surely had warrant to designate Egypt as "the gift of the river."

1. POLITICAL HISTORY UNDER THE PHARAOHS

Foundation of Egypt's advanced civilization

The ancient history of Egypt is usually divided into six eras: the archaic period (c. 3100-c. 2770 B.C.), the Old Kingdom (c. 2770-c. 2200 B.C.), the first intermediate period (c. 2200-c. 2050 B.C.), the Middle Kingdom (c. 2050–1786 B.C.), the second intermediate period (c. 1786-c. 1560 B.C.), and the New Kingdom (c. 1560–1087 B.C.). Even before the beginning of the archaic period, the Egyptians had taken some fundamental steps in the direction of creating an advanced civilization. Above all, they had begun to engage in settled farming; they had learned to use copper tools in addition to stone ones; and shortly before 3100 B.C., they had developed a system of writing known as *hieroglyphic* (Greek for "priestly carving"). Experts are uncertain whether the Egyptians arrived at the idea of writing on their own, or whether the idea came to them from Mesopotamia. The strongest argument for the former position is that the hieroglyphic system is very different from Mesopotamian cuneiform, but the sudden appearance of hieroglyphic suggests that certain Egyptian administrator-priests decided to work out a record-keeping system on the basis of their knowledge of a foreign precedent. Whatever the case, writing surely allowed for greater governmental efficiency and apparently was a precondition for the greatest event in ancient Egyptian political history, the unification of the north and the south.

Narmer Palette. Dating from about 3100 B.C., this stone carving shows a warrior-ruler from the south who was thought to be Narmer, subduing his counterpart from the north with a mace. The falcon probably represents the God Horus, who looks with approval on the birth of Egyptian unification in violence.

Egyptian unification, and therewith the beginning of the archaic period, occurred around 3100 B.C. Until then separate powers had ruled in Upper (or southern) Egypt, and Lower (or northern) Egypt, but unity was essential for Egypt's future because a single government was necessary to ensure the free flow of traffic along the entire length of the Nile, as well as to provide centralized direction of irrigation projects. Tradition attributes the unification of Egypt to a warrior from the south called Narmer, the first of the *pharaohs* (kings), who brought all of Egypt northward to the Mediterranean delta under his control. (Egyptian rulers are called "pharaohs" as the result of biblical usage, even though the ancient Egyptians themselves did not use this term.) It may be that the process was somewhat more gradual, but there is little doubt that for roughly four hundred years after about 3100 B.C. a succession of two ruling dynasties held sway over a united Egypt.

Zoser and the founding of the Old Kingdom

The first two Egyptian dynasties were succeeded around 2770 B.C. by the rule of the mighty Zoser, the first king of the Third Dynasty and the founder of the Old Kingdom. While the details of how the governmental system of the Old Kingdom differed from that of the archaic period will never be known, it is certain that Zoser's reign initiated a period of vastly greater state power and royal absolutism, best witnessed by the fact that

Zoser presided over the building of the first pyramid. Under Zoser and his leading successors of the Old Kingdom the power of the pharaoh was virtually unlimited. The pharaoh was considered to be the child of the sun god, and by custom married one of his sisters to keep the divine blood from becoming contaminated. No separation of religious and political life existed. The pharaoh's chief subordinates were priests, and he himself was the chief priest.

See color map facing page 45

The government of the Old Kingdom was founded upon a policy of peace. In this respect it was virtually unique among ancient states. The pharaoh had no standing army, nor was there anything that could be called a national militia. Each local area had its own militia, but militias were commanded by civil officials, and when called into active service generally devoted their energies to labor on the public works. In case of a threat of invasion the various local units were assembled at the call of the pharaoh and placed under the command of one of his civil subordinates. At no other time did the head of the government have a military force at his disposal. The Egyptians of the Old Kingdom were content for the most part to work out their own destinies and to let other nations alone. The reasons for this attitude lie in the protected position of their country, in their possession of land of inexhaustible fertility, and in the fact that their state was a product of cooperative need instead of being grounded in exploitation.

The nonmilitaristic character of the Old Kingdom

After centuries of peace and relative prosperity the Old Kingdom came to an end with the downfall of the Sixth Dynasty about 2200 B.C. Several causes were responsible. Governmental revenues became exhausted because the pharaohs invested heavily in such grandiose projects as pyramid-building. To make matters worse, overall Egyptian prosperity was adversely affected by climatic disasters that precipitated crop failures. In the meantime provincial nobles usurped more and more power until central authority virtually disappeared. The era that followed is called the first intermediate period. Anarchy now prevailed. The nobles created their own rival principalities, and political chaos was aggravated by internal brigandage and invasion by desert tribes. The first intermediate period did not end until the rise of the Eleventh Dynasty, which restored centralized rule around 2050 B.C. from its base in Thebes (Upper Egypt). The next great stage of Egyptian history, known as the Middle Kingdom, ensued.

End of the Old Kingdom

Throughout most of its life the government of the Middle Kingdom was more socially responsible than that of the Old Kingdom. Although the Eleventh Dynasty could not withstand the power of the nobles, the Twelfth, which followed around 1990 B.C., and which lasted until 1786 B.C., ruled strongly by means of an alliance with a middle class composed of officials, merchants, artisans, and farmers. This alliance kept the nobility in check and laid the foundations for unprecedented prosperity. During the rule of the Twelfth Dynasty there were advances in social justice and much intellectual achievement. Public works that benefited the whole population, such as extensive drainage and irrigation projects, replaced the building of pyramids, which had no practical use. There was also a democratization of religion, which extended to common people a hope for salvation

The Middle Kingdom

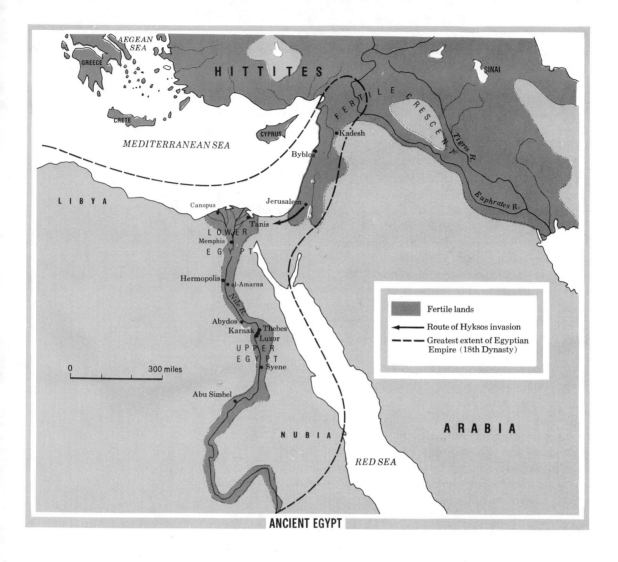

ANCIENT EGYPT

that they had not been granted before. Religion now emphasized proper moral conduct instead of ritual dependent on wealth. For all these reasons the reign of the Twelfth Dynasty is commonly considered to be Egypt's classical or golden age.

Immediately afterward, however, Egypt entered its second intermediate period. This was another era of internal chaos and foreign invasion lasting *The invasion of the Hyksos* for more than two centuries, or from 1786 to about 1560 B.C. The contemporary records are scanty, but they seem to show that the internal disorder was the result of a counterrevolt of the nobles. The pharaohs were again reduced to impotence, and much of the social progress of the Twelfth Dynasty was destroyed. About 1750 B.C. the land was invaded by the Hyksos, or "Rulers of Foreign Lands," a mixed horde originating in western Asia. Their military prowess is commonly ascribed to the fact that they possessed horses and war chariots, but their victory was certainly made easier by the dissension among the Egyptians themselves. Their rule had profound effects upon Egyptian history. Not only did they introduce the Egyptians to new methods of warfare, but by providing them with a common grievance in the face of foreign tyranny they also enabled them to forget their differences and unite in a common cause.

Near the end of the seventeenth century B.C. the rulers of southern (Upper) Egypt launched a revolt against the Hyksos, a movement that was eventually joined by all of Egypt. By about 1560 B.C. the last conquerors who had not been killed or enslaved had been driven from the country. The hero of this victory, Ahmose, founder of the Eighteenth Dynasty, thereafter established a regime that was much more highly consolidated than any that had hitherto existed. In the great outpouring of patriotism that had accompanied the struggle against the Hyksos, local loyalties were reduced, and with them the power of the nobles.

The period that followed the accession of Ahmose is called the New Kingdom, and by some, the period of the Empire. It lasted from about 1560 to 1087 B.C., during which time Egypt was ruled by three dynasties of pharaohs in succession: the Eighteenth, Nineteenth, and Twentieth. No longer was the prevailing state policy pacific and isolationist; a spirit of aggressive imperialism pervaded the nation, for the military ardor generated by the successful war against the Hyksos whetted an appetite for further victories. Moreover, a vast military machine had been created to expel the invader, which proved to be too valuable an adjunct to the pharaoh's power to be discarded.

The first steps in the direction of the new policy were taken by the immediate successors of Ahmose in making extensive raids into Palestine and claiming sovereignty over Syria. With one of the most formidable armies of ancient times, the new pharaohs speedily eliminated all opposition in Syria and eventually made themselves masters of a vast domain extending from the Euphrates to the southern parts of the Nile. But they never succeeded in welding the conquered peoples into loyal subjects, and this weakness was the signal for widespread revolt in Syria. Although their successors suppressed the uprising and managed to hold the Empire together

Ramses II (19th Dynasty)

Failures of the Empire

A Pharoah of the New Kingdom. Ramses II (who reigned from 1295 to 1225 B.C.) brought Egyptian rule temporarily into Syria by means of lightning military campaigns with war chariots.

for some time, ultimate disaster could not be averted. More territory had been annexed than could be managed successfully. The influx of wealth into Egypt weakened the national fiber by fostering corruption, and the constant revolts of the vanquished eventually sapped the strength of the state beyond hope of recovery. By the twelfth century most of the conquered provinces had been permanently lost.

The government of the Empire

The government of the New Kingdom or Empire resembled that of the Old Kingdom, but it was even more absolute. Military power now provided the basis of the pharaoh's rule. A professional army was always available with which to overawe his subjects. Most of the former nobles now became courtiers or members of the royal bureaucracy under the complete domination of the king.

The last of the great pharaohs

The last of the great pharaohs was Ramses III, who ruled from 1182 to 1151 B.C. He was succeeded by a long line of nonentities who inherited his name but not his ability. By the end of the twelfth century Egypt had fallen prey to renewed barbarian invasions. About the same time the Egyptians appear to have lost most of their creative talents. To win immortality by magic devices was now the commanding interest of people of every class. The process of decline was hastened by the growing power of the priests, who usurped the royal prerogatives and dictated the pharaoh's decrees.

The end of Egyptian independence

From the middle of the tenth century B.C. until the end of the eighth century B.C. a dynasty of Libyan barbarians held power. They were followed briefly by a line of Nubians, who overran Egypt from the deserts east of the Upper Nile. In 671 B.C. Egypt was conquered by the Assyrians, but the latter held their ascendancy for only eight years. After the collapse of Assyrian rule the Egyptians regained their independence, and a revival of traditionalism ensued. This was doomed to an untimely end, however, for in 525 B.C. Persian invaders defeated a defending Egyptian army in pitched battle. Egypt thence was absorbed into the Persian Empire and subsequently was ruled by Greeks and Romans.

2. EGYPTIAN RELIGION

The early religious evolution

Religion played a very influential role in the life of the ancient Egyptians, leaving its impress on politics, literature, architecture, art, and the conduct of daily affairs. The evolution of Egyptian religion went through various stages: from simple polytheism to the earliest known expression of monotheism, and then back to polytheism. In the beginning each city or district appears to have had its local deities, who were guardian gods of the locality or personifications of nature powers. The unification of the country resulted not only in a consolidation of territory but in a fusion of divinities as well. All of the guardian deities were merged into the great sun god Re. Under the Theban rulers of the Middle Kingdom, this deity was called Amon or Amon-Re from the name of the chief god of Thebes. The gods who personified the vegetative powers of nature were fused into a deity called Osiris, who was also the god of the Nile. Thereafter these two great powers who ruled the universe, Amon and Osiris, vied with each other for supremacy. Other deities, as we shall see, were recognized also, but they occupied a distinctly subordinate place.

During the period of the Old Kingdom the solar faith, embodied in the worship of Re, was the dominant system of belief. It served as an official religion whose chief function was to give immortality to the state and to the people collectively. The pharaoh was the living representative of this faith on earth; through his rule the rule of the god was maintained. But Re was not only a guardian deity, he was in addition the god of righteousness, justice, and truth, and the upholder of the moral order of the universe. He offered no spiritual blessings or even material rewards to people as individuals. The solar faith was not a religion for the masses, except insofar as their welfare coincided with that of the state.

The solar faith

The cult of Osiris, as already observed, began its existence as a nature religion. Osiris personified the growth of vegetation and the life-giving powers of the Nile. His career was marked by elaborate legend. In the remote past, according to belief, he had been a benevolent ruler, who taught his people agriculture and other practical arts and gave them laws. After a time he was treacherously slain by his wicked brother Seth, and his body cut into pieces. His wife Isis, who was also his sister, went in search of the pieces, put them together, and miraculously restored his body to life. The

The cult of Osiris

The Gods Isis, Osiris, and Horus

Funerary Papyrus. The scene shows the heart of a princess of the Twenty-First Dynasty being weighed in a balance before the god Osiris. On the other side of the balance are the symbols for life and truth.

risen god regained his kingdom and continued his beneficent rule for a time, but eventually he descended to the underworld to serve as judge of the dead. Then his son Horus avenged his father's death.

Originally this legend seems to have been little more than a nature myth. The death and resurrection of Osiris symbolized the drying of the Nile in the autumn and the coming of the flood in the spring. But in time the Osiris legend began to take on a deeper significance. The human qualities of the deities concerned—the paternal solicitude of Osiris for his subjects, the faithful devotion of his wife and son—appealed to the emotions of average Egyptians, who were now able to see their own tribulations and triumphs mirrored in the lives of the gods. More important still, the death and resurrection of Osiris came to be regarded as conveying a promise of personal immortality. As the god had triumphed over death, so might the individual who worshiped him inherit everlasting life. Finally, the victory of Horus appeared to foreshadow the ultimate ascendancy of good over evil.

Egyptian ideas of the hereafter attained their full development in the later history of the Middle Kingdom. Because of their belief in an afterlife, elaborate preparations were made to prevent the loss of their earthly remains. Not only were bodies mummified, but wealthy men left rich endowments to provide their mummies with food and other essentials. As the religion advanced toward maturity, however, a less naive conception of the afterlife was adopted. The dead were now believed to appear before Osiris to be judged according to their deeds on earth. All of the departed who met the tests entered a realm of physical delights. In marshes of lotus-flowers they would hunt geese and quail with never-ending success. Or they might build houses in the midst of orchards with luscious fruits of unfailing yield. They would find lily-lakes on which to sail, pools of sparkling water in which to bathe, and shady groves inhabited by singing birds. But the un-

Significance of the Osiris legend

Egyptian ideas of the hereafter

fortunate victims whose hearts revealed their vicious lives were utterly destroyed.

The Egyptian religion attained its fullest development about the end of the Middle Kingdom. By this time the solar faith and the cult of Osiris had been merged in such a way as to preserve the best features of both. The province of Amon as the god of the living, as the champion of good in this world, was accorded almost equal importance with the functions of Osiris as the judge of the dead and giver of immortality. The religion was now quite clearly an ethical one. People repeatedly avowed their desire to do justice because such conduct was pleasing to the great sun god.

Soon after the establishment of the Empire, however, the ethical quality of Egyptian religion became diminished. The chief cause seems to have been that the bitter war to expel the Hyksos fostered the growth of irrational attitudes. Whatever the reason, people started preferring magical practices in a search for personal rewards. For example, priests started selling magical charms that were supposed to have the effect of preventing the heart of the deceased from betraying his or her real character. They also sold formulas that were alleged to be effective in facilitating the passage of the dead to the realm of the blessed.

Akhenaton. A full-sized weathered bust.

This trend toward the predominance of magical practices finally resulted in a great religious upheaval. The leader of this movement was the Pharaoh Amenhotep IV, who began his reign about 1375 B.C. and died or was murdered about fifteen years later. He drove the priests from the temples, hacked the names of the traditional deities from the public monuments, and initiated the worship of a new god whom he called "Aton," an ancient designation for the physical sun. He changed his own name from Amenhotep ("Amon rests") to Akhenaton, which meant "Aton is satisfied." His wife Nefertiti became Nefer-nefru-aton, which meant "beautiful is the beauty of Aton." In keeping with his desire to begin all over, Akhenaton built a new capital, El-Amarna, which he dedicated to the worship of the new deity.

Religion of Aton

More important than these physical changes was the set of doctrines enunciated by the reforming pharaoh. He taught first of all a religion of qualified monotheism. Aton and Akhenaton himself were the only gods in existence. Like none of the gods before him, Aton had no human or animal shape but was to be conceived in terms of the life-giving, warming rays of the sun. He was the creator of all, and thus god not merely of Egypt but of the whole universe. Akhenaton deemed himself to be Aton's heir and co-regent; while the pharaoh and his wife worshiped Aton, others were to worship Akhenaton as a living deity. Aside from this important qualification, Akhenaton reemphasized the ethical quality of Egyptian religion by insisting that Aton was the author of the moral order of the world and the rewarder of humanity for integrity and purity of heart. He envisaged the new god as the sustainer of all that is beneficial, and as a heavenly father who watches with benevolent care over all his creatures. Conceptions like these of the unity, righteousness, and benevolence of God were not attained again until the time of the Hebrew prophets 600 years later.

Akhenaton, His Wife Nefertiti, and Their Children. The god Aton is depicted here as a sundisk, raining down his power on the royal family.

Qualified monotheism

Older modes of worship restored

See color plates following page 76

Despite the energy with which Akhenaton pursued his religious revolution it was still a failure. The religion of Aton gained little popular following because the masses remained devoted to their old gods. The new religion was too strange for them and lacked the greatest attraction of the older faith: the promise of an afterlife. Moreover, the pharaohs who followed Akhenaton were allied with the priests of Amon and accordingly restored the older modes of worship. Akhenaton's successor, the pharaoh whom we refer to as "King Tut," changed his name from Tutankhaton to Tutankhamen, abandoned El-Amarna for the old capital of Thebes, and presided over a return to all the old ways. His own burial was a lavish demonstration of commitment to the old rituals and belief in life after death. Thereafter Egyptian religion was characterized by growing faith in ritualism and magic. Priests sold formulas and charms that were supposed to trick the gods into granting salvation. Thus even the cult of Osiris lost most of its moral quality.

3. EGYPTIAN INTELLECTUAL ACHIEVEMENTS

Nature of Egyptian writing

Aside from the varied richness of their religious thought, the greatest intellectual accomplishments of the Egyptians lay in their system of writing and in the realm of certain practical sciences. We have seen that Egyptian writing, hieroglyphic, emerged after the appearance of cuneiform writing in Mesopotamia, perhaps even with an awareness of the Mesopotamian precedent. Thus it is not so much the idea of writing as the particular nature of Egyptian writing that is worth consideration here. Specifically, as early as the time of the Old Kingdom, Egyptian hieroglyphic was based on three types of characters: the pictographic, the syllabic, and the alphabetic. The first two were already components of cuneiform, but the last was a crucially significant innovation. Had the Egyptians taken the step of separating their alphabetic characters—twenty-four symbols, each representing a single consonant sound of the human voice—from their nonalphabetic ones and using the former exclusively in their written communication they would have developed a writing system that was fully modern. Since conservatism kept them from doing this, it was left for a Semitic people of the eastern Mediterranean shore, the Phoenicians, to devise the first exclusively alphabetical system around 1400 B.C. The Phoenician alphabet in turn became the model for the alphabets of the Hebrews, Arabs, Greeks, and Romans. Nevertheless, since the Phoenicians definitely borrowed the idea of using single symbols for denoting single sounds from the Egyptians, and since they even modeled many of their letters on Egyptian exemplars, there is warrant for viewing the Egyptian alphabetical system as the parent of every alphabet that has been used in the Western world.

Significance of papyrus

Blessed with a plant, the papyrus reed, that grew abundantly in the Nile delta region (papyrus in Lower Egypt was so plentiful that it was the pictographic symbol in hieroglyphic for "Lower Egypt"), the Egyptians possessed a cheap material on which to write. Strips of the papyrus reed, when flattened and dried, could be used for setting down hieroglyphic and then rolled up into scrolls for storage or transport. The advantage of writing on papyrus over writing on clay tablets was that papyrus rolls were less cumbersome and vastly lighter: hence they not only became the standard writing material in Egypt but their use spread from the Egyptians to the civilizations of ancient Greece and Rome. (Could the Roman Empire have established its vast administrative system on clay tablets? It is doubtful.)

Perhaps because it was so easy to write things down, the Egyptians experimented in several forms of literature. The Egyptians of the Middle Kingdom are considered by many literary historians to have been the fathers of the short story. Various kinds of short narratives were written at that time: a surviving papyrus roll from the nineteenth century B.C. contains a tall tale about a shipwrecked sailor; a somewhat later narrative describes the plight of a man who cannot sleep because of the bellowing of hippopotamuses on the Nile; and an ancient Egyptian bawdy tale tells of a lustful woman who says to the hero, "Come, let us spend an hour lying together, it will be good for you!" At the other extreme are collections of maxims offering practical wisdom and enjoining moderation and justice. Finally, there is at least one surviving Egyptian approximation of a political treatise, *The Plea of the Eloquent Peasant,* written around 2050 B.C. In this the author sets forth the ideal of a ruler committed to benevolence and justice for the good of his subjects. Although no single work of Egyptian literature approaches the Mesopotamian *Gilgamesh* epic, parts of the Hebrew Bible, or the Greek *Iliad* and *Odyssey* for enduring literary quality, Egyptian writing nonetheless has its entertaining features.

As for science, the Egyptians were most interested in those branches that aimed particularly at practical ends—astronomy, medicine, and mathematics. In the realm of astronomy the Egyptians' greatest achievement was their discovery of a way to avoid the imprecisions of a lunar calendar. We have seen that the peoples of ancient Mesopotamia remained limited in marking the passage of seasons and years to working with the cycles of the moon. In contrast, by around 2000 B.C. the Egyptians noticed that the brightest star in the sky, Sirius, rose in the morning once a year in direct alignment with the sun. Constructing a calendar on this observation, wherein "New Year's Day" began with Sirius's solar alignment, they could foretell the coming of the Nile's floods and produced the best calendar in antiquity before that devised by Julius Caesar. Indeed, Caesar's calendar itself rested on the Egyptian precedent.

Ancient Egyptian medical practice was distinguished by the view that diseases came from natural rather than supernatural causes and hence that physicians should provide accurate diagnoses and predictably reliable treatments. Among diagnostic methods was the taking of the pulse and the listening to the heartbeat. As for therapeutics, surviving papyrus documents show that some treatments must have been predictably reliable and others not. For example, Egyptian doctors prescribed castor oil as a cathartic but offered whipped ostrich eggs mixed with tortoise shells and thorns to cure internal ulcers. Concerned with hygiene as well as health, they proposed the following remedy for sweaty feet: "take uadu-plant-of-the-Fields and eel-from-the-Canal, warm in oil, and smear both feet therewith." While it is easy to smile at such prescriptions, the Egyptian attempt to alleviate pain and enhance health by natural means deserves respect, not to mention the fact that some Egyptian medicinal remedies, carried to Europe by the Greeks, are still employed today.

(3) mathematics and measurement

In mathematics the Egyptians excelled in methods of measurement. For example, they were the first to mark off 360 degrees to a circle and the first to notice that the ratio of the circumference of a circle to its diameter is the same for all circles (today this is known as the "pi" ratio). They also devised means for computing the areas of triangles and the volumes of pyramids, cylinders, and hemispheres. Such accomplishments obviously were interrelated with the Egyptians' spectacular building projects, to which we may now turn.

4. THE SPLENDOR OF EGYPTIAN ART

The pyramids

The most famous of all Egyptian visual monuments are of course the pyramids—vast constructions of towering simplicity, built at the dawn of recorded time to serve as tombs of the pharaohs. Awe for the pyramids must extend from amazement at their stark beauty to astonishment regarding the circumstances of their construction. The earliest pyramid, the step-pyramid of the pharaoh Zoser, was erected around 2770 B.C. at a time when nothing remotely resembling its scale had ever been attempted by

The Pyramids of Gizeh with the Sphinx in the Foreground

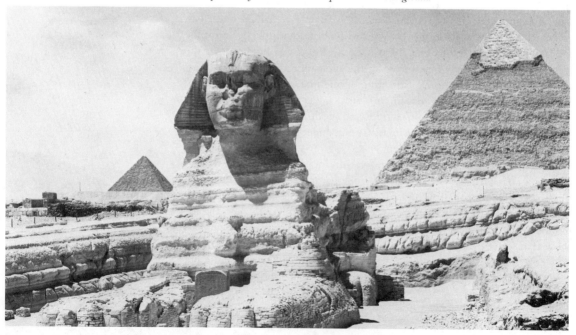

humanity. Whereas contemporary Sumerians built solely with mud bricks and prior Egyptians had gone no further than erecting edifices from a few tons of limestone, all of a sudden, under the guidance of Zoser's chief builder, Imhotep, one million tons of limestone were quarried, hauled without wheeled vehicles, and fitted precisely into place to a summit about 200 feet high. And that was just the beginning. Soon after, in the century from roughly 2700 to roughly 2600 B.C., a total of some 25 million tons of limestone were hewn out of rock cliffs, dressed, hauled, and piled in the course of building a series of pyramids that are the most famous and beautiful of all. Of these the gem of gems is no doubt the pyramid of Khufu (a pharaoh known to the Greeks as Cheops), which rose to a height of 482 feet at the "perfect" angle of 52°, making its pinnacle stand in relation to its circumference as in the "pi" ratio of circles. When the Greeks decided to count the seven wonders of the world, they unhesitatingly ranked the pyramid of "Cheops" as the first.

While the great pyramids remain for us to see, many questions arise as to how and why they were built. By a conservative estimate some 70,000 laborers were needed to put up a pyramid. These were almost certainly seasonal laborers. During the summer months, when the Nile was at its flood stage, there was little or nothing for farmers to do, so they could be employed on massive building projects without detrimental effect to the Egyptian agricultural economy. But one summer does not make a pyramid. Rather, it has recently been concluded that pyramid laborers must have worked summer after summer, starting on a new pyramid after the last one was finished, without reference to whether a reigning pharaoh had died or not, because that is the only way to account for the transformation of 25 million tons of stone into several enormous pyramids during the course of one century. Thus for thousands of people, hewing and hauling limestone in the raging heat of an Egyptian summer was a yearly way of life without prospect of termination.

The perennial summer's work

Why did 70,000 laborers endure this? Brute coercion is surely not the answer, for Egypt at this time did not know slavery (aside from a small number of war captives); moreover, it is impossible to imagine that a handful of rulers could have forced tens of thousands of subjects to labor against their wills year after year without cowing them by any extraordinary weaponry. Religious psychology and group dynamics instead seem to provide the best explanations. The Egyptian laborers who built the pyramids apparently believed that their pharaohs were living gods who could ascend to eternal life upon their earthly exits solely by means of proper burial. Zoser's step-pyramid was thus in a literal sense a "stairway to heaven" and the later pyramids were simply straight-angle embodiments of the same ascent-to-heaven conception. The laborers who sweated to build these enormous monuments on the hot sands believed their own well-being was inextricably tied to that of their god-rulers: if the pharaohs journeyed well to their eternal glory, life on earth would flourish. In addition, collaborative labor must have given the individual toiler a sense of uplifting comradeship and team accomplishment. This point seems borne out by marks found on

The laborer's motivation: Religious psychology and group dynamics

Temples of Karnak and Luxor

various pyramid stones reading "vigorous team," "enduring team," and so forth. Farmers who were relatively isolated during most of the year must have found teamwork on the most prestigious and exalted projects of the day to be a source of pride and emotional reward that made their heaving and sweating seem almost pleasurable.

Ultimately pyramid building was recognized by Egyptian leaders of state to be a wasteful occupation. Since concern for personal salvation became the major religious trend during the time of the Middle Kingdom, the temple, then and afterwards, replaced the pyramid as Egypt's leading architectural form. The most noted Egyptian temples are those of Karnak and Luxor, built during the period of the New Kingdom. Many of their gigantic, richly carved columns still stand as silent witness to a splendid architectural talent. Egyptian temples were characterized by massive size. The temple at Karnak, with a length of about 1,300 feet, covered the largest area of any religious edifice ever built. Its central hall alone could contain almost any of the cathedrals of Europe. The columns used in the temples had stupendous proportions. The largest were seventy feet high, with diameters in excess of twenty feet. It has been estimated that the capitals surmounting them could furnish standing room for a hundred men.

Egyptian sculpture and painting

Egyptian sculpture and painting served primarily as adjuncts to architecture. Sculpture was characterized by set conventions governing its style and meaning. Statues of pharaohs were commonly of colossal size. Those produced during the New Kingdom ranged in height from seventy-five to ninety feet. Some of them were colored to enhance the portrait, and the eyes were frequently inlaid with rock crystal. The figures were nearly always rigid, with the arms folded across the chest or fixed to the sides of the

The Temple at Karnak. Most of this building has collapsed or been carried away, but the huge columns give an idea of the massiveness of Egyptian temples.

body, and with the eyes staring straight ahead. Countenances were generally represented as slightly smiling but otherwise devoid of emotional expression. Anatomical distortion was frequently practiced: the natural length of the thighs might be increased, the squareness of the shoulders accentuated, or all of the fingers of the hand made equal in length. A familiar example of nonnaturalistic sculpture was the Sphinx, of which there were thousands in Egypt; the best-known example was the Great Sphinx at Gizeh. This represented the head of a pharaoh on the body of a lion. The purpose was probably to symbolize the notion that the pharaoh possessed the lion's qualities of strength and courage. The figures of sculpture in relief were even less in conformity with nature. The head was presented in profile, with the eyes full-face; the torso was shown in the frontal position, while the legs were rendered in profile.

The meaning of Egyptian sculpture is not hard to perceive. The colossal size of the statues of pharaohs was doubtless intended to symbolize their power and the power of the state they represented. It is significant that the size of these statues increased as the Empire expanded and the government became more absolute. The conventions of rigidity and impassiveness were meant to express the timelessness and stability of the national life. Here was an empire that was not to be torn loose from its moorings by the uncertain mutations of fortune but was to remain fixed and imperturbable. The portraits of its chief men consequently must betray no anxiety, fear, or triumph, but an unvarying calmness throughout the ages. In similar fashion, the anatomical distortion can probably be interpreted as an attempt to express some national ideal.

An intriguing exception to the mainstream of Egyptian artistic development is the art produced during the reign of Akhenaton. Because the pharaoh wished to break with all manifestations of the ancient Egyptian religion, including its artistic conventions, he presided over an artistic revolution. The new style he patronized was naturalistic because his new religion revered nature as the handiwork of Aton. Accordingly portrait busts of the pharaoh himself and his queen Nefertiti abandoned the earlier grandiloquent impassivity and distortion in favor of more realistic detail. A surviving bust of Nefertiti that reveals her slightly quizzical and haunting femininity is one of the greatest monuments in the history of art. For the same reasons painting under the patronage of Akhenaton also emerged as a highly expressive art form. Murals of this period display the world of experience above all in terms of movement. They catch the instant action of the wild bull leaping in the swamp, the headlong flight of the frightened stag, and the effortless swimming of ducks in a pond. But just as Akhenaton's religious reform was not lasting, neither was the more naturalistic art of his reign.

Pharaoh Mycerinus and His Queen. Above: Sculpture from the Fourth Dynasty, c. 2590 B.C.—an example of the impassive, grandiloquent style. Below: A comparison of their profiles leaves little doubt that they were brother and sister as well as husband and wife.

5. SOCIAL AND ECONOMIC LIFE

During the greater part of the history of Egypt the population was divided into five classes: the royal family; the priests; the nobles; the middle class of

*The principal classes of
Egyptian society*

scribes, merchants, artisans, and wealthy farmers; and the peasants, who comprised by far the bulk of the population. During the New Kingdom a sixth class, the professional soldiers, was added, ranking immediately below the nobles. Thousands of slaves were also captured in this period, and for a time these formed a seventh class. Despised by all, they were forced to labor in the government quarries and on the temple estates. Gradually, however, they were allowed to enlist in the army and even in the personal service of the pharaoh. With these developments they ceased to constitute a separate class. The position of the various ranks of society shifted from time to time. In the Old Kingdom the nobles and priests among all of the pharaoh's subjects were supreme. During the Middle Kingdom the classes of commoners came into their own. Merchants, artisans, and farmers gained concessions from the government. Particularly impressive is the dominant role played by the merchants and artisans in this period. The establishment of the Empire, accompanied as it was by the extension of government functions, resulted in the ascendancy of a new nobility, primarily made up of officials. The priests also gained more power with the growth of magic and ritualism.

The gulf that separated the standards of living of the upper and lower classes of Egypt was perhaps even wider than it is today in Europe and America. The wealthy nobles lived in splendid villas that opened onto fragrant gardens and shady groves. Their food had all the richness and variety of sundry kinds of meat, poultry, cakes, fruit, wine, and sweets. They ate from vessels of alabaster, gold, and silver, and adorned themselves with expensive fabrics and costly jewels. By contrast, the life of the poor was wretched. The laborers in the towns inhabited congested quarters composed of mud-brick hovels whose only furnishings were stools, boxes, and a few crude pottery jars. The peasants on the great estates enjoyed a less crowded but no more abundant life.

Although polygamy was permitted, normally the basic social unit was the monogamous family. Even the pharaoh, who could keep a harem of secondary wives and concubines, had a chief wife. Concubinage, however, was a socially reputable institution. Yet compared to women in most other ancient societies, Egyptian women were not entirely subordinated to men. Wives were not secluded; women could own and inherit property and engage in business. The Egyptians also permitted women to succeed to the throne: Queen Sobeknofru reigned during the Twelfth Dynasty and Queen Hatshepsut during the Eighteenth.

Nefertiti. The famous portrait bust executed in Akhenaton's studios at El-Amarna.

*Agriculture, trade, and
industry*

The Egyptian economic system rested primarily upon an agrarian basis. Agriculture was diversified and highly developed, and the soil yielded excellent crops of wheat, barley, millet, vegetables, fruits, flax, and cotton. Theoretically the land was the property of the pharaoh, but in the earlier periods he granted most of it to his subjects, so that in actual practice it was largely in the possession of individuals. Commerce grew steadily after about 2000 B.C. to a position of first-rate importance. A flourishing trade was carried on with the island of Crete, and with Lebanon on the eastern Mediterranean shore. Gold mines in Libya controlled by Egypt were an

Fishing and Fowling: Wall Painting, Thebes, Eighteenth Dynasty. Most of the women appear to belong to the prosperous classes, while the simple garb and insignificant size of the men indicates that they are probably slaves.

important source of wealth. The chief articles of export consisted of gold, wheat, and linen fabrics, with imports being confined primarily to silver, ivory, and lumber. Of no less significance than commerce was manufacturing. As early as 3000 B.C. large number of people were engaged in artisanal crafts. Later, factories were established, employing twenty or more persons under one roof, and with some degree of division of labor. The leading industries were shipbuilding and the manufacture of pottery, glass, and textiles.

From an early date the Egyptians made progress in the development of instruments of business. They knew the elements of accounting and bookkeeping. Their merchants issued orders and receipts for goods. They invented deeds for property, written contracts, and wills. While they had no system of coinage, they had rings of copper or gold of set weight circulated as exchange, in effect the oldest known currency in the history of civilizations. The simple dealings of the peasants and poorer townsfolk, however, were doubtless based on barter.

The development of instruments of business

The Egyptian economic system was primarily collective. From the very beginning the energies of the people had been drawn into socialized channels. The interests of the individual and the interests of society were conceived as identical. The productive activities of the entire nation revolved around huge state enterprises, and the government remained by far the largest employer of labor. But this collectivism was not all-inclusive; a considerable sphere was left for private initiative. Merchants conducted their own businesses; many of the craftsmen had their own shops; and as time went on, larger and larger numbers of peasants gained the status of inde-

Economic collectivism

Egyptian Slaves at Work. Left: Sculptors at work in a tomb of the Sixth Dynasty, c. 2300 B.C. Right: A wall painting done around 1550 B.C. displays slave-laborers making bricks.

pendent farmers. The government continued to operate the quarries and mines, to build pyramids and temples, and to farm the royal estates.

6. THE EGYPTIAN ACHIEVEMENT

Peace and self-sufficiency

When a party of Greeks visited the Nile valley around 500 B.C. a dignified Egyptian priest supposedly told them, "You Greeks are always children; there is not an old man among you." The point of course is that members of a civilization that had outlasted two and a half millennia considered the Greeks to be mere whippersnappers: Egypt was into its Twenty-sixth Dynasty when the Greeks were just beginning to organize their thoughts. Seen from today's perspective, the relatively untroubled longevity of Egyptian civilization still commands respect. Apparently the ancient Egyptians had found a way to cooperate with nature and each other in order to live in peace and self-sufficiency for centuries at a stretch. The Greeks, who conquered the Egyptians in 332 B.C., were vastly more experimental and creative, but they also introduced continual upheaval into an Egyptian world that until then had been characterized by stability.

Egypt's unique circumstances

The ancient Egyptian success formula was so closely bound to the annual flooding of the Nile that it could not easily be transported. Hence, aside from a few specific accomplishments, such as the solar calendar or the reckoning of cubic space, the Egyptian achievement is not best estimated by the directness of its influence on subsequent thought or events. Rather, Egyptian patterns of living, thinking, sculpting, painting, and building are fascinating for their own sake. There is something in all of us that makes us wish we could go back in time to view Nefertiti, listen to King Tut's priests intone their timeless hymns, or float on a barge down the Nile past lotus-flowers while the pyramids are rising. This is understandable awe for a civilization that found its place in the sun when history's sun was still at its dawn.

SELECTED READINGS

• *Items so designated are available in paperback editions.*

• Aldred, Cyril, *Akhenaton: King of Egypt,* New York, 1988. The standard treatment; particularly strong in its use of artistic evidence.
• ———, *The Egyptians,* rev. ed., London, 1984. A short but reliable treatment of political history and cultural accomplishments.
  Bibby, Geoffrey, *Four Thousand Years Ago,* Baltimore, 1961. Egyptian developments from 2000 to 1000 B.C., seen from the perspective of contemporary events elsewhere in the ancient world.
  Breasted, James H., *History of Egypt,* New York, 1912. By America's first great Egyptologist. A classic, although now regarded as out of date in its extreme claims for Egyptian originality and influence.
• Butzer, Karl W., and Leslie G. Freeman, eds., *Early Hydraulic Civilization in Egypt,* Chicago, 1976. A careful analysis of the Nile valley as an eco-system. Downplays grandeur in favor of examining the essential circumstances of daily existence.
  Cambridge Ancient History (3rd ed., vols. I–II), Cambridge, 1971–1975.
  Cottrell, Leonard, *Life under the Pharaohs,* New York, 1960. Fascinating recreation of life under the Empire.
• Emery, Walter, *Archaic Egypt,* Baltimore, 1961. Controversial account of the earliest period.
• Frankfort, Henri, *Ancient Egyptian Religion: An Interpretation,* New York, 1948. A penetrating, profound study.
• Hayes, William C., *The Scepter of Egypt,* 2 vols., New York, 1953–1959. Written with special reference to the Egyptian holdings of the Metropolitan Museum of Art in New York.
• Mendelssohn, Kurt, *The Riddle of the Pyramids,* London, 1974. A lucid account of how the pyramids were built and a persuasive interpretation of why they were built.
• Mertz, Barbara, *Temples, Tombs and Hieroglyphs,* rev. ed., New York, 1978. Intriguing approach by means of archeological discoveries.
• Redford, Donald B., *Akhenaten: The Heretic King,* Princeton, 1987. Takes a more negative view of the controversial pharaoh than that offered by Aldred.
• Smith, W. S., *The Art and Architecture of Ancient Egypt,* rev. ed., Baltimore, 1965.
• Steindorff, George, and Keith C. Seele, *When Egypt Ruled the East,* rev. ed., Chicago, 1963. The political history of the Empire.
• Trigger, B. G., et al., *Ancient Egypt: A Social History,* London, 1983. A guide to current directions in Egyptology; exciting research, but unexciting prose.

• Wilson, John A., *The Burden of Egypt,* Chicago, 1951. (Paperback edition under title of *The Culture of Ancient Egypt.*) In a class by itself as the one book to read if the student wishes to read just one. Scintillating and masterful.

SOURCE MATERIALS

Grayson, A. Kirk, and D. B. Redford, *Papyrus and Tablet,* Englewood Cliffs, N.J., 1973. The best short collection.

• Lichtheim, M., *Ancient Egyptian Literature,* 3 vols., Berkeley, 1973–1980. The standard selection of representative works, many of which are highly entertaining.

• Pritchard, James B., ed., *The Ancient Near East: An Anthology of Texts and Pictures,* Princeton, 1965. Covers both Egypt and Mesopotamia.

Chapter 4

THE HEBREW AND EARLY GREEK CIVILIZATIONS

I am the Lord thy God, which brought thee out of the land of Egypt
    from the house of bondage.
Thou shalt have none other gods before me. . . .
Thou shalt not take the name of the Lord thy God in vain.

—Deuteronomy 5:6–11

Then Agamemnon awoke from slumber . . . and put on a soft tunic,
fair and new, and he threw a great cloak about him; about his shining
feet he bound fair sandals. . . . Then he grasped his ancestral sceptre,
indestructible forever.

—Homer, *The Iliad*

D warfed by the great empires of Mesopotamia and Egypt in territory
and military prowess, the civilizations of the Hebrews and the
early Greeks nonetheless merit full consideration. The extraordinary historical significance of the Hebrews lies beyond challenge, for despite their political insignificance, the Hebrews exerted the greatest influence of any ancient western Asian peoples on the thought and life of the
modern world. As for the ancient Greek civilizations (as will be seen, there
were two of them), they are memorable for their grace and sophistication
and for being the earliest civilizations of Europe.

Importance of the Hebrew civilization

1. HEBREW BEGINNINGS

The first known appearance of the Hebrews, who were members of the
Semitic language family, was in Mesopotamia, for according to the Bible
the Hebrew patriarch Abraham's family was native to Sumer. Since the
Hebrews originally were a wandering pastoral people it is not surprising
that thereafter their exact whereabouts are often difficult to locate. Suffice
it to say that between roughly 1900 and 1500 B.C. they gradually migrated

Hebrew migrations

A Canaanite Deity. Thought to be an image of Baal, a god of storms and fertility, this statuette was discovered in a thirteenth century B.C. temple in northern Palestine.

The struggle for Canaan

Invasion of Philistines

from Mesopotamia to southern Syria (a land then known as Canaan) and thence into Egypt. During those centuries a tribe of Hebrews who claimed descent from Abraham's grandson Jacob began to call themselves "Israelites" after Jacob's alternative name. (According to the Book of Genesis, after Jacob wrestled through the night with an angel he received the name "Israel," which means "soldier of God.") After sojourning for about three centuries in Egypt the Hebrews were enslaved during the time when the pharaohs of the New Kingdom were attempting to create an Egyptian Empire and seeking ever more slaves to keep their home economy running. It was then, around 1250 B.C., that the Hebrews found a leader in the heroic Moses, who led their exodus out of Egyptian bondage into the Sinai peninsula (a desert land located between Egypt and Canaan) and persuaded them to become worshipers of Yahweh, a god whose name was much later written as Jehovah. It was then too that all Hebrews became Israelites because Moses persuaded them that Yahweh had been the god of Abraham, Isaac, and Jacob, and that accordingly the god of Israel was the god now worshiped by them all.

After wandering for about a generation in the Sinai desert the Hebrews resolved to move back into the much richer land of Canaan, a land indeed so much richer than the arid Sinai that it seemed a land "flowing with milk and honey." Yet it was impossible simply to move in and settle down because Canaan was already occupied by another Semitic language people, the Canaanites. Hence the Hebrews had to fight their way into Canaan, and that proved to be a slow and difficult process, misrepresented by the famous line that "Joshua fit the battle of Jericho and the walls came a tumbling down." Moses' successor Joshua did indeed gain some territory in Canaan, but not very much because the pastoral Israelites were generally not well equipped to reduce the well-fortified Canaanite cities by siege warfare. Moreover, after Joshua's death the Israelites fared even less well because they lost their ability to pursue concerted military action as a result of the revival of tribal particularism. Thus after a century of fighting they had gained no more than some of Canaan's hills and a few of the less fertile valleys. Worse, just around that time they were forced to defend themselves, not only against the Canaanites, who hoped to recoup their losses, but against a mighty foreign invasion.

The invasion was that of the Philistines, a non-Semitic people of unknown origins who quickly conquered so much of Canaan around 1050 B.C. that the region became known alternatively as Palestine, in effect meaning "the Philistine country." Faced with the threat of extinction, the Hebrews now intensified their struggle. Whereas hitherto they had preserved a tribal form of organization whereby wise men ("judges") in each tribe were chosen when there was a need to resolve conflicts, it now became clear that a tighter, "national" form of government was necessary to meet the Philistine challenge. Accordingly, around 1025 B.C., Samuel, a tribal judge with the force of personality to gain adherence from all the Israelite tribes, selected for all of them a king, Saul, who would make them a united people.

2. THE RECORD OF POLITICAL HOPES AND FRUSTRATIONS

Although the reign of King Saul marked the beginning of Hebrew national unity, it was not in itself a happy reign, either for the Hebrews or for the ruler himself. Only a few hints of the reasons are given in the Old Testament account. Evidently, soon after he began acting assertively as king, Saul incurred the anger of Samuel, who had expected to remain the power behind the throne. So Samuel began to lend his support to an energetic young warrior, David, who carried on skillful maneuvers to draw popular support away from Saul. Waging his own military campaigns, David achieved one triumph over the Philistines after another. (His victory over "Goliath" would have been accomplished with more than a slingshot.) In contrast, the armies of Saul met frequent reverses. Finally the king, being critically wounded, ended the rivalry by slaying himself. The date would have been roughly 1005 B.C.—close enough to the millennium marker to make it easy to remember.

The reign of King Saul

With Saul in his grave, David now became king and initiated the most glorious period in Hebrew political history—at least until modern times. Advancing relentlessly against the Philistines, he reduced their territory to a narrow strip of coast in the south. He compelled the Canaanites to recognize his rule, with the effect that during the next few generations they lost their separate identity and became fully merged with the Hebrew people. As this process of amalgamation progressed, the Hebrews increasingly put aside pastoralism and took up either farming or urban occupations. Once David fully established his position as absolute monarch, he exacted forced labor from some of his subjects, instituted a census as a basis for collecting taxes, and then actually started to collect taxes. His ultimate goal was to build a splendid capital and religious center at Jerusalem, but although he made some progress in this enterprise he died before the work was completed.

David as absolute monarch

David was succeeded by his son Solomon, who ruled from 973 to 933 B.C., the last of the three kings of the united Hebrew monarchy. Solomon was determined to finish his father's work in building Jerusalem. The purpose, inherited from his father, was twofold. First, if the Israelites were to take their place among the great nations of western Asia, they had to have a magnificent capital as a visual manifestation of their greatness. And secondly, they also needed a splendid temple to reaffirm their national religious commitment. Until then the "Ark of the Covenant," the biblical name for the chest containing the stone tablets supposedly given by Yahweh to Moses on Mount Sinai, had been carried by the Israelites in their wanderings in a "tabernacle," actually no more than a portable tent. To house an exalted shrine in a tent may have been barely satisfactory for a nomadic people, but not for settled agriculturalists of a great nation. Instead, the Ark, the physical token of Israel's special relationship with Yahweh, had to be located in a mighty capital and housed properly in the innermost precincts of a splendid temple. For these reasons Solomon spared

Star of David. This emblem from the kingdom of the Hebrews was dug up in the 1980s in Jerusalem.

Solomon, Jerusalem, and the Temple

no expense in building his capital, and especially in building the temple that would be the central monument of Hebrew national and religious life. In the long run this policy contributed fundamentally to the survival of the Hebrews, for Solomon indeed succeeded in erecting a splendid temple and Solomon's Temple thereafter served as an inspiring symbol whenever Israel was faced with the possibility of national and cultural obliteration. But in the short term the king's lavish building projects caused trouble because Palestine was poor in natural resources needed for basic building materials, not to mention lacking in the gold and gems needed to adorn these projects. When, despite mountingly oppressive taxation, Solomon found himself unable to pay his construction debts, he first ceded territory to his main supplier, the bordering country (to the north) of Phoenicia, and then he drafted and deported Hebrews to work in Phoenicia's forests and mines.

Northern antagonism and secession

Not surprisingly, such tyrannical behavior provoked bitter antagonism among many of Solomon's subjects, especially those of the north. The northerners were the ones who saw their sons forcibly sent to Phoenicia, and they were least sympathetic to the building projects in Jerusalem, which lay more to the south of the Hebrew kingdom. (Apparently the northerners were also less ardent in exclusive dedication to Yahweh than the southerners, still another reason why they would have been less enthusiastic about making personal sacrifices to import gold for the Ark of the Covenant.) While Solomon remained alive his northern subjects remained obedient to him, but his death was the signal for open revolt. Refusing to pay taxes to Solomon's son Rehoboam, the northerners quickly seceded from the united Hebrew state and set up their own kingdom.

The fragility and fate of the Kingdoms of Israel and Judah

The northern kingdom came to be known as the Kingdom of Israel, having its capital in Samaria, while the remnant in the south was the Kingdom of Judah, with its capital in Jerusalem. Even as a united state the Hebrew realm would not have been impressively strong, but split in half, the realm was pitifully weak. More by luck and the forbearance of its neighbors than by intrinsic viability the Kingdom of Israel managed to survive (usually paying tribute) for two centuries until 722 B.C., when it was annihilated by the Assyrians. Since the Assyrians followed a policy of leveling all the important buildings of conquered nations and scattering their populations, the Kingdom of Israel was never heard from again. As for the Kingdom of Judah, it just barely eluded the Assyrian menace, partly because of its very insignificance, but in 586 B.C. it was conquered by the Babylonians under Nebuchadnezzar, who plundered and burned Jerusalem and its Temple, deporting Judah's leading citizens to Babylon. For a half-century thereafter the Judeans—from this point customarily called the Jews by historians—suffered their "Babylonian Captivity," fearing that they would never again see their homeland.

Palestine: From Persian overlordship to Roman annexation

As events would have it, they were mistaken, for upon conquering Babylon in 539 B.C. Cyrus the Persian magnanimously allowed the Jews to return to Palestine and to establish their rule there semi-independently under Persian overlordship. The returnees wasted no time in rebuilding the Jerusalem Temple (accomplished from 520 to 516 B.C.), and their heirs

PALESTINE AFTER THE DEATH OF KING SOLOMON

lived more or less peacefully within the Persian sphere of influence until 332 B.C., when Palestine was conquered by the Greek, Alexander the Great. Since Alexander died soon afterwards the Jews then passed under the rule of successive Greek-speaking overlords. In 168 B.C., one of them, Antiochus Epiphanes, attempted to destroy the Jewish faith by desecrating the Temple and prohibiting all worship in it, but this ruthlessness resulted in provoking a Jewish revolt led by the inspiring fighter Judas Maccabeus. After two decades of struggle the Jews of Palestine finally succeeded in gaining political independence under the rule of a native Maccabean dynasty, but that situation lasted only until 63 B.C., when the Roman general Pompey took advantage of the dynasty's internal feuding to turn Palestine

Roman Coin Celebrating the Destruction of Jerusalem. The inscription IVDAEA CAPTA means "Judea Captured," and "S. C." is a standard abbreviation for "with consent of the Senate." A triumphant Roman soldier lords it over a female personification of the Jews shown in an attitude of dejection.

into a Roman protectorate. Discontented under Roman rule, the Jews revolted in 66 C.E.* in a desperate attempt to recreate the victory over Antiochus. But this time they faced the mightiest of all ancient empires and lost all they had. In 70 C.E. the Roman Emperor Titus put down the Jewish uprising mercilessly and razed the Temple, which has never been rebuilt since. Palestine then was annexed by the Romans outright, and the Jews gradually left for other parts of the vast Roman Empire. The diaspora, or migration of the Jews away from Palestine to country after country through the centuries, became the central fact of Jewish existence from then until the twentieth century.

3. HEBREW RELIGIOUS DEVELOPMENT

Even during King David's time the ancient Hebrews were no more than a second-rate political power, and after Solomon's reign they were not even that. Hence the Hebrews would not be worth more than passing consideration here were it not for their achievements in religion. Today Judaism, the religion of the Jews, is a coherent body of beliefs, customs, and liturgical practices, all of which are founded in passages from the Jewish Bible (known to Christians as the Old Testament). The student of history, however, must recognize that Judaism did not spring suddenly into place in one moment but was the product of a long process of change transpiring between the time of Moses and that of the Maccabees.

Four stages can be distinguished in the growth of the Hebrew religion. In the first, known only by inference, the Hebrews were *polytheists* (worshipers of many gods), like all other contemporary western Asian peoples. Then came the stage of national *monolatry,* initiated by Moses around 1250 B.C. and lasting until about 750 B.C. Monolatry means the exclusive worship of one god, without denying the existence of others. Under Moses the people of Israel adopted as their national deity a god whose name was written "Yhwh" and was probably pronounced as if spelled "Yahweh," and they agreed to worship no other gods. During the time of national monolatry Yahweh was conceived mainly in anthropomorphic terms. He possessed a physical body and was sometimes capricious or irascible, occasionally punishing someone who had sinned accidentally. For example, he struck someone dead merely for placing his hand on the Ark of the Covenant to steady it while it was being carried to Jerusalem (I Chronicles 13:9–10). Nor was Yahweh omnipotent, for his power was limited to the territory occupied by the Hebrews.

Despite these holdovers from more primitive religious systems, some of the Hebrews' most important contributions to subsequent Western thought

Stage of national monolatry

---

*In this edition we have shifted from the antiquated "A.D." to the abbreviation "C.E." to indicate dates after the birth of Christ. C.E. stands for "common era."

Egyptian Bronze Cat. This elegant creature from roughly a millennium before the birth of Christ prefers a style in earrings that has regained popularity in the late twentieth century.

Throne of "King Tut." Dating from about 1360 B.C., this relief in gold and silver is part of the back of the young pharaoh's throne. The sun god Aton shines down on Tutankhamen and his queen. The relaxed lounging position of the pharaoh's right arm is typical of the stylistic informality of the period. (Lee Boltin)

Tomb of Tutankhamen. This solid–gold coffin weighing 2,500 pounds was placed in Tutankhamen's pyramid after his death. Inside the coffin was the mummified body of King Tut, preserved to prevent the body from decaying. (Lee Boltin)

Minoan Snake Goddess. A statuette in ivory and gold discovered near the palace of Knossus and dating from about 1550 B.C. (Lee Boltin)

emerged during this time. One was their unique *transcendent theology*. In their view God was not part of nature but entirely outside of it; thus he could become understood in purely intellectual or abstract terms. Complementing the principle of divine transcendence was the principle that humans were rulers of nature by divine mandate. This is stated explicitly in the famous line from Genesis in which God tells Adam and Eve: "be fruitful and multiply, and replenish the earth and subdue it, and have dominion over . . . every living thing." The quotation contrasts strikingly with parallel Babylonian creation accounts in which humans are created merely to serve the gods, "that they might be at ease." Finally, while not fully developed, ethical considerations are already present in this period. According to the Babylonian flood story a certain petulant god decides to destroy humanity on the grounds that their noise deprives him of sleep, whereas Yahweh in Genesis sends a flood because of human wickedness and saves only Noah and his family because "Noah was a just man."

Transcendent theology

The Hebrews honored Yahweh during the period of monolatry by subscribing to moral precepts, rituals, and tabus. Although it is uncertain whether the exact form of the Ten Commandments, as they became known from the seventh century B.C. onwards (the form found in Exodus 20:3–17), existed before the Babylonian Captivity, the Hebrews certainly observed some set of commandments, including ethical ones such as injunctions against murder, adultery, bearing false witness, and "coveting anything that is thy neighbor's." In addition they observed ritualistic demands, such as celebrating feasts and offering sacrifices, and prohibitions, such as refraining from labor on the seventh day or boiling a kid in its mother's milk. Although moral standards may have been observed within the Hebrew community, however, they were not always considered applicable when dealing with outsiders. Thus even in regard to murder the Hebrews were no more averse to slaughtering civilians in warfare than were the Assyrians. When Joshua conquered territories in Canaan his troops

Moral precepts, rituals, and tabus

Menorah Mosaic from a Synagogue Pavement. After the Romans destroyed the Second Temple the seven-branched candelabrum (*menorah*) became the identifying emblem for Judaism because the candelabrum formerly had been placed next to the "Ark of the Covenant" in the Temple and now stood for the missing Temple itself. In this mosaic from a synagogue of Jericho (twenty-five miles east of Jerusalem), done around 500 C.E., the menorah is complemented by a branch associated with the Harvest Festival and a ram's horn (*shofar*) sounded at the New Year. The inscription reads "Peace upon Israel."

"took for a prey unto themselves all the spoil of the cities, and every man they smote with the sword . . . until they had destroyed them, neither left they any to breathe." Rather than having any doubts about such a brutal policy, the Israelites believed it had been ordered by their Lord himself—indeed that Yahweh had inspired the Canaanites to offer resistance so that there would be reason to slaughter them: "For it was of the Lord to harden their hearts, that they should come against Israel in battle, that he might destroy them utterly" (Joshua 11:20).

The prophetic revolution

In comparison to such dubious notions of divine justice, the ideas advanced during the third stage of Hebrew religious development can be deemed revolutionary; in fact the stage is customarily called that of the *prophetic revolution*. The "prophets" who effected this revolution in religious thought lived at the time of the threat to Hebrew nationhood coming from Assyria and Babylonia and during the period of the exile in Babylon, that is, from roughly 750 to roughly 550 B.C. Although the word "prophet" has come to mean someone who predicts the future, its original meaning is closer to "preacher"—more exactly someone who has an urgent message to proclaim, in the belief that his message derives from divine inspiration. The foremost Hebrew prophets were Amos and Hosea, who "prophesied" (i.e., preached and exhorted) in the Kingdom of Israel shortly before its fall in 722 B.C.; Isaiah and Jeremiah, who prophesied in Judah before its fall in 586 B.C.; and Ezekiel and the second Isaiah (the Book of Isaiah was probably written by three different authors) who prophesied "by the waters of Babylon." Initially warning of imminent disaster to Israelites who worshiped and behaved improperly, and then announcing the justice of God's retribution, these men's messages were sufficiently similar to each other to warrant treating them as if they formed a single coherent body of religious thought.

The prophets' teachings

Three doctrines made up the core of the prophets' teachings: (1) thoroughgoing monotheism—Yahweh is the ruler of the universe; He even makes use of nations other than the Hebrews to accomplish His purposes; the gods of others are false gods; (2) Yahweh is exclusively a god of righteousness; He wills only the good, and evil in the world comes from humanity, not from Him; (3) since Yahweh is righteous, He demands ethical behavior from His Israelite children more than anything else; He cares less for ritual and sacrifice than that His followers should "seek justice, relieve the oppressed, protect the fatherless, and plead for the widow." Merged with the Canaanites and practicing settled agriculture after the time of David, some Israelites had reverted to offering sacrifices to Canaanite fertility gods in the hope that such sacrifices would ensure rich harvests, while others who remained thoroughly loyal to Yahweh dedicated themselves ever more to ritualism as a demonstration of their loyalty. In fierce opposition to such practices, the prophet Amos summed up the prophetic revolution and marked one of the epoch-making moments in human cultural development when he expressed Yahweh's resounding warning:

> I hate, I despise your feasts,
>   and I take no delight in your solemn assemblies.

Even though you offer me your burnt offer-
    ings and cereal offerings,
     I will not accept them,
and the peace offerings of your fatted beasts
     I will not look upon.
Take away from me the noise of your songs;
    to the melody of your harps I will not listen.
But let justice roll down like waters,
    and righteousness like an ever-flowing
      stream.   —Amos 5:21–24

   The last stage in the shaping of Judaism took place during the four centuries after the return of the Jews from Babylon; thus it is called the postexi-
ilic stage. The major contribution of postexilic religious thinkers was a set
of eschatological doctrines, writings on "last things" or what will happen at
the end of time. Under the indirect or direct sway of Persians and Greeks,
and during the years of the Maccabean revolt, Jewish thinkers in Palestine
began to wonder ever more about what role their small and politically
weak nation would play in the divine plan for the world, and hence began
to fix upon messianic and millenarian expectations. In other words, they
came to believe that God would soon send them a national savior or "messiah" (meaning "anointed one"), who would not only lift up the Jews to
greatness but would spread the worship of Yahweh to the entire world
during a millennium of peace and justice before the end of time. At first
they assumed that the millennial kingdom of peace would be "this-
worldly"—that humans would live to see and enjoy it, as in the words of
the third Isaiah, "for as the earth bringeth forth her bud . . . so the Lord
God will cause righteousness and praise to spring forth before nations" (Isaiah 61:11). But as time went on, the likelihood that the millennial kingdom would arise naturally "as the earth brings forth its bud" seemed for
some ever more remote, with the alternative of otherworldly triumph

The postexilic stage

Jewish Sarcophagus. A wealthy Jew commis-sioned this sarcophagus around 100 C.E. Today he would emblemize his reli-gion with a Star of David, but then the standard em-blem for Judaism was the menorah. Under the menorah are the three He-brew children in the fiery furnace from the Book of Daniel, probably meant here to stand for the im-mortality of the soul and the patron's own hope for eternal life.

seeming to them more inescapable. The fullest statement of otherworldly eschatology in the Old Testament appears in the Book of Daniel, written not by a Daniel who may have lived at the time of Nebuchadnezzar, but instead by someone who wrote under Daniel's name during the time of the revolt of the Maccabees. In the view of this seer, the messiah, called by him "the Son of Man," would come "with the clouds of heaven," and would have an "everlasting dominion, which shall not pass away" (Daniel 7:13–14). Integral to this otherworldly view was the belief that the messiah would preside over a "last judgment"; in other words, that by supernatural means all the human dead would be resurrected to stand at judgment before the messiah for the quality of their lives, evil men and women being condemned to eternal suffering, "saints" remaining to serve in the "greatness of the kingdom under the whole heaven" (Daniel 7:26–28).

*Hopes for the coming of the
messiah*

The Jewish expectation of a messiah has obvious bearing on the career of Jesus, a Jew who was considered to be the messiah by Jewish and Gentile followers, who thereafter became known as Christians. (Further treatment of the split-off of Christianity from Judaism will be found in Chapter 8.) The Jews who denied that Jesus was the messiah continued to expect that the messiah would come. Some thought of him as coming in the clouds, as in Daniel, but most expected him to be an earthly savior who would exalt the nation of Israel and rebuild the Temple. Either way the expectation of the miraculous coming of the messiah motivated the Jewish people to maintain all their other beliefs and practices steadfastly even when they were forced to live thousands of miles away from the Holy Land. To a large degree it accounts for the real Jewish miracle—the capacity of an otherwise insignificant nation to endure until the present despite appalling adversity, enriching the world by its accomplishments in myriad ways.

4. HEBREW LAW AND LITERATURE

The ancient Hebrews were not great scientists, builders, or artists. So far as can be judged, even Solomon's Temple was not really a Hebrew building accomplishment, for it appears that Phoenician masons and artisans were called in to address the most challenging construction tasks involved in the project. Since the Hebrew religious code prohibited the making of any "graven image" or "likeness" of anything in heaven, earth, or water (Exodus 20:4), there was no sculpture and no painting. Instead it was in law and literature that ancient Hebrew culture found its most estimable expressions.

*Hebrew culture: Limitations
and accomplishments*

The major repository of Hebrew law is the Deuteronomic Code, which forms the core of the biblical Book of Deuteronomy. Although partly based on very ancient traditions that display kinship with the legal thought of the Old Babylonians, the Deuteronomic Code in its present form undoubtedly dates from the time of the prophetic revolution. In general its provisions are more altruistic and equitable than the laws found in the Old Babylonian Code of Hammurabi. As examples of altruism, it not only en-

*Hebrew law: The
Deuteronomic Code*

Hebrew Inscription from a Synagogue Pavement. The Hebrew people created no statuary because of the biblical injunction against "graven images," and the same injunction apparently prohibited all figural art until roughly the time of Christ. Here, in a mosaic pavement from Palestine dating from about 900 C.E., a dedication and prayer take the place of art. Note that Hebrew writing moves from right to left.

joins generosity to the poor and to the stranger, but it prescribes that the Hebrew slave who had served six years should be freed and given some provisions to start his own life, and it requires that every seven years all debtors be released from their debts. Fairness is found in principles dictating that children should not be held responsible for the guilt of their fathers and that judges under no circumstances should be allowed to accept gifts. Above all the Deuteronomic Code upholds the stringent ideal of what is "altogether just," for Yahweh demands no less, and only by living "altogether justly" could the Hebrews consider themselves worthy of inheriting the promised land.

Taken in total the literature of the Hebrews was the finest produced by any ancient civilization of western Asia. All of it that survives is found in the Old Testament and in the books of the Apocrypha (ancient Hebrew works not recognized as scriptural because of doubtful religious authority). Except for a few fragments like the Song of Deborah in Judges 5, the Old Testament is not really so old as is commonly supposed. Scholars now recognize that it was created from a series of collections and revisions in which old and new parts were merged and generally assigned to an ancient author—Moses, for example. But the oldest of these revisions was not prepared any earlier than 850 B.C. The majority of the books of the Old Testament were of still later origin, excepting some of the chronicles. Although the bulk of the Psalms were ascribed to King David, a good many of them refer to events of the Babylonian Captivity, and it is certain that the collection of Psalms as a whole was the work of several centuries.

Hebrew literature

Granted that parts of the Old Testament consist of long lists of names or arcane ritual prohibitions, others, whether biographical or military narratives, thanksgiving prayers, battle hymns, prophetic exhortations, love lyrics, or dialogues, are rich in rhythm, evocative imagery, and emotional vigor. Few passages in any language can surpass the chaste beauty of the

Old Testament literary qualities

Twenty-third Psalm: "the Lord is my shepherd, I shall not want. He maketh me to lie down in green pastures, he leadeth me beside the still waters. He restoreth my soul . . ."; or the vision of peace in Isaiah: "and they shall beat their swords into plowshares, and their spears into pruninghooks; nation shall not lift up sword against nation, neither shall they learn war any more."

Song of Songs

Among the most beautiful of all the world's love lyrics is the biblical Song of Songs. Although generations of readers have sought to find figurative spiritual meaning in it (and some modern critics tell us we are free to find any meaning in any text we like), the Song of Songs surely originated around the fifth century B.C. as a collection of purely secular wedding poems. The bridegroom praises his bride as his "dove," and she regards him as her "king." Together they rejoice in the prospect of sharing caresses and a loving life together in the orchards and the vineyards: "Rise up, my love, my fair one, and come away. For lo, the winter is past, the rain is over and gone; the flowers appear on the earth . . . and the vines with the tender grape give a good smell. . . . Behold, thou art fair, my love . . . thou hast doves' eyes . . . thy teeth are like a flock of sheep that are even shorn. . . . My beloved is gone down into his garden, to the beds of spices, to feed in the gardens and to gather lilies. I am my beloved's, and my beloved is mine."

The Book of Job

An entirely different variety of Hebrew literary achievement is the Book of Job, written sometime between 500 to 300 B.C. In form the work is a drama of the tragic struggle between man and fate. Its central theme is the problem of evil: how it can be that the righteous suffer while the wicked prosper. The story was an old one, adapted very probably from an Old Babylonian writing of similar content. But the Hebrews introduced into it a much deeper realization of philosophical possibilities. The main character, Job, a man of virtue, is suddenly overtaken by a series of disasters: he is despoiled of his property, his children are killed, and his body is afflicted with disease. His attitude at first is one of stoic resignation; the evil must be accepted along with the good. But as his sufferings increase he is plunged into despair. He curses the day of his birth and praises death, where "the wicked cease from troubling and the weary be at rest."

The problem of evil in Job

Then follows a lengthy debate between Job and his friends over the meaning of evil. The latter take the view that all suffering is a punishment for sin, and that those who repent are forgiven and strengthened in character. But Job is not satisfied with any of their arguments. Torn between hope and despair, he strives to review the problem from every angle. He even considers the possibility that death may not be the end, that there may be some adjustment of the balance hereafter. But the mood of despair returns, and he decides that God is an omnipotent demon, destroying without mercy wherever His caprice or anger directs. Finally, in his anguish he appeals to the Almighty to reveal Himself and make known His ways to him. God answers him out of the whirlwind with a magnificent exposition of the tremendous works of nature. Convinced of his own insignificance and of the unutterable majesty of God, Job despises himself and repents in dust and ashes. In the end no solution for the problem of individual suffering is given. No promise is made of recompense in a life hereafter, nor does God make any effort to refute the hopeless pessimism of Job. Humans must take comfort in the philosophic reflection that the universe is greater than themselves, and that God in the pursuit of His sublime purposes cannot really be limited by human standards of equity and goodness.

As different as the lyric Song of Songs and the tragic Book of Job are from each other, the bleakly worldly wise Book of Ecclesiastes is different from both. Unquestionably this book, attributed to Solomon but surely written no earlier than the third century B.C., contains some of the Bible's most pithy and forceful quotations. Yet its doctrine contradicts all the elevated presuppositions found in the rest of the Hebrew Bible, for the author of Ecclesiastes was a skeptic and a materialist. According to him humans die just like beasts, no afterlife being granted to either, and human history is no more than the successive passing away of generations. Everything is cyclical, and nothing adds up to lasting achievement, for "the sun also rises and the sun goeth down, and hasteth to the place where he arose . . . and there is nothing new under the sun." On top of all this purposeless repetition, in the realm of human affairs, blind fate rather than merit predominates, for "the race is not to the swift, nor the battle to the strong . . . nor yet riches to men of understanding, nor yet favor to men of skill, but time and chance happen to them all." In light of these circumstances the author proposes taking life as it comes without excess: "be not righteous overmuch, neither make thyself over wise . . . be not over much wicked, neither be thou foolish: why shouldest thou die before thy time?" Surprisingly in view of his bleakness he also "commends mirth," on the grounds that "a man hath no better thing under the sun than to eat, and drink, and to be merry."

Book of Ecclesiastes

How it came about that a text which offers the maxim "be not righteous overmuch" crept into the Hebrew Bible remains uncertain, but it cannot be stressed overmuch that it is exceptional. Therefore, rather than ending this survey of Hebrew literature with Ecclesiastes, it is best to point out that the last book of the Hebrew Bible, Malachi, ends on a highly characteristic note, both in terms of its prophetic-eschatological message and its vigorously affirmative expression, when it has Yahweh state: "unto you that fear my name shall the Sun of righteousness arise with healing in his wings . . . and ye shall tread down the wicked . . . Behold, I will send you Elijah the prophet before the coming of the great and dreadful day of the Lord."

Old Testament ultimately affirmative

5. THE MAGNITUDE OF THE HEBREW INFLUENCE

The history of Western existence during the past two thousand years has been profoundly influenced by the Hebrew heritage, partly because of the activities of the Jews and partly because Judaism was the matrix from

The Hebrew legacy

whence sprang Christianity. (As will be seen in Chapter 9, a third great world religion, Islam, grew from both Judaism and Christianity.) Virtually all religious believers in the West today are monotheists—descendants in belief, therefore, from Moses and the Hebrew prophets. In addition Hebrew transcendent theology has given westerners the sense of assurance that they are masters of nature and need not waver in cutting down trees or changing the courses of rivers for fear of angering forest or water deities. Whether in its religious version or its secular adaptations, this worldview has surely contributed enormously to Western technological initiative. The morality shaped by the great Hebrew prophets remains the morality most ethically sensitive people today cherish: "Love thy neighbor as thyself" (Leviticus 19:18) speaks better than any paraphrase. And the vision of a world united in peace, when "the wolf shall dwell with the lamb, and the leopard shall lie down with the kid" (Isaiah 11:6), is a vision that we all know must be implemented soon or else no tradition will mean anything to anyone.

6. THE MINOAN AND MYCENAEAN CIVILIZATIONS

Before 1870 no one guessed that great civilizations flourished in the Greek archipelago many hundreds of years before the rise of Athens. Students of the Greek epic, Homer's *Iliad,* of course knew that a mighty Greek king, Agamemnon, was supposed to have led all the Greeks to victory in the "Trojan War" long before the eighth century B.C., when the *Iliad* was first set down in writing. But it was simply assumed that Homer's entire plot was fictional. Today, however, scholars are certain that Greek history—and thus European history—began well over one thousand years before Socrates started discussing the nature of truth in the Athenian marketplace.

The breakthrough into certain knowledge of these ancient Greek civilizations came about as the result of the most famous "storybook triumph" in the annals of archeology. In the middle of the nineteenth century the German businessman, Heinrich Schliemann, fascinated from youth by the narrative in the *Iliad,* determined to prove his hunch that there was substantial truth in it as soon as he had gained sufficient income. Luckily Schliemann accumulated a fortune in his business ventures and thereupon retired to spend his time and his money in pursuit of Agamemnon. Although he had no archeological or scholarly training, in 1870 he began excavating in western Asia Minor at a site he felt confident was that of ancient Troy, and, amazingly enough, soon after he began digging he uncovered portions of nine different ancient cities, each built upon the ruins of its predecessor. Schliemann identified the second of these cities as the Troy of the *Iliad*, but scholars now believe that Troy was probably the seventh city. Encouraged by his success, he started excavations in Greece in 1876, and lo and behold, he struck gold again—this time literally as well as figuratively because he hit upon a grave site containing gold in staggering quantities. Since Schliemann's dig of 1876 was located at a deserted Greek site called Mycenae (pronounced Myseénee), he felt completely vindicated because the *Iliad* stated that Mycenae was Agamemnon's place of residence and termed it "Mycenae rich in gold." It is sad to report that Schliemann's excavations were not unqualifiedly beneficial to the study of the distant past because in his zealous enthusiasm and disregard of scientific procedures he destroyed evidence as he dug and scorned meticulous record-keeping. Yet all told his discoveries were so exciting and momentous that they themselves almost merit being memorialized in an epic.

Once Schliemann demonstrated that there was some truth in what formerly had been regarded as legend, others rushed to add to his discoveries. His most important successor in this regard was the Englishman Arthur Evans. In 1899 Evans began looking for "Minos" as Schliemann had been looking for Agamemnon—which meant that Evans began excavating on the Greek island of Crete because legend had identified the city of Knossos on Crete as the capital of a mighty empire ruled over by a ruler named Minos. Again, legend proved to have some kernel of fact, for Evans soon found remains as rich (and indeed more beautiful) than anything dug up by Schliemann. Although Evans's work (which earned him a knighthood) followed after Schliemann's, the civilization he found at Knossos dates back earlier than the Greek civilization uncovered by Schliemann. Hence we should look at the "world of Minos" before we see how it became drawn into the "world of Agamemnon."

The earliest traces of the *Minoan civilization,* so called by modern scholars after the legendary Cretan ruler Minos, date from the period around 2000 B.C. Around that time the Minoans, whose origins before they inhabited Crete are unknown, had begun to build cities and to develop a unique form of writing. The half-millennium from about 2000 to 1500 B.C. saw Minoan civilization at its peak. Rather than being the center of an empire, Knossos was one of several thriving cities on Crete that coexisted so har-

Cretan Labyrinth Coin. According to legend, King Minos of Crete built a labyrinth to pen in the Minotaur, part man, part bull. This coin from about 300 B.C. shows the labyrinth as the emblem of Knossos.

Flowering of Minoan civilization

Central Staircase of the Palace at Knossos

THE EARLY AEGEAN WORLD

moniously that none of them found it necessary to build protective walls. Only earthquakes, which periodically shook the island, interrupted the Minoans' serene existence. These natural disasters caused much devastation, but after each the Minoans set about rebuilding their cities and usually managed to found more splendid ones than those that had just been destroyed. At Knossos Sir Arthur Evans found not just beautiful stonework and paintings but humanity's first known flush-toilet. Later excavations at another Minoan site, Kato Zakros, unearthed a huge palace with 250 rooms, a swimming pool, and parquet floors.

Origins of the Mycenaean civilization

While the Minoan civilization was flourishing on Crete, potential rivals were gaining strength on the mainland of Greece. Around 2200 B.C. Indo-European peoples who spoke the earliest form of Greek invaded the Greek peninsula, and by 1600 B.C. they had begun to form small cities. Primarily owing to trading relations, these peoples gradually became influenced in their cultural development by Minoan Crete. The civilization that resulted from the fusion of Greek and Minoan elements is called Mycenaean after Mycenae, the leading city of Greece from about 1600 to 1200 B.C. It was this civilization that became dominant in the Aegean world (the Aegean Sea is that part of the Mediterranean lying between Greece and Asia Minor) after about 1500 B.C. and even gained predominance on Crete itself.

One of the greatest scholarly accomplishments of the twentieth century radically altered our understanding of Cretan and Greek history in the century between 1500 and 1400 B.C. It was once thought that Greece throughout that time was still a semibarbarous economic colony of splendid Crete and that internal changes on Crete between 1500 and 1400 B.C. could be attributed to the rise of a "new dynasty." It was known that numerous specimens of the same linear script (called "Linear B") could be found on both Crete and the Greek mainland, but it was simply assumed that the script was Cretan in origin and spread from Crete to Greece. But in 1952 a brilliant young Englishman, Michael Ventris, who was then only thirty years old (and tragically died in an automobile accident four years later), succeeded in deciphering Linear B and demonstrating that it expressed an early form of Greek. Ventris's discovery revolutionized preclassical Greek studies by showing that the mainlanders dominated Crete in the late Minoan period and not vice versa.

Linear B

Wall Painting from Thera. The volcanic eruption on the island of Thera preserved many splendid paintings. Here an elegant priestess is burning incense.

Scholars now agree that the Mycenaeans supplanted the Minoans as rulers of the Aegean world shortly after 1500 B.C., although they are uncertain exactly how that happened. A fascinating source of speculation concerns the effects of an immense volcanic eruption on the island of Thera, some seventy miles distant from Crete. It is certain that around 1500 an eruption on Thera was so great that it buried all the island's dwellings under several feet of volcanic ash; possibly this event formed the historical basis for the later Greek legend of Atlantis, a mythic island said to have been struck by an earthquake that sank it far under the sea. Without doubt, the eruption of the volcano on Thera caused tremors and floods on Crete that damaged coastal settlements and many buildings in Knossos. Yet, so far as can be told, rebuilding efforts were swift, and life quickly returned to normal. Perhaps some degree of local political weakness caused by the disaster allowed Greek mainlanders to take control of Crete around this time, but it seems more likely that for unrelated reasons the Mycenaeans had become strong enough to conquer Crete with minimal fighting. In either event, between about 1475 and 1400 B.C., the Mycenaeans presided over an era of prosperity and artistic accomplishment on Crete.

*Mycenaeans supplant
Minoans*

A Linear B Tablet from Knossos

Mycenaeans succumb to
Dorians

A Minoan Vase, c. 1400 B.C. Minoan potters glorified in creating
a great variety of shapes.

The Minoan king as
economic overseer

Minoan state as bureaucratic
monarchy

Around 1400 B.C., however, another wave of Mycenaeans crossed over to Crete, destroyed Knossos, and put a sudden end to the Minoan civilization. Why this invasion was so destructive remains unknown, but it left mainland Greece unrivaled as the dominant power of the Aegean world for about another two hundred years. Around 1250 B.C., the Mycenaeans waged their successful war with the Trojans of western Asia Minor, but their own downfall was now on the horizon. In the course of the century between 1200 and 1100 B.C., the Mycenaeans succumbed to the Dorians—barbaric northern Greeks who had iron weapons. (Iron weapons may not at first have been much superior to the bronze ones used by the Mycenaeans, but since iron ore was found far more widely in western Asia and eastern Europe than the copper and tin needed for bronze, iron weapons were much cheaper, thereby allowing many more fighters to wield them.) Because the Dorians were primitive in all but their weaponry, their ascendancy constituted a dark age in Greek history that lasted until about 800 B.C.

As can be seen from the foregoing account, the Minoan and Mycenaean civilizations were closely interrelated; even the greatest experts have difficulty in determining exactly where one left off and the other began. The problem is complicated by the fact that two forms of writing that predate Linear B and have been found on Crete alone have not yet been deciphered. (Anyone who wishes to become as famous as Schliemann, Evans, or Ventris may take the decipherment of Minoan writing as his or her goal.) Accordingly, discussions of Minoan civilization before about 1500 B.C. rely exclusively on visual and archeological evidence, leaving much to the realm of speculation. Such evidence, however, does suggest that Minoan civilization was one of the most progressive in all of early history.

The Minoan ruler was not a bristling warlord like the Assyrian king. He does seem to have commanded a large navy, but this was not for war but for the maintenance of trade. In fact, the king was the chief entrepreneur in the country. The workshops located near his palace turned out great quantities of fine pottery, textiles, and metal goods. Although private enterprise apparently was not prohibited, it seems to have been heavily taxed. Nevertheless, there were some privately owned workshops, especially in smaller towns, and much agriculture was also in private hands.

The Minoan state is best described as a bureaucratic monarchy. The ruler of each leading city and its surrounding territory appears to have been absolute, and toward the end of Minoan history (exactly when is hard to say) the ruler of Knossos appears to have taken over the entire island. The absolute ruler governed by means of a large administrative class. Scribes, who seem to have had a monopoly on learning, kept close accounts of all aspects of economic life. All agricultural production and manufacturing were closely supervised for purposes of gathering or taxing whatever was owed to the king. Foreign trade too seems to have been closely supervised; most likely the Minoan ships that put into ports as far away as Syria and Egypt were owned or at least heavily taxed by the ruler and carefully watched over by the bureaucratic administration.

Despite such close supervision, the Minoan people of nearly all classes appear to have led fairly prosperous lives. Although there were great social and economic distinctions between the rulers and the ruled, there were apparently few gradations of wealth or status among the common people. If slavery existed at all, it certainly occupied an unimportant place. The dwellings in the poorest urban quarters were well built and spacious, often with as many as six or eight rooms, but we do not know how many families resided in them. Women seem to have enjoyed equality with men. Regardless of class, there was no public activity from which they were debarred, and no occupation that they could not enter. In this the Minoans were the exception in the ancient world. Crete had female bullfighters and even female boxers. Women of the upper strata devoted much time to fashion and other leisure activities.

The natives of Crete delighted in games and sports. Dancing, running races, and boxing rivaled each other as main attractions. The Minoans were the first to build stone theaters where processions and music entertained large audiences. Archeological discoveries on the island of Crete indicate that the Minoans were also gifted inventors and engineers. They built excellent stone roads about eleven feet wide. Many of the principles of modern sanitary engineering were known to the designers of the palace of Knossos, with the result that the royal family of Crete in the seventeenth century B.C. enjoyed comforts and conveniences, such as indoor running water, that were not available to the royalty of Western Europe even in the seventeenth century C.E.

The religion of the Minoans was outstanding among those of the ancient world for being dominantly matriarchal. The chief deity was not a god but a goddess who was the ruler of the entire universe—the sea and the sky as

Prosperity and equality

Sports, theater, engineering

Scenes from the Bull Ring: Minoan Mural, c. 1500 B.C. Evident are the youth, skill, and agility of the Minoan athletes, the center one a male, the other two female. The body and horns of the bull are exaggerated, as are the slenderness of the athletes and their full-face eyes in profile heads. There is probably also some exaggeration in content: modern experts in bullfighting insist that it is impossible to somersault over the back of a charging bull.

*The matriarchal nature of
Minoan religion*

*The elegance of Minoan
painting*

"La Parisienne"

See color plates facing
page 77

*Similarities between the
Minoan and Mycenaean
civilizations*

well as the earth. Originally no male deity seems to have been worshiped at all, but later a god emerged who was associated with the great goddess as her son and consort. Nonetheless, this male figure was never regarded by the Minoans as having any independent importance. Although the mother goddess was considered to be the source of evil as well as good, even her evil powers were not morbid or terrifying: though she brought the storm and spread destruction, such acts served for the replenishment of nature as death served as the prerequisite for life. Mortals on earth were expected to make sacrifices to the goddess, as well as to her sacred animals, such as bulls and snakes. Minoan rites were administered by priestesses instead of priests in keeping with the female orientation of the entire belief system.

If any achievement of the Minoans best demonstrates the vitality of their civilization, it was their genius in painting. With the exception of the artistic attainments of the classical Greeks and Romans that evolved a millennium later, no art of the ancient world was its equal. The distinguishing features of Minoan painting were delicacy, spontaneity, and naturalism. It served, not to glorify the ambitions of an arrogant ruling class or to inculcate the doctrines of a religion, but to express the delight of the individual in the beauty of the Minoan world. Most of Minoan painting consisted of murals done in fresco, but painted reliefs were occasionally to be found. The murals in the palaces of Crete are surely the best that have survived from ancient times, revealing instincts for the dramatic and rhythmic and the capturing of nature in its changing moods. So sophisticated and elegant was Minoan art that a Frenchman who was unearthing the remains of a fresco at Knossos could not help exclaiming when he saw a painting of a striking woman portrayed with curls, vivid eyes, and sensuous lips: "Mais, c'est la Parisienne!" ("Why, she's just like a woman from Paris!").

Not surprisingly for a people dedicated to elegance, artistic excellence among the Minoans extended from painting to sculpture and even to household objects of everyday use. Perhaps the most noteworthy fact about Minoan sculpture is that its scale is always reduced. One looks in vain among Minoan remains for equivalents of giant Mesopotamian kings smiting their puny enemies or colossal pharaohs of Egypt advancing toward the beholder like enormous zombies, for the ancient Minoans were averse to relying on size for creating stunning effects. Instead, Minoan statues of human figures are almost always smaller than life-size, and they rely on naturalism and delicacy to engage the imagination of the viewer. Similarly, carved gems, gold-work and bronze-work, and ceramics down to the humblest crockery utensils are invariably finely wrought and sometimes wryly humorous.

Mycenaean civilization appears to have been more warlike and less refined than the Minoan, but recent scholarship warns us to beware of exaggerating these differences. Trade still flourished: Mycenaean artifacts have been found in areas as far distant as Britain and Egypt. As on Crete, so on mainland Greece, the city was the center of civilization—the leading Mycenaean cities being Mycenae itself, Pylos, and Tiryns. Each city and its surrounding area was ruled over by a king called a *wanax.* As on Crete, the

Mycenaean state was a bureaucratic monarchy. We know about some of the workings of this monarchy because of the decipherment of numerous Linear B tablets, all of which are records of a highly regulatory bureaucratic apparatus. Linear B tablets from Pylos report the minutest details of the economic lives of the king's subjects: the exact acreage of a given estate; the number of cooking utensils owned by so-and-so; the personal names given to somebody's two oxen ("Glossy" and "Blackie"). Such detailed inventories show us that the state was highly centralized and that it was supreme in its control over the economic activities of its citizens.

Although the bureaucratic monarchies of the Minoans and the Mycenaeans were similar, there were still at least a few notable differences between the two related civilizations. One was that the Mycenaeans definitely had a slave system. Mycenaean society too was geared much more toward warfare. Because Mycenaean cities frequently fought with one another they were built on hilltops and were heavily fortified. In keeping with a somewhat more rugged and barbaric style of life than that of Crete, Mycenaean kings built themselves ostentatious graves in which they buried their best inlaid bronze daggers and other signs of power and wealth.

It is also true that Mycenaean art is less elegant than Minoan art. Without question the Mycenaeans never equaled the artistic delicacy and grace of the Minoans. Nevertheless, Myceanaean artwork done in Knossos between 1500 and 1400 B.C., while stiffer and more symmetrical in composition than earlier Minoan work, is by no means wholly different in kind. Moreover, the "Parisian woman" of Minoan Knossos has some very close stylistic relatives in a female procession fresco from about 1300 B.C. found in Mycenaean Tiryns. Nor should it be thought that all the best traits of Mycenaean art can merely be seen as debased borrowings from the Minoans: the superbly executed and exquisite Mycenaean inlaid daggers have no antecedents anywhere on Crete.

The significance of the Minoan and the Mycenaean civilizations should not be estimated primarily in terms of subsequent influences. Minoan culture hardly influenced any peoples other than the Mycenaeans, and it was then destroyed more or less without a trace after about 1400 B.C. The Mycenaeans left behind a few more traces, but still not very many. Later Greeks retained some Mycenaean gods and goddesses like Zeus, Hera, and Poseidon, but they completely altered their role in the religious pantheon. It may also be that the later Greeks gained from the Mycenaeans their devotion to athletics and their system of weights and measures, but these connections remain uncertain. Homer definitely remembered the successful Mycenaean siege of Troy, but it is just as important to realize how much Homer forgot: writing in the eighth century B.C. Homer (actually several different writers who have come down to us under that name) entirely forgot the whole pattern of Mycenaean bureaucracy that we know from the Linear B tablets. It may well be that the break between the Mycenaeans and the later Greeks was all for the good. Some historians maintain that the destruction of despotic Mycenae by the Dorians was a necessary prelude to the emergence of the freer and more enlightened later Greek outlook.

Mycenaean departures from the Minoan social model

Detail from a Procession Fresco at Tiryns, c. 1300 B.C. Note the similarity of this Mycenaean female profile to the Minoan "La Parisienne" shown on p. 90.

Influence of the Minoan and Mycenaean civilizations

Although the Minoan and Mycenaean civilizations had little subsequent influence, they are still noteworthy for at least four reasons. First of all, they were the earliest civilizations of Europe. Before the Minoan accomplishments all civilizations had existed farther east, but afterward Europe was to witness the development of one impressive civilization after another. Second, in some respects the Minoans and the Mycenaeans seem to have looked forward to certain later European values and accomplishments even if they did not directly influence them. Minoan and Mycenaean political organization was similar to that of many Asian states, but Minoan art in particular seems very different and more characteristic of later European patterns. Third, the Minoan civilization, and to a lesser degree also the Mycenaean one, is significant for its worldly and progressive outlook. This is exemplified in the devotion of the Aegean peoples to comfort and opulence, in their love of amusement, zest for life, and courage for experimentation. And finally, whereas ancient Assyria, ancient Babylon, and even ancient Egypt all breathed their last as "corpses in armor," ancient Crete breathed its last amid joyous festivals celebrated in cities without walls.

SELECTED READINGS

• *Items so designated are available in paperback editions.*

HEBREWS

• Albright, W. F., *From the Stone Age to Christianity,* New York, 1957. Emphasizes the development of Hebrew monotheism.

  Anderson, Bernhard W., *Understanding the Old Testament,* 4th ed., Englewood Cliffs, N.J., 1986.

  Baron, Salo W., *A Social and Religious History of the Jews,* rev. ed., 18 vols., New York, 1952–1980. A modern classic: almost all work on Jewish history takes Baron as a point of departure.

• Bickerman, Elias J., *From Ezra to the Last of the Maccabees: Foundations of Post-Biblical Judaism,* New York, 1962.

  Bright, John, *A History of Israel,* 3rd ed., Philadelphia, 1981. A standard account.

  Hermann, Siegfried, *A History of Israel in Old Testament Times,* London, 1975. Iconoclastic and challenging.

• Kaufmann, Yehezkel, *The Religion of Israel,* New York, 1972. Stresses the uniqueness of the Hebrew religious accomplishment.

• McCullough, W. S., *The History and Literature of the Palestinian Jews from Cyrus to Herod, 550 B.C. to 4 B.C.,* Toronto, 1976.

  Noth, Martin, *The History of Israel,* 2nd ed., New York, 1960. A provocative reappraisal.

• Orlinsky, H. M., *Ancient Israel,* 2nd ed., Ithaca, N.Y., 1960. A good brief overview of ancient Hebrew history.

  Rowley, H. H., *Growth of the Old Testament,* New York, 1963. A helpful survey of scholarly opinion concerning the circumstances of origin of the various Old Testament books.

- Schürer, E., *The History of the Jewish People in the Age of Jesus Christ* (*175 B.C.–A.D.135*), rev. ed., 3 vols., Edinburgh, 1973–1983. A new edition of an irreplaceable nineteenth-century narrative.
- Vaux, Roland de, *Ancient Israel: Its Life and Institutions,* New York, 1962. Especially valuable for archaeological data.

MINOANS AND MYCENAEANS

Alsop, Joseph, *From the Silent Earth: A Report on the Greek Bronze Age,* New York, 1964. An enthusiastic account by a modern political reporter of some of the most exciting discoveries and hypotheses. Favors the Mycenaeans in discussions of their relationships to the Minoans.

Blegen, Carl W., *Troy and the Trojans,* New York, 1963. The most reliable archeological appraisal.

- Chadwick, John, *The Decipherment of Linear B,* 2nd ed., New York, 1968. Chadwick was a research colleague of Michael Ventris and here gives the most accessible account of Ventris's brilliant work.

———, *The Mycenaean World,* New York, 1976. A lively account of the society based on the evidence of the Linear B tablets.

- Finley, M. I., *Early Greece: The Bronze and Archaic Ages,* New York, 1970. An excellent survey that spans two different eras.
- Higgins, Reynold, *Minoan and Mycenaean Art,* rev. ed., London, 1981.

History of the Hellenic World, Vol. I, Prehistoric and Protohistory, University Park, Pa., 1974.

Hood, Sinclair, *The Minoans,* London, 1971.

MacDonald, William A., *Progress into the Past: The Rediscovery of Mycenaean Civilization,* New York, 1967.

Palmer, L. R., *Mycenaeans and Minoans,* New York, 1962. Includes both statements on many debatable problems of interpretation.

- Starr, Chester G., *The Origins of Greek Civilization,* New York, 1961.
- Vermeule, Emily, *Greece in the Bronze Age,* Chicago, 1964. The best book on the subject.

SOURCE MATERIALS

Baron, Salo W., and J. L. Blau, eds. *Judaism: Post-Biblical and Talmudic Periods,* New York, 1954.

- The *Old Testament* and the *Apocrypha,* many editions.
- Pritchard, J. B., ed., *Ancient Near Eastern Texts Relating to the Old Testament,* 3rd ed., Princeton, 1969.

Part Two

THE CLASSICAL CIVILIZATIONS OF GREECE AND ROME

After about 600 B.C. the once mighty civilizations of Mesopotamia and Egypt became overshadowed and then dominated by the classical civilizations of Greece and Rome. The word classical comes from the Latin classicus, meaning "of the first class," and is customarily used to denote the civilization that flourished in Greece between about 600 B.C. and 300 B.C. and the one centered in Rome between about 300 B.C. and 300 C.E. Although the classical Roman civilization gradually began to take shape around the time when the classical Greek civilization was losing its independent identity, "Rome" did not directly supplant "Greece." Rather, transpiring chronologically between the heyday of the Greek and Roman civilizations was the time of the Hellenistic civilization, a hybrid composed of elements derived from Greece and western Asia. Based territorially on conquests of Alexander the Great completed in 323 B.C., the Hellenistic civilization extended over all of Greece, all of Egypt, and most of Asia up to the borders of India, and it maintained its separate identity from 323 B.C. until shortly before the birth of Christ. The outstanding characteristic that distinguishes the three civilizations in question from those that had gone before was their secularism. No longer did religion absorb the interests and expend the wealth of humans to the extent that it did in ancient Mesopotamia and Egypt. The state now became much more independent of the priesthood, and the life of the mind was freed from the dictates of organized belief-systems. In addition, ideals of human freedom and an emphasis on the welfare of the individual superseded the despotism and collectivism that characterized the civilizations of the Tigris, Euphrates, and Nile. Only late in the development of Roman civilization did despotism begin to reassert itself. Around that time too, a new religion, Christianity, began to reshape the lives of those who lived in the Roman world.

The Classical Civilizations of Greece and Rome

POLITICS	PHILOSOPHY AND SCIENCE	
Dark Ages of Greek history, 1150–800		
		800 *B.C.*
Beginning of city-states in Greece, c. 800		
Rome founded, c. 753		
Shift from cavalry to infantry in Greece, c. 650	Thales of Miletus, c. 600	
Reforms of Solon in Athens, 594		
Cyrus the Great of Persia, 559–529	Pythagoras, c. 530	
Darius the Great of Persia, 521–486		
Reforms of Clisthenes in Athens, 507		
Establishment of Roman Republic, c. 500	Protagoras, c. 490–c. 420	*500* *B.C.*
Greco-Persian War, 490–479	Socrates, 469–399	
Delian League, 478–404		
Perfection of Athenian democracy, 487–429	Hippocrates, 460–c. 377	
Law of the Twelve Tables, Rome, c. 450	The Sophists, c. 450–c. 400	
Peloponnesian War, 431–404	Plato, c. 429–347	
	Aristotle, 384–322	*400* *B.C.*
	Epicurus, 342–270	
Macedonian conquest of Greece, 338	Herophilus, c. 335–c. 280	
Conquests of Alexander the Great, 334–323	Zeno the Stoic, c. 320–c. 250	
Division of Alexander's empire, 323	Euclid, c. 323–285	
	Aristarchus, 310–230	
	Archimedes, c. 287–212	*300* *B.C.*
	Eratosthenes, c. 276–c. 196	
Punic Wars between Rome and Carthage, 264–146	Polybius, c. 205–118	
	The Skeptics, c. 200	*200* *B.C.*
Reforms of the Gracchi, 133–121	Introduction of Greek philosophy into Rome, c. 140–c. 60	
Dictatorship of Julius Caesar, 46–44	Cicero, 106–43	*100* *B.C.*
	Lucretius, 98–55	
Principate of Augustus Caesar, 27 B.C.–14 C.E.	Seneca, 4 B.C.–65 C.E.	
"Five Good Emperors," 96–180	Epictetus, 60–120	*100* *C.E.*
	Marcus Aurelius, 121–180	
	Galen, 130–c. 200	*200* *C.E.*
Civil war in Roman Empire, 235–284	Plotinus, c. 204–270	
Diocletian, 284–305		
Constantine I, 306–337		
Theodosius I, 379–395		
Visigoths sack Rome, 410		*300* *C.E.*
Deposition of last of Western Roman emperors, 476		*400* *C.E.*
Theodoric the Ostrogoth king of Italy, 493–526	Boethius, c. 480–524	*500* *C.E.*
Justinian, 527–565		
Corpus of Roman law, c. 550		

The Classical Civilizations of Greece and Rome (continued)

	ECONOMICS	RELIGION	ARTS AND LETTERS
			Invention of Greek alphabet, c. 800
800 B.C.			
	Greek overseas expansion, c. 750–c. 600	Zoroaster formulates Zoroastrian religion in Persia, c. 625	*Iliad* and *Odyssey,* c. 750
	Invention of coinage by Lydians, c. 600		Sappho, c. 550
500 B.C.	Royal Road of Persians, c. 500		Aeschylus, 525–456
400 B.C.			Sophocles, 496–406
			Herodotus, c. 484–c. 420
			Euripides, 480–406
			Thucydides, c. 460–c. 400
			The Parthenon, c. 460
			Aristophanes, c. 448–c. 380
300 B.C.	Hellenistic international trade and growth of large cities, c. 300–c. 100	Emergence of Mithraism, c. 300	Theocritus, c. 300–c. 250
	Growth of slavery, decline of small farmer in Rome,		
200 B.C.	c. 250–100	Eastern mystery cults in Rome, c. 250–50	
100 B.C.		Spread of Mithraism in Rome, 27 B.C.–270 C.E.	Virgil, 70–19
			Horace, 65–8
		The Crucifixion, c. 30 C.E.	Livy, 59 B.C.–17 C.E.
100 C.E.	Decline of slavery in Rome, c. 120–c. 476	St. Paul's missionary work, c. 35–c. 67	Ovid, c. 43 B.C.–17 C.E.
			Tacitus, c. 55 C.E.–c. 117 C.E.
			The Colosseum, c. 80 C.E.
200 C.E.	Economic contraction in Rome, c. 200–c. 300		The Pantheon, c. 120
		Beginning of toleration of Christians in the Roman Empire, 311	Height of Roman portrait statuary, c. 120–c. 250
300 C.E.			
		St. Augustine, 354–430	
400 C.E.		Christianity made sole religion of Roman Empire, 392	
500 C.E.		Benedictine monastic rule, c. 520	

Chapter 5

GREEK CIVILIZATION

We love beauty without extravagance, and wisdom without weakness of will. Wealth we regard not as a means for private display but rather for public service; and poverty we consider no disgrace, although we think it is a disgrace not to try to overcome it. We believe a man should be concerned about public as well as private affairs, for we regard the person who takes no part in politics not as merely uninterested but as useless.

          —Pericles, *Funeral Oration,* on the ideals of Athens

Now, what is characteristic of any nature is that which is best for it and gives most joy. Such to man is the life according to reason, since it is this that makes him man.

          —Aristotle, *Nicomachean Ethics*

Among all the peoples of the ancient world, the one whose culture most clearly exemplified the spirit of Western society was the Greek or Hellenic. No other people had so strong a devotion to freedom or so firm a belief in the nobility of human achievement. The Greeks glorified humanity as the most important creation in the universe and refused to submit to the dictates of priests or despots. The Greek view of the world was predominantly secular and rationalistic; it exalted the spirit of free inquiry and preferred knowledge to faith. With only a limited cultural inheritance from the past upon which to build, the Greeks produced intellectual and artistic monuments that have served ever since as standards of achievement. "Wonders are many on earth, and the greatest of these are humans," the Greek tragic poet Sophocles proposed, to which we might well respond: "wonders were many in the ancient world, and the greatest of these were the Greeks."

The character of Greek civilization

1. THE GREEK DARK AGES

The fall of the Mycenaean civilization resulted in catastrophic change for the Hellenic world (*Hellas* is the Greek for Greece). It ushered in a period

The Early Greek Smile. Greek statues dating from the period when the city-states were taking shape already show a bemused view of human existence.

usually called the Dark Ages, which lasted from about 1150 to 800 B.C. Written records disappeared, and culture reverted to simpler forms. Toward the end of the period some decorated pottery and skillfully crafted metal objects began to appear on the islands of the Aegean Sea, but basically the period was a long night. Given the lack of writing or physical remains, our knowledge of Greek society during the Dark Ages is scanty, almost all of it coming from inferences drawn from the *Iliad* and the *Odyssey.* Since these epic poems, mistakenly attributed by the Greeks of later centuries to a single blind genius named Homer, evolved from oral traditions during the Dark Ages, they tell us the most we can hope to know of how the Greeks then lived.

Political patterns were very simple. Village communities were autonomous. The ruler of each, called *basileus* (Greek for king), was little more than a tribal leader who commanded the local army. Whatever assemblies existed were gatherings of warriors, convened informally to decide where and how to fight the next battle. Occasionally when warriors came together at such times they conferred about other matters of common concern, and they did what they could to put their decisions into effect. Formal legal institutions were entirely lacking—murder was punished (if at all) when the family of the victim took its revenge. A good illustration of the indifference of Greeks during the Dark Ages to organized government comes from the *Odyssey:* when Ulysses, king of Ithaca, was absent for twenty years, no regent replaced him, no assemblies were convened, and no one seemed to think that the absence of government was a matter of importance.

Forms of social and economic life toward the end of the Dark Ages were equally simple. Everyone lived on the land. The kings and warriors, who together owned most of the land, were steadily occupied in the daily administration of their estates. Otherwise agriculture and herding were the basic occupations of free men. Although slavery existed, male slaves were relatively few in number because the source of supply was war prisoners, and males were usually slaughtered rather than taken prisoner. Almost all women, including the rulers' wives, worked in the home: in the *Odyssey* Ulysses' wife Penelope occupies her time with weaving during her husband's absence. But women were not secluded; on the evidence of the *Iliad* and *Odyssey* they were free to receive male guests and could walk outdoors among men without causing comment. Every household raised its own food, manufactured its own clothing, and even produced most of its tools. Among the rare skilled craftsmen were wagonmakers and swordsmiths, paid not with cash but by barter. Indeed, the Greeks of this time were so far from being a trading people that they had no word in their language for "merchant."

Social and economic life

To the Greeks of the Dark Ages religion meant chiefly a polytheistic system for explaining the workings of the physical world and for obtaining such earthly benefits as health, offspring, and abundant harvests. The Greeks did not expect that their religion would endow them with goodness of heart or grant them everlasting rewards. Since piety was only a matter of pleasing the numerous gods by means of gifts and sacrifices, and modes of worship varied greatly, Greek religion lacked commandments, dogmas, or sacraments. The multiplicity of gods and goddesses in early Greek religion arose from the belief that different deities ruled over different natural phenomena and hence could help humans deal with these phenomena. Zeus, the mightiest of the gods, ruled the skies and gathered the storms; if one wished to bring on rains, one gave gifts to him. Similarly, Poseidon, god of the seas, might calm the waves; Aphrodite, goddess of love, might grant progeny; and Ares, god of war, might bring military victory.

Poseidon. The naked god brandishing his trident which raises storms. A coin of about 540 B.C. from the Greek city of Posidonia (southern Italy), named for Poseidon.

Religious conceptions in the Dark Ages

Left: *Zeus.* Right: *Aphrodite.* Both works of sculpture date from about 470 B.C. The male god communicates masculine majesty. Aphrodite (her Roman name was Venus) is shown rising from the sea in one of the earliest Greek works of art to exhibit naturalistic attention to the female body.

Myths

Persephone

Human qualities of the deities

Man Carrying a Calf for Sacrifice. A life-size Athenian sculpture from about 570 B.C.

In addition to this system of assigning different functions to different gods, the Greeks gradually formulated a collection of myths that helped explain nature's mysteries. One particularly poetic example is the myth of Persephone (pronounced Perséfonee), which explained why crops grew for half the year. Originally crops grew all the time. Then they stopped growing entirely when Hades, god of the underworld, raped Persephone, daughter of the goddess of vegetation, and carried her off to his infernal abode. The grief-stricken mother, Demeter, searched for Persephone in vain for many years. Because Demeter was so bereaved, nothing grew at all. Then Zeus took pity on Demeter and ruled that Persephone should return to earth, provided she had eaten nothing below. Because the girl had eaten a few pomegranate seeds a compromise was reached: Persephone would remain in the underworld for half the year and with Demeter in the sunlight for the other. Ever since, Demeter rejoices every spring when her daughter returns, making the earth fruitful; but every fall Demeter mourns and whatever crops are not harvested shrivel.

As can be seen from this story (and even more from many others), the gods of Hellas behaved much like humans. Thus individual believers could not rely on the gods' benevolence; rather they had to take divine jealousies and anger for granted. Truly chilling is the opening scene of the *Iliad*, wherein the god Apollo's implacable fury is vented on the whole Greek army because one of their leaders had offered a personal slight: "Phoebus Apollo came down from Olympus with a storm in his heart, descending black like the night. . . . With his arrows he shot at the pack-animals first, then at the dogs, then at the men, over and over again. Pyres burned for the dead day after day." With deities so terrible, the individual could only hope to ingratiate himself with them by offering sacrifices and prayers as often and opportunely as possible. Despite this need for religious ceremonies, however, the Greeks perceived no need for a professional priesthood or houses of worship. Venerable members of a clan or community often presided over collective rites, but they did so only as a part-time duty; individuals could also sacrifice or pray alone. As for the well-known Greek temples, these were places where the gods were supposed to take up temporary residence rather than locations for human religious assemblage. Instead, rites were performed out of doors or at home.

Because the modern understanding of religion is so closely tied to hopes for the afterlife it may come as a surprise that the Greeks were largely indifferent to their fate after death. They did assume that shades or ghosts survived for a while after bodily death, yet all went to the same abode, a murky realm called Hades (after the name of its ruling deity) situated beneath the earth. This was neither a paradise nor a hell: no one was rewarded for good deeds, no one punished for sins. Since the shades in Hades gradually faded away, the only true immortality one might attain was earthly remembrance for one's earthly accomplishments.

Indeed, the theme of human accomplishment bulks the largest in early Greek thought. The Greeks were convinced that life was worth living for its own sake and that glory resided not in self-abasement but in practicing human virtues such as bravery, wisdom (in the sense of cunning), and service to one's family and community. The Greeks also loved human beauty (according to the *Iliad,* the entire Trojan War was fought for the beautiful Helen) and sang songs in praise of great men and women. Whereas other early civilizations considered humanity contemptible in comparison to the omnipotent gods, the Greeks were well aware of forces beyond their control but did what they could to strike a balance between awe of their gods and pride in themselves. This confidence in human greatness was to characterize Hellenic civilization for centuries to come.

Confidence in human greatness

2. THE EMERGENCE OF THE CITY-STATES

About 800 B.C. the village communities, which rested mainly on tribal or clan organization, started growing into larger units centered on towns. Most often the towns were built on hills, and were little more than fortifications with marketplaces. As time went on they gained more and more permanent residents and came to look more and more like cities. Thus emerged the *polis,* or city-state, consisting usually of a single city and all its surrounding territory. This was the unit that not only was to become the standard form of Hellenic political organization but created the modern notion of *political* life. (Our word *political* comes from polis.) In the years after 800 city-states emerged throughout the Greek world: Athens, Sparta, Thebes, and Corinth on the mainland; Miletus on the shore of Asia Minor; Naxos and Samos on the islands of the Aegean. The city-states varied greatly in area and population. Sparta with more than 3,000 square miles and Athens with 1,060 had the greatest territorial extent; the others averaged less than 100 square miles. Athens and Sparta, each with populations of 300,000 to 350,000 inhabitants at the peak of their power, had approximately three times the numbers of most of their neighbors.

The origin and nature of the city-states

Behind the rise of the polis lay two interrelated developments: the revival of trade and the invention of the Greek alphabet. During the eighth century B.C., for reasons that remain unclear, the Greeks reestablished trading links with western Asia, using new trading bases on Cyprus and the coast of Syria to gain access to commerce with wealthy Mesopotamia. As the Greeks' horizons broadened, they learned artisanal skills, especially of metalcraft. Most importantly, they also learned how to write—and now in a form entirely different from their writing of centuries earlier. Whereas the Bronze Age script assigned symbols for syllables, the Greeks now drew on the Phoenician system, which assigned symbols for individual sounds. But since the Phoenicians had no symbols for vowels, only consonants (this is still true of modern Arabic and Hebrew), the Greeks added letters to make up for that defect. The result was an alphabet consisting of separate signs for every consonant and vowel, a principle so familiar today it seems amazing it ever had to be invented.

Coin of the Gorgon Medusa. Viewing the face of Medusa supposedly turned men into stone. This Greek coin may have been meant to ward off evil spirits as well as to serve as an instrument of trade.

Because the Greek alphabet was so simple, literacy became widespread

The Greek colonization movement

See color map facing page 109

Political consequences of new military techniques

rather than being monopolized by a scribal caste. Consequently many Greeks learned how to keep records, sometimes for trading purposes, sometimes for estate management. This trend spurred the Greek economy ever more, producing greater wealth, as well as an expanding population. The result was the Greek colonization movement. At first, in the early eighth century B.C., Greek colonization was of a purely commercial nature: warehouses and marketplaces would be established in overseas coastal settlements in order for small numbers of Greeks to carry on trade. But, as the eighth century progressed and the Greek population at home began to outstrip its food supply, Greek settlers began to migrate abroad to establish new lives in farming rather than trade. This migration, which reached its peak during the period from about 735 until about 600 B.C., centered on southern Italy and Sicily, areas then thinly populated and agriculturally fertile. It resulted in the foundation of many autonomous city-states abroad, among them Croton and Posidonia (named for the god Poseidon) on the mainland, and Syracuse on Sicily. The modern Italian city of Naples takes its name from the Greek for "new city": *Neapolis*.

As time went on the Greek city-states at home and abroad changed their forms of government, the general trend being toward a larger share in government for greater numbers of people. Expanding trade contributed to this trend, with newly rich elements in society seeking and gaining a greater share of the power. But a transformation in military techniques may have been even more influential. Around 650 B.C., Greek warfare gradually began to see a shift from dominance of cavalry fighting from horse-drawn chariots to dominance of infantry amassed on foot in tight formations known as *phalanxes*. Since the phalanxes were manned by comparatively large numbers of modest farmers, instead of the aristocrats who had fought in chariots (chariot warfare was inherently aristocratic since only the rich could afford horses), the shift gradually had profound political consequences. Simply stated, those who provided military service ultimately gained their say in Greek government.

Greek Infantry Advancing into Combat. From a vase of about 650 B.C.

Before looking more closely at the political and social structures of the two leading Greek city-states, Sparta and Athens, it is worth pointing out two profound differences between Greek city-state government and our own. In the first place, government in the city-states was participatory, with no difference existing whatsoever between the state and its citizens. In every polis all the citizens did all the governmental work; rather than employing people specifically as civil servants, judges, or professional soldiers, all citizens shared in collective decision-making, judiciary functions, and fighting. Thus one could never say "Sparta fought Athens," since no one conceived of such abstract political entities; instead one would say that "the Spartans fought the Athenians." Secondly, it followed from the participatory dimension of citizenship that Greek political life was solely the preserve of males. As the Greeks saw things, biology made women weaker than men for the battlefield and relegated women to the home for long periods of pregnancy, delivery, and child-rearing. It need not have been this way, but the Greeks never began to consider alternatives. Consequently women were never citizens and were not asked for their political opinions; worse, they often were denied legal rights such as being able to sue or to own property. If born to free parents they were technically free, but for practical purposes they were chained to the home.

3. THE ARMED CAMP OF SPARTA

A story told by the later Greek writer Plutarch evokes the most famous quality of the Spartans, their tenacious militarism. According to Plutarch, when the Spartans met for public festivals the old men would sing: "We once were young, and brave, and strong"; then the young men would sing: "And we're so now"; and then the children would chime in: "But we'll be strongest soon enough." Sparta's governmental system and culture was heavily conditioned by the fact that the Spartans were originally Dorians who in the twelfth century B.C. had entered the Peloponnesian peninsula of southern Greece as an invading army. Instead of mingling with the local peoples in Laconia, the region they had conquered, the Spartans forced the natives to do all the farming while they remained full-time soldiers. Around 735 B.C., the Spartans' military superiority enabled them to annex neighboring Messenia and to force the Messenians into becoming subject agricultural laborers. About 650 B.C., the oppressed Messenians launched a revolt with the aid of the Peloponnesian city-state of Argos, and a bitter struggle ensued for several years before the Spartans achieved total victory. During this fighting and its aftermath the victors forged a repressive governmental and social system meant to ensure that no challenge to their power would occur again.

Seen from the point of view of the Spartan rulers, their government was wonderfully equitable. The Spartan system of checks and balances was probably the first known to human history. The Spartans retained their ancient hereditary kingship as a concession to military necessity, for they thought that a supreme leader, well-experienced in war, was necessary on the battlefield. But rather than having one king they had two, thereby balancing the influence of two great families. When wartime came, an assembly of all the Spartan citizens would decide which king would lead the army into battle, and he then would assume full military powers. Otherwise the government depended entirely on the combined workings of three bodies: a council of elders, the citizen assembly, and a panel of magistrates. The elders numbered thirty—the two kings and twenty-eight others chosen for life by the citizen assembly from a pool of Spartans over the age of sixty (throughout the ancient world the eldest people were presumed to be the wisest). The job of the elders was to propose motions to be voted upon by the assembly, which numbered about 8,000 and so was too large to formulate motions itself. The magistrates, who numbered five and were replaced annually by a vote in the assembly, were the executives who implemented the assembly's motions, performed all judicial business, and negotiated with outsiders.

With its large assembly and dual kingship, the Spartan political system emphasized equality; indeed the Spartan citizens actually called themselves "the equals." In fact, had there been no inhabitants in the territories of Laconia and Messenia other than the citizens, the Spartans might have been said to have had a perfect direct democracy. But the roughly 8,000 Spartan citizens were a mere handful in a total population of roughly 400,000, the vast majority of whom were the unfree farm laborers called *helots*. This circumstance helps account for the shared power among the Spartan elite, for they wished to make certain that no faction among them might feel a lack of power and seek alliance with elements of the oppressed. For the same motive the Spartans saw to it that most of their land was divided equally, and that the helots were attached to the land rather than owned individually. Helot families worked their own plots, from which they could never be moved, giving most of their produce to their masters and saving what was left to feed themselves.

With a certain ironic justice the determination of the Spartan elite to keep the mass of the population in a state of subjugation led to a life bearing some resemblance to slavery even for themselves. Their culture prized toughness and iron discipline above all. Puny infants were immediately put to death, and Spartan boys from an early age were taught to endure pain. Once the boys reached the age of twelve they were taken from their families and forced to live together out of doors, covering themselves with the down of thistles in the winter, and sleeping on rushes (thick plant stems) they broke off with their hands since knives would have made the job too easy. Later they moved to barracks where they lived collectively until age thirty. Since wives were selected for them and since they were allowed to visit their wives only at night for a single obvious purpose, it sometimes happened that men became fathers before they ever saw their wives' faces in daylight. Once they were age thirty they could finally live at home, but they were still obliged to eat together in military messes on rations of the coarsest food. (Supposedly a certain Greek king, having heard of the Spartans' famous black soup, asked a Spartan cook to make him some and found it truly awful; when the king complained, the cook replied, "Sir, the soup is delicious only if you've bathed in Spartan rivers.")

Intent on never turning "soft," the Spartans not only shunned tasty food but any sort of outward show. This meant that they were indifferent to elegant crafts and had little need for imported goods. Sparta thus had relatively few artisans and very little foreign commerce. Although one effect was that the Spartan economy remained static, another was that the Spartans avoided overseas political entanglements. Indeed, militaristic Sparta generally managed better than most other Greek states to stay out of war. Contemptuous of foreign customs, and hoping to avoid any occasion upon which the helots might take advantage of their absence or weakness, the members of the Spartan elite struck defensive alliances that allowed them to remain behind their own frontiers. But when foreign war became inevitable—and this happened in the fifth century—they were well prepared, for, as the other Greeks said, the Spartans were "the only people to whom war might give repose."

4. THE ATHENIAN POLITICAL PARTNERSHIP

While Sparta was becoming a bastion of military repression, Athens was evolving in the direction of true democracy. The very word *democracy* is a Greek coinage, meaning "people power," and Athens was the city-state that cultivated democracy to the fullest. One explanation for the political differences between Sparta and Athens is that the district of Attica in which Athens is situated was never the scene of an armed invasion or conflict between opposing peoples. Consequently, no military caste imposed its rule upon a huge number of vanquished natives. In addition, Attica's natural resources were more varied, with mineral deposits and good harbors. This allowed Athens to develop a prosperous trade and a greater emphasis on urban life as the framework for democratic politics.

Although little is known about the nature of government in Athens from about 750 B.C. until about 600 B.C., it seems clear that throughout this time Athens was ruled by a hereditary aristocracy. Economic trends that gained momentum toward the end of the period, together with the shift from cavalry to infantry, produced strains in that system. In 594 B.C. a grave economic crisis brought matters to a head. The growth of commerce had made the cultivation of grapes and olives more profitable than raising grain, a circumstance that led to the rise of new wealth and the impoverishment of farmers who had been unable to invest in vineyards or olive orchards. With the poor farmers apparently on the verge of revolt because

107

The Athenian Political Partnership

Athena. A relief dating from about 450 B.C., discovered in the ruins of ancient Athens. The mourning goddess is contemplating a list of citizens who had died fighting for her city.

Owl of Athens. In addition to the wide-awake bird, sacred to Athena, coins of Athens bore olive leaves and the Greek letters AΘE for the name of the city.

Threats of revolt and the reforms of Solon

they were being forced into semi-slavery for not paying their debts, the ruling aristocrats attempted to forestall class warfare by granting emergency powers to a merchant named Solon, who was renowned for his wisdom and fairness. Solon rescued the poor by cancelling all debts, and he mollified the rich by instituting a new governmental system that gave them the greatest political power. By this system wealth rather than hereditary status became the main qualification for ruling privileges: the richest Athenians carried the greatest weight, and they alone could hold office. But Solon also introduced a democratic principle for the first time into Athenian government by allowing even the poor (excluding women, resident foreigners, and slaves) to have some veto power in a general assembly of citizens.

An interval of tyranny

Supposedly Solon, who lived on in legend as the Athenian George Washington, was later asked whether he had given the Athenians the best laws he could give them and replied "the best laws they could observe." In fact Solon's system by no means solved all the state's problems; elements among the old aristocracy were disgruntled about having lost their hereditary privileges, and the poor remained a volatile force. Quarrelling among Athens's ruling elite created such instability that finally, in 546 B.C., all factions seemed relieved when an Athenian strongman named Pisistratus seized dictatorial power. Ruling until 527, Pisistratus proved to be a benevolent tyrant. He aided poor farmers by granting them lands from confiscated estates and offering them advantageous loans. In addition, he patronized culture, bringing poets and sculptors to his court, and engaging—as dictators will—in ambitious building projects. His son Hippias, however, to whom he bequeathed his powers, was a ruthless oppressor who was overthrown in 510 B.C. by an Athenian faction that was aided by Sparta.

The reforms of Clisthenes

Renewed factional strife then briefly threatened to tear the Athenian state apart once more until a shrewd aristocrat, Clisthenes, enlisted enough support from the lower classes in 507 B.C. to eliminate his rivals from the scene and introduce lasting stability. Having promised concessions to the poorer elements as a reward for their help, Clisthenes, as the Greek historian Herodotus put it, "took the people into partnership." His major innovation was to implement a system for electing magistrates based on geography rather than on leagues of families. By this system, he divided all of Attica into ten regions for the purpose of nominating candidates for the most important offices in the state. Since every free man participated in the regional selection processes, every free man had some role in influencing Athenian affairs.

The assembly and the council

Clisthenes ruled for only one year, but the effects of his system were so profound that he properly counts as the father of Athenian democracy. After the system was perfected in 487 B.C. it worked as follows. Sovereign power resided in an assembly of all the male citizens: when matters of the greatest magnitude had to be settled, such as going to war, or raising emergency financial levies, the assembly would decide. Since the assembly was extraordinarily large (in the middle of the fifth century B.C. about 40,000

Wedding Procession, ca. 540 B.C. A detail of a black-figure vase showing a newly married couple standing in a chariot and being greeted by a woman or goddess while Apollo plays the kithera.

Battle Scenes, ca. 450 B.C. This terracotta bowl for mixing wine and water shows two principal scenes: on the neck of the bowl is a battle between Greeks and Centaurs, and on the body of the bowl is a battle between Athenians and Amazons.

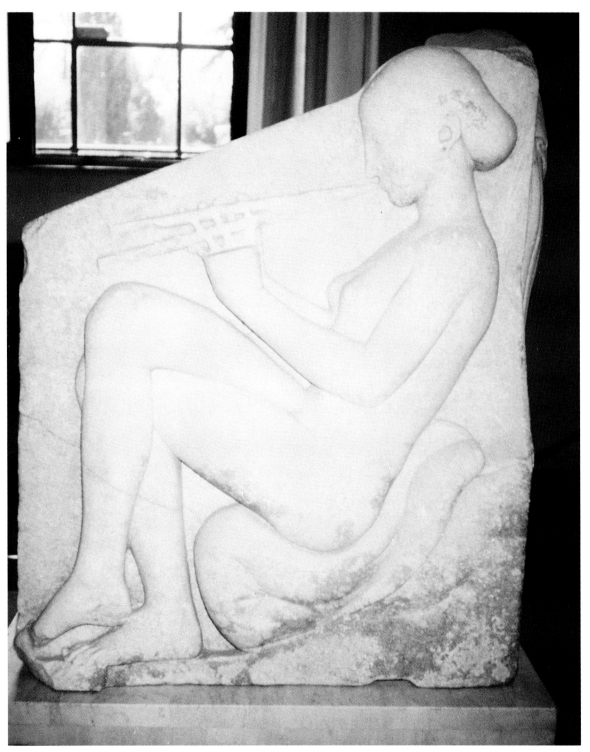

Flute Player. An Athenian marble relief dating from about 470 B.C. The relaxed pose (reclining position, crossed legs) and naturalistic representation of the naked female form were unprecedented in human art before the classical age of the Greeks.

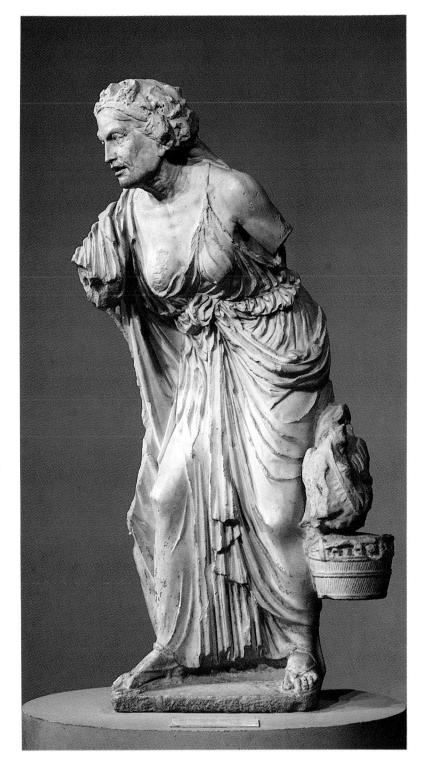

Old Market Woman, 2nd cent. B.C. Sculptures of this period often showed ordinary people engaged in ordinary activities. This realistic marble sculpture is of an old, tired woman who is carrying a basket of fruits and vegetables and chickens to market.

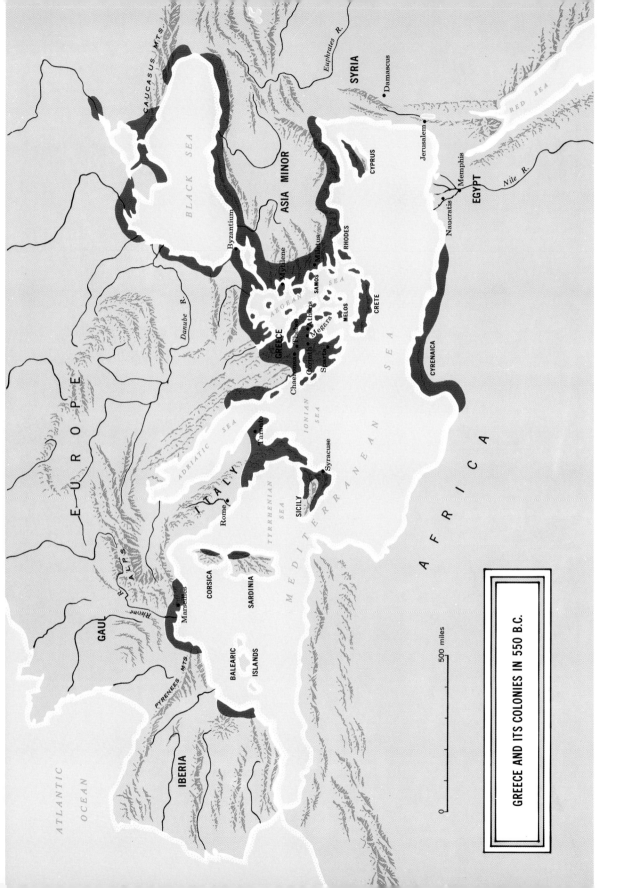

ATLANTIC
OCEAN

EUROPE

GAUL

IBERIA

PYRENEES MTS.

Rhône R.

ALPS

Marseilles

BALEARIC
ISLANDS

CORSICA

SARDINIA

Rome

ITALY

TYRRHENIAN
SEA

Taranto

SICILY

Syracuse

ADRIATIC
SEA

IONIAN
SEA

MEDITERRANEAN
SEA

Danube R.

CAUCASUS MTS.

BLACK SEA

Byzantium

GREECE

Chaeronea
Thebes
Corinth Athens Megara
Sparta

AEGEAN SEA

Mytilene

SAMOS

Miletus

MELOS

CRETE

ASIA MINOR

RHODES

CYPRUS

SYRIA

Damascus

Euphrates R.

RED SEA

Jerusalem

Memphis
Naucratis

EGYPT

Nile R.

AFRICA

CYRENAICA

500 miles

0

GREECE AND ITS COLONIES IN 550 B.C.

men were entitled to participate, and some 5,000 were likely to do so on any given occasion), measures were submitted to it by a council, which had supreme control over executive and administrative activities. Membership in the council was established annually by lot from lists prepared in the regional meetings instituted by Clisthenes, any male citizen over thirty being eligible for service. Since the council itself numbered 500 men, and service was limited to a year, large numbers of Athenian men gained governmental experience.

Obviously even a body of 500 people cannot make administrative decisions or exercise executive powers efficiently. Taking this into account, the Athenians gave special powers to a small number of magistrates, rotated in and out of office by lot for terms of one year. These magistrates had various duties, including the oversight of judicial panels mustered individually from lists of citizens for every different case. In all these matters the Athenians never supposed that any specialized training or particular gifts were prerequisites for office holding. But they did make an exception for military functions. Whereas magistrates were chosen by lot, generals were elected annually from lists submitted by the regions, and whereas magistrates could not serve for more than two nonconsecutive terms, generals could be reelected as frequently as the assembly wished. When certain generals were reelected frequently they became, for practical purposes, policymakers and leaders of the Athenian state. Nonetheless the citizens were always free to vote them out of office, and even to exercise the peculiar Athenian device of ostracism, whereby anyone considered a potential threat to the balanced workings of the constitution could be sent into honorable ten-year exile by vote of the citizen assembly.

In several ways Athenian democracy was quite different from democracies of today. The Athenian form was much more limited in one crucial respect, namely, that all women, resident aliens, and slaves were excluded. These exclusions deprived roughly three-quarters of the adult population of Athens of any role in government. For the remainder, however, the system was as fully participatory as might be imagined. Everyone, rich or poor, had an opportunity to do everything with the possible exception of becoming a general. So averse were the Athenians to being governed by a few men of wealth or reputation, so confident were they of the political capacities of all their citizens, and so determined were they to ensure equality of service, that they provided small payments when it became clear that poor people were declining office because they could not afford the unpaid time. More remarkably still, every important political decision was made by majority vote of each and every citizen who decided to attend the general assembly. This uncompromising adherence to the principle of majority rule had advantages and disadvantages. The most obvious advantage was fairness and the most obvious disadvantage the role that unreflective emotionalism might play in decision making. The modern word *demagogue* comes from the Greek orator who was effective at swaying public opinion insincerely for his own gain; indeed, many Greek philosophers, including

Ostracism. The system took its name from the potsherds (Greek: *ostraka*) on which the names of unpopular citizens were scratched. Many of the "ballots" have survived. Here we see "Aristeides," "Kimon," and "Themistokles."

Majority rule

Plato and Aristotle, considered democracy no different from mob rule. Yet the system worked extremely well for about a century and brought Athens to its greatest triumphs in both foreign affairs and cultural achievements.

5. THE PERSIAN WAR AND THE PELOPONNESIAN WAR

While Sparta and Athens were developing their different forms of government they became engaged in life-or-death wars. In the first of these they were allies; in the second, the bitterest of enemies.

The Persian War

A Spartan-Athenian alliance gained a dramatic victory for all the Greek peoples in two campaigns known collectively as the Persian War. As we have seen in an earlier chapter, the Persians had replaced the Babylonians in 539 B.C. as the mightiest power in western Asia. One result was that the Persians came to rule all of Asia Minor, including formerly independent Greek city-states on the western coast. After turning their attentions to conquering Egypt, the Persians crossed over to Europe in 512 and occupied the northernmost Greek territory of Thrace. It is unclear whether they had designs on the rest of Greece, but many of the Greek city-states surely felt uncomfortable living under the Persian shadow. Moreover, the Greek-speaking cities in Asia Minor began to chafe under Persian rule and unsuccessfully tried to gain their independence in a revolt that lasted from 499 until 494 B.C. During this time Athens, for motives both economic and patriotic, dispatched a number of ships and troops to aid the rebels. (The Athenians shared with the Greeks of Asia Minor a common dialect, and thus a special sense of kinship.) Once the Persians had put down the revolt, they decided to teach the Athenians a lesson.

Greek Forces Defeat Persians. This piece from a fifth century B.C. Attic bowl depicts an Athenian soldier standing over a defeated Persian soldier from Xerxes's army.

The two campaigns of the Persian War followed, one in 490 B.C., and the other extending from 480 to 479. In the first a Persian expeditionary force sent by sea to Attica was defeated by the Athenians in the battle of Marathon. Recognizing that a much greater military enterprise was necessary, the Persian ruler, Xerxes, sent an enormous army by the European land route to bring all Greece under his rule. At first his army was successful, conquering all of northern Greece down to Athens itself. The Athenians withdrew and watched from afar while their city was burned. But Sparta came to Athens's aid, and heroic resistance by the allies, first in the sea battle of Salamis (480) and then in the land battle of Platea (479) sent the Persians off and packing. The Greek exploits in these campaigns testified to their military resourcefulness and their heroism. Among the many stirring incidents, none is more stirring than the retort of a Spartan general trying to hold off a huge Persian force at the pass at Thermopylae with just 300 men: when a scout warned him that the Persians were so numerous that the mass of their arrows would darken the sun, he replied "so much the better, we will fight in the shade." He and the others then went down fighting to the last man.

Campaigns of the Persian War

Without becoming misty-eyed it is possible to view the Persian War as one of the most significant in the history of the world, for it was a victory for Hellenic ideals of freedom against Persian autocracy, and it allowed the Greek city-states, above all Athens, to preserve these ideals for themselves and for posterity. And yet, for Athens the glorious war led relentlessly to an inglorious one, almost as if plotted by an Athenian tragic playwright. The first step was the creation by Athens in 478 B.C. of a naval confederacy meant to carry on the war against Persia and liberate the Greek cities of Asia Minor. Sparta, a land power, had no interest in joining, but Athens gained the support of many other Greek city-states, each of which was obliged to contribute annually a fixed number of ships or monetary payments. Since the expense was great the island of Naxos asked to withdraw from the confederation in 467, but Athens refused to grant permission and made the point clear by taking punitive military action. By mid-century the league had lost its original purpose because the Asian Greek cities had all been freed. Just then Athens moved the league's treasury from the island of Delos to Athens itself, demonstrating that the confederation had been transformed into an empire shaped for Athenian financial and commercial interests. Meanwhile, the Spartans looked on, and, not surprisingly, began strengthening a defensive alliance out of fear that Athenian hegemony might be extended over all of Greece.

The immediate origins of the Peloponnesian War, fought between Athens and Sparta between 431 and 404 B.C., lay in a confrontation between the respective alliance systems. Athens needed desperately to maintain ports on the Gulf of Corinth because that waterway led to Italy, a source of imported grain for the Athenian populace and timber for its shipbuilding. This meant that Athens had to extend alliances to areas near the Peloponnesian peninsula, Sparta's bastion, bringing tensions to a height. Each time a smaller city under the thumb of either Athens or Sparta tried to revolt, it gained help from the opposing power. Finally a relatively minor incident of this sort became the cause of all-out war. Athenian strategy, shaped by Pericles, the city's charismatic political and military leader of the time, was defensive. Pericles feared that the Athenian infantry could never match the well-drilled Spartan one, and thus he ordered that all Athenians living in the country abandon their land to the invading Spartans and take refuge behind newly constructed Athenian walls. His hope was that the navy would ultimately win the day by coastal campaigns against Sparta. Unfortunately for Athens, however, not only did the Spartans lay waste to Attica, but crowding behind the walls led to an outbreak of plague in 430 B.C. that wiped out about a quarter of the population.

One of the most famous scenes in Greek history, reported by the contemporary Athenian historian of the Peloponnesian War, Thucydides, was the Funeral Oration delivered by Pericles to commemorate the war dead after the first year of battle. In words of simple dignity (at least as Thucydides recorded them) Pericles proposed that the death of so many had not been in vain because they had fought for splendid ideals: democracy, an open society, and "beauty without extravagance." While this was surely true, Athens was also fighting to enforce its will on others, and as the war

Growth of Athenian hegemony

The Peloponnesian War

Bust of Pericles. A Roman copy of a Greek work possibly done from life.

progressed Athens became ever more ruthless in its quest for total victory. Pericles, who himself succumbed to the plague in 429 B.C., was succeeded by leaders more unscrupulous than he; they began to balance the military score with Sparta but also embarked on overly ambitious imperialistic ventures and a policy of forcing neutral states to join forces with Athens or face extermination. Having lost its own sense of mission and become weakened by internal divisions, Athens was finally deserted by so many of its allies as the war dragged on that when it lost a naval battle to Sparta in 404 it had to surrender rather than starve. The terms then imposed by the victorious Spartans were harsh: Athens had to destroy all of its fortifications, surrender all of its foreign possessions, and submit to Sparta as a subject state.

The defeat of Athens

The outcome of the Peloponnesian War led to political trials for all of Greece. At first Sparta assumed supremacy throughout the Greek world, installing dictatorships in cities formerly allied with Athens and governed by democracy. Yet it slowly became clear that Sparta lacked the will or the governmental strength to maintain hegemony beyond its earlier boundaries. The result was civil strife in several Greek cities, anti-Spartan democrats rising against Spartan-backed oligarchs, as well as attempts by Athens and Thebes—cities in which democrats had taken power—to wrest domination over Greece from Sparta. In 371 B.C. Thebes accomplished that goal by a victory over Spartan troops at the battle of Leuctra, but Thebes soon proved no more able to rule Greece firmly. Consequently from 371 until 338 B.C. shifting alliances between cities led to interminable warfare. Although the splendor of Greek culture had hardly dimmed (Plato and Aristotle, the greatest of Greek philosophers, flourished successively from about 390 to about 330 B.C.), all the leading cities of Greece had become militarily and politically exhausted.

Continuing strife among the city-states

6. WOMEN AND MEN IN THE DAILY LIFE OF ANCIENT ATHENS

Toward the end of his stirring Funeral Oration, the Athenian leader Pericles briefly addressed the married women in his audience and urged them to remember three things: they should strive to rear more children for the sake of Athens; they should not show more weakness than is "natural to their sex"; and they should act in such a way as to avoid gossip, good or bad. Only recently have scholars become sensitive to such belittling remarks, recognizing that they cast a shadow on the glories of Athenian accomplishments.

Belittling of women

Far from leading to greater equality among the sexes, as might perhaps have been thought, the growth of democracy throughout Greece had precisely the opposite result. The Greeks of the Dark Ages had no difficulty in conceiving of awe-inspiring goddesses and heroic women. Part of the reason for this may be that female divinities often have a prominent role in societies where fertility is at a premium. Furthermore, in the primarily aris-

Role of women in Dark Ages

GREECE AT THE END OF THE AGE OF PERICLES

tocratic society of the Dark Ages it was possible to conceive of a few select women as possessing extraordinary traits—of beauty, wisdom, or of courage—that placed them above all others. Thus the Trojan War was allegedly fought over the beauteous Helen, and the wise Andromache offered her husband shrewd military advice. No one would wish to idealize the situation of either character because Helen was merely an object of conquest and Andromache was immediately told by her husband to go back to her loom. Nonetheless, assuming that the epics represent some aspects of real life, such women did not exist entirely in the shadows.

But as aristocratic ideals gave way to more democratic ones throughout Greece, life in the shadows became ever more women's lot. Limiting the present discussion to Athens, for which we have the most evidence, it seems that an emphasis on the infantry and its spirit of equality interrelated with an emphasis on men training together and developing close relationships, often of a homosexual nature. In addition, the ostentation of individual aristocratic women was frowned upon and the rearing of children to

Women relegated to domestic roles

supply the infantry and serve the state was made almost a requirement. Finally, as town life became the norm, husbands thought it ever more urgent to keep their wives away from the desirous glances of male neighbors. Thus public spaces were located in towns for "male activities" such as athletics and political gatherings, and private spaces were delimited for female activities such as child rearing and domestic chores.

Women treated like property

The result of these trends was that almost all Athenian women were kept in domestic seclusion. Married women were to bring into the world enough children to ensure the continued existence of the state. Thus girls would be married at age fourteen—as soon as they were biologically ready for childbearing—to husbands about twice their age (younger men were supposed to dedicate themselves more fully to war). A girl's father would arrange the marriage without caring about his daughter's preferences, and provide her with a dowry that her husband was expected to use for her support without rapidly depleting the principal. In such ways the girl was treated rather like a piece of property. Shortly after she entered her new surroundings, a regular schedule of childbearing would begin. Typically the interval between births was about two years, meaning that the average young wife was either pregnant or nursing most of the time. The rigors of childbirth also affected the female death rate: scientists studying Greek skeletal remains estimate (not without controversy) that the average age of death for men was forty-five and for women thirty-six.

Male lack of respect for women

Women seldom went out of doors, partly because it was thought immodest to be seen frequently by other men, and partly because nursing and advanced stages of pregnancy made it difficult to attend public festivals. At home, women were expected to do "women's work"—mostly food preparation and cloth production. Since the ideology of democratic Athens opposed excessive displays of wealth or leisure, women were not supposed to sit around idly; but since "women's work" was basically menial and akin to that of slaves, men looked down on women for engaging in it. In fact, male lack of respect for women was often blatant; a medical precept had it, for example, that "a pregnant woman has a good complexion if the child is male; a poor one if the child is female."

Little emotional attachment of husbands to wives

While we can never know how husbands and wives felt about each other from case to case, much evidence suggests that husbands customarily had little emotional attachment to their wives because they took them to be their natural inferiors. In a revealing passage the historian Herodotus says of a certain king: "this Candaules fell in love with his own wife, a fancy that had strange consequences. . . ." Athenian men of the fifth and fourth centuries tended to idealize male homosexual rather than heterosexual relationships, assuming that since men were superior to women love between men was more exalted; when the sage Socrates was forced to take his own life, he sent his wife home because he wished to die solely among male companions. Athenian men did seek physical pleasure as well, but for the purest sexual gratifications a man could always rely on household slaves of either sex, or on whores. Thus an Athenian orator once remarked, "prostitutes we have for pleasure, concubines for daily physical attendance, wives to bear us legitimate children and be our faithful housekeepers."

Music and Poetry in Everyday Greek Life. The Greeks proudly used pottery design to depict their daily activities. Here a musician entertains a boy while a poet writes verses for another boy. The homoerotic implications of such scenes were intentional.

Another great shadow on Greek life in the fifth and fourth centuries was slavery. None of the extraordinary Greek accomplishments in politics, thought, or art would have been possible had slaves not been forced to do the heavy labor while free men debated policy in assemblies, or discussed the true and beautiful while banqueting or strolling in the countryside. For modern lovers of democracy there is an awkward relationship between the rise of democratic government in Greece, especially in Athens, and the increase in slavery as compared with the Dark Ages. The Athenian ideal of division and rotation of governmental functions among all free men was founded on the assumption that slaves would be widely available to perform a variety of chores in the fields, in small businesses, and in the homes, while free men lavished time in political activities. In fact, the Athenian democratic system only began to function fully when the Athenians "struck it rich," coming upon a rich vein of silver in the Laurion mines of Attica just around the year 500 B.C. Whereas the supply of slaves had previously been limited to war captives, the newly found silver enabled the Athenians collectively to buy slaves in larger numbers from Eastern slave dealers or barbarian tribes.

Increase in slavery

Although widespread, Athenian slavery was small in scale. The only exception was the state-owned silver mines, where large numbers of slaves toiled to produce enough wealth so that the Athenians could buy more slaves and thus keep the slave system solvent. Otherwise, however, slaves were distributed about equally in small numbers among Athenian families, rather than working in large teams on plantations or in industries. Typically every family would own a slave or two to perform its hardest and most menial work, tilling the soil or doing the laundry. In such circumstances slaves would seldom be treated cruelly, although their masters surely looked down on them as semi-human brutes or scoundrels and were free to punish them with blows. The very notion that slaves were not entirely human, perpetuated by such remarks as "the ox is the poor man's slave," made it easier for Athenian free men to assume that nature had chosen some for servile labor, and others, like themselves, for political life.

Slaves distributed among Athenian families

Men Weighing Goods on a Balance-Scale. From a pottery decoration of about 550 B.C.

Social and economic equality of male citizens

If one puts aside the subjection of women and slaves—admittedly no small qualifications—daily life in ancient Athens had numerous attractive features. The male citizens enjoyed considerable social and economic equality. Small-scale farming and commerce were the norms, and what little industry existed—pottery and armaments manufacture—was also limited in scale, being carried on in shops owned by individual craftsmen who produced their own wares. Factories employing large numbers of workers were virtually unknown: one of the largest in fifth-century Athens, a shield factory, was staffed by only 120 workers and owned not by a citizen but by a resident alien. Some citizens were of course richer than others, but the richest were required to donate some of their wealth to support public festivals or equip the navy.

Simplicity of life

The social equality of citizens brought with it an extraordinary simplicity in their ways of life. In part, this simplicity was owing to the climate. Since the weather in Greece is predominantly warm and dry (300 days of sunshine) there was no need for elaborate housing or heavy overcoats. The democratic ideal and the absence of extremes in wealth reinforced this simplicity, which allowed the Athenians to make do with the barest essentials. Their beds had no springs, their houses had no drains, and their food consisted chiefly of cereals, handfuls of figs and olives, some goat's cheese, and perhaps some dried fish, washed down with diluted wine. A rectangular piece of wool wrapped around the body and fastened with pins at the shoulders and with a rope around the waist served as the main garment. One could sleep in this, shake it out at dawn, and fasten it again for the day's wear, without a thought for changing fashions.

Leisure and sociability

All told, Athenian male citizens not only enjoyed a life full of simplicity, but also one in which the main qualities were leisure and sociability. Since Athenians demanded so little, they did not have to work very hard. This would have been true even if they did not have slaves (although of course to a lesser extent) since their main form of agriculture, raising olive trees and grapevines, only called for a total of about seventy days' work per year.

Since they did not care about working hard for frills such as pajamas or pin-striped suits, when Athens was at peace they had plenty of time to spend in assemblies and festivals, as well as in games and athletics, or simply standing around chatting or arguing with each other. When Athens was at war—which it often was—its male citizens were obliged to fight, and then they might get killed, maimed, or taken into slavery. But in times of peace the average free Athenian male lived a fulfilling existence of work and play.

7. GREEK PHILOSOPHY

The Greeks invented philosophy. The word itself comes from the Greek, meaning "love of wisdom." It is a mystery why the Greeks, beginning around the sixth century B.C., were the first to pursue sustained philosophical inquiry. But since they lacked palace bureaucracies or professional priests, no vested interests stood opposed to free speculation and observation. In addition, because literacy was widespread—owing to the simplified Greek alphabet—and because new military tactics and governmental institutions gradually strengthened their ideals of equality, the Greeks came to believe that they were different from others, especially their Persian neighbors, and began ever more to speculate on the reasons for the differences. Finally, their relative indifference to material needs and the availability of leisure time offered the Greeks unprecedented opportunities for reflection.

Greeks pursue philosophical inquiry

From the sixth century B.C. until the fourth century B.C. Greek thinkers throughout the Hellenic world started addressing a wide range of questions about the nature of the universe and the meaning of life. The earliest Greek philosophers were the "Pre-Socratics" (so called because they preceded Socrates), all of whom lived during the sixth century in the city of Miletus in Asia Minor. Like their contemporaries, the New Babylonians, the Pre-Socratics studied the course of the stars as a way to observe the predictable regularities of nature. Thus the earliest of the Pre-Socratics, Thales (exact dates unknown), predicted a solar eclipse in 585 B.C. But whereas the New Babylonians interrelated their astronomy with supernatural doctrines about occult forces inherent in the stars, the Pre-Socratics excluded occult explanations for natural events and extended their strictly nonreligious inquiries into the workings of the entire physical universe. They believed that all things could be reduced to some primary substance and differed only about what it was. Thales, perceiving that all things contained moisture, believed that the basic substance was water, but one of his students insisted that it was primal, indestructible matter. Although the various conclusions of the Pre-Socratics would not stand up to later questioning and testing, their insistence on looking for natural laws and rational explanations was pathfinding and would remain characteristic of the Greeks.

The Pre-Socratics

After the Persians conquered Asia Minor some of the Pre-Socratics became silent and others fled to distant Sicily in order to retain their personal independence. Philosophical speculation thus continued in the Greek "Far

West," but it was now tinged with a pessimism and religious coloration that reflected Greek distress at seeing their freedoms crushed and a diminished trust in the strength of human rationality. Typifying this reaction was the system of Pythagoras, a thinker who migrated around 530 B.C. from the island of Samos near Asia Minor to southern Italy, where he founded a sect—half-philosophical, half-mystical—in the city of Croton. Pythagoras and his followers held the speculative life to be the highest good, but they believed that in order to pursue it, the individual must be purified of evil fleshly desires. They also believed that the essence of things is not a material but an abstract principle, number. Accordingly they concentrated on the study of mathematics, dividing numbers up into various categories such as odd and even, and devising the famous "Pythagorean theorem"—that the square of the hypotenuse of any right-angled triangle is equal to the sum of the squares of the other two sides. Thus even though the Pythagoreans turned away from the material world, they still exhibited the characteristic Greek quest for regularities and predictabilities in the abstract world.

The Pythagoreans

Victory in the Persian War enabled the Greeks to overcome the failure of nerve exemplified by the Pythagoreans. Above all in Athens, a state that became exuberantly optimistic after the victory over the Persians and the creation of a Greek naval empire, the increasing power of the individual citizen motivated inquiry into how the individual might best act in the here and now. Roughly around 450 B.C., to fulfill the demand to cultivate such worldly wisdom, teachers emerged who were called *Sophists,* a term simply meaning "those who are wise," or perhaps "those who know things." Unlike the Pre-Socratics or the Pythagoreans, the Sophists were professional teachers, the first in the history of the West who made a living from selling their knowledge. Because they were later opposed bitterly by Socrates and Plato, the term "Sophist" became one of abuse, meaning someone who deviously employs false reasoning, and their entire movement acquired a poor reputation. But modern research has shown that the Sophists were often impressive thinkers and educators.

The Sophists

The Sophists did not comprise a coherent philosophical school; indeed some were paid teachers of such practical matters as public speaking who were not engaged at all in philosophy as commonly understood. But their work displayed certain common threads, as shown by that of Protagoras, who was active in Athens from about 445 until about 420 B.C. and was the most prototypic of the intellectually ambitious Sophists. His famous dictum, "man is the measure of all things," meant that goodness, truth, and justice are relative to the needs and interests of man. (Protagoras and all other thinkers in the male-dominated world of ancient Greece had males in mind when they said "man," unless they specified to the contrary.) In religious matters Protagoras was completely agnostic; in a second famous remark he said that he did not know whether or not the gods existed or what they did—"for there are many hindrances to such knowledge—the obscurity of the subject and the brevity of life." Since he knew nothing of the gods, he found that there were no absolute truths or eternal standards

Protagoras

of right. Sense perception being the only source of knowledge, there can be only particular truths valid for the individual knower.

Such teachings could be progressive and liberating or corrosive of social cohesion, depending on who phrased them and the circumstances in which they were phrased. Sophists such as Protagoras were courageous in calling into doubt outmoded traditions and encouraging Athenians to examine each situation afresh to see what might work best in each case. With their urgings and precepts everyday life became for the first time the subject of systematic discussion. Yet it is also true that the relativism of Sophists like Protagoras could easily degenerate into the doctrine that the wise man is the one who knows best how to manipulate others and gratify his own desires. Since the Sophists competed with each other for students and fees, some apparently went so far as to teach nothing more than debating skills as a way of getting ahead in the shifting sands of Athenian politics.

Relativism of Sophists

Inevitably the relativism and occasional opportunism of the Sophists aroused strenuous opposition. In the judgment of conservative critics the Sophists were pointing the way straight to atheism and anarchy. If there is no final truth, and if goodness and justice are merely relative to the whims of the individual, then religion, morality, the state, and society itself cannot long be maintained. This conviction led to the growth of a new philosophic movement grounded upon the theory that truth is real and that absolute standards do exist. The leaders of this movement were perhaps the three most famous individuals in the history of thought—Socrates, Plato, and Aristotle.

Opposition to Sophists

Socrates was born in Athens in 469 B.C. and drew on sufficient income so that he never had to teach for a living. Having twice fought in battle with the Athenian infantry, he was an ardent patriot who believed Athens was being corrupted by what he considered the shameful doctrines of the Sophists. Yet far from being an unthinking patriot who cherished slogans,

Socrates

Socrates Gaining Wisdom from the Wise-Woman Diotima. In Plato's *Symposium* Socrates learns the philosophical meaning of love from Diotima, an ethereal female being, wiser than he. In this sculptural representation of the scene the winged figure between Diotima and Socrates is probably a personification of love itself.

Socrates. According to Plato, Socrates looked like a goatman but spoke like a god.

he wished to submit every slogan to rigorous questioning in order to build the life of the Athenian state on the firm basis of ethical certainties. It is bitterly ironic that such a dedicated idealist was put to death by his own countrymen. Shortly after the end of the Peloponnesian War, in 399 B.C., while Athens was recovering from the shock of defeat and from violent internal upheavals, a democratic faction determined that Socrates was a threat to the state, and condemned him to death on a charge of "corrupting the youth and introducing new gods." Although his friends made arrangements for him to flee, Socrates decided to accept the popular judgment and died by calmly taking a cup of poison.

Teaching of Socrates

Because Socrates wrote nothing himself, it is difficult to determine exactly what he taught. Contemporary reports, however, especially by his student Plato, make a few points clear. First, Socrates wished to subject all inherited assumptions to reexamination. In his view the complacent people who went around thinking they knew everything really knew nothing. Acting as a gadfly, he continually engaged such people in conversation and managed to show them by "Socratic" questioning that all their supposed certainties were nothing more than unthinking prejudices resting on false assumptions. According to Plato, an oracle once said that Socrates was the wisest person in the world and Socrates agreed: everyone else thought he knew something, but he was wiser because he knew he knew nothing. Secondly, he wished to build an edifice of the firmest truth by means of utilizing sound definitions. Others went around mouthing such words as justice, love, or piety without quite knowing what they meant by them; one had to establish clear and mutually agreed upon meaning to such words or else they could not be used to build any system at all. Thirdly, he wished to advance to a new system of truth by examining ethics rather than by studying the physical world. He shunned discussions of why things exist, why they grow, and why they perish, urging people instead to reflect on principles of conduct both for their own sake and for that of society. One should think of the meaning of one's life and actions at all times, for according to one of his most memorable sayings, "the unexamined life is not worth living."

Absolute standards

So far, Socrates might seem rather like a Sophist; indeed, some archconservatives in his own day thought he was just that. Together with the Sophists, he was a "philosopher of the marketplace" who held tradition and clichés up to doubt, and like them he treated daily affairs in order to help people improve their lives. But the overwhelming differences between Socrates and the Sophists lay in his belief in certainties—even if he avoided saying what they were—and in the standard of absolute good rather than expediency. To defeat the Sophists, however, it was necessary to go further and construct a system that offered a positive framework of truth and reality. This was the task accomplished by Socrates' most brilliant student, Plato.

Plato seeks to vindicate Socrates

Born in Athens around 429 B.C., Plato joined Socrates' circle as a young man and soon saw his mentor condemned to death. This experience made such an indelible impression on Plato that from then on until his own death around 349 B.C. he sought to vindicate Socrates by constructing a philosophical system based on Socratic precepts. Plato set forth this system by teaching in Athens in an informal school (no buildings, tuition, or set curriculum) called the Academy, and also by writing a series of dialogues (treatises expressed in dramatic form) in which Socrates was the main speaker. The Platonic dialogues, among which some of the most important are the *Phaedo,* the *Symposium,* and the *Republic,* are enduringly great works of literature as well as the earliest surviving complete works of philosophy.

Plato's doctrine of Ideas

Plato understood that in order to combat skepticism and refute the Sophists he needed to provide a secure foundation for ethics. This he did by means of his doctrine of Ideas. He granted that relativity and change are characteristics of the world we perceive with our senses, but he denied that this world is the entire universe. A higher, spiritual realm exists, composed of eternal forms or Ideas that only the mind can grasp. The Ideas are not mere abstractions but have a real existence. Each is the pattern of some class of objects or relation between objects on earth. Thus there are Ideas of chair, tree, shape, color, proportion, beauty, and justice. Highest is the Idea of the Good, the cause and guiding purpose of the universe. The things we perceive through our senses are merely imperfect copies of the supreme realities, the Ideas, and relate to them as shadows relate to material objects.

Plato's moral philosophy

Plato's moral philosophy was founded on his doctrine of Ideas. Since earthly life is delusive and corruptible, as opposed to the realm of Ideas, which is true and eternal, the goal of human existence must be to enter as fully as possible into the realm of Ideas. And since that realm is spiritual, one can attain it only by subduing the material side of one's earthly existence and cultivating the intellectual or spiritual side. Plato's thought regarding the body seems to have undergone some evolution, for at first he granted that physical sensations might legitimately serve as a basis for ascending to spiritual heights, but he later taught a more ascetic doctrine associating the flesh and its appetites with evil. At all times, however, he taught the superiority of soul to body, and insisted that the virtuous life on earth would prepare the soul for rising to the heights of eternal truth and beauty. Those who live rightly might possibly gain some glimpse of the Idea of the Good in the here and now; even if not, such a life will prepare the soul for union with the Idea of the Good in the afterlife. As may be gathered, Plato's "Good" resembled the Judeo-Christian conception of an omnipotent God; in fact, some Christians wondered later whether Plato had not somehow been instructed by the Jewish prophets. (Of course he never was.) On the other hand, Plato neither portrayed his "Good" as an interventionist force in human affairs nor proposed any system of worship.

Plato

Plato's political philosophy

Understanding that the virtuous life would be difficult to attain in a society full of turbulence, Plato addressed himself to politics in his most famous dialogue, the *Republic,* the earliest systematic treatment of political philosophy ever written. Since Plato sought social harmony and efficiency rather than liberty or equality, he argued for an elitist state in which most of the people—the farmers, artisans, and traders—would be governed by intellectually superior "guardians." The guardian class itself would be divided. All guardians would serve first as soldiers, living together without private property, but then those found to be the wisest would receive more education and ultimately become Plato's famous "philosopher-kings." In Plato's view neither wealth nor hereditary title equipped one properly to rule but only the greatest intelligence, enhanced by the best possible education. Once philosophers were in power they would always choose the wisest to succeed them and see to it that everyone in the state be subordinated to the Idea of the Good. Later commentators have usually found this ideal of rule by the wisest to be seductive, but they ask of Plato: "who will guard the guardians?" In other words, Plato's elitist system seems to founder not only on the controversial assumption that people are born with unequal intelligence but also on the assumption that just because some rulers may be very wise they will never be corrupted by the lures of wealth or family ties.

Aristotle

Such practical considerations were typical of the thought of Plato's best student, Aristotle (384–322 B.C.), a philosopher who sought never to have his "head in the clouds." Aristotle was the son of a physician from Stagira in northern Greece and apparently learned from his father the importance of careful observation of natural phenomena. Migrating as a young man to Athens in order to study with Plato, he accepted Plato's assumption that there are some things that only the mind can grasp, but then he constructed his own philosophical system based on his confidence in human abilities to understand the universe by the rational ordering of sense experience. As opposed to Plato, who taught that everything we see and touch is but an untrustworthy reflection of some intangible truth, Aristotle believed in the objective reality of material objects and taught that systematic investigation of tangible things, combined with rational inquiry into how they functioned, could yield full comprehension of nature and nature's plan.

Aristotle's logic and metaphysics

Aristotle surveyed a wide variety of subjects in numerous separate but interrelated treatises. Among the most insightful and influential were those devoted to logic, metaphysics, ethics, and politics. Aristotle was the earliest formal logician known to human history, and probably the greatest. He established rules for the *syllogism,* a form of reasoning in which certain premises inevitably lead to a valid conclusion, and he established precise categories for underpinning all philosophical and scientific analysis, such as substance, quantity, relation, and place. Using his own logical methods he then constructed a rigorously ordered system of metaphysics. (The word *metaphysics* meaning "next to physics" was invented by Aristotle and means the study of the nature and causes of things, free from appeals to divine intervention or the supernatural.) Aristotle's central metaphysical belief was that all things in the universe consist of the imprint of *form* upon matter. This was a compromise between Platonism, which tended to ignore matter, and the purest materialism, which saw no patterns in the universe other than the accidents of matter impinging on matter. Forms are the purposeful forces that shape the world of matter; thus the presence of the form of humanity molds and directs the human embryo until it ultimately becomes a human being. Since everything has a purposeful form, the universe for

Aristotle is *teleological,* that is, every item and every class of items is inherently aiming toward an end.

Aristotle's moral philosophy, expressed in his *Nicomachean Ethics* (often known simply as *Ethics*), was concerned solely with life in this world rather than as a path to otherworldly salvation. Aristotle taught that the highest good consists in human self-realization, the harmonious functioning of soul and body. Humans differ from the animals by means of their rational capacities and find happiness by means of exercising these appropriately. For most this means exercising reason in practical affairs. Good conduct is virtuous conduct, and virtue resides in aiming for the *golden mean:* for example, courage rather than rashness or cowardice, temperance rather than excessive indulgence or ascetic denial. Better even than the practical life, however, is the contemplative life, for such a life allows men (here Aristotle meant to say males alone) the possibility of exercising their rational capacities to the utmost. Aristotle thus believed that philosophers were the happiest of men, but he understood that even they could not engage in contemplation without interruption. As a practical person, moreover, he deemed it necessary for them to intersperse their speculative activities with practical life in the real world.

Aristotle's moral philosophy

Whereas Plato conceived of politics as a means to an end, the orderly pursuit of the supernatural Good, Aristotle thought of politics as an end in itself, the collective exercise of the good life. An enormous qualification is that Aristotle, like Plato, was an elitist; he took it for granted that some people—"barbarians"—were not quite human and were meant by nature to be slaves. Similarly, he assumed that women were outside politics and should dedicate themselves to raising children and managing domestic concerns for the family. By implication Aristotle believed that women could not be happy to the same degree as men since they could not share in the life of the state in which human rational faculties enjoyed their fullest exercise. All male citizens, on the other hand, were indeed meant to share in it, for, as Aristotle proposed, "man is by nature a political animal." This view by no means implied that the best form of government was democracy, for Aristotle saw that as a "debased" form of government. What he preferred was the *polity,* the well-functioning *polis* in which monarchical, aristocratic, and democratic elements are combined by means of checks and balances. Such a government would allow all free men to realize their rational potential, showing themselves to be located in nature's hierarchy right above the animals and right below the gods.

Aristotle's political philosophy

Strange though it may seem, two subjects that today are hardly thought of as "philosophical" were closely interrelated with the earliest developments of philosophy in Greece. One was medicine. We have seen that Aristotle's father was a physician, and that this may have influenced Aristotle to emphasize observation based on sense experience. Greek medicine itself was inseparable from the emergence of orderly philosophy, for it rested on the unprecedented assumption that regularities divorced from supernatural causes existed in human health and illness. By general consent the father of scientific medicine was the Greek physician Hippocrates

Medicine

(c. 460–377 B.C.), who dinned into the ears of his pupils the precept that "every disease has a natural cause, and without natural causes, nothing ever happens." Using methods of careful study and comparison of symptoms he laid the foundations for clinical diagnosis and also discovered the phenomenon of crisis in disease. Unfortunately, however, he thought his examinations proved that the body consists of four "humors"—yellow bile, black bile, blood, and phlegm—and that illness occurs from excess amounts of any of these. The practice of bleeding the patient, most damaging to women, was the sad consequence of this theory.

History-writing

The other subject that was closely related to philosophy was the writing of history. Like so many other words we take for granted, *history* is a Greek coinage meaning nothing more than "inquiry" or "research." As this fact suggests, Greek history-writing was an original form of gathering knowledge that began by asking questions about human affairs, rather than just reporting data such as lists of kings or outcomes of battles. As an "inquirer" or "researcher," moreover, the historian looked for evidence rather than making things up himself or reporting legends. Another original feature of Greek history was that it was humanistic: the characters were always humans, never gods, and explanations were usually found in the realm of human decision-making.

Herodotus writes about the Persian War

As Hippocrates was the father of medicine, so Herodotus (c. 484–c. 420 B.C.) was the "father of history." Indeed, Herodotus was the first who employed the word "history" in its current sense. The questions he asked were about the Persian War: Why did the Greeks and Persians fight each other? Why did the outcome fall out as it did? To gain answers Herodotus traveled all over the Mediterranean world collecting evidence by interviews. Since these netted him a wealth of wonderful stories, he could not resist repeating them, even if they were often digressive and sometimes obviously legendary. (Some think that his fascination with the legendary traditions of foreign peoples allows Herodotus to rank as the father of anthropology as well as the father of history.) Yet in its main lines his narrative adheres to the theme of the great war between the Greeks and the Persians seen as an epic struggle for liberty against despotism. In his conception, liberty inspires valor and ultimately triumphs.

Thucydides writes about the Peloponnesian War

In contrast to Herodotus his younger contemporary, Thucydides (c. 460–c. 400 B.C.), who wrote a history of the Peloponnesian War, wished to reconstruct events as scientifically as possible by rejecting legends and untrustworthy hearsay in favor of only the most reliable evidence. Much like a physician of the body politic, Thucydides sought to diagnose the causes of human social diseases, such as war and civil strife, by dispassionate observation and comparison of symptoms. By presenting an accurate record of the greatest war of his own day he believed he could be useful to statesmen and generals of all time. Although his dispassionate tone and single-minded emphasis on war and politics often make him difficult to read, Thucydides' feat in presenting a coherent and accurate analysis of a highly complex event is beyond comparison in the writing of history until modern times. Individual passages of his history are so keenly insightful that they rank among the all-time classics not just of history but of social science.

8. LITERATURE AND ART

Just as it is extremely difficult to account for the sudden emergence of philosophy among the Greeks, so is it difficult to account for the emergence among them of the most profoundly beautiful and awe-inspiring works of literature and art. Doubtless the economic and political factors adduced to explain the appearance of philosophy help to explain the Greek accomplishments in the literary and artistic realms too. But when all is said and done the simultaneous achievements of the Greeks in the activities of mind and imagination can only be thought of as the "Greek miracle."

The Homeric epics

Any consideration of the Greek triumphs in literature must begin with the Homeric epics, the *Iliad* and the *Odyssey,* set down in writing around 750 B.C. The first deals with the Trojan War, concentrating on the exploits of the Greek hero Achilles; the second describes the adventurous homeward journey after the Trojan War of the Greek hero Odysseus (also known as Ulysses). Both epics emphasize memorable deeds: in the case of the *Iliad,* of military prowess; in the case of the *Odyssey,* of a wily protagonist cleverly coping with adversities by stratagem. In both epics the characters are seldom reflective; they are intent on avoiding shame and live entirely for their public reputation, showing no notion of conscience, self-discovery, or psychological growth. On the other hand, the Homeric epics excel in their exuberant descriptions of battles, personal confrontations, and a full range of fierce passions. Written in verse, they also are studded with interludes of quiet beauty: a ship skimming the seas, water being heated for a bath, preparations for bedtime, the washing of clothing in a stream. Declaimed publicly on ceremonial occasions for decade after decade, century after century, the Homeric epics exerted an enormous in-

Interior of a Greek Cup. Depicted is the friendship of leading characters from the *Iliad:* Patroklus and Achilles. Here Achilles is bandaging Patroklus's wounds.

fluence upon subsequent Greek thought and expression, continually reinforcing a faith in human greatness and a delight in the beautiful.

Lyric poetry

Both traits found a new and different mode of expression in the Greek lyric poetry of the sixth century B.C. Lyric poetry, so named because it was sung to the music of the lyre rather than being declaimed to large groups, was more gentle and personal than epic poetry, musing over disappointments and disillusionments, singing of love or of wine or the starlit summer night. One of the most gifted of the Greek lyric poets of this period was a woman named Sappho, who lived on the island of Lesbos, off the shore of Asia Minor. The few surviving examples of her poetry apparently address themselves to other women. (At this time women on Lesbos were not secluded as they were in Athens later, and many gained a reputation for female homosexuality from whence derives the word *lesbian,* but we know too little about Sappho to be certain whether she herself was a lesbian in that sense.) Sappho's poetry sings with a distinctly feminine voice, as in the splendid lines: "On the black earth, some say, the thing most lovely/is a host of horsemen, and others infantry/or a host of ships, but I say whatever anyone loveth."

Tragic drama

Stirring as was the epic, and lovely as was the lyric, the supreme literary achievement of the Greeks was the tragic drama. This form of poetic expression, invented by the Athenians, took shape around 500 B.C. as part of the outdoor public festivals that played a central role in the life of the state. Although Greek tragedy was the ancestor of modern theater, it differed from most plays we know today in many respects. All the characters wore masks, men played the roles of women, and several actors played the "chorus," chanting poetic lines in unison as a way of commenting on the action and driving home certain conclusions. Initially there was only a chorus and a single actor; later a few more actors were added. Plot was always central and straightforward, without subplots or subsidiary incidents. The reason for this was that tragedy was meant to inspire the audience with "pity or fear," and this could only be done—especially in outdoor theaters that might hold 17,000 people—by concentrating relentlessly on a single highly dramatic line of action. The ideal tragic plot inspired pity or fear by depicting a terrible change in the central character's fortunes, thereby leading the audience to feel a "catharsis" or cleansing.

Aeschylus

Although Greek tragedy focused on plot, it was not indifferent to ideas or character. Those two elements were always present, with greater emphasis on ideas at the beginning of the fifth century and on character by the end of the century. The first of the great Greek tragedians, Aeschylus (525–456 B.C.), used the simplest dramatic means for primarily patriotic purposes. His tragedies were poetic dialogues between a chorus and no more than two characters on the stage at a single time. Having fought in the Persian War, Aeschylus was an ardent Athenian patriot whose primary purpose was to express high-minded, uplifting ideas. Although he managed surprisingly well in plot, given his limited means, he was less concerned about inspiring pity or fear than in arousing enthusiasm for sentiments of societal harmony. Aeschylus's *The Persians* is the only surviving Greek

Greek Theater in Epidauros. The construction, to take advantage of the slope of the hill, and the arrangement of the stage are of particular interest. Greek dramas were invariably presented in the open air.

Epidauros Plan

Sophocles

Euripides

tragedy about recent current events and celebrates the victory of freedom; his *Agamemnon* is a stripped-down narrative of the penalties for crime and the inevitable triumph of justice.

With Sophocles (496–406 B.C.) comes the perfection of the most "classic" traits of Greek tragedy. In his plays in particular we witness the fullest exemplification of the dramatic plot creating pity or fear and leading the audience to catharsis. Sophocles was able to accomplish this partly because his plots had more complexity than those of Aeschylus. Mostly, however, Sophocles heightened the sense of tragedy in his plays by paying more attention to character. For example, whereas the central character of *The Persians* was the ranting "barbarian" Xerxes, with whom no Athenian could ever have felt real sympathy, the titular hero of Sophocles' *Oedipus the King,* was a fairly decent human being with no exceptional virtues or vices. Thus the audience was able to identify with Oedipus and feel deep pity when, by a twist in Sophocles' plot, he is stripped of power and blinded. Sophocles, of course, is still interested in driving home ideas: *Oedipus* teaches humans to avoid the complacency that comes with transitory material success and to recognize an order in the universe higher than any individual. This interest in ideas, moreover, leads Sophocles to emphasize universal qualities of human nature rather than nuanced particular ones.

A shift to the particular was one of the accomplishments of Euripides (480–406 B.C.), the third of the great Athenian tragedians. Unlike his predecessors, Euripides was a strong critic of established ways, and this led him to theatrical innovation. He was the first to introduce elements of satiric wit into tragic writing, and the first to present sympathetic lower-class characters who used lower-class speech instead of the customary elevated poetic diction. Most notably, Euripides displayed a sense of sympathy for women. He made women his central characters in such plays as *Alcestis, Medea, Electra,* and *Helen;* in *Medea* he proposed that "esteem shall come to women," and that if the gods had allowed them to play the lyre, women would have "sung an answer to the male sex." Euripides' critical intellect led him to look for nuance in character more than universal qualities; thus he seems the most psychological and in this sense the most "modern" of the three great tragedians.

Greek comedy

No discussion of the great literary achievements of classical Greece can end without mention of comedy, brought to its perfection by the Athenian playwright, Aristophanes (c. 448–c. 380 B.C.). Greek comedy lacked all "politeness" and subtlety, for it was performed in the open air before large crowds by actors in masks who shouted to be heard. Instead it was very broad—full of slapstick, absurdity, and vulgarity. Aristophanes delighted in ridiculing "newfangled" trends: the philosophy of Socrates, the tragedy of Euripides, the imperialistic warmongering of contemporary politicians. His satire often was so exaggerated that it verged on travesty, as when he had Socrates explain thunder as "bathroom noises of the clouds." Some of his humor is now hard to follow because of its topicality, but some is timeless, as in his masterwork, *Lysistrata,* in which women of enemy cities bring an end to a stupid war by refusing to have sex with their husbands until a peace agreement is signed. The idea has yet to be tried.

Greek Sculptor at Work. The Greeks were not prudish.

Greek visual arts

The same Greeks who were so innovative and accomplished in both comedy and tragedy showed a similar range of genius in the visual arts. Their comic gift—exuberance, cheerful sensuality, and often coarse wit—can be seen especially in their pottery. In "black figure" vases and jugs done throughout the Greek world in the sixth and fifth centuries B.C., the characters often look like glinting rascals up to some sort of mischief, often sexual. More dignified and uplifting were the marble statuary and sculptured reliefs the Greeks made for temples and public places. Here Athens once more took the lead in a series of extraordinary artistic accomplishments. Athenian sculptors took human greatness as their main theme, depicting even gods or goddesses as humans. Their statuary shows that the Athenians could conceive of nothing more beautiful or awe-inspiring than the human form.

Naturalistic statues of human figure

Perhaps the most miraculous aspect of the Greek "miracle" is the nearly sudden appearance of the well-proportioned, naturalistic statue of the naked human figure. This happened in Athens in the years around 490 to 480 B.C., perhaps not coincidentally the time of the Greek victory over Persia. Until then Greek statuary had been dominated by Egyptian influence; rigid figures with square shoulders met the viewer frontally, one foot slightly advanced. Then there suddenly appeared well-proportioned, well-modeled figures, resting their weight gracefully and naturally. Nothing like this had ever been seen in the entire human record, and it is hard to avoid the conclusion that the triumph of Greek ideals of human dignity in the Persian War had something to do with it. Convinced that all Persians bowed down to their rulers like slaves, while they themselves enjoyed political and social equality, the Greeks expressed their idea of human great-

See color plates following page 108

Apollo of Tenea; Apollo of Piombino; "The Critian Boy." These three statues, dating from about 560, 500, and 480 B.C. respectively, display the progressive "unfreezing" of Greek statuary art. The first stiff and symmetrical statue is imitative of Egyptian sculpture (see statue of the Pharoah Mycerinus, p. 65 above). Roughly half a century later it is succeeded by a figure that begins to display motion, as if awakening from a sleep of centuries in a fairy tale. The last figure introduces genuine naturalism in its delicate twists and depiction of the subject's weight resting on one leg.

ness by commemorating the dignity of the naked human form. The fact that women too were shown naked and beautiful makes clear that the ideal was not strictly political, for as we have seen, women played no role in the life of the state. But sculptors attuned to depicting natural human beauty reveled in displaying the loveliness of women as well as men.

The sudden appearance of naturalistic statuary in Athens coincided not only with the victory over Persia but also with the earliest tragedies of Aeschylus. On that basis it is tempting to draw specific analogies between the development of Athenian tragic theater and Athenian sculpture. To a certain extent these analogies are valid since the most "classic" of the Athenian sculptors whose names survive, Phidias and Myron, were contemporaries of the most "classic" tragedian, Sophocles (that is, they all flourished in the middle of the fifth century B.C.), and achieved similar qualities of universality. They all sought to portray humans who were deeply and recognizably human, and yet not so unique in physical features as to be identifiable as any particular human. On the other hand, Phidias and Myron differed from Sophocles in their idealizing: if showing an athlete or a poet

Universalized qualities in statues

they depicted the perfect athletic body or the most poetic-looking face rather than specimens that were less than perfect for their type. In addition, since their aesthetic values were always those of balance and restraint, the notion of instilling "pity or fear" as did the tragedians was totally foreign to them. Finally, although some Greek sculptors were the rough equivalents of Euripides in emphasizing particularity rather than universality, they came much later than he did. It is certain, for example, that no portrait statuary of specific humans was done from life in the entire Greek world before the middle of the fourth century B.C. And not until Lysippus, who worked at the very end of the century, can we find a truly great master of the realistic portrait.

Greek architecture

Almost as if all the citizens of Athens met together on some bright morning in the fifth century B.C. and agreed to excel in as many forms of artistic expression as possible, the Athenians made exceptionally fine contributions to architecture as well as to literature and representational art. Actually the "classic" Greek temple was not an Athenian invention; it emerged gradually throughout the entire Greek world in the period from about 550 to 500 B.C. Nonetheless, of all the Greek temples ever built, the Parthenon of Athens, constructed between 447 and 438 B.C., while Sophocles was writing his plays, and with statuary and reliefs by Phidias, is gener-

Left: *The Discobolus or Discus Thrower of Myron.* The statue reflects the glorification of the human body characteristic of Athens in the Golden Age. Now in the Vatican Museum. Right: *Hermes with the Infant Dionysus, by Praxiteles, Fourth Century* B.C. Original in the Olympia Museum, Greece.

The Parthenon. The largest and most famous of Athenian temples, the Parthenon is considered the classic example of Doric architecture. Its columns were made more graceful by tapering them in a slight curve toward the top. Its friezes and pediments were decorated with lifelike sculptures of prancing horses, fighting giants, and confident deities.

ally considered the finest. Greek temple architecture was dramatically different from the massive temples that aimed for the skies of western Asia or Egypt. Stressing the horizontal rather than the vertical, the Greeks sought to create an impression of harmony and repose. The most characteristic feature of the Greek temple was the imposing yet graceful fluted column, surmounted by a plain capital in the so-called *Doric order,* and by a scroll-shaped one in the *Ionic order.* When the Athenians built the Parthenon, a temple dedicated to their patron goddess Athena and intended as the most prominent visual expression of their civic accomplishments, they chose for it the more restrained Doric order as if to demonstrate to all the world that "less is more."

9. THE GREEK ACHIEVEMENT

It is necessary to be on guard against uncritical admiration of the ancient Greeks. The Spartans kept the mass of their population in serf-like subjugation, and the Athenians took slavery for granted, subjecting slaves who toiled in the mines to the most brutal treatment. Women throughout the Greek world were exploited by what today would be called a "patriarchy"—a repressive system managed by fathers and husbands. Greek state-

Doric

Ionic

Details of the Doric and Ionic Orders

The Acropolis. A model of the highest and most sacred part of the city of Athens at the time of its greatest splendor, about 420 B.C. The dominating central temple is the Parthenon.

craft was not sufficiently enlightened to avoid imperialism and aggressive war, and the Greeks made no great advances in economic enterprise. Finally, not even the Athenians were unfailingly tolerant: Socrates was put to death for nothing more than expressing his opinions.

And yet, where would we be without the ancient Greeks? The profound significance of the Greek adventure for the history of the world can be seen with particular clarity by a comparison of Greek cultural traits with those of Mesopotamia and Egypt. The Mesopotamian and Egyptian civilizations were dominated by autocracy, supernaturalism, and the subjection of the individual to the group. The Greek word for freedom—*eleutheria*—cannot be translated into any ancient Near Eastern language, not even Hebrew. The typical political regime of western Asia was that of an absolute monarch supported by a powerful priesthood. Culture served mainly as an instrument to enhance the prestige of rulers and priests. In contrast, the civilization of Greece, notably in its Athenian form, was founded upon ideals of freedom, optimism, secularism, rationalism, measured beauty, the glorification of body and mind, and a high regard for the dignity and worth of the individual. The culture of the Greeks was the first to be based upon the primacy of intellect; there was no subject they feared to investigate. As Herodotus has a Greek (in this case a Spartan) say to a Persian: "You understand how to be a slave, but you know nothing of freedom. . . . if you had but tasted it you would counsel us to fight for it not only with spears but with axes."

Another way of appreciating the uniqueness of Greek civilization and its enduring importance is to recall some of the words that come to us from this civilization: politics, democracy, philosophy, metaphysics, history, tragedy. These are all ways of thinking and acting that have helped enrich human life immeasurably but that had hardly been known to humanity before the Greeks invented them. To a startling degree the very concept of "humanity" itself—the exalted role within nature of the human race in general and the individual human in particular—comes to us from the Greeks. For them the aim of existence was the fullest development of one's human potential: the work of becoming a person, called in Greek *paideia,* meant that everyone was supposed to be the sculptor of his or her own statue. When the Roman civilization later took up this ideal from the Greeks, the Romans called it *humanitas,* from which we gain our word "humanity." The Romans admitted the fact when they said that "Greece was where humanity was invented," and it is hard to doubt that they were right.

SELECTED READINGS

• *Items so designated are available in paperback editions.*

• Andrewes, Anthony, *The Greeks,* New York, 1967. An excellent, up-to-date account of archaic and classical Greek history from about 750 to 350 B.C.
• Austin, M., and P. Vidal-Naquet, *The Economic and Social History of Ancient Greece,* Berkeley, 1977.
• Boardman, J., *Greek Art,* rev. ed., New York, 1985.
• ———, *The Greeks Overseas,* rev. ed., London, 1982. The standard treatment of Greek colonization.
• Burkert, Walter, *Greek Religion,* Cambridge, Mass., 1985. Up-to-date and encyclopedic. Best used as a reference work.
   Burn, A. R., *The Lyric Age of Greece,* New York, 1961. A lively introduction to the seventh and sixth centuries B.C.
• Davies, J. K., *Democracy and Classical Greece,* Glasgow, 1978. Lucid and authoritative.
• Dodds, Eric R., *The Greeks and the Irrational,* Berkeley, 1963. A novel approach to classical Greek culture.
• Dover, K. J., *Greek Homosexuality,* Cambridge, Mass., 1978. A serious analysis of a basic aspect of classical Greek life.
• ———, et al., *Ancient Greek Literature,* Oxford, 1980.
• Finley, M. I., *The Ancient Greeks: An Introduction to Their Life and Thought,* New York, 1963. An expert, brief introduction to the Greeks.
• ———, *The World of Odysseus,* rev. ed., New York, 1978. Attempts to use the Homeric poems as a guide to Dark-Age Greece.
   Foley, H. P., *Reflections of Women in Antiquity,* New York, 1981.
   Forrest, W. G., *The Emergence of Greek Democracy,* London, 1966. An engaging account of the origins of democratic ideas and practices.
• ———, *A History of Sparta, 950–192 B.C.,* London, 1969.
• Kagan, Donald, *Pericles of Athens and the Birth of Democracy,* New York, 1991.
• Kitto, H. D. F., *The Greeks,* Baltimore, 1957. A delightfully written, highly personal interpretation.
• Lloyd, G. E. R., *Early Greek Science: Thales to Aristotle,* London, 1970.
• Marrou, H. I., *A History of Education of Antiquity,* New York, 1964. A modern classic that covers the entire ancient world.
• Meiggs, R., *The Athenian Empire,* Oxford, 1979. The major study of fifth-century Athenian imperialism; a monumental work.

- Murray, O., *Early Greece,* Glasgow, 1980. An excellent analytical narrative of early Greek history before the fifth century B.C.

  Nilsson, M. P., *A History of Greek Religion,* New York, 1964.

- Pollitt, J. J., *Art and Experience in Classical Greece,* Cambridge, Mass., 1972. The best introduction to the social and intellectual forces behind Greek art.

- Pomeroy, Sarah B., *Goddesses, Whores, Wives, and Slaves: Women in Classical Antiquity,* New York, 1975. The best treatment of the role of women in Greece and Rome. Relies on a variety of source material and covers women of all classes.

  Rose, H. J., *A Handbook of Greek Literature,* New York, 1960.

- ———, *A Handbook of Greek Mythology,* New York, 1959.

- Sealey, Raphael, *A History of the Greek City States, ca. 700–338 B.C.,* Berkeley, 1977. A provocative account that reconsiders older assumptions about Greek political life.

  Sinclair, T. A., *A History of Greek Political Thought,* London, 1951.

  Snell, Bruno, *The Discovery of the Mind: The Greek Origins of European Thought,* Cambridge, Mass., 1953. Stimulating essays.

- Snodgrass, A. M., *Archaic Greece,* London, 1980.

- Starr, C. G., *The Economic and Social Growth of Early Greece: 800–500 B.C.,* New York, 1977. An excellent study of this difficult but important topic.

- ———, *The Origins of Greek Civilization, 1100–650 B.C.,* New York, 1961. The best detailed treatment of the early periods.

- Stockton, D., *The Classical Athenian Democracy,* Oxford, 1990. A nontechnical, clearly written summary of recent research; highly recommended.

SOURCE MATERIALS

Most Greek authors have been translated in the appropriate volumes of the Loeb Classical Library, Harvard University Press.

In addition the following may be helpful:

- Barnstone, Willis, tr., *Greek Lyric Poetry,* New York, 1962.

  Kagan, Donald, *Sources in Greek Political Thought,* Glencoe, Ill., 1965.

- Lattimore, R., tr., *Greek Lyrics,* Chicago, 1960.

- ———, tr., *The Iliad,* Chicago, 1961.

- ———, tr., *The Odyssey,* New York, 1968.

Chapter 6

THE HELLENISTIC CIVILIZATION

Alexander wept when he heard from Anaxarchus that there was an infinite number of worlds. When his friends asked if any accident had befallen him, he answered: "Do you not think it a matter worthy of lamentation that when there is such a vast multitude of them, we have not yet conquered one?"

—Plutarch, *On the Tranquillity of the Mind*

The supreme tragedy of the Greeks was their failure to solve the problem of political conflict. Gravely weakened by the wars between cities that transpired from 431 B.C. until 338 B.C. Greek civilization was simultaneously rescued and transformed by one of the most remarkable characters who ever trod the world's stage, a young man later known as Alexander the Great. In 338 B.C. Alexander's father, Philip of Macedon, a semi-barbarian chieftain from the rocky wildernesses north of Greece, took over all of Greece by decisively defeating a combined Athenian-Theban force in pitched battle. Two years later Philip was killed in a family feud, and his dashingly handsome and energetic son Alexander succeeded him at the age of twenty. Swiftly consolidating his rule throughout Greece by putting to death all possible rivals, in 334 B.C. Alexander felt secure enough to leave behind a deputy and cross into Asia with an army of 48,000 troops to carve out some additional territory. The Persians may first have looked askance at this brash twenty-two-year-old advancing in their direction, but within four years, as the victor of three brilliantly fought battles—the Granicus (334), Issus (333), and Gaugamela (331)—Alexander had conquered the entire Persian Empire. During this campaign Alexander's troops performed some of the most stunning feats in the annals of military history. In the midst of hot and arid Persian terrain, for example, they marched with heavy packs on their backs from sundown until noon in sixteen-hour stretches, averaging a march rate of 33 miles per day. Rather than returning home or residing peacefully in the Persian capital of Persepolis after this whirlwind campaign, Alexander then marched farther east to conquer Bactria (modern Afghanistan) and cross the Indus River into India, spending two years (327–326 B.C.) in an attempt to destroy Hindu

The exploits of Alexander the Great

Marble Head of Alexander. Alexander the Great was reputed to have been very handsome, but all surviving representations doubtless make him more handsome still. This one dates from about 180 B.C. and is typical in showing Alexander with "lion's-mane hair."

armies equipped with war elephants. When his troops finally refused to fight any more in such distant lands, he took them back to the Persian heartland and died in Babylon of an infectious disease in 323 B.C. while preparing for another aggressive campaign—this time to Arabia. Although Alexander supposedly wept because he had not conquered the globe, he still had traversed some 20,000 miles, fighting as he went, to become in his twenties the ruler of the largest empire the world had ever seen.

Alexander the Great's conquests laid the foundations for the *Hellenistic civilization,* a civilization that endured from his own time until roughly the beginning of the Christian era in all the lands of the eastern Mediterranean and western Asia. The term *Hellenistic* means "Greek-like," and stands in contrast to *Hellenic,* or purely Greek. Hellenistic civilization was "Greek-like" because it was a hybrid, composed of Greek and Asian elements. Alexander himself spoke Greek and had been educated by none other than the great Greek philosopher Aristotle, yet he ignored the Greek precepts of modesty and living according to the "golden mean." Similarly, during the Hellenistic era Greek became the language of government in Mesopotamia, Syria, and Egypt, and Greek philosophy and literature were cultivated throughout western Asia, yet Greek-speaking rulers insisted upon being adored as divinities. We will presently see that Hellenistic culture was not just a hodgepodge but had its own distinctive traits. Before we examine the fascinating Hellenistic civilization itself, however, it is necessary to take account of its Persian background because, just as the Hellenistic world could not have existed without Alexander the Great and the Greeks, so it could not have existed without the prior accomplishments of Cyrus the Great and the Persians.

1. THE PERSIAN EMPIRE

The rise of Cyrus

Almost nothing is known of the Persians before the middle of the sixth century B.C., other than that they lived on the eastern shore of the Persian Gulf, spoke an Indo-European language, and were subject to the Medes, a kindred people who inhabited territories east and north of the River Tigris. Out of this obscurity the Persians emerged suddenly into the spotlight of history owing to the extraordinary exploits of a prince named Cyrus, who succeeded to the rule of a southern Persian tribe in 559 B.C. Swiftly thereafter Cyrus made himself ruler of all the Persians, and around 549 B.C. he threw off the lordship of the Medes, taking over their domination of lands that stretched from the Persian Gulf to the Halys River in Asia Minor.

By occupying part of Asia Minor Cyrus became a neighbor of the kingdom of Lydia, which then comprised the western half of Asia Minor up to the Halys. The Indo-European Lydians had created one of the successor states of the Hittites and had attained great prosperity as a result of gold-prospecting and acting as intermediaries for overland commerce passing between Mesopotamia and the Aegean Sea. In connection with their com-

An Early Lydian Coin, Probably Struck during the Reign of Croesus

THE PERSIAN EMPIRE UNDER DARIUS I • 521-486 B.C.

mercial enterprises the Lydians invented the use of metallic coinage as a medium of exchange for goods and services. When Cyrus reached their border, the reigning king of the Lydians was Croesus (pronounced Creesus), so rich that the simile "rich as Croesus" remains embedded in our language. Distrusting the newcomer, Croesus decided in 546 B.C. to wage a preventive war in order to preserve his kingdom from conquest. According to the Greek historian Herodotus, Croesus consulted the oracle at Delphi as to the advisability of an immediate attack and gained the reply that if he would cross the Halys he would destroy a great nation. He did, but the nation he destroyed was his own. His forces were completely overwhelmed, and his prosperous realm was annexed as a province of the Persian state.

The annexation of Lydia

Cyrus invaded Mesopotamia in 539 B.C. and struck so quickly that he was able to take Babylon without a fight. Once in Babylon the entire New Babylonian Empire was his. We have seen earlier that Cyrus allowed the Jews who had been held captive in Babylon to return to Palestine and set up a semi-independent vassal state; here it can be added that Cyrus allowed other conquered peoples considerable self-determination as well. Dying in 529 of wounds incurred in a minor skirmish with barbarian tribes to the north of his realms near the Aral Sea, Cyrus left behind him an empire

Cyrus's conquests and the policy of self-determination

The Great Palace of Darius and Xerxes at Persepolis. Persian architecture made use of fluted columns, copied from the Greeks, and reliefs resembling those of the Assyrians.

vaster than any that had previously existed. Yet shortly afterward, in 525, the Persian Empire became vaster still when Cyrus's son Cambyses conquered all of Egypt.

Consolidation of the Persian Empire under Darius the Great

Cambyses's successor, Darius I, who ruled Persia from 521 to 486 B.C., concentrated on consolidating his predecessors' military gains by improving the administration of the Persian state. Darius the Great, as he is usually called, presided over the division of the empire into provinces, known as *satrapies,* administered by governors called *satraps,* who were accorded extensive powers but who were obliged to send fixed annual tributes to the central government. (Vassal states such as the Jewish kingdom were obliged to send the Persian government annual tributes as well.) Adhering to the tolerant policy of Cyrus, Darius allowed the various non-Persian peoples of the Persian Empire to retain most of their local institutions while enforcing a standardized currency and system of weights and measures. For example, Darius's satrap of Egypt restored ancient Egyptian temples and codified Egyptian laws in consultation with native priests.

Darius as a builder

Darius was also a great builder. He erected a new royal residence, called by the Greeks Persepolis ("Persian City"), which thereafter became the Persian ceremonial capital. Additionally he dug a canal from the Nile to the Red Sea and installed irrigation systems on the Persian plateau and on the fringe of the Syrian desert. Most impressive of Darius's public works was his system of roads, intended to enhance trade and communications in his far-flung realms. Justly the most famous was the "Royal Road" spanning 1,600 miles from Susa near the Persian Gulf to Sardis near the Aegean.

Government couriers along this road comprised the first "postal system" because they passed messages and goods in relay stages from one *post* to another, with each post measured by the distance traversable in a day's horseback ride: a fresh horse and rider would be ready at each post to carry what had been brought by the "postman" before him. Few people today realize that the motto of the U.S. Post Office is borrowed from Herodotus's praise for the Persian messengers on the Royal Road: "neither snow nor rain nor heat nor gloom of night stays these couriers from the swift completion of their appointed rounds."

Extraordinarily gifted as an administrator, Darius the Great made one enormous mistake in geopolitical strategy: his attempt to extend Persian hegemony into Greece. After Cyrus's conquest of Lydia had made Persia the ruler of Greek-speaking cities on the western coast of Asia Minor, no matter how tolerant Persia's rule was, these cities continued to yearn for the freedom of all other Greek city-states. Consequently, between 499 and 494 B.C. the Greeks on the Asian mainland waged a war for independence and briefly gained the support of troops from Athens, who joined the Asian Greeks in burning Sardis, the Persian regional administrative center. After Darius had quelled the uprising he decided to be certain that his Greek subjects would never again receive foreign aid by sending a force across the Aegean in 490 to punish Athens and let all European Greeks know that henceforth he intended to be their overlord. At the battle of Marathon in 490, the Athenians dealt Darius the only major setback he ever experienced. Although in 480 his son and successor, Xerxes, attempted to avenge the humiliation by crushing all Greece with a tremendous army, heroic resistance by Athens and Sparta forced him to retreat and abandon his plans a year later. At that point the Persians must have realized that the limits of their expansionism had been reached, and that they now had to beware of the European Greeks as their implacable enemies.

Greek resistance to Persian overlordship

In fact from 479 B.C. until Alexander the Great's invasion of Asia Minor in 334 B.C. the Greeks were usually too embroiled by internal rivalries to pose any aggressive challenge to Persia. From the Persian perspective that was extremely fortunate, for during the period in question the Persian Empire was beset by mounting governmental instability caused by intrigues for the throne and rebellions in various provinces. Thus by the time of Alexander, although the empire had survived intact, it had become extremely rickety. Nonetheless, when Alexander gained the expanses won by Cyrus he also gained two intangible legacies—one religious, the other broadly cultural.

Persia's increasing governmental instability

Persia's religious legacy was Zoroastrianism, which along with Buddhism and Judaism, was one of the three major *universal* and *personal* religions known to the world before Christianity and Islam. Although distant origins of Zoroastrianism can be traced back as far as the sixteenth century B.C., the religion's real founder, and the one who gave it its name, was Zoroaster (the Greek form of the Persian name Zarathustra), a Persian who seems to have lived shortly before 600 B.C. (There is scholarly disagreement on when Zoroaster lived, with some authorities arguing for a date many

The founding of Zoroastrianism

centuries earlier.) Zoroaster was probably the first real theologian in history, the first known person to devise a fully developed system of religious belief. He seems to have conceived it as his mission to purify the traditional customs of the Persian tribes—to eradicate polytheism, animal sacrifice, and magic—and to establish their worship on a more coherent and ethical plane.

A universal religion characterized by dualism

Zoroastrianism was a universal religion inasmuch as Zoroaster taught that there was one supreme god in the universe, whom he called Ahura-Mazda, meaning "the wise lord." Ahura-Mazda embodied the principles of light, truth, and righteousness; there was nothing wrathful, let alone evil, about him, and his light shone everywhere, not just upon one tribe or another. In view of the fact that sin or sorrow in the world could not be explained by reference to Ahura-Mazda, Zoroaster posited the existence of a counter-deity, Ahriman, treacherous and malignant, who presided over the forces of darkness and evil. Apparently in Zoroaster's own view Ahura-Mazda was vastly stronger than Ahriman, whom Ahura-Mazda allowed to exist almost by absentmindedness, but the priests of Zoroastrianism, known as *magi,* gradually came to emphasize the dualistic aspect of the founder's thought by insisting that Ahura-Mazda and Ahriman were about evenly matched, and were engaged in a desperate struggle for supremacy. According to them, only on the last great day would "light" decisively triumph over "darkness," when Ahura-Mazda would overpower Ahriman and cast him down into the abyss.

A personal religion

In both its less dualistic and more dualistic forms Zoroastrianism was a thoroughly personal religion, by which is meant that it made private rather than public demands and offered private rewards. Specifically, Zoroastrianism assumed that Ahura-Mazda patronized neither tribes nor states but only individuals who served his cause of truth and justice. Humans possessed free will and were free to sin or not to sin. Of course Zoroastrianism urged them not to sin but to be truthful, to love and help one another to the best of their powers, to aid the poor, and to practice generous hospitality. Those who did so would be rewarded in an afterlife, for the religion assumed the resurrection of the dead on "judgment day" and their consignment either to a realm of bliss or of flames. In the scriptures of the Zoroastrian faith known as the *Avesta* (a work compiled by accretion over the course of many centuries) the rewards for righteousness are explicit: "Whosoever shall give meat to one of the faithful . . . he shall go to Paradise."

Persian Gold Drinking Cup. Persian fondness for lions probably derived from the art of the Assyrians.

The brief recital of Zoroastrianism's tenets makes clear that the religion bore numerous similarities to Judaism and Christianity. Zoroastrianism's ethical content resembles the teachings of the Jewish prophets, its eschatology resembles aspects of postexilic Judaism, and its heaven and hell resemble aspects of the afterlife teaching of Christianity. Even the existence of authoritative scriptures is reminiscent of the weight accorded by Jews to the Old Testament and by Christians to the Old Testament and the New. Unfortunately it is not possible to determine with any precision in what direction influences may have flown because of nearly insuperable chronological complexities. Yet it is surely not coincidental that central aspects of Jewish religious thought took shape in an Asian world dominated by Cyrus and Darius—both convinced Zoroastrians—or that later Jewish beliefs about a judgment day, which themselves influenced Christianity, evolved in a Hellenistic world in which Zoroastrianism continued to exert influence. Furthermore, entirely aside from likely Zoroastrian influence on Judaism, the Persian faith exerted some influence on western Asia's Greek conquerors in encouraging them to think of religion in ever more universalistic and personal terms.

Universalism is also the expression that best characterizes Persia's cultural contribution to the Hellenistic synthesis. Unlike the Assyrians, the New Babylonians, and the Egyptians, all of whom tried to impose their own customs on conquered peoples (when they did not simply enslave them), the Persians adopted a tolerant "One World" policy, by which they conceived themselves to be the guiding force over an assemblage of united nations. Whereas Mesopotamian potentates characteristically called themselves "true king," the rulers of the Persian Empire took the title "King of Kings," thereby implying that they recognized the continued existence of various peoples with various rulers under the canopy of their rule. Moreover, the greatest Persian monarchs, Cyrus and Darius, continually sought to learn whatever they could from the customs and the science of the peoples they conquered. For example, they adopted and diffused the Lydian invention of metallic coinage, learned to chart the night skies from Babylonian astronomers, and commissioned Phoenician sailors to embark on exploratory voyages.

Persian Griffin. Typical Persian ornamentation dating from about 500 B.C.

The Persian habit of borrowing ideas from others, known technically as *eclecticism,* can be observed particularly clearly in the evidence of architecture. The Persians copied the raised platform and the terraced building style that had been standard in Babylonia, and they also imitated the winged bulls, the brilliantly colored glazed bricks, and other decorative motifs of Mesopotamian architecture. Yet in place of the Mesopotamian arch and

Two Reliefs from the Staircase of the Great Palace at Persepolis

vault they adopted the column and the colonnade from Egypt. In addition, interior arrangement and the use of palm and lotus designs at the base of columns also derived from Egyptian influence. Finally, the fluting of the columns and the scrolls beneath the capitals were not Egyptian, but Greek, adopted not from the mainland of Greece but from the Greek cities of Asia Minor. With Alexander's arrival the Persians would become directly subject to the mainland Greeks, but the Greeks would immediately begin borrowing from the Persians.

2. PHILIP OF MACEDON AND ALEXANDER THE GREAT

Political division in Greece

Throughout the first two-thirds of the fourth century B.C. many Greeks took to heart a verse from Euripides' play *Andromache*, "In Greece, alas! how ill things ordered are!" but none seemed able to do much about it. Greece's "ill order" was its political division: city fought city and faction fought faction. As Thebes warred with Sparta and Athens warred with Thebes, ever more Greeks began to long for a national "strong man" to quell all strife, however much imperialism and tyranny were at variance with pristine Greek ideals. Finally a strong man appeared in the person of Philip of Macedon.

Macedon transformed under Philip

Had Philip's fame not been overshadowed by that of his son Alexander, he surely would have been known as Philip the Great. Before he assumed rule in Macedon in 359 B.C. the Greek-speaking territory north of Greece had no cities, little agriculture, and no political stability, being little more than a warring-ground for rival clans. Yet by sheer force of will Philip transformed Macedon into a major power within two decades. First he eliminated all his rivals, then he introduced autocratic institutions of government, and then he began to expand his frontiers by a combination of military skill and "divide and conquer" diplomacy. Philip's fighting style led to a revolution in the art of warfare, as contemporaries themselves recognized. Hitherto the Greeks had formed their armies almost exclusively from citizen-volunteers and conscripts, all of whom could fight for only part of the year because they could not abandon their crops during farming seasons. With limited periods of training, almost all soldiers in such Greek armies fought the same way, as massed infantry with heavy arms. In contrast, drawing partly on mercenaries and partly on loyal Macedonians who had no farming commitments, Philip built a professional army.

The Macedonian professional army

The advantages of the Macedonian professional army, an army that later served Alexander the Great as well as Philip, were manifold. For one, the commander of such a force could count on a wide range of "specialists." Philip's army had an effective mobile cavalry and it had *skirmishers*—fighters whose goal was to demoralize and confuse the enemy at the onset of battle by distracting them with a rain of projectiles coming from the wrong part of the field. Not least among Philip's specialists were well-trained spies and counter-spies, adept at the art of spreading "disinformation." Another advantage of professionalism was that one could impose the strictest disci-

Macedonian Phalanx. Philip of Macedon's infantry—and Alexander the Great's thereafter—was armed with two-handed pikes and massed in squares sixteen rows deep and wide. Members of the phalanx were trained to wheel in step in any direction or to double their front by filing off in rows of eight.

pline. Free Greeks who volunteered for service might, from idealism, have imposed some discipline on themselves, yet it would have been difficult for a commander to address them peremptorily, and their idealism would have tended to diminish in inverse proportion to the length of campaigns. Philip's army, on the other hand, invariably took orders without flinching, having no doubts about the consequences of insubordination: supposedly Philip once murdered a sleeping sentry on the spot, stating coolly as he walked off, "I left him as I found him." Finally, professionalism allowed Philip to eliminate large numbers of noncombatant servants who carried provisions. Earlier Greek forces moved slowly from site to site and were hampered by logistical problems because they were swelled with men who carried food and arms for other men, but Philip forced his fighters to carry their necessities for themselves as much as strength allowed. All of Philip's innovations were considered uncouth by the "gentlemanly" Greeks of the city-states, but his indifference to military "good manners" allowed him to engage in lightning strikes and ensured his total victory in 338 B.C. over combined Athenian and Theban forces at the battle of Chaeronea.

That victory ended Greek city-state freedom once and for all because after Chaeronea Philip installed his despotic rule throughout Greece and his son Alexander thereafter maintained that despotism as the springboard for the conquest of half of Asia. Much irony resides in the fact that Alexander's tutor during his early teenage years had been Aristotle, the very Greek philosopher who insisted that humans are so designed by nature for life in city-states that "he who can live without one must be either a beast or a god," for Alexander proved indifferent to this teaching and proceeded to act as if his tutor had not been a Greek but a Persian. Some historians used to think that Alexander's amazing march through Asia Minor, Egypt, Mesopotamia, Persia, and Afghanistan, to the borders of India was motivated by an urgent sense of mission to bring Greek enlightenment to presumably benighted Asians, but it is now widely agreed upon that Alexander was driven forward solely by a quest for power and glory that verged on

Despotism and conquest

Alexander in Battle. A scene from a sarcophagus of about 300 B.C. Alexander is shown on horseback at the left.

megalomania. (He named several cities "Alexandria" after himself.) In his own day the story was told that a sea pirate taken captive by the mighty conqueror told him that the only difference between them was one of scale. If we put aside motives, however, it was Alexander's conquests, and not the pirate's, that provided the foundations for the Hellenistic civilization.

Intermarriage encouraged

Alexander's pattern of rule itself was Hellenistic in mixing Greek and Asiatic traits. For propaganda purposes the young Macedonian claimed to be punishing Persia for insults inflicted earlier on Greeks, and in fact he not only customarily replaced Persian governors with Greek-speaking ones, but he imported Greek settlers to inhabit newly founded cities as a means of keeping conquered populations in a state of subordination. Yet Alexander also recognized that he and his Greeks could never hope to rule a gigantic Asian empire as hated foreigners, and hence encouraged intermarriage. In keeping with this policy Alexander himself married a Bactrian princess, Roxane (his ultimate preferences were homosexual), and divided a loaf of bread with his bride at the wedding as a gesture of deference to local custom.

Alexander's Asian trappings

What inspired Alexander most about the ways of Asia were not princesses or loaves of bread, but any Asian customs that might enhance his autocracy and his glamour. The traditions of Greece, of course, were thoroughly at odds with flattery and ostentation. Well known is the story that when Alexander first assumed rule in Greece he met the philosopher Diogenes sitting in a wooden tub that served as his home and asked the sage if he would like a favor. "Yes," said Diogenes, "move out of my sun." Determined not to be spoken to this way if he could possibly help it, Alexander adopted lavish Persian dress as he moved through Asia and commanded subjects to approach him, depending on their rank, on bended knee or fully prostrate. Most extreme was Alexander's decision to proclaim himself a god. Although he did this only in Egypt, where the pharaohs had been worshiped as offspring of the sun-god Amon for millennia, claiming divinity was an extraordinary measure for a Greek who was expected to move out of the sun when an unkempt philosopher told him to do so.

3. POLITICAL AND ECONOMIC TRENDS

When Alexander died in 323 B.C., he left no legitimate heir to succeed him save a feeble-minded half-brother. Tradition relates that when his friends requested him on his deathbed to designate a successor, he replied "to the strongest." After his death his highest-ranking generals proceeded to divide the empire among them. Some of the younger commanders contested this arrangement, and a series of wars followed culminating in the decisive battle of Ipsus in 301 B.C. The result was a new division among the victors. Seleucus took possession of Persia, Mesopotamia, and Syria; Lysimachus assumed control over Asia Minor and Thrace; Cassander established himself in Macedonia; and Ptolemy added Phoenicia and Palestine to his original domain of Egypt. Twenty years later these four states were reduced to three when Seleucus defeated and killed Lysimachus in battle and

Alexander the Great. Hellenistic rulers depicted Alexander on their coins in order to stress their connection with the revered hero. This dramatic profile was struck by Lysimachus of Thrace around 300 B.C.

The Hellenistic states

ALEXANDER THE GREAT AND THE HELLENISTIC WORLD

Antiochus I, "Soter." A Hellenistic ruler of Syria (281–261 B.C.), whose chosen title of *soter* meant "savior." The faraway stare connotes supernatural inspiration.

Woman Playing a Lyre. A marble relief from mainland Greece, first century B.C.

appropriated his territory in Asia Minor. In the meantime most of the Greek cities had revolted against Macedonian rule. By banding together in defensive leagues, several of them succeeded in maintaining some independence in federalist form for nearly a century. Finally, between 146 and 30 B.C. nearly all of the Hellenistic territory passed under Roman rule, except the easternmost part, which reverted to rule under native Persians.

The dominant form of government in the Hellenistic Age throughout all the lands once conquered by Alexander, except for most of mainland Greece, was the despotism of rulers who represented themselves as at least semi-divine. Alexander's most powerful successors, the Seleucid kings in western Asia and the Ptolemies in Egypt, made systematic attempts to deify themselves. A Seleucid monarch, Antiochus IV, adopted the title "Epiphanes" or "God Manifest." The later members of the dynasty of the Ptolemies signed their decrees "Theos" (God) and revived the practice of sister marriage that had been followed by the pharaohs as a means of preserving the divine blood of the royal family from contamination. Needless to say, rulers such as these brooked no formal opposition, yet the inevitable consequence of untrammeled autocracy was frequent palace intrigue, leading to stabbings, poisonings, conspirings with foreign rivals, invasions, and wars. Following a policy of kill or be killed, Ptolemy IV of Egypt (221–204 B.C.) put to death his mother, his uncle, and his brother. Generations later his descendant, the beauteous Cleopatra (69–30 B.C.), intrigued with Romans in a vain attempt to maintain some semblance of Hellenistic Egyptian independence.

The only viable alternative to Oriental despotism during the Hellenistic era was the city-state federalism developed in mainland Greece. After having gained independence from the Hellenistic state of Macedon, several Greek cities formed defensive alliances that rapidly evolved into two confederations: the Aetolian League and the Achaean League. These leagues dominated all of Greece until 146 B.C., when they were supplanted by Roman imperial rule. The organization of both leagues was basically the same. Each had a federal council that was composed of representatives of the member cities and that had power to enact laws on subjects of general concern. An assembly that all of the citizens of the member cities could attend decided questions of war and peace and elected officials. Executive and military authority was vested in the hands of a general, elected for one year and eligible for reelection only in alternate years. The leagues were certainly not unified states, for the central authority depended upon the local governments for contributions of revenue and troops. Nonetheless, they constituted the nearest approach ever made in Greece to voluntary national union before modern times.

In regard to economics, the Hellenistic world was generally prosperous, owing to the growth of long-distance trade, finance, and cities. The growth of trade may be explained by reference to several factors, first among which was the opening up of a vast trading area as the result of Alexander's conquests. Long before the time of Alexander, Greeks had been energetic long-distance traders, but they were hampered in trading with Persian realms and with areas east of Persia because Persian emperors and satraps preferred to act in their own economic interests rather than in Greek ones. But when Greek rulers became ensconced throughout Egypt and western Asia after 323 B.C., and when Greek-speaking communities dotted the terrain from Alexandria in Egypt, to another Alexandria in northern Syria, to yet another Alexandria at the head of the Persian Gulf, steady trading connections were facilitated from the eastern Mediterranean to central Asia. Moreover, with bases in Egypt, Asia Minor, Persia, and Bactria, Greek traders could fan out further, venturing into the hinterland of Africa, Russia, and India. Secondly, Alexander unwittingly stimulated a growth of intensive investment when he placed in circulation hoards of Persian gold and silver in the form of coins, jewelry, and luxury utensils. And thirdly, in addition to commerce, manufacturing industries aimed at providing items for trade were now more consciously promoted by autocratic rulers as a means of increasing their revenues.

New trading ventures were particularly vigorous and lucrative in Ptolemaic Egypt and the area of western Asia ruled over by the Seleucid monarchs, the heartland of which was Syria. Every facility was provided by the Ptolemies and the Seleucids for the encouragement of trade. Harbors were improved, warships were sent out to police the seas, and roads and canals were built. Moreover, the Ptolemies employed geographers to discover new routes to distant lands and thereby open up valuable markets. As a result of such methods Egypt developed a flourishing commerce in the widest variety of products. Into the port of Alexandria came spices from Arabia, copper from Cyprus, gold from Ethiopia and India, tin from Britain, elephants and ivory from Nubia, silver from Spain, fine carpets from Asia Minor, and even silk from China. Profits for the government and for some of the merchants were often as high as 20 or 30 percent.

Further evidence of the significant economic development of the Hellenistic Age is to be found in the growth of finance. An international money economy, based upon gold and silver coins, now became general throughout the eastern Mediterranean and western Asia. Banks, usually owned by the government, developed as the chief institutions of credit for business ventures of every description. Speculation, cornering of markets, intense competition, the growth of large business houses, and the development of insurance were other phenomena of this remarkable age.

Finally, cities grew enormously during the Hellenistic Age, for a combination of noneconomic and economic reasons. Entirely aside from economic motives, Greek rulers imported Greek officials and especially Greek soldiers to maintain their control over non-Greek populations. Often this policy resulted in the creation of urban settlements from nothing. Alexander the Great himself had founded some seventy cities as outposts of Greek domination, and in the next two centuries his successors founded about two hundred more. Yet urbanization also increased because of the expansion of commerce and industry and the proliferation of governmental bureaus responsible for economic oversight. Hence the growth of populations in some urban centers was truly explosive. The population of Antioch in Syria quadrupled during a single century. Seleucia on the Tigris grew from nothing to a metropolis of several hundred thousand in less than two cen-

147

Philip of Macedon and Alexander the Great

Dynamic aspects of Hellenistic economy: (1) the growth of trade

The Marble Streets of Ephesus. Taken from the Persians by Alexander in 334 B.C., this cosmopolitan city on the west coast of Asia Minor was noted for its splendor.

(2) the growth of finance

(3) the growth of cities

turies. The largest and most famous of all the Hellenistic cities was Alexandria in Egypt, with about 500,000 inhabitants. No other city in ancient times before imperial Rome surpassed it in size or in magnificence. Its streets were well paved and laid out in regular order. It had splendid public buildings and parks, a museum, and a library of 700,000 scrolls. The masses of its people, however, had no share in the brilliant and luxurious life around them, although it was paid for in part out of the fruits of their labor.

The predominance of agriculture and the advance of manual industry

While the Hellenistic economy was basically a dynamic one, throughout the Hellenistic period agriculture remained the major form of occupation and the primary source of wealth. (Only within the last century did trade and industry replace agriculture as the major source of wealth in Western Europe and North America.) Furthermore, although industry advanced in Hellenistic Egypt and parts of western Asia, nowhere did a true "industrial revolution" based on any technological breakthrough occur. Rather, all industry was based on manual labor rather than being power driven.

The uneven impact of prosperity

Despite the overall growth and prosperity of the Hellenistic economy, prosperity was by no means enjoyed by everyone. Quite to the contrary, for some people sudden wealth was followed by sudden penury, and for others poverty was a constant. Individual merchants and speculators were those most subject to drastic fluctuations in their fortunes, owing to the natural precariousness of mercantile endeavors. For example, a trader who did very well selling a luxury cloth might have decided to invest heavily in it, only to find that tastes had changed, or that a ship he had dispatched to convey his wares had sunk. Merchants were also particularly exposed to what economists now recognize as the "boom and bust" syndrome. A merchant, thinking he would make a fortune during an upward price spiral, might go into debt in order to take advantage of the upward trend, only to find that supply in the commodity he traded suddenly exceeded demand, leaving him nothing with which to pay back his creditors. Among those whose poverty remained unchanged were small-scale farmers who grew crops for sale in regional markets. (In Greece they may have become poorer because Greece suffered during the Hellenistic era from a negative balance of payments, having little to offer for long-distance trade except objects of art.) Those who immigrated to cities in most cases probably also did not improve their economic status, and many of them became subject to badly overcrowded living conditions. All told, therefore, it seems clear that the economic landscape of the Hellenistic world was one of contrasting extremes, an image worth remembering in moving to a consideration of Hellenistic thought and culture.

4. HELLENISTIC CULTURE: PHILOSOPHY AND RELIGION

Hellenistic philosophy exhibited two trends that ran almost parallel throughout the civilization. The major trend, exemplified by Stoicism and

Epicureanism, showed a fundamental regard for reason as the key to the solution of human problems. This trend was a manifestation of Greek influence, though philosophy and science, as combined in Aristotle, had now come to a parting of the ways. The minor trend, exemplified by the Cynics, Skeptics, and various Asian cults, tended to reject reason, to deny the possibility of attaining truth, and in some cases to turn toward mysticism and reliance upon faith. Despite the differences in their teachings, the philosophers and religious enthusiasts of the Hellenistic Age generally agreed upon one thing: the necessity of finding some release from the trials of human existence, for with the decline of free civic life as a means for the expression of human idealism, alternatives needed to be found to make life seem meaningful, or at least endurable.

The earliest of the new Hellenistic philosophical movements was that of the Cynics, who emerged about 350 B.C. Their foremost leader, Diogenes, won fame by his ceaseless quest for an "honest" man. The Cynics argued for living a "natural" life and repudiating everything conventional and artificial. (The word *cynic* comes from the Greek for "dog" and connoted the idea that people should live as naturally as beasts.) Their principal goal was self-sufficiency: everyone should cultivate within himself the ability to satisfy his own needs. Obviously the Cynics bore some resemblance to other movements that have cropped up through the ages—the hippie movement of the 1960s, for example. There were notable differences, however. The Cynics spurned music and art as manifestations of artificiality, and they were not representative of a youth generation. But all such movements seem to reflect a sense of frustration with the constraints and goals of society. According to one story, Alexander the Great once asked Diogenes' disciple Crates whether the city of Thebes, recently destroyed in war, should be rebuilt: "Why?" replied the Cynic, "Another Alexander will surely tear it down again."

Epicureanism and Stoicism both originated about 300 B.C. The founders were, respectively, Epicurus (c. 342–270) and Zeno (fl. after 300), both residents of Athens. Epicureanism and Stoicism had several features in common. Both were individualistic, concerned not with the welfare of society but with the good of the individual. Both were materialistic, denying categorically the existence of any spiritual substances; even divine beings and the soul were declared to be formed of matter. Moreover, Stoicism and Epicureanism alike contained elements of universalism since both taught that people are the same the world over and recognized no distinctions between Greeks and non-Greeks.

But in many ways the two systems were quite different. The Stoics believed that the cosmos is an ordered whole in which all contradictions are resolved for ultimate good. Evil is, therefore, relative; the particular misfortunes that befall human beings are but necessary incidents to the final perfection of the universe. Everything that happens is rigidly determined in accordance with rational purpose. No individual is master of his fate; human destiny is a link in an unbroken chain. People are free only in the sense that they can accept their fate or rebel against it. But whether they

Trends in philosophy and religion

The Cynics

Epicureanism and Stoicism

The Stoics' pursuit of tranquillity of mind through fatalism

accept or rebel, they cannot overcome it. Their supreme duty is to submit to the order of the universe in the knowledge that this order is good; in other words, to resign themselves as graciously as possible to their fate. Through such an act of resignation the highest happiness will be attained, which consists in tranquillity of mind. The individual who is most truly happy is therefore the one who by the assertion of his rational nature has accomplished a perfect adjustment of his life to the cosmic purpose and has purged his soul of all bitterness and whining protest against evil turns of fortune.

The ethical and social teachings of the Stoics

The Stoics developed an ethical and social theory that accorded well with their general philosophy. Believing that the highest good is serenity of mind, they emphasized duty and self-discipline as cardinal virtues. Recognizing the prevalence of particular evils, they taught tolerance for and forgiveness of one another. Unlike the Cynics, they did not recommend withdrawal from society but urged participation in public affairs as a duty for those of rational mind. They condemned slavery and war, but it was far from their purpose to preach any crusade against these evils. They believed that the results that might arise from violent measures of social change would be worse than the diseases they were meant to cure. Besides, what difference did it make if the body were in bondage so long as the mind was free? Despite its partly negative character, the Stoic philosophy was one of the noblest products of the Hellenistic Age in teaching equalitarianism, pacifism, and humanitarianism.

Epicureans and pleasure

Epicurus and the Epicureans based their philosophy on the materialistic "atomism" of an earlier Greek thinker named Democritus, who lived in the latter part of the fifth century B.C. According to this theory the ultimate constituents of the universe are atoms, infinite in number, indestructible, and indivisible. Every individual object or organism in the universe is the product of a fortuitous concourse of atoms. Taking this as given, Epicurus and his followers proposed that since there is no ultimate purpose in the universe, the highest good is pleasure—the moderate satisfaction of bodily appetites, the mental pleasure of contemplating excellence and satisfactions previously enjoyed, and above all, serenity of soul. The last end can be best achieved through the elimination of fear, especially fear of the supernatural, since that is the greatest source of mental pain. The individual must understand that the soul is material and therefore cannot survive the body, that the universe operates of itself, and that no gods intervene in human affairs. The Epicureans thus came by a different route to the same general conclusion as the Stoics—there is nothing better than tranquillity of mind.

The ethical and political theories of the Epicureans

The practical moral teachings and the politics of the Epicureans rested upon utilitarianism. In contrast to the Stoics, they did not insist upon virtue as an end in itself but taught that the only reason why one should be good is to increase one's own happiness. In like manner, they denied that there is any such thing as absolute justice: laws and institutions are just only insofar as they contribute to the welfare of the individual. Certain rules have been found necessary in every society for the maintenance of order. These rules should be obeyed solely because it is to each individual's advantage to do so. Epicurus considered the state as a mere convenience and taught that the wise man should take no active part in politics. Unlike the Cynics, he did not propose that civilization should be abandoned; yet his conception of the happiest life was essentially passive and defeatist. Epicurus taught that the thinking person will recognize that evils in the world cannot be eradicated by human effort; the individual will therefore withdraw to study philosophy and enjoy the fellowship of a few congenial friends.

A more radically defeatist philosophy was that propounded by the Skeptics. Skepticism reached the zenith of its popularity about 200 B.C. under the influence of Carneades. The chief source of its inspiration was the Sophist teaching that all knowledge is derived from sense perception and therefore must be limited and relative. From this was deduced the conclusion that we cannot prove anything. Since the impressions of our senses deceive us, no truth can be certain. All we can say is that things *appear* to be such and such; we do not know what they really *are*. We have no definite knowledge of the supernatural, of the meaning of life, or even of right and wrong. It follows that the sensible course to pursue is suspension of judgment; this alone can lead to happiness. If we will abandon the fruitless quest for absolute truth and cease worrying about good and evil, we will attain peace of mind, which is the highest satisfaction that life affords. The Skeptics were even less concerned than the Epicureans with political and social problems. Their ideal was the typically Hellenistic one of escape from a world neither reformable nor understandable.

The defeatist philosophy of the Skeptics

Hellenistic religion similarly tended to offer vehicles of escape from collective political commitments. Although Greek religion in the age of the city-states had emphasized the worship of gods associated with given cities to advance the fortunes of those cities, such civic-oriented worship now lost its vitality. Its place was taken for many of society's leaders by the philosophies of Stoicism, Epicureanism, and Skepticism. Most ordinary people, on the other hand, tended to embrace emotional personal religions offering elaborate ritual in this world and salvation in the next. In Greek-speaking communities cults that stressed extreme ascetic atonement for sin, ecstatic mystical union with divinity, and otherworldly salvation attracted ever more followers. Among these *mystery cults,* so-called because their membership was secret and their rites held in private, one of the most popular was the Orphic cult, based on the myth of the death and resurrection of the god Dionysius. Even today the word *Dionysian* connotes dedication to ecstatic religious practices bordering on the orgiastic. In Persian communities Zoroastrianism became ever more extreme in its dualism, with Zoroastrian priests, the magi, insisting that everything physical and material was evil and demanding that believers practice austerities in order to ready their immaterial souls for ethereal joy in the afterlife. Finally, among Greeks and non-Greeks alike, an offshoot of Zoroastrianism known as Mithraism gained ever more popularity.

The appeal of emotional personal religions

Exactly when Mithraism became an independent religion is unknown, but it was certainly not later than the fourth century B.C. The cult gained its name from Mithras, a lieutenant of Zoroastrianism's omnipotent god

The spread and influence of Mithraism

Cupid and Psyche. Hellenistic tastes often inclined toward "dainty" representations of eroticism. Cupid's right hand conveys a studied sensuality held in check only by his fig leaf.

Ahura-Mazda. At first only a minor deity in Zoroastrianism, Mithras gradually became recognized by many as the god most deserving of worship, probably because of his emotional appeal. He was believed to have lived an earthly existence involving great suffering and sacrifice. He performed miracles giving bread and wine to humanity and ending a drought and also a disastrous flood. He proclaimed Sunday as the most sacred day of the week since the sun was the giver of light. He declared the twenty-fifth of December as the most sacred day of the year because, as the approximate date of the winter solstice, it marked the return of the sun from its long journey south of the Equator. This was the "birthday" of the sun since on that day its life-giving powers began to increase for the benefit of humankind. Drawing its converts mostly from the lower classes of Hellenistic society, Mithraism offered them an elaborate ritual, contempt for life in this world, and a clearly defined doctrine of redemption through Mithras, a personal savior. Not surprisingly it outlasted the Hellenistic period, becoming after about 100 C.E. one of the most popular religions in the Roman Empire and exerting a slight influence on Christianity.

5. HELLENISTIC CULTURE: LITERATURE AND ART

Both the literature and the art of the Hellenistic Age were characterized by a tendency to take aspects of earlier Greek accomplishments to extremes. It is hard to be sure of the reasons for this, but apparently writers and artists wished to demonstrate their purely formal skills in order to please their autocratic patrons. Furthermore, the greater uncertainties of existence in Hellenistic times may have led consumers of art to seek gratification from more dramatic and less subtle forms of artistic expression. Whatever the case, rather than being an integral expression of civic activities, art definitely became ever more of a commodity, which meant that much of it was ephemeral or even trash: we know the names of at least 1,100 Hellenistic authors, yet hardly more than a handful of these possessed any true literary distinction. Nonetheless, rising above the numerous mediocre works of literature and art dating from the Hellenistic period, a few stand out as enduring masterpieces.

The two most prominent forms of Hellenistic literature were the drama, an established genre, and the pastoral, a new one. The greatest Hellenistic dramatist was the Athenian comic playwright Menander (c. 343–c. 291 B.C.), who worked within a genre previously brought to perfection by Aristophanes. Menander learned much from Aristophanes, but in contrast to him Menander was not a satirist and was indifferent to politics (something unimaginable for any Athenian writer until then). The exclusive subject of Menander's comedies was romantic love, with its pains and pleasures, its intrigues and seductions, and its culmination in happy marriage. Plots of this sort, set within the context of everyday life, succeeded well in engaging the attention of Menander's audiences. Yet Menander was more

Hellenistic literature: (1) the comedies of Menander

than a writer of mere "soap opera," for he was skilled in creating humorous situations and in portraying the foibles of human character.

Romance was also the subject of the pastoral, but rather than being set against a realistic backdrop the pastoral was located in a make-believe world of shepherds, nymphs, and pipes of Pan. The inventor of this genre was a Greek named Theocritus, who was born in Sicily yet lived and wrote in the big city of Alexandria (writing from roughly 270 to roughly 250 B.C.). Theocritus was a model author of prototypically escapist literature. In the midst of urban bustle, faced with arrogant autocratic rulers demanding to be worshiped, and within sight of overcrowded, almost slum-like living conditions for the poor, he celebrated the charm of hazy or sun-drenched country vales and idealized the "simple pleasures" of rustic folk. "Begin my country song, sweet Muses, begin,/I am Thrysis from Etna, this is Thrysis's lovely voice." So might one of his pastorals commence. The artificiality of such verse cannot be denied, but neither can its frequent lush effectiveness. Moreover, in creating the pastoral, Theocritus was the founder of an enduring tradition later taken up by such poetic masters as Virgil and Milton, and one that also provided a wealth of themes for painters and sculptors. Even composers of modern concert music, such as Claude Debussy in his *Afternoon of a Faun,* bear a debt to the escapist poet from Alexandria.

(2) the pastorals of Theocritus

The field of Hellenistic prose literature was dominated by the historians, the biographers, and the authors of utopias. By far the most profound of the writers of history was the mainland Greek, Polybius, who lived during the second century B.C. According to Polybius, historical development proceeds in cycles, nations passing so inevitably through stages of growth and decay that it is possible to predict exactly where a nation is heading if one knows what has happened to it in the past. From the standpoint of his scientific approach, Polybius deserves to be ranked second only to Thucydides among all the historians of ancient times, and he even surpassed Thucydides in his grasp of the importance of social and economic forces.

(3) history

Although most biographies of the time were of a light and gossipy character, their tremendous popularity bears eloquent testimony to the literary tastes of the Hellenistic period. Even more significant was the popularity of the *utopias,* descriptive accounts of ideal states. Virtually all of them depicted a life of social and economic equality, free from greed, oppression, and strife, on an imaginary island or in some distant, unfamiliar region. Generally in these paradises money was considered to be unknown, trade was prohibited, all property was held in common, and all were required to work with their hands to produce the necessities of life. We are probably justified in assuming that the profusion of this utopian literature was a response to the economic and social tensions inherent in Hellenistic society, offering either escapism, similar to that of the pastorals, or perhaps a latent consciousness of the need for reform.

(4) biography and utopias

The very magniloquence implicitly criticized by the utopias is best observed in the main traits of Hellenistic architecture. In place of the balance and restraint that had distinguished Greek architecture of the fifth and early

Hellenistic architecture

The Corinthian Order of Architecture. Note how much more ornate this Hellenistic style is in comparison to the earlier Doric and Ionic orders depicted on p. 131.

fourth centuries B.C., a stress on grandeur and luxuriance, partly derived from standards set by Egyptian pharaohs and Persian emperors, became dominant. Two examples (both of which unfortunately no longer survive) are the great lighthouse of Alexandria, which rose to a height of nearly four hundred feet and had three diminishing stories and eight columns to support the light at the top, and the citadel of Alexandria, which was dedicated to the god Serapis, built of stone covered with blue-tinted plaster, and was said by a contemporary to have "risen into mid-air." In Pergamon, a Greek site in Asia Minor, an enormous altar to Zeus (transported in modern times to Berlin) and an enormous open-air theater looked out over a high hill. In Ephesus, not far away, the streets were paved with marble. Of course not every building in the Hellenistic world was constructed on an enormous scale, yet the "signature" of Hellenistic architecture of whatever dimension was the Corinthian column, a form of column more ornate than the simple and dignified Doric and Ionic alternatives that had predominated in earlier Greek building.

Dying Gaul Seen from Front and Back. A famous example of Hellenistic realism and pathos, this statue was executed around 230 B.C. in the court of Pergamon in Asia Minor. (The original is lost; shown here is a faithful Roman copy.) The sculptor clearly wished to exhibit skill in depicting an unusual human posture and succeeded remarkably in evoking the thin line that separates human dignity from unappeasable loneliness and physical suffering.

Left: *The Winged Victory of Samothrace*. In this figure, done around 200 B.C., a Hellenistic sculptor preserved some of the calmness and devotion to grace and proportion characteristic of Hellenic art in the Golden Age. Right: *Laocoön*. In sharp contrast to the serenity of the Winged Victory is this famous sculpture group from the late second century B.C., depicting the death of Laocoön. According to legend, Laocoön warned the Trojans not to touch the wooden horse sent by the Greeks and was punished by Poseidon, who sent two serpents to kill him and his sons. The intense emotionalism of this work later had a great influence on Western European art from Michelangelo onward. See, for example, the painting by El Greco on page 517.

In the final analysis, probably the most influential of all products of Hellenistic culture, and almost certainly the most congenial to modern tastes, were works of sculpture. Whereas earlier Greek sculpture had sought to idealize humanity and to express Greek ideals of modesty by understated restraint, Hellenistic sculpture emphasized extreme naturalism and unashamed extravagance. In practice this meant that sculptors went to great lengths to recreate facial furrows, muscular distensions, and complex folds of drapery. Awkward human postures were considered to offer the greatest challenges to the artist in stone, to the degree that sculptors might prefer to show people stretching themselves or balancing themselves on one leg in ways that hardly ever occur in real life. Since most Hellenistic sculpture was executed for wealthy private patrons, it is clear that the goal was to create something unique in terms of its conception and craftsmanship—something a collector could show off as the only one of its type. Not surprisingly, therefore, complexity came to be admired for its own sake, and extreme naturalism sometimes teetered on the brink of distorted stylization.

Hellenistic sculpture

Top: *Hellenistic Aphrodite.* This figure, dating from the fourth century B.C., displays the Hellenistic fascination with ungainly, "unnatural," postures. Bottom: *French Bather.* This statuette done by Edgar Degas around 1890 shows some evident continuities between Hellenistic and modern art.

Yet when moderns see such works they frequently experience a shock of recognition, for the bizarre and exaggerated postures of Hellenistic sculptures later exerted an enormous influence on Michelangelo and his followers, and later inspired some of the most "modern" sculptors of the nineteenth and twentieth centuries. Three of the most famous examples of Hellenistic sculpture may be cited here which reveal different aspects of Hellenistic aesthetic ideals: the *Dying Gaul,* done in Pergamon around 220 B.C., shows consummate skill in portraying a distended human body; the *Winged Victory of Samothrace,* of about 200 B.C., displays flowing drapery as if it were not stone but real cloth; and the *Laocoön* group, of the first century B.C., offers one of the most intensely emotional as well as complex compositions known in the entire history of sculptural art.

6. THE FIRST GREAT AGE OF SCIENCE

The most brilliant age in the history of science prior to the seventeenth century C.E. was the period of the Hellenistic civilization. Indeed, some modern scientific achievements would not have been possible without the discoveries of the scientists of Alexandria, Pergamon, and other Hellenistic cities. There are two major reasons for the impressive development of science in the centuries after Alexander's conquest of the Persian Empire. One was the enormous stimulus given to intellectual inquiry by the fusion of Mesopotamian and Egyptian science with the learning and the curiosity of the Greeks. The other was that many Hellenistic rulers were generous patrons of scientific research, subsidizing scientists who belonged to their retinues just as they subsidized sculptors. It was once thought that the motive for such patronage was purely practical—that rulers believed the progress of science would enhance the growth of industry in their territories and would also improve their own material comforts. Yet students of Hellenistic civilization now agree that it is anachronistic to think that any ruler was hoping for an "industrial revolution" in the sense of applying technology to save human labor, for labor was cheap and autocratic princes were completely indifferent to the pains and sufferings of the laboring classes. As for the supposed connection between science and the enhancement of material comfort, Hellenistic rulers in fact hardly thought along those lines because they had adequate numbers of slaves to fan them and were not inclined to introduce mechanical devices that would have lessened the public grandeur of being fanned by deferential subordinates. To be sure, practical aims motivated the patronage of science in some areas, above all in medicine and anything that might relate to military technology. Yet it has become clear that the autocrats who financed the scientific endeavors did so primarily for motives of prestige: sometimes a scientist might fashion a splendid gadget for a ruler that he could show off to visitors as he would show off his sculptures; and even if not, purely theoretical achievements were so much admired among the Greek-speaking leisured classes that a Hellenistic prince who subsidized a theoretical breakthrough would share the prestige for it in the way the mayor of an American city might bask in prestige today if his city's baseball team were to win the World Series.

The major Hellenistic sciences were astronomy, mathematics, geography, medicine, and physics. The most renowned of the earlier Hellenistic astronomers was Aristarchus of Samos (310–230 B.C.), sometimes called the "Hellenistic Copernicus." His primary accomplishment was his deduction that the earth and the other planets revolve around the sun. This view was not accepted by his successors because it conflicted with the teachings of Aristotle and with the conviction of the Greeks that humanity, and therefore the earth, must be at the center of the universe. Later the fame of Aristarchus was overshadowed by that of Ptolemy of Alexandria (second century C.E.). Although Ptolemy made few original discoveries, he systematized the work of others. His principal writing, the *Almagest,* based upon the geocentric theory (the view that all heavenly bodies revolve around the earth), was handed down to medieval Europe as the classic summary of ancient astronomy.

Astronomy

Closely allied with astronomy were mathematics and geography. The most influential Hellenistic mathematician was Euclid, the master of geometry. Until the middle of the nineteenth century his *Elements of Geometry* (written around 300 B.C. as a synthesis of the work of others) remained the accepted basis for the study of that branch of mathematics. The most original of the Hellenistic mathematicians were probably Hipparchus (second century B.C.), who laid the foundations of both plane and spherical trigonometry, and Archimedes, who was primarily a physicist, but who also discovered the integral calculus. Hellenistic geography owed most of its development to Eratosthenes (c. 276–c. 196 B.C.), astronomer and librarian of Alexandria. By means of sundials placed some hundreds of miles apart, he calculated the circumference of the earth with an error of less than 200 miles. Eratosthenes was also the first to suggest the possibility of reaching eastern Asia by sailing west. One of his successors divided the earth into the five climatic zones that are still recognized, and explained the ebb and flow of the tides as due to the influence of the moon.

Mathematics and geography

Perhaps none of the Hellenistic advances in science surpassed in importance the progress in medicine. Especially significant was the work of Herophilus of Chalcedon (c. 335–c. 280 B.C.), who conducted his researches in Alexandria at about the beginning of the third century B.C. Herophilus was the greatest anatomist of antiquity and probably the first to practice human dissection. Among his achievements were a detailed description of the brain, with an insistence (against Aristotle) that the brain is the seat of human intelligence; the discovery of the significance of the pulse, and its use in diagnosing illness; and the discovery that the arteries contain blood alone (not a mixture of blood and air as Aristotle had taught), and that their function is to carry blood from the heart to all parts of the body.

Herophilus and anatomy

The ablest of the colleagues of Herophilus was Erasistratus, who flourished in Alexandria at about the middle of the third century B.C. He is considered the founder of physiology as a separate science. Not only did he practice dissection, but he is believed to have gained much of his knowledge of bodily functions from vivisection. He discovered the valves of the heart, distinguished between motor and sensory nerves, and taught that the ultimate branches of the arteries and veins are connected. In addition, he rejected Hippocrates's theory that the body consists of four "humors" and consequently criticized excessive bloodletting as a method of cure. Unfortunately the humoral theory and an emphasis on bloodletting were revived by Galen, the great encyclopedist of medicine who lived in the Roman Empire in the second century C.E.

Erasistratus and physiology

Prior to the third century B.C. physics had been a branch of philosophy. It was made a separate experimental science by Archimedes of Syracuse (c. 287–212 B.C.), who discovered the law of floating bodies, or specific gravity, and formulated with scientific exactness the principles of the lever, the pulley, and the screw. Among his memorable inventions were the compound pulley and the screw propeller for ships. Although he has been considered the greatest technical genius of antiquity, in fact he placed no emphasis on his mechanical contraptions and preferred to devote his time instead to pure scientific research. Tradition relates that he discovered "Archimedes' principle" (specific gravity) while pondering possible theories in his bath: when he reached his stunning insight he dashed out naked into the street crying "Eureka" ("I have found it").

Archimedes and physics

7. THE BALANCE SHEET

Judged from the vantage of classical Greece, Hellenistic civilization may at first seem no more than a degenerate phase of Greek civilization. Doubtless the autocratic governments of the Hellenistic Age appear debased and repugnant in contrast to Athenian democracy, and doubtless the Hellenistic penchant for extravagance appears debased in contrast to the earlier Greek taste for chaste beauty. It must also be admitted that the best Hellenistic literary works lack the inspired majesty of the great Greek tragedies and that none of the Hellenistic philosophers matched the profundity of Plato and Aristotle. Yet the Hellenistic civilization had its own accomplishments to offer. For example, most Hellenistic cities offered a greater range of public facilities, such as museums and libraries, than earlier Greek cities did, and we have seen that numerous Hellenistic thinkers, writers, and artists left to posterity important new ideas, impressive new genres, and imaginative new styles. Above all, the fact that Hellenistic science was the most advanced in the Western world until the seventeenth century demonstrates that the Hellenistic civilization was by no means retrograde on all fronts.

The Hellenistic contribution

Probably the most important contribution of the Hellenistic era to subsequent historical development was the role it played as intermediary between Greece and Rome. In some cases the Hellenistic contribution was simply that of preservation. For example, most of the familiarity the ancient

Intermediary between Greece and Rome

Romans had with classical Greek thought came to them by way of copies of Greek philosophical and literary texts preserved in Hellenistic libraries. In other areas, however, transfer involved transmutation. A case in point is architecture and art: as we have seen, Hellenistic art evolved from earlier Greek art into something related but quite different, and it was this "Greek-like" art that exerted the greatest influence on the tastes and artistic accomplishments of the Romans.

In conclusion, two particularly remarkable aspects of Hellenistic culture deserve special comment—Hellenistic cosmopolitanism and Hellenistic "modernity." Not only does the word "cosmopolitan" itself come from Greek *cosmopolis,* meaning "universal city," but it was the Greeks of the Hellenistic period who came the closest among westerners to turning this ideal of cosmopolitanism into reality. Specifically, around 250 B.C. a leisure-class Greek could have traveled from Sicily to the borders of India, always meeting people who "spoke his language," both literally and in terms of shared ideals. Moreover, this same Greek would not have been a nationalist in the sense of professing any deep loyalty to a city-state or kingdom. Rather, he would have considered himself a "citizen of the world." Hellenistic cosmopolitanism was partly a product of the cosmopolitanism of Persia, and it helped in turn to create the cosmopolitanism of Rome, but in contrast to both it was not imperial—that is, it was entirely divorced from constraints imposed by a supranational state—although unfortunately it was achieved by means of Greek exploitation of subject peoples. Finally, although cosmopolitanism is surely not an obvious condition of the present, other aspects of Hellenistic civilization must seem very familiar to observers today. Authoritarian governments, ruler worship, economic instability, extreme skepticism existing side by side with intense religiosity, rational science existing side by side with irrational superstition, flamboyant art and ostentatious art collecting: all these traits might make the thoughtful student of history wonder whether the Hellenistic Age is not one of the most relevant in the entire human record for comparison with our own.

Young Athlete. Hellenistic sculptors felt challenged to take "snapshots" of fleeting moments from real life.

Hellenistic cosmopolitanism and Hellenistic "modernity"

SELECTED READINGS

- *Items so designated are available in paperback editions.*

- Boyce, Mary, *The History of Zoroastrianism,* Leiden, 1975.
  Cambridge History of Iran, vol. II, Cambridge, 1985. The most up-to-date large-scale treatment of affairs relating to the Persian Empire during the centuries covered by this chapter.
- Cary, Max, *The Legacy of Alexander: A History of the Greek World from 323 to 146 B.C.,* New York, 1932. A firm guide to the complicated political history of the period.
- Clagett, Marshall, *Greek Science in Antiquity,* rev. ed., New York, 1971. A dependable introduction.
- Engels, Donald W., *Alexander the Great and the Logistics of the Macedonian Army,* Berkeley, 1978. Treats Alexander's amazing campaigns.

Ferguson, John, *The Heritage of Hellenism: The Greek World from 323 to 31 B.C.,* New York, 1973. An engagingly written and lavishly illustrated exposition of typical characteristics of Hellenistic culture.

• Finley, M. I., *The Ancient Economy,* Berkeley, 1973. A fundamental topical treatment by a brilliant scholar. Seeks to emphasize what was truly ancient about the ancient economy.

Frye, R. N., *The Heritage of Persia,* New York, 1963. A fascinating and authoritative history of Persia from earliest times to the triumph of Islam in the seventh century C.E.

• Grant, F. C., *Hellenistic Religions,* New York, 1953. A standard work.

• Grant, Michael, *From Alexander to Cleopatra: The Hellenistic World,* New York, 1982. A useful elementary introduction.

Green, Peter, *Alexander to Actium: The Historical Evolution of the Hellenistic Age,* Berkeley, 1990. A rich, panoramic account.

———, *Alexander of Macedon,* rev. ed., Baltimore, 1974. The best concise biography.

Lane Fox, Robin, *Alexander the Great,* London, 1973. Very long, very interpretative, very good.

Larsen, J. A. O., *Greek Federal States,* Oxford, 1968.

Lewis, Naphtali, *Greeks in Ptolemaic Egypt,* New York, 1986. Studies Greek colonists as a ruling class.

• Tarn, W. W., *Alexander the Great,* Cambridge, 1948. Tarn was the leading English expert on Hellenistic history of the earlier part of this century.

Tarn, W. W., and G. T. Griffith, *Hellenistic Civilisation,* 3rd ed., London, 1952. Still indispensable.

• Walbank, R. W., *The Hellenistic World,* Cambridge, Mass., 1982. An excellent college-level survey.

Zaehner, Robert C., *The Dawn and Twilight of Zoroastrianism,* New York, 1961.

SOURCE MATERIAL

• Austin, M. M., *The Hellenistic World from Alexander to the Roman Conquest: A Selection of Ancient Sources in Translation,* Cambridge, 1981.

• Bagnall, R. S., and P. Derow, *Greek Historical Documents: The Hellenistic Period,* Chico, Calif., 1981.

• Boyce, Mary, *Textual Sources for the Study of Zoroastrianism,* Totowa, N.J., 1984.

Chapter 7

ROMAN CIVILIZATION

My city and country, so far as I am Antoninus, is Rome, but so far as I am
a man, it is the world.

—Marcus Aurelius Antoninus, *Meditations*

For the categories into which you divide the world are not Hellenes and
Barbarians. . . . The division which you substituted is one into Romans
and non-Romans. To such a degree have you expanded the name of your
city.

—Aelius Aristides, *Oration to Rome*

Well before the glory that was Greece had begun to fade, another
civilization, ultimately much influenced by Greek culture, had
started its growth in the West on the banks of the Tiber.
Around the time of Alexander's conquests the emerging power of Rome
was already a dominant force on the Italian peninsula. For five centuries
thereafter Rome's power increased. By the end of the first century B.C. it
had imposed its rule over most of the Hellenistic world as well as over
most of Western Europe. By conquering Hellenistic territory and destroying the North African civilization of Carthage, Rome was able to make the
Mediterranean a "Roman lake." In so doing it brought Greek institutions
and ideas to the western half of the Mediterranean world. And by pushing
northward to the Rhine and Danube Rivers it brought Mediterranean urban culture to lands still sunk in the Iron Age. Rome, then, was the builder
of a great historical bridge between East and West.

Of course Rome would not have been able to play this role had it not
followed its own peculiar course of development. This was marked by the
tension between two different cultural outlooks. On the one hand, Romans throughout most of their history tended to be conservative: they
revered their old agricultural traditions, household gods, and ruggedly warlike ways. But they also strove to be builders and could not resist the attractions of Greek culture. For a few centuries their greatness was based on
a synthesis of these different traits: respect for tradition, order, and military
prowess, together with Greek urbanization and cultivation of the mind.

The Roman synthesis

161

The synthesis could not last forever, but as long as it did the glory that was Greece was replaced by the grandeur that was Rome.

1. EARLY ITALY AND THE ROMAN MONARCHY

The geographical character of the Italian peninsula contributed significantly to the course of Roman history. Except for some excellent marble and small quantities of tin, copper, iron, and gold, Italy has no mineral resources. The extensive coastline is broken by few good harbors. On the other hand, the amount of fertile land in Italy is greater than that in Greece. As a result, the Romans remained a predominantly agrarian people through the greater part of their history. They seldom enjoyed the intellectual stimulus that comes from extensive trading with other areas. In addition, the Italian peninsula was more open to invasion than was Greece. The Alps posed no effective barrier to the influx of peoples from central Europe, and the low-lying coast in many places invited conquest by sea. Domination of the territory by force was therefore more common than peaceful intermingling of immigrants with original settlers. The Romans became absorbed in military pursuits almost from the moment of their settlement on Italian soil, for they were forced to defend their own conquests against other invaders.

Left: *An Etruscan Musician*. Right: *Etruscan Winged Horses*. Both the well-coordinated flutist dating from about 480 B.C., and the proud horses (carved from terra cotta) dating from about 300 B.C. reflect the Etruscans' delight in fluid movement.

Etruscan Sarcophagus. This highly naturalistic statuary depicting a gravely pensive husband and wife dates from roughly 300 B.C. The use of terra cotta (clay) instead of stone allowed easier modeling and enabled the Etruscans to achieve startling visual effects.

Among the many peoples who inhabited Italy before the establishment of Roman hegemony, the most dominant were the Etruscans, the Greeks, and gradually, the Romans themselves. In all probability the Etruscans were natives of the Italian peninsula: certainly they were not members of the Indo-European language group. Whatever their origins, by the sixth century B.C. they had established a confederation of cities that stretched over most of northern and central Italy. Although their writing has never been completely deciphered, enough materials survive to indicate the nature of their culture. They had an alphabet based upon the Greek, much skill in metalwork, great artistic talents, a flourishing trade with the East, and a religion based upon the worship of gods in human form. They bequeathed to the Romans a knowledge of the arch and the vault, the cruel amusement of gladiatorial combats, and the practice of foretelling the future by supernatural means such as studying the entrails of animals or the flight of birds. One of the most distinctive Etruscan traits was the comparatively great respect they showed for women. Etruscan women, some of whom knew how to read, participated in public life, attending dramatic performances and dancing in ways that shocked the contemporary Greeks and Romans. Etruscan wives, unlike those in other contemporary societies, ate with their husbands, reclining together with them on the banqueting couch, and some Etruscan families listed descent through the maternal line.

The Greeks in Italy were immigrants who began to arrive in the eighth century B.C. and who settled mainly in the south, as well as on the island of Sicily. Greek civilization in Italy and Sicily, centered on independent Greek city-states, was as advanced as in Greece itself. Such famous Greeks as Pythagoras, Archimedes, and even Plato for a time, lived in the "Italian West." From the Greeks the Romans derived their alphabet, some of their religious concepts, and much of their art and mythology.

See color plates following page 172

Coins from Greek Colonies in Italy. Above is a coin from Syracuse depicting the nymph Arethusa surrounded by dolphins. Below, a bull from Sybaris, a Greek colony so famous for its easy living that "sybaritic" remains a word in the English language.

As for the Romans themselves, they descended from a cluster of peoples of the Indo-European language group who entered Italy by way of the Alps between 2000 and 1000 B.C. Recent archeological research places the founding of the city of Rome by Latin-speaking people, thereafter known as Romans, quite near the traditional date of 753 B.C. Party because of their strategic location on the Tiber River, the Romans soon began to exercise hegemony over several neighboring cities. One conquest followed another until, by the sixth century B.C. Rome came to dominate most of the surrounding area.

Founding of Rome

Initially Roman government was monarchical—aimed far more at establishing stability and military efficiency than at creating liberty. The earliest Roman political system was an application of the idea of the patriarchal family to the whole community, with the king exercising a jurisdiction over his subjects comparable to that of the head of the family over the members of his household. A *Senate,* or council of elders (*senex* is Latin for "old man"), was composed of the heads of the various clans that formed the community. So far as we know (and we know extremely little about Roman government in this period), the Senate could exercise veto power over royal actions when it seemed absolutely necessary, also providing some government when the royal office became vacant.

The Senate and the assembly

Legend has it that in 534 B.C. an Etruscan tyrant, Tarquin the Proud, managed to gain control of the kingship in Rome. Supposedly Tarquin lorded it over the Romans with extreme cruelty, the final indignity occurring in 510 B.C. when his son raped a virtuous Roman wife, Lucretia. When Lucretia committed suicide rather than living on "in dishonor," the Romans rose up in revolt, overthrowing not only the Etruscan tyranny but the monarchical form of government itself. Almost all of this is patriotic

End of the monarchy

The Diver. A painted tomb-covering from about 480 B.C., unearthed near Paestum, a Greek settlement in southern Italy.

Roman Battle Sarcophagus. This relief displays the glories of war and expresses the Roman military ideal.

myth, but it is possible that the Etruscans had gained some temporary dominion over Rome around the time indicated, and it is all but certain that there was a change in government in Rome around 500 B.C. (whether gradual or sudden is unknown) that ended the kingship and replaced it with a republic. It is also evident that Etruscan power throughout Italy began to decline after 500 and that the Romans gradually cultivated a conviction that kingship was dangerous.

2. THE EARLY REPUBLIC

The history of the Roman Republic for more than two centuries after its establishment was one of practically annual warfare. At first the Romans were on the defensive because rival cities took advantage of the confusion accompanying the change of regime by invading Roman territory. After Rome managed to ward off these attacks the city began to shift to the offensive; as time went on the Romans steadily conquered all the Etruscan territories and then took over all the Greek cities in the south on the Italian mainland. Not only did the latter conquests add to the Roman domain, they also brought the Romans into fruitful contact with Greek culture. As the Romans conquered new areas they were confronted with revolts of the newly subjected populations; the suppression of these revolts whetted the appetite of the victors for further triumphs. Thus new wars followed each other in relentless succession, until by 265 B.C. Rome had conquered almost the entire Italian peninsula.

Early Roman expansion

See color map facing page 172

This long series of conflicts reinforced both the agrarian and military character of the Roman nation. The acquisition of new lands enabled needy Romans to engage in agricultural pursuits in the Roman colonies. As a consequence Romans saw no need for the development of industry and commerce. In addition, the continual warfare served to confirm among

Effects of the early military conflicts

the Romans a steely military ideal. Many of the most familiar Roman legends of martial heroism date from this period. The brave Horatio, for example, supposedly held off an entire army with only two friends in front of a bridge; the retired soldier Cincinnatus supposedly left his farm at a moment's notice for the battlefield.

King replaced by two consuls

During this same period of the early Republic, Rome underwent some glacial political evolution. The replacement of the monarchy was about as conservative a political change as it is possible for any political change to be. Its chief effect was to substitute two elected officials called *consuls* for the king and to exalt the position of the aristocratic Senate by granting it control over the public funds. Although the consuls were chosen by a citizen assembly, the assembly itself was controlled by the aristocracy. The consuls as a result were usually senators who acted as the agents of aristocratic interests. Each consul was supposed to possess the full executive and judicial authority that had previously been wielded by the king, limited by the right each possessed to veto the action of the other. If a conflict arose between them, the Senate might be called upon to decide; or in time of grave emergency a dictator might be appointed for a term not greater than six months.

The struggle between patricians and plebeians

After the establishment of the Republic the political dominance of the aristocracy, known in the Rome of this period as the *patricians,* began to be challenged by the *plebeians*. The latter were mostly small farmers, and occasionally tradesmen, although plebeian ranks also included some wealthy families who were barred from the patriciate because of recent foreign origin. The grievances of the plebeians were numerous. Forced to serve in the army in time of war, they were nevertheless excluded from all officeholding. Moreover, they felt themselves the victims of discriminatory decisions in judicial trials. They did not even know what legal rights they were supposed to enjoy, for the laws were unwritten, and the patricians alone had the power to interpret them. Worst was the oppression that could stem from debt because a debtor could be sold into slavery outside Rome by the creditor.

The victories of the plebeians

To obtain a redress of these grievances the plebeians rebelled soon after the beginning of the fifth century B.C. At that time they forced the patricians to agree to the election of a number of officers known as *tribunes* with power to protect the plebeians by means of a veto over unlawful patrician acts. This victory was followed by a successful demand for codification of the laws about 450 B.C. The result was the issuance of the famous Law of the Twelve Tables, so called because it was written on tablets ("tables") of wood. Although this came to be revered by the Romans of later times as a kind of charter of the people's liberties, it was really nothing of the sort, for it mostly perpetuated ancient custom without even abolishing enslavement for debt. Nevertheless at least there was now a clear definition of law. Roughly a generation later the plebeians won eligibility to positions as lesser magistrates, and about 367 B.C. the first plebeian consul was elected. Since ancient custom provided that, upon completing their terms of office, consuls should automatically enter the Senate, the patrician monopoly of seats in that body was broken. The final plebeian victory came in 287 with the passage of a law which provided that measures enacted by the citizen assembly (now balanced in its composition between patricians and plebeians) should become binding upon the Roman government whether the Senate approved them or not.

All told, the significance of these changes was not great. Their aim was not to gain more liberty for the individual but merely to curb the power of the patriciate and to win for the plebeians a larger share in government. Indeed, as the great Roman historian Theodor Mommsen once put it, the Romans of the early Republic "never really abandoned the principle that the people were not to govern but to be governed." Because of this attitude the grant of full legislative powers to the assembly was little more than a formality, for the Senate continued to wield the real power. Nor did the admission of plebeians to membership in the Senate have any effect in liberalizing that body. So high was its prestige and so deep the veneration of the Romans for authority, that the new members were soon swallowed up in the conservatism of the old. Moreover, the fact that the magistrates received no salaries prevented most of the poorer citizens from seeking public office.

As political changes in Rome moved glacially, so did intellectual and cultural ones. Though writing had been adopted as early as the sixth century B.C., little use was made of it except for the copying of laws, treaties, and funerary inscriptions. Inasmuch as education was limited to instruction imparted by fathers to sons in manly sports, practical arts, and soldierly virtues, the great majority of the people remained illiterate. War and agriculture continued to be the chief occupations for the bulk of the population. A few craftsmen were found in the cities, and a minor development of trade had occurred. But the fact that the Republic had no standard system of coinage until 269 B.C. reflects the comparative insignificance of Roman commerce at this time.

Roman society and culture still rather primitive

During the period of the early Republic Roman religion assumed the character it retained through the greater part of Roman history. In several ways this religion resembled that of the Greeks, partly because the Etruscan religion was deeply indebted to the Greek, and the Romans, in turn, were influenced by the Etruscans. Both the Greek and Roman religions emphasized the performances of rites in order to gain benefits from the gods or keep them from anger. Roman and Greek deities performed similar functions: Jupiter corresponded to Zeus as god of the sky, Venus to Aphrodite as goddess of love, Neptune to Poseidon as god of the sea, and so on. The Roman religion, like the Greek, had no dogmas or sacraments or belief in rewards and punishments in an afterlife.

The religion of the Romans compared with that of the Greeks

But there were significant differences also. The Roman religion was decidedly more political. It served not to glorify humanity or establish a comfortable relationship between human beings and their world but to protect the state from its enemies and to augment its power and prosperity. The gods were less human; indeed, it was only as a result of Greek influences that they were made personal deities at all, having previously been wor-

Contrasts with Greek religion

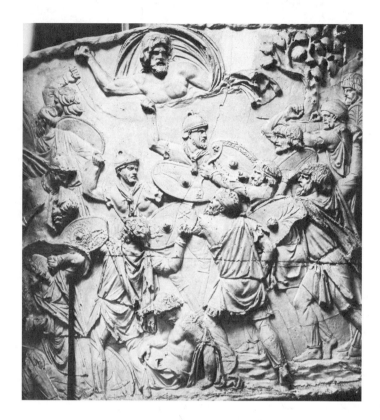

Intervention of Jupiter. This scene from the first century C.E. depicts Jupiter, god of the sky, support-ing the Romans in a battle against Germanic barbarians.

shiped as animistic spirits. The Romans never conceived of their deities as quarreling among themselves or mingling with human beings after the fashion of Greek divinities. Finally, the Roman religion contained a stronger element of religious interaction with public political life than the Greek. A committee of priests known as pontiffs formed a branch of the government, presiding over public sacrifices and serving as guardians of sa-cred traditions that they alone were allowed to interpret. It must be stressed, however, that these religious officials were not priests in a profes-sional sense. Instead, they were aristocrats who served as pontiffs for limited terms of office before or after assuming other governmental duties and without having been trained in any specialized manner for a religious call-ing. Furthermore their role was strictly public, for they heard no confes-sions, forgave no sins, and administered no sacraments.

Morality in the early Republic

The morality of the Romans in this as in later periods had almost no connection with religion. The Romans did not ask their gods to reward them for virtue, but to bestow upon the community and their families ma-terial blessings. Morality lay in patriotism and respect for authority and tra-dition. The chief virtues were bravery, honor, self-discipline, reverence for one's ancestors, and loyalty to country and family. Loyalty to Rome took precedence over everything else. For the good of the Republic, citizens had to be ready to sacrifice not only their own lives but, if necessary, those of their family and friends. The cold-bloodedness of certain consuls who put their sons to death for breaches of military discipline was a matter of deep admiration. Few people in European history, with the exception of the Spartans and modern totalitarians, have ever considered the national interest so paramount or subordinated the individual so completely to the welfare of the state.

3. THE FATEFUL WARS WITH CARTHAGE

By 265 B.C. the Romans had conquered almost the entire Italian mainland. Proud and confident of their strength, they were poised to strike out into overseas terrain. The prosperous island of Sicily was not yet within their grasp, nor could they be indifferent to opportunities for conquest in other parts of the Mediterranean world. Rome was now prone to interpret almost any change in the status quo as a threat to its own security. Accordingly it soon became involved in a series of wars with other great nations which decidedly altered the course of its history.

The beginning of imperialism on a major scale

By far the most important was the struggle with Carthage, a great maritime empire that stretched along the northern coast of Africa from modern-day Tunisia to the Straits of Gibraltar. Carthage had been founded about 800 B.C. as a Phoenician colony. In the sixth century B.C. it gradually developed into a rich and powerful independent state. The prosperity of its upper classes was founded upon commerce and the exploitation of North African natural resources. Carthaginian government was oligarchic. The real rulers were thirty merchant princes who constituted an inner council of the Senate. Despite a cruel religion that demanded blood sacrifices, Carthage during the third century B.C. had a civilization superior in luxury and scientific achievement to that of Rome.

Carthage

The protracted struggles between Rome and Carthage are known collectively as the Punic Wars since the Romans called the Carthaginians *Poeni,* that is, Phoenicians. The initial clash began in 264 B.C. because of Roman resentment about Carthaginian expansion in Sicily. Carthage already controlled the western portion of the island and now was threatening to take over the eastern coast, nearer to the Italian mainland. Unwilling to see Carthage rule all of Sicily and become a threatening next-door neighbor, Rome declared war upon Carthage with the hope of forcing its enemy back into North Africa. Twenty-three years of bitter fighting finally brought victory to the Roman generals. Carthage was compelled to surrender all of its holdings in Sicily and to pay a very large indemnity.

Causes of the First Punic War

Because the Romans had fought so long and hard to defeat Carthage, they became determined not to let their enemy become dominant in other Mediterranean areas. Accordingly, in 218 B.C. the Romans interpreted Carthage's attempt to expand its rule in Spain as a threat to Roman interests and responded with a declaration of war. The renewed struggle, known as the Second Punic War, raged for sixteen years. At first Rome was entirely thrown off guard by the brilliant exploits of the famous

The Second Punic War

Hannibal. A coin from Carthage representing Hannibal as a victorious general, with an elephant on the reverse.

Carthaginian commander, Hannibal. Already commanding an army in Spain, Hannibal in a truly remarkable military feat, brought this force, including war elephants, through southern France and then over the Alps into Italy. (Scholars are uncertain through which Alpine pass Hannibal brought his troops and elephants but continue to investigate this urgent subject on many a happy vacation in the French mountains.) With Carthaginian troops on Italian soil, Rome escaped defeat by the narrowest of margins. Only "delaying tactics" ultimately saved the day, for time was on the side of those who could keep an invader short of supplies and worn down by harrassment. Such tactics called for iron discipline, but this was Rome's greatest strength. As pursued by the Roman general Fabius, known as "Fabius the Delayer" (whence the modern term "Fabianism," meaning gradualism), delaying tactics robbed Hannibal of his advantage until a more aggressive Roman general, Scipio Africanus, finally defeated Hannibal in pitched battle at Zama (202 B.C.).

With Scipio's victory, the Second Punic War came to an end. Carthage was now more completely humbled than before, being compelled to abandon all its possessions except the city of Carthage itself and its surrounding territory in Africa, and to pay an indemnity three times greater than that paid at the end of the First Punic War. Yet Roman suspicion of Carthage remained obsessive. About the middle of the second century B.C. Carthage had recovered some of its former prosperity—and this was enough to provoke the displeasure of the Romans. Nothing now would satisfy the most influential Roman senators but the total demolition of the Carthaginian state. In 150 B.C. the Roman warhawk Cato the Censor ended every speech he made in the Senate with the same words: "Carthage must be destroyed." Not surprisingly, in the following year the Senate seized on a minor pretext to demand that the Carthaginians abandon their city and settle at least ten miles from the coast. Since this demand amounted to a death sentence for a nation dependent upon commerce, it was refused—as the Romans probably realized it would be. The result was the Third Punic War, a conflict fought between 149 and 146 B.C. The final Roman assault was carried into the city of Carthage, and a frightful butchery took place. When the victorious Roman general saw Carthage going up in flames he said: "It is a glorious moment, but I have a strange feeling that some day the same fate will befall my own homeland." With the might of the Carthaginians completely broken, the 55,000 that remained alive were sold into slavery, their once magnificent city was razed, and the ground was plowed over with salt.

The wars with Carthage had momentous effects on Rome's development. Most obvious was an enormous increase in Roman territory. The Roman victories over Carthage led to the creation of overseas provinces in Sicily, North Africa, and Spain. This not only brought Rome great new wealth—above all from Sicilian and African grain, and Spanish silver—but in the case of Spain was the beginning of a policy of westward expansion that proved to be one of the great formative influences on the history of Europe. Then too the wars brought Rome into conflict with eastern

The Third Punic War and the destruction of Carthage

Results of the wars with Carthage: (1) conquest of Spain and the Hellenistic East

Mediterranean powers and thereby paved the way for still greater dominion. During the Second Punic War, Philip V of Macedon had entered into an alliance with Carthage and was said to have had designs on Egypt. Declaring a disinterested intention to forestall Philip's moves, Rome sent an army to the East, although the extension of Roman rule was evidently the real item on the Roman agenda. The result was the conquest of Greece and Asia Minor and the reduction of Egypt into a Roman sphere of influence. Thus before the end of the second century B.C. virtually the entire Mediterranean world had been brought under Roman control.

As Roman tentacles stretched out over the Mediterranean, a host of fundamental economic and social changes ensued. One was a huge increase in slavery due to the capture and sale of prisoners of war. We have seen that 55,000 Carthaginians were enslaved in 146 B.C.; not long before, 150,000 Greeks had met the same fate. By the end of the second century about a million slaves toiled in Italy, mainly in the fields, making Rome one of the most slave-based economies known to history. Concomitant with this development was the decline of the small farmer as a result of the establishment of the plantation system based on slave labor and the influx of cheap grain from the provinces. Small farmers, in turn, took refuge in the cities, above all the city of Rome itself, creating a large new urban element. Inevitably this trend, along with the incorporation of overseas areas long oriented to trade, and the need for an administrative apparatus, led to the appearance of a middle class comprising merchants, moneylenders, and men who held government contracts to operate mines, build roads, or collect taxes. Yet the cities were also full of impoverished drifters because Rome never made a transition to industrialism; with slaves to do all the hard work, a great disincentive existed for the technological initiative that might have led to industrialism, and without large-scale manufacture the urban population remained underemployed. Thus a traveler to Italy around 150 B.C. would have found a countryside full of slaves and cities full of disgruntled ex-farmers, living from hand to mouth.

(2) a social and economic revolution

Yet another change that accompanied the acquisition of new territories was a change in the nature of family life and the status of women. In earlier times the Roman family was based on the husband's legal and financial authority, which gave him nearly absolute powers. The wife was subordinated and served as custodian of the home while the husband managed outside affairs and expected to be treated with reverence. In the second century B.C., however, two legal innovations greatly altered this pattern. One was the introduction of so-called "free marriage," whereby the wife's share of her father's property remained her own instead of passing to her husband and reverted to her father or her father's heirs upon her death. Together with that came new rules for divorce, whereby either side, instead of just the man, could initiate proceedings, and adultery was not needed as the sole justification. Apparently the motive of both legal novelties was to prevent the transfer of property from one family to another, which would diminish the size of the large estates created with the influx of slaves. Yet both changes obviously resulted in giving the wife greater le-

Free marriage and divorce

gal independence. In addition, the slave system itself gave wealthier women greater practical independence, for slaves could now take over tasks of child-rearing and household maintenance. Upper-class Roman women accordingly spent more time away from the home and began to engage in a range of social, intellectual, and artistic activities.

Introduction of Greek ideas and customs

Cultivated upper-class life for both men and women had been made possible by a final change attendant on Roman expansion, the introduction of Greek ideas and customs. These flowed more easily to Rome with the conquest of the Hellenistic East and were adopted once upper-class Romans began to become really wealthy as a result of their conquests. In particular, children were given much more education, theater and literature became ever more the mode, and the creature comforts that Hellenistic Greeks had begun to prize in Syria and Egypt became equally prized in turn by the Roman conquerors of the Mediterranean world. Some conservative Roman males viewed such changes with repugnance. For them the "good old Roman ways" with emphasis on family life based on fatherly authority and sober military discipline were giving way to the collapse of the family and the debilitating lures of soft living. But whether they liked it or not, they could not turn the clock back, for Rome had now become irreversibly transformed from a republic of farmers into a complex society with vast gaps between rich and poor and new habits, at least among the well-to-do, of greater personal autonomy.

4. THE SOCIAL STRUGGLES OF THE LATE REPUBLIC

The new period of turbulence

The period from the end of the Punic War in 146 B.C. to about 30 B.C. was one of enormous turbulence. Social conflicts, assassinations, struggles between rival dictators, wars, and insurrections were the common occurrences of the time. Slave uprisings were also part of the general disorder. Some 70,000 slaves defeated a Roman army in Sicily in 134 B.C. before this revolt was put down by further Roman reinforcements, with slaves again ravaging Sicily in 104 B.C. But the most threatening slave revolt of all was one led by a slave named Spartacus from 73 to 71 B.C. Spartacus, who was being trained to become a gladiator (which meant certain death in the arena), escaped with a band of fugitives to Mount Vesuvius near Naples, there attracting a huge host of other fugitive slaves. For two years the escapees under his leadership held off Roman armies and overran much of southern Italy until they were finally defeated and Spartacus was slain in battle. Six thousand of those captured were left crucified along the length of a road from Capua to Rome (about 150 miles) to provide a terrible warning.

Meanwhile an extended conflict between elements of the Roman governing class began in 133 B.C. with the attempts at social and economic reform instituted by the two Gracchi brothers. Though of aristocratic lineage themselves, they proposed to alleviate social and economic stress by grant-

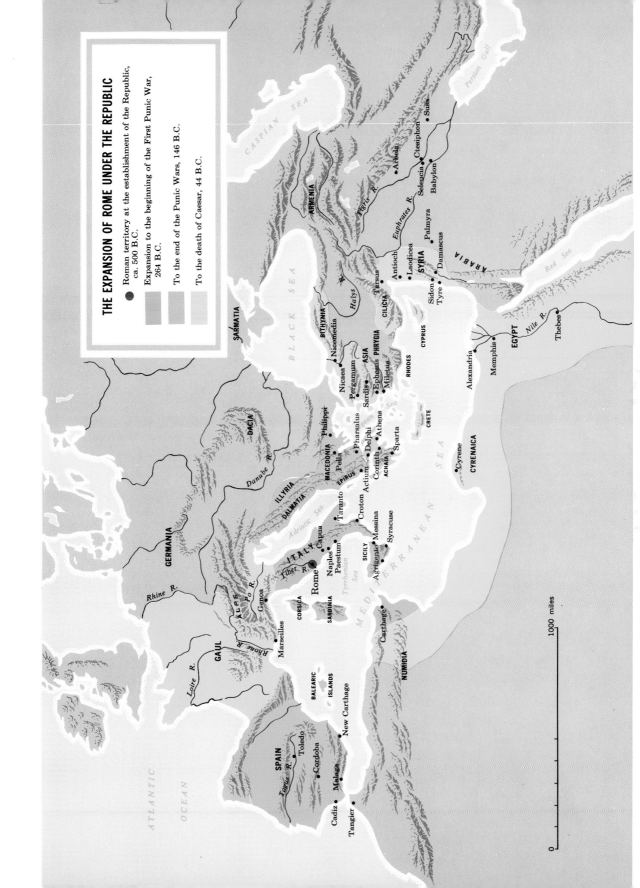

THE EXPANSION OF ROME UNDER THE REPUBLIC

- Roman territory at the establishment of the Republic, ca. 500 B.C.
- Expansion to the beginning of the First Punic War, 264 B.C.
- To the end of the Punic Wars, 146 B.C.
- To the death of Caesar, 44 B.C.

1000 miles

0

ATLANTIC OCEAN

SPAIN
Tangier
Cadiz
Malaga
Cordoba
Toledo
Tagus R.

Loire R.
GAUL
Rhône R.
Marseilles
Rhine R.
GERMANIA
ALPS
Po R.
Genoa
CORSICA
SARDINIA
BALEARIC ISLANDS
New Carthage

DACIA
Danube R.
ILLYRIA
DALMATIA
Adriatic Sea
ITALY
Tiber R.
Rome
Naples
Capua
Paestum
Taranto
Croton
Tyrrhenian Sea
SICILY
Agrigento Messina
Syracuse
Carthage
NUMIDIA

SARMATIA

BLACK SEA
BITHYNIA
Nicomedia
Nicaea
Pergamum
Sardis
ASIA
Ephesus PHRYGIA
Miletus
RHODES
Halys R.
CILICIA
Tarsus

MACEDONIA
Philippi
Pella
Pharsalus
Delphi
EPIRUS
Actium
Corinth Athens
ACHAIA Sparta
Aegean Sea
CRETE

MEDITERRANEAN SEA
CYRENAICA
Cyrene
Alexandria

CASPIAN SEA
ARMENIA
Tigris R.
Euphrates R.
Arbela
Ctesiphon
Seleucia
Babylon
Susa
Persian Gulf

Antioch
Laodicea
SYRIA
Palmyra
Damascus
Sidon
Tyre
ARABIA
Red Sea

EGYPT
Memphis
Nile R.
Thebes

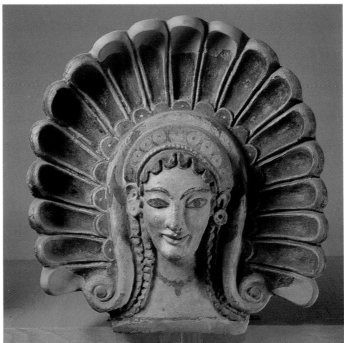

Etruscan Grotesques. These building ornaments of about 500 B.C. were meant to frighten away evil spirits. (Art Resource)

Etruscan Sarcophagus. Etruscan culture was unusual in the ancient world for the dignity it offered women.

Roman Mystery Rites. The so-called "Villa of the Mysteries" in Pompeii preserves an astonishing cycle of wall-paintings done around 50 B.C. The exact meaning is debatable, but the most persuasive interpretation is that it shows a succession of cult rites. Here a young woman is being whipped, probably in an initiation ceremony, while a cult member performs a solemn dance in the nude. (Art Resource)

Unidentified Man, 1st cent. C.E. The Romans excelled in portraits of sharp individuality and realistic details.

Young Roman Woman with Pen. This wall-painting, originally from Pompeii, demonstrates that wealthy Roman women could lead lives of great cultivation. It is unknown whether the portrait was meant to represent a real woman or an imaginary poetess, but in either case it displays an ideal of elegance, pensiveness, and literary accomplishment. (Art Resource)

Wall Painting of a Satyr Mask, 1st cent. B.C. The belief in satyrs, thought to inhabit forests and pastures, was taken over from the Greeks.

Mummy Portrait, 2nd cent. C.E. A Roman woman buried in Egypt.

Mosaic, 1st cent. C.E. A floor design composed of small pieces of colored marble fitted together to form a picture.

Diana. A Roman painting depicting the goddess of the hunt. Roman art was often gentle and impressionistic; far from the military grandeur most often associated to-day with the Romans. (Art Resource)

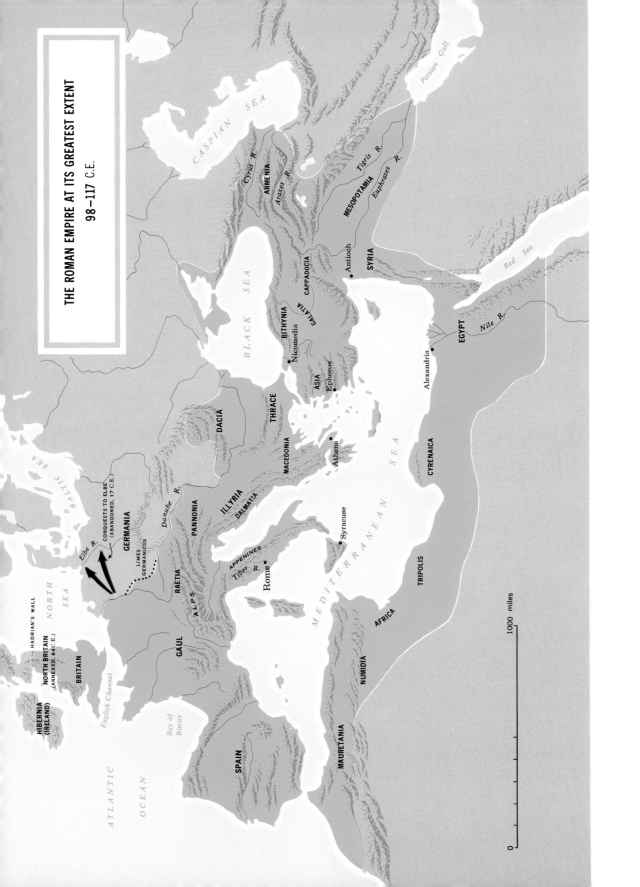

THE ROMAN EMPIRE AT ITS GREATEST EXTENT
98–117 C.E.

CASPIAN SEA

Cyrus R.

ARMENIA

Araxes R.

Tigris R.

Euphrates R.

MESOPOTAMIA

Persian Gulf

CAPPADOCIA

Antioch

SYRIA

GALATIA

BITHYNIA

Nicomedia

Red Sea

BLACK SEA

ASIA

Ephesus

EGYPT

Nile R.

Alexandria

THRACE

MACEDONIA

Athens

CYRENAICA

DACIA

MEDITERRANEAN SEA

BALTIC SEA

ILLYRIA

DALMATIA

Danube R.

PANNONIA

Syracuse

CONQUESTS TO ELBE
(ABANDONED, 17 C.E.)

GERMANIA

Elbe R.

LIMES
GERMANICUS

RAETIA

APPENINES

Tiber R.

TRIPOLIS

Rome

ALPS

AFRICA

HADRIAN'S WALL

NORTH SEA

GAUL

NUMIDIA

NORTH BRITAIN
(ANNEXED, 84 C.E.)

BRITAIN

HIBERNIA
(IRELAND)

English Channel

Bay of Biscay

SPAIN

MAURETANIA

ATLANTIC OCEAN

1000 miles

0

ing government lands to the landless. In 133 Tiberius Gracchus, as tribune, proposed a law that restricted the current renters or holders of state lands to a maximum of 300 acres per citizen plus 150 acres for each child in the family. The excess was to be given to the poor in small plots. Conservative aristocrats bitterly opposed this proposal and engineered its veto by Octavius, Tiberius's fellow tribune. Tiberius removed Octavius from office, and when his own term expired attempted to stand for reelection. Both of these moves seemed to threaten a dictatorship and offered the conservative senators an excuse for resistance. Armed with clubs, they went on a rampage during the elections and murdered Tiberius and many of his followers.

The land program of Tiberius Gracchus

Nine years later Tiberius's younger brother, Gaius Gracchus, renewed the struggle. Though Tiberius's land law had finally been enacted by the Senate, Gaius believed that the campaign had to go further. Elected tribune in 123 B.C., and reelected in 122, he enacted several laws for the benefit of the less privileged. One provided for stabilizing the price of grain in Rome. For this purpose public granaries were built along the Tiber. Another exercised controls on governors suspected of exploiting the provinces for their own advantage. These and similar measures provoked so much anger among the vested interests that they resolved to eliminate their enemy. The Roman Senate proclaimed Gaius Gracchus an outlaw and authorized the consuls to take all necessary steps for the defense of the Republic. In the ensuing conflict Gaius was killed and about 3,000 of his followers lost their lives in vengeful purges.

Gaius Gracchus and the renewed fight for reform

The Gracchan turbulence demonstrated that the Roman Republic had outgrown its constitution. Over the years the assembly had gained powers almost equal to those of the Senate. Instead of working out a peaceful accommodation to these changes, both sides resorted to violence. By so doing they set a precedent for the use of force by any politician ambitious for supreme power and thereby paved the way for the destruction of the Republic. The Romans had shown a remarkable capacity for organizing an empire and for adapting the Greek idea of a city-state to a large territory, but the narrow conservatism of their upper classes was a fatal hindrance to the health of the state. Regarding all reform as evil, they failed to understand the reasons for internal discord and seemed to think that repression was its only remedy.

Significance of the Gracchan attempts at reform

After the downfall of the Gracchi, two military leaders who had won fame in foreign wars successively made themselves rulers of the state. The first was Marius, who was elevated to the consulship by the plebeian party in 107 B.C. and reelected six times. Unfortunately, Marius was no statesman and accomplished nothing for his followers beyond demonstrating the ease with which a general with an army at his back could override opposition. Following his death in 86 B.C. the aristocrats took a turn at government by force. Their champion was Sulla, another victorious commander. Appointed dictator in 82 B.C. for an unlimited term, Sulla ruthlessly proceeded to exterminate his opponents and extend the powers of the Senate. Even the senatorial veto over acts of the assembly was revived, and the au-

Marius and Sulla

Pompey

Julius Caesar

Caesar's achievements

thority of the tribunes was sharply curtailed. After three years of rule Sulla decided to exchange the pomp of power for the pleasures of the senses and retired to a life of luxury on his country estate.

The actions of Sulla did not stand unchallenged after he relinquished his office, for the effect of his decrees was to give control to a selfish aristocracy. Several new leaders now emerged to espouse the cause of the people. The most famous of them were Pompey (106–48 B.C.) and Julius Caesar (100–44 B.C.). For a time they cooperated in a plot to gain control of the government, but later they became rivals and sought to outdo each other in bids for popular support. Pompey won fame as the conqueror of Syria and Palestine, while Caesar devoted his talents to a series of brilliant forays against the Gauls, adding to the Roman state the territory of modern Belgium, Germany west of the Rhine, and France. In 52 B.C., after protracted mob disorders in Rome, the Senate turned to Pompey and engineered his election as sole consul. Caesar, stationed in Gaul, was branded an enemy of the state, and Pompey conspired with the senatorial faction to deprive him of political power. The result was a deadly war between the two men. In 49 B.C. Caesar crossed the Rubicon River into Italy (ever since then an image for a fateful decision) and marched on Rome. Pompey fled to the East in the hope of gathering an army large enough to regain control of Italy. In 48 B.C. the forces of the rivals met at Pharsalus in Greece. Pompey was defeated and soon afterward murdered by schemers in favor of Caesar.

Caesar then intervened in Egyptian politics at the court of Cleopatra (whom he left pregnant). Then he conducted another military campaign in Asia Minor in which victory was so swift that he could report "I came, I saw, I conquered" (*veni, vidi, vici*). After that Caesar returned to Rome. No one now dared challenge his power. With the aid of his veterans he cowed the Senate into granting his every desire. In 46 B.C. he became dictator for ten years, and two years later for life. In addition, he assumed nearly every other title that could augment his power. He obtained from the Senate full authority to make war and peace and to control the revenues of the state. For all practical purposes he was above the law, and rumors spread that he intended to make himself king. Such fears led to his assassination on the Ides of March in 44 B.C. by a group of conspirators, under the leadership of Brutus and Cassius, who hoped to return Rome to republican government.

Although Caesar was once revered by historians as a superhuman hero, he is now often dismissed as insignificant. But both extremes of interpretation should be avoided. Certainly he did not "save Rome" and was not the greatest statesman of all time, for he treated the Republic with contempt and made the problem of governing more difficult for those who came after him. Yet some of the measures he took as dictator did have lasting effects. With the aid of a Greek astronomer he revised the calendar so as to make a year last for 365 days (with an extra day added every fourth year). This "Julian" calendar—subject to adjustments made by Pope Gregory XIII in 1582—is still with us. It is thus only proper that the seventh month is named after Julius as "July." By conferring citizenship upon thousands of Spaniards and Gauls, Caesar took an important step toward eliminating the distinction between Italians and provincials. He also helped relieve economic inequities by settling many of his veterans and some of the urban poor on unused lands. Vastly more important than these reforms, however, was Caesar's farsighted resolve, made before he seized power, to invest his efforts in the West. While Pompey, and before him Alexander, went to the East to gain fame and fortune, Caesar was the first great leader to recognize the potential significance of northwestern Europe. By incorporating Gaul into the Roman world he brought Rome great agricultural wealth and helped bring urban life and culture to what was then the wild West. Western European civilization, later to be anchored in just those regions that Caesar conquered, might not have been the same without him.

5. ROME BECOMES SOPHISTICATED

The culture that Rome brought to Gaul was itself taken from the Greek East, for during the time between the end of the Punic Wars and the death of Julius Caesar Rome came ever more under the influence of Hellenistic civilization. One result was the adoption of Hellenistic schools of thought, especially Epicureanism and Stoicism, by the upper classes, and another was the flowering of intellectual activity. The most renowned of the Roman exponents of Epicureanism was Lucretius (98–55 B.C.), author of a book-length philosophical poem entitled *On the Nature of Things.* In writing this work Lucretius wished to explain the universe in such a way as to remove all fear of the supernatural, which he regarded as the chief obstacle to peace of mind. Worlds and all things in them, he taught, are the result of fortuitous combinations of atoms. Though he admitted the existence of the gods, he conceived of them as living in eternal peace, neither creating nor governing the universe. Everything is a product of mechanical evolution, including human beings, and their habits and beliefs. Since mind is indissolubly linked with matter, death means utter extinction; consequently, no part of the human personality can survive to be rewarded or punished in an afterlife. Lucretius's conception of the good life was simple: what one needs, he asserted, is not enjoyment but "peace and a pure heart." Whether one agrees with Lucretius's philosophy or not, there is no doubt that he was an extraordinarily fine poet. In fact his musical cadences, sustained majesty of expression, and infectious enthusiasm earn him a rank among the greatest poets who ever lived.

Stoicism was introduced into Rome about 140 B.C. and soon came to include among its converts numerous influential leaders of public life. The greatest of these was Cicero (106–43 B.C.), the "father of Roman eloquence." Although Cicero adopted doctrines from a number of philosophers, including both Plato and Aristotle, he derived more of his ideas from the Stoics than from any other source. Cicero's ethical philosophy was based on the Stoic premises that virtue is sufficient for happiness and that tranquillity of mind is the highest good. He conceived of the ideal human

Ides of March Coin. This coin was struck by Brutus to commemorate the assassination of Julius Caesar. Brutus is depicted on the obverse; on the reverse is a liberty cap between two daggers and the Latin abbreviation for the Ides of March.

Roman Epicureanism: Lucretius

The Stoic philosophy of Cicero

being as one who has been guided by reason to an indifference toward sorrow and pain. Cicero diverged from the Greek Stoics in his greater approval of the active, political life. To this degree he still spoke for the older Roman tradition of service to the state. Cicero never claimed to be an original philosopher but rather conceived his goal to be that of bringing the best of Greek philosophy to the West. In this he was remarkably successful, for he wrote in a rich and elegant Latin prose style that has never been surpassed. Cicero's prose immediately became a standard for composition and has remained so until the present century. Thus even though not a truly great thinker Cicero was the most influential Latin transmitter of ancient thought to the medieval and modern Western European worlds.

Works of Plautus, Catallus, and Julius Caesar

Lucretius and Cicero were the two leading exponents of Greek thought but not the only two fine writers of the later Roman Republic. It now became the fashion among the upper classes to learn Greek and to strive to reproduce in Latin some of the more popular forms of Greek literature. Some results of enduring literary merit were the ribald comedies of Plautus (257?–184 B.C.), the passionate love poems of Catullus (84?–54? B.C.), and the crisp military memoirs of Julius Caesar.

Social conditions in the late Republic

In addition to its intellectual effects, Roman interaction with the Hellenistic world accelerated the process of social change, foremost of which was the cleavage between classes. The Italian people, numbering about eight million on the death of Caesar, had come to be divided into four main social orders: the senatorial aristocracy, the equestrians, the common

Left: *Atrium of an Upper-Class House in Pompeii, Seen from the Interior.* Around the atrium or central court were grouped suites of living rooms. The marble columns and decorated walls still give an idea of the luxury and refinement enjoyed by the privileged minority. Right: *Orpheus Floor Mosaic.* This luxurious adornment to an upper-class Roman dwelling, in what is today Arles in southern France, represents the inspired musician soothing lions and tigers as well as numerous other representatives of the animal kingdom.

citizens, and the slaves. The senatorial aristocrats numbered 300 citizens and their families. Most of the aristocrats gained their living as officeholders and as owners of great landed estates. The equestrian order was made up of propertied aristocrats who were not in the Senate. Originally this class had been composed of those citizens with incomes sufficient to enable them to serve in the cavalry at their own expense, but the term *equestrian* came to be applied to all outside of the senatorial class who possessed property in substantial amount. The equestrians were the chief offenders in the exploitation of the poor. As moneylenders they often charged exorbitant interest rates. By far the largest number of the citizens were mere commoners. Most of these were independent farmers, a few were industrial workers, and some were indigent city dwellers who lived by intermittent employment and public relief. When Julius Caesar became dictator, 320,000 citizens were receiving free grain from the state.

The Roman slaves were scarcely considered people at all but instruments of production like cattle or horses. Notwithstanding the fact that some of them were cultivated foreigners taken as prisoners of war, the standard policy of their owners was to get as much work out of them as possible during their prime until they died of exhaustion or were released to fend for themselves. Although domestic slaves might from time to time have been treated decently, and some slave artisans in the city of Rome were relatively free to run their own businesses, the general lot of the slave was horrendous. Moreover, it is a sad commentary on Roman civilization that most of its productive labor was done by slaves. They produced much of the food supply, for the amount contributed by the few surviving independent farmers was quite insignificant, and did much of the work in the urban shops as well. In addition, slaves were employed in numerous nonproductive activities. A lucrative form of investment for the business classes was ownership of slaves trained as gladiators, who could be slaughtered by wild animals for the amusement of the people. The growth of luxury also required the employment of thousands of slaves in domestic service. The man of great wealth insisted on having his doorkeepers, his litter-bearers, his couriers (for the government of the Republic had no postal service), his valets, and his tutors for his children. In some great households there were special servants with no other duties than to rub the master down after his bath or to care for his sandals.

The status of the slaves

The religious beliefs of the Romans were altered in various ways in the last two centuries of the Republic—again mainly because of Rome's interaction with the Hellenistic world. Most pronounced was the spread of Eastern mystery cults, which satisfied the craving for a more emotional religion than traditional Roman worship and offered the reward of immortality to the wretched of the earth. From Egypt came the cult of Osiris (or Serapis, as the god was now more commonly called), while from Asia Minor was introduced the worship of the Great Mother, with her eunuch priests and ritualistic orgies. Most popular of all at the end of the period was the Persian cult of Mithraism, which offered awe-inspiring underground rites and a doctrine of the afterlife of the soul.

Changes in religion

6. THE PRINCIPATE OR EARLY EMPIRE (27 B.C.–180 C.E.)

An alliance to avenge Caesar's death

Shortly before his death in 44 B.C., Julius Caesar had adopted as his sole heir his grandnephew Octavian (63 B.C.–14 C.E.), then a young man of eighteen acting in this uncle's service in Illyria across the Adriatic Sea. Upon learning of Caesar's death, Octavian hastened to Rome to see if he could claim his inheritance. He soon found that he had to join forces with two of Caesar's powerful friends, Mark Antony and Lepidus. The following year the three formed an alliance for the purpose of crushing the power of the aristocratic group responsible for Caesar's murder. The methods employed were not to the new leaders' credit. Prominent members of the aristocracy were hunted down and slain and their property confiscated. The most noted of the victims was Cicero, brutally slain by Mark Antony's thugs though he had taken no part in the conspiracy against Caesar's life. Caesar's real murderers, Brutus and Cassius, escaped and organized an army, but they were defeated by Octavian and his colleagues near Philippi in 42 B.C.

Struggle between East and West

Thereafter a quarrel developed between the members of the alliance, inspired primarily by Antony's jealousy of Octavian. The subsequent struggle became a contest between East and West. Antony went to the East and made an alliance with Cleopatra that was dedicated to introducing principles of Oriental despotism into Roman rule. Octavian consolidated the forces of the West and came forward as the champion of Greek cultural traditions. As in the earlier contest between Caesar and Pompey the victory again went to the West. In the naval battle of Actium (31 B.C.) Octavian's

View of Rome. This aerial photo shows the Colosseum in the commanding central position and the ruins of the Forum (the ancient civic center) fanning out from the Colosseum in a diagonal toward the bottom right.

forces defeated those of Antony and Cleopatra, both of whom soon afterward committed suicide. It was now clear that Rome would not be swallowed up by the East. Octavian's victory guaranteed that there would be several more centuries for the consolidation of Greek ideals and urban life, a development important above all for the future of Western Europe.

The victory at Actium ushered in a new period in Roman history, the most glorious and the most prosperous that Rome ever experienced. Although problems of peace and order were still far from being completely solved, the deadly civil strife was over, and the people now had their first opportunity to show what their talents could achieve. Octavian was determined to preserve the forms if not the substance of constitutional government. He accepted the titles of Augustus and emperor (which then only meant "victorious general") conferred upon him by the Senate and the army. He held the authority of proconsul and tribune permanently, but he refused to make himself dictator or even consul for life, despite the pleas of the populace that he do so. Theoretically the Senate and the people were the supreme sovereigns, as they had been under the early Republic. The title by which he preferred to have his authority designated was *princeps,* or first citizen of the state. For this reason the period of his rule and that of his successors is properly called the Principate, or early Empire, to distinguish it from the periods of the Republic (sixth century B.C. to 27 B.C.), the time of upheavals (180 C.E. to 284 C.E.), and the period of the late Empire (284 C.E. to 610 C.E.).

Octavian. When Octavian gained sole rule he became known as Augustus. Many statues of him survive, all of them idealized.

Octavian, or Augustus as he was now more commonly called, ruled over Italy and the provinces for forty-four years (31 B.C.–14 C.E.). At the beginning of the period he governed by military power and by common consent, but in 27 B.C. the Senate bestowed upon him the series of offices and titles described above. His work as a statesman at least equaled in importance that of Julius Caesar. Among the reforms of Augustus were the establishment of a new coinage system for use throughout the entire Roman Empire; the introduction within Rome itself of a range of public services, including police and fire fighting; and more self-government for cities and provinces than they had enjoyed before. He also abolished the old system of farming out the collection of financial dues. Whereas previously tax collectors were remunerated solely by being allowed to keep a percentage of their intake, a system that led inevitably to graft and extortion, Augustus now appointed his own representatives as tax collectors, paid them regular salaries, and kept them under strict supervision. Above all, Augustus instituted a program of incentives for colonization of the provinces in order to shift the excess free population out of Italy and thereby remove a major source of social tensions and political upheaval. All told, such measures in fact contributed to bringing about the enhancement of local peace.

Reforms of Augustus

After the death of Augustus in 14 C.E. until almost the end of the century, Rome had no really capable rulers, with the single exception of Claudius (41–54). Several of Augustus's successors, most infamously Caligula (37–41) and Nero (54–68), were brutal tyrants who squandered the resources of the state and kept the city of Rome in an uproar by their

Augustus's successors

Trajan

Expansion of Roman Empire

Hadrian

See color map facing page 173

deeds of bloody violence. But starting in 96 C.E., a period of strong and stable government returned with the advent of "five good emperors": Nerva (96–98), Trajan (98–117), Hadrian (117–138), Antoninus Pius (138–161), and Marcus Aurelius (161–180). These five ruled in harmony with the Senate, displayed great gifts as administrators, and each in turn was able to bequeath a well-ordered and united realm to his designated successor.

From the time of Augustus until that of Trajan, the Roman Empire continued to expand. Augustus gained more land for Rome than did any other Roman ruler. His generals advanced into central Europe, conquering the territories known today as Switzerland, Austria, and Bulgaria. Only in modern-day central Germany did Roman troops meet defeat, a setback that convinced Augustus to hold the Roman borders at the Rhine and Danube. Subsequently, in 43 C.E., the Emperor Claudius began the conquest of Britain, and at the beginning of the next century Trajan pushed beyond the Danube to add Dacia (now Rumania) to the Roman realms. Trajan also conquered territories in Mesopotamia but thereby incurred the enmity of the Persians, causing his successor Hadrian to embark on a defensive policy. The Roman Empire had now reached its ultimate territorial limits; in the third century these limits would begin to recede.

Rome's peaceful sway over a vast empire for about two centuries, from the time of Augustus to that of Marcus Aurelius, was certainly one of its most impressive accomplishments. As the historian Gibbon said, "the Empire of Rome comprehended the fairest part of the earth and the most civilized portion of mankind." The celebrated *Pax Romana,* or Roman peace, was unprecedented. The Mediterranean was now under the control of one power (as it has never been before or since) and experienced the passage of centuries without a single naval battle. On land Roman officials ruled from the borders of Scotland to those of Persia. A contemporary orator justly boasted that "the whole civilized world lays down the arms which were its ancient load, as if on holiday . . . all places are full of gymnasia, fountains, monumental approaches, temples, workshops, schools; one can say that the civilized world, which had been sick from the beginning . . . , has been brought by the right knowledge to a state of health." But much of this health, as we will see, proved illusory.

7. CULTURE AND LIFE IN THE PERIOD OF THE PRINCIPATE

Roman Stoics: Seneca, Epictetus, and Marcus Aurelius

The intellectual and artistic achievements of the Principate outshone those of all other ages in the history of Rome. Three eminent apostles of Stoicism lived and taught in Rome in the two centuries that followed the rule of Augustus: Seneca (4 B.C.–65 C.E.), wealthy advisor for a time to Nero; the slave Epictetus (60?–120 C.E.); and the Emperor Marcus Aurelius (121–180 C.E.). All of them agreed that inner serenity is the ultimate human goal, that true happiness can be found only in surrender to the benevolent order of the universe. They preached the ideal of virtue for virtue's

Marcus Aurelius. This equestrian statue is one of the few surviving from the ancient world: the Christians destroyed most Roman equestrian statues because they found them idolatrous, but they spared this one because they mistakenly believed that it represented Constantine, the first Christian Roman Emperor. The statue stood outdoors in Rome from the second century until 1980, when it was taken into storage to protect it from air pollution.

sake, deplored the sinfulness of human nature, and urged obedience to conscience as the voice of duty. Seneca and Epictetus both expressed deep mystical yearnings as part of their philosophy, making it almost a religion. They worshiped the cosmos as divine, governed by an all-powerful Providence who ordains all that happens for ultimate good. The last of the Roman Stoics, Marcus Aurelius, was more fatalistic and less hopeful. Although he did not reject the conception of an ordered and rational universe, he shared neither the faith nor the dogmatism of the earlier Stoics. He did not believe that immortality would balance suffering on earth and was inclined to think of humans as creatures buffeted by evil fortune for which no distant perfection of the whole could fully atone. He urged, nevertheless, that people should continue to live nobly, that they should neither abandon themselves to gross indulgence nor break down in angry protest, but that they should derive what contentment they could from dignified resignation to suffering and tranquil submission to death.

Roman literature of the Principate is conventionally divided into two periods: works of the *golden age,* written during the reign of Augustus, and works of the *silver age,* written during the first century C.E. Most of the literature of the golden age was vigorous, affirmative, and uplifting. The poetry of the greatest of all Roman poets, Virgil (70–19 B.C.), was prototypic. In a set of pastoral poems, the *Eclogues,* Virgil expressed an idealized vision of human life led in harmony with nature. The *Eclogues* also implicitly extolled Augustus as the bringer of peace and abundance. Virgil's masterpiece, the *Aeneid,* is an epic poem about a Trojan hero, Aeneas, understood to have been the distant ancestor of the Roman people and the model of Roman greatness. Written in elevated, yet sinewy and stirring metrical verse ("Arms and the man, I sing. . . ."), the *Aeneid* tells of the founding of a great state by dint of warfare and toil and foretells Rome's glorious future.

Golden-age literature: Virgil

Golden-age literature:
Horace, Livy, Ovid

Silver-age literature

Achievements in art

See color plates following
page 172

Other major golden-age writers were Horace (65–8 B.C.), Livy (59 B.C.–17 C.E.), and Ovid (43 B.C.–17 C.E.). Of these, Horace was the most philosophical. His *Odes* drew from the practical teachings of both Epicureans and Stoics, combining the Epicurean justification of pleasure with the Stoic passivity in the face of trouble. The chief claim to fame of Livy, a narrative historian, rests on his skill as a prose stylist. His *History of Rome,* starting "from the founding of the city," is factually unreliable but replete with dramatic and picturesque narrative designed to appeal to patriotic emotions. Ovid was the least typical of the Latin golden-age writers insofar as his outlook tended to be more satiric than heroically affirmative. His main poetic accomplishment was a highly sophisticated retelling of Greek myths in a long poem of fifteen books, the *Metamorphoses,* full of wit and eroticism. Whereas the Emperor Augustus delighted in the *Aeneid,* he found the mocking and dissolute tone of Ovid's verses to be so repellant that he banished Ovid from his court.

The literature of the silver age was typically less calm and balanced than that of the golden age. Its effects derived more often from self-conscious artifice. The tales of Petronius and Apuleius describe the more exotic and sometimes sordid aspects of Roman life. The aim of the authors is less to instruct or uplift than to tell an entertaining story or turn a witty phrase. An entirely different viewpoint is presented in the works of the other most important writers of this age: Juvenal, the satirist (60?–140 C.E.), and Tacitus, the historian (55?–117? C.E.). Juvenal wrote under the influence of the Stoics but with narrow vision. Convinced that the troubles of the nation were due to moral degeneracy, he censured the vices of his countrymen with the fury of an evangelist. A somewhat similar attitude characterized the writing of his younger contemporary, Tacitus. The best-known of Roman historians, Tacitus described the events of his age not with a view to dispassionate analysis but largely for the purpose of moral indictment. His description of the customs of the ancient Germans in his *Germania* served to heighten the contrast between the manly virtues of an unspoiled race and the effeminate vices of the decadent Romans. Whatever his failings as a historian, he was a master of ironic wit and brilliant aphorism. Referring to the boasted *Pax Romana,* he makes a barbarian chieftain say: "They create a wilderness and call it peace."

Roman art first assumed its distinctive character during the period of the Principate. Before this time what passed for an art of Rome was really an importation from the Hellenistic East. Conquering armies brought back to Italy wagonloads of statues, reliefs, and marble columns as part of the plunder from Greece and Asia Minor. These became the property of wealthy businessmen and were used to embellish their sumptuous mansions. As the demand increased, hundreds of copies were made, with the result that by the end of the Republic Rome came to have a profusion of objects of art that had no more cultural significance than the Picassos in the home of a modern stockbroker. The aura of national glory that surrounded the early Principate, however, also stimulated the growth of an art that was more indigenous. Augustus himself boasted that he found Rome a city of brick and left it a city of marble. Nevertheless, much of the old Hellenistic influence remained until the talent of the Romans themselves was exhausted.

The arts most truly expressive of the Roman character were architecture and sculpture. Architecture was monumental, designed to symbolize power and grandeur. It contained as its leading elements the round arch, the vault, and the dome, although at times the Corinthian column was employed, especially in the construction of temples. The materials most commonly used were brick, squared stone blocks, and concrete. (The Romans were the first to use concrete for large-scale building projects.) As a further adornment of public buildings, sculptured entablatures and facades, built up of tiers of colonnades or arcades, were frequently added. Roman architecture was devoted primarily to utilitarian purposes. The foremost examples were government buildings, amphitheaters, baths, race courses, and private houses. Nearly all were of massive proportions and solid construction. Among the largest and most noted were the Pantheon, with its dome hav-

Architecture and sculpture

The Pantheon in Rome. Built by the Emperor Hadrian it boasted the largest dome without interior supports of the ancient world. The dome forms a perfect sphere, exactly as high as it is wide.

ing a diameter of 142 feet, and the Colosseum, which could accommodate 50,000 spectators at the gladiatorial combats. Roman sculpture included as its main forms triumphal arches and columns, narrative reliefs, altars, and portrait busts and statues. Its distinguishing characteristics were individuality and naturalism. Sometimes Roman statues and busts served only to express the vanity of the aristocracy, but the best Roman sculptured portraiture succeeded in conveying qualities of simple human dignity similar to those espoused in the philosophy of the Stoics.

Engineering and public services

Closely related to their achievements in architecture were Roman triumphs in engineering and public services. The imperial Romans built marvelous roads and bridges, many of which still survive. In the time of Trajan eleven aqueducts brought water into Rome from the nearby hills and provided the city with 300 million gallons daily for drinking and bathing as well as for flushing a well-designed sewage system. Water was cleverly funneled into the homes of the rich for their private gardens, fountains, and pools. Romans also established the first hospitals in the Western world and the first system of state-supported medicine.

Lack of scientific accomplishments

For all their achievements in engineering, the Romans accomplished little in science. They excelled, as has been jokingly but not inaccurately said, in drains, not brains. Few original scientific discoveries of fundamental importance were made by the Romans. This fact seems strange when we consider that the Romans had the advantage of Hellenistic science as a foundation upon which to build. But they neglected their opportunity almost completely. Roman writers on scientific subjects were largely devoid of critical intelligence. The most renowned and typical of them was Pliny

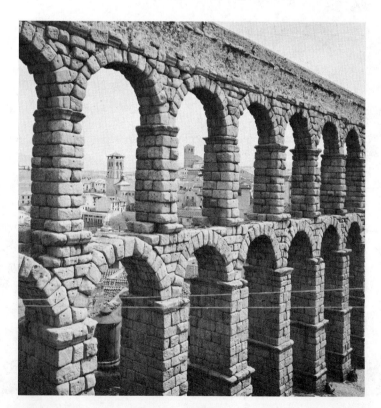

Roman Aqueduct at Segovia, Spain. Aqueducts conveyed water from mountains to the larger cities.

the Elder (23–79 C.E.), who completed about 77 C.E. a voluminous encyclopedia of "science" which he called *Natural History*. The subjects discussed varied from cosmology to economics. Despite the wealth of material it contains, Pliny's work is of limited value, for he was totally unable to distinguish between fact and fable.

One of the more impressive aspects of Roman society under the Principate was the role played by upper-class women. We have seen that under the Republic wealthier women were less confined to domesticity and obscurity than their counterparts in Athens, and this trait became even more pronounced in the early Empire. It is true that Roman women were assigned the names of their fathers with feminine endings—for example, Julia from Julius, Claudia from Claudius, Marcia from Marcus. Yet unlike women in most modern societies they did not change their names when they were married. This was a reflection of the fact that wealthier Roman women had a status quite independent from that of their husbands. With numerous slaves to take care of their households and wealth of their own to draw on, upper-class Roman women customarily were educated in the liberal arts and were free to engage in intellectual and artistic pursuits. Some wrote poetry, others studied philosophy, and others presided over literary salons. Aristocratic Roman women often had their portraits painted or chiseled in stone, revealing their cultivation of physical elegance. The busts of several emperors' wives or daughters even appeared on the Roman coinage, partly because the emperors wished to proclaim the greatness of their families, and partly because some of these women really did play an influential role (albeit an informal one) in affairs of state. Of course, women wielded none of the power and had none of the freedom of men, yet by the standards of the ancient world they were relatively liberated.

For most modern sensibilities, the most repellant aspect of Roman culture during the period of the Principate was the passion for cruelty. Whereas the Greeks entertained themselves with theater, the Romans more and more preferred "circuses," which were really exhibitions of human slaughter. During the Principate the spectacles became bloodier than ever. The Romans could no longer obtain a sufficient thrill from mere exhibitions of athletic prowess: pugilists were now required to have their hands wrapped with thongs of leather loaded with iron or lead. The most popular amusement of all was watching the gladiatorial combats in the Colosseum or in other amphitheaters capable of accommodating thousands of spectators. Fights between gladiators were nothing new, but they were now presented on a much more elaborate scale. Not only the common people attended them, but also wealthy aristocrats, and frequently the head of the government himself. The gladiators fought to the accompaniment of savage cries and curses from the audience. When one went down with a disabling wound, the crowd was asked to decide whether his life should be spared or whether the weapon of his opponent should be plunged into his heart. One contest after another, often featuring the sacrifice of men to wild animals, was staged in the course of a single exhibition. Should the arena become too sodden with blood, it was covered over with a fresh

Portrait Bust of a Roman Lady. The ostentatiousness of upper-class culture during the period of the Principate is well displayed by this sculpture, done around 90 C.E.

Upper-class Roman women

Coin Depicting Emperor's Wife. This Roman coin bears the image of Julia Domna, the wife of emperor Septimius Severus and mother of emperor Caracalla (Aurelius Antonius).

The Colosseum. Built by the Roman emperors between 75 and 80 C.E. as a place of entertainment, it was the scene of gladiatorial combats. The most common form of Greek secular architecture was the theater (see p. 127), but the most common Roman form was the amphitheater.

(see p. 127)

Gladiatorial combat

layer of sand, and the revolting performance went on. Most of the gladiators were condemned criminals or slaves, but some were volunteers even from the respectable classes. Commodus, the worthless son of Marcus Aurelius, entered the arena several times for the sake of the plaudits of the mob; this was his idea of a Roman holiday.

The spread of Mithraism and Christianity

Notwithstanding its low moral tone, the age of the Principate was characterized by an even deeper interest in salvationist religions than that which had prevailed under the Republic. Mithraism now gained adherents by the thousands, absorbing many of the followers of the cults of the Great Mother and of Serapis. About 40 C.E. the first Christians appeared in Rome. The new sect grew steadily and eventually succeeded in displacing Mithraism as the most popular of the salvationist faiths.

Unhealthy economic order

The establishment of stable government by Augustus ushered in a period of prosperity for Italy that lasted for more than two centuries. Trade was now extended to all parts of the known world, even to Arabia, India, and China. Manufacturing increased somewhat, especially in the production of pottery, textiles, and articles of metal and glass. In spite of all this, the economic order was far from healthy. Prosperity was not evenly distributed but was confined primarily to the upper classes. Since the stigma attached to manual labor persisted as strongly as ever, production was bound to decline as the supply of slaves diminished. Perhaps worse was the fact that Italy had a decidedly unfavorable balance of trade. The meager industrial development was by no means sufficient to provide enough articles of export to meet the demand for luxuries imported from the provinces and from the outside world. As a consequence, Italy was gradually drained of its supply of precious metals. By the third century the Western Roman economy began to collapse.

8. ROMAN LAW

There is general agreement that one of the most important legacies that the Romans left to succeeding cultures was their system of law. This resulted from a gradual evolution that began roughly with the publication of the Twelve Tables about 450 B.C. In the later centuries of the Republic the law of the Twelve Tables was transformed by the growth of new precedents and principles. These emanated from different sources: from changes in custom, from the teachings of the Stoics, from the decisions of judges, but especially from the edicts of the *praetors,* magistrates who had authority to define and interpret the law in a particular suit and issue instructions to judges.

The early development of Roman law

Roman law attained its highest stage of development under the Principate. This resulted in part from the extension of the law over a wider field of jurisdiction, over the lives and properties of aliens in strange environments as well as over the citizens of Italy. But the major reason was the fact that Augustus and his successors gave to certain eminent jurists the right to deliver opinions on the legal issues of cases under trial in the courts. The most prominent of the men thus designated from time to time were Gaius, Ulpian, Papinian, and Paulus. Although most of them held high judicial office, they had gained their reputations primarily as lawyers and writers on legal subjects. The responses of these jurists came to embody a science and philosophy of law and were accepted as the basis of Roman jurisprudence.

Roman law under the Principate; the great jurists

The Roman law as it was developed under the influence of the jurists comprised three great branches or divisions: the civil law, the law of peoples, and the natural law. The civil law was the law of Rome and its citizens. As such it existed in both written and unwritten forms. It included the statutes of the Senate, the decrees of the princeps, the edicts of the praetors, and also certain ancient customs operating with the force of law. The law of peoples was the law held to be common to all people regardless of nationality. This law authorized slavery and private ownership of property and defined the principles of purchase and sale, partnership, and contract. It was not superior to the civil law but supplemented it as especially applicable to the alien inhabitants of the Empire.

The three divisions of Roman law

The most interesting and in many ways the most important branch of the Roman law was the natural law, a product not of judicial practice, but of philosophy. The Stoics had developed the idea of a rational order of nature that is the embodiment of justice and right. They had affirmed that all men are by nature equal, and that they are entitled to certain basic rights that governments have no authority to transgress. The father of the law of nature as a legal principle, however, was not one of the Hellenistic Stoics, but Cicero. "True law," he declared, "is right reason consonant with nature, diffused among all men, constant, eternal. To make enactments infringing this law, religion forbids, neither may it be repealed even in part, nor have we power through Senate or people to free ourselves from it." This law is prior to the state itself, and any ruler who defies it automatically becomes a tyrant. Most of the great jurists subscribed to conceptions of the law of nature very similar to those of the philosophers. Although the jurists did not regard this law as an automatic limitation upon the civil law, they thought of it as an ideal to which the statutes and decrees of men ought to conform. This development of the concept of abstract justice as a legal principle was one of the noblest achievements of the Roman civilization.

The natural law

9. THE CRISIS OF THE THIRD CENTURY (180–284 C.E.)

With the death of Marcus Aurelius in 180 C.E. the period of beneficent imperial rule came to an end. One reason for the success of the "five good emperors" was that the first four designated particularly promising young men, rather than sons or close relatives, for the succession. But Marcus Aurelius broke this pattern with results that were to prove fateful. Although he was one of the most philosophic and thoughtful rulers who ever reigned, he was not wise enough to recognize that his son Commodus was a vicious incompetent. Made emperor by his father's wishes, Commodus indulged his taste for perversities, showed open contempt for the Senate, and ruled so brutally that a palace clique finally had him murdered by strangling in 192. Matters thereafter became worse. With the lack of an obvious successor to Commodus, the armies of the provinces raised their own candidates and civil war ensued. Although a provincial general, Septimius Severus (193–211), emerged victorious, it now became clear that provincial armies could interfere in imperial politics at will. Severus and some of his successors aggravated the problem by eliminating even the theoretical rights of the Senate and ruling frankly as military dictators. Once the role of brute force was openly revealed any aspiring general could try his luck at seizing power. Hence civil war became endemic. From 235 to 284 there were no less than twenty-six "barracks emperors," of whom only one managed to escape a violent death.

End of political stability

Commodus. The self-deluded ruler encouraged artists to portray him as the equal of the superhuman Hercules.

The half-century between 235 and 284 was certainly the worst for Rome since its rise to world power. In addition to political chaos, a number of other factors combined to bring the Empire to the brink of ruin. One was that civil war had disastrous economic effects. Not only did con-

Consequences of civil war

stant warfare interfere with agriculture and trade, but the rivalry of aspirants to rule led them to drain the wealth of their territories in order to gain favor with their armies. Following the maxim of "enriching the soldiers and scorning the rest," they could only raise funds by debasing the coinage and by nearly confiscatory taxation of civilians. Landlords, small tenants, and manufacturers thus had little motive to produce at a time when production was most necessary. In human terms the poorest, as is usual in times of economic contraction, suffered the most. Often they were driven to the most abject destitution. In the wake of war and hunger, disease then became rampant. Already in the reign of Marcus Aurelius a terrible plague had swept through the Empire, decimating the army and the population at large. In the middle of the third century pestilence returned and struck at the population with its fearful scythe for fifteen years.

The resulting strain on human resources came at a time when Rome could least afford it, for still another threat to the Empire in the middle of the third century was the advance of Rome's external enemies. With Roman ranks thinned by disease and Roman armies fighting each other, Germans in the West and Persians in the East broke through the old Roman defense lines. In 251 the Goths defeated and slew the Emperor Decius, crossed the Danube, and marauded at will in the Balkans. A more humiliating disaster came in 260 when the Emperor Valerian was captured in battle by the Persians and made to kneel as a footstool for their ruler. When he died his body was stuffed and hung on exhibition. Clearly the days of Caesar and Augustus were very far off.

Understandably enough the culture of the third century was marked by pervasive anxiety. One can even see expressions of worry in the surviving statuary, as in the bust of the Emperor Philip (244–249) who appears almost to realize that he would soon be killed in battle. Suiting the spirit of the age, the Neoplatonic philosophy of otherworldlyism came to the fore. *Neoplatonism* (meaning "New Platonism") drew the spiritualist tendency of Plato's thought to extremes. The first of its basic teachings was emanationism: everything that exists proceeds from the divine in a continuing stream of emanations. The initial stage in the process is the emanation of the world-soul. From this come the divine Ideas or spiritual patterns, and then the souls of particular things. The final emanation is matter. But matter has no form or quality of its own; it is simply the privation of spirit, the residue that is left after the spiritual rays from the divine have burned themselves out. It follows that matter is to be despised as the symbol of evil and darkness. The second major doctrine was mysticism. The human soul was originally a part of God, but it has become separated from its divine source through its union with matter. The highest goal of life should be mystic reunion with the divine, which can be accomplished through contemplation and through emancipation of the soul from bondage to matter. Human beings should be ashamed of the fact that they possess a physical body and should seek to subjugate it in every way possible. Asceticism was therefore the third main teaching of this philosophy.

The real founder of Neoplatonism was Plotinus, who was born in Egypt

The Emperor Decius. The extreme naturalism and furrowed brow is typical of the portraits of this period.

Advance of Rome's external enemies

Neoplatonism and otherworldlyism

The Emperor Philip the Arab. An artistic legacy of the Roman "age of anxiety."

about 204 C.E. In the later years of his life he taught in Rome and won many followers among the upper classes before he died in 270. His principal successors diluted the philosophy with more and more bizarre superstitions. In spite of its antirational viewpoint and its utter indifference to the state, Neoplatonism became so popular in Rome in the third and fourth centuries C.E. that it almost completely supplanted Stoicism. No fact could have expressed more eloquently the turn of Rome away from the realities of the here and now.

10. CAUSES FOR ROME'S DECLINE

As Rome was not built in a day, so it was not lost in one. As we will see in the next chapter, strong rule returned in 284. Thereafter the Roman Empire endured in the West for two hundred years more and in the East for a millennium. But the restored Roman state differed greatly from the old one—so much so that it is proper to end the story of characteristically Roman civilization here and review the reasons for Rome's decline.

More has been written on the fall of Rome than on the death of any other civilization. The theories offered to account for the decline have been many and varied. A popular recent one is that Rome fell from the effects of lead ingested from cooking utensils, but if this were true one would have to ask why Rome did so well for so long. Moralists have found the explanation for Rome's fall in the descriptions of lechery and gluttony presented in the writings of such authors as Juvenal and Petronius. Such an approach, however, overlooks the facts that much of this evidence is patently overdrawn, and that nearly all of it comes from the period of the early Principate: in the later centuries, when the Empire was more obviously collapsing, morality became more austere through the influence of ascetic religions. One of the simplest explanations is that Rome fell only because of the severity of German attacks. But barbarians had always stood ready to attack Rome throughout its long history: German pressures indeed mounted at certain times but German invasions would never have succeeded had they not come at moments when Rome was already weakened internally.

It is best then to concentrate on Rome's most serious internal problems. Some of these were political. The most obvious political failing of the Roman constitution under the Principate was the lack of a clear law of succession. Especially when a ruler died suddenly, there was no certainty about who was to follow him. In modern America the deaths of a Lincoln or Kennedy might shock the nation, but people at least knew what would happen next; in imperial Rome no one knew and civil war was generally the result. From 235 to 284 such warfare fed upon itself. Civil war was also nurtured by the lack of constitutional means for reform. If regimes became unpopular, as most did after 180, the only means to alter them was to overthrow them. But the resort to violence always bred more violence. In addition to those problems, imperial Rome's greatest political weakness may ultimately have been that it did not involve enough people in the work of government. The vast majority of the Empire's inhabitants were subjects who did not participate in the government in any way. Hence they looked on the Empire at best with indifference and often with hostility, especially when tax collectors appeared. Loyalty to Rome was needed to keep the Empire going, but when the tests came such loyalty was lacking.

Even without political problems the Roman Empire would probably have been fated to extinction for economic reasons. Rome's worst economic problems derived from its slave system and from manpower shortages. Roman civilization was based on cities, and Roman cities existed largely by virtue of an agricultural surplus produced by slaves. Slaves were worked so hard that they did not normally reproduce to fill their own ranks. Until the time of Trajan Roman victories in war and fresh conquests provided fresh supplies of slaves to keep the system going, but thereafter the economy began to run out of human fuel. Landlords could no longer be so profligate of human life, barracks slavery came to an end, and the countryside produced less of a surplus to feed the towns. The fact that no technological advance took up the slack may also be attributed to slavery. Later in Western history agricultural surpluses were produced by technological revolutions, but Roman landlords were indifferent to technology because interest in it was thought to be demeaning. As long as slaves were present to do the work there was no interest in labor-saving devices, and attention to any sort of machinery was deemed a sign of slavishness. Landlords proved their nobility by their interest in "higher things," but while they were contemplating these heights their agricultural surpluses gradually became depleted.

Manpower shortages greatly aggravated Rome's economic problems. With the end of foreign conquests and the decline of slavery there was a

Economic causes of decline

Slaves Towing a Barge. This relief shows very graphically how heavily Roman civilizations relied on slave labor.

Inadequate manpower

Lack of civic ideals

pressing need for people to stay on the farm, but because of constant barbarian pressures there was also a steady need for men to serve in the army. The plagues of the second and third centuries sharply reduced the population just at the worst time. It has been estimated that between the reign of Marcus Aurelius and the restoration of strong rule in 284 the population of the Roman Empire was reduced by one-third. (Demoralization seems also to have lowered the birthrate.) The result was that there were neither sufficient forces to work the land nor men to fight Rome's enemies. No wonder Rome began to lose battles as it had seldom lost them before.

Enormous dedication and exertion on the part of large numbers might just possibly have saved Rome, but few were willing to work hard for the public good. For this, cultural explanations may be posited. Most simply stated, the Roman Empire of the third century could not draw upon commonly shared civic ideals. By then the old republican and senatorial traditions had been rendered manifestly obsolete. Worse, provincials could hardly be expected to fight or work hard for Roman ideals of any sort, especially when the Roman state no longer stood for beneficent peace but only brought recurrent war and oppressive taxation. Regional differences,

The Forum. The civic center of imperial Rome consisted of avenues, public squares, triumphal arches, temples, and government buildings. The arch of Titus, erected to celebrate Rome's final victory over Hebrew rebels, is in the background at the far right. Roman streets and buildings were arranged in rectilinear patterns to emphasize a sense of order and to facilitate triumphal processions. Note the contrast with ancient Athens where buildings stood more freely (see the model of the Athenian Acropolis on p. 132).

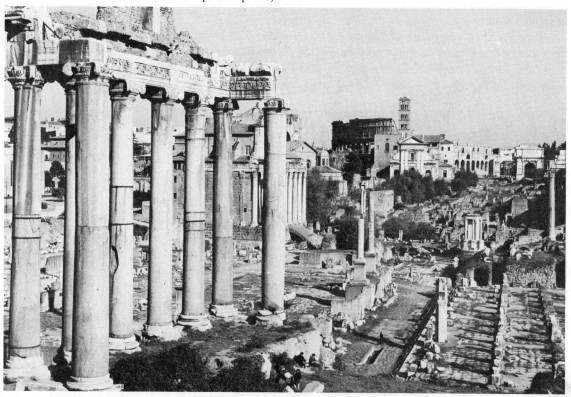

the lack of public education, and social stratification were further barriers to the development of any unifying public spirit. As the Empire foundered new ideals indeed emerged, but these were religious, otherworldly ones. Ultimately, then, the decline of Rome was accompanied by disinterest, and the Roman world slowly came to an end not so much with a bang as with a whimper.

11. THE ROMAN HERITAGE

It is tempting to believe that we today have many similarities to the Romans: first of all, because Rome is nearer to us in time than any of the other civilizations of antiquity; and second, because Rome seems to bear such a close kinship to the modern temper. The resemblances between Roman history and the history of Great Britain or the United States in the nineteenth and twentieth centuries have often been noted. The Roman economic evolution progressed all the way from a simple agrarianism to a complex urban system with problems of unemployment, gross disparities of wealth, and financial crises. The Roman Empire, in common with the British, was founded upon conquest. It must not be forgotten, however, that the heritage of Rome was an ancient heritage and that consequently the similarities between the Roman and modern civilizations are not so important as they seem. As noted already, the Romans disdained industrial activities, and they were not interested in science. Neither did they have any idea of the modern national state; the provinces were really colonies, not integral parts of a body politic. The Romans also never developed an adequate system of representative government. Finally, the Roman conception of religion was vastly different from our own. Their system of worship, like that of the Greeks, was external and mechanical, not inward or spiritual. What Christians consider the highest ideal of piety—an emotional attitude of love for the divine—the Romans regarded as gross superstition.

Comparison of Rome with the modern world

Nevertheless, the civilization of Rome exerted a great influence upon later cultures. The form, if not the spirit, of Roman architecture was preserved in the ecclesiastical architecture of the Middle Ages and survives to this day in the design of many of our government buildings. The sculpture of the Augustan Age also lives on in the equestrian statues, the memorial arches and columns, and in the portraits in stone of statesmen and generals that adorn our streets and parks. Although subjected to new interpretations, the law of the great jurists became an important part of the Code of Justinian and was thus handed down to the Middle Ages and modern times. American judges frequently cite maxims originally invented by Gaius or Ulpian. Further, the legal systems of nearly all continental European countries today incorporate much of the Roman law. This law was one of the grandest of the Romans' achievements and reflected their genius for governing a vast and diverse empire. It should not be forgotten either that Ro-

The influence of Roman civilization

man literary achievements furnished much of the inspiration for the revival of learning that spread over Europe in the twelfth century and reached its zenith in the Renaissance. Perhaps not so well known is the fact that the organization of the Catholic Church, to say nothing of part of its ritual, was adapted from the structure of the Roman state and the complex of the Roman religion. For example, the pope still bears the title of supreme pontiff (*pontifex maximus*), which was used to designate the authority of the emperor as head of the civic religion.

Rome's role as conveyor of Greek civilization

Most important of all Rome's contributions to the future was the transmission of Greek civilization to the European West. The development in Italy of a culture that was highly suffused by Greek ideals from the second century B.C. onward was in itself an important counterweight to the earlier predominance of Greek-oriented civilization in the East. Then, following the path of Julius Caesar, this culture advanced still further west. Before the coming of Rome the culture of northwestern Europe (modern France, the Benelux countries, western and southern Germany, and England) was tribal. Rome brought cities and Greek ideas, above all conceptions of human freedom and individual autonomy, that went along with the development of highly differentiated urban life. It is true that ideals of freedom were often ignored in practice—they did not temper Roman dependence on slavery, or prevent Roman rule in conquered territories from being exploitive and sometimes oppressive. Nonetheless, Roman history is the real beginning of Western history as we now know it. Greek civilization brought to the East by Alexander was not enduring, but the same civilization brought west by the work of such men as Caesar, Cicero, and Augustus was the starting point for many of the subsequent accomplishments of Western Europe. As we will see, the development was not continuous, and there were many other ingredients to later European success, but the influence of Rome was no less profound.

SELECTED READINGS

• *Items so designated are available in paperback editions.*

POLITICAL HISTORY

Bloch, Raymond, *The Origins of Rome,* New York, 1960.
Cary, M., and H. H. Scullard, *A History of Rome,* 3rd ed., New York, 1975. A basic college-level textbook.
• Chambers, M., ed., *The Fall of Rome,* 2nd ed., New York, 1970. A collection of readings on this perennially fascinating subject.
• Crawford, Michael H., *The Roman Republic,* Atlantic Heights, N.J., 1978.
• Crook, J. A., *Law and Life of Rome,* 90 B.C.–A.D. 212, Ithaca, N.Y., 1977.
Grant, M., *The Etruscans,* New York, 1980.
Gruen, Erich S., *The Last Generation of the Roman Republic,* Berkeley, 1964.
• Harris, William V., *War and Imperialism in Republican Rome,* Oxford, 1979. A searching and original examination of why the Romans became expansionists.

Haywood, R. M., *The Myth of Rome's Fall,* New York, 1958.

Millar, F., *The Emperor in the Roman World: 31 B.C.–A.D. 337,* Ithaca, N.Y., 1977.

Mommsen, Theodor, *The History of Rome,* Chicago, 1957. An abridged reissue of one of the greatest historical works of the nineteenth century. Emphasizes personalities, especially that of Julius Caesar.

Ogilvie, R. M., *Early Rome and the Etruscans,* Atlantic Heights, N.J., 1976. The best specialized review of the earliest period.

Pallottino, M., *The Etruscans,* rev. ed., Baltimore, 1978. The standard introduction.

• Scullard, H. H., *From the Gracchi to Nero,* 5th ed., London, 1982. Good survey of events in this central period.

• Syme, Ronald, *The Roman Revolution,* New York, 1939. A pathfinding work on the late Republic and early Empire that stresses power politics and the role of factions rather than the clash of institutional principles. Also extremely well written.

• Taylor, Lily Ross, *Party Politics in the Age of Caesar,* Berkeley, 1949. Still the best introduction to society and politics in the late republican period.

Warmington, B. H., *Carthage,* Baltimore, 1965.

ECONOMIC, SOCIAL, AND CULTURAL HISTORY

Africa, T., *Rome of the Caesars,* New York, 1965. An entertaining approach to the history of imperial Rome by means of short biographies.

Arnold, E. V., *Roman Stoicism,* New York, 1911.

Balsdon, J. P. V. D., *Life and Leisure in Ancient Rome,* New York, 1969.

• Brunt, P. A., *Social Conflicts in the Roman Republic,* London, 1971.

• Carcopino, Jerome, *Daily Life in Ancient Rome,* New Haven, Conn., 1960.

Duff, J. W., *A Literary History of Rome in the Golden Age,* New York, 1964.

———, *A Literary History of Rome in the Silver Age,* New York, 1960.

• Earl, Donald, *The Moral and Political Tradition of Rome,* Ithaca, N.Y., 1967.

Frank, T., *An Economic Survey of Ancient Rome,* 6 vols., Baltimore, 1933–1940. Remains the basic work of reference on its subject.

• Hopkins, K., *Conquerors and Slaves,* Cambridge, 1978. Interconnected essays that approach the world of the Roman Empire from an innovative sociological perspective.

Laistner, M. L. W., *The Greater Roman Historians,* Berkeley, 1947.

MacMullen, Ramsey, *Enemies of the Roman Order,* Cambridge, Mass., 1966.

• ———, *Paganism in the Roman Empire,* New Haven, Conn., 1981.

• ———, *Roman Social Relations: 50 B.C. to A.D. 284,* New Haven, Conn., 1974.

• Pomeroy, Sarah B., *Goddesses, Whores, Wives, and Slaves: Women in Classical Antiquity,* New York, 1975. A superb review of the lives and status of women in the Roman world.

Rostovtzeff, Mikhail I., *Social and Economic History of the Roman Empire,* 2nd ed., 2 vols., New York, 1957. By one of the greatest historians of the early twentieth century. Important both for its interpretations and the wealth of information it contains.

• Sandbach, F. H., *The Stoics,* London, 1975.

Scullard, H. H., *The Etruscan Cities and Rome,* Ithaca, N.Y., 1967.

• Starr, Chester G., *Civilization and the Caesars,* Ithaca, N.Y., 1954. Surveys Roman
  intellectual developments in the four centuries after Cicero.
  Toynbee, Arnold J., *Hannibal's Legacy,* 2 vols., London, 1965.
  Westermann, W. L., *The Slave Systems of Greek and Roman Antiquity,* Philadel-
  phia, 1955. The best overview of this basic subject.
• Wheeler, Mortimer, *The Art of Rome,* New York, 1964.
  Yavetz, Z., *Plebs and Princeps,* London, 1969.

SOURCE MATERIALS

Translations of Roman authors are available in the appropriate volumes of the Loeb
  Classical Library, Harvard University Press.

See also:

  Gruen, E. S., *The Image of Rome,* Englewood Cliffs, N.J., 1969.
• Lewis, Naphtali, and M. Reinhold, *Roman Civilization,* 2 vols., New York, 1955.

Chapter 8

CHRISTIANITY AND THE TRANSFORMATION OF THE ROMAN WORLD

Who will hereafter credit the fact . . . that Rome has to fight within her own borders not for glory but for bare life? . . . The poet Lucan describing the power of the city in a glowing passage says: "If Rome be weak, where shall we look for strength?" We may vary his words and say: "If Rome be lost, where shall we look for help?"

For mortals this life is a race: we run it on earth that we may receive our crown elsewhere. No one can walk secure amid serpents and scorpions.

—St. Jerome, *Letters*

T he Roman Empire declined after 180 C.E., but it did not collapse. In 284 the vigorous soldier-emperor Diocletian began a reorganization of the Empire that gave it a new lease on life. Thereafter, throughout the fourth century the Roman state continued to surround the Mediterranean. In the fifth century the western half of the Empire did fall to invading Germans, but even then Roman institutions were not entirely destroyed, and in the sixth century the eastern half of the Empire managed to reconquer a good part of the western Mediterranean shoreline. Only in the seventh century did it become fully evident that the Roman Empire could only hope to survive by turning away from the West and consolidating its strength in the East. When that happened antiquity clearly came to an end.

The protracted decline of the Roman Empire

Historians used to underestimate the longevity of Roman institutions and begin their discussions of medieval history in the third, fourth, or fifth century. Since historical periodization is always approximate and depends largely on which aspects of development a historian wishes to emphasize, this approach cannot be dismissed. Certainly the transition from the ancient to the medieval world was gradual and many "medieval" ways were slowly emerging in the West as early as the third century. But it is now more cus-

The age of late antiquity (284–610)

197

tomary to conceive of ancient history as continuing after 284 and lasting until the Roman Empire lost control over the Mediterranean in the seventh century. The period from 284 to about 610, although transitional (as, of course, all ages are), has certain themes of its own and is perhaps best described as neither Roman nor medieval but as the age of late antiquity.

The major cultural trend of late-antique history was the spread and triumph of Christianity throughout the Roman world. At first Christianity was just one of several varieties of otherworldlyism that appealed to increasing numbers of persons during the later Empire. But in the fourth century it was adopted as the Roman state religion and thereafter became one of the greatest shaping forces in the development of the West. While Christianity was spreading, the Roman Empire was indubitably declining. Central to this decline was a contraction of the urban life on which the Empire had been based. As the Empire began to experience severe pressures, urban contraction was most pronounced in the European northwest because city civilization there was least deeply rooted and most distant from the Empire's major trade and communications lifelines on the Mediterranean. Contraction was also felt in parts of the West that were closer to the Mediterranean because Western cities depended far more on declining agricultural production than did Eastern cities, which relied more on trade in luxury goods and industry. Consequently the entire period saw a steady shift in the weight of civilization and imperial government from West to East. The most visible manifestations of this shift were the German successes of the fifth century. These surely helped open a new chapter in Western political history, but their immediate impact should not be exaggerated. Even with the influx of Germans, Roman institutions continued to decline gradually. Particularly in areas that were on or close to the Mediterranean, Roman city life persisted, albeit with steadily declining vigor, until the Mediterranean was no longer a Roman lake.

1. THE REORGANIZED EMPIRE

Diocletian. His short hair is in the Roman military style.

Before we examine the emergence and triumph of Christianity, it is best to survey the nature of the government and society in which the new religion became a dominant force. The fifty years of chaos that threatened to destroy Rome in the third century were ended by the energetic work of a remarkable soldier named Diocletian, who ruled as emperor from 284 to 305. Conscious of some of the more obvious problems that had undone his predecessors, Diocletian embarked on a number of fundamental political and economic reforms. Recognizing that the dominance of the army in the life of the state had hitherto been too great, he introduced measures to separate military from civilian administrative chains of command. Aware that new pressures, both external and internal, had made it nearly impossible for one man to govern the entire Roman Empire, he divided his realm in half, granting the western part to a trusted colleague, Maximian, who recognized Diocletian as the senior ruler. The two then chose lieutenants, called *caesars,* to govern large subsections of their territories. This system was also meant to provide for an orderly succession, for the caesars were supposed to inherit the major rule of either East or West and then appoint new caesars in their stead. In the economic sphere Diocletian stabilized the badly debased currency, introduced a new system of taxation, and issued legislation designed to keep agricultural workers and town-dwellers at their jobs so that the basic work necessary to support the Empire would continue to be done.

Although Diocletian's program of reorganization was remarkably successful in restoring an empire that had been on the verge of expiring, it also transformed the Empire by "orientalizing" it in three primary and lasting ways. Most literally, Diocletian began a geographical orientalization of the empire by shifting its administrative weight toward the East. Since he was a "Roman" emperor we might assume that he ruled from Rome, but in fact between 284 and 303 he was never there, ruling instead from Nicomedia, a city in modern-day Turkey. This he did in tacit recognition of the fact that the wealthier and more vital part of the Empire was clearly in the East. Second, as befitting one who turned his back on Rome, Diocletian adopted the titles and ceremonies of an Oriental potentate. Probably he did this less because he had Eastern tastes than because he wished to avoid the fate of his predecessors who were insufficiently respected. Most likely he thought that if he were feared and worshiped he would stand a greater chance of dying in bed. Accordingly, Diocletian completely abandoned Augustus's policy of appearing to be a constitutional ruler and came forward as an undisguised autocrat. He took the title not of *princeps,* or first citizen, but of *dominus,* or lord, and he introduced Oriental ceremony into his court. He wore a diadem and a purple gown of silk interwoven with gold. Those who gained an audience had to prostrate themselves before him; a privileged few were allowed to kiss his robe.

The third aspect of orientalization in Diocletian's policy was his growing reliance on an imperial bureaucracy. By separating civilian from military commands and legislating on a wide variety of economic and social matters, Diocletian created the need for many new officials. Not surprisingly, by the end of his reign subjects were complaining that "there were more tax-collectors than taxpayers." The officials did keep the Empire going, but the new bureaucracy was prone to graft and corruption; worse, the growth of officialdom called for reservoirs of manpower and wealth at a time when the Roman Empire no longer had large supplies of either. Taken together, the various aspects of Diocletian's easternizing made him seem more like a pharaoh than a Roman ruler: it was almost as if the defeat of Antony and Cleopatra at Actium was now being avenged.

The new coercive regime of Diocletian left no room for the cultivation of individual spontaneity or freedom. The results can be seen most clearly in the architecture and art of the age. Diocletian himself preferred a colossal, bombastic style of building that was meant to emphasize his own power. The baths he had constructed in Rome, when he finally arrived there in 303, were the largest yet known, encompassing about thirty acres. When he retired in 305 Diocletian built a palace for himself in what is now

Diocletian's Palace in Split.
An artistic reconstruction.

The Emperor Honorius. An example of the impassive portrait sculpture brought in by the age of Diocletian. Compare the lack of individuality of this bust to the portraits of Decius and Philip the Arab, above, p. 189.

The reign of Constantine

Split (Croatia) that was laid out along a rectilinear grid like an army camp. A plan of this palace shows clearly how Diocletian favored regimentation in everything.

Also in the age of Diocletian, Roman portrait statuary, which had hitherto featured striking naturalism and individuality, became impersonal. Human faces became impassive and symmetrical rather than reflecting a free play of emotions. Porphyry, a particularly hard and dark stone that had to be imported from Egypt—itself a sign of easternization—often replaced marble for imperial busts. Sculpted in porphyry, groups of statues of Diocletian, Maximian, and their two caesars show the new hardness and symmetry at their fullest, for the figures were made to look so similar that they are indistinguishable from each other.

In 305 Diocletian decided to abdicate to raise cabbages—an unprecedented achievement for a late-Roman ruler. At the same time he obliged his colleague Maximian to retire as well, and their two caesars moved peacefully up the ladders of succession. Such concord, however, could not last. Soon civil war broke out among Diocletian's successors and continued until Constantine, the son of one of the original caesars, emerged victorious. From 312 until 324 Constantine ruled only in the West, but from the latter year until his death in 337 he did away with power sharing and ruled over a reunited Empire. Except for the fact that he favored Christianity, an epoch-making decision to be examined in the next section, Constantine otherwise continued to govern along the lines laid down by Diocletian. Bureaucracy proliferated and the state became so vigilant in keeping town-dwellers and agricultural laborers at their posts that society began to harden into a caste system. Although Constantine was a Christian, he never thought for a moment of acting with any Christlike humility: on the contrary, he made court ceremonial more elaborate and generally behaved as if he were a god. In keeping with this he built a new capital in 330 and named it Constantinople, after himself. Although he declared that he moved his government from Rome to Constantinople in order to demonstrate his abandonment of paganism, self-esteem was no doubt a major factor, and the shift was the most visible manifestation of the continued move of Roman civilization to the East. Situated on the border of Europe and Asia, Constantinople had commanding advantages as a center for Eastern-oriented communications, trade, and defense. Surrounded on three sides by water and protected on land by walls, it was to prove nearly impregnable and would remain the center of "Roman" government for as long as the Roman Empire was to endure.

Constantine also made the succession hereditary. By so doing he brought Rome back to the principle of dynastic monarchy that it had thrown off about eight hundred years earlier. But Constantine, who treated the Empire as if it were his private property, did not pass on united rule to one son. Instead he divided his realm among three of them. Not surprisingly his three sons started fighting each other upon their father's death, a conflict exacerbated by religious differences. The warfare and succeeding dynastic squabbles that continued on and off for most of the fourth century need not detain us here. Suffice it to say that they were not as serious as the civil wars of the third century, and that from time to time one or another contestant was able to reunite the empire for a period of years. The last to do

Dynastic squabbles

Left: *Porphyry Sculptures of Diocletian and His Colleagues in Rule.* Every effort is made to make the two senior rulers and their two junior colleagues look identical by means of stylization. Note also the emphasis on military strength. Right: *Colossal Head of Constantine.* In the head of Constantine the eyes are enlarged as if to emphasize the ruler's spiritual vision. The head is approximately seven times larger than life and weighs about nine tons.

Two Contemporary Representations of Theodosius. Above is a detail from a silver plate. Theodosius is shown here with an orb in his hand, symbolizing his worldly power, and a halo, symbolizing his supernatural strength. In both the plate and the coin shown below the emperor is depicted in military garb.

Jesus of Nazareth; his milieu

so was Theodosius I (379–395), who butchered thousands of innocent citizens of Thessalonica in retribution for the death of one of his officers, but whose energies in preserving the Empire by holding off Germanic barbarians still gave him some claim to his surname "the Great."

The period between Constantine and Theodosius saw the hardening of earlier tendencies. With Constantinople now the leading city of the Empire, the center of commerce and administration was located clearly in the East. Regionalism too grew more pronounced: the Latin-speaking West was losing a sense of rapport and contact with the Greek-speaking East, and in both West and East local differences were becoming accentuated. In economic life the hallmark of the age was the growing gap between rich and poor. In the West large landowners were able to consolidate their holdings, and in the East some individuals became prosperous by rising through the bureaucracy and enriching themselves with graft, or by trading in luxury goods. But the taxation system initiated by Diocletian and maintained throughout the fourth century weighed down heavily on the poor, forcing them to carry the burden of supporting the bureaucracy, the army, and the lavish imperial court or courts. The poor, moreover, had no chance to escape their poverty, for legislation demanded that they and their heirs stay at their unrewarding and heavily taxed jobs. Since most people in the fourth century were poor, most lived in desperate and unrelenting poverty against a backdrop of ostentatious wealth. The Roman Empire may have been restored in the years from 284 to 395, but it was nonetheless a fertile breeding ground for a new religion of otherwordly salvation.

2. THE EMERGENCE AND TRIUMPH OF CHRISTIANITY

Christian beginnings of course go back several centuries before Constantine to the time of Jesus. Christianity was formed primarily by Jesus and St. Paul and gained converts steadily thereafter. But the new religion only became widespread during the chaos of the third century and only triumphed in the Roman Empire during the demoralization of the fourth century. At the time of its humble beginnings nobody could have known that Christianity would be decreed the sole religion of the Roman Empire by the year 392.

Jesus of Nazareth was born in Judea sometime near the beginning of the Christian era (but not exactly in the "year one"—we owe this mistake in our dating system to a sixth-century monk). While Jesus was growing up, Judea was under Roman overlordship. The atmosphere of the region was charged with religious emotionalism and political discontent. Some of the people, notably the *Pharisees,* concentrated on preserving the Jewish law and looked forward to the coming of a political messiah who would rescue the Jews from Rome. Most extreme of those who sought hope in politics were the *Zealots,* who wished to overthrow the Romans by means of armed force. Some groups, on the other hand, were not interested in politics at all. Typical of these were the *Essenes,* who hoped for spiritual deliv-

erance through asceticism, repentance, and mystical union with God. The
ministry of Jesus was clearly more allied to this pacific orientation.

In considering the story of Jesus' career as an historical event, it is important to recognize that virtually the only sources of information are the first
four books of the New Testament, the Gospels, the earliest of which (the
Gospel of Mark) was written some thirty years after Jesus' death. Inevitably
these sources are full of inaccuracies, in part because they were not eyewitness accounts, and even more because they were never meant to be strictly
factual reports but were intended as proclamations of supernatural faith.
Bearing in mind that more or less anything in the Gospel record may not
be true in the historical sense, so far as we know, when Jesus was about
thirty years old he was acclaimed by a preacher of moral reform, John the
Baptist, as one "mightier than I, whose shoes I am not worthy to stoop
down and unloose." For about three years thereafter Jesus' career was a
continuous course of preaching, healing the sick, "casting out devils," and
teaching humility by precepts, parables, and by his own example.

Jesus. An artist's conception from
a sixth-century mosaic in Ravenna.

Believing he had a mission to save humanity from sin, Jesus denounced
greed and licentiousness and urged love of God and neighbor. Additionally, it seems reasonably clear that he taught the following: (1) the father-
hood of God and the brotherhood of humanity; (2) the Golden Rule ("do
unto others as you would have others do unto you"); (3) forgiveness and
love of one's enemies; (4) repayment of evil with good; (5) shunning of
hypocrisy; (6) opposition to religious ceremonialism; (7) the imminent approach of the kingdom of God; (8) the resurrection of the dead and the establishment of the kingdom of heaven.

The teachings of Jesus

The Gospel record is particularly controversial when it reaches the story
of Jesus' death because aspects of it, which may or may not be true, fueled
Christian persecutions of Jews in subsequent eras. Purportedly when Jesus
began to preach in Jerusalem, Judea's major city and religious center, the
city's religious leaders quickly became antagonistic to him because of his
contempt for form and ceremony. Moving swiftly to silence the troublemaker, they arrested him, tried him in their highest court for blasphemy,
condemned him, and handed him over to Pontius Pilate, the Roman governor, for sentencing and execution of the sentence. Some scholars hold
that this version of Jesus' last days is a fabrication, designed to shift blame
for his death from the Romans, who were really responsible, to the Jews,
who were not. Others believe that it is substantially correct. All that can be
said here is that whoever arrested, tried, condemned, and executed Jesus,
he did indeed die in agony by crucifixion.

*The Gospel record and the
death of Jesus*

The crucifixion of Jesus certainly marked a decisive moment in Christian
history. At first Jesus' death was viewed by his followers as the end of their
hopes. Yet after a few days their despair began to dissipate, for rumors began to spread that the Master was alive and had been seen by some of his
faithful disciples. In short order Jesus' followers became convinced that
Jesus not only had risen from the dead but that he had walked on earth
thereafter for forty days and hence that he truly was a divine being. With
their courage restored, they fanned out to preach the good news of Jesus'

*The crucifixion of Jesus and
belief in the resurrection*

St. Paul. From a Ravenna mosaic.

The Apostle Paul and Christianity as universal

The beginnings of Church organization

Preeminence of religions emphasizing otherworldlyness

divinity and to testify in the name of their martyred leader. Soon belief in Jesus' godliness and resurrection became articles of faith for thousands: Jesus was the "Christ" (Greek for "the anointed one"), the divine Son of God who was sent to earth to suffer and die for the sins of humanity, and who, after three days in the tomb, had risen from the dead and ascended into heaven, whence he would come again to judge the world at the end of time.

Christianity was broadened and invested with a more elaborate theology by some of the successors of Jesus, above all the Apostle Paul, originally known as Saul of Tarsus (c. 10–c. 67 C.E.). Paul was not a native of Palestine but a Jew born in the city of Tarsus in southeastern Asia Minor. Originally a persecutor of Christians, he later converted to Christianity and devoted his limitless energy to propagating that faith throughout the Near East. It would be almost impossible to overestimate the significance of his work. Denying that Jesus was sent merely as the redeemer of the Jews, Paul proclaimed Christianity to be a universal religion. Furthermore, he placed major emphasis on the idea of Jesus as the Christ, as the anointed God-man whose death on the cross was an atonement for the sins of humanity. Not only did he reject the works of the Law (i.e., Jewish ritualism) as of primary importance in religion, but he declared them to be utterly worthless in procuring salvation. Sinners by nature, human beings can be saved only by faith and by the grace of God "through the redemption that is in Christ Jesus." It follows, according to Paul, that human fate in the life to come is almost entirely dependent upon the will of God, for "hath not the potter power over the clay, of the same lump to make one vessel unto honor, and another unto dishonor?" (Romans 9:21). God has mercy "on whom He will have mercy, and whom He will He hardeneth" (Romans 9:18).

Although it may be something of a simplification, it seems basically true to say that whereas Jesus proclaimed the imminent coming of the kingdom of God, Paul laid the basis for a religion of personal salvation through Christ and the ministry of the Church. Therefore, after Paul Christianity developed both ceremonies, or sacraments, to bring the believer closer to Christ and an organization of priests to administer those sacraments. In teaching that priests who administered sacraments were endowed with supernatural powers, Christianity gradually posited a distinction between clergy and laity much sharper than that which had existed in most earlier religions. This would become the basis of subsequent Western controversies and divisions between "Church" and "State." In the meantime, Christianity's emphasis on otherworldly salvation ministered by a priestly organization helped it greatly to grow.

Christianity only began to gain substantial numbers in the third century after Christ. To understand this we must recall that in Roman history the third century was an "age of anxiety." During a time of extreme political turbulence and economic hardship people began to treat life on earth as an illusion and place their hopes in the beyond. The human body and the material world were more and more regarded as either evil or basically unreal. As the philosopher Plotinus wrote, "when I come to myself, I wonder how it is that I have a body . . . by what deterioration did this happen?"

Plotinus devised a philosophical system to answer this question, but this was far too abstruse to have much meaning for large numbers of people. Instead, several religions that emphasized the dominance of spiritual forces in this world and the absolute preeminence of otherworldly salvation gained hold as never before.

At first Christianity was just another of these religions; Mithraism and the cult of Serapis were others. It is natural to ask, therefore, why Christianity gained converts in the third century at the expense of its rivals. A number of answers may be posited. One of the simplest, but not the least important, is that even though Christianity borrowed elements from older religions—above all, Judaism—it was new and hence possessed a sense of dynamism lacking among the salvationist religions, which had existed for centuries. Christianity's dynamism was also enhanced by its rigorous exclusiveness. Hitherto people had adopted religions as people today take on insurance policies, piling one on another in order to feel more secure. The fact that Christianity prohibited this, demanding that the Christian God be worshiped alone, made the new religion most appealing at a time when people were searching desperately for absolutes. Similarly, Christianity alone among its rivals had an all-embracing theory to explain evil on earth, namely as the work of demons governed by the devil. When Christian missionaries sought converts they successfully emphasized the new faith's ability to combat these demons by reputed miracles.

Although Christianity's novelty, exclusiveness, and theory of evil help greatly to explain its success, probably the greatest attractions of the religion had to do with three other traits: its view of salvation, its social dimensions, and its organizational structure. Exorcism of demons might help to make life more tolerable on earth, but ultimately people in the later Roman Empire were most concerned with otherworldly salvation. Rival religions also promised an afterlife, but Christianity's doctrine on this subject was the most far-reaching. Christian preachers who warned that nonbelievers would "liquefy in fierce fires" for eternity and that believers would enjoy eternal blessedness understandably made many converts in an age of fears. They made converts too among all classes because Christianity had from its origins been a religion of the humble—carpenters, fishermen, and tentmakers—that promised the exaltation of the lowly. As the religion grew it gained a few wealthy patrons, but it continued to find its greatest strength among the lower and middle classes who comprised the greatest numbers in the Roman Empire. Moreover, while Christianity forbade women to become priests or discuss the faith and, as we will see, adopted many attitudes hostile to women, it at least accorded women some rights of participation in worship and equal hope for salvation. This fact gave it an advantage over Mithraism, which excluded women from its cult entirely. In addition to all these considerations, a final reason for Christianity's success lay in its organization. Unlike the rival mystery religions, by the third century it had developed an organized hierarchy of priests to direct the life of the faith. More than that, Christian congregations were tightly knit communities that provided services to their members—such as nursing, support

Altar of Mithras. Dating from the third century C.E., this altar used for Mithraic services in an underground chamber in the heart of Rome depicts Mithras slaying a bull. A century later, when Christianity triumphed in the Roman Empire, a Christian church was built over the Mithraic sanctuary.

An Early-Christian Woman. A wall-painting from the catacomb of Priscilla, Rome, third century C.E.

of the unprotected, and burial—that went beyond strictly religious concerns. Those who became Christians found human contacts and a sense of mission while the rest of the world seemed to be collapsing about them.

Christians were never as brutally persecuted by the Roman state as used to be thought. In fact the attitude of Rome was usually one of indifference: Christians were customarily tolerated unless certain magistrates decided to prosecute them for refusing to worship the official state gods. From time to time there were more concerted persecutions, but these were too intermittent and short-lived to do irreparable damage: on the contrary, they served to give Christianity some helpful publicity. To this degree the blood of martyrs really was the seed of the Church, but only because the blood did not flow too freely. One last great persecution took place toward the end of the reign of Diocletian and was continued by one of his immediate successors, a particularly bitter enemy of Christianity named Galerius. But by then the religion had gained too many converts to be wiped out by persecution, a fact that Galerius finally recognized by issuing an edict of toleration just before his death in 311.

Despite all that has been said, the triumph of Christianity in the Roman Empire was by no means inevitable. Although exact statistics are impossible to come by, estimates of the number of Christians in the Empire around 300 range from 1 percent to 5 percent of the total population. Thus it was only the conversion of the Emperor Constantine in 312 that ensured the success of the new faith. Exactly why Constantine became a Christian will never be known; most likely he thought he saw a cross in the sky while preparing for battle and then switched allegiance to the new faith, hoping that it would yield him victory in a contest for political supremacy. Cer-

Jonah under the Gourd. A Christian marble statue done around the time of Constantine's conversion. Jonah resting after leaving the whale's belly was a symbol for the risen Christ.

tainly, as Constantine did in fact gain military victories and ultimately rose to become sole emperor, his commitment to Christianity became ever more pronounced. By the time of his death in 337 he had showered favors on the Christian clergy and patronized the building of churches throughout the Empire. This was the turning point, for although Constantine did not yet prohibit paganism, his sons and emperors after them were raised as Christians and were ever less inclined to tolerate competing faiths. A brief exception was the reign from 360 to 363 of Julian, "the Apostate," an emperor who attempted to launch a pagan revival. But after Julian was killed in battle with the Persians, his pro-pagan edicts were revoked, and by the end of the century Theodosius the Great had completed Constantine's work by prohibiting pagan worship of any sort, public or private. Meanwhile most citizens of the Roman Empire had converted to Christianity because of the environment of official support.

3. THE NEW CONTOURS OF CHRISTIANITY

Once the new faith became dominant within the Roman Empire it underwent some major changes in forms of thought, organization, and conduct. These changes all bore relationships to earlier tendencies, but the triumph of the faith greatly accelerated certain trends and altered the course of others. The result was that in many respects the Christianity of the late fourth century was a very different religion from the one persecuted by Diocletian and Galerius.

One consequence of Christianity's triumph was the flaring up of bitter doctrinal disputes. These brought great turmoil to the Church but resulted in the hammering out of dogma and discipline. Before the conversion of Constantine there had of course been disagreements among Christians about doctrinal matters, but as long as Christianity was a minority religion it managed to control its internal divisions in order to present a united front against hostile outsiders. As soon as the new faith emerged victorious, however, sharp splits developed within its own ranks. These were due partly to the fact that there had always been a tension between the intellectual and emotional tendencies within the religion that could now come more fully into the open, and partly to the fact that different regions of the Empire tried to preserve a sense of their separate identities by preferring different theological formulas.

Controversy over doctrinal matters

The first of the bitter disputes was between the Arians and Athanasians over the nature of the Trinity. The Arians—not to be confused with Aryans (a racial term)—were followers of a priest named Arius and were the more intellectual group. Under the influence of Greek philosophy they rejected the idea that Christ could be equal with God. Instead they maintained that the Son was created by the Father and therefore was not co-eternal with Him or formed of the same substance. The followers of St. Athanasius, indifferent to apparent logic, held that even though Christ was the Son he was fully God: that Father, Son, and Holy Ghost were all abso-

Division between Arians and Athanasians

lutely equal and composed of an identical substance. After protracted struggles Athanasius's side won out and the Athanasian doctrine became the Christian dogma of the Trinity, as it remains today.

Consequences of successive doctrinal disputes

The struggle between the Arians and Athanasians was followed by numerous other doctrinal quarrels during the next few centuries. The issues at stake were generally too abstruse to warrant explaining here, but the results were momentous. One was that the dogmas of the Catholic faith gradually became fixed. Granted, this was a slow development and many basic tenets of Catholicism were only defined much later (for example, the theory of the Mass was not formally promulgated until 1215; the doctrine of the Immaculate Conception of the Virgin Mary until 1854; and that of the Bodily Assumption of the Virgin until 1950). Nonetheless, the faith was beginning to take on a sharply defined form unprecedented in the history of earlier religions. Above all, this meant that anyone who differed from a certain formulation would be excluded from the community and often persecuted as a heretic. In the subsequent history of Christianity this concern for doctrinal uniformity was to result in both strengths and weaknesses for the Church.

Regionalism

A second result of the doctrinal quarrels was that they aggravated regional hostilities. In the fourth century differences among Christians increased alienation between West and East and also aggravated hostilities among regions within the East. Although the Roman Empire was evolving toward regionalism for many different reasons, including economic and administrative ones, and although regionalism was partly a cause of religious differences, the sharper and more frequent doctrinal quarrels became, the more they served to intensify regional hostilities.

Imperial involvement in religious conflicts

Finally, the doctrinal quarrels provoked the interference of the Roman state in the governance of the Church. Because Constantine had hoped that Christianity would be a unifying rather than a divisive force in the Empire, he was horrified by the Arian conflict and intervened in it by calling the Council of Nicea (325), which condemned Arius. It is noteworthy that this council—the first general council of the Church—was convened

Christ Separating the Sheep from the Goats as an Image for the Last Judgment. This early Christian sarcophagus (fourth century C.E.) illustrates a verse from the New Testament: "And before Him shall be gathered all nations: and He shall separate them one from another, as a shepherd divideth his sheep from his goats" (Matthew 25:31). The theme was obviously appropriate for a burial repository.

by a Roman emperor and that Constantine served during its meetings as a presiding officer. Thereafter secular interference in Church matters continued, above all in the East. There were two major reasons for this. First, religious disputes were more prevalent in the East than the West and quarreling parties often appealed to the emperor for support. Second, the weight of imperial government was generally heavier in the East, and after 476 there were no Roman emperors in the West at all. When Eastern emperors were not appealed to by quarreling parties they interfered in religious disputes themselves, as Constantine had done before them, in order to preserve unity. The result was that in the East the emperor assumed great religious authority and control, while in the West the future of relations between State and Church was more open.

Even while emperors were interfering in religious matters, however, the Church's own internal organization was becoming more complex and articulated. We have seen that a clear distinction between clergy and laity was already a hallmark of the early Christian religion after the time of St. Paul. The next step was the development of a hierarchical organization within the ranks of the clergy. The superiority of bishops over priests was recognized before Christianity's triumph. Christian organization was centered in cities, and one bishop in each important city became the authority to which all the clergy in the surrounding vicinity answered. This organization was sufficient for a minority religion, but as the number of congregations multiplied and as the influence of the Church increased due to the adoption of Christianity as the official religion of Rome, distinctions of rank among the bishops themselves began to appear. Those who had their headquarters in the larger cities came to be called *metropolitans* (today known in the West as *archbishops*), with authority over the clergy of an entire province. In the fourth century the still higher rank of *patriarch* was established to designate those bishops who ruled over the oldest and largest of Christian communities—such cities as Rome, Jerusalem, Constantinople, Antioch, and Alexandria, and their surrounding districts. Thus the Christian clergy by 400 C.E. had come to embrace a definite hierarchy of patriarchs, metropolitans, bishops, and priests.

The organization of the clergy

The climax of all this development would be the growth of the primacy of the bishop of Rome, or the rise of the papacy. For several reasons the bishop of Rome enjoyed a preeminence over the other patriarchs of the Church. The city in which he ruled was venerated by the faithful as a scene of the missionary activities of the Apostles Peter and Paul. The tradition was widely accepted that Peter had founded the bishopric of Rome and that therefore all of his successors were heirs of his authority and prestige. This tradition was supplemented by the theory that Peter had been commissioned by Christ as his vicar on earth and had been given the keys of the kingdom of heaven with power to punish people for their sins and even to absolve them from guilt (Matthew 16:18–19). This theory, known as the doctrine of the Petrine Succession, has been used by popes ever since as a basis for their claims to authority over the Church. The bishops of Rome had an advantage also in the fact that after the transfer of the impe-

The rise of the papacy

rial capital to Constantinople there was seldom any emperor with effective sovereignty in the West. Finally, in 445 the Emperor Valentinian III issued a decree commanding all Western bishops to submit to the jurisdiction of the pope. It must not be supposed, however, that the Church was by any means yet under a monarchical form of government. The patriarchs in the East regarded the extreme assertions of papal claims as brazen effrontery, and even many bishops in the West continued to ignore them for some time. The clearest example of the papacy's early weakness is the fact that the popes did not even attend the first eight general councils of the Church (from 325 to 869), although later they were to convene and preside over all the others.

Effects of the rationalization of ecclesiastical administration

The growth of ecclesiastical organization helped the Church to conquer the Roman world in the fourth century and to minister to the needs of the faithful thereafter. The existence of an episcopal administrative structure was particularly influential in the West as the Roman Empire decayed and finally collapsed in the fifth century. Since every city had a bishop trained to some degree in the arts of administration, the Church in the West took over many of the functions of government and helped to preserve order amid the deepening chaos. But the new emphasis on administration also had its inevitably detrimental effects: as the Church developed its own rationalized administrative structure it inevitably became more worldly and distant in spirit from the simple faith of Jesus and the Apostles.

The rise of monasticism

The clearest reaction to this trend was expressed in the spread of monasticism. Today we are accustomed to thinking of monks as groups of priests who live communally in order to dedicate themselves primarily to lives of contemplation and prayer. In their origins, however, monks were not priests but laymen who almost always lived alone and who sought extremes of self-torture rather than ordered lives of spirituality. Monasticism began

A Monastery near Assisi, in Italy. One can see well how monks attempted to be as isolated as possible.

to emerge in the third century as a response to the anxieties of that age, but it only became a dominant movement within Christianity in the fourth century. Two obvious reasons for this fact stand out. First of all, the choice of extreme hermitlike asceticism was a substitute for martyrdom. With the conversion of Constantine and the abandonment of persecution, most chances of winning a crown of glory in heaven by undergoing death for the faith were eliminated. But the desire to prove one's religious ardor by self-abasement and suffering was still present. Second, as the fourth century progressed the priesthood became more and more immersed in worldly concerns. Those who wished to avoid secular temptations fled to the deserts and woods to practice an asceticism that priests and bishops were forgetting. (Monks customarily became priests only later during the Middle Ages.) In this way even while Christianity was accommodating itself to practical needs, monasticism satisfied the inclinations of ascetic extremists.

Monasticism first emerged in the East, where for about one hundred years after Constantine's conversion it spread like a mania. Hermit monks of Egypt and Syria vied with each other in their pursuit of the most inhuman and humiliating excesses. Some grazed in the fields after the manner of cows, others penned themselves into small cages, and others hung heavy weights around their necks. A monk named Cyriacus stood for hours on one leg like a crane until he could bear it no more. The most extravagant of these monastic ascetics was St. Simeon Stylites, who performed self-punishing exercises—such as touching his feet with his head 1,244 times in succession—on top of a high pillar for thirty-seven years, while crowds gathered below to worship "the worms that dropped from his body."

In time such ascetic hysteria subsided, and it became recognized that monasticism would be more enduring if monks lived in a community and did not concentrate on self-torture. The most successful architect of communal monasticism in the East was St. Basil (c. 330–379), who started his monastic career as a hermit and ascetic extremist but came to prefer communal and more moderate forms of life. Basil expressed this preference in writings for monks that laid down the basic guidelines for Eastern monasticism down to the present. Rather than encouraging extremes of self-torture, Basil encouraged monks to discipline themselves by useful labor. Although his teachings were still extremely severe by modern standards, he prohibited monks from engaging in prolonged fasts or lacerating their flesh. Instead he urged them to submit to obligations of poverty and humility, and to spend many hours of the day in silent religious meditation. With the triumph of St. Basil's ideas, Eastern monasticism became more organized and subdued, but even so Basilian monks preferred to live as far away from the "world" as they could and never had the same civilizing influence on external society as did their brothers in Western Europe.

Monasticism did not at first spread quickly in the West because the appeal of asceticism was much weaker there. This situation changed only in the sixth century when St. Benedict (c. 480–c. 547) drafted his famous Latin rule, which ultimately became the guide for nearly all Western monks. Modern scholarship has shown that Benedict copied much of his

Monks Chopping Down Trees (above) *and Harvesting Grain* (below) *From a twelfth-century French manuscript.*

The Benedictine rule

St. Benedict Offering His Rule to Grateful Monks. A late-medieval conception from an Austrian manuscript of about 1355.

rule from an earlier Latin text known as the "Rule of the Master," but he still produced a document notable for its brevity, flexibility, and moderation. The Benedictine rule imposed obligations similar to those laid down by St. Basil: poverty, obedience, labor, and religious devotion. Yet Benedict prescribed less austerity than Basil did: the monks were granted a sufficiency of simple food, clothing, and enough sleep; they were even allowed to drink a small amount of wine, although meat was only granted to the sick. The abbot's authority was absolute, and the abbot was allowed to flog monks for disobedience, yet Benedict urged him to try "to be loved rather than feared," and ordained that the abbot gather advice before making decisions "because the Lord often reveals to a younger member what is best." For such reasons the Benedictine monastery became a home of religious enrichment rather than a school for punishment.

We will have occasion for continuing the story of Benedictine monasticism later on, but here we may point in advance to some of its greatest contributions to the development of Western civilization. One was that Benedictine monks were committed from an early date to missionary work: they were primarily responsible for the conversion of England and later most of Germany. Such activities not only helped to spread the faith but also served to create a sense of cultural unity for Western Europe. Another positive contribution lay in the attitude of the Benedictines toward work. Whereas the highest goal for ancient philosophers and aristocrats was to have enough leisure time for unimpeded contemplation, St. Benedict wanted his monks always to keep busy, for he believed that "idleness is an enemy of the soul." Therefore he prescribed that they should be occupied at certain times in manual labor, a prescription that would have horrified most thinkers of earlier times. Accordingly, early Benedictines worked hard themselves and spread the idea of the dignity of labor to others. With

The significance of Benedictine monasticism: (1) missionary activities; (2) attitude toward manual labor

Benedictine support, this idea would become one of the most distinctive traits of Western culture. We read of Benedictines who gladly milked cows, threshed, plowed, and hammered: in so doing they increased the prosperity of their own monasteries and provided good examples for others. Benedictine monasteries became particularly successful in farming and later in estate-managing. Thus they often helped to advance the level of the Western European economy and sometimes even to provide wealth that could be drawn upon by emerging Western European states.

The fact that Benedictine monasteries were often islands of culture when literacy and learning were all but forgotten in the secular world is better known. St. Benedict himself was no admirer of classical culture. Quite to the contrary, he wanted his monks to serve only Christ—not literature or philosophy. But he did assume that monks would have to read well enough to say their prayers. That meant that some teaching in the monasteries was necessary because it was seldom available outside and because boys were often given over from birth to the monastic profession. Once there was teaching there would obviously be at least a few writing implements and books. This explains why Benedictines always maintained some literacy but not why some of them became devoted to perpetuating classical culture. The impetus behind the latter development was the work of a monastic thinker named Cassiodorus (c. 477–c. 570). Inspired by St. Augustine, whom we will treat in more detail later, Cassiodorus believed that some basic classical learning was necessary for the proper understanding of the Bible; this justified the study of the classics by monks. Furthermore, Cassiodorus recognized that copying manuscripts was in itself "manual labor" (literally work with the hands) and might be even more appropriate for monks than hard work in the fields. As Benedictines began to subscribe to these ideas, Benedictine monasteries became centers for learning and transcribing that were without rival for centuries. No work of classical Latin literature, including such "licentious" writings as the poems of Catullus and Ovid, would survive today had they not been copied and preserved during the early Middle Ages by Benedictine monks.

(3) the preservation of classical culture; Cassiodorus

Cassiodorus. This frontispiece of a Bible executed around 700 C.E. in an English Benedictine monastery depicts Cassiodorus as a copyist and as a preserver of books. (Since books were exceedingly rare until the invention of printing in the fifteenth century, they customarily were stored in cupboards, lying flat.)

Returning to our original subject—the changes that took place in Christian institutions and attitudes during the fourth century—a final fateful trend was the development of a negative attitude toward women. Compared to most other religions, Christianity was favorable to women. Female souls were regarded as equal to male souls in the eyes of God, and human nature was deemed to be complete only in both sexes. St. Paul even went so far as to say that after baptism "there is neither male nor female" (Galatians 3:28), a spiritual equalitarianism which meant that women could be saved as fully as men. But Christians from earliest times shared the view of their contemporaries that in everyday life and in marriage women were to be strictly subject to men. Not only did early Christians believe, with all male supremacists of the ancient world, that women should be excluded from positions of leadership or decision-making, meaning that they should be "silent in Church" (I Corinthians 14:34–35) and could never be priests, but they added to this the view that women were more "fleshly" than men

Christianity's negative attitude toward women

and therefore should be subjected to men as the flesh is subjected to the spirit (Ephesians 5:21–33).

With the growth of the ascetic movement in the third and fourth centuries, the denigration of women as dangerously "fleshly" creatures became more and more pronounced. Since sexual abstinence lay at the heart of asceticism, the most perfect men were expected to shun women. Monks, of course, shunned women the most. This was a primary reason why they fled to deserts and forests. One Eastern ascetic was struck by the need for virginity in the midst of his marriage ceremony, ran off to a hermit's cell, and blocked the entrance; another monk who was forced to carry his aged mother across a stream swaddled her up as thoroughly as he could so that he would not catch any "fire" and no thoughts of other women would attack him. With monks taking such an uncompromising attitude, the call for continence was extended to the priesthood. Originally priests could be married; it seems that even some of the Apostles had wives (I Corinthians 9:5). But in the course of the fourth century the doctrine spread that priests could not be married after ordination, and that those already married were obliged to live continently with their wives afterward.

Once virginity was accepted as the highest standard, marriage was taken to be only second best. St. Jerome expressed this view most earthily when he said that virginity was wheat, marriage barley, and fornication cow-dung: since people should not eat cow-dung he would permit them barley. The major purposes of marriage were to keep men from "burning" and to propagate the species. (Jerome went so far as to praise marriage above all because it brought more virgins into the world!) Thus Christianity reinforced the ancient view that woman's major earthly purpose was to serve as mother. Men and women were warned not to take pleasure even in marital intercourse but to indulge in it only for the purpose of procreation. Women were to be "saved in childbearing" (I Timothy 2:15). Since they could not become priests and only a very few could become nuns (female monasticism was regarded as a very expensive luxury in the premodern world), almost all women were expected to become submissive wives and mothers. As wives they were not expected to have their own careers and were not meant to be educated or even literate. Hence even though they had full hopes for salvation, they were treated as inferiors in the everyday affairs of the world, a treatment that would endure until modern times.

4. THE GERMANIC INVASIONS AND THE FALL OF THE ROMAN EMPIRE IN THE WEST

While Christianity was conquering the Roman Empire from within, another force, that of the Germanic barbarians, was threatening it from without. The Germans, who had already almost brought Rome to its knees in the third century, were held off from the time of Diocletian until shortly before the reign of Theodosius the Great. But thereafter they demolished

Western Roman resistance and, by the end of the fifth century, succeeded in conquering all of the Roman West. Germanic kingdoms then became the new form of government in territories once ruled over by Caesar and Augustus.

It was once customary to think that the Germans were fierce and thoroughly uncouth savages who wantonly destroyed the Western Roman Empire out of sheer hatred for civilization. But that is a misunderstanding. The Germans were barbarians in Roman eyes because they did not live in cities and were illiterate, but they were not therefore savages. On the contrary, they often practiced settled agriculture—although they preferred hunting and grazing—and were adept in making iron tools and weapons as well as lavish jewelry. Physically they looked enough like Romans to intermarry without causing much comment, and their Indo-European language was related to Latin and Greek. Prolonged interaction with the Romans had a decisive civilizing influence on the Germans before they started their final conquests. Germans and Romans who shared common borders along the Rhine and Danube had steady trading relations with each other. Even during times of war Romans were often allied with some German tribes while they fought others. By the fourth century, moreover, German tribes often served as auxiliaries of depleted Roman armies and were sometimes allowed to settle on borderlands of the Empire where Roman farmers had given up trying to cultivate the land. Finally, many German tribes had been converted to Christianity in the fourth century, although the Christianity they accepted was of the heretical Arian version. All these interactions made the "barbarians" very familiar with Roman civilization and substantially favorable to it.

The Germans began their final push not to destroy Rome but to find more and better land. The first breakthrough occurred in 378 when one tribe, the Visigoths, which had recently settled on some Roman lands in the Danube region, revolted against mistreatment by Roman officials and then decisively defeated a punitive Roman army in the Battle of Adrianople. The Visigoths did not immediately follow up this victory because they were cleverly bought off and made allies of the Empire by Theodosius the Great. But when Theodosius died in 395 he divided his realm between his two sons, neither of whom was as competent as he, and both halves of the Empire were weakened by political intrigues. The Visigoths under their leader Alaric took advantage of this situation to wander through Roman realms almost at will, looking for the best land and provisions. In 410 they sacked Rome itself—a great shock to some contemporaries—and in the following years marched into southern Gaul. Meanwhile, in December of 406, a group of allied Germanic tribes led by the Vandals crossed the frozen Rhine and capitalized on Roman preoccupation with the Visigoths by streaming through Gaul into Spain. Later they were able to cross the straits into Northwest Africa, then one of the richest agricultural regions of the Empire. From Africa they took control of the central Mediterranean, even sacking Rome from the sea in 455. By 476 the entirely ineffectual Western Roman emperor, a mere boy derisively nicknamed Augustulus

A Roman Empress of the Mid-Fifth Century. The long headdress is possibly a sign of Germanic influence.

("little Augustus"), was easily deposed by a leader of a mixed band of Germans who then assumed the title of king of Rome. Accordingly, 476 is conventionally given as the date for the end of the Western Roman Empire. But it must be remembered that a Roman emperor, who maintained some claims to authority in the West, continued to rule in Constantinople.

Two questions that historians of the German invasions customarily ask are: How did the Germans manage to triumph so easily? Why was it that they were particularly successful in the West rather than the East? The ease of the German victories appears particularly striking when it is recognized that the German armies were remarkably small: the Visigoths who won at Adrianople numbered no more than 10,000 men, and the total number of the Vandal "hordes" (including women and children) was about 80,000—a population about the same as that of an average-sized American suburb. But the Roman armies themselves were depleted because of declining population and the need for manpower in other occupations, above all in the new bureaucracies. More than that, German armies often won by default (Adrianople was one of the few pitched battles in the history of their advance) because the Romans were no longer zealous about defending themselves. Germans were seldom regarded with horror—many German soldiers had even risen to positions of leadership within Roman ranks—and the coercive regime begun by Diocletian was not deemed to be worth fighting for.

The reasons why the Germans fared best in the West are complex—some having to do with personalities and mistakes of the moment, and others with geographical considerations. But the primary explanation why the Eastern Roman Empire survived while the Western did not is that the East was simply richer. By the fifth century most Western Roman cities had shrunk in terms of both population and space to a small fraction of their earlier size, and they were often little more than empty administrative shells or fortifications. The economy of the West was becoming more and more strictly agricultural, and agricultural produce served only to feed farm laborers and keep rich landlords in luxuries. In the East, on the other hand, cities like Constantinople, Antioch, and Alexandria remained teeming metropolises because of their trade and industry. Because the Eastern State had greater reserves of wealth to tax, it was more vigorous. It could also afford to buy off the barbarians with tribute money, which it did with increasing regularity. So Constantinople was able to stay afloat while Rome floundered and then sank.

The effects of the Germanic conquests in the West were not cataclysmic. The greatest difference between the Germans and the Romans had been that the former did not live in cities, but since the Western Roman cities were already in a state of decline, the invasions only served at most to accelerate the progress of urban decay. On the land Germans replaced Roman landlords without interrupting basic Roman agricultural patterns. Moreover, since the Germans never comprised very large numbers, they usually never took over more than a part of Roman lands. Germans also tried to avail themselves of Roman administrative apparatuses, but these

Political divisions of Western Europe

THE BARBARIAN INVASIONS IN THE FIFTH AND SIXTH CENTURIES

tended to diminish gradually because of the diminishing of wealth and literacy. Thus the only major German innovation was to create separate tribal kingdoms in the West in place of a united empire.

The map of Western Europe around the year 500 reveals the following major political divisions. Germanic tribes of Anglo-Saxons, who had crossed the English Channel in the middle of the fifth century, were extending their rule on the island of Britain. In the northern part of Gaul, around Paris and east to the Rhine, the growing kingdom of the Franks was ruled by a crafty warrior named Clovis. South of the Franks stood the Visigoths, who ruled the southern half of Gaul and most of Spain. South of them were the Vandals, who ruled throughout previously Roman North-

Mosaic of Theodoric's Palace at Ravenna. At the right is a stylized conception of the ruler's palace, with the Latin inscription PALA TIVM; to the left of it is a row of saints, who would be indistinguishable were it not for the initials on their clothing: for early Christian artists, supernatural merits rather than individual personality traits were of the essence.

Theodoric the Ostrogoth. The barbarian ruler is shown here in Roman dress, with an ornate Roman hairstyle and a Roman symbol of victory in his hand. The inscription reads REX THEODERICVS PIVS PRINCIS. Latin for King Theodoric, pious prince.

west Africa. In all of Italy the Ostrogoths, Eastern relatives of the Visigoths, held sway under their impressive King Theodoric. Of these kingdoms that of the Franks would be the most promising for the future (for that reason it will be taken up in the next chapter) and the seemingly strongest for the present was that of the Ostrogoths.

Theodoric the Ostrogoth, who ruled in Italy from 493 to 526, was a great admirer of Roman civilization; this he tried to preserve as best he could. He fostered agriculture and commerce, repaired public buildings and roads, patronized learning, and maintained a policy of religious toleration. In short he gave Italy a more enlightened rule than it had known under most of its earlier emperors. But since Theodoric and his sparsely numbered Ostrogoths were Arian Christians while the local bishops and native population were Catholics, his rule, no matter how tolerant and benign, was viewed with some hostility. The "Roman" rulers in Constantinople were also hostile to Theodoric because he was an Arian and because they had not given up hopes of reconquering Italy themselves. All these circumstances led to the demise of Theodoric's Ostrogothic kingdom not long after his death. In fact, none of the Continental barbarian kingdoms would last long except for that of the Franks.

5. THE SHAPING OF WESTERN CHRISTIAN THOUGHT

The period of the decline and fall of the Roman Empire in the West was also the time when a few Western Christian thinkers formulated an approach to the world and to God that was to guide the thought of the West for roughly the next 800 years. This concurrence of political decline and theological advance was not coincidental. With the Empire falling and being replaced by barbarian kingdoms, it seemed clearer than ever to thinking Christians both that the classical inheritance had to be reexamined and that God had not intended the world to be anything more than a transitory testing place. The consequences of these assumptions accordingly became urgent questions. Between about 380 and 525, answers were worked out by Western Christian thinkers whose accomplishments were intimately interrelated. The towering figure among them was St. Augustine, but some others had great influence as well.

The advance of Western Christian thought

Three contemporaries who knew and influenced each other—St. Jerome (c. 340–420), St. Ambrose (c. 340–397), and St. Augustine (354–430)—count as three of the four greatest "fathers" of the Western, Latin Church. (The fourth, St. Gregory the Great, came later and will be discussed in the next chapter.) St. Jerome's greatest single contribution was his translation of the Bible from Hebrew and Greek into Latin. His version, known as the *Vulgate* (or "common" version), became the standard Latin Bible used throughout the Middle Ages; with minor variations it continued to be used long afterward by the Roman Catholic Church. Fortunately Jerome was one of the best writers of his day, and he endowed his translation with vigorous, often colloquial prose and, occasionally, fine poetry. Since the Vulgate was the most widely read work in Latin for centuries, Jerome's writing had as much influence on Latin style and thought as the King James Bible has had on English literature. Jerome, who was the least original thinker of the great Latin fathers, also influenced Western Christian thought by his contentious but eloquent formulations of contemporary views. Among the most important of these were the beliefs that much of the Bible was to be understood allegorically rather than literally, that classical learning could be valid for Christians if it was thoroughly subordinated to Christian aims, and that the most perfect Christians were rigorous ascetics. In keeping with the last position Jerome avidly supported monasticism. He also taught that women should not take baths so that they would not see their own bodies naked.

St. Jerome

Unlike Jerome, who was primarily a scholar, St. Ambrose was most active in the concerns of the world. As archbishop of Milan, Ambrose was the most influential Church official in the West—more so even than the pope. Guided by practical concerns, he wrote an ethical work, *On the Duties of Ministers,* which followed closely upon Cicero's *On Duties* in title and form, and also drew heavily on Cicero's Stoic ethics. But Ambrose differed from Cicero and most of traditional classical thought on two major points. One was that the beginning and end of human conduct should be reverence for God rather than any self-concern or interest in social adjustment. The other—Ambrose's most original contribution—was that God helps some Christians but not others in this pursuit by the gift of grace, a point that was to be greatly refined and amplified by St. Augustine. Ambrose put his concern for proper conduct into action by his most famous act, his con-

St. Ambrose

frontation with the Emperor Theodosius the Great over the massacring of innocent civilians. Ambrose argued that by violating divine commandments Theodosius had made himself subject to Church discipline. Remarkably the archbishop succeeded in forcing the sovereign emperor to do penance. This was the first time that a churchman had subordinated the Roman secular power in matters of morality. Consequently it symbolized the Church's claim to preeminence in this sphere, and particularly the Western Church's developing sense of autonomy and moral superiority that would subsequently make it so much more independent and influential on the secular world than the Eastern Church.

St. Augustine

St. Ambrose's disciple, St. Augustine, was the greatest of all the Latin fathers; indeed he was one of the most powerful Christian intellects of all time. Augustine's influence on subsequent medieval thought was incalculable. Even after the Middle Ages his theology had a profound influence on the development of Protestantism; in the twentieth century many leading Christian thinkers have called themselves Neo-Augustinians. Augustine's Christianity may have been so searching because he began his career by searching for it. Nominally a Christian from birth, he hesitated until the age of thirty-three to be baptized, passing from one system of thought to another without being able to find intellectual or spiritual satisfaction in any. Only increasing doubts about all other alternatives, the appeals of St. Ambrose's teachings, and a mystical experience movingly described in his *Confessions* led Augustine to embrace the faith wholeheartedly in 387. Thereafter he advanced rapidly in ecclesiastical positions, becoming bishop of the North African city of Hippo in 395. Although he led a most active life in this office, he still found time to write a large number of profound, complex, and powerful treatises in which he set forth his convictions concerning the most fundamental problems of Christian thought and action.

Augustine's theology

St. Augustine's theology revolved around the principles of the profound sinfulness of humanity and divine omnipotence. Ever since Adam and Eve turned away from God in the Garden of Eden humans have remained basically sinful. One of Augustine's most vivid illustrations of human depravity appears in the *Confessions,* where he tells how he and some other boys once were driven to steal pears from a neighbor's garden, not because they were hungry or because the pears were beautiful, but for the sake of the evil itself. God would be purely just if He condemned all human beings to hell, but since He is also merciful He has elected to save a few. Ultimately human will has nothing to do with this choice: although one has the power to choose between good and evil, one does not have the power to decide whether he will be saved. God alone, from eternity, predestined a portion of the human race to be saved and sentenced the rest to be damned. In other words, God fixed for all time the number of human inhabitants of heaven. If any mere mortals were to respond that this seems unfair, the answer is first that strict "fairness" would confine all to perdition, and second that the basis for God's choice is a mystery shrouded in His omnipotence— far beyond the realm of human comprehension.

Even though it might seem to us that the practical consequences of this rigorous doctrine of predestination would be lethargy and fatalism, Augustine and subsequent medieval Christians did not see it that way at all. Humans themselves must do good, and if they are "chosen" they usually will do good; since no one knows who is chosen and who is not, all should try to do good in the hope that they are among the chosen. For Augustine the central guide to doing good was the doctrine of "charity," which meant leading a life devoted to loving God and loving one's neighbor for the sake of God, rather than a life of "cupidity," of loving earthly things for their own sake. Put in other terms, Augustine taught that humans should behave on earth as if they were travelers or "pilgrims," keeping their eyes at all times on their heavenly home and avoiding all materialistic concerns.

Augustine built an interpretation of history on this view in one of his major works, *On the City of God.* In this, he argued that the entire human race from the Creation until the Last Judgment was and will be composed of two warring societies, those who "live according to man" and love themselves, and those who "live according to God." The former belong to the "City of Earth" and will be damned, while the blessed few who compose the "City of God" will on Judgment Day put on the garment of immortality. As for the time when the Last Judgment would come, Augustine argued vehemently that no human could know its exact date; nonetheless since the Judgment might come at any time, and since no other world-historical events were in store for humans that mattered, all mortals should devote their utmost efforts to preparing for it by leading lives of righteousness.

Although St. Augustine formulated major new aspects of Christian theology, he believed that he was doing no more than drawing out truths found in the Bible. Indeed, he was convinced that the Bible alone con-

"The City of the Earth." A medieval illustration for Augustine's *City of God* showing Cain slaying Abel and Romulus slaying Remus. The point is that all human society on earth is a product of sin.

Augustine's view of classical learning

tained all the wisdom worth knowing. But he also believed that much of the Bible was expressed obscurely, and that it was therefore necessary to have a certain amount of education in order to understand it thoroughly. This conviction led him to a modified acceptance of classical learning. The ancient world had already worked out an educational system based on the "liberal arts," or those subjects necessary for the worldly success and intellectual growth of free men. Augustine argued that privileged Christians could learn the fundamentals of these subjects, but only in a limited way and for a completely different end—study of the Bible. Since nonreligious schools existed in his day which taught these subjects, he permitted a Christian elite to attend them; later, when such schools died out, their place was taken by schools in monasteries and cathedrals. Thus Augustine's teaching laid the groundwork for some continuity of educational practice as well as for the theory behind the preservation of some classical treatises. But we must qualify this by remarking that Augustine intended liberal education only for an elite; all others were simply to be catechized, or drilled, in the faith. He also thought it far worse that anyone should become engaged in classical thought for its own sake than that someone might not know any classical thought at all. The true wisdom of mortals, he insisted, was piety.

Augustine had many followers, of whom the most interesting and influential was Boethius, a Roman aristocrat who lived from about 480 to 524. Until recently, it was not customary to say that Boethius was a follower of St. Augustine because some of Boethius's works do not make explicit mention of Christianity. Indeed, since Boethius was indisputably interested in ancient philosophy, wrote in a polished, almost Ciceronian style, and came from a noble Roman family, it has been customary to view him as the "last of the Romans." But in fact he intended the classics to serve Christian purposes, just as Augustine had prescribed, and his own teachings were basically Augustinian.

Boethius. A twelfth-century artist's conception of Boethius as a musician, a reputation he earned because of his treatise on music.

Boethius's intellectual contributions

Because Boethius lived a century after Augustine he could see far more clearly that the ancient world was coming to an end. Therefore he made it his first goal to preserve as much of the best ancient learning as possible by a series of handbooks, translations, and commentaries. Accepting a contemporary division of the liberal arts into seven subjects—grammar, rhetoric, logic, arithmetic, geometry, astronomy, and music—he wrote handbooks on two: arithmetic and music. These summaries were meant to convey all the basic aspects of the subject matter that a Christian might need to know. Had Boethius lived longer he probably would have written similar treatments of the other liberal arts, but as it was he concentrated his efforts on his favorite subject: logic. In order to preserve the best of classical logic, he translated from Greek into Latin some of Aristotle's logical treatises as well as an introductory work on logic by Porphyry (another ancient philosopher). He also wrote his own explanatory commentaries on these works in order to help beginners. Since Latin writers had never been interested in logic, even in the most flourishing periods of Roman culture, Boethius's translations and commentaries became a crucial link between the thought of the Greeks and that of the Middle Ages. Boethius helped endow the Latin language with a logical vocabulary, and when interest in logic was revived in the twelfth-century West it rested first on a Boethian basis.

Although Boethius was an exponent of Aristotle's logic, his worldview was not Aristotelian but Augustinian. This can be seen both in his several orthodox treatises on Christian theology and above all in his masterpiece, *The Consolation of Philosophy*. Boethius wrote the *Consolation* at the end of his life, after he had been condemned to death for treason by Theodoric the Ostrogoth, whom he had served as an official. (Historians are unsure about the justice of the charges.) In it Boethius asks the age-old question of what is human happiness and concludes that it is not found in earthly rewards such as riches or fame but only in the "highest good," which is God. Human life, then, should be spent in pursuit of God. Since Boethius speaks in the *Consolation* as a philosopher rather than a theologian, he does not refer to Christian revelation or to the role of divine grace in salvation. But his basically Augustinian message is unmistakable. *The Consolation of Philosophy* became one of the most popular books of the Middle Ages because it was extremely well written, because it showed how classical expression and some classical ideas could be appropriated and subordinated into a clearly Christian framework, and most of all, because it seemed to offer a real meaning to life. In times when all earthly things really did seem crude or fleeting it was genuinely consoling to be told eloquently and "philosophically" that life has purpose if led for the sake of God.

At a climactic moment in the *Consolation* Boethius retold in verse the myth of Orpheus in a way that might stand for the common position of

The Consolation of Philosophy

Orpheus and Eurydice. Although dating from the Later Middle Ages, this manuscript illumination may still intend to deliver Boethius's message that he who turns to look on the joys of earthly life is "turning toward hell" (note the devil standing at the far right).

the four writers just discussed; i.e., how Christian thinkers were willing to accept and maintain some continuity with the classical tradition. But Boethius also made new sense of the story. According to Boethius Orpheus's wife, Eurydice, symbolized hell; since Orpheus could not refrain from looking at her he was forced to die and was condemned to hell himself. In other words, Orpheus was too worldly and material; he should not have loved a woman but should have sought God. True Christians, on the other hand, know that "happy is he who can look into the shining spring of good [i.e., the divine vision]; happy is he who can break the heavy chains of earth."

6. EASTERN ROME AND THE WEST

Boethius's execution by Theodoric the Ostrogoth in 524 was in many ways an important historical turning point. For one, Boethius was both the last noteworthy philosopher and last writer of cultivated Latin prose the West was to have for many hundreds of years. Then too Boethius was a layman, and for hundreds of years afterward almost all Western European writers would be priests or monks. In the political sphere Boethius's execution was symptomatic as well because it was the harbinger of the collapse of the Ostrogothic kingdom in Italy. Whether or not he was justly con-

Justinian and Theodora. Sixth-century mosaics from the church of San Vitale, Ravenna. The emperor and empress are conceived here to have supernatural, almost priestly powers: they are advancing toward the altar, bringing the communion dish and chalice respectively. Both rulers are set off from their retinues by demned, Boethius's execution showed that the Arian Ostrogoths could not live in perfect harmony with Catholic Christians. Soon afterward, therefore, the Ostrogoths were overthrown by the Eastern Roman Empire. That event in turn was to be a major factor in the ultimate divorce between East and West and the consequent final disintegration of the old Roman world.

The conquest of the Ostrogoths was part of a larger plan for Roman revival conceived and directed by the Eastern Roman Emperor Justinian (527–565). Eastern Rome, with its capital at Constantinople, had faced many external pressures from barbarians and internal religious dissensions since the time of Theodosius. But throughout the fifth century it had managed to weather these, and by the time of Justinian's accession had regained much of its strength. Although the Eastern Roman Empire—which then encompassed the modern-day territories of Greece, Turkey, most of the Middle East, and Egypt—was largely Greek- and Syriac-speaking, Justinian himself came from a westernmost province (modern-day Serbia) and spoke Latin. Not surprisingly, therefore, he concentrated his interests on the West. He saw himself as the heir of imperial Rome, whose ancient power and western territory he was resolved to restore. Aided by his astute and determined wife Theodora, who, unlike earlier imperial Roman consorts, played an influential role in his reign, Justinian took great strides toward this goal. But ultimately his policy of recovering the West proved unrealistic.

One of Justinian's most impressive and lasting accomplishments was his

The Emperor Justinian

See color map facing page 236

their haloes. The observant viewer is also meant to note the representation of the "three wise kings from the East" at the hem of Theodora's gown: just as the "three magi" once had supernatural knowledge of Christ, so now do their counterparts, Justinian and Theodora.

Codification and revision of Roman law; the Corpus Juris Civilis

codification of Roman law. This project was part of his attempt to emphasize continuities with earlier imperial Rome and was also meant to enhance his own prestige and absolute power. Codification of the law was necessary because between the third and sixth centuries the volume of statutes had continued to grow, with the result that the vast body of enactments contained many contradictory or obsolete elements. Moreover, conditions had changed so radically that many of the old legal principles could no longer be applied, due to the establishment of an Oriental despotism and the adoption of Christianity as the official religion. When Justinian came to the throne in 527, he immediately decided upon a revision and codification of the existing law to bring it into harmony with the new conditions and to establish it as an authoritative basis of his rule. To carry out the actual work he appointed a commission of lawyers under the supervision of his minister, Tribonian. Within two years the commission published the first result of its labors. This was the *Code,* a systematic revision of all of the statutory laws that had been issued from the reign of Hadrian to the reign of Justinian. The *Code* was later supplemented by the *Novels,* which contained the legislation of Justinian and his immediate successors. By 532 the commission had completed the *Digest,* a summary of all of the writings of the great jurists. The final product of the work of revision was the *Institutes,* a textbook of the legal principles reflected in both the *Digest* and the *Code.* All four volumes together constitute the *Corpus Juris Civilis,* or the body of the civil law.

General significance of Justinian's Corpus

Justinian's *Corpus* was a brilliant achievement in its own terms: the *Digest* alone has been justly called "the most remarkable and important lawbook that the world has ever seen." In addition, the *Corpus* had an extraordinarily great influence on subsequent legal and governmental history. Revived and restudied in Western Europe from the eleventh century on, Justinian's *Corpus* became the basis of all the law and jurisprudence of European states, exclusive of England (which followed its own "common law"). The nineteenth-century Napoleonic Code, which provided the basis for the laws of modern European countries and also of Latin America, is fundamentally the *Institutes* of Justinian in modern dress.

Other influences

Only a few of the more specific influences of Justinian's legal work can be enumerated here. One is that in its basic governmental theory it was a bastion of absolutism. Starting from the maxim that "what pleases the prince has the force of law," it granted untrammeled powers to the imperial sovereign and therefore was adopted with alacrity by later European monarchs and autocrats. But the *Corpus* also provided some theoretical support for constitutionalism because it maintained that the sovereign originally obtained his powers from the people rather than from God. Since government came from the people it could in theory be given back to them. Perhaps most important and influential was the *Corpus*'s view of the state as an abstract public and secular entity. In the Middle Ages rival views of the state as the private property of the ruler or as a supernatural creation meant to control sin often predominated. The modern conception of the state as a public entity concerned not with the future life but with everyday affairs gained strength toward the end of the Middle Ages largely because of the revival of assumptions found in Justinian's legal compilations.

Justinian aimed to be a full Roman emperor in geographical practice as well as in legal theory. To this end he sent out armies to reconquer the West. At first they were quickly successful. In 533 Justinian's brilliant general Belisarius conquered the Vandal kingdom in Northwest Africa, and in 536 Belisarius seemed to have won all Italy, where he was welcomed by the Catholic subjects of the Ostrogoths. But the first victories of the Italian campaign were illusory. After their initial defeats the Ostrogoths put up stubborn resistance and the war dragged on for decades until the exhausted Eastern Romans finally reduced the last Gothic outposts in 563. Shortly before he died Justinian became master of all Italy as well as Northwest Africa and coastal parts of Spain that his troops had also managed to recapture. The Mediterranean was once more briefly a "Roman" lake. But the cost of the endeavor was soon going to call the very existence of the Eastern Roman Empire into question.

Justinian's policy of reconquest in the West

There were two major reasons why Justinian's Western campaigns were ill-advised. One was that his realm really could not afford them. Belisarius seldom had enough troops to do his job properly: he began his Italian campaign with only 8,000 men. Later, when Justinian did grant his generals enough troops, it was only at the cost of oppressive taxation. But additional troops would probably have been insufficient to hold the new lines in the West because the Empire had greater interests, as well as enemies, to the East. While the Eastern Roman Empire was exhausting itself in Italy the Persians were gathering strength. Justinian's successors had to pull away from the West in order to meet the threat of a revived Persia, but even so, by the beginning of the seventh century, it seemed as if the Persians would be able to march all the way to the waters that faced Constantinople. Only a heroic reorganization of the Empire after 610 saved the day, but it was one that helped withdraw Eastern Rome from the West and helped the West begin to lead a life of its own.

The Western campaigns unwise

In the meantime Justinian's wars had left most of Italy in a shambles. In the course of the protracted fighting much devastation had been wrought. Around Rome aqueducts were cut and parts of the countryside returned to marshes not drained until the twentieth century. In 568, only three years after Justinian's death, another Germanic tribe, the Lombards, invaded the country and took much of it away from the Eastern Romans. They met little resistance because the latter were now paying more attention to the East, but the Lombards were still too weak to conquer the whole Italian peninsula. Instead, Italy became divided between Lombard, Eastern Roman, and papal territories. At the same time Slavs took advantage of Eastern Roman weakness to sweep into the Balkans. Farther west the Franks in Gaul were fighting among themselves, and it would be only a matter of time before Northwest Africa and most of Spain would fall to Arabs. So the Roman unity had finally come to an end. The future in this decentralized world may have looked bleak, but new forces in the separate areas would soon be gathering strength.

The end of Roman unity

See color plates following page 236

SELECTED READINGS

- *Items so designated are available in paperback editions.*

  Anderson, Hugh, *Jesus,* Englewood Cliffs, N.J., 1967. An excellent collection of readings displaying many different scholarly points of view.

  Bonner, Gerald, *St. Augustine of Hippo,* London, 1963. The best biography for beginners.

- Brown, Peter, *Augustine of Hippo,* Berkeley, 1967. An extremely subtle study.

- ———, *The Body and Society: Men, Women and Sexual Renunciation in Early Christianity,* New York, 1988. Exquisitely written and sensitive treatment of sexual asceticism.

- ———, *The World of Late Antiquity,* New York, 1971. A survey that approaches the period in its own terms rather than as a prelude to the Middle Ages.

- Bultmann, Rudolf, *Primitive Christianity in Its Contemporary Setting,* New York, 1956. Summarizes the ideas of one of our century's most important biblical scholars.

- Bury, J. B., *The Invasion of Europe by the Barbarians,* London, 1928. A straightforward narrative.

- Chadwick, Henry, *The Early Church,* Baltimore, 1967.

  Daniélou, Jean, and Henri I. Marrou, *The Christian Centuries; Vol. I: The First Six Hundred Years,* London, 1964. A survey from the Roman Catholic perspective.

- Dodds, E. R., *Pagan and Christian in an Age of Anxiety,* Cambridge, 1965. A short but brilliant study of what pagans and Christians had in common as well as what made Christianity ultimately successful.

- Enslin, M. S., *The Prophet from Nazareth,* New York, 1961.

- Katz, Solomon, *The Decline of Rome,* Ithaca, N.Y., 1955. One of the best brief introductions.

- Knowles, David, *Christian Monasticism,* New York, 1969.

- Lane Fox, Robin, *Pagans and Christians,* New York, 1987. A highly acclaimed major study of religion in the Late Roman world.

- L'Orange, H. P., *Art Forms and Civic Life in the Late Roman Empire,* Princeton, 1965. An imaginative and stimulating essay displaying how developments in art reflected developments in political and social life.

  Lot, Ferdinand, *The End of the Ancient World,* New York, 1931. Detailed treatment of the political history of the period.

- MacMullen, Ramsay, *Constantine,* New York, 1969. A good popular biography.

  Markus, Robert A., *Christianity in the Roman World,* New York, 1974.

- Mattingly, Harold, *Christianity in the Roman Empire,* New York, 1967.

  Metzger, Bruce, *The Canon of the New Testament,* New York, 1987. A careful survey of the process of composition of the New Testament.

- Pelikan, Jaroslav, *The Christian Tradition; Vol. I: The Emergence of the Catholic Tradition,* Chicago, 1971. An advanced survey of doctrine.

- Rand, E. K., *Founders of the Middle Ages,* Cambridge, Mass., 1928. A thoroughly engaging account of the early Christian reactions to the classics.

- Riché, Pierre, *Education and Culture in the Barbarian West,* Columbia, S.C., 1976. A magisterial survey of learning in the Christian West from the fall of Rome to about 800.

  Thompson, E. A., *Romans and Barbarians: The Decline of the Western Empire,* Madison, Wis., 1982. A collection of essays, organized geographically. For advanced readers.

- White, Lynn T., Jr., *The Transformation of the Roman World,* Berkeley, 1966. Stimulating essays.

  Williams, Stephen, *Diocletian and the Roman Recovery,* New York, 1985. A well-informed "life and times."

  Workman, Herbert B., *The Evolution of the Monastic Ideal,* London, 1913. Highly interpretative but still one of the best works on the subject.

SOURCE MATERIALS

- St. Augustine, *City of God,* tr. H. Bettenson, Baltimore, 1972.
- ———, *Confessions,* tr. R. S. Pine-Coffin, Baltimore, 1961.
- ———, *The Enchiridion on Faith, Hope and Love,* ed. H. Paolucci, Chicago, 1961.
- ———, *On Christian Doctrine,* tr. D. W. Robertson, Jr., New York, 1958.
- Boethius, *The Consolation of Philosophy,* tr. R. Green, Indianapolis, 1962.
- Cassiodorus, *An Introduction to Divine and Human Readings,* tr. L. W. Jones, New York, 1946.
- *Early Christian Writings: The Apostolic Fathers,* tr. M. Staniforth, Baltimore, 1968.
- Eusebius, *The History of the Church,* tr. G. A. Williamson, Baltimore, 1965.
- Procopius, *The Secret History,* tr. G. A. Williamson, Baltimore, 1966.

Part Three

THE MIDDLE AGES

The term "Middle Ages" was coined by Europeans in the seventeenth century to express their view that a long and dismal period of interruption extended between the glorious accomplishments of classical Greece and Rome and their own "modern age." Because the term became so widespread, it is now an ineradicable part of our historical vocabulary; but no serious scholar uses it with the sense of contempt it once had. Between about 600 and 1500—the rough opening and closing dates of the Middle Ages—too many different things happened to be characterized in any single way. In the eastern parts of the old Roman Empire two new civilizations emerged, the Byzantine and the Islamic, which rank among the most impressive civilizations of all time. Although the Byzantine civilization came to an end in 1453, the Islamic one has continued to exist without major interruption right up to the present. Seen from an Islamic perspective, therefore, the "Middle Ages" was not a middle period at all but a marvelous time of birth and vigorous early youth. The history of Western Europe in the Middle Ages is conventionally divided into three parts: the Early Middle Ages, the High Middle Ages, and the Later Middle Ages. Throughout the Early, High, and Later Middle Ages the Christian religion played an extraordinarily important role in human life, but otherwise there are few common denominators. The Early Middle Ages, from about 600 to about 1050, came closest to seeming to be an interval of darkness, for the level of material and intellectual accomplishment was, in fact, very low. Nonetheless, even during the Early Middle Ages important foundations were being laid for the future: above all, Western Europe was beginning to develop its own distinct sense of cultural identity. The High Middle Ages, from about 1050 to 1300, was one of the most creative epochs in the history of human endeavor. Europeans greatly improved their standard of living, established enduring national states, developed new institutions of learning and modes of thought, and created magnificent works of literature and art. During the Later Middle Ages, from about 1300 to 1500, the survival of many high-medieval accomplishments was threatened by numerous disasters, particularly profound economic depression and lethal plague. But people in the Later Middle Ages rose above adversity, tenaciously held on to what was most valuable in their inheritance, and, where necessary, created new institutions and thought patterns to fit their altered circumstances. The Middle Ages thus were really many hundred years of enormous diversity. They may be studied profitably both for their own intrinsic interest and for the fundamental contributions they made to the development of the modern world.

The Middle Ages

POLITICS	PHILOSOPHY AND SCIENCE	
Byzantine Emperor Heraclius, 610–641		600
Muhammad enters Mecca in triumph, 630		
Muslims conquer Syria, Persia, and Egypt, 636–651		700
Muslims conquer Spain, 711		
Muslim attack on Constantinople repulsed, 717		
Charles Martel defeats Muslims at Poitiers, 732		
Abbasid dynasty in Islam, 750–1258		
Pepin the Short anointed king of the Franks, 751		
Charlemagne, 768–814		
Charlemagne crowned emperor, 800		800
Carolingian Empire disintegrates, c. 850–911		
Alfred the Great of England, 871–899		
High point of Viking raids in Europe, c. 880–911		
Otto the Great of Germany, 936–973		900
Foundation of Kievan state, c. 950	Al-Farabi, d. 950	
Norman Conquest of England, 1066	Avicenna, d. 1037	1000
Seljuk Turks defeat Byzantines at Manzikert, 1071	Peter Abelard, 1079–1142	
Penance of Henry IV at Canossa, 1077		
Henry I of England, 1100–1135	Origins of universities in the West, c. 1100–c. 1300	1100
Louis VI of France, 1108–1137	Translation of Aristotle's works into Latin, c. 1140–c. 1260	
Frederick I (Barbarossa) of Germany, 1152–1190	Peter Lombard's *Sentences,* c. 1155–1157	
Henry II of England, 1154–1189	Robert Grosseteste, c. 1168–1253	
Philip Augustus of France, 1180–1223	Windmill invented, c. 1180	
	Averroës, d. 1198	
Crusaders take Constantinople (Fourth Crusade), 1204	Maimonides, d. 1204	1200
Spanish victory over Muslims at Las Navas de Tolosa, 1212		
Frederick II of Germany and Sicily, 1212–1250	Roger Bacon, c. 1214–1294	
Magna Carta, 1215	St. Thomas Aquinas, 1225–1274	
Louis IX (St. Louis) of France, 1226–1270	Height of Scholasticism, c. 1250–c. 1277	
Edward I of England, 1272–1307	William of Ockham, c. 1285–1349	
Philip IV (the Fair) of France, 1285-1314	Mechanical clock invented, c. 1290	
Hundred Years' War, 1337–1453	Master Eckhart, active c. 1300–c. 1327	1300
	Height of nominalism, c. 1320–c. 1500	
Political chaos in Germany, c. 1350–c. 1450		
		1400
Appearance of Joan of Arc, 1429–1431	Printing with movable type, c. 1450	
Rise of princes in Germany, c. 1450–c. 1500	Heavy artillery helps Turks capture Constantinople and French end Hundred Years' War, 1453	
Capture of Constantinople by Ottoman Turks, 1453		
Reassertion of royal power in France, c. 1453–c. 1513		
Wars of the Roses in England, 1455–1485		
Peace among northern Italian states, 1454–1485		
Marriage of Ferdinand and Isabella, 1469		
Ivan III lays groundwork for Russian Empire, 1462–1505		
Strong Tudor dynasty in England, 1485–1603		

	ECONOMICS	RELIGION	ARTS AND LETTERS
600	Decline of towns and trade in the West, c. 500–c. 700	Muhammad, c. 570–632 Pope Gregory I, 590–604 Muhammad's *Hijrah,* 622 Split in Islam between Shiites and Sunnites, c. 656	Byzantine church of Santa Sophia, 532–537
700	Height of Islamic commerce and industry, c. 700–c. 1300 Predominantly agrarian economy in the West, c. 700–c. 1050	Missionary work of St. Boniface in Germany, c. 715–754 Iconoclasm in Byzantine Empire, 726–843	The Venerable Bede, d. 735 *Beowulf,* c. 750 Irish *Book of Kells,* c. 750
800 **900**	Height of Byzantine commerce and industry, c. 800–c. 1000	Foundation of Cluny, 910 Byzantine conversion of Russia, c. 988	Carolingian Renaissance, c. 800–c. 850
1000	Destruction of Byzantine free peasantry, c. 1025–c. 1100 Agricultural advance, revival of towns and trade in the West, c. 1050–c. 1300	Beginning of Reform Papacy, 1046 Schism between Roman and Eastern Orthodox Churches, 1054 Pope Gregory VII, 1073–1085 St. Bernard of Clairvaux, 1090–1153 First Crusade, 1095–1099	Romanesque style in architecture and art, c. 1000–c. 1200 *Song of Roland,* c. 1095 Troubadour poetry, c. 1100–c. 1220
1100 **1200**		Height of Cistercian monasticism, c. 1115–c. 1153 Concordat of Worms ends investiture struggle, 1122 Crusaders lose Jerusalem to Saladin, 1187 Pope Innocent III, 1198–1216	*Rubaiyat* of Umar Khayyam, c. 1120 Gothic style in architecture and art, c. 1150–c.1500 Poetry of Chrétien de Troyes, c. 1165–c. 1190
		Albigensian Crusade, 1208–1213 Founding of Franciscan Order, 1210 Fourth Lateran Council, 1215 Founding of Dominican Order, 1216 Fall of last Christian outposts in Holy Land, 1291 Pope Boniface VIII, 1294–1303	Wolfram von Eschenbach, c. 1200 Gottfried von Strassburg, c. 1210 Persian poetry of Sadi, c. 1250 *Romance of the Rose,* c. 1270
1300 **1400**	European economic depression, c. 1300–c. 1450 Floods through Western Europe, 1315 Black Death, 1347–1350 Height of Hanseatic League, c. 1350–c. 1450 English Peasants' Revolt, 1381 Medici Bank, 1397–1494	Babylonian Captivity of papacy, 1305–1378 John Wyclif, c. 1330–1384 Great Schism of papacy, 1378–1417 John Hus preaches in Bohemia, c. 1408–1415 Council of Constance, 1414–1417 Hussite Revolt, 1420–1434 *Imitation of Christ,* c. 1427 Council of Basel, defeat of conciliarism 1431–1449	Paintings of Giotto, c. 1305 –1337 Dante's *Divine Comedy,* c. 1310 Boccaccio's *Decameron,* c. 1350 Persian poetry of Hafiz, c. 1370 Chaucer's *Canterbury Tales,* c. 1390 Paintings of Jan van Eyck, c. 1400–c. 1441

Chapter 9

ROME'S THREE HEIRS: THE BYZANTINE, ISLAMIC, AND EARLY-MEDIEVAL WESTERN WORLDS

Constantinople is a bustling city, and merchants come to it from all over, by sea or land, and there is none like it in the world except Baghdad, the great city of Islam. In Constantinople is the church of Santa Sophia, and the seat of the Pope of the Greeks, since the Greeks do not obey the Pope of Rome. There are also as many churches as there are days of the year. A quantity of wealth is brought to them from the islands, and the like of this wealth is not to be found in any other church in the world.

—Benjamin of Tudela, *Travels*

You have become the best community ever raised up for mankind, enjoining the right and forbidding the wrong, and having faith in God.

—The Koran, III, 110

He who ordains the fate of kingdoms and the march of events, the almighty Disposer, having destroyed one extraordinary image, that of the Romans, which had feet of iron, or even feet of clay, then raised up among the Franks the golden head of a second image, just as remarkable, in the person of the glorious Charlemagne.

—A monk of St. Gall

A new period in the history of Western civilizations began in the seventh century, when it became clear that there would no longer be a single empire ruling over all the territories bordering on the Mediterranean. By about 700 C.E., in place of a united Rome, there were three successor civilizations that stood as rivals on different Mediterranean shores: the Byzantine, the Islamic, and the Western Christian. Each of these had its own language and distinctive forms of life. The Byzantine

The successors of Rome

235

civilization, which descended directly from the Eastern Roman Empire, was Greek-speaking and dedicated to combining Roman governmental traditions with intense pursuit of the Christian faith. The Islamic civilization was Arabic-speaking and inspired in government as well as culture by the idealism of a dynamic new religion. Western Christian civilization in comparison to the others was a laggard. It was the least economically advanced and faced organizational weaknesses in both government and religion. But it did have some base of unity in Christianity and the Latin language, and would soon begin to find greater political and religious cohesiveness.

Reappraisal of the Byzantine and Islamic civilizations

Because the Western Christian civilization ultimately outstripped its rivals, Western writers until recently have tended to denigrate the Byzantine and Islamic civilizations as backward and even irrational. Of the three, however, the Western Christian was certainly the most backward from about the seventh to the eleventh centuries. For some four or five hundred years the West lived in the shadow of Constantinople and Mecca. Scholars are only now beginning to recognize the full measure of Byzantine and Islamic accomplishments. These greatly merit our attention both for their own sakes and because they influenced Western European development in many direct and indirect ways.

1. THE BYZANTINE EMPIRE AND ITS CULTURE

The Byzantine achievement impressive despite weaknesses

Once dismissed by the historian Gibbon as "a tedious and uniform tale of weakness and misery," the story of Byzantine civilization is today recognized as a most interesting and impressive one. It is true that the Byzantine Empire was in many respects not very innovative; it was also continually beset by grave external threats and internal weaknesses. Nonetheless it managed to survive for a millennium. In fact the empire did not just survive, it frequently prospered and greatly influenced the world around it. Among many other achievements, it helped preserve ancient Greek thought, created magnificent works of art, and brought Christian culture to pagan peoples, above all the Slavs. Simply stated it was one of the most enduring and influential empires the world has ever known.

Problems of periodization in Byzantine history

It is impossible to date the beginning of Byzantine history with any precision because the Byzantine Empire was the uninterrupted successor of the Roman state. For this reason different historians prefer different beginnings. Some argue that "Byzantine" characteristics had already emerged in Roman history as a result of the easternizing policy of Diocletian, and others that Byzantine history began when Constantine moved his capital from Rome to Constantinople, the city that subsequently became the center of the Byzantine world. (The old name for the site on which Constantinople was built was Byzantium, from which we get the adjective Byzantine; it would be more accurate but cumbersome to say Constantinopolitine.) Diocletian and Constantine, however, continued to rule a united Roman

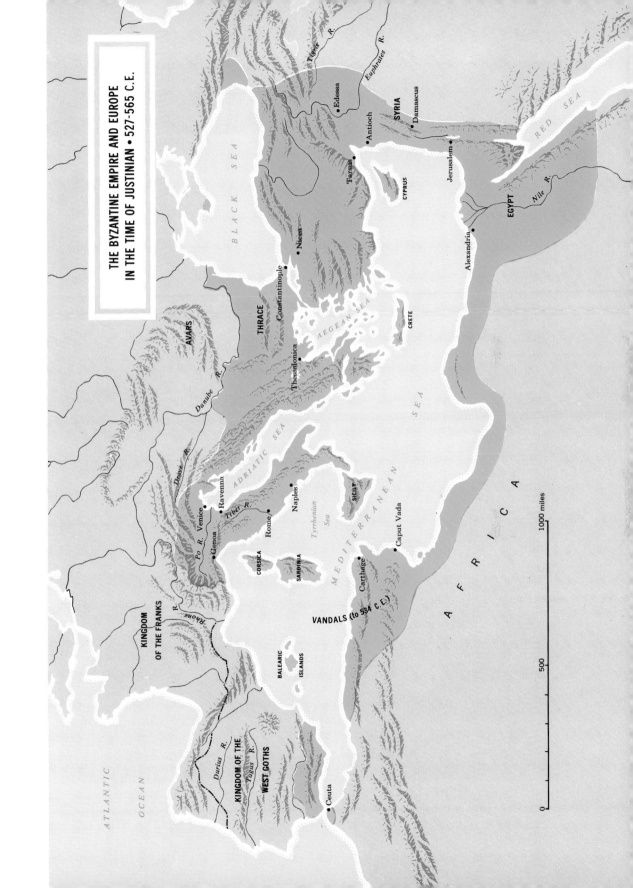

THE BYZANTINE EMPIRE AND EUROPE
IN THE TIME OF JUSTINIAN • 527-565 C.E.

ATLANTIC
OCEAN

KINGDOM
OF THE FRANKS

KINGDOM OF THE
WEST GOTHS

Durius R.

Tagus R.

Rhone R.

Po R.

Genoa

Venice

Ravenna

Tiber R.

Rome

Naples

CORSICA

SARDINIA

BALEARIC
ISLANDS

Ceuta

Carthage

Caput Vada

VANDALS (to 534 C.E.)

SICILY

Tyrrhenian
Sea

MEDITERRANEAN

AFRICA

ADRIATIC SEA

Drave R.

Danube R.

AVARS

THRACE

Thessalonica

Constantinople

BLACK SEA

AEGEAN SEA

Nicæa

SEA

CRETE

CYPRUS

Tarsus

Antioch

Edessa

Tigris R.

Euphrates R.

SYRIA

Damascus

Jerusalem

Alexandria

EGYPT

Nile R.

RED SEA

0   500   1000 miles

Hen and Chicks. North Italian small figures from the sixth century made from silver overlaid with gold. The purpose of this luxurious and seemingly humorous work dating from a time of economic decline and grave political crisis is unknown; there are as many theories offered for it as there are chicks. (Art Resource)

Iron Crown. This splendidly bejewelled iron chaplet may have been used to crown the Lombard kings of Italy.

Book Cover. The cover of a gospel book encrusted with jewels and ivory cameos presented by Pope Gregory the Great to a Lombard queen around the year 600.

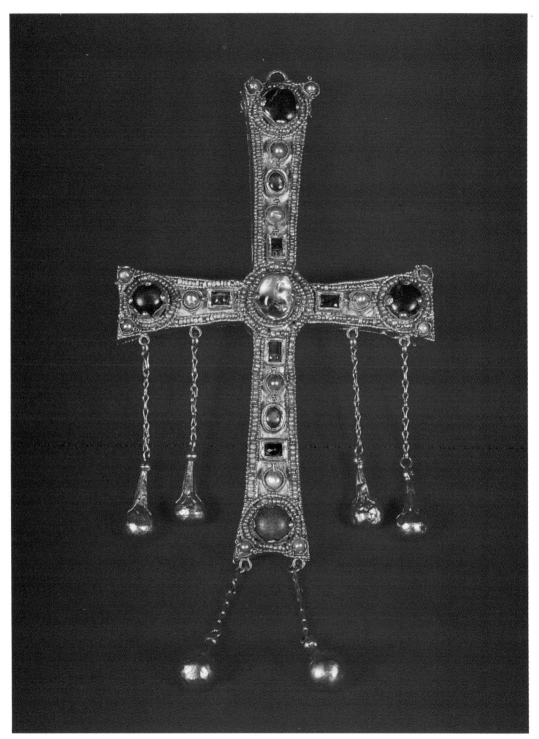

Decorative Cross. Lombard work from the seventh century.

Empire. As we have seen, as late as the sixth century, after the western part of the empire had fallen to the Germans, the Eastern Roman Emperor Justinian thought of himself as an heir to Augustus and fought hard to win back the West. Justinian's reign was clearly an important turning point in the direction of Byzantine civilization because it saw the crystallization of new forms of thought and art that can be considered more "Byzantine" than "Roman." But this still remains a matter of subjective emphasis: some scholars emphasize these newer forms, while others respond that Justinian continued to speak Latin and dreamed of restoring old Rome. Only after 610 did a new dynasty emerge that came from the East, spoke Greek, and maintained a fully Eastern or properly "Byzantine" policy. Hence although good arguments can be made for beginning Byzantine history with Diocletian, Constantine, or Justinian, we will begin here with the accession in 610 of the Emperor Heraclius.

The Byzantine Emperor Heraclius and His Son. Comparison to coins of Trajan and Theodosius (pp. 180, 202) shows that a new style of civilization had emerged with much less attachment to naturalistic portraiture.

It is also convenient to begin in 610 because from then until 1071 the main lines of Byzantine military and political history were determined by resistance against successive waves of invasions from the East. When Heraclius came to the throne the very existence of the Byzantine Empire was being challenged by the Persians, who had conquered almost all of the empire's Asian territories. As a symbol of their triumph the Persians in 614 even carried off the relic believed to be part of the original cross from Jerusalem. By enormous effort Heraclius rallied Byzantine strength and turned the tide, routing the Persians and retrieving the cross in 627. Persia was then reduced to subordination and Heraclius reigned in glory until 641. But in his last years new armies began to invade Byzantine territory, swarming out of hitherto placid Arabia. Inspired by the new religion of Islam and profiting from Byzantine exhaustion after the struggle with Persia, the Arabs made astonishingly rapid gains. By 650 they had taken most of the Byzantine territories the Persians had occupied briefly in the early seventh century, had conquered all of Persia itself, and were making their way westward across North Africa. Having become a Mediterranean power, the Arabs also took to the sea. In 677 they tried to conquer Constantinople with a fleet. Failing that, they attempted to take the city again in 717 by means of a concerted land and sea operation.

The reign of Heraclius; the rise of Islam

The Arab threat to Constantinople in 717 marked a new low in Byzantine fortunes, but the threat was countered by the Emperor Leo the Isaurian (717–741) with as much resolution as Heraclius had met the Persian threat a century before. With the help of a secret incendiary device known as "Greek fire" (a mixture of sulphur, naphtha, and quicklime aimed at the enemy from the prows of ships) and great military ability, Leo was able to defeat the Arab forces on sea and land. Leo's relief of Constantinople in 717 was one of the most significant battles in European history, not just because it allowed the Byzantine Empire to endure for centuries more, but also because it helped to save the West: had the Islamic armies taken Constantinople there would have been little to stop them from sweeping through the rest of Europe. Over the next few decades the Byzantines were able to reconquer most of Asia Minor. This territory, to-

Byzantine revival prior to the Battle of Manzikert

ωρρικῶν· Ἡραῖο δὲ Καιπασοκλασιῶπ̅ρ̅σ̅ολοωι̅πυρὶ

ἐ̄ρω̄μ̄η̄ π̅υρ̅π̅ολ̅ τον τωνι̅ηαη̅π̅γ̅λον·

Greek Fire

The Emperor John I (969–976) Being Crowned by Christ. Byzantine rulers characteristically used coins as objects of propaganda designed to show that their powers came to them supernaturally.

gether with Greece, became the heartland of their empire for the next three hundred years. A stalemate with the Islamic forces prevailed until the Byzantines were able to take the offensive against a decaying Islamic power in the second half of the tenth century. In that period—the greatest in Byzantine history—Byzantine troops reconquered most of Syria. But in the eleventh century a different Islamic people, the Seljuk Turks, cancelled out all the prior Byzantine gains. In 1071 the Seljuks annihilated a Byzantine army at Manzikert in Asia Minor, a stunning victory that allowed them to overrun the remaining Byzantine eastern provinces. Constantinople was now thrown back upon itself more or less as it had been in the days of Heraclius and Leo.

After Manzikert the Byzantine Empire managed to survive, but it never regained its earlier vigor. One major reason for this was the fact that, from 1071 until the final destruction of the empire in 1453, Byzantine fortunes were greatly complicated by the rise of Western Europe. Hitherto the West had been far too weak to present any major challenge to Byzantium, but that situation changed entirely in the course of the eleventh century. In 1071, the same year that saw the victory of the Seljuks over the Byzantines in Asia Minor, westerners known as Normans expelled the Byzantines from their last holdings in southern Italy. Despite this clear sign of Western enmity, in 1095 a Byzantine emperor named Alexius Comnenus issued a call for Western help against the Turks. He could hardly have made a worse mistake: his call helped inspire the Crusades, and the Crusades became a major cause for the fall of the Byzantine state. Westerners on the First Crusade did help the Byzantines win back Asia Minor, but they also carved out territories for themselves in Syria, which the Byzantines considered to be their own. As time went on frictions mounted and the westerners, now militarily superior, looked more and more upon Constantinople as a fruit ripe for the picking. In 1204 they finally picked it: Crusaders who should have been intent on conquering Jerusalem conquered Constantinople instead and sacked the city with ruthless ferocity. A greatly reduced Byzantine government was able to survive nearby and return to Constantinople in 1261, but thereafter the Byzantine state was an "empire" in name and recollection of past glories only. After 1261 it eked out a reduced existence in parts of Greece until 1453, when powerful Turkish successors to the Seljuks, the Ottomans, completed the Crusaders' work of destruction by conquering the last vestiges of the empire and taking Constantinople. Turks rule in Constantinople—now Istanbul—even today.

*Crusaders sack
Constantinople*

That Constantinople was finally taken was no surprise. What is a cause for wonder is that the Byzantine state survived for so many centuries in the face of so many different hostile forces. This wonder becomes all the greater when it is recognized that the internal political history of the empire was exceedingly tumultuous. Because Byzantine rulers followed their late-Roman predecessors in claiming the powers of divinely appointed absolute monarchs, there was no way of opposing them other than by intrigue and violence. Hence Byzantine history was marked by repeated palace revolts; mutilations, murders, and blindings were almost commonplace. Byzantine politics became so famous for their behind-the-scenes complexity that we still use the word "Byzantine" to refer to highly complex and devious backstage machinations. Fortunately for the empire, some very able rulers did emerge from time to time to wield their untrammeled powers with efficiency, and, even more fortunately, a bureaucratic machinery continued to function during times of palace upheaval.

*Factors contributing to the
stability of the Byzantine
Empire: (1) occasional able
rulers*

Efficient bureaucratic government indeed was one of the major elements of Byzantine success and longevity. The Byzantines could count on having an adequate supply of manpower for their bureaucracy because Byzantine civilization preserved and encouraged the practice of education for the laity. This was one of the major differences between the Byzantine East and the early Latin West: from about 600 to about 1200 there was practically no literate laity in Western Christendom, while lay literacy in the Byzantine East was the basis of governmental accomplishment. Byzantine officialdom regulated many aspects of life, far more than we would think proper today. Bureaucrats helped supervise education and religion and presided over all forms of economic endeavor. Urban officials in Constantinople, for example, regulated prices and wages, maintained systems of licensing, controlled exports, and enforced the observance of the Sabbath. What is more, they usually did this with comparative efficiency and did not stifle business initiative. Bureaucratic methods too helped regulate the army and navy, the courts, and the diplomatic service, endowing them with organizational strengths incomparable for their age.

*(2) efficient bureaucratic
administration*

Another explanation for Byzantine endurance was the comparatively sound economic base of the state until the eleventh century. As the historian Sir Steven Runciman has said, "if Byzantium owed her strength and security to the efficiency of her Services, it was her trade that enabled her

(3) firm economic base

to pay for them." While long-distance trade and urban life all but disappeared in the West for hundreds of years, commerce and cities continued to flourish in the Byzantine East. Above all, in the ninth and tenth centuries Constantinople was a vital trade emporium for Far Eastern luxury goods and Western raw materials. The empire also nurtured and protected its own industries, most notably that of silk-making, and it was renowned until the eleventh century for its stable gold and silver coinage. Among its great urban centers was not only Constantinople, which at times may have had a population of close to a million, but also in certain periods Antioch, and up until the end of Byzantine history the bustling cities of Thessalonica and Trebizond.

The significance of Byzantine agricultural history

Historians emphasize Byzantine trade and industry because these were so advanced for the time and provided most of the surplus wealth that supported the state. But agriculture was really at the heart of the Byzantine economy as it was of all premodern ones. The story of Byzantine agricultural history is mainly one of a struggle of small peasants to stay free of the encroachments of large estates owned by wealthy aristocrats and monasteries. Until the eleventh century the free peasantry just managed to maintain its existence with the help of state legislation, but after 1025 the aristocracy gained power in the government and began to transform the peasants into impoverished tenants. This had many unfortunate results, not the least of which was that the peasants became less interested in resisting the enemy. The defeat at Manzikert was the inevitable result. The destruction of the free peasantry was accompanied and followed in the last centuries of Byzantine history by foreign domination of Byzantine trade. Primarily the Italian cities of Venice and Genoa established trading outposts and privileges within Byzantine realms after 1204, which channeled off much of the wealth on which the state had previously relied. In this way the empire was defeated by the Venetians from within before it was destroyed by the Turks from without.

Preoccupation with religion

So far we have spoken about military campaigns, government, and economics as if they were at the center of Byzantine survival. Seen from hindsight they were, but what the Byzantines themselves cared about most was usually religion. Remarkable as it might seem, Byzantines fought over abstruse religious questions as vehemently as we today might argue about politics and sports—indeed more vehemently because the Byzantines were often willing to fight and even die over some words in a religious creed. The intense preoccupation with questions of doctrine is well illustrated by the report of an early Byzantine writer who said that when he asked a baker for the price of bread, the answer came back, "the Father is greater than the Son," and when he asked whether his bath was ready, was told that "the Son proceeds from nothing." Understandably such zealousness could harm the state greatly during times of religious dissension, but it could also endow it with a powerful sense of confidence and mission during times of religious concord.

Byzantine religious dissensions were greatly complicated by the fact that the emperors took an active role in them. Because the emperors carried great power in the life of the Church—emperors were sometimes deemed by churchmen to be "similar to God"—they exerted great influence in religious debates. Nonetheless, especially in the face of provincial separatism, rulers could never force all their subjects to believe what they did. Only after the loss of many eastern provinces and the refinement of doctrinal formulae did religious peace seem near in the eighth century. But then it was shattered for still another century by what is known as the *Iconoclastic Controversy.*

The Iconoclasts were those who wished to prohibit the worship of icons—that is, images of Christ and the saints. Since the Iconoclastic movement was initiated by the Emperor Leo the Isaurian, and subsequently directed with even greater energy by his son Constantine V (740–775), historians have discerned in it different motives. One was certainly theological. The worship of images seemed to the Iconoclasts to smack of paganism. They believed that nothing made by human beings should be worshiped by them, that Christ was so divine that he could not be conceived of in terms of human art, and that the prohibition of worshiping "graven images" in the Ten Commandments (Exodus 20:4) placed the matter beyond dispute.

In addition to these theological points, there were probably other considerations. Since Leo the Isaurian was the emperor who saved Constantinople from the onslaught of Islam, and since Muslims zealously shunned images on the grounds that they were "the work of Satan" (Koran, V. 92), it has been argued that Leo's Iconoclastic policy was an attempt to answer one of Islam's greatest criticisms of Christianity and thereby deprive Islam of some of its appeal. There may also have been certain internal political and financial motives. By proclaiming a radical new religious movement the emperors may have wished to reassert their control over the Church and combat the growing strength of monasteries. As events turned out, the monasteries did rally behind the cause of images, and as a result, they were bitterly persecuted by Constantine V, who took the opportunity to appropriate much monastic wealth.

The Iconoclastic Controversy was resolved in the ninth century by a return to the status quo, namely the worship of images, but the century of turmoil over the issue had some profound results. One was the destruction by imperial order of a large amount of religious art. Pre-eighth-century Byzantine religious art that survives today comes mostly from places like Italy or Palestine, which were beyond the easy reach of the Iconoclastic emperors. When we see how great this art is we can only lament the destruction of the rest. A second consequence of the controversy was the opening of a serious religious breach between East and West. The pope, who until the eighth century had usually been a close ally of the Byzantines, could not accept Iconoclasm for many reasons. The most important of these was that extreme Iconoclasm tended to question the cult of saints, and the claims of papal primacy were based on an assumed descent from St. Peter. Accordingly, the eighth-century popes combated Byzantine Iconoclasm and turned to the Frankish kings for support. This "about-face of the

Imperial participation in religious controversies

Iconoclasts' Cross. The Iconoclasts covered over beautiful apse mosaics with unadorned crosses. This example survives in St. Irene's church, Istanbul, Turkey.

Political and financial motives

Significance of the Iconoclastic Controversy

Christ as Ruler of the Universe. A twelfth-century Byzantine mosaic from the cathedral of Cefalù in Sicily. Although the Byzantines did not rule in Sicily in the twelfth century, the Norman rulers employed Byzantine workmen. Note the use of Greek—the Byzantine language—on the left-handed Bible page and Latin—the Norman language—on the right.

papacy" was both a major step in the worsening of East-West relations and a landmark in the history of Western Europe.

In contrast to the above consequences of Iconoclasm's temporary victory, a major consequence of its defeat was the reassertion of some major traits of Byzantine religiosity, which from the ninth century until the end of Byzantine history remained predominant. One of these was the reemphasis of a faith in traditionalism. Even when Byzantines were experimenting in religious matters they consistently stated that they were only restating or developing the implications of tradition. Now, after centuries of turmoil, they abandoned experiment almost entirely and reaffirmed tradition more than ever. As one opponent of Iconoclasm said: "If an angel or an emperor announces to you a gospel other than the one you have received, close your ears." This view gave strength to Byzantine religion internally by ending controversy and heresy, and it helped it gain new adherents in the ninth and tenth centuries. But it also inhibited free speculation not just in religion but also in related intellectual matters.

Other results:(1) reaffirmation of tradition

Allied to this development was the triumph of Byzantine contemplative piety. Supporters defended the use of icons not on the grounds that they were meant to be worshiped for themselves but because they helped lead the mind from the material to the immaterial. The emphasis on contemplation as a road to religious enlightenment thereafter became the hallmark of Byzantine spirituality. While westerners did not by any means reject such a path, the typical Western saint was an activist who saw sin as a vice and sought salvation through good works. Byzantine theologians on the other hand saw sin more as ignorance and believed that salvation was to be found in illumination. This led to a certain religious passivity and mysticism in Eastern Christianity, which makes it seem different from Western varieties up to the present time.

(2) the triumph of Byzantine contemplative piety

Since religion was so dominant in Byzantine life, certain secular aspects of Byzantine civilization often go unnoticed, but there are good reasons why some of these should not be forgotten. One is Byzantine cultivation of the classics. Commitment to Christianity by no means inhibited the Byzantines from revering their ancient Greek heritage. Byzantine schools based their instruction on classical Greek literature to the degree that educated people could quote Homer more extensively than we today can quote Shakespeare. Byzantine scholars studied and commented on the philosophy of Plato and Aristotle, and Byzantine writers imitated the prose of Thucydides. Such dedicated classicism both enriched Byzantine intellectual and literary life, which is too often dismissed entirely by moderns because it generally lacked originality, and it helped preserve the Greek classics for later ages. The bulk of classical Greek literature that we have today survives only because it was copied by Byzantine scribes.

Byzantine classicism

Byzantine classicism was a product of an educational system for the laity that extended to the education of women as well as men. Given attitudes and practices in the contemporary Christian West and in Islam, Byzantine commitment to female education was truly unusual. Girls from aristocratic or prosperous families did not go to schools but were relatively well educated at home by private tutors. We are told, for example, of one Byzantine woman who could discourse like Plato or Pythagoras. The most famous Byzantine female intellectual was the Princess Anna Comnena, who described the deeds of her father Alexius in an urbane biography in which she copiously cited Homer and Euripides. In addition to such literary figures there were women doctors in the Byzantine Empire, a fact of note given their scarcity in Western society until recent times.

The education of women

Byzantine achievements in the realms of architecture and art are more familiar. The finest example of Byzantine architecture was the Church of Santa Sophia (Holy Wisdom), built at enormous cost in the sixth century.

Santa Sophia. The greatest monument of Byzantine architecture. The four minarets were added after the fall of the Byzantine Empire, when the Turks turned the church into a mosque.

Diagram of Santa Sophia Dome

Novel structural design

Byzantine art

Conversion of Slavic people

Although built before the date taken here as the beginning of Byzantine history, it was typically Byzantine in both its style and subsequent influence. Though designed by architects of Hellenic descent, it was vastly different from any Greek temple. Its purpose was not to express human pride in the power of the individual, but to symbolize the inward and spiritual character of the Christian religion. For this reason the architects gave little attention to the external appearance of the building. Nothing but plain brick covered with plaster was used for the exterior walls; there were no marble facings, graceful columns, or sculptured entablatures. The interior, however, was decorated with richly colored mosaics, gold leaf, colored marble columns, and bits of tinted glass set on edge to refract the rays of sunlight after the fashion of sparkling gems. To emphasize a sense of the miraculous, the building was constructed in such a way that no light appeared to come from the outside at all but to be manufactured within.

The structural design of Santa Sophia was something altogether new in the history of architecture. Its central feature was the application of the principle of the dome to a building of square shape. The church was designed in the form of a cross that would have a magnificent dome over its central square. The main problem was how to fit the round circumference of the dome to the square area it was supposed to cover. The solution consisted in having four great arches spring from pillars at the four corners of the square. The rim of the dome was then made to rest on the keystones of the arches, with the curved triangular spaces between the arches filled in with masonry. The result was an architectural framework of marvelous strength, which at the same time made possible a style of imposing grandeur and even some delicacy of treatment. The great dome of Santa Sophia has a diameter of 107 feet and rises to a height of nearly 180 feet from the floor. So many windows are placed around its rim that the dome appears to have no support at all but to be suspended in midair.

As in architecture, so in art the Byzantines profoundly altered the earlier Greek classical style. Byzantines excelled in ivory-carving, manuscript illumination, jewelry-making, and, above all, the creation of mosaics—that is, designs of pictures produced by fitting together small pieces of colored glass or stone. Human figures in these mosaics were usually distorted and elongated in a very unclassical fashion to create the impression of intense piety or extreme majesty. Most Byzantine art is marked by highly abstract, formal, and jewel-like qualities. For this reason many consider Byzantine artistic culture to be a model of timeless perfection. The modern poet W. B. Yeats expressed this point of view most eloquently when he wrote in his "Sailing to Byzantium" of artificial birds made by Byzantine goldsmiths ". . . to sing/To lords and ladies of Byzantium/Of what is past, or passing, or to come."

Probably the single greatest testimony to the vitality of Byzantine civilization at its height was the conversion of many Slavic peoples, especially those of Russia. According to the legend, which has a basic kernel of fact, an east-Slavic prince named Vladimir who ruled most of Russia and the Ukraine decided around 988 to abandon the paganism of his ancestors. Accordingly, he sent emissaries to report on the religious practices of Islam,

Roman Catholicism, and Byzantine Christianity. When they returned to tell him that only among the Byzantines did God seem to "dwell among men," he promptly agreed to be baptized by a Byzantine missionary. The event was momentous because Russia thereupon became a cultural province of Byzantium. From then until the twentieth century Russia remained a bastion of the Eastern Orthodox religion.

After Constantinople fell in 1453 Russians began to feel that they were chosen to carry on both the faith and the imperial mission of the fallen Byzantine Empire. Thus their ruler took the title of *tsar*—which simply means caesar—and Russians asserted that Moscow was "the third Rome": "Two Romes have fallen," said a Russian spokesman, "the third is still standing, and a fourth there shall not be." Such ideology helps explain in part the later growth of Russian imperialism. Byzantine traditions also may help explain the dominance of the ruler in the Russian state. Without question Byzantine stylistic principles influenced Russian religious art, and Byzantine ideas influenced the thought of modern Russia's greatest writers, Dostoevsky and Tolstoy.

Unfortunately, just at the time when relations between Constantinople and Russia were solidifying, relations with the West were deteriorating to a point of no return. After the skirmishes of the Iconoclastic period relations between Eastern and Western Christians remained tense, partly because Constantinople resented Western claims (initiated by Charlemagne in 800) of creating a rival empire, but most of all because cultural and religious differences between the two were growing. From the Byzantine point of view westerners were uncouth and ignorant, while to Western European eyes Byzantines were effeminate and prone to heresy. Once the West started to revive, it began to take the offensive against a weakened East in theory and practice. In 1054 extreme papal claims of primacy over the Eastern Church provoked a religious schism that has never been healed. Thereafter the Crusades drove home the dividing wedge.

After the sack of Constantinople in 1204 Byzantine hatred of westerners became understandably intense. "Between us and them," one Byzantine wrote, "there is now a deep chasm: we do not have a single thought in common." Westerners called easterners "the dregs of the dregs . . . unworthy of the sun's light," while easterners called westerners the children of darkness, alluding to the fact that the sun sets in the West. The beneficiaries of this hatred were the Turks, who not only conquered Constantinople in 1453, but soon after conquered most of southeastern Europe up to Vienna.

In view of this sad history of hostility it is best to end our treatment of Byzantine civilization by recalling how much we owe to it. In simple physical terms the Byzantine Empire acted as a bulwark against Islam from the seventh to the eleventh centuries, thus helping to preserve an independent West. If the Byzantines had not prospered and defended Europe, Western Christian civilization might well have been snuffed out. Then too we owe an enormous amount in cultural terms to Byzantine scholars who helped preserve classical Greek learning. The most famous moment of communication between Byzantine and Western European scholars came

Russian Icon. This early-seventeenth-century Russian painting depicts an angel in a distinctly Byzantine style.

Tense relations between Eastern and Western Christians

Turks benefit from hostility between East and West

The Byzantine contribution to Western civilization

St. Mark's Church, Venice. The most splendid example of Byzantine architecture in Italy.

during the Italian Renaissance, when Byzantines helped introduce Italian humanists to the works of Plato. But westerners had been learning from Byzantines even before then, and they continued to gain riches from Byzantine manuscripts until the sixteenth century. Similarly, Byzantine art exerted a great influence on the art of Western Europe over a long period of time. To take only some of the most famous examples, St. Mark's basilica in Venice was built in close imitation of the Byzantine style, and the art of such great Western painters as Giotto and El Greco owes much in different ways to Byzantine influences. Nor should we stop at listing influences because the great surviving monuments of Byzantine culture retain their imposing appeal in and of themselves. Travelers who view Byzantine mosaics in such cities as Ravenna and Palermo are continually awestruck; others who make their way to Istanbul still find Santa Sophia to be a marvel. In such jeweled beauty, then, the light from the Byzantine East, which once glowed so brightly, continues to shimmer.

2. THE FLOWERING OF ISLAM

In contrast to Byzantine history, which has no clearly datable beginning but a definite end in 1453, the history of Islamic civilization has a clear point of origin, beginning with the career of Muhammad in the seventh century, but no end since Islam, Muhammad's religion, is still a major force in the modern world. Believers in Islam, known as Muslims, currently comprise about one-seventh of the global population: in their greatest concentrations they extend from Africa through the Middle East and the states of the former Soviet Union to India, Bangladesh, and Indonesia. All these Muslims subscribe both to a common religion and a common way of life, for Islam has always demanded from its followers not just adherence to certain forms of worship but also adherence to set social and cultural norms. Indeed, more than Judaism or Christianity, Islam has been a great experiment in trying to build a worldwide society based on the fullest harmony between religious requirements and precepts for everyday existence. In practice, of course, that experiment has differed in its success and quality according to time and place, but it is still being tested, and it accounts for the fact that there remains an extraordinary sense of community between all Muslims regardless of race, language, and geographical distribution. In this section we will trace the early history of the Islamic experiment, with primary emphasis on its orientation toward the West. Nonetheless it must be remembered that Islam expanded in many directions and that it ultimately had as much influence on the history of Africa and India as it did on that of Europe or western Asia.

Although Islam spread to many lands it was born in Arabia, so the story of its history must begin there. Arabia, a peninsula of deserts, had been so backward before the founding of Islam that the two dominant neighboring empires, the Roman and the Persian, had not deemed it worthwhile to extend their rule over Arabian territories. Most Arabs were Bedouins, wandering camel herdsmen who lived off the milk of their animals and the produce, such as dates, that was grown in desert oases. In the second half of the sixth century there was a quickening of economic life owing to a shift in long-distance trade routes. The protracted wars between the Byzantine and Persian empires made Arabia a safer transit route for caravans going between Africa and Asia than were other alternatives, and some towns grew to direct and take advantage of this growth of trade. The most prominent of these was Mecca, which not only lay on the junction of major trade routes, but also had long been a local religious center. In Mecca was located the *Kabah,* a pilgrimage shrine that served as a central place of worship for many different Arabian clans and tribes. (Within the Kabah was the Black Stone, a meteorite worshiped as a miraculous relic by adherents of many different divinities.) The men who controlled this shrine and also directed the economic life of the Meccan area belonged to the tribe of Quraish, an aristocracy of traders and entrepreneurs who provided the area with whatever little government it knew.

Muhammad, the founder of Islam, was born in Mecca to a family of the Quraish about 570. Orphaned early in life, he entered the service of a rich widow whom he later married, thereby attaining financial security. Until middle age he lived as a prosperous trader, behaving little differently from his fellow townsmen, but around 610 he underwent a religious experience that changed the course of his life and ultimately that of a good part of the

The Kabah. It contains the black stone which was supposed to have been miraculously sent down from heaven, and rests in the courtyard of the great mosque in Mecca.

world. Although most Arabs until then had been polytheists who recognized at most the vague superiority of a more powerful god they called Allah, Muhammad in 610 believed he heard a voice from heaven tell him that there was no god but Allah alone. In other words, as the result of a conversion experience he became an uncompromising monotheist. Thereafter he received further messages that served as the basis for a new religion and that commanded him to accept the calling of "Prophet" to proclaim the monotheistic faith to the Quraish. At first he was not very successful in gaining converts beyond a limited circle, perhaps because the leading Quraish tribesmen believed that establishment of a new religion would deprive the Kabah, and therewith Mecca, of its central place in local worship. The town of Yathrib to the north, however, had no such concerns, and its representatives invited Muhammad to emigrate there so that he could serve as a neutral arbiter of local rivalries. In 622 Muhammad and his followers accepted the invitation. Because their migration—called in Arabic the *Hijrah* (or Hegira)—saw the beginning of an advance in Muhammad's fortunes, it is considered by Muslims to mark the beginning of their era: as Christians begin their era with the birth of Christ so Muslims begin their dating system with the *Hijrah* of 622.

Muhammad changed the name of Yathrib to Medina (the "city of the Prophet") and quickly succeeded in establishing himself as ruler of the town. In the course of doing this he consciously began to organize his converts into a political as well as religious community. But he still needed to find some means of support for his original Meccan followers, and he also desired to wreak vengeance on the Quraish for not heeding his calls for

The consolidation of Muhammad's religion

conversion. Accordingly, he started leading his followers in raids on Quraish caravans traveling beyond Mecca. The Quraish endeavored to defend themselves, but after a few years Muhammad's band, fired by religious enthusiasm, succeeded in defeating them. In 630, after several desert battles, Muhammad entered Mecca in triumph. The Quraish thereupon submitted to the new faith and the Kabah was not only preserved but made the main shrine of Islam, as it remains today. With the taking of Mecca other tribes throughout Arabia in turn accepted the new faith. Thus, although Muhammad died in 632, he lived long enough to see the religion he had founded become a success.

The doctrines of Islam are straightforward. The word *islam* itself means submission, and the faith of Islam called for absolute submission to God. Although the Arabic name for the one God is Allah, it is mistaken to believe that Muslims worship a god like Zeus or Jupiter who is merely the first among many: Allah for Muslims means the Creator God Almighty— the same omnipotent deity worshiped by Christians and Jews. Instead of saying, then, that Muslims believe "there is no god but Allah," it is more correct to say they believe that "there is no divinity but God." In keeping with this, Muslims believe that Muhammad himself was God's last and greatest prophet, but not that he was God himself. In addition to strict monotheism Muhammad taught above all that men and women must surrender themselves entirely to God because divine judgment was imminent. Mortals must make a fundamental choice about whether to begin a new life of divine service: if they decide in favor of this, God will guide them to blessedness, but if they do not, God will turn away from them and they will become irredeemably wicked. On judgment day the pious will be granted eternal life in a fleshly paradise of delights, but the damned will be sent to a realm of eternal fire and torture. The practical steps the believer can take are found in the *Koran,* the compilation of the revelations purportedly sent by God to Muhammad, and hence the definitive Islamic scripture. These steps include thorough dedication to moral rectitude and compassion, and fidelity to set religious observances: i.e., a regimen of prayers and fasts, pilgrimage to Mecca, and frequent recitation of parts of the Koran.

The fact that much in the religion of Islam resembles Judaism and Christianity is not just coincidental; Muhammad was definitely influenced by the two earlier religions. (There were many Jews in Mecca and Medina; Christian thought was also known to Muhammad, although more indirectly.) Islam most resembles the two earlier religions in its strict monotheism, its stress on personal morality and compassion, and its reliance on written, revealed scripture. Muhammad proclaimed the Koran as the ultimate source of religious authority but accepted both the Old and New Testaments as divinely inspired. From Christianity Muhammad seems to have derived his doctrines of the last judgment, the resurrection of the body with subsequent rewards and punishments, and his belief in angels (he thought that God's first message to him had been sent by the angel Gabriel). But although Muhammad accepted Jesus Christ as one of the greatest of a long line of prophets, he did not believe in Christ's divinity and laid claim to no miracles himself other than the writing of the Koran. He also preached a religion without sacraments or priests. For Muslims every believer has direct responsibility for living the life of the faith without intermediaries; instead of priests there are only religious scholars who may comment on problems of Islamic faith and law. Muslims are expected to pray together in mosques, but there is nothing like a Muslim mass. The absence of clergy makes Islam more like Judaism, a similarity that is enhanced by Islamic stress on the inextricable connection between the religious and sociopolitical life of the divinely inspired community. But, unlike Judaism, Islam laid claim to a unique role in uniting the world as it started to spread far beyond the confines of Arabia.

The unification of Arabia after Muhammad: The caliphs

This move toward world influence began immediately upon Muhammad's death. Since he had made no provision for the future, and since the Arabs had no clear concept of political succession, it was unclear whether Muhammad's community would survive at all. But his closest followers, led by his father-in-law Abu-Bakr and a zealous early convert named Umar, quickly took the initiative by naming Abu-Bakr *caliph,* meaning "deputy of the Prophet." Thereafter, for about three hundred years, the caliph was to serve as the supreme religious and political leader of all Muslims. Immediately after becoming caliph Abu-Bakr began a military campaign to subdue various Arabian tribes that had followed Muhammad but were not willing to accept his successor's authority. In the course of this thoroughly successful military action Abu-Bakr's forces began to spill northward over the borders of Arabia. Probably to their surprise they found that they met minimal resistance from Byzantine and Persian forces.

Arab expansion and conquests

Abu-Bakr died two years after his accession but was succeeded as caliph by Umar, who continued to direct the Arabian invasions of the neighboring empires. In the following years triumph was virtually uninterrupted. In 636 the Arabs routed a Byzantine army in Syria and then quickly swept

The Archangel Gabriel Brings Revelation to Muhammad. A much later Persian conception.

Two Views of the Dome of the Rock, Jerusalem. According to Muslim tradition, Muhammad made a miraculous journey to Jerusalem before his death and left a footprint in a rock. The mosque that was erected over the site in the seventh century is, after the Kabah, Islam's second-holiest shrine.

over the entire area, occupying the leading cities of Antioch, Damascus, and Jerusalem; in 637 they destroyed the main army of the Persians and marched into the Persian capital of Ctesiphon. Once the Persian administrative center was taken, the Persian Empire offered scarcely any more resistance: by 651 the Arabian conquest of the entire Persian realm was complete. Since Byzantium was centered around distant Constantinople, the Arabs were not similarly able to stop its imperial heart from beating. But they did quickly manage to deprive the Byzantine Empire of Egypt by 646 and then swept west across North Africa. In 711 they crossed from there into Spain and quickly took almost all of that area too. Thus within less than a century Islam had conquered all of ancient Persia and much of the old Roman world.

How can we explain this prodigious expansion? The best approach is to see first what impelled the conquerors and then to see what circumstances helped to ease their way. Contrary to widespread belief the early spread of Islam was not achieved through a religious crusade. At first the Arabs were not at all interested in converting other peoples: instead, they hoped that conquered populations would not convert so that they could maintain their own identity as a community of rulers and tax-gatherers. But although their motives for expansion were not religious, religious enthusiasm played

Reasons for the spread of Islam

a crucial role in making the hitherto unruly Arabs take orders from the caliph and in instilling a sense that they were carrying out the will of God. What really moved the Arabs out of the desert was the search for richer territory and booty, and what kept them moving ever farther was the ease of acquiring new wealth as they progressed.

Weakness of enemies

Fortunately for the Arabs their inspiration by Islam came just at the right time in terms of the weakness of their enemies. The Byzantines and Persians had become so exhausted by their long wars that they could hardly rally for a new effort. Moreover, Persian and Byzantine local populations were hostile to the financial demands made by their bureaucratic empires; also, in the Byzantine lands of Syria and Egypt "heretical" Christians were at odds with the persecuting orthodoxy of Constantinople. Because the Arabs did not demand conversion and exacted fewer taxes than the Byzantines and Persians, they were often welcomed as preferable to the old rulers. One Christian writer in Syria went so far as to say "the God of vengeance delivered us out of the hands of the Romans [i.e., the Byzantine Empire] by means of the Arabs." For all these reasons Islam quickly spread over the vast extent of territory between Egypt and Iran, and has been rooted there ever since.

Division between Shiites and Sunnites

While the Arabs were extending their conquests they ran into their first serious political divisions. In 644 the Caliph Umar died; he was replaced by one Uthman, a weak ruler who had the added drawback for many of belonging to the Umayyad family, a wealthy clan from Mecca that had not at first accepted Muhammad's call. Those dissatisfied with Uthman rallied around the Prophet's cousin and son-in-law Ali, whose blood, background, and warrior spirit made him seem a more appropriate leader of the cause. When Uthman was murdered in 656 by mutineers, Ali's partisans raised him up as caliph. But Uthman's powerful family and supporters were unwilling to accept Ali. In subsequent disturbances Ali was murdered and Uthman's party emerged triumphant. In 661 a member of the Umayyad family took over as caliph and that house ruled Islam until 750. Even then, however, Ali's followers did not accept defeat. As time went on they hardened into a minority religious party known as *Shiites* (*Shi'a* is Arabic for party, or faction); this group insisted that only descendants of Ali could be caliphs or have any authority over the Muslim community. Those who stood instead for the actual historical development of the caliphate and became committed to its customs were called *Sunnites* (*Sunna* is Arabic for religious custom). The cleft between the two parties has been a lasting one in Islamic history. Often persecuted, Shiites developed great militancy and a deep sense of being the only true preservers of the faith. From time to time they were able to seize power in one or another area, but they never succeeded in converting the majority of Muslims. Today they rule in Iran and are very numerous in Iraq but comprise only about one-tenth of the worldwide population of Islam.

The triumph of the Umayyads in 661 began a more settled period in the history of the caliphate, lasting until 945. During that time there were two major governing orientations: that represented by the rule of the

THE EXPANSION OF ISLAM

At the death of Muhammad, 632 C.E.

After the conquests of the first four caliphs, 661 C.E.

After the conquests of the Umayyad caliphs, 750 C.E.

Outer limits of the Byzantine Empire

1000 miles

0

ATLANTIC OCEAN

SPAIN
Toledo
Cordova
Cadiz
Tangier
Barcelona
PYRENEES
Poitiers
FRANKS
BERBERS
Tunis
SARDINIA
CORSICA
LOMBARDS
Ravenna
Rome
SICILY
Tripoli
MEDITERRANEAN SEA
CRETE
AVARS
MAGYARS
Danube R.
BULGARIANS
Constantinople
BYZANTINE EMPIRE
BLACK SEA
CYPRUS
Alexandria
Cairo
EGYPT
Nile R.
Jerusalem
Damascus
Antioch
SYRIA
ARMENIA
CAUCASUS MTS.
CASPIAN SEA
ARAL SEA
PERSIA
Baghdad
Tigris R.
Euphrates R.
Indus R.
PERSIAN GULF
ARABIA
Medina
Mecca
RED SEA

Umayyads, and that represented by their successors, the Abbasids. The Umayyads centered their strength in the old Byzantine territories in Syria and continued to use local officials who were not Muslims for their administration. For these reasons the Umayyad caliphate appears to some extent like a Byzantine successor state. With their more Western orientation the Umayyads concentrated their energies on dominating the Mediterranean and conquering Constantinople. When their most massive attack on the Byzantine capital failed in 717, Umayyad strength was seriously weakened; it was only a matter of time before a new orientation would develop.

This was represented by the takeover of a new family, the Abbasids, in 750. Their rule may be said to have stressed Persian more than Byzantine elements. Characteristic of this change was a shift in capitals, for the second Abbasid caliph built his new capital of Baghdad in Iraq near the ruins of the old Persian capital and even appropriated stones from the ruins. The Abbasids developed their own Muslim administration and imitated Persian absolutism. Abbasid caliphs ruthlessly cut down their enemies, surrounded themselves with elaborate court ceremonies, and lavishly patronized sophisticated literature. This is the world described in the *Arabian Nights,* a collection of stories of dazzling Oriental splendor written in Baghdad under the Abbasids. The dominating presence in those stories, Harun al-Rashid, actually reigned as caliph from 786 to 809 and behaved as extravagantly as he was described, tossing coins in the streets, passing out sumptuous gifts to his favorites and severe punishments to his enemies. From a Western point of view the Abbasid caliphate was of significance not just in creating legends and literature but also because its Eastern orientation took much pressure off the Mediterranean. The Byzantine state, accordingly, was able to revive, and the Franks in the West began to develop some strength of their own. (The greatest Frankish ruler, Charlemagne, maintained diplomatic relations with the caliphate of Harun al-Rashid, who patronizingly sent the much poorer westerner a gift of an elephant.)

When Abbasid power began to decline in the tenth century there followed an extended period of decentralization. The major cause for growing Abbasid weakness was the gradual impoverishment of their primary economic base, the agricultural wealth of the Tigris–Euphrates basin. Their decline was further accelerated by the later Abbasids' practice of surrounding themselves with Turkish soldiers, who soon realized that they could take over actual power in the state. In 945 the Abbasid Empire fell apart when a Shiite tribe seized Baghdad. Thereafter the Abbasids became powerless figureheads until their caliphate was completely destroyed with the destruction of Baghdad by the Mongols in 1258. From 945 until the sixteenth century Islamic political life was marked by localism, with different petty rulers, most often Turkish, taking command in different areas. It was once thought that this decentralization also meant decay, but in fact Islamic civilization greatly prospered in the "middle period," above all from about 900 to about 1250, a time also when Islamic rule expanded into modern-day Turkey and India. Later, new Islamic empires developed, the leading one in the West being that of the Ottoman Turks, who controlled much of eastern Europe and western Asia from the fifteenth century until 1918. It is therefore entirely false to believe that Islamic history descended upon an ever-downward course sometime shortly after the reign of Harun al-Rashid.

For those who approach Islamic civilization with modern preconceptions, the greatest surprise is to realize that from the time of Muhammad until at least about 1500 Islamic culture and society was extraordinarily cosmopolitan and dynamic. Muhammad himself was not a desert Arab but a town-dweller and trader imbued with advanced ideals. Subsequently, Muslim culture became highly cosmopolitan for several reasons: it inherited the sophistication of Byzantium and Persia; it remained centered at the crossroads of long-distance trade between the Far East and West; and the prosperous town life in most Muslim territories counterbalanced agriculture. Because of the importance of trade there was much geographical mobility. Muhammad's teachings furthermore encouraged social mobility because the Koran stressed the equality of all Muslims. The result was that at the court of Baghdad, and later at those of the decentralized Muslim states, careers were open to those with talent. Since literacy was remarkably widespread—a rough estimate for around the year 1000 is 20 percent of all Muslim males—many could rise through education. Offices were seldom regarded as being hereditary and "new men" could arrive at the top by enterprise and skill. Muslims were also remarkably tolerant of other religions. As stated above, they rarely sought forced conversions, and they generally allowed a place within their own states for Jews and Christians, whom they accepted as "people of the book" because the Bible was seen as a precursor of the Koran. In keeping with this attitude of toleration an early caliph employed a Christian as his chief secretary, the Umayyads patronized a Christian who wrote poetry in Arabic, and Muslim Spain saw the greatest flowering of Jewish culture between ancient and modern times. The greatest fruit of this Jewish flowering was the work of Moses Maimonides (1135–1204), a profound religious thinker, sometimes called "the second Moses," who wrote both in Hebrew and Arabic.

There was one major exception to this rule of Muslim equalitarianism and tolerance: the treatment of women. Perhaps because social status was so fluid, successful men were extremely anxious to preserve and enhance their positions and their "honor." They could accomplish this by maintaining and/or expanding their worldly possessions, which category included women. For a man's females to be most "valuable" to his status, their inviolability had to be assured. The Koran allowed a man to marry four wives, so women were at a premium, and married ones were segregated from other males. A prominent man would also have a number of female servants and concubines, and he kept all these women in a part of his residence called the harem, where they were guarded by eunuchs, i.e., castrated men. Within these enclaves women vied with each other for preeminence and engaged in intrigues to advance the fortunes of their children. Although large harems could be kept only by the wealthy, the system was imitated as far as possible by all classes. Based on the principle that

The character of Islamic culture and society

Women in Islam

women were chattel, these practices did much to debase women and to emphasize attitudes of domination in sexual life. Male homosexual relations were tolerated in upper-class society, yet they too were based on patterns of domination, usually that of a powerful adult over an adolescent.

Islamic religious life: The ulama *and the* sufis

There were two major Islamic avenues for devotion to the particularly religious life. One was that of the *ulama,* learned men who came closest to being like priests. Their job was to study and offer advice on all aspects of religion and religious law. Not surprisingly they usually stood for tradition and rigorous maintenance of the faith; most often they exerted great influence on the conduct of public life. But complementary to them were the *sufis,* religious mystics who might be equated with Christian monks were it not for the fact that they were not committed to celibacy and seldom withdrew from the life of the community. Sufis stressed contemplation and ecstasy as the ulama stressed religious law; they had no common program and in practice behaved very differently. Some sufis were "whirling dervishes," so known in the West because of their dances; others were *faqirs,* associated in the West with snake-charming in marketplaces; and others were quiet, meditative men who practiced no exotic rites. Sufis were usually organized into "brotherhoods," which did much to convert outlying areas such as Africa and India. Throughout the Islamic world sufism provided a channel for the most intense religious impulses. The ability of the ulama and sufis to coexist is in itself a remarkable index of Islamic cultural pluralism.

Islamic philosophy

More remarkable still is the fact that these two groups often coexisted with representatives of yet another worldview, students and practitioners of philosophy and science. Islamic philosophers were actually called *faylasufs* in Arabic because they were dedicated to the cultivation of what the Greeks had called *philosophia.* Islamic philosophy was based on the study of earlier Greek thought, above all the Aristotelian and Neoplatonic strains. Around the time when the philosophical schools were closed in Athens by order of the Emperor Justinian, Greek philosophers migrated east, and the works of Aristotle and others were translated into Syriac, a Semitic dialect. From that point of transmission Greek philosophy gradually entered the life of Islam and became cultivated by the class of *faylasufs,* who believed that the universe is rational and that a philosophical approach to life was the highest God-given calling. The *faylasufs'* profound knowledge of Aristotle can be seen, for example, in the fact that Avicenna (d. 1037), one of the greatest of *faylasufs,* read practically all of Aristotle's works in the Far Eastern town of Bukhara before he reached the age of eighteen.

The problem of reconciling Greek ideas with Islamic religion

The most serious problem faced by the *faylasufs* was that of reconciling Greek philosophy with Islamic religion because they followed their Greek sources in believing—in opposition to Islamic doctrine—that the world is eternal and that there is no immortality for the individual soul. Different *faylasufs* reacted to this problem in different ways. Of the three greatest, Al-Farabi (d. 950), who lived mainly in Baghdad, was least concerned by it; he taught that an enlightened elite could philosophize without being distracted by the binding common beliefs of the masses. Even so, he never attacked these beliefs, considering them necessary to hold society together.

Unlike Al-Farabi, Avicenna, who was active farther east, taught a less rationalistic philosophy that came close in many points to sufi mysticism. (A later story held that Avicenna said of a sufi "all I know, he sees," while the sufi replied "all I see, he knows.") Finally, Averroës (1126–1198) of Cordova, in Spain, was a thoroughgoing Aristotelian who led two lives, one in private as an extreme rationalist and the other in public as a believer in the official faith, indeed even as an official censor. Averroës was the last really important Islamic philosopher: after him rationalism either blended into sufism, the direction pointed to by Avicenna, or became too constrained by religious orthodoxy to lead an independent existence. But in its heyday between about 850 and 1200 Islamic philosophy was far more advanced and sophisticated than anything found in either the Byzantine or Western Christian realms.

Avicenna and Averroës

Before their decline Islamic *faylasufs* were as distinguished in studying natural science as they were in philosophical speculation. Usually the same men were both philosophers and scientists because they could not make a living by commenting on Aristotle (there were no universities in which to teach) but could rise to positions of wealth and power by practicing astrology and medicine. Astrology sounds to us today less like science than superstition, but among the Muslims it was an "applied science" intimately related to accurate astronomical observation. After an Islamic astrologer carefully studied and foretold the courses of the heavenly bodies, he would endeavor to apply his knowledge to the course of human events, particu-

Islamic science; the practice of astrology

The Planetary Constellation of Andromeda as Visualized by the Muslims. This manuscript illumination executed in western Iran in 1009 C.E. shows clearly how Muslim culture reconceived Greek learning.

larly the fortunes of wealthy patrons. In order to account most simply for heavenly motions, some Muslims considered the possibilities that the earth rotates on its axis and revolves around the sun, but these theories were not accepted because they did not fit in with ancient preconceptions such as the assumption of circular planetary orbits. It was therefore not in these suggestions that Muslim astrologers later influenced the West, but rather in their extremely advanced observations and predictive tables that often went beyond the most careful work of the Greeks.

Islamic accomplishments in medicine were equally remarkable. *Faylasufs* serving as physicians appropriated the knowledge contained in the medical writings of the Hellenistic Age but were rarely content with that. Avicenna discovered the contagious nature of tuberculosis, described pleurisy and several varieties of nervous ailments, and pointed out that disease can be spread through contamination of water and soil. His chief medical writing, the *Canon of Medicine,* was accepted in Europe as authoritative until late in the seventeenth century. Avicenna's older contemporary, Rhazes (865–925), was the greatest clinical physician of the medieval world. His major achievement was the discovery of the difference between measles and smallpox. Other Islamic physicians discovered the value of cauterization and of styptic agents, diagnosed cancer of the stomach, prescribed antidotes for cases of poisoning, and made notable progress in treating diseases of the eyes. In addition, they recognized the infectious character of bubonic plague, pointing out that it could be transmitted by clothes. Finally, the Muslims excelled over all other medieval peoples in the organization of hospitals and in the control of medical practice. There were at least thirty-four great hospitals located in the principal cities of Persia, Syria, and Egypt, which appear to have been organized in a strikingly modern fashion. Each had wards for particular cases, a dispensary, and a library. The chief physicians and surgeons lectured to the students and graduates, examined them, and issued licenses to practice. Even the owners of leeches, who in most cases were also barbers, had to submit them for inspection at regular intervals.

Other great Islamic scientific achievements were in optics, chemistry, and mathematics. Islamic physicists founded the science of optics and drew a number of significant conclusions regarding the theory of magnifying lenses and the velocity, transmission, and refraction of light. Islamic chemistry was an outgrowth of alchemy, an invention of the Hellenistic Greeks, the system of belief that was based upon the principle that all metals were the same in essence, and that baser metals could therefore be transmuted into gold if only the right instrument, the philosopher's stone, could be found. But the efforts of scientists in this field were by no means confined to this fruitless quest; some even denied the whole theory of transmutation of metals. As a result of experiments by Muslim scientists, various new substances and compounds were discovered, among them carbonate of soda, alum, borax, nitrate of silver, saltpeter, and nitric and sulphuric acids. In addition, Islamic scientists were the first to describe the chemical processes of distillation, filtration, and sublimation. In mathematics Islam's greatest accomplishment was to unite the geometry of the Greeks with the number science of the Hindus. Borrowing what westerners know as "Arabic numerals," including the zero, from the Hindus, Islamic mathematicians were able to develop an arithmetic based on the decimal system and also make advances in algebra (itself an Arabic word). Building upon Greek geometry with reference to heavenly motions, they made great progress in spherical trigonometry. Thus they brought together and advanced all the areas of mathematical knowledge that would later be further developed in the Christian West.

In addition to its philosophers and scientists Islam had its poets too. The primitive Arabs themselves had excelled in writing poetry, and literary accomplishment became recognized as a way to distinguish oneself at court. Probably the greatest of Islamic poets were the Persians (who wrote in their own language), the best known of whom in the West is Umar Khayyam (d. 1123) because his *Rubaiyat* was turned into a popular English poem by the Victorian Edward Fitzgerald. Although Fitzgerald's translation distorts much, Umar's hedonism ("a jug of wine, a loaf of bread—and thou") shows us that all Muslims were by no means dour puritans. Actually Umar's poetry was excelled by the works of Sadi (1193–1292) and Hafiz (d. 1389). And far from Persia lush poetry was cultivated as well in the courts of Muslim Spain. This poetry too was by no means inhibited, as can be seen from lines like "such was my kissing, such my sucking of his mouth/that he was almost made toothless."

In their artistic endeavors Muslims were highly eclectic. Their main source of inspiration came from the art of Byzantium and Persia. The former contributed many of the structural features of Islamic architecture, es-

Islamic poets

The Court of the Lions in the Alhambra, Granada, Spain. The palace-fortress of the Alhambra is one of the finest monuments of the Islamic architectural style. Notable are the graceful columns, the horseshoe arches, and the delicate tracery in stone that surmounts the arches.

pecially the dome, the column, and the arch. Persian influence was probably responsible for the intricate, nonnaturalistic designs that were used as decorative motifs in practically all of the arts. From both Persia and Byzantium came the tendency to subordinate form to rich and sensuous color. Architecture was the most important of the Islamic arts; the development of both painting and sculpture was inhibited by religious prejudice against representation of the human form. By no means all of the examples of this architecture were mosques; many were palaces, schools, libraries, private dwellings, and hospitals. Indeed, Islamic architecture had a much more decidedly secular character than any in medieval Europe. Among its principal elements were bulbous domes, minarets, horseshoe arches, and twisted columns, together with the use of tracery in stone, alternating stripes of black and white, mosaics, and Arabic script as decorative devices. As in the Byzantine style, comparatively little attention was given to exterior ornamentation. The so-called minor arts of the Muslims included the weaving of gorgeous pile carpets and rugs, magnificent leather tooling, and the making of brocaded silks and tapestries, inlaid metalwork, enameled glassware, and painted pottery. Most of the products of these arts were embellished with complicated patterns of interlacing geometric designs, plants and fruits and flowers, Arabic script, and fantastic animal figures. In general, art laid particular emphasis on pure visual design. Separated from any role in religious teaching, it became highly abstract and nonrepresentational. For these reasons Islamic art often seems more secular and "modern" than any other art of premodern times.

The economic life of the Islamic world varied greatly according to time and place, but underdevelopment was certainly not one of its primary characteristics. On the contrary, in the central areas of Islamic civilization from

Interior of the Great Mosque at Cordova, Spain. This splendid specimen of Moorish architecture gives an excellent view of the cusped arches and alternating stripes of black and white so commonly used by Islamic architects.

the first Arab conquests until about the fourteenth century mercantile life was extraordinarily advanced. The principal reason for this was that the Arabs inherited in Syria and Persia an area that was already marked by an enterprising urban culture and that was at the crossroads of the world, lying athwart the major trade routes between Africa, Europe, India, and China. Islamic traders and entrepreneurs built venturesomely on these earlier foundations. Muslim merchants penetrated into southern Russia and even into the equatorial regions of Africa, while caravans of thousands of camels traveled to the gates of India and China. (The Muslims used camels as pack animals instead of building roads and drawing wheeled carts.) Ships from Islam established new routes across the Indian Ocean, the Persian Gulf, and the Caspian Sea. For periods of time Islamic ships also dominated parts of the Mediterranean. Indeed, one reason for subsequent Islamic decline was that the Western Christians took hold of the Mediterranean in the eleventh and twelfth centuries and wrested control of the Indian Ocean in the sixteenth century.

The great Islamic expansion of commerce would scarcely have been possible without a corresponding development of industry. It was the ability of the people of one region to turn their natural resources into finished products for sale to other regions that provided a basis for a large part of the trade. Nearly every one of the great cities specialized in some particular variety of manufactures. Mosul, in Syria, was a center of the manufacture of cotton cloth; Baghdad specialized in glassware, jewelry, pottery, and silks; Damascus was famous for its fine steel and for its "damask" or woven figured silk; Morocco was noted for the manufacture of leather; and Toledo, in Spain, for its excellent swords. The products of these cities did not exhaust the list of manufactures. Drugs, perfumes, carpets, tapestries, brocades, woolens, satins, metal products, and a host of others were turned out by the craftsmen of many cities. From the Chinese the Muslims learned the art of papermaking, and the products of that industry were in great demand, not only within the empire itself but in Europe as well.

In all the areas we have reviewed Islamic civilization so overshadowed that of the Christian West until about the twelfth century that there can be no comparison. When the West did move forward it was able to do so partly because of what it learned from Islam. In the economic sphere westerners profited from absorbing many accomplishments of Islamic technology, such as irrigation techniques, the raising of new crops, papermaking, and the distillation of alcohol. The extent of our debt to Islamic economic influence is well mirrored in the large number of common English words that were originally of Arabic or Persian origin. Among these are traffic, tariff, magazine, alcohol, muslin, orange, lemon, alfalfa, saffron, sugar, syrup, and musk. (Our word admiral also comes from the Arabic—in this case deriving from the title of emir.)

The West was as much indebted to Islam in intellectual and scientific as in economic life. In those areas, too, borrowed words tell some of the story: algebra, cipher, zero, nadir, amalgam, alembic, alchemy, alkali, soda, almanac, and names of many stars such as Aldebaran and Betelgeuse. Is-

The economic development of the Islamic world: (1) commerce

(2) industry

Islamic economic influence on the West

Intellectual and scientific contributions

The Great Mosque, Qayrawan, Tunisia. This ninth-century minaret, from which the criers call the faithful to prayer, is a leading monument of the North African Islamic architectural style.

lamic civilization both preserved and expanded Greek philosophical and scientific knowledge when such knowledge was almost entirely forgotten in the West. All the important Greek scientific works surviving from ancient times were translated into Arabic, and most of these in turn were translated in the medieval West from Arabic into Latin. Above all, the preservation and interpretation of the works of Aristotle was one of Islam's most enduring accomplishments. Not only was Aristotle first reacquired in the West by means of the Arabic translations, but Aristotle was interpreted with Islamic help, above all that of Averroës, whose prestige was so great that he was simply called "the Commentator" by medieval Western writers. Of course Arabic numerals, too, rank as a tremendously important intellectual legacy, as anyone will discover by trying to balance a checkbook with Roman ones.

Aside from all these specific contributions, the civilization of Islam probably had its greatest influence on the West merely by standing as a powerful rival and spur to the imagination. Byzantine civilization was at once too closely related to the Christian West and too weak to serve this function. Westerners usually, for right or wrong, looked down on the Byzantine Greeks, but they more often respected and feared the Muslims. And right they were as well, for Islamic civilization at its zenith (to use another Arabic word) was surely one of the world's greatest. Though loosely organized, it united peoples as diverse as Arabs, Persians, Turks, various African tribes, and Hindus by means of a great religion and common institutions. Unity within multiplicity was an Islamic hallmark, which created both a splendid, diverse society and a splendid legacy of original discoveries and achievements.

3. WESTERN CHRISTIAN CIVILIZATION IN THE EARLY MIDDLE AGES

The shaping of a cultural unity in the early-medieval West

Western Europeans in the Early Middle Ages (the period between about 600 and 1050) were so backward in comparison to their Byzantine and Islamic neighbors that a tenth-century Arabic geographer could write of them that "they have large bodies, gross natures, harsh manners, and dull intellects . . . those who live farthest north are particularly stupid, gross, and brutish." Material conditions throughout this period were so primitive that one can almost speak of five centuries of camping-out. Yet new and promising patterns were definitely taking shape. Above all, a new center of civilization was emerging in the North Atlantic regions. Around 800 the Frankish monarchy, based in agriculturally rich northwestern Europe, managed to create a Western European empire in alliance with the Western Christian Church. Although this empire did not last long, it still managed to hew out a new Western cultural unity that was to be an important building block for the future.

Once the Eastern Romans under Justinian had destroyed the Ostrogothic and Vandal kingdoms in Italy and Africa, and the Arabs had eliminated the Visigothic kingdom in Spain, the Frankish rulers in Gaul remained as the major surviving barbarian power in Western Europe. But it took about two centuries before they began to exercise their full hegemony. The founder of the Frankish state was the brutal and wily chieftain Clovis, who conquered most of modern-day France and Belgium around 500 and cleverly converted to Western Catholic Christianity, the religion of the local bishops and indigenous population. Clovis founded the Merovingian dynasty (so called from Merovech, the founder of the family to which he belonged). He did not, however, pass on a united realm but followed the typical barbarian custom of dividing up his kingdom among his sons. More or less without interruption for the next two hundred years sons fought sons for a larger share of the Merovingian inheritance. Toward the end of that period the line also began to degenerate, and numerous so-called do-nothing kings left their government and fighting to their chief ministers, known as "mayors of the palace." Throughout this era, one of the darkest in the recorded history of Europe, trade contracted, towns declined, literacy was almost forgotten, and violence was endemic. Minimal agricultural self-sufficiency coexisted with the rule of the battle-axe.

*The kingdom of the Franks:
The Merovingian period*

Largely unnoticed, however, some hope for the future was coalescing around the institutions of the Roman papacy and Benedictine monasticism. The architect of a new Western European religious policy that was based on an alliance between these two institutions was Pope Gregory I (590–604),* known as St. Gregory the Great. Until his time the Roman popes were generally subordinate to the emperors in Constantinople and to the greater religious prestige of the Christian East, but Gregory sought to counteract this situation by creating a more autonomous Western-oriented Latin Church. This he tried to do in many ways. As a theologian—the fourth great "Latin father" of the Church—he built upon the work of his three predecessors, Jerome, Ambrose, and especially Augustine, in articulating a theology that had its own distinct characteristics. Among these were emphasis on the idea of penance and the concept of purgatory as a place for purification before admission into heaven. (Western belief in purgatory was thereafter to become one of the major differences in the dogmas of the Eastern and Western Churches.) In addition to his theological work, Gregory pioneered in the writing of a simplified unadorned Latin prose that corresponded to the actual spoken language of his contemporaries, and presided over the creation of a powerful Latin liturgy. If Gregory did not actually invent the "Gregorian chant," it was under his impetus that this new plainsong—later a central part of the Roman Catholic ritual—developed. All of these innovations helped to make the Christian West religiously and culturally more independent of the Greek-speaking East than it had ever been before.

Gregory the Great was as much a statesman as he was a theologian and

Pope Gregory the Great. In this tenth-century German ivory panel the pope is receiving inspiration from the Holy Spirit in the form of a dove.

---

* Here, and throughout, the dates following a pope's name refer to the dates of his pontificate.

shaper of Latin. Within Italy he assured the physical survival of the papacy in the face of the barbarian Lombard threat of his day by clever diplomacy and expert management of papal landed estates. He also began to reemphasize earlier claims of papal primacy, especially over Western bishops, that were in danger of being forgotten. Above all, he patronized the order of Benedictine monks and used them to help evangelize new Western territories. Gregory himself had been a Benedictine—perhaps the first Benedictine monk to become pope—and he wrote the standard life of St. Benedict. Because the Benedictine order was still very young and the times were turbulent, Gregory's patronage helped the order to survive and later to become for centuries the only monastic order in the West. In return the pope could profit from using the Benedictines to carry out special projects. The most significant of these was the conversion of Anglo-Saxon England to Christianity. This was a long-term project that took about a century to complete, but its great result was that it left a Christian outpost to the far northwest that was thoroughly loyal to the papacy and that would soon help to bring together the papacy and the Frankish state. Gregory the Great himself did not live to see that union, but it was his policy of invigorating the Western Church that most helped to bring it about.

Around 700, when the Benedictines were completing their conversion of England, the outlook for Frankish Gaul was becoming somewhat brighter. The most profound reason for this was that the long, troubled period of transition between the ancient and medieval worlds was finally coming to an end. The ancient Roman civilization of cities and Mediterranean trade was in its last gasps in Gaul in the time after Clovis. Then, when the Arabs conquered the southern Mediterranean shore and took to the sea in the seventh century, northwestern Europe was finally thrown back upon itself and forced to look away from the Mediterranean. In fact the lands of the north—modern-day northern France, the Low Countries, Germany, and England—were extremely fertile: with adequate farming implements they could yield great natural wealth. Given the proper circumstances, a new power could emerge in the north to make the most of a new pattern of life based predominantly on agrarianism instead of urban commerce and Mediterranean trade. Around 700 that is exactly what happened in Merovingian Gaul.

The proper circumstances were the triumph of a succession of able rulers and their alliance with the Church. In 687 an energetic Merovingian mayor of the palace, Pepin of Heristal, managed to unite all the Frankish lands under his rule and build a new power base for his own family in the region of Belgium and the Rhine. He was succeeded by his aggressive son, Charles Martel ("the Hammer"), who is sometimes considered a second founder of the Frankish state. Charles's claim to this title is twofold. First, in 732 he turned back a Muslim force from Spain at the Battle of Tours, some 150 miles from Paris. Although the Muslim contingent was not a real army but merely a marauding band, the incursion was the high-water mark of their progress toward the northwest and Charles's victory won him great prestige. Equally important, around the end of his reign Charles began to develop an alliance with the Church, particularly with the Benedictines of England. Having finished most of their conversion work on their island, the Benedictines, under their idealistic leader St. Boniface, were moving across the English Channel in an attempt to convert central Germany. Charles Martel realized that he and they had common interests, for after he had guarded his southern flank against the Muslims he was seeking to direct Frankish expansion eastward in the direction of Germany. Missionary work and Frankish expansion could go hand in hand, so Charles offered St. Boniface and his Benedictines material aid in return for their support of his territorial aims.

Once allied with the Franks, St. Boniface provided further service in the next reign in helping to contribute to one of the most momentous events in Western history. Charles Martel had never assumed the royal title, but his son, Pepin the Short, wished to take it. Even though Pepin and not the reigning "do-nothing king" was the real power, Pepin needed the prestige of the Church for supporting a change in dynasties. Fortunately for him the times were highly propitious for obtaining Church support. St. Boniface supported Pepin because the young ruler continued his father's policy of collaborating with the Benedictines in Germany. And Boniface had great influence in Rome because the Anglo-Saxon Benedictines had remained in close touch with the papacy since the time of Gregory the Great.

Solidification of the alliance in the time of Pepin the Short

The papacy was now fully prepared to cast its own lots with a strong Frankish ruler because it was in the midst of a bitter fight with the Byzantine emperors over Iconoclasm. The Byzantines until then had offered papal territories in Italy some protection against the Lombards, but the increasingly powerful Franks were now fully able to take over that role. The papacy accordingly made an epochal about-face, turning once and for all to the West. In 750 the pope encouraged Pepin to depose the Merovingian figurehead, and in 751 St. Boniface, acting as papal emissary, anointed Pepin as a divinely sanctioned king. Thus the Frankish monarchy attained a spiritual mandate and was fully integrated into the papal-Benedictine orbit. Shortly afterward Pepin paid his debt to the pope by conquering the Lombards in Italy. The West was now achieving its own unity based on the Frankish state and the Latin Church, not coincidentally just at the time when the Abbasid caliphate was being founded in the East and the Byzantines were going their own fully Greek way.

The "about-face" of the papacy

The ultimate consolidation of the new pattern took place in the reign of Pepin's son, Carolus Magnus or Charlemagne (768–814), from whom the new dynasty takes its name of "Carolingian." Without question Charlemagne ranks as one of the most important rulers of the whole medieval period. Had it been possible to ask him what his greatest accomplishment was, he almost certainly would have replied that it lay in greatly increasing the Frankish realm. Except for the English, there was scarcely a people of Western Europe against whom he did not fight. Most of his campaigns were successful; he annexed the greater part of central Europe and northern and central Italy to the Frankish domain. To rule this vast area he bestowed all the powers of local government upon his own appointees, called

Charlemagne. A silver penny struck between 804 and 814 in Mainz (as indicated by the letter M at the bottom) showing Charlemagne in a highly stylized fashion as emperor with Roman military cloak and laurel. The inscription reads KAROLVS IMP AVG (Charles, Emperor, Augustus). See p. 180, above, for the variety of late-Roman coin portraiture that must have served as the Carolingian minter's model.

counts, and tried to remain in control of them by sending representatives of the court to observe them. Among the counts' many duties were the administration of justice and the raising of armies. Although Charlemagne's system in practice was far from perfect, it led to the best government that Europe had seen since the Romans. Because of the military triumphs and internal peace of his reign, Charlemagne was long remembered and revered as a Western European folk hero.

Primarily to aid his territorial expansion and help administer his realm Charlemagne presided over a revival of learning known as the "Carolingian Renaissance." Charlemagne extended his rule into Germany in the name of Christianity, but in order to proselytize he needed educated monks and priests. More than that, in order to administer his far-flung territories he needed at least a few people who could read and write. Amazing as it may seem to us, at first hardly any people in his entire realm were literate, so thoroughly had the rudiments of learning been forgotten since the decay of Roman city life. Only in Anglo-Saxon England had literacy been cultivated by the Benedictine monks. The reason for this was that the Anglo-Saxons spoke a form of German but the monks needed to learn Latin in order to say their offices and study the Bible. Since they knew no Latin to begin with they had to go about learning it by a very self-conscious program of studies. The greatest Anglo-Saxon Benedictine scholar before Charlemagne's time was the Venerable Bede (d. 735), whose *History of the English Church and People* written in Latin, was one of the best historical writings of the early-medieval period and can still be read with pleasure. When Charlemagne came to the throne he invited the Anglo-Saxon Benedictine Alcuin—a student of one of Bede's students—to direct a revival of studies on the Continent. With Charlemagne's active support Alcuin helped establish new schools to teach reading, directed the copying and correcting of important Latin works, including many Roman classics, and inspired the formulation of a new clear handwriting that is the ancestor of

Carolingian Handwriting. Even the untrained reader has little difficulty in reading this excerpt from a Carolingian manuscript.

THE EMPIRE OF CHARLEMAGNE 814 C.E.

our modern "Roman" print. These were the greatest achievements of the Carolingian Renaissance, which stressed practicality rather than original literary or intellectual endeavors. Thoroughly unpretentious as they were, they established a bridgehead for literacy on the Continent which thereafter would never be completely lost. They also helped to preserve Latin literature, and they made the Latin language the language of state and diplomacy for all of Western Europe, as it remained until comparatively recent times.

The climax of Charlemagne's career came in the year 800 when he was crowned emperor on Christmas Day in Rome by the pope. Historians continue to debate whether this was Charlemagne's or the pope's idea, but there is no doubt that the pope did not gain any immediate power from it. Once the Franks ruled Italy they came to dominate the papacy, and indeed the whole Church, to such a degree that by 800 the pope was very close to being Charlemagne's puppet. Charlemagne did not gain any actual new power by taking the imperial title either, but the significance of the event is nonetheless great. Up until 800 the only emperor ruled in Constantinople

Charlemagne's coronation as emperor

and could lay claim to being the direct heir of Augustus. Although the Byzantines had lost most of their interest in the West, they still continued to regard it vaguely as an outlying province and were actively opposed to any westerner calling himself emperor. Charlemagne's assumption of the title was virtually a declaration of Western self-confidence and independence. Since Charlemagne's vast realm was fully as large as that of the Byzantines, had great reserves of agricultural wealth, and was defining its own culture based on Western Christianity and the Latin linguistic tradition, the claim to empire was largely justified. More than that, it was never forgotten. Both for its symbolism and for its contribution toward giving westerners a sense of unity and purpose it was a major landmark on the road to the making of a great Western Europe.

Although the claim to empire was bold and memorable, Charlemagne's actual empire disintegrated quickly after his death for many reasons. The simplest was that hardly any of his successors were as competent and decisive as he was. In order to rule an empire in those still extremely primitive times, one had to have enormous reserves of strength and energy—one had to travel on horseback over enormous distances, fight and win battles at the head of unruly armies, and know how to delegate power to others yet guard against its abuse. Unfortunately for Western Europe few of Charlemagne's heirs had such combinations of energy and talent. To make matters worse, Charlemagne's sole surviving son, Louis the Pious, who inherited the Frankish realm intact, divided his inheritance among his own three sons, thereby bringing civil war back to Frankish Europe. And to make matters worst of all, new waves of invasions began just as Charlemagne's grandsons and great-grandsons started fighting each other: from the north came the Scandinavian Vikings; from the east came the Asiatic Magyars (or Hungarians); and from the south came new attacks by marauding Muslims, attacking now from the sea. Under these pressures the Carolingian Empire completely fell apart and a new political map of Europe was drawn in the tenth century.

Viking Dragon Head. Wooden carvings like these on the stemposts of Viking ships were calculated to inspire terror.

As the Carolingian period was crucial for marking the beginnings of a common North Atlantic, Western European civilization, so the tenth century was crucial for marking the beginnings of the major modern European political entities. England, which never had been part of Charlemagne's empire, and which hitherto had been divided among smaller warring Anglo-Saxon states, became unified in the late ninth and the tenth century owing to the work of King Alfred the Great (871–899) and his direct successors. Alfred and his heirs reorganized the army, infused new vigor into local government, and codified the English laws. In addition, Alfred founded schools and fostered an interest in Anglo-Saxon writing and other elements of a national culture.

England in the time of Alfred the Great

Political conditions in France and Germany

Across the Channel, France (now the name for the main part of Roman Gaul because it was the original seat of the Frankish monarchy) was devastated by the invasions of Vikings, who had sailed up the French rivers. For that reason France broke up into small principalities rather than developing a strong national monarchy on the pattern of England. Nonetheless there

Byzantine Gold Cup, 6th–9th cent. The relief shows Constantinople personified as a queen holding the sceptre of imperial rule (MMA)

Merovingian Fibule or Brooch, 7th cent. A fabulous gold-plated animal set with garnets and colored paste. (MMA)

Sienese Madonna and Child, Byzantine School, 13th cent. The painters of Siena in Italy imitated the opulent style of Byzantine art. Their madonnas were not earthly mothers, but celestial queens reigning in dignified splendor. (National Gallery)

Christ and the Apostles. A German manuscript illumination from the tenth century showing Christ appointing the apostles to become "princes over all the earth." The leader of the apostles is Peter, as shown by the letters "PETRVS" on the staff. (Koninklijke Bibliotheek)

Romanesque Annunciation. An angel arrives to tell the Virgin Mary, shown here spinning, that she will bear the Christ child. In between is a dove representing the Holy Spirit. This twelfth-century manuscript illumination bears many typically non-naturalistic features of Romanesque art, such as Mary's contorted position (meant to show that she is being taken by surprise), her awkward seating on her three-legged throne, and the spilling of the angel's wings over the border. (Badische Landesbibliothek)

was a king in France, who, however weak, was recognized as the ruler of the western part of Charlemagne's former territories. Directly to the east, the kings of Germany were the strongest Continental monarchs of the tenth century, ruling over an essentially united realm. In addition to Germany, their lands encompassed most of the Low Countries and a good part of modern eastern France.

The most important German ruler of the period was Otto the Great. He became king in 936, resoundingly defeated the Hungarians in 955—thereby relieving Germany of its greatest foreign threat—and took the title of emperor in Rome in 962. By this last act Otto strengthened his claim to being the greatest Continental monarch since Charlemagne. Otto and his successors, who continued to call themselves emperors, tried to rule over Italy but barely succeeded in doing so. Instead, Italy in the tenth century saw the greatest Western European development of urban life, a pattern on which the Italians would subsequently build.

Otto the Great of Germany

Although Italy did develop some city life in the tenth century, this was by no means typical of the early-medieval period in Western Europe as a whole. Quite to the contrary, from the eighth to the eleventh century the European economy was based almost entirely on agriculture and very limited local trade. Roads deteriorated and barter widely replaced the use of money. Whatever cities survived from Roman days were usually empty shells that served at most as administrative centers for bishops and fortified places in case of common danger. The main economic unit throughout the period was the self-supporting, large landed estate, usually owned by kings, warrior aristocrats, or large-scale monasteries. Although the northern European soil was rich, farming tools in most places were still too primitive to bring in a fully adequate return on the enormous investment of effort expended by the laboring masses. Agricultural yields in all but the most fertile Carolingian heartlands (and often even in them) were pitifully low, and Europeans, except the rulers and the higher clergy, lived on the edge of subsistence. It is true that some increase in agricultural income had underpinned the Carolingian successes, and some progress in farming might have continued had the peace of Charlemagne's reign endured. But the subsequent invasions of the ninth and tenth centuries set agricultural life back and new beginnings would have to be made in the years thereafter.

The economy of Western Europe in the Early Middle Ages

Irish Art. The opening of a gospel page that shows the Irish style at its most surrealistic.

Given the low level of early-medieval economic life, it is not surprising that the age was not a prosperous time for learning or the arts: with scarcely enough wealth to keep most people alive, there was not much to support schools or major artistic projects. Throughout the period, even in the best of years, learning was a privilege for the few: the masses received no formal education, and even most members of the secular aristocracy were illiterate. Learning also consisted mostly of memorization, without regard for criticism or refutation. We have seen that there was some revival of learning under Charlemagne that may be called a "renaissance" but that it did not issue into any real intellectual creativity. Its major accomplishment was the founding of enough schools to educate the clergy in the rudiments of reading and the training of enough monastic scribes to recopy

The low level of intellectual life

Carolingian Art. The fountain of life: an illuminated manuscript page from Gottschalk's Evangeliary (book with four gospels), dating from 781.

and preserve some major works of Roman literature. Even this accomplishment was jeopardized in the period of invasions that accompanied the fall of the Carolingian Empire. Fortunately just enough schools and manuscripts survived to become the basis for another—far greater—revival of learning that began in the eleventh and twelfth centuries.

Literature in the Early Middle Ages

In the realm of literature the Early Middle Ages had an extremely meager production. This was because few Christians could write and those who could were usually monks and priests, who were not supposed to engage in purely literary endeavors. There was some impressive writing of history in Latin, most notably that of Bede and Charlemagne's eloquent biographer, Einhard, but otherwise Latin composition was little cultivated. Toward the close of the period, however, the vernacular languages, which were either Germanic or based on different regional dialects of Latin (the "Romance" languages, so-called because they were based on "Roman" speech), began to be employed for crude poetic expression, usually first by oral transmission.

Beowulf

The best-known example of this literature in the vernacular is the Anglo-Saxon epic poem *Beowulf*. First put into written form about the eighth century, this poem incorporates ancient legends of the Germanic peoples of northwestern Europe. It is a story of fighting and seafaring and of heroic adventure against deadly dragons and the forces of nature. The background of the epic is pre-Christian, but the author of the work introduced into it some qualities of Christian idealism. *Beowulf* is important not only as one of the earliest specimens of Anglo-Saxon or Old English poetry but also for the picture it gives of the society of the English and their ancestors in the Early Middle Ages.

The artistic history of the Early Middle Ages was a story of isolated and interrupted accomplishments because artistic life relied most of all on brief moments of local peace or royal patronage. The earliest enduring monuments of early-medieval art were those created by monks in Ireland—which had its own unique culture—between the sixth and the eighth centuries. Above all in manuscript illumination (i.e., painted illustrations) the Irish monks developed a thoroughly anticlassical and almost surrealistic style, whose origins are most difficult to account for. The greatest surviving product from this school is the stunning *Book of Kells,* an illuminated Gospel book that has been called "the most sophisticated work of decorative art in the history of painting." The Irish school declined without subsequent influence and was followed by artistic products of the Carolingian Renaissance.

For much of its inspiration, the art of Charlemagne's period returned to classical models, yet it also retained some of the spontaneous vitality of barbarian decoration. When Charlemagne's empire declined and disintegrated there was a corresponding decline and then interruption in the history of Western art. In the tenth century, however, new regional schools emerged.

Book of Kells

Regional variations in early-medieval art

Left: *Utrecht Psalter.* This Carolingian manuscript of the Psalms from about 820 later provided the basis for the "nervous expressiveness" of the tenth-century English regional school. Right: *Bamberg Apocalypse.* In this manuscript illumination from about 1000 C.E. the fall of Babylon in the Book of Revelation (18:1–20) is displayed by depicting the city upside down. This is an example of the grave regional German style.

The greatest of these were the English, which emphasized restless fluency in manuscript illumination; the German, which was more grave but still managed to communicate extreme religious ecstasy; and the northern Spanish, which, though Christian, created a rather strange and independent style mostly influenced by the decorative style of Islamic art.

Undoubtedly, there is no single, obvious terminal date for early-medieval history as a whole. The date 1000 is sometimes given because it is a convenient round number, but even as late as 1050 Europe had not changed on the surface very much from the way it had been since the end of the Carolingian period. Indeed, looking at Europe as late as 1050 it would at first seem that not much progress had been made over the entire course of the early-medieval centuries. Except for Germany, there was hardly any centralized government, for by 1050 the Anglo-Saxon English state created by King Alfred and his successors was falling apart. Throughout Europe, all but the most privileged individuals continued to live on the brink of starvation, and cultural attainments were minimal and sparse. But actually much had been accomplished. By shifting its main weight to the Atlantic northwest, European civilization became centered in lands that would soon harvest great agricultural wealth. By preserving some of the traditions developed by Gregory the Great, St. Boniface, Pepin, and Charlemagne, European civilization had also developed an enduring sense of cultural unity based on Western Christianity and the Latin inheritance. And in the tenth century the beginnings of the future European kingdoms and city-states started to coalesce. Western European civilization was thus for the first time becoming autonomous and distinctive. From then on it would become a leading force in the history of the world.

A distinct Western European civilization evident in 1050

See color plates facing page 268

SELECTED READINGS

• *Items so designated are available in paperback editions.*

BYZANTINE CIVILIZATION

Beckwith, John, *The Art of Constantinople,* 2nd ed., London, 1968. A standard account.
• Diehl, Charles, *Byzantium: Greatness and Decline,* New Brunswick, N.J., 1957. Evaluates strengths and weaknesses of Byzantine civilization.
Hussey, Joan M., *The Byzantine World,* London, 1957. Half-narrative, half-topical; a useful short introduction.
• Krautheimer, R., *Early Christian and Byzantine Architecture,* Baltimore, 1970.
• Magoulias, H. J., *Byzantine Christianity: Emperor, Church and the West,* Chicago, 1970. Limited to the three themes mentioned in the title.
• Ostrogorsky, George, *History of the Byzantine State,* New Brunswick, N.J., 1957. The most authoritative longer account of political developments; very scholarly.
• Pelikan, Jaroslav, *The Christian Tradition; Vol. II: The Spirit of Eastern Christendom,* Chicago, 1974. An advanced treatment of religious doctrines.

Runciman, Steven, *Byzantine Civilization,* New York, 1933. A topical approach; well written but in parts outdated.
• ———, *Byzantine Style and Civilization,* Baltimore, 1975. A fine study of Byzantine art.
• Vasiliev, A. A., *History of the Byzantine Empire,* 2 vols., Madison, Wis., 1928. Supplements Ostrogorsky; valuable for its detail on social and intellectual as well as political history.
Vryonis, Speros, *Byzantium and Europe,* New York, 1967. Noteworthy for its illustrations.

ISLAMIC CIVILIZATION

Arnold, Thomas, and A. Guillaume, *The Legacy of Islam,* New York, 1931.
Gibb, H. A. R., *Arabic Literature: An Introduction,* 2nd ed., Oxford, 1963. An excellent survey.
• ———, *Mohammedanism: An Historical Survey,* 2nd ed., Oxford, 1953. The best brief interpretation of Islamic religion.
• Goitein, S. D., *Jews and Arabs, Their Contacts through the Ages,* New York, 1955.
Grube, E. J., *The World of Islam,* New York, 1966.
• Hodgson, M., *The Venture of Islam,* 3 vols., Chicago, 1974. A masterwork. One of the greatest works of history written by a modern American. Advanced and sometimes difficult, but always rewarding.
Kennedy, Hugh, *The Early Abbasid Caliphate: A Political History,* Totowa, N.J., 1981.
• ———, *The Prophet and the Age of the Caliphates,* London, 1986. A lucid introduction to the political history of Islam from the sixth through the eleventh centuries.
• Lewis, Bernard, *The Arabs in History,* rev. ed., New York, 1966. The best short survey of the conquests and political fortunes of the Arabs.
Lombard, Maurice, *The Golden Age of Islam,* New York, 1975.
Peters, F. E., *Aristotle and the Arabs,* New York, 1968. A well-written and engaging account.
• Watt, W. Montgomery, *Islamic Philosophy and Theology,* 2nd ed., Edinburgh, 1988.
• ———, *Muhammad: Prophet and Statesman,* Oxford, 1961. A good short biography.
• Watt, W. Montgomery, and P. Cachia, *A History of Islamic Spain,* Edinburgh, 1965. Briefly covers an undeservedly neglected subject.

EARLY-MEDIEVAL WESTERN CHRISTIAN CIVILIZATION

• Barraclough, Geoffrey, *The Crucible of Europe: The Ninth and Tenth Centuries in European History,* Berkeley, 1976. A controversial, but clear and stimulating interpretation of political developments.
• Dawson, Christopher, *The Making of Europe,* London, 1932. A brilliant interpretation that emphasizes cultural and religious developments by one of this century's most eminent Catholic historians.
• Duby, G., *The Early Growth of the European Economy,* Ithaca, N.Y., 1974. Emphasizes role of lords and peasants; very sophisticated economic history.
• Fichtenau, H., *The Carolingian Empire,* Oxford, 1957. A highly interpretative account that aims to whittle its subject down to size.

Ganshof, Francois L., *Frankish Institutions under Charlemagne*, Providence, 1958. A straightforward, technical exposition.

• Kitzinger, Ernst, *Early Medieval Art*, 2nd ed. Bloomington, Ind., 1983. A very short but masterful introduction.

• Laistner, M. L. W., and King, H. H., *Thought and Letters in Western Europe*, A.D. *500–900*, 2nd ed., Ithaca, N.Y., 1966. An old-fashioned but standard account; should be supplemented by Wolff.

McKitterick, Rosamond, *The Frankish Kingdoms under the Carolingians, 751–987*, New York, 1983.

• Pirenne, Henri, *Mohammed and Charlemagne*, New York, 1939. A bold interpretation, now no longer widely accepted but still thought-provoking.

• Stenton, Frank, *Anglo-Saxon England*, 3rd ed., Oxford, 1971. A standard work.

• Sullivan, Richard E., *Heirs of the Roman Empire*, Ithaca, N.Y., 1960. An elementary introduction.

• Wallace-Hadrill, J. M., *The Barbarian West: The Early Middle Ages*, A.D. *400–1000*, 2nd ed., London, 1962. A sophisticated, short account that emphasizes analysis of the historical sources and questions earlier scholarly assumptions.

• Wemple, Suzanne F., *Women in Frankish Society: Marriage and the Cloister, 500–900*, Philadelphia, 1981. Describes changing attitudes toward marriage among the early Franks.

• Wolff, Philippe, *The Awakening of Europe*, Baltimore, 1968. The "new intellectual history": emphasizes interrelations between the development of thought and material foundations. Masterfully written and organized.

SOURCE MATERIALS

• Arberry, A. J., *The Koran Interpreted*, 2 vols., London, 1955.

• Bede, *A History of the English Church and People*, tr. L. Sherley-Price, Baltimore, 1955.

Brand, Charles M., ed., *Icon and Minaret: Sources of Byzantine and Islamic Civilization*, Englewood Cliffs, N.J., 1969.

• Brentano, Robert, ed., *The Early Middle Ages: 500–1000*, New York, 1964. The best shorter anthology of the Western Christian sources, enlivened by the editor's subjective commentary.

• Einhard and Notker the Stammerer, *Two Lives of Charlemagne*, tr. L. Thorpe, Baltimore, 1969.

• Gregory Bishop of Tours, *History of the Franks*, tr. E. Brehaut, New York, 1965.

Chapter 10

THE HIGH MIDDLE AGES (1050–1300): ECONOMIC, SOCIAL, AND POLITICAL INSTITUTIONS

I judge those who write at this time to be in a certain measure happy. For, after the turbulence of the past, an unprecedented brightness of peace has dawned again.

—The historian Otto of Freising, writing around 1158

The period between about 1050 and 1300, termed by historians the High Middle Ages, was the time when Western Europe first clearly emerged from backwardness to become one of the greatest powers on the globe. Around 1050 the West was still less developed in most respects than the Byzantine Empire or the Islamic world, but by 1300 it had forged ahead of these two rivals. From a global perspective, only China was its equal in economic, political, and cultural prosperity. Given the sorry state of Western Europe around 1050, this startling leap forward was certainly one of the most impressive achievements of human history. Those who think that the entire Middle Ages were times of stagnation could not be more wrong.

Western Europe emerges from backwardness

The reasons for Europe's enormous progress in the High Middle Ages are predictably complex, yet medieval historians agree upon certain broad lines of interpretation. One is that Europe between 900 and 1050 was already poised for growth and could finally begin to live up to its potential once the devastating invasions of Vikings, Hungarians, and Muslims had ceased. Most of these invasions had tapered off by around 1000, but in the eleventh century England was still troubled by the Danes: the year 1066, more famous as the year of the Norman Conquest, was also the year of the last Viking invasion of England. Once foreign invasions were no longer imminent, Western Europeans could concentrate on developing their economic life with much less fear of interruption than before. Because of the relative continuity allowed by this change, extraordinarily important technological breakthroughs were made, above all those that contributed to the

Reasons for the "great leap forward"

first great Western European "agricultural revolution." The revolution in agriculture made food more bountiful and provided a solid basis for economic development and diversification in other spheres. Population grew rapidly, and towns and cities grew to such a degree that we can speak also of an "urban revolution," even though Western Europe remained predominantly agrarian. At the same time political life in the West became more stable. In the course of the High Middle Ages strong new secular governments began to provide more and more internal peace for their subjects and became the foundations of our modern nation-states. In addition to all these advances, there were also striking new religious and intellectual developments, to be treated in the next chapter, which helped give the West a new sense of mission and self-confidence. Although in this chapter we will treat only the economic, social, and political accomplishments of the High Middle Ages, it is well to bear in mind that religion played a pervasive role in all of medieval life, and that all aspects of the high-medieval "great leap forward" were inextricably interrelated.

1. THE FIRST AGRICULTURAL REVOLUTION

*The state of agriculture
before 1050*

The agricultural worker, the "Man with the Hoe," supported European civilization materially by his labors more than anyone else until the industrialization of modern times. Yet, amazing as it seems, until about 1050 he had hardly so much as a hoe. Inventories of farm implements from the Carolingian period reveal that metal tools on the wealthiest rural estates were extremely rare, and even wooden implements were so few in number that many laborers must have had to grapple with nature quite literally with only their bare hands. Between about 1050 and 1250 all that changed. In roughly those two centuries an agricultural revolution took place that entirely altered the nature and vastly increased the output of Western European farming.

*Prerequisites for the medieval
agricultural revolution:
(1) shift in area of cultivation*

———Many of the prerequisites for the medieval agricultural revolution had been present before the middle of the eleventh century. The most important was the shift in the weight of European civilization from the Mediterranean to the North Atlantic regions. Most of northern Europe from southern England to the Urals is a vast, wet, and highly fertile alluvial plain. The Romans had hardly begun to cultivate this area because they only ruled part of it, because it lay too far away from the center of their civilization, and because they did not have the proper tools and systems to work the soil. Starting around the time of the Carolingians much more attention was paid to colonizing and cultivating the great alluvial plain. The Carolingians opened up all of western and central Germany to agricultural settlement and started experimenting with new tools and methods that would be most appropriate for cultivating the newly settled lands. The results helped support other Carolingian achievements, but the Carolingian peace, as we have seen, was too brief to allow for any cumulative development. After the invasions of the tenth century, it was necessary to start again in a systematic attempt to exploit the potential wealth of the north. As long as Western civilization was centered in England, northern France, the Low Countries, and Germany, however, the rich lands remained available for cultivation.

Another prerequisite for agricultural development was improved climate. We know far less about European climatic patterns in past centuries than we would like to, but historians of climate are reasonably certain that there was an "optimum," or period of improved climate for Western Europe, lasting from about 700 to 1200. This meant not only that during those centuries the temperature on the average was somewhat warmer than it had been before (at most only a rise of about 1° Centigrade), but also that the weather was somewhat drier. Dryness was of primary advantage to northern Europe, where lands were, if anything, usually too wet for good farming, whereas it was disadvantageous to the Mediterranean south, which was already dry enough. Among other things, the occurrence of this optimum helps explain why there was more agricultural cultivation in northern climes such as Iceland than there has been since then. (Also, with fewer icebergs in the northern seas, Norsemen were able to reach Greenland and Newfoundland, and Greenland then was probably indeed more green than white.) Although the optimum began around 700 and continued through the ninth and tenth centuries, it could not by itself counteract the deleterious effects of the tenth-century invasions. Fortunately the weather stayed propitious when Europeans again were able to take advantage of it. *(2) improved climate*

Similar remarks apply to the fact that the Carolingians knew about many of the technological devices to be discussed presently that later helped Western Europeans accomplish their first agricultural revolution. Although the most basic new devices were known before 1050, all came into widespread use and were brought to greatest perfection between then and about 1200 because only then was there a conjunction of the most favorable circumstances. Not only did the invasions end and good climate continue, but better government gradually provided the more lasting peace necessary for agricultural expansion. Landlords too became more interested in profit-making than mere consumption. Above all, from about 1050 to 1200 there was a greater consolidation of wealth for further investment as one advance helped support another; quite simply, technological devices could now be afforded. *(3) technology in conjunction with favorable circumstances*

One of the first and most important breakthroughs in agriculture was the use of the heavy plow. The plow itself, of course, is an ancient tool, but the Romans knew only a light "scratch plow" that broke up the surface of the ground without fully turning it over. This implement was sufficient for the light soil of the Mediterranean regions but was virtually useless with the much heavier, wetter soil of the European north. During the course of the Early Middle Ages a much heavier and more efficient plow was developed that could cultivate the northern lands. Not only could this heavier plow deal with heavier soils, but it was fitted with new parts that enabled it to *Technological innovations: (1) the heavy plow*

Light Plow and Heavy Plow. Note that the peasant using the light plow had to press his foot on it to give it added weight. The major innovation of the heavy plow (often wheeled, as shown here) was the long moldboard, which turned over the

turn over furrows and fully aerate the ground. The benefits were immeasurable. In addition to the fact that the plow allowed for the cultivation of hitherto unworkable lands, the furrows it made provided excellent drainage systems for water-logged territories. It also saved labor: whereas the Roman scratch plow had to be dragged over the fields twice in two different directions, the heavy plow did more thorough work in one operation. In short, the opening up of northern Europe for intensive agriculture and everything that followed would have been inconceivable without the heavy plow.

Closely allied to the use of the heavy plow was the introduction of the three-field system of crop rotation. Before modern times, farmers always let a large part of their arable land lie fallow for a year to avoid exhaustion of the soil because there was not enough fertilizer to support more intensive agriculture, and nitrogen-fixing crops such as clover and alfalfa were almost unknown. But the Romans were especially unproductive due to their inability to cultivate any more than half of their arable land in any year. The medieval innovation was to reduce the fallow to one-third by introducing a three-field system. In a given year one-third of the land would lie fallow, one-third would be given to cereal that was sown in the fall and harvested in early summer, and one-third to a new crop—oats, barley, or legumes— that would be planted in the late spring and harvested in August or September. The fields were then rotated over a three-year cycle. The major innovation was the planting of the new crop which grew over the summer. The Romans could not have supported this system because their lands were poorer and especially because the Mediterranean area is too dry to support much summer growth at all. In this respect the wetter north obviously had a great advantage. The benefits of the new crop were that it did

(2) the three-field system of
crop rotation

ground after the plowshare cut into it. The picture on the right depicts a second crucial medieval invention as well—the padded horse collar, which allowed horses to throw their full weight into pulling.

not deplete the soil as much as cereal like wheat and rye (in fact, it restored nitrogen taken from the soil by these crops); that it provided some insurance against loss from natural disasters by diversifying the growth of the fields; and that it produced new types of food. If the third field was planted with oats, the crop could be consumed by both humans and horses; if planted with legumes, it helped to balance the human diet by providing a source of protein to balance the major intake of cereal carbohydrates. Since the new system also helped to diversify labor over the course of the year and raised production from one-half to two-thirds, it was nothing short of an agricultural miracle.

A third major innovation was the use of mills. The Romans had known about water mills but hardly used them, partly because they had enough slaves to be indifferent to labor-saving devices and partly because most Roman territories were not richly endowed with swiftly flowing streams. Starting around 1050, however, there was a veritable craze in northern Europe for building increasingly efficient water mills. One French area saw a growth from 14 water mills in the eleventh century to 60 in the twelfth; in another part of France about 40 mills were built between 850 and 1080, 40 more between 1080 and 1125, and 245 between 1125 and 1175. Once Europeans had mastered the complex technology of building water mills, they turned their attention to harnessing the power of wind: around 1170 they constructed the first European windmills. Thereafter, in flat lands like Holland that had no swiftly flowing streams, windmills proliferated as rapidly as water-powered ones had spread elsewhere. Although the major use of mills was to grind grain, they were soon adapted for a variety of other important functions: for example, they were employed to drive saws, process cloth, press oil, brew beer, provide power for iron forges, and crush pulp for

(3) use of mills

Medieval Windmill. The peasant on the left is bringing his grain in a sack to be ground into flour. Note that the mill is built on a pivot so that it can rotate in the direction of any prevailing wind.

manufacturing paper. Paper had been made in China and the Islamic world before this but never with the aid of paper mills, which is evidence of the technological sophistication the West was achieving in comparison to other advanced civilizations.

(4) other technological developments

Other important technological breakthroughs that gathered force around 1050 should be mentioned. Several related to providing the means for using horses as farm animals. Around 800 a padded collar was first introduced into Europe; this allowed the horse to put his full weight into pulling without choking himself. Roughly a century later iron horseshoes were first used to protect hooves, and perhaps around 1050 tandem harnessing was developed to allow horses to pull behind each other. With these advances and the greater abundance of oats due to the three-field system, horses replaced oxen as farm animals in some parts of Europe and brought with them the advantages of working more quickly and working longer hours. Further inventions were the wheelbarrow and the harrow, a tool drawn over the field after the plow to level the earth and mix in the seed. Important for most of these inventions was the greater use of iron in the High Middle Ages to reinforce all sorts of agricultural implements, most crucially the parts of the heavy plow that came into contact with the soil.

Extension and intense cultivation of arable land

So far we have been speaking of technological developments as if they alone account for the high-medieval agricultural revolution. But that is by no means the case. Along with improved technology came a great extension in the amount of land made arable and more intensive cultivation of the land already cleared. Although the Carolingians had begun to open the rich plain of northwestern Europe to tillage, they had only chosen to clear the most easily workable patches: a map of Carolingian agricultural settlements would show numerous tiny islands of cultivated lands surrounded by vast stretches of forests, swamps, and wastes. Starting around 1050, and greatly accelerating in the twelfth century, movements of land-clearing entirely changed the topography of northern Europe. First, greater peace and stability allowed farm workers in northern France and western Germany to begin pushing beyond the islands of settlement, clearing little bits of land at a time. At first they did this surreptitiously because they were poaching on territories that were actually owned by aristocratic lords. In time the aristocratic landowners gave their support to the clearing activities because they demanded their own profits from them. When that happened the work of clearing forests and draining swamps was carried on more swiftly. Thus, as the twelfth century progressed the isolated arable islands of Carolingian times expanded to meet each other. While this was going on, and continuing somewhat later, entirely new areas were colonized and opened to cultivation, for example, in northern England, Holland, and above all the eastern parts of Germany. Finally, in the twelfth and thirteenth centuries, peasants began working all the lands they had cleared more efficiently and intensively in order to gain more income for themselves. They harrowed after plowing, hoed frequently to keep down weeds, and added extra plowings to their yearly cycle, thereby greatly helping to renew the fertility of the soil.

The result of all these changes was an enormous increase in agricultural production. With more land opened for cultivation obviously more crops were raised, but the increase was magnified by the introduction of more efficient farming methods. Thus, average yields from grains of seed sown increased from at best twofold in Carolingian times to three- or fourfold by around 1300. And all the additional grain could be ground far more rapidly than before because a mill could grind grain in the same time that it would have taken forty men or women to do the same job. Europeans, therefore, could for the first time begin to rely on a regular and stable food supply.

"Dawn." A medieval peasant, up with the roosters, returns from outdoors after attending to some early-morning business. The woman overhead is "dawn" herself.

That fact in turn had the profoundest consequences for the further development of European history. To begin with, it meant that more land could be given over to uses other than raising grain. Accordingly, as the High Middle Ages progressed, there was greater agricultural diversification and specialization. Large areas were turned over to sheep-raising, others to viniculture, and others to raising cotton and dyestuffs. Many of the products of these new enterprises were consumed locally, but many were also traded over long distances or used to provide the raw materials for new industries—above all those of cloth-making. The growth of this trade and manufacturing helped initiate and support, as we will see, the growth of towns. The agricultural boom also helped sustain the growth of towns in another way: by supporting a great spurt in population. With more food and a better diet (above all the increase in proteins) life expectancy increased from perhaps as low as an average of thirty years for the poor of Carolingian Europe to between forty and fifty years in the High Middle Ages. Healthier people also increased their birthrate. For these reasons the population of the West grew about threefold between about 1050 and 1300. More people and more labor-saving devices meant that not everybody had to stay on the farm: some could migrate to new towns and cities where they found a new way of life.

Consequences of the agricultural revolution

Still other results of the agricultural revolution were that it raised the incomes of lords, thereby underpinning a great increase in the sophistication of aristocratic life, and raised the incomes of monarchs, underpinning the

Raised incomes

growth of states. European-wide prosperity also helped support the growth of the Church and paid the way for the burgeoning of schools and intellectual enterprises. One final, more intangible, result was that Europeans apparently became more optimistic, more energetic, and more willing to experiment and take risks than any of their rivals on the world scene.

2. LORD AND SERF: SOCIAL CONDITIONS AND QUALITY OF LIFE IN THE MANORIAL REGIME

The meaning of the term manorialism

While agriculture was being transformed, social and economic conditions began to change for both landowners and agricultural laborers. Since for much of the High Middle Ages, however, rural life revolved around the institution of the manor owned by lords and worked by serfs, it is best to describe this manorial regime in its most typical form before describing basic changes. In reading the following it should be understood that the term manorialism is not synonymous with feudalism: *manorialism* was an economic system in which large agricultural estates were worked by serfs, whereas *feudalism*, in the sense the word is used by most medieval historians, was a political system in which government was greatly decentralized (see the fourth section of this chapter). It should also be borne in mind that when scholars talk about manorialism based on a "typical manor" they are resorting to a historical approximation: no two manors were ever exactly alike; indeed many differed enormously in size and basic characteristics. Moreover, in those parts of Europe farthest away from the original centers of Carolingian settlement between the Seine and the Rhine, there were few, if any, manors at all. In Italy there was still much agriculture based on slavery, and in central and eastern Germany there were many smaller farms worked by free peasants.

Manor worked by serfs

The manor first clearly emerged in Carolingian times and continued to be the dominant form of agrarian social and economic organization in most of northwestern Europe until about the thirteenth century. It descended from the large Roman landed estate, but, unlike the Roman estate, the manor was worked by *serfs* (sometimes called villeins) and not slaves. Serfs were definitely not free in the modern sense: above all, they could not leave their lands, were forced to work for their lords regularly without pay, and were subject to numerous humiliating dues and to the jurisdiction of the lord's court. But they were much better off than slaves insofar as they were allocated land that they cultivated to support themselves and that normally could not be taken away from them. Thus, when agricultural improvements took place the serfs themselves could hope to profit at least a little from them. More than that, although the lord theoretically had the right to levy dues at will, in practice obligations tended to remain fixed. Although the lot of the serfs was surely terribly hard, they were seldom entirely at their lord's whim.

The lands of the manor, which might run from several hundred to sev-

Diagram of a Manor

eral thousand acres, were divided into those that belonged to the lord and those that were allocated to the serfs. The former, called the lord's *demesne* (pronounced demean), usually comprised between a third and a half of the arable land. It was worked by the serfs on certain days, perhaps three days a week. The demesne did not consist of big parcels but was made up of narrow strips alternating with strips belonging to different peasants (and sometimes also strips set aside for the Church). All these strips were long and narrow because a heavy plow drawn by a yoke of horses or oxen could not

Open-field system

Sowing Seed. **When the peasant sows his seed broadcast, the crows are not far off to help themselves. Here, one is bold enough to peck at the sack while another is momentarily chased off by a dog.**

be turned around easily. Because all the strips were generally separated only by a narrow band of unplowed turf, the whole regime is sometimes called the *open-field system*. Even when the serfs tilled their own lands they almost always worked together because they usually owned farm animals and implements in common. For the same reason, grazing lands were called *commons* because the commonly owned herds grazed there together. In addition to cultivated fields and pastures, the serfs usually had their own small gardens. Most manors also had forests set aside primarily for the lord's hunting which were also useful for the foraging of pigs and the gathering of firewood. Insofar as serfs were allowed to take advantage of such opportunities they did that too in common: indeed, the entire manorial system emphasized communal enterprise and solidarity.

Living conditions of serfs

Communalism must have helped make a barely endurable life seem slightly more bearable. Even though the lot of the medieval serf was surely far superior to that of the Roman slave, and even though it improved from around 1050 to 1300, it was still primitive and pitiful beyond modern comprehension. Dwellings were usually miserable hovels constructed of wattle—braided twigs—smeared over with mud. As late as the thirteenth century an English peasant was convicted of destroying his neighbor's house simply by sawing apart one central beam. The floors of most huts were usually no more than the bare earth, often cold or damp. For beds there was seldom more than bracken—large, coarse ferns—and beyond that there was hardly any furniture. Not entirely jokingly it may be said that a good meal often consisted of two courses: one a porridge very much like

gruel and the other a gruel very much like porridge. Fruit was almost unheard of, and meager vegetables were limited to such fare as onions, leeks,
turnips, and cabbages—all boiled to make a thin soup. Meat came at most a
few times a year, either on holidays or deep in winter, when all the fodder
for a scrawny ox or pig had run out. Cooking utensils were never cleaned,
so as to make sure that there was never any waste. In addition, there was
always the possibility of crop failures, which affected the serfs far more than
their lords since the lords demanded the same income as always. At such
times the serfs were forced to surrender whatever grain they had and
watched their children die slowly of starvation. It is particularly heart-rend-
ing to realize that children might be dying while there was still a bit of
grain in the granaries: but that grain could not be touched because it was
set aside as next year's seed, and without that there would be no future at
all.

To counterbalance this grim picture we may now turn to patterns of
change and improvement. One, as we have already seen, was dietary. In
the High Middle Ages famines were actually far rarer than before, and people grew stronger because some protein, mostly in the form of legumes,
was added to their fare. There was also a widespread enfranchisement (i.e.,
freeing) of serfs for many reasons. Once landlords started opening up new
lands, they could only attract laborers by guaranteeing their freedom. Such
areas of free labor usually attracted runaway serfs and became models of a
new system whereby landlords asked for fixed rents rather than demanding
services. Then, even on the old manors, lords began to realize that they
might be able to raise profits by demanding rents instead of duties. Alterna-

*Improvements in the
condition of serfs*

*Medieval Peasants Slaughtering a
Pig.* Deep in winter, probably
around Christmas, it is finally
time to slaughter the household pig. But nothing can be
wasted, so even the blood is
caught in a pan to make
blood pudding.

The decline of serfdom

tively, by selling their excess produce at free markets serfs might become sufficiently rich to buy their freedom.

In these different ways serfdom gradually came to an end throughout most of Europe in the course of the thirteenth century. The process, however, moved more or less swiftly in different areas—it was somewhat delayed in England and was seldom so complete that former serfs did not owe some remnant of labor service and dues to powerful local lords. In France some of these obligations continued to exist as nagging indignities right down to the French Revolution in 1789. Serfs who became enfranchised often continued to work communally, but they were now free peasants who produced more for the open market than for their own subsistence.

Benefits of the agricultural revolution for lords

The lords profited even more than their serfs from the agricultural revolution for several reasons. One was that whenever lords enfranchised serfs they obtained large sums of cash, usually about all the wealth that the serfs had hitherto amassed. Afterward the lords lived mainly on their rents. Since some of these were levied on lands that the lords had once owned but had never cultivated, noble income rose greatly. Even more than that, once the lords began to prefer rents to services, they found that rents were easier to increase. In their capacity as rent-collectors the lords did not personally supervise their lands as much as before but traveled more freely, sometimes going off crusading and sometimes living at royal courts. Consequently, added wealth allowed them to live better, and greater mobility gave them new ideas for improving their style of life.

The rise of chivalry

Increased sophistication of the nobility was much enhanced by the fact that in the High Middle Ages there was less tumultuous local warfare than before. Until around 1100 the typical European noble was a crude and brutal warrior who spent most of his time engaging in combat with his neighbors and pillaging the defenseless. Much of this violence decreased in

An Aristocratic Family of the Twelfth Century. Warm family feelings existed among medieval people as they did at any other time. Here a mother is telling her two boys to bid good-bye to their father who is about to depart on the Third Crusade.

Jousting in a Tournament

the twelfth century because of ecclesiastical constraints, because emerging states were more effectively enforcing local peace, and because the nobles themselves were beginning to enjoy a more settled existence. Nobles continued to go on crusades and to fight in national wars, but they engaged in petty quarrels with each other less frequently. Apparently as an unconscious surrogate for the old fighting spirit the code of *chivalry* was developed. This channeled martial conduct into relatively benign activities. Chivalry literally means "horsemanship," and the chivalrous noble was expected to be thoroughly adept at the equestrian arts. Chivalry also imposed the obligation of fighting in defense of honorable causes; if none was to be found there were opportunities for combat in tournaments, mock battles that at first were quite savage but later became elaborate ceremonial affairs. Above all, the chivalric lord—typically a "knight" who owned less land than the upper aristocracy—was expected to be not only brave and loyal but generous, truthful, reverent, and disdainful of unfair advantage or sordid gain.

By-products of the increase in noble wealth and the rise of chivalry were improvements in the quality of living conditions and the treatment of women. Until around 1100 most noble dwellings were made of wood, and burned down frequently because of primitive heating and cooking methods. With increasing wealth and more advanced technology, castles after 1100 were usually built of stone and were thus far less flammable. Moreover, they were now equipped with chimneys and mantled fireplaces, both medieval inventions, which meant that instead of having one large fire in a central great hall, individual rooms could be heated and individuals gained some privacy. Nobles customarily ate fewer vegetables than peasants, but

Improvements in the quality of noble life

Aristocratic Table Manners. There are knives but no forks or napkins on the table. The large stars mark these nobles as members of a chivalric order.

their diet was laden with meat; increased luxury trade also brought costly exotic spices like pepper and saffron to their tables. Although table manners were still atrocious—all used only knives and spoons but no forks and blew their noses on their sleeves—nobles tried to show their superiority to others by dressing elegantly, indeed ostentatiously. During this period snug-fitting clothing also became available because both knitting and the button and buttonhole had just been invented.

Changes in noble attitudes toward women

The history of noble attitudes toward women in the High Middle Ages is somewhat controversial for two reasons. One is that most of our evidence comes from literature, and historians differ as to what degree literature actually reflects life. The other is that according to some scholars women were at best put on a pedestal, itself a position of constraint. Nonetheless, there can be no question that as the material quality of noble life improved it did so for women as well as men. More than that, there definitely was a revolution in some verbalized attitudes toward the female sex. Until the twelfth century, aside from a few female saints, women were virtually ignored in literature: the typical French epic told of bloody warlike deeds that either made no mention of women or portrayed them only in passing as being totally subservient. But within a few decades after 1100 noblewomen were suddenly turned into objects of veneration by lyric poets and writers of romances (see the following chapter). A typical troubadour poet could write of his lady that "all I do that is fitting I infer from her beautiful body," and that "she is the tree and the branch where joy's fruit ripens."

Changes in the status of noblewomen

Although the new "courtly" literature was extremely idealistic and somewhat artificial, it surely expressed the values of a gentler culture wherein upper-class women were in practice more respected than before. Moreover, there is no question that certain royal women in the twelfth and thirteenth centuries actually did rule their states on various occasions when their husbands or sons were dead or unable to do so. The indomitable Eleanor of Aquitaine, wife of Henry II, for example, helped rule England even though she was over seventy years old when her son Richard I went on a crusade from 1190 to 1194, and the strong-willed Blanche of Castile ruled France extremely well twice in the thirteenth century, once during the minority of her son Louis IX and again when he was off crusading. No doubt from a modern perspective high-medieval women were still very constrained, but from the point of view of the past the High Middle Ages was a time of progress for the women of the upper classes. The most striking symbol comes from the history of the game of chess: before the twelfth century chess was played in Eastern countries, but there the equivalent of the queen was a male figure, the king's chief minister, who could only move diagonally one square at a time; in twelfth-century Western Europe, however, this piece was turned into a queen, and sometime before the end of the Middle Ages she began to move all over the board.

3. THE REVIVAL OF TRADE AND THE URBAN REVOLUTION

Inseparable from the agricultural revolution, the freeing of serfs, and the growing sophistication of noble life was the revival of trade and the burgeoning of towns. Reviving trade was of many different sorts. Most fundamental was the mundane trade at local markets, where serfs or free peasants sold their excess grain or perhaps a few dozen eggs. But with growing specialization, produce like wine or cotton might be shipped over longer distances. River and sea routes were used wherever possible, but land transport was also necessary, and this was aided by improvements in road-building, the introduction of packhorses and mules, and the building of bridges. Whereas the Romans were really only interested in land *communications,* medieval people, starting in the eleventh century, concentrated on land *transport* to the degree that they were much better able to maintain a vigorous land-based trade. And that is not to say that they ignored Mediterranean transport either. On the contrary, starting again in the eleventh century they began to make the former Roman "lake" the intermediary for an extensive seaborne trade that stretched over shorter and longer distances. Between 1050 and 1300 the Italian city-states of Genoa, Pisa, and Venice freed much of the Mediterranean from Muslim control, started monopolizing trade on formerly Byzantine waters, and began to establish in eastern Mediterranean outposts a flourishing commerce with the Orient. As a result, luxury goods such as spices, gems, perfumes, and fine cloths began to appear in Western markets and stimulated economic life by inspiring nobles to accelerate the agricultural revolution in order to pay for them.

Patterns of trade

This revival of trade called for new patterns of payment and the development of new commercial techniques. Most significantly, Western Europe returned to a money economy after about four centuries when coined money was hardly used as a medium of exchange. The traditional manor had been almost self-sufficient and the few external items needed could be bartered for. But with the growth of markets coins became indispensable. At first these were coins of only the smallest denominations, but as luxury

The revival of a money economy

MEDIEVAL TRADE ROUTES

trade grew in the West the denominations increased apace; by the thirteenth century gold coins were minted by Italian states such as Florence
and Venice.

In a similar pattern of development, long-distance trade at first consisted
of little more than peddlers crisscrossing over dusty roads with pack-laden
Trade fairs mules. But during the course of the twelfth century such peddlers evolved
into more prosperous merchants who managed to decrease their year-
round traveling and to offer their wares instead at international trade fairs.
The most prominent of these fairs, reaching the pinnacle of their prosperity
in the thirteenth century, were held in the French region of Champagne, a
meeting place between north and south, where Flemish merchants sold
cloth to Italians, and Italian merchants sold Eastern spices to Flemings. By
such means a unified European economy came into being. Thereafter even
the trade fairs became outmoded because around 1300 Italian merchants
succeeded in replacing costly overland transport over the Alps by means of
dispatching shipping fleets via the Straits of Gibraltar and the Atlantic di-

rectly to the ports of northern Europe. Now staying at home entirely themselves, such large-scale trading entrepreneurs perfected modern techniques of business partnerships, accounting, and letters of credit. Because they invested in trade intentionally for profit and devised and used sophisticated credit mechanisms, most modern historians agree in calling them the first Western commercial capitalists.

In addition to the expansion of money and credit, trade was vastly facilitated by the rapid growth of towns. If we could imagine an aerial view of twelfth-century Europe, the mushrooming of towns would be the most strikingly visible phenomenon after the clearing of forests and wastes. Some historians misleadingly include under the heading of towns the numerous new agricultural village communities of peasants that were established in clearings. These, however, were not really urban in any sense. Putting them aside, many urban agglomerations were built from the ground up in the High Middle Ages, and existing towns that had barely survived from the Roman period grew enormously in size. To take some examples, in central and eastern Germany, which had not been part of the old Roman area of settlement, new towns such as Freiburg, Lübeck, Munich, and Berlin were founded in the twelfth century. Farther west, where old Roman towns had become little more than episcopal residences or stockades, formerly small towns like Paris, London, and Cologne roughly doubled in size between 1100 and 1200 and doubled again in the next century. Urban life was above all concentrated in Italy, which encompassed most of Europe's largest cities: Venice, Genoa, Milan, Bologna, Palermo, Florence, and Naples. In the thirteenth century the population of the largest of these—Venice, Genoa, and Milan—was in the range of 100,000 each. We lack accurate statistics for most Italian cities, but it seems likely that many at least trebled in population between about 1150 and 1300, because we do know that the smaller Italian town of Imola, near Bologna, grew from some 4,200 in 1210 to 11,500 in 1312. Considering that town life had come very close to disappearing in most of Europe between 750 and 1050, it is warranted to speak of a high-medieval urban revolution. Moreover, from the High Middle Ages until now a vigorous urban life has been a major characteristic of Western European and subsequently modern world civilization.

It was once thought that the primary cause of the medieval urban revolution was the revival of long-distance trade. Theoretically, itinerant peddlers, who had no secure place in the dominantly agrarian society of Europe, gradually settled together in towns in order to offer each other much-needed protection and establish markets to sell their wares. In fact, the picture is far more complicated than that. While some towns did receive great stimulus from long-distance trade, and the growth of a major city such as Venice would have been unthinkable without it, most towns relied for their origin and early economic vitality far more on the wealth of their surrounding areas. These brought them surplus agricultural goods, raw materials for manufacture, and an influx of population. In other words, the quickening of economic life in general was the major cause of urban

Medieval Tollbooth. Whoever made use of a medieval road for transporting merchandise had to pay tolls to pay for its upkeep.

Growth of towns

Venetian Coin. The patron saint of Venice, Saint Mark, grants a banner symbolizing worldly rule to the Venetian doge. The Venetians consciously imitated Byzantine coinage (see p. 238) as part of a successful effort to replace the Byzantine Empire as the dominant trading power in the Mediterranean basin.

View of Paris. **The city looked this way at the end of the Middle Ages, around 1480.** Note the prominence of the cathedral of Notre Dame in the center and the large number of other church spires; note, too, how closely all the buildings are packed behind the walls.

Causes of the urban revolution

growth: towns existed in a symbiotic relationship with the countryside by providing markets and also wares made by artisans, while they lived off the rural food surplus and grew with the migration of surplus serfs or peasants who were seeking a better life. (Escaped serfs were guaranteed their freedom if they stayed in a town a year and a day.) Once towns started to flourish, many of them began to specialize in certain enterprises. Paris and Bologna gained considerable wealth by becoming the homes of leading universities; Venice, Genoa, Cologne, and London became centers of long-distance trade; and Milan, Ghent, and Bruges specialized in manufactures. The most important urban industries were those devoted to cloth-making. Cloth manufacturers sometimes developed techniques of large-scale production and investment that are ancestors of the modern factory system and industrial capitalism. Nonetheless large industrial enterprises were atypical of medieval economic life as a whole.

Medieval cities and towns were not smaller-scale facsimiles of modern ones; to our own eyes they would still have seemed half-rural and uncivilized. Streets were often unpaved, houses had gardens for raising vegetables, and cows and pigs were kept in stables and pigsties. Passing along the streets of a major metropolis one might be stopped by a flock of bleating sheep or a crowd of honking geese. Sanitary conditions were often very poor and the air must often have reeked of excrement—both animal and human. Town-dwellers were cursed by the frequency of fires that swept quickly through closely settled wooden or straw quarters and went unstopped by the lack of fire stations. People were also highly susceptible to contagious diseases bred by unsanitary conditions and crowding. Still another problem was that economic tensions and family rivalries could lead to bloody riots. Yet for all this, urban folk took great pride in their new cities and ways of life. A famous paean to London, for example, written by a twelfth-century denizen of that city, boasted of its prosperity, piety, and perfect climate (!), and claimed that except for frequent fires, London's only nuisance was "the immoderate drinking of fools."

Old Houses in Strassburg. In the Middle Ages food was stored in attics, with special openings for ventilation, as insurance against famine. Of course there was still much spoilage.

The most distinctive form of economic and social organization in the medieval towns was the *guild*. This was, roughly speaking, a professional association organized to protect and promote special interests. The main types were merchant guilds and craft guilds. The primary functions of the merchant guild were to maintain a monopoly of the local market for its members and to preserve a stable economic system. To accomplish these ends the merchant guild severely restricted trading by foreigners in the city, guaranteed to its members the right to participate in sales offered by other members, enforced uniform pricing, and did everything possible to ensure that no individual would corner the market for goods produced by its members.

Craft guilds similarly regulated the affairs of artisans. Usually their only full-fledged voting members were so-called master craftsmen, who were experts at their trades and ran their own shops. Hence if these guilds were anything like modern trade unions, they were unions of bosses. Second-class members of craft guilds were journeymen, who had learned their trades but still worked for the masters (*journeyman* is from the French *journeé,* meaning "day," or by extension "day's work"), and apprentices. Terms of apprenticeship were carefully regulated: if an apprentice wished to become a master he often had to produce a "masterpiece" for judging by the masters of the guild. Craft guilds, like merchant guilds, sought to preserve monopolies and to limit competition. Thus they established uniformity of prices and wages, prohibited working after hours, and formulated detailed regulations governing methods of production and quality of materials. In addition to all their economic functions, both kinds of guilds served important social ones. Often they acted in the capacity of religious

A City on Fire. Once a fire began to spread in a medieval city, women, children, and priests were swiftly evacuated and servants of the rich would start carrying out their masters' possessions. Here the Swiss city of Bern is shown in flames: although a "bucket-brigade" tried desperately to extinguish the fire with water taken from the town moat, chronicles report that the city was leveled by flames in less than half an hour.

The Seal of a Leprosarium. Lepers with their crutches were common sights in medieval cities. This seal of a French leper house dates from 1208.

Medieval attitudes toward merchants

Significance of the urban revolution: (1) development of the economy and government

(2) towns as a foundation for intellectual life

associations, benevolent societies, and social clubs. Wherever possible guilds tried to minister to the human needs of their members. Thus in some cities they came close to becoming miniature governments.

Town merchants and artisans were particularly concerned to protect themselves because they had no accepted role in the older medieval scheme of things. Usually merchants were disdained by the landed aristocracy because they could claim no ancient lineages and were not versed in the ways of chivalry. Worst of all, they were too obviously concerned with pecuniary gain. Although nobles too were gradually becoming interested in making profits, they displayed this less openly: they paid little attention in their daily lives to accounts and made much of their free-spending largesse. Still another reason why medieval merchants were on the defensive was that the Church, opposed to illicit gain, taught a doctrine of the "just price" that was often at variance with what the merchants thought they deserved. Clergymen too condemned usury—i.e., the lending of money for interest—even though it was often essential for doing business. A decree of the Second Lateran Council of 1139, to take one example, excoriated the "detestable, shameful, and insatiable rapacity of moneylenders." As time went on, however, attitudes slowly changed. In Italy it often became hard to tell merchants from aristocrats because the latter customarily lived in towns and often engaged in trade themselves. In the rest of Europe, the most prosperous town-dwellers, called patricians, developed their own sense of pride verging on that of the nobility. The medieval Church never abandoned its prohibition of usury, but it did come to approve making profits on commercial risks, which was often close to the same thing. Moreover, starting around the thirteenth century leading churchmen came to speak more favorably of merchants. St. Bonaventure, a leading thirteenth-century churchman, argued that God showed special favors to shepherds like David in the time of the Old Testament, to fishers like Peter in the time of the New, and to merchants like St. Francis in the thirteenth century.

All in all, the importance of the high-medieval urban revolution can scarcely be overestimated. The fact that the new towns were the vital pumps of the high-medieval economy has already been sufficiently emphasized: in providing markets and producing wares they kept the entire economic system thriving. In addition, cities and towns made important contributions to the development of government because in many areas they gained their own independence and ruled themselves as city-states. Primarily in Italy, where urban life was by far the most advanced, city governments experimented with new systems of tax-collecting, record-keeping, and public participation in decision-making. Italian city-states were particularly advanced in their administrative techniques and thereby helped influence a general European-wide growth in governmental sophistication.

Finally, the rise of towns contributed greatly to the quickening of intellectual life in the West. New schools were invariably located in towns because towns afforded domiciles and legal protection for scholars. At first, students and teachers were always clerics, but by the thirteenth century the needs of merchants to be trained in reading and accounting led to the

Medieval Walled City of Carcassonne, France. These walls date from 1240 to 1285.

foundation of numerous lay primary schools. Equally momentous for the future was the fact that the stimulating urban environment helped make advanced schools more open to intellectual experimentation than any in the West since those of the Greeks. Not coincidentally, Greek intellectual life too was based on thriving cities. Thus it seems that without commerce in goods there can be little exciting commerce in ideas.

4. FEUDALISM AND THE RISE OF THE NATIONAL MONARCHIES

If any Western European city of around 1200 epitomized Europe's greatest new accomplishments it was Paris: that city was not only a bustling commercial center and an important center of learning, it was also the capital of what was becoming Europe's most powerful government. France, like England and the new Christian kingdoms of the Iberian peninsula, was taking shape in the twelfth and thirteenth centuries as a *national monarchy,* a new form of government that was to dominate Europe's political future. Because the developing national monarchies were the most successful and promising European governments we will concentrate on them. But before we do it is well to see what was happening from the political point of view in Germany and Italy.

Around 1050 Germany was unquestionably the most centralized and best-ruled territory in Europe, but by 1300 it had turned into a snake pit of warring petty states. Since most other areas of Europe were gaining stronger rule in the very same period, the political decline of Germany is an intriguing historical problem. It is also a problem of fundamental impor-

The political decline of medieval Germany an intriguing historical problem tance because from a political point of view Germany only caught up with the rest of Europe in the nineteenth century, and its belated efforts to gain its full place in the European political system created difficulties that have just come to be resolved in our own age.

The German monarchy in the tenth and eleventh centuries

The major sources of Germany's strength from the reign of Otto the Great in the middle of the tenth century until the latter part of the eleventh century were its succession of strong rulers, its resistance to political fragmentation, and the close alliance of its crown with the Church. By resoundingly defeating the Hungarians and taking the title of emperor, Otto kept the country from falling prey to further invasions and won great prestige for the monarchy. For over a century afterward there was a nearly uninterrupted succession of rulers as able and vigorous as Otto. Their nearest political rivals were the dukes, military leaders of five large German territories (Lorraine, Saxony, Franconia, Swabia, and Bavaria), but throughout most of this period the dukes were overawed by the emperors' greater power. In order to rule their wide territories—which included Switzerland, eastern France, and most of the Low Countries, as well as claims to northern Italy—the emperors relied heavily on cooperation with the Church. The leading royal administrators were archbishops and bishops whom the emperors appointed without interference from the pope and who often came from their own families. The German emperors were so strong that, when they chose to do so, they could march down to Italy and name their own popes. The archbishops and bishops ran the German government fairly well for the times without any elaborate administrative machinery, and they counterbalanced the strength of the dukes. In the course of the eleventh century the emperors were starting tentatively to develop their own secular administration. Had they been allowed to continue this policy, it might have provided a really solid governmental foundation for the future. But just then the whole system shaped by Otto the Great and his successors was dramatically challenged by a revolution within the Church.

The struggle between Henry IV and Gregory VII

The challenge to the German government came in the reign of Henry IV (1056–1106) and was directed by Pope Gregory VII (1073–1085). For reasons that will be discussed in the next chapter, Gregory wished to free the Church from secular control and launched a struggle to achieve this aim against Henry IV. Gregory immediately placed Henry on the defensive by forging an alliance with the dukes and other German princes, who only needed a sufficient pretext to rise up against their ruler. When the princes threatened to depose Henry because of his disobedience to the pope, the hitherto mighty ruler was forced to seek absolution from Gregory VII in one of the most melodramatic scenes of the Middle Ages. In the depths of winter in 1077 Henry hurried over the Alps to abase himself before the pope in the north Italian castle of Canossa. As Gregory described the scene in a letter to the princes: "There on three successive days, standing before the castle gate, laying aside all royal insignia, barefooted and in coarse attire, Henry ceased not with many tears to beseech the apostolic help and comfort." No German ruler had ever been so humiliated. Although the events at Canossa forestalled Henry's deposition, they robbed him of his great prestige. By the time his struggle with the papacy, continued by his son, was over, the princes had won far more practical independence from the crown than they had ever had. More than that, in 1125 they made good their claims to be able to elect a new ruler regardless of hereditary succession—a principle that would thereafter often lead them to choose the weakest successors or to embroil the country in civil war. Meanwhile, the crown had lost much of its control of the Church and thus in effect had its administrative rug pulled out from under it. While France and England were gradually consolidating their centralized governmental apparatuses, Germany was losing its own.

A major attempt to stem the tide running against the German monarchy was made in the twelfth century by Frederick I (1152–1190), who came from the family of Hohenstaufen. Frederick, called "Barbarossa" (meaning "red beard"), tried to reassert his imperial dignity by calling his realm the "Holy Roman Empire," on the theory that it was a universal empire descending from Rome and blessed by God. Laying claim to Roman descent, he promulgated old Roman imperial laws—preserved in the Code of Justinian—that gave him much theoretical power. But he could not hope to enforce such laws unless he had his own material base of support. Therefore the major policy of his reign was to balance the power of the princes by carving out his own geographical domain from which he might draw wealth and strength.

Frederick Barbarossa. A stylized contemporary representation.

Unfortunately for Frederick, his ancestral lands were located in Swabia, a poorer part of Germany that even today still consists of relatively unproductive hill country and the Black Forest. So Frederick decided to make northern Italy his power base in addition to Swabia. In this he could hardly have made a worse decision. Northern Italy was certainly wealthy, but it was also fiercely independent. Its rich towns and cities, led by Milan, offered stiff resistance. The papacy, which had no wish to see a strong German emperor ruling powerfully in Italy, further lent them helpful moral support. Frederick came very close to overpowering the urban-papal alliance but ultimately the Alps proved to be too great a barrier to allow him to enforce his will in Italy and hope to rule in Germany as well. Whenever he subdued the towns he would shortly afterward have to leave for home, and the towns, with papal encouragement, would then rise up again. Finally, in 1176, insufficient German imperial forces were resoundingly defeated by the troops of a north Italian urban coalition—the Lombard League—at Legnano, and Barbarossa was forced to concede the area's de facto independence. In the meantime, the princes in Germany were continuing to gather strength, especially by colonizing the rich agricultural lands east of the Elbe where Frederick really should have busied himself, and the emperor's struggle with the popes further alienated elements within the German Church. Because Barbarossa was a dashing figure he was well remembered by Germans, but his reign virtually made it certain that the German Empire would not rise again during the medieval period.

Frederick's Italian policy

The reign of Barbarossa's equally famous grandson, Frederick II (1212–1250), was merely a playing out of Germany's fate. In terms of his

The Emperor Frederick II. He is
shown holding a *fleur de lis,* as a
symbol of rule, with a falcon, his
favorite bird, at his side.

*Frederick II's personality
and policies*

*The political situation in
high-medieval Italy*

personality Frederick was probably the most fascinating of all medieval rulers. Because his father, Henry VI, had inherited through marriage the kingdom of southern Italy and Sicily (later called the Kingdom of the Two Sicilies), Frederick grew up in Palermo, where he absorbed elements of Islamic culture. (Arabs had ruled in Sicily for two and a half centuries, from 831 to 1071.) Frederick II spoke five or six languages, was a patron of learning, and wrote his own book on falconry, which takes an honored place in the early history of Western observational science. He also performed bizarre and brutal "experiments," such as disemboweling men to observe the comparative effects of rest and exercise upon digestion. Such practices corresponded to Frederick's overall policy of trying to rule like an Oriental despot. In his autonomous kingdom of southern Italy he introduced Eastern forms of absolutist and bureaucratic government. He established a professional army, levied direct taxation, and promulgated uniform Roman law. Typically, Frederick tried to create a ruler cult and decreed it an act of sacrilege even to discuss his statutes or judgments. For a while these policies seemed successful in ruling southern Italy, but Frederick's power base in Italy led to renewed conflicts with the papacy and the northern Italian cities. These dragged on indecisively until his death, but thereafter the papacy was resolved to see no further Hohenstaufens ruling in Italy and proceeded to eliminate the remaining contenders from the line by calling crusades against them. Overtaxed by Frederick's ruthlessness and subsequent wars, southern Italy gradually sank into the backwardness from which it is only barely emerging today. And Frederick's reign was damaging to Germany as well. Bent on pursuing his Italian policies without hindrance, Frederick formally wrote Germany off to the princes by granting them large areas of sovereignty. Although titular "emperors" afterward continued to be elected, the princes were the real rulers of the country. Yet they fought with each other so much that peace was rare, and they subdivided their lands among their heirs to such an extent that the map of Germany began to look like a jigsaw puzzle. As the French writer Voltaire later said, the German "Holy Roman Empire" had become neither holy, nor Roman, nor an empire.

The story of high-medieval Italian politics may be told more quickly. Southern Italy and Sicily had been welded together into a strong monarchical state in the twelfth century by Norman-French descendants of the Vikings. But then, as we have seen, the area went to the Hohenstaufens and was subsequently brought to ruin. Central Italy was largely ruled by the papacy in the High Middle Ages, but the popes were seldom strong enough to create a really well-governed state, partly because they were at constant loggerheads with the German emperors. Farthest north were the rich commercial and manufacturing cities that had successfully fought off Barbarossa. These were usually organized politically in the form of republics or "communes." They offered much participation in governmental life to their more prosperous inhabitants. But because of diverse economic interests and family antagonisms, the Italian cities were usually riven with internal strife. Moreover, although they could unite in leagues against for-

GERMAN EMPIRE c. 1200

eign threats such as those represented by Barbarossa or Frederick II, the cities often fought each other when foreign threats were absent. The result was that although economic and cultural life was very far advanced in the Italian cities, and although the cities made important experiments in administrative techniques, political stability was widely lacking in northern Italy throughout most of the high-medieval period.

If one looks for the centers of growing political stability in Europe, then one has to seek them in high-medieval France and England. Ironically,

Feudalism defined

Political feudalism

some of the most basic foundations for future political achievement in France were established without any planning just when that area was most politically unstable. These foundations were aspects of a level of political decentralization often referred to by historians as the system of *feudalism*. The use of this word is controversial because, ever since Marx, some historians prefer to use it as a term to describe an agrarian economic and social system wherein large estates are worked by a dependent peasantry. The difficulty with this usage is that it is too imprecise, for such large estates existed in many times and places beyond the European Middle Ages and the medieval agrarian system can best be called *manorialism*. Some historians on the other extreme argue that even if the word "feudalism" is used to describe a medieval political system, medieval realities were so diverse that no one definition of feudalism can accurately or even usefully be extended to cover more than a single case. Nonetheless, for convenience we can retain the use of the word here and apply it to a specific point in medieval political development so long as we bear in mind that, like manorialism, it is only meant to serve as an approximation and that other historians may use it as a term for economic or sociological analysis.

Political feudalism was essentially a system of extreme political decentralization wherein what we today would call public power was widely vested in private hands. From a historical perspective it was most fully experienced in France during the tenth century when the Carolingian Empire had disintegrated and the area was being buffeted by devastating Viking invasions. The Carolingians had maintained a modicum of public authority, but they proved to be no help whatsoever in warding off the invasions. So local landlords had to fend for themselves. In the end, the landlords turned out to offer the best defense against the Vikings and accordingly were able to acquire practically all the old governmental powers. They raised their own small armies, dispensed their own crude justice, and occasionally issued their own primitive coins. Despite such decentralization, however, it was never forgotten that there once had been higher and larger units of government. Above all, no matter how weak the king was (and he was indeed usually very weak), there always remained a king in France who descended directly or indirectly from the western branch of the Carolingians. There also were scattered remaining dukes or counts, who in theory were supposed to have more power and authority than petty landlords or knights. So, by a complicated and hard-to-trace process of rationalization, a vague theory was worked out in the course of the tenth and eleventh centuries that tried to establish some order within feudalism. According to this, minor feudal lords did not hold their powers outright but only held them as so-called *fiefs* (rhymes with reefs), which could be revoked upon noncompliance with certain obligations. In theory—and much of this theory was ignored in practice for long periods of time—the king or higher lords granted fiefs, that is, governmental rights over various lands, to lesser lords in return for a stipulated amount of military service. In turn, the lesser lords could grant some of those fiefs to still lesser lords for military services until the chain stopped at the lowest level of knights. The holder of a fief was called a *vassal* of the granter, but this term had none of the demeaning connotations that it has gained today. Vassalage—much unlike serfdom—was a purely honorable status and all fief-holders were "noble."

Since feudalism was originally a form of decentralization, it once was considered by historians to have been a corrosive or divisive historical force; in common speech today many use the word "feudal" as a synonym for backward. But scholars more recently have come to the conclusion that feudalism was a force for progress and a fundamental point of departure for the growth of the modern state. They note that in areas such as Germany and Italy, where there was hardly any feudalism, political stabilization and unification came only in later times, whereas in the areas of France and England, which saw full feudalization, stabilization and governmental centralization came rapidly afterward. Scholars now posit several reasons for this. Because feudalism was originally spontaneous and makeshift, it was highly flexible. Local lords, instead of being bound by anachronistic, procrustean principles, could rule as seemed best at the moment, or could bend to the dictates of particular local customs. Thus their governments, however crude, worked the best for their times and could be used for building an even stronger government as time went on. A second reason for the effectiveness of feudalism was that it drew more people into direct contact with the actual workings of political life than had the old Roman or Carolingian systems. Government on the most local level could most easily be seen or experienced; as it became tangible people began to appreciate and identify with it far more than they had identified with empires. The result was that feudalism inculcated growing governmental loyalty, and once that loyalty was developed it could be drawn upon by still larger units. Third, feudalism helped lead to certain more modern institutions by its emphasis on courts. As the feudal system became more regularized, it became customary for vassals to appear at the court of their overlords at least once a year. There they were expected to "pay court," i.e., show certain ceremonial signs of loyalty, and also to serve on "courts" in the sense of participating in trials and offering counsel. Thus they became more and more accustomed to performing governmental business and began to behave more like courtiers or politicians. As the monarchical states of France and England themselves developed, kings saw how useful the feudal court was and made it the administrative kernel of their expanding governmental systems. A final reason why feudalism led to political progress is not really intrinsic to the system itself. Because the theory of larger units was never forgotten, it could be drawn upon by greater lords and kings when the right time came to reacquire their rights.

The greatest possibilities for the use of feudalism were first demonstrated in England after the Norman Conquest of 1066. We have seen that England became unified and enjoyed strong kingship under the Saxon Alfred and his successors in the late ninth and tenth centuries. But then the Saxon kingship began to weaken, primarily as the result of renewed Viking invasions and poor leadership. In 1066 William, the duke of Normandy (in northwestern France), laid claim to the English crown and crossed the

Battle of Hastings. A scene from the Bayeux tapestry, embroidered shortly after William the Conqueror's victory. The inscription reads in translation: "Here the English and French have fallen together in battle."

Channel to conquer what he had claimed. Fortunately for him the newly installed English king, Harold, had just warded off a Viking attack in the north and thus could not offer resistance at full strength. At the Battle of Hastings Harold and his Saxon troops fought bravely, but ultimately could not withstand the onslaught of the fresher Norman troops. As the day waned Harold fell, mortally wounded by a random arrow, his forces dispersed, and the Normans took the field and with it, England. Duke William now became King William, the Conqueror, and proceeded to rule his new prize as he wished.

With hindsight we can say that the Norman Conquest came at just the right time to preserve and enhance political stability. Before 1066 England was threatened with disintegration under warrior aristocrats called earls, but William destroyed their power entirely. In its place he substituted the feudal system, whereby all the land in England was newly granted in the form of fiefs held directly or indirectly from the king. Fief-holders had most of the governmental rights they had obtained less formally on the Continent, but William retained the prerogatives of coining money, collecting a land tax, and supervising justice in major criminal cases. He also retained the Anglo-Saxon officer of local government, known as the *sheriff,* to help him administer and enforce these rights. In order to make sure that none of his barons (the English term for major fief-holders) became too powerful, William was careful to scatter the fiefs granted to them throughout various parts of the country. In these ways William used feudal practices to help govern England when there were not yet enough trained administrators to allow any real governmental professionalization. But he also retained much royal power and kept the country thoroughly unified under the crown.

The history of English government in the two centuries after William is primarily a story of kings tightening up the feudal system to their advantage

The feudal system under William the Conqueror

until they superseded it and created a strong national monarchy. The first to take steps in this direction was the Conqueror's energetic son Henry I (1100–1135). One of his most important accomplishments was to start a process of specialization at the royal court whereby certain officials began to take full professional responsibility for supervising financial accounts; these officials became known as clerks of the *Exchequer*. Another accomplishment was to institute a system of traveling circuit-judges to administer justice as direct royal representatives in various parts of the realm.

After an intervening period of civil war Henry I was succeeded by his grandson Henry II (1154–1189), who was very much in his grandfather's activist mold. Henry II's reign was certainly one of the most momentous in all of English history. One reason for this was that it saw a great struggle between the king and the flamboyant archbishop of Canterbury, Thomas Becket, over the status of Church courts and Church law. In Henry's time priests and other clerics were tried for any crimes in Church courts under the rules of canon law. Punishment in these courts was notoriously lax. Even murderers were seldom sentenced to more than penance and loss of their clerical status. Also, decisions handed down in English Church courts could be appealed to the papal *curia* in Rome. Henry, who wished to have royal law prevail as far as possible and maintain judicial standards for all subjects in his realm, tried to limit these practices by the Constitutions of Clarendon of 1164. On the matter of clerics accused of crime he was willing to compromise by allowing them to be judged in Church courts but then have them sentenced in royal courts. Becket, however, resisted all attempts at change with great determination. The quarrel between king and archbishop was made more bitter by the fact that the two had earlier been close friends. It reached a tragic climax when Becket was murdered in Canterbury Cathedral by four of Henry's knights, after the king, in an outburst of anger, had rebuked them for doing nothing to rid him of his antagonist. The crime so shocked the English public that Becket was quickly revered as a martyr and became the most famous English saint. More important for the history of government, Henry had to abandon most of his program of bringing the Church courts under royal control, and his aims were only fulfilled in the sixteenth century with the coming of the English Reformation.

Despite this major setback, Henry II made enormous governmental gains in other areas, so much so that some historians maintain that Henry was the greatest king that England has ever known. His most important contributions were judicial. He greatly expanded the use of the itinerant judges instituted by Henry I and began the practice of commanding sheriffs to bring before these judges groups of men who were familiar with local conditions. These were then required to report under oath every case of murder, arson, robbery, or other major crimes known to them to have occurred since the judges' last visit. This was the origin of the grand jury. Henry also for the first time allowed parties in civil disputes to obtain royal justice. In the most prevalent type of case, someone who claimed to have been recently dispossessed of his land could obtain a writ from the crown, which would

The growth of national monarchy in England; The reign of Henry I

The struggle between Henry II and Thomas Becket

Medieval Justice. Medieval sentencing was usually harsh. Here a convicted offender pays for his crime with the loss of his right hand.

The judicial reforms of Henry II

Martyrdom of Thomas Becket. From a thirteenth-century English Psalter. One of the knights has struck Becket so mightily that he has broken his sword.

order the sheriff to bring twelve men who were assumed to know the facts before a judge. The twelve were then asked under oath if the plaintiff's claim was true, and the judge rendered his decision in accordance with their answers. Out of such practices grew the institution of the trial jury, although the trial jury was not used in criminal cases until the thirteenth century.

Henry II's legal innovations benefited both the crown and the country in several ways. Most obviously, they made justice more uniform and equitable throughout the realm. They also thereby made royal justice sought after and popular. Particularly in disputes over land—the most important and frequent disputes of the day—the weaker party was no longer at the mercy of a strong-arming neighbor. Usually the weaker parties were knights, with whom the crown before then had not been in close touch. In helping defend their rights Henry gained valuable allies in his policy of keeping the stronger barons in tow. Finally, the widespread use of juries in Henry's reign brought more and more people into actual participation in royal government. In so doing it got them more interested in government and more loyal to government. Since these people served without pay, Henry brilliantly managed to expand the competence and popularity of his government at very little cost.

The most concrete proof of Henry II's success is that after his death his government worked so well that it more or less ran on its own. Henry's

The benefits of Henry's legal work

son, the swashbuckling Richard I, the "Lionhearted," ruled for ten years, from 1189 to 1199, but in that time he only stayed in England for six months because he was otherwise engaged in crusading or defending his possessions on the Continent. Throughout the time of Richard's absence governmental administration actually became more efficient, owing to the work of capable ministers. The country also raised two huge sums for Richard by taxation: one to pay for his crusade to the Holy Land and the other to buy his ransom when he was captured by an enemy on his return. But later when a new king needed still more money, most Englishmen were disinclined to pay it.

The new king was Richard's brother, John (1199–1216), who has the reputation of being a villain but was more a victim of circumstances. Ever since the time of William the Conqueror, English kings had continued to rule in large portions of modern-day France, but by John's reign the kings of France were becoming strong enough to take back much of these territories. John had the great misfortune of facing the able French King Philip Augustus, who won back Normandy and neighboring lands by force of arms in 1204 and reinsured this victory by military successes in 1214. John needed money both to govern England and to fight in France, but his defeats made his subjects disinclined to give it to him. The barons particularly resented John's financial exigencies and in 1215 they made him renounce these in the subsequently famous Magna Carta (Great Charter), a document that was also designed to redress all the other abuses the barons could think of. Most common conceptions of Magna Carta are erroneous. It was not intended to be a bill of rights or a charter of liberties for the common people. On the contrary, it was basically a feudal document in which the king as overlord pledged to respect the traditional rights of his vassals. Nonetheless, it did enunciate in writing the important principles that large sums of money could not be raised by the crown without consent given by the barons in a common council, and that no free man could be punished by the crown without judgment by his equals and by the law of the land. Above all, Magna Carta was important as an expression of the principle of limited government and of the idea that the king is bound by the law.

As the contemporary American medievalist J. R. Strayer has said, "Magna Carta made arbitrary government difficult, but it did not make centralized government impossible." In the century following its issuance, the progress of centralized government continued apace. In the reign of John's son, Henry III (1216–1272), the barons vied with the weak king for control of the government but did so on the assumption that centralized government itself was a good thing. Throughout that period administrators continued to perfect more efficient legal and administrative institutions. Whereas in the reign of Henry I financial administration began to become a specialized bureau of the royal court, in the reign of Henry III this became true of legal administration (the creation of permanent High Courts) and administration of foreign correspondence (the so-called Chancery). English central government was now fully developing a trained officialdom.

Efficient governmental administration during Richard's absence

King John and Magna Carta

The progress of centralized government in the reign of Henry III

Edward I. A contemporary representation forming part of the initial "E" in a document that re-granted Magna Carta.

The last and most famous branch of the medieval English governmental system was Parliament. This gradually emerged as a separate branch of government in the decades before and after 1300, above all owing to the wishes of Henry III's son, Edward I (1272–1307). Although Parliament later became a check against royal absolutism, nothing could be further from the truth than to think that its first meetings were "demanded by the people." In its origins Parliament actually had little to do with popular representation, but was rather the king's feudal court in its largest gathering. Edward I was a strong king who called Parliaments frequently to raise money as quickly and efficiently as possible in order to help finance his foreign wars. Those present at Parliaments were not only expected to give their consent to taxation—in fact, it was virtually inconceivable for them to refuse—but while they were there they were told why taxes were necessary so that they would pay them less grudgingly. They could also agree upon details of collection and payment. At the same meetings Edward could take advice about pressing concerns, have justice done for exceptional cases, review local administration, and promulgate new laws. Probably the most unusual trait of Edward's Parliaments in comparison to similar assemblies on the Continent was that they began to include representatives from the counties and towns in addition to the higher nobility. These representatives, however, scarcely spoke for "the people" because most of the people of England were unenfranchised serfs and peasants—not to mention women—who were never consulted in any way. Most likely, Edward had predominantly financial motives for calling representatives from the "commons." He probably also realized the propaganda value of overawing local representatives with royal grandeur at impressive parliamentary meetings so that they would then spread a favorable impression of the monarchy back home. As time went on, commoners were called to Parliament so often that they became a recognized part of its organization: by the middle of the fourteenth century they sat regularly in their own "house." But they still represented only the prosperous people of countryside and towns and were usually manipulated by the crown or the nobles.

The English monarchy under Edward I

Edward I's reign also saw the culmination of the development of a strong national monarchy in other aspects. By force of arms Edward nearly unified the entire island of Britain, conquering Wales and almost subduing Scotland (which, however, was to rise up again soon after his death). Edward began the practice of regularly issuing statute law, that is, original public legislation designed to apply indefinitely to the entire realm. Because of his role as a lawgiver, Edward is sometimes referred to as the "English Justinian." Most important, Edward also curtailed the feudal powers of his barons by limiting their rights to hold private courts and to grant their own lands as fiefs. Thus, by the end of his reign much of the independent power once consciously vested with the barons by William the Conqueror was being taken away from them. The explanation for this is that in the intervening high-medieval centuries the king was developing his own royal institutions of government to the degree that old-fashioned feudalism was now no longer of any real service. Because Edward pressed his strong government and financial demands somewhat excessively for the spirit of the age, there was an antimonarchical reaction after his death. But it is striking that after Edward's time whenever there were baronial rebellions they were always made on the assumption that England would remain a unified country, governed by the basic high-medieval monarchical institutions. England was unified around the crown in the High Middle Ages and would remain a basically well-governed and unified country right up to modern times.

While the process of governmental centralization was making impressive strides in England, it developed more slowly in France. But by around 1300 it had come close to reaching the same point of completion. French governmental unification proceeded more slowly because France in the eleventh century was more decentralized than England and faced greater problems. The last of the weak Carolingian monarchs was replaced in 987 by Hugh Capet, the count of Paris, but the new Capetian dynasty—which

The process of political centralization in France

ENGLAND AND FRANCE C. 1000

was to rule without interruption until 1328—was at first no stronger than the old Carolingian one. Even through most of the twelfth century the kings of France ruled directly only in a small area around Paris known as the Ile-de-France, roughly the size of Vermont. Beyond that territory the kings had shadowy claims to being the feudal overlords of numerous counts and dukes throughout much of the area of modern France, but for practical purposes those counts and dukes were almost entirely independent. It was said that when the king of France demanded homage from the first duke of Normandy, the duke had one of his warriors pretend to kiss the king's foot but then seize the royal leg and pull the king over backwards, to the mockery of all those present. While the French kingship was so weak, the various parts of France were developing their own distinct local traditions and dialects. Thus, whereas William the Conqueror inherited in England a country that had already been unified and was just on the verge of falling apart, the French kings of the High Middle Ages had to unify their country from scratch, with only a vague reminiscence of Carolingian unity to build upon.

*Factors facilitating the growth
of the French monarchy*

In many respects, however, luck was on their side. First of all, they were fortunate for hundreds of years in having direct male heirs to succeed them. Consequently, there were no deadly quarrels over the right of succession. In the second place, most of the French kings lived to an advanced age, the average period of rule being about thirty years. That meant that sons were already mature men when they came to the throne and there were few regencies to squander the royal power during the minority of a prince. More than that, the kings of France were always highly visible, if sometimes not very imposing, when there were power struggles elsewhere, so people in neighboring areas became accustomed to thinking of the kingship as a force for stability in an unstable world. A third favorable circumstance for the French kings was the growth of agricultural prosperity and trade in their home region; this provided them with important sources of revenue. A fourth fortuitous development was that the kings were able to gain the support of the popes because the latter usually needed allies in their incessant struggles with the German emperors. The popes lent the French kings prestige, as they earlier had done for the Carolingians, and they also allowed them much direct power over the local Church, thereby bringing the kings further income and influence from patronage. A fifth factor in the French kings' favor was the growth in the twelfth and thirteenth centuries of the University of Paris as the leading European center of studies. As foreigners came flocking to the university, they learned of the French kings' growing authority and spread their impressions when they returned home. Finally, and by no means least of all, great credit must be given to the shrewdness and vigor of several of the French kings themselves.

*Foundations of the French
monarchy; Louis VI and
Philip Augustus*

The first noteworthy Capetian king was Louis VI, "the Fat" (1108–1137). While accomplishing nothing startling, Louis at least managed to pacify his home base, the Ile-de-France, by driving out or subduing its turbulent "robber barons." Once this was accomplished, agriculture and trade could prosper and the intellectual life of Paris could start to flourish. Thereafter, the French kings had a geographical source of power of exactly the kind that the German ruler Barbarossa sought but never found. The really startling additions to the realm were made by Louis's grandson, Philip Augustus (1180–1223). Philip was wily enough to know how to take advantage of certain feudal rights in order to win large amounts of western French territory from the English King John. He was also decisive enough to know how to defend his gains in battle. Most impressive of all, Philip worked out an excellent formula for governing his new acquisitions. Since these increased his original lands close to fourfold, and since each new area had its own highly distinct local customs, it would have been hopeless to try to enforce strict governmental standardization by means of what was then a very rudimentary administrative system. Instead, Philip allowed his new provinces to maintain most of their indigenous governmental practices but superimposed on them new royal officials known as *baillis*. These officials were entirely loyal to Philip because they never came from the regions in which they served and were paid impressive salaries for the day. They had full judicial, administrative, and military authority in their bailiwicks: on royal orders they tolerated regional diversities but guided them to the king's advantage. Thus there were no revolts in the conquered territories and royal power was enhanced. This pattern of local diversity balanced against bureaucratic centralization was to remain the basic pattern of French government. Thus Philip Augustus can be seen as an important founder of the modern French state.

In the brief reign of Philip's son, Louis VIII (1223–1226), almost all of southern France was added to the crown in the name of intervention against religious heresy. Once incorporated, this territory was governed largely on the same principles laid down by Philip. The next king, Louis IX (1226–1270), was so pious that he was later canonized by the Church and is commonly referred to as St. Louis. He ruled strongly and justly (except for great intolerance of Jews and heretics), decreed a standardized coinage for the country, perfected the judicial system, and brought France a long, golden period of internal peace. Because he was so well-loved, the monarchy lived off his prestige for many years afterward.

That prestige, however, came close to being squandered by St. Louis's more ruthless grandson, Philip IV, "the Fair" (1285–1314). Philip fought many battles at once, seeking to round out French territories in the northeast and southwest and to gain full control over the French Church instead of sharing it with the pope in Rome. All these activities forced him to accelerate the process of governmental centralization, especially with the aim of trying to raise money. Thus his reign saw the quick formulation of many administrative institutions that came close to completing the development of medieval French government, as the contemporary reign of Edward I did in England. Philip's reign also saw the calling of assemblies that were roughly equivalent to the English Parliaments, but these—later called "Estates-General"—never played a central role in the French governmental system. Philip the Fair was successful in most of his ventures; above all, as we will later see, in reducing the pope to the level of a virtual French fig-

A Seal Depicting Philip Augustus

King Philip the Fair of France. An author is presenting a copy of his book to the mighty king, enthroned on a pedestal.

*Comparison of England
and France*

Medieval Spain

urehead. After his death there would be an antimonarchical reaction, as there was at the same time in England, but by his reign France was unquestionably the strongest power in Europe. With only a sixteenth-century interruption, it would remain so until the nineteenth century.

While England and France followed certain similar processes of monarchical centralization and nation-building, they were also marked by basic differences that are worth describing because they were to typify differences in development for centuries after. England, a far smaller country than France, was much better unified. Aside from Wales and Scotland, there were no regions in Britain that had such different languages or traditions that they thought of themselves as separate territories. Correspondingly, there were no aristocrats who could move toward separatism by drawing on regional resentments. This meant that England never really had to face the threat of internal division and could develop strong institutions of united national government such as Parliament. It also meant that the English kings, starting primarily with Henry II, could rely on numerous local dignitaries, above all, the knights, to do much work of local government without pay. The obvious advantage was that local government was cheap, but the hidden implication of the system was that government also had to be popular, or else much of the voluntary work would grind to a halt. This doubtless was the main reason why English kings went out of their way to seek formal consent for their actions. When they did not they could barely rule, so wise kings learned the lesson and as time went on England became most clearly a limited monarchy. The French kings, much to the contrary, ruled a richer and larger country, which gave them—at least in times of peace—sufficient wealth to pay for a more bureaucratic, salaried administration at both the central and local levels. French kings therefore could rule more absolutely. But they were continually faced with serious threats of regional separatism. Different regions continued to cherish their own traditions and often veered toward separatism in league with the upper aristocracy. So French kings often had to struggle with attempts at regional breakaways and take various measures to subdue their aristocrats. Up to around 1700 the monarchy had to fight a steady battle against regionalism, but it had the resources to win consistently and thereby managed to grow from strength to strength.

The only continental state that would rival France until the rise of Germany in the nineteenth century was Spain. The foundations of Spain's greatness were also laid in the High Middle Ages on the principle of national monarchy, but in the Middle Ages there was not yet one monarchy that ruled through most of the Iberian peninsula. After the Christians started pushing back the forces of Islam around 1100 there were four Spanish Christian kingdoms: the tiny northern mountain state of Navarre, which would always remain comparatively insignificant; Portugal in the west; Aragon in the northeast; and Castile in the center. The main Spanish occupation in the High Middle Ages was the *Reconquista,* i.e., the reconquest of the peninsula for Christianity. This reached its culmination in the year 1212 in a major victory of a combined Aragonese-Castilian army over

Bullfighting in a Thirteenth-Century Spanish Arena. Times do not seem to have changed much, although here the spectators are taking a rather unsporting part in the action.

the Muslims at Las Navas de Tolosa. The rest was mostly mopping up. By the end of the thirteenth century all that remained of earlier Muslim domination was the small state of Granada in the extreme south, and Granada existed mostly because it was willing to pay tribute to the Christians. Because Castile had the largest open frontier, it became by far the largest Spanish kingdom, but it was balanced in wealth by the more urban and trade-oriented Aragon. Both kingdoms developed institutions in the thirteenth century that roughly paralleled those of France. But until the union of Aragon and Castile under King Ferdinand and Queen Isabella in the fifteenth century, the Iberian states individually could not hope to be as strong as the much richer and more populous France.

Before concluding this chapter it is best to assess the general significance of the rise of the national monarchies in high-medieval Western Europe. Until their emergence there had been two basic patterns of government in Europe: city-states and empires. City-states had the advantage of drawing heavily upon citizen participation and loyalty and thus were able to make highly efficient use of their human potential. But they were often divided by economic rivalries, and they were not sufficiently large or militarily strong to defend themselves against imperial forces. The empires, on the other hand, could win battles and often had the resources to support an efficient bureaucratic administrative apparatus, but they drew on little voluntary participation and were too far-flung or rapacious to inspire any deep loyalties. The new national monarchies were to prove the "golden mean" between these extremes. They were large enough to have adequate military strength, and they developed administrative techniques that would ri-

Historical role of the national monarchies

val and eventually surpass those of the Roman or Byzantine empires. More than that, building at first upon the bases of feudalism, they drew upon sufficient citizen participation and loyalty to help support them in times of stress when empires would have foundered. By about 1300 the monarchies of England, France, and the Iberian peninsula had gained the primary loyalties of their subjects, superseding loyalties to communities, regions, or to the government of the Church. For all these reasons they brought much internal peace and stability to large parts of Europe where there had been little stability before. Thus they contributed greatly to making life fruitful. The medieval national monarchies were also the ancestors of the modern nation-states—the most effective and equitable governments of our day (the former Soviet Union was more like an empire). In short, they were one of the Middle Ages' most beneficial bequests to modern times.

SELECTED READINGS

• *Items so designated are available in paperback editions.*

GENERAL STUDIES

• Bloch, Marc, *Feudal Society,* Chicago, 1961. A modern classic, first published in France in 1940. Full of valuable insights but outdated in some respects.
• Southern, Richard W., *The Making of the Middle Ages,* New Haven, 1953. A subtle and brilliant reading of eleventh- and twelfth-century developments. Difficult but most rewarding.
• Strayer, J. R., *Western Europe in the Middle Ages,* 3rd ed., Glenview, 1982. In a class by itself as the best short introduction to medieval political and cultural history.
• Wood, Charles T., *The Age of Chivalry* (also published as *The Quest for Eternity*), London, 1970. A lively work for the beginner that supplements Strayer in its emphasis on economic and social history.

ECONOMIC AND SOCIAL CONDITIONS

• Duby, G., *Rural Economy and Country Life in the Medieval West,* London, 1968. The best work on agrarian history. Highly recommended as an example of French historiography at its highest level.
  Ennen, E., *The Medieval Town,* New York, 1979. Complements Duby on urban development.
• Gies, Joseph, and Frances Gies, *Life in a Medieval City,* New York, 1973. An engaging popular account concentrating on life in thirteenth-century Troyes.
• ———, *Women in the Middle Ages,* New York, 1978. An engaging account of women's lives in many different walks of life.
• Herlihy, David, *Medieval Households,* Cambridge, Mass., 1985. Covers family history from late antiquity until the end of the Middle Ages.
• Keen, Maurice, *Chivalry,* New Haven, 1984.
• Labarge, Margaret W., *A Small Sound of the Trumpet: Women in Medieval Life,* London, 1986. A lively survey.

- Lopez, Robert S., *The Commercial Revolution of the Middle Ages, 950–1350,* Englewood Cliffs, N.J., 1971.
- Pirenne, H., *Economic and Social History of Medieval Europe,* London, 1936. Many of Pirenne's ideas are no longer accepted but this is still an extremely useful brief account.
- Postan, M. M., *The Medieval Economy and Society: An Economic History of Britain, 1100–1500,* Berkeley, 1972.
- Power, Eileen, *Medieval Women,* Cambridge, 1975. Very brief but informative.
- White, Lynn, Jr., *Medieval Technology and Social Change,* Oxford, 1962. Controversial but excellently written and thought-provoking.

POLITICAL DEVELOPMENTS

Baldwin, John W., *The Government of Philip Augustus,* Berkeley, 1986. A landmark of scholarship.
- Barraclough, Geoffrey, *The Origins of Modern Germany,* 2nd ed., Oxford, 1947. Highly interpretative.
Davies, R. G., and J. H. Denton, eds., *The English Parliament in the Middle Ages,* Manchester, England, 1981. Essays communicating up-to-date knowledge about the history of Parliament.
Douglas, David, *The Norman Achievement, 1050–1100,* Berkeley, 1969.
———, *The Norman Fate, 1100–1154,* Berkeley, 1976.
Duby, Georges, *France in the Middle Ages: 987–1460,* Oxford, 1991. An innovative approach by a modern master organized around the evolution of shifting power relationships.
- Fawtier, R., *The Capetian Kings of France,* London, 1962. The best traditional account of medieval French royal history.
- Fuhrmann, Horst, *Germany in the High Middle Ages,* Cambridge, 1986. The best short introduction to the "hinge" period of medieval German history.
Hyde, J. K., *Society and Politics in Medieval Italy,* New York, 1973. An excellent survey that integrates political and social history.
- Loyn, H. R., *The Norman Conquest,* London, 1965.
- O'Callaghan, Joseph F., *A History of Medieval Spain,* Ithaca, N.Y., 1975.
Poole, Austin L., *From Domesday Book to Magna Carta, 1087–1216,* 2nd ed., Oxford, 1955. Very detailed yet clear.
- Sayles, George O., *The King's Parliament of England,* New York, 1974. Emphasizes the role of the crown and downplays the importance of the commons.
———, *The Medieval Foundations of England,* London, 1952. An excellent interpretation of medieval English political developments.
- Strayer, J. R., *On the Medieval Origins of the Modern State,* Princeton, 1970. A distillation of the ideas of one of America's greatest medievalists.
Warren, W. L., *The Governance of Norman and Angevin England, 1086–1272,* Stanford, 1987. A masterly recent synthesis.

SOURCE MATERIALS

- Herlihy, David, ed., *The History of Feudalism,* New York, 1970.
- Lopez, Robert S., and I. W. Raymond, eds., *Medieval Trade in the Mediterranean World,* New York, 1955.

- Lyon, Bryce, ed., *The High Middle Ages,* New York, 1964.
- Otto, Bishop of Freising, *The Deeds of Frederick Barbarossa,* tr. C. C. Mierow, New York, 1953. A contemporary chronicle that is interesting enough to read from start to finish.
- Strayer, J. R., ed., *Feudalism,* Princeton, 1965.

Chapter 11

THE HIGH MIDDLE AGES (1050–1300): RELIGIOUS AND INTELLECTUAL DEVELOPMENTS

You would see men and women dragging carts through marshes . . . everywhere miracles daily occurring, jubilant songs rendered to God. . . . You would say that the prophecy was fulfilled, "The Spirit of Life was in the wheels."

—Abbot Robert of Torigni, on the building of the
cathedral of Chartres, 1145

T he religious and intellectual changes that transpired in the West between 1050 and 1300 were as important as the economic, social, and political ones. In the sphere of religion, the most fundamental organizational development was the triumph of the *papal monarchy*. Before the middle of the eleventh century certain popes had laid claim to primacy within the Church, but very few were able to come close to making good on such claims. Indeed, most popes before about 1050 were hardly able to rule effectively as bishops of Rome. But then, most dramatically, the popes emerged as the supreme religious leaders of Western Christendom. They centralized the government of the Church, challenged the sway of emperors and kings, and called forth the crusading movement. By 1300 the temporal success of the papacy had proven to be its own nemesis, but the popes still ruled the Church internally, as they continue to rule the Roman Catholic Church today.

Religious changes

While the papacy was assuming power, a new vitality infused the Christian religion itself, enabling Christianity to capture the human imagination as never before. At the same time too there was a remarkable revival of intellectual and cultural life. In education, thought, and the arts, as in economics and politics, the West before 1050 had been a backwater. Thereafter it emerged swiftly from backwardness to become an intellectual and artistic leader of the globe. Westerners boasted that learning and the arts had moved northwest to them from Egypt, Greece, and Rome—a boast that was largely true. In the High Middle Ages Europeans first started

Intellectual changes

building on ancient intellectual foundations and also contributed major intellectual and artistic innovations of their own.

1. THE CONSOLIDATION OF THE PAPAL MONARCHY

*The sorry state of religious
life in the tenth and
early eleventh centuries*

To understand the origins and appreciate the significance of the Western European religious revival of the High Middle Ages it is necessary to have some idea of the level to which religion had sunk in the tenth and early eleventh centuries. Around 800 the Emperor Charlemagne had made some valiant attempts to enhance the religious authority of bishops, introduce the parish system into rural regions where there had hardly been any priests before, and provide for the literacy of the clergy. But with the collapse of the Carolingian Empire, religious decentralization and ensuing corruption prevailed throughout most of Europe. Most churches and monasteries became the private property of strong local lords. The latter disposed of Church offices under their control as they wished, often by selling them or by granting them to close relatives. Obviously this was not the best way to find the most worthy candidates, and many priests were quite unqualified for their jobs. They were almost always illiterate, and often they lived openly with concubines. When archbishops or bishops were able to control appointments the results were not much better because such officials were usually close relatives of secular lords who followed their practices of financial or family aggrandizement. As for the popes, they were usually incompetent or corrupt, the sons or tools of powerful families who lived in or around the city of Rome. Some were astonishingly debauched. John XII may have been the worst of them. He was made pope at the age of eighteen in 955 because of the strength of his family. It is certain that he ruled for nine years as a thorough profligate, but there is some uncertainty about the cause of his death: either he was caught *in flagrante delicto* by a jealous husband and murdered on the spot, or else he died in the midst of a carnal act from sheer amorous exertion.

Once Europe began to catch its breath from the wave of external invasions that peaked in the tenth century, the wide extent of religious corruption or indifference was bound to call forth some reaction. Bishops could do little to effect change because the work of a bishop was limited to what he could do in his lifetime, and even more because most archbishops and bishops were unable to disentangle themselves from the political affairs of their day. The first successful measures of reform were taken in the monasteries because monasteries could be somewhat more independent and could count more on the support of their reforms by lay lords, insofar as lords feared for the health of their souls if monks did not serve their proper function in saying offices (i.e., prayers). The movement for monastic reform began with the foundation of the monastery of Cluny in Burgundy in 910 by a pious nobleman. Cluny was a Benedictine house but it introduced two constitutional innovations. One was that, in order to remain free from domination by either local secular or ecclesiastical powers, it was made directly subject to the pope. The other was that it undertook the reform or foundation of numerous "daughter monasteries": whereas formerly all Benedictine houses had been independent and equal, Cluny founded a monastic "family," whose members were subordinate to it. Owing to the succession of a few extremely pious, active, and long-lived abbots, the congregation of Cluniac houses grew so rapidly that there were sixty-seven by 1049. In all of them dedicated priors were chosen who followed the dictates of the abbot of Cluny rather than being responsible to local potentates. Cluniac monks accordingly became famous for their industry in the saying of offices. And Cluny was only the most famous of the new congregations. Other similar ones spread just as rapidly in the years around 1000 and succeeded in making the reformed monasteries vital centers of religious life and prayer.

Around the middle of the eleventh century, after so many monasteries had been taken out of the control of secular authorities, the leaders of the monastic reform movement started to lobby for the reform of the clerical hierarchy as well. They centered their attacks upon *simony*—i.e., the buying and selling of positions in the Church—and they also demanded celibacy for all levels of clergy. Their entire program was directed toward depriving secular powers of their ability to dictate appointments of bishops, abbots, and priests, and toward making the clerical estate as "pure" and as distinct from the secular one as possible. Once this reform program was appropriated by the papacy, it would begin to change the face of the entire Church.

*(2) reform of the clerical
hierarchy*

Considering that the reformers were greatly opposed to lay interference, it is ironic that the first reformer was installed in the papacy by a German emperor, namely Henry III. In 1046 this ruler came to Italy, deposed three rival Italian claimants to the papal title, and named as pope a German reformer from his own retinue. Henry III's act brought in a series of reforming popes, who started to promulgate decrees against simony, clerical marriage, and immorality of all sorts throughout the Church. These popes also insisted upon their own role as primates and universal spiritual leaders in order to give strength to their actions. One of the most important steps they took was the issuance in 1059 of a decree on papal elections. This vested the right of naming a new pope solely with the cardinals, thereby depriving the Roman aristocracy or the German emperor of the chance to interfere in the matter. The decree preserved the independence of papal elections thereafter. In granting the right of election to cardinals the decree also became a milestone in the evolution of a special body within the Church. Ever since the tenth century a number of bishops and clerics, known as cardinals, from churches in and near Rome had taken on an important role as advisors and administrative assistants of the popes, but the election decree of 1059 first gave them their clearest powers. Thereafter the "college of cardinals" took on more and more administrative duties and helped create continuity in papal policy, especially when there was a quick succession of pontiffs. The cardinals still elect the pope today.

*Emperor Henry III and reform
of the papacy*

A new and most momentous phase in the history of the reform move-

*The ideals of Pope
Gregory VII*

ment was initiated during the pontificate of Gregory VII (1073–1085). Scholars disagree about how much Gregory was indebted to the ideas and policies of his predecessors in the reform movement and how much he departed from them. The answer seems to be that Gregory supported reform as much as others, indeed he explicitly renewed his predecessors' decrees against simony and clerical marriage. Yet he was not only more zealous in trying to enforce these decrees—a contemporary even called him a "Holy Satan"—but he brought with him a basically new conception of the role of the Church in human life. Whereas the older Christian ideal had been that of withdrawal, and the perfect "athlete of Christ" had been a passive contemplative, or ascetic monk, Gregory VII conceived of Christianity as being much more activist and believed that the Church was responsible for creating "right order in the world." To this end he demanded absolute obedience and strenuous chastity from his clergy: some of his clerical opponents complained that he wanted clerics to live like angels. Equally important, he thought of kings and emperors as his inferiors, who would carry out his commands obediently and help him reform and evangelize the world. Gregory allowed that secular princes would continue to rule directly and make their own decisions in purely secular matters, but he expected them to accept ultimate papal overlordship. Put in other terms, in contrast to his predecessors who had sought merely a duality of ecclesiastical and secular authority, Gregory VII wanted to create a papal monarchy over both. When told that his ideas were novel, he and his immediate followers replied: "The Lord did not say 'I am custom'; the Lord said 'I am truth.' " Since no pope had spoken like this before, it is proper to accept the judgment of a modern historian who called Gregory "the great innovator, who stood quite alone."

The investiture struggle

Gregory's actual conduct as pope was nothing short of revolutionary. From the start he was determined to enforce a decree against "lay investiture," the practice whereby secular rulers ceremonially granted clerics the symbols of their office. The German Emperor Henry IV was bound to resist this because the ceremony was a manifestation of his long-accepted rights to appoint and control churchmen: without these his own authority would be greatly weakened. The ensuing fight is often called "the investiture struggle" because the problem of investitures was a central one, but the struggle was really about the relative obedience and strength of pope and emperor. The larger issue was immediately joined when Henry IV flouted Gregory's injunctions against appointing prelates. Whereas earlier popes might have tried to deal with such insubordination diplomatically, Gregory rapidly took the entirely unprecedented step of excommunicating the emperor and suspending him from all his powers as an earthly ruler. This bold act amazed all who learned of it. Between 955 and 1057 German emperors had deposed five and named twelve out of twenty-five popes; now a pope dared to dismiss an emperor! We have seen in the previous chapter that in 1077 Henry IV abased himself before the pope in order to forestall a formal deposition: that act amazed contemporaries even more. Thereafter Henry was able to rally some support and sympathy for himself and a terrible war of words ensued, while on the actual battlefield the emperor was able to place troops supporting the pope on the defensive. In 1085 Gregory died, seemingly defeated. But Gregory's successors continued the struggle with Henry IV and later with his son, Henry V.

The long and bitter contest on investiture only came to an end with the Concordat of Worms (a city in Germany) of 1122. Under this compromise the German emperor was forbidden to invest prelates with the religious symbols of their office but was allowed to invest them with the symbols of their rights as temporal rulers because the emperor was recognized as their temporal overlord. That settlement was ultimately less significant than the fact that the struggle had lastingly impaired the prestige of the emperors and raised that of the popes. In addition, the dramatic struggle helped rally the Western clergy behind the pope and galvanized the attentions of all onlookers. As one contemporary reported, nothing else was talked about "even in the women's spinning-rooms and the artisans' workshops." This meant that people who had earlier been largely indifferent to or excluded from religious issues became much more absorbed by them.

Gregory VII's successors and most of the popes of the twelfth century were fully committed to the goal of papal monarchy. But they were far less impetuous than Gregory had been and were more interested in the everyday administration of the Church. They apparently recognized that there was no point in claiming to rule as papal monarchs unless they could avail themselves of a governmental apparatus to support their claims. To this end they presided over an impressive growth of law and administration. Under papal guidance the twelfth century saw the basic formulation of the *canon law* of the Church. Canon law claimed ecclesiastical jurisdiction for all sorts of cases pertaining not only to the clergy but also to problems of marriage, inheritance, and rights of widows and orphans. Most of these cases were supposed to originate in the courts of bishops, but the popes insisted that they alone could issue dispensations from the strict letter of the law and that the papal *consistory*—comprised of the pope and cardinals—should serve as a final court of appeals. As the power of the papacy and the prestige of the Church mounted, cases in canon law courts and appeals to Rome rapidly increased; after the middle of the twelfth century legal expertise became so important for exercising the papal office that most popes were trained canon lawyers, whereas previously they had usually been monks. Concurrent with this growth of legalism was the growth of an administrative apparatus to keep records and collect income. As the century wore on, the papacy developed a bureaucratic government that was far in advance of most of the secular governments of the day. This allowed it to become richer, more efficient, and ever stronger. Finally, the popes asserted their powers within the Church by gaining greater control over the election of bishops and by calling general councils in Rome to promulgate laws and demonstrate their leadership.

By common consent the most capable and successful of all high-medieval popes was Innocent III (1198–1216). Innocent, who was elected at the age of thirty-seven, was one of the youngest and most vigorous indi-

Pope Innocent III. A mosaic dating from the thirteenth century.

Innocent's policies in action

Problems for Innocent's successors

viduals ever to be raised to the papacy; more than that, he was expertly trained in theology and had also studied canon law. His major goal was to unify all Christendom under papal hegemony and to bring in the "right order in the world" so fervently desired by Gregory VII. He never questioned the right of kings and princes to rule directly in the secular sphere but believed that he could step in and discipline kings whenever they "sinned," a wide opening for interference. Beyond that, he saw himself as the ultimate overlord of all. In his own words he said that "as every knee is bowed to Jesus . . . so all men should obey His Vicar [i.e., the pope]."

Innocent sought to implement his goals in many different ways. In order to give the papacy a solid territorial base of support, like the one drawn upon by the French kings, he tried to initiate strong rule in the papal territories around Rome by consolidating them where possible and providing for efficient and vigilant administration. For this reason Innocent is often considered to be the real founder of the Papal States. But because some urban communities tenaciously sought to maintain their independence, he never came close to dominating the papal lands in Italy so completely as the French kings controlled the Ile-de-France. In other projects he was more completely successful. He intervened in German politics assertively enough to engineer the triumph of his own candidate for the imperial office, the Hohenstaufen Frederick II. He disciplined the French King Philip Augustus for his marital misconduct and forced John of England to accept an unwanted candidate as archbishop of Canterbury. To demonstrate his superiority and also gain income, Innocent forced John to grant England to the papacy as a fief, and he similarly gained the feudal overlordship of Aragon, Sicily, and Hungary. When southern France was threatened by the spread of the Albigensian heresy (to be discussed later) the pope effectively called a crusade that would extinguish it by force. He also levied the first income tax on the clergy to support a crusade to the Holy Land. The crown of Innocent's religious achievement was the calling of the Fourth Lateran Council in Rome in 1215. This defined central dogmas of the faith and made the leadership of the papacy within Christendom more apparent than ever. The pope was now clearly both disciplining kings and ruling over the Church without hindrance.

Innocent's reign was certainly the zenith of the papal monarchy, but it also sowed some of the seeds of future ruin. Innocent himself could administer the Papal States and seek new sources of income without seeming to compromise the spiritual dignity of his office. But future popes who followed his policies had less of his stature and thus began to appear more like ordinary acquisitive rulers. Moreover, because the Papal States bordered on the Kingdom of Sicily, Innocent's successors quickly came into conflict with the neighboring ruler, who was none other than Innocent's protégé Frederick II. Although Innocent had raised up Frederick, he did not suppose that Frederick would later become an inveterate opponent of papal power in Italy.

At first these and other problems were not fully apparent. The popes of the thirteenth century continued to enhance their powers and centralize the government of the Church. They gradually asserted the right to name candidates for ecclesiastical positions, both high and low, and they asserted control over the curriculum and doctrine taught at the University of Paris. But they also became involved in a protracted political struggle that led to their own demise as temporal powers. This struggle began with the attempt of the popes to destroy Frederick II. To some degree they were acting in self-defense because Frederick threatened their own rule in central Italy. But in combating him they overemployed their spiritual weapons. Instead of merely excommunicating and deposing Frederick, they also called a crusade against him—the first time a crusade was called on a large scale for blatantly political purposes.

Popes become involved in political struggle

After Frederick's death in 1250 a succession of popes made a still worse mistake by renewing and maintaining their crusade against all of the emperor's heirs, whom they called the "viper brood." In order to implement this crusade they became preoccupied with raising funds, and they sought and won as their military champion a younger son from the French royal house, Charles of Anjou. But the latter only helped the popes for the purely political motive of winning the Kingdom of Sicily for himself. Charles in fact won Sicily in 1268 by defeating the last of Frederick II's male heirs. But he then taxed the realm so excessively that the Sicilians revolted in the "Sicilian Vespers" of 1282 and offered their crown to the king of Aragon, who had married Frederick II's granddaughter. The king of Aragon accordingly entered the Italian arena and came close to winning Frederick's former kingdom for himself. To prevent this Charles of Anjou and the reigning pope prevailed upon the king of France—then Philip III (1270–1285)—to embark on a crusade against Aragon. This crusade was a terrible failure and Philip III died on it. In the wake of these events Philip's son, Philip IV, resolved to alter the traditional French pro-papal policy. By that time France had become so strong that such a decision was fateful. More than that, by misusing the institution of the crusade and trying to raise increasingly large sums of money to support it, the popes had lost much of their prestige. The denouement would be played out at the very beginning of the next century.

Popes lose prestige

The temporal might of the papacy was toppled almost melodramatically in the reign of Boniface VIII (1294–1303). Many of Boniface's troubles were not of his own making. His greatest obstacle was that the national monarchies had gained more of their subjects' loyalties than the papacy could draw upon because of the steady growth of royal power and erosion of papal prestige. Boniface also had the misfortune to succeed a particularly pious, although inept, pope who resigned his office within a year. Since Boniface was entirely lacking in conventional piety or humility, the contrast turned many Christian observers against him. Some even maintained—incorrectly—that Boniface had convinced his predecessor to resign and had murdered him shortly afterward. Boniface ruled assertively and presided over the first papal "jubilee" in Rome in 1300. This was an apparent, but, as events would show, hollow demonstration of papal might.

Charles of Anjou. One of the earliest known medieval statues that may be done from life.

Boniface VIII

Two disputes with the kings of England and France proved to be Boni-

Pope Boniface VIII. Boniface was so far lacking in humility that he had a statue of himself erected during his lifetime on the side of the cathedral of Anagni, overlooking the town square.

Two crucial disputes: (1) the issue of clerical taxation

face's undoing. The first concerned the clerical taxation that had been initiated by Innocent III. Although Innocent had levied this tax to support a crusade and had collected it himself, in the course of the thirteenth century the kings of England and France had begun to levy and collect clerical taxes on the pretext that they would use them to help the popes on future crusades to the Holy Land or aid in papal crusades against the Hohenstaufens. Then, at the end of the century, the kings started to levy their own war taxes on the clergy without any pretexts at all. Boniface understandably tried to prohibit this step, but quickly found that he had lost the support of the English and French clergy. Thus when the kings offered resistance he had to back down.

(2) quarrel with the king of France

Boniface's second dispute was with the king of France alone. Specifically it concerned Philip IV's determination to try a French bishop for treason. As in the earlier struggle between Gregory VII and Henry IV of Germany, the real issue was the comparative strength of papal and secular power, but this time the papacy was decisively defeated. As before, there was a bitter propaganda war, but now hardly anyone listened to the pope. The king instead pressed absurd charges of heresy against Boniface and sent his minions to arrest the pope to stand trial. At the papal residence of Anagni in 1303 Boniface, who was in his seventies, was captured and mistreated before he was released by the local citizens. These events exhausted the old man's strength and he died a month later. Immediately thereupon it was said that he had entered the papacy like a fox, reigned like a lion, but died like a dog.

Beneficial effects of the papal monarchy

After Boniface VIII's death the papacy became virtually a pawn of French temporal authority for most of the fourteenth century. But the emergence and success of the papal monarchy in the High Middle Ages had several beneficial effects during the course of that period. One was that the international rule of the papacy over the Church enhanced international communications and uniformity of religious practices. Another was that the papal cultivation of canon law led to a growing respect for law of all sorts and often helped protect the causes of otherwise defenseless subjects, like widows and orphans. The popes also managed to achieve some success in their campaigns to eliminate the sale of Church offices and to raise the morals of the clergy. By centralizing appointments they made it easier for worthy candidates who had no locally influential relatives to gain advancement. There was of course corruption in the papal government too, but in an age of entrenched localism the triumph of an international force was mainly beneficial. Finally, as we will see later, the growth of the papal monarchy helped bring vitality to popular religion and helped support the revival of learning.

2. THE CRUSADES

The rise and fall of the crusading movement was closely related to the fortunes of the high-medieval papal monarchy. The First Crusade was initiated by the papacy, and its success was a great early victory for the papal monarchy. But the later decline of the crusading movement helped undermine the pope's temporal authority. Thus the Crusades can be seen as part of a chapter in papal and religious history. In addition, the Crusades opened the first chapter in the history of Western colonialism.

Crusading movement affects authority of pope

The immediate cause of the First Crusade was an appeal for aid in 1095 by the Byzantine Emperor Alexius Comnenus. Alexius hoped to reconquer Byzantine territory in Asia Minor which had recently been lost to the Turks. Since he had already become accustomed to using Western mercenaries as auxiliary troops, he asked the pope to help rally some Western military support. But the emperor soon found, no doubt to his great surprise, that he was receiving not just simple aid but a *crusade*. In other words, instead of a band of mercenaries to fight in Asia Minor, the West sent forth an enormous army of volunteers whose goal was to wrest Jerusalem away from Islam. Since the decision to turn Alexius's call for aid into a crusade was made by the pope, it is well to examine the latter's motives.

The direct cause of the First Crusade

The reigning pope in 1095 was Urban II, an extremely competent disciple of Gregory VII. Without question, Urban called the First Crusade to help further the policies of the Gregorian papacy. Urban's very patronage of Christian warfare was Gregorian. Early Christianity had been pacifistic: St. Martin, for example, a revered Christian saint of the fourth century, gave up his career as a soldier when he converted with the statement "I am Christ's soldier; I cannot fight." The Latin fathers St. Augustine and St. Gregory worked out theories to justify Christian warfare, but only in the eleventh century, with the triumph of the Gregorian movement, were these put into practice. Gregory VII engineered papal support for the Norman Conquest even before he became pope, and he, or popes under his

The Gregorian theory of Christian warfare

THE MAJOR CRUSADES

Map legend:

- Population predominantly Christian
- Population predominantly Muslim
- → First Crusade
- +++++→ Second Crusade
- – – –→ Third Crusade
- ·······→ Fourth Crusade

Political boundaries shown are those of the time of the First Crusade.

0 — 500 miles

influence, blessed Christian campaigns against Muslims in Spain, Greeks in Italy, and Slavs in the German east. All these campaigns were considered by Gregory VII and his followers to be steps toward gaining "right order in the world."

Urban II's motives

Following in Gregory VII's footsteps, Urban II probably conceived of a great crusade to the Holy Land as a means for achieving at least four ends. One was to bring the Greek Orthodox Church back into the fold. By sending a mighty volunteer army to the East, Urban might overawe the Byzantines with Western strength and convince them to reaccept Roman primacy. If he was successful in that, he would gain a great victory for the Gregorian program of papal monarchy. A second motive was to embarrass the pope's greatest enemy, the German emperor. In 1095 Henry IV had become so militarily strong that Urban had been forced to flee Italy for France. By calling a mighty crusade, Urban might hope to show up the emperor as a narrow-minded, un-Christian persecutor, and demonstrate his own ability to be the spiritual leader of the West. Third, by sending off a large contingent of fighters Urban might help to achieve peace at home. Earlier, the local French Church had supported a "peace movement" which prohibited attacks on noncombatants (the "Peace of God") and then prohibited fighting on certain holy days (the "Truce of God"). Right before he called the First Crusade Urban promulgated the first full papal approval and extension of this peace movement. Clearly the crusade was linked to the call for peace: in effect, Urban told unruly warriors that if they really wished to fight they could do so justly for a Christian cause overseas. Finally, the goal of Jerusalem itself must have genuinely inspired Urban. Jerusalem was thought to be the center of the earth and was the most sacred shrine of the Christian religion. It must have seemed only proper that pilgrimages to Jerusalem should not be impeded and that Christians should rule the city directly. "Right order in the world" could scarcely mean less.

When Urban called his crusade at a Church council in the French town of Clermont in 1095, the response was more enthusiastic than he could possibly have expected. Many in the crowd interrupted the pope's speech with spontaneous cries of "God wills it," and many impetuously rushed off to the East shortly thereafter. All told, there were probably about a hundred thousand men in the main crusading army, an enormous number for the day. Accordingly, the question arises as to why Urban's appeal was so remarkably successful. Certainly there were economic and political reasons. Many of the poorer people who went crusading came from areas that by 1095 were already becoming overpopulated: these Crusaders may have hoped to do better for themselves in the East than they could on their crowded lands. Similarly, some lords were feeling the pressures of growing political stability and a growing acceptance of *primogeniture* (inheritance limited to the eldest male heir). Hitherto younger sons might have hoped to make their own fortune in endemic warfare, or at least inherit a small piece of territory for themselves, but now there were more and longer-lived siblings, warfare was becoming limited, and only the eldest son inherited his father's lands. Clearly, leaving for the East was an attractive alternative to chafing at home.

Economic and political causes of the First Crusade

But the dominant motive for going on the First Crusade was definitely religious. Nobody could have gone crusading out of purely calculating motives because nobody could have predicted for certain that new lands would be won. Indeed, any rational calculation would have predicted at best an unremunerative return trip, or, more likely, death at the hands of the Muslims. But the journey offered great solace for the Christian soul. For centuries pilgrimages had been the most popular type of Christian penance, and the pilgrimage to Jerusalem was considered to be the most sacred and efficacious one of all. Obviously the greatest of all spiritual rewards would come from going on an armed pilgrimage to Jerusalem in order to win back the holiest of sacred places for Christianity. To make this point explicit, Urban II at Clermont promised that Crusaders would be freed from all other penances imposed by the Church. Immediately after-

Religion the dominant motive; crusades as armed pilgrimages

Burning of Jews. From a late-medieval German manuscript. After the persecutions of the First Crusade, treatment of Jews in Western Europe became worse and worse. These Jews were set upon by the populace because they were suspected of poisoning wells.

ward some Crusade preachers went even further by promising, without Urban's authorization, what became known as a *plenary indulgence.* This was the promise that all Crusaders would be entirely freed from other-worldly punishments in purgatory and that their souls would go straight to heaven if they died on the Crusade. The plenary indulgence was a truly extraordinary offer and crowds streamed in to take advantage of it. As they flocked together they were further whipped up by preachers into a religious frenzy that approached mass hysteria. They were convinced that they had been chosen to cleanse the world of unbelievers. One terrible consequence was that even before they had fully set out for the East they started slaughtering European Jews in the first really virulent outbreak of Western anti-Semitism.

The brutal conduct of the Crusaders

Against great odds the First Crusade was a thorough success. In 1098 the Crusaders captured Antioch and with it most of Syria; in 1099 they took Jerusalem. Their success came mainly from the facts that their Muslim opponents just at that time were internally divided and that the appearance of the strange, uncouth, and terribly savage Westerners took the Muslims by surprise. From the start the Crusaders in the Holy Land acted like imperialists. As soon as they conquered new territories they claimed them as property for themselves, carving out their acquisitions into four different principalities. They also exulted in their own ferocity. When they captured Antioch, instead of taking prisoners they killed all the Turks they laid their hands on. Similarly, when they conquered Jerusalem they ignored Christ's own pacifistic precepts, mercilessly slaughtering all the Muslim inhabitants of the city. Some Crusaders actually boasted in a joint letter home that "in Solomon's Porch and in his temple our men rode in the blood of the Saracens up to the knees of their horses." Those Crusaders who stayed on in the Holy Land gradually became more civilized and tolerant, but new waves of armed pilgrims from the West continued to act brutally. Moreover, even the settled Crusaders never became fully integrated with the local population but remained a separate, exploiting foreign element in the heart of the Islamic world.

Given the fact that the Christian states comprised only an underpopulated, narrow strip of colonies along the coastline of Syria and Palestine, it was only a matter of time before they would be won back for Islam. By 1144 the northernmost principality fell. When Christian warriors led by the king of France and emperor of Germany came East in the Second Crusade to recoup the losses, they were too internally divided to win any victories. Not long afterward the Islamic lands of the region were united from the base of Egypt by the Sultan Saladin, who recaptured Jerusalem in 1187. Again a force from the West tried to repair the damages: this was the Third Crusade, led by the German Emperor Frederick Barbarossa, the French King Philip Augustus, and the English King Richard the Lionhearted. Even this glorious host, however, could not triumph, above all because rival leaders again quarreled among themselves. When Innocent III became pope his main ambition was to win back Jerusalem. He called the Fourth Crusade to that end, but that crusade was an unprecedented disaster from the point of view of a united Christendom. The pope could not control its direction and the Crusaders in 1204 wound up seizing Orthodox Christian Constantinople instead of marching on the Holy Land. As we have seen, the ultimate result of this act was to help destroy the Byzantine Empire and open up eastern Europe to the Ottoman Turks. Innocent convened the Fourth Lateran Council in 1215 partially to prepare for yet another crusade that would be more directly under papal guidance. That crusade, the fifth,

Failure of subsequent crusades; the triumph of Frederick II's diplomacy

King Louis VII of France and His Queen, Eleanor of Aquitaine, Embarking for the Second Crusade. This late-medieval conception is idealized inasmuch as Louis did not travel to the Holy Land by sea but took a land route.

was launched from the sea against Egypt in order to penetrate Muslim power at its base, but after a promising start it too was a failure. Only the Sixth Crusade, led from 1228 to 1229 by the Emperor Frederick II, was a success; this, however, was not for any military reasons. Frederick, who knew Arabic and could communicate easily with the Egyptian sultan, did not fight but skillfully negotiated a treaty whereby Jerusalem and a narrow access route were restored to the Christians. Thus diplomacy triumphed where warfare had failed. But the Christians could not hold on to their gains and Jerusalem fell again in 1244, never to be recaptured by the West until 1917. The Christian "states" were now only a small enclave around the Palestinian city of Acre.

The papacy's sacrifice of the crusading ideal to political interests

While Frederick II was negotiating for Jerusalem, he was under excommunication by the pope; therefore, when he entered the city, he had to crown himself king of Jerusalem in the Church of the Holy Sepulcher with his own hands. This was indicative of the fact that by then the papacy was becoming more intent on advancing European political aims than on reconquering the Holy Land. The victory of the First Crusade had greatly enhanced the prestige and strength of the papal monarchy, but the subsequent failures were increasingly calling into question the papal ability to unite the West for a great enterprise. The Albigensian Crusade, called by Innocent III in 1208, established the crucial precedent that a believer could receive the same spiritual rewards by crusading within Europe as by going on a much longer and more risky crusade to the East. The Albigensian Crusade did not damage the papacy's religious image, however, because the Albigensian heretics (whose beliefs will be discussed later) were a clear religious threat to the Church. Once the papacy launched its crusade against Frederick II and his heirs, however, it fully sacrificed the crusading ideal to political interests.

The decline of the crusading movement and the decline of the papacy interrelated

It was then that the decline of the crusading movement and the decline of the papacy became most closely interrelated. In the crusades against Frederick and his successors, and later against the king of Aragon, the popes offered the same plenary indulgence that was by then officially offered to all Crusaders against Islam. Worse, they granted the same indulgence to anyone who simply contributed enough money to arm a Crusader for the enterprise. This created a great inflation in indulgences. By 1291 the last Christian outposts in the Holy Land had fallen without any Western help while the papacy was still trying to salvage its losing crusade against Aragon. Boniface VIII's papal jubilee of 1300, which offered a plenary indulgence to all those who made a pilgrimage to Rome, was a tacit recognition that the Eternal City and not the Holy Land would henceforth have to be the central goal of Christian pilgrimage. Boniface fell from power three years later for many reasons, but one was certainly that the prestige of the papacy had become irreparably damaged by the misuses and failure of crusading.

So, while the crusading idea helped build up the papal monarchy, it also helped destroy it. Other than that, what practical significance did the Crusades have? On the credit side, the almost incredible success of the First

Krak des Chevaliers. This Crusader castle in northern Syria is one of the best preserved fortresses of the Middle Ages. The word *krak* comes from the Arabic *karak,* meaning strong fort.

Crusade greatly helped raise the self-confidence of the medieval West. For centuries Western Europe had been on the defensive against Islam; now a Western army could march into a center of Islamic power and take a coveted prize seemingly at will. This dramatic victory contributed to making the twelfth century an age of extraordinary buoyancy and optimism. To Western Christians it must have seemed as if God was on their side and that they could accomplish almost anything they wished. The Crusades also helped broaden Western horizons. Few westerners in the Holy Land ever bothered to learn Arabic or profit from specific Islamic institutions or ideas—the most profitable cultural communications between Christians and Muslims took place in Spain and Sicily—but Crusaders who traveled long distances through foreign lands were bound to become somewhat more sophisticated. The Crusades certainly stimulated interest in hitherto unknown luxury goods and presented a wealth of subjects for literature and fable.

Positive effects of the Crusades

From an economic point of view, the success of the First Crusade helped open up the eastern Mediterranean to Western commerce. The Italian cities of Venice and Genoa particularly began to dominate trade in that area, thereby helping to enhance Western prosperity as a whole. The need to transfer money over long distances also stimulated early experiments in banking techniques. Politically, the precedent of taxing the clergy for financing the Crusades was not only quickly turned to the advantage of the Western monarchies, it also stimulated the development of various forms of national taxation. More than that, the very act of organizing a country to help support a royal crusade by raising funds and provisions was an important stimulus to the development of efficient administrative institutions in the emerging nation-states.

Commerce and taxation

But there was a debit as well as a credit side to the crusading balance sheet. There is no excusing the Crusaders' savage butchery—of Jews at home and of Muslims abroad. As we have seen too in Chapter 9, the Cru-

Negative consequences

sades greatly accelerated the deterioration of Western relations with the Byzantine Empire and contributed fundamentally to the destruction of that realm, with all the disastrous consequences that followed. And Western colonialism in the Holy Land was only the beginning of a long history of colonialism that has continued until modern times.

3. THE OUTBURST OF RELIGIOUS VITALITY

The awakening of religious interest

The First Crusade would never have succeeded if westerners had not become enthusiastic about religion. The growth of that enthusiasm itself was a most remarkable development. Had the First Crusade been called about fifty years earlier it is doubtful that many people would have joined it. But the eleventh-century reform movement and the pontificate of Gregory VII awakened interest in religion in all quarters. Thereafter the entire high-medieval period was to be marked by extraordinary religious vitality.

The impact of the Gregorian reform movement on religious revival

The reformers and Gregory VII stimulated a European religious revival for two reasons. One was that the campaign to cleanse the Church actually achieved a large measure of success: the laity could now respect the clergy more and increasingly large numbers of people were inspired to join the clergy themselves. According to a reliable estimate, the number of people who joined monastic orders in England increased tenfold between 1066 and 1200, a statistic that does not include the increase in priests. The other reason why the work of Gregory VII in particular helped inspire a revival was that Gregory explicitly called upon the laity to help discipline their priests. In letters of great propagandistic power he denounced the sins of "fornicating priests" (by which he really meant just married ones) and urged the laity to drive them from their pulpits or boycott their services. Not surprisingly, this touched off something close to a vigilante movement in many parts of Europe. This excitement, taken together with the fact that the papal struggle with Henry IV was really the first European event of universal interest, increased religious commitment immensely. Until about 1050 most Western Europeans were Christians in name, but religious commitment seems to have been lukewarm and attendance at church services quite rare; after the Gregorian period Christianity was becoming an ideal and practice that really began to direct human lives.

St. Bernard of Clairvaux. From a wall painting in a church in Italy.

The new piety: the Carthusian and Cistercian orders; St. Bernard of Clairvaux

One of the most visible manifestations of the new piety was the spread of the Cistercian movement in the twelfth century. By around 1100 no form of Benedictine monasticism seemed fully satisfactory to aspirants to holiness who sought great asceticism and, above all, intense "interiority"—unrelenting self-examination and meditative striving toward knowledge of God. The result was the founding of new orders to provide for the fullest expression of monastic idealism. One was the Carthusian order, whose monks were required to live in separate cells, abstain from meat, and fast three days each week on bread, water, and salt. The Carthusians never sought to attract great numbers and therefore remained a small group. But the same was by no means true of the Cistercians. The latter were monks who were first organized around 1100 and who sought to follow the Benedictine Rule in the purest and most austere way possible. In order to avoid the worldly temptations to which the Cluniacs had succumbed, they founded new monasteries in forests and wastelands as far away from civilization as possible. They shunned all unnecessary church decoration and ostentatious utensils, abandoned the Cluniac stress on an elaborate liturgy in favor of more contemplation and private prayer, and seriously committed themselves to hard manual labor. Under the charismatic leadership of St. Bernard of Clairvaux (1090–1153), a spellbinding preacher, brilliant writer, and the most influential European religious personality of his age, the Cistercian order grew exponentially. There were only 5 houses in 1115 but no less than 343 on St. Bernard's death in 1153. This growth not only meant that many more men were becoming monks—the older houses did not disappear—but that many pious laymen were donating funds and lands to support the new monasteries.

As more people were entering or patronizing new monasteries, the very nature of religious belief and devotion was changing. One of many examples was a shift away from the cult of saints to emphasis on the worship of Jesus and veneration of the Virgin Mary. Older Benedictine monasteries encouraged the veneration of the relics of local saints that they housed in order to attract pilgrims and donations. But the Cluniac and Cistercian orders were both centralized congregations that allowed only one saintly patron for all their houses: respectively, St. Peter (to honor the founder of the papacy) and the Virgin. Since these monasteries contained few relics (the

New forms of religious belief and practice

See color plate facing page 269

Mary and Eve. The "correct" medieval theological view of women. On the left (Latin: *sinister*) side of the naked Adam the naked Eve takes the apple of sin from the serpent and feeds it to erring mortals while a skeleton waits to carry them to hell. On Adam's right Mary counteracts Eve by feeding a different "fruit"—the eucharistic wafer—to the devout.

Mary and Christ. The sculpture over the main entrance to the cathedral of Senlis (northern France), dating from about 1180, shows perhaps for the first time in Western history a woman represented in a position equal in dignity with a man.

Virgin was thought to have been taken bodily into heaven, so there were no corporeal relics for her at all) they deemphasized their cult. The veneration of relics was replaced by a concentration on the Eucharist, or the sacrament of the Lord's Supper. Of course celebration of the Eucharist had always been an important part of the Christian faith, but only in the twelfth century was it made really central, for only then did theologians fully work out the doctrine of *transubstantiation*. According to this the priest during mass cooperates with God in the performance of a miracle whereby the bread and wine on the altar are changed or "transubstantiated" into the body and blood of Christ. Popular reverence for the Eucharist became so great in the twelfth century that for the first time the practice of elevating the consecrated host was initiated so that the whole congregation could see it. The new theology of the Eucharist greatly enhanced the dignity of the priest and also encouraged the faithful to meditate on the sufferings of Christ. As a result many developed an intense sense of identification with Christ and tried to imitate his life in different ways.

The cult of the Virgin Mary

Coming a very close second to the renewed worship of Christ in the twelfth century was veneration of the Virgin Mary. This development was more unprecedented because until then the Virgin had been only negligibly honored in the Western Church. Exactly why veneration of the Virgin became so pronounced in the twelfth century is not fully clear, but, whatever the explanation, there is no doubt that in the twelfth century the cult

"Monkey in the Middle." A lively portrayal of a children's game from a medieval songbook of roughly 1280. (Montpellier, Faculté de Medecine)

Rabbit on the Hunt. Marginal illustrations in medieval manuscripts (this one dates from about 1340) often exhibit ironic humor. (Bodleian Library)

Building Operations. From a French picture Bible, c. 1300. Note the treadmill, with wheel, ropes, and pulley, by means of which a basket of stones is brought to the construction level. (Morgan Library)

Siege of a City, c. 1470. The use of cannon would soon put an end to traditional medieval fortifications. (Morgan Library)

Illuminated Manuscript Initial. The joy taken by medieval monks in splendid ornamentation is nowhere more apparent than in this letter B, opening a book of psalms. From a French manuscript of the later twelfth century. (Theresa Gross-Diaz)

The Virgin and Chancellor Rolin, Jan van Eyck (1390–1444). The early Flemish painters loved to present scenes of piety in the sumptuous surroundings of wealthy burghers. (Louvre)

Armorial Insignia of the Tailors' Guild of Perugia. The rampant griffin is the emblem of Perugia (central Italy) and the scissors denote the city's guild of tailors. A striking example of bourgeois pride expressed in aristocratic terms found in a manuscript dating from the year 1368. (British Library)

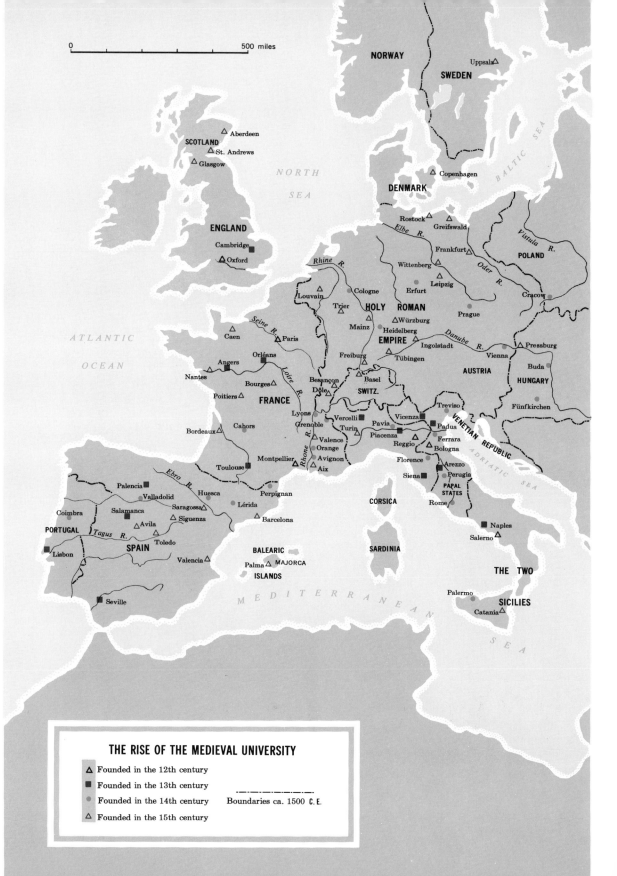

0   500 miles

NORWAY

SWEDEN

Uppsala

BALTIC SEA

SCOTLAND
Aberdeen
St. Andrews
Glasgow

Copenhagen

NORTH SEA

DENMARK

Rostock
Greifswald

Elbe R.

Frankfurt

Vistula R.

POLAND

ENGLAND

Cambridge
Oxford

Rhine R.

Wittenberg

Leipzig

Oder R.

Cracow

Louvain
Cologne

Erfurt

Trier

HOLY ROMAN

Prague

ATLANTIC

Seine R.

Caen

Paris

Mainz
Würzburg
Heidelberg

EMPIRE

Danube R.

Ingolstadt

Pressburg

OCEAN

Orléans

Freiburg

Tübingen

Vienna

AUSTRIA

Buda

HUNGARY

Angers

Nantes

Loire R.

Bourges

Besançon
Dôle

Basel

SWITZ.

Treviso

Fünfkirchen

Poitiers

FRANCE

Lyons
Grenoble

Vercelli
Turin

Vicenza

Pavia

Padua

VENETIAN REPUBLIC

Bordeaux

Cahors

Valence
Orange

Piacenza

Ferrara
Reggio

Bologna

ADRIATIC SEA

Montpellier

Rhône R.

Avignon
Aix

Florence

Arezzo

Toulouse

Siena

Perugia

PAPAL
STATES

Palencia

Ebro R.

Huesca

Perpignan

CORSICA

Rome

Valladolid
Coimbra
Salamanca
Saragossa
Siguenza
Avila

Lérida

Barcelona

Naples

Salerno

PORTUGAL

Tagus R.

Toledo

SPAIN

Valencia

BALEARIC

Palma

MAJORCA

SARDINIA

THE TWO

Lisbon

ISLANDS

Palermo

Seville

MEDITERRANEAN

SICILIES

Catania

SEA

THE RISE OF THE MEDIEVAL UNIVERSITY

△ Founded in the 12th century

■ Founded in the 13th century

● Founded in the 14th century   ―――・―――・―――

                       Boundaries ca. 1500 C.E.

△ Founded in the 15th century

of Mary blossomed throughout all of Western Europe. The Cistercians made her their patron saint, St. Bernard constantly taught about her life and virtues, and practically all the magnificent new cathedrals of the age were dedicated to her: there was Notre Dame ("Our Lady") of Paris, and also a "Notre Dame" of Chartres, Rheims, Amiens, Rouen, Laon, and many other places. Theologically, Mary's role was that of intercessor with her son for the salvation of human souls. It was held that Mary was the mother of all, an infinite repository of mercy who urged the salvation even of sinners so long as they were loving and ultimately contrite. Numerous stories circulated about seeming reprobates who were saved because they venerated Mary and because she then spoke for them at the hour of death.

The significance of the new cult was manifold. For the first time a woman was given a central and honored place in the Christian religion. Theologians still taught that sin had entered the world through the woman, but they now counterbalanced this by explaining how the triumph over sin transpired with the help of Mary. Moreover, this emphasis on Mary gave women a religious figure with whom they could identify, thereby enhancing their own religiosity. A third result was that artists and writers who portrayed Mary were able to concentrate on femininity and scenes of human tenderness and family life. This contributed greatly to a general softening of artistic and literary style. But perhaps most important of all, the rise of the cult of Mary was closely associated with a general rise of hopefulness and optimism in the twelfth-century West.

Sometimes the great religious enthusiasm of the twelfth century went beyond the bounds approved by the Church. After Gregory VII had called upon the laity to help discipline their clergy it was difficult to control lay enthusiasm. As the twelfth century progressed and the papal monarchy concentrated on strengthening its legal and financial administration, some lay people began to wonder whether the Church, which had once been so inspiring, had not begun to lose sight of its idealistic goals. Another difficulty was that the growing emphasis on the miraculous powers of priests tended to inhibit the religious role of the laity and place it in a distinct position of spiritual inferiority. The result was that in the second half of the twelfth century large-scale movements of popular heresy swept over Western Europe for the first time in its history. The two major twelfth-century heresies were Albigensianism and Waldensianism. The former, which had its greatest strength in Italy and southern France, was a recrudescence of Eastern dualism. The Albigensians believed that all matter was created by an evil principle and that therefore the flesh should be thoroughly mortified. This teaching was completely at variance with Christianity, but it seems that most Albigensians believed themselves to be Christians and subscribed to the heresy mainly because it challenged the authority of insufficiently zealous Catholic priests and provided an outlet for intense lay spirituality. More typical of twelfth-century religious dissent was Waldensianism, a movement that originated in the French city of Lyons and spread to much of southern France, northern Italy, and Germany. Waldensians were layfolk who wished to imitate the life of Christ and the Apostles to

The Virgin in Majesty. A representation from a stained-glass window in the cathedral of Chartres.

Heresies: Albigensianism and Waldensianism

the fullest. They therefore translated and studied the Gospels, and dedicated themselves to lives of poverty and preaching. Since the earliest Waldensians did not attack any Catholic doctrines, the Church hierarchy did not at first interfere with them. But it was soon recognized that they were becoming too independent and that their voluntary poverty was proving an embarrassing contrast to the luxurious lives of worldly prelates. So the papacy forbade them to preach without authorization and condemned them for heresy when they refused to obey. At that point they became more radical and started to create an alternative church, which they maintained offered the only route to salvation.

*Innocent III's response
to heresy*

When Innocent III became pope in 1198 he was faced with a very serious challenge from growing heresies. His response was characteristically decisive and fateful for the future of the Church. Simply stated it was two-pronged. On the one hand, Innocent resolved to crush all disobedience to papal authority, but on the other, he decided to patronize whatever idealistic religious groups he could find that were willing to acknowledge obedience. Papal monarchy could thus be protected without frustrating all dynamic spirituality within the Church. Innocent not only launched a full-scale crusade against the Albigensians, he also encouraged the use against heresy of judicial procedures that included ruthless techniques of religious "inquisition." In 1252 the papacy first approved the use of torture in inquisitorial trials, and burning at the stake became the prevalent punishment for religious disobedience. Neither the crusade nor the inquisitorial procedures were fully successful in uprooting the Albigensian heresy in Innocent's own lifetime, but the extension of such measures did result in destroying the heresy by fire and sword after about the middle of the thirteenth century. Waldensians, like Albigensians, were hunted down by inquisitors and their numbers reduced, but scattered Waldensian groups did manage to survive until modern times.

*Innocent III's emphasis
on the sacraments*

Another aspect of Innocent's program was to pronounce formally the new religious doctrines that enhanced the special status of priests and the ecclesiastical hierarchy. Thus at the Fourth Lateran Council of 1215 he reaffirmed the doctrine that the sacraments administered by the Church were the indispensable means of procuring God's grace, and that no one could be saved without them. The decrees of the Lateran Council emphasized two sacraments: the Eucharist and penance. The doctrine of transubstantiation was formally defined and it was made a requirement—as it remains today—that all Catholics confess their sins to a priest and then take Communion at least once a year. The council also promulgated other doctrinal definitions and disciplinary measures that served both to oppose heresy and to assert the unique dignity of the clergy.

The new orders of friars

As stated above, the other side of Innocent's policy was to support obedient idealistic movements within the Church. The most important of these were the new orders of *friars*—the Dominicans and the Franciscans. Friars resembled monks in vowing to follow a rule, but they differed greatly from monks in their actual conduct. Above all, they did not retreat from society into monasteries. Assuming that the way of life originally followed by Christ and the Apostles was the most holy, they wandered through the countryside and especially the towns, preaching and offering spiritual guidance. They also accepted voluntary poverty and begged for their subsistence. In these respects they resembled the Waldensian heretics, but they professed unquestioning obedience to the pope and sought to fight heresy themselves.

The Dominican order, founded by the Spaniard St. Dominic and approved by Innocent III in 1216, was particularly dedicated to the fight against heresy and also to the conversion of Jews and Muslims. At first the Dominicans hoped to achieve these ends by preaching and public debate. Hence they became intellectually oriented. Many members of the order gained teaching positions in the infant European universities and contributed much to the development of philosophy and theology. The most influential thinker of the thirteenth century, St. Thomas Aquinas, was a Dominican who addressed one of his major theological works to converting the "gentiles" (i.e., all non-Christians). The Dominicans always retained their reputation for learning, but they also came to believe that stubborn heretics were best controlled by legal procedures. Accordingly, they became the leading medieval administrators of inquisitorial trials.

In its origins the Franciscan order was quite different from the Dominican, being characterized less by a commitment to doctrine and discipline and more by a sense of emotional fervor. Whereas St. Dominic and his earliest followers had been ordained priests who were licensed to preach by their office, the founder of the Franciscans, the Italian St. Francis of Assisi (1182–1226), was a layman who behaved at first remarkably like a social rebel and a heretic. The son of a rich merchant, he became dissatisfied with the materialistic values of his father and determined to become a servant of the poor. Giving away all his property, he threw off his clothes in public, put on the tattered garb of a beggar, and began without official approval to preach salvation in town squares and minister to outcasts in the darkest corners of Italian cities. He rigorously imitated the life of Christ and displayed indifference to doctrine, form, and ceremony, except for reverencing the sacrament of the Eucharist. But he did wish to gain the support of the pope. One day in 1210 he appeared in Rome with a small ragged band to request that Innocent III approve a primitive "rule" that was little more than a collection of Gospel precepts. Some other pope might have rejected the layman Francis as a hopelessly unworldly religious anarchist. But Francis was thoroughly willing to profess obedience, and Innocent had the genius to approve Francis's rule and grant him permission to preach. With papal support, the Franciscan order spread, and though it gradually became more "civilized," conceding the importance of administrative stability and doctrinal training for all its members, it continued to specialize in revivalistic outdoor preaching and in offering a model for "apostolic living" within an orthodox framework. Thus Innocent managed to harness a vital new force that would help maintain a sense of religious enthusiasm within the Church.

Until the end of the thirteenth century both the Franciscans and Do-

The Earliest Known Portrait of St. Francis. Dating from the year 1228, this fresco shows the saint without the "stigmata," the wounds of Christ's crucifixion he was believed to have received miraculously toward the end of his life.

A Portrait of St. Francis by the Florentine Painter Cimabue. Although this conception, dating from about 1285, may have been modeled on the one shown above, it clearly depicts the stigmata: notice the nail wound in the saint's hand and the lance wound in his side.

Four major intellectual accomplishments

The spread of primary education

minicans worked closely together with the papal monarchy in a mutually supportive relationship. The popes helped the friars establish themselves throughout Europe and often allowed them to infringe on the duties of parish priests. On their side, the friars combated heresy, helped preach papal crusades, were active in missionary work, and otherwise undertook special missions for the popes. Above all, by the power of their examples and by their vigorous preaching, the friars helped maintain religious intensity throughout the thirteenth century.

The entire period from 1050 to 1300 was hence unquestionably a great "age of faith." The products of this faith were both tangible and intangible. We will examine the tangible products—works of theology, literature, art, and architecture—presently. Great as these were, the intangible products were equally important. Until the Christian religion became deeply felt in the High Middle Ages hardly any common ideals inspired average men and women. Life in the Middle Ages was extraordinarily hard, and until about 1050 there was not much to give it meaning. Then, when people began to take Christianity more seriously, an impetus was provided for performing hard work of all sorts. As we have seen in the last chapter, Europeans after 1050 literally had better food than before, and now we have seen that they were better fed figuratively as well. With more spiritual as well as material nourishment they accomplished great feats in all forms of human endeavor.

4. THE MEDIEVAL INTELLECTUAL REVIVAL

The major intellectual accomplishments of the High Middle Ages were of four related but different sorts: the spread of primary education and literacy; the origin and spread of universities; the acquisition of classical and Islamic knowledge; and the actual progress in thought made by westerners. Any one of these accomplishments would have earned the High Middle Ages a signal place in the history of Western learning; taken together they began the era of Western intellectual predominance that became a hallmark of modern times.

Around 800 Charlemagne ordered that primary schools be established in every bishopic and monastery in his realm. Although it is doubtful that this command was carried out to the letter, many schools were certainly founded during the Carolingian period. But their continued existence was later endangered by the Viking invasions. Primary education in some monasteries and cathedral towns managed to survive, but until around 1050 the extent and quality of basic education in the European West were meager. Thereafter, however, there was a blossoming that paralleled the efflorescence we have seen in other human activities. Even contemporaries were struck by the rapidity with which schools sprang up all over Europe. One French monk writing in 1115 stated that when he was growing up around 1075 there was "such a scarcity of teachers that there were almost none in the villages and hardly any in the cities," but that by his maturity

Two Medieval Conceptions of Elementary Education. On the left, an illumination from a fourteenth-century manuscript depicts a master of grammar who simultaneously points to the day's lesson and keeps order with a cudgel. Grammar school education is portrayed more gently on the right, a late-medieval scene in which a woman personifying the alphabet leads a willing boy into a tower of learning wherein the stories ascend from grammar through logic and rhetoric to the heights of theology.

there was "a great number of schools," and the study of grammar was "flourishing far and wide." Similarly, a Flemish chronicle referred to an extraordinary new passion for the study and practice of rhetoric around 1120. Clearly, the economic revival, the growth of towns, and the emergence of strong government allowed Europeans to dedicate themselves to basic education as never before.

The high-medieval educational boom was more than merely a growth of schools, for the nature of the schools changed, and as time went on so did the curriculum and the clientele. The first basic mutation was that monasteries in the twelfth century abandoned their practice of educating outsiders. Earlier, monasteries had taught a few privileged nonmonastic students how to read because there were no other schools for such pupils. But by the twelfth century sufficient alternatives existed. The main centers of European education became the cathedral schools located in the growing towns. The papal monarchy energetically supported this development by ordering in 1179 that all cathedrals should set aside income for one schoolteacher, who could then instruct all who wished, rich or poor, with-

Changes in medieval education: (1) the development of cathedral schools

*(2) the broadening of the
curriculum*

out fee. The papacy believed correctly that this measure would enlarge the number of well-trained clerics and potential administrators.

At first the cathedral schools existed almost exclusively for the basic training of priests, with a curriculum designed to teach only such literacy necessary for reading the Church offices. But soon after 1100 the curriculum was broadened, for the growth of both ecclesiastical and secular governments created a growing demand for trained officials who had to know more than how to read a few prayers. The revived reliance on law especially made it imperative to improve the quality of primary education in order to train future lawyers. Above all, a thorough knowledge of Latin grammar and composition began to be inculcated, often by studying some of the Roman classics such as the works of Cicero and Virgil. The revived interest in these texts, and attempts to imitate them, have led scholars to refer to a "renaissance of the twelfth century."

(3) the growth of lay education

Until about 1200 the students in the urban schools remained predominantly clerical. Even those who hoped to become lawyers or administrators rather than mere priests usually found it advantageous to take Church orders. But afterward more pupils entered schools who were not in the clergy and never intended to be. Some were children of the upper classes who began to regard literacy as a badge of status. Others were future notaries (i.e., men who drew up official documents) or merchants who needed some literacy and/or computational skills to advance their own careers. Customarily, the latter groups would not go to cathedral schools but to alternate ones that were more practically oriented. Such schools grew rapidly in the course of the thirteenth century and became completely independent of ecclesiastical control. Not only were their students recruited from the laity, their teachers were usually laymen as well. As time went on instruction ceased being in Latin, as had hitherto been the case, and was offered in the European vernacular languages instead.

*Significance of the rise of
lay education*

The rise of lay education was an enormously important development in Western European history for two related reasons. The first was that the Church lost its monopoly over education for the first time in almost a millennium. Learning and resultant attitudes could now become more secular, and they did just that increasingly over the course of time. Laymen could not only evaluate and criticize the ideas of priests, they could also pursue entirely secular lines of inquiry. Western culture therefore ultimately became more independent of religion, and much of the traditionalism associated with religion, than any other culture in the world. Second, the growth of lay schools, taken together with the growth of church schools that trained the laity, led to an enormous growth of lay literacy: by 1340 roughly 40 percent of the Florentine population could read; by the later fifteenth century about 40 percent of the total population of England was literate as well. (These figures include women, who were usually taught to read by paid tutors or male family members at home rather than in schools.) When one considers that literacy around 1050 was almost entirely limited to the clergy and that the literate comprised less than 1 percent of the population of Western Europe, it can be appreciated that an astonishing revolution had taken place. Without it, many of Europe's other accomplishments would have been inconceivable.

The emergence of universities was part of the same high-medieval educational boom. Originally, universities were institutions that offered instruction in advanced studies that could not be pursued in average cathedral schools: advanced liberal arts and the professional studies of law, medicine, and theology. The earliest Italian university was that of Bologna, an institution that took shape during the course of the twelfth century. Although liberal arts were taught at Bologna, the institution gained its greatest prominence from the time of its twelfth-century origins until the end of the Middle Ages as Europe's leading center for the study of law. North of the Alps, the earliest and most prominent university was that of Paris. The University of Paris started out as a cathedral school like many others, but in the twelfth century it began to become a recognized center of northern intellectual life. One reason for this was that scholars there found necessary conditions of peace and stability provided by the increasingly strong French kingship; another was that food was plentiful because the area was rich in agricultural produce; and another was that the cathedral school of Paris in the first half of the twelfth century boasted the most charismatic and controversial teacher of the day, Peter Abelard (1079–1142). Abelard, whose intellectual accomplishments we will discuss later, attracted students from all over Europe in droves. According to an apocryphal story that was told at the time, he was such an exciting teacher that when he was forbidden to teach in French lands because of his controversial views, he climbed a tree and students flocked under it to hear him lecture; when he was then forbidden to teach from the air he started lecturing from a boat and students massed to hear him from the banks. As a result of his reputation many other teachers settled in Paris and began to offer much more varied and advanced instruction than anything offered in other French cathedral schools. By 1200 Paris was evolving into a university that specialized in liberal arts and theology. Around then Innocent III, who had studied in Paris himself, called the school "the oven that bakes the bread for the entire world."

The origins of universities

See color map facing page 333

Abelard. A late-medieval conception.

It should be emphasized that the institution of the university was really a medieval invention. Of course advanced schools existed in the ancient world, but they did not have fixed curricula or organized faculties, and they did not award degrees. At first, medieval universities themselves were not so much places as groups of scholars. The term "university" originally meant a corporation or guild. In fact, all of the medieval universities were corporations, either of teachers or students, organized like other guilds to protect their interests and rights. But gradually the word "university" came to mean an educational institution with a school of liberal arts and one or more faculties in the professional subjects of law, medicine, and theology. After about 1200 Bologna and Paris were regarded as the prototypic universities. During the thirteenth century such famous institutions as Oxford, Cambridge, Montpellier, Salamanca, and Naples were founded or granted formal recognition. In Germany there were no universities until the fourteenth century—a reflection of the disorganized condition of that area—

Nature of the medieval university

but in 1385 Heidelberg, the first university on German soil, was founded and many others quickly followed.

Every university in medieval Europe was patterned after one or the other of two different models. Throughout Italy, Spain, and southern France the standard was generally the University of Bologna, in which the students themselves constituted the corporation. They hired the teachers, paid their salaries, and fined or discharged them for neglect of duty or inefficient instruction. The universities of northern Europe were modeled after Paris, which was not a guild of students but of teachers. It included four faculties—arts, theology, law, and medicine—each headed by a dean. In the great majority of the northern universities arts and theology were the leading branches of study. Before the end of the thirteenth century separate colleges came to be established within the University of Paris. The original college was nothing more than an endowed home for poor students, but eventually the colleges become centers of instruction as well as residences. While most of these colleges have disappeared from the Continent, the universities of Oxford and Cambridge still retain the pattern of federal organization copied from Paris. The colleges of which they are composed are semi-independent educational units.

Most of our modern degrees as well as our modern university organization derive from the medieval system, but actual courses of study have been greatly altered. No curriculum in the Middle Ages included history or anything like the modern social sciences. The medieval student was assumed to know Latin grammar thoroughly before entrance into a university—this he learned in the primary, or "grammar," schools. Upon admission, limited to males, he was required to spend about four years studying the basic liberal arts, which meant doing advanced work in Latin grammar and rhetoric,

A Lecture Class in a Medieval University. Some interesting similarities and contrasts may be observed between this scene and a modern classroom.

and mastering the rules of logic. If he passed his examinations he received the preliminary degree of bachelor of arts (the prototype of our B.A.), which conferred no unusual distinction. To assure himself a place in professional life he then usually had to devote additional years to the pursuit of an advanced degree, such as master of arts (M.A.), or doctor of laws, medicine, or theology. For the M.A. degree three or four years had to be given to the study of mathematics, natural science, and philosophy. This was accomplished by reading and commenting on standard ancient works, such as those of Euclid and especially Aristotle. Abstract analysis was emphasized and there was no such thing as laboratory science. The requirements for the doctor's degrees included more specialized training. Those for the doctorate in theology were particularly arduous: by the end of the Middle Ages the course for the doctorate in theology at the University of Paris had been extended to twelve or thirteen years after the roughly eight years taken for the M.A.! Continuous residence was not required, and it was accordingly rare to become a doctor of theology before the age of forty; statutes in fact forbade awarding the degree to anyone under thirty-five. Strictly speaking, doctor's degrees, including even the one in medicine, only conferred the right to teach. But in practice university degrees of all grades were recognized as standards of attainment and became pathways to nonacademic careers.

Student life in medieval universities was often rowdy. Many students were very immature because it was customary to begin university studies between the ages of twelve and fifteen. Moreover, all university students believed that they comprised an independent and privileged community, set aside from that of the local townspeople. Since the latter tried to reap financial profits from the students and the students were naturally boisterous, there were frequent riots and sometimes pitched battles between "town" and "gown." But actual study was very intense. Because the greatest emphasis was placed on the value of authority and also because books were prohibitively expensive (they were handwritten and made from rare parchment), there was an enormous amount of rote memorization. As students advanced in their disciplines they were also expected to develop their own skills in formal, public disputations. Advanced disputations could become extremely complex and abstract; sometimes they might also last for days. The most important fact pertaining to medieval university students was that, after about 1250, there were so many of them. The University of Paris in the thirteenth century numbered about seven thousand students, and Oxford somewhere around two thousand in any given year. This means that a relatively appreciable proportion of male Europeans who were more than peasants or artisans were gaining at least some education at the higher levels.

As the numbers of those educated at all levels vastly increased during the High Middle Ages, so did the quality of learning. This was owing first and foremost to the reacquisition of Greek knowledge and to the absorption of intellectual advances made by the Muslims. Since practically no Western Europeans knew Greek or Arabic, works in those languages had to be

A Scribe with a Sense of Humor. An English scribe of around 1300, having noticed that he left out a whole line in a luxurious prayerbook, devised this ingenious way to rectify the error.

Student life in medieval universities

Acquisition of Greek and Arabic scientific knowledge

Medicine as Monkey Business. Even after a medieval physician had studied Galen, he was equipped with only two fairly reliable diagnostic methods: taking the pulse and examining urine. A visual parody from a French manuscript of 1316 makes this observation dryly.

The growth of Western scientific and speculative thought; Robert Grosseteste and Roger Bacon

The meaning of Scholasticism

transmitted by means of Latin translations. But there were very few of these before about 1140: of all the many works of Aristotle only a few logical treatises were available in Latin translations before the middle of the twelfth century. But then, suddenly, an enormous burst of translating activity made almost all of ancient Greek and Arabic scientific knowledge accessible to Western Europeans. This activity transpired in Spain and Sicily because Christians there lived in close proximity with Arabic speakers, or Jews who knew Latin and Arabic, either of whom could aid them in their tasks. Greek works were first translated into Latin from earlier Arabic translations; then many were retranslated directly from the Greek by a few westerners who had managed to learn that language, usually by traveling in Greek-speaking territories. The result was that by about 1260 almost the entire Aristotelian corpus that is known today was made available in Latin. So also were basic works of such important Greek scientific thinkers as Euclid, Galen, and Ptolemy. Only the milestones of Greek literature and the works of Plato were not yet translated because they had not been made available to the Arabs; they existed only in inaccessible Byzantine manuscripts. But in addition to the thought of the Greeks, Western scholars became familiar with the accomplishments of all the major Islamic philosophers and scientists such as Avicenna and Averroës.

Having acquired the best of Greek and Arabic scientific and speculative thought, the West was able to build on it and make its own advances. This progress transpired in different ways. When it came to natural science, westerners were able to start building on the acquired learning without much difficulty because it seldom conflicted with the principles of Christianity. But when it came to philosophy, the basic question arose as to how thoroughly Greek and Arabic thought was compatible with the Christian faith. One of the most advanced thirteenth-century scientists was the Englishman Robert Grosseteste (c. 1168–1253), who was not only a great thinker but was also very active in public life as bishop of Lincoln. Grosseteste became so proficient at Greek that he translated all of Aristotle's *Ethics.* More important, he made very significant theoretical advances in mathematics, astronomy, and optics. He formulated a sophisticated scientific explanation of the rainbow, and he posited the use of lenses for magnification. Grosseteste's leading disciple was Roger Bacon (c. 1214–1294), who is today more famous than his teacher because he seems to have predicted automobiles and flying machines. Bacon in fact had no real interest in machinery, but he did follow up on Grosseteste's work in optics, discussing, for example, further properties of lenses, the rapid speed of light, and the nature of human vision. Grosseteste, Bacon, and some of their followers at the University of Oxford argued that natural knowledge was more certain when it was based on sensory evidence than when it rested on abstract reason. To this degree they can be seen as early forerunners of modern science. But the important qualification remains that they did not perform any real laboratory experiments.

The story of the high-medieval encounter between Greek and Arabic philosophy and Christian faith is basically the story of the emergence of

Scholasticism. This word can be, and has been, defined in many ways. In its root meaning Scholasticism was simply the method of teaching and learning followed in the medieval schools. That meant that it was highly systematic and also that it was highly respectful of authority. Yet Scholasticism was not only a method of study: it was a worldview. As such, it taught that there was a fundamental compatibility between the knowledge humans can obtain naturally, i.e., by experience or reason, and the teachings imparted by Divine Revelation. Since medieval scholars believed that the Greeks were the masters of natural knowledge and that all revelation was in the Bible, Scholasticism consequently was the theory and practice of reconciling classical philosophy with Christian faith.

The Creator as Architect. An underlying assumption of thirteenth-century philosophy and theology was that God created the universe according to scientific principles. This scene from a late-thirteenth century French Bible shows God working on His Creation with a draftsman's compass.

One of the most important thinkers who paved the way for Scholasticism without yet being fully a Scholastic himself was the stormy Peter Abelard, who was active in and around Paris in the first half of the twelfth century. Probably the first Western European who consciously sought to forge a career as an intellectual (rather than being merely a cleric who taught on the side or a schoolteacher who had no goal of adding to knowledge), Abelard was so adept at logic and theology that even as a student he easily outshone the experts of his day who had the misfortune to be his teachers. Others might have been tactful about such superiority, but Abelard gloried in openly humiliating his elders in public debate, thereby making himself many enemies. To complicate matters, in 1118 he seduced a brilliant seventeen-year-old girl, Heloise, who had been taking private lessons with him. When a child was the issue, Abelard married Heloise, but the two decided to keep the marriage secret for the sake of his career. This, however, enraged Heloise's uncle because he thought that Abelard was planning to abandon Heloise; therefore he took revenge for his family's honor by having Abelard castrated. Seeking refuge as a monk, Abelard soon witnessed his enemies engineer his first conviction for heresy. Still restless and cantankerous, he found no spiritual solace in monasticism and after quarreling and breaking with the monks of two different monastic communities he returned to life in the world by setting himself up as a teacher in Paris from about 1132 to 1141. This was the peak of his career. But in 1141 he again was charged with heresy, now by the highly influential St. Bernard, and condemned by a Church council. Not long afterward the persecuted thinker abjured, and in 1142 he died in retirement.

Peter Abelard

Abelard told of many of these trials in a letter called *The Story of My Calamities,* one of the first autobiographical accounts written in the West since St. Augustine's *Confessions.* On first reading, this work appears atypically modern because the author seems to defy the medieval Christian virtue of humility by constantly boasting about himself. But actually Abelard did not write about his calamities in order to boast. Rather, his main intention was to moralize about how he had been justly punished for his "lechery" by the loss of those parts which had "offended" and for his intellectual pride by the burning of his writings after his first condemnation. Since Abelard urged intense self-examination and analysis of human motives in an ethical treatise programmatically entitled *Know Thyself,* it

The Story of My Calamities

Sic et Non and the Scholastic method

Peter Lombard

Reacquisition of classical philosophy

seems wisest to conclude that he never intended to recommend egotism but rather was one of several prominent twelfth-century thinkers (ironically including his mortal enemy St. Bernard) who sought to take stock of the human personality by means of personal introspection.

Abelard's greatest contributions to the development of Scholasticism were made in his *Sic et Non* (Yes and No) and in a number of original theological works. In the *Sic et Non* Abelard prepared the way for the Scholastic method by gathering a collection of statements from the Church fathers that spoke for both sides of 150 theological questions. It was once thought that the brash Abelard did this in order to embarrass authority, but the contrary is true. What Abelard really hoped to do was begin a process of careful study whereby it could be shown that the Bible was infallible and that other authorities, despite any appearances to the contrary, really agreed with each other. Later Scholastics would follow his method of studying theology by raising fundamental questions and arraying the answers that had been put forth in authoritative texts. Abelard did not propose any solutions of his own in the *Sic et Non,* but he did start to do this in his original theological writings. In these he proposed to treat theology like a science, by studying it as comprehensively as possible and by applying to it the tools of logic, of which he was a master. He did not even shrink from applying logic to the mystery of the Trinity, one of the excesses for which he was condemned. Thus he was one of the first to try to harmonize religion with rationalism and was in this capacity a herald of the Scholastic outlook.

Immediately after Abelard's death two further steps were taken to prepare for mature Scholasticism. One was the writing of the *Book of Sentences* between 1155 and 1157 by Abelard's student Peter Lombard. This raised all the most fundamental theological questions in rigorously consequential order, adduced answers from the Bible and Christian authorities on both sides of each question, and then proposed judgments on every case. By the thirteenth century Peter Lombard's work became a standard text. Once formal schools of theology were established in the universities, all aspirants to the doctorate were required to study and comment upon it; not surprisingly, theologians also followed its organizational procedures in their own writings. Thus the full Scholastic method was born.

The other basic step in the development of Scholasticism was the reacquisition of classical philosophy that occurred after about 1140. Abelard would probably have been glad to have drawn upon the thought of the Greeks, but he could not because few Greek works were yet available in translation. Later theologians, however, could avail themselves fully of the Greeks' knowledge, above all, the works of Aristotle and his Arabic commentators. By around 1250 Aristotle's authority in purely philosophical matters became so great that he was referred to as "the Philosopher" pure and simple. Scholastics of the mid-thirteenth century accordingly adhered to Peter Lombard's organizational method, but added the consideration of Greek and Arabic philosophical authorities to that of purely Christian theological ones. In doing this they tried to construct systems of understanding the entire universe that most fully harmonized the earlier separate realms of faith and natural knowledge.

By far the greatest accomplishments in this endeavor were made by St. Thomas Aquinas (1225–1274), the leading Scholastic theologian of the University of Paris. As a member of the Dominican order, St. Thomas was committed to the principle that faith could be defended by reason. More important, he believed that natural knowledge and the study of the created universe were legitimate ways of approaching theological wisdom because "nature" complements "grace." By this he meant to say that because God created the natural world He can be approached through its terms even though ultimate certainty about the highest truths can only be obtained through the supernatural revelation of the Bible. Imbued with a deep confidence in the value of human reason and human experience, as well as in his own ability to harmonize Greek philosophy with Christian theology, Thomas was the most serene of saints. In a long career of teaching at the University of Paris and elsewhere he indulged in few controversies and worked quietly on his two great Summaries of theology: the *Summa contra Gentiles* and the much larger *Summa Theologica*. In these he hoped to set down all that could be said about the faith on the firmest of foundations.

St. Thomas Aquinas. A fifteenth-century painting by Justus of Ghent, after an earlier copy.

St. Thomas's Summaries

Most experts think that St. Thomas came extremely close to fulfilling this extraordinarily ambitious goal. His vast Summar*i*es are awesome for their rigorous orderliness and intellectual penetration. He admits in them that there are certain "mysteries of the faith," such as the doctrines of the Trinity and the Incarnation, that cannot be approached by the unaided human intellect; otherwise, he subjects all theological questions to philosophical inquiry. In this, St. Thomas relied heavily on the work of Aristotle, but he was by no means merely "Aristotle baptized." Instead, he fully subordinated Aristotelianism to basic Christian principles and thereby created his own original philosophical and theological system. Scholars disagree about how far this system diverges from the earlier Christian thought of St. Augustine, but there seems little doubt that Aquinas placed a higher value on human reason, on human life in this world, and on the abilities of humans to participate in their own salvation. Not long after his death St. Thomas was canonized, for his intellectual accomplishments seemed like miracles. His influence lives on today insofar as he helped to revive confidence in rationalism and human experience. More directly, philosophy in the modern Roman Catholic Church is supposed to be taught according to the Thomistic method, doctrine, and principles.

With the achievements of St. Thomas Aquinas in the middle of the thirteenth century, Western medieval thought reached its pinnacle. Not coincidentally, other aspects of medieval civilization were reaching their pinnacles at the same time. France was enjoying its ripest period of peace and prosperity under the rule of St. Louis, the University of Paris was defining its basic organizational forms, and the greatest French Gothic cathedrals were being built. Some ardent admirers of medieval culture have fixed on these accomplishments to call the thirteenth the "greatest of centuries."

Western medieval thought reaches its pinnacle

Such a judgment, of course, is a matter of taste, and many might respond that life was still too harsh and requirements for religious orthodoxy too great to justify this extreme celebration of the lost past. Whatever our individual judgments, it seems wise to end this section by correcting some false impressions about medieval intellectual life.

It is often thought that medieval thinkers were excessively conservative, but in fact the greatest thinkers of the High Middle Ages were astonishingly receptive to new ideas. As committed Christians they could not allow doubts to be cast upon the principles of their faith, but otherwise they were glad to accept whatever they could from the Greeks and Arabs. Considering that Aristotelian thought differed radically from anything accepted earlier in its emphasis on rationalism and the fundamental goodness and purposefulness of nature, its rapid acceptance by the Scholastics was a philosophical revolution. Another false impression is that Scholastic thinkers were greatly constrained by authority. Certainly they revered authority more than we do today, but Scholastics like St. Thomas did not regard the mere citation of texts—except biblical revelation concerning the mysteries of the faith—as being sufficient to clinch an argument. Rather, the authorities were brought forth to outline the possibilities, but reason and experience then demonstrated the truth. Finally, it is often believed that Scholastic thinkers were "antihumanistic," but modern scholars are coming to the opposite conclusion. Scholastics unquestionably gave primacy to the soul over the body and to otherworldly salvation over life in the here and now. But they also exalted the dignity of human nature because they viewed it as a glorious divine creation, and they believed in the possibility of a working alliance between themselves and God. Moreover, they had extraordinary faith in the powers of human reason—probably more than we do today.

5. THE BLOSSOMING OF LITERATURE, ART, AND MUSIC

The literature of the High Middle Ages was as varied, lively, and impressive as that produced in any other period in Western history. The revival of grammatical studies in the cathedral schools and universities led to the production of some excellent Latin poetry. The best examples were secular lyrics, especially those written in the twelfth century by a group of poets known as the *Goliards*. How these poets got their name is uncertain, but it possibly meant followers of the devil. That would have been appropriate because the Goliards were riotous poets who wrote parodies of the liturgy and burlesques of the Gospels. Their lyrics celebrated the beauties of the changing seasons, the carefree life of the open road, the pleasures of drinking and sporting, and especially the joys of love. The authors of these rollicking and satirical songs were mainly wandering students, although some were men in more advanced years. The names of most are unknown. Their poetry is particularly significant both for its robust vitality and for being the first clear counterstatement to the ascetic ideal of Christianity.

Charlemagne Weeping for His Knights. A scene from the *Song of Roland*.

In addition to the use of Latin, the vernacular languages of French, German, Spanish, and Italian became increasingly popular as media of literary expression. At first, most of the literature in the vernacular languages was written in the form of the heroic epic. Among the leading examples were the French *Song of Roland,* the Norse eddas and sagas, the German *Song of the Nibelungs,* and the Spanish *Poem of the Cid.* Practically all of these works were originally composed between 1050 and 1150, although some were first set down in writing afterward. These epics portrayed a virile but unpolished warrior society. Blood flowed freely, skulls were cleaved by battle-axes, and heroic warfare, honor, and loyalty were the major themes. If women were mentioned at all, they were subordinate to men. Brides were expected to die for their betrotheds, but husbands were free to beat their wives. In one French epic a queen who tried to influence her husband met with a blow to the nose; even though blood flowed she replied: "Many thanks, when it pleases you, you may do it again." Despite the repugnance we find in such passages, the best of the vernacular epics have much unpretentious literary power. Above all, the *Song of Roland,* though crude, is like an uncut gem.

The growth of vernacular literature; the epic

In comparison to the epics, an enormous change in both subject matter and style was introduced in twelfth-century France by the troubadour poets and the writers of courtly romances. The dramatic nature of this change represents further proof that high-medieval culture was not at all conservative. The troubadours were courtier poets who came from southern France and wrote in a language related to French known as Provençal. The origin of their inspiration is debated, but there can be no doubt that they initiated a movement of profound importance for all subsequent Western literature. Their style was far more finely wrought and sophisticated than that of the epic poets, and the most eloquent of their lyrics, which were meant to be

The love songs of the troubadours

sung to music, originated the theme of romantic love. The troubadours idealized women as marvelous beings who could grant intense spiritual and sensual gratification. Whatever greatness the poets found in themselves they usually attributed to the inspiration they found in love. But they also assumed that their love would lose its magic if it were too easily or frequently gratified. Therefore, they wrote more often of longing than of romantic fulfillment.

Other troubadour poems

In addition to their love lyrics, the troubadours wrote several other kinds of short poems. Some were simply bawdy. In these, love is not mentioned at all, but the poet revels in thoughts of carnality, comparing, for example, the riding of his horse to the "riding" of his mistress. Other troubadour poems treat of feats of arms, others comment on contemporary political events, and a few even meditate on matters of religion. But whatever the subject matter, the best troubadour poems were always cleverly and innovatively expressed. The literary tradition originated by the southern French troubadours was continued by the *trouvères* in northern France and by the *minnesingers* in Germany. Thereafter many of their innovations were developed by later lyric poets in all Western languages. Some of their poetic devices were consciously revived in the twentieth century by such "modernists" as Ezra Pound.

*The Arthurian romances;
Chrétien de Troyes*

An equally important twelfth-century French innovation was the composition of longer narrative poems known as *romances*. These were the first clear ancestors of the modern novel: they told engaging stories, they often excelled in portraying character, and their subject matter was usually love and adventure. Some romances elaborated on classical Greek themes, but the most famous and best were "Arthurian." These took their material from the legendary exploits of the Celtic hero King Arthur and his many chivalrous knights. The first great writer of Arthurian romances was the northern Frenchman Chrétien de Troyes, who was active between about 1165 and 1190. Chrétien did much to help create and shape the new form, and he also introduced innovations in subject matter and attitudes. Whereas the troubadours exalted unrequited, extramarital love, Chrétien was the first to hold forth the ideal of romantic love within marriage. He also described not only the deeds but the thoughts and emotions of his characters.

"Courtly Love." Although authors of medieval romances did not themselves use the term courtly love, they did propagate the ideal of intense romantic feeling between a knightly lover and his faraway beloved. From a manuscript of the romance *Willehalm* by Wolfram von Eschenbach.

A generation later, Chrétien's work was continued by the great German poets Wolfram von Eschenbach and Gottfried von Strassburg. These are recognized as the greatest writers in the German language before the eighteenth century. Wolfram's *Parzival,* a story of love and the search for the Holy Grail, is more subtle, complex, and greater in scope than any other high-medieval literary work except Dante's *Divine Comedy.* Like Chrétien, Wolfram believed that true love could only be fulfilled in marriage, and in *Parzival,* for the first time in Western literature since the Greeks, one can see a full psychological development of the hero. Gottfried von Strassburg's *Tristan* is a more somber work, which tells of the hopeless adulterous love of Tristan and Isolde. Indeed, it might almost be regarded as the prototype of modern tragic romanticism. Gottfried was one of the first to develop fully the idea of individual suffering as a literary theme and to point out the indistinct line that separates pleasure from pain. For him, to love is to yearn, and suffering and unfulfilled gratification are integral chapters of the book of life. Unlike the troubadours, he could only see complete fulfillment of love in death. *Parzival* and *Tristan* have become most famous today in the form of their operatic reconceptions by the nineteenth-century German composer Richard Wagner.

Not all high-medieval narratives were so elevated as the romances in either form or substance. A very different new narrative form was the *fabliau,* or verse fable. Although *fabliaux* derived from the moral animal tales of Aesop, they quickly evolved into short stories that were written less to edify or instruct than to amuse. Often they were very coarse, and sometimes they dealt with sexual relations in a broadly humorous and thoroughly unromantic manner. Many were also strongly anticlerical, making monks and priests the butts of their jokes. Because the *fabliaux* are so "uncourtly" it was once thought that they were written solely for the new urban classes. But there is now little doubt that they were addressed at least equally to the "refined" aristocracy who liked to have their laughs too. They are significant as expressions of growing worldliness and as the first manifestations of the robust realism that was later to be perfected by Boccaccio and Chaucer.

The fabliaux

Completely different in form but similar as an illustration of growing worldliness was the sprawling *Romance of the Rose.* As its title indicates, this was begun as a romance, specifically around 1230 by the courtly Frenchman William of Lorris. But William left his rather flowery, romantic work unfinished, and it was completed around 1270 by another Frenchman, John of Meun. The latter changed its nature greatly. He inserted long, biting digressions in which he skewered religious hypocrisy, and made his major theme the need for procreation. Not love, but the service of "Dame Nature" in sexual fecundity is urged in numerous witty but extremely earthy images and metaphors. At the climax the originally dreamy hero seizes his mistress, who is allegorically depicted as a rose, and rapes her. Since the work became enormously popular, it seems fair to conclude that tastes, then as now, were very diverse.

Nature Perpetuates the Species. A miniature from a manuscript of the *Romance of the Rose.*

Romance of the Rose

In a class by itself as the greatest work of medieval literature is Dante's *Divine Comedy.* Not much is known about the life of Dante Alighieri (1265–1321), except that he was active during the early part of his career in the political affairs of his native city of Florence. Despite his engagement in politics and the fact that he was a layman, he managed to acquire an awesome mastery of the religious, philosophic, and literary knowledge of his time. He not only knew the Bible and the Church fathers, but—most unusual for a layman—he also absorbed the most recent Scholastic theology. In addition, he was thoroughly familiar with Virgil, Cicero, Boethius, and numerous other classical writers, and was fully conversant with the poems of the troubadours and the Italian poetry of his own day. In 1302 he was expelled from Florence after a political upheaval and was forced to live the rest of his life in exile. The *Divine Comedy,* his major work, was written during this final period.

Dante

Dante's *Divine Comedy* is a monumental narrative in powerful rhyming

*Dante and Virgil Journey through
Hell.* From an Italian manuscript
of the late fourteenth century.

Italian verse, which describes the poet's journey through hell, purgatory, and paradise. At the start Dante tells of how he once found himself in a "dark wood," his metaphor for a deep personal mid-life crisis. He is led out of this forest of despair by the Roman Virgil, who stands for the heights of classical reason and philosophy. Virgil guides Dante on a trip through hell and purgatory, and afterward Dante's deceased beloved, Beatrice, who stands for Christian wisdom and blessedness, takes over and guides him through paradise. In the course of this progress Dante meets both historical beings and the poet's contemporaries, all of whom have already been assigned places in the afterlife, and he is instructed by them and his guides as to why they met their several fates. As the poem progresses the poet himself leaves the condition of despair to grow in wisdom and ultimately to reach assurance of his own salvation.

Every reader finds a different combination of wonder and satisfaction in Dante's magnificent work. Some—especially those who know Italian—marvel at the vigor and inventiveness of Dante's language and images. Others are awed by his subtle complexity and poetic symmetry; others by his array of learning; others by the vitality of his characters and individual stories; and still others by his soaring imagination. The historian finds it particularly remarkable that Dante could sum up the best of medieval learning in such an artistically satisfying manner. Dante stressed the precedence of salvation, but he viewed the earth as existing for human benefit. He allowed humans free will to choose good and avoid evil, and accepted Greek philosophy as authoritative in its own sphere; for example, he called Aristotle "the master of them that know." Above all, his sense of hope and his ultimate faith in humanity—remarkable for a defeated exile—most powerfully expresses the dominant mood of the High Middle Ages and makes Dante one of the two or three most stirringly affirmative writers who ever lived.

*Medieval architecture: (1) the
Romanesque style*

The closest architectural equivalents of the *Divine Comedy* are the great high-medieval Gothic cathedrals, for they too have qualities of vast scope, balance of intricate detail with careful symmetry, soaring height, and affir-

A Romanesque Vision of Original Sin. One of the masterpieces of Romanesque style, this sculptural relief, dating from about 1100, appears on a bronze door of the cathedral of Hildesheim (Germany) and depicts the moment of punishment in the Garden of Eden. Anatomical distortion and spare abstraction create a haunting effect of tremulous human vulnerability. Caught in the profoundest act of disobedience the first humans hope to shift the blame for their own actions.

Worms Cathedral, Eleventh-Century Romanesque

mative religious grandeur. But before we approach the Gothic style, it is best to introduce it by means of its high-medieval predecessor, the style of architecture and art known as the *Romanesque*. This style had its origins in the tenth century, but became fully formed in the eleventh and first half of the twelfth centuries, when the religious reform movement led to the building of many new monasteries and large churches. The Romanesque was primarily a building style: it aimed to manifest the glory of God in ecclesiastical construction by rigorously subordinating all architectural details to a uniform system. In this it was very severe: we may think of it as the architectural analogue of the unadorned hymn. Aside from its primary stress on systematic construction, the essential features of the Romanesque style were the rounded arch, massive stone walls, enormous piers, small windows, and the predominance of horizontal lines. The plainness of interiors was sometimes relieved by mosaics or frescoes in bright colors and, a very important innovation for Christian art, the introduction of sculptural decoration, both within and without. For the first time, full-length human figures appeared on facades. These are usually grave and elongated far beyond natural dimensions, but they have much evocative power and represent the first manifestations of a revived interest in sculpting the human form.

In the course of the twelfth and thirteenth centuries the Romanesque style was supplanted throughout most of Europe by the *Gothic*. Although trained art historians can see how certain traits of the one style led to the development of the other, the actual appearance of the two styles is enormously different. In fact, the two seem as different as the epic is different

A Romanesque Vision of the Last Judgment. A detail from the reliefs made for the cathedral of Autun (central France) around 1135 shows an angel sounding his trumpet while one of the human elect ascends to heaven. Extreme vertical elongation here creates a sense of dramatic intensity.

(2) the development of the Gothic style

from the romance, an appropriate analogy because the Gothic style emerged in France in the mid-twelfth century exactly when the romance did, and because it was far more sophisticated, graceful, and elegant than its predecessor, in the same way that the romance compared with the epic. The rapid development and acceptance of the Gothic shows for a last time—if any more proof be needed—that the twelfth century was experimental and dynamic, at least as much as the twentieth. When the abbey church of St. Denis, venerated as the shrine of the French patron saint and burial place of French kings, was torn down in 1144 in order to make room for a much larger one in the strikingly new Gothic style, it was as if the president of the United States were to tear down the White House and replace it with a Mies van der Rohe or Helmut Jahn edifice. Such an act today would be highly improbable, or at least would create an enormous uproar. But in the twelfth century the equivalent actually happened and was taken in stride.

Elements of the Gothic style

Gothic architecture was one of the most intricate of building styles. Its basic elements were the pointed arch, groined and ribbed vaulting, and the flying buttress. These devices made possible a much lighter and loftier construction than could ever have been achieved with the round arch and the

Left: *Rheims Cathedral.* Built between 1220 and 1299, this High Gothic cathedral places great stress on the vertical elements. The gabled portals, the windows above the doorways, the gallery of royal statues, and the multitude of pinnacles all accentuate the height of the structure. Right: *The High Chapel of La Sainte-Chapelle, Paris.* High Gothic is here carried to its logical extreme. Slender columns, tracery, and stained-glass windows take the place of walls.

engaged pier of the Romanesque. In fact, the Gothic cathedral could be described as a skeletal framework of stone enclosed by enormous windows. Other features included lofty spires, rose windows, delicate tracery in stone, elaborately sculptured facades, multiple columns, and the use of gargoyles, or representations of mythical monsters, as decorative devices. Ornamentation in the best of the cathedrals was generally concentrated on the exterior. Except for the stained-glass windows and the intricate carving on woodwork and altars, interiors were kept rather simple and occasionally almost severe. But the inside of the Gothic cathedral was never somber or gloomy. The stained-glass windows served not to exclude the light but to glorify it, to catch the rays of sunlight and suffuse them with a richness and warmth of color that nature itself could hardly duplicate even in its happiest moods.

Many people still think of the Gothic cathedral as the expression of purely ascetic otherworldliness, but this estimation is highly inaccurate. Certainly all churches are dedicated to the glory of God and hope for life everlasting, but Gothic ones sometimes included stained-glass scenes of daily life that had no overt religious significance at all. More important, Gothic sculpture of religious figures such as Jesus, the Virgin, and the saints was becoming far more naturalistic than anything hitherto created in the medieval West. So also was the sculptural representation of plant and animal life, for interest in the human person and in the world of natural beauty was no longer considered sinful. Moreover, Gothic architecture was also an expression of the medieval intellectual genius. Each cathedral, with its mass of symbolic figures, was a kind of encyclopedia of medieval knowledge carved in stone for those who could not read. Finally, Gothic cathedrals were manifestations of urban pride. Always located in the growing medieval cities, they were meant to be both centers of community life and expressions of a town's greatness. When a new cathedral went up the people of the entire community participated in erecting it, and rightfully regarded it as almost their own property. Many of the Gothic cathedrals were the products of urban rivalries. Each city or town sought to overawe its neighbor with ever bigger or taller buildings, to the degree that ambitions sometimes got out of bounds and many of the cathedrals were left unfinished. But most of the finished ones are still vast enough. Built to last into eternity, they provide the most striking visual manifestation of the soaring exuberance of their age.

The significance of Gothic architecture

Surveys of high-medieval accomplishments often omit drama and music, but such oversights are unfortunate. Our own modern drama descends at least as much from the medieval form as from the classical one. Throughout the medieval period some Latin classical plays were known in manuscript but were never performed. Instead drama was born all over again within the Church. In the early Middle Ages certain passages in the liturgy began to be acted out. Then, in the twelfth century, primarily in Paris, these were superseded by short religious plays in Latin, performed inside the Church. Rapidly thereafter, and still in twelfth-century Paris, the Latin plays were supplemented or supplanted by ones in the vernacular so that the whole congregation could understand them. Then, around 1200,

The revival of drama

Gothic Scuplture. The three kings bearing gifts, from the thirteenth-century cathedral of Amiens. Note the greater naturalism in comparison to the Romanesque sculptural scenes shown on pages 350 and 351.

these started to be performed outside, in front of the Church, so that they would not take time away from the services. As soon as that happened, drama entered the everyday world: nonreligious stories were introduced, character portrayal was expanded, and the way was fully prepared for the Elizabethans and Shakespeare.

As the drama grew out of developments within the liturgy and then moved far beyond them, so did characteristically Western music. Until the High Middle Ages Western music was *homophonic,* as is most non-Western music even today. That is, it developed only one melody at a time without any harmonic background. The great high-medieval invention was *polyphony,* or the playing of two or more harmonious melodies together. Some experiments along these lines may have been made in the West as early as the tenth century, but the most fundamental breakthrough was achieved in the cathedral of Paris around 1170, when the Mass was first sung by two voices weaving together two different melodies in "counterpoint." Roughly concurrently, systems of musical notation were invented and perfected so that performance no longer had to rely on memory and could become more complex. All the greatness of Western music followed from these first steps.

It may have been noticed that many of the same people who made such important contributions to learning, thought, literature, architecture, drama, and music, must have intermingled with each other in the Paris of the High Middle Ages. Some of them no doubt prayed together in the

Medieval music: Polyphony

The enduring achievements of the High Middle Ages

cathedral of Notre Dame. The names of the leading scholars are remembered, but the names of most of the others are forgotten. Yet taken together they did as much for civilization and created as many enduring monuments as their counterparts in ancient Athens. If their names are forgotten, their achievements in many different ways live on still.

SELECTED READINGS

- *Items so designated are available in paperback editions.*

RELIGION AND THE CRUSADES

- Barraclough, Geoffrey, *The Medieval Papacy,* New York, 1968. A forcefully argued analytical treatment. Noteworthy too for its illustrations.

  Blumenthal, Uta-Renate, *The Investiture Controversy,* Philadelphia, 1988. A clear review of a complicated subject.

  Erdmann, Carl, *The Origin of the Idea of Crusade,* Princeton, 1977. A brilliant advanced work on the background to the First Crusade.

  Lambert, Malcolm, *Medieval Heresy,* 2nd ed., London, 1992. The standard synthesis.

  Leclercq, Jean, *Bernard of Clairvaux and the Cistercian Spirit,* Kalamazoo, Mich., 1976.

- Mayer, Hans Eberhard, *The Crusades,* 2nd ed., New York, 1988. The best one-volume survey.

  Moorman, J. R. H., *A History of the Franciscan Order from Its Origins to the Year 1517,* Oxford, 1968. Exhaustive.

  Morris, Colin, *The Papal Monarchy: The Western Church from 1050 to 1250,* Oxford, 1989. An encyclopedic survey.

- Runciman, Steven, *A History of the Crusades,* 3 vols., Cambridge, 1951–1954. Colorful and engrossing.

  Southern, Richard W., *Western Society and the Church in the Middle Ages,* Baltimore, 1970. An extremely insightful and well-written interpretation of the interplay between society and religion.

  Tellenbach, Gerd, *Church, State and Christian Society at the Time of the Investiture Contest,* Oxford, 1940. Stresses revolutionary aspects of Gregory VII's thought and career.

THOUGHT, LETTERS, AND THE ARTS

- Baldwin, John W., *The Scholastic Culture of the Middle Ages,* Lexington, Mass., 1971. A fine introduction.

  Bergin, Thomas G., *Dante,* New York, 1965.

  Cobban, Alan B., *The Medieval Universities,* London, 1975. The best shorter treatment in English.

  _____, *The Medieval English Universities,* Berkeley, 1988.

- Curtius, E. R., *European Literature and the Latin Middle Ages,* New York, 1953. An exhaustive treatment of medieval Latin literature in terms of its classical background and influence on later times.

  Fox, John, *A Literary History of France, I: The Middle Ages,* London, 1974. The best general history.

- Gilson, E., *Reason and Revelation in the Middle Ages,* New York, 1938. A brief but illuminating treatment by the greatest modern student of Scholasticism.
- Henderson, George, *Gothic,* Baltimore, 1967.

  Hoppin, Richard H., *Medieval Music,* New York, 1978.
- Knowles, David, *The Evolution of Medieval Thought,* 2nd ed., London, 1988. A very authoritative and well-written but often difficult survey.
- Leclercq, Jean, *The Love of Learning and the Desire for God,* New York, 1961. About monastic culture, with special reference to St. Bernard.

  Leff, G., *Paris and Oxford Universities in the Thirteenth and Fourteenth Centuries,* New York, 1968. Covers both thought and institutions of learning.
- Lewis, C. S., *The Discarded Image,* Cambridge, 1964.
- Lindberg, David C., ed., *Science in the Middle Ages,* Chicago, 1978. A collection of introductory essays by leading authorities in their respective fields.
- Mâle, Emile, *The Gothic Image,* New York, 1913.
- Morris, Colin, *The Discovery of the Individual,* London, 1972. A provocative interpretation that sees "individualism" as a twelfth-century discovery.
- Smalley, B., *The Study of the Bible in the Middle Ages,* 3rd ed., Oxford, 1983. A standard work that is also gracefully written and original in its argumentation.

  Southern, Richard W., *Medieval Humanism,* New York, 1970. A collection of essays, almost all of which are exciting. Most exciting is the title piece.

  Ullmann, Walter, *Medieval Political Thought,* rev. ed., Baltimore, 1976. The best short survey.

  Van Steenberghen, F., *Aristotle in the West,* New York, 1970. A short account of the recovery of Aristotelian thought in the High Middle Ages.
- Von Simson, O., *The Gothic Cathedral,* New York, 1956. A controversial argument that Gothic architecture was meant to be "scientific."
- Weisheipl, J. A., *Friar Thomas d'Aquino: His Life, Thought, and Works,* 2nd ed., Washington, D.C., 1983.

SOURCE MATERIALS

- *An Aquinas Reader,* ed. Mary T. Clark, New York, 1972.
- Chrétien de Troyes, *Arthurian Romances,* tr. W. W. Kibler, New York, 1991.
- Dante, *The Divine Comedy,* tr. J. Ciardi, New York, 1977.
- Goldin, F., ed., *Lyrics of the Troubadours and Trouvères,* New York, 1973.
- Gottfried von Strassburg, *Tristan,* tr. A. T. Hatto, Baltimore, 1960.
- Joinville and Villehardouin, *Chronicles of the Crusades,* tr. M. R. B. Shaw, Baltimore, 1963.
- *The Letters of Abelard and Heloise* (includes Abelard's *Story of My Calamities*), tr. B. Radice, Baltimore, 1974.
- Peters, Edward, ed., *The First Crusade: The Chronicle of Fulcher of Chartres and Other Source Materials,* Philadelphia, 1971.
- *The Romance of the Rose,* tr. Harry W. Robbins, New York, 1962.
- *The Song of Roland,* tr. F. Goldin, New York, 1978.
- Thorndike, Lynn, ed., *University Records and Life in the Middle Ages,* New York, 1944.
- Tierney, Brian, ed., *The Crisis of Church and State, 1050–1300,* Englewood Cliffs, N.J., 1964. An excellent anthology of readings introduced and connected by masterful commentary.
- Wolfram von Eschenbach, *Parzival,* tr. H. M. Mustard and C. E. Passage, New York, 1961.

Chapter 12

THE LATER MIDDLE AGES
(1300–1500)

My lot has been to live amidst a storm
Of varying disturbing circumstances.
For you . . . a better age awaits.
Our descendants—the darkness once dispersed—
Can come again to the old radiance.

        —The poet Petrarch,

           writing in the 1340s

I f the High Middle Ages were "times of feasts," then the late Middle Ages were "times of famine." From about 1300 until the middle or latter part of the fifteenth century calamities struck throughout Western Europe with appalling severity and dismaying persistence. Famine first prevailed because agriculture was impeded by soil exhaustion, colder weather, and torrential rainfalls. Then, on top of those "acts of God," came the most terrible natural disaster of all: the dreadful plague known as the "Black Death," which cut broad swaths of mortality throughout Western Europe. As if all that were not enough, incessant warfare continually brought hardship and desolation. Common people suffered most because they were most exposed to raping, stabbing, looting, and burning by soldiers and organized bands of freebooters. After an army passed through a region one might see miles of smoldering ruins littered with putrefying corpses; in many places the desolation was so great that wolves roamed the countryside and even entered the outskirts of the cities. In short, if the serene Virgin symbolized the High Middle Ages, the grinning death's-head symbolized the succeeding period. For these reasons we should not look to the Later Middle Ages for the dramatic progress we saw transpiring earlier; but this is not to say that there was no progress at all. In the last two centuries of the Middle Ages Europeans displayed a tenacious perseverance in the face of adversity. Instead of abandoning themselves to apathy, they resolutely sought to adjust themselves to changed circumstances. Thus there was no collapse of civilization as there was with the fall of the Roman Em-

The Later Middle Ages: Catastrophe and adaptation

pire, but rather a period of transition that resulted in preserving and build-ing upon what was most solid in Europe's earlier legacy.

1. ECONOMIC DEPRESSION AND THE EMERGENCE OF A NEW EQUILIBRIUM

Economic crisis

By around 1300 the agricultural expansion of the High Middle Ages had reached its limits. Thereafter yields and areas under cultivation began to decline, causing a decline in the whole European economy that was accel-erated by the disruptive effects of war. Accordingly, the first half of the fourteenth century was a time of growing economic depression. The com-ing of the Black Death in 1347 made this depression particularly acute be-cause it completely disrupted the affairs of daily life. Subsequent recur-rences of the plague and protracted warfare continued to depress most of the European economy until deep into the fifteenth century. But between roughly 1350 and 1450 Europeans learned how to adjust to the new eco-nomic circumstances and succeeded in placing their economy on a sounder basis. This became most evident after around 1450, when the tapering off of disease and warfare permitted a slow, but steady economic recovery. All told, therefore, despite a prolonged depression of roughly 150 years, Eu-rope emerged in the later fifteenth century with a healthier economy than it had known earlier.

Agricultural adversity

The limits to agricultural expansion reached around 1300 were natural ones. There was a limit to the amount of land that could be cleared and a limit to the amount of crops that could be raised without the introduction of scientific farming. In fact, Europeans had gone further in clearing and cultivating than they should have: in the enthusiasm of the high-medieval colonization movement, marginal lands had been cleared that were not rich enough to sustain intense cultivation. In addition, even the best plots were becoming overworked. To make matters worse, after around 1300 the weather deteriorated. Whereas Western Europe had been favored with a drying and warming trend in the eleventh and twelfth centuries, in the fourteenth century the climate became colder and wetter. Although the av-erage decline in temperature over the course of the century was only at most 1° Centigrade, this was sufficient to curtail viticulture in many north-ern areas such as England. Cereal farming too became increasingly imprac-tical in far northern regions because the growing season became too short: in Greenland and parts of Scandinavia agricultural settlements were aban-doned entirely. Increased rainfall also took its toll. Terrible floods that del-uged all of northwestern Europe in 1315 ruined crops and caused a pro-longed, deadly famine. For three years peasants were so driven by hunger that they ate their seed grain, ruining their chances for a full recovery in the following season. In desperation they also ate cats, dogs, and rats. Many peasants were so exposed to unsanitary conditions and weakened by mal-nutrition that they became highly susceptible to disease. Thus there was an appalling death rate. In one Flemish city a tenth of the population was

Death at the Baptism. In the Later Middle Ages recurrent outbreaks of plague, coupled with other natural and manmade disasters, led to an obsession with the omnipresence of death. This chilling illumination from a fifteenth-century German manuscript shows a friar baptizing a newborn child while death stands ready to "dry him off." The point is that death stands waiting for all of us, even from the first minute of life.

buried within a six-month period of 1316 alone. Relatively settled farming conditions returned after 1318, but in many parts of Europe heavy rains or other climatic disasters came again. In Italy floods swept away Florentine bridges in 1333 and a tidal wave destroyed the port of Amalfi in 1343. With nature so recurrently capricious economic life could only suffer.

Although ruinous wars combined with famine to kill off many, Europe remained overpopulated until the middle of the fourteenth century. The reason for this was that population growth was still outstripping food supply. Since people continued to multiply while cereal production declined, there was just not enough food to go around. Accordingly, grain prices soared and the poor throughout Europe paid the penalty in hunger. And then a disaster struck that was so appalling that it seemed to many to presage the end of the world.

The pressure of population

This was the Black Death, a combined onslaught of bubonic and pneumonic plague that first swept through Europe from 1347 to 1350, and returned at periodic intervals for roughly the next hundred years. This calamity was fully comparable—in terms of the death, dislocation, and horror it wrought—to the two world wars of the twentieth century. The clinical effects of the plague were hideous. Once infected with bubonic plague by a flea-bite, the diseased person would develop enormous swellings in the groin or armpits; black spots might appear on the arms and legs, diarrhea would ensue, and the victim would die between the third and fifth day. If the infection came in the pneumonic form, i.e., caused by inhalation, there would be coughing of blood instead of swellings, and death

Black Death decimates population

Bubonic Plague. This representation from a late-fifteenth-century French painting shows a man in the throes of death from the plague. The swelling on his neck is a "bubo," a form of lymphatic swelling that gave the bubonic plague its name.

would follow within three days. Some people went to bed healthy and were dead the next morning after a night of agony; ships with dead crews floated aimlessly on the seas. Although the successive epidemics left a few localities unscathed, the overall demographic effects of the plague were devastating. To take just a few examples: the population of Toulouse declined from roughly 30,000 in 1335, to 26,000 in 1385, to 8,000 in 1430; the total population of eastern Normandy fell by 30 percent between 1347 and 1357, and again by 30 percent before 1380; in the rural area around Pistoia a population depletion of about 60 percent occurred between 1340 and 1404. Altogether, the combined effects of famine, war, and, above all, plague reduced the total population of Western Europe by at least one-half and probably more like two-thirds between 1300 and 1450.

At first, the Black Death caused great hardships for most of the survivors. Since panic-stricken people wished to avoid contagion, many fled from their jobs to seek isolation. Town-dwellers fled to the country and country-dwellers fled from each other. Even the pope retreated to the interior of his palace and allowed no one entrance. With large numbers dead and others away from their posts, harvests were left rotting, manufacturing was disrupted, and conveyance systems were abandoned. Hence basic commodities became scarcer and prices rose. For these reasons the onslaught of the plague greatly intensified Europe's economic crisis.

But after around 1400 the new demographic realities began to turn prices around and alter basic economic patterns. Particularly, the prices of staple foodstuffs began to decline because production gradually returned to normal and there were fewer mouths to feed. Recurrent reappearances of the plague or natural disasters sometimes caused prices to fluctuate greatly

A Late-Medieval Funeral Scene

PROGRESS OF THE BLACK DEATH, 14th CENTURY

in certain years, but overall prices of basic commodities throughout most of the fifteenth century went down or remained stable. This trend led to new agricultural specialization. Since cereals were cheaper, people could afford to spend a greater percentage of their income on comparative luxuries such as dairy products, meat, and wine. Hitherto farmers all over Europe had concentrated on cereals because bread was the staff of life, but now it was wisest, particularly in areas of poorer soil or unpropitious climate, to shift to specialized production. Depending upon whatever seemed most feasible, land might be used for the raising of livestock for milk, grapes for wine, or malt for beer. Specialized regional economies resulted: parts of England were given over to sheep-raising or beer production, parts of France concentrated on wine, and Sweden traded butter for cheap German grain. Most areas of Europe turned to what they could do best, and reciprocal

Economic consequences of the Black Death: (1) agricultural specialization

(2) the growth in importance of urban centers

An Artisan Making Chain Mail. One can easily see why late-medieval knightly armor was terribly expensive.

(3) growth in trade

The growth of advanced business and financial techniques

trade of basic commodities over long distances created a sound new commercial equilibrium.

Another economic result of the Black Death was an increase in the relative importance of towns and cities. Urban manufacturers usually could respond more flexibly than landlords to drastically changed economic conditions because their production capabilities were more elastic. When markets shrank, manufacturers could cut back supply more easily to match demand; they could also raise production more easily when circumstances warranted. Thus urban entrepreneurs bounced back from disaster more quickly than landowners. Often they took advantage of their greater strength to attract rural labor by means of higher salaries. Thereby the population balance between countryside and town was shifted slightly in favor of the latter.

Certain urban centers, especially those in northern Germany and northern Italy, profited the most from the new circumstances. In Germany a group of cities and towns under the leadership of Lübeck and Bremen allied in the so-called Hanseatic League to control long-distance trade in the Baltic and North Seas. Their fleets transported German grain to Scandinavia and brought back dairy products, fish, and furs. The enhanced European per capita ability to buy luxury goods brought new wealth to the northern Italian trading cities of Genoa and, especially, Venice because these cities controlled the importation of spices from the East. Greater expenditures on luxury also aided the economies of Florence, Venice, Milan, and other neighboring cities because those cities concentrated on the manufacture of silks and linens, light woolens, and other fine cloths. Milan, in addition, prospered from its armaments industry, which kept the warring European states supplied with armor and weapons. Because of varying local conditions, some cities and towns, above all those of Flanders, became economically depressed, but altogether European urban centers profited remarkably well from the new economic circumstances and emphasis on specialization.

The changed circumstances also helped stimulate the development of sophisticated business, accounting, and banking techniques. Because sharp fluctuations in prices made investments precarious, new forms of partnerships were created to minimize risks. Insurance contracts were also invented to take some of the risk out of shipping. Europe's most useful accounting invention, double-entry bookkeeping, was first put into use in Italy in the mid-fourteenth century and spread rapidly thereafter north of the Alps. This allowed for quick discovery of computational errors and easy overview of profits and losses, credits and debits. Large-scale banking had already become common after the middle of the thirteenth century, but the economic crises of the Later Middle Ages encouraged banks to alter some of their ways of doing business. Most important was the development of prudent branch-banking techniques, especially by the Florentine house of the Medici. Earlier banks had built branches, but the Medici bank, which flourished from 1397 to 1494, organized theirs along the lines of a modern holding company. The Medici branches, located in London,

Bruges, and Avignon, as well as several Italian cities, were dominated by senior partners from the Medici family who followed common policies. Formally, however, each branch was a separate partnership which did not carry any other branch down with it if it collapsed. Other Italian banks experimented with advanced credit techniques. Some even allowed their clients to transfer funds between each other without any real money changing hands. Such "book transfers" were at first executed only by oral command, but around 1400 they started to be carried out by written orders. These were the earliest ancestors of the modern check.

In surveying the two centuries of late-medieval economic history, both the role of nature and that of human beings must be emphasized. The premodern history of all parts of the globe tends to show that whenever population becomes excessive natural controls manage to reduce it. Bad weather and disease may come at any time, but when humans are already suffering from hunger and conditions of overcrowding, the results of natural disasters will be particularly devastating. That certainly is what happened in the fourteenth century. Nature intervened cruelly in human affairs, but no matter how cruel the immediate effects, the results were ultimately beneficial. By 1450 a far smaller population had a higher average standard of living than the population of 1300. In this result humans too played their part. Because people were determined to make the best of the new circumstances and avoid a recurrence of economic depression, they managed to reorganize their economic life and place it on a sounder footing. The gross European product of about 1450 was probably smaller than it was in 1300, but this is not surprising given the much smaller population. In fact, per capita output had risen with per capita income, and the European economy was ready to move on to new conquests.

The interaction of man and nature in late-medieval economic history

2. SOCIAL AND EMOTIONAL DISLOCATION

Before the healthy new equilibrium was reached, the economic crises of the Later Middle Ages contributed from about 1300 to 1450 to provoking a rash of lower-class rural and urban insurrections more numerous than Europe had ever known before or has ever known since. It was once thought that these were all caused by extreme deprivation, but as we will see, that was often not the case.

Economic crises lead to lower-class revolts

The one large-scale rural uprising that was most clearly caused by economic hardship was the northern French "Jacquerie" of 1358. This took its name from the prototypical French peasant, "Jacques Bonhomme," who had suffered more than he could endure. In 1348 and 1349 the Black Death had brought its terror and wreaked havoc with the economy. Then a flare-up of war between England and France had spread great desolation over the countryside. The peasants, as usual in late-medieval warfare, suffered most from the pillaging and burning carried out by the rapacious soldiers. To make matters even less endurable, after the English decisively de-

Rural insurrections: The Jacquerie

feated the French in 1356 at the Battle of Poitiers the French king, John II, and numerous aristocrats had to be ransomed. As always in such cases, the peasants were asked to bear the heaviest share of the burden, but by 1358 they had had enough and rose up with astounding ferocity. Without any clear program they burned down castles, murdered their lords, and raped their lords' wives. Undoubtedly their intense economic resentments were the major cause for the uprising, but two qualifications remain in order. The first is that the peasants who participated in the Jacquerie were, comparatively speaking, among the richest in France: apparently those who suffered most abjectly were entirely unable to organize themselves for revolt. The other qualification is that political factors surely help account for the Jacquerie as well as economic ones. While the king was in captivity in England, groups of townsmen were trying to reform the governmental system by limiting monarchical powers, and aristocratic factions were plotting to seize power. Since nobody quite knew which element was going to rule where, the peasants seem to have sensed an opportunity to take advantage of France's political confusion. But in fact the opportunity was not as great as they may have thought: within a month the privileged powers closed ranks, massacred the rebels, and quickly restored order.

Background of the English Peasants' Revolt

The English Peasants' Revolt of 1381—the most serious lower-class rebellion in English history—is frequently bracketed with the Jacquerie, but its causes were very different. Instead of being a revolt of desperation, it was one of frustrated rising expectations. By 1381 the effects of the Black Death should have been working in favor of the peasants. Above all, a shortage of labor should have placed their services in demand. In fact, the incidence of the plague did help to increase manumissions (i.e., freeings) of serfs and raise salaries or lower rents of free farm laborers. But aristocratic landlords fought back to preserve their own incomes. They succeeded in passing legislation that aimed to keep wages at pre-plague levels and force landless laborers to work at the lower rates. Aristocrats furthermore often tried to exact all their old dues and unpaid services. Because the peasants were unwilling to be pushed down into their previous poverty and subservience, a collision was inevitable.

The course of the revolt

The spark that ignited the great revolt of 1381 was an attempt to collect a national tax levied equally on every head instead of being made proportional to wealth. This was an unprecedented development in English tax-collecting that the peasants understandably found unfair. Two head-taxes were levied without resistance in 1377 and 1379, but when agents tried to collect a third in 1381 the peasantry rose up to resist and seek redress of all their grievances. First they burned local records and sacked the dwellings of those they considered their exploiters; then they marched on London, where they executed the lord chancellor and treasurer of England. Recognizing the gravity of the situation, the fifteen-year-old king, Richard II, went out to meet the peasants and won their confidence by promising to abolish serfdom and keep rents low; meanwhile, during negotiations, the peasant leader, Wat Tyler, was murdered in a squabble with the king's escort. Lacking leadership, the peasants, who mistakenly thought they had

The Flight into Egypt, Giotto (1276–1337). Giotto is regarded as the founder of the modern tradition in painting. A fresco in the Arena Chapel, Padua. (MMA)

The Poet Dante Driven into Exile. On the left Dante is expelled from Florence; on the right he begins work on his great poem, the *Divine Comedy.* From a mid-fifteenth-century Florentine manuscript. (The nearly completed dome of Florence's cathedral can be seen at the far left.) (British Library)

The Marriage at Cana, by Giotto.
The miracle in which Christ
(seen blessing at the far left) turns
water into wine. (Art Resource)

The Adoration of the Magi, by
Giotto. The Star of Bethlehem is
actually Halley's comet, which
Giotto would have seen in the
night skies in 1301; the fact that
this fresco was executed in 1303
or 1304 indicates that Giotto
must have made sketches from
nature that he saved for future
use. (Art Resource)

Charles the Bold, Roger van der Weyden (c. 1400–1464). The mighty duke of Burgundy, shown with the insignia of the chivalric Order of the Golden Fleece as his pendant. Command of the order passed to Charles's Habsburg descendants; thus the fleece can be seen, for example, around the neck of the Emperor Charles V as painted by Titian (color-plate facing p. 429). (Germäldegalerie, Staatliche Museen, Preussischer Kulturbesitz, Berlin)

Young Knight in the Countryside, Carpaccio (c. 1455–c. 1526). A specimen of the delight in sumptuous color of the Venetian school of Renaissance painting. (Collection Thyssen-Bornemisza)

achieved their aims, rapidly dispersed. But once the boy-king was no longer in danger of his life he kept none of his promises. Instead, the scattered peasant forces were quickly hunted down and a few alleged troublemakers were executed without any mass reprisals. The revolt itself therefore accomplished nothing, but within a few decades the natural play of economic forces caused serfdom to disappear and considerably improved the lot of the rural wage laborer.

Other rural revolts took place in other parts of Europe, but we may now look at some urban ones. Conventionally, the urban revolts of the Later Middle Ages are viewed as uprisings of exploited proletarians who were more oppressed than ever because of the effects of economic depression. But this is probably too great a simplification because each case differed and complex forces were always at work. For example, an uprising in the north German town of Brunswick in 1374 was much less a movement of the poor against the rich than a political upheaval in which one political alliance replaced another. A different north German uprising, in Lübeck in 1408, has been aptly described as a "taxpayer's" revolt. This again was less a confrontation of the poor versus the rich than an attempt of a faction that was out of power to initiate less costly government.

Urban revolts

The nearest thing to a real proletarian revolt was the uprising in 1378 of the Florentine *Ciompi* (pronounced "cheeompi"). The Ciompi were woolcombers who had the misfortune to be engaged in an industry that had become particularly depressed. Some of them had lost their jobs and others were frequently cheated or underpaid by the masters of the woolen industry. The latter wielded great political power in Florence, and thus could pass economic legislation in their own favor. This fact in itself meant that if there were to be economic reforms, they would have to go together with political changes. As events transpired it was a political crisis that called the Ciompi into direct action. In 1378 Florence had become exhausted by three years of war with the papacy. Certain patrician leaders overthrew the old regime to alter the war policy and gain their own political advantage. Circumstances led them to seek the support of the lower classes and, once stirred up, the Ciompi became emboldened after a few months to launch their own far more radical rebellion. This was inspired primarily by economic hardship and grievances, but personal hatreds also played a role. The Ciompi gained power for six weeks, during which they tried to institute tax relief, fuller employment, and representation of themselves and other proletarian groups in the Florentine government. But they could not maintain their hold on power and a new oligarchical government revoked all their reforms.

If we try to draw any general conclusions about these various uprisings, we can certainly say that few if any of them would have occurred had there not been an economic crisis. But political considerations always had some influence, and the rebels in some uprisings were more prosperous than in others. It is noteworthy that all the genuinely lower-class uprisings of economically desperate groups quickly failed. This was certainly because the upper classes were more accustomed to wielding power and giving orders;

Tombstone of a Leader of a Fourteenth-Century German Peasant Uprising. In 1336 a petty knight from Franconia (central Germany) marched at the head of impoverished peasants who vented their resentments by robbing and murdering all the Jews they could find in the nearby towns. After several months of leading this rampage the knight was finally apprehended and executed by governing authorities. His tombstone shows him with bound hands at the moment of his beheading, but the inscription calls him "blessed," a sign that some wished to view him as a martyred saint.

even more important, they had access to the money and troops necessary to quell revolts. Sometimes elements within the lower classes might fight among themselves, whereas the privileged always managed to rally into a united front when faced by a lower-class threat to their domination. In addition, lower-class rebels were usually more intent on redressing immediate grievances than on developing fully coherent long-term governmental programs; inspiring ideals for cohesive action were generally lacking. The case of the Hussite Revolution in Bohemia—to be treated later—shows that religion in the Later Middle Ages was a more effective rallying ground for large numbers of people than political, economic, and social demands.

Although the upper classes succeeded in overcoming popular uprisings, they perceived the economic and emotional insecurities of the Later Middle Ages and the possibility of revolt as a constant threat, and became obsessed with maintaining their privileged social status. Late-medieval aristocrats were in a precarious economic position because they gained most of their income from land. In times when grain prices and rents were falling and wages rising, landowners were obviously in economic trouble. Some aristocrats probably also felt threatened by the rapid rise of merchants and financiers who could make quick killings because of sharp market fluctuations. In practice, really wealthy merchants bought land and were absorbed into the aristocracy. Moreover, most landowning aristocrats were able to stave off economic threats by expert estate management; in fact, many of them actually became richer than ever. But most still felt more exposed to social and economic insecurities than before. The result was that they tried to set up artificial barriers behind which they separated themselves from other classes.

A Party of Late-Medieval Aristocrats. Notice the pointed shoes and the women's pointed hats, twice as high as their heads.

Two of the most striking examples of this separation were the aristocratic emphasis on luxury and the formation of exclusive chivalric orders. The Later Middle Ages was the period par excellence of aristocratic ostentation. While famine or disease raged, aristocrats regaled themselves with lavish banquets and magnificent pageants. At one feast in Flanders in 1468 a table decoration was forty-six feet high. Aristocratic clothing too was extremely ostentatious: men wore long, pointed shoes, and women ornately festooned headdresses. Throughout history rich people have always enjoyed dressing up, but the aristocrats of the Later Middle Ages seem to have done so obsessively to comfort themselves and convey the message that they were entirely different from others. The insistence on maintaining a sharply defined social hierarchy also accounts for the late-medieval proliferation of chivalric orders, such as those of the Knights of the Garter or the Golden Fleece. By joining together in exclusive orders that prescribed special conduct and boasted special insignia of membership, aristocrats who felt threatened by social pressures again tried to set themselves off from others, in effect, by putting up a sign that read "for members only."

Another explanation for the exorbitant stress on luxury is that it was a form of escapism. Aristocrats who were continually exposed to the sight and smell of death must have found it emotionally comforting to retreat into a dream-world of elegant manners, splendid feasts, and multicolored clothes. In a parallel fashion, nonaristocrats who could not afford such luxuries often sought relief from the vision of death in crude public entertainments: for example, crowds would watch blind beggars try to catch a squealing pig but beat each other with clubs instead, or they would cheer on boys to clamber up greasy poles in order to win prizes of geese.

It must not be thought, however, that late-medieval Europeans gave themselves over to riotous living without interruption. In fact, the same people who sought elegant or boisterous diversions just as often went to the other emotional extreme when faced by the psychic stress caused by the troubles of the age, and abandoned themselves to sorrow. Throughout the period grown men and women shed tears in abundance. The queen mother of France wept in public when she first viewed her grandson; the great preacher Vincent Ferrer had to interrupt his sermons on Christ's Passion and the Last Judgment because he and his audience were sobbing too convulsively; and the English king, Edward II, supposedly wept so much when imprisoned that he gushed forth enough hot water for his own shave. The last story taxes the imagination, but it does illustrate well what contemporaries thought was possible. We know for certain that the Church encouraged crying because of the survival of moving statuettes of weeping St. Johns, which were obviously designed to call forth tears from their viewers.

People also were encouraged by preachers to brood on the Passion of Christ and on their own mortality. Fearsome crucifixes abounded, and the figure of the Virgin Mary was less a smiling madonna than a sorrowing mother: now she was most frequently depicted slumping with grief at the foot of the cross, or holding the dead Christ in her lap. The late-medieval

Duke Philip the Good of Burgundy. The duke proudly wears the emblem of the Order of the Golden Fleece around his neck.

A Late-Medieval Crucifixion Scene. The Virgin has to be held up to keep from swooning, and the angels are weeping.

Left: *A Dead Man Before His Judge*. A late-medieval reminder of human mortality. Right: *Tomb of François de la Sarra*. This late-fourteenth-century Swiss nobleman is shown with snakes around his arms and toads littering his face.

Obsession with mortality

obsession with mortality can also still be seen in sculptures, frescoes, and book illustrations that reminded viewers of the brevity of life and the torments of hell. The characteristic tombs of the High Middle Ages were mounted with sculptures that either showed the deceased in some action that had been typical of his or her accomplishments in life, or else in a state of repose that showed death to be nothing more than peaceful sleep. But in the late fourteenth century, tombs appeared that displayed the physical ravages of death in the most gruesome ways imaginable: emaciated corpses were displayed with protruding intestines or covered with snakes or toads. Some tombs bore inscriptions stating that the viewer would soon be "a fetid cadaver, food for worms"; some warned chillingly: "What you are, I was; what I am, you will be." Omnipresent illustrations displayed figures of grinning Death, with his scythe, carrying off elegant and healthy men and women, or sadistic devils roasting pain-wracked humans in hell. Because people who painted or brooded on such pictures might the next day indulge in excessive revels, late-medieval culture often seems to border on the manic-depressive. But apparently such extreme reactions were necessary to help people cope with their fears.

3. TRIALS FOR THE CHURCH AND HUNGER FOR THE DIVINE

The intense concentration on the meaning of death was also a manifestation of a very deep and pervasive religiosity. The religious enthusiasm of the High Middle Ages by no means flagged after 1300; if anything, it became more intense. But religious enthusiasm took on new forms of expression because of the institutional difficulties of the Church and the turmoils of the age.

After the humiliation and death of Pope Boniface VIII in 1303, the Church experienced a period of institutional crisis that was as severe and prolonged as the contemporary economic crisis. We may distinguish three phases: the so-called Babylonian Captivity of the papacy, 1305–1378; the Great Schism, 1378–1417; and the period of the Italian territorial papacy, 1417–1517. During the Babylonian Captivity the papacy was located in Avignon instead of Rome and was generally subservient to the interests of the French crown. There were several reasons for this: the most obvious was that since the test of strength between Philip the Fair and Boniface VIII had resulted in a clear victory for the French king, subsequent popes were unwilling to risk French royal ire. In fact, once the popes recognized that they could not give orders to the French kings, they found that they could gain certain advantages from currying their favor. One was a safe home in southern France, away from the tumult of Italy. Central Italy and the city of Rome in the fourteenth century had become so politically turbulent and rebellious that the pope could not even count on finding personal safety there, let alone sufficiently peaceful conditions to maintain orderly ecclesiastical administration. But no such danger existed in Avignon. Even though Avignon was not then part of the French kingdom—it was the major city of a small papal territory—French military might was close enough to guarantee the pope his much-needed security. Another advantage of papal subservience to French power was help from the French in pursuing mutually advantageous policies in Germany and southern Italy. Perhaps most important was a working agreement whereby the French king would propose his own candidates to become bishops and the pope would then name them, thereby gaining sizable monetary payments. After 1305 the pro-French system became so entrenched that a majority of cardinals and all the popes until 1378 were themselves French.

At Avignon the popes were more successful than ever in pursuing their policy of centralizing the government of the Church. For the first time they worked out a really sound system of papal finance, based on the systematization of dues collected from the clergy throughout Europe. The papacy also succeeded in appointing more candidates to vacant benefices than before (in practice often naming candidates proposed by the French and English kings), and they proceeded against heresy with great determination, indeed with ruthlessness. But whatever the popes achieved in power they

The Prince of the World. A stone figure from the church of St. Sebald, Nuremberg, from about 1330. From the front the man is smiling and master of all he surveys; from the rear he is crawling with vermin.

lost in respect and loyalty. The clergy became alienated as a result of being asked to pay so much money, and much of the laity was horrified by the corruption and unbridled luxury displayed at the papal court: there the cardinals lived more splendidly than lords, dining off peacocks, pheasants, grouse, and swans, and drinking from elaborately sculptured fountains that spouted the finest wines. Most of the Avignonese popes themselves were personally upright and abstemious, but one, Clement VI (1342–1352), was worse than his cardinals. Clement was ready to offer any spiritual benefit for money, boasted that he would appoint even a jackass as bishop if political circumstances warranted, and defended his incessant sexual transgressions by insisting that he fornicated on doctors' orders.

As time went on the pressures of informed public opinion forced the popes to promise that they would return to Rome. After one abortive attempt by Urban V in 1367, Pope Gregory XI finally did return to the Holy City in 1377. But he died a year later and then disaster struck. The college of cardinals, surrounded in Rome by clamoring Italians, yielded to local sentiment by naming an Italian as pope, who took the title of Urban VI. But most of the cardinals were Frenchmen and quickly regretted their decision, especially because Urban VI immediately began quarreling with them and revealing what were probably paranoid tendencies. Therefore, after only a few months, the French cardinals met again, declared the previous election void, and replaced Urban with one of their own number, who called himself Clement VII.

Unfortunately, however, Urban VI did not meekly resign. On the contrary, he named an entirely new Italian college of cardinals and remained entrenched in Rome. Clement VII quickly retreated with his own party to Avignon and the so-called Great Schism ensued. France and other countries in the French political orbit—such as Scotland, Castile, and Aragon—recognized Clement, while the rest of Europe recognized Urban as the true pope. For three decades Christians looked on helplessly while the rival pontiffs hurled curses at each other and the international monastic orders became divided into Roman and Avignonese camps. The death of one or the other pope did not end the schism; each camp had its own set of cardinals which promptly named either a French or Italian successor. The desperateness of the situation led a council of prelates from both camps to meet in Pisa in 1409 to depose both popes and name a new one instead. But neither the Italian nor the French pope accepted the council's decision, and both had enough political support to retain some obedience. So after 1409 there were three rival claimants hurling curses instead of two.

The Great Schism was finally ended in 1417 by the Council of Constance, the largest ecclesiastical gathering in medieval history. This time the assembled prelates made certain to gain the crucial support of secular powers and also to eliminate the prior claimants before naming a new pope. After the council's election of Martin V in 1417, European ecclesiastical unity was thus fully restored. But a struggle over the nature of Church government followed immediately. The members of the Council of Constance challenged the prevailing medieval theory of papal monarchy by calling for balanced, "conciliar," government. In two momentous decrees they stated that a general council of prelates was superior in authority to the pope, and that such councils should meet regularly to govern the Church. Not surprisingly, subsequent popes—who had now returned to Rome—sought to nullify these decrees. When a new council met in Basel in 1431, in accordance with the principles laid down at Constance, the reigning pope did all he could to sabotage its activities. Ultimately he was successful: after a protracted struggle the Council of Basel dissolved in 1449 in abject failure, and the attempt to institute constitutional government in the Church was completely defeated. But the papacy only won this victory over conciliarism by gaining the support of the rulers of the European states. In separate concordats with kings and princes the popes granted the secular rulers much authority over the various local churches. The popes thus became assured of theoretical supremacy at the cost of surrendering much real power. To compensate for this they concentrated on consolidating their own direct rule in central Italy. Most of the fifteenth-century popes ruled very much like any other princes, leading armies, jockeying for alliances, and building magnificent palaces. Hence, although they did succeed for the first time in creating a viable political state, their reputation for disinterested piety remained low.

While the papacy was undergoing these vicissitudes, the local clergy throughout Europe was undergoing a loss of prestige for several reasons. One was that the pope's greater financial demands forced the clergy to demand more from the laity, but such demands were bitterly resented, especially during times of prevailing economic crisis. Then too during outbreaks of plague the clergy sometimes fled their posts just like everyone else, but in so doing they lost whatever claim they had for being morally superior. Probably the single greatest reason for growing dissatisfaction with the clergy was the increase in lay literacy. The continued proliferation of schools and the decline in the cost of books—a subject we will treat later—made it possible for large numbers of lay people to learn how to read. Once that happened, the laity could start reading parts of the Bible, or, more frequently, popular religious primers. These made it clear that their local priests were not living according to the standards set by Jesus and the Apostles. In the meantime, the upheavals and horrors of the age drove people to seek religious solace more than ever. Finding the conventional channels of church attendance, confession, and submission to clerical authority insufficient, the laity sought supplementary or alternate routes to piety. These differed greatly from each other, but they all aimed to satisfy an immense hunger for the divine.

The decline of clerical prestige

The most widely traveled route was that of performing repeated acts of external devotion in the hope that they would gain the devotee divine favor on earth and salvation in the hereafter. People flocked to go on pilgrimages as never before and participated regularly in barefooted religious processions: the latter were often held twice a month and occasionally as often as once a week. Men and women also eagerly paid for thousands of masses to be said by full-time "mass priests" for the souls of their dead rela-

The growth of lay piety: (1) devotional practices

A German Flagellant Procession. These penitents hoped they could ward off the Black Death by their mutually inflicted tortures.

tives and left legacies for the reading of numerous requiem masses to save their own souls after death. Obsession with repeating prayers reached a peak when some pious individuals tried to compute the number of drops of blood that Christ shed on the cross so that they could say the same number of Our Fathers. The most excessive and repugnant form of religious ritual in the later Middle Ages was flagellation. Some women who lived in communal houses beat themselves with the roughest animal hides, chains, and knotted thongs. A young girl who entered such a community in Poland in 1331 suffered extreme internal injuries and became completely disfigured within eleven months. Flailings were not usually performed in public, but during the first onslaught of the Black Death in 1348 and 1349, whole bands of lay people marched through northern Europe chanting and beating each other with metal-tipped scourges in the hope of appeasing the apparent divine wrath.

(2) mysticism

An opposite route to godliness was the inward path of mysticism. Throughout the European continent, but particularly in Germany and England, male and female mystics, both clerical and lay, sought union with God by means of "detachment," contemplation, or spiritual exercises. The most original and eloquent late-medieval mystical theorist was the German Dominican, Master Eckhart (c. 1260–1327), who taught that there was a power or "spark" deep within every human soul that was really the dwelling-place of God. By renouncing all sense of selfhood one could retreat into one's innermost recesses and there find divinity. Eckhart did not recommend ceasing attendance at church—he hardly could have because he preached in churches—but he made it clear that outward rituals were of comparatively little importance in reaching God. He also gave the impression to his lay audiences that they might attain godliness largely on their own volition. Thus ecclesiastical authorities charged him with inciting "ignorant and undisciplined people to wild and dangerous excesses." Although Eckhart pleaded his own doctrinal orthodoxy, some of his teachings were condemned by the papacy.

That Eckhart's critics were not entirely mistaken in their worries is shown by the fact that some lay people in Germany who were influenced by him did fall into the heresy of believing that they could become fully united with God on earth without any priestly intermediaries. But these so-called heretics of the Free Spirit were few in number. Much more numerous were later orthodox mystics, sometimes influenced by Eckhart and sometimes not, who placed greater emphasis on the divine initiative in the meeting of the soul with God and made certain to insist that the ministrations of the Church were a necessary contribution to the mystic way. Even they, however, believed that "churches make no man holy, but men make churches holy." Most of the great teachers and practitioners of mysticism in the fourteenth century were clerics, nuns, or hermits, but in the fifteenth century a modified form of mystical belief spread among lay people. This "practical mysticism" did not aim for full ecstatic union with God, but rather for an ongoing sense of some divine presence during the conduct of daily life. The most popular manual that pointed the way to this goal was the Latin *Imitation of Christ,* written around 1427, probably by the north German canon Thomas à Kempis. Because this was written in a simple but forceful style and taught how to be a pious Christian while still living actively in the world, it was particularly attractive to lay readers. Thus it quickly became translated into the leading European vernaculars. From then until today it has been more widely read by Christians than any other religious work outside of the Bible. The *Imitation* urges its readers to participate in one religious ceremony—the sacrament of the Eucharist—but otherwise it emphasizes inward piety. According to its teachings, the individual Christian is best able to become the "partner" of Jesus Christ both by taking communion and also by engaging in biblical meditation and leading a simple, moral life.

A third distinct form of late-medieval piety was outright religious protest or heresy. In England and Bohemia especially, heretical movements became serious threats to the Church. The initiator of heresy in late-medieval England was an Oxford theologian named John Wyclif (c. 1330–1384). Wyclif's rigorous adherence to the theology of St. Augustine led him to believe that a certain number of humans were predestined to be saved while the rest were irrevocably damned. He thought the predestined would naturally live simply, according to the standards of the New Testament, but in fact he found most members of the Church hierarchy indulging in splendid extravagances. Hence he concluded that most Church officials were damned. For him the only solution was to have secular rulers

*(3) heresy: John Wyclif and
the Lollards*

Death at the Stake. This fifteenth-century Italian painting reflects a pervasive late-medieval obsession with heresy. The man being burned is made to look hideous and in league with the demon flying above his head. Meanwhile a priest is elevating the host (the eucharistic wafer) to reemphasize the true faith.

appropriate ecclesiastical wealth and reform the Church by replacing corrupt priests and bishops with men who would live according to apostolic standards. This position was obviously attractive to the aristocracy of England, who may have looked forward to enriching themselves with Church spoils and at least saw nothing wrong with using Wyclif as a bulldog to frighten the pope and the local clergy. Thus Wyclif at first received influential aristocratic support. But toward the end of his life he moved from merely calling for reform to attacking some of the most basic institutions of the Church, above all the sacrament of the Eucharist. This radicalism frightened off his influential protectors, and Wyclif probably would have been formally condemned for heresy had he lived longer. His death brought no respite for the Church, however, because he had attracted numerous lay followers—called Lollards—who zealously continued to propagate some of his most radical ideas. Above all, the Lollards taught that pious Christians should shun the corrupt Church and instead study the Bible and rely as far as possible on their individual consciences. Lollardy gained many adherents in the last two decades of the fourteenth century, but after the introduction in England of the death penalty for heresy in 1399 and the failure of a Lollard uprising in 1414 the heretical wave greatly receded. Nonetheless, a few Lollards did continue to survive underground, and their descendants helped contribute to the Protestant Reformation of the sixteenth century.

John Hus

Much greater was the influence of Wyclifism in Bohemia. Around 1400, Czech students who had studied in Oxford brought back Wyclif's ideas to the Bohemian capital of Prague. There Wyclifism was enthusiastically adopted by an eloquent preacher named John Hus (c. 1373–1415), who had already been inveighing in well-attended sermons against "the world, the flesh, and the devil." Hus employed Wyclifite theories to back up his own calls for the end of ecclesiastical corruption, and rallied many Bohemians to the cause of reform in the years between 1408 and 1415. Never alienating anyone as Wyclif had done by criticizing the doctrine of the Eucharist, Hus gained support from many different directions. The politics of the Great Schism prompted the king of Bohemia to lend Hus his protection, and influential aristocrats supported Hus for motives similar to those of their English counterparts. Above all, Hus gained a mass following because of his eloquence and concern for social justice. Accordingly, most of Bohemia was behind him when Hus in 1415 agreed to travel to the Council of Constance to defend his views and try to convince the assembled prelates that only thoroughgoing reform could save the Church. But although Hus had been guaranteed his personal safety, this assurance was revoked as soon as he arrived at the Council: rather than being given a fair hearing, the betrayed idealist was tried for heresy and burned.

Hus's supporters in Bohemia were justifiably outraged and quickly raised the banner of open revolt. The aristocracy took advantage of the situation to seize Church lands, and poorer priests, artisans, and peasants rallied together in the hope of achieving Hus's goals of religious reform and social justice. Between 1420 and 1424 armies of lower-class Hussites, led by a brilliant blind general, John Zizka, amazingly defeated several invading forces of well-armed "crusading" knights from Germany. In 1434 more conservative, aristocratically dominated Hussites overcame the radicals, thereby ending attempts to initiate a purified new religious and social dispensation. But even the conservatives refused to return to full orthodoxy. Thus Bohemia never came back to the Catholic fold until after the Catholic Reformation in the seventeenth century. The Hussite declaration of religious independence was both a foretaste of what was to come one hundred years later with Protestantism and the most successful late-medieval expression of dissatisfaction with the government of the Church.

The Hussite revolt

4. POLITICAL CRISIS AND RECOVERY

The story of late-medieval politics at first seems very dreary because throughout most of the period there was incessant strife. Almost everywhere neighbors fought neighbors and states fought states. But on closer inspection it becomes clear that despite the turmoil there was ultimate improvement in almost all the governments of Europe. In the course of the fifteenth century peace returned to most of the Continent, the national monarchies in particular became stronger, and the period ended on a new note of strength just as it had from the point of view of economics.

Progress in late-medieval politics despite turmoil

Starting our survey with Italy, it must first be explained that the Kingdom of Naples in the extreme south of the Italian peninsula was sunk in endemic warfare or maladministration more or less without interruption throughout the fourteenth and fifteenth centuries. Otherwise, Italy emerged from the prevailing political turmoil of the Late Middle Ages earlier than any other part of Europe. The fourteenth century was a time of troubles for the Papal States, comprising most of central Italy, because

The political situation in Italy

forces representing the absent or divided papacy were seldom able to overcome the resistance of refractory towns and rival leaders of marauding military bands. But after the end of the Great Schism in 1417 the popes concentrated more on consolidating their own Italian territories and gradually became the strong rulers of most of the middle part of the peninsula. Farther north some of the leading city-states—such as Florence, Venice, Siena, and Genoa—had experienced at least occasional and most often prolonged social warfare in the fourteenth century because of the economic pressures of the age. But sooner or later the most powerful families or interest groups overcame internal resistance. By around 1400 the three leading cities of the north—Venice, Milan, Florence—had fixed definitively upon their own different forms of government: Venice was ruled by a merchant oligarchy, Milan by a dynastic despotism, and Florence by a complex, supposedly republican system that was actually controlled by the rich. (After 1434 the Florentine republic was in practice dominated by the banking family of the Medici.)

Peace established in the fifteenth century

Having settled their internal problems, Venice, Milan, and Florence proceeded from about 1400 to 1454 to expand territorially and conquer almost all the other northern Italian cities and towns except Genoa, which remained prosperous and independent but gained no new territory. Thus, by the middle of the fifteenth century Italy was divided into five major parts: the states of Venice, Milan, and Florence in the north; the Papal States in the middle; and the backward Kingdom of Naples in the south. A treaty of 1454 initiated a half-century of peace between these states: whenever one threatened to upset the "balance of power," the others usually allied against it before serious warfare could break out. Accordingly, the last half of the fifteenth century was a fortunate age for Italy. But in 1494 a French invasion initiated a period of renewed warfare in which the French attempt at dominating Italy was successfully countered by Spain.

Germany: The triumph of the princes

North of the Alps political turmoil prevailed throughout the fourteenth century and lasted longer into the fifteenth. Probably the worst instability was experienced in Germany. There the virtually independent princes continually warred with the greatly weakened emperors, or else they warred with each other. Between about 1350 and 1450 near-anarchy prevailed, because while the princes were warring and subdividing their inheritances into smaller states, petty powers such as free cities and knights who owned one or two castles were striving to shake off the rule of the princes. Throughout most of the German west these attempts met with enough success to fragment political authority more than ever, but in the east after about 1450 certain stronger German princes managed to assert their authority over divisive forces. After they did so they started to govern firmly over middle-sized states on the model of the larger national monarchies of England and France. The strongest princes were those who ruled in eastern territories such as Bavaria, Austria, and Brandenburg, because there towns were fewer and smaller and the princes had earlier been able to take advantage of imperial weakness to preside over the colonization of large tracts of land. Especially the Habsburg princes of Austria and the Hohenzollern princes of Brandenburg—a territory joined in the sixteenth century with the easternmost lands of Prussia—would be the most influential powers in Germany's future.

The great nation-states did not escape unscathed from the late-medieval turmoil either. France was strife-ridden for much of the period, primarily in the form of the Hundred Years' War between France and England. The Hundred Years' War was actually a series of conflicts that lasted for even more than one hundred years—from 1337 to 1453. There were several different causes for this prolonged struggle. The major one was the longstanding problem of French territory held by the English kings. At the beginning of the fourteenth century the English kings still ruled much of the rich southern French lands of Gascony and Aquitaine as vassals of the French crown. The French, who since the reign of Philip Augustus had been expanding and consolidating their rule, obviously hoped to expel the English, making war inevitable. Another cause for strife was that the English economic interests in the woolen trade with Flanders led them to support the frequent attempts of Flemish burghers to rebel against French rule. Finally, the fact that the direct Capetian line of succession to the French throne died out in 1328, to be replaced thereafter by the related Valois dynasty, meant that the English kings, who themselves descended from the Capetians as a result of intermarriage, laid claim to the French crown itself.

France: Causes of the Hundred Years' War

France should have had no difficulty in defeating England at the start: it was the richest country in Europe and outnumbered England in population by some fifteen million to fewer than four million. Nonetheless, throughout most of the first three-quarters of the Hundred Years' War the English won most of the pitched battles. One reason for this was that the English had learned superior military tactics, using well-disciplined archers to fend off and scatter the heavily armored mounted French knights. In the three greatest battles of the long conflict—Crécy (1346), Poitiers (1356), and Agincourt (1415)—the outnumbered English relied on tight discipline and effective use of the longbow to inflict crushing defeats on the French. Another reason for English success was that the war was always fought on French soil. That being the case, English soldiers were eager to fight because they could look forward to rich plunder, while their own homeland suffered none of the disasters of war. Worst of all for the French was the fact that they often were badly divided. The French crown always had to fear provincial attempts to assert autonomy: especially during the long period of warfare, when there were several highly inept kings and the English encouraged internal French dissensions, many aristocratic provincial leaders took advantage of the confusion to ally with the enemy and seek their own advantage. The most dramatic and fateful instance was the breaking away of Burgundy, whose dukes from 1419 to 1435 allied with the English, an act that called the very existence of an independent French crown into question.

The course of the war: Factors in the initial English success

It was in this dark period that the heroic figure of Joan of Arc came forth to rally the French. In 1429 Joan, an illiterate but extremely devout peasant girl, sought out the uncrowned French ruler, Charles VII, to announce that she had been divinely commissioned to drive the English out of France. Charles was persuaded to let her take command of his troops, and her piety and sincerity made such a favorable impression on the soldiers that their morale was raised immensely. In a few months Joan had liberated much of central France from English domination and had brought Charles to Rheims, where he was crowned king. But in May 1430 she was captured by the Burgundians and handed over to the English, who accused her of being a witch and tried her for heresy. Condemned in 1431 after a predetermined trial, she was publicly burned to death in the market square at Rouen. Nonetheless, the French, fired by their initial victories, continued to move on the offensive. When Burgundy withdrew from the English alliance in 1435, and the English king, Henry VI, proved to be totally incompetent, there followed an uninterrupted series of triumphs for the French side. In 1453 the capture of Bordeaux, the last of the English strongholds in the southwest, finally brought the long war to an end. The English now held no land in France except for the Channel port of Calais, which they ultimately lost in 1558.

French monarchy becomes stronger

More than merely expelling the English from French territory, the Hundred Years' War resulted in greatly strengthening the powers of the French crown. Although many of the French kings during the long war had been ineffective personalities—one, Charles VI, suffered periodic bouts of insanity—the monarchy demonstrated remarkable staying power because it provided France with the strongest institutions it knew and therefore offered the only realistic hope for lasting stability and peace. Moreover, warfare emergencies allowed the kings to gather new powers, above all, the rights to collect national taxes and maintain a standing army. Hence after Charles VII succeeded in defeating the English, the crown was able to renew the high-medieval royal tradition of ruling the country assertively. In the reigns of Charles's successors, Louis XI (1461–1483) and Louis XII (1498–1515), the monarchy became ever stronger. Its greatest single achievement was the destruction of the power of Burgundy in 1477 when the Burgundian duke, Charles the Bold, fell in the battle of Nancy at the hands of the Swiss, whom Charles had been trying to dominate. Since Charles died without a male heir, Louis XI of France was able to march into Burgundy and reabsorb the breakaway duchy. Later, when Louis XII gained Brittany by marriage, the French kings ruled powerfully over almost all of what is today included in the borders of France.

Louis XI of France. A portrait by Fouquet.

Internal turmoil in England

Although the Hundred Years' War was fought on French instead of English soil, England also experienced great turmoil during the Later Middle Ages because of internal instability. Indeed, England was a hotbed of insurrection: of the nine English kings who came to the throne between 1307 and 1485, five died violently because of revolts or conspiracies. Most of these slain kings had proven themselves to be incapable rulers, but there were other reasons for England's political troubles as well. One was that the crown had been too ambitious in trying both to hold on to its territories in France and also to subdue Scotland. This policy often made it necessary to resort to heavy taxation and to grant major political concessions to the aristocracy. When English arms in France were successful, the crown rode the crest of popularity and the aristocracy prospered from military spoils and ransoms; but whenever the tides of battle turned to defeat, the crown became financially embarrassed and thrown on the political defensive. To make matters worse, the English aristocracy was particularly unruly throughout the period, not just because the aristocrats often had reason to distrust the inept kings, but because the economic pressures of the age made them seek to enlarge their agricultural estates at the expense of each other. This led to factionalism, and factionalism often led to civil war.

The Wars of the Roses

After the English presence in France was virtually eradicated and the aristocracy could no longer hope to enrich itself on the spoils of foreign warfare, England's political situation became particularly desperate. As bad luck would have it, the reigning king, Henry VI (1422–1461), was one of the most incompetent that England has ever had. According to one authority, Henry "paralyzed and confused the whole process of English government with a royal irresponsibility and inanity which had no precedent." Henry's willfulness helped provoke the Wars of the Roses that flared on and off from 1455 to 1485. These wars received their name from the emblems of the two competing factions: the red rose of Henry's family of Lancaster and the white rose of the rival house of York. The Yorkists for a time gained the kingship, under such monarchs as Richard III, but in 1485 they were replaced by a new dynasty, that of the Tudors, who began a new period in English history. The first Tudor king, Henry VII, steadily eliminated rival claimants to the throne, avoided expensive foreign wars, built up a financial surplus, and gradually reasserted royal power over the aristocracy. When he died in 1509 he was therefore able to pass on to his son, Henry VIII (1509–1547), a royal power as great as it had ever been before.

Henry VII. A 1505 portrait by M. Sittow.

It is tempting to view the entire period of English history between 1307 and the accession of Henry VII in 1485 as one long, dreary interregnum that accomplished nothing positive. But that would not quite be doing justice to the time: in the first place, the fact that England did not entirely fall apart during the recurrent turbulence was an accomplishment in itself. Remarkably, the rebellious aristocrats of the Later Middle Ages never tried to proclaim the independence of any of their regions; only once, in 1405, did they seek unsuccessfully to divide the country between them. Discounting that insignificant exception, aristocratic rebels always sought to control the central government rather than destroy or break away from it. Thus when Henry VII came to the throne, he did not have to win back any English territories as Louis XI of France had had to win back Burgundy. More than that, the antagonisms of the Hundred Years' War had the ultimately beneficial effect of strengthening English national identity. From the Norman Conquest until deep into the fourteenth century, French was the preferred language of the English crown and aristocracy, but mounting anti-French sentiment contributed to the complete triumph of English by around 1400. The loss of lands in France was also ultimately beneficial because thereafter the crown was freed from the inevitability of war with the French. This

The positive aspects of English political developments, 1307–1485

freedom gave England more diplomatic maneuverability in sixteenth-century Continental politics and later helped strengthen England's ability to invest its energies in overseas expansion in America and elsewhere. Yet another positive development was the steady growth of effective governmental institutions; despite the shifting fortunes of kings, the central governmental administration expanded and became more sophisticated. Parliament too became stronger, largely because both the crown and the aristocracy believed that they could use it for their own ends. In 1307 Parliament had not yet become a regular part of the English governmental system, but by 1485 it definitely had. Later kings who tried to govern without it ran into severe difficulties.

The consolidation of royal power in Spain

While Louis XI of France and Henry VII of England were reasserting royal power in their respective countries, the Spanish monarchs, Ferdinand and Isabella, were doing the same on the Iberian peninsula. In the latter area there had also been incessant strife in the Later Middle Ages; Aragon and Castile had often fought each other, and aristocratic factions within those kingdoms had continually fought the crown. But in 1469 Ferdinand, the heir of Aragon, married Isabella, the heiress of Castile, and thereby created a union that laid the basis for modern Spain.

Ferdinand and Isabella

Although Spain did not become a fully united nation until 1716 because Aragon and Castile retained their separate institutions, at least warfare between the two previously independent kingdoms ended and the new country was able to embark on united policies. Isabella and Ferdinand, ruling respectively until 1504 and 1516, subdued their aristocracies, and, in the same year (1492), annexed Granada, the last Muslim state in the peninsula, and expelled all of Spain's Jews. Some historians believe that the expulsion of the Jews was motivated by religious bigotry, others that it was a cruel but dispassionate act of state that aimed to keep Spanish *conversos* (Jews who had previously converted to Christianity) from backsliding. Either way, the forced Jewish exodus led Ferdinand and Isabella to suppose that they had eliminated an internal threat to cohesive nationhood and emboldened them to initiate an ambitious foreign policy: not only did they turn to overseas expansion, as most famously in their support of Christopher Columbus, but they also entered decisively into the arena of Italian politics. Enriched by the influx of American gold and silver after the conquest of Mexico and Peru, and nearly invincible on the battlefields, Spain quickly became Europe's most powerful state in the sixteenth century.

The triumph of the national monarchies

Ultimately the clearest result of political developments throughout Europe in the Late Middle Ages was the preservation of basic high-medieval patterns. The areas of Italy and Germany that had been politically divided before 1300 remained politically divided thereafter. The emergence of middle-sized states in both of these areas in the fifteenth century brought more stability than had existed before, but events would show that Italy and Germany would still be the prey of the Western powers. The latter were clearly much stronger because they were consolidated around stronger national monarchies. The trials of the Later Middle Ages put the existence of these monarchies to the test, but after 1450 they emerged stronger than ever. The clearest illustration of their superiority is shown by the history of Italy in the years immediately following 1494. Until then the Italian states appeared to be relatively well governed and prosperous. They experimented with advanced techniques of administration and diplomacy. But when France and Spain invaded the peninsula the Italian states fell over like houses of cards. The Western monarchies could simply draw on greater resources and thus inherited the future of Europe.

5. THE FORMATION OF THE EMPIRE OF RUSSIA

Just as the half century after 1450 witnessed the definitive consolidation of the power of the Western European nation-states, so it saw the rise to prominence of the state that henceforth was to be the dominant power in the European East—Russia. But Russia was not at all like a Western nation-state; rather, by about 1500 Russia had taken the first decisive steps on its way to becoming Europe's leading Eastern-style empire.

Had it not been for a combination of late-medieval circumstances, one or several east-Slavic states might well have developed along typical Western lines. Indeed, the founders of the first political entity located in the territories of modern-day Russia, Ukraine, and Belarus were themselves westerners—Swedish Vikings who in the tenth century established a principality centered around Kiev for the purposes of protecting their lines of trade between Scandinavia and Constantinople. Within two or three generations these Vikings became linguistically assimilated by their Slavic environment, but the Kievan state they founded remained until about 1200 very much part of the greater European community of nations. Since Kiev lay on the westernmost extremity of the Russian plain (today it is the capital of Ukraine), it was natural for the Kievan state of the High Middle Ages to maintain close and cordial diplomatic and trading relations with Western Europe. For example, in the eleventh century King Henry I of France was married to a Kievan princess, Anne, and their son was consequently given the Kievan name of Philip, a christening that marked the introduction of this hitherto foreign first name into the West. Aside from such direct links with Western culture, Kievan government bore some similarity to Western limited monarchy inasmuch as the ruling power of the Kievan princes was limited by the institution of the *veche,* or popular assembly.

But after 1200 four epoch-making developments conspired to drive a wedge between Russia and Western European civilization. The first was the conquest of most of the east-Slavic states by the Mongols, or Tartars, in the thirteenth century. As early as the mid-twelfth century Kiev had been buffeted by the incursions of an Asiatic tribe known as Cumans, but Kiev and other loosely federated Russian principalities ultimately managed to hold the Cumans at bay. The utterly savage Mongols, who crossed the Urals from Asia into Russia in 1237, however, were quite another matter. Commanded by Batu, a grandson of the dreaded Genghis Khan, the Mon-

The Kievan state's ties to the West

Signature of Anne of Kiev. The Kievan princess who became queen of France must have learned how to write her name in her native land, for the letters at the bottom of this document dating from 1063 spell out "Queen Anne" in the Russian (Cyrillic) alphabet. Her son Philip, however, could only make his "sign," as indicated on the top.

Kievans Chasing Cumans.
From a fifteenth-century
Russian manuscript.

Reasons for retreat from the West: (1) the Mongol conquests in Russia

gols cut such swaths of devastation as they advanced westward that, according to one contemporary, "no eye remained open to weep for the dead." In 1240 the Mongols overran Kiev, and two years later they created their own state on the lower Volga River—the Khanate of the Golden Horde—that exerted suzerainty over almost all of Russia for roughly the following two centuries. Unwilling or unable to institute governmental arrangements that would permit them to rule the vast expanses of Russia directly, the Mongol Khans instead tolerated the existence of several native Slavic states, from whom they demanded obeisance and regular monetary tribute. Under this "Tartar yoke," the normal course of Russian political development was inevitably impeded.

(2) the emergence of Moscow as a unifying force

The native principality that finally emerged to defeat the Mongols and unify much of Russia in the fifteenth century was the Grand Duchy of Moscow, situated deep in the northeastern Russian interior. Inasmuch as Moscow was located very far away from the Mongol power base on the lower Volga, the Muscovite dukes had greater freedom of initiative to consolidate their strength free from Mongol interference than did some of their rivals, and when the Mongol Khans began to realize what was happening, it was too late to stem the Muscovite tide. But Moscow's remote location also placed it extremely far from Western Europe: about 600 miles (often snow covered) farther away from France or Italy than the distance separating those countries from Kiev. This added distance alone would have presented an appreciable obstacle to the establishment of close relations between Moscow and the West, but, to make matters far worse, the rise of Poland-Lithuania after 1386 and the fall of Constantinople in 1453 rendered cordial relations all but impossible.

Throughout most of the Middle Ages the Kingdom of Poland had been a second-rate power, usually on the defensive against German encroachments. But in the fourteenth century that situation changed dramatically, partly because German strength had by then become a ghost of its former self, and above all because the marriage in 1386 of Poland's reigning queen, Jadwiga, to Jagiello, grand duke of Lithuania, more than doubled Poland's size and enabled it to beome a major expansionist state. Even before 1386 the Grand Duchy of Lithuania had begun to carve out an extensive territory for itself, not just on the shores of the Baltic where the present territory of Lithuania lies, but in Belarus and the Ukraine. Obviously, Lithuania's expansionist momentum increased after the union with Poland: in 1410 combined Polish-Lithuanian forces in the battle of Tannenberg inflicted a stunning defeat on the German military order of Teutonic Knights who ruled neighboring Prussia, and Poland-Lithuania extended its borders so far east in the early fifteenth century that the new power seemed on the verge of conquering all of Russia. But Poland-Lithuania subscribed to Roman Catholicism in religion, whereas many of the Slavic peoples it had conquered were Eastern Orthodox who accordingly resented the sway of their new rulers. Eastern Orthodox Moscow was the obvious beneficiary of such discontent, becoming a center of religious resistance to Poland. Thus when Moscow was able to move on the offensive against Poland-Lithuania in the late fifteenth century, it appealed to religious as well as national sentiments. Prolonged warfare ensued, greatly exacerbating antagonisms, and since Poland-Lithuania stood in the Muscovites' minds for all the West, Moscow's attitude toward all of Western civilization became ever more etched by hostility.

*(3) resentment of Catholic
Poland's expansion*

Finally, interrelated with this trend were the incalculable effects wrought by the fall of Constantinople to the Turks in 1453. We have seen in Chapter 9 that missionaries from the Byzantine Empire had been responsible for converting the Kievan Slavs to the Eastern Orthodox faith in the late tenth century. During the Kievan period Russia's commitment to Eastern Orthodoxy posed no barrier to cordial communications with Western Europe because there was as yet no insuperable religious enmity between Orthodox Byzantium and the West. But embittered hatred is the only expression to describe Byzantine attitudes toward Rome after 1204 when the Western Fourth Crusaders sacked Constantinople. Eastern Orthodox Russians came to sympathize with their Byzantine mentors thereafter, and felt all the more that they had extraordinarily good reason to shun the "Roman infection" after the debacle of 1453. This was because in 1438 the Byzantines in Constantinople, sensing correctly that a mighty Turkish onslaught was in the offing, swallowed their pride and agreed to a submissive religious compromise with the papacy in the hope that this might earn them Western military support for their last-ditch stand. But despite this submission, no Western help was forthcoming and Constantinople fell to the Turks in 1453 without any Roman Catholic knight lifting a hand. Meanwhile, however, the Orthodox hierarchy of Moscow had refused to follow Byzantium in its religious submission for the obvious reason that Moscow was in no way threatened by the Turks. Once Constantinople fell, therefore, the Muscovites reached the conclusion that the Turkish victory was a divine chas-

*(4) impact of the fall of
Constantinople*

NORWAY

SWEDEN

NORWAY

WHITE
SEA

• Archangel

FINLAND

BALTIC SEA

LIVONIA

TEUTONIC
ORDERS

REP. OF NOVGOROD
• Novgorod

URAL MOUNTAINS

TEUTONIC
ORDER

LITHUANIA

KAZAN

Tannenberg

BELARUS

DUCHY OF
MOSCOW

Smolensk •   • Moscow

Nizhny
Novgorod

Kazan •

POLAND

KINGDOM OF POLAND
AND LITHUANIA

Cracow •

KHANATE OF
THE GOLDEN HORDE

UKRAINE

Kiev •

Dnieper R.

Volga R.

HUNGARY

MOLDAVIA

	Moscow c. 1300
	Expansion to 1389
	Expansion to 1462
	Expansion to 1505
- - -	Kievan State (10th-11th centuries)

VALLACHIA

ASTRAKHAN

CRIMEA

BLACK SEA

CASPIAN

OTTOMAN

Constantinople •

SEA

EMPIRE

RUSSIAN EMPIRE TO 1505

tisement for the Byzantines' religious perfidy, and the Muscovite state became the center of a particularly zealous anti-Roman ideology.

It is against this backdrop that we can examine the reign of the man who did the most to turn the Grand Duchy of Moscow into the nascent empire of Russia, Ivan III (1462–1505), customarily known as Ivan the Great. Ivan's immediate predecessor, Vasily II, had already gained the upper hand in Moscow's struggle to overthrow the domination of the Mongols, but Ivan was the one who completed this process by formally renouncing all subservience to the Mongol Khanate in 1480, by which time the Mongols were too awed by Muscovy's strength to offer any resistance. Concurrently, between 1462 and 1485, Ivan annexed one by one all the independent Russian principalities that remained between Moscow and Poland-Lithuania. And finally, as the result of two successive invasions of Lithuania (1492 and 1501), the mighty conqueror wrested away most of Belarus and the Ukraine along his western border. Thus when Ivan the Great died in 1505, it had become clear that Muscovy was a power to be reckoned with on the European scene.

But it also would have been clear to any observer that Russian culture and government were now very non-Western. Having been divorced from the West for all practical purposes since about 1200, Russia had not kept up with the most basic Western intellectual and cultural developments. For example, there was virtually no secular literature, arithmetic was barely known, Arabic numerals were not used, and merchants made their calculations with the abacus. Nor were manners and customs comparable to those of the West. Women of the upper classes were veiled and secluded, and flowing beards and skirted garments were universal for men.

Perhaps most important, during the reign of Ivan III Russia was evolving in the direction of Eastern-style political autocracy and imperialism. This can be seen most clearly in Ivan's assumption of the title "tsar of all the Russias." The word *tsar* (sometimes spelled czar) is Russian for caesar, and Ivan's appropriation of it meant that he was claiming to be the successor of the defunct Byzantine emperors, who themselves had been heirs of the Roman caesars. To reinforce this claim, Ivan married the niece of the last Byzantine ruler, adopted as his insignia the Byzantine double-headed eagle, and rebuilt Moscow's fortified princely residence, the Kremlin, in magnificent style to display his imperial splendor. Ivan's appropriation of the Byzantine model was fateful for Russia's future political development because it enabled him and his successors to imitate the Byzantine emperors in behaving like Oriental despots who assumed without discussion that "what pleases the prince has the force of law." Moreover, as "tsar of all the Russias," Ivan conceived of himself as the autocratic potentate not just of the Russians of Moscow but of all Russians, and even of Belarussians and Ukrainians. As the subsequent course of events would show, this was the beginning of an expansionist policy by which future Russian tsars would incorporate both Russian and a wide variety of non-Russian peoples into Europe's largest empire.

Ivan the Great

Russia's isolation from the West

Toward political autocracy and imperialism

6. THOUGHT, LITERATURE, AND ART

Although it might be guessed that the extreme hardships of the Later Middle Ages in Western Europe should have led to the decline or stagnation of intellectual and artistic endeavors, in fact the period was an extremely fruitful one in the realms of thought, literature, and art. In this section we will postpone treatment of certain developments most closely related to the early history of the Italian Renaissance, but will discuss some of Western Europe's other important late-medieval intellectual and artistic accomplishments.

Crisis in theology and philosophy

Theology and philosophy after about 1300 faced a crisis of doubt. This doubt did not concern the existence of God and His supernatural powers, but was rather doubt about human ability to comprehend the supernatural. St. Thomas Aquinas and other Scholastics in the High Middle Ages had serenely delimited the number of "mysteries of the faith" and believed that everything else, both in heaven and earth, could be thoroughly understood by humans. But the floods, frosts, wars, and plagues of the fourteenth century helped undermine such confidence in the powers of human understanding. Once human beings experienced the universe as arbitrary and unpredictable, fourteenth-century thinkers began to wonder whether there was not far more in heaven and earth than could be understood by their philosophies. The result was a thoroughgoing reevaluation of the prior theological and philosophical outlook.

William of Ockham; nominalism

The leading late-medieval abstract thinker was the English Franciscan William of Ockham, who was born around 1285 and died in 1349, apparently from the Black Death. Traditionally, Franciscans had always had greater doubts than Dominicans like St. Thomas concerning the abilities of human reason to comprehend the supernatural; Ockham, convinced by the events of his age, expressed these most formidably. He denied that the existence of God and numerous other theological matters could be demonstrated apart from scriptural revelation, and he emphasized God's freedom and absolute power to do anything He wished. In the realm of human knowledge per se Ockham's searching intellect drove him to look for absolute certainties instead of mere theories. In investigating earthly matters he developed the position, known as *nominalism,* that only individual things, but not collectivities, are real, and that one thing therefore cannot be understood by means of another: to know a chair one has to see and touch it rather than just know what several other chairs are like. Ockham also formulated a logic that was based upon the assumption that words stood only for themselves rather than for real things. Such logic might not say much about the real world, but at least it could not be refuted, since it was as internally valid in its own terms as Euclidean geometry.

Ockham's outlook, which gained widespread adherence in the late-medieval universities, today often seems overly methodological and verging on the arid, but it had several important effects on the development of Western thought. Ockham's concern about what God *might* do led his followers to raise some of the seemingly absurd questions for which medieval theology has been mocked, for example, asking whether God can undo the past, or whether an infinite number of pure spirits can simultaneously inhabit the same place (the nearest medieval thinkers actually came to asking how many angels can dance on the head of a pin). Nonetheless, Ockham's emphasis on preserving God's autonomy led to a stress on divine omnipotence that became one of the basic presuppositions of sixteenth-century Protestantism. Further, Ockham's determination to find certainties in the realm of human knowledge ultimately helped make it possible to discuss human affairs and natural science without reference to supernatural explanations—one of the most important foundations of the modern scientific method. Finally, Ockham's opposition to studying collectivities and his refusal to apply logic to real things helped encourage *empiricism,* or the belief that knowledge of the world should rest on sense experience rather than abstract reason. This too is a presupposition for scientific progress: thus it is probably not coincidental that some of Ockham's fourteenth-century followers made significant advances in the study of physics.

The significance of Ockham's thought

Ockham's search for reliable truths finds certain parallels in the realm of late-medieval literature, although Ockham surely had no direct influence in that field. The major trait of the best late-medieval literature was *naturalism,* or the attempt to describe things the way they really are. This was more a development from high-medieval precedents—such as the explorations of human conduct pursued by Chrétien de Troyes, Wolfram von Eschenbach, and Dante—than a reaction against them. The steady growth of a lay reading public furthermore encouraged authors to avoid theological and philosophical abstractions and seek more to entertain by portraying people realistically with all their strengths and foibles. Another main characteristic of late-medieval literature, the predominance of composition in the European vernaculars instead of Latin, also developed out of high-medieval precedents but gained great momentum in the Later Middle Ages for two different reasons. One was that international tensions and hostilities, including the numerous wars of the age and the trials of the universal papacy, led to need for security and a pride of self-identification reflected by the use of vernacular tongues. Probably more important was the fact that the continued spread of education for the laity greatly increased the number of people who could read in a given vernacular language but not in Latin. Hence although much poetry had been composed in the vernacular during the High Middle Ages, in the Later Middle Ages use of the vernacular was widely extended to prose. Moreover, countries such as Italy and England, which had just begun to cultivate their own vernacular literatures around 1300, subsequently began to employ their native tongues to the most impressive literary effect.

The naturalism of late-medieval literature

The greatest writer of vernacular prose fiction of the Later Middle Ages was the Italian Giovanni Boccaccio (1313–1375). Although Boccaccio would have taken an honored place in literary history for some of his lesser works, which included courtly romances, pastoral poems, and learned treatises, by far the most impressive of his writings is the *Decameron,* written

Boccaccio

between 1348 and 1351. This is a collection of one hundred stories, mostly about love and sex, adventure, and clever trickery, supposedly told by a sophisticated party of seven young ladies and three men who are sojourning in a country villa outside Florence in order to escape the ravages of the Black Death. Boccaccio by no means invented all one hundred plots, but even when he borrowed the outlines of his tales from earlier sources he retold the stories in his own characteristically exuberant, masterful, and extremely witty fashion. There are many reasons why the *Decameron* must be counted as epoch-making from a historical point of view. The first is that it was the earliest ambitious and successful work of vernacular creative literature ever written in Western Europe in narrative prose. Boccaccio's prose is "modern" in the sense that it is brisk, for unlike the medieval authors of flowery romances, Boccaccio purposely wrote in an unaffected, colloquial style. Simply stated, in the *Decameron* he was less interested in being "elevated" or elegant than in being unpretentiously entertaining. From the point of view of content, Boccaccio wished to portray men and women as they really are rather than as they ought to be. Thus when he wrote about the clergy he showed them to be as susceptible to human appetites and failings as other mortals. His women are not pallid playthings, distant goddesses, or steadfast virgins, but flesh-and-blood creatures with intellects, who interact more comfortably and naturally with men and with each other than any women in Western literature had ever done before. Boccaccio's treatment of sexual relations is often graphic, often witty, but never demeaning. In his world the natural desires of both women and men are not meant to be thwarted. For all these reasons the *Decameron* is a robust and delightful appreciation of all that is human.

Similar in many ways to Boccaccio as a creator of robust, naturalistic vernacular literature was the Englishman Geoffrey Chaucer (c. 1340–1400). *Chaucer* Chaucer was the first major writer of an English that can still be read today with relatively little effort. Remarkably, he was both a founding father of England's mighty literary tradition and one of the four or five greatest contributors to it: most critics rank him just behind Shakespeare, and in a class with Milton, Wordsworth, and Dickens. Chaucer wrote several highly impressive works, but his masterpiece is unquestionably the *Canterbury Tales,* dating from the end of his career. Like the *Decameron,* this is a collection of stories held together by a frame, in Chaucer's case the device of having a group of people tell stories while on a pilgrimage from London to Canterbury. But there are also differences between the *Decameron* and the *Canterbury Tales.* Chaucer's stories are told in sparkling verse instead of prose, and they are recounted by people of all different classes—from a chivalric knight to a dedicated university student to a thieving miller with a wart on his nose. Lively women are also represented, most memorably the gaptoothed, oft-married "Wife of Bath," who knows all "the remedies of love." Each character tells a story that is particularly illustrative of his or her own occupation and outlook on the world. By this device Chaucer is able to create a highly diverse "human comedy." His range is therefore greater than Boccaccio's. And although he is as witty, frank, and lusty as the Italian, he is sometimes more profound.

As naturalism was a dominant trait of late-medieval literature, so it was of late-medieval art. Already by the thirteenth century Gothic sculptors were paying far more attention than their Romanesque predecessors had done to the way plants, animals, and human beings really looked. Whereas medieval art had previously emphasized abstract design, the stress was now increasingly on realism: thirteenth-century carvings of leaves and flowers must have been done from direct observation and are the first to be clearly recognizable as distinct species. Statues of humans also gradually became more naturally proportioned and realistic in their portrayals of facial expressions. By around 1290 the concern for realism had become so great that a sculptor working on a tomb-portrait of the German Emperor Rudolf of Habsburg allegedly made a hurried return trip to view Rudolf in person, because he had heard that a new wrinkle had appeared on the emperor's face.

Naturalism in late-medieval art

In the next two centuries the trend toward naturalism continued in sculpture and was extended to manuscript illumination and painting. The latter was in certain basic respects a new art. Ever since the caveman, painting had been done on walls, but walls of course were not easily movable. The art of wall-painting continued to be cultivated in the Middle Ages and long afterward, especially in the form of *frescoes,* or paintings done on wet plaster. But in addition to frescoes, Italian artists in the thirteenth century first started painting pictures on pieces of wood or canvas. These were first done in tempera (pigments mixed with water and natural gums or egg-whites), but around 1400 painting in oils was introduced in the European north. These new technical developments created new artistic opportunities. Artists were now able to paint religious scenes on altarpieces for churches and for private devotions practiced by the wealthier laity at home. Artists also painted the first Western portraits, which were meant to gratify the self-esteem of monarchs and aristocrats. The earliest surviving example of a naturalistic, painted portrait is one of a French king, John the Good, executed around 1360. Others followed quickly, so that within a short time the art of portraiture done from life was highly developed. Visitors to art museums will notice that some of the most realistic and sensitive portraits of all time date from the fifteenth century.

Painting

The most pioneering and important painter of the Later Middle Ages was the Florentine Giotto (c. 1267–1337). He did not engage in individual portraiture, but he brought deep humanity to his religious images done on both walls and movable panels. Giotto was preeminently a naturalist, i.e., an imitator of nature. Not only do his human beings and animals look more natural than those of his predecessors, they seem to do more natural things. When Christ enters Jerusalem on Palm Sunday, boys climb trees to get a better view; when St. Francis is laid out in death, one onlooker takes the opportunity to see whether the saint had really received Christ's wounds; and when the Virgin's parents, Joachim and Anna, meet after a long separation, they actually embrace and kiss—perhaps the first deeply tender kiss in Western art. It was certainly not true, as one fanciful story-teller later reported, that an onlooker found a fly Giotto had painted so real that he attempted to brush it away with his hand, but Giotto in fact ac-

The naturalistic style of Giotto

See color plates facing page 364 for *The Flight into Egypt, Adoration of the Magi,* and *Marriage at Cana,* all by Giotto

The Meeting of Joachim and Anna at the Golden Gate. A fresco by Giotto. Note how the haloes merge: this old and barren couple will soon miraculously have a child, none other than Mary, the mother of Jesus.

See color plates following page 364 for *Charles the Bold* by van der Weyden and *Young Knight in the Countryside* by Carpaccio

The Flemish painters

See color plate following page 332 for *The Virgin and Chancellor Rolin* by Jan van Eyck

complished something more. Specifically, he was the first to conceive of the painted space in fully three-dimensional terms: as one art historian has put it, Giotto's frescoes were the first to "knock a hole into the wall." After Giotto's death a reaction in Italian painting set in. This was probably caused by a new reverence for the awesomely supernatural brought about by the horrors of the plague. Whatever the explanation, artists of the mid-fourteenth century briefly moved away from naturalism and painted stern, forbidding religious figures who seemed to float in space. But by around 1400 artists came back down to earth and started to build upon Giotto's influence in ways that led to the great Italian renaissance in painting.

In the north of Europe painting did not advance impressively beyond manuscript illumination until the early fifteenth century, but then it suddenly came very much into its own. The leading northern European painters were Flemish, first and foremost Jan van Eyck (c. 1380–1441), Roger van der Weyden (c. 1400–1464), and Hans Memling (c. 1430–1494). These three were the greatest early practitioners of painting in oil, a medium that allowed them to engage in brilliant coloring and sharp-focused realism. Van Eyck and van der Weyden excelled most at two things: communicating a sense of deep religious piety and portraying minute details of familiar everyday experience. These may at first seem incompatible, but it should be remembered that contemporary manuals of practical mysticism such as *The Imitation of Christ* also sought to link deep piety with everyday existence. Thus it was by no means blasphemous when a Flemish painter would portray behind a tender Madonna and Child a vista of contemporary life with people going about their usual business and a man even urinating against a wall. This union between the sacred and profane tended to fall apart in the work of Memling, who excelled in either straightforward religious pictures or secular portraits, but it would return in the work of the greatest painters of the Low Countries, Brueghel and Rembrandt.

7. ADVANCES IN TECHNOLOGY

No account of enduring late-medieval accomplishments would be complete without mention of certain epoch-making technological advances. Sadly, but probably not unexpectedly, treatment of this subject has to begin with reference to the invention of artillery and firearms. The prevalence of warfare stimulated the development of new weaponry. Gunpowder itself was a Chinese invention, but it was first put to particularly devastating uses in the late-medieval West. Heavy cannons, which made terrible noises "as though all the dyvels of hell had been in the way," were first employed around 1330. The earliest cannons were so primitive that it often was more dangerous to stand behind than in front of them, but by the middle of the fifteenth century they were greatly improved and began to revolutionize the nature of warfare. In one year, 1453, heavy artillery played a leading role in determining the outcome of two crucial conflicts: the Ottoman Turks used German and Hungarian cannons to breach the defenses of Constantinople—hitherto the most impregnable in Europe—and the

The Earliest Known Depiction of a Cannon. A fourteenth-century manuscript shows a primitive cannon firing an arrow rather than a cannonball.

Cannons Being Used to Breach the Walls of a Castle. This scene depicts a late engagement of the Hundred Years' War.

Late-medieval technological achievements:
(1) the weapons of war

(2) optical and navigational instruments

Devil with Eyeglasses. Once spectacles became common they were even sported by devils in hell.

(3) mechanical clocks

French used heavy artillery to take the city of Bordeaux, thereby ending the Hundred Years' War. Cannons thereafter made it difficult for rebellious aristocrats to hole up in their stone castles, and thus they aided in the consolidation of the national monarchies. Placed aboard ships, cannons enabled European vessels to dominate foreign waters in the subsequent age of overseas expansion. Guns, also invented in the fourteenth century, were gradually perfected afterward. Shortly after 1500 the most effective new variety of gun, the musket, allowed foot-soldiers to end once and for all the earlier military dominance of heavily armored mounted knights. Once lance-bearing cavalries became outmoded and fighting could more easily be carried on by all, the monarchical states that could turn out the largest armies completely subdued internal resistance and dominated the battlefields of Europe.

Other late-medieval technological developments were more life-enhancing. Eyeglasses, first invented in the 1280s, were perfected in the fourteenth century. These allowed older people to keep on reading when near-sightedness would otherwise have stopped them. For example, the great fourteenth-century scholar Petrarch, who boasted excellent sight in his youth, wore spectacles after his sixtieth year and was thus enabled to complete some of his most important works. Around 1300 the use of the magnetic compass helped ships to sail farther away from land and venture out into the Atlantic. One immediate result was the opening of direct sea commerce between Italy and the North. Subsequently, numerous improvements in shipbuilding, map making, and navigational devices contributed to Europe's ability to start expanding overseas. In the early fourteenth century the Azores and Cape Verde Islands were reached; then, after a long pause caused by Europe's plagues and wars, the African Cape of Good Hope was rounded in 1487, the West Indies reached in 1492, India reached by the sea route in 1498, and Brazil sighted in 1500. Partly as a result of technology the world was thus suddenly made much smaller.

Among the most familiar implements of our modern life that were invented by Europeans in the Later Middle Ages were clocks and printed books. Mechanical clocks were invented shortly before 1300 and proliferated in the years immediately thereafter. The earliest clocks were too expensive for private purchase, but towns quickly vied with each other to install the most elaborate clocks in their prominent public buildings. These clocks not only told the time but showed the courses of sun, moon, and planets, and performed mechanical tricks on the striking of the hours. The new invention ultimately had two profound effects. One was the further stimulation of European interest in complex machinery of all sorts. This interest had already been awakened by the high-medieval proliferation of mills, but clocks ultimately became even more omnipresent than mills because after about 1650 they became quite cheap and were brought into practically every European home. Household clocks served as models of marvelous machines. Equally if not more significant was the fact that clocks began to rationalize the course of European daily affairs. Until the advent of clocks in the Late Middle Ages time was flexible. Men and women had

Horloge de Sapience. This miniature, from an early-fifteenth-century French manuscript, reflects the growing fascination with machines of all sorts and clocks in particular.

only a rough idea of how late in the day it was and rose and retired more or less with the sun. Especially people who lived in the country performed different jobs at different rates according to the rhythm of the seasons. Even when hours were counted, they were measured at different lengths according to the amount of light in the different seasons of the year. In the fourteenth century, however, clocks first started relentlessly striking equal hours through the day and night. Thus they began to regulate work with new precision. People were expected to start and end work "on time" and many came to believe that "time is money." This emphasis on time-keeping brought new efficiencies but also new tensions: Lewis Carroll's white rabbit, who is always looking at his pocket watch and muttering, "how late it's getting," is a telling caricature of time-obsessed Western man.

The invention of printing with movable type was equally momentous. The major stimulus for this invention was the replacement of parchment by paper as Europe's primary writing material between 1200 and 1400. Parchment, made from the skins of valuable farm animals, was extremely expensive: since it was possible to get only about four good parchment leaves from one animal, it was necessary to slaughter between two to three hundred sheep or calves to gain enough parchment for a Bible! Paper, made from rags turned into pulp by mills, brought prices down dramatically. Late-medieval records show that paper sold at one-sixth the price of parchment. Accordingly, it became cheaper to learn how to read and write. With literacy becoming ever more widespread, there was a growing market for still cheaper books, and the invention of printing with movable type around 1450 fully met this demand. By greatly saving labor, the invention made printed books about one-fifth as expensive as handwritten ones within about two decades.

(4) the invention of printing

Left: *Paper-Making at a Paper Mill.* Right: *A Printing Press.* From a title page of a Parisian printer, 1520.

The effects of printing

As soon as books became easily accessible, literacy increased even more and book-culture became a basic part of the European way of life. After about 1500 Europeans could afford to read and buy books of all sorts—not just religious tracts, but instructional manuals, light entertainment, and, by the eighteenth century, newspapers. Printing ensured that ideas would spread quickly and reliably; moreover, revolutionary ideas could no longer be easily extinguished once they were set down in hundreds of copies of books. Thus the greatest religious reformer of the sixteenth century, Martin Luther, gained an immediate following throughout Germany by employing the printing press to run off pamphlets: had printing not been available to him, Luther might have died like Hus. The spread of books also helped stimulate the growth of cultural nationalism. Before printing, regional dialects in most European countries were often so diverse that people who supposedly spoke the same language often could barely understand each other. Such a situation hindered governmental centralization because a royal servant might be entirely unable to communicate with inhabitants of the provinces. Shortly after the invention of printing, however, each European country began to develop its own linguistic standards, which were disseminated uniformly by books. The "King's English" was what was printed in London and carried to Yorkshire or Wales. Thus communications were enhanced and governments were able to operate ever more efficiently.

In conclusion it may be said that clocks and books as much as guns and ocean-going ships helped Europe to dominate the globe after 1500. The habits inculcated by clocks encouraged Europeans to work efficiently and to plan precisely; the prevalence of books enhanced communications and the flow of progressive ideas. Once accustomed to reading books, Europeans communicated and experimented intellectually as no other peoples in the world. Thus it was not surprising that after 1500 Europeans could start to make the whole world their own.

SELECTED READINGS

• *Items so designated are available in paperback editions.*

• Allmand, Christopher, *The Hundred Years War,* Cambridge, 1988. The standard account.

Breisach, E., *Renaissance Europe, 1300–1517,* New York, 1973. The best college-level textbook.

Bridbury, A. R., *Economic Growth: England in the Later Middle Ages,* 2nd ed., New York, 1975. A controversial argument against the dominant theory of economic depression.

• Brucker, G., *Renaissance Florence,* New York, 1969. An excellent introduction by one of America's foremost experts.

Bynum, Caroline W., *Holy Feast and Holy Fast: The Religious Significance of Food to Medieval Women,* Berkeley, 1987. A highly original study, full of rich insights into late-medieval religion and the place of women in society.

• Cipolla, C. M., *Clocks and Culture, 1300–1700,* London, 1967. Treats both technological developments and the importance of clocks as items of trade.

• Cole, Bruce, *Giotto and Florentine Painting, 1280–1375,* New York, 1976. A clear and stimulating introduction.

• Crummey, Robert O., *The Formation of Muscovy, 1304–1613,* New York, 1987. Now the standard detailed treatment.

Florinsky, M. T., *Russia: A History and Interpretation,* Vol. I, New York, 1961. The best narrative in English of early Russian developments.

Geremek, Bronislaw, *The Margins of Society in Late Medieval Paris,* New York, 1987. A pioneering study of late-medieval "drifters," first published in Polish in 1971 by a historian who then helped lead Poland's breakaway from the Soviet Union.

• Hanawalt, Barbara, *The Ties That Bound: Peasant Families in Medieval England,* New York, 1986. Indispensable for understanding late-medieval English rural society.

• Herlihy, David, *Opera Muliebria: Women and Work in Medieval Europe,* New York, 1990. Proposes an original argument about a decline in vocational opportunities for women in the Later Middle Ages.

• Hilton, R. H., and T. H. Aston, *The English Rising of 1381,* Cambridge, 1984. A collection of articles that includes treatment of the *Jacquerie* and the *Ciompi.*

• Huizinga, Johan, *The Waning of the Middle Ages,* London, 1924. An evocatively written classic on forms of thought and art in the Low Countries.

Kaminsky, Howard, *A History of the Hussite Revolution,* Berkeley, 1967. Detailed and difficult but far and away the best treatment of the subject.

———, *Simon de Cramaud and the Great Schism,* New Brunswick, N.J., 1983. A brilliant materialist interpretation of the Schism and the activities of one of the foremost ecclesiastical politicians who helped bring it to a close.

• Lerner, Robert E., *The Age of Adversity: The Fourteenth Century,* Ithaca, N.Y., 1968.

———, *The Heresy of the Free Spirit in the Later Middle Ages,* 2nd ed., Notre Dame, 1991.

Lewis, P. S., *Later Medieval France: The Polity,* London, 1968.

• McFarlane, K. B., *The Nobility of Later Medieval England,* Oxford, 1973. An excellent collection of essays by a late master of the field.

McKisack, May, *The Fourteenth Century: 1307–1399,* Oxford, 1959. A volume in the older "Oxford History of England" series; out of date in some respects, but still the best synthesis available.

• Meiss, M., *Painting in Florence and Siena After the Black Death,* Princeton, 1951. A stimulating attempt to relate art history to the spirit of an age.

• Miskimin, H. A., *The Economy of Early Renaissance Europe, 1300–1460,* Englewood Cliffs, N.J., 1969. The best short work on the subject.

Mollat, G., *The Popes at Avignon, 1305–1378,* London, 1963.

Mollat, M., and P. Wolff, *The Popular Revolts of the Late Middle Ages,* London, 1973.

• Oakley, F., *The Western Church in the Later Middle Ages,* Ithaca, N.Y., 1979.

• Panofsky, E., *Early Netherlandish Painting,* 2 vols., Cambridge, Mass., 1953. A brilliant specialized history by a master art historian.

• Pernoud, R., *Joan of Arc,* New York, 1966. Joan viewed through the eyes of her contemporaries.

• Smart, Alastair, *The Dawn of Italian Painting, 1250–1400,* Ithaca, N.Y., 1978. More detailed than Cole

Vaughan, Richard, *Valois Burgundy,* London, 1975.

SOURCE MATERIALS

Allmand, Christopher. T., ed., *Society at War: The Experience of England and France During the Hundred Years War,* Edinburgh, 1973. An outstanding collection of documents.

• Boccaccio, G., *The Decameron,* tr. M. Musa and P. E. Bondanella, New York, 1977.

• Chaucer, G., *The Canterbury Tales.* (Many editions.)

Colledge, E., ed., *The Medieval Mystics of England,* New York, 1961.

• Froissart, J., *Chronicles,* tr. G. Brereton, Baltimore, 1968. A selection from the most famous contemporary account of the Hundred Years' War.

The Imitation of Christ, tr. L. Sherley-Price, Baltimore, 1952.

John Hus at the Council of Constance, tr. M. Spinka, New York, 1965. The translation of a Czech chronicle with an expert introduction and appended collection of documents.

• *Meister Eckhart,* eds. E. Colledge and B. McGinn, 2 vols., New York, 1981–1986. A rich collection of Eckhart's basic works, expertly introduced and annotated.

Memoirs of a Renaissance Pope: The Commentaries of Pius II (abridged ed.), tr. F. A. Gragg, New York, 1959. A fascinating insight into the Renaissance papacy.

A Parisian Journal, 1405–1449, tr. J. Shirley, Oxford, 1968. A marvelous panorama of Parisian life recorded by an eyewitness.

Part Four

THE EARLY-MODERN WORLD

Historians tend to agree that the Middle Ages ended sometime roughly around 1500 and were followed by an "early-modern" period of European history that lasted until the concurrent outbreaks of the French and Industrial Revolutions at the very end of the eighteenth century. As early as about 1350 in Italy representatives of a new cultural movement, usually called the Renaissance, began to challenge certain basic medieval assumptions and offer alternatives to medieval modes of literary and artistic expression. By around 1500 Renaissance ideals had not only triumphed fully in Italy, but they were also spreading to northern Europe where they were reconceived to produce the highly influential movement of Christian humanism. At the same time, in the early sixteenth century Western Europe lost much of its medieval appearance by expanding and dividing. Intrepid mariners and conquistadores *ended Europe's millennium of geographical self-containment by venturing onto the high seas of the Atlantic and Indian Oceans and by planting Europe's flag throughout the world. Concurrently, however, Europe lost its religious uniformity as a result of the Protestant Reformation, which divided the Continent up into hostile religious camps. Thereafter, from about 1560 to about 1660, Western Europe experienced a period of grave economic, political, and spiritual crisis but emerged from this century of testing with renewed energy and confidence. A commercial revolution spurred the development of overseas colonies and trade, and encouraged agricultural and industrial expansion. Though monarchs continued to meet with opposition from the various estates within their realms, they asserted their power as absolute rulers, stabilizing domestic unrest by continually expanding state bureaucracies. Warfare remained the chief instrument of their foreign policies; yet by the end of the period, the mutually recognized goal of those policies was more often the maintenance of a general balance of power than the pursuit of unrestrained aggrandizement. Finally, in the later seventeenth century the scientific revolution, initiated earlier by Copernicus, was completed by Sir Isaac Newton, and was followed during the eighteenth century by the "Enlightenment," or enthronement of a new secular faith in humanity's ability to master nature and better itself by its own efforts.*

The Early-Modern World

POLITICS	PHILOSOPHY AND SCIENCE	
	Civic humanism in Italy, c. 1400–c. 1450	*1400*
Renaissance popes, 1447–1521	Lorenzo Valla, 1407–1457	
French invade Italy, 1494	Florentine Neoplatonism, c. 1450–c. 1600	
	Erasmus, c. 1466–1536	
	Machiavelli, 1469–1527	
Henry VIII of England, 1509–1547	Nicholas Copernicus, 1473–1543	
Charles V, Holy Roman Emperor, 1519–1546	Andreas Vesalius, 1514–1564	*1500*
Troops of Charles V sack Rome, 1527	Thomas More's *Utopia,* 1516	
Spanish gain supremacy in Italy, 1529	Jean Bodin, 1530–1596	
	Michel de Montaigne, 1533–1592	
Philip II of Spain, 1556–1598		
Elizabeth I of England, 1558–1603	Francis Bacon, 1561–1626	
Revolt of the Netherlands, 1566–1609	Galileo, 1564–1642	
Defeat of Spanish Armada, 1588	Johann Kepler, 1571–1630	
Henry IV of France, 1589–1610	William Harvey, 1578–1657	
Edict of Nantes, 1598	Thomas Hobbes, 1588–1679	
	René Descartes, 1596–1650	
James I of England, 1603–1625		*1600*
Thirty Years' War, 1618–1648	Bacon's *Novum Organum,* 1620	
Supremacy of Richelieu in France, 1624–1642	Blaise Pascal, 1623–1662	
Frederick William, Elector of Brandenburg,	John Locke, 1632–1704	
1640–1688	Descartes' *Discourse on Method,* 1637	
English Civil War, 1642–1649	Isaac Newton, 1642–1727	
Louis XIV of France, 1643–1715		
Fronde revolts in France, 1648–1653		
Commonwealth and Protectorate in England,		
1649–1660		
Leopold I, Habsburg emperor, 1658–1705		
Restoration of Stuart dynasty in England, 1660		
Charles II of England, 1660–1685		
Peter the Great of Russia, 1682–1725		
Revocation of the Edict of Nantes, 1685		
James II of England, 1685–1688	Newton's *Mathematical Principles of Natural*	
"Glorious Revolution" in England, 1688	*Philosophy,* 1687	
War of the League of Augsburg, 1688–1697	Montesquieu, 1689–1755	
John Locke, *Two Treatises of Government,* 1690	Voltaire, 1694–1778	
War of the Spanish Succession, 1702–1714		*1700*
Treaty of Utrecht, 1713	David Hume, 1711–1776	
Frederick William I of Prussia, 1713–1740	Jean-Jacques Rousseau, 1712–1778	
Louis XV of France, 1715–1774	Denis Diderot, 1713–1784	
Ascendancy of Robert Walpole as Britain's	Immanuel Kant, 1724–1804	
"first minister," 1720–1742		
Frederick the Great of Prussia, 1740–1786		
Maria Theresa of Austria, 1740–1780		
Seven Years' War, 1756–1763	Condorcet, 1743–1794	
George III of Britain, 1760–1820	Antoine Lavoisier, 1743–1794	
Catherine the Great of Russia, 1762–1796	French *Encyclopedia,* 1751–1772	
Louis XVI of France, 1774–1792	Edward Jenner introduces vaccination, 1796	
War of American Independence, 1776–1783		
Joseph II of Austria, 1780–1790		
Beginning of the French Revolution, 1789		

The Early-Modern World (continued)

	ECONOMICS	RELIGION	ARTS AND LETTERS
			Francis Petrarch, 1304–1374
			Italian Renaissance, c. 1350–c. 1550
1400			Masaccio, 1401–1428
		Martin Luther, 1483–1546	Botticelli, 1444–1510
		Ulrich Zwingli, 1484–1531	Leonardo da Vinci, 1452–1519
	Portugal gains control of East Indian	Ignatius Loyola, 1491–1556	Erasmus, c. 1466–1536
	spice trade, 1498–1511		Albrecht Dürer, 1471–1528
			Ariosto, 1474–1533
			Michelangelo, 1475–1564
1500		John Calvin, 1509–1564	Raphael, 1483–1520
		Letters of Obscure Men, 1515	Rabelais, c. 1490–1553
		Erasmus's Greek New Testament,	Michelangelo's main work on
		1516	Sistine Chapel, 1508–1512
		Luther attacks indulgences, 1517	Peter Brueghel, c. 1525–1569
		Henry VIII of England breaks	Palestrina, c. 1525–1594
	Spain gains control of Central and	with Rome, 1527–1534	El Greco, c. 1541– 1614
	South America, c. 1520–c. 1550		Miguel de Cervantes, 1547–1616
		Anabaptists seize Münster, 1534	William Shakespeare, 1564–1616
		Loyola's Society of Jesus approved	Claudio Monteverdi, 1567–1643
		by Pope Paul III, 1540	Peter Paul Rubens, 1577–1640
		Calvin takes over Geneva, 1541	Gionlorenzo Bernini, 1598–1680
		Council of Trent, 1545–1563	Diego Velázquez, 1599–1660
	"Price Revolution" in Europe,	Peace of Augsburg divides	
	c. 1560–c. 1600	Germany into Lutheran and	
	Economic decline of Italy, c. 1580–	Catholic areas, 1555	
	c. 1700	Elizabethan religious compromise	
1600	Chartering of English East India	in England, c. 1558–c. 1570	
	Company, 1600		
	English Poor Law, 1601		
	Chartering of Dutch East India		
	Company, 1602		Rembrandt, 1606–1669
	Settlement of Jamestown, 1607		John Milton, 1608–1674
	Height of mercantilism in Europe,		Jean Baptiste Molière, 1622–1673
	1650–1750		Christopher Wren, 1632–1723
	Colbert's economic reforms in France,		
	1664–1683		Antoine Watteau, 1684–1721
	Founding of Bank of England, 1694		J. S. Bach, 1685–1750
	Introduction of maize and potato		G. F. Handel, 1685–1759
1700	crops in Europe, c. 1700		Voltaire, 1694–1778
	Mississippi Bubble, 1715–1720	John Wesley, 1703–1789	The Enlightenment, c. 1700–
	South Sea Bubble, 1720		c. 1790
	Last appearance of bubonic plague		Henry Fielding, 1707–1754
	in Western Europe, 1720		
	Enclosure movement in England,		Joseph Haydn, 1732–1809
	1730–1810		Edward Gibbon, 1737–1794
	General European population		
	increase beginning 1750		W. A. Mozart, 1756–1791
	Adam Smith, *The Wealth of Nations,*		Jane Austen, 1775–1817
	1776		

Chapter 13

THE CIVILIZATION OF THE RENAISSANCE (c. 1350–c. 1550)

Now may every reflecting spirit thank God he has chosen to live in this new age, so full of hope and promise, which already exults in a greater array of nobly-gifted souls than the world has seen in the thousand years before.

—Matteo Palmieri, *On the Civil Life,* c. 1435

Whatever was done by man with genius and with a certain grace he held to be almost divine.

—L. B. Alberti, *Self-Portrait,* c. 1460

T he prevalent modern notion that a "Renaissance period" followed Western Europe's medieval age was first expressed by numerous Italian writers who lived between 1350 and 1550. According to them, one thousand years of unrelieved darkness had intervened between the Roman era and their own times. During these "dark ages" the Muses of art and literature had fled Europe before the onslaught of barbarism and ignorance. Almost miraculously, however, in the fourteenth century the Muses suddenly returned, and Italians happily collaborated with them to bring forth a glorious "renaissance of the arts."

Ever since this periodization was advanced historians have taken for granted the existence of some sort of "renaissance" intervening between medieval and modern times. Indeed, in the late nineteenth and early twentieth centuries many scholars went so far as to argue that the Renaissance was not just an epoch in the history of learning and culture but that a unique "Renaissance spirit" transformed all aspects of life—political, economic, and religious, as well as intellectual and artistic. Today, however, most experts no longer accept this characterization because they find it impossible to locate any truly distinctive "Renaissance" politics, economics, or religion. Instead, scholars tend to agree that the term "Renaissance" should be reserved to describe certain exciting trends in thought, literature, and the arts that emerged in Italy from roughly 1350 to 1550 and then

"A renaissance of the arts"

Limits of the term "Renaissance"

spread to northern Europe during the first half of the sixteenth century. That is the approach that will be followed here: accordingly, when we refer to a "Renaissance period" in this chapter we mean to limit ourselves to an epoch in intellectual and cultural history.

Further qualifications

Granted this restriction, some further qualifications are still necessary. Since the word *renaissance* literally means "rebirth," it is sometimes thought that after about 1350 certain Italians who were newly cognizant of Greek and Roman cultural accomplishments initiated a classical cultural rebirth after a long period of "death." In fact, however, the High Middle Ages witnessed no "death" of classical learning. St. Thomas Aquinas, for example, considered Aristotle to be "the Philosopher" and Dante revered Virgil. Similarly, it would be completely false to oppose an imaginary "Renaissance paganism" to a medieval "age of faith" because however much most Renaissance personalities loved the classics, none went so far as to worship classical gods. And finally, all discussions of the post-medieval Renaissance must be qualified by the fact that there was no single Renaissance position on any given subject.

The continuing rediscovery and spread of classical learning

Nonetheless, in the realms of thought, literature, and the arts important distinguishing traits may certainly be found that make the concept of a "Renaissance" meaningful for intellectual and cultural history. First, regarding knowledge of the classics, there was indubitably a significant quantitative difference between the learning of the Middle Ages and that of the Renaissance. Medieval scholars knew many Roman authors, such as Virgil, Ovid, and Cicero, but in the Renaissance the works of others such as Livy, Tacitus, and Lucretius were rediscovered and made familiar. Equally if not more important was the Renaissance discovery of the literature of classical Greece. In the twelfth and thirteenth centuries Greek scientific and philosophical treatises were made available to westerners in Latin translations, but none of the great Greek literary masterpieces and practically none of the major works of Plato were yet known. Nor could more than a handful of medieval westerners read the Greek language. In the Renaissance, on the other hand, large numbers of Western scholars learned Greek and mastered almost the entire Greek literary heritage that is known today.

New uses for classical learning

Second, Renaissance thinkers not only knew many more classical texts than their medieval counterparts, but they used them in new ways. Whereas medieval writers tended to employ their ancient sources for the purposes of complementing and confirming their own preconceived Christian assumptions, Renaissance writers customarily drew on the classics to reconsider their preconceived notions and alter their modes of expression. Firm determination to learn from classical antiquity, moreover, was even more pronounced in the realms of architecture and art, areas in which classical models contributed most strikingly to the creation of fully distinct "Renaissance" artistic styles.

A secular Renaissance culture

Third, although Renaissance culture was by no means pagan, it certainly was more secular in its orientation than the culture of the Middle Ages. The evolution of the Italian city-states in the fourteenth and fifteenth centuries created a supportive environment for attitudes that stressed the attainment of success in the urban political arena and living well in this world. Inevitably such secular ideals helped create a culture that was increasingly non-ecclesiastical. To be sure, the Church retained its wealth and some of its influence, but it adjusted to the spread of secularity by becoming more secular itself.

One word above all comes closest to summing up the most common and basic Renaissance intellectual ideals, namely *humanism*. This word has two different meanings, one technical and one general, but both apply to the cultural goals and ideals of a large number of Renaissance thinkers. In its technical sense humanism was a program of studies that aimed to replace the medieval Scholastic emphasis on logic and metaphysics with the study of language, literature, history, and ethics. Ancient literature was always preferred: the study of the Latin classics was at the core of the curriculum, and, whenever possible, the student was expected to advance to Greek. Humanist teachers argued that Scholastic logic was too arid and irrelevant to the practical concerns of life; instead, they preferred the "humanities," which were meant to make their students virtuous and prepare them for contributing best to the public functions of the state. (Women, as usual, were generally ignored, but sometimes aristocratic women were given humanist training in order to make them appear more polished.) In a broader sense, humanism stressed the "dignity" of man as the most excellent of all God's creatures below the angels. Some Renaissance thinkers argued that man was excellent because he alone of earthly creatures could obtain knowledge of God; others stressed man's ability to master his fate and live happily in the world. Either way, Renaissance humanists had a firm belief in the nobility and possibilities of the human race.

Humanism

1. THE ITALIAN BACKGROUND

The Renaissance originated in Italy for several reasons. The most fundamental was that Italy in the Later Middle Ages encompassed the most advanced urban society in all of Europe. Unlike aristocrats north of the Alps, Italian aristocrats customarily lived in urban centers rather than in rural castles and consequently became fully involved in urban public affairs. Moreover, since the Italian aristocracy built its palaces in the cities, the aristocratic class was less sharply set off from the class of rich merchants than in the north. Hence whereas in France or German there was never any appreciable variation from the rule that aristocrats lived off the income from their landed estates while rich town-dwellers (bourgeois) gained their living from trade, in Italy so many town-dwelling aristocrats engaged in banking or mercantile enterprises and so many rich mercantile families imitated the manners of the aristocracy that by the fourteenth and fifteenth centuries the aristocracy and upper bourgeoisie were becoming virtually indistinguishable. The noted Florentine family of the Medici, for example, emerged as a family of physicians (as the name suggests), made its fortune in banking,

The erosion of distinctions between the aristocracy and upper bourgeoisie in Italy and rose imperceptibly into the aristocracy in the fifteenth century. The results of these developments for the history of education are obvious: not only was there a great demand for education in the skills of reading and counting necessary to become a successful merchant, but the richest and most prominent families sought above all to find teachers who would impart to their offspring the knowledge and skills necessary to argue well in the public arena. Consequently, Italy produced a large number of secular educators, many of whom not only taught students but demonstrated their learned attainments in the production of political and ethical treatises and works of literature. The schools of these educators, moreover, created the best-educated upper-class public in all of Europe and inevitably therewith a considerable number of wealthy patrons who were ready to invest in the cultivation of new ideas and new forms of literary and artistic expression.

A second reason why late-medieval Italy was the birthplace of an intellectual and artistic Renaissance lay in the fact that it had a far greater sense of rapport with the classical past than any other territory in Western Europe. Given the Italian aristocratic commitment to an educational curriculum that stressed success in urban politics, the best teachers understandably sought inspiration from ancient Latin and Greek texts because politics and political rhetoric were classical rather than medieval arts. Elsewhere, resort to classical knowledge and classical literary style might have seemed intol-

The special appeal of the classical past

Bernabò Visconti. The funeral monument of a magnificent lord who ruled Milan from 1354 to 1385.

erably antiquarian and artificial, but in Italy the classical past appeared most "relevant" because ancient Roman monuments were omnipresent throughout the peninsula and ancient Latin literature referred to cities and sites that Renaissance Italians recognized as their own. Moreover, Italians became particularly intent on reappropriating their classical heritage in the fourteenth and fifteenth centuries because Italians then were seeking to establish an independent cultural identity in opposition to a Scholasticism most closely associated with France. Not only did the removal of the papacy to Avignon for most of the fourteenth century and then the prolonged Great Schism from 1378 to 1417 heighten antagonisms between Italy and France, but during the fourteenth century there was an intellectual reaction against Scholasticism on all fronts which made it natural for Italians to prefer the intellectual alternatives offered by classical literary sources. Naturally too, once Roman literature and learning became particularly favored in Italy, so did Roman art and architecture, for Roman models could help Italians create a splendid artistic alternative to French Gothicism just as Roman learning offered an intellectual alternative to French Scholasticism.

Finally, the Italian Renaissance obviously could not have occurred without the underpinning of Italian wealth. Oddly enough, the Italian economy as a whole was probably more prosperous in the thirteenth century than it was in the fourteenth and fifteenth. But late-medieval Italy was wealthier in comparison to the rest of Europe than it had been before, a fact that meant that Italian writers and artists were more likely to stay at home than seek employment abroad. Moreover, in late-medieval Italy unusually intensive investment in culture arose from an intensification of urban pride and the concentration of per capita wealth. Although these two trends overlapped somewhat, most scholars tend to agree that a phase of predominantly public urban support for culture came first in Italy from roughly 1250 to about 1400 or 1450, depending on place, with the private sector taking over thereafter. In the first phase the richest cities vied with each other in building the most splendid public monuments and in supporting writers whose role was to glorify the urban republics in letters and speeches as full of magniloquent Ciceronian prose as possible. But in the course of the fifteenth century, when most Italian city-states succumbed to the hereditary rule of princely families, patronage was monopolized by the princely aristocracy. It was then that the great princes—the Visconti and Sforza in Milan, the Medici in Florence, the Este in Ferrara, and the Gonzaga in Mantua—patronized art and literature in their courts to glorify themselves, while lesser aristocratic families imitated those princes on a smaller scale. Not least of the great princes in Italy from about 1450 to about 1550 were the popes in Rome, who were dedicated to a policy of basing their strength on temporal control of the Papal States. Hence the most worldly of the Renaissance popes—Alexander VI (1492–1503); Julius II (1503–1513); and Leo X (1513–1521), son of the Florentine ruler Lorenzo de' Medici—obtained the services of the greatest artists of the day and for a few decades made Rome the unrivaled artistic capital of the Western world.

Patronage of the arts rooted in urban pride and private wealth

Pope Julius II by Raphael. The acorns at the top of the throne posts are visual puns for the pope's family name "della Rovere" ("of the oak").

2. THE RENAISSANCE OF THOUGHT AND LITERATURE IN ITALY

Petrarch, the first humanist

In surveying the greatest accomplishments of Italian Renaissance scholars and writers it is natural to begin with the work of Francis Petrarch (1304–1374), the earliest of the humanists in the technical sense of the term. Petrarch was a deeply committed Christian who believed that Scholasticism was entirely misguided because it concentrated on abstract speculation rather than teaching people how to behave properly and attain salvation. Petrarch thought that the Christian writer must above all cultivate literary eloquence so that he could inspire people to do good. For him the best models of eloquence were to be found in the ancient literary classics, which he thought repaid study doubly inasmuch as they were filled with ethical wisdom. So Petrarch dedicated himself to searching for undiscovered ancient Latin texts and writing his own moral treatises in which he imitated classical style and quoted classical phrases. Thereby he initiated a program of "humanist" studies that was to be influential for centuries. Petrarch also has a place in purely literary history because of his poetry. Although he prized his own Latin poetry over the poems he wrote in the Italian vernacular, only the latter have proved enduring. Above all, the Italian sonnets—later called Petrarchan sonnets—which he wrote for his beloved Laura in the chivalrous style of the troubadours, were widely imitated in form and content throughout the Renaissance period.

Civic humanism

Because he was a very traditional Christian, Petrarch's ultimate ideal for human conduct was the solitary life of contemplation and asceticism. But in subsequent generations, from about 1400 to 1450, a number of Italian thinkers and scholars, located mainly in Florence, developed the alternative of what is customarily called *civic humanism*. Civic humanists like the Florentines Leonardo Bruni (c. 1370–1444) and Leon Battista Alberti (1404–1472) agreed with Petrarch on the need for eloquence and the study of classical literature, but they also taught that man's nature equipped him for action, for usefulness to his family and society, and for serving the state—ideally a republican city-state after the classical or contemporary Florentine model. In their view ambition and the quest for glory were noble impulses that ought to be encouraged. They refused to condemn the striving for material possessions, for they argued that the history of human progress is inseparable from mankind's success in gaining mastery over the earth and its resources. Perhaps the most vivid of the civic humanists' writings is Alberti's *On the Family* (1443), in which he argued that the nuclear family was instituted by nature for the well-being of humanity. Not surprisingly, however, Alberti consigned women to purely domestic roles within this framework, for he believed that "man [is] by nature more energetic and industrious," and that woman was created "to increase and continue generations, and to nourish and preserve those already born."

In addition to differing with Petrarch in their preference for the active over the solitary or contemplative life, the civic humanists went far beyond

Leon Battista Alberti. A contemporary medal.

him in their study of the ancient literary heritage. Some discovered important new Latin texts, but more important was their success in opening up the field of classical Greek studies. In this they were aided by several Byzantine scholars who had migrated to Italy in the first half of the fifteenth century and gave instruction in the Greek language. Coming to recognize the glories of ancient Greek literature, Italian scholars traveled to Constantinople and other Eastern cities in search of forgotten Greek masterpieces. In 1423 one Italian, Giovanni Aurispa, alone brought back 238 manuscript books, including works of Sophocles, Euripides, and Thucydides. Soon followed the work of translation into Latin, not word for word, but sense for sense in order to preserve the literary force of the original. In this way most of the Greek classics, particularly the writings of Plato, the dramatists, and the historians, were first made available to Western Europe.

Related in his textual interests to the civic humanists, but by no means a full adherent of their movement, was the atypical yet highly influential Renaissance thinker, Lorenzo Valla (1407–1457). Born in Rome and active primarily as a secretary in the service of the king of Naples, Valla had no inclination to espouse the ideas of republican political engagement as the Florentine civic humanists did. Instead, he preferred to advertise his skills as an expert in grammar, rhetoric, and the painstaking analysis of Greek and Latin texts by showing how the thorough study of language could discredit old verities. Most decisive in this regard was Valla's brilliant demonstration that the so-called Donation of Constantine was a medieval forgery. Whereas papal propagandists had argued ever since the early thirteenth century that the papacy possessed rights to temporal rule in Western Europe on the grounds of a charter purportedly granted by the Emperor Constantine in the fourth century, Valla proved beyond dispute that the document in question was full of nonclassical Latin usages and anachronistic terms. Hence he concluded that the "Donation" was the work of a medieval forger whose "monstrous impudence" was exposed by the "stupidity of his language." This demonstration not only discredited a prize specimen of "medieval ignorance," but, more importantly, introduced the concept of anachronism into all subsequent textual study and historical thought. Valla also employed his skills in linguistic analysis and rhetorical argumentation to challenge a wide variety of philosophical positions, but his ultimate goals were by no means purely destructive, for he revered the literal teachings of the Pauline Epistles. Accordingly, in his *Notes on the New Testament* he applied his expert knowledge of Greek to elucidating the true meaning of St. Paul's words, which he believed had been obscured by the Latin Vulgate translation. This work was to prove an important link between Italian Renaissance scholarship and the subsequent Christian humanism of the north.

From about 1450 until about 1600 dominance in the world of Italian thought was assumed by a school of Neoplatonists, who sought to blend the thought of Plato, Plotinus, and various strands of ancient mysticism with Christianity. Foremost among these were Marsilio Ficino (1433–1499) and Giovanni Pico della Mirandola (1463–1494), both of whom

Pico della Mirandola. When the young nobleman Pico arrived in Florence at age nineteen he was said to have been "of beauteous feature and shape." This contemporary portrait may have been done by the great Florentine painter Botticelli.

Machiavelli

Niccolò Machiavelli

were members of the Platonic Academy founded by Cosimo de' Medici in Florence. The academy was a loosely organized society of scholars who met to hear readings and lectures. Their hero was unquestionably Plato: sometimes they celebrated Plato's birthday by holding a banquet in his honor, after which everybody gave speeches as if they were characters in a Platonic dialogue. Ficino's greatest achievement was the translation of Plato's works into Latin, thereby making them widely available to Western Europeans for the first time. It is debatable whether Ficino's own philosophy may be called humanist because he moved away from ethics to metaphysics and taught that the individual should look primarily to the other world. In Ficino's opinion, "the immortal soul is always miserable in its mortal body." The same problem holds for Ficino's disciple Giovanni Pico della Mirandola, whose most famous work is the *Oration on the Dignity of Man.* Pico was certainly not a civic humanist since he saw little worth in mundane public affairs. But he did believe that there is "nothing more wonderful than man" because he believed that man is endowed with the capacity to achieve union with God if he so wills.

Hardly any of the Italian thinkers between Petrarch and Pico were really original: their greatness lay mostly in their manner of expression, their accomplishments in technical scholarship, and their popularization of different themes of ancient thought. The same, however, can by no means be said of Renaissance Italy's greatest political philosopher, Niccolò Machiavelli (1469–1527), who belonged to no school and stood in a class by himself. No man did more than Machiavelli to overturn all earlier views of the ethical basis of politics or to pioneer in the dispassionate direct observation of political life. Machiavelli's writings reflect the unhappy condition of Italy in his time. At the end of the fifteenth century Italy had become the cockpit of international struggles. Both France and Spain had invaded the peninsula and were competing with each other for the allegiance of the Italian states, which in many cases were torn by internal dissension making them easy prey for foreign conquerors. In 1498 Machiavelli became the second chancellor and secretary of the newly founded republic of Florence. His duties largely involved diplomatic missions to other states. While in Rome he became fascinated with the achievements of Cesare Borgia, son of Pope Alexander VI, in cementing a solidified state out of scattered elements. He noted with approval Cesare's combination of ruthlessness with shrewdness and his complete subordination of morality to political ends. In 1512 the Medici returned to overthrow the republic of Florence, and Machiavelli was deprived of his position. Disappointed and embittered, he spent the remainder of his life at his country estate, devoting his time primarily to writing. In his *Discourses on Livy* he praised the ancient Roman republic as a model for all time. He lauded constitutionalism, equality, liberty, in the sense of freedom from outside interference, and subordination of religion to the interests of the state. But Machiavelli also wrote *The Prince* in which he described the policies and practices of government, not in accordance with some lofty ideal, but as they actually were. The supreme obligation of the ruler, he avowed, was to maintain the power and safety of the country over which he ruled. No consideration of justice or mercy or the sanctity of treaties should be allowed to stand in his way. Cynical in his views of human nature, Machiavelli maintained that all men are prompted exclusively by motives of self-interest, particularly by desires for personal power and material prosperity. The head of the state should therefore not take for granted the loyalty or affection of his subjects. The one ideal Machiavelli kept before him in his later years was the unification of Italy. But this he believed could only be achieved through ruthlessness.

Far more congenial to contemporary tastes than the shocking political theories of Machiavelli were the guidelines for proper aristocratic conduct offered in *The Book of the Courtier* (1516) by the diplomat and count Baldassare Castiglione. This cleverly written forerunner of modern handbooks of etiquette stands in sharp contrast to the earlier civic humanist treatises of Bruni and Alberti, for whereas they taught the sober "republican" virtues of strenuous service in behalf of the city-state and family, Castiglione, writing in an Italy dominated by magnificent princely courts, taught how to attain the elegant and seemingly effortless qualities necessary for acting like a "true gentleman." More than anyone else, Castiglione popularized the ideal of the "Renaissance man": one who is accomplished in many different pursuits and is also brave, witty, and "courteous," meaning civilized and learned. By no means ignoring the female sex, Castiglione, unlike Alberti, was silent about women's role in "hearth and home," but stressed instead the ways in which court ladies could be "gracious entertainers." Thereby he was one of the first European male writers to offer women an independent role outside of the household, a fact that should not be underrated even though he was offering such a role merely to the richest of the rich and even though his stress on "pleasing affability" today seems demeaning. Widely read throughout Europe for over a century after its publication, Castiglione's *Courtier* spread Italian ideals of "civility" to princely courts north of the Alps, resulted in the ever-greater patronage of art and literature by the European aristocracy, and gave currency to the hitherto novel proposition that some women other than nuns were not fated to be passive vessels of reproduction and nutrition.

Castiglione's ideal courtier
and court lady

Had Castiglione's ideal courtier wished to show off his knowledge of contemporary Italian literature, he would have had many works from which to choose, for sixteenth-century Italians were highly accomplished in the creation of imaginative prose and verse. Among the many impressive writers who might be mentioned, Machiavelli himself wrote a delightful short story, "Belfagor," and an engaging bawdy play, *Mandragola;* the great artist Michelangelo wrote many moving sonnets; and Ludovico Ariosto (1474–1533), the most eminent of sixteenth-century Italian epic poets, wrote a lengthy verse narrative called *Orlando Furioso* (*The Madness of Roland*). Although woven substantially from materials taken from the medieval Charlemagne cycle, this work differed radically from any of the medieval epics because it introduced elements of lyrical fantasy and above all because it was totally devoid of heroic idealism. Ariosto wrote to make readers laugh and to charm them with felicitous descriptions of the quiet

Other sixteenth-century
Italian literary achievements

splendor of nature and the passions of love. His work represents the disillusionment of the late Renaissance, the loss of hope and faith, and the tendency to seek consolation in the pursuit of pleasure and aesthetic delight.

3. THE ARTISTIC RENAISSANCE IN ITALY

Secular art

Despite numerous intellectual and literary advances, the most long-lived achievements of the Italian Renaissance were made in the realm of art. Of all the arts, painting was undoubtedly supreme. We have already seen that around 1300 very impressive beginnings were made in the history of Italian painting by the artistic genius of Giotto, but it was not until the fifteenth century that Italian painting began to attain its majority. One reason for this was that in the early fifteenth century the laws of linear perspective were discovered and first employed to give the fullest sense of three dimensions. Fifteenth-century artists also experimented with effects of light and shade (*chiaroscuro*) and for the first time carefully studied the anatomy and proportions of the human body. By the fifteenth century, too, increase in private wealth and the partial triumph of the secular spirit had freed the domain of art to a large extent from the service of religion. As we have noted above, the Church was no longer the only patron of artists. While subject matter from biblical history was still commonly employed, it was frequently infused with nonreligious themes. The painting of portraits for the purpose of revealing the hidden mysteries of the soul now became popular. Paintings intended to appeal primarily to the intellect were paralleled by others whose main purpose was to delight the eye with gorgeous color and beauty of form. The fifteenth century was characterized also by the introduction of painting in oil, probably from Flanders. The use of the new technique doubtless had much to do with the artistic advance of this period. Since oil does not dry so quickly as fresco pigment, the painter could now work more leisurely, taking time with the more difficult parts of the picture and making corrections if necessary as he went along.

The Expulsion of Adam and Eve from the Garden of Eden. Masaccio built on the artistic tradition established by Giotto in stressing emotion and psychological study.

The majority of the painters of the fifteenth century were Florentines. First among them was the precocious Masaccio (1401–1428). Although he died at the age of twenty-seven, Masaccio inspired the work of Italian painters for a hundred years. Masaccio's greatness as a painter is based on his success in "imitating nature," which became a primary value in Renaissance painting. To achieve this effect he employed perspective, perhaps most dramatically in his fresco of the Trinity; he also used *chiaroscuro* with originality, leading to a dramatic and moving outcome. In the *Expulsion of Adam and Eve from the Garden,* he records the shame and guilt felt by the individuals in the biblical story.

Botticelli

The best known of the painters who directly followed the tradition begun by Masaccio was the Florentine Sandro Botticelli (1444–1510), who depicted both religious and classical themes. Botticelli's work excels in beautiful and accurate depiction of natural detail; he was a master, for example, at painting the female nude. But his major contribution to Renaissance painting derives from the philosophical basis of much of his work, for he was closely associated with the Florentine Neoplatonists. Two of his most famous paintings are *The Allegory of Spring* and *The Birth of Venus,* which illustrate Neoplatonic concepts regarding the classical goddess of love, Venus or Aphrodite. Later in his life Botticelli became a follower of the evangelical priest Savonarola, who came to Florence from Ferrara to preach fire-and-brimstone sermons against worldliness. Botticelli's *Mystic Nativity* was probably painted as a result of Savonarola's influence; it is a profoundly moving religious painting, in which he anticipates the end of the world. The last years of Botticelli's life are shadowy; his popularity declined, and it is believed he died in poverty.

Perhaps the greatest of the Florentine artists was Leonardo da Vinci (1452–1519), one of the most versatile geniuses who ever lived. Leonardo was practically the personification of the "Renaissance man": he was a painter, architect, musician, mathematician, engineer, and inventor. The illegitimate son of a lawyer and a peasant woman, Leonardo set up an artist's shop in Florence by the time he reached twenty-five and gained the patronage of the Medici ruler of the city, Lorenzo the Magnificent. But if Leonardo had any weakness, it was his slowness in working and difficulty in finishing anything. This naturally displeased Lorenzo and other Florentine patrons, who thought an artist was little more than an artisan, commissioned to produce a certain piece of work of a certain size for a certain price on a certain date. Leonardo, however, strongly objected to this view because he considered himself to be no menial craftsman but an inspired creator. Therefore in 1482 he left Florence for the Sforza court of Milan where he was given freer rein in structuring his time and work. He remained there until the French invaded Milan in 1499; after that he wandered about Italy, finally accepting the patronage of the French king, Francis I, under whose auspices Leonardo lived and worked in France until his death.

The paintings of Leonardo da Vinci began what is known as the High Renaissance in Italy. His approach to painting was that it should be the most accurate possible imitation of nature. Leonardo was like a naturalist, basing his work on his own detailed observations of a blade of grass, the wing of a bird, a waterfall. He obtained human corpses for dissection—by which he was breaking the law—and reconstructed in drawing the minutest features of anatomy, which knowledge he carried over to his paintings. Leonardo worshiped nature, and was convinced of the essential divinity in all living things. It is not surprising, therefore, that he was a vegetarian, and that he went to the marketplace to buy caged birds, which he released to their native habitat.

It is generally agreed that Leonardo's masterpieces are the *Virgin of the Rocks* (which exists in two versions), the *Last Supper,* and the *Mona Lisa.* The first represents not only his marvelous technical skill but also his passion for science and his belief in the universe as a well-ordered place. The figures are arranged geometrically, with every rock and plant depicted in

Lorenzo de' Medici, Known as Lorenzo the Magnificent. A detail from *The Adoration of the Magi* by Benozzo Gozzoli showing the future Florentine ruler and patron of art.

See color plates following page 428 for the *Birth of Venus* by Botticelli

Studies of the Shoulder by Leonardo da Vinci

St. Francis in the Desert by Giovanni Bellini

accurate detail. The *Last Supper,* painted on the walls of the refectory of Santa Maria delle Grazie in Milan, is a study of psychological reactions. A serene Christ, resigned to his terrible fate, has just announced to his disciples that one of them will betray him. The artist succeeds in portraying the mingled emotions of surprise, horror, and guilt in the faces of the disciples as they gradually perceive the meaning of their master's statement. The third of Leonardo's major triumphs, the *Mona Lisa,* reflects a similar interest in the varied moods of the human soul. Although it is true that the *Mona Lisa* is a portrait of an actual woman, the wife of Francesco del Giocondo, a Neapolitan, it is more than a mere photographic likeness. The distinguished art critic Bernard Berenson has said of it, "Who like Leonardo has depicted . . . the inexhaustible fascination of the woman in her years of mastery? . . . Leonardo is the one artist of whom it may be said with perfect literalness: 'Nothing that he touched but turned into a thing of eternal beauty.' "

See color plates following page 428 for the *Virgin of the Rocks,* the *Last Supper,* and the *Mona Lisa* by Leonardo da Vinci

The beginning of the High Renaissance around 1490 also witnessed the rise of the so-called Venetian school, the major members of which were Giovanni Bellini (c. 1430–1516), Giorgione (1478–1510), and Titian (c. 1490–1576). The work of all these men reflected the luxurious life and the pleasure-loving interests of the thriving commercial city of Venice. Most Venetian painters had little of the concern with philosophical and psychological themes that characterized the Florentine school. Their aim was to appeal primarily to the senses rather than to the mind. They delighted in painting idyllic landscapes and gorgeous symphonies of color. For their subject matter they chose not merely the natural beauty of Venetian sunsets and the shimmering silver of lagoons in the moonlight but also the artificial splendor of sparkling jewels, richly colored satins and velvets, and gorgeous palaces. Their portraits were invariably likenesses of the rich and the powerful. In the subordination of form and meaning to color and elegance

The Venetian painters

See color plates facing page 429 for *Pope Paul III and His Nephews* and *Charles V* by Titian there were mirrored not only the sumptuous tastes of wealthy merchants, but also definite traces of Eastern influence which had filtered through from Byzantium during the Middle Ages.

The remaining great painters of the High Renaissance all accomplished their most important work in the first half of the sixteenth century when Renaissance Italian art reached its peak. Rome was now the major artistic center of the Italian peninsula, although the traditions of the Florentine school still exerted a potent influence. Among the eminent painters of this period at least two must be given more than passing attention. One was Raphael (1483–1520), a native of Urbino, and perhaps the most beloved artist of the entire Renaissance. The lasting appeal of his style is due primarily to his ennobling humanism, for he portrayed the members of the human species as temperate, wise, and dignified beings. Although Raphael was influenced by Leonardo da Vinci and copied many features of his work, he cultivated a much more symbolical or allegorical approach. His *Disputà* symbolized the dialectical relationship between the Church in heaven and the Church on earth. In a worldly setting against a brilliant sky, theologians debate the meaning of the Eucharist, while in the clouds above, saints and the Trinity repose in the possession of a holy mystery. Raphael's *School of Athens* depicts a harmony between the Platonist and Aristotelian philosophies. Plato (painted as a portrait of Leonardo) is shown pointing upward to emphasize the spiritual basis of his world of Ideas, while Aristotle stretches a hand forward to exemplify his teaching that human life should be led in accordance with ethical moderation. Raphael is noted also for his portraits and Madonnas. To the latter, especially, he gave a softness and warmth that seemed to endow them with a sweetness and piety quite different from the enigmatic and somewhat distant Madonnas of Leonardo da Vinci.

The painters of the late Renaissance: Raphael

See color plates facing page 429 for the *Madonna of the Chair* by Raphael

The last towering figure of the High Renaissance was Michelangelo (1475–1564) of Florence. If Leonardo was a naturalist, Michelangelo was

The School of Athens by Raphael

The Creation of Adam by Michelangelo. One of a series of frescoes on the ceiling of the Sistine Chapel in Rome. Inquiring into the meaning of life and the universe, it represents Renaissance realism at its height.

Michelangelo's paintings

an idealist; where the former sought to recapture and interpret fleeting natural phenomena, Michelangelo, who embraced Neoplatonism as a philosophy, was more concerned with expressing enduring, abstract truths. Michelangelo was a painter, sculptor, architect, and poet—and he expressed himself in all these forms with a similar power and in a similar manner. At the center of all of his paintings is the human figure, which is always powerful, colossal, magnificent. If humanity, and the potential of the individual, lay at the center of Italian Renaissance culture, then Michelangelo, who depicted the human, and particularly the male, figure without cease, is the supreme Renaissance artist.

The Sistine Chapel

Michelangelo's greatest achievements in painting appear in a single location—the Sistine Chapel in Rome—yet they are products of two different periods in the artist's life and consequently exemplify two different artistic styles and outlooks on the human condition. Most famous are the sublime frescoes Michelangelo painted on the ceiling of the Sistine Chapel from 1508 to 1512, depicting scenes from the book of Genesis. All the panels in this series, including *God Dividing the Light from Darkness, The Creation of Adam,* and *The Flood,* exemplify the young artist's commitment to classical Greek aesthetic principles of harmony, solidity, and dignified restraint. Correspondingly, all exude as well a sense of sublime affirmation regarding Creation and the heroic qualities of mankind. But a quarter of a century later, when Michelangelo returned to work in the Sistine Chapel, both his style and mood had changed dramatically. In the enormous *Last Judgment,* a fresco done for the Sistine Chapel's altar wall in 1536, Michelangelo repudiated classical restraint and substituted a style that emphasized tension and distortion in order to communicate the older man's pessimistic conception of a humanity wracked by fear and bowed by guilt.

In the realm of sculpture the Italian Renaissance took a great step forward by creating statues that were no longer carved as parts of columns or doorways on church buildings or as effigies on tombs. Instead, Italian sculptors for the first time since antiquity carved free-standing statues "in the round." These freed sculpture from its bondage to architecture and established its status as a separate art frequently devoted to secular purposes.

The first great master of Renaissance sculpture was Donatello (c. 1386–1466). He emancipated his art from Gothic mannerisms and introduced a new vigorous note of individualism. His bronze statue of David triumphant over the body of the slain Goliath, the first free-standing nude since antiquity, established a precedent of glorifying the life-size nude. Donatello's *David,* moreover, represents a first step in the direction of imitating classical sculpture, not just in the depiction of a nude body, but also in the subject's posture of resting his weight on one leg. Yet this David is clearly a lithe adolescent rather than a muscular Greek athlete. Later in his career, Donatello more fully imitated ancient statuary in his commanding portrayal of the proud warrior Gattamelata—the first monumental equestrian statue in bronze executed in the West since the time of the Romans. Here, in addition to drawing very heavily on the legacy of antiquity, the sculptor most clearly expressed his dedication to immortalizing the earthly accomplishments of a contemporary secular hero.

Certainly the greatest sculptor of the Italian Renaissance—indeed, probably the greatest sculptor of all time—was Michelangelo. Believing with Leonardo that the artist was an inspired creator, Michelangelo pursued this belief to the conclusion that sculpture was the most exalted of the arts because it allowed the artist to imitate God most fully in recreating human forms. Furthermore, in Michelangelo's view the most God-like sculptor disdained slavish naturalism, for anyone could make a plaster cast of a hu-

David by Donatello. The first free-standing nude statue executed in the West since antiquity.

Gattamelata by Donatello. Note the debt to the Roman equestrian statue of Marcus Aurelius, shown above, p. 181.

Left: *Moses* by Michelangelo. Far less classical in style than Michelangelo's *David,* this statue stresses a sense of drama. (Moses was depicted with horns in medieval and renaissance art on account of a faulty translation of a passage from the Book of Exodus.) Right: *Descent from the Cross* by Michelangelo. This portrayal of tragedy was made by the sculptor for his own tomb. Note the distortion for effect exemplified by the elongated body and left arm of the figure of Christ. The figure in the rear is Nicodemus, but was probably intended to represent Michelangelo himself.

David by Michelangelo. Over thirteen feet high, this serenely self-confident affirmation of the beauty of the human form was placed prominently by the Florentine government in front of Florence's city hall to proclaim the city's humanistic values.

man figure, but only an inspired creative genius could endow his sculpted figures with a sense of life. Accordingly, Michelangelo subordinated naturalism to the force of his imagination and sought restlessly to express his ideals in ever more arresting forms.

As in his painting, Michelangelo's sculpture followed a course from classicism to anticlassicism, that is, from harmonious modeling to dramatic distortion. The sculptor's most noted early work, his *David,* executed in 1501 when he was just twenty-six, is surely his most perfect classical statue in style and inspiration. Choosing, like Donatello, to depict a life-size male nude, Michelangelo nonetheless decided to make his own *David* heroic rather than merely graceful and hence conceived his nude in the purest, well-proportioned Greek terms. The resulting portrait in marble epitomizes for many the Italian Renaissance's facility for employing classical style to express the serenest confidence in human attainments. Deep serenity, however, is no longer prominent in the works of Michelangelo's middle period; rather, in a work such as his *Moses* of about 1515, the sculptor has begun to explore the use of anatomical distortion to create effects of emotional intensity—in this case, the biblical prophet's righteous rage.

While such statues remained awesomely heroic, as Michelangelo's life drew to a close he experimented ever more with exaggerated stylistic mannerisms for the purpose of communicating moods of brooding pensiveness or outright pathos. The culmination of this trend in Michelangelo's statuary in his moving *Descent from the Cross,* a depiction of an old man resembling the sculptor himself grieving over the distended, slumping body of the dead Christ.

Michelangelo's sculpture

To a much greater extent than either sculpture or painting, Renaissance architecture had its roots in the past. The new building style was eclectic, a compound of elements derived from the Middle Ages and from antiquity. It was not the Greek or the Gothic, however, but the Roman and the Romanesque which provided the inspiration for the architecture of the Italian Renaissance. Neither the Greek nor the Gothic had ever found a congenial soil in Italy. The Romanesque, by contrast, was able to flourish there, since it was more in keeping with Italian traditions, while the persistence of a strong admiration for Latin culture made possible a revival of the Roman style. Accordingly, the great architects of the Renaissance generally adopted their building plans from the Romanesque churches and monasteries and copied their decorative devices from the ruins of ancient Rome. The result was an architecture based on the cruciform floor plan of transept and nave and embodying the decorative features of the column and arch, or the column and lintel, the colonnade, and frequently the dome. Horizontal lines predominated. Though many of the buildings were churches, the ideals they expressed were the secular ones of joy in this life and pride in human achievement. Renaissance architecture also emphasized harmony and proportion because Italian builders, under the influence of Neoplatonism, concluded that perfect proportions in man reflect the harmony of the universe, and that, therefore, the parts of a building should be related to

Renaissance architecture

St. Peter's, Rome. Built to a square cross plan originally conceived by Bramante and revised by Michelangelo. Completed in 1626, the church rises to a total height of 450 feet.

The Villa Rotonda of Palladio. A highly influential Renaissance private dwelling near Vicenza. Note how Palladio drew for inspiration on the Roman Pantheon, pictured above, p. 183.

each other and to the whole in the same way as the parts of the human body. A fine example of Renaissance architecture is St. Peter's Basilica in Rome, built under the patronage of Popes Julius II and Leo X and designed by some of the most celebrated architects of the time, including Donato Bramante (c. 1444–1514) and Michelangelo. Equally impressive are the artfully proportioned aristocratic country houses designed by the northern Italian architect Andrea Palladio (1508–1580), who created secular miniatures of ancient temples such as the Roman Pantheon to glorify the aristocrats who dwelled within them.

4. THE WANING OF THE ITALIAN RENAISSANCE

Political factors in the decline of the Italian Renaissance: The French invasion of 1494

Around 1550 the Renaissance in Italy began to decline after some two hundred glorious years. The causes of this decline were varied. Perhaps at the head of the list should be placed the French invasion of 1494 and the incessant warfare that ensued. The French king Charles VIII, who ruled the richest and most powerful kingdom in Europe, viewed Italy as an attractive prey for his grandiose ambitions. Accordingly, in 1494 he led an army of 30,000 well-trained troops across the Alps. The Medici of Florence fled before him, abandoning their city to immediate capture. Halting only long enough to establish peace with a subservient new republican government, the French resumed their advance and conquered Naples. By so doing, however, they aroused the suspicions of the rulers of Spain, who feared an attack on Sicily, which was their possession. An alliance among Spain, the Papal States, the Holy Roman Empire, Milan, and Venice finally forced Charles to withdraw from Italy. Yet upon his death his successor, Louis XII, launched a second invasion, and from 1499 until 1529 warfare in Italy was virtually uninterrupted. Alliances and counteralliances followed each other in bewildering succession, but they only managed to prolong the hostilities. The French won a great victory at Marignano in 1515, but they were decisively defeated by the Spanish at Pavia in 1525. The worst disaster came in 1527 when unruly Spanish and German troops, nominally under the command of the Spanish ruler and Holy Roman Emperor Charles V, but in fact entirely out of control, sacked the city of Rome, causing irreparable destruction. Only in 1529 did Charles finally manage to gain control over most of the Italian peninsula, putting the fighting to an end for a time. Once triumphant, Charles retained two of the largest portions of Italy for Spain—the Duchy of Milan and the Kingdom of Naples—and installed favored princes as the rulers of almost all the other Italian political entities exclusive of Venice and the Papal States. These protégés of the Spanish crown continued to preside over their own courts, to patronize the arts, and to adorn their cities with luxurious buildings, but in fact they were puppets of a foreign power and unable to inspire their retinues with a sense of vigorous cultural independence.

To the Italian political disasters was added a waning of Italian prosperity. Whereas Italy's virtual monopoly of trade with Asia in the fifteenth century had been one of the chief economic supports for the cultivation of Italian Renaissance culture, the gradual shifting of trade routes from the Mediterranean to the Atlantic region following the overseas discoveries of around 1500 slowly but surely cost Italy its supremacy as the center of world trade.

The waning of Italian prosperity

THE STATES OF ITALY DURING THE RENAISSANCE C. 1494

*The Church asserts control over
thought and art*

Giordano Bruno

Disciplining of Galileo

*Continued flourishing of
Italian art and music*

Since the incessant warfare of the sixteenth century also contributed to Italy's economic hardships, as did Spanish financial exactions in Milan and Naples, there was gradually less and less of a surplus to support artistic endeavors.

A final cause of the decline of the Italian Renaissance was the Counter-Reformation. During the sixteenth century the Roman Church sought increasingly to exercise firm control over thought and art as part of a campaign to combat worldliness and the spread of Protestantism. In 1542 the Roman Inquisition was established; in 1564 the first Index of Prohibited Books was published. The extent of ecclesiastical interference in cultural life was enormous. For example, Michelangelo's great *Last Judgment* in the Sistine Chapel was criticized by some straitlaced fanatics for looking like a bordello because it showed too many naked bodies. Therefore, Pope Paul IV ordered a second-rate artist to paint in clothing wherever possible. (The unfortunate artist was afterward known as "the underwear-maker.") While this incident may appear merely grotesquely humorous, the determination of ecclesiastical censors to enforce doctrinal uniformity could lead to death, as in the case of the unfortunate Neoplatonic philosopher Giordano Bruno, whose insistence that there may be more than one world in contravention of the book of Genesis resulted in his being burned at the stake by the Roman Inquisition in 1600.

The most notorious example of inquisitorial censorship of free intellectual speculation was the disciplining of the great scientist Galileo, whose achievements we will discuss in more detail later on. In 1616 the Holy Office in Rome condemned the new astronomical theory that the earth moves around the sun as "foolish, absurd, philosophically false, and formally heretical." Accordingly, the Inquisition proceeded immediately against Galileo when he published a brilliant defense of the heliocentric system in 1632. In short order the Inquisition made Galileo recant his "errors" and sentenced him to house arrest for the duration of his life. Galileo was not willing to face death for his beliefs, but after he publicly retracted his view that the earth revolves around the sun he supposedly whispered, "despite everything, it still moves." Not surprisingly, Galileo was the last great Italian contributor to the development of astronomy and physics until modern times.

In conclusion, it should be emphasized that cultural and artistic achievement was by no means extinguished in Italy after the middle of the sixteenth century. On the contrary, an impressive new artistic style known as Mannerism was cultivated between about 1550 and 1600 by painters who drew on traits found in the later work of Michelangelo, and in the seventeenth century Mannerism was supplanted by the dazzling Baroque style, which was born in Rome under ecclesiastical auspices. Similarly, Italian music registered enormous accomplishments virtually without interruption from the sixteenth to the twentieth century. But whatever seemed threatening to the Church could not be tolerated, and the free spirit of Renaissance culture was found no more.

5. THE RENAISSANCE IN THE NORTH

It was inevitable that after about 1500 the Renaissance, which originated in Italy, should have spread to other European countries. Throughout the fifteenth century a continuous procession of northern European students went to Italy to study in Italian universities such as Bologna or Padua, and an occasional Italian writer or artist traveled briefly north of the Alps. Such interchanges helped spread ideas, but only after around 1500 did most of northern Europe become sufficiently prosperous and politically stable to provide a truly congenial environment for the widespread cultivation of art and literature. Intellectual interchanges, moreover, became much more extensive after 1494, when France and Spain started fighting on Italian battlefields. The result of this development was that more and more northern Europeans began to learn what the Italians had been accomplishing (Spain's forces came not just from Spain but also from Germany and the Low Countries). Then too leading Italian thinkers and artists, like Leonardo, began to enter the retinues of northern kings or aristocrats. Accordingly, the Renaissance became an international movement and continued to be vigorous in the north even as it started to wane on its native ground.

The diffusion of the Renaissance outside Italy

The Renaissance outside Italy, however, was by no means identical to the Renaissance within Italy. Above all, the northern European Renaissance was generally less secular. The main explanation for this difference lies in the different social and cultural traditions Italy and northern Europe had inherited from the Middle Ages. As we have seen, late-medieval Italy's vigorous urban society fostered a secular educational system that led, in union with a revival of classicism, to the evolution of new and more secular forms of expression. The north, on the other hand, had a far less mercantile and urban-oriented economy than did Italy and no northern cities ever attained the political dominance of their surrounding countrysides as did Florence, Venice, and Milan. Instead, political power was coalescing around the nation-states (or in Germany the princedoms), whose rulers were willing until about 1500 to acknowledge the educational and cultural hegemony of the clergy. Consequently, northern European universities tended to specialize in theological studies, and the most prominent buildings in almost all the leading northern European towns were cathedrals.

The religious roots of the northern Renaissance

Simply stated, the northern Renaissance was the product of an engrafting of certain Italian Renaissance ideals upon preexisting northern traditions. This can be seen very clearly in the case of the most prominent northern Renaissance intellectual movement, *Christian humanism*. Agreeing with Italian humanists that medieval Scholasticism was too ensnarled in logical hair-splitting to have any value for the practical conduct of life, northern Christian humanists nonetheless looked for practical guidance from purely biblical, religious precepts. Like their Italian counterparts, they sought wisdom from antiquity, but the antiquity they had in mind was Christian rather than pagan—the antiquity, that is, of the New Testament

Northern Christian humanism

and the early Christian fathers. Similarly, northern Renaissance artists were moved by the accomplishments of Italian Renaissance masters to turn their backs on medieval Gothic artistic styles and to learn instead how to employ classical techniques. Yet these same artists depicted classical subject matter far less frequently than did the Italians, and inhibited by the greater northern European attachment to Christian asceticism, virtually never dared to portray completely undressed nudes.

Erasmus

Any discussion of northern Renaissance accomplishments in the realm of thought and literary expression must begin with the career of Desiderius Erasmus (c. 1466–1536), "the prince of the Christian humanists." The illegitimate son of a priest, Erasmus was born near Rotterdam in Holland, but later, as a result of his wide travels, became in effect a citizen of all northern Europe. Forced into a monastery against his will when he was a teenager, the young Erasmus found there little religion or formal instruction of any kind but plenty of freedom to read what he liked. He devoured all the classics he could get his hands on and the writings of many of the Church fathers. When he was about thirty years of age, he obtained permission to leave the monastery and enroll in the University of Paris, where he completed the requirements for the degree of bachelor of divinity. But Erasmus subsequently rebelled against what he considered the arid learning of Parisian Scholasticism. In one of his later writings he reported the following exchange: "Q. Where do you come from? A. The College of Montaigu. Q. Ah, then you must be bowed down with learning. A. No, with lice." Erasmus also never entered into the active duties of a priest, choosing rather to make his living by teaching and writing. Ever on the lookout for new patrons, he changed his residence at frequent intervals, traveling often to England, staying once for three years in Italy, and residing in several different cities in the Netherlands before settling finally toward the end of his life in Basel, Switzerland. By means of a voluminous correspondence he kept up with learned friends he made wherever he went, Erasmus became the leader of a northern European humanist coterie. And by means of the popularity of his numerous publications, he became the arbiter of "advanced" northern European cultural tastes during the first quarter of the sixteenth century.

Erasmus's literary accomplishments

Erasmus's many-sided intellectual activity may best be appraised from two different points of view: the literary and the doctrinal. As a Latin prose stylist, Erasmus probably was unequaled since the days of Cicero. Extraordinarily learned and witty, he revelled in tailoring his mode of discourse to fit his subject, creating dazzling verbal effects when appropriate, and coining puns that took on added meaning if one knew Greek as well as Latin. Above all, Erasmus excelled in the deft use of irony, poking fun at all and sundry, including himself. For example, in his *Colloquies* (Latin for *Discussions*) he had a fictional character lament the evil signs of the times thus: "kings make war, priests strive to line their pockets, theologians invent syllogisms, monks roam outside their cloisters, the commons riot, and Erasmus writes colloquies."

But although Erasmus's urbane Latin style and wit earned him a wide audience for purely literary reasons, he by no means thought of himself as a mere entertainer. Rather, he intended everything he wrote to propagate in one form or another what he called the "philosophy of Christ." The essence of Erasmus's Christian humanist convictions was his belief that the entire society of his day was caught up in corruption and immorality as a result of having lost sight of the simple teachings of the Gospels. Accordingly, he offered to his contemporaries three different categories of publication: clever satires meant to show people the error of their ways, serious moral treatises meant to offer guidance toward proper Christian behavior, and scholarly editions of basic Christian texts.

Erasmus's "philosophy of Christ"

In the first category belong the works of Erasmus that are still most widely read today—*The Praise of Folly* (1509), in which he pilloried Scholastic pedantry and dogmatism as well as the ignorance and superstitious credulity of the masses; and the *Colloquies* (1518), in which he held up contemporary religious practices for examination in a more serious but still pervasively ironic tone. In such works Erasmus let fictional characters do the talking, and hence his own views can only be determined by inference. But in his second mode Erasmus did not hesitate to speak clearly in his own voice. The most prominent treatises in this second genre are the quietly eloquent *Handbook of the Christian Knight* (1503), which urged the laity to pursue lives of serene inward piety, and the *Complaint of Peace* (1517), which pleaded movingly for Christian pacifism.

The satires and moral treatises

Despite this highly impressive literary production, however, Erasmus probably considered his textual scholarship his single greatest achievement. Revering the authority of the early Latin Fathers, Augustine, Jerome, and Ambrose, he brought out reliable editions of all their works, and revering the authority of the Bible most of all, he applied his extraordinary skills as a student of Latin and Greek to producing a reliable edition of the New Testament. After reading Lorenzo Valla's *Notes on the New Testament* in 1505, Erasmus became convinced that nothing was more imperative than divesting the text of the entire New Testament of the myriad errors in transcription and translation that had piled up during the Middle Ages, for no one could be a good Christian without being certain of exactly what Christ's message really was. Hence he spent ten years studying and comparing all the best early Greek biblical manuscripts he could find in order to establish an authoritative text. Finally appearing in 1516, Erasmus's Greek New Testament, published together with explanatory notes and his own new Latin translation, was one of the most important landmarks of biblical scholarship of all time.

Erasmus's edition of the New Testament

One of Erasmus's closest friends, and a close second to him in distinction among the ranks of the Christian humanists, was the Englishman Sir Thomas More (1478–1535). Following a successful career as a lawyer and as speaker of the House of Commons, in 1529 More was appointed lord chancellor of England. He was not long in this position, however, before he incurred the wrath of his royal master, King Henry VIII, because More, who was loyal to Catholic universalism, opposed the king's design to establish a national church under subjection to the state. Finally, in 1534, when

Sir Thomas More and Utopia

A Map of Thomas More's Imaginary Island of Utopia. "Utopia's" fictional discoverer, Hythlodaeus, whose name means "dispenser of nonsense" in Greek, points to the island of Utopia, which means "no place." From an early edition.

More refused to take an oath acknowledging Henry as head of the Church of England, he was thrown into the Tower, and a year later met his death on the scaffold as a Catholic martyr. Much earlier, however, in 1516, long before More had any inkling of how his life was to end, he published the one work for which he will ever be best remembered, the *Utopia*. Creating the subsequently popular genre of "utopian fiction," More's *Utopia* expressed an Erasmian critique of contemporary society. Purporting to describe an ideal community on an imaginary island, the book is really an indictment of the glaring abuses of the time—of poverty undeserved and wealth unearned, of drastic punishments, religious persecution, and the senseless slaughter of war. The inhabitants of Utopia hold all their goods in common, work only six hours a day so that all may have leisure for intellectual pursuits, and practice the natural virtues of wisdom, moderation, fortitude, and justice. Iron is the precious metal "because it is useful," war and monasticism are abolished, and toleration is granted to all who recognize the existence of God and the immortality of the soul. Although More advanced no explicit arguments in his *Utopia* in favor of Christianity, he clearly meant to imply that if the "Utopians" could manage their society so well without the benefit of Christian Revelation, Europeans who knew the Gospels ought to be able to do even better.

Whereas Erasmus and More were basically conciliatory in their tempera-ments and preferred to express themselves by means of wry understate-ments, a third representative of the Christian humanist movement, Eras-mus's German disciple Ulrich von Hutten (1488–1523) was of a much more combative disposition. Dedicated to the cause of German cultural na-tionalism, von Hutten, in translating the Roman historian Tacitus, em-ployed his command of classical scholarship to demonstrate how "proud and free" Germanic tribes had once triumphed heroically over Roman le-gions. In other writings he spoke up truculently in his own words to de-fend the German people against foreigners. But von Hutten's chief claim to fame was his collaboration with another German humanist, Crotus Ru-bianus, in the authorship of the *Letters of Obscure Men* (1515), one of the most stinging satires in the history of literature. This was written as part of a propaganda war in favor of a scholar named Johann Reuchlin who wished to pursue his study of Hebrew writings, above all, the Talmud. When Scholastic theologians from the University of Cologne and the Ger-man inquisitor general tried to have all Hebrew books in Germany de-stroyed, Reuchlin and his party strongly opposed the move. After a while it became apparent that direct argument was accomplishing nothing, so Reuchlin's supporters resorted to ridicule. Von Hutten and Rubianus pub-lished a series of letters, written in intentionally bad Latin, purportedly by some of Reuchlin's Scholastic opponents from the University of Cologne. These were given such ridiculous names as Goatmilker, Baldpate, and Dungspreader, and shown to be learned fools who paraded forth examples of absurd religious literalism or grotesque erudition. Heinrich Sheep's-mouth, for example, the supposed writer of one of the letters, professed to be worried that he had sinned grievously by eating on Friday an egg that contained the yolk of a chick. The author of another boasted of his "bril-liant discovery" that Julius Caesar could not have written Latin histories because he was too busy with his military exploits ever to have learned Latin. Although immediately banned by the Church, the letters circulated nonetheless and were widely read, giving ever more currency to the Eras-mian proposition that Scholastic theology and Catholic religious ritual had to be set aside in favor of the most earnest dedication to the pursuit of apostolic Christianity.

Ulrich von Hutten and the Letters of Obscure Men

With Erasmus, More, and von Hutten the list of energetic and eloquent Christian humanists is by no means exhausted, for the Englishman John Colet (c. 1467–1519), the Frenchman Jacques Lefèvre d'Étaples (c. 1455–1536), and the Spaniards Cardinal Francisco Ximénez de Cisneros (1436–1517) and Juan Luis Vives (1492–1540), among still many others, all made signal contributions to the collective enterprise of editing biblical and early Christian texts and expounding Gospel morality. But despite a host of achievements, the Christian humanist movement, which possessed such an extraordinary degree of international solidarity and vigor from about 1500 to 1525, was thrown into disarray by the rise of Protestantism and subse-quently lost its momentum. The irony here is obvious, for the Christian humanists' emphasis on the literal truth of the Gospels and their devastating criticisms of clerical corruption and excessive religious ceremonialism cer-

The decline of Christian humanism

tainly helped pave the way for the Protestant Reformation initiated by Martin Luther in 1517. But, as will be seen in the following chapter, very few Christian humanists were willing to go the whole route with Luther in rejecting the most fundamental principles on which Catholicism was based, and the few who did became such ardent Protestants that they lost all the sense of quiet irony that earlier had been a hallmark of Christian humanist expression. Most Christian humanists tried to remain within the Catholic fold while still espousing their ideal of nonritualistic inward piety. But as time went on, the leaders of Catholicism had less and less tolerance for them because lines were hardening in the war with Protestantism and any suggestion of internal criticism of Catholic religious practices seemed like giving covert aid to "the enemy." Erasmus himself, who remained a Catholic, died early enough to escape opprobrium, but several of his less fortunate followers lived on to suffer as victims of the Spanish Inquisition.

Northern Renaissance poetry

Yet if Christian humanism faded rapidly after about 1525, the northern Renaissance continued to flourish throughout the sixteenth century in primarily literary and artistic forms. In France, for example, the highly accomplished poets Pierre de Ronsard (c. 1524–1585) and Joachim du Bellay (c. 1522–1560) wrote elegant sonnets in the style of Petrarch, and in England the poets Sir Philip Sidney (1554–1586) and Edmund Spenser (c. 1552–1599) drew impressively on Italian literary innovations as well. Indeed, Spenser's *The Faerie Queene,* a long chivalric romance written in the manner of Ariosto's *Orlando Furioso,* communicates as well as any Italian work the gorgeous sensuousness typical of Italian Renaissance culture.

François Rabelais

More intrinsically original than any of the aforementioned poets was the French prose satirist François Rabelais (c. 1490–1553), probably the best loved of all the great European creative writers of the sixteenth century. Like Erasmus, whom he greatly admired, Rabelais was educated as a monk, but soon after taking holy orders he left his monastery to study medicine. Becoming thereafter a practicing physician in Lyons, Rabelais from the start interspersed his professional activities with literary endeavors of one sort or another. He wrote almanacs for the common people, satires against quacks and astrologers, and burlesques of popular superstitions. But by far his most enduring literary legacy consists of his five volumes of "chronicles" published under the collective title of *Gargantua and Pantagruel.*

Rabelais' affirmativeness

Rabelais' account of the adventures of Gargantua and Pantagruel, originally the names of legendary medieval giants noted for their fabulous size and gross appetites, served as a vehicle for his lusty humor and his penchant for exuberant narrative as well as for the expression of his philosophy of naturalism. To some degree, Rabelais drew on the precedents of Christian humanism. Thus, like Erasmus, he satirized religious ceremonialism, ridiculed Scholasticism, scoffed at superstitions, and pilloried every form of bigotry. But much unlike Erasmus, who wrote in a highly cultivated classical Latin style comprehensible to only the most learned readers, Rabelais chose to address a far wider audience by writing in an extremely down-to-earth French, often loaded with the crudest vulgarities. Likewise, Rabelais wanted to avoid seeming in any way "preachy" and therefore eschewed all

Madonna of Mercy, Piero della Francesca (c. 1420–1492). This fresco, painted in central Italy in the middle of the fifteenth century, depicts the Virgin Mary protecting her faithful. Piero della Francesca was considered provincial by the Florentines of his day because his severe style lacked the fluidity and charm then fashionable in Florence. Today, however, connoisseurs place his painting in the very highest rank. (Art Resource)

Christ Appears to the Magdalen, Fra Angelico (1387–1455). The Florentine painter Fra Angelico's work is characterized by its grace of line and delicacy of color. (Art Resource)

The Birth of Venus, Sandro Botticelli (1444–1510). Botticelli was a mystic as well as a lover of beauty and the painting is most often interpreted as a neo-Platonic allegory. (Scala)

The Virgin of the Rocks, Leonardo da Vinci (1452–1519). This painting reveals not only Leonardo's interest in human character, but also his absorption in the phenomenon of nature. (Louvre)

Mona Lisa, Leonardo da Vinci. Unlike most other Renaissance painters who sought to convey an understandable message, Leonardo created questions to which he gave no answer. Nowhere is this more evident than in the enigmatic countenance of Mona Lisa. (Louvre)

The Last Supper, Leonardo da Vinci. This great fresco depicts the varying reactions of Jesus' disciples when He announces that one of them will betray Him. (Santa Maria della Grazie, Milan)

Above: *The Madonna of the Chair,* Raphael (1483–1520). Raphael's art was distinguished by warmth, serenity, and tenderness. (Pitti Palace, Florence) Right: "Christ and Madonna." From *The Last Judgment,* Michelangelo (1475–1564). This painting above the altar in the Sistine Chapel, Rome, shows Christ as judge. (Sistine Chapel)

Pope Paul III with His Nephews, Titian (1488–1576). This painting emphasizes action far more than its forebear, Raphael's portrait of Pope Leo X with his nephews. (National Museum, Naples)

The Emperor Charles V, Titian. (Alte Pinakothek)

Chambord. Built in the early sixteenth century by an Italian architect in the service of King Francis I of France, this magnificent Loire Valley château combines Gothic and Renaissance architectural traits.

suggestions of moralism in favor of giving the impression that he wished merely to offer his readers some rollicking good fun. Yet, aside from the critical satire in *Gargantua and Pantagruel,* there runs through all five volumes a common theme of glorifying the human and the natural. For Rabelais, whose robust giants were really life-loving human beings writ very large, every instinct of humanity was healthy, provided it was not directed toward tyranny over others. Thus in his ideal community, the utopian "abbey of Thélème," there was no repressiveness whatsoever, but only a congenial environment for the pursuit of life-affirming, natural human attainments, guided by the single rule of "do what thou wouldst."

Were we to imagine what Rabelais' fictional abbey of Thélème might have looked like, we would do best to picture it as resembling one of the famous sixteenth-century French Renaissance châteaux built along the River Loire, for the northern European Renaissance had its own distinctive architecture that often corresponded in certain essentials to its literature. Thus, just as Rabelais recounted stories of medieval giants in order to express an affirmation of Renaissance values, so French architects who constructed such splendid Loire châteaux as Amboise, Chenonceaux, and Chambord, combined elements of the late-medieval French flamboyant Gothic style with an up-to-date emphasis on classical horizontality to produce some of the most impressively distinctive architectural landmarks ever constructed in France. Yet much closer architectural imitation of Italian models occurred in France as well, for just as Ronsard and du Bellay modeled their poetic style very closely on Petrarch, so Pierre Lescot, the French architect who began work on the new royal palace of the Louvre in Paris

Northern Renaissance architecture

The West Side of the Square Court of the Louvre by Pierre Lescot. The enlargement of the Louvre, begun by Lescot in 1546, took more than a century to complete. Drawing on the work of Bramante (see above, p. 419), he achieved a synthesis of the traditional château and the Renaissance palace.

Albrecht Dürer

See color plates facing page 492 for *Self-Portrait* by Dürer and *Erasmus* by Hans Holbein the Younger

in 1546, hewed closely to the classicism of Italian Renaissance masters in constructing a facade that emphasized classical pilasters and pediments.

It only remains to treat the accomplishments of northern Renaissance painting, another realm in which links between thought and art can be discerned. Certainly the most moving visual embodiments of the ideals of Christian humanism were conceived by the foremost of northern Renaissance artists, the German Albrecht Dürer (1471–1528). From the purely technical and stylistic points of view, Dürer's greatest significance lies in the fact that, returning to his native Nuremberg after a trip to Venice in 1494, he became the first northerner to master Italian Renaissance techniques of proportion, perspective, and modeling. Dürer also shared with contemporary Italians a fascination with reproducing the manifold works of nature down to the minutest details and a penchant for displaying various postures of the human nude. But whereas Michelangelo portrayed his naked David or Adam entirely without covering, Dürer's nudes are seldom lacking their fig leaves, in deference to more restrained northern traditions. Moreover, Dürer consistently refrained from abandoning himself to the pure classicism and sumptuousness of much Italian Renaissance art because he was inspired primarily by the more traditionally Christian ideals of Erasmus. Thus Dürer's serenely radiant *St. Jerome* expresses the sense of accomplishment that Erasmus or any other contemporary Christian humanist may have had while working quietly in his study, his *Knight, Death, and Devil* offers a stirring visual depiction of Erasmus's ideal Christian knight, and his *Four Apostles* intones a solemn hymn to the dignity and penetrating insight of Dürer's favorite New Testament authors, Saints Paul, John, Peter, and Mark.

Dürer would have loved nothing more than to have immortalized Erasmus in a major painted portrait, but circumstances prevented him from doing this because the paths of the two men crossed only once, and after Dürer started sketching his hero on that occasion his work was interrupted by Erasmus's press of business. Instead, the accomplishment of capturing Erasmus's pensive spirit in oils was left to the second greatest of northern Renaissance artists, the German Hans Holbein the Younger (1497–1543). As good fortune would have it, during a stay in England Holbein also painted an extraordinarily acute portrait of Erasmus's friend and kindred spirit, Sir Thomas More, which enables us to see clearly why a contemporary called More "a man of . . . sad gravity; a man for all seasons." These two portraits in and of themselves point up a major difference between medieval and Renaissance culture because, whereas the Middle Ages produced no convincing naturalistic likenesses of any leading intellectual figures, Renaissance culture's greater commitment to capturing the essence of human individuality created the environment in which Holbein was able to make Erasmus and More come to life.

Sir Thomas More. Portrait by Hans Holbein the Younger.

Left: *St. Jerome in His Study* by Dürer. St. Jerome, a hero for both Dürer and Erasmus, represents inspired Christian scholarship. Note how the scene exudes contentment, even down to the sleeping lion which seems rather like an overgrown tabby cat. Right: *The Four Apostles* by Dürer. This painting in two separate panels is a moving statement of the artist's intense religious faith.

Knight, Death, and Devil by Dürer. This engraving of 1513 illustrates the ideal figure of Erasmus's *Handbook of a Christian Knight*. The Steadfast Knight is able to advance through the world on his charger, his loyal dog at his side, despite intimations of mortality and the snares of the devil.

6. RENAISSANCE DEVELOPMENTS IN MUSIC

The evolution of music as an independent art

Music in Western Europe in the fifteenth and sixteenth centuries reached such a high point of development that it constitutes, together with painting and sculpture, one of the most brilliant aspects of Renaissance endeavor. While the visual arts were stimulated by the study of ancient models, music flowed naturally from an independent evolution that had been in progress in medieval Christendom. As earlier, leadership came from men trained in the service of the Church, but secular music was now valued as well, and its principles were combined with those of sacred music to bring a decided gain in color and emotional appeal. The distinction between sacred and profane became less sharp; most composers did not restrict their activities to either field. Music was no longer regarded merely as a diversion or an adjunct to worship but came into its own as a serious independent art.

Leadership provided by Italy and France

Different sections of Europe vied with one another for musical leadership. As with the other arts, advances were related to the generous patronage afforded by the prosperous cities of Italy and the northern European princely courts. During the fourteenth century a pre- or early Renaissance musical movement called Ars Nova (new art) flourished in Italy and France. Its outstanding composers were Francesco Landini (c. 1325–1397) and Guillaume de Machaut (1300–1377). The madrigals, ballads, and other songs composed by the Ars Nova musicians testify to a rich secular art, but the greatest achievement of the period was a highly complicated yet delicate contrapuntal style adapted for ecclesiastical motets. Machaut, moreover, was the first known composer to provide a polyphonic version for the singing of the Mass.

The fifteenth century was ushered in by a synthesis of French, Flemish, and Italian elements in the ducal court of Burgundy. This music was melodious and gentle, but in the second half of the century it hardened a little as northern Flemish elements gained in importance. As the sixteenth century opened, Franco-Flemish composers appeared in every important court and cathedral all over Europe, gradually establishing regional-national schools, usually in attractive combinations of Flemish with German, Spanish, and Italian musical cultures. The various genres thus created show a close affinity with Renaissance art and poetry. In the second half of the sixteenth century the leaders of the nationalized Franco-Flemish style were the Flemish Roland de Lassus (1532–1594), the most versatile composer of the age, and the Italian Giovanni Pierluigi da Palestrina (c. 1525–1594), who specialized in highly intricate polyphonic choral music written for Catholic church services under the patronage of the popes in Rome. Music also flourished in sixteenth-century England, where the Tudor monarchs Henry VIII and Elizabeth I were active in patronizing the arts. Not only did the Italian madrigal, imported toward the end of the sixteenth century,

Renaissance Trumpeters and Singers. Reliefs by Luca della Robbia.

take on remarkable new life in England, but songs and instrumental music of an original cast anticipated future developments on the Continent. In William Byrd (1543–1623) English music produced a master fully the equal of the great Flemish and Italian composers of the Renaissance period. The general level of musical proficiency seems to have been higher in Queen Elizabeth's day than in ours: the singing of part-songs was a popular pastime in homes and at informal social gatherings, and the ability to read a part at sight was expected of the educated elite.

The greatness of the Renaissance musical achievement

In conclusion, it may be observed that while accomplishments in counterpoint were already very advanced in the Renaissance period, our modern harmonic system was still in its infancy, and thus there was much room for later experimentation. At the same time one should realize that the music of the Renaissance constitutes not merely a stage in evolution but a magnificent achievement in itself, with masters who rank among the great of all time. The composers Lassus, Palestrina, and Byrd are as truly representative of the artistic triumph of the Renaissance as are the painters Leonardo, Raphael, and Michelangelo. Their heritage, long neglected, has within recent years begun to be appreciated, and is now gaining in popularity as interested groups of musicians devote themselves to its revival.

7. THE SCIENTIFIC ACCOMPLISHMENTS OF THE RENAISSANCE PERIOD

The nonscientific orientation of Renaissance humanism

Some extraordinarily important accomplishments were made in the history of science during the sixteenth and early seventeenth centuries, but these were not preeminently the achievements of Renaissance humanism. The educational program of the humanists placed a low value on science because it seemed irrelevant to their aim of making people more eloquent and moral. Science for humanists like Petrarch, Leonardo Bruni, or Erasmus was part and parcel of the "vain speculation" of the Scholastics which they attacked and held up to ridicule. Accordingly, none of the great scientists of the Renaissance Age belonged to the humanist movement.

Renaissance foundations of modern science: (1) Neoplatonism

Nonetheless, at least two intellectual trends of the period did prepare the way for great new scientific advances. One was the currency of Neoplatonism. The importance of this philosophical system to science was that it proposed certain ideas, such as the central position of the sun and the supposed divinity of given geometrical shapes, that would help lead to crucial scientific breakthroughs. Although Neoplatonism seems very "unscientific" from the modern perspective because it emphasizes mysticism and intuition instead of empiricism or strictly rational thought, it helped scientific thinkers to reconsider older notions that had impeded the progress of medieval science; in other words, it helped them to put on a new "thinking cap." Among the most important of the scientists who were influenced by Neoplatonism were Copernicus and Kepler.

A second trend that contributed to the advance of science was very different: the growth in popularity of a *mechanistic* interpretation of the universe. Renaissance mechanism owed its greatest impetus to the publication in 1543 of the works of the great Greek mathematician and physicist Archimedes. Not only were his concrete observations and discoveries among the most advanced and reliable in the entire body of Greek science, but Archimedes taught that the universe operates on the basis of mechanical forces, like a great machine. Because his view was diametrically opposed to the occult outlook of the Neoplatonists, who saw the world as inhabited by spirits and driven by supernatural forces, it took some time to gather strength. Nonetheless, mechanism did gain some very important late Renaissance adherents, foremost among whom was the Italian scientist Galileo. Ultimately mechanism played an enormous role in the development of modern science because it insisted upon finding observable and measurable causes and effects in the world of nature.

(2) *a mechanistic view of the universe*

One other Renaissance development that contributed to the rise of modern science was the breakdown of the medieval separation between the realms of theory and practice. In the Middle Ages Scholastically trained clerics theorized about the natural world but never for a moment thought of tinkering with machines or dissecting corpses because this empirical approach to science lay outside the Scholastic framework. On the other hand, numerous technicians who had little formal education and knew little of abstract theories had much practical expertise in various aspects of mechanical engineering. Theory and practice began to come together in the fifteenth century. One reason for this was that the highly respected Renaissance artists bridged both areas of endeavor: not only were they marvelous craftsmen, but they advanced mathematics and science when they investigated the laws of perspective and optics, worked out geometric methods for supporting the weight of enormous architectural domes, and studied the dimensions and details of the human body. In general, they helped make science more empirical and practically oriented than it had been earlier. Other reasons for the integration were the decline in prestige of the overly theoretical universities and a growing interest in alchemy and astrology among the leisured classes. Thus although alchemy and astrology are today properly dismissed as unscientific superstitions, in the sixteenth and seventeenth centuries their vogue led some wealthy amateurs to start building laboratories and measuring the courses of the stars. Thereby scientific practice was rendered eminently respectable. When that happened modern science was on the way to some of its greatest triumphs.

A Cannon Foundry by Leonardo da Vinci

(3) *the integration of theory and practice*

The actual scientific accomplishments of the Renaissance period were international in scope. The achievement par excellence in astronomy—the formulation and proof of the heliocentric theory that the earth revolves around the sun—was primarily the work of the Pole Copernicus, the German Kepler, and the Italian Galileo. Until the sixteenth century the Ptolemaic theory that the earth stands still at the center of the universe went virtually unchallenged in Western Europe. Nicholas Copernicus (1473–1543), a Polish clergyman who had absorbed Neoplatonism while studying in Italy, was the first to posit an alternative system. Copernicus made few new

Copernicus and heliocentric theory

The Ptolemaic System of the Universe

Kepler's laws of planetary motion

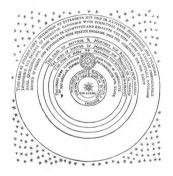

The Copernican System. A diagram devised by Copernicus himself. Note that the planetary orbits are still circular, as they were in the Ptolemaic system. It was Johann Kepler who proved that all the planets move in elliptical orbits.

Galileo's confirmation of the Copernican revolution

observations, but he thoroughly reinterpreted the significance of the old astronomical evidence. Inspired by the Neoplatonic assumptions that the sphere is the most perfect shape, that motion is more nearly divine than rest, and that the sun sits "enthroned" in the midst of the universe, "ruling his children the planets which circle around him," Copernicus worked out a new heliocentric theory. Specifically, in his *On the Revolutions of the Heavenly Spheres*—which he completed around 1530 but did not publish until 1543—he argued that the earth and the planets move around the sun in concentric circles. Copernicus's system itself was still highly imperfect: by no means did it account without difficulties for all the known facts of planetary motion. Moreover, it asked people to reject their common-sense assumptions: that the sun moves since they observe it moving across the sky and that the earth stands still since no movement can be felt. More serious, Copernicus contradicted passages in the Bible, such as the one wherein Joshua commands the sun to stand still. As a result of such problems, believers in Copernicus's heliocentric theory remained distinctly in the minority until the early seventeenth century.

It was Kepler and Galileo who ensured the triumph of Copernicus's revolution in astronomy. Johann Kepler (1571–1630), a mystical thinker who was in many ways more like a magician than a modern scientist, studied astronomy in order to probe the hidden secrets of God. His basic conviction was that God had created the universe according to mathematical laws. Relying on the new and impressively accurate astronomical observations of the Dane Tycho Brahe (1546–1601), Kepler was able to recognize that two assumptions about planetary motion that Copernicus had taken for granted were simply not in accord with the observable facts. Specifically, Kepler replaced Copernicus's view that planetary orbits were circular with his "First Law" that the earth and the other planets travel in elliptical paths around the sun, and he replaced Copernicus's belief in uniform planetary velocity with his own "Second Law" that the speed of planets varies with their distance from the sun. He also argued that magnetic attractions between the sun and the planets keep the planets in orbital motion. That approach was rejected by most seventeenth-century mechanistic scientists as being far too magical, but in fact it paved the way for the law of universal gravitation formulated by Isaac Newton at the end of the seventeenth century.

As Kepler perfected Copernicus's heliocentric system from the point of view of mathematical theory, so Galileo Galilei (1564–1642) promoted acceptance for it by gathering further astronomical evidence. With a telescope that he manufactured himself and raised to a magnifying power of thirty times, he discovered the moons of Jupiter and spots on the sun. He was also able to determine that the Milky Way is a collection of celestial bodies independent of our solar system and to form some idea of the enormous distances of the fixed stars. Though many held out against them, Galileo's discoveries gradually convinced the majority of scientists that the main conclusion of Copernicus was true. The final triumph of this idea is commonly called the *Copernican Revolution*. Few more significant events have occurred in the intellectual history of the world, for it overturned the medieval worldview and paved the way for modern conceptions of mechanism, skepticism, and the infinity of time and space. Some thinkers believe that it contributed also to the degradation of man, since it swept man out of his majestic position at the center of the universe and reduced him to a mere particle of dust in an endless cosmic machine.

In the front rank among the physicists of the Renaissance were Leonardo da Vinci and Galileo. If Leonardo da Vinci had failed completely as a painter, his contributions to science would still entitle him to considerable fame. Not the least of these were his achievements in physics. Though he actually made few complete discoveries, his conclusion that "every weight tends to fall toward the center by the shortest way" contained the kernel of the law of gravity. In addition, he worked out the principles of an astonishing variety of inventions, including a diving board, a steam engine, an armored tank, and a helicopter. Galileo is especially noted as a physicist for his law of falling bodies. Skeptical of the traditional theory that bodies fall with a speed directly proportional to their weight, he taught that bodies dropped from various heights would fall at a rate of speed that increases with the square of the time involved. Rejecting the Scholastic notions of absolute gravity and absolute levity, he taught that these are purely relative terms, that all bodies have weight, even those which, like the air, are invisible, and that in a vacuum all objects would fall with equal velocity. Galileo seems to have had a broader conception of a universal force of gravitation than Leonardo da Vinci, for he perceived that the power that holds the moon in the vicinity of the earth and causes the satellites of Jupiter to circulate around that planet is essentially the same as the force that enables the earth to draw bodies to its surface. He never formulated this principle as a law, however, nor did he realize all of its implications, as did Newton some fifty years later.

The record of Renaissance achievements in medicine and anatomy is also impressive. Attention must be called above all to the work of the German Theophrastus von Hohenheim, known as Paracelsus (1493–1541), the Spaniard Michael Servetus (1511–1553), and the Belgian Andreas Vesalius (1514–1564). The physician Paracelsus resembled Copernicus and Kepler in believing that spiritual rather than material forces governed the workings of the universe. Hence he was a firm believer in alchemy and astrology. Nevertheless, Paracelsus relied on observation for his knowledge of diseases and their cures. Instead of following the teachings of ancient authorities, he traveled widely, studying cases of illness in different environments and experimenting with many drugs. Above all, his insistence on the close relationship of chemistry and medicine foreshadowed and sometimes directly influenced important modern achievements in pharmacology and healing. Michael Servetus, whose major interest was theology but who practiced medicine for a living, discovered the pulmonary circulation of the blood, in an attempt to prove the veracity of the Virgin birth. He described how the blood leaves the right chambers of the heart, is carried to the lungs to be purified, then returns to the heart and is conveyed from that organ to all

Galileo. A portrait by Ottavio Leoni.

Leonardo da Vinci and Galileo as physicists

Michael Servetus

Two Plates from Vesalius's On the Structure of the Human Body. On the left is a portrait of Vesalius himself displaying the sinews of the forearm. Note the striking similarity to the anatomical drawings of Leonardo, shown above, p. 413. On the right we see "the human skeleton shown from the side." The presence of the sarcophagus with the Latin warning "we live by the spirit, all else will die" shows that scientific illustrations still had to be justified by moralistic sententiousness in the early-modern period.

parts of the body. But Servetus had no idea that the blood returned to the heart through the veins, a discovery that was made by the Englishman William Harvey in the early seventeenth century.

Vesalius

Purely by coincidence the one sixteenth-century scientific treatise that came closest to rivaling in significance Copernicus's work in astronomy, Vesalius's *On the Structure of the Human Body,* was published in 1543, the same year that saw the issuance of Copernicus's *Revolutions of the Heavenly Spheres.* Vesalius was born in Brussels and studied in Paris but later migrated to Italy where he taught anatomy and surgery at the University of Padua. He approached his research from the correct point of view that much of ancient anatomical doctrine was in error. For him the ancient anatomy of Galen (so to speak, the Ptolemy of medicine) could only be corrected on the basis of direct observation. Hence he applied himself to frequent dissections of human corpses to see how various parts of the body actually appear when the skin covering is stripped away. Not content with merely describing in words what he saw, Vesalius then collaborated with an artist—Jan van Calcar, a fellow Belgian who had come to Italy to study under the Renaissance master Titian—in portraying his observations in detailed engravings. Art historians are uncertain as to whether van Calcar was directly inspired in executing his illustrations for Vesalius by knowledge of earlier anatomical drawings of Leonardo da Vinci, but even if he was not, he certainly relied on a cumulative tradition of expert anatomical depiction bequeathed to him by Italian Renaissance art. Gathered in Vesalius's *Structure of the Human Body* of 1543, van Calcar's plates offered a new map of the human anatomy just when Copernicus was laying out a new map of the heavens. Since Vesalius in the same work offered basic explanations of how parts of the body move and interact, in addition to discussing and illustrating how they look, he is often counted as the father of modern physiology as well as the father of modern anatomy. With his landmark treatise we come to a fitting end to our survey of Renaissance accomplishments inasmuch as his *Structure of the Human Body* represented the fullest degree of fruitful international intellectual exchanges as well as the fullest merger of theory and practice, and art and science.

SELECTED READINGS

• *Items so designated are available in paperback editions.*

Baker, Herschel, *The Image of Man: A Study of the Idea of Human Dignity in Classical Antiquity, the Middle Ages, and the Renaissance,* Cambridge, Mass., 1947. An outstanding and engagingly written survey from the perspective of a modern liberal.

• Baxandall, Michael, *Painting and Experience in Fifteenth Century Italy,* Oxford, 1972.

Benesch, Otto, *The Art of the Renaissance in Northern Europe,* rev. ed., New York, 1965.

• Boas, Marie, *The Scientific Renaissance: 1450–1630,* New York, 1962. An excellent, straightforward survey.

• Burckhardt, Jacob, *The Civilization of the Renaissance in Italy,* many eds. The nineteenth-century work that formulated the modern view of the Renaissance.

Burke, Peter, *Culture and Society in Renaissance Italy, 1420–1540,* New York, 1972.

• Butterfield, Herbert, *The Origins of Modern Science,* rev. ed., New York, 1965. Clear and wide ranging. Shows how science developed from major changes in intellectual orientations.

• Chambers, R. W., *Thomas More,* London, 1936. A spirited defense of the view that More was a lifelong committed Catholic.

• Clark, Kenneth M., *Leonardo da Vinci,* 2nd ed., Cambridge, 1952.

• De Tolnay, C., *Michelangelo: Sculptor, Painter, Architect,* Princeton, 1975.

Ferguson, Wallace, ed., *The Renaissance: Six Essays,* rev. ed., New York, 1962.

• Fox, Alistair, *Thomas More: History and Providence,* Oxford, 1982. More reliable in its judgments than Chambers.

• Gilmore, Myron, *The World of Humanism, 1453–1517,* New York, 1952. A well-written survey.

Gould, Cecil, *An Introduction to Italian Renaissance Painting,* London, 1957.

Hale, J. R., *Machiavelli and Renaissance Italy,* New York, 1960.

• ———, *Renaissance Europe: The Individual and Society, 1480–1520,* London, 1971. A different kind of survey that does not treat the great events but examines the quality of life.

• Hay, D., ed., *The Renaissance Debate,* New York, 1965. A collection of readings on the question of how to define the Renaissance.

Herlihy, David, and Christiane Klapisch-Zuber, *Tuscans and Their Families,* New Haven, 1985. Best on the social context of Florentine culture.

• Kearney, Hugh, *Science and Change, 1500–1700,* New York, 1971. Supplements Butterfield in arguing that science progressed as the result of contributions made by three different "schools."

• Kristeller, Paul O., *Eight Philosophers of the Italian Renaissance,* Stanford, 1964. Admirably clear.

• ———, *Renaissance Thought: The Classic, Scholastic, and Humanistic Strains,* New York, 1961. Very helpful in defining main trends of Renaissance thought.

- Kuhn, Thomas S., *The Copernican Revolution: Planetary Astronomy in the Development of Western Thought,* Cambridge, Mass., 1957. Admirably clear.

  Larner, John, *Culture and Society in Italy, 1290–1420,* New York, 1971.
- Levey, M., *Early Renaissance (Style and Civilization),* Baltimore, 1967. Art history.
- Panofsky, E., *The Life and Art of Albrecht Dürer,* 4th ed., Princeton, 1955.
- ———, *Renaissance and Renascences in Western Art,* Stockholm, 1960. A difficult but rewarding attempt to distinguish the Italian Renaissance from its medieval predecessors.

  Phillips, Margaret M., *Erasmus and the Northern Renaissance,* London, 1949.
- Pope-Hennessy, John, *The Portrait in the Renaissance,* Princeton, 1966.
- Ralph, Philip L., *The Renaissance in Perspective,* New York, 1973. Both a useful summary and a stimulus to thought.

  Reese, Gustave, *Music in the Renaissance,* rev. ed., New York, 1959. The leading work on the subject.
- Rice, Eugene F., Jr., *The Foundations of Early Modern Europe, 1460–1559,* New York, 1970.
- ———, *Saint Jerome in the Renaissance,* Baltimore, 1985. Employs a fascinating strategy for estimating Renaissance values.

  Seigel, J., *Rhetoric and Philosophy in Renaissance Humanism,* Princeton, 1968. Treats a basic tension in the thought of early Renaissance thinkers.

  Stechow, Wolfgang, *Northern Renaissance Art: 1400–1600,* Englewood Cliffs, N.J., 1966.

  Tracy, James, *Erasmus: The Growth of a Mind,* Geneva, 1972. The best intellectual biography.
- Whitfield, J. H., *A Short History of Italian Literature,* Baltimore, 1960.
- Wittkower, Rudolf, *Architectural Principles in the Age of Humanism,* rev. ed., New York, 1965. An art-historical classic.

SOURCE MATERIALS

  Alberti, Leon Battista, *The Family in Renaissance Florence,* tr. R. N. Watkins, Columbia, S.C., 1969.
- Cassirer, E., et al., eds., *The Renaissance Philosophy of Man,* Chicago, 1948. Leading works of Petrarch, Pico, etc.
- Castiglione, B., *The Book of the Courtier,* tr. C. S. Singleton, New York, 1959.
- Erasmus, D., *The Praise of Folly,* tr. J. Wilson, Ann Arbor, Mich., 1958.
- ———, *Ten Colloquies,* tr. C. R. Thompson, Indianapolis, 1957.
- Kohl, B. G., and R. G. Witt, eds., *The Earthly Republic: Italian Humanists on Government and Society,* Philadelphia, 1978. New translations with excellent introductions.
- Machiavelli, N., *The Prince,* tr. R. M. Adams, New York, 1976. In addition to Machiavelli's text, this edition provides related documents and an excellent selection of scholarly interpretations.
- More, Sir Thomas, *Utopia,* tr. R. M. Adams, 2nd. ed., New York, 1992. In the same series as Adams's translation of Machiavelli's *Prince;* provides background materials and selected scholarly interpretations as well as the text.
- Rabelais, F., *Gargantua and Pantagruel,* tr. J. M. Cohen, Baltimore, 1955. A robust modern translation.

Chapter 14

EUROPE EXPANDS AND DIVIDES: OVERSEAS DISCOVERIES AND PROTESTANT REFORMATION

Formerly we were at the end of the world, and now we are in the middle of it, with an unprecedented change in our fortunes.

—Hernán Pérez de Oliva, addressing the city fathers
of Cordova, Spain, 1524

Since then your serene majesty and your lordships seek a simple answer, I will give it in this manner, neither horned nor toothed: unless I am convinced by the testimony of Scripture or by clear reason . . . I am bound by the Scripture I have quoted, and my conscience is captive to the Word of God. I cannot and I will not retract anything, since it is neither safe nor right to violate one's conscience. I cannot do otherwise, here I stand, may God help me. Amen.

—Martin Luther, addressing the Diet of Worms, 1521

Much as the civilization of the Renaissance made fundamental contributions toward the shaping of the modern world, the two most dramatic developments in the transition from the Middle Ages to the early-modern period of Western European history were the overseas ventures of Spain and Portugal, and the Protestant Reformation. More or less overnight, these two developments changed the course of European history. Whereas European Christian civilization had been geographically self-contained throughout the thousand years of its prior history (excepting the relatively brief Crusade episode), in just a few decades, from about 1490 to about 1520, Europeans sailed over the open seas to take commanding positions in Southeast Asia and lay claim to the whole Western Hemisphere. Ever since, the course of European history has been inseparable from interactions between events on the land mass of Europe and European engagements in the rest of the world.

But just when Europe was expanding it was also dividing. Up until the early sixteenth century, despite growing national differences, there remained a distinct European "Community of Christendom," presided over

Overseas expansion of Spain and Portugal

by the pope. Wherever one traveled one could hear the same Latin Mass, see infants baptized and couples wed according to the same ecclesiastical formulae, and receive blessings from priests who were all ordained by virtue of the same papal authority. As quickly as Europeans took hold of the world, however, they lost their spiritual unity. The Protestant Reformation initiated by Martin Luther in 1517, as well as the Catholic response to it, were both to have numerous progressive effects, but the most obvious immediate results were that Europe rapidly became divided along several different religious lines and that Europeans quickly started warring with one another in the name of faith.

Although the overseas discoveries and Protestant Reformation were roughly contemporaneous, it is important to recognize that in their origins they had nothing directly to do with each other. The early explorers sailed prior to or in disregard of European religious dissensions, and the early Protestants gave little thought to the opening up of new trade routes or the discovery of continents. Yet there is warrant for treating the discoveries, the Protestant Reformation, and the Catholic Counter-Reformation all in the same chapter because their effects very quickly became interrelated, and also because all these movements were marked by incidents of great heroism. As Columbus sailed fearlessly into the unknown and Balboa viewed a new ocean, "silent, upon a peak in Darien," so Luther struggled fearlessly for a new understanding of "the justice of God" and the crippled soldier Ignatius Loyola found inspiration by inward "spiritual exercises," thereby opening up new vistas of their own.

1. THE OVERSEAS DISCOVERIES AND CONQUESTS OF PORTUGAL AND SPAIN

At first glance the speed with which Europeans in the years around 1500 began to traverse the high seas appears bewildering and almost incomprehensible. With good reason most contemporaries perceived Christian civilization to be on the defensive, not the offensive, in the second half of the fifteenth century. In 1453 Constantinople, a hitherto impregnable barrier to Islamic advance, fell to the Turks, commanded by Sultan Muhammad II "the Conqueror"; Serbia was lost in 1459, and Albania followed in 1470. Most frightening of all to Western Europeans was a Turkish landing on the Italian peninsula itself in 1480, which saw the city of Otranto occupied and half the inhabitants slaughtered. Only the death of Sultan Muhammad in 1481 caused the Turks to abandon their Italian foothold, but many feared that the "Infidels" might soon return. In the midst of an unsuccessful attempt to organize united European resistance to the Turks, Pope Pius II (1458–1464) observed: "I see nothing good on the horizon."

Yet Pius II could hardly have been more wrong, for while Christians remained on the defensive against the Turks in eastern Europe until the later sixteenth century, Portuguese and Spanish sailing ships on the Atlantic horizon soon made Christians lords of much of the world. A few facts speak eloquently for themselves: in 1482 the Portuguese built a fortress at Elmina, in modern-day Ghana, which quickly dominated trade on the West African "Gold Coast"; in 1492 Columbus sighted the West Indies; in 1500 the Portuguese established their first trading base on the west coast of India; and in the two years from 1519 to 1521 the Spaniard Cortés seized hold of the Mexican empire of Montezuma.

How did this all happen so quickly? Two different schools of scholarly interpretation offer substantially different responses. Proponents of what may be called the "Renaissance School" point out that the Portuguese and Spanish voyages of discovery occurred at the same time as the spread of Renaissance civilization (Columbus was a direct contemporary of Leonardo da Vinci) and argue that European overseas expansion can only be explained as a manifestation of allegedly new Renaissance principles of curiosity and self-reliance in practical affairs. But this interpretation assumes falsely that medieval people were not curious and self-reliant. Proponents of the Renaissance school also call attention to the fact that many of the mariners who sailed for Portugal and Spain were Italian born, but here they dodge the reality that some Italian voyagers, like Columbus himself, came from Genoa, a city that hardly participated in Italian Renaissance civilization. More important, the Renaissance interpretation seems weak because the leading Italian Renaissance states did not patronize the voyages of discovery at all. Undeniably some bits of classical geographical knowledge acquired in Italy by Renaissance humanists strengthened the resolve of some explorers to pursue certain ocean routes, but otherwise the alternative to the Renaissance explanation, namely the view that the movement of overseas expansion came from medieval preparations, seems far preferable.

Simply stated, the motives, the knowledge, and the wherewithal for the great discoveries were all essentially medieval. Certainly the single most dominant motive for the oceanic voyages was economic—the quest for Asiatic spices and other luxury goods. Pepper, cinnamon, nutmeg, ginger, and cloves could all be grown only in the tropical climates of Southeast Asia, and all were greatly prized throughout the High and Late Middle Ages because of their preservative qualities. (Imagine a civilization without refrigeration and one can easily understand why wealthy Europeans hankered after tangy spices to keep their food from putrifying and to relieve the monotony of salt.) In the Late Middle Ages, Asiatic spices, as well as luxury cloths and precious gems, reached European households by means of the enterprise of Islamic, Venetian, and Genoese middlemen. But the costs were exorbitant, and a fortune was to be made by anyone who could go directly to the source by sea. (Land routes were out of the question because turbulent conditions in central Asia made them extremely unsafe; moreover, until the invention of railroads it normally was vastly more expensive to transport goods by land than by water.) Complementing the economic motives for overseas exploration were religious ones—hopes for converting unbaptized heathens and of finding imagined "lost Christians" in the East who might serve as allies against Islam. Needless to say, these

Explanations for voyages: "Renaissance School"

Medieval background to voyages: Economic motives

OVERSEAS EXPLORATIONS IN THE 15TH AND 16TH CENTURIES

ARCTIC OCEAN

PACIFIC OCEAN

GREENLAND

ICELAND
Vikings 983

Vikings(?) c. 1000

LABRADOR

ATLANTIC OCEAN

AZORES IS.

Columbia 1492

Columbus 1493–150M

HISPANIOLA

WEST INDIES

St. Augustine
FLORIDA

Havana

Cortés 1519
Mexico
AZTEC EMPIRE

PACIFIC OCEAN

Panama

Pizarro 1531
Lima
INCA EMPIRE
Cuzco
Potosi
Santiago

Buenos Aires

Magellan 1521

Vespucci 1502
Rio de Janeiro
Bahia

Vespucci 1501

CAPE VERDE IS.

Magellan 1519

CANARY IS.

PORTUGAL
CASTILLE
Seville
Ceuta

Genoa
ITALY
Otranto

EMPIRE

A F R I C A

GOLD COAST
Elmina

Da Gama 1489

Da Gama 1498

Diaz 1487

CAPE OF GOOD HOPE
Magellan's Ship 1522

Sofala

KENYA

MADAGASCAR

Magellan 1522

I N D I A N   O C E A N

CEYLON

Goa
Calicut

INDIA

CHINESE EMPIRE

JAPAN

Macao

SUMATRA
MALAY PEN.
Malacca

BORNEO
EAST INDIES
Java

PHILIPPINES

MOLUCCAS

NEW GUINEA

Magellan 1521

P A C I F I C   O C E A N

EXPLORERS

Columbus; first voyage
Columbus; next three voyages
Bartholomew Diaz
Vasco de Gama
Amerigo Vespucci
Magellan & Magellan's ship
Vikings

CONQUISTADORES:

Cortes
Pizarro

OUTPOSTS & SETTLEMENTS:

Portuguese
Spanish

hopes, like the lust for spices, flourished in the Middle Ages quite independently of the Italian Renaissance.

Then too the most important knowledge that lay behind the great discoveries and also the technological means to execute them were as medieval as the motivations. The popular notion that Europeans before Columbus believed the earth to be flat is simply a mistake: it would have been impossible after the twelfth century to have found an educated person or a mariner who did not accept the fact that the earth is a sphere. Nor did this knowledge remain solely in the realm of theory. As early as 1291 two Genoese, the Vivaldi brothers, sailed out on the Atlantic with the aim of reaching the East Indies by a "westward route." Although the Vivaldis never came back, by the middle of the fourteenth century Portuguese mariners were sailing regularly back and forth on the Atlantic as far west as the Azores Islands. These Portuguese sailings offer proof that by about 1350 European shipbuilding and navigational technology were fully up to the challenge of reaching new continents. Since the Azores are one-third of the distance between Europe and America, from the strictly technological point of view any ship that could sail from Portugal to the Azores could have sailed all the way to the New World.

Why, then, was America not discovered a century before it actually was? Historians are at their greatest disadvantage in trying to explain things that did not happen, but two hypotheses may be offered. One relates to the fact that the fourteenth and fifteenth centuries were times of acute economic depression and political turmoil throughout Western Europe. Since the major states of the Atlantic—France, England, and Castile (the dominant kingdom on the Spanish peninsula)—were all weakened by economic contraction and caught up in seemingly interminable wars, it is no wonder that none of them commissioned expensive and risky sailing ventures to the west. The second, less speculative hypothesis pertains to the change in routes pursued by Portugal, the one Atlantic state already deeply involved in ambitious seaward expeditions. After establishing colonies in the second half of the fourteenth century on the Atlantic islands of the Azores and Madeira that yielded a lucrative trade in sugar and wine, the Portuguese in the early fifteenth century quite understandably turned their attention to exploring the coast of West Africa because Africa promised even greater wealth in gold and slaves. Thereafter one Portuguese African discovery led to another until the Cape of Good Hope was rounded in 1488 and the race for Asiatic spices that led to the most dramatic of European overseas exploits had begun. Thus seen from the perspective of late-medieval Portuguese sailing and trading history, the great discoveries look much less startlingly revolutionary than they do at first glance.

The fifteenth-century Portuguese voyages that served as the major connecting link to the dramatic achievements of the years around 1500 were commissioned by Portugal's Prince Henry "the Navigator" from 1418 until his death in 1460. Starting from an initial base of Ceuta in North Africa, Portuguese ships advanced steadily southward along the West African coastline, braving the ever-hotter sun and establishing forts and trading

Medieval background to voyages: Technology

Timing of voyages of discovery

Prince Henry the Navigator. By a fifteenth-century Portuguese painter.

Portuguese voyages along African coastline

posts as they went. The extraordinary heroism of the sailors on these ships can easily be appreciated from a mid-fifteenth-century account, according to which four galleys "were provisioned for several years and were away three years, but only one galley returned and even on that galley most of the crew had died. And those which survived could hardly be recognized as human. They had lost flesh and hair, the nails had gone from hands and feet. Their eyes were sunk deep in their heads and they were as black as Moors. They spoke of heat so incredible that it was a marvel that ships and crews were not burnt. They said also that they found no houses or land and they could sail no farther. The farther they sailed, so the sea became more furious and the heat grew more intense. They thought that the other ships had sailed too far and it was impossible that they should be able to return." But return they did, and despite the terrifying tales that such crews told, new expeditions continually were sent out that ventured still farther.

Discovery of Cape of Good Hope

After Henry the Navigator's death in 1460 some slackening in the Portuguese enterprise ensued, but it regained vigor with the accession of King John II (1481–1495). Inasmuch as the Portuguese had already gained full control of the African Gold Coast and slave trade, they naturally began to set their sights on reaching the wealth of Asia. The literal as well as figurative turning point in this effort was the accidental rounding of the tip of southernmost Africa by the Portuguese captain Bartholomew Dias in 1488. Since Dias had only accomplished this feat by being caught in a gale, he pessimistically called this promontory the "Cape of Storms," but John II took a more optimistic view of the matter and renamed it the Cape of Good Hope. Furthermore, John resolved to organize a major naval expedition designed to travel beyond the cape all the way to India.

Vasco da Gama's voyage to India

After several delays John's successor, Manuel I (1495–1521), finally sent off a fleet in 1497 captained by Vasco da Gama which accomplished all that was planned. Da Gama's exploits were so heroic that they later became the basis for the Portuguese national epic, *The Lusiads*. After four months beyond sight of land the intrepid captain rounded Africa, sailed up Africa's east coast to Kenya, and then crossed the Indian Ocean to western India, where he loaded his ships with spices. Two years after his departure da Gama returned, having lost half of his fleet and one-third of his men. But his pepper and cinnamon were so valuable that they made his losses seem worthwhile. Now master of the quickest route to riches in the world, King Manuel swiftly capitalized on da Gama's accomplishment. After 1500 Portuguese trading fleets sailed regularly to India; by 1510 Portuguese arms had established full control of the western Indian coastline, and in 1511 Portuguese ships seized Malacca, a center of the spice trade on the Malay peninsula. The Cape of Good Hope thus had lived up to John II's prophetic name, and Europeans had arrived in the Far East to stay.

Reasons for Columbus's westward voyage

The decision of the Spanish rulers to underwrite Columbus's famous voyage was directly related to the progress of the Portuguese ventures. Specifically, given the strong likelihood that the Portuguese would dominate the sea lanes leading to Asia by the east in the wake of Dias's successful return in 1488, the only alternative for Portugal's Spanish rivals was to fi-

Left: *The Tower of Belem*. Right: *A Portuguese Galleon*. The Tower of Belem, a fifteenth-century fort, stands at the beach where Vasco da Gama departed in 1497 to sail beyond the Cape of Good Hope to India. The galleon shown at the right is the sort of ship da Gama might have sailed in.

nance someone bold enough to try to reach Asia by sailing west. The popular image of Christopher Columbus (1451–1506) as a visionary who struggled to convince hardened ignoramuses that the world was round does not bear up under scrutiny. In fact the sphericity of the earth was never in doubt. Rather the stubborn Genoese seaman who had settled in Spain erred in vastly underestimating the distance westward from Europe to Asia. Had Columbus known the actual circumference of the earth, even he would not have dared to set out because he would have realized that the distance to Asia, assuming no barriers lay between, was too great for ships of his day to traverse. America, then, was discovered as the result of a colossal error in reckoning, but when Columbus, with the financial backing of Queen Isabella of Castile, reached what we know today as the Bahamas and the island of Hispaniola in 1492 after only a month's sailing, he felt fully vindicated.

Strictly speaking, it cannot be said that Columbus "discovered America" for two reasons. In the first place, experts now agree that the earliest Europeans to reach the Western Hemisphere were the Vikings, who touched on present-day Newfoundland, Labrador, and perhaps New England in voyages made around the year 1000. Second, Columbus did not "discover America" because he never knew what he found, dying in the conviction that all the new land he encountered was merely the outer reaches of Asia.

The "discovery" of America

Ferdinand and Isabella Worshiping the Virgin. A contemporary Spanish painting: the royal pair are shown with two of their children in the company of saints from the Dominican order.

Yet neither of these arguments diminishes Columbus's achievement because the Viking landings had been forgotten or ignored throughout Europe for hundreds of years, and if Columbus did not know what he had found, others, following immediately in his path, came to the realization soon thereafter. Although Columbus brought back no Asiatic spices from his voyage of 1492, he did return with some small samples of gold and a few natives who gave promise of entire tribes that might be enslaved. (Columbus and most of his contemporaries saw no conflict between converting heathen to Christianity and enslaving them.) This provided sufficient incentive for the Spanish monarchs, Ferdinand and Isabella, to finance three more expeditions by Columbus and many more by others. Soon the mainland was discovered as well as islands, and although Columbus refused until his death to accept the truth, the conclusion quickly became inescapable around 1500 that a new world had indeed been found. Since the recognition that Columbus had really stumbled upon a new world was most widely publicized by the Italian geographer Amerigo Vespucci (one of Vespucci's writings of 1504 was actually called *Mundus novus* or *A New World*), the Western Hemisphere soon became known as "America" after Vespucci's first name.

One might well think that the discovery of a new world around 1500 would have delighted the Spanish rulers who had invested in it, but in fact it came as a disappointment, for with a major land mass standing between Europe and Asia, Spain hardly could hope to beat Portugal in the race for spices. Any remaining doubt that two vast oceans separated Europe from East Asia instead of one was completely removed when Vasco Núñez de Balboa first viewed the Pacific from the Isthmus of Panama in 1513. Not entirely admitting defeat, Ferdinand and Isabella's grandson King Charles accepted Ferdinand Magellan's offer in 1519 to see whether a feasible route to Asia could be found by sailing around South America. But Magellan's voyage merely demonstrated that the perils of a journey around southern Argentina were simply too great: of five ships that left Spain, only one returned three years later, having been forced to circumnavigate the globe. Nor did Magellan himself live to tell this tale; instead, eighteen survivors out of an original crew of about two hundred and sixty-five reported that most of their comrades had died from scurvy or starvation and that their captain had been killed in a skirmish with East Indian natives. After this fiasco, all hope for an easy "southwest passage" came to an end.

But if it was disappointing that America loomed as a barricade to the East, it gradually became clear to the Spanish that the New World had much wealth of its own. From the start Columbus's gold samples, in themselves rather paltry, had nurtured hopes that somewhere in America gold might lie piled in ingots, and rumor fed rumor until a few Spanish adventurers really did strike it rich beyond their most avaricious imaginings. At first riches were seized by dint of astonishing feats of arms. In two years, from 1519 to 1521, the *conquistador* (Spanish for conqueror) Hernando Cortés, commanding six hundred men, subjugated the Aztec empire of Mexico which numbered a million, and carried off all of the Aztecs' fabu-

The search for a "southwest passage" to Asia

The conquistadores *plunder the New World for gold*

Left: *An Early Conception of the Encounter between Europeans and American Natives.* This sixteenth-century engraving shows how overseas voyaging was reconceived at home as a mixture of truth and fantasy. Note, for example, the small mermaid to the left of the ship in the foreground. Right: *The Silver Mines of Spanish America.* An engraving of 1602. Some of the miners work naked because of the heat.

lous wealth. Then in 1533 another *conquistador,* Francisco Pizarro, this time with a mere hundred eighty men, plundered the fabled gold of the Incas in conquering Peru. Cortés and Pizarro had the advantage of some cannon and a few horses, but they achieved their victories primarily by sheer courage, treachery, and cruelty. Never before or since have so few men won such great realms against such enormous odds, but seldom have men acted in so ruthless and repugnant a manner.

Economic rewards for Spain in the New World

Cortés, Pizarro, and their fellow *conquistadores* fought only for themselves, not for Spain, and knew only how to plunder, not produce, but by the middle of the sixteenth century the Spanish crown had taken governmental control of all Central and South America (except for Brazil, which was colonized by Portugal), and great quantities of bullion were being mined instead of stolen. Most important by far was the mining of silver. Gold, of course, was the more sought-after metal, but after quickly hauling off the stores of gold amassed for centuries by pre-Columbian native civilizations, the Spanish were able to mine only small quantities of gold on their own. On the other hand, however, they soon realized that in areas of Bolivia and Mexico they were sitting on some of the richest silver deposits in the world. By means of forced native labor and new refining techniques, Spanish overlords produced such vast quantities of silver bars by the second half of the sixteenth century that the relative lack of gold was hardly a disappointment. Since livestock farming and the production of sugar cane in sixteenth-century Spanish America also became highly remunerative, the Spanish crown could have had no regrets after all that Columbus had lighted on a new world instead of Asia.

Consequences of European expansion overseas

Subsequent chapters will pursue the continued development of European overseas expansion and colonization; here it may be said that the overall results of the initial achievements were extremely profound in their implications for at least three reasons. First of all, the emergence of Portugal and Spain as Europe's leading long-distance traders in the sixteenth century permanently moved the center of gravity of European economic power away from Italy and the Mediterranean toward the Atlantic. Deprived of their role as conduits of Oriental trade, Genoa became Spain's banker and Venice gradually a tourist attraction, while Atlantic ports bustled with vessels and shone with wealth. Admittedly the prosperity of Portugal and Spain themselves was fleeting, but the other Atlantic states of England, Holland, and France quickly inherited their mantle as the preeminent economic powers of the world. Second, throughout Europe the increase in the circulation of imported goods and the sudden influx of bullion stimulated entrepreneurial ambitions. Simply stated, the opening of the seas around 1500 provided marvelous opportunities for people with ability and daring to make new fortunes, inspiring a sense that success could only lead to success. Thus not only were many enterprising individuals enriched overnight, but the entire sixteenth century was one of great overall economic growth for Western Europe.

Unfortunately, however, the enormous riches of America were gained only at an appalling cost in human life. Although exact figures are not

A Spaniard Kicking an Indian. As this sixteenth-century drawing makes clear, the Spanish treatment of the indigenous American population was brutal.

available, of an estimated indigenous population of 250,000 on the island of Hispaniola in 1492, only about 500 remained in 1538. As for the far larger population of Mexico, it declined by about 90 percent in the first century of Spanish rule. Not all this loss of life was due to conscious ruthlessness; on the contrary, huge numbers of natives died from epidemic diseases unwittingly introduced by the Europeans, for the natives had no biological resistance to such diseases as smallpox and measles. But countless innocent people also died as the result of merciless exploitation—literally worked so hard by their conquerors that they expired from exhaustion and lack of care. Thus, however much Europeans profited from their colonization of the New World, for the original inhabitants the appearance of the white man was an unmitigated disaster.

The human costs

2. THE LUTHERAN UPHEAVAL

While the Portuguese and Spanish were plowing new paths on the seas, a German monk named Martin Luther (1483–1546) was searching for a new path to the understanding of human salvation, and though his discoveries were made in the quiet of a monastic cell rather than in exotic tropical climes, their effects were no less momentous. Indeed, many Europeans felt the impact of Luther's activities much more immediately and directly than they did the results of the overseas discoveries, because once the German monk started attacking the institutions of the contemporary Roman Church he set off a chain reaction that rapidly resulted in the secession of

Impact of Martin Luther

Martin Luther. A portrait by Lucas Cranach.

much of northern Europe from the Catholic faith, thereby quickly affecting the religious practices of millions.

In searching for the causes of the Lutheran revolt in Germany, three main questions arise: (1) why Martin Luther instigated a break with Rome; (2) why large numbers of Germans rallied to his cause; and (3) why several ruling German princes decided to put the Lutheran Reformation into effect. Reduced to the barest essentials, the answers to these questions are that Luther broke with Rome because of his doctrine of justification by faith, that the German masses followed him primarily because they were swept away by a surge of religious nationalism, and that the princes were moved to institute Lutheranism particularly because of their quest for governmental sovereignty. Within a decade preacher, populace, and princes, so to speak, would all sing the same stirring Lutheran hymn, "A Mighty Fortress Is Our God," in the same church, but they arrived there by rather different paths.

Many people think that Luther rebelled against Rome because he was disgusted with contemporary religious abuses—superstitions, frauds, and the offer of salvation for money—but that is only part of the story. Certainly abuses in Luther's day were grave and intensely upsetting to religious idealists. In a world beset by disease and disaster, frail mortals clutched at supernatural straws to seek health on earth and salvation in the hereafter. Some superstitious men and women, for example, believed that viewing the consecrated host during Mass in the morning would guard them from death throughout the day, and others neglected to swallow the consecrated wafer so that they could use it later either as a charm to ward off evil, an application to cure the sick, or a powder to fertilize their crops. Similarly, belief in the miraculous curative powers of saints was hard to distinguish from belief in magic. Every saint had his or her specialty: "for botches and biles, Cosmas and Damian; St. Clare for the eyes, St. Apolline for teeth, St. Job for pox. And for sore breasts, St. Agatha." Because alleged relics of Christ and the saints were thought to radiate marvelous healing effects, traffic in relics boomed. Even Luther's patron, the Elector Frederick the Wise of Saxony, had a collection in his castle church at Wittenberg of 17,000 relics, including a supposed remnant of Moses' burning bush, pieces of the holy cradle, shreds from Christ's swaddling clothes, and thirty-three fragments of the holy cross. As Mark Twain once sardonically observed, there were indeed enough splinters of the holy cross throughout Europe "to shingle a barn."

Background to Luther's revolt: Superstition

Superstitions and gross credulity were offensive enough to religious idealists of Luther's stamp, but worse still were the granting of dispensations and the promises of spiritual benefits for money. If a man wished to marry his first cousin, for example, he could usually receive an official religious dispensation allowing the marriage for a fee, and annulments of marriage—divorce being prohibited—similarly came for a price. Most malodorous to many, however, was the sale of indulgences. In Catholic theology, an indulgence is a remission by papal authority of all or part of the temporal punishment due for sin—that is, of the punishment in this life and in pur-

Background to Luther's revolt: Sale of dispensations and indulgences gatory—after the guilt of sin itself is absolved by sacramental confession. As we have seen, the practice of granting indulgences began at the end of the eleventh century as an incentive for encouraging men to become Crusaders. Once it became accepted in the course of the High Middle Ages that the pope could dispense grace from a "Treasury of Merits" (that is, a storehouse of surplus good works piled up by Christ and the saints), it soon was taken for granted that the pope could promise people time off in purgatory as well. But indulgences originally granted for extraordinary deeds gradually came to be sold for money; by the fourteenth century, popes started granting indulgences to raise money for any worthy cause whatsoever, such as the building of cathedrals or hospitals; and finally, in 1476 Pope Sixtus IV (the patron of the Sistine Chapel) took the extreme step of declaring that the benefits of indulgences could be extended to the dead already in purgatory as well as to the living. Money, then, could not only save an individual from works of penance but could save his dearest relatives from eons of agonizing torments after death.

Certainly Luther was horrified by the traffic in relics and the sale of indulgences; indeed, the latter provided the immediate grounds for his revolt against Rome. But it was by no means the abuses of the late-medieval Church so much as medieval Catholic theology itself that he came to find thoroughly unacceptable. To this degree the term "Lutheran Reformation" is misleading, for Luther was no mere "reformer" who wanted to cleanse the current religious system of its impurities. Many Christian humanists of Luther's day were reformers in just that sense, but they shrank from breaking with Rome because they had no objections to the basic principles of medieval Catholicism. Luther, on the other hand, by no means would have been satisfied with the mere abolition of abuses because it was the entire Catholic "religion of works" that appalled him.

Luther's opposition to medieval Catholic theology

Simply stated, Luther preferred a rigorously Augustinian system of theology to a medieval Thomistic one. As we have seen, around the year 400 St. Augustine of Hippo had formulated an uncompromising doctrine of predestination which maintained that God alone determined human salvation and that His decisions concerning whom to save and whom to damn were made from eternity, without any regard to merits that given humans might show while sojourning on earth. This extreme view, however, left so little room for human freedom and responsibility that it was modified greatly in the course of the Middle Ages. Above all, during the twelfth and thirteenth centuries theologians such as Peter Lombard and St. Thomas Aquinas (hence the term "Thomistic") set forth an alternative belief system that rested on two assumptions: (1) since God's saving grace is not irresistible, humans can freely reject God's advances and encompass their own doom; and (2) since the sacramental ministrations of the Church communicate ongoing grace, they help human sinners improve their chances of salvation. Except in emergencies, none of the sacraments could be administered by persons other than priests. Having inherited this power from the Apostle Peter, the members of the clergy alone had the authority to cooperate with God in forgiving sins and in performing the miracle of the Eu-

Augustinian and Thomistic theological systems

charist, whereby the bread and wine were transubstantiated into the body and blood of the Saviour. In Luther's opinion, all of this amounted to saying that humans could be saved by the performance of "good works," and it was this theology of works that he became prepared to resist even unto death.

Martin Luther may ultimately have been a source of inspiration for millions, but at first he was a terrible disappointment to his father. The elder Luther, who had risen from Thuringian German peasant stock and gained prosperity by leasing some mines, wanted his son Martin to rise still further. The father thus sent young Luther to the University of Erfurt to study law, but while there in 1505, possibly as the result of unconscious psychological rebellion against parental pressure, Martin shattered his father's ambitions by becoming a monk instead. Afterward, throughout his life Martin Luther was never to "put on airs." Even at the time of his greatest fame he lived simply and always expressed himself in the vigorous and sometimes earthy vernacular of the German peasantry.

Luther's early life

Like many great figures in the history of religion, Luther arrived at what he conceived to be the truth by a dramatic conversion experience. As a monk, young Martin zealously pursued all the traditional medieval means for achieving his own salvation. Not only did he fast and pray continuously, but he confessed so often that his exhausted confessor would sometimes jokingly say that his sins were actually trifling and that if he really wanted to have a rousing confession he should go out and do something dramatic like committing adultery. Yet, try as he might, Luther could find no spiritual peace because he feared that he could never perform enough good deeds to placate an angry God. But then, in 1513 he hit upon an insight that granted him relief and changed the course of his life.

Luther's search for religious solace

Luther's guiding insight pertained to the problem of the justice of God. For years he had worried that God seemed unjust in issuing commandments that He knew men would not observe and then in punishing them with eternal damnation for not observing them. But after becoming a professor of biblical theology at the University of Wittenberg (many members of his monastic order were expected to teach), he was led by the Bible to a new understanding of the problem. Specifically, while meditating on the words in the Psalms "deliver me in thy justice," it suddenly struck him that God's justice had nothing to do with His disciplinary power but rather with His mercy in saving sinful mortals through faith. As Luther later wrote, "At last, by the mercy of God, I began to understand the justice of God as that by which God makes us just in his mercy and through faith . . . and at this I felt as though I had been born again, and had gone through open gates into paradise." Since the fateful moment of truth came to Luther in the tower room of his monastery, it is customarily called his "tower experience."

Luther's "tower experience"

After that, everything seemed to fall into place. Lecturing on the Pauline Epistles in Wittenberg in the years immediately following 1513, Luther dwelled on the text of St. Paul to the Romans (1:17) "the just shall live by faith" to reach his central doctrine of "justification by faith alone." By this

Justification by faith

Left: *Luther with Dove and Halo*. Right: *The Pope as a Donkey Playing Bagpipes*. Two specimens of Lutheran visual propaganda concerning "true" and "false" spiritual insight. While Luther was still a monk (before the end of 1522), the artist Hans Baldung Grien portrayed him as a saint whose insight into Scripture was sent by the Holy Spirit in the form of a dove. At the right is a 1545 woodcut depicting Luther's view that "the pope can interpret Holy Scripture just as well as he can play the bagpipes."

he meant that God's justice does not demand endless good works and religious ceremonies, for no one can hope to be saved by his own works. Rather, humans are "justified"—that is, granted salvation—by God's saving grace alone, offered as an utterly unmerited gift to those predestined for salvation. Since this grace is manifested in humans in thoroughly passive faith, men and women are justified from the human perspective by faith alone. In Luther's view those who had faith would do good works anyway, but it was the faith that came first. Although the essence of this doctrine was not original but harked back to the predestinarianism of St. Augustine, it was new for Luther and the early sixteenth century, and if followed to its conclusions could only mean the dismantling of much of the contemporary Catholic religious structure.

At first Luther remained merely an academic lecturer, teaching within the realm of theory, but in 1517 he was goaded into attacking some of the actual practices of the Church by a provocation that was too much for him to bear. The story of the indulgence campaign of 1517 in Germany is col-

The scandalous indulgence campaign

Pope Leo X. A portrait by the Italian Renaissance master, Raphael.

orful but unsavory. The worldly Albert of Hohenzollern, archbishop of Mainz and youngest brother of the elector of Brandenburg, had sunk himself into enormous debt for several discreditable reasons. In 1513 he had to pay large sums for gaining dispensations from the papacy to hold the bishoprics of Magdeburg and Halberstadt concurrently, and for assuming these offices even though at twenty-three he was not old enough to be a bishop at all. Not satisfied, when the see of Mainz fell vacant in the next year, Albert gained election to that too, even though he knew full well that the costs of becoming archbishop of Mainz meant still larger payments to Rome. Obtaining the necessary funds by loans from the German banking firm of the Fuggers, he then struck a bargain with Pope Leo X (1513–1521). According to this, Leo proclaimed an indulgence in Albert's ecclesiastical territories on the understanding that half of the income raised would go to Rome for the building of St. Peter's Basilica, with the other half going to Albert so that he could repay the Fuggers. Luther did not know the sordid details of Albert's bargain, but he did know that a Dominican friar named Tetzel soon was hawking indulgences throughout much of northern Germany with Fugger banking agents in his train, and that Tetzel was deliberately giving people the impression that the purchase of an indulgence regardless of contrition in penance was an immediate ticket to heaven for oneself and one's dear departed in purgatory. For Luther this was more than enough because Tetzel's advertising campaign flagrantly violated his own conviction that people are saved by faith, not works. So on October 31, 1517, the earnest theologian offered to his university colleagues a list of ninety-five theses objecting to Catholic indulgence doctrine, an act by which the Protestant Reformation is conventionally thought to have begun.

In circulating his theses within the University of Wittenberg, Luther by no means intended to bring his criticism of Tetzel to the public. Quite to the contrary, he wrote his objections in Latin, not German, and meant them only for academic dispute. But some unknown person translated and published Luther's theses, an event that immediately gained the hitherto obscure monk wide notoriety. Since Tetzel and his allies outside the university did not mean to let the matter rest, Luther was immediately called upon to withdraw his theses or defend himself. At that point, far from backing down, he became ever bolder in his attacks on the government of the Church. In 1519 in public disputation before throngs in Leipzig, Luther defiantly maintained that the pope and all clerics were merely fallible men and that the highest authority for an individual's conscience was the truth of Scripture. Thereupon Pope Leo X responded by charging the monk with heresy, and after that there was no alternative for Luther but to break with the Catholic faith entirely.

Luther's year of greatest creative activity came in 1520 when, in the midst of the crisis caused by his defiance, he composed three seminal pamphlets formulating the outlines of what was soon to become the new Lutheran religion. In these writings he put forth his three theological premises: justification by faith, the primacy of Scripture, and "the priesthood of all believers." We have already examined the meaning of the first. By the second he simply meant that the literal meaning of Scripture was always to be preferred to the accretions of tradition, and that all beliefs (such as purgatory) or practices (such as prayers to saints) not explicitly grounded in Scripture were to be rejected. As for "the priesthood of all believers," that meant that the true spiritual estate was the congregation of all the faithful rather than a special club of ordained priests.

From these premises a host of practical consequences followed. Since works themselves had no intrinsic value for salvation, Luther discarded such formalized practices as fasts, pilgrimages, and the veneration of relics. Far more fundamentally, he recognized only baptism and the Eucharist as sacraments (in 1520 he also included penance, but he later changed his mind on this), denying that even these had any supernatural effect in bringing down grace from heaven. For Luther, Christ was really present in the consecrated elements of the Lord's Supper, but there was no grace in the sacrament as such; rather, faith was essential to render the Eucharist effective as a means for aiding the believer along the road to eternal life. To make the meaning of the ceremony clear to all, Luther proposed the substitution of German for Latin in church services, and, to emphasize that those who presided in churches had no supernatural authority, he insisted on calling them merely ministers or pastors rather than priests. On the same grounds there was to be no ecclesiastical hierarchy since neither the pope nor anyone else was a custodian of the keys to heaven, and monasticism was to be abolished since it served no purpose whatsoever. Finally, firm in the belief that no sacramental distinction existed between clergy and laity, Luther argued that ministers could marry, and in 1525 he took a wife himself.

Luther and his Wife, Katherine von Bora. Portraits done by Cranach for the couple's wedding in 1525.

Widely disseminated by means of the printing press, Luther's pamphlets of 1520 electrified much of Germany, gaining him broad and enthusiastic popular support. Because this response played a crucial role in determining the future success of the Lutheran movement—emboldening Luther to persevere in his defiance of Rome and soon encouraging some ruling princes to convert to Lutheranism themselves—it is appropriate before continuing to inquire into its causes. Of course, different combinations of motives influenced different people to rally behind Luther, but the uproar in Germany on Luther's behalf was above all a national religious revolt against Rome.

Ever since the High Middle Ages many people throughout Europe had resented the centralization of Church government because it meant the interference of a foreign papacy in local ecclesiastical affairs and the siphoning off of large amounts of ecclesiastical fees and commissions to the papal court. But certain concrete circumstances made Germany in the early sixteenth century particularly ripe for religious revolt. Perhaps greatest among these was the fact that the papacy of that time had clearly lost the slightest hint of apostolic calling but was demanding as much, if not more money from German coffers as before. Although great patrons of the arts, successive popes of Luther's day were worldly scoundrels or sybarites. As Luther

Pope Alexander VI: "Appearance and Reality." Even before Luther initiated the German Reformation, anonymous critics of the dissolute Alexander VI surreptitiously spread propaganda showing him to be a devil. By lifting a flap Alexander is transformed into a monster who proclaims "I am the pope."

Anti-Roman propaganda

was growing up, the Borgia pope, Alexander VI (1492–1503), bribed the cardinals to gain the papacy, used the money raised from the jubilee of 1500 to support the military campaigns of his son Cesare, and was so lascivious in office that he was suspected of seeking the sexual favors of his own daughter Lucrezia. Alexander's scandals could hardly have been outdone, but his successor, Julius II (1503–1513), was interested only in enlarging the papal states by military means (a contemporary remarked that he would have gained the greatest glory had he been a secular prince), and Leo X, the pope obliged to deal with Luther's defiance, was a self-indulgent esthete who, in the words of a modern Catholic historian, "would not have been deemed fit to be a doorkeeper in the house of the Lord had he lived in the days of the apostles." Under such circumstances it was bad enough for Germans to know that fees sent to Rome were being used to finance papal politics and the upkeep of luxurious courts, but worse still to pay money in the realization that Germany had no influence in Italian papal affairs, for Germans, unlike the French or Spaniards, were seldom represented in the College of Cardinals and practically never gained employment in the papal bureaucracy.

In this overheated atmosphere, reformist criticisms voiced by both traditional clerical moralists and the new breed of Christian humanists exacerbated resentments. Ever since about 1400 prominent German critics of the papacy had been saying that the entire Church needed to be reformed "in head and members," and as the fifteenth century progressed, anonymous prophecies mounted to the effect, for example, that a future heroic emperor would reform the Church by removing the papacy from Rome to the Rhineland. Then in the early years of the sixteenth century, Christian humanists began to chime in with their own brand of satirical propaganda. Most eloquent of these humanists, of course, was Erasmus, who lampooned the religious abuses of his day with no mercy for Rome. Thus in *The Praise of Folly,* first published in 1511 and frequently reprinted, Erasmus stated that if popes were ever forced to lead Christlike lives, no one would be more disconsolate than themselves, and in his more daring pamphlet called *Julius Excluded,* published anonymously in Basel in 1517, the clever satirist imagined a dialogue held before the pearly gates in which Pope Julius II was locked out of heaven by Saint Peter because of his transgressions.

In addition to the objective reality of a corrupt Rome and the circulation of anti-Roman propaganda, a final factor that made Germany ready for revolt in Luther's time was the belated growth of universities. All revolts need to have some general headquarters; universities were the most natural centers for late-medieval religious revolts because assembled there were groups of enthusiastic, educated young people accustomed to working together, who could formulate doctrinal positions with assurance, and who could turn out militant manifestoes at a moment's notice. There had hardly been any universities on German soil until a spate of new founda-

The role of the German universities

Left: *The Seven-Headed Papal Beast*. Right: *The Seven-Headed Martin Luther*. Around 1530 a Lutheran cartoon was circulated in Germany which turned the papacy into the "seven-headed beast" of the Book of Revelation. The papacy's "seven heads" consist of pope, cardinals, bishops, and priests; the sign on the cross reads "for money, a sack full of indulgences"; and a devil is seen emerging from an indulgence treasure chest below. In response, a German Catholic propagandist showed Luther as Revelation's "beast." In the Catholic conception Luther's seven heads show him by turn to be a hypocrite, a fanatic, and "Barabbas"—the thief who should have been crucified instead of Jesus.

tions between 1450 and 1517 provided many spawning grounds for cultural nationalism and religious resistance to Rome. Luther's own University of Wittenberg was founded as late as 1502, but soon enough it became the cradle of the Lutheran Reformation, offering immediate support to its embattled hero.

Still, of course, there would have been no Lutheran Reformation without Luther himself, and the daring monk did the most to enflame Germany's dry kindling of resentment in his pamphlets of 1520, above all in one entitled *To the Christian Nobility of the German Nation*. Here, in highly intemperate colloquial German, Luther stated that "if the pope's court were reduced ninety-nine percent it would still be large enough to give decisions on matters of faith"; that "the cardinals have sucked Italy dry and now turn to Germany"; and that, given Rome's corruption, "the reign of Antichrist could not be worse." Needless to say, once this savage indictment was lodged, everyone wanted to read it. Whereas the average press run of a printed book before 1520 had been one thousand copies, the first run of *To the Christian Nobility* was four thousand, and these copies were sold out in a few days with many more thousands following.

Meanwhile, even as Luther's pamphlets were selling so rapidly, his personal drama riveted all onlookers. Late in 1520 the German rebel responded to Pope Leo X's bull ordering his recantation by casting not only the bull but all of Church law as well onto a roaring bonfire in front of a huge crowd. With the lines so drawn, events moved with great swiftness. Since in the eyes of the Church Luther was now a stubborn heretic, he was formally "released" to his lay overlord, the Elector Frederick the Wise, for proper punishment. Normally this would have meant certain death at the stake, but in this case Frederick was loath to silence the pope's antagonist. Instead, claiming that Luther had not yet received a fair hearing, he brought him early in 1521 to be examined by a "diet" (that is, a formal assembly) of the princes of the Holy Roman Empire convening in the city of Worms.

At Worms the initiative lay with the presiding officer, the newly elected Holy Roman Emperor, Charles V. Charles was not a German; rather, as a member of the Habsburg family by his paternal descent, he had been born and bred in his ancestral holding of the Netherlands. Since he additionally held Austria, and as grandson of Ferdinand and Isabella by his maternal descent, all of Spain, including extensive Spanish possessions in Italy and America, the emperor had primarily international rather than national interests and surely thought of Catholicism as a sort of glue necessary to hold together all his far-flung territories. Thus from the start Charles had no sympathy for Luther, and since Luther fearlessly refused to back down before the emperor, declaring instead "here I stand," it soon became clear that Luther would be condemned by the power of state as well as by the Church. But just then Frederick the Wise once more intervened, this time by arranging a "kidnapping" whereby Luther was spirited off to the elector's castle of the Wartburg and kept out of harm's way for a year.

Thereafter Luther was never again to be in danger of his life. Although

The Wartburg. The castle in central Germany where Luther was hidden after the Diet of Worms.

the Diet of Worms did issue an edict shortly after his disappearance proclaiming him an outlaw, the Edict of Worms was never properly enforced because, with Luther in hiding, Charles V soon left Germany to conduct a war with France. In 1522 Luther returned in triumph from the Wartburg to Wittenberg to find that all the changes in ecclesiastical government and ceremonial he had called for had spontaneously been put into practice by his university cohorts. Then, in rapid succession, several German princes formally converted to Lutheranism, bringing their territories with them. Thus by around 1530 a considerable part of Germany had been brought over to the new faith.

Lutheranism triumphant

At this point, then, the last of the three major questions regarding the early history of Lutheranism arises: Why did German princes, secure in their own powers, heed Luther's call by establishing Lutheran religious practices within their territories? The importance of this question should by no means be underestimated, because no matter how much intense admiration Luther may have gained from the German populace, his cause surely would have failed had it not been for the decisive intervention and support of constituted political authorities. There had been heretics aplenty in Europe before, but most of them had died at the stake, as Luther would have without the intervention of Frederick the Wise. And even had Luther lived, spontaneous popular expressions of support alone would not have succeeded in instituting Lutheranism because such could easily have been put down by the power of the state. In fact, although in the early years of

Importance of German princely support

Luther's revolt he was more or less equally popular throughout Germany, only in those territories where rulers formally established Lutheranism (mostly in the German north) did the new religion prevail, whereas in the others Luther's sympathizers were forced to flee, face death, or conform to Catholicism. In short, the word of the prince in religious matters was simply law.

Economic motives for adoption of Lutheranism

The distinction between populace and princes should not obscure the fact that the motivations of both for turning to Lutheranism were similar, with the emphasis on the princely side being the search for sovereignty. As little as common people liked the idea of money being pumped off to Rome, princes liked it less: German princes assembled at the Diet of Augsburg in 1500, for example, went so far as to demand the refund of some of the ecclesiastical dues sent to Rome on the grounds that Germany was being drained of its coin. Since such demands fell on deaf ears, many princes were quick to perceive that if Lutheranism were adopted, ecclesiastical dues would not be sent to support ill-loved foreigners and much of the savings would directly or indirectly wind up in their own treasuries.

Political motives

Yet the matter of taxation was only part of the larger issue of the search for absolute governmental sovereignty. Throughout Europe the major political trend in the years around 1500 was toward making the state dominant in all walks of life, religious as well as secular. Hence rulers sought to control the appointments of Church officials in their own realms and to limit or curtail the independent jurisdictions of Church courts. Because the papacy in this period had to fight off the attacks of internal clerical critics who wanted recognition of the "conciliarist" principle that general councils of prelates rather than popes should rule the Church (see Chapter 12), many popes found it advantageous to sign concordats with the most powerful rulers in the West—primarily the kings of France and Spain—whereby they granted the rulers much of the sovereignty they wanted in return for support against conciliarism. Thus in 1482 Sixtus IV conceded to the Spanish monarchs Ferdinand and Isabella the right to name candidates for all major Church offices. In 1487 Innocent VIII consented to the establishment of a Spanish Inquisition controlled by the crown which gave the rulers extraordinary powers in dictating religious policies. And in 1516, by the Concordat of Bologna, Leo X granted the choice of bishops and abbots in France to the French king, Francis I. In Germany, however, primarily because there was no political unity, princes were not strong enough to gain such concessions. Hence what they could not achieve by concordats some decided to wrest by force.

The princes seize their opportunity

In this determination they were fully abetted by Luther. Certainly as early as 1520 the fiery reformer recognized that he could never hope to institute new religious practices without the strong arm of the princes behind him, so he implicitly encouraged them to disappropriate the wealth of the Catholic Church as an incentive for creating a new order. At first the princes bided their time, but when they realized that Luther had enormous public support and that Charles V would not act swiftly to defend the Catholic faith, several moved to introduce Lutheranism into their territories. Motives of personal piety surely played their role in individual cases, but the common aim of gaining sovereignty by naming pastors, cutting off fees to Rome, and curtailing the jurisdiction of Church courts probably was the most decisive consideration. Given the added fact that under Lutheranism monasteries could be shut down and their wealth simply pocketed by the princes, the temptation to ordain the new faith regardless of any deeply felt religious convictions must have been overwhelming.

Once safely ensconced in Wittenberg as the protégé of princes, Luther began to express ever more vehemently his own profound conservatism in political and social matters. In a treatise of 1523, *On Temporal Authority,* he insisted that "godly" rulers must always be obeyed in all things and that even ungodly ones should never be actively resisted since tyranny "is not to be resisted but endured." Then, in 1525, when peasants throughout Germany rose up in economic revolt against their landlords—in some places encouraged by the religious radical Thomas Müntzer (c. 1490–1525), who urged the use of fire and sword against "ungodly" powers—Luther responded with intense hostility. In his vituperative pamphlet of 1525, *Against the Thievish, Murderous Hordes of Peasants,* he went so far as to urge all who could to hunt the rebels down like mad dogs, to "strike, strangle, stab secretly or in public, and remember that nothing can be more poisonous than a man in rebellion." Once the princes had ruthlessly put down the Peasants' Revolt of 1525, the firm alliance of Lutheranism with the powers of the state helped ensure social peace. In fact, after the bloody punishment of the peasant rebels there was never again to be a mass lower-class uprising in Germany.

As for Luther himself, he concentrated in his last years on debating with younger, more radical, religious reformers, and on offering spiritual counsel to all who sought it. Never tiring in his amazingly prolific literary activity, he wrote an average of one treatise every two weeks for twenty-five years. To the end Luther was unswerving in his faith: on his deathbed in 1546 he responded to the question "Will you stand firm in Christ and the doctrine which you have preached?" with a resolute "Yes."

3. THE SPREAD OF PROTESTANTISM

Originating as a term applied to Lutherans who "protested" an action of a German Imperial Diet of 1529, the word "Protestant" has come to mean any non-Catholic, non-Eastern Orthodox Christian. In fact, it was soon applied to non-Lutherans after 1529 because the particular form of Protestantism developed by Luther did not prove to be popular much beyond its native environment of Germany. To be sure, Lutheranism was instituted as the state religion of Denmark, Norway, and Sweden by official decrees of rulers made during the 1520s, and remains the religion of most Scandinavians today. But elsewhere early Protestantism spread in different forms. In England a break with Rome was introduced from above, just as in Ger-

RELIGIOUS SITUATIONS IN EUROPE c.1560

Legend:

- Anglican
- Calvinist and areas of Calvinist influence
- Eastern Orthodox
- Lutheran
- Roman Catholic

ATLANTIC OCEAN

SCOTLAND — Edinburgh

IRELAND

ENGLAND — Cambridge, Oxford, London

NORTH SEA

NETHERLANDS

Calais

FRANCE — Noyon, Paris, La Rochelle, Avignon

NAVARRE — Manresa

SPAIN — Madrid, Seville

PORTUGAL

MEDITERRANEAN SEA

NORWAY

SWEDEN — Stockholm

DENMARK — Copenhagen

BALTIC SEA

FINLAND

TEUTONIC ORDER

PRUSSIA

LITHUANIA

POLAND — Warsaw, Cracow

RUSSIA

Approximate limit of Eastern Orthodox Church

HOLY ROMAN EMPIRE — Berlin, Wittenberg, Leipzig, Prague, Münster, Cologne, Mainz, Worms, Erfurt, THURINGIA, SAXONY, Augsburg, Munich, Vienna

Elbe R.

Rhine R.

SWITZ. — Zürich, Basel, Geneva

PIEDMONT

Trent

Bologna

PAPAL STATES

Rome

ITALY

HUNGARY — Budapest

Danube R.

OTTOMAN EMPIRE

BLACK SEA

MUS[LIM]

many and Scandinavia, but since Lutheranism appeared too radical for the reigning English monarch, a compromise variety of religious belief and practice, subsequently known as Anglicanism (in America, Episcopalianism), was worked out. On the other extreme, Protestantism spread more spontaneously in several cities of Switzerland and there soon took on forms that were more radical than Lutheranism.

Although the original blow against the Roman Church in England was struck by the head of the government, King Henry VIII (1509–1547), in breaking with Rome the English monarch had the support of most of his subjects. For this there were at least three reasons. First, in England, as in Germany, many people in the early sixteenth century had come to resent Rome's corruption and the siphoning off of the country's wealth to pay for the worldly pursuits of foreign popes. Second, England had already been the scene of protests against religious abuses voiced by John Wyclif's heretical followers known as Lollards. The Lollards had indeed been driven underground in the course of the fifteenth century, but numbers of them survived in pockets throughout England, where they promulgated their anticlerical ideas whenever they could and enthusiastically welcomed Henry VIII's revolt from Rome when it occurred. Finally, soon after the outbreak of the Reformation in Germany, Lutheran ideas were brought into England by travelers and by the circulation of printed tracts. As early as 1520 a Lutheran group was meeting at the University of Cambridge, and Lutheranism began to gain more and more clandestine strength as the decade progressed.

Henry VIII. Portrait by Hans Holbein.

Despite all this, England would never have broken with Rome had Henry VIII not issued the command because of his marital difficulties. In 1527 the imperious Henry had been married for eighteen years to Ferdinand and Isabella's daughter, Catherine of Aragon, yet all the offspring of this union had died in infancy, save only the Princess Mary. Since Henry needed a male heir to preserve the succession of his Tudor dynasty, and since Catherine was now past childbearing age, Henry had good reasons of state to rid himself of her, and in 1527 an immediate incentive arose when he became infatuated with the dark-eyed lady-in-waiting, Anne Boleyn, who would not give in to his advances out of wedlock. The king hence appealed to Rome to allow the severance of his marriage to Catherine so that he could make Anne his queen. Although the law of the Church did not sanction divorce, it did provide that a marriage might be annulled if proof could be given that conditions existing at the time of the wedding had made it unlawful. Accordingly, the king's representatives, recalling that Queen Catherine had previously been married to Henry's older brother, who had died shortly after the ceremony was performed, rested their case on a passage from the Bible which pronounced it "an unclean thing" for a man to take his brother's wife and cursed such a marriage with childlessness (Leviticus 20:31).

King Henry VIII's divorce suit

Henry's suit put the reigning pope, Clement VII (1523–1534), in a quandary. If he rejected the king's appeal, England would probably be lost to Catholicism, for Henry was indeed firmly convinced that the Scriptural curse had blighted his chances of perpetuating his dynasty. On the other

Henry's break with Rome

hand, if the pope granted the annulment he would provoke the wrath of the Emperor Charles V, Catherine of Aragon's nephew, for Charles was then on a military campaign in Italy and threatening the pope with a loss of his temporal power. There seemed nothing for Clement to do but to procrastinate. At first he made a pretense of having the question settled in England, empowering his officials to hold a court of inquiry to determine whether the marriage to Catherine had been legal. Then, after a long delay, he suddenly transferred the case to Rome. But meanwhile Henry had lost patience and resolved to take matters into his own hands. In 1531 the king obliged an assembly of English clergy to recognize him as "the supreme head" of the English Church. Next he induced Parliament to enact a series of laws abolishing all payments to Rome and proclaiming the English Church an independent, national unit, subject alone to royal authority. With the passage of the parliamentary Act of Supremacy (1534), declaring "the King's highness to be supreme head of the Church of England [having] the authority to redress all errors, heresies, and abuses," the last bonds uniting the English Church to Rome had been cut.

The conservative nature of the Henrician Reformation

Yet these enactments did not yet make England a Protestant country. Quite to the contrary, although the break with Rome was followed by the dissolution of all of England's monasteries, with their lands and wealth being sold to many of the king's loyal supporters, the system of Church government by bishops (episcopalianism) was retained, and the English Church remained Catholic in doctrine. The Six Articles, promulgated by Parliament in 1539 at Henry VIII's behest, left no room for doubt as to official orthodoxy: oral confession to priests, masses for the dead, and clerical celibacy were all confirmed; moreover, the Catholic doctrine of the Eucharist was not only confirmed but its denial made punishable by death.

The consolidation of English Protestantism

Nonetheless, the influence of Protestantism in the country at large at this time was growing, and during the reign of Henry's son, Edward VI (1547–1553), Protestantism gained the ascendancy. Since the new king (born from Henry's union with his third wife, Jane Seymour) was only nine years old when he inherited the crown, it was inevitable that the policies of the government should be dictated by powers behind the throne. The men most active in this regard were Thomas Cranmer, archbishop of Canterbury, and the dukes of Somerset and Northumberland, who successfully dominated the regency. Inasmuch as all three had strong Protestant leanings, the creeds and ceremonies of the Church of England were soon drastically altered. Priests were permitted to marry; English was substituted for Latin in the services; the veneration of images was abolished; and new articles of belief were drawn up repudiating all sacraments except baptism and communion and affirming the Lutheran doctrine of justification by faith alone. Thus when the youthful Edward died in 1553 it seemed as if England had definitely entered the Protestant camp.

But Edward's pious Catholic successor, Mary (1553–1558), Henry VIII's daughter by Catherine of Aragon, thought otherwise. Because Mary associated the revolt against Rome with her mother's humiliations and her own removal from direct succession, upon coming to the throne she attempted

Philip of Spain and Mary Tudor. This double portrait was done on the occasion of the royal marriage.

to turn the clock back. Not only did she restore the celebration of the Mass and the rule of clerical celibacy, but she prevailed upon Parliament to vote the unconditional return of England to papal allegiance. Yet her policies ended in failure for several reasons. First of all, not only had Protestantism by then already sunk in deeply among the English masses, but many of the leading families that had profited from Henry VIII's dissolution of the monasteries had become particularly committed to Protestantism because a restoration of Catholic monasticism would have meant the loss of their newly acquired wealth. Then too, although Mary ordered the burning of Cranmer and a few hundred Protestant extremists, these executions were insufficient to wipe out religious resistance—indeed, Protestant propaganda about "Bloody Mary" and the "fires of Smithfield" soon actually hardened resistance to Mary's rule, making her seem like a vengeful persecutor. But perhaps the most serious cause of Mary's failure was her marriage to Philip, Charles V's son and heir to the Spanish throne. Although the marriage treaty stipulated that in the event of Mary's death Philip could not succeed her, patriotic Englanders never trusted him. Hence when the queen allowed herself to be drawn by Philip into a war with France on Spain's behalf, in which England lost Calais, its last foothold on the European continent, many English people became highly disaffected. No one knows what might have happened next because death soon after ended Mary's troubled reign.

Popular resistance to Queen Mary's Catholicism

The Burning of Archbishop Cranmer. In this Protestant conception an ugly Catholic, "Friar John," directs the proceedings, while the martyred Cranmer repeats Christ's words, "Lord, receive my spirit." John Foxe's *Book of Martyrs* (1563), in which this engraving first appeared, was an extraordinarily successful piece of English Protestant propaganda.

The Elizabethan religious settlement

The question of whether England was to be Catholic or Protestant was thereupon settled definitively in favor of Protestantism by Elizabeth I (1558–1603). Daughter of Anne Boleyn and one of the most capable and popular monarchs ever to sit on the English throne, Elizabeth was predisposed in favor of Protestantism by the circumstances of her father's marriage as well as by her upbringing. But Elizabeth was no zealot, and wisely recognized that supporting radical Protestantism in England posed the danger of provoking bitter sectarian strife because some English people were still Catholic and others resisted extremism. Accordingly, she presided over what is customarily known as "the Elizabethan compromise." By a new Act of Supremacy (1559), Elizabeth repealed all of Mary's Catholic legislation, prohibited the exercise of any authority by foreign religious powers, and made herself "supreme governor" of the English Church—a more Protestant title than Henry VIII's "supreme head" insofar as most Protestants believed that Christ alone was the head of the Church. At the same time she accepted most of the Protestant ceremonial reforms instituted in the reign of her brother Edward. On the other hand, she retained Church government by bishops and left the definitions of some controversial articles of the faith, especially the meaning of the Eucharist, vague enough so that all but the most extreme Catholics and Protestants could accept them. Long after Elizabeth's death this settlement remained in effect. Indeed, as a result of the Elizabethan compromise, the Church of England today is broad enough to include such diverse elements as the "Anglo-Catholics," who differ from Roman Catholics only in rejecting papal supremacy, and the "low-church" Anglicans, who are as thoroughgoing in their Protestant practices as members of most other modern Protestant denominations.

If the English compromise came about through royal decision-making, in Switzerland more spontaneous movements to establish Protestantism resulted in the victory of greater radicalism. In the early sixteenth century Switzerland was neither ruled by kings nor dominated by all-powerful territorial princes; instead, prosperous Swiss cities were either independent or on the verge of becoming so. Hence when the leading citizens of a Swiss municipality decided to adopt Protestant reforms no one could stop them, and Protestantism in Switzerland could usually take its own course. Although religious arrangements tended at first to vary in detail from city to city, the three main forms of Protestantism that emerged in Switzerland from about 1520 to 1550 were Zwinglianism, Anabaptism, and, most fateful for Europe's future, Calvinism.

Protestantism in Switzerland

Zwinglianism, founded by Ulrich Zwingli (1484–1531) in Zürich, was the most moderate form of the three. Although Zwingli was at first a somewhat indifferent Catholic priest, around 1516 he was led by close study of the Bible, as Luther was, to conclude that contemporary Catholic theology and religious observances conflicted with the Gospel. But he did not speak out until Luther set the precedent. Then, in 1522, Zwingli started attacking the authority of the Catholic Church in Zürich, and soon all Zürich and much of northern Switzerland had accepted his leadership in instituting reforms that closely resembled those of the Lutherans in Germany. Yet Zwingli did differ from Luther concerning the theology of the Eucharist: whereas Luther believed in the real presence of Christ's body, for Zwingli Christ was present merely in spirit. Thus for him the sacrament conferred no grace at all and was to be retained merely as a memorial service. This disagreement may seem trifling to many of us today, but at the time it was enough to prevent Lutherans and Zwinglians from uniting in a common Protestant front. Fighting independently, Zwingli fell in battle against Catholic forces in 1531, whereupon his successors in Zürich lost their leadership over Swiss Protestantism, and the Zwinglian movement was soon after absorbed by the far more radical Protestantism of John Calvin.

Zwinglianism

Before that happened, however, the phenomenon of *Anabaptism* briefly flared up in Switzerland and also Germany. The first Anabaptists were members of Zwingli's circle in Zürich, but they quickly broke with him around 1525 on the issues of infant baptism and their conception of an exclusive Church of true believers. The name Anabaptism means "rebaptism," and stemmed from the Anabaptists' conviction that baptism should only be administered to adults because infants have no understanding of the meaning of the service. Yet this was only one manifestation of the Anabaptists' main belief that men and women were not born into any Church. Although Luther and Zwingli alike taught the "priesthood of all believers," they still insisted that everyone, believer or not, should attend services and be part of one and the same officially instituted religious community. But the Anabaptists were sectarians or separatists, firm in the conviction that joining the true Church should be the product of an individual's inspired decision. For them, one had to follow the guidance of one's own "inner light" in opting for Church membership, and the rest of the world could

Anabaptism

The turning point at Münster

go its own way. Since this was a hopelessly apolitical doctrine in an age when almost everyone assumed that Church and state were inextricably connected, Anabaptism was bound to be anathema to the established powers, both Protestant and Catholic. Yet in its first few years the movement did gain numerous adherents in Switzerland and Germany, above all because it appealed to sincere religious piety in calling for extreme simplicity of worship, pacifism, and strict biblical morality.

Unhappily for the fortunes of Anabaptism, an unrepresentative group of Anabaptist extremists managed to gain control of the German city of Münster in 1534. These zealots combined sectarianism with millenarianism, or the belief that God wished to institute a completely new order of justice and spirituality throughout the world before the end of time. Determined to help God bring about this goal, the extremists attempted to turn Münster into a new Jerusalem. A former tailor named John of Leyden assumed the title of "King of the New Temple," proclaiming himself the successor of David. Under his leadership Anabaptist religious practices were made obligatory, private property was abolished, the sharing of goods was introduced, and even polygamy was instituted on the grounds of Old Testament precedents. Nonetheless, Münster succumbed to a siege by Catholic forces little more than a year after the Anabaptist takeover, and the new David,

The Anabaptists' Cages, Then and Now. After the three Anabaptist leaders who had reigned in Münster for a year were executed in 1535, their corpses were prominently displayed in cages hung from a tower of the marketplace church. As can be seen from the photo on the right, the bones are now gone but the iron cages remain to this very day as a grisly reminder of the horrors of sixteenth-century religious strife.

together with two of his lieutenants, was put to death by excruciating tortures. Given that Anabaptism had already been proscribed by many governments, this episode thoroughly discredited the movement, and all of its adherents were subjected to ruthless persecution throughout Germany, Switzerland, and wherever else they could be found. Among the few who survived were some who banded together in the Mennonite sect, named for its founder, the Dutchman Menno Simons (c. 1496–1561). This sect, dedicated to the pacifism and simple "religion of the heart" of original Anabaptism, has continued to exist until the present. Various Anabaptist tenets were also revived later by religious groups such as the Quakers and different Baptist and Pentecostal sects.

A year after events in Münster sealed the fate of Anabaptism, a twenty-six-year-old French Protestant named John Calvin (1509–1564), who had fled to the Swiss city of Basel to escape religious persecution, published the first version of his *Institutes of the Christian Religion,* a work that was soon to prove the most influential systematic formulation of Protestant theology ever written. Born in Noyon in northern France, Calvin originally had been trained for the law and around 1533 was studying the Greek and Latin classics while living off the income from a Church benefice. But then, as he later wrote, while he was "obstinately devoted to the superstitions of Popery," a stroke of light made him feel that God was extricating him from "an abyss of filth," and he thereupon opted for becoming a Protestant theologian and propagandist. Though some of these details resemble the early career of Luther, there was one essential difference: namely, whereas Luther was always a highly volatile personality, Calvin remained a cool legalist through and through. Thus, whereas Luther never wrote systematic theology but only responded to given problems as they arose or as the impulse struck him, Calvin resolved in his *Institutes* to set forth all the principles of Protestantism comprehensively, logically, and consistently. Accordingly, after several revisions and enlargements (the definitive edition appeared in 1559), Calvin's *Institutes of the Christian Religion* became the most theologically authoritative statement of basic Protestant beliefs and the nearest Protestant equivalent of St. Thomas Aquinas's *Summa Theologica.*

John Calvin. A recently discovered anonymous portrait.

The hallmark of Calvin's rigorous theology in the *Institutes* is that he started with the omnipotence of God and worked downward. For Calvin the entire universe is utterly dependent on the will of the Almighty, who created all things for His greater glory. Because of the original fall from grace, all human beings are sinners by nature, bound hand and foot to an evil inheritance they cannot escape. Nevertheless, the Lord for reasons of His own has predestined some for eternal salvation and damned all the rest to the torments of hell. Nothing that human beings may do can alter their fate; their souls are stamped with God's blessing or curse before they are born. But this does not mean, in Calvin's opinion, that Christians should be indifferent to their conduct on earth. If they are among the elect, God will implant in them the desire to live right. Upright conduct is a sign, though not an infallible one, that whoever practices it has been chosen to sit at the throne of glory. Public profession of faith and participation in the

Calvin's theology

sacrament of the Lord's Supper are also presumptive signs of election to be saved. But most of all, Calvin required an active life of piety and morality as a solemn obligation resting upon members of the Christian commonwealth. For him, good Christians should conceive of themselves as chosen instruments of God with a mission to help in the fulfillment of His purposes on earth, not striving for their souls' salvation but for the glory of God. In other words, Calvin clearly did not encourage his readers to sit with folded hands, serene in the knowledge that their fate was sealed.

Calvinism and Lutheranism compared

Although Calvin always acknowledged a great theological debt to Luther, his religious teachings differed from those of the Wittenberg reformer in several essentials. First of all, Luther's attitude toward proper Christian conduct in the world was much more passive than Calvin's: for the former, the good Christian should merely endure the trials of this life in suffering, whereas for the latter the world was to be mastered in unceasing labor for God's sake. Second, Calvin's religion was more legalistic and more nearly an Old Testament faith than Luther's. This can be illustrated in the attitude of the two men toward Sabbath observance. Luther's conception of Sunday was similar to that which prevails among most Christians today. He insisted, of course, that his followers attend church, but he did not demand that during the remainder of the day they refrain from all pleasure or work. Calvin, on the other hand, revived the Jewish Sabbath with its strict taboos against anything faintly resembling worldliness. Finally, the two men differed explicitly on basic matters of Church government and ritual. Although Luther broke with the Catholic system of a gradated ecclesiastical hierarchy, Lutheran district superintendents were not unlike bishops, and Luther also retained a good many features of Catholic worship such as altars and vestments (special clothing for the clergy). In contrast, Calvin rejected everything that smacked to him of "popery." Thus he argued for the elimination of all traces of the hierarchical system, instead having congregational election of ministers and assemblies of ministers and "elders" (laymen responsible for maintaining proper religious conduct among the faithful) governing the entire Church. Further, he insisted on the barest simplicity in church services, prohibiting all ritual, vestments, instrumental music, images, and stained-glass windows. When these teachings were put into practice, Calvinist services became little more than "four bare walls and a sermon."

Calvinist theocracy in Geneva

Not content with mere theory, Calvin was intent upon putting his teachings into practice. Sensing an opportunity to influence the course of events in the French-speaking Swiss city of Geneva, then in the throes of combined political and religious upheaval, he moved there late in 1536 and began preaching and organizing immediately. In 1538 his activities caused him to be expelled, but in 1541 he returned, with the city coming to be completely under his sway. Under Calvin's guidance Geneva's government became theocratic. Supreme authority in the city was vested in a "Consistory," made up of twelve lay elders and five ministers. (Although Calvin himself was seldom the presiding officer, he usually dominated the Consistory's decisions until his death in 1564.) In addition to passing on legisla-

Services in a Calvinist Church. "Four bare walls and a sermon."

tion submitted to it by a congregation of ministers, the Consistory had as its main function the supervision of morals. This activity was carried out not merely by the punishment of antisocial conduct but by a persistent snooping into the private life of every individual. Geneva was divided into districts, and a committee of the Consistory visited every household without warning to check on the habits of its members. Even the mildest forms of self-indulgence were strictly prohibited. Dancing, card-playing, attending the theater, working or playing on the Sabbath—all were outlawed as works of the devil. Innkeepers were forbidden to allow anyone to consume food or drink without first saying grace, or to permit any patron to stay up after nine o'clock. Needless to say, penalties were severe. Not only were murder and treason classified as capital crimes, but also adultery, "witchcraft," blasphemy, and heresy. During the first four years after Calvin gained control in Geneva, there were no fewer than fifty-eight executions out of a total population of only 16,000.

As reprehensible as such interference in the private sphere may seem today, in the middle of the sixteenth century Calvin's Geneva appeared as a beacon of thoroughgoing Protestantism to thousands throughout Europe. Calvin's disciple John Knox, for example, who brought Calvinism to Scotland, declared that Geneva under Calvin was "the most perfect school of Christ that ever was on earth since the days of the Apostles." Accordingly, many foreigners flocked to the "perfect school" for refuge or instruction, and usually returned home to become ardent proselytizers of Calvinism. Moreover, since Calvin himself thought of Geneva as merely a way station

Proselytizing from Geneva

Calvin as Seen by His Friends and His Enemies. Above, an idealized contemporary portrait of Calvin as a pensive scholar. Below, a Catholic caricature in which Calvin's face is a composite made from fish, a toad, and a chicken drumstick.

Renaissance and Reformation

for bringing Calvinism to France and the rest of the world, he encouraged the dispatching of missionaries and propaganda into hostile territories, with the result that from about the middle of the sixteenth century Geneva became the center of a concerted and militant attempt to spread the new faith far and wide. Soon Calvinists became a majority in Scotland, where they were known as Presbyterians; a majority in Holland, where they founded the Dutch Reformed Church; a substantial minority in France, where they were called Huguenots; and a substantial minority in England, where they were called Puritans. In addition, Calvinist preachers zealously tried to make converts in most other parts of Europe. But just as the Calvinists were fanning out through Europe, the forces of Catholicism were hardening in their determination to head off any further Protestant advances. The result, as we will see in the next chapter, was that many parts of a hitherto united Christendom became mired in bloody religious wars for decades after.

4. THE PROTESTANT HERITAGE

Inasmuch as Luther's revolt from Rome and the spread of Protestantism occurred after the height of the civilization of the Renaissance and before some particularly fundamental advances in modern European political, economic, and social development, it is tempting to think of historical events unfolding in an inevitably cumulative way: Renaissance, Reformation, "Triumphs of the Modern World." But history is seldom as neat as that. Although scholars will continue to disagree on points of detail, most agree that the Protestant Reformation inherited little from the civilization of the Renaissance, that indeed in certain basic respects Protestant principles were completely at odds with major assumptions of Renaissance humanists. As for the relationship between "Protestantism and Progress," the most apt formulation appears to be a statement from a book of that title by the great German religious historian Ernst Troeltsch, according to which "Protestantism has furthered the rise of the modern world . . . [but nowhere] does it appear as its actual creator."

In considering the relationship between the Renaissance and the origins of the Protestant Reformation, it would admittedly be false to say that the one had absolutely nothing to do with the other. Certainly, criticisms of religious abuses by Christian humanists helped prepare Germany for the Lutheran revolt. Furthermore, close humanistic textual study of the Bible led to the publication of new, reliable biblical editions used by the Protestant reformers. In this regard a direct line ran from the Italian humanist Lorenzo Valla to Erasmus to Luther insofar as Valla's *Notes on the New Testament* inspired Erasmus to produce his own Greek edition and accompanying Latin translation of the New Testament in 1516, and that in turn enabled Luther in 1518 to reach some crucial conclusions concerning the literal biblical meaning of penance. For these and related reasons, Luther addressed Erasmus in 1519 as "our ornament and our hope."

But in fact Erasmus quickly showed that he had no sympathy whatsoever with Luther's first principles, and most other Christian humanists shunned Protestantism as soon as it became clear to them what Luther and other Protestant reformers actually were teaching. The reasons for this were that most humanists believed in free will while Protestants believed in predestination, that humanists tended to think of human nature as basically good while Protestants found it unspeakably corrupt, and that most humanists favored urbanity and tolerance while the followers of Luther and Calvin emphasized faith and conformity. Thus when Erasmus, for example, defended *The Freedom of the Will* in a treatise of 1524, Luther attacked it vehemently in his *Bondage of the Will* of the following year, insisting that original sin makes all humans "bound, wretched, captive, sick, and dead." And when Henry VIII introduced the Reformation into England, England's foremost Christian humanist, Sir Thomas More, resisted the break with Rome even unto martyrdom, mounting the scaffold with some stirring words about the primacy of the individual conscience.

If the Protestant Reformation, then, was by no means the natural outgrowth of the civilization of the Renaissance, it very definitely contributed to certain traits most characteristic of modern European historical development. Foremost among these was the rise of the untrammeled powers of the sovereign state. As we have seen, those German princes who converted to Protestantism were moved to do so primarily by the search for sovereignty, and the kings of Denmark, Sweden, and England followed suit for the same reasons. Not at all accidentally, the earliest act of the English Parliament announcing Henry VIII's break with Rome, the Act in Restraint of Appeals of 1533, put forth the earliest official statement that England is a completely independent country, "governed by one supreme head and king," possessed of "plenary, whole, and entire power . . . to render and yield justice and final determination to all manner of folk." Since Protestant leaders—Calvin as well as Luther—preached absolute obedience to "godly" rulers, and since the state in Protestant countries assumed direct control of the Church, the spread of Protestantism definitely resulted in the growth of state power. But, as we have also seen, the power of the state was growing anyway, and it continued to grow in Catholic countries like France and Spain where kings were granted most of the same rights over the Church that were forcibly seized by Lutheran German princes or Henry VIII.

As for the growth of nationalism, a sense of national pride was already present in sixteenth-century Germany that Luther played upon in his appeals of 1520. But Luther himself then did the most to foster German cultural nationalism by translating the entire Bible into a vigorous German idiom. Up until then Germans from some regions spoke a language so different from that of Germans from other areas that they could not understand each other, but the form of German given currency by Luther's Bible soon became the linguistic standard for the entire nation. Religion did not help to unite the German nation politically because the non-German Charles V opposed Lutheranism and as a result Germany soon became po-

The Christian humanists' opposition to Protestantism

Catholic and Protestant Views of a Cardinal. A genuine papal medal (shown above) depicted a cardinal (right-side up) merged with a bishop (upside down). In response, a Protestant replica (shown below), probably struck in the Netherlands, depicted a cardinal merged with a grinning fool.

Protestantism and the rise of the modern state

litically divided into Protestant and Catholic camps. But elsewhere, as in Scotland and Holland, where Protestants fought successfully against Catholic overlords, Protestantism enhanced a sense of national identity. And perhaps the most familiar case of all is that of England, where a sense of nationhood had existed before the advent of Protestantism even more markedly than it had in Germany, Scotland, or Holland, but where the new faith, as we shall see, helped underpin the greatest accomplishments of the Elizabethan Age.

Protestantism and modern economic development

The problem of Protestantism's relationship to modern commercial and industrial economic development is more controversial. Around 1900 the great German sociologist Max Weber, noticing that the economically advanced territories of England, Holland, and North America had all been Protestant, argued that Protestantism, particularly in its Calvinist forms, was especially conducive to acquisitive economic enterprise. According to Weber, this was because Calvinistic theology, as opposed to Catholicism, sanctified the ventures of profit-oriented traders and moneylenders, and gave an exalted place in its ethical system to the business virtues of thrift and diligence. But historians have found shortcomings in Weber's thesis. Although Calvin did indeed praise diligence and acknowledge that merchants could be "sanctified in their calling," he no more approved of exorbitant interest rates than Catholics did. Moreover Calvin argued vehemently that people should put their excess wealth at the service of the poor rather than piling up capital for the sake of gain or subsequent investments. Thus it appears that the "work ethic" necessary for economic success in commercial ventures did have some Calvinistic roots, but that Calvin's ideal merchant would by no means have been a great speculator or maker of fortunes. Bearing in mind that the European economy had already made great strides forward in the High Middle Ages and was advancing again in the early-modern period, not least because of the overseas ventures initiated by the Catholic powers of Portugal and Spain, Calvinism thus was at most just one of many contributory factors to the triumph of modern capitalism and the Industrial Revolution.

Protestantism's effects on relations between the sexes

Finally, there arises the subject of Protestantism's effects on social relationships, specifically those between the sexes. As opposed to the question of Protestantism and economic development, this topic is still relatively unstudied. What is certain is that Protestant men as individuals could be just as ambivalent about women as Catholics, heathens, or Turks. John Knox, for example, inveighed against the Catholic regent of Scotland, Mary Stuart, in a treatise called *The First Blast of the Trumpet Against the Monstrous Regiment of Women,* yet maintained deeply respectful relationships with women of his own faith. But if one asks how Protestantism as a belief system that rose above individual vagaries affected women's lot, the answer appears to be that it enabled women to become just a shade more equal to men, albeit still clearly within a framework of subjection. Above all, since Protestantism, with its stress on the primacy of Scripture and the priesthood of all believers, called on women as well as men to undertake serious Bible study, it sponsored primary schooling for both sexes and thus enhanced female as well as male literacy. But Protestant male leaders never hesitated to insist that women were naturally inferior to men and thus should always defer to men in case of arguments. As Calvin himself said, "let the woman be satisfied with her state of subjection and not take it ill that she is made inferior to the more distinguished sex." Both Luther and Calvin appear to have been happily married, but that clearly meant being happily married on their own terms.

5. CATHOLIC REFORM

The historical novelty of Protestantism in the sixteenth century inevitably tends to cast the spotlight on such religious reformers as Luther and Calvin, but it must be emphasized that a powerful internal reform movement within the Catholic Church exercised just as profound an effect on the course of European history as Protestantism did. Historians differ about whether to call this movement the "Catholic Reformation" or the "Counter-Reformation." Some prefer the former term because they wish to show that significant efforts to reform the Catholic Church from within antedated the posting of Luther's theses and that therefore Catholic reform in the sixteenth century was no mere counterattack to check the growth of Protestantism. Others, however, insist quite properly that for the main part sixteenth-century Catholic reformers were indeed inspired primarily by the urgency of resisting what they regarded as heresy and schism. Fortunately the two interpretations are by no means irreconcilable, for they allude to two complementary phases: a Catholic Reformation that came before Luther and a Counter-Reformation that followed.

Catholic reform before and after Luther

The Catholic Reformation beginning around 1490 was primarily a movement for moral and institutional reform inspired by the principles of Christian humanism and carried on with practically no help from the dissolute Renaissance papacy. In Spain around the turn of the fifteenth century, reform activities directed by Cardinal Francisco Ximénes de Cisneros (1436–1517) with the cooperation of the monarchy led to the imposition of strict rules of behavior for Franciscan friars and the elimination of abuses prevalent among the diocesan clergy. Although Ximénes aimed primarily at strengthening the Church in its rivalry with Jews and Muslims, his work had considerable effect in regenerating the spiritual life of the nation. In Italy there was no similarly centralized reform movement, but a number of earnest clerics in the early sixteenth century labored on their own to make the Italian Church more worthy of its calling. The task was a difficult one on account of the entrenchment of abuses and the example of profligacy set by the papal court, but despite these obstacles, the Italian reformers did manage to establish some new religious orders dedicated to high ideals of piety and social service. Finally, it cannot be forgotten that such leading Christian humanists as Erasmus and Thomas More were in their own way Catholic reformers, for in criticizing abuses and editing sacred texts, men like these certainly helped to enhance spirituality.

The Catholic Reformation

The Counter-Reformation popes

Once Protestantism began threatening to sweep over Europe, however, Catholic reform of the earlier variety clearly became inadequate to defend the Church, let alone turn the tide of revolt. Thus a second, more aggressive, phase of reform under a new style of vigorous papal leadership gained momentum during the middle and latter half of the sixteenth century. The leading Counter-Reformation popes—Paul III (1534–1549), Paul IV (1555–1559), St. Pius V (1566–1572), and Sixtus V (1585–1590)—were collectively the most zealous crusaders for reform who had presided over the papacy since the High Middle Ages. All led upright personal lives. Indeed, some were so grimly ascetic that contemporaries were unsure whether they were not too holy: as a Spanish councillor wrote in 1567, "We should like it even better if the present Holy Father were no longer with us, however great, inexpressible, unparalleled, and extraordinary his holiness may be." But in the circumstances of the Protestant onslaught, a pope's reputation for excessive asceticism was vastly preferable to a reputation for profligacy. More than that, becoming fully dedicated to activist revitalization of the Church, the Counter-Reformation popes reorganized their finances and filled ecclesiastical offices with bishops and abbots as renowned for austerity as themselves, and these appointees in turn set high standards for their own priests and monks.

The Council of Trent: Doctrinal matters

These papal activities were supplemented by the actions of the Council of Trent, convoked by Paul III in 1545 and meeting at intervals thereafter until 1563. This general council was one of the most important in the history of the Church. Concerning basic matters of doctrine, the Council of Trent without exception reaffirmed all the tenets challenged by the Protestant Reformers. Good works were held to be as necessary for salvation as

A Session of the Council of Trent. The pope is not present, but the cardinals who represent him are enthroned, facing the semicircle of bishops. The orator with a raised right hand is a theologian advancing an opinion.

faith. The theory of the sacraments as indispensable means of grace was up- held. Likewise, transubstantiation, the apostolic succession of the priest- hood, the belief in purgatory, the invocation of saints, and the rule of celibacy for the clergy were all confirmed as essential elements in the Catholic system. On the question as to the proper source of Christian be- lief, the Bible and the traditions of apostolic teaching were held to be of equal authority. Not only was papal supremacy over every bishop and priest expressly maintained, but the supremacy of the pope over the Church council itself was taken for granted in a way that left the monar- chical government of the Church undisturbed. The Council of Trent also reaffirmed the doctrine of indulgences which had touched off the Lutheran revolt, although it did condemn the worst scandals connected with the sell- ing of indulgences.

The legislation of Trent was not confined to matters of doctrine, but also included provisions for the elimination of abuses and for reinforcing the discipline of the Church over its members. Bishops and priests were forbid- den to hold more than one benefice, so that absentees could not grow rich from a plurality of incomes. To eliminate the evil of an ignorant priest- hood, it was provided that a theological seminary must be established in every diocese. Toward the end of its deliberations the council decided upon a censorship of books to prevent heretical ideas from corrupting those who still remained in the faith. A commission was appointed to draw up an index, or list of writings that ought not to be read. The publication of this list in 1564 resulted in the formal establishment of the Index of Pro- hibited Books as a part of the machinery of the Church. Later, a permanent agency known as the Congregation of the Index was set up to revise the list from time to time. Altogether more than forty such revisions have been made. The majority of the books condemned have been theological trea- tises, and probably the effect in retarding the progress of learning has been slight. Nonetheless, the establishment of the Index must be viewed as a symptom of the intolerance that had come to infect both Catholics and Protestants.

The Council of Trent: Practical reform and discipline

In addition to the independent activities of popes and the legislation of the Council of Trent, a third main force propelling the Counter-Reforma- tion was the foundation of the Society of Jesus, commonly known as the Jesuit order, by St. Ignatius Loyola (1491–1556). In the midst of a youthful career as a worldly soldier, the Spanish nobleman Loyola was wounded in battle in 1521 (the same year in which Luther defied Charles V at Worms), and while recuperating, he decided to change his ways and become a spiri- tual soldier of Christ. Shortly afterward he lived as a hermit in a cave near the Spanish town of Manresa for ten months, during which time, instead of reading the Bible as Luther or Calvin might have done, he experienced ec- static visions and worked out the principles of his subsequent meditational guide, *The Spiritual Exercises*. This manual, completed in 1535 and first published in 1541, offered practical advice on how to master one's will and serve God by a systematic program of meditations on sin and the life of Christ. Soon made a basic handbook for all Jesuits, and widely studied by

St. Ignatius Loyola

numerous Catholic lay people as well, Loyola's *Spiritual Exercises* had an influence second only to Calvin's *Institutes* of all the religious writings of the sixteenth century.

Nonetheless, St. Ignatius's founding of the Jesuit order itself was certainly his greatest single accomplishment. Originating as a small group of six disciples who gathered around Loyola in Paris in 1534 to serve God in poverty, chastity, and missionary work, Ignatius's Society of Jesus was formally constituted as an order of the Church by Pope Paul III in 1540, and by the time of Loyola's death it already numbered fifteen hundred members. The Society of Jesus was by far the most militant of the religious orders fostered by the Catholic reform movements of the sixteenth century. It was not merely a monastic society but a company of soldiers sworn to defend the faith. Their weapons were not to be bullets and spears but eloquence, persuasion, instruction in the right doctrines, and if necessary, more worldly methods of exerting influence. The organization was patterned after that of a military company, with a general as commander-in-chief and iron discipline enforced on all members. Individuality was suppressed, and a soldierlike obedience to the general was exacted of the rank and file. The Jesuit general, sometimes known as "the black pope" (from the color of the order's habit), was elected for life and was not bound to take advice offered by any other member. But he did have one clear superior, namely the Roman pope himself, for in addition to the three monastic vows of poverty, chastity, and obedience, all senior Jesuits took a "fourth vow" of strict obedience to the Vicar of Christ and were held to be at the pope's disposal at all times.

The activities of the Jesuits consisted primarily of proselytizing not just heathens but Christians, and establishing schools. Originally founded with the major aim of engaging in missionary work abroad, the early Jesuits by no means abandoned this goal, preaching to the heathen in India, China, and Spanish America. For example, one of St. Ignatius's closest early associates, St. Francis Xavier (1506–1552), baptized thousands of natives and covered thousands of miles missionizing in the Indies. Yet, although Loyola had not at first conceived of his society as comprising shock troops against Protestantism, that is what primarily became of it as the Counter-Reformation mounted in intensity. Working by means of preaching and diplomacy—sometimes at the risk of their lives—Jesuits in the second half of the sixteenth century fanned out through Europe in direct confrontation with Calvinists. In many places the Jesuits succeeded in keeping rulers and their subjects loyal to Catholicism, in others they met martyrdom, and in some others—notably Poland and parts of Germany and France—they actually succeeded in regaining territory temporarily lost to the Protestant faith. Wherever they were allowed to settle, the Jesuits set up schools and colleges, for they firmly believed that a vigorous Catholicism could rest only on widespread literacy and education. Indeed their schools were often so efficient that, after the fires of religious hatred began to subside, upper-class Protestants would sometimes send their children to receive a Jesuit education.

The Inspiration of St. Jerome by Guido Reni. In 1546 the Council of Trent declared St. Jerome's Latin translation of the Bible, known as the Vulgate, to be the official version of the Catholic Church; then, in 1592, Pope Clement VIII chose one edition of the Vulgate to be authoritative above all others. Since Biblical scholars had known since the early sixteenth century that St. Jerome's translation contained numerous mistakes, Counter-Reformation defenders of the Vulgate insisted that even his mistakes had been divinely inspired and thus were somehow preferable to the original meaning of Scripture. The point is made visually in Guido Reni's painting of 1635.

From the foregoing it should be self-evident that there is a "Counter-Reformation Heritage" every bit as much as there is a Protestant one. Needless to say, for committed Catholics, the greatest achievement of sixteenth-century Catholic reform was the defense and revitalization of the faith. Without any question, Catholicism would not have swept over the globe and reemerged in Europe as the vigorous spiritual force it remains today had it not been for the determined efforts of the sixteenth-century reformers. But there were more practical results stemming from the Counter-Reformation as well. One was the spread of literacy in Catholic countries due to the educational activities of the Jesuits, and another was the growth of intense concern for acts of charity. Since Counter-Reformation Catholicism continued to emphasize good works as well as faith, charitable activities took on an extremely important role in the revitalized religion: hence spiritual leaders of the Counter-Reformation such as St. Francis de Sales (1567–1622) and St. Vincent de Paul (1581–1660) urged alms-giving in their sermons and writings, and a wave of founding of orphanages and houses for the poor swept over Catholic Europe.

Results of the Counter-Reformation

Two other areas in which the Counter-Reformation had less dramatic but still noteworthy effects were in the realm of women's history and intellectual developments. Whereas Protestantism encouraged female literacy for the purpose of making women just a little bit more like men in the

Catholicism and a female religious elite

ability to read the Bible, reinvigorated Catholicism pursued a different course. Most Catholic women were kept in a more subordinate position in the life of the faith than women under Protestantism, but Catholicism fostered a distinctive role for a female religious elite—countenancing the mysticism of a St. Teresa of Avila (1515–1582), or allowing the foundation of new orders of nuns such as the Ursulines and the Sisters of Charity. Under both Protestantism and Catholicism women remained subordinate, but in the latter model they were able to pursue their religious impulses more independently.

The Counter-Reformation and reason

Finally, it unfortunately cannot be said that the Counter-Reformation perpetuated the tolerant Christianity of Erasmus, for Christian humanists lost favor with Counter-Reformation popes and all of Erasmus's writings were immediately placed on the Index. But sixteenth-century Protestantism was just as intolerant as sixteenth-century Catholicism, and far more hostile to the cause of rationalism. Indeed, because Counter-Reformation theologians returned for guidance to the Scholasticism of St. Thomas Aquinas, they were much more committed to acknowledging the dignity of human reason than their Protestant counterparts who emphasized pure Scriptural authority and blind faith. Thus although a hallmark of the subsequent seventeenth-century scientific revolution was the divorce between spirituality of any variety and strict scientific work, it does not seem entirely coincidental that René Descartes, one of the founders of the scientific revolution who coined the famous phrase "I think, therefore I am," was trained as a youth by the Jesuits.

SELECTED READINGS

• *Items so designated are available in paperback editions.*

OVERSEAS EXPANSION

• Boxer, C. R., *The Portuguese Seaborne Empire, 1415–1825,* New York, 1969. The standard work on the subject.
• Elliott, J. H., *The Old World and the New, 1492–1650,* Cambridge, 1970. A superb short analysis of the many ways in which the discovery of the New World affected life in the Old.
• Hale, J. R., *Renaissance Exploration,* New York, 1968. A scintillating brief introduction. Highly recommended as a point of departure.
• Morison, S. E., *Christopher Columbus, Mariner,* New York, 1955. A convenient abridgment of the master storyteller's definitive biography of Columbus, *Admiral of the Ocean Sea* (1942).
• Parry, J. H., *The Age of Reconnaissance,* London, 1963. Probably the best one-volume survey of the entire subject of early-modern European expansion; particularly strong on details of shipbuilding and navigation.
• ———, *The Spanish Seaborne Empire,* London, 1966. The counterpart to Boxer for the early Spanish colonial experience.
• Phillips, J. R. S., *The Medieval Expansion of Europe,* Oxford, 1988. Makes the strongest case for continuity between medieval and Renaissance expansion.

• Bainton, Roland H., *Here I Stand: A Life of Martin Luther,* Nashville, Tenn., 1950. The best introductory biography in English: absorbing and authoritative, though clearly partisan in Luther's favor.

———, *Women of the Reformation,* 3 vols., Minneapolis, 1970–1977. Full of interesting narrative, but little analysis.

• Bouwsma, William, *John Calvin,* Oxford, 1987. Now the best biography available.

Brandi, K., *The Emperor Charles V,* New York, 1939. The standard narrative biography of the emperor who faced Luther and ruled much of Europe as well.

• Davis, Natalie Z., *Society and Culture in Early Modern France,* Stanford, 1975. A collection of pioneering essays in historical anthropology, including a brilliant piece on the role of women in sixteenth-century religious movements.

• Dickens, A. G., *The English Reformation,* New York, 1964. The best introduction.

• ———, *Reformation and Society in Sixteenth-Century Europe,* London, 1966. A highly stimulating introductory survey, with the added advantage of being profusely illustrated.

• Erikson, E. H., *Young Man Luther,* New York, 1958. A classic psychobiography that analyzes the young Luther's "identity crisis."

Grimm, Harold J., *The Reformation Era: 1500–1650,* 2nd ed., New York, 1973. The best college-level text; consistently informative, balanced, and reliable.

• Harbison, E. H., *The Age of Reformation,* Ithaca, N.Y., 1955. A fine elementary introduction by a master of the field.

———, *The Christian Scholar in the Age of the Reformation,* New York, 1956. Discusses the relationship between Christian humanism and early Protestantism.

• Hillerbrand, H., *The World of the Reformation,* London, 1975. A stimulating overview.

McGrath, A., *The Intellectual Origins of the English Reformation,* New York, 1987. Concise and lucid exposition of complicated material.

McNeill, John T., *The History and Character of Calvinism,* New York, 1945. A basic, reliable, older work.

Monter, E. William, *Calvin's Geneva,* New York, 1967. Standard on the history of Calvin's Geneva.

Mullett, M., *Radical Religious Movements in Early Modern Europe,* London, 1980. Thematic analysis of some of the major effects of Protestantism, with as much attention given to the seventeenth as to the sixteenth century. Contains a particularly valuable annotated bibliography.

Po-Chia Hsia, R., ed., *The German People and the Reformation,* Ithaca, 1988. A collection of essays representative of the most original and important work in this area.

Samuelsson, K., *Religion and Economic Action,* New York, 1961. The standard critical evaluation of Max Weber's thesis that Calvinism fostered the modern "spirit of capitalism."

• Scribner, R. W., *The German Reformation,* Atlantic Heights, N.J., 1986. A brief survey of recent work on Church reform in its social and cultural context. Includes superb bibliographies.

• Skinner, Q., *The Foundations of Modern Political Thought: 2. The Age of Reformation,* Cambridge, 1978. The best analysis of Reformation and Counter-Reformation trends in political theory.

- Smith, Lacey B., *Henry VIII: The Mask of Royalty,* Boston, 1971. A breathtaking interpretation of the last years of Henry VIII and the age in which he lived.
- Spitz, Lewis W., *The Protestant Reformation: 1517–1559,* New York, 1985. A thorough recent survey.

  Tawney, Richard H., *Religion and the Rise of Capitalism,* New York, 1926. The most sophisticated and elegantly written defense of the "Weber thesis."
- Troeltsch, E., *Protestantism and Progress,* New York, 1931. An enduring classic.

  Williams, George H., *The Radical Reformation,* Philadelphia, 1962. Detailed account of Anabaptism and the "left wing" of the Protestant Reformation.

CATHOLIC REFORM

  Broderick, James, *The Origin of the Jesuits,* London, 1940. An older work, but still unsurpassed.

  Delumeau, J., *Catholicism between Luther and Voltaire: A New View of the Counter-Reformation,* Philadelphia, 1977. A sympathetic account stressing the positive aspects of Reformed Catholicism.
- Dickens, A. G., *The Counter-Reformation,* London, 1968. A splendid counterpart to Dickens's *Reformation and Society;* like its companion, profusely illustrated.

  Janelle, P., *The Catholic Reformation,* Milwaukee, 1949. A reliable brief introduction.

  Jedin, H., *A History of the Council of Trent,* 2 vols., London, 1957–1961. Authoritative and exhaustive.

  Knowles, D., *From Pachomius to Ignatius: A Study in the Constitutional History of the Religious Orders,* Oxford, 1966. In less than one hundred masterful pages Knowles places the organizational principles of the Jesuits in historical perspective.

SOURCE MATERIALS

- Dillenberger, J., ed., *John Calvin: Selections from His Writings,* Garden City, N.Y., 1971.
- ———, *Martin Luther: Selections from His Writings,* Garden City, N.Y., 1961.
- Hillerbrand, H. J., ed., *The Protestant Reformation,* New York, 1967.

  St. Ignatius Loyola, *The Spiritual Exercises,* tr. R. W. Gleason, Garden City, N.Y., 1964.

  Ziegler, D. J., *Great Debates of the Reformation,* New York, 1969.

Chapter 15

A CENTURY OF CRISIS FOR EARLY-MODERN EUROPE (c. 1560–c. 1660)

I do not wish to say much about the customs of the age in which we live.
I can only state that this age is not one of the best, being a century of iron.

—R. Mentet de Salmonet, *History of the Troubles in Great Britain* (1649)

What in me is dark
Illumine, what is low raise and support.

—John Milton, *Paradise Lost*

O n the night before St. Bartholomew's Day in August of 1572 the Catholic queen mother of France, Catherine de Medici, authorized the ambush of French Protestant leaders who had come to Paris to attend a wedding. Thereupon, during the hours after midnight, unsuspecting people were awakened and stabbed to death or thrown out of windows. Soon all the targeted Protestants were eliminated, but the killing did not stop because roving bands of Parisian Catholics seized the opportunity of licensed carnage to slaughter at will any enemies they happened upon, Protestant or otherwise. By morning the River Seine was clogged with corpses and scores of bodies hung from gibbets in witness to an event known ever since as the Massacre of St. Bartholomew's Day.

A massacre in Paris

Had this lamentable incident been an isolated event it hardly would be worth mentioning, but in fact throughout the hundred years from roughly 1560 to roughly 1660 outbreaks of religious mayhem—with Protestants the ruthless killers in certain cases as Catholics were in others—recurred in many parts of Europe. Moreover, to make matters far worse, economic hardships and prolonged wars accompanied religious riots to result in a century of pronounced crisis for European civilization. Granted that Europe's early-modern period of crisis was much less uniform in its nature

A century of crisis

The St. Bartholomew's Day Massacre. A contemporary painting depicts the merciless slaughter of Huguenots in Paris. At the top left (in front of the large gate next to the Seine) the Queen Mother Catherine looks over a pile of naked dead bodies; to the right a Huguenot leader is being pushed out of a window.

and extent than the terrible times of the Later Middle Ages, seen from the broadest perspective the period from 1560 to 1660 was Western Europe's "iron century"—an age of great turbulence and severe trials.

1. ECONOMIC, RELIGIOUS, AND POLITICAL TESTS

Impending crisis

Europe's time of troubles crept up on contemporaries unawares. For almost a century before 1560 most of the West had enjoyed steady economic growth, and the discovery of the New World seemed the basis of greater prosperity to come. Political trends too seemed auspicious, since most Western European governments were becoming ever more efficient and providing more internal peace for their subjects. Yet around 1560 thunderclouds were gathering in the skies that would soon burst into terrible storms.

Soaring prices

Although the causes of these storms were interrelated, each may be examined separately, starting with the great price inflation. Nothing like the upward price trend that affected Western Europe in the second half of the sixteenth century had ever happened before. The cost of a measure of wheat in Flanders, for example, tripled from 1550 to 1600, grain prices in Paris quadrupled, and the overall cost of living in England advanced well over 100 percent during the same period. Certainly the twentieth century has seen much more dizzying inflations than this, but since the skyrocketing of prices in the later sixteenth century was a novelty, most historians agree on calling it the "price revolution."

If experts agree on the terminology, however, very few of them agree on the exact combination of circumstances that caused the price revolution, for early-modern statistics are patchy and many areas of economic theory remain under dispute. Nonetheless, for present purposes two explanations for the great inflation may be offered with confidence. The first is demographic. Starting in the later fifteenth century, Europe's population began to mount again after the plague-induced fall-off: roughly estimated, there were about 50 million people in Europe around 1450 and 90 million around 1600. Since Europe's food supply remained more or less constant owing to the lack of any noteworthy breakthrough in agricultural technology, food prices inevitably were driven sharply higher by greater demand. Although the prices of manufactured goods did not rise as steeply because there was a greater match between supply and demand, the prices of manufactured items did rise, especially in cases where the supply of agricultural raw materials crucial to the manufacturing process remained relatively inelastic.

Causes of inflation: (1) population increase

Population trends explain much, but since Europe's population did not grow nearly as rapidly in the second half of the sixteenth century as prices, other explanations for the great inflation are still necessary. Foremost among these is the enormous influx of bullion from Spanish America. Around 1560 a new technique of extracting silver from silver ore made the working of newly discovered mines in Mexico and Bolivia highly practical, soon transforming the previous trickle of silver entering the European economy into a flood. Whereas in the five years between 1556 and 1560 roughly 10 million ducats worth of silver passed through the Spanish entry point of Seville, between 1576 and 1580 that figure had doubled, and between 1591 and 1595 it had more than quadrupled. Inasmuch as most of this silver was used by the Spanish crown to pay its foreign creditors and its armies abroad, or by private individuals to pay for imports from other countries, Spanish bullion quickly circulated throughout Europe, where much of it was minted into coins. This dramatic increase in the volume of money in circulation further fueled the spiral of rising prices. "I learned a proverb here," said a French traveler in Spain in 1603, "everything costs much here except silver."

(2) influx of silver

Aggressive entrepreneurs and landlords profited most from the changed economic circumstances, while the masses of laboring people were hurt the worst. Obviously, merchants in possession of sought-after goods were able to raise prices at will, and landlords either could profit directly from the rising prices of agricultural produce or, if they did not farm their own lands, could always raise rents. But laborers in country and town were caught in a squeeze because wages rose far more slowly than prices, owing to the pres-

Effects of inflation on the laboring poor

ence of a more-than-adequate labor supply. Moreover, because the cost of food staples rose at a sharper rate proportionately than the cost of most other items of consumption, poor people had to spend an ever-greater percentage of their paltry income on necessities. In normal years they barely managed to survive, but when disasters such as wars or poor harvests drove grain prices out of reach, some of the poor literally starved to death. The picture that thus emerges is one of the rich getting richer and the poor getting poorer—splendid feasts enjoyed amid the most appalling suffering.

Political results

In addition to these direct economic effects, the price inflation of the later sixteenth century had significant political effects as well because higher prices placed new pressures on the sovereign states of Europe. The reasons for this were simple. Since the inflation depressed the real value of money, fixed incomes from taxes and dues in effect yielded less and less. Thus merely to keep their incomes constant governments would have been forced to raise taxes. But to compound this problem, most states needed much more real income than previously because they were undertaking more wars, and warfare, as always, was becoming increasingly expensive. The only recourse, then, was to raise taxes precipitously, but such draconian measures incurred great resentments on the part of subject populations—especially the very poor who were already strapped more than enough by the effects of the inflation. Hence governments faced continuous threats of defiance and potential armed resistance.

Economic stagnation after 1600

Less need be said about the economic stagnation that followed the price revolution because it interfered little with most of the trends just discussed. When population growth began to ease and the flood of silver from America began to abate around 1600, prices soon leveled off. Yet because the most lucrative economic exploitation of the New World only began in the late seventeenth century and Europe experienced little new industrial development, the period from about 1600 to 1660 was at best one of very limited overall economic growth, even though a few areas—notably Holland—bucked the trend. Within this context the rich were usually able to hold their own, but the poor as a group made no advances since the relationship of prices to wages remained fixed to their disadvantage. Indeed, if anything, the lot of the poor in many places deteriorated because the mid-seventeenth century saw some particularly expensive and destructive wars, causing helpless civilians to be plundered either by rapacious tax collectors, looting soldiers, or sometimes by both.

Religious wars

It goes without saying that most people would have been far better off had there been fewer wars during Europe's iron century, but given prevalent attitudes, newly arisen religious rivalries made wars inevitable. Simply stated, until religious passions began to cool toward the end of the period, most Catholics and Protestants viewed each other as minions of Satan who could not be allowed to live. Worse, sovereign states attempted to enforce religious uniformity on the grounds that "crown and altar" offered each other mutual support and in the belief that governments would totter where diversity of faith prevailed. Rulers on both sides felt certain that religious minorities, if allowed to survive in their realms, would inevitably engage in sedition; nor were they far wrong since militant Calvinists and Jesuits were indeed dedicated to subverting constituted powers in areas where they had not yet triumphed. Thus states tried to extirpate all potential religious resistance, but in the process sometimes provoked civil wars in which both sides tended to assume there could be no victory until the other was exterminated. And of course civil wars might become international in scope when one or more foreign powers resolved to aid embattled religious allies elsewhere.

Compounding the foregoing problems were more strictly political ones: namely, while strapped by price trends and racked by religious wars, governments brought certain provincial and constitutional grievances down upon themselves. Regarding the provincial issue, most of the major states of early-modern Europe had been built up by conquests or dynastic unions with the result that many smaller territories had been subjected to rule by foreign governors. At first some degree of provincial autonomy was usually preserved and hence the inhabitants of such territories did not object too much to their annexation. But in the iron century, when governments were making ever-greater financial claims on all their subjects or trying to enforce religious uniformity, rulers customarily moved to destroy all remnants of provincial autonomy in order to implement their financial or religious policies. Naturally the province-dwellers were usually not inclined to accept total subjugation without a fight, so rebellions might break out on combined patriotic and economic or religious grounds. Nor was that all, since most governments seeking money and/or religious uniformity tried to rule their subjects with a firmer hand than before, and thus sometimes provoked armed resistance in the name of traditional constitutional liberties. Given this bewildering variety of motives for revolt, it is by no means surprising that the century between 1560 and 1660 was one of the most turbulent in all European history.

Governmental crises

2. A HALF CENTURY OF RELIGIOUS WARS

The greatest single cause of warfare in the first half of Europe's iron century was religious rivalry. Indeed, wars between Catholics and Protestants began as early as the 1540s when the Catholic Holy Roman Emperor Charles V tried to reestablish Catholic unity in Germany by launching a military campaign against several German princes who had instituted Lutheran worship in their principalities. At times thereafter it appeared as if Charles was going to succeed in reducing his German Protestant opponents to complete submission, but since he was also involved in fighting against France, he seldom was able to devote concerted attention to affairs in Germany. Accordingly, religious warfare sputtered on and off until a compromise settlement was reached in the Religious Peace of Augsburg (1555). This rested on the principle of *cuius regio, eius religio* ("as the ruler, so the religion"), which meant that in those principalities where Lutheran princes

Religious wars in Germany until the Peace of Augsburg

EUROPE c. 1560

ruled, Lutheranism would be the sole state religion, and the same for those with Catholic princes. Although the Peace of Augsburg was a historical milestone inasmuch as Catholic rulers for the first time acknowledged the legality of Protestantism, it boded ill for the future in assuming that no sovereign state larger than a free city (for which it made exceptions) could tolerate religious diversity. Moreover, in excluding Calvinism it ensured that Calvinists would become aggressive opponents of the status quo.

Even though wars in the name of religion were fought in Europe before 1560, those that raged afterward were far more brutal, partly because the combatants had become more fanatical (intransigent Calvinists and Jesuits customarily took the lead on their respective sides), and partly because the later religious wars were aggravated by political and economic resentments.

Background of the French wars of religion

Since Geneva bordered on France, since Calvin himself was a Frenchman who longed to convert his mother country, and since Calvinists had no wish to displace German Lutherans, the next act in the tragedy of Europe's confessional warfare was played out on French soil. Calvinist missionaries had already made much headway in France in the years between Calvin's rise to power in Geneva in 1541 and the outbreak of religious warfare in 1562. Of the greatest aid to the Calvinist (Huguenot) cause was the conversion of many aristocratic French women to Calvinism because such women often won over their husbands, who in turn maintained large private armies. The foremost example is that of Jeanne d'Albret, queen of the tiny Pyrenean kingdom of Navarre, who brought over to Calvinism her husband, the prominent French aristocrat Antoine de Bourbon, and her brother-in-law, the prince de Condé. Not only did Condé take command of the French Huguenot party when civil war broke out in 1562, but he later was succeeded in this capacity by Jeanne's son, Henry of Navarre, who came to rule all of France at the end of the century as King Henry IV. In addition to aristocrats, many people from all walks of life became Huguenots for a variety of motives, with Huguenot strength greatest in areas of the south which had long resented the dominance of northern rule from Paris. In short, by 1562 Calvinists comprised between 10 and 20 percent of France's population of roughly 16 million, and their numbers were swelling every day.

Since both Catholics and Protestants assumed that France could have only a single *roi, foi,* and *loi* (king, faith, and law), civil war was inevitable, and no one was surprised when a struggle between the Huguenot Condé and the ultra-Catholic duke of Guise for control of the government during a royal minority led in 1562 to a show of arms. Soon all France was aflame. Rampaging mobs, often incited on either side by members of the clergy, ransacked churches and settled local scores. After a while it became clear that the Huguenots were not strong or numerous enough to gain victory, but they were also too strong to be defeated. Hence, despite intermittent truces, warfare dragged on at great cost of life until 1572. Then, during an interval of peace, the cultivated queen mother Catherine de Medici, normally a woman who favored compromise, plotted with members of the Catholic Guise faction to kill all the Huguenot leaders while they were assembled in Paris for the wedding of Henry of Navarre. In the early morning of St. Bartholomew's Day (August 24) most of the Huguenot chiefs were murdered in bed and two to three thousand other Protestants were slaughtered in the streets or drowned in the Seine by Catholic mobs. When word of the Parisian massacre spread to the provinces, some ten thousand more Huguenots were killed in a frenzy of blood lust that swept through France.

The St. Bartholomew's Day episode effectively broke the back of Huguenot resistance, but even then warfare did not cease because the neurotic King Henry III (1574–1589)[*] tried to play off Huguenots against the

Jeanne D'Albret

French warfare: The St. Bartholomew's Day Massacre

---

[*]Here, as elsewhere, dates following a ruler's name refer to dates of reign.

dominant Catholic Guise family and because die-hard Huguenots sometimes were able to ally with Catholics revolting against overburdensome taxes or inequities in tax assessments. Only when the politically astute Henry of Navarre succeeded to the French throne as Henry IV (1589–1610), initiating the Bourbon dynasty that would rule until 1792, did civil war finally come to an end. In 1593 Henry abjured his Protestantism in order to placate France's Catholic majority ("Paris is worth a mass") and then, in 1598, he offered limited religious freedom to the Huguenots by the Edict of Nantes. According to the terms of this proclamation, Catholicism was recognized as the official religion, but Huguenot nobles were allowed to hold Protestant services privately in their castles, other Huguenots were allowed to worship at specified places (excluding Paris and all cities where bishops and archbishops resided), and the Huguenot party was permitted to fortify some towns, especially in the south, for military defense if the need arose. Thus, although the Edict of Nantes certainly did not countenance absolute freedom of worship, it nevertheless represented a major stride in the direction of toleration. With religious peace established, France quickly began to recover from decades of devastation, but Henry IV himself was cut down by the dagger of a Catholic fanatic in 1610.

Contemporaneous with the religious warfare in France was equally bitter religious strife between Catholics and Protestants in the neighboring Netherlands, where national resentments gravely compounded religious hatreds. For almost a century the Netherlands (or Low Countries), comprising modern-day Holland in the north and Belgium in the south, had been ruled by the Habsburg family. Particularly the southern part of the Netherlands prospered greatly from trade and manufacture: southern Netherlanders had the greatest per capita wealth of all Europe, and their metropolis of Antwerp was northern Europe's leading commercial and fi-

The Assassination of Henry IV. This contemporary engraving shows Henry seated in an open carriage without any concern for his personal danger while his assassin climbs on the spoke of the carriage wheel to attack him. The entire composition conveys a vivid impression of early-modern Paris.

Self-Portrait, Albrecht Dürer (1471–1528). Dürer was the first major artist to paint self-portraits at different phases of his life. Here, aged twenty-eight, he makes himself seem almost Christlike. Note also the prominent initials "A.D." under the date of the painting at the upper left. (Alte Pinakothek)

Erasmus, Hans Holbein the Younger (1497–1543). This portrait is generally regarded as the most telling visual characterization of "the prince of the Christian humanists." (Louvre)

The Harvesters, Peter Brueghel (c. 1525–1569). Brueghel chose to depict both the hard work and recreation of the peasantry. (MMA)

The Crucifixion, Tintoretto (1518–1594). This Venetian master of Mannerism combined typically Venetian richness of color with an innovative concern for movement and emotion. (Scala)

Saint Andrew and St. Francis, El Greco (c. 1541–1614). A striking exemplification of the artist's penchant for elongation as well as his profound psychological penetration. (The Prado)

View of Toledo, El Greco. Light breaks where no sun shines. One of the most awesomely mysterious paintings in the entire Western tradition. (MMA)

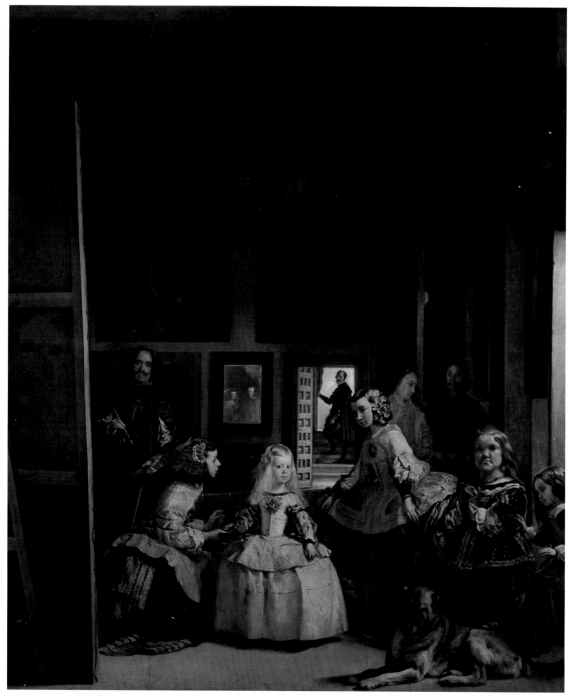

The Maids of Honor, Diego Velázquez (1599–1660). The artist himself is at work on a double portrait of the king and queen of Spain (who may be seen in the rear mirror), but reality is more obvious in the foreground in the persons of the delicately impish princess, her two maids, and a misshapen dwarf. The twentieth-century Spanish artist Picasso gained great inspiration from this work. (The Prado)

Pope Innocent X, Velázquez. A trenchant portrait of a decisive man of affairs. (Doria–Pamphili Collection)

England and Scotland Crowning Charles I, Peter Paul Rubens (1577–1640). A typical piece of Baroque propaganda, in this case painted to glorify the English monarch of the Stuart family in the years before his ill-fated demise. (Minneapolis Institute of Art)

The Horrors of War, Rubens. The war god Mars here casts aside his mistress Venus and threatens humanity with death and destruction. In his old age Rubens took a far more critical view of war than he did for most of his earlier career. (Gallery Palatina)

Aristotle Contemplating the Bust of Homer, Rembrandt van Rijn (1606–1669). One of the greatest painters' view of one of the greatest of philosophers caught up by the aura of one of the greatest poets. (MMA)

The Calling of St. Matthew, Caravaggio (1565–1609). Among the earliest of the great Baroque painters, Caravaggio special-ized in contrasts of light and shade (*chiaroscuro*), and preferred to conceive of religious scenes in terms of everyday life. Here Christ (extreme right), whose halo is the only supernatural detail in the composition, enters a tavern to call St. Matthew (pointing doubtfully at himself) to his service. (Art Resource)

RUSSIA

SWEDEN

Stockholm•

Christiania•

DENMARK

Copenhagen•

NORTH
SEA

BALTIC
SEA

Danzig•

E. PRUSSIA

Warsaw•

Vistula R.

POLAND

Kiev•

SCOTLAND

Edinburgh•

Liverpool•

IRELAND

Dublin•

ENGLAND

London•

Bristol•

English Channel

ATLANTIC

OCEAN

Hamburg•

UNITED
PROVINCES

Amsterdam•

SPANISH
NETH.

Paris•

Seine R.

FRANCE

Loire R.

Bordeaux•

Garonne R.

MECKLEN-
BURG

HANOVER

HESSE

Rhine R.

LORRAINE

FRANCHE
COMTÉ

SWITZ.

SAVOY

PIEDMONT

Marseilles•

Rhone R.

Avignon•

BRANDENBURG

Berlin•

SAXONY

WÜRTEM-
BERG

BAVARIA

Vienna•

AUSTRIA

Elbe R.

Budapest•

HUNGARY

Danube R.

VENICE

MILAN

GENOA

PARMA

MODENA

TUSCANY

Florence•

PAPAL
STATES

Rome•

CORSICA
(To Genoa)

SARDINIA
(To Spain)

BALEARIC
ISLANDS

Zara•

Ragusa•

Cattaro•

Adriatic Sea

Naples•

KINGDOM

OF THE

TWO SICILIES

MEDITERRANEAN

SEA

OTTOMAN EMPIRE

Constantinople•

BLACK SEA

AEGEAN SEA

CRETE
(To Venice)

CYPRUS
(To Ottoman Empire)

(To Venice)

(To Venice)

SPAIN

Madrid•

Tagus R.

PORTUGAL

Lisbon•

Strait of Gibraltar

**EUROPE AT THE END
OF THE THIRTY YEARS' WAR • 1648**

The Church

Spain

Austria

Brandenburg-
Prussia

——— Boundary of the Holy Roman Empire

miles

The Emperor Charles V. This portrait by the Venetian painter Titian depicts the emperor in a grandiloquent equestrian pose. (Another depiction of Charles V by Titian appears in the section of color plates facing p. 429.)

nancial center. Moreover, the half-century-long rule of the Habsburg Charles V (1506–1556) had been popular because Charles, who had been born in the Belgian city of Ghent, felt a sense of rapport with his subjects, and allowed them a large degree of local self-government.

But around 1560 the good fortune of the Netherlands began to ebb. When Charles V retired to a monastery in 1556 (dying two years later) he ceded all his vast territories outside of the Holy Roman Empire and Hungary—not only the Netherlands, but Spain, Spanish America, and close to half of Italy—to his son Philip II (1556–1598). Unlike Charles, Philip had been born in Spain, and thinking of himself as a Spaniard, made Spain his residence and the focus of his policy. Thus he viewed the Netherlands primarily as a potentially rich source of income necessary for pursuing Spanish affairs. (Around 1560 silver was only beginning to flood through Seville.) But in order to tap the wealth of the Netherlands Philip had to rule it more directly than his father had, and such attempts were naturally resented by the local magnates who until then had dominated the government. To make matters worse, a religious storm also was brewing, for after a treaty of 1559 ended a long war between France and Spain, French Calvinists had begun to stream over the Netherlandish border, making converts wherever they went. Soon there were more Calvinists in Antwerp than in Geneva, a situation that Philip II could not tolerate because he was an ardent Catholic who subscribed wholeheartedly to the goals of the Counter-Reformation. Indeed, as he wrote to Rome on the eve of conflict: "rather than suffer the slightest harm to the true religion and service of God, I would lose all my

Philip II of Spain. Titian's portrait shows Philip's resemblance to his father, Charles V, particularly in the protruding lower jaw of the Habsburgs.

The Duke of Alva. The gaunt
Spanish general who attempted
in vain to extirpate Calvinism in
the Netherlands.

states and even my life a hundred times over because I am not and will not be the ruler of heretics."

Evidence of the complexity of the Netherlandish situation is found in the facts that the leader of resistance to Philip, William the Silent, was at first not a Calvinist and that the territories that ultimately succeeded in breaking away from Spanish rule were at first the most Catholic ones in the Low Countries. William "the Silent," a prominent nobleman with large landholdings in the Netherlands, was in fact very talkative, receiving his nickname rather from his ability to hide his true religious and political feelings when the need arose. In 1566, when still a nominal Catholic, he and other local nobles not formally committed to Protestantism appealed to Philip to allow toleration for Calvinists. But while Philip momentarily temporized, radical Protestant mobs proved to be their own worst enemy—ransacking Catholic churches throughout the country, methodically desecrating hosts, smashing statuary, and shattering stained-glass windows. Though local troops soon had the situation under control, Philip II nonetheless decided to dispatch an army of ten thousand commanded by the steely Spanish duke of Alva to wipe out Protestantism in the Low Countries forever. Alva's tribunal, the "Council of Blood," soon examined some twelve thousand persons on charges of heresy or sedition, of whom nine thousand were convicted and one thousand executed. William the Silent fled the country, and all hope for a free Netherlands seemed lost.

But the tide turned quickly for two related reasons. First, instead of giving up, William the Silent converted to Protestantism, sought help from Protestants in France, Germany, and England, and organized bands of sea rovers to harass Spanish shipping on the Netherlands coast. And second, Alva's tyranny helped William's cause, especially when the hated Spanish

Protestants Ransacking a Catholic Church in the Netherlands. The "Protestant fury" of 1566 was responsible for the large-scale destruction of religious art and statuary in the Low Countries, provoking the stern repression of Philip II.

governor attempted to levy a repressive 10 percent sales tax. With internal disaffection growing, in 1572 William, for tactical military reasons, was able to seize the northern Netherlands even though the north until then had been predominantly Catholic. Thereafter geography played a major role in determining the outcome of the conflict. Spanish armies repeatedly attempted to win back the north, but they were stopped by a combination of impassable rivers and dikes that could be opened to flood out the invaders. Although William the Silent was assassinated by a Catholic in 1584, his son continued to lead the resistance until the Spanish crown finally agreed by a truce in 1609 to stop fighting and thus implicitly recognized the independence of the northern Dutch Republic. Meanwhile, the pressures of war and persecution had made the whole north Calvinistic, whereas the south—which remained Spanish—returned to uniform Catholicism.

Religious strife could thus take the form of civil war, as in France, or war for national liberation, as in the Netherlands. But it could also take the form of warfare between sovereign states, as in the case of the late-sixteenth-century struggle between England and Spain. After narrowly escaping domination by the Catholic Queen Mary and her Spanish husband Philip II, English Protestants rejoiced in the rule of Queen Elizabeth I (1558–1603) and naturally harbored great antipathy toward Philip II and the Counter-Reformation. Furthermore, English economic interests were directly opposed to those of the Spanish. A seafaring and trading people, the English in the later sixteenth century were steadily making inroads into Spanish naval and commercial domination, and were also determined to resist any Spanish attempt to block England's lucrative trade with the Low Countries. But the greatest source of antagonism lay in naval contests in the Atlantic, where English privateers, with the tacit consent of Queen Elizabeth, could not resist raiding silver-laden Spanish treasure ships. Beginning around 1570, and taking as an excuse Spanish oppression of Protestants in the Netherlands, English admirals or pirates (the terms were really interchangeable) such as Sir Francis Drake and Sir John Hawkins began plundering Spanish vessels on the high seas. In a particularly dramatic sailing exploit lasting from 1577 to 1580, lust for booty and prevailing winds propelled Drake all the way around the world, to return with stolen Spanish treasure worth twice as much as Queen Elizabeth's annual revenue.

All this would have been sufficient provocation for Philip II to have retaliated against England, but because he had his hands full in the Netherlands he resolved to invade the island only after the English openly allied with the Dutch rebels in 1585. And even then Philip did not act without extensive planning and a sense of assurance that nothing could go wrong. Finally, in 1588 he dispatched an enormous fleet, confidently called the "Invincible Armada," to punish insolent Britannia. After an initial standoff in the English Channel, however, English fireships outmaneuvered the Spanish fleet, setting some Spanish galleons ablaze and forcing the rest to break formation. "Protestant gales" did the rest and a battered flotilla soon limped home with almost half its ships lost.

Left: *The Defeat of the Spanish Armada*. Right: *Queen Elizabeth I*. The contemporary English oil painting of the great sea battle gives only a schematic idea of its turbulence. Note, however, the prominence of the papal insignia (tiara over crossed keys of St. Peter) on the ship in the middle foreground. Englishmen were convinced that had they not defeated the Spanish Armada in 1588 the pope would have planted his banner on their shores. At the right is a typically overblown portrait of Queen Elizabeth, known to her admiring subjects as "Gloriana," standing on a map of England.

The salvation of Protestantism

The defeat of the Spanish Armada was one of the most decisive battles of Western history. Had Spain conquered England it is quite likely that the Spanish would have gone on to crush Holland and perhaps even to destroy Protestantism everywhere. But, as it was, the Protestant day was saved, and not long afterward Spanish power began to decline, with English and Dutch ships taking ever-greater command of the seas. Moreover, in England itself patriotic fervor became intense. Popular even before then, "Good Queen Bess" was virtually revered by her subjects until her death in 1603, and England embarked on its golden "Elizabethan Age" of literary endeavor. War with Spain dragged on inconclusively until 1604, but the fighting never brought England any serious harm and was just lively enough to keep the English people deeply committed to the cause of their queen, their country, and the Protestant religion.

3. YEARS OF TREMBLING

With the promulgation of the Edict of Nantes in 1598, the peace between England and Spain of 1604, and the truce between Spain and Holland of

1609, religious warfare tapered off and came to an end in the early seventeenth century. But in 1618 a major new war broke out, this time in Germany. Since this struggle raged more or less unceasingly until 1648 it bears the name of the Thirty Years' War. Far from returning to enduring peace, Spain and France became engaged in the conflict in Germany and in war with each other, and internal resentments in Spain, France, and England flared up in the decade of the 1640s in concurrent outbreaks of uprisings and civil turmoil. As an English preacher said in 1643, "these are days of shaking, and this shaking is universal." He might have added that while in some instances religion remained one of the contested issues, secular disputes about powers of government were now becoming predominant.

The clearest example is that of the Thirty Years' War, which began in a welter of religious passions as a war between Catholics and Protestants but immediately raised basic German constitutional issues and ended as an international struggle in which the initial religious dimension was almost entirely forgotten. Between the Peace of Augsburg in 1555 and the outbreak of war in 1618, Calvinists had replaced Lutherans in a few German territories, but the overall balance between Protestants and Catholics within the Holy Roman Empire had remained undisturbed. In 1618, however, when a Protestant uprising against Habsburg Catholic rule in Bohemia (not a German territory, yet part of the Holy Roman Empire) threatened to upset the balance, German Catholic forces ruthlessly counterattacked, first in Bohemia and then in Germany proper. Led by Charles V's Habsburg descendant, Ferdinand II, who was archduke of Austria, king of Hungary, and from 1619 to his death in 1637, Holy Roman Emperor, a German Catholic league seized the military initiative and within a decade seemed close to extirpating Protestantism throughout Germany. But Ferdinand,

A new phase of turmoil

The Thirty Years' War

See color map facing page 493

Two Artistic Broadsides from the Thirty Years' War. On the left the German peasantry is ridden by the soldiery; on the right is an allegorical representation of "the monstrous beast of war."

Gustavus Adolphus at the Battle of Leipzig. This engraving celebrates a victory won by the king of Sweden in 1631. One of the angels trumpets "German freedom," but the city of Leipzig is partly in flames and the Thirty Years' War would continue mercilessly for another seventeen years.

who was intent on pursuing political goals, imposed firm direct rule in Bohemia in order to build up the strength of his own Austro-Hungarian state, and attempted to revive the faded authority of the Holy Roman Empire in whatever ways he could.

The involvement of Sweden and France

Thus when the Lutheran king of Sweden, Gustavus Adolphus, the "Lion of the North," marched into Germany in 1630 to champion the nearly lost cause of Protestantism, he was welcomed by several German Catholic princes who preferred to see the former religious balance restored rather than stand the chance of surrendering their sovereignty to Ferdinand II. To make matters still more ironic, Gustavus's Protestant army was secretly subsidized by Catholic France, then governed by a cardinal of the Church, Cardinal Richelieu. This was because Habsburg Spain had been fighting in Germany on the side of Habsburg Austria, and Richelieu was determined to resist any possibility of France being surrounded by a strong Habsburg alliance on the north, east, and south. In the event, the military genius Gustavus Adolphus started routing the Habsburgs, but when he fell in battle in 1632, Cardinal Richelieu had little choice but to send ever-greater support to the remaining Swedish troops in Germany, until in 1635 French armies entered the war directly on Sweden's side. From then until 1648 the struggle was really one of France and Sweden against Austria and Spain, with most of Germany a helpless battleground.

The toll of warfare in Germany

The result was that Germany suffered more from warfare in the terrible years between 1618 and 1648 than it ever did before or after until the twentieth century. Several German cities were besieged and sacked nine or ten times over, and soldiers from all nations, who often had to sustain themselves by plunder, gave no quarter to defenseless civilians. With plague and disease adding to the toll of outright butchery, some parts of Germany lost more than half their populations, although it is true that others went relatively unscathed. Most horrifying was the loss of life in the last four years, when the carnage continued unabated even while peace negotiators had already arrived at broad areas of agreement and were dickering over subsidiary clauses.

Nor did the Peace of Westphalia, which finally ended the Thirty Years' War in 1648, do much to vindicate anyone's death, even though it did establish some abiding landmarks in European history. Above all, from the international perspective, the Peace of Westphalia marked the reemergence of France as the predominant power on the continental European scene, replacing Spain—a position France was to hold for two centuries more. In particular, France moved its eastern frontier directly into German territory by taking over large parts of Alsace. As for strictly internal German matters, the greatest losers were the Austrian Habsburgs, who were forced to surrender all the territory they had gained in Germany and to abandon their hopes of using the office of Holy Roman Emperor to dominate central Europe. Otherwise, something very close to the German status quo of 1618 was reestablished, with Protestant principalities in the north balancing Catholic ones in the south, and Germany so hopelessly divided that it could play no united role in European history until the nineteenth century.

Still greater losers from the Thirty Years' War than the Austrian Habsburgs were their Spanish cousins, for Spain had invested in the struggle vast sums it could not afford and ceased being a great power forever after. The story of Spain's swift fall from grandeur is almost like a Greek tragedy in its relentless unfolding. Despite the defeat of the "Invincible Armada" in 1588, around 1600 the Spanish empire—comprising all of the Iberian

The Recapture of Bahía. The Spanish constantly had to defend their overseas holdings from the Dutch. In 1625 a Spanish fleet recaptured the Brazilian port of Bahía, taken by the Dutch the year before. A Spanish propaganda painting combines realism and allegory by showing Spain's governing minister, the count of Olivares, proudly pointing to a painting of King Philip IV, while the returning inhabitants of Bahía nurse a wounded soldier.

peninsula (including Portugal, which had been annexed by Philip II in 1580), half of Italy, half of the Netherlands, all of Central and South America, and even the Philippine Islands—was still the mightiest power not just in Europe but in the world. Yet a bare half century later this empire on which the sun never set had come close to falling apart.

Economic causes of Spain's decline

Spain's greatest underlying weakness was economic. At first this may seem like a very odd statement considering that in 1600, as in the three or four previous decades, huge amounts of American silver were being unloaded on the docks of Seville. Yet as contemporaries themselves recognized, "the new world that Spain had conquered was conquering Spain in turn." Lacking either rich agricultural or mineral resources, Spain desperately needed to develop industries and a balanced trading pattern as its rivals England and France were doing. But the dominant Spanish nobility had prized ideals of chivalry over practical business ever since the medieval days when Spanish nobles were engaged in reconquering Christian territory from the Muslims. Thus the Spanish governing class was only too glad to use American silver to buy manufactured goods from other parts of Europe in order to live in splendor and dedicate itself to military exploits. Thus bullion left the country as soon as it entered, virtually no industry was established, and when the influx of silver began to decline after 1600 the Spanish economy remained with nothing except increasing debts.

Spain's continued aggressiveness

Nonetheless, the crown, dedicated to supporting the Counter-Reformation and maintaining Spain's international dominance, would not cease fighting abroad. Indeed, the entire Spanish budget remained on such a warlike footing that even in the relatively peaceful year of 1608 four million out of a total revenue of seven million ducats were paid for military expenditures. Thus when Spain became engaged in fighting France during the Thirty Years' War it overextended itself. The clearest visible sign of this was that in 1643 French troops at Rocroi inflicted a stunning defeat on the famed Spanish infantry, the first time that a Spanish army had been overcome in battle since the reign of Ferdinand and Isabella. Yet worse still was the fact that by then two territories belonging to Spain's European empire were in open revolt.

Internal revolts against the Castilian government

In order to understand the causes of these revolts one must recognize that in the seventeenth century the governing power of Spain lay entirely in Castile. After the marriage of Isabella of Castile and Ferdinand of Aragon in 1469, geographically central Castile emerged as the dominant partner in the Spanish union, becoming even more dominant when Castile conquered the Muslim kingdom of Granada in southern Spain in 1492 and annexed Portugal in 1580. In the absence of any great financial hardships, semi-autonomous Catalonia (the most fiercely independent part of Aragon) endured Castilian hegemony. But in 1640, when the strains of warfare induced Castile to limit Catalonian liberties in order to raise more money and men for combat, Catalonia revolted and drove off Castilian governors. Immediately afterward the Portuguese learned of the Catalonian uprising and revolted as well, followed by southern Italians who revolted against Castilian viceroys in Naples and Sicily in 1647. At that point only the mo-

The Escorial. Philip II of Spain ordered the building between 1563 and 1584 of this somber retreat—part royal residence, part monastery—on an isolated spot, well removed from Madrid. Conceived on a grid-iron plan to honor the grid-iron martyrdom of St. Lawrence (on whose feast day Philip had won a decisive victory against the French), the Escorial symbolizes for many the Spanish crown's dedication to the ideals of the Counter-Reformation as well as its attempt to impose rationalized central government on the refractory outlying provinces of the Spanish Empire.

mentary inability of Spain's greatest external enemies, France and England, to take advantage of its plight saved the Spanish Empire from utter collapse. Nothing if not determined, the Castilian government quickly put down the Italian revolts and by 1652 also brought Catalonia to heel. But Portugal retained its independence forever, and by the Peace of the Pyrenees, signed with France in 1659, Spain in effect conceded that it would entirely abandon its ambitions of dominating Europe.

A comparison between the fortunes of Spain and France in the first half of the seventeenth century is highly instructive because some striking similarities existed between the two countries, but in the end differences turned out to be most decisive. Spain and France were of almost identical territorial extent, and both countries had been created by the same process of accretion. Just as the Castilian crown had gained Aragon in the north, Granada in the south, and then Portugal, so the kingdom of France had grown by adding on such diverse territories as Languedoc, Dauphiné, Provence, Burgundy, and Brittany. Since the inhabitants of all these territories cherished traditions of local independence as much as the Catalans or Portuguese, and since the rulers of France, like those of Spain, were determined to govern their provinces ever more firmly—especially when the financial stringencies of the Thirty Years' War made ruthless tax-collecting urgently necessary—a direct confrontation between the central government and the provinces in France became inevitable, just as in Spain. But France weathered the storm whereas Spain did not, a result largely attributable to France's greater wealth and the greater prestige of the French crown.

Spain and France compared

In good times most French people, including those from the outlying provinces, tended to revere their king. Certainly they had excellent reason to do so during the reign of Henry IV. Having established religious peace

The reign of Henry IV

Cardinal Richelieu. A contemporary portrait emphasizing the cardinal's austere bearing.

Cardinal Richelieu

The Fronde

in 1598 by the Edict of Nantes, the affable Henry, who declared that there should be a chicken in every French family's pot each Sunday, set about to restore the prosperity of a country devastated by four decades of civil war. Fortunately France had enormous economic resiliency, owing primarily to its extremely rich and varied agricultural resources. Unlike Spain, which had to import food, France normally had been able to export it, and Henry's finance minister, the duke of Sully, quickly saw to it that France became a food exporter once more. Among other things, Sully distributed throughout the country free copies of a guide to recommended farming techniques and financed the rebuilding or new construction of roads, bridges, and canals to help expedite the flow of goods. In addition, Henry IV was not content to see France rest its economic development on agri-cultural wealth alone; instead he ordered the construction of royal factories to manufacture luxury goods such as crystal glass and tapestries, and he also supported the growth of silk, linen, and woolen cloth industries in many different parts of the country. Moreover, Henry's patronage allowed the explorer Champlain to claim parts of Canada as France's first foothold in the New World. Thus Henry IV's reign certainly must be counted as one of the most benevolent in all French history.

Far less benevolent was Henry's *de facto* successor as ruler of France, Car-dinal Richelieu (1585–1642), yet Richelieu fully managed to maintain France's forward momentum. The cardinal, of course, was never the real king of France—the actual title was held from 1610 to 1643 by Henry IV's ineffectual son Louis XIII. But as first minister from 1624 to his death in 1642 Richelieu governed as he wished, and what he wished most of all was to enhance centralized royal power at home and expand French influence in the larger theater of Europe. Accordingly, when Huguenots rebelled against restrictions placed on them by the Edict of Nantes, Richelieu put them down with an iron fist and emended the Edict in 1629 by depriving them of all their political and military rights. Since his armed campaigns against the Huguenots had been very costly, the cardinal then moved to gain more income for the crown by abolishing the semi-autonomy of Bur-gundy, Dauphiné, and Provence so that he could introduce direct royal taxation in all three areas. Later, to make sure all taxes levied were effi-ciently collected, Richelieu instituted a new system of local government by royal officials known as *intendants* who were expressly commissioned to run roughshod over any provincial obstructionism. By these and related meth-ods Richelieu made French government more centralized than ever and managed to double the crown's income during his rule. But since he also engaged in an ambitious foreign policy directed against the Habsburgs of Austria and Spain, resulting in France's costly involvement in the Thirty Years' War, internal pressures mounted in the years after Richelieu's death.

A reaction against French governmental centralization manifested itself in a series of revolts between 1648 and 1653 collectively known as "the slingshot tumults," or in French, the *Fronde*. By this time Louis XIII had been succeeded by his son Louis XIV, but because the latter was still a boy, France was governed by a regency consisting of Louis's mother Anne of

Austria and her paramour Cardinal Mazarin. Considering that both were foreigners (Anne was a Habsburg and Mazarin originally an Italian adventurer named Giulio Mazarini), it is not surprising that many of their subjects, including some extremely powerful nobles, hated them. Moreover, nationwide resentments were greater still because the costs of war and several consecutive years of bad harvests had brought France temporarily into a grave economic plight. Thus when cliques of nobles expressed their disgust with Mazarin for primarily petty and self-interested reasons, they found much support throughout the country, and uncoordinated revolts against the regency flared on and off for several years.

France, however, was not Spain, and thus did not come close to falling apart. Above all, the French crown itself, which retained great reservoirs of prestige owing to a well-established national tradition and the undoubted achievements of Henry IV and Richelieu, was by no means under attack. On the contrary, neither the aristocratic leaders of the *Fronde* nor the commoners from all ranks who joined them in revolt claimed to be resisting the young king but only the alleged corruption and mismanagement of Mazarin. Some of the rebels, it is true, insisted that part of Mazarin's fault lay in his pursuance of Richelieu's centralizing, antiprovincial policy. But since most of the aristocrats who led the *Fronde* were merely "outs" who wanted to be "in," they often squabbled among themselves—sometimes even arranging agreements of convenience with the regency or striking alliances with France's enemy, Spain, for momentary gain—and proved completely unable to rally any unified support behind a common program. Thus when Louis XIV began to rule in his own name in 1651 and pretexts for revolting against "corrupt ministers" no longer existed, all opposition was soon silenced. As so often happens, the idealists and poor people paid the greatest price for revolt: in 1653 a defeated leader of popular resistance in Bordeaux was broken on a wheel, and not long afterward a massive new round of taxation was proclaimed. Remembering the turbulence of the *Fronde* for the rest of his life, Louis XIV resolved never to let his aristocracy or his provinces get out of hand again and ruled as the most effective royal absolutist in all of French history.

Compared to the civil disturbances of the 1640s in Spain and France, those in England proved the most momentous in their results for the history of limited government. Whereas all that the revolts against Castile accomplished was the achievement of Portuguese independence and the crippling of an empire that was already in decline, and all that happened in France was a momentary interruption of the steady advance of royal power, in England a king was executed and barriers were erected against royal absolutism.

England around 1600 was caught up in a trend toward the growth of centralized royal authority characteristic of all Western Europe. Not only had Henry VIII and Elizabeth I brought the English Church fully under royal control, but both monarchs employed so-called prerogative courts wherein they could proceed against subjects in disregard of traditional English legal safeguards for the rights of the accused. Furthermore, although

French absolutism triumphant

The case of England

Henry VIII and Elizabeth I increase royal power

James I. "The wisest fool in
Christendom."

*Causes of antagonism to
James I*

The Puritans

Parliament met regularly during both reigns, members of Parliament were
far less independent than they had been in the fifteenth century: any parliamentary representative who might have stood up to Henry VIII would
have lost his head, and almost all parliamentarians admired Elizabeth
enough to abide by her policies. Thus when the Stuart dynasty succeeded
Elizabeth, the last of the Tudors, it was only natural that the Stuarts would
try to increase royal power still more. And indeed they might have succeeded had it not been for their ineptness and an extraordinary combination of forces ranged against them.

Lines of contention were drawn immediately at the accession of Elizabeth's nearest relative, her cousin James VI of Scotland, who in 1603 retained his Scottish crown but also became king of England as James I
(1603–1625). Homely but vain, addled but erudite, James fittingly was
called by Henry IV of France "the wisest fool in Christendom," and presented the starkest contrast to his predecessor. Whereas Elizabeth knew
how to gain her way with Parliament without making a fuss about it, the
schoolmasterish foreigner insisted on lecturing parliamentarians that he was
semi-divine and would brook no resistance: "As it is atheism and blasphemy to dispute what God can do, so it is presumption and high contempt in a subject to dispute what a king can do." Carrying these sentiments further, in a speech to Parliament of 1609 he proclaimed that "kings
are not only God's lieutenants on earth . . . but even by God Himself they
are called gods."

That such extreme pretentions to divine authority would arouse strong
opposition was a result even James should have been able to foresee, for the
English ruling groups were still intensely committed to the theory of parliamentary controls on the crown. Yet not just theory was at stake, for the
specific policies of the new king antagonized large numbers of his subjects.
For example, James insisted upon supplementing his income by modes of
money-raising that had never been sanctioned by Parliament; and when
the leaders of that body remonstrated, he angrily tore up their protests and
dissolved their sessions. Worse, he interfered with the freedom of business
by granting monopolies and lucrative privileges to favored companies.
And, worst of all in the eyes of most patriotic Englishmen, James quickly
put an end to the long war with Spain and refused thereafter to become involved in any foreign military entanglements. Today many of us might
think that James's commitment to peace was his greatest virtue; certainly
his pacifism was justifiable financially since it spared the crown enormous
debts. But in his own age James was hated particularly for his peace policy
because it made him seem far too friendly with England's traditional enemy, Spain, and because "appeasement" meant leaving seemingly heroic
Protestants in Holland and Germany in the lurch.

Although almost all English people (except for a small minority of clandestine Catholics) objected to James I's pacific foreign policy, those who
hated it most were a group destined to play the greatest role in overthrowing the Stuarts, namely, the Puritans. Extremist Calvinistic Protestants, the
Puritans believed that Elizabeth I's religious compromises had not broken

fully enough with the forms and doctrines of Roman Catholicism. Called Puritans from their desire to "purify" the English Church of all traces of Catholic ritual and observance, they most vehemently opposed the English "episcopal system" of church government by bishops. But James I was as committed to retaining episcopalianism as the Puritans were intent on abolishing it because he viewed royally appointed bishops as one of the pillars of a strong monarchy: "No bishop, no king." Since the Puritans were the dominant faction in the House of Commons and many Puritans were also prosperous merchants who opposed James's monopolistic policies and money-raising expediencies, throughout his reign James remained at loggerheads with an extremely powerful group of his subjects for a combination of religious, constitutional, and economic reasons.

Nonetheless, James survived to die peacefully in bed in 1625, and had it not been for mistakes made by his son Charles I (1625–1649), England might have gone the way of absolutist France. Charles held the same inflated notions of royal power and consequently was quickly at odds with the Puritan leaders of Parliament. Soon after his accession to the throne Charles became involved in a war with France and needed revenue desperately. When Parliament refused to make more than the customary grants, he resorted to forced loans from his subjects, punishing those who failed to comply by quartering soldiers in their homes or throwing them into prison without a trial. In reaction to this, Parliament forced the Petition of Right on the king in 1628. This document declared all taxes not voted by Parliament illegal, condemned the quartering of soldiers in private houses, and prohibited arbitrary imprisonment and the establishment of martial law in time of peace.

Charles I. This portrait by Van Dyck vividly captures the ill-fated monarch's arrogance.

Angered rather than chastened by the Petition of Right, Charles I soon resolved to rule entirely without Parliament—and nearly succeeded. From 1629 to 1640 no Parliaments were called. During this "eleven-years' tyranny," Charles's government lived off a variety of makeshift dues and levies. For example, the crown sold monopolies at exorbitant rates, revived highly antiquated medieval financial claims, and admonished judges to collect the stiffest of fines. Though technically not illegal, all of these expedients were deeply resented. Most controversial was the collection of "ship money," a levy taken on the pretext of a medieval obligation of English seaboard towns to provide ships (or their worth in money) for the royal navy. Extending the payment of ship money from coastal towns to the whole country, Charles threatened to make it a regular tax in contravention of the Petition of Right, and was upheld in a legal challenge of 1637 brought against him on these grounds by the Puritan squire John Hampden.

The eleven-years' tyranny

By such means the king managed to make ends meet without the aid of taxes granted by Parliament. But he became ever more hated by most of his subjects, and above all the Puritans, not just because of his constitutional and financial policies but also because he seemed to be pursuing a course in religion that came much closer to Catholicism than to Calvinism. Whether the English Puritans would have risen up in revolt on their own

The Scottish uprising

is a moot question, but they were ultimately emboldened to do so by a chain of events beginning with a revolt in Scotland. The uprising in Scotland of 1640 against the policy of an English king was not unlike those in Catalonia and Portugal of the same year against the Spanish crown except that the Scottish rising was not just nationalistic but also explicitly religious in nature. Like his father, Charles believed in the adage "no bishop, no king" and hence foolhardily decided to introduce episcopalian church government into staunchly Presbyterian Scotland. The result was armed resistance by Charles's northern subjects and the first step toward civil war in England.

The convening of Parliament

In order to obtain the funds necessary to punish the Scots, Charles had no other choice but to summon Parliament and soon found himself the target of pent-up resentments. Knowing full well that the king was helpless without money, the Puritan leaders of the House of Commons determined to take England's government into their own hands. Accordingly, they not only executed the king's first minister, the earl of Strafford, but they abolished ship money and the prerogative courts that ever since the reign of Henry VIII had served as instruments of arbitrary rule. Most significantly, they enacted a law forbidding the crown to dissolve Parliament and requiring the convening of sessions at least once every three years. After some indecision, early in 1642 Charles replied to these acts with a show of force. He marched with his guard into the House of Commons and attempted to arrest five of its leaders. All of them escaped, but an open conflict between crown and Parliament could no longer be avoided. Both parties collected troops and prepared for an appeal to the sword.

*Civil war: The Cavaliers
vs. the Roundheads*

These events initiated the English Civil War, a conflict at once political and religious, which lasted from 1642 to 1649. Arrayed on the royal side were most of England's most prominent aristocrats and largest landowners, who were almost all "high-church" Anglicans. Opposed to them, the followers of Parliament included smaller landholders, tradesmen, and manufacturers, the majority of whom were Puritans. The members of the king's party were commonly known by the aristocratic name of Cavaliers. Their opponents, who cut their hair short in contempt for the fashionable custom of wearing curls, were derisively called Roundheads. At first the royalists, having obvious advantages of military experience, won most of the victories. In 1644, however, the parliamentary army was reorganized, and soon afterward the fortunes of battle shifted. The Cavalier forces were badly beaten, and in 1646 the king was compelled to surrender.

Oliver Cromwell

The struggle would now have ended had not a quarrel developed within the parliamentary party. The majority of its members, who had allied with the Presbyterian Scots, were ready to restore Charles to the throne as a limited monarch under an arrangement whereby a uniform Calvinistic Presbyterian faith would be imposed on both Scotland and England as the state religion. But a radical minority of Puritans, commonly known as Independents, distrusted Charles and insisted upon religious toleration for themselves and all other non-Presbyterian Protestants. Their leader was Oliver Cromwell (1599–1658), who had risen to command the Roundhead army. Taking advantage of the dissension within the ranks of his opponents, Charles renewed the war in 1648, but after a brief campaign was forced to surrender. Cromwell now resolved to end the life of "that man of blood," and, ejecting all the Presbyterians from Parliament by force of arms, obliged the remaining so-called Rump Parliament to vote an end to the monarchy. On 30 January 1649 Charles I was beheaded; a short time later the hereditary House of Lords was abolished, and England became a republic.

But founding a republic was far easier than maintaining one, and the new form of government, officially called a Commonwealth, did not last long. Technically the Rump Parliament continued as the legislative body, but Cromwell, with the army at his command, possessed the real power and soon became exasperated by the attempts of the legislators to perpetuate themselves in office and to profit from confiscating the wealth of their opponents. Accordingly, in 1653 he marched a detachment of troops into the Rump Parliament and saying "Come, I will put an end to your prating," ordered the members to disperse. Thereby the Commonwealth ceased to exist and was soon followed by the "Protectorate," or virtual dictatorship established under a constitution drafted by officers of the army. Called the Instrument of Government, this text was the nearest approximation of a written constitution England has ever had. Extensive powers were given to Cromwell as Lord Protector for life, and his office was made hereditary. At first a Parliament exercised limited authority in making laws and levying taxes, but in 1655 its members were abruptly dismissed by the Lord Protector. Thereafter the government became a thinly disguised autocracy, with Cromwell now wielding a sovereignty even more absolute than any the Stuart monarchs would have dared to claim.

Given the choice between a Puritan military dictatorship and the old royalist regime, when the occasion arose England unhesitatingly opted for the latter. Above all, years of Calvinistic austerities such as the prohibition of any public recreation on Sundays—then the workingperson's only holiday—had discredited the Puritans, making most people long for the milder Anglicanism of the original Elizabethan settlement. Thus not long after Cromwell's death in 1658, one of the deceased Protector's generals seized power and called for elections for a new Parliament which met in the spring of 1660 and proclaimed as king Charles I's exiled son, Charles II. With the reign of Charles II (1660–1685) Anglicanism was immediately restored, but by no means the same was true for untrammeled monarchical power. Rather, stating with characteristic good humor that he did not wish to "resume his travels," Charles agreed to respect Parliament and observe the Petition of Right. Of greatest constitutional significance was the fact that all the legislation passed by Parliament immediately before the outbreak of the Civil War, including the requirement to hold Parliaments at least once every three years, remained as law. Thus in striking contrast to absolutist France, England became a limited monarchy. Putting its constitutional struggles behind it after one brief further test in the late seventeenth century, the realm of England would soon live up to the poet Milton's prediction of "a noble and puissant nation rousing herself like a strong man after sleep."

4. QUESTS FOR LIGHT OUT OF DARKNESS

Witchcraft and philosophy

Caught up in economic uncertainty, religious rivalries, and political turmoil, many Europeans between 1560 and 1660 understandably cast about for emotional or intellectual resolutions of their most pressing problems. Sometimes, as in the case of the great witchcraft delusion, this quest led merely to an intensification of hysteria. But in the case of more dispassionate reflections, the search for ways of resolving Europe's crises led to some of the most enduring statements of moral and political philosophy of all time.

The origins of the witchcraft delusion

Although no one simple explanation can be offered for the outbreak of Western Europe's fearful witchcraft hysteria that reached its peak between 1580 and 1660, it is certain that persecutions of witches in those years were fiercest during times of greatest disaster and that people who burned witches genuinely thought they were fighting the powers of darkness. Looking for the origins of the great early-modern witchcraft delusion, historians recognize that peasant culture throughout the Middle Ages included belief in the possibilities of sorcery. In other words, most simple rural people assumed that certain unusual individuals could practice good, or "white," magic in the form of healing, divination for lost objects, and for-

Supposed Witches Worshiping the Devil in the Form of a Billy-Goat. In the background other "witches" ride bareback on flying demons. This is one of the earliest visual conceptions of witchcraft, dating from around 1460.

Burning of Witches at Dernberg in 1555. From a sixteenth-century German pamphlet denouncing witchcraft.

tune-telling, or perhaps also evil, "black" magic that might, for example, call up tempests or ravage crops. Yet only in the Later Middle Ages did learned authorities begin to insist on theological grounds that black magic could be practiced only as a result of pacts with the devil. Naturally, once this belief became accepted, judicial officers soon found it urgent to prosecute all "witches" who practiced black magic because warfare against the devil was paramount to Christian society and "the evil one" could not be allowed to hold any sway. Accordingly, as early as 1484 Pope Innocent VIII ordered papal inquisitors to root out alleged witchcraft with all the means at their disposal, and the pace of witch hunts gained momentum in the following decades. Nor were witch trials curtailed in areas that broke with Rome, for Protestant reformers believed in the insidious powers of Satan just as much as Catholics did. Indeed, Luther himself once threw an inkpot at a supposed apparition of the devil, and Calvin saw Satan's evil workings wherever he looked. Thus both urged that alleged witches be tried more peremptorily and sentenced with less leniency than ordinary criminals, and persecutions of innocent people continued apace in Protestant as well as Catholic lands.

Yet the outbreak of a real mania for catching and killing "witches" did not begin until about 1580. Therefore it can only be supposed that the witchcraft hysteria was connected in some way with Europe's general crisis—all the more since it continued for about as long as the age of crisis itself and was most severe in just those localities where warfare or economic dislocation was most intense. In such places, whenever crops failed or cattle sickened people assumed that a "witch"—usually a defenseless old woman—was responsible, and rushed to put her to death. If not always old, the victims were most frequently women, no doubt in part because preachers had encouraged their flocks to believe that evil had first come into the world with Eve and in part because men in authority felt psychologically most ambivalent about members of the opposite sex. Pure sadism

Witchcraft hysteria and the European crisis

certainly cannot have been the original motive for such proceedings, but once trials began, horrendous sadism very often was unleashed. Thus old women, young girls, and sometimes even mere children might be brutally tortured by having needles driven under their nails, fires placed at their heels, or their legs crushed under weights until marrow spurted from their bones, in order to make them confess to having had filthy orgies with demons. The final death toll will never be known, but in the 1620s there was an average of one hundred burnings a year in the German cities of Würzburg and Bamberg, and around the same time it was said the town square of Wolfenbüttel "looked like a little forest, so crowded were the stakes."

The end of the witch hunts

Why persecution quickly ended in the years immediately after 1660 will remain a matter for scholarly speculation. Aside from the fact that better times returned to most of Europe around then, probably the best explanation is that shortly after 1660 educated magistrates began to adhere to a mechanistic view of the universe. In other words, once the leaders of society came to believe that storms and epidemics arose from natural rather than supernatural causes, they ceased to countenance witch hunts.

Fortunately, other attempts of Europeans between 1560 and 1660 to master the darkness around them were not in themselves so dark. Indeed, one of the most "enlightened" of all European moral philosophers was the Frenchman Michel de Montaigne (1533–1592), who wrote during the height of the French wars of religion. The son of a Catholic father and a Huguenot mother of Jewish ancestry, the well-to-do Montaigne retired from a legal career at the age of thirty-eight to devote himself to a life of leisured reflection. The *Essays* that resulted were a new literary form originally conceived as "experiments" in writing (French *essai* simply means "trial"). Because they are extraordinarily well written as well as being searchingly reflective, Montaigne's *Essays* ever since have ranked securely among the most enduring classics of French literature and thought.

Michel de Montaigne

Scepticism and need for
tolerance

Although the range of subjects of the *Essays* runs a wide gamut from "The Resemblance of Children to Their Fathers" to "The Art of Conversing," two main themes are dominant. One is a pervasive skepticism. Making his motto *"Que sais-je?"* (What do I know?), Montaigne decided that he knew very little for certain. According to him, "it is folly to measure truth and error by our own capacities" because our capacities are severely limited. Thus, as he maintained in one of his most famous essays, "On Cannibals," what may seem indisputably true and proper to one nation may seem absolutely false to another because "everyone gives the title of barbarism to everything that is not of his usage." From this Montaigne's second main principle followed—the need for tolerance. Since all people think they know the perfect religion and the perfect government, no religion or government is really perfect and consequently no belief is worth fighting for to the death.

Essays *help combat*
religious intolerance

If the foregoing description makes Montaigne sound surprisingly modern, it must be emphasized that he was by no means a rationalist. On the contrary, he believed that "reason does nothing but go astray in everything," and that intellectual curiosity "which prompts us to thrust our noses into everything" is a "scourge of the soul." Moreover, concerning practical affairs Montaigne was a fatalist who thought that in a world governed by unpredictable "fortune" the best human strategy is to face the good and the bad with steadfastness and dignity. Lest people begin to think too highly of their own abilities, he reminded them that "sit we upon the highest throne in the world, yet we do sit upon our own behinds." Nonetheless, despite his passive belief that "fortune, not wisdom, rules the life of mankind," the wide circulation of Montaigne's *Essays* did help combat fanaticism and religious intolerance in his own and subsequent ages.

If Montaigne sought refuge from the trials of his age in skepticism, tolerance, and resigned dignity, his contemporary, the French lawyer Jean Bodin (1530–1596), looked for more light to come out of darkness from the powers of the state. Like Montaigne, Bodin was particularly troubled by the upheavals caused by the religious wars in France—he had even witnessed the frightful St. Bartholomew's Day Massacre of 1572 in Paris. But instead of shrugging his shoulders about the bloodshed, he resolved to offer a political plan to make sure turbulence would cease. This he did in his monumental *Six Books of the Commonwealth* (1576), the earliest fully developed statement of governmental absolutism in Western political thought. According to Bodin, the state arises from the needs of collections of families, but once constituted should brook no opposition, for maintaining order is paramount. Whereas writers on law and politics before him had groped toward a theory of governmental sovereignty, Bodin was the first to offer a succinct definition; for him, sovereignty was "the most high, absolute, and perpetual power over all subjects," consisting principally in the power "to give laws to subjects without their consent." Although Bodin acknowledged the theoretical possibility of government by aristocracy or democracy, he assumed that the nation-states of his day would be ruled by monarchs and insisted that such monarchs could in no way be limited, either by legislative or judicial bodies, or even by laws made by their predecessors or themselves. Expressing the sharpest opposition to contemporary Huguenots who were saying (in contravention of the original teachings of Luther and Calvin) that subjects had a right to resist "ungodly princes," Bodin maintained that a subject must trust in his ruler's "mere and frank good will." Even if the ruler proved a tyrant, Bodin insisted that the subject had no warrant to resist, for any resistance would open the door "to a licentious anarchy which is worse than the harshest tyranny in the world." Since in his own day Bodin knew much "licentious anarchy" but had hardly any notion of how harsh the "harshest tyranny" could be, his position is somewhat understandable. Yet in the next century his *Commonwealth* would become the grounds for justifications of an increasingly oppressive French royal absolutism.

Quite understandably, just as the French civil wars of the sixteenth century provoked a variety of responses, so did the English Civil War of the seventeenth. Drawing on a tradition of resistance to untrammeled state power expressed by French Huguenots and earlier English parliamentarians

A "Camel-Leopard." In the sixteenth century burgeoning overseas travel led to proliferating rumors of strange sights. This "camel-leopard" is obviously a crude conception of what was really a giraffe. Uncertain of absolute truth and falsity, Montaigne concluded that what seemed true one day might be cast into doubt tomorrow.

Jean Bodin

*The Title Page of Hobbes's Levia-
than*

and Puritans, the great English Puritan poet John Milton enunciated a stirring defense of freedom of the press in his *Areopagitica* (1644). Similarly
bold upholders of libertarianism were a party of Milton's Puritan contemporaries known as Levellers, the first exponents of democracy since Greek
times. Organizing themselves as a pressure group within Cromwell's army
in the later 1640s when Charles I's monarchy seemed clearly doomed, the
Levellers—who derived their name from their advocacy of equal political
rights for all classes—agitated in favor of a parlimentary republic based on
nearly universal manhood suffrage. For them, servants and other wage-
laborers had no right to vote because they formed part of their employer's
"family" and allegedly were represented by the family head. Moreover, the
Levellers did not even deign to argue about women's rights. Otherwise,
however, in the immortal words of one of their spokesmen, they argued
that "the poorest He that is in England hath a life to live as the greatest He,
and therefore . . . every man that is to live under a government ought first
by his own consent to put himself under that government." But since
Oliver Cromwell, who believed that the only grounds for suffrage was sufficient property, would have none of this, once Cromwell assumed virtually dictatorial powers the Leveller party disintegrated. More radical still
were the communistic Diggers, so called from their attempts to cultivate
common lands in 1649. Claiming to be "true Levellers," the Diggers argued that true freedom lies not in votes, but "where a man receives his
nourishment," and hence argued for the redistribution of property.
Cromwell, however, dispersed them quickly, and thus the Diggers have
merely historical interest as vanguards of movements to come.

Far to the other extreme of the libertarian Puritans was the political
philosopher Thomas Hobbes (1588–1679), whose reactions to the English
Civil War led him to become the most forceful advocate of unrestrained
state power of all time. Like Bodin, who was moved by the events of St.
Bartholomew's Day to formulate a doctrine of political absolutism, Hobbes
was moved by the turmoil of the English Civil War to do the same in his
classic of political theory entitled *Leviathan* (1651). Yet Hobbes differed
from Bodin in several respects. For one, whereas Bodin assumed that the
absolute sovereign power would be a royal monarch, the more radical
Hobbes, writing without any respect for tradition in Cromwell's England
two years after the beheading of a king, thought the sovereign could be
any ruthless dictator whatsoever. Then too, whereas Bodin defined his state
as "the lawful government of families" and hence did not believe that the
state could abridge private property rights because families could not exist
without property, Hobbes's state existed to rule over atomistic individuals
and thus was licensed to trample over both liberty and property.

But the most fundamental difference between Bodin and Hobbes lay in
the latter's uncompromisingly pessimistic view of human nature. Hobbes
posited that the "state of nature" that existed before civil government came
into being was a condition of "war of all against all." Since man naturally
behaves as "a wolf" toward man and increasing fear of violent death in the
state of nature makes human life "solitary, poor, nasty, brutish, and short,"

people for their own good at some purely theoretical point in time surrender their liberties to a sovereign ruler in exchange for his agreement to keep the peace. Having granted away their liberties, subjects have no right whatsoever to seek them back, and the sovereign can tyrannize as he likes —free to oppress his charges in any way other than to kill them, an act that would negate the very purpose of his rule. It is a measure of the relentless logic and clarity of Hobbes's abstract exposition that his *Leviathan* is widely regarded as one of the four or five greatest political treatises ever written, for practically nobody really likes what he says. Indeed, even in his own age Hobbes's views were vastly unpopular—libertarians detested them for obvious reasons, and royalists hated them as much because Hobbes was contemptuous of dynastic claims based on blood lineage and rationalized absolutistic rule not on the grounds of powers granted from God, as most royalists did, but on powers surrendered by society. Yet because many important thinkers felt compelled to argue against Hobbes, he had enormous influence, if only in provoking the responses of others.

Perhaps the most moving attempt to bring light out of pervasive darkness was that of the seventeenth-century French moral and religious philosopher Blaise Pascal (1623–1662). Pascal began his career as a mathematician and scientific rationalist. A modern computer language has been named for him because he constructed the first calculating machine. (He did this when he was nineteen years old.) But at age thirty Pascal abandoned science as the result of a conversion experience and became a firm adherent of Jansenism, a puritanical faction within French Catholicism. From then till his death he worked on a highly ambitious philosophical-religious project meant to persuade doubters of the truth of Christianity by appealing simultaneously to their intellects and their emotions. Unfortunately, because of his premature death all that came of this was his *Pensées* (*Thoughts*), a collection of fragments and short informal pieces about religion written with great literary power. In these he argued that faith alone could show the way to salvation and that "the heart has its reasons of which reason itself knows nothing." Pascal's *Pensées* express the author's own sense of terror and anguish in the face of evil and eternity, but make the awe itself a sign of the existence of God. Individuals today will be moved by this work in varying degrees according to their own convictions, but few of any persuasion will dispute Pascal's proposition that "man knows he is wretched; he is therefore wretched because he is so; but he is very great because he knows it."

Blaise Pascal

5. LITERATURE AND THE ARTS

The combined wretchedness and greatness of humanity may be taken as the theme for the extraordinary profusion of towering works of literature and art produced during Western Europe's period of crisis from 1560 to 1660. Of course not every single writing or painting of the era expressed

Grappling with the human condition

the same message. During a hundred years of extraordinary literary and artistic creativity, works of all genres and sentiments were produced, ranging from the frothiest farces to the darkest tragedies, the serenest still lifes to the most grotesque scenes of religious martyrdom. Nonetheless, the greatest writers and painters of the period all were moved by a realization of the ambiguities and ironies of human existence not unlike that expressed in different ways by Montaigne and Pascal. They all were fully aware of the horrors of war and human suffering so rampant in their day, and all were directly or indirectly aware of the Protestant conviction that men are "vessels of iniquity," but they also inherited a large degree of Renaissance affirmativeness, and most of them accordingly preferred to view life on earth as a great dare.

From the host of remarkable writers who flourished during what was probably the most extraordinary century in the entire history of Western European poetry and drama, we may take the very greatest: Cervantes, the Elizabethan dramatists—Shakespeare to the fore—and John Milton. Although Miguel de Cervantes (1547–1616) was not strictly speaking either a poet or a dramatist, his masterpiece, the satirical romance *Don Quixote,* exudes great lyricism and drama. The plot recounts the adventures of a Spanish gentleman, Don Quixote of La Mancha, who has become slightly unbalanced by constant reading of chivalric epics. His mind filled with all kinds of fantastic adventures, he sets out at the age of fifty upon the slippery road of knight-errantry, imagining windmills to be glowering giants and flocks of sheep to be armies of infidels whom it is his duty to rout with his spear. In his distorted fancy he mistakes inns for castles and serving girls for courtly ladies on fire with love. Set off in contrast to the "knight-errant" is the figure of his faithful squire, Sancho Panza. The latter represents the ideal of the practical man, with his feet on the ground and content with the modest but substantial pleasures of eating, drinking, and sleeping. Yet Cervantes clearly does not wish to say that the realism of a Sancho Panza is categorically preferable to the "quixotic" idealism of his master. Rather, the two men represent different facets of human nature. Without any doubt, Don Quixote is a devastating satire on the anachronistic chivalric mentality that would soon help hasten Spain's decline. But for all that, the reader's sympathies remain with the protagonist, the man from La Mancha who dares to "dream the impossible dream."

Directly contemporaneous with Cervantes were the English Elizabethan dramatists who collectively produced the most glorious age of theater known in the Western world. Writing after England's victory over the Spanish Armada, when national pride was at a peak, all exhibited great exuberance but none was by any means a facile optimist. In fact a strain of reflective seriousness pervades all their best works, and a few, like the tragedian John Webster (c. 1580–c. 1625), who "saw the skull beneath the skin," were if anything morbid pessimists. Literary critics tend to agree that of a bevy of great Elizabethan playwrights the most outstanding were Christopher Marlowe (1564–1593), Ben Jonson (c. 1572–1637), and, of course, William Shakespeare (1564–1616). Of the three, the fiery Mar-

Miguel de Cervantes

Elizabethan drama

lowe, whose life was cut short in a tavern brawl before he reached the age of thirty, was the most youthfully energetic. In plays such as *Tamburlaine* and *Doctor Faustus* Marlowe created larger-than-life heroes who seek and come close to conquering everything in their path and feeling every possible sensation. But they meet unhappy ends because, for all his vitality, Marlowe knew that there are limits on human striving, and that wretchedness as well as greatness lies in the human lot. Thus though Faustus asks a reincarnated Helen of Troy, conjured up by Satan, to make him "immortal with a kiss," he dies and is damned in the end because immortality is not awarded by the devil or found in earthly kisses. In contrast to the heroic tragedian Marlowe, Ben Jonson wrote corrosive comedies that expose human vices and foibles. In the particularly bleak *Volpone* Jonson shows people behaving like deceitful and lustful animals, but in the later *Alchemist* he balances an attack on quackery and gullibility with admiration for resourceful lower-class characters who cleverly take advantage of their supposed betters.

Incomparably the greatest of the Elizabethan dramatists, William Shakespeare, was born into the family of a tradesman in the provincial town of Stratford-on-Avon. His life is enshrouded in more mists of obscurity than the careers of most other great people. It is known that he left his native village, having gained little formal education, when he was about twenty, and that he drifted to London to find employment in the theater. How he eventually became an actor and still later a writer of plays is uncertain, but by the age of twenty-eight he had definitely acquired a reputation as an author sufficient to excite the jealousy of his rivals. Before he retired to his native Stratford about 1610 to spend the rest of his days in ease, he had written or collaborated in writing nearly forty plays, over and above 150 sonnets and two long narrative poems.

As everyone knows, Shakespeare's plays rank as a kind of secular Bible wherever the English language is spoken. The reasons lie not only in the author's unrivaled gift of expression, and in his scintillating wit, but most of all in his profound analysis of human character seized by passion and tried by fate. Shakespeare's dramas fall rather naturally into three groups. Those written during the playwright's earlier years are characterized by a sense of confidence. They include a number of history plays, which recount England's struggles and glories leading up to the triumph of the Tudor dynasty; the lyrical romantic tragedy *Romeo and Juliet;* and a wide variety of comedies including the magical *Midsummer Night's Dream* and Shakespeare's greatest creations in the comic vein—*Twelfth Night, As You Like It,* and *Much Ado about Nothing.* Despite the last-named title, few even of the plays of Shakespeare's early, lightest period are "much ado about nothing." Rather, most explore with wisdom as well as wit fundamental problems of psychological identity, honor and ambition, love and friendship. Occasionally they also contain touches of deep seriousness, as in *As You Like It,* when Shakespeare has a character pause to reflect that "all the world's a stage, and all the men and women merely players" who pass through seven "acts" or stages of life.

William Shakespeare. Portrait made for the First Folio edition of his works, 1623.

Shakespeare's three periods: (1) confidence

(2) crisis

Such touches, however, never obscure the restrained optimism of Shakespeare's first period, whereas the plays from his second period are far darker in mood. Apparently around 1601 Shakespeare underwent a crisis during which he began to distrust human nature profoundly and to indict the whole scheme of the universe. The result was a group of dramas characterized by bitterness, frequent pathos, and a troubled searching into the mysteries of things. The series begins with the tragedy of indecisive idealism represented by *Hamlet,* goes on to the cynicism of *Measure for Measure* and *All's Well That Ends Well,* and culminates in the cosmic tragedies of *Macbeth* and *King Lear,* wherein characters assert that "life's but a walking shadow . . . a tale told by an idiot, full of sound and fury signifying nothing," and that "as flies to wanton boys are we to the gods; they kill us for their sport." Despite all this gloom, however, the plays of Shakespeare's second period generally contain the dramatist's greatest flights of poetic grandeur.

(3) reconciliation

Although *Macbeth* and *Lear* suggest an author in the throes of deep depression, Shakespeare managed to resolve his personal crisis and end his dramatic career with a third period characterized by a profound spirit of reconciliation. Of the three plays (all idyllic romances) written during this final period, the last, *The Tempest,* is the greatest. Here ancient animosities are buried and wrongs are righted by a combination of natural and supernatural means, and a wide-eyed, youthful heroine rejoices on first seeing men with the words "O brave new world, that has such people in it!" Here, then, Shakespeare seems to be saying that for all humanity's trials life is not so unrelentingly bitter after all, and the divine plan of the universe is somehow benevolent and just.

Though less versatile than Shakespeare, not far behind him in eloquent grandeur stands the Puritan poet John Milton (1608–1674). The leading publicist of Oliver Cromwell's regime, Milton wrote the official defense of the beheading of Charles I as well as a number of treatises justifying Puritan positions in contemporary affairs. But he was also a man full of contradictions who loved the Greek and Latin classics at least as much as the Bible. Hence he could write a perfect pastoral elegy, *Lycidas,* mourning the loss of a dear friend in purely classical terms. Later, when forced into retirement by the accession of Charles II, Milton, though now blind, embarked on writing a classical epic, *Paradise Lost,* out of material found in Genesis concerning the creation of the world and the fall of man. This magnificent poem, which links the classical tradition to Christianity more successfully than any literary work written before or since, is surely one of the greatest epics of all time. Setting out to "justify the ways of God to man," Milton in *Paradise Lost* first plays "devil's advocate" by creating the compelling character of Satan, who defies God with boldness and subtlety. But Satan is more than counterbalanced in the end by the real "epic hero" of *Paradise Lost,* Adam, who learns to accept the human lot of moral responsibility and suffering, and is last seen leaving Paradise with Eve, the world "all before them."

John Milton. From the First Edition of his poems, 1645.

The ironies and tensions inherent in human existence also were portrayed with extraordinary eloquence and profundity by several immortal masters of the visual arts who flourished between 1560 and 1660. The dominant style in painting in Italy and Spain in the second half of the sixteenth century was Mannerism. Originally a term of opprobrium for alleged imitators—supposedly second-rate artists who painted in the "manner" of Michelangelo's late phase—the term Mannerism in current analysis has come to mean much more than that; indeed art historians now rank some Mannerist painters among the West's greatest masters. Unquestionably Mannerism did take as its point of departure Michelangelo's tendency toward anticlassicism and distortion of nature for emotional effects, but Mannerist painters went so much further in emphasizing restlessness, imbalance, and distortion that they left Michelangelo far behind. Admittedly many of them lacked skill and depth of vision, contenting themselves with protraying brawn instead of muscle, melodrama instead of drama. But some others fully succeeded in balancing great artistic virtuosity with the communication of radiant inner light.

Fray Felix Hortensio Paravicino, by El Greco. More restrained in composition than most of the artist's other work, this portrait nonetheless communicates a sense of deep spiritual intensity.

Of the latter, the two most outstanding are the Venetian Tintoretto (1518–1594) and the Spaniard El Greco (c. 1541–1614). Combining Manneristic distortion and restlessness with a traditionally Venetian taste for rich color, Tintoretto produced an enormous number of monumentally large canvases devoted to religious themes that still inspire awe with their broodingly shimmering light and gripping theatricality. More emotional still is the work of Tintoretto's disciple, El Greco. Born Domenikos Theotokopoulos on the Greek island of Crete, this extraordinary painter absorbed some of the stylized elongation characteristic of Greco-Byzantine icon painting before traveling to Italy to learn from great contemporary Mannerist painters such as Tintoretto. He then finally settled in Spain, where he was nicknamed "El Greco"—Spanish for "the Greek." El Greco's paintings were too bizarre to be greatly appreciated in his own age, and even now they often appear so unbalanced as to seem the work of one almost deranged. Yet such a view slights El Greco's deeply mystical Catholic fervor

The Laocoön, by El Greco. An extreme example of Manneristic stress on restlessness and distortion. Note that the Spanish painter here drew for inspiration on the famous Hellenistic sculpture group shown on p. 155.

Left: *David,* by Bernini. Whereas the earlier conceptions of David by the Renaissance sculptors Donatello and Michelangelo were reposeful (see pp. 417 and 418), the Baroque sculptor Bernini chose to portray his young hero at the peak of physical exertion. Right: *St. Theresa in Ecstasy,* by Bernini. As David is seen at the peak of bodily exertion, St. Theresa is shown at the peak of spiritual transport.

See color plates following page 492 for the *Crucifixion* by Tintoretto and the *View of Toledo* by El Greco

Baroque style

as well as his technical achievements. Best known today is his transfigured landscape, the *View of Toledo,* with its somber but awesome light breaking where no sun shines. But equally inspiring are his swirling religious scenes such as *The Burial of Count Orgaz* (thought by the painter to be his masterpiece), and his myriad stunning portraits in which gaunt, dignified Spaniards radiate a rare blend of austerity and spiritual insight.

The dominant artistic school of southern Europe succeeding Mannerism was that of the Baroque, a school not just of painting but of sculpture and architecture, lasting from about 1600 until the early 1700s. The term *Baroque* is derived from a Portuguese word for an irregular, rough pearl, and this reveals much about its meaning. Picking up where Mannerism left off, the Baroque style emphasized the emotional and the swirling as much as Mannerism, but Baroque works of art characteristically were less shrouded by somber mystery and were far more affirmative than Manneristic paintings. One major explanation for this is that Baroque art in all genres was usually semipropagandistic. Originating in Rome as an expression of the ideals of the Counter-Reformation papacy and the Jesuit order, Baroque architecture in particular aimed to gain adherence for a specific worldview. Similarly, Baroque painting often was done in the service of the Counter-Reformation Church, which at its high tide around 1620 seemed everywhere to be on the offensive. When Baroque painters were not celebrating Counter-Reformation ideals, most of them worked in the service of monarchs who sought their own glorification.

Indubitably the most imaginative and influential figure of the original Roman Baroque was the architect and sculptor Gianlorenzo Bernini (1598–1680), a frequent employee of the papacy who created one of the most magnificent celebrations of papal grandeur in the sweeping colonnades leading up to St. Peter's Basilica. Breaking with the serene Renaissance classicism of Palladio, Bernini's architecture retained the use of classical elements such as columns and domes, but combined them in ways meant to express both aggressive restlessness and great power. In addition Bernini was one of the first to experiment with church facades built "in depth"—building frontages not conceived as continuous surfaces but that jutted out at odd angles and seemingly invaded the open space in front of them. If the purpose of these innovations was to draw the viewer emotionally into the ambit of the work of art, the same may be said for Bernini's aims in sculpture. Harking back to the restless motion of Hellenistic statuary—particularly the Laocoön group—and building on tendencies already present in the later sculpture of Michelangelo, Bernini's statuary emphasizes drama and incites the viewer to respond to it rather than serenely to observe.

The Church of S. Carlo alle Quattro Fontane, Rome. Built by Bernini's contemporary Francesco Borromini in 1665, the facade of S. Carlo well exemplifies the frontage "in depth" characteristic of Baroque architecture.

Since most Italian Baroque painters lacked Bernini's artistic genius, to view the very greatest masterpieces of southern European Baroque painting one must look to Spain and the work of Diego Velázquez (1599–1660). Unlike Bernini, Velázquez, a court painter in Madrid just when Spain hung on the brink of ruin, was not an entirely typical exponent of the

The Surrender of Breda, by Velázquez. Celebrating a Spanish victory over the Dutch in an early phase of the Thirty Years' War, the Spanish lances point proudly skyward in contrast to the desolate Dutch smoke, but the Spanish commander displays magnanimity for the defeated enemy.

A Dwarf, by Velázquez. The great Spanish artist had an enduring fascination with the less favored of the earth.

See color plates following page 492 for *Maids of Honor* and *Pope Innocent X* by Velázquez and *Harvesters* by Brueghel

Baroque style. Certainly many of his canvases display a characteristically Baroque delight in motion, drama, and power, but Velázquez's best work is characterized by a more restrained thoughtfulness than is usually found in the Baroque. Thus his famous *Surrender of Breda* shows muscular horses and splendid Spanish grandees on the one hand, but un–Baroque humane and deep sympathy for defeated, disarrayed troops on the other. Moreover, Velázquez's single greatest painting, *The Maids of Honor,* done around 1656 after Spain's collapse, radiates thoughtfulness rather than drama and is one of the most probing artistic examinations of illusion and reality ever executed.

Southern Europe's main northern rival for artistic laurels in the "iron century" was the Netherlands, where three extremely dissimilar painters all explored the theme of the greatness and wretchedness of man to the fullest. The earliest, Peter Brueghel (c. 1525–1569), worked in a vein related to earlier Netherlandish realism. But unlike his predecessors, who favored quiet urban scenes, Brueghel exulted in portraying the busy, elemental life of the peasantry. Most famous in this respect are his rollicking *Peasant Wedding* and *Peasant Wedding Dance,* and his spacious *Harvesters,* in which guzzling and snoring fieldhands are taking a well-deserved break from their heavy labors under the noon sun. Such vistas give the impression of uninterrupted rhythms of life, but late in his career Brueghel became appalled by the intolerance and bloodshed he witnessed during the time of the Calvinist riots and the Spanish repression in the Netherlands and expressed his criticism in an understated yet searing manner. In *The Blind Leading the Blind,* for example, we see what happens when ignorant fanatics start showing the way to each other. More powerful still is Brueghel's *Massacre of the Innocents,* which from a distance looks like a snug scene of a Flemish village buried in snow. In fact, however, heartless soldiers are methodically breaking into homes and slaughtering babies, the simple peasant folk are fully at their mercy, and the artist—alluding to a Gospel forgotten by war-

The Massacre of the Innocents. This painting by Brueghel shows how effectively art can be used as a means of social commentary. Many art historians believe that Brueghel was tacitly depicting the suffering of the Netherlands at the hands of the Spanish in his own day.

The Triumph of the Eucharist, by Rubens. A typical Baroque work, this painting proclaims the victory of the Cross and the Eucharistic Chalice, symbols of Counter-Reformation Catholicism.

ring Catholics and Protestants alike—seems to be saying "as it happened in the time of Christ, so it happens now."

Vastly different from Brueghel was the Netherlandish Baroque painter Peter Paul Rubens (1577–1640). Since the Baroque, unlike Mannerism, was an international movement closely linked to the spread of the Counter-Reformation, it should offer no surprise that Baroque style was extremely well represented in just that part of the Netherlands which, after long warfare, had been retained by Spain. In fact, Rubens of Antwerp was a far more typical Baroque artist than Velázquez of Madrid, painting literally thousands of robust canvases that glorified resurgent Catholicism or exalted second-rate aristocrats by portraying them as epic heroes dressed in bearskins. Even when Rubens's intent was not overly propagandistic he customarily revelled in the sumptuous extravagance of the Baroque manner, being perhaps most famous today for the pink and rounded flesh of his well-nourished nudes. But unlike a host of lesser Baroque artists, Rubens was not entirely lacking in subtlety and was a man of many moods. His gentle portrait of his son Nicholas catches unaffected childhood in a moment of repose, and though throughout most of his career Rubens had celebrated martial valor, his late *Horrors of War* movingly portrays what he himself called "the grief of unfortunate Europe, which, for so many years now, has suffered plunder, outrage, and misery."

In some ways a blend of Brueghel and Rubens, the greatest of all Netherlandish painters, Rembrandt van Rijn (1606–1669), defies all attempts at facile characterization. Living across the border from the Spanish Netherlands in staunchly Calvinistic Holland, Rembrandt belonged to a society that was too austere to tolerate the unbuckled realism of a Brueghel

See color plates following page 492 for the *Horrors of War* and *England and Scotland Crowning Charles I* by Rubens

Rubens's Portrait of his Son Nicholas.

The Polish Rider, by Rembrandt. Unlike Titian's equestrian Charles V (above, p. 493), Rembrandt's rider is self-reflective and hence more humane.

See color plates following page 492 for *Aristotle Contemplating the Bust of Homer* by Rembrandt

or the fleshy Baroque pomposity of a Rubens. Yet Rembrandt managed to put both realistic and Baroque traits to new uses. In his early career he gained fame and fortune as the painter of biblical scenes that lacked the Baroque's fleshiness but retained its grandeur in their swirling forms and stunning experiments with light. In this early period too Rembrandt was active as a realistic portrait painter who knew how to flatter his self-satisfied subjects by emphasizing their Calvinistic steadfastness, to the great advantage of his purse. But gradually his prosperity faded, apparently in part because he grew tired of flattering and definitely because he made some bad investments. Since personal tragedies also mounted in the painter's middle and declining years his art inevitably became far more pensive and sombre, but it gained in dignity, subtle lyricism, and awesome mystery. Thus his later portraits, including those of himself, are imbued with introspective qualities and a suggestion that only the half is being told. Equally moving are explicitly philosophical paintings such as *Aristotle Contemplating the Bust of Homer,* in which the supposedly earthbound philosopher seems spellbound by the otherworldly luminous radiance of the epic poet, and *The Polish Rider,* in which realistic and Baroque elements merge into a higher synthesis portraying a pensive young man setting out fearlessly into a perilous world. Like Shakespeare, Rembrandt knew that life's journey is full of perils, but his most mature paintings suggest that these can be mastered with poetry and courage.

• *Items so designated are available in paperback editions.*

• Aston, T., ed., *Crisis in Europe: 1560–1660,* London, 1965. A collection of highly valuable essays.
• Braudel, F., *The Mediterranean and the Mediterranean World in the Age of Philip II,* 2 vols., New York, 1972. One of the most brilliant history books of our age. Treats life in the Mediterranean regions in the second half of the sixteenth century with particular emphasis on how geography determines the course of human history.
• Chute, M., *Shakespeare of London,* New York, 1949. The best popular biography.
• Dean, Leonard F., ed., *Shakespeare: Modern Essays in Criticism,* New York, 1958. A variety of scholarly appraisals.
• Dunn, Richard S., *The Age of Religious Wars, 1559–1715,* 2nd ed., New York, 1979. The best college-level text on this period. Extremely well written.
• Elliott, J. H., *Imperial Spain, 1469–1716,* London, 1963. A splendid work of synthesis.
• ———, *Europe Divided: 1559–1598,* London, 1968. An extremely lucid narrative of complex events.
• ———, *Richelieu and Olivares,* New York, 1984. Brilliant comparative history setting off similarities and differences between seventeenth-century France and Spain.
• Elton, G. R., *England under the Tudors,* 2nd ed., London, 1977. Engagingly written and authoritative.
• Frame, D., *Montaigne: A Biography,* New York, 1965. By far the best study in English.
• Fraser, Lady Antonia, *Cromwell: The Lord Protector,* London, 1973. A popular biography.
• Held, J. S., and D. Posner, *17th and 18th Century Art: Baroque Painting, Sculpture, Architecture,* New York, 1979. The most complete introductory review of the subject in English.
• Hibbard, Howard, *Bernini,* Baltimore, 1965. The basic study in English of this central figure of Baroque artistic activity.
• Hill, Christopher, *A Century of Revolution: 1603–1714,* 2nd ed., New York, 1982. A valuable survey of English developments that holds narrative to a minimum and stresses economic and social trends.
• Hirst, Derek, *Authority and Conflict: England, 1603–1658,* London, 1986. Integrates recent interpretations. The best survey out of several available.
• Kahr, M. M., *Velázquez: The Art of Painting,* New York, 1976.
  Kamen, Henry, *The Iron Century: Social Change in Europe, 1559–1660,* New York, 1971. One of the most detailed and persuasive statements of the view that there was a "general crisis" in many different aspects of European life.
  Le Roy Ladurie, Emmanuel, *Carnival in Romans,* New York, 1979. A close-up view of social turmoil in France in 1580.
• Levack, Brian P., *The Witch-Hunt in Early Modern Europe,* New York, 1987.
• Mattingly, Garrett, *The Armada,* Boston, 1959. Fascinating narrative; thoroughly reliable but reads like a novel.

- Monter, E. W., ed., *European Witchcraft,* New York, 1969. Selected readings with fine introductions by one of the world's leading experts.
- Parker, Geoffrey, *The Dutch Revolt,* rev. ed., Ithaca, N.Y., 1989. The standard survey in English on the revolt of the Netherlands.
- ———, *Europe in Crisis: 1598–1648,* Brighton, Sussex, 1980. A primarily political narrative of war and revolution in Europe exclusive of England.
- Pennington, D. H., *Seventeenth-Century Europe,* London, 1970. An extremely thorough and reliable survey that follows the conventional periodization of treating a century bounded by the round numbers 1600 and 1700.

  Pierson, Peter, *Philip II of Spain,* London, 1975. An absorbing attempt to study Philip's personality and actions in terms of the dominant assumptions of his age.
- Rabb, T. K., *The Struggle for Stability in Early Modern Europe,* New York, 1975. A stimulating essay arguing for a shift from crisis to stability around 1660.

  Roots, Ivan, ed., *Cromwell, A Profile,* New York, 1973. A collection of readings on problems in interpretation; complements Fraser.
- Rosenberg, Jakob, *Rembrandt: Life and Work,* London, 1964.
- Russell, Conrad, *The Crisis of Parliaments: English History, 1509–1660,* New York, 1971. The best survey covering this broad range of time.
- Shearman, John, *Mannerism,* Baltimore, 1967. Treats trends in late-sixteenth-century architecture and sculpture as well as Manneristic painting.
- Steinberg, S. H., *The Thirty Years' War and the Conflict for European Hegemony, 1600–1660,* New York, 1966. The best scholarly account.
- Stone, Lawrence, *The Causes of the English Revolution, 1529–1642,* New York, 1972. A judicious analysis by one of the foremost social historians of our age.
- Thomas, Keith, *Religion and the Decline of Magic,* London, 1971. A marvelously insightful broad-gauged study of popular belief in England.
- Walzer, Michael, *The Revolution of the Saints: A Study in the Origins of Radical Politics,* Cambridge, Mass., 1965. An attempt by a political scientist to demonstrate that English Puritanism was the earliest form of modern political radicalism.
- Wedgwood, C. V., *William the Silent,* London, 1944. A laudatory and urbanely written biography.

SOURCE MATERIALS

- Cervantes, Miguel de, *Don Quixote,* tr. Walter Starkie, New York, 1957.

  Hobbes, Thomas, *Leviathan,* abridged by F. B. Randall, New York, 1964.
- Montaigne, Michel de, *Essays,* tr. J. M. Cohen, Baltimore, 1958.

  Pascal, Blaise, *Pensées,* French-English ed., H. F. Stewart, London, 1950.

  Sprenger, Jakob, and H. Kramer, *The Malleus Maleficarum,* tr. M. Summers, 2nd ed., London, 1948. A frightful yet fascinating work, the *Malleus* ("The Hammer of Witches") was the most frequently used handbook of early-modern witchcraft prosecutors.

Chapter 16

THE ECONOMY AND SOCIETY OF EARLY-MODERN EUROPE

We ought to esteem and cherish those trades which we have in remote or far countries, for besides the increase in shipping and mariners thereby, the wares also sent thither and received from thence are far more profitable unto the kingdom than by our trades near at hand.

—Thomas Mun, *England's Treasure by Foreign Trade,* 1630

In nearly every state in Europe citizens are divided into the three orders of nobles, clergy, and people. . . . Even Plato, although he intended all his citizens to enjoy an equality of rights and privileges, divided them into the three orders of guardians, soldiers and labourers. All this goes to show that there never was a commonwealth, real or imaginary, even if conceived in the most popular terms, where citizens were in truth equal in all rights and privileges. Some always have more, some less than the rest.

—Jean Bodin, *Six Books of the Commonwealth,* 1570

A ny study of early-modern European society must concern itself with change, with the factors that in the two hundred years after 1600 were powerful enough to produce the political upheaval of the French Revolution and the economic stimulus for the Industrial Revolution. Arguably, the most profound change during that period was economic. By the latter part of the eighteenth century, the freebooting overseas expansionism that had begun in the sixteenth century with the Spanish *conquistadors* had ended with Europe at the center of a vast system of worldwide trade. Commerce on this increasingly global scale had given birth to institutions fashioned for its support, and had altered patterns of living among those caught up in its overpowering dynamic. Banks and joint-stock companies financed international commercial ventures. New urban workshops responded to the intensified demand for manufactured goods. As international banking developed into a highly sophisticated profession, its practitioners became powerful men. As urban workshops imposed new

Economic change

525

*New economic realities and
old social forms*

conditions and habits, the urban artisan was forced to bend uncomfortably to unfamiliar demands.

European society as a whole found bending no more comfortable. Change was imposed upon national communities which, in many cases, were still defined according to the hierarchies of the Middle Ages: landlord and peasant, nobleman and serf. Each order was expected to acknowledge its inherent obligations and responsibilities, as each was assumed to be part of an organic and divinely sanctioned communal whole. Where, within this preordained structure, was the independent commercial entrepreneur or the dispossessed laborer supposed to fit? Tension of this sort between old forms and new realities was further exacerbated by the general crisis that we analyzed in the preceding chapter. Change produced by economic expansion and dislocation occurred against the background of civil and religious turmoil that tore much of Europe to pieces in the seventeenth century, and against an equally disruptive cycle of demographic swings caused by warfare and disease, by good weather one year, bad weather—and hence famine—the next. Those were the changes closest to the lives of most Europeans, the men and women still bound to the land, for whom, as the French historian Pierre Goubert has observed, "death was at the center of life, just as the graveyard was at the center of the village." The concerns of this chapter are thus both the economic and social circumstances that produced change over a period of almost two hundred years, and the habits and traditions that were making change complex and difficult.

1. LIFE AND DEATH: PATTERNS OF POPULATION

No facts better illustrate the degree to which the two hundred years of European history between 1600 and 1800 were subject to chance and change than those having to do with life and death—patterns of population, as they imprinted themselves across the early-modern period.

The threat of famine

The pattern of life for most Europeans centered on the struggle to stay alive. They lived and worked within a subsistence economy, considering themselves extremely fortunate if they could grow or earn what it took to survive. In most instances their enemy was not an invading army, but famine; it is not surprising that one's well-being was measured simply by one's girth. At least once a decade, climatic conditions—usually a long period of summer rainfall—would produce a devastatingly bad harvest, which in turn would result in widespread malnutrition often leading to serious illness and death. A family might survive for a time by eating less; but eventually, with its meager stocks exhausted and the cost of grain high, the human costs would mount. The substitution of grass, nuts, and tree bark for grain on which the peasants depended almost entirely for nourishment was as inadequate for them as it appears pathetic to us.

Widespread crop failures occurred at fairly regular intervals—the worst in France, for example, about every thirty years (1597, 1630, 1662, 1694).

They helped to cause the series of population crises that are the outstanding feature of early-modern demographic history. Poor harvests and the high prices produced by a scarcity of grain meant not only undernourishment and possible starvation, but increasing unemployment: with fewer crops to be harvested, more money was spent on food and, consequently, less on manufactured goods. The despair such conditions could easily breed would in turn contribute to a postponement of marriage and of births, and thus to a population decline. The patterns of marriages and births revealed in local parish registers indicate that throughout Europe the populations of individual communities rose and fell dramatically in rhythm with the fortunes of the harvest.

Population crises

An undernourished population is a population particularly susceptible to disease. Bubonic plague ravaged seventeenth-century Europe. Severe outbreaks occurred in Seville in 1649, in Amsterdam in 1664, and in London the following year. By 1700 it had all but disappeared; it last appeared in Western Europe in a small area of southern France in 1720, though Moscow suffered an outbreak as late as 1771. Despite the gradual retreat of the plague, however, other diseases took a dreadful toll, in an age when available medical treatment was little more than crude guesswork, and in any event, beyond the reach of the poor. Epidemics of dysentery, small-pox, and typhus occurred with savage regularity. As late as 1779, over 100,000 people died of dysentery in the French province of Brittany. Most diseases attacked rich and poor impartially. Water supplies in towns and in the country were contaminated by heedless disposal of human waste and by

Health and sanitation

Left: *A Plague Hospital in Vienna*. The efforts to contain outbreaks of plague by gathering the sick in establishments such as this and burying the dead on the site proved unsuccessful. Right: *A Physician's Mask*. This German device containing smelling salts in its curved beak was designed to combat the plague, which physicians incorrectly believed was spread by poisonous vapors.

"Summer Amusement: Bugg Hunting." In this joking treatment of
one of the facts of everyday life
the bedbugs meet sudden death
in a full chamber pot.

*Implications of the European
marriage pattern*

all manner of garbage and urban filth. Bathing, feared at one time as a
method of spreading disease, was by no means a weekly habit, whatever
the social status of the household. Samuel Pepys, a prosperous servant of
the crown in seventeenth-century London, recorded in his diary that his
housemaid was in the habit of picking the lice from his scalp, that he took
his first bath only after his wife had taken hers and experienced the pleasures of cleanliness, and that he had, on occasion, thought nothing of using
the fireplace in his bedroom as a toilet, the maid having failed to provide
him with a chamberpot. If such was Pepys's attitude toward hygiene and
sanitation, imagine that of the poverty-stricken peasant, and the threat to
health implicit in such attitudes.

The precariousness of life helped encourage most men and women in
early-modern Europe to wed much later than in traditional societies in Asia
and Africa. Men and women were unwilling to risk binding their fortunes
to others' until assured to a degree of their own ability to survive. This exceptional pattern found women marrying, on average, at twenty-five years
of age, men at twenty-seven or twenty-eight, by which time they hoped to
have accumulated sufficient resources to establish a household. Young couples lived on their own, and not, as in societies elsewhere, as part of "extended" families of three generations. Since a son could not inherit until
his father died, he was compelled to establish himself independently, and to
postpone starting his own family until he had done so. Though historians
have failed to find a clear explanation for this pattern of later marriages, it
may have resulted from a growing desire on the part of younger men and
women for a higher standard of living. Late marriage helped to control the
birth rate. Once married, however, a couple generally produced their first
child within a year. Although subsequent children appeared with annual or
biennial regularity, long periods of breastfeeding, which tends to reduce

Eighteenth-Century   Sanitation.
"Nightmen" moved through city
streets after dark emptying the
refuse of privies.

the mother's fertility, and community disapproval of extramarital sexual relations went some way toward limiting childbirth.

Until the middle of the eighteenth century, populations continued to
wax and wane according to the outbreak of warfare, famine, and disease.
From about 1750 on, however, there was a steady and significant population increase, with almost all countries experiencing major growth. In
Russia, where territorial expansion added further to the increases, the population rate may have tripled in the second half of the eighteenth century.
Gains elsewhere, while not usually as spectacular, were nevertheless significant. The population of Prussia doubled; Hungary's more than tripled; and
England's population, which was about 5.5 million in 1700, reached 9 million in 1800. France, already in 1700 the most heavily populated country
in Europe (about 20 million), added a further 6 million before 1790.
Spaniards multiplied from 7.6 million in 1717 to 10.5 million in 1797. Although reasons for the population increase remain something of a mystery,
historians are inclined to agree that it was the cumulative result of a decrease in infant mortality and a very gradual decline in the death rate, due
in large measure to an equally gradual increase in the food supply. Better
transportation facilitated the shipment of food over greater distances. Land
clearances, particularly in England, and in Prussia and Russia, where territories were opened to colonization, provided an essential ingredient for increased production. New staples—the potato and maize—supplemented
the diets of the very poor. And although evidence here is only fragmentary,
it appears that whereas the climate of seventeenth-century Europe was ab-
normally bad, that of the succeeding hundred years was on the whole favorable.

Population increase brought with it new problems and new attitudes.
For example, in France, it meant pressure on the land, as more peasants attempted to wring survival from an overpopulated countryside. The consequence was migration from the country to the city. The decline in the
death rate among infants—along with an apparent increase in illegitimacy
at the end of the eighteenth century—created a growing population of unwanted babies among the poor. Some desperate women resorted to infanti-
cide, though since children murdered at birth died without benefit of baptism, the crime was stigmatized as especially heinous by the Church as well
as by society in general. More often, babies were abandoned at the door of
foundling hospitals. As an English benefactor of several such institutions,
Jonas Hanway, remarked in 1766, "it is much less difficult to the human
heart and the dictates of self-preservation to drop a child than to kill it." In
Paris during the 1780s from seven to eight thousand children were being
abandoned out of a total of thirty thousand new births. Paradoxically, some
historians now argue that during this same period the decrease in infant and
child mortality encouraged many parents to lavish care and affection on
their offspring in a way that they had not when the repeated early deaths of
their sons and daughters had taught them the futility of that emotional
bond.

Although somewhere between 80 and 90 percent of the population

*The "rise" of towns and
cities*

Shifts in urban population

*Ebb and flow of urban
growth*

*Growth of administrative
centers*

lived in small rural communities, towns and cities were coming to play an increasingly important role in the life of early-modern Europe. One must speak of the "rise" of towns and cities with caution, however, since the pace of urbanization varied greatly across the Continent. Russia remained almost entirely rural: only 2.5 percent of its population lived in towns in 1630, and that percentage had risen by only 0.5 percent by 1774. In Holland, on the other hand, 59 percent of the population was urban in 1627 and 65 percent in 1795.

The total number of urban dwellers did not vary markedly after the end of the sixteenth century, when there were approximately 200 cities in Europe with a population of over 10,000. What did change between 1600 and 1800 was, first, the way in which those cities were distributed across the map, concentrated increasingly in the north and west; and second, the growing proportion of very large cities to the whole. The patterns of trade and commerce had much to do with these shifts. Cities like Hamburg in Germany, Liverpool in England, Toulon in France, and Cadiz in Spain grew by about 250 percent between 1600 and 1750. Amsterdam, the hub of early-modern international commerce, increased from 30,000 in 1530 to 115,000 in 1630 and 200,000 by 1800. Naples, the busy Mediterranean port, went from a population of 300,000 in 1600 to nearly half a million by the late eighteenth century. Where goods were traded, processed, and manufactured, fleets built and provisioned, people flocked to work. An eighteenth-century commentator noted that the laborers in Paris were "almost all foreigners"—that is, men and women born outside the city: carpenters from Savoy, water carriers from Auvergne, porters from Lyons, stonecutters from Normandy, wigmakers from Gascony, shoemakers from Lorraine.

As some cities expanded, others stagnated or declined as a result of commercial changes. Norwich, in England, grew at the expense of older industrial centers on the English Channel when the manufacture of woolen goods shifted north. The population of the important German market center of Frankfurt declined during and after the period of the Thirty Years' War, when difficulties of communication and the general instability caused by frequent military campaigns diverted much of its former business to Amsterdam.

The most spectacular urban population growth occurred in the administrative capitals of the increasingly centralized nations of Europe. By the middle of the eighteenth century, Madrid, Berlin, and St. Petersburg all had populations of over 100,000. London grew from 674,000 in 1700 to 860,000 a century later. Paris, a city of approximately 180,000 in 1600, increased to over half a million by 1800. Berlin grew from a population of 6,500 in 1661, to 60,000 in 1721, to 140,000 in 1783. Its increase was due in part to the fact that successive Prussian rulers undertook to improve its position as a trade center by the construction of canals that linked it with Breslau and Hamburg. Its population rose as well, however, because of the marked increase in Prussian army and bureaucratic personnel based in the capital city. Of the 140,000 citizens of Berlin in 1783, approximately 65,000 were state employees or members of their families.

2. THE DYNAMICS OF AGRICULTURE AND INDUSTRY

The dramatic shifts in population we have been tracing were in some cases the cause, in others the effect, of equally important changes occurring in agriculture and industry. Throughout most of the two-hundred-year period under review, agricultural production was generally carried on according to traditional techniques that kept the volume of production low, yet by the end of the eighteenth century, tradition in some areas had yielded to innovation, with the result that production was increasing dramatically.

Traditional techniques yield to innovation

Most of the agricultural regions of seventeenth-century Europe consisted of open fields. In the north, these fields were usually large sections of land, divided into long, narrow strips; in the south, the strips tended to reflect the more irregular shape of local landscapes. Although one or two rich proprietors might own as much as three-fourths of the land in an open-field village, that land did not comprise one solid block. Instead it was made up of a great many plots, seldom contiguous, within the various open fields that surrounded the village. Landholding was further complicated by local usage. In France, for example, a *seigneur* might own a group of estates (*seigneury*) whose boundaries were not contiguous with any one parish. A parish, in turn, might be dependent on more than one *seigneur*. A property owner's *desmesne* farm—which he worked with hired laborers for his own direct profit—and his tenant farms—those that he leased out to peasants—all consisted of bits and pieces of land that lay alongside other bits and pieces that belonged to other landowners—very often small peasant proprietors. Each large open field thus resembled a patchwork quilt. Under these circumstances, in order for the fields to be cultivated with any degree of ef-

The open-field system

The Open-Field System in Northern France, 1738. Note the subdivision of large tracts into narrow strips, each owned by different proprietors.

ficiency, all the "patches" had to be planted with the same crop, and sown, cultivated, and harvested together.

The inefficiency inherent in the management of a multitude of plots by many farmers was a price small peasant proprietors were willing to pay in return for the social utility of communal decision-making and the right to graze livestock on common land. Once landlords, particularly in England and Holland, began to compete for markets as capitalist agricultural entrepreneurs, however, they looked for ways to overcome the inefficiency of traditional practices, so as to improve the yield on their land.

Communal decision-making

By the end of the eighteenth century a great many English and Dutch landlords had resolved the problem of low production by adopting a full range of innovative farming techniques, the most drastic of which was the enclosure of open fields to allow for more systematic and therefore more productive farming. "Enclosure" was the term for land reorganization within a traditional village community. The earliest enclosures in England took place in the fifteenth and sixteenth centuries and entailed the conversion of lands into fenced-off sheep meadows. Because of the great profits to be accrued from wool, some landlords converted common pastures that hitherto had supported peasant livestock into their own preserves for sheep-raising, thus threatening the livelihood of entire peasant communities.

Enclosure

Enclosure was more easily accomplished in those countries—England most notably—where there was a system of absolute property rights and wage labor. Where the tradition of "common" rights to grazing and foraging was strong, as in France, landlords found it far more difficult to impose a new economic order. In France, as well, a large peasantry owned small plots of land outright, adding up to approximately one-third of all agricultural land. It had neither an interest in nor the financial capacity for change. Monarchs tended to oppose enclosure since it promised to enrich further a rival noble class. In seventeenth-century France the monarchy needed an economically stable peasantry to support its expanding tax programs, and therefore worked to secure peasants in the customary tenure of their farms. Thus defended, the peasants were better able to resist effectively attempts at enclosure launched by large landholders. English property owners were more fortunate, taking advantage of the absence of royal opposition during the Cromwellian period to enclose on a broad scale.

*Absolute vs. common
property rights*

The really dramatic enclosure movement in England took place, however, at the end of the early-modern period, between 1710 and 1810. Landlords began to engage in the practice of "scientific farming." They realized that by introducing new crops and farming methods they could reduce the amount of land kept fallow, and bring in higher yields, and thus higher profits. The most important new crops with which landowners experimented were clover, alfalfa, and related varieties of leguminous plants. These reduced fertility much less than cereal grains and helped to improve the quality of the soil by gathering nitrogen and making the ground more porous. Another new crop that had a similar effect was the turnip. The greatest propagandist for the planting of this unattractive vegetable was Vis-

Scientific farming

count Charles Townshend (1674–1738), a prominent aristocrat and politician, who toward the end of his life gained the nickname of "Turnip" Townshend because of his dedication to the use of the turnip in new crop-rotation systems.

Clover, alfalfa, and turnips not only helped do away with fallow lands; they also provided excellent winter food for animals, thereby aiding the production of more and better livestock. More livestock also meant more manure. Accordingly, intensive manuring became another way in which scientific farmers could eliminate the need for fallow land. Other improvements in farming methods introduced in the period were more intensive hoeing and weeding, and the use of the seed drill for planting grain. The latter eliminated the old wasteful method of sowing grain by hand, much of it remaining on top to be eaten by birds.

Scientific farming necessitated enclosures because the "improving" landlord needed flexibility to experiment as he wished. He could not plant one narrow open strip with turnips while peasants were continuing to rotate all the contiguous areas on the basis of the age-old system. Instead, he had to organize his land into fenced-off compact plots, to leave no doubt as to which territory was his own, to maximize efficiency in experimentation, and to exclude stray grazing animals. With the introduction of fodder crops such as clover the large landowner no longer needed common pastures, since he could now graze his livestock on his own fields; he was therefore likely to press for the enclosure of what had previously been set aside as common land.

Enclosure was a change that had major social consequences where it occurred. Village life under the open-field system was communal to the extent that decisions as to which crops were to be grown where and when had to be arrived at jointly. Common land afforded the poor not only a place to tether a cow, to fish, or to gather firewood, but to breathe at least a bit of the air of social freedom. Enclosure cost villagers their modest freedoms, as well as the traditional right to help determine how the community's subsistence economy was to be managed. Cottagers (very small landholders) and squatters, who had over generations established a customary right to the use of common lands, were reduced to the rank of landless laborers.

On the Continent, except for Holland, there was nothing comparable to the English advance in scientific farming. Nor, with the notable exception of Spain, was there a pronounced enclosure movement as in England and the Low Countries. Yet despite that fact, European food production became increasingly capitalistic in the seventeenth and eighteenth centuries. Landlords leased farms to tenants and reaped profits as rent. Often they allowed tenants to pay rent in the form of half their crops. This system of sharecropping was most prevalent in France, Italy, and Spain. Farther east, in Prussia, Poland, Hungary, and Russia, landowners continued to rely on unpaid serfs to till the land. But wherever the scale of production and marketing was altered to increase profits, it brought change in its wake.

The eighteenth century saw the introduction of two crops from the

The Title Page of One of Many Agricultural Tracts Available to Capitalist Farmers Interested in Improving Their Output

The social consequences of enclosure

The increasingly capitalistic basis of European agriculture

New World, maize (Indian corn) and the potato, which eventually resulted in the provision of a more adequate diet for the poor. Since maize can only be grown in areas with substantial periods of sunny and dry weather, its cultivation spread through Italy and the southeastern part of the Continent. Whereas an average ear of grain would yield only about four seeds for every one planted, an ear of maize would yield about seventy or eighty. That made it a "miracle" crop, filling granaries where they had been almost empty before. The potato was an equally miraculous innovation for the European north. Its advantages were numerous: potatoes could be grown on the poorest, sandiest, or wettest of lands where nothing else could be raised; they could be fitted into the smallest of patches. Raising potatoes even in small patches was profitable because the yield of potatoes was extraordinarily abundant. Finally, the potato provided an inexpensive means of improving the human diet. It is rich in calories, and contains many vitamins and minerals. Northern European peasants initially resisted growing and eating potatoes. Clergymen taught them to fear the plant because it is not mentioned in the Bible. Some claimed that it transmitted leprosy. Still others insisted that it was a cause of flatulence, a property acknowledged by the French *Encyclopédie* in 1765, although the writers added: "What is a little wind to the vigorous organs of the peasants and workers?" Yet in the course of the eighteenth century the poor grew accustomed to the potato, although sometimes after considerable pressure. Frederick the Great compelled Prussian peasants to cultivate potatoes until the crop achieved acceptance and became a staple throughout much of northern Germany. By about 1800 the average north German peasant family ate potatoes as a main course at least once a day.

Agriculture was not the only commercial enterprise in early-modern rural Europe. Increasingly, manufactured goods—particularly textiles—were being produced in the countryside, as entrepreneurs battled to circumvent artisanal and guild restrictions that limited production in urban manufacturing centers. Unfettered rural industry was a response to the constantly growing demand of new markets created by the increase in regional, national, and international commerce. Entrepreneurs made use of the so-called putting-out system to address this demand and to reap large profits. Unhampered by guild regulations, which in medieval times had restricted the production and distribution of textiles to maintain price levels, merchants would buy up a stock of raw material, most often wool or flax, which they would then "put out," or supply, to rural workers for carding (combing the fibers) and spinning. Once spun, the yarn or thread was collected by the merchant and passed to rural weavers, who wove it into cloth. Collected once more, the material was processed by other workers at bleaching or dyeing shops, and collected for a final time by the entrepreneur who then either sold it to a wholesaler or directly to retail customers.

Although the putting-out phenomenon—or, as it is often referred to, the process of *proto-industrialization*—occurred throughout Europe, it was usually concentrated regionally. Most industrial areas specialized in the production of particular commodities, based on the availability of raw materials. Flanders was a producer of linens; Verviers (in present-day Belgium) of woolens; Silesia of linens. As markets—regional, national, and international—developed, these rural manufacturing areas grew accordingly. Industries employed homeworkers by the thousands. A major mid-eighteenth century textile firm in Abbéville, France, provided work to 1,800 in central workshops but to 10,000 in their own homes. One of the largest woolen manufacturers in Linz, Austria, in 1786 was employing 35,000, of whom over 29,000 were domestic spinners. These figures emphasize once more the fact that change is the hallmark of the early-modern period. Proto-industrialization, as it occurred over a timespan of more than one hundred years, made Abbéville and Linz very different places in 1780 from what they had been in 1650.

Rural workers accepted this system of manufacture as a means of staving off poverty, or possible starvation in years of particularly bad harvests. Domestic textile production involved the entire family. Even the youngest children could participate in the process of cleaning the raw wool. Older children carded. Wives and husbands spun or wove. Spinning, until the invention of the jenny at the end of the eighteenth century (see below, p.

Left: *"Rustic Courtship."* This detail from an etching (1785) by the English satirist Thomas Rowlandson suggests the advantages of doorstep domestic industry: natural lighting, improved ventilation, and a chance to converse with visitors. Work under these self-paced conditions, though usually long and hard, was carried on to a personal rhythm. Right: *Artisan and Family* by Gerard ter Borch. This seventeenth-century wheelwright, though a skilled artisan, is nevertheless depicted as living on the brink of poverty. Sickness, a bad harvest, unemployment—any of these might easily drive him and his family over the edge.

699) was a far more time-consuming process than weaving, which had been speeded considerably by the Englishman John Kay's early-eighteenth-century invention of the fly-shuttle, a mechanical device that automatically returned the shuttle to its starting place after it had been "thrown" across the loom.

Advantages of putting-out

In addition to providing extra income, the putting-out system brought other advantages to rural homeworkers. They could regulate the pace of their labor to some degree, and could abandon it altogether when farm work was available during the planting and harvest seasons. Their ability to work at home was a mixed blessing, however, for conditions in cottages that were wretchedly built and poorly ventilated were often exceedingly cramped and unpleasant, especially when workers were compelled to accommodate a bulky loom within their already crowded living quarters. But domestic labor, however unpleasant, was preferable to work away from home in a shop, where conditions might be even more oppressive under the watchful eye of an unsympathetic master. There were also advantages for the merchant-entrepreneur, who benefited not only from the absence of guild restrictions, but from the fact that none of his capital was tied up in expensive equipment. (Spinners usually owned their spinning wheels; weavers either owned or rented their looms.) Governments appreciated the advantages of the system too, viewing it as one way to alleviate the ever-present problem of rural poverty. The French abolished the traditional privileges of urban manufacturers in 1762, acknowledging by law what economic demand had long since established: the widespread practice of unrestricted rural domestic production. By that time, proto-industrialization prevailed not only in northern France, but in the east and northeast of England, in Flanders, and in much of northern Germany—all areas where a mixed agricultural and manufacturing economy made economic sense to those engaged in it as entrepreneurs and producers.

Quality of life under the family system

Later generations, looking back nostalgically on the putting-out system, often compared it favorably to the factory system that displaced it. Life within the system's "family economy" was seldom other than hard, however. While workers could set their own pace to some extent, they remained subject to the demands of small, often inexperienced entrepreneurs who, misjudging their markets, might overload spinners and weavers with work at one moment, then abandon them for lack of orders the next. Though it often kept families from starvation, the system did little to mitigate the monotony and harshness of their lives. Its pressures are crudely if eloquently expressed in an English ballad, in which the weaver husband responds to his wife's complaint that she has no time to sit at the "bobbin wheel," what with the washing and baking and milking she must do. No matter, the husband replies. She must "stir about and get things done./ For all things must aside be laid,/ when we want help about our trade."

Textiles were not the only manufactured goods produced in the countryside. In France, for example, metal-working was as much a rural as an urban occupation, with migrant laborers providing a work force for small, self-contained shops. In various parts of Germany, the same sort of unregulated domestic manufacturing base prevailed: in the Black Forest for clock making, in Thuringia for toys. English production of iron grew fivefold from the mid-sixteenth to the late seventeenth century. The phenomenon of proto-industrialization increased demand for raw materials. Pressure on timber reserves for fuel led to widespread deforestation, with a resulting exploitation of coal reserves, particularly in the Rhineland, England, and the south Netherlands. In 1550 the English mined 200,000 tons of coal. By 1800 that figure had risen to 3 million.

Rural industry flourished despite the fact that for most of the early-modern period transportation systems remained rudimentary. In all but a very few cases, roads were little more than ill-defined tracks, full of holes as much as four feet deep, and all but impassable in the rain, when carts and carriages might stay mired in deep ruts for days. One of the few paved roads ran from Paris to Orléans, the main river port of France, but that was a notable exception. In general, no one could travel more than 12 miles an hour—"post haste" at a gallop on horseback—and speed such as that could be achieved only at the expense of fresh horses at each stage of the ride. In the late seventeenth century, a journey of 60 miles over good roads could be accomplished in twenty-four hours, provided that the weather was fair. To travel by coach from Paris to Lyons, a distance of approximately 250 miles, took ten days. Merchants ran great risks when they shipped perishable goods. Breakables were not expected to survive for more than 15 miles. Transportation of goods by boat along coastal routes was far more reliable than shipment overland, though in both cases the obstacle of excessive tolls was frequently inhibiting. In 1675, English merchants calculated that it was cheaper to ship coal 300 miles by water than to send it 15 miles overland, so impassable were the roads to heavy transport. Madrid, without

Other rural manufacturing activities

Rudimentary transportation systems

Roadside Inn by Thomas Rowlandson. Coaching inns brought the outside world into the lives of isolated villagers. Note the absence of any clearly defined roadway.

The Duke of Bridgewater Canal

a river, relied upon mules and carts for its supplies. By the mid-eighteenth century, the city required the services of over half a million mules and 150,000 carts, all forced to labor their way into town over rugged terrain. In 1698, a bronze statue of Louis XIV was sent on its way from the river port of Auxerre, southeast of Paris, to the town of Dijon. The cart in which it was dispatched was soon stuck in the mud, however, and the statute remained marooned in a wayside shed for twenty-one years, until the road was improved to the point that it could continue its belated journey.

Gradually in the eighteenth century transportation improved. The French established a Road and Bridge Corps of civil engineers, with a separate training school, in 1747. Work began in the 1670s on a series of canals that eventually linked the English Channel to the Mediterranean. In England, private investors, spearheaded by that inveterate canal builder the duke of Bridgewater, constructed a network of waterways and turnpikes tying provincial towns to each other and to London. With improved roads came stagecoaches, feared at first for their speed and recklessness much as automobiles were feared in the early twentieth century. People objected to being crowded into narrow carriages designed to reduce the load pulled by the team of horses. "If by chance a traveller with a big stomach or wide shoulders appears," an unhappy passenger lamented, "one has to groan or desert." But improvements such as stagecoaches and canals, much as they might increase the profits or change the pattern of life for the wealthy, meant little to the average European. Barges plied the waterways from the north to the south of France, but most men and women traveled no farther than to their neighboring market town, on footpaths or on rutted cart

Transportation improvements

tracks eight feet wide, which had served their ancestors much as they served them.

That industry flourished to the extent it did, despite the hazards and inefficiencies of transport, is a measure of the strength of Europe's ever-increasing commercial impulse. Rural proto-industrialization did not prevent the growth of important urban manufacturing centers. In northern France, many of the million or so men and women employed in the textile trade lived and worked in cities such as Amiens, Lille, and Rheims. The eighteenth-century rulers of Prussia made it their policy to develop Berlin as a manufacturing center, taking advantage of an influx of French Protestants to establish the silk-weaving industry there. Even in cities, however, work was likely to be carried out in small shops, where anywhere from five to twenty journeymen labored under the supervision of a master to manufacture the particular products of their craft. Despite the fact that manufacturing was centered in homes and workshops, by 1700 these industries were increasing significantly in scale as many workshops grouped together to form a single manufacturing district. Textile industries led this trend, but it was true as well of brewing, distilling, soap and candle-making, tanning, and the manufacturing of various chemical substances for the bleaching and dying of cloth. These and other industries might often employ several thousand men and women congregated together into towns—or larger communities of several towns—all dedicated to the same occupation and production.

Techniques in some crafts remained much as they had been for centuries. In others, however, inventions changed the pattern of work as well as the nature of the product. Knitting frames, simple devices to speed the manufacture of textile goods, made their appearance in England and Holland. Wire-drawing machines and slitting mills, the latter enabling nailmakers to convert iron bars into rods, spread from Germany into England. Mechanically powered saws were introduced into shipyards and elsewhere across Europe in the seventeenth century. The technique of calico printing, the application of colored designs directly to textiles, was imported from the Far East. New and more efficient printing presses appeared, first in Holland and then elsewhere. The Dutch invented a machine, called a "camel," by which the hulls of ships could be raised in the water so that they could be more easily repaired.

Innovations of this kind were not readily accepted by workers. Labor-saving machines such as mechanical saws threw men out of work. Artisans, especially those organized into guilds, were by nature conservative, anxious to protect not only their restrictive "rights," but the secrets of their trade. Often, too, the state would intervene to block the widespread use of machines if they threatened to increase unemployment. The Dutch and some German states for example, prohibited the use of what was described as a "devilish invention," a ribbon loom capable of weaving sixteen or more ribbons at the same time. Sometimes the spread of new techniques was curtailed by states in order to protect the livelihood of powerful commercial interest groups. On behalf of both domestic textile manufacturers and importers of Indian goods, calico printing was for a time outlawed in both France and England. The cities of Paris and Lyons and several German states banned the use of indigo dyes because they were manufactured abroad.

Changes that occurred in trade, commerce, agriculture, and industry, though large-scale phenomena, nevertheless touched individual men and women directly. Enclosure stripped away customary rights. An English cottager by 1780 might well have lost his family's age-old right to tether a cow on the common, which was now an enclosed and "scientifically" manured corn field. Markets developed to receive and transmit goods from around the world altered the lives of those whose work now responded to their rhythms. A linen weaver in rural Holland in 1700, whose peasant father had eked out a meager living from his subsistence farm, now supplemented his income by working for an Amsterdam entrepreneur, and paid progressively less for his food as a result of the cheap grain imported to the Low Countries across the Baltic Sea from eastern Europe. A carpenter in an early-eighteenth-century Toulon shipyard lost his job when his employer purchased a mechanical saw that did the work of five men. A sailor on one of the ships built in that Toulon shipyard died at sea off the French colony of Martinique, an island of which he had never heard, at a distance so far from home as to be inconceivable to those who mourned his death when they learned of it months later. Meanwhile, in vast areas of southern and eastern Europe, men and women led lives that followed the same patterns they had for centuries, all but untouched by the changes taking place elsewhere. They clung to the life they knew, a life which, if harsh, was at least predictable.

3. THE COMMERCIAL REVOLUTION

Hand in hand with changes in agriculture and industry came an alteration in the manner in which commerce was organized and trade conducted. So extensive were changes in these areas over the course of two hundred years that it is accurate to speak of them as comprising a commercial revolution. The early-modern world of commerce and industry grew increasingly to be governed by the assumptions of capitalism and mercantilism. Reduced to its simplest terms, *capitalism* is a system of production, distribution, and exchange, in which accumulated wealth is invested by private owners for the sake of gain. Its essential features are private enterprise, competition for markets, and business for profit. Generally it involves the wage system as a method of payment of workers; that is, a mode of payment based not on the amount of wealth workers create, but rather upon their willingness to compete with one another for jobs. Capitalism represented a direct challenge to the semi-static economy of the medieval guilds, in which production and trade were—in theory, at least—conducted for the benefit of society and with only a reasonable charge for the service rendered, instead of unlimited profits. Capitalism is a system designed to encourage commercial expansion beyond the local level, on a national and international scale. Guildmasters had neither the money (capital) to support nor the knowledge to organize and direct commercial enterprises beyond their own towns. Activity on that wider scale demanded the resources and expertise of wealthy and experienced entrepreneurs. The capitalist studied patterns of international trade. He knew where markets were and how to manipulate them to his advantage.

Capitalism is a system designed to reward the individual. In contrast, *mercantilist* doctrine emphasized direct governmental intervention in economic policy to enhance the general prosperity of the state and to increase political authority. Mercantilism was by no means a new idea. It was in fact a variation on the medieval notion that the populace of any particular town comprised a community with a common wealth, and that the economic well-being of such communities depended on the willingness of that populace to work at whatever task God or their rulers assigned them to benefit the local community as a whole.

The medieval origins of mercantilism

The mercantilism of the seventeenth and eighteenth centuries translated this earlier concept of community as a privileged, but regimented, economic unit from the level of towns to the level of the entire state. This translation represented not so much a complete change as it did the extension and elaboration of theories and practices that had governed the policies of earlier rulers. The conquest and subsequent plundering of the New World by Spain was an earlier instance of mercantilism at work on a grand scale. The theory and practice of mercantilism reflected the expansion of state power. Responding to the needs of war, rulers enforced mercantilist policies, often by increasingly autocratic methods, certain that the needs of the state must take precedence over those of individuals.

Mercantilism and the state

Mercantilist theory held that a state's power depended on its actual, calculable wealth. The degree to which a state could remain self-sufficient, importing as little as necessary while exporting as much as possible, was the clearest gauge not only of its economic prosperity but of its power. This doctrine had profound effects on state policy. First, it led to the establishment and development of overseas colonies. Colonies, mercantilists reasoned, would, as part of the national community, provide it with raw materials, including precious metals in some instances, which would otherwise have to be obtained outside the community. Second, the doctrine of mercantilism inspired state governments to encourage industrial production and trade, both sources of revenue that would increase the state's income.

Mercantilism in theory

Although most Western European statesmen were prepared to endorse mercantilist goals in principle, the degree to which their policies reflected those goals varied according to national circumstance. Spain, despite its insistence on closed colonial markets and its determination to amass a fortune in bullion, never succeeded in attaining the economic self-sufficiency that mercantilist theory demanded. Since they were unable to supply their own manufactured goods to meet the demand at home or in their colonies, the Spaniards found it necessary to exchange their bullion for Flemish, French,

Mercantilism in practice

and English manufactured goods. But mercantilism, which appealed at least in theory to the rulers in Madrid, had little attraction for the merchants of Amsterdam. The Dutch rejected the governmental centralization implicit in the mercantilist notion of the sovereign state as an economic unit since they associated it with the hated regime of Philip II of Spain. They further recognized that the United Provinces were too small to permit them to achieve economic self-sufficiency. Throughout the seventeenth and eighteenth centuries the Dutch remained dedicated in principle and practice to free trade, often investing, contrary to mercantilist doctrine, in the commercial enterprises of other countries and promoting national prosperity by encouraging the rest of Europe to rely upon Amsterdam as a hub of international finance and trade. Nonetheless the Dutch commitment to free trade did not extend to their colonial preserves, which remained closed to their commercial rivals. It was the French and the English who combined, in differing degrees, governmental centralization and independent commercial enterprise most consistently and effectively.

*Effects of capitalism and
mercantilism on individuals*

Capitalism and mercantilism were economic systems that produced important consequences to individuals as well as to nations and regions. Laboring men and women frequently found themselves the victims of the policies and programs of those who, either as individuals or state functionaries, managed and controlled dynamic, expansionist national economies. For example, capitalists could afford to invest in large quantities of manufactured goods, and if necessary, hold them unsold until they could command a high price, favorable to them but damaging to the budget of humbler consumers. Mercantilism persuaded policy-makers to discourage domestic consumption, since goods purchased on the home market reduced the goods available for export. Government policy was thus to keep wages low, so that laborers would not have money to spend for more than it took to provide them with basic food and shelter. While some suffered, others prospered. Although mercantilism put the state before the individual, many individuals nonetheless profited handsomely from mercantilism as they collected taxes, administered the finances of the armed forces, or otherwise worked to enhance the financial power of the central government.

*International centers and
commercial routes*

Together, governments and entrepreneurs designed new institutions that facilitated the expansion of global commerce during the seventeenth and eighteenth centuries to effect the commercial revolution of early-modern Europe. While local and regional markets continued to flourish, international centers such as Antwerp, Amsterdam, and London became hubs for a flourishing and complex system of international trade. Commercial routes linking one country to another developed along river systems: the Volga, Don, and Dvina in the east; the Oder, Weser, and Rhine in the west. An increasing number of European men and women grew dependent upon the commerce that brought both necessities and luxuries into their lives. The eighteenth-century essayist Joseph Addison sang the praises of the beneficent merchant prince. "There are not more useful members in the Commonwealth," he wrote. "They distribute the gifts of nature, find work for the poor, and wealth to the rich, and magnificence to the great."

Enterprise on this new scale depended on the availability of capital for investment. And that capital was generated primarily by a gradual increase in agricultural prices throughout much of the period. Had that increase been sharp, it would probably have produced enough hunger and suffering to retard rather than stimulate economic growth. Had there been no increase, however, the resulting stagnation produced by marginal profits would have proved equally detrimental to expansion. Agricultural entrepreneurs had surplus capital to invest in trade; bankers put that surplus to use to expand their commercial enterprises. Together, capitalist investors and merchants profited.

Banks played a vital role in the history of this expansion. Strong religious and moral disapproval of lending money at interest meant that banking had enjoyed a dubious reputation in the Middle Ages. Because the Church did come to allow profit-making on commercial risks, however, banks in Italy and Germany were organized under family auspices, the most notable examples being the fourteenth- and fifteenth-century operations of the Medici in Florence and the Fuggers of Augsburg. The Fuggers lent money to kings and bishops, and served as broker to the pope for the sale of indulgences. The rise of these private financial houses was followed by the establishing of government banks, reflecting the mercantilist goal of serving the monetary needs of the state. The first such institution, the Bank of Sweden, was founded in 1657. The Bank of England was established in

Elements of the Commercial Revolution: (1) *increased capital*

(2) *the rise of banking*

Merchants' Houses in Seventeenth-Century Amsterdam. This engraving depicts not only the opulence of middle-class life in a thriving commercial capital, but also the spirit of civic unity, expressed by the crowds gathered for a public celebration. (Several of the principal thoroughfares of Amsterdam are canals.)

The Lyons Stock Exchange. Built in 1749, the stylish and impressive facade of the structure bespeaks the prominent role of commerce in French society.

1694, at a time when England's emergence as a world commercial power guaranteed that institution a leading role in international finance.

(3) expansion of credit facilities

The growth of banking was necessarily accompanied by the adoption of various aids to financial transactions on a large scale, further evidence of a commercial revolution. Credit facilities were extended in such a way that a merchant in Amsterdam could purchase goods from a merchant in Venice by means of a bill of exchange issued by an Amsterdam bank. The Venetian merchant would obtain his money by depositing the bill of exchange in his local bank. Later, the two banks would settle their accounts by comparing balances. Among the other facilities for the expansion of credit were the adoption of a system of payment by check in local transactions and the issuance of bank notes as a substitute for gold and silver. Both of these devices were invented by the Italians and were gradually adopted in northern Europe. The system of payment by check was particularly important in increasing the volume of trade, since the credit resources of the banks could now be expanded far beyond the actual amounts of cash in their vaults.

(4) changes in business organization; the growth of regulated companies

International commercial expansion called forth larger units of business organization. The prevailing unit of production and trade in the Middle Ages was the workshop or store owned by an individual or a family. Partnerships were also quite common, in spite of the grave disadvantage of unlimited liability of each of its members for the debts of the entire firm. Obviously no one of these units was well adapted to business involving heavy risks and a huge investment of capital. The attempt to devise a more suitable business organization resulted in the formation of *regulated companies,* which were associations of merchants banded together for a common venture. Members did not pool their resources but agreed merely to cooperate for their mutual advantage and to abide by certain definite regulations.

The commercial revolution was facilitated in the seventeenth century when the regulated company was largely superseded by a new type of organization at once more compact and broader in scope. This was the *joint-stock company,* formed through the issuance of shares of capital to a considerable number of investors. Those who purchased the shares might or might not take part in the work of the company. Whether they did or not, they were joint owners of the business and therefore entitled to share in its profits in accordance with the amount they had invested. The joint-stock company had advantages over the partnership and the regulated company. First, it was a permanent unit, not subject to reorganization every time one of its members died or withdrew. And second, it made possible a much larger accumulation of capital, through a wide distribution of shares. Its organization and methods resembled to a degree those of the modern corporation. Yet the joint-stock company of the early-modern period is best understood not so much as a conscious precursor of capitalist endeavor as a pragmatic attempt at commercial expansion by both individuals and the state, its structure dictated by present opportunity and circumstance. Initially, for example, the Dutch United East India Company, one of the early joint-stock ventures, had expected to pay off its investors ten years after its founding in 1602, much as regulated companies had. Yet when that time came, the directors recognized the impossibility of the plan. By 1612, the company's assets were scattered—as ships, wharves, warehouses, and cargoes—across the globe. As a result, the directors urged those anxious to realize their profits to sell their shares on the Amsterdam exchange to other eager investors, thereby ensuring the sustained operation of their enterprise and, in the process, establishing a practice of continuous financing that was soon to become common.

Joint-stock companies

While most of the early joint-stock companies were founded for commercial ventures, some were organized later in industry. A number of the outstanding trading combinations were also *chartered companies.* They held charters from the government granting a monopoly of the trade in a certain locality and conferring extensive authority over the inhabitants, and were thus an example of the way capitalist and mercantilist interests might coincide. Through a charter of this kind, the British East India Company undertook the exploitation of vast territories on the Indian subcontinent, and remained virtual ruler there until the end of the eighteenth century.

Chartered companies

Joint-stock companies in France were more directly dependent on the state than was the case elsewhere, a reflection of French dedication to mercantilist theory. In most cases French companies were floated under governmental auspices; courtiers—and the king himself—were heavy investors. Agents of the state played a direct role in their management, sometimes to the company's ultimate disadvantage. The French East India Company, for example, was compelled by state direction to govern its colonies in accordance with the laws of Paris, a fact which, one historian has remarked, "reminds one of the complaint that French progress in the Sahara was retarded by the refusal of the camel to accommodate its habits to administrative regulations made in Paris."

Even though companies elsewhere were less subject to governmental regulation than they were in France, government and commerce generally worked to promote each other's interests. The exceptions were the Dutch, who almost exclusively put their capital to work not for the state but for the rest of Europe. In time of war, governments called upon commercial capitalists to assist in the financing of their campaigns. When England went to war against France in 1689, for example, the government had no long-range borrowing mechanism available to it; during the next quarter century the merchant community, through the Bank of England, assisted the government in raising over £170 million and in stabilizing the national debt at £40 million. In return, trading companies used the war to increase long-distance commercial traffic at the expense of their French enemy, and exerted powerful pressure on the government to secure treaties that would work to their advantage. This partnership between state and commerce was never an easy one, however. A large gap remained between a state's ambitions and its ability to realize them economically. National mercantilism, and the wars that were so often its most striking feature, created a demand for money that could not be satisfied within governmental structures bound up in the practices of the past.

A final important feature of the commercial revolution was the development of a more efficient money economy. Money had been used widely since the revival of trade in the eleventh century. Nevertheless, there were few coins with a value that was recognized other than locally. By 1300, the gold ducat of Venice and the gold florin of Florence had come to be accepted in Italy and also in the international markets of northern Europe. But no country could be said to have had a uniform monetary system. The growth of trade and industry in the commercial revolution accentuated the need for more stable and uniform monetary systems. The problem was solved by the adoption of a standard system of money by every important state to be used for all transactions within its borders. Much time elapsed, however, before the reform was complete. England began the construction of a uniform coinage during the reign of Queen Elizabeth, but the task was not finished until late in the seventeenth century. Indeed, the French did not succeed in reducing their money to its modern standard of simplicity and convenience until the early nineteenth century.

The history of coinage illustrates the degree to which fluctuation and change were among the few constants throughout the extremely unstable seventeenth and eighteenth centuries. The economic institutions just described never remained static, but rather existed in a continuously volatile state of development. Their volatility, in turn, had a direct effect on the lives of individual men and women. One major result of overseas expansion, for example, was the severe inflation caused by the increase in the supply of silver, which plagued Europe at the end of the sixteenth century (see above, pp. 486–488). Price fluctuations, in turn, produced further economic instability. Businessmen were tempted to expand their enterprises too rapidly; bankers extended credit so liberally that their principal borrowers, especially noblemen, often defaulted on loans. In both Spain and Italy, wages failed to keep pace with rising prices, which brought severe and continuing hardships to the lower classes. Impoverishment was rife in the cities, and bandits flourished in the rural areas.

Speculative greed could, and sometimes did, threaten to bring a nation to its knees. Though feverish speculation characterized the period as a whole, the most notorious bouts of that particular economic disease occurred in the early eighteenth century. The so-called South Sea Bubble was the result of deliberate inflation of the stock of the South Sea Company in England, whose offer to assume the national debt led to unwarranted confidence in the company's future. When buoyant hopes gave way to fears, investors made frantic attempts to dispose of their shares for whatever they would bring. A crash which came in 1720 was the inevitable result.

During the years when the South Sea Bubble was being inflated in England, the French were engaged in a similar wave of speculative madness. In 1715 a Scotsman by the name of John Law, compelled to flee from British soil for killing his rival in a love intrigue, settled in Paris, after various successful gambling adventures in other cities. He persuaded the regent of France to adopt his scheme for paying off the national debt through the issuance of paper money and to grant him the privilege of organizing the Mississippi Company for the colonization and exploitation of Louisiana. As happened in England, stock prices soared in response to an alluring but basically unrealistic scheme. Stories were told of butchers and tailors who made fortunes from their few initial shares. Ultimately, however, panic set in, and in 1720 the Mississippi Bubble burst in a wild panic. Thousands who had invested at fantastically high prices were ruined, victims of the violent unpredictability that so characterized the period.

4. COLONIZATION AND OVERSEAS TRADE

The institutions of the commercial revolution—banks, credit facilities, joint-stock companies, monetary systems—were designed specifically to assist both capitalist entrepreneurs and mercantilist policy-makers in the development and exploitation of trade. Despite the existence of increasingly profitable European commercial routes and centers, the most visible evidence of the economic expansionism of early-modern Europe were the overseas colonies and trading posts developed and exploited during the seventeenth and eighteenth centuries. Following the exploits of the *conquistadores,* the Spanish established colonial governments in Peru and in Mexico, which they controlled from Madrid in proper mercantilist fashion by a Council of the Indies. The governments of Philip II and his successors were determined to defend their monopoly in the New World. They issued trading licenses to none but Spanish merchants; exports and imports passed only through the port of Seville (later the more navigable port of Cadiz), where they were registered at the government-operated Casa de Contratación, or customs house. In their heyday, Spanish traders circled the globe. Because of the lucrative market for silver in East Asia, they found it well worth their while to establish an outpost in far-off Manila in the Philippines, where Asian silk was exchanged for South American bul-

GREENLAND

BRITAIN

HUDSON
BAY
COMPANY

Québec
NEW FRANCE
ACADIA
NEWFOUNDLAND

Bristol
Amsterdam
NETHERLANDS

FRANCE

Boston
New Amsterdam
(New York after 1667)

LOUISIANA

VIRGINIA
Jamestown

PORTUGAL
Madrid
Lisbon
SPAIN
Cadiz

Charlestown

FLORIDA

A T L A N T I C

O C E A N

A F R I C A

NEW
SPAIN

Gulf of
Mexico

Mexico

CUBA

HISPANIOLA

SPANISH MAIN
See enlargement below

St. Louis

Panama

GAMBIA

NEW
GRANADA

SURINAM
FR. GUYANA

GOLD
COAST
GUINEA

SLAVES

P A C I F I C
Lima

BRAZIL

KENYA

O C E A N

ANGOLA

Rio de Janeiro

MADAGASCAR

MOZAMBIQUE

PERU

CAPE OF
GOOD HOPE

Buenos Aires

Havana
Bahamas (Br.)

CUBA
Puerto
Rico

St. Domingue
(Fr.)
HISPANIOLA
Guadeloupe (Fr.)

Belize (Br.)
Jamaica (Br.)
Martinique (Fr.)

	Spanish
	Portuguese
	French
	British
	Dutch

C A R I B B E A N   S E A

Barbados (Br.)

NEW SPAIN

Curaçao (Dutch)
Trinidad (Sp.)
Tobago

NEW GRANADA

THE ATLANTIC WORLD IN 1713

lion. The silk was then shipped back to Spain by way of the Mexican ports of Acapulco and Veracruz. The search for gold and silver was accompanied by the establishment of permanent colonies in Central and South America and on the east and west coasts of North America in what are now the states of Florida and California.

Spain's predominance did not deter other countries from attempting to win a share of the treasure for themselves. Probably the boldest challengers were the English, and their leading buccaneer the "sea dog" Sir Francis Drake, who three times raided the east and west coasts of Spanish America and who, in 1587, the year before the Armada set sail on its ill-fated voyage north, "singed the beard of the Spanish king" by attacking the Spanish fleet at its anchorage in Cadiz harbor. Yet despite dashing heroics of that sort, the English could do no more than dent the Spanish trade.

Challenges to Spanish predominance

English colonists sought profits elsewhere by establishing agricultural settlements in North America and the Caribbean basin. Their first permanent, though ultimately unsuccessful, colony was Jamestown, in Virginia, founded in 1607. Over the next forty years, 80,000 English emigrants sailed to over twenty autonomous settlements in the New World. In this instance, however, religious freedom, as well as economic gain, was often the motive of the settlers. The renowned band of "pilgrim fathers" that landed on the New England shores in 1620 was but one of a large number of dissident groups that sought to escape the attempts of the English Kings, James I and Charles I, to impose religious conformity on their subjects. Religion also played a role in the efforts of the Spanish to colonize Central and South America, and of the French to penetrate the hinterlands of North America. Roman Catholic Jesuit missionaries, intent upon the conversion of native Americans to Christianity, joined fur traders in journeys across the continent to the Great Lakes and the Mississippi.

English colonization

Both England and France were quick to extract profit from their expanding colonial empires. England's agricultural colonies were producing crops in high demand throughout Europe. The success of colonial planters encouraged the governments of both Oliver Cromwell and Charles II to intervene in the management of their overseas economy. Navigation Acts, passed in 1651 and 1660, and rigorously enforced thereafter, decreed that all exports from English colonies to the mother country be carried in English ships, and forbade the direct exporting of certain "enumerated" products directly from the colonies to Continental ports.

The growth of English colonial regulation

The most valuable of those products were sugar and tobacco. Sugar, virtually unknown in Europe earlier, had become a popular luxury by the end of the sixteenth century. Where once it had been considered no more than a medicine, one observer now noted that the wealthy were "devouring it out of gluttony." Sugarcane was raised in the West Indies after 1650 in ever-larger amounts. In the eighteenth century, the value of the sugar that England imported from its small island colonies there—Barbados, Jamaica, St. Kitts, and others—exceeded the value of its imports from the vast subcontinents of China and India. Although the tobacco plant was imported into Europe by the Spaniards about fifty years after the discovery of Amer-

Sugar and tobacco

ica, another half century passed before Europeans took up the habit of smoking. At first the plant was believed to possess miraculous healing powers and was referred to as "divine tobacco" and "our holy herb nicotian." (The word "nicotine" derives from the name of the French ambassador to Portugal, Jean Nicot, who brought the tobacco plant to France.) The practice of smoking was popularized by English explorers, especially by Sir Walter Raleigh, who had learned to smoke while living among the Indians of Virginia. It spread rapidly through all classes of European society. Governments at first joined the Church in condemning the use of tobacco because of its socially and spiritually harmful effects, but by the end of the seventeenth century, having realized the profits to be made from its production, they were encouraging its use.

The French in America

French colonial policy matured during the administration of Louis XIV's mercantilist finance minister, Jean Baptiste Colbert (1619–1683), who perceived of overseas expansion as an integral part of state economic policy. He organized joint-stock companies to compete with those of the English. He encouraged the development of lucrative sugar-producing colonies in the West Indies, the largest of which was St. Dominique (present-day Haiti). France also dominated the interior of the North American continent. Frenchmen traded furs and preached Christianity to the Indians in a vast territory that stretched from Acadia and the St. Lawrence River in the northeast to Louisiana in the west. Yet the financial returns from these lands were hardly commensurate with their size. Furs, fish, and tobacco were exported to home markets, but not in sufficient amounts to match the profits from the sugar colonies of the Caribbean or from the line of trading posts the French maintained in India.

The Dutch East India Company Warehouse and Timber Wharf at Amsterdam. The substantial warehouse, the stockpiles of lumber, and the company ship under construction in the foreground illustrate the degree to which overseas commerce could stimulate the economy of the mother country.

The Dutch were even more successful than the English and the French in establishing a flourishing commercial empire in the seventeenth century. Their joint-stock East India Company, founded in 1602, rivaled its English counterpart in Asia, gaining firm control of Sumatra, Borneo, and the Moluccas, or Spice Islands, and driving Portuguese traders from an area where they had heretofore enjoyed an undisturbed commercial dominion. The result was a Dutch monopoly in pepper, cinnamon, nutmeg, mace, and cloves. The Dutch also secured an exclusive right to trade with the Japanese, and maintained outposts in China and India as well. In the Western Hemisphere, their achievements were less spectacular. Following a series of trade wars with England, they surrendered their North American colony of New Amsterdam (subsequently renamed New York) in 1667, retaining Surinam, off the northern coast of South America, as well as the islands of Curaçao and Tobago in the West Indies in compensation.

The fortunes of these commercial empires rose and fell in the course of the seventeenth and eighteenth centuries. The Spanish, mired in persistent economic stagnation and embroiled in a succession of expensive wars and domestic rebellions, were powerless to prevent losses to their empire. Their merchant marine, once a match for cunning pirate-admirals like Drake, was by the middle of the seventeenth century unable to protect itself from attack by its more spirited commercial rivals. In a war with Spain in the 1650s, the English captured not only the island of Jamaica but treasure ships lying off the Spanish harbor of Cadiz. Further profit was obtained by bribing Spanish customs officials on a grand scale. During the second half of the century, two-thirds of the imported goods sold in Spanish colonies were smuggled in by Dutch, English, and French traders. By 1700, though Spain still possessed a colonial empire, it was one that lay at the mercy of its more dynamic rivals. A brief revival of its fortunes under more enlightened leadership in the mid-eighteenth century did nothing to prevent its ultimate eclipse.

Portugal, too, found it impossible to prevent foreign penetration of its colonial economies. The English worked diligently and successfully to win commercial advantages there. They obtained concessions to export woolens duty-free into Portugal itself in return for similar preferential treatment for Portuguese wines. (The notorious affection of the English upper class for port wine dates from the signing of the Treaty of 1703.) English trade with the mother country led in time to English trade with the Portuguese colony of Brazil, indeed to the opening of commercial offices in Rio de Janeiro.

The Dutch, whose merchant fleet of over 16,000 vessels was the largest in Europe, were the masters of world trade throughout most of the seventeenth century. Dutch ships—about half the European total—not only sailed the high seas, but dominated the coastal carrying trade as well. To reduce the time of ocean voyages, Amsterdam shipyards developed the *fluitschip*. Longer and shallower than conventional craft, it was flat-bottomed and built of lightweight fir or pine, rather than oak. The *fluitschip* required only half the crew of regular ships, and cost half as much to build.

The Dutch merchant marine ensured the position of Amsterdam as the world's premier trading center, and the volume of Dutch commerce allowed Amsterdam merchants to undersell their English and French rivals. During the eighteenth century, however, a growing Anglo–French rivalry in India stole the commercial spotlight from the Dutch spice monopoly in the Far East. The French and English East India Companies employed mercenaries to establish and expand trading areas such as Madras, Bombay, and Pondichéry. By exploiting indigenous industries, European capitalists continued to increase the flow of fine cotton textiles, tea, and spices, which passed through these commercial depots on their way to Europe. The struggle for worldwide economic dominance reached a peak in the mid-eighteenth century (see below, p. 605). At that time the Anglo–French rivalry in India was resolved in England's favor. As a sign of France's defeat, in 1769 the French East India Company was dissolved.

*Increasing dominance of
western trade routes*

Despite the commercial importance of India, however, patterns of world trade came increasingly to be dominated by western routes that had developed in response to the lucrative West Indian sugar industry, and to the demand for slaves from Africa to work the plantations in the Caribbean. Here Britain again eventually assumed the lead. Typically, a ship might begin its voyage from New England with a consignment of rum and sail to Africa, where the rum would be exchanged for a cargo of slaves. From the west coast of Africa the ship would then cross the South Atlantic to the sugar colonies of Jamaica or Barbados, where slaves would be traded for molasses, which would make the final leg of the journey to New England, where it would be made into rum. A variant triangle might see cheap manufactured goods move from England to Africa, where they would be traded for slaves. Those slaves would then be shipped to Virginia and exchanged for tobacco, which would be shipped to England and processed there for sale in Continental markets. Other eighteenth-century trade

The Rewards of Commercial Exploitation. An English employee of the East India Company, enjoying his ease and his opium, as depicted by an eighteenth-century Indian artist.

routes were more direct: the Spanish, French, Portuguese, and Dutch all engaged in the slave trade between Africa and Central and South America; the Spanish attempted, vainly, to retain a mercantilist monopoly on direct trade between Cadiz and their South American colonies; others sailed from England, France, or North America to the Caribbean and back again. And of course trade continued to flourish between Europe and the Near and Far East. But the triangular western routes, dictated by the grim economic symbiosis of sugar and slaves, remained dominant.

The cultivation of sugar and tobacco depended on slave labor; and as demand for those products increased, so did the traffic in black slaves, without whose labor those products could not be raised or harvested. At the height of the Atlantic slave trade in the eighteenth century, somewhere between 75,000 and 90,000 blacks were shipped across the Atlantic yearly: 6 million in the eighteenth century, out of a total of over 9 million for the entire history of the trade. About 35 percent went to English and French Caribbean plantations, 5 percent (roughly 450,000) to North America, and the rest to the Portuguese colony of Brazil and to Spanish colonies in South America. Although run as a monopoly by various governments in the sixteenth and early seventeenth centuries, in its heyday the slave trade was open to private entrepreneurs, who operated ports on the West African coast. Traders exchanged cheap Indian cloth, metal goods, rum, and firearms with African slave merchants in return for their human cargo. Already disoriented and degraded by their capture at the hands of rival tribes, black men, women, and children were packed by the hundreds into the holds of slave ships for the gruesome "middle passage" across the Atlantic (so called to distinguish it from the ship's voyage from Europe to Africa, and from the slave colony back to Europe again). Shackled to the decks, without sanitary facilities, the black "cargo" suffered horribly; the mortality rate, however, remained at about 10 or 11 percent, not much higher than the rate for a normal sea voyage of one hundred days or more. Since traders had to invest as much as £10 per slave in their enterprise, they ensured that their consignment would reach its destination in good enough shape to be sold for a profit.

The trade was risky, dependent as it was on a good wind and fair weather, and competition was increasingly keen. Yet profits could run high, occasionally as much as 300 percent. Demand for slaves remained constant throughout the eighteenth century. By the 1780s, there were over 500,000 slaves on the largest French plantation island, St. Dominique, and 200,000 or more on the English counterpart, Jamaica. Those numbers reflected the expanding world market for slave-grown crops. As long as there was a market for the crops cultivated by slaves—as long as the economy relied to the extent it did upon slave labor—governments would remain unwilling to put an end to the system that, as one Englishman wrote in 1749, provided "an unexhaustible fund of wealth to this nation."

Philosophers argued that though there was reason to rejoice that slavery had been banished from the continent of Europe (forgetting, apparently, the extent to which it continued to exist east of the Elbe in the form of

The slave trade

Female Slave Being Whipped. After capture by rival tribes, black men, women, and children could expect further suffering, both during the middle passage and after reaching their final destinations.

High profits from slaves

How Slaves Were Stowed Aboard Ship during the Middle Passage. Men were "housed" on the right; women on the left; children in the middle. The human cargo was jammed onto platforms six feet wide without sufficient headroom to permit an adult to sit up. This diagram is from evidence gathered by English abolitionists and depicts conditions on the Liverpool slave ship *Brookes.*

The ending of the trade

serfdom), it remained a necessity in other parts of the world. Not until the very end of the eighteenth century did Europeans begin to protest the ghastly traffic. Public pressure, first from Quakers and then from others motivated either by religious or humanitarian zeal, helped put an end to the trade in England in 1807, and to slavery itself in British colonies in 1833. Slavery in French colonies was abolished in 1793, but only after slaves had risen in massive revolt on St. Dominique. Elsewhere, in Latin and North America, slavery lasted well into the nineteenth century—in the United States, until the Civil War of 1861–1865.

The continuing rise of commerce

The slave trade was an integral part of the history of the dramatic rise of English and French commerce during the eighteenth century. French colonial trade, valued at 25 million livres in 1716, rose to 263 million livres in 1789. In England, during roughly the same period, foreign trade increased in value from £10 million to £40 million, the latter amount more than twice that for France. These figures suggest the degree to which statecraft and private enterprise were bound to each other. If merchants depended on their government to provide a navy to protect and defend their overseas investments, governments depended equally on entrepreneurship, not only to generate money to build ships, but to sustain the trade upon which national power had come to rely so heavily.

5. LIFE WITHIN A SOCIETY OF ORDERS

Orders, privilege, and freedom

Despite the economic and demographic shifts that were occurring in early-modern Europe, it remained a society divided into traditional orders or ranks. The changes we have been concerned with occurred against the continuity of long-accepted social divisions based upon birth and occupation. As circumstances altered, the fluid patterns of economic reorganization clashed with older, rigid assumptions about the place of men and women within a preordained—to many, a divinely ordained—social hierarchy. Jean Bodin, the French philosopher, wrote in 1570 that the division of the citizenry into "the three orders of nobles, clergy and people" was no more than natural. "There never was a commonwealth, real or imaginary, where citizens were in truth equal in all rights and privileges. Some always have more, some less than the rest." And some had none. Most would have recognized infinitely subtle subdivisions among and between the three orders Bodin specified. Ranks were demarcated by rights and privileges. "Freedom" was understood as one such privilege, as a benefit, bestowed not upon all men and women, but upon special groups whose position "freed" them to do certain things others could not do, or freed them from the burden of doing certain things that were required of others. An English landowner was, because of the position his property conferred upon him, privileged, and therefore "free," to participate directly in the election of his government. A French nobleman was privileged, and therefore "free," to avoid the heavy burden of taxation levied upon the unprivileged orders. A German tailor who had served out his seven-year apprenticeship was free to set up his own shop for profit, something an unapprenticed man was not traditionally "at liberty" to do, no matter what his degree of skill with needle and thread. The master tailor's position conferred his freedom, just as the position of aristocrat and property owner conferred theirs.

The members of the higher orders attempted at all times to live their lives in a particular style that accorded with their rank. The nobility was taught from birth to consider itself above and apart from the rest of society. Merchants and manufacturers were just as insistent upon maintaining the traditional marks of privilege that separated them from artisans and peas-

The theater of a society of orders

Middle-Class Fashion. In this seventeenth-century portrait of a Dutch burgomaster and his family, the patriarch and his wife are wearing the costume of an earlier generation, while the children are clothed in the current style. All display the opulence characteristic of their prosperous class.

Banquet Given in Paris by the Spanish Duke of Alva in Honor of the Prince of Asturias. The scene illustrates the ostentatious display this powerful nobleman believed suitable to his rank and fortune.

ants. Sumptuary laws decreed what could be worn and by whom. An edict promulgated in the German principality of Brunswick in 1738, for example, forbade servant girls to use silk dress materials, to wear gold or silver ornaments, or shoes of anything but plain black leather. A similar seventeenth-century law in the Polish city of Posen prohibited the wives of burghers from wearing capes or long hair. Style was not simply a matter of current whim. It was a badge of status and was carefully adhered to as such. An aristocratic lady powdered her hair and rouged her cheeks as a sign that she was an aristocrat. Life within a society of orders demanded a certain degree of theatricality, especially from those at the top of the social hierarchy. Aristocrats "acted" their part in a calculatedly self-conscious way. Their manner of speech, their dress, the ceremonial sword they were privileged to wear, the title by which they were addressed, were the props of a performance that constantly emphasized the distinctions between those above and those below. Noble families lived in castles, chateaux, or country houses whose size and antiquity were a further proclamation of superiority. When they built new mansions, as the *nouveau riche* capitalist English gentry did in the eighteenth century, they made certain their elaborate houses and spacious private parks declared their newfound power. The English politician Robert Walpole had an entire village moved to improve the view from his grand new residence.

The vast majority of men and women defined and understood social hierarchy in terms of the rural communities in which they lived. At the head of those communities, in all likelihood, stood a representative of the noble elite. The nobility probably numbered about 3 percent of the total population of Europe. The percentage was higher in Russia, Poland, Hungary, and Spain; lower in Germany, France, and England. Ownership of a landed estate was proof of one's elevated rank. Generally speaking, the more land one possessed, the higher one stood within the social hierarchy. In Hungary, five noble families owned about 14 percent of the entire country; the greatest of these, Prince Esterházy, controlled the lives of over half a million peasants. Most noblemen were not nearly so rich and powerful. Some, indeed, could rely on little more than inherited privilege to distinguish themselves from peasants.

The nobility

Tradition had it that noble service meant military service; yet, as we shall see, that tradition—like so many others—was increasingly breached during the early-modern period. Noble title was granted by a monarch, in theory for service to the state. But such service was more and more frequently defined as nonmilitary, as support, financial and political, for the expanding apparatus of local and central government. The pattern of noble life varied considerably from country to country. In England and Prussia, the nobility tended to reside on its estates; in south and west Germany, and in France, they were more likely to leave the management of their estates to stewards and to live at the royal court or in cities. Despite the traditional assumption that noblemen need not, and therefore must not, soil their aristocratic reputation by commercial dealing, by the end of the eighteenth century they were involving themselves in increasing numbers in a variety of entrepreneurial enterprises. Some exploited mineral deposits on their estates; others invested in overseas trade. In France, two of the four largest coal mines were owned and operated by noblemen, while the duke of Orléans was an important investor in the newly established chemical dye industry. In Eastern Europe, because there were few middle-class merchants, noblemen frequently undertook to market their agricultural produce themselves.

Nobility and commerce

In no country was the nobility a completely closed order. Men who proved of use to the crown as administrators or lawyers, men who amassed large fortunes as a consequence of judicious—and often legally questionable—financial transactions, moved into the ranks of the nobility with increasing frequency during the late seventeenth and eighteenth century. Joseph II of Austria was making financiers into noblemen by the dozen in the late eighteenth century. In France, it was possible to attain nobility through the purchase of expensive offices from the crown. There was also a growing legal nobility of the "robe," headed by members of the thirteen provincial *parlements* whose function it was to record, and thereby sanction, the laws of the kingdom, and who performed administrative and judicial duties as well.

An "open" nobility

Land ownership brought the nobility into direct relationship with the peasants and laborers who worked the land and over whose lives their masters exercised dominion. The status of the peasantry varied greatly across

The peasantry

the face of rural Europe. In the east—Russia, Poland, Hungary, and in parts of Germany beyond the Elbe—the desire for profit in agriculture and the collusion of the state with the nobility led to the growth of a "second serfdom," a serf system much stronger than that which had existed during the Middle Ages. In East Prussia, serfs often had to work from three to six days a week for their lord, and some had only late evening or night hours to cultivate their own lands.

*Peasant subordination in
Eastern Europe*

Peasants throughout Eastern Europe found their destinies controlled in almost all respects by their masters. Noble landlords dispensed justice in manorial courts and even ruled in cases to which they were themselves interested parties. These men were a combination of sheriff, chief magistrate, and police force in one, able to sentence their "subjects" to corporal punishment, imprisonment, exile, or in many cases death, without right of appeal. Peasants could not leave their land, marry, or learn a trade unless permitted to do so by their lord. In Russia, where half the land was owned by the state, peasants were bound to work in mines or workshops if their masters so ordered, and could be sold to private owners. Although Russian peasant serfs were said to possess a "legal personality" that distinguished them from slaves, the distinction was obscured in practice. They lived as bound to their masters as had their great-grandfathers.

Peasant obligations

In Western Europe, the position of the peasantry reflected the fact that serfdom had all but disappeared by the sixteenth century. Peasants might theoretically own land, although the vast majority were either tenants or laborers. Hereditary tenure was in general more secure than in the east; peasants could dispose of their land and had legal claim to farm buildings and implements. Although far freer than their Eastern European counterparts, the peasantry of Western Europe still lived to a great degree under the domination of landowners. They were in many cases responsible for the payment of various dues and fees: an annual rent paid to landlords by those who might otherwise own their land outright; a special tax on recently cleared land; a fee, often as much as one-sixth of the assessed value of the land, collected by the manorial lord whenever peasant property changed hands; and charges for the use of the lord's mill, bakery, or wine press. In France, peasants were compelled to submit to the *corvée,* a requirement that they labor for several weeks a year maintaining local roads. Even access to the often questionable justice meted out in the manorial courts, which endured throughout the early-modern period in almost all of Western Europe, was encumbered with fees and commissions. To many peasants, however, the most galling badge of their inferiority was their inability to hunt within the jurisdiction of their landlord's manor. The slaughter of game was a privilege reserved to the nobility, a circumstance generating sustained resentment on the part of a population that looked upon deer and pheasant not as a symbol of aristocratic status but as a necessary supplement to its meager diet. Noble landlords rarely missed an opportunity to extract all the money they could from their peasants while constantly reminding them of the degree to which their destiny was controlled by the lord of the manor.

A French Peasant. Tattered and overworked, this peasant farmer is shown feeding his livestock as the tax collector at his door relieves him of all of his profits.

Market Scene by Jean Michelin. Peasant women and children bringing produce to a nearby market town.

Despite their traditional subservience, however, Western European peasants found themselves caught up directly in the process of economic change. The growth of centralized monarchies intensified the states' need for income, with the result that peasants were more burdened than ever with taxes and required services. They responded by accepting a new role as wage-earners in an expanding market economy, some as agricultural day laborers on enclosed estates, others as part of the work force in expanding rural industries. A few were genuinely independent, literate, influential members of the communities where they lived, owning not only land but considerable livestock. In France, some acted as intermediaries between their landlords, from whom they leased several large farms, and the share-croppers who actually worked the land. Most, however, were far less fortunate. Those with claim to a small piece of property usually worked it into infertility in the course of one or two generations as they scrambled to make it produce as much as possible.

Poor peasants often lived, contrary to the biblical injunction, by bread alone—two pounds a day if they were lucky, the dark dough a mixture of wheat and rye flour. According to region, bread was supplemented by peas and beans, beer, wine, or, far less often, skimmed milk. Peasant houses usually contained no more than one or two rooms, and were constructed of wood, plastered with mud or clay. Roofs were most often thatched with straw, which was used as fertilizer when replaced, and provided fodder for animals at times of scarcity. Furnishings seldom consisted of more than a table, benches, pallets for sleeping, a few earthenware plates, and simple tools—an axe, a wooden spade, a knife.

Peasant women tended livestock and vegetables, and managed the dairy, if there was one. Women went out as field workers, or worked at home at knitting, spinning, or weaving in order to augment the family income. A

Peasants and economic change

Peasant bread and board

Peasant women

popular seventeenth-century poem has a laborer's wife lamenting her lot with a refrain that has echoed down the ages: ". . . my labor is hard,/ And all my pleasures are debarr'd;/ Both morning, evening, night and noon,/ I am sure a woman's work is never done."

The spread of proto-industrialization broke down the previously sharp demarcations between town and country, between the life lived inside a city's medieval walls and that lived outside. Suburbs merged urban and rural existence. In some, textile workers labored. In others, families of fashion took their ease, creating an environment "where the want of London smoke is supplied by the smoke of Virginia tobacco," as one Englishman remarked wryly. Houses in areas inhabited by the wealthy were increasingly built of brick and stone, which replaced the wood, lath, and plaster of the Middle Ages. This change was a response to the constant danger of fire. The great fire of London in 1666, which destroyed three-quarters of the town—12,000 houses—was the largest of the conflagrations that swept cities with devastating regularity. Urban dwellings of the laboring poor remained firetraps. Workers' quarters were badly overcrowded; entire families lived in one-room accommodations in basements and attics that were infested with bugs and fleas.

Urban society was, like its rural counterpart, a society of orders. In capital cities, noble families occupied the highest social position, as they did in the countryside, living a parasitic life of conspicuous consumption. The majority of cities and towns were dominated by a nonnoble *bourgeoisie*. That French term originally designated a burgher or townsman who was a long-term, resident property owner or leaseholder and taxpayer. By the eighteenth century it had come to mean a townsman of some means who aspired to be recognized as a person of local importance, and evinced a willingness to work hard, whether at counting-house or government office, and a desire to live a comfortable, if by no means extravagant, existence. A bourgeois gentleman might derive his income from rents; he might, as well, be an industrialist, banker, or merchant, lawyer, or physician. If he served in the central bureaucracy, he would consider himself the social superior of those provincials whose affairs he administered. Yet he would himself be looked down upon by the aristocracy, many of whom enjoyed thinking of the *bourgeoisie* as a class of vulgar social climbers, often conveniently forgetting their own commercial origins a generation or two previously. The French playwright Molière's comedy *The Bourgeois Gentleman* (1670) reflected this attitude, ridiculing the manners of the class who were trying to ape their betters. "Bourgeois," another French writer observed, "is the insult given by noblemen to anybody they deem slow-witted or out of touch with the court." The *bourgeoisie* usually constituted about 20 to 25 percent of a town's population. As its economic elite, these men were almost always its governing elite as well.

Surprisingly, given the increase of commercial and industrial activity in the early-modern period, many cities witnessed a decline in the relative size of their *bourgeoisies*. For example, Frenchmen who made their money in trade could purchase land, and by paying fees to the king, gain the right to

Urban living conditions

The *"Bon Ton."* This English cartoon mocks the rage for French fashion and illustrates the affluence of a middle class able to afford the changing dictates of fashion.

*Urban society: The
bourgeoisie*

*Upper bourgeoisie purchase
land*

an ennobling office. In seventeenth-century Amiens, a major textile center, the upper *bourgeoisie* deserted trade and derived the majority of its income from land or bonds. Where the *bourgeoisie* thrived, it more often than not did so as the result of a burgeoning state or regional bureaucracy.

Next within the urban hierarchy was a vast middle range of shopkeepers and artisans. Many of the latter continued to learn and then to practice their craft as members of guilds, which in turn contained their own particular ascending hierarchy of apprentice, journeyman, and master, thus preserving a society of orders. Throughout the early-modern period, however, commercial expansion threatened the rigid hierarchy of the guild structure. The expense and curtailed output resulting from restrictive guild practices met with serious opposition in big cities such as Paris and London, and in the industrial hinterlands of France and Germany, where expanding markets called for cheaper and more readily available goods. Journeymen tailors and shoemakers in increasing numbers set up shops without benefit of mastership and produced cheaper coats and shoes in defiance of guild regulations. In the silk workshops of Lyons, both masters and journeymen were compelled to labor without distinction of status for piece rates (wages paid per finished article, rather than per hour) set by merchandising middlemen and far below an equitable level in the opinion of the silk workers. Artisans like these, compelled to work for low wages at the behest of profiteering middlemen, grew increasingly restive. In France and Germany, journeymen's associations had originated as social and mutual-aid organizations for young men engaged in "tramping" the country to gain experience in their trade. In some instances, however, these associations fostered the development of a trade consciousness that led to strikes and boycotts against masters and middlemen over the issues of wages and working conditions. An imperial law passed in Germany in 1731 deprived the associations of their right to organize, and required journeymen to carry a certificate of identification as testimony of their respectability during their travels.

Urban society: Shopkeepers and artisans

At the bottom of urban society was a mass of semi-skilled and unskilled workers: carters and porters; stevedores and dockers; water carriers and sweepers; seamstresses, laundresses, cleaners, and domestic servants. These men and women, like their rural counterparts, lived on the margins of life, constantly battling the trade cycles, seasonal unemployment, and epidemics that threatened their ability to survive. A number existed in shanties on the edge of towns and cities. In Genoa, the homeless poor were sold as galley slaves each winter. In Venice, the poor lived on decrepit barges under the city's bridges. A French ordinance of 1669 ordered the destruction of all houses "built on poles by vagabonds and useless members of society." Deprived of the certainty of steady work, these people were prey not only to economic fluctuations and malevolent "acts of God," but to a social system that left them without any "privilege" or "freedom" whatsoever.

Urban society: The poor

Attitudes toward poverty varied from country to country. Most localities extended the concept of orders to include the poor: "the deserving"—usually orphans, the insane, the aged, the infirm; and "the undeserving"— able-bodied men and women who were out of work or who, even though

Attitudes toward poverty

Hanging Thieves. This seventeenth-century engraving is designed to teach a lesson. Troops stand by and priests bless the condemned criminals as they are executed by the dozen. "At last," the engraver's caption reads, "these infamous lost souls are hung like unhappy fruit."

Ifrael ex. Cum Priul. Reg.

employed, could not support themselves and their families. The authorities tended to assume in the latter case that poverty was the result of personal failings; few made a connection between general economic circumstances and the plight of the individual poor. For the deserving, private charitable organizations, such as those in France, founded by the order of St. Vincent de Paul and by the Sisters of Charity, provided assistance. For the undeserving, there was harsh treatment at the hands of the state whose concern to alleviate extreme deprivation arose more from a desire to avert public disorder than from motives of human charity. Food riots were common occurrences. In times of scarcity the French government frequently intervened to reduce the price of grain, hoping thereby to prevent an outbreak of rioting. Yet riots nevertheless occurred. When property damage resulted, the ringleaders were always severely punished, usually by hanging. The remainder of the crowd was often left untouched by the law, a fact suggesting the degree to which governments were prepared to tolerate rioting itself as a means of dealing with the chronic problem of poverty.

The treatment of paupers

Poor vagrants were perceived as a serious threat to social tranquility. They were therefore frequently rounded up at harvest time to keep them from plundering the fields. Vagrants and other chronically unemployed persons were placed in poorhouses where conditions were little better than those in prisons. Often the very young, the very old, the sick, and the insane were housed together with hardened criminals. Poor relief in England was administered parish by parish in accordance with a law passed in 1601. Relief was tied to a "law of settlement," which stipulated that paupers might receive aid only if still residing in the parish of their birth. An unemployed weaver who had migrated fifty miles in search of work could thus expect assistance only if he returned home again. In the late eighteenth century, several European countries established modest public works programs in an attempt to relieve poverty by reducing unemployment. France, for example, undertook road-building projects in the 1770s under the auspices of its progressive finance minister, Turgot. But generally speaking, indigence was perceived not as a social ill for which a remedy might be sought, but as an indelible stigma demarking the lowest of a community's social orders.

Early-modern Europe fashioned its institutions to reflect the patterns of social hierarchy. Nowhere was this more apparent than in the field of education. One barrier—a knowledge of Latin—separated nobles and a fair number of scholars and professionals from the commercial middle ranks; a second—the ability to read and write—separated the middle from the rest. Noblemen were generally educated by private tutors; though they might attend university for a time, they did so not in preparation for a profession but to receive further educational "finishing." Indeed during the late seventeenth and eighteenth centuries, universities more or less surrendered intellectual leadership to various academies established with royal patronage by European monarchs to enhance their own reputations as well as to encourage the advancement of science and the arts: the Royal Society of London, founded by Charles II in 1660; the French Academy of Sciences, a project upon which Louis XIV lavished a good deal of ostentatious attention; and the Berlin Royal Academy of Science and Letters, patronized by Frederick the Great of Prussia in the eighteenth century. Few noblemen had the interest or the intelligence to participate in the activities of these august organizations, which were not, in any case, teaching institutions. Far

Louis XIV Visiting the French Academy of Sciences. Royal patronage sustained such academies by guaranteeing members rewards suitable to their station.

better suited to their needs and inclinations was "the grand tour," often of many months' duration, which led the nobleman through the capitals of Europe, and during which he was expected to acquire a kind of international *politesse*. One observer, commenting on the habits of young English noblemen abroad, remarked: "they game; purchase pictures, mutilated statues, and mistresses to the astonishment of all beholders."

Training for government service

Endowed, fee-charging institutions for the training of a governmental elite existed in France (the *collège*) and Spain (the *colegio mayor*) and in Germany and Austria (the *gymnasium*). Here the emphasis was by no means on "practical" subjects such as modern language or mathematics, but on the mastery of Greek and Latin translation and composition, the intellectual badge of the educated elite. An exception was the Prussian University of Halle, designed to teach a professional elite; a contemporary described that institution as teaching only what was "rational, useful, and practical."

Education for the middle orders

Male children from the middle orders destined to enter the family business or profession as a rule attended small private academies where the curriculum included the sort of "useful" instruction ignored in the *collèges* and *gymnasia*. Female children, from both the upper and middle orders, were almost invariably educated at home, receiving little more than rudimentary instruction in gentlewomanly subjects such as modern language, belles lettres, and music, if from the noble ranks; and a similar, if slightly more practical training, if from the bourgeoisie.

Education for the poor

No European country undertook the task of providing primary education to all its citizens until the mid-eighteenth century, when Frederick the Great in Prussia and the Habsburg monarchs Maria Theresa and her son Joseph II in Austria instituted systems of compulsory attendance. Available evidence suggests that their results fell far short of expectation. An early-nineteenth-century survey from the relatively enlightened Prussian province of Cleves revealed dilapidated schools, poorly attended classes, and an incompetent corps of teachers. Educational conditions were undoubtedly worse in most other European communities.

Increasing literacy

Although educational opportunities for peasants and workers remained meager by modern standards, literacy rates increased considerably in the seventeenth and eighteenth centuries; in England, from one in four males in 1600 to one in two by 1800; in France, from 29 percent of the male population in 1686 to 47 percent in 1786. Literacy among women increased as well, though their rate of increase generally lagged behind that of men: only 27 percent of the female population in France was literate in 1786. Naturally, such rates varied according to particular localities and circumstances, and from country to country. Literacy was higher in urban areas that contained a large proportion of artisans. In rural Eastern Europe, literacy remained extremely low (20–30 percent) well into the nineteenth century. Notwithstanding state-directed efforts in Prussia and Austria, the rise in literacy was largely the result of a growing determination on the part of religiously minded reformers to teach the poor to read and write as a means of encouraging obedience to divine and secular authority. A Sunday-school movement in eighteenth-century England and similar activities among the Christian Brotherhood in France are clear evidence of this trend.

Though the majority of the common people were probably no more than barely literate, they possessed a flourishing culture of their own. Village life, particularly in Roman Catholic countries, centered about the church, to which men and women would go on Sundays not only to worship but to socialize. Much of the remainder of their day of rest would be devoted to participation in village games. Religion provided the opportunity for association and for a welcome break from the daily work routines. Pilgrimages, for example, to a nearby shrine would include a procession of villagers led by one of their number carrying an image of the village's patron saint and accompanied by drinking, dancing, and picnicking. In towns, Catholics joined organizations, called *confraternities* in France, Italy, Austria, and the Netherlands, which provided mutual aid and a set of common rituals and traditions centered upon a patron saint. Religious community was expressed as well in popular Protestant movements that arose in the eighteenth century: Pietism on the Continent and Methodism in England. Both emphasized the importance of personal salvation through faith and the potential worth of every human soul regardless of station. Both therefore appealed particularly to people whose position within the community had heretofore been presumed to be without any value. Though Methodism's founder, John Wesley (1703–1791), preached obedience to earthly authority, his willingness to rely on working men and women as preachers and organizers gave them a new sense of personal importance.

While much popular culture was directly linked to religious traditions and practices, much was now growing secular. Carnival, that vibrant pre-Lenten celebration indigenous not only to Mediterranean Europe but to

Cockfight by William Hogarth. This London scene suggests the degree to which men from different social orders came together for sport, drinking, and adventure. Here a clergyman and a young gentleman consort with the London riffraff.

French Tavern. Often located outside the city limits so as to avoid the payment of municipal taxes, taverns such as this provided a gathering place for workers to drink, gossip, and relax after the day's labors. The tavern also served as a convenient place for public readings and for airing common grievances.

Carnival and other amusements

Germany and Austria as well, represented an opportunity for common folk to cast aside the burdens and restraints imposed upon their order by secular authority. Performances and processions celebrated a "world turned upside down," a theme popular throughout much of Europe from the Later Middle Ages, appealing to commoners for a variety of ambiguous psychological reasons, but in large part, certainly, as a way of avenging symbolically the economic and social oppression under which they lived. For a few days, the oppressed played the role of the oppressor and rulers were made to look like fools and knaves. In parades, men dressed as kings walked barefoot while peasants rode on horseback or in carriages; the poor threw pretend money to the rich. These occasions, although emphasizing social divisions, worked to hold communities to a common cultural center, since, through most of the early-modern period, both rich and poor celebrated together, as they did on major religious holidays. Annual harvest festivals, once sponsored by the Church, were also increasingly secular celebrations of release from backbreaking labor, punctuated by feasting, drinking, sporting, and lovemaking. Fairs and traveling circuses brought something of distant places and people into lives bound to one spot. The drudgery of everyday life was also relieved by horse races, cock fights, and bear baiting. Taverns played an even more constant role in the daily life of the village, providing a place for men to gather over tobacco and drink to gossip and gamble.

Laboring men and women depended on an oral tradition of myth, leg-

end, and superstition to steady their lives, and give them point and purpose. Stories in books sold at fairs by peddlers were passed on by those who
could read. They told of heroes and saints, and of kings like Charlemagne
whose paternal concern for his common subjects led him into battle against
his selfish nobility. Belief in villains matched belief in heroes. Witchcraft, as
we have seen, was a reality for much of the period to superstitious men and
women. So was Satan. So was any supernatural force, whether for good or
evil, which could help them make sense of a world in which they, more
than any, were victims of events beyond their control.

Though increasingly secularized, popular customs, celebrations, and beliefs remained a stabilizing force in early-modern Europe. They were the
cultural expression of that social order to which the vast majority of Europeans belonged. Popular culture in the main tended to reinforce the traditions and assumptions of order and hierarchy. Peasants and urban workers
worshiped saints and venerated heroic rulers, thereby accepting the authority of the established, ordered society of which they were a part. They
were seldom satisfied with their lot, yet they were as seldom willing to
question the social structure they saw as a bulwark against the swift changes
so often surrounding them. Popular culture helped to bind men and
women to what civilization had been, as capitalism and mercantilism impelled them in the direction of what it would become.

SELECTED READINGS

• *Items so designated are available in paperback editions.*

• Blum, Jerome, *Lord and Peasant in Russia,* Princeton, 1961. A good study of Russian society.
• Braudel, F., *Capitalism and Material Life, 1400–1800,* London, 1973. A fascinating
review of evidence pertaining to the entire world.
• ———, *The Structures of Everyday Life: The Limits of the Possible,* New York,
1981. A survey of the material conditions of life; profusely illustrated.
• Burke, Peter, *Popular Culture in Early Modern Europe,* London, 1978. Synthesizes
the most recent work on the period between 1500 and 1800; fascinating.
• Chambers, J. D., and G. E. Mingay, *The Agricultural Revolution, 1750–1880,* London, 1966. Now the standard work.
• Cipolla, C. M., *Before the Industrial Revolution: European Economy and Society,
1000–1700,* 2nd ed., New York, 1980. Wide-ranging and full of deft observations.
• Curtin, Philip D., *The Atlantic Slave Trade,* Madison, Wisc., 1969. Reinterprets
the character of the trade.
• Darnton, Robert, *The Great Cat Massacre and Other Episodes in French Cultural History,* New York, 1984. Fascinating explorations into early-modern French
mentalities.
• Davis, D. B., *The Problem of Slavery in Western Culture,* Ithaca, N.Y., 1966. A brilliant analysis of Western attitudes and assumptions.
• Davis, Natalie Z., *Society and Culture in Early Modern France,* Stanford, 1975. Eight

scintillating essays by a pioneer in the use of anthropological methods for the study of early-modern European history.

Forster, Robert, *The Nobility of Toulouse in the Eighteenth Century,* Baltimore, 1960. A careful analysis of the extent and nature of aristocratic power.

• Foucault, M., *The History of Sexuality: An Introduction,* Vol. I, New York, 1978. Useful material on the early-modern period.

Hufton, Olwen H., *The Poor of Eighteenth Century France,* Oxford, 1974. One of the first studies of a preindustrial "underclass."

Heckscher, E., *Mercantilism,* rev. ed., 2 vols., London, 1955. The most influential, but controversial, work on the subject.

Kaplow, Jeffry, *The Names of Kings: The Parisian Laboring Poor in the Eighteenth Century,* New York, 1972. A valuable study of the urban poor.

• Laslett, Peter, and Richard Wall, eds., *Household and Family in Past Times,* New York, 1972. A suggestive collection of essays.

Le Roy Ladurie, Emmanuel, *The Peasants of Languedoc,* Urbana, Ill., 1974. A classic on peasant life and demography.

Levine, David, *Family Formation in an Age of Nascent Capitalism,* New York, 1977. A thoughtful treatment of patterns of social formation.

Lougee, Carolyn C., *Le Paradis des Femmes: Women, Salons, and Social Stratification in Seventeenth-Century France.* Princeton, 1976. Women's role in the intellectual life of the Old Regime.

• Mousnier, R., *Peasant Uprisings in Seventeenth-Century France, Russia and China,* New York, 1970. A comparative analysis.

Parry, J. H., *Trade and Dominion: The European Overseas Empires in the Eighteenth Century,* New York, 1971. A comparative overview.

• Ranum, Orest, *Paris in the Age of Absolutism,* New York, 1968. A useful view of urban life.

Rich, E. E., and C. H. Wilson, eds., *The Cambridge Economic History of Europe:* Volume 5, *The Economic Organization of Early Modern Europe,* New York, 1977. An indispensable guide to the study of the period's economy and society.

• Stone, Lawrence, *The Family, Sex and Marriage in England, 1500–1800,* New York, 1977. An important, controversial book which argues important changes in attitudes over the course of three centuries.

• Wilson, Charles, *England's Apprenticeship, 1603–1763,* London, 1965. A reliable economic survey.

• Wrigley, E. A., *Population and History,* New York, 1969. A good introduction to family history.

SOURCE MATERIALS

Barnett, G. E., ed., *Two Tracts by Gregory King,* Baltimore, 1936. An introduction to the work of the modern world's first real statistician.

• Goubert, P., *The Ancien Régime: French Society, 1600–1750,* London, 1973. Particularly strong in its descriptions of rural life. Includes selections from illuminating documents.

Young, Arthur, *Travels in France during the Years 1787, 1788, 1789,* London, various editions. Vivid observations by an English traveler.

Chapter 17

THE AGE OF ABSOLUTISM (1660–1789)

There are four essential characteristics or qualities of royal authority.
First, royal authority is sacred.
Second, it is paternal.
Third, it is absolute.
Fourth, it is subject to reason.

    —Jacques Bossuet, *Politics Drawn from the Very Words of Holy Scripture*

T he period from the accession to personal rule of Louis XIV of France (1651) until the French Revolution (1789) is known as the age of absolutism. The label is accurate if we define *absolutism* as the conscious attempt by state sovereigns—sometimes successful; more often not—to extend their legal and administrative power over their subjects, and over the vested interests of the social and economic orders in which those subjects were ranked. The dates are suggestive in that for the period as a whole the activities of French monarchs most clearly expressed the intentions of absolutist government. Yet both the dates and the label need to be treated with some caution. We have already noted that from about 1500 on, a general trend to make the state more powerful had manifested itself in England and on the Continent. Sixteenth-century kings saw in Protestantism a way of asserting the sovereignty of their states over the power of the papacy and the aristocracy. And political thinkers such as Jean Bodin were championing absolutist theory in their writings well before Louis XIV assumed personal rulership of France. By establishing the French monarchs as prototypical early-modern rulers, we risk ignoring other modes of centralized government instituted by the rulers of Prussia, Russia, and Austria. And we exclude the crucially important exception of England, where after 1688, absolutist tendencies gave way to oligarchy.

The term "absolutism" needs qualification. As practiced by Western European eighteenth-century rulers, absolutism was not despotism. They did

Absolutism defined

The limits of absolutism

not understand it as a license for untrammeled and arbitrary rule, such as that practiced by Oriental potentates. Despite the best efforts of these European monarchs to consolidate their authority, they could not issue irresponsible decrees and achieve lasting compliance. Aristocrats, churchmen, merchants, and entrepreneurs remained strong enough within their respective orders to ensure that kings and queens would need to justify the actions they took. Moreover, rulers tended to respect not only the strength of their political adversaries but the processes of law; they quarreled openly and broke with tradition only under exceptional circumstances. No matter how "absolute" monarchs might wish to be, they were limited as well by rudimentary systems of transportation and communication from interfering with any degree of consistency and efficiency in the daily lives of their subjects.

The relationship between state power and economic innovation

Although the emphasis in this chapter is largely upon political, diplomatic, and military events, absolutism cannot be fully understood without relating it to the commercial and industrial trends we have just analyzed. Tariff legislation, industrial regulations, wars of trade, currency manipulation, tax laws—all were useful tools in the construction of a new economic order. And all were tools that could be employed only by a strongly centralized state. Governments might take active steps to manage production and exportation, as the English did when they imposed the Navigation Acts in 1660, which restricted imports to material transported on English ships or those of their country of origin, and required colonial goods to pass through English ports before being sold elsewhere. Other governments (the French, for example), in their determination to finance expanding bureaucratic and military establishments, imposed new taxes and exacted an increasingly high price for the privileges they meted out. The state's expanding financial demands placed considerable pressure on both urban middle orders and peasantry to make more money. And the result of that pressure, in turn, was entrepreneurship and wage labor.

Bearing in mind, then, the important symbiotic relationship between state power and economic innovation, we shall, in this chapter, measure the extent of royal power throughout Europe in the late seventeenth and eighteenth centuries, examine the varieties of absolutism as instituted and practiced by different monarchs, and take note of the way in which the centralization of power contributed to the rise of an international state system.

1. THE APPEAL AND JUSTIFICATION OF ABSOLUTISM

Absolutism's appeal

Absolutism appealed to many Europeans for the same reason that mercantalism did. In theory and practice, it expressed a desire for an end to the constant alarms and confusions of Europe's "iron century." The French religious wars, the Thirty Years' War in Germany, and the English Civil War all had produced great turbulence. The alternative, domestic order, absolutists argued, could come only with strong, centralized government. Just as mercantilists maintained that economic stability would result from regimentation, so absolutists contended that social and political harmony would be realized when subjects recognized their duty to obey their divinely sanctioned rulers.

Absolutist monarchs insisted, in turn, upon *their* duty to teach their subjects, even against their will, how to order their domestic affairs. As Margrave Karl Friedrich, eighteenth-century ruler of the German principality of Baden, expressed it: "We must make them, whether they like it or not, into free, opulent and law-abiding citizens." Looking back to the seventeenth-century wars that had torn Europe apart, rulers can be excused for believing that absolutism's promise of stability and prosperity—"freedom and opulence"—presented an attractive as well as an imperative alternative to disorder. Louis XIV of France remembered the *Fronde* (see above, pp. 502–503) as a threat to the welfare of the nation that he had been appointed by God to rule wisely and justly. When marauding Parisians entered his bedchamber one night in 1651 to discover if he had fled the city with Mazarin, Louis saw the intrusion as a horrid affront not only to his own person, but to the state. Squabbles among the nobility and criticisms of royal policy in the Paris Parlement during his minority left him convinced that he must exercise his powers and prerogatives rigorously if France was to survive and prosper as a great European state.

The duties of the monarch

In order to achieve that objective, absolutist monarchs worked to control the disposition of the state's armed forces, the administration of its legal system, and the collection and distribution of its tax revenues. This ambitious goal required an efficient bureaucracy that owed its primary allegiance, not to some particular social or economic order with interests antithetical to the monarchy, but to the institution of the monarchy itself. One hallmark of absolutist policy was its determination to construct a set of institutions strong enough to withstand, if not destroy, the privileged interests that had stood in the path of royal power in the past. The Church and the nobility, the semiautonomous regions, and the would-be independent representative bodies (the English Parliament and the French Estates-General) were all obstacles to the achievement of strong, centralized monarchical government. And the history of absolutism is, as much as anything, the history of the attempts of various rulers to bring these institutions to heel.

Goals of absolute monarchs: Army, administration, and revenue

In those major European countries where Roman Catholicism still remained the state religion—France, Spain, and Austria—successive monarchs throughout the eighteenth century made various attempts to "nationalize" the Church and its clergy. We have already noted the way in which in the fifteenth and sixteenth centuries, popes had conceded certain powers to the temporal rulers of France and Spain. Later absolutists, building on those earlier precedents, wrested further power from the Church in Rome. Even Charles III, the devout Spanish king who ruled from 1759 to 1788, pressed successfully for a papal concordat granting the state control over ecclesiastical appointments, and established his right to sanction the proclamation of papal bulls.

Absolutism and the control of the Church and its clergy

Powerful as the Church was, it did not rival the nobility as an opponent of a centralized state. Monarchs combatted the noble orders in various ways. Louis XIV attempted to control the ancient French aristocracy by depriving it of political power while increasing its social prestige. Peter the Great, the talented and erratic tsar of early eighteenth-century Russia, co-opted the nobility into government service. Later in the century, Catherine II struck a bargain whereby in return for the granting of vast estates and a variety of social and economic privileges such as exemption from taxation, the Russian nobility virtually surrendered the administrative and political power of the state into the empress's hands. In Prussia under Frederick the Great, the army was staffed by nobles; here again, as in Peter's Russia, was a case of co-option. Yet in late-eighteenth-century Austria, the emperor Joseph II adopted a policy of confrontation rather than accommodation, denying the nobility exemption from taxation and deliberately blurring the distinctions between nobles and commoners.

These struggles between monarchs and nobles had implications for the additional struggle between local privileges and centralized power. Absolutists in France waged a constant and never-entirely-successful war against the autonomy of provincial institutions, often headed by nobles, much as Spanish rulers in the sixteenth century had battled independent-minded nobles in Aragon and Catalonia. Prussian rulers intruded into the governance of formerly "free" cities, assuming police and revenue powers over their inhabitants. These various campaigns, constantly waged and usually successful for a time, were evidence of the nature of absolutism and of its continuing success.

Absolutism had its theoretical apologists as well as its able practitioners. In addition to the political philosophies of men such as Bodin, defenders of royal power could rely on treatises such as Bishop Jacques Bossuet's *Politics Drawn from the Very Words of Scripture* (1708), written during the reign of Louis XIV, to sustain the case for extended monarchical control. Bossuet argued that absolute government was not the same as arbitrary government, since God, in whom "all strength and all perfection were united," was united as well with the person of the king. "God is holiness itself, goodness itself, and power itself. In these things lies the majesty of God. In the image of these things lies the majesty of the prince." It followed that the king was answerable to no one but God himself, and that the king was as far above other mortals as God was above the king. "The prince, as prince, is not regarded as a private person; he is a public personage, all the state is in him. . . . As all perfection and all strength are united in God, all the power of individuals is united in the Person of the prince. What grandeur that a simple man should embody so much." What grandeur indeed! Bossuet's treatise was the most explicit and extreme statement of the theory of the divine right of kings, the doctrine that James I had tried to foist upon the English. Unlikely as it may sound to modern ears, the political philosophy of Bossuet was comforting to men and women in the upper orders of society who craved peace and stability after a century or more of international and domestic turmoil, and who found themselves embarked upon bold economic adventures that required a strong and stable polity.

Bishop Jacques Bossuet

2. THE ABSOLUTISM OF LOUIS XIV

Examine a portrait of Louis XIV* (1643–1715) in court robes; it is all but impossible to discern the human being behind the facade of the absolute monarch. That facade was carefully and artfully constructed by Louis, who recognized, perhaps more clearly than any other early-modern ruler, the importance of theater as a means of establishing authority. Well into the eighteenth century, superstitious commoners continued to believe in the power of the king's magic "touch" to cure disease. Louis and his successors manipulated the theater of their sovereignty so as to enhance their position as divine-right rulers endowed with God-like powers and far removed from common humanity.

Absolutism as theater: Louis XIV

The advantages of strategic theater were expressed most clearly in Louis's palace at Versailles, the town outside of Paris to which he moved his court. The building itself was a stage upon which Louis attempted to mesmerize the aristocracy into obedience by his performance of the daily rituals of absolutism. The main facade of the palace was a third of a mile in length. Inside, tapestries and paintings celebrated French military victories and royal triumphs. Outside, in gardens containing 1400 fountains, statues of Apollo, god of the sun, recalled Louis's claim to be the "Sun King" of the French. Noblemen vied to attend him when he arose from bed, ate his meals (usually stone-cold, having traveled the distance of several city blocks from royal kitchen to royal table), strolled in his gardens, or rode to the hunt. As Louis called himself the Sun King, so his court was the epicenter of his

Versailles

*Here, as elsewhere, dates following a ruler's name refer to dates of reign.

The Château of Versailles. Dramatically expanded by Louis XIV in the 1660s from a hunting lodge to the principal royal residence and the seat of government, the château became a monument to the international power and prestige of the Grand Monarch.

One of the 140 Fountains in the Gardens at Versailles. The grounds as well as the palace were part of the backdrop for the theater of absolutism.

royal effulgence. Its glitter, in which France's leading nobles were required by their monarch to share, was deliberately manufactured so as to blind them to the possibility of disobedience to the royal will. Instead of plotting some sort of minor treason on his estate, a marquis enjoyed the pleasure of knowing that on the morrow he was to be privileged to engage the king in two or three minutes of vapid conversation as the royal party made its stately progress through the vast palace halls (whose smells were evidence of the absence of sanitation facilities and of the seamy side of absolutist grandeur).

Louis XIV on his duties

Louis understood this theater as part of his duty as sovereign, a duty that he took with utmost seriousness. Though far from brilliant, he was hard-working and conscientious. Whether or not he actually remarked *"L'état, c'est moi"* ("I am the State"), he believed himself personally responsible for the well-being of his subjects. "The deference and the respect that we receive from our subjects," he wrote in a memoir he prepared for his son on the art of ruling, "are not a free gift from them but payment for the justice and the protection that they expect from us. Just as they must honor us, we must protect and defend them."

The administration of French absolutism: Intendants and revenue

Louis defined this responsibility in absolutist terms: as a need to concentrate royal power so as to produce general domestic tranquillity. While taming the nobility, he conciliated the upper bourgeoisie by enlisting its members to assist him in the task of administration. He appointed them as intendants, responsible for the administration and taxation of the thirty-six *generalités* into which France was divided. Intendants usually served outside the region where they were born, and were thus unconnected with the local elites over which they exercised authority. They held office at the king's pleasure, and were clearly "his" men. Other administrators, often from families newly ennobled as a result of administrative service, assisted in directing affairs of state from Versailles. These men were not actors in the theater of Louis the Sun King; they were the hard-working assistants of Louis the royal custodian of his country's welfare. Much of the time and energy of Louis's bureaucrats were expended on the collection of taxes, necessary above all in order to finance the large standing army on which France's ambitious foreign policy depended. Absolutism, it must never be forgotten, was a mechanism designed to assist ambitious monarchs in their determination to increase their power through conquest. In addition to the *taille,* or land tax, which increased throughout the seventeenth century and upon which a surtax was levied as well, the government introduced a *capitation* tax (head tax), payable by all, and pressed hard for the collection of indirect taxes such as that on salt (the *gabelle*) and on wine and tobacco. Since the nobility was exempt from the *taille,* its burden fell most heavily on the peasantry, whose periodic local revolts Louis easily crushed.

Regional opposition—and indeed regionalism generally—was curtailed, but by no means eliminated, during Louis's reign. Although intendants and lesser administrators came from afar, did not speak the local dialect, and ignored local custom, they were generally obeyed. The semiautonomous outer provinces of Brittany, Languedoc, and Franche Comté (a part of that territory known collectively as the *pays d'états*) suffered the crippling of their provincial Estates. To put an end to the power of regional *parlements,*

Curbing regional opposition

Louis XIV, the Sun King. This portrait by Rigaud illustrates the degree to which absolute monarchy was defined in terms of studied performance.

Louis decreed that members of those bodies that refused to register his laws would be summarily exiled. The Estates-General, the national French representative assembly last summoned in 1614 during the troubled regency that followed the death of Henry IV, did not meet again until 1789.

Louis was equally determined, for reasons of state and of personal conscience, to impose religious unity upon the French. That task proved to be difficult and time-consuming. The Huguenots were not the only source of theological heterodoxy. Quietists and Jansenists—both claiming to represent the "true" Roman faith—battled among themselves for adherents to their particular brand of Catholicism. Quietists preached retreat into personal mysticism that emphasized a direct relationship between God and the individual human heart. Such doctrine, dispensing as it did with the intermediary services of the Church and of the orthodox authority those services represented, was suspect in the eyes of absolutists wedded to the doctrine of *un roi, une loi, une foi* (one king, one law, one faith). Jansenism—a movement named for its founder Cornelius Jansen, a seventeenth-century bishop of Ypres—challenged the authority of the state church with an unorthodox doctrine of predestination, proclaiming the salvation of no more than an elected few. Louis persecuted Quietists and Jansenists, offering them the choice of recanting or of prison and exile. Against the Huguenots he waged an even sterner war. Protestant churches and schools were destroyed; Protestant families were forced to convert. In 1685, Louis revoked the Edict of Nantes, the legal foundation of the toleration Huguenots had enjoyed since 1598. French Protestants were thereafter denied civil rights, and their clergy was exiled. Thousands of religious refugees fled France for England, Holland, the Protestant states of Germany, and America, where their particular professional and artisanal skills made a significant contribution to economic prosperity. (The silk industry of Berlin and of Spitalfields, an urban quarter of London, was established by Huguenots.)

Louis's drive for unification and centralization was assisted by his ability to rely upon increased revenues. Those revenues were largely the result of policies and programs initiated by Jean Baptiste Colbert (1619–1683), the country's finance minister from 1664 until his death. Colbert was an energetic and committed mercantilist who believed that until France could put its fiscal house in order it could not achieve economic greatness. He tightened the process of tax collection, and he eliminated wherever possible the practice of tax farming, the system whereby collection agents were permitted to withhold a certain percentage of what they gathered for themselves. When Colbert assumed office, only about 25 percent of the taxes collected throughout the kingdom was reaching the treasury. By the time he died, that figure had risen to 80 percent.

Jean Baptiste Colbert

Colbert's efforts were not limited to managing the public debt and wringing the inefficiencies out of the tax system, however. During this period the state also merchandised government positions and privileges on an increasing scale. Judgeships, mayoralities and other public offices were sold, and guilds purchased the right to enforce trade regulations. The state extracted direct profit from every office it created and every privilege it controlled, demonstrating once again the way in which economy and politics were inextricably intertwined.

As a mercantilist, Colbert did all he could to increase the nation's income by means of protection and regimentation. Tariffs he imposed in 1667 and 1668 were designed to discourage the importation of foreign goods into France. He invested in the improvement of France's roads and waterways. And he used state money to promote the growth of national industry, in particular the manufacture of goods such as silk, lace, tapestries, and glass, which had long been imported. Yet Colbert's efforts to achieve national economic stability and self-sufficiency could not withstand the insatiable demands of Louis XIV's increasingly expensive wars. By the end of Louis's reign, indeed, the limitations of his absolutist ambitions were strikingly evident. As we shall see, his aggressive foreign policy lay in ruins. The country's finances were enfeebled by the economic demands that policy exacted. Colbert himself foreshadowed Louis's ultimate failure when he lectured him in 1680: "Trade is the source of public finance and public finance is the vital nerve of war. . . . I beg your Majesty to permit me only to say to him that in war as in peace he has never consulted the amount of money available in determining his expenditures."

Colbert as mercantilist

3. ABSOLUTISM IN CENTRAL AND EASTERN EUROPE, 1660–1720

Whatever success Louis XIV did enjoy as an absolute monarch was in part the result of his own abilities, and of those of his advisors. Yet it was due as well to the fact that he could claim to stand as the supreme embodiment of the will of all of his people. Despite its internal division into territories and orders that continued to claim some right to independence, France was already unified before the accession of Louis XIV and possessed a sense of itself as a nation. In this, it differed from the empires, kingdoms, and principalities to the east, where rulers faced an even more formidable task than did Louis as they attempted to weld their disparately constructed monarchies into a united, centralized whole. The Thirty Years' War had delivered a final blow to the pretensions of the Holy Roman Empire, which the French philosopher Voltaire dubbed neither holy, Roman, nor an empire. Power, in varying degrees, passed to the over three hundred princes, bishops, and magistrates who governed the assorted states of Germany throughout the remainder of the seventeenth and eighteenth centuries.

Absolutism and national unity

Despite the minute size of their domains, many of these petty monarchs attempted to establish themselves as absolutists in miniature, building lesser versions of Louis XIV's Versailles. They remodeled cities to serve as explicit expressions of their power. Broad avenues led to monumental squares and eventually to the grand palace of the monarch. Medieval cities had masked the inequalities of the social order in their crowded, twisted streets and passageways, where social ranks often lived jumbled together in close

Absolutism in the German states

physical proximity. Absolutist capital cities, in contrast, celebrated inequality, their planning and architecture purposely emphasizing the vast distance separating the ruler from the ruled. European absolutists followed the French example by maintaining standing armies, and paying for their expensive pretensions by tariffs and tolls that severely hampered the development of any sort of economic unity within the region as a whole. Although these rulers often prided themselves on their independence from imperial control, in many instances they were client states of France. A sizable portion of the money Louis devoted to the conduct of foreign affairs went to these German princelings. States like Saxony, Brandenburg-Prussia, and Bavaria, which were of a size to establish themselves as truly independent, were not averse to forming alliances against their own emperor.

The absolutism of Frederick
William of Brandenburg

Most notable among these middle-sized German states was Brandenburg-Prussia, whose emergence as a power of consequence during this period was the result of the single-minded determination of its rulers, principally Frederick William, elector of Brandenburg from 1640 to 1688, whose abilities have earned him the title of "Great Elector." The rise of Brandenburg-Prussia from initial insignificance, poverty, and devastation in the wake of the Thirty Years' War resulted from three basic achievements that can be credited to the Great Elector. First, he pursued an adroit foreign policy that enabled him to establish effective sovereignty over the widely dispersed and underdeveloped territories under his rule: Brandenburg, a large but not particularly productive territory in north-central Germany; Prussia, a duchy to the east that was dangerously exposed on three sides to Poland; and a sprinkling of tiny states—Cleves, Mark, and Ravensberg—to the west. By siding with Poland in a war against Sweden in the late 1650s, the Great Elector obtained the Polish king's surrender of nominal overlordship in East Prussia. And by some crafty diplomatic shuffling in the 1670s, he secured his western provinces from French interference by returning Pomerania, captured in a recent war, to France's Swedish allies.

The establishment of a large
standing army

Frederick William's second achievement was the establishment of a large standing army, the primary instrument of his diplomatic successes. By 1688, Brandenburg-Prussia had 30,000 troops permanently under arms. That he was able to sustain an army of this size in a state with comparatively limited resources was a measure of the degree to which the army more than repaid its costs. It ensured the elector and his successors absolute political control by fostering obedience among the populace, an obedience they were prepared to observe if their lands might be spared the devastation of another Thirty Years' War.

Taxation and bureaucracy:
Bargaining with the Junkers

The third factor contributing to the emergence of the Great Elector's state as an international power was his imposition of an effective system of taxation and his creation of a government bureaucracy to administer it. Here he struck an important bargain with the powerful and privileged landlords (*Junkers*) without whose cooperation his programs would have had no chance of success. In return for an agreement that allowed them to reduce their peasant underlings to the status of serfs, the Junkers gave away their right to oppose a permanent tax system, provided, of course, that they

Prussians Swearing Allegiance to the Great Elector at Königsberg, 1663. The occasion upon which the Prussian estates first acknowledged the overlordship of their ruler. This ceremony marked the beginning of the centralization of the Prussian state.

were made immune from the payment of taxes themselves. (As in other European countries, taxes in Prussia fell most heavily on the peasantry.)

Henceforth, the political privileges of the landlord class diminished; secure in their right to manage their own estates as they wished, the Junkers were content to surrender management of the Hohenzollern possessions into the hands of a centralized bureaucracy. Its most important department was a military commissariat, whose functions included not only the dispensing of army pay and matériel, but the development of industries to manufacture military equipment. Frederick William's success was due primarily to his ability to gain the active cooperation of the Junker class, something he needed even more than Louis XIV needed the support of the French nobility. Without it, Frederick William could never have hammered together a state from the disparate territories that were his political raw material. To obtain it, he used the army, not only to maintain order, but as a way of co-opting Junker participation. The highest honor that could befall a Brandenburg squire was commission and promotion as a military servant of the state.

Like Brandenburg-Prussia, the Habsburg monarchy was confronted with the task of transforming four different regions into a cohesive state. In the

The Junkers and the army

Absolutism in the Habsburg Empire

case of Austria, this effort was complicated by the fact that these areas were ethnically and linguistically diverse: the southernmost Germanic lands that roughly comprised the present-day state of Austria; the northern Czech- (Slavic-) speaking provinces of Bohemia and Moravia; the German-speaking Silesia, inherited in 1527; and Hungary (where the Magyar population spoke a non-Slavic, Finno-Ugric language), also acquired in 1527 but largely lost to Turkish invasion just a few years afterward. For the next 150 years the Habsburgs and the Turks vied for control of Hungary. Until 1683 Turkish pashas ruled three-fourths of the Magyar kingdom, extending to within eighty miles of the Habsburg capital of Vienna. In 1683 the Turks beseiged Vienna itself, but were repulsed by the Austrians, assisted by a mixed German and Polish army under the command of King John Sobieski of Poland. This victory was a prelude to the Habsburg reconquest of virtually all of Hungary by the end of the century.

Bargaining with Bohemia and Moravia

The task of constructing an absolutist state from these extraordinarily varied territories was tackled with limited success by the seventeenth-century Habsburg emperors Ferdinand III (1637–1657) and Leopold I (1658–1705). Most of their efforts were devoted to the establishment of productive agricultural estates in Bohemia and Moravia, and to taming the independent nobility there and in Hungary. Landlords were encouraged to farm for export, and were supported in this effort by a government decree that compelled peasants to provide three days of unpaid *robot* service per week to their masters.* For this support, Bohemian and Moravian landed elites exchanged the political independence that had in the past expressed itself in the activities of their territorial legislative Estates.

Problems with the Hungarian nobility

Habsburg rulers tried to effect this same sort of bargain in Hungary as well. But there the tradition of independence was stronger and died harder. Hungarian (or Magyar) nobles in the west claimed the right to elect their king, a right they eventually surrendered to Leopold in 1687. But the central government's attempts to reduce the country further by administering it through the army, by granting large tracts of land to German aristocrats and settlers, and by persecuting non-Catholics were an almost total failure. The result was a powerful nobility that remained fiercely determined to retain its traditional constitutional and religious "liberties." The Habsburg emperors could boast that they too, like absolutists elsewhere, possessed a large standing army and an educated (in this case, German-speaking) bureaucracy. But the exigencies imposed by geography and ethnicity kept them at some distance from the absolutist goal of a unified, centrally controlled and administered state.

Peter the Great. An eighteenth-century mosaic.

Undoubtedly the most dramatic episode in the history of early-modern absolutist rule was the dynamic reign of Tsar Peter I of Russia (1682–1725). Peter's accomplishments alone would clearly have earned him his history-book title, Peter the Great. But his imposing height—he was nearly seven feet tall—as well as his mercurial personality—jesting one moment, raging the next—certainly helped. Peter is best remembered as

---

*The English usage of the term *robot* derives from the Czech designation of a serf.

the tsar whose policies brought Russia into the world of Western Europe. Previously the country's rulers had set their faces firmly against the West, disdaining a civilization at odds with the Eastern Orthodox culture that was their heritage, while laboring to keep the various ethnic groups—Russians, Ukrainians, and a wide variety of nomadic tribes—within their ever-growing empire from destroying not only each other but the tsarist state itself. Since 1613 Russia had been ruled by members of the Romanov dynasty, who had attempted with some success to restore political stability following the chaotic "time of troubles" that had occurred after the death of the bloodthirsty, half-mad Tsar Ivan the Terrible in 1584. Tsar Alexis I (1645–1676) took a significant step toward unification in 1654 when he secured an agreement with the Ukrainians to incorporate that portion of the Ukraine lying east of the Dneiper River into the Muscovy state. But the early Romanovs were faced with a severe threat to this unity and their rule between 1667 and 1671, when a Cossack leader (the Russian Cossacks were semi-autonomous bands of peasant cavalrymen) named Stenka Razin led much of southeastern Russia into rebellion. Stenka Razin's uprising found widespread support from serfs who had been oppressed by their masters as well as from non-Russian tribes in the lower Volga area who longed to cast off domination from Moscow. But ultimately Tsar Alexis and the Russian nobility whose interests were most at stake were able to raise an army capable of defeating Razin's zealous but disorganized bands. Before the rebellion was finally crushed, over 100,000 rebels had been slaughtered.

These campaigns were but a prelude to the deliberate and ruthless drive to absolutist power launched by Peter after he overthrew the regency of his half-sister Sophia and assumed personal control of the state in 1689. Within ten years he had scandalized nobility and churchmen alike by traveling to Holland and England to recruit highly skilled foreign workers and to study the craft of shipbuilding. Upon his return he distressed them still further by declaring his intention to westernize Russia, and initiating this campaign by cutting off the "Eastern" beards and flowing sleeves of leading noblemen at court. Determined to "civilize" the nobility, he published a book of manners which forbade spitting on the floor and eating with one's fingers, and encouraged the cultivation of the art of polite conversation between the sexes.

Peter Cutting a Nobleman's Beard. In this Russian woodcut Peter the Great is portrayed as a diminutive pest.

Much as Peter wished to consider himself a westerner, his particular brand of absolutism differed from that of other contemporary monarchs. As we have seen, the autocracy imposed by Ivan III in the fifteenth century had a decidedly Eastern caste. Peter was the willing heir to much of that tradition. He considered himself above the law and thus his own absolute master to a degree that was alien to the absolutist theories and traditions of the Habsburgs and Bourbons. Autocrat of all the Russias, he ruled despotically, with a ferocious individual power that Western European rulers did not possess. Armed with such arbitrary power in theory, and intent on realizing its full potential in practice, Peter set out to turn Russia to the West and to modernize his state. He would brook no opposition.

Confronted with a rebellion among the *streltsy,* the politically active,

Peter the Great's Execution of the Streltsy. This contemporary print shows scores of corpses gibbeted outside the walls of the Kremlin. Peter kept the rotting bodies on display for months to discourage his subjects from opposing his efforts to westernize Russian society.

The suppression and reconstruction of the army

elite corps of the army who were most opposed to his innovations and who favored the restoration of his half-sister to the throne, Peter reacted with a savagery that astonished his contemporaries. Roughly 1200 suspected conspirators were summarily executed, many of them gibbeted outside the walls of the Kremlin, where their bodies remained for months as a graphic reminder of the fate awaiting those who would dare to challenge his absolute authority. Applying a lesson from the West, Peter proceeded to create a large standing army recruited from the ranks of the peasantry and scrupulously loyal to the tsar. One of every twenty males was conscripted for lifelong service. He financed his army, as did other absolutists, by increasing taxes, with their burden falling most heavily on the peasantry. To equip his new military force, he fostered the growth of the iron and munitions industries. Factories were built and manned by peasant laborers whose position was little better than that of slaves. Serfs were also commandeered for other public works projects, such as road and canal building, necessary for the modernization of the state.

Absolutism and the new bureaucracy

In an effort to further consolidate his absolute power, he replaced the Duma—the nation's rudimentary national assembly—with a rubber-stamp senate, and appointed a procurator, or agent, dependent directly on him, to manage the affairs of the tradition-bound Russian Orthodox Church, which essentially became an extension of the state. At the same time, Peter was fashioning new, larger, and more efficient administrative machinery to cope with the demands of his modernization program. Although he preferred to draw "new" men, whose loyalty to the tsar would be unerring, into the bureaucracy, he was compelled to rely upon the services of the noble—or *boyar*—class as well, rewarding them by increasing their control over their serfs. Nevertheless, membership in his new bureaucracy did not depend on birth. One of his principal advisors, Alexander Menshikov, began his career as a cook and finished as a prince. Bureaucratic status replaced noble rank as the key to power. The administrative machinery devised by Peter furnished Russia with its ruling class for the next two hundred years.

Peter the Great's Eurocentric worldview also manifested itself in his foreign policy, as witnessed by his bold drive to gain a Russian outlet on the Baltic Sea. Previous battles with the Turks to secure a port on the Black Sea, and thus a southern passage to the West, had failed. Now he engaged in a war with Sweden's meteoric soldier-king Charles XII (1697–1718), who devoted most of his reign to campaigns in the field against the Danes, the Poles, and the Russians. By defeating Charles decisively at the battle of Poltava in 1709, Peter was able to secure his window to the West. He promptly outdid his absolutist counterparts in Europe, who had moved their courts to the outskirts of their capital cities, by moving the Russian capital from Moscow to an entirely new city on the Gulf of Finland. An army of serfs was employed to erect the baroque city of St. Petersburg around a palace intended to imitate and rival Louis XIV's Versailles.

The influence of foreign and domestic policy

The St. Petersburg Palaces The first of six versions of the Winter Palace here depicted (left) was erected in 1711. It quickly proved to be too modest for Peter's needs. Within a decade he had created a far more elaborate complex called Peterhof (right), complete with fountains fashioned after those of Versailles.

Not surprisingly, Peter's drastic programs met with concerted resistance. Resentment smoldered under his imposing hand, even within the palace. His son Alexis, who had dared to declare himself opposed to his father's innovations, became a rallying point for the forces of resistance to the tsar and his policies, and died under torture inflicted at his father's command in 1718. Upon Peter's death in 1725, *boyar* determination to undo his reforms surfaced during the succession struggle. There followed a series of ineffective tsars, creatures of the Palace guard, thus allowing the resentful nobles to rescind many of his reforms. In 1762, the crown passed to Catherine II, a ruler whose ambitions and determination were equal to those of her august predecessor.

Peter the Great of Russia, Leopold I of Austria, Frederick William of Brandenburg-Prussia, and above all Louis XIV of France: these were the "great" seventeenth-century absolutists. Elsewhere, the fortunes of absolutism fared far less well. The ineffectual, weak-minded Spanish monarch Charles II found himself besieged by rebellions in Portugal and Sicily. In 1668, after years of fighting, he was forced to recognize Portuguese independence. In Sweden, Charles X and Charles XI managed to extend their territories at the expense of the Danes and to quell the independence of the aristocracy by confiscating their fiefdoms. During the reign of Charles XII, however, that legacy was dissipated by an adventurous but ultimately unproductive foreign policy. In Poland, the opposition of the landed gentry—or *szlachta*—to any form of centralized government produced a political stalemate that amounted to little more than anarchy. Foreign powers took advantage of this situation to intervene in Polish affairs and, in the eighteenth century, to carve up the country and distribute it among themselves.

4. THE ENGLISH EXCEPTION

But what of England, which had experienced a taste of absolutist centralization under the Tudors and early Stuarts, and indeed under Oliver Cromwell, but which possessed in its Parliament the longest tradition and most highly developed form of representative government in Western Europe? England's political history in the late seventeenth century provides the most striking contrast to Continental absolutism. Charles II, son of the beheaded Charles I, who returned from exile and ascended the throne in 1660, was initially welcomed by most English men and women. He pledged himself not to reign as a despot, but to respect Parliament and to observe Magna Carta and the Petition of Right, for he admitted that he was not anxious to "resume his travels." His delight in the unbuttoned moral atmosphere of his court and the culture it supported (risque plays, dancing, and marital infidelity) mirrored a public desire to forget the restraints of the Puritan past. The wits of the time suggested that Charles, "that known enemy to virginity and chastity," played his role as the father of his country to the fullest. However, as Charles's admiration of things French grew to include the absolutism of Louis XIV, he came to be regarded as a threat to more than English womanhood by a great many powerful Englishmen. However anxious to restore the monarchy, they were not about to surrender their traditional rights to another Stuart autocrat. By the late 1670s, the country found itself divided politically into those who supported the king (called by their opponents "Tories," a popular nickname for Irish Catholic bandits) and those opposed to him (called by *their* opponents "Whigs," a similar nickname for Scottish Presbyterian rebels).

Charles II of England

As the new party labels suggest, religion remained an exceedingly divisive national issue. Charles was sympathetic to Roman Catholicism, even to the point of a deathbed conversion in 1685. He therefore opposed the stiff code of ecclesiastical regulations, known as the Clarendon Code, which had reestablished Anglicanism as the official state religion and which penalized Catholics and Protestant dissenters. In 1672, Charles suspended the Clarendon Code, although the public outcry against this action compelled him to retreat. This controversy, and rising opposition to the probable succession of Charles's ardent Roman Catholic brother James, led to a series of Whig electoral victories between 1679 and 1681. But Charles found that increased revenues, plus a secret subsidy he was receiving from Louis XIV, enabled him to govern without resort to Parliament, to which he would otherwise have had to go for money. In addition to ignoring Parliament, Charles further infuriated and alarmed Whig politicians by arranging the execution of several of their most prominent leaders on charges of treason, and by remodeling local government in such a way as to make it more dependent on royal favor. Charles died in 1685 with his power enhanced, but he left behind him a political and religious legacy that was to be the undoing of his successor.

Charles suspends Clarendon Code

James II was the very opposite of his brother. A zealous Catholic convert, he alienated his Tory supporters, all of whom were of course Anglicans, by dismissing them in favor of Roman Catholics, and by once again suspending the penal laws against Catholics and dissenters. His stubbornness, as one historian has remarked, made it all but impossible for him to take "yes" for an answer. Whereas Charles had been content to defeat his political enemies, James was determined to humiliate them. Like Charles, James interfered in local government, but his appointments were so personally distasteful and so mediocre as to arouse active opposition. James made no attempt to disguise his Roman Catholicism. He publicly declared his wish that all his subjects might be converted, and paraded papal legates through the streets of London. When, in June 1688, he ordered all Anglican clergymen to read his decree of toleration from their pulpits, seven bishops refused and were clapped into prison on charges of seditious libel. At their trial, however, they were declared not guilty, to the vast satisfaction of the English populace.

James II as religious zealot

The trial of the bishops was one event that brought matters to a head. The other was the birth of a son in 1688 to James and his second wife, the Roman Catholic daughter of the duke of Modena. This male infant, who

The succession question

William III

William and Mary; joint sovereigns of England

A "glorious" revolution?

was to be raised a Catholic, replaced James's much older Protestant daughter Mary as heir to the British throne. Despite a rumor that the baby boy was an imposter smuggled into the royal bedchamber in a warming pan, political leaders of both parties were prepared not only to believe in the legitimacy of the child but to take active steps to prevent the possibility of his succession. A delegation of Whigs and Tories crossed the Channel to Holland with an invitation to Mary's husband William of Orange, the *stadholder* or chief executive of the United Provinces and the great-grandson of William the Silent. William was asked to cross to England with an invading army to restore English religious and political freedom. As leader of a Continental coalition determined to thwart Louis XIV's expansionist policies, he accepted, welcoming the chance such a move represented to bring England into active opposition to the French (see below, p. 590).

William's "conquest" was a bloodless coup. James fled the country in 1688, thereby allowing Parliament to declare the throne vacant and clearing the way for the accession of William and Mary as joint sovereigns of England. A Bill of Rights, passed by Parliament and accepted by the new king and queen in 1689, reaffirmed English civil liberties such as trial by jury, habeas corpus (guaranteeing the accused a speedy trial), and the right of petition and redress, and established that the monarchy was subject to the law of the land. An Act of Toleration, passed in 1689, granted dissenters the right to worship, though not the right to full political protection. In 1701, with the son of the exiled James II now reaching maturity in France, an Act of Succession ordained that the English throne was to pass first to Mary's childless sister Anne, who ruled from 1702 to 1714, and then to George, elector of the German principality of Hanover, who was the great-grandson of James I. The connection was a distant one, but the Hanoverian dynasty was Protestant, and George reputed to be a capable enough ruler. The act was further evidence of the degree to which Parliament could dictate its terms. Henceforth, all English sovereigns were to be communicants of the Church of England. If foreign born, they could not engage England in the defense of their native land, nor leave the country, without Parliamentary consent.

The events of 1688 and 1689 were soon referred to by the English as "the Glorious Revolution." Glorious for the English in that it occurred without bloodshed (although James is reputed to have been suffering from a nosebleed at the moment of crisis). Glorious, too, for defenders of Parliamentary prerogative. Although William and Mary and their royal successors continued to enjoy a large measure of executive power, after 1688 no king or queen attempted to govern without Parliament, which met annually from that time on. Parliament strengthened its control over the collection and expenditure of public money. Future sovereigns were henceforth unable to conduct the country's business without recourse to the House of Commons for the funds to do so. Glorious, finally, for advocates of the civil liberties now guaranteed within the Bill of Rights.

Yet 1688 was not all glory. It was a revolution that consolidated the position of large property holders, local magnates whose political and economic power base in their rural constituencies and on their estates had been threatened by the interventions of Charles II and James II. If it was a revolution, it was one designed to restore the *status quo* on behalf of a wealthy social and economic order that would soon make itself even wealthier as it drank its fill of government patronage and war profits. And it was a revolution that brought nothing but misery to the Roman Catholic minority in Scotland, which joined with England and Wales in the union of Great Britain in 1707, and the Catholic majority in Ireland where, following the Battle of the Boyne in 1690, repressive military forces imposed the exploitive will of a self-interested Protestant minority upon the Catholic majority.

Although the "Glorious Revolution" was an expression of immediate political circumstance, it was a reflection as well of anti-absolutist theories that had risen in the late seventeenth century to challenge the ideas of writers such as Bodin, Hobbes, and Bossuet. Chief among these opponents of absolutism was the Englishman John Locke (1632–1704), whose *Two Treatises of Civil Government,* written prior to the revolution, though published in 1690, was used to justify the events of the previous two years. Locke maintained that originally all humans had lived in a theoretical state of nature in which absolute freedom and equality prevailed, and in which there was no government of any kind. The only law was the law of nature, which individuals enforced for themselves in order to protect their natural rights to life, liberty, and property. It was not long, however, before they began to perceive that the inconveniences of the state of nature greatly outweighed its advantages. With individuals attempting to enforce their own rights, confusion and insecurity were the unavoidable results. Accordingly, the people agreed among themselves to establish a civil society, to set up a government, and to surrender certain powers to it. But they did not make that government absolute. The only power they conferred upon it was the executive power of the law of nature. Since the state was nothing but the joint power of all the members of society, its authority could "be no more than those persons had in a state of nature before they entered into society, and gave it up to the community." All powers not expressly surrendered were reserved to the people themselves. If the government exceeded or abused the authority explicitly granted in the political contract, it became tyrannical; the people then had the right to dissolve it or to rebel against it and overthrow it.

Locke condemned absolutism in every form. He denounced despotic monarchy, but he was no less severe in his strictures against the absolute sovereignty of parliaments. Though he defended the supremacy of the lawmaking branch, with the executive primarily an agent of the legislature, he nevertheless refused to concede to the representatives of the people an unlimited power. Arguing that state government was instituted among people for the preservation of property, he denied the authority of any political agency to invade the natural rights of a single individual. The law of nature, which embodied these rights, was an automatic limitation upon every branch of the government. Locke's theoretical defense of political liberties

1688 as a defense of status quo

John Locke

Defense of 1688: The political theories of John Locke

Locke and limited sovereignty

emerged in the late eighteenth century as an important element in the intellectual background of the American and French Revolutions. In 1688, however, it served a far less radical purpose. The landed magnates responsible for the exchange of James II for William and Mary could read Locke as an apologia for their conservative revolution. James II, rather than protecting their property and liberties, had encroached upon them; hence they had every right to overthrow the tyranny he had established and to replace it with a government that would, by ensuring their rights, defend their interests.

5. WARFARE AND DIPLOMACY: THE EMERGENCE OF A STATE SYSTEM

To the extent that absolute monarchs succeeded in attaining their goals of unification and centralization, their states took shape as individual, identifiable political and economic entities. Often, it is true, the interests of a monarch might clash with those of the country over which he ruled. Bourbon kings and Habsburg emperors worried about the future of their family dynasties to the detriment of the future of France or Austria. And religion, the factor that had torn Europe apart in the preceding century, remained an international issue in 1700. But increasingly, both dynasty and religion were superseded by newer "interests"—commerce and international balance and stability.

Emergence of state system

The result was the emergence of a state system. Although the achievements of various monarchs were limited, they were significant enough to encourage diplomats to speak more commonly than in the past of the "interests" of a particular state, as if that state somehow had a corporate personality of its own, and of the way in which those interests might coincide or conflict with the interests of another state. What followed was a significant redefinition of the aims and calculations of diplomacy and warfare.

The growth of diplomacy

The organization of diplomatic bureaucracies was a major accomplishment of absolutist monarchies. Had most foreign ministers and ambassadors read the Dutchman Hugo Grotius's treatise on *The Law of War and Peace* (1625), they would have agreed with him about the necessity of establishing a body of rules that would help to bring reason and order to relations between governments. In practice, of course, reason and order gave way to bribery and improvisation. Yet the rationalization of diplomatic processes and the establishment of foreign ministries and embassies in European capitals, with their growing staffs of clerks and ministers, reflected a desire to bring order out of the international chaos that had gripped Europe during the early seventeenth century. International relations in the late 1600s was, among other things, a history of diplomatic coalitions, an indication of the degree to which negotiation was now a weapon in the armory of the absolutist state.

Warfare, however, continued to play an integral and almost constant

The Capture of Cambrai by Louis XIV in 1677. This print illustrates the tactics of siege warfare as practiced by early-modern armies. Louis is shown receiving an emissary from the city, whose walls have been breached by siege guns.

role in the international arena. The armies of the period grew dramatically. When Louis XIV acceded to power in 1661, the French army numbered 20,000 men; by 1688, it stood at 290,000; by 1694, 400,000. These armies were increasingly professional organizations, controlled directly by the state, and under the command of trained officers recruited from the nobility. In Prussia, common soldiers were mostly conscripts; in other European countries they were volunteers, either native or foreign, though often "volunteers" in no more than name, having been coerced or tricked into service. Increasingly, however, enlistment was perceived by common soldiers as an avenue to a career, one that included the possibility of promotion to corporal or sergeant, and in the case of France, the promise of a small pension at the end of one's service. However recruited, common soldiers became part of an increasingly elaborate and efficient fighting force. The maneuvers of infantry, cavalry, and artillery were coordinated as never before. Soldiers were drilled with a thoroughness necessitated by tactics that depended on the accurate firepower of cannon and flintlock muskets. They were taught to stand their ground in formations of long, rigid lines in the face of direct enemy assault. They mastered the bayonet (a short steel spike attached to the end of muskets, first manufactured in Bayonne, France, in the seventeenth century); the most effective procedure for its use was stabbing a man in his left side as he raised his right arm to fire. Above all, they were made to understand the dire consequences of disobedience, breaking rank, or desertion. Soldiers were expected to obey instantly and

The growth of professional armies

unquestioningly. Failure to do so resulted in brutal punishment, often flogging, sometimes execution. Commissioned and noncommissioned officers carried sticks and prods with which to "encourage" correct military behavior in their men. Drill, not only on the battlefield but on the parade ground, in brilliant, elaborate uniforms and intricate formations, was designed to reduce individuals to automaton-like parts of an army whose regiments were moved across battlefields as a chess player moves pawns across the board—and with about the same concern for loss of human life.

The foreign policies of Louis XIV

The patterns of international relations during the period from 1660 to 1715 show European monarchs making use of the new machinery of diplomacy and warfare to resolve the conflicting interests of dynasty, stability, and commerce. At the center of that pattern, as at the center of Europe, stood Louis XIV. From 1661 until 1688, in a quest for glory, empire, and even revenge, he waged war across his northern and eastern frontiers on the pretext that the lands in question belonged both to the Bourbons and to the French by tradition, by former treaty, or by dynastic inheritance. His aggressively expansionist policies, alarming to other European rulers, led William of Orange, in 1674, to form an anti-French coalition with Austria, Spain, and various smaller German states. Yet Louis continued to push his frontiers eastward, invading territories that had been Germanic for centuries, and capturing Strassburg in 1681 and Luxembourg in 1684. Louis's seizure of Strassburg (subsequently called Strasbourg by the French), completing the conquest of the German-speaking province of Alsace begun in 1634 by Richelieu, irreversibly incorporated the seeds of a Franco-German animosity centered on this region that would bear bitter fruit in the great wars of the nineteenth and twentieth centuries. A second coalition, the so-called League of Augsburg (1686)—Holland, Austria, Sweden, and further German allies—was only somewhat more successful than the first.

Europe on the verge of war

These allies were concerned above all to maintain some sort of European balance of power. They feared an expansionist France would prove insatiable, as it pressed its boundaries farther and farther into Germany and the Low Countries. Louis, mistakenly expecting that William would be forced to fight an English army under James to establish his right to his new throne and would therefore be too preoccupied to devote his full attention to developments on the Continent, kept up the pressure. In September 1688 he invaded the Palatinate and occupied the city of Cologne. The following year the French armies crossed the Rhine and continued their eastward drive, burning Heidelberg and committing numerous atrocities throughout the middle Rhine area. Aroused at last to effective action, the coalition, led by William and now including in addition to its former members both England and Spain, engaged Louis in a war that was to last until 1697.

War of the League of Augsburg

The major campaigns of this War of the League of Augsburg were fought in the Low Countries. William managed to drive an army under his predecessor, James II, from Ireland in 1690; from that point on, he took command of the allied forces on the Continent. By 1694 Louis was pressed hard, not only by his allied foes, but by a succession of disastrous harvests that crippled France. Fighting remained stalemated until a treaty was signed at Ryswick in Holland in 1697, which compelled Louis to return most of France's recent gains, except for Alsace, and to recognize William as the rightful king of England.

Ryswick did nothing, however, to resolve the dynastic tangle known as the Spanish Succession. Since Charles II of Spain had no direct heirs, and since he appeared to be on his deathbed in 1699, European monarchs and diplomats were obsessed by the question of who would succeed to the vast domain of the Spanish Habsburgs: not only Spain itself, but also its overseas empire, as well as the Spanish Netherlands, Naples, Sicily, and other territories in Italy. Both Louis XIV and Leopold I of Austria were married to sisters of the decrepit, unstable Charles; and both, naturally, eyed the succession to the Spanish inheritance as an exceedingly tempting dynastic plum. Yet it is a measure of the degree to which even absolutists were willing to keep their ambitions within bounds that both Leopold and Louis agreed to William's suggestion that the lion's share of the Habsburg lands should go to six-year-old Joseph Ferdinand, the prince of Bavaria, who was Charles II's grandnephew. Unfortunately, in 1699 the child died. Though the chances of war increased, William and Louis were prepared to bargain further and arranged a second treaty that divided the Spanish empire between Louis's and Leopold's heirs. Yet at the same time, Louis's diplomatic agents in Madrid persuaded Charles to sign a will in which he stipulated that the entire Spanish Habsburg inheritance should pass to Louis's grandson Philip of Anjou. This option was welcomed by many influential Spaniards, willing to endure French hegemony in return for the protection France could provide to the Spanish empire. For a time, Louis contemplated an alternative agreement that would have given France direct control of much of Italy. When Charles finally died in November 1700, Louis decided to accept the will. As if this was not enough to drive his former enemies back to war, he sent troops into the Spanish Netherlands and traders to the Spanish colonial empire, while declaring the late James II's son—the child of the warming pan myth—the legitimate king of England.

The problem of the Spanish Succession

Once it was clear to the allies that Louis intended to treat Spain as if it were his own kingdom, they again united against him in the cause of balance and stability. William died in 1702, just as the War of the Spanish Succession was beginning. His position as first general of the coalition passed to two brilliant strategists, the Englishman John Churchill, duke of Marlborough, and his Austrian counterpart, Prince Eugene of Savoy, an upper-class soldier of fortune who had been denied a commission by Louis. Under their command the allied forces engaged in battle after fierce battle in the Low Countries and Germany, including an extraordinary march deep into Bavaria, where the combined forces under Marlborough and Eugene smashed the French and their Bavarian allies decisively at Blenheim (1704). While the allies pressed France's armies on land, the English navy

War: The battle of Blenheim

captured Gibraltar and the island of Minorca, thus establishing a strategic and commercial foothold in the Mediterranean, and helping to open a fourth major military theater in Spain itself.

Military stalemate

The War of the Spanish Succession was a "professional" war that tested the highly trained armies of the combatants to the fullest. At the battle of Malplaquet in northeastern France in 1709, 80,000 French soldiers faced 110,000 allied troops. Though Marlborough and Eugene could claim to have won that battle, in that they forced the French to retreat, they suffered 24,000 casualties, twice those of the French. Neither Malplaquet nor other such victories brought the allies any closer to their final goal, which now appeared to be not the containment, but the complete destruction of the French military force. Queen Anne of England (Mary's sister and William's successor), once Marlborough's staunchest defender, grew disillusioned with the war and fired her general.

Dynastic changes and the pursuit of peace

More than war weariness impelled the combatants toward negotiation, however. The War of the Spanish Succession had begun as a conflict about the balance of power in Europe and the world. Yet dynastic changes had by 1711 compelled a reappraisal of allied goals. Leopold I had died in 1705. When his elder son and successor Joseph I died in 1711, the Austrian monarchy fell to Leopold's youngest son, the Archduke Charles, who had been the allies' candidate for the throne of Spain. With Charles now the Austrian and the Holy Roman Emperor as Charles VI (1711–1740), the prospect of his accession to the Spanish inheritance conjured up the ghost of Charles V and threatened to give him far too much power. International stability therefore demanded an end to hostilities and diplomatic negotiation toward a solution that would reestablish some sort of general balance.

The Treaty of Utrecht

The Treaty of Utrecht settled the conflict in 1713 by redistributing territory and power in equitable portions. No one emerged a major winner or loser. Philip, Louis's grandson, remained on the throne of Spain, but Louis agreed that France and Spain would never be united under the same ruler. Austria gained territories in the Netherlands and Italy. The Dutch, victims of French aggression during the war, were guaranteed protection of their borders against future invasion. The English retained Gibraltar and Minorca, as well as territory in America: Newfoundland, Acadia, Hudson Bay, and in the Caribbean, St. Kitts. Perhaps most valuable of all, the English extracted the *asiento* from Spain which gave them the right to supply Spanish America with African slaves. The settlement reflected the degree to which new interests had superseded old. Balance of power and stability among states were the major goals of the negotiations, goals that reflected a departure from the world of seventeenth-century turmoil when religious fanaticism had been a major factor in international conflict. The eventual "winners" were undoubtedly the English, whose dynastic concerns were limited to a general acceptance of the Hanoverian settlement, and who could therefore concentrate their efforts on amassing overseas territories that would contribute to the growth of their economic prosperity and hence their international power.

Treaty sites, 1697-1721
Boundary of the German Empire
Habsburg dominions

AGE OF ABSOLUTISM

6. ENLIGHTENED ABSOLUTISM AND LIMITED MONARCHY IN THE EIGHTEENTH CENTURY

Eighteenth-century absolutism was a series of variations on the dominant themes composed in the previous century by Louis XIV. That it has earned itself the historical distinction of "enlightened" absolutism suggests that those variations were of some consequence. Eighteenth-century rulers backed their sovereign claims not in the language of divine right, but in terms of their determination to act, as Frederick the Great of Prussia declared, as "first servant of the state." That phrase meant not so much service to the people as it did service to the goal of further strengthening the authority of the state over institutions that sought to challenge its corporate well-being. Enlightened rulers moved to curtail the privileges of old institutions. The Roman Catholic Church, for example, was compelled to suffer the expulsion of the Jesuits from most Catholic countries. Customary laws benefiting particular orders or interests were reformed. To strengthen the state community, innovative policies in the areas of taxation, economic

"Enlightened" absolutism

Louis XV

Absolutism under the successors of Louis XIV

Resurgence of the parlements

The achievements of Frederick I of Prussia

development, and education were instituted. As we shall see in Chapter 18, rational schemes of this sort reflected the spread of Enlightenment ideals as manifested in the writings of thinkers such as Beccaria, Diderot, and Voltaire. (The last was, in fact, a guest at Frederick's court for several years.) Assisting enlightened "first servants" in the implementation of these changes was a growing cadre of lesser servants: bureaucrats, often recruited from the nobility, but once recruited, expected to declare primary allegiance to their new master, the state. Despite innovation, "enlightened" absolutists continued to insist, as their predecessors had, that state sovereignty rested with the monarchy. Authority remained their overriding concern, and to the extent that they combatted efforts by the estates of their realms to dilute that authority, they declared their descent from their seventeenth-century forebears.

Louis XIV's successors, his great-grandson Louis XV (1715–1774) and that monarch's grandson Louis XVI (1774–1792), were unable to sustain the energetic drive toward centralization that had taken place under the Sun King. Indeed, during his last years, while fighting a desperate defensive war against his allied enemies, Louis XIV had seen his own accomplishments begin to crumble under the mounting pressure of military expenses. His heir was only five years old when he assumed the throne. As he grew up, Louis XV displayed less single-minded determination than had his great-grandfather to act the role of Sun King. The heroic, baroque grandeur of the main palace at Versailles yielded to the rococo grace of the Grand and Petit Trianons, pleasure pavillions built by Louis XV in the palace gardens.

During the minority of Louis XV, the French *parlements,* those courts of record responsible for registering and thereby legalizing royal decrees, enjoyed a resurgence of power which they retained throughout the century. No longer tame adjuncts of absolutist governmental machinery as they had been under Louis XIV, these bodies now proclaimed themselves the protectors of French "liberties." In the late 1760s, encouraged by his chancellor René Maupeou, Louis XV issued an edict effectively ending the right of *parlements* to reject decrees. Protest on the part of the magistrates resulted in their imprisonment or banishment. The *parlements* themselves were replaced by new courts charged not only with the responsibility of rubber-stamping legislation but also with administering law more justly and less expensively. When Louis XVI ascended the throne in 1774, his ministers persuaded him to reestablish the *parlements* as a sign of his willingness to conciliate his trouble-making aristocracy. This he did, with the result that government—particularly the management of finances—developed into a stalemated battle.

Stalemate was what the Prussian successors to Frederick William, the Great Elector, were determined to avoid. Frederick I (1688–1713), the Great Elector Frederick William's immediate successor, enhanced the appearance and cultural life of Berlin. As the Roman numeral by his name attests, he also succeeded in bargaining his support to the Austrians during the War of the Spanish Succession in return for the coveted right to style himself king. (The Austrian monarch was the Holy Roman Emperor and therefore had the right to create kings.)

Frederick William I (1713–1740), cared little for the embellishments his father had made to the capital city. His overriding concern was the building of a first-rate army. So single-minded was his attention to the military that he came to be called "the sergeant king." Military display became an obsession. His private regiment of "Potsdam Giants" was comprised exclusively of soldiers over six feet in height. The king traded musicians and prize stallions for such choice specimens and delighted in marching them about his palace grounds. Frederick William I's success as the builder of a military machine can be measured in terms of numbers: 30,000 men under arms when he came to the throne; 83,000 when he died twenty-seven years later, commander of the fourth-largest army in Europe, after France, Russia, and Austria. Since he could hardly count on volunteers, most of his soldiers were conscripts, drafted from the peasantry for a period of years and required to attend annual training exercises lasting three months. Conscription was supplemented by the kidnapping of forced recruits in neighboring German lands. To finance his army, Frederick William I increased taxes and streamlined their collection through the establishment of a General Directory of War, Finance, and Domains. In 1723, he instituted a system of administration by boards, hoping thereby to eliminate individual inefficiency through collective responsibility and surveillance. In addition, he created an inspectorate to uncover and report to him the mistakes and inefficiencies of his officialdom. Even then, he continued to supervise personally the implementation of state policy while shunning the luxuries of court life; for him, the "theater" of absolutism was not the palace but the office, which placed him at the helm of the state and the army. Perceiving the resources of the state to be too precious to waste, he pared costs at every turn to the point where, it was said, he had to invite himself to a nobleman's table in order to enjoy a good meal.

Frederick William I

Frederick William I builds first-rate army

A hard, unimaginative man, Frederick William I had little use for his son, whose passion was not the battlefield but the flute, and who admired French culture as much as his father disdained it. Not surprisingly, young Frederick rebelled; in 1730, when he was eighteen, he ran away from court with a friend. Apprehended, the companions were returned to the king, who welcomed the fledgling prodigal with something other than a fatted calf. Before Frederick's eyes, he had the friend executed. The grisly lesson took. Thenceforward Frederick, though he never surrendered his love of music and literature, bound himself to his royal duties, living in accordance with his own image of himself as "first servant of the state," and earning himself history's title of Frederick the Great.

The apprenticeship of Frederick the Great

Frederick William I's zealous austerity and his compulsion to build an efficient army and administrative state made Prussia a strong state. Frederick the Great, building on the work of his father, raised his country to the status of a major power. As soon as he became king in 1740, Frederick mobilized the army his father had never taken into battle and occupied the poorly protected Austrian province of Silesia to which Prussia had no legit-

The seizure of Silesia

Frederick the Great and Voltaire. Although Frederick offered asylum to the French philosophe, this "enlightened despot" did not permit his intellectual pursuits to interfere with matters of state.

imate claim. Although he had earlier vowed to make morality rather than expediency the hallmark of his reign, he seemingly had little difficulty in sacrificing his youthful idealism in the face of an opportunity to make his Prussian state a leading power. The remaining forty-five years of his monarchy were devoted to the consolidation of this first bold stroke.

Such a daring course required some adjustments within the Prussian state. The army had to be kept at full strength, and to this end, Frederick staffed its officer corps with young noblemen. In expanding the bureaucracy, whose financial administration kept his army in the field, he relied on the nobility as well, reversing the policy of his father, who had recruited his civil servants according to merit rather than birth. But Frederick was not one to tolerate mediocrity; he fashioned the most highly professional and efficient bureaucracy in Europe. The degree to which both army and bureaucracy were staffed by the nobility is a measure of his determination to secure the unflagging support of the most privileged order in his realm, in order to ensure a united front against Prussia's external foes.

The Prussian army and the nobility

Frederick's domestic policies reflected that same strategy. In matters where he ran no risk of offending the nobility, he followed his own rationalist bent, prohibiting the torture of accused criminals, putting an end to the bribing of judges, and establishing a system of elementary schools. He promoted religious toleration, declaring that he would happily build a mosque in Berlin if he could find enough Muslims to fill it. (Yet he was strongly anti-Semitic, levying special taxes on Jews and making efforts to close the professions and the civil service to them.) On his own royal estates he was a model "enlightened" monarch. He abolished capital punish-

Frederick the Great as an enlightened absolutist

ment, curtailed the forced labor services of his peasantry, and granted them long leases on the land they worked. He fostered scientific forestry and the cultivation of new crops. He opened new lands in Silesia and brought in thousands of immigrants to cultivate them. When wars ruined their farms, he supplied the peasants with new livestock and tools. Yet he never attempted to extend these reforms to the estates of the Junker elite, since to have done so would have alienated that social and economic group upon which Frederick was most dependent.

Although the monarchs of eighteenth-century Austria eventually proved themselves even more willing than Frederick the Great to undertake significant social reform, the energies of Emperor Charles VI (1711–1740) were concentrated on guaranteeing the future dynastic and territorial integrity of the Habsburg lineage and domain. Without a male heir, Charles worked to secure the right of his daughter Maria Theresa to succeed him as eventual empress. By his death in 1740 Charles had managed to persuade not only his subjects but all the major European powers to accept his daughter as his royal heir—a feat known as the "pragmatic sanction." Yet his painstaking efforts were only partially successful. As we have seen, Frederick the Great used the occasion of Charles's death to seize Silesia. The French, unable to resist the temptation to grab what they could, joined the coalition against the new empress, Maria Theresa (1740–1780).

Charles VI and the "pragmatic sanction"

With most of her other possessions already occupied by her enemies, Maria Theresa appealed successfully to the Hungarians for support. The empress was willing to play the role of the wronged woman when, as on this occasion, it suited her interests to do so. Hungary's vital troops combined with British financial assistance helped to enable her to battle Austria's enemies to a draw, although she never succeeded in regaining Silesia. The experience of those first few years of her reign persuaded Maria

Maria Theresa: Adversity and centralization

Maria Theresa of Austria. This portrait was painted to suggest, correctly, that the empress, shown here reviewing her troops, was a formidable monarch and a match for Frederick the Great.

Theresa, who was both capable and tenacious, to reorganize her dominions along the tightly centralized lines characteristic of Prussia and France. Ten new administrative districts were established, each with its own "war commissar" appointed by and responsible to the central administration in Vienna—an Austrian equivalent of the French intendant. Property taxes were increased to finance an expanded army, which was modernized and professionalized so as to remain on a par with the military establishments of the other great powers. Centralization, finances, army: once more those three crucial elements in the formula of absolute rule came into play.

"Enlightened" absolutism in Austria

Reform did not stop there, however. Together Maria Theresa and her son Joseph II, with whom she ruled jointly from 1765 to 1780, and who then succeeded her for another ten years, instituted a series of significant social reforms. Although both mother and son were devout Roman Catholics, they moved to assert their control over the Church, removing the clergy's exemption from taxation and decreeing the state's ability to block the publication of papal bulls in Austria. In 1773, following the papal suppression of the Jesuits, they used the order's assets to finance a program of state-wide primary education. Although the General Schools Ordinance of 1774 never achieved anything like a universally literate population, it did succeed in educating hundreds of thousands, and in financing not only schools for children but schools as well for those who taught the children. Joseph followed these reforms with an "Edict on Idle Institutions" in 1780, which resulted in the closing of hundreds of monastic houses, whose property went to support charitable institutions now under state control. These reforms and others—liberalization of punishment for criminal offenses, a relaxation of censorship, the abolishing of serfdom and feudal dues, and an attempt to eradicate superstition by curbing the practice of pilgrimages and celebration of saint's days—made Joseph more enemies than friends, among

Joseph II of Austria Visiting a Farm. The royal estates provided Joseph with the opportunity to experiment with agrarian reforms by raising the serfs to the status of free peasants.

both the noble elite and the common people. "Enlightened" though Joseph II was, however, he nevertheless remained a staunch absolutist, as concerned with the maintenance of a strong army and an efficient bureaucracy as with the need to educate his peasantry. Joseph's brother Leopold II, who succeeded him in 1790, attempted to maintain the reformist momentum. His death two years later and the accession of his reactionary son Francis II (1792–1835), put an end to liberalizing experiments.

Unlike Joseph II, Catherine the Great of Russia (1762–1796) felt herself compelled to curry the favor of her nobility by involving them directly in the structure of local administration, by exempting them from military service and taxation, and probably most important, by granting them absolute control over the serfs on their estates. Her policy grew out of her strong ties to powerful nobles and her involvement in the conspiracy that led to the assassination of her husband, Tsar Peter III, the last of a series of weak rulers who followed Peter the Great. Catherine was herself a German, and prided herself on her devotion to Western principles of government. Ambitious to establish a reputation as an intellectual and enlightened monarch, she corresponded with French philosophers, wrote plays, published a digest of William Blackstone's *Commentaries on the Laws of England,* and began a history of Russia. Her contributions to social reform did not extend much beyond the founding of hospitals and orphanages, and the expression of a pious hope that someday the serfs might be liberated. Although she did summon a commission in 1767 to codify Russian law, its achievements were modest: a minor extension of religious toleration, a slight restriction of the use of torture by the state. Catherine's interest in theories of reform did, however, stimulate the development of a social conscience among certain gentry intellectuals, foreshadowing a more widespread movement in the nineteenth century.

Any plans Catherine may have had for improving the lot of the peasants, however, were abruptly cancelled after their frustration with St. Petersburg's centralization efforts erupted in a violent peasant-serf rebellion in 1773–1774. Free peasants in the Volga valley region found themselves compelled to provide labor services to nobles sent by the crown to control them, Cossacks were subjected to taxation and conscription for the first time, and factory workers and miners were pressed into service in the state's industrial enterprises. These and other disparate but dissatisfied groups, including serfs, united under the rebel banner of Emelyan Pugachev, an illiterate Cossack who claimed to be the late Tsar Peter III. The hapless Peter, who had spoken as a reformer in life, in death became a larger-than-life hero for those opposed to the determined absolutism of his successor. As Pugachev marched, he encouraged his followers to strike out not only against the empress but also against the nobility and the church. Over 1500 landlords and priests were murdered, and the ruling classes were terrified as the revolt spread. While Catherine's forces initially had little success against the rebel army, the threat of famine plagued Pugachev's advance and finally led to disarray among his troops. Betrayed in 1774, he was captured and taken in an iron cage to Moscow, where he was tortured

Catherine the Great

Emelyan Pugachev Shackled and Encaged after His Capture

The significance of Catherine the Great

and killed. Catherine responded to this uprising with further centralization and tightening of aristocratic authority over the peasantry.

The brutal suppression and punishment of the rebels reflected the ease with which the German-born Catherine took to the despotic authoritarianism that characterized Russian absolutism. She was as outsized in her tastes and personality as was Peter the Great. Her sexual appetite was voracious; her current chief officers of state as often as not were also her current lovers. But Catherine continued the work of Peter the Great in introducing Russia to Western ideas; she came to terms with the nobility in a way that brought stability to the state; and she made the country a formidable power in European affairs by extending its boundaries to include not only most of Poland but also lands on the Black Sea.

The absolutist worldview

Eighteenth-century monarchs shared a desire to pursue policies that would mark their regimes as befitting a world that was leaving obscurantism and fanaticism behind. They were determined to press ahead with the task, begun by their seventeenth-century predecessors, of building powerful, centralized states by continuing to attempt the elimination or harnassing of the ancient privileges of still-powerful noble orders and provincial estates. The notion of a limited monarchy, in which power was divided between local and central authorities and shared by monarchs, nobles, and legislative assemblies, struck them as a dangerous anachronism. Yet as the century progressed, they found that conviction challenged by the emergence of England, under limited monarchy, as the world's leading commercial and naval power.

Hanoverians as English kings

England (or Britain, as the country was called after its union with Scotland in 1707) prospered as a state in which power was divided between the king and Parliament. This division of political power was guaranteed by a constitution which, though unwritten, was grounded in common law and strengthened by precedent and by particular legal settlements such as those that had followed the restoration of the Stuarts in 1660 and the overthrow of James II in 1688. The Hanoverians George I (1714–1727) and his son George II (1727–1760) were by no means political nonentities. Though George I could not speak English, he could converse comfortably enough with his ministers in French. The first two Georges made a conscientious and generally successful effort to govern within their adopted kingdom. They appointed the chief ministers who remained responsible to them for the creation and direction of state policy. Yet because Parliament, after 1688, retained the right to legislate, tax, and spend, its powers were far greater than those of any European parlement, estate, or diet. During the reign of the first two Hanoverians, politics was on most occasions little more than a struggle between factions within the Whig party, composed of wealthy—and in many cases newly rich—landed magnates who were making fortunes in an expanding economy based on commercial and agricultural capitalism.

George I of England

The Tories, because of their previous association with the Stuarts, remained political "outs" for most of the century. To the Whigs, national politics was no longer a matter of clashing principles. Those principles had

The House of Commons. Despite its architectural division into two "sides," the House was composed of men of property whose similar economic interests encouraged them to agree on political fundamentals.

been settled—to their satisfaction—in 1688. Nor was politics a matter of legislating in the national interest. Britain was governed locally, not from the center as in an absolutist state. Aristocrats and landed gentry administered the affairs of the particular counties and parishes in which their estates lay, as lords lieutenant, as justices of the peace, as overseers of the poor, unhampered, to a degree unknown on the Continent, by legislation imposed uniformly throughout the kingdom. The quality of local government varied greatly. Some squires were as "allworthy" as Henry Fielding's fictional character of that name in the novel *Tom Jones*. Others cared for little beyond the bottle and the chase. A French traveler noted in 1747 that the country gentleman was "naturally a very dull animal" whose favorite after-dinner toast was "to all honest fox hunters in Great Britain." These men administered those general laws that did exist—the Poor Law, game laws—which were drawn in such a way as to leave their administrators wide latitude, a latitude that they exercised in order to enhance the appearance of their own local omnipotence. Thus in Britain there was no attempt to pass a law establishing a state-wide system of primary education. Centralizing legislation of that sort, the hallmark of absolutist states, was anathema to the British aristocracy and gentry. They argued that education, if it was to be provided, should be provided at their expense, in village schoolrooms by schoolmasters in their employ. Those instructors would make it their business to teach their pupils not only rudimentary reading, writing, and figur

Local government

Left: *Sir Robert Walpole with Members of His Cabinet.* Right: *Walpole as a Roman Emperor.*

Robert Walpole as chief minister

ing, but the deferential behavior that bespoke the obligation of the poor to their rich benefactors. As the Church of England catechism had it, they were "to do their duty in that station of life unto which it shall please God to call them."

Politics, then, was neither first principles nor national legislation. It was "interest" and "influence," the weaving of a web of obligations into a political faction powerful enough to secure jobs and favors—a third secretaryship in the foreign office from a minister, an Act of Enclosure from Parliament. The greatest master of this game of politics was Robert Walpole (1676–1745) who was England's leading minister from the early 1720s until 1742. Walpole is sometimes called Britain's first prime minister, a less than entirely accurate distinction, since officially that position did not exist until the nineteenth century. Prime minister or not, he wielded great political power. He took advantage of the king's frequent absences in Hanover to assert control over the day-to-day governance of the country. He ruled as chief officer of his cabinet, a small group of like-minded politicians whose collective name derived from the room in which they met. In time the cabinet evolved into the policy-making executive arm of the British political system; Britain is governed today by cabinet and Parliament, the cabinet being composed of leading politicians from the majority party in Parliament.

Walpole was a member of a Norfolk gentry family who had risen to national prominence on the fortune he amassed while serving as paymaster-general to the armed forces during the War of the Spanish Succession. Adept at bribery and corruption, he used his ability to reward his supporters with appointments to ensure himself a loyal political following. By the end of his career, grossly fat and stuffed seemingly with the profits of his years in office, he was being depicted by cartoonists and balladeers as Britain's most accomplished robber. "Little villains must submit to Fate," lamented a typical lampoon, "while great ones do enjoy the world in state." Walpole was no more corrupt, however, than the political process over which he presided. Most seats in Parliament's lower House of Commons were filled by representatives from boroughs that often had no more than two or three dozen electors. Hence it was a relatively simple task to buy votes, either directly or with promises of future favors. Walpole cemented political factions together into an alliance that survived for about twenty years. During that time, he worked to ensure domestic tranquillity by refusing to press ahead with any legislation that might arouse national controversy. He withdrew what was perhaps his most innovative piece of legislation—a scheme that would increase excise taxes and reduce import duties as a means of curbing smugglers—in the face of widespread popular opposition.

Other Whig politicians succeeded Walpole in office in the 1740s and 1750s, but only one, William Pitt, later elevated to the House of Lords as the earl of Chatham, commanded public attention as Walpole had. George III (1760–1820), who came to the throne as a young man in 1760, resented the manner in which he believed his royal predecessors had been treated by the Whig oligarchy. Whether or not, as legend has it, his mother fired his determination with the constant injunction "George, be king!" he began his reign convinced that he must assert his rightful prerogatives. He dismissed Pitt, and attempted to impose ministers of his own choosing on Parliament. King and Parliament battled this issue of prerogative throughout the 1760s. In 1770, Lord North, an aristocrat satisfactory to the king and with a large enough following in the House of Commons to ensure some measure of stability, assumed the position of first minister. His downfall occurred a decade later, as a result of his mismanagement of the overseas war that resulted in Britain's loss of its original thirteen North American colonies. A period of political shuffling was followed by the king's appointment, at the age of twenty-three, of another William Pitt, Chatham's son, and this Pitt directed Britain's fortunes for the next twenty-five years—a political reign even longer than Walpole's. Although the period between 1760 and 1780 witnessed a struggle between crown (as the king and his political following were called) and Parliament, it was a very minor skirmish compared with the titanic constitutional struggles of the seventeenth century. Britain saw the last of absolutism in 1688. What followed was the mutual adjustment of the two formerly contending parties to a settlement both considered essentially sound.

The history of European diplomacy and warfare after 1715 is one in which the twin goals of international stability and economic expansion remained paramount. The fact that those objectives often conflicted with each other set off further frequent wars, in which the ever-growing standing armies of absolutist Europe were matched against each other and in which the deciding factor often turned out to be not Continental military strength, but British naval power. The major conflict at mid-century, known as the Seven Years' War in Europe and the French and Indian War in North America, reflects the overlapping interests of power balance and commercial gain. In Europe, the primary concern was balance. Whereas in the past France had seemed the major threat, now Prussia loomed—at least in Austrian eyes—as a far more dangerous interloper. Under these circumstances, in 1756 the Austrian foreign minister, Prince Wenzel von Kaunitz, effected the so-called diplomatic revolution, which put an end to the enmity between France and Austria, and resulted in a formidable threat to the Prussia of Frederick the Great. Frederick, meanwhile, was taking steps to protect his flanks. While anxious not to arouse his French ally, he nevertheless signed a neutrality treaty with the British, who were concerned to secure protection for their sovereign's Hanoverian domains. The French read Frederick's act as a hostile one, and thus fell all the more readily for Kaunitz's offer of an alliance. The French indeed perceived a pressing need for trustworthy European allies, since they were already engaged in an undeclared war with England in North America. By mid-1756 Kaunitz could count France, Russia, Sweden, and several German states as likely allies against Prussia. Rather than await retribution from his enemies, Frederick invaded strategic but neutral Saxony and then Austria itself, thus once again playing the role of aggressor.

The configurations in this diplomatic gavotte are undoubtedly confusing. They are historically important, however, because they indicate the way in which the power balance was shifting, and the attempts of European states to respond to those shifts by means of new diplomatic alliances. Prussia and Britain were the volatile elements: Prussia on the Continent; Britain overseas. The war from 1756 to 1763 in Europe centered upon Frederick's attempts to prevent the dismemberment of his domain at the hands of the French-Austrian-Russian alliance. Time and again the Prussian army's superiority and Frederick's own military genius frustrated his enemies' attacks. Ultimately, Prussia's survival against these overwhelming odds—"the miracle of the House of Brandenburg"—was ensured by the death of the Tsarina Elizabeth (1741–1762), daughter of Peter the Great, and by the accession of Peter III (1762), whose admiration for Frederick was as great as was his predecessor's hostility. Peter withdrew from the war, returning the conquered provinces of East Prussia and Pomerania to his country's erstwhile enemy. The peace that followed, though it compelled Frederick to

The Battle of Québec, 1759. Most often remembered for the fact that the British and French commanders, Generals Wolfe and Montcalm, were killed on the bluffs above the St. Lawrence River (the Plains of Abraham), this battle was most notable for the success of the British amphibious assault, a measure of Britain's naval superiority.

relinquish Saxony, recognized his right to retain Silesia, and hence put an end to Austria's hope of one day recapturing that rich prize.

Overseas, battles occurred not only in North America but in the West Indies and in India, where Anglo-French commercial rivalry had resulted in sporadic, fierce fighting since the 1740s. Ultimate victory would go to that power possessing a navy strong enough to keep its supply routes open—that is, to Britain. Superior naval forces resulted in victories along the North American Great Lakes, climaxing in the Battle of Québec in 1759 and the eventual surrender of all of Canada to the British. By 1762 the French sugar islands, including Martinique, Grenada, and St. Vincent, were in British hands. Across the globe in India, the defeat of the French in the Battle of Plassey in 1757 and the capture of Pondichéry four years later made Britain the dominant European presence on the subcontinent. In the Treaty of Paris in 1763 which brought the Seven Years' War to an end, France officially surrendered Canada and India to the British, thus affording them an extraordinary field for commercial exploitation.

The success of the British in North America in the Seven Years' War was itself a major cause of the war that broke out between the mother country and her thirteen original colonies in 1775. To pay for the larger army the British now deemed necessary to protect their vastly expanded colonial possessions, they imposed unwelcome new taxes on the colonists.

The North Americans protested that they were being taxed without representation. The home government responded that, like all British subjects, they were "virtually" if not actually represented by the present members of the House of Commons. Colonists thundered back that the present political system in Britain was so corrupt that no one but the Whig oligarchs could claim that their interests were being looked after.

The American Revolution

Meanwhile the British were exacting retribution for rebellious acts on the part of colonists. East India Company tea shipped to be sold in Boston at prices advantageous to the company was dumped in Boston harbor. The port of Boston was thereupon closed, and representative government in the colony of Massachusetts curtailed. The British garrison clashed with colonial civilians. Colonial "minutemen" formed a counterforce. By the time war broke out in 1775, most Americans were prepared to sever ties with Britain and declare themselves an independent nation, which they did the following year. Fighting continued until 1781 when a British army surrendered to the colonists at Yorktown to the tune of a song entitled "A World Turned Upside Down." The French, followed by Spain and the Netherlands, determined to do everything possible to inhibit the further growth of Britain's colonial empire, had allied themselves with the newly independent United States in 1778. A peace treaty signed in Paris in 1783 recognized the sovereignty of the new state. Though the British lost direct control of their former colonies, they reestablished their transatlantic commercial ties with America in the 1780s. Indeed, the brisk trade in raw cotton between the slave-owning southern states and Britain made possible the industrial revolution in textiles that began in the north of England at this time, and that carried Britain to worldwide preeminence as an economic power in the first half of the nineteenth century. This ultimately profitable arrangement lay in the future. At the time, the victory of the American colonists seemed to contemporary observers to right the world balance of commercial power, which had swung so far to the side of the British. In this instance, independence seemed designed to restore stability.

Poland and the balance of power in Eastern Europe

In Eastern Europe, however, the very precariousness of Poland's independence posed a threat to stability and the balance of power. As an independent state, Poland functioned, at least in theory, as a buffer among the major Central European powers—Russia, Austria, and Prussia. Poland was the one major Central European territory whose landed elite had successfully opposed introduction of absolutist centralization and a consequent curtailment of its "liberties." The result, however, had not been anything like real independence for either the Polish nobility or the country as a whole. Aristocrats were quite prepared to accept bribes from foreign powers in return for their vote in elections for the Polish king. And their continued exercise of their constitutionally guaranteed individual veto (the *liberum veto*) in the Polish Diet meant that the country remained in a perpetual state of weakness that made it fair game for the land-hungry absolutist potentates who surrounded its borders.

In 1764 Russia intervened to influence the election of King Stanislaus Poniatowski, an able enough nobleman who had been one of Catherine

Dividing the Royal Cake. A contemporary cartoon showing the monarchs of Europe at work carving up a hapless Poland.

the Great's lovers. Thereafter Russia continued to meddle in the affairs of Poland—and of Turkey as well—often protecting both countries' Greek Orthodox Christian minority. When war finally broke out with Turkey in 1769, resulting in large Russian gains in the Balkans, Austria made known its opposition to further Russian expansion, lest it upset the existing balance of power in Eastern Europe. In the end Russia was persuaded to acquire territory in Poland instead, by joining Austria and Prussia in a general partition of that country's lands. Though Maria Theresa opposed the dismemberment of Poland, she reluctantly agreed to participate in the partition in order to maintain the balance of power, an attitude that prompted a scornful Frederick the Great to remark that "She weeps, but she takes her share." According to the agreement of 1772, Poland lost about 30 percent of its kingdom and about half of its population.

The first partition of Poland

Following this first partition, the Russians continued to exercise virtual control of Poland. King Stanislaus, however, took advantage of a new Russo-Turkish war in 1788 to press for a more truly independent state with a far stronger executive than had existed previously. A constitution adopted in May 1791 established just that; but this rejuvenated Polish state was to be short-lived. In January 1792, the Russo-Turkish war ended, and Catherine the Great pounced. Together the Russians and Prussians took two more enormous bites out of Poland in 1793, destroying the new constitution in the process. A rebellion under the leadership of Thaddeus

The second and third partitions of Poland

Kosciuszko, who had fought in America, was crushed in 1794 and 1795. A final swallow by Russia, Austria, and Prussia in 1795 left nothing of Poland at all. After this series of partitions of Poland, each of the major powers was a good deal fatter; but on the international scales by which such things were measured, they continued to weigh proportionately the same.

European upheaval

The final devouring of Poland occurred at a time when the Continent was once again engaged in a general war. Yet this conflict was not just another military attempt to resolve customary disputes over commerce or problems of international stability. It was the result of violent revolution that had broken out in France in 1789, that had toppled the Bourbon dynasty there, and that threatened to do the same to other monarchs across Europe. The second and third partitions of Poland were a final bravura declaration of power by monarchs who already feared for their heads. Henceforth, neither foreign nor domestic policy would ever again be dictated as they had been in absolutist Europe by the convictions and determinations of kings and queens alone. Poland disappeared as Europe fell to pieces, as customary practice gave way to new and desperate necessity.

Though absolutism met its death in the years immediately after 1789, the relevance of its history to that of the modern world is greater than it might appear. First, centralization provided useful precedents to nineteenth-century state-builders. Modern standing armies—be they made up of soldiers or bureaucrats—are institutions whose origins rest in the age of absolutism. Second, absolutism's centripetal force contributed to an economic climate that gave birth to industrial revolution. Factories built to produce military matériel, capitalist agricultural policies designed to provide food for burgeoning capital cities, increased taxes that drove peasants to seek work in rural industries: these and other programs pointed to the future. Third, in their constant struggle to curb the privileges of nobility and oligarchy, absolute monarchs played out one more act in a drama that would continue into the nineteenth century. French nobles, Prussian junkers, and Russian boyars all bargained successfully to retain their rights to property and its management while surrendering to some degree their role as governors. But as long as their property rights remained secure, their power was assured. The French Revolution would curb their power for a time, but they were survivors. Their adaptability, whether as agricultural entrepreneurs or as senior servants of the state, ensured their order an important place in the world that lay beyond absolutism.

SELECTED READINGS

• *Items so designated are available in paperback editions.*

Anderson, M. S., *Historians and Eighteenth-Century Europe,* Oxford, 1979. Contains recent scholarly debate.
———, *Peter the Great,* London, 1978. A good, thorough biography.

- Avrich, Paul, *Russian Rebels, 1600–1800,* New York, 1972. A study of revolts against absolutist power.

  Baxter, Stephen, *William III and the Defense of European Liberty, 1650–1702,* New York, 1966. The best study of the Dutchman who became England's king.

  Bernard, Paul, *Joseph II,* New York, 1968.

- Brewer, John, *Party Ideology and Popular Politics at the Accession of George III,* Cambridge, 1976. A revisionist interpretation of political alignments and party.

  Churchill, Winston S., *Marlborough,* New York, 1968. An abridged edition of Churchill's magnificently written biography of his ancestor.

- Cobban, Alfred, *A History of Modern France,* New York, 1961. A survey with a point of view.

  Corvisier, André, *Armies and Societies in Europe, 1494–1789,* Bloomington, Ind., 1979. Focuses on the French army.

- Dukes, Paul, *Catherine the Great and the Russian Nobility,* Cambridge, 1967. A study of the limits of absolutism.

- Dunn, Richard S., *The Age of Religious Wars, 1559–1715,* 2nd ed., New York, 1979. A detailed and up-to-date survey, useful for the history of late seventeenth- and early eighteenth-century absolutism.

  Ford, Franklin, *Robe and Sword: The Regrouping of the French Aristocracy after Louis XIV,* Cambridge, Mass., 1953. An important social study of the nobility of the robe and its striving for dominance before the Revolution.

- Fraser, Antonia, *Royal Charles: Charles II and the Restoration,* New York, 1979. A readable, reliable life of the king and his times.

- Goubert, Pierre, *Louis XIV and Twenty Million Frenchmen,* New York, 1972. A valuable study, the starting point for an understanding of the Sun King's reign.

- Hatton, R. H., *Europe in the Age of Louis XIV,* New York, 1969. Thoughtful interpretation of the period; excellent illustrations.

- Herr, Richard, *The Eighteenth Century Revolution in Spain,* Princeton, 1958. The best introduction to Spain in this period.

- Holborn, Hajo, *The Age of Absolutism,* New York, 1964. The best survey for Germany. Second volume of Holborn's *History of Modern Germany.*

- Krieger, Leonard, *Kings and Philosophers, 1689–1789,* New York, 1970. A thorough survey of the political and intellectual developments of this century.

- Lewis, W. H., *The Splendid Century: Life in the France of Louis XIV,* New York, 1953. A delightfully written survey.

- Palmer, R. R., *The Age of the Democratic Revolution: A Political History of Europe and America, 1760 1800,* Vol. I, Princeton, 1964. Argues in favor of a general European aristocratic reaction prior to 1789.

  Plumb, John H., *Sir Robert Walpole,* 2 vols., Boston, 1956, 1961. A well-written, sympathetic biography of England's leading eighteenth-century politician.

- Riasanovsky, Nicholas V., *A History of Russia,* 4th ed., Oxford, 1984. A useful introduction.

- Ritter, Gerhard, *Frederick The Great: A Historical Profile,* Berkeley, 1968. A readable biography.

- Rudé, George, *Europe in the Eighteenth Century: Aristocracy and the Bourgeois Challenge,* New York, 1972. A survey that stresses social stratification and tension.

- Speck, W. A., *Stability and Strife: England, 1714–1760,* Cambridge, Mass., 1977. A good, recent survey.

  Spielman, John P., *Leopold I of Austria,* New Brunswick, N.J., 1977. The only biography of the monarch in English.

- Wangermann, Ernst, *The Austrian Achievement, 1700–1800,* London, 1973. A suggestive introductory survey.

• Wolf, John B., *Louis XIV,* New York, 1968. The standard biography in English.
———, *The Emergence of the Great Powers, 1685–1715,* New York, 1951. A useful general survey of this critical period.
• Woloch, Isser, *Eighteenth Century Europe: Tradition and Progress, 1715–1789,* New York, 1982. A thoughtful, well-organized survey.

SOURCE MATERIALS

• Locke, John, *Two Treatises of Government.* (Many editions.) The argument against absolutism.
• Saint-Simon, Louis, *Historical Memoirs.* (Many editions.) A brilliant source for evidence about life at the court of Louis XIV.

Chapter 18

THE SCIENTIFIC REVOLUTION AND ENLIGHTENMENT

This is the age wherein philosophy comes in with a spring-tide. . . . Methinks I see how all the old rubbish must be thrown away, and the rotten buildings be overthrown, and carried away with so powerful an inundation.

—Henry Power, *Experimental Philosophy* (1663)

Enlightenment is humanity's departure from its self-imposed immaturity. Immaturity is the inability to use one's intellect without the guidance of others. This immaturity is self-imposed when its cause is not a lack of intelligence but a failure of determination and courage to think without the guidance of someone else. Dare to know! This then is the slogan of the Enlightenment.

—Immanuel Kant, *What Is Enlightenment?* (1784)

The years between roughly 1660 and 1789, which witnessed the prevalence of absolutism in Western Europe, witnessed as well the most important mutation in all of European intellectual and cultural history to occur between the Middle Ages and the present. Just as the sweep of fresh winds can greatly change the weather, so in the last few decades of the seventeenth century the sweep of new ideas led to a bracing change in Europe's "climate of opinion." For purposes of analysis it is convenient to refer to two phases within the larger period: the triumph of the scientific revolution in the second half of the seventeenth century and the age of "Enlightenment" which followed for most of the eighteenth century. But without any doubt the same intellectual winds that swept into Europe during the later seventeenth century prevailed for well over a hundred years. Indeed, their influence is still felt today.

New ideas: 1660–1789

How did the new intellectual climate differ from the old? Concentrating on essentials, three points may be stressed. First, whereas medieval, Renaissance, and Reformation thinkers all assumed that past knowledge was the most reliable source of wisdom, the greatest thinkers from the seventeenth

Changes in intellectual environment

century onward rejected any obeisance to ancient authority and resolved to rely on their own intellects to see where knowledge would lead them. Making their motto "dare to know," they stressed the autonomy of science and the free play of the mind in ways unheard of in the West since the golden age of Greece. Second, the new breed of thinkers believed strongly that knowledge was valueless if it could not be put to use. For a Plato, an Aristotle, or a St. Thomas Aquinas alike, the greatest wisdom was the most abstract wisdom since such wisdom helped to turn the human mind away from all earthly "corruptibility" and supposedly brought happiness by its sheer resemblance to timeless divinity. But after the change in Europe's climate of opinion in the late seventeenth century, all knowledge without practical value was belittled and thinkers from every realm of intellectual endeavor aimed directly or indirectly at achieving "the relief of man's estate." Finally, the new climate of opinion was characterized by the demystification of the universe. Up until the mid-seventeenth century, most people, learned and unlearned, assumed that the universe was driven and inhabited by occult forces that humans could barely understand and surely never control unless they were magicians. But around 1660 a mechanistic worldview swept away occultism, and pixies became consigned to the realm of children's storybooks. Thereafter nature was believed to work like the finest mechanical clock—consummately predictable and fully open to human understanding.

Causes of change Why such a dramatic change in basic patterns of thought took place when it did will long remain a subject for speculation. Certainly the prior Scholastic stress on human rationality and the Renaissance reacquisition of classical Greek texts helped to bring European thought to a scientific threshold. Probably the most direct causes of the intellectual mutations, however, were the twin challenges to conventional assumptions introduced in the sixteenth century by the discovery of the New World and the realization that the earth revolves around the sun rather than vice versa, for neither the Bible nor ancient science allowed room for what one bewildered contemporary called "new islands, new lands, new seas, new peoples, and what is more, a new sky and new stars." At first many thinkers, daunted by all this novelty, experienced a sense of intellectual crisis. Some took refuge in skepticism, others in relativism, and others in a return to blind faith. Speaking for several generations, the poet John Donne lamented in 1611 that "new philosophy calls all in doubt, the element of fire is quite put out, the sun is lost, and the earth, and no man's wit can well direct him where to look for it. . . . 'tis all in pieces, all coherence gone." But just as Europe surmounted its early-modern political crisis around 1660, so did it surmount its intellectual one, above all because the last stages of a profound scientific revolution gave a new, completely convincing "coherence" to things. As Alexander Pope wrote in the early eighteenth century, almost as if in response to Donne: "Nature and Nature's Law's lay hid in night:/God said, Let Newton Be! and all was light."

1. THE SCIENTIFIC REVOLUTION

Even though Europe did not begin to resolve its intellectual crisis until about 1660, the groundwork for that resolution was prepared earlier in the seventeenth century by four great individuals—Kepler, Galileo, Bacon, and Descartes. Kepler and Galileo—both practicing scientists—have been discussed earlier; suffice it here to say that they removed all doubts about the Copernican heliocentric theory of the solar system and helped lead the way to Sir Isaac Newton's theory of universal gravitation. As for Bacon and Descartes, their main achievements were not in the realm of original scientific discovery but rather in propagating new attitudes toward learning and the nature of the universe.

Sir Francis Bacon (1561–1626), lord chancellor of England, was also an extremely influential philosopher of science. In Bacon's view, expressed most fully in his *Novum Organum (New Instrument)* of 1620, science could not advance unless it departed entirely from the inherited errors of the past and established "progressive stages of certainty." For Bacon this meant proceeding strictly on the basis of empirical knowledge (knowledge gained solely by the senses) and by means of the "inductive method," meaning the arrival at truth by proceeding upward from particular observations to generalizations. Insisting that "the corruption of philosophy by superstition and an admixture of theology . . . does the greatest harm," and that thinking people thus should be "sober-minded, and give to faith that only which is faith's," Bacon advocated the advancement of learning as a cooperative venture proceeding by means of meticulously recorded empirical experiments. Unlike the arid speculations of the past, collective scientific research and observation would produce useful knowledge and result in bettering the human lot. Much of Bacon's ideology is vividly evoked in the cover illustration of his *Novum Organum,* wherein intrepid ships venture out beyond the Pillars of Hercules (Straits of Gibraltar) onto a fathomless sea in pursuit of unknown but great things to come.

Bacon's later contemporary, the French philosopher René Descartes (1596–1650), agreed with him on two points: that all past knowledge should be discarded, and that the worth of any idea depended on its usefulness. Yet Descartes otherwise proposed some very different approaches to science, for unlike the empiricist Bacon, Descartes was a rationalist and a champion of mathematics. In his *Discourse on Method* (1637), Descartes explained how, during a period of solitude, he resolved to submit all inherited doctrines to a process of systematic doubting because he knew that the "strangest or most incredible" things had previously been set down in learned books. Taking as his first rule "never to receive anything as a truth which [he] did not clearly know to be such," he found himself doubting everything until he came to the recognition that his mere process of thought proved his own existence ("I think, therefore I am"). Thereupon making rationality the point of departure for his entire philosophical enter-

Title Page of Bacon's Novum Organum. Underneath the ship sailing out into the ocean is a quotation from the Book of Daniel: "Many shall venture forth and science shall be increased."

René Descartes

A Diagram Illustrating Cartesian Principles. Descartes maintained that the pineal gland, seen here at the back of the head, transmitted messages from the eyes to the muscles in purely mechanical fashion. But the pineal gland was also the link between the material body and the nonmaterial human mind. From the 1677 edition of Descartes' *De Homine.*

Descartes' influence

The English and French traditions

prise, Descartes rebuilt the universe on largely speculative grounds that differed in almost every detail from the universe conceived by the Greeks, yet conformed fully to the highest principles of human rationality as expressed in the laws of mathematics. That most of his theories were not empirically verifiable did not trouble him at all, because he was confident that "natural processes almost always depend on parts so small that they utterly elude our senses."

Predictably, the details of Descartes' scientific system are now regarded as mere curiosities, but the French philosopher nonetheless was enormously influential in contributing to the advance of science and in creating a new climate of opinion for several reasons. First of all, even though his systematic doubting did not succeed in establishing any solid new scientific truths, it did contribute to the discrediting of all the faulty science of the ancients. Then too, Descartes' stress on mathematics was salutary because mathematics has indeed proven to be an indispensable handmaiden to the pursuit of natural science. But undoubtedly Descartes' single most influential legacy was his philosophy of dualism, according to which God created only two kinds of reality—mind and matter. In Descartes' view, mind belonged to man alone, and all else was matter. Thus he insisted that all created existence beyond man—organic and inorganic alike—operated solely in terms of physical laws, or the interplay of "extension and motion." In other words, for Descartes every single entity from the solar system to the realm of animals and plants was a self-operating machine propelled by a force arising from the original motion given to the universe by God. Indeed, Descartes thought that man himself was a machine—although, in this sole exception, a machine equipped with a mind. From this it followed that the entire universe could be studied objectively, without any aid from theology or appeals to the occult. Moreover, all apparent attributes of matter, such as light, color, sound, taste, or smell, which had no "extension" were to be classified as mere subjective impressions of the human mind unfit for proper scientific analysis. Based on such assumptions the pursuit of science could be dispassionate as never before.

Roughly speaking, for about a century after the work of Bacon and Descartes the English scientific community was Baconian and the French Cartesian (a name given to followers of Descartes). This is to say that the English concentrated primarily on performing empirical experiments in many different areas of physical science leading to concrete scientific advances, whereas the French tended to remain more oriented toward mathematics and philosophical theory. Among the numerous great seventeenth-century English laboratory scientists were the physician William Harvey (1578–1657), the chemist Robert Boyle (1627–1691), and the biologist Robert Hooke (1635–1703). Pursuing the earlier work of Vesalius and Servetus, but daring, unlike them, to practice vivisection, Harvey was the first to observe and describe the circulation of the blood through the arteries and back to the heart through the veins. Similarly committed to empirical experiment, Boyle used an air pump to establish "Boyle's law"—namely, that under constant temperature the volume of a gas decreases in proportion to the pressure placed on it. Boyle also was the first chemist to distinguish between a mixture and a compound (wherein the chemical combination occurs), and accomplished much to discredit alchemy. As for Hooke, although he conducted research in astronomy and physics as well as biology, he is best known for having used the microscope to discover the cellular structure of plants. Meanwhile, in France, Descartes himself pioneered in analytical geometry, Blaise Pascal worked on probability theory and invented a calculating machine before his conversion to religion, and Pierre Gassendi (1592–1655) sought to demonstrate the truth of the atomic theory. Also within the French realm of thought was the Dutch Jew Baruch Spinoza (1632–1677), a philosopher who tried to apply geometry to ethics and believed that he advanced beyond Descartes by interpreting the universe as being composed of a single substance—simultaneously God and nature—instead of two.

The dichotomy between English Baconianism and French Cartesianism, however, breaks down when one approaches the man commonly considered to have been the greatest scientist of all time, Sir Isaac Newton (1642–1727). A highly unattractive personality in his daily conduct—being secretive, petty, and vindictive—Newton was nonetheless a towering genius who drew on both the Baconian and Cartesian heritages. For example, following Bacon, and in the sharpest opposition to Descartes, Newton refused to dismiss the phenomenon of light as a mere subjective impression of "mind." Instead, by means of laboratory experiments he demonstrated that light behaves differently when filtered through different media, and hence offered an interpretation of light as a stream of particles that solidly established optics as an empirical branch of physics. Yet, on the other hand, Newton thoroughly approved of Descartes' stress on mathematics, and once in a burst of purely theoretical inspiration discovered one of modern mathematics' most basic tools, the calculus.

Sir Isaac Newton

Newton's law of gravitation

Of course Newton's supreme accomplishment lay in his formulation of the law of universal gravitation, which, as expressed in his monumental Latin *Principia Mathematica* (*Mathematical Principles of Natural Philosophy*) of 1687, integrated Copernican astronomy with Galileo's physics. In the *Principia* Newton broached the two major scientific questions of his day: (1) What keeps the heavy earth in motion? (before Copernicus the earth had been thought immobile), and (2) Why do terrestrial bodies tend to fall to the earth's center whereas planets stay in orbital motion? (before Copernicus the planets were thought to be embedded in crystalline spheres moved by angels or "divine intelligences"). In the early seventeenth century Kepler had already suggested the possibility of mutual attractions between all bodies in the solar system that kept the earth and other planets moving, but the Cartesians attacked this explanation as being too occult since attraction over space left out the crucial Cartesian ingredient of matter. Disregarding these Cartesian doubts because he saw no alternative, Newton returned to consider Kepler's theory of mutual attractions, and uniting Baconian observations with Cartesian mathematics, arrived at a single law of universal gravitation according to which "every particle of matter in the universe attracts every other particle with a force varying inversely as the square of the distance between them and directly proportional to the product of their masses." Since this law was verified by experience in both terrestrial and celestial realms, there could be no doubt that it explained all motion. Indeed, Newton's law was so reliable that it was employed immediately to predict the ebb and flow of tides. Later, in 1846, astronomers, noting irregularities in the motion of the planet Uranus, were able to deduce on Newtonian grounds the presence of the more distant planet Neptune before Neptune was actually located with the aid of high-power telescopes.

The impact of Newton's
Principia

Historians of science consider Newton's law of gravity to be "the most stupendous single achievement of the human mind," finding that "no other work in the whole history of science equals the *Principia* either in originality and power of thought or in the majesty of its achievement." Certainly the publication of the *Principia* was the crowning event of the scientific revolution because it confirmed the most important astronomical and physical theories previously set forth by Copernicus, Kepler, and Galileo, and resolved beyond quarrel the major problems that Copernicus's heliocentric theory had created. Needless to say, scientific work did not thereafter come to a standstill. Quite to the contrary, since Newton's accomplishment proved inspirational to researchers in many other fields, scientific work advanced steadily after 1687. But a fundamental reconception of the nature of the physical universe had been made, and thinkers in all areas could proceed with their work confident that science rather than superstition was the new order of the day.

2. THE FOUNDATIONS OF THE ENLIGHTENMENT

The Enlightenment: The
major pattern of eighteenth-
century thought

Although the presuppositions for the Enlightenment were set by the triumph of the scientific revolution in the late seventeenth century, the Enlightenment itself was an eighteenth-century phenomenon, lasting for close to the entire century until certain basic Enlightenment postulates were challenged around 1790 by the effects of the French Revolution and the new movement of romanticism. Of course not every thinker who lived and worked in the eighteenth century was equally "enlightened." Some, such as the Italian philosopher of history G. B. Vico (1668–1744), were opposed to almost everything the Enlightenment stood for, and others, most notably Jean-Jacques Rousseau, accepted certain Enlightenment values but sharply rejected others. Moreover, patterns of Enlightenment ideology tended to vary from country to country and to change in each country over the course of the century. Yet, despite these qualifications, most thinkers of the eighteenth century definitely shared the sense of living in an exciting new intellectual environment in which "the party of humanity" would prevail over traditionalism and obscurantism by dint of an unflinching commitment to the primacy of the intellect.

Most Enlightenment thought stemmed from three basic premises: (1) the entire universe is fully intelligible and governed by natural rather than su-pernatural forces; (2) rigorous application of "scientific method" can an-swer fundamental questions in all areas of inquiry; and (3) the human race can be "educated" to achieve nearly infinite improvement. The first two of these premises were products of the scientific revolution and the third pri-marily an inheritance from the psychology of John Locke.

Regarding the substitution of a natural for a supernatural worldview, ex-planations must start with the euphoria that greeted Isaac Newton's discov-ery of a single law whereby all motion in the heavens and earth became in-telligible and predictable. If Newton could deal so authoritatively and elegantly with motion, it seemed to follow that all nature is governed nei-ther by mysterious divine intervention nor by caprice, but by humanly per-ceivable universal laws. Hence most serious thinkers from about 1690 to 1790 became inveterate opponents of belief in miracles, and considered all varieties of revealed religion to be not just irrelevant to the pursuit of sci-ence, but positively antithetical to it. This is not to say that the Enlighten-ment abandoned belief in the existence of God: to the contrary, only the smallest number of Enlightenment thinkers were atheists, and very few even were avowed agnostics. Rather, most adhered to a religious outlook known as Deism which assumed that God existed but, having once created a perfect universe, no longer took an active interest in it. Expressed in the language of the Deists themselves, God was the "divine clockmaker" who, at the beginning of time, constructed a perfect timepiece and then left it to run on with predictable regularity. Most Deists continued to attend the churches of their ancestors (either Protestant or Catholic) from time to time, but they made little secret of their doubts about the efficacy of ritual and spoke out against all forms of religious intolerance.

As for the second Enlightenment premise, the accomplishments of the scientific revolution inspired a deep sense of assurance that "scientific method" was the only valid means for pursuing research in all areas of hu-man inquiry. By scientific method Enlightenment thinkers usually meant the dispassionate, empirical observation of particular phenomena in order to arrive at general laws. Given the acknowledged triumph of Newtonian physics, it is not surprising that around 1700 Western Europe was struck by a virtual mania for applying scientific method in studying all the workings of nature. Since most scientific work was still simple enough to be under-stood by amateurs without the benefit of years of specialized education, European aristocrats and prosperous people in all walks of life began to dabble in "research"—buying telescopes, chasing butterflies, or building home laboratories in the hope of participating in some new scientific breakthrough. Writing in 1710, the English essayist Joseph Addison sati-rized such pursuits by imagining a will written by one "Sir Nicholas Gim-crack," an earnest amateur who left his "recipe for preserving dead caterpil-lars" to his daughters, his "rat's testicles" to a "learned and worthy friend," and who disinherited his son for "having spoken disrespectfully of his little sister," whose mortal remains Sir Nicholas kept near his desk in "spirits of wine." Of course most of the aristocratic "Gimcracks" never progressed

The Study of an Amateur Scientist. This late-seventeenth-century aristocratic dilettante collected all sorts of specimens from the natural world. The mounting of his crocodile must have offered some challenge.

beyond pickling, but their enthusiasm for following the latest developments in scientific research led them to patronize the work of truly gifted scientists and contributed to creating an atmosphere wherein science was prized as humanity's greatest attainment.

The scientific method applied to human concerns

Inevitably, in turn, such an atmosphere was conducive to an assumption that became dominant in the course of the eighteenth century—that scientific method was the only proper means for studying human affairs as well as natural phenomena. Since the world of physical nature seemed well on the way to being mastered, Enlightenment thinkers considered it mere common sense that the world of human nature could soon be mastered as well by scientific means. Thus students of religion started collecting myths from numerous different traditions, not to find any occult truth in them, but to classify their common traits and learn the steps by which humanity supposedly freed itself from superstition. Similarly, historians collected evidence to learn the laws governing the rise and fall of nations, and students of politics compared governmental constitutions to arrive at an ideal and universally applicable political system. In other words, as the English poet Alexander Pope stated in his *Essay on Man* of 1733, "the science of human nature [may be] like all other sciences reduced to a few clear points," and Enlightenment thinkers became determined to learn exactly what those "few clear points" were.

John Locke's psychology and human perfectibility

It must be stressed, however, that if most thinkers of the Enlightenment supposed that the empirical study of human conduct could reduce society's working to a few laws, most also believed that human conduct was not immutable but highly perfectible. In this they were inspired primarily by the psychology of John Locke (1632–1704), who was not only a very influential political philosopher, as we have seen, but also the formulator of an extremely influential theory of knowledge. In his *Essay Concerning Human Understanding* (1690) Locke rejected the hitherto dominant assumption that ideas are innate, maintaining instead that all knowledge originates from sense perception. According to Locke, the human mind at birth is a "blank tablet" (Latin: *tabula rasa*) upon which nothing is inscribed: not until the infant begins to experience things, that is, to perceive the external world with its senses, is anything registered on its mind. From this point of departure, Enlightenment thinkers concluded that environment determines everything. For example, in their view, if some aristocrats were better than ordinary mortals it was not because they had inherited any special knowledge or virtues, but only because they had been better trained. It therefore followed that all people could be educated to become the equals of the most perfect aristocrats, and that there were no limits to the potential for universal human progress. Indeed, a few Enlightenment thinkers became so optimistic as to propose that all evil might be eradicated from the world, since whatever evil existed was not the result of some divine plan but only the product of a faulty environment that humans had created and humans could change.

3. THE WORLD OF THE PHILOSOPHES

France, the dominant country in eighteenth-century Europe, was the center of the Enlightenment movement, and thus it is customary to refer to the leading exponents of the Enlightenment, regardless of where they lived, by the French term *philosophe,* meaning philosopher. In fact the term philosophe is slightly misleading inasmuch as hardly any of the philosophes—with the exceptions, to be seen, of David Hume and Immanuel Kant—were really philosophers in the sense of being highly original abstract thinkers. Rather, most were practically oriented publicists who aimed to reform society by popularizing the new scientific interpretation of the universe and applying dispassionate "scientific method" to a host of contemporary problems. Since they sought most of all to gain converts and alter what they regarded as outmoded institutions, they shunned all forms of expression that might seem incomprehensible or abstruse, priding themselves instead on their clarity, and occasionally even expressing their ideas in the form of stories or plays rather than treatises.

General characteristics of the philosophes

By common consent the prince of the philosophes was the Frenchman born François Marie Arouet, who called himself Voltaire (1694–1778). Virtually the personification of the Enlightenment, much as Erasmus two centuries earlier had embodied Christian humanism, Voltaire commented on an enormous range of subjects in a wide variety of literary forms. Probably his greatest single accomplishment lay in championing the cause of English empiricism in previously Cartesian France. Having as a young man been exiled to England for the crime of insulting a pompous French nobleman, Voltaire returned after three years a thorough and extremely persua-

Voltaire

Voltaire by Houdon

sive convert to the ideas of Bacon and Locke. Not only did this mean that he persuaded other French thinkers to accept Newton's empirically verifiable scientific system in place of Descartes' unverifiable one, but he also encouraged them to be less abstract and theoretical in all their intellectual inclinations and more oriented toward the solving of everyday problems. To be sure, throughout the eighteenth century France's intellectual world remained more rationalistic than England's, but Voltaire's lifelong campaign on behalf of empiricism nonetheless had a very salutary effect in making French thinkers more practically oriented than before.

Continually engaged in commenting on contemporary problems himself, Voltaire was an ardent spokesman for civil liberties. In this regard his battlecry was *Écrasez l'infâme*—"crush infamy"—meaning by "infamy" all forms of repression, fanaticism, and bigotry. In his own words, he believed that "the individual who persecutes another because he is not of the same opinion is nothing less than a monster." Accordingly, he wrote an opponent a line that forever after has been held forth as the first principle of civil liberty: "I do not agree with a word you say, but I will defend to the death your right to say it." Of all forms of intolerance Voltaire hated religious bigotry most of all because it seemed based on silly superstitions: "the less superstition, the less fanaticism; and the less fanaticism, the less misery." In addition to attacking religious repression, Voltaire also frequently criticized the exercise of arbitrary powers by secular states. In particular, he thought that the English parliamentary system was preferable to French absolutism and that all states acted criminally when their policies resulted in senseless wars. "It is forbidden to kill," he maintained sardonically, "therefore all murderers are punished unless they kill in large numbers and to the sound of trumpets."

Although Voltaire exerted the greatest effect on his age as a propagandist for the basically optimistic Enlightenment principle that by "crushing infamy" humanity could take enormous strides forward, the only one of his works still widely read today, the satirical story *Candide* (1759), is atypically subdued. Writing not long after the disastrous Lisbon earthquake of 1755, in which over 20,000 lives were lost for no apparent reason, Voltaire drew back in this work from some of his earlier faith that mankind by its own actions could limitlessly improve itself. Lulled into false security concerning what life has in store for him by the fatuous optimism of his tutor, Dr. Pangloss, the hero of the story, Candide, journeys through the world only to experience one outrageous misfortune after another. Storms and earthquakes are bad enough, but worse still are wars and rapacity caused by uncontrollable human passions. Only in the golden never-never land of "Eldorado" (clearly a spoof of the perfect world most philosophes saw on the horizon), where there are no priests, law courts, or prisons, but unlimited wealth and a "palace of sciences . . . filled with instruments of mathematics and physics," does Candide find temporary respite from disaster. Being a naturally restless mortal, however, he quickly becomes bored with Eldorado's placid perfection and leaves for the renewed buffetings of the real world. After many more lessons in "the school of hard knocks," he finally

Landscape with the Burial of Phocion, Nicolas Poussin (1594–1665). An outstanding example of the classical style in painting. As opposed to the Baroque stress on swirling movement, here there is practically no movement at all. Instead, nature is conceived in rigorously geometrical terms to convey a sense of permanence. Note too the presence of ancient classical buildings, making it seem as if the past is enduring. (Louvre)

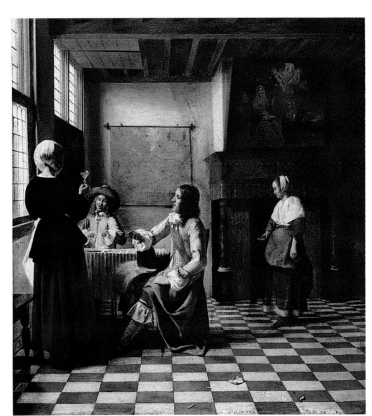

A Dutch Interior, Pieter de Hooch (c. 1629–c. 1679). Seventeenth-century Dutch painters excelled at indoor genre compositions bathed in light. The restraint of the scene itself stands in contrast to the melodramatic Baroque painting in the background. (National Gallery, London)

Le Mezzetin, Antoine Watteau (1684–1721). Mezzetin was a popular character from Italian comedy. In portraying him in a relaxed pose Watteau succeeded in conveying a sense of dreamy elegance. (MMA)

The Blue Boy, Thomas Gainsborough (1727–1788). Gainsborough, eighteenth-century England's greatest portrait painter, combined Watteau's lushness with more traditional English gravity. (Huntington Library)

Madame de Pompadour, François Boucher (1703–1770). A characteristically frilly French Rococo portrait. Madame de Pompadour, King Louis XV's mistress, was a patroness of arts and letters, and for a time the virtual ruler of France. (The Wallace Collection, London)

The Stonemason's Yard, Canaletto (1697–1768). A quiet scene of everyday life, in strong contrast to the scene below. (National Gallery, London)

Marriage à la Mode, William Hogarth (1697–1764). A satirical look at the arranged marriage: the financial needs of the nobleman and the social aspirations of his middle-class counterpart dominate the negotiations. (National Gallery, London)

Sarah Siddons as the Tragic Muse, Sir Joshua Reynolds (1723–1792). Mrs. Siddons, a famous actress of the seventeenth century, is here portrayed as the Queen of Tragedy, in accordance with Reynolds's habit of depicting wealthy patrons in impressive classical poses. (Huntington Library)

Madame Recamier, Jacques Louis David (1748–1825). David was the exponent of a new classicism during and after the French Revolution. The couch, the lamp, and the costume are copied from Rome and Pompeii. (Louvre)

learns one basic truth by the end of the story: settling down on a modest farm with his once-beautiful but now hideously disfigured wife, he shrugs when Dr. Pangloss repeats for the hundredth time that "this is the best of all possible worlds," and replies: "that's as may be, but we must cultivate our garden." In other words, according to Voltaire, life is not perfect and probably never will be, but humans will succeed best if they ignore vapid theorizing and buckle down to unglamorous but productive hard work.

In addition to Voltaire, the most prominent French philosophes were Montesquieu, Diderot, and Condorcet. The baron de Montesquieu (1689–1755) was primarily a political thinker. In his major work, *The Spirit of Laws* (1748), Montesquieu sought to discover the ways in which differing environments and historical and religious traditions influence governmental institutions. Finding that unalterable differences in climates and geographic terrains affect human behavior, and hence governmental forms, Montesquieu throughout much of *The Spirit of Laws* seems to be saying that external conditions force humans to behave in different ways and that there is nothing they can do about this. But ultimately he was an idealist who preferred one particular political system, the English, and hoped that all nations might overcome whatever environmental handicaps they faced to imitate it. For him, the greatest strength of the English system was that it consisted of separate and balanced powers—executive, legislative, and judicial: thus it guaranteed liberty inasmuch as no absolute sovereignty was given to any single governing individual or group. This idealization of "checks and balances" subsequently influenced many other Enlightenment political theorists and played a particularly dominant role in the shaping of the United States Constitution in 1787.

Unlike Voltaire, who was not a very systematic thinker, and Montesquieu, who wrote in a somewhat ambiguous and primarily reflective mode, the most programmatic of the philosophes was Denis Diderot (1713–1784). As a young firebrand Diderot was clapped into solitary confinement for his attacks on religion and thereafter he worked under the ever-present threat of censorship and imprisonment. Yet throughout his life he never shrank from espousing a fully materialistic philosophy or criticizing what he considered to be backwardness or tyranny wherever he found it. Although, like Voltaire, Diderot wrote on a wide range of subjects in numerous different forms, including stories and plays, he exerted his greatest influence as the organizer of and main contributor to an extremely ambitious publishing venture, the *Encyclopedia*. Conceived as a summation and means for dissemination of all the most advanced contemporary philosophical, scientific, and technical knowledge, with articles written by all the leading philosophes of the day (including Voltaire and Montesquieu), the *Encyclopedia* first appeared between 1751 and 1772 in installments totaling seventeen large volumes and eleven more of illustrative plates. Whereas modern encyclopedias serve primarily as reference works, Diderot thought of his *Encyclopedia* as a set of volumes that people would read at length rather than merely using to look up facts. Therefore he hoped that it would "change the general way of thinking." Above all,

Montesquieu

Montesquieu's The Spirit of Laws

Diderot. A contemporary portrait by Van Loo.

A Laboratory, from Diderot's *Encyclopedia.* Each printed number refers to a detailed discussion in the text. Note the far greater stress on practical instruction here than in the illustration of the amateur scientist's study shown above, p. 618.

p. 618.

Diderot and the Encyclopedia

by popularizing the most recent achievements in science and technology, Diderot intended to combat "superstition" on the broadest front, aid the further advance of science, and thereby help alleviate all forms of human misery. Dedicated to the proposition that all traditional beliefs had to be re-examined "without sparing anyone's sensibilities," he certainly would have excoriated all "irrational" religious dogmas openly if left to himself. But since strict censorship made explicitly antireligious articles impossible, Diderot thumbed his nose at religion in such oblique ways as offering the laconic cross-reference for the entry on the Eucharist: "see cannibalism." Not surprisingly, gibes like this aroused storms of controversy when the early volumes of the *Encyclopedia* appeared. Nonetheless, the project was not only completed in the face of prominent opposition, but as time went on the complete work became so popular that it was reprinted several times and helped spread the ideas of the philosophes not just in France but all over Europe.

Condorcet and faith in progress

One of the youngest of the contributors to the *Encyclopedia,* the marquis de Condorcet (1743–1794), is customarily termed "the last of the philosophes" because his career, and the philosophes' activities in general, was cut short by the excesses of the French Revolution. In his early career Condorcet gained prominence as a brilliant mathematician, but he is best known as the most extreme Enlightenment exponent of the idea of progress. Already in the late seventeenth century, particularly as the result of the triumphs of science, several thinkers began arguing that the intellectual accomplishments of their own day were superior to any of the past and that greater intellectual progress in the future was inevitable. But since it was less clear to some that modern literature was superior to the Greek and

Latin classics, around 1700 an argument raged concerning the relative claims of "ancients" and "moderns" wherein so able a critic as the English writer Jonathan Swift could regard what he called the "battle of the books" as a standoff. In the eighteenth century, however, the conviction grew that the present had advanced in all aspects of human endeavor beyond the accomplishments of any earlier time, and that the future was bound to see unlimited further progress on all fronts. Condorcet's *Outline of the Progress of the Human Mind* (1794) was the ultimate expression of this point of view. According to Condorcet, progress in the past had not been uninterrupted—the Middle Ages had been an especially retrogressive era—but, given the victories of the scientific revolution and Enlightenment, indefinite and uninterrupted progress in the future was assured. Venturing into prophecy, Condorcet confidently stated not only that "as preventive medicine improves . . . the average human life-span will be increased and a more healthy and stronger physical constitution guaranteed," but that "the moment will come . . . when tyrants and slaves . . . will exist only in history or on the stage." Ironically, even while Condorcet was writing such optimistic passages he was hiding out from the agents of the French Revolution, who in fact soon counted him among the victims of their "reign of terror."

One other French thinker of the eighteenth century, Jean-Jacques Rousseau (1712–1778), must be considered here, for even though Rousseau was an "outsider," who quarreled with the philosophes and contradicted many of their assumptions, he was still inescapably part of their world. Rousseau's central concerns were similar to those of Voltaire and Diderot: the reform of society, the dissemination of useful knowledge, the search for freedom. Like the philosophes, he despised inherited privilege and believed optimistically that a just and moral society could be created by "crushing the infamy" of tyrannical and repressive government. Yet Rousseau's proposals for creating a just society, which he customarily expressed with the deepest passion, were founded on an almost mystical respect for "nature" as opposed to reason and thus differed greatly from those of his primarily rationalistic allies. Considered a boor and almost a madman in his own day, Rousseau was a forerunner of the French Revolution, nineteenth-century romanticism, and perhaps (although this is debatable) twentieth-century totalitarianism.

Jean-Jacques Rousseau

The two fields in which Rousseau exerted the greatest influence were those of education and political theory. Rousseau's treatise on education, *Émile* (1762), is the ultimate source of all "progressive" pedagogy. Here he laid down as a maxim that "the first impulses of nature are always right." Accordingly, he insisted that children are not to be treated as miniature or incomplete adults, but must be allowed their own natural development proper to children. In practice this meant that they were not to be subjected to discipline and drilling; instead they should be encouraged to employ their keen youthful sense impressions and healthy young bodies to discover useful knowledge by themselves and "learn by doing." It was pointless to force a child to reason since reason is the human faculty that

Émile

develops last. Teaching from books was postponed until adolescence since "books teach us only to talk about things we do not know." Ultimately such education was designed to create moral and useful citizens, those who would be inclined to do good and serve society by engaging in useful vocations. For women, however, it meant staying at home and being "useful" to men, since Rousseau was convinced that this was nature's plan for the female sex.

The Social Contract

Rousseau's most important treatise on politics, *The Social Contract,* came out in the same year as *Émile,* 1762, and complemented it in its aim of creating a moral society. Here the author argued that humans were "born free." In the state of nature, that is, all had been equal (although we have seen that Rousseau believed women inferior to men) until the institution of private property led owners to protect their property by creating instruments of repression: law, police, slavery. To remedy this situation, Rousseau proposed the altogether new solution of government by the "general will." Supreme authority should be held by all the people, acting in collective assemblies rather than through institutions of representative democracy, whose rule would be absolute and indivisible. The people would act together as legislators, executors, and judges, and in doing so would become transformed into more than the sum of their parts. With the "general will" thus creating a "moral and collective person," individuals would surrender all their rights to the collectivity, yet they would be perfectly free since the general will inevitably would be just and would express their own will. In case any individuals became determined to resist the general will, they would be forced to obey, or, as Rousseau stated the matter, they would be "forced to be free." It has frequently been observed that the ideals of *The Social Contract* were distilled thirty years later in the French Revolution's slogan of "liberty, equality, fraternity." The obvious paradox lies in the fact that the emphasis on liberty and equality looks forward to institutions of modern democracy, but the emphasis on fraternity (the individual sinking into the mass) has ominous undertones of totalitarianism.

Edward Gibbon

Beyond France, philosophes in other countries also made significant contributions to the Enlightenment legacy. After France, the most "enlightened" country of Europe was Great Britain, where the most noteworthy philosophes were Gibbon, Hume, and Adam Smith. Edward Gibbon (1737–1794) was a man of letters and historian whose *Decline and Fall of the Roman Empire* (1776–1788) remains among the two or three most widely read history books of all time. Scintillatingly written, the *Decline and Fall* covers Roman and Byzantine history from Augustus to the fall of Constantinople in 1453. According to Gibbon, the Roman Empire was brought down by "the triumph of barbarism [i.e., the Germanic invasions] and religion [i.e., Christianity]," but the Europe of his day was no longer "threatened with a repetition of those calamities." For him the rise of Christianity was the greatest calamity because "the servile and pusillanimous reign of the monks" replaced Roman philosophy and science with a credulity that "debased and vitiated the faculties of the mind." Certainly

Gibbon's antireligious bias vitiated the quality of his own work. He is therefore read today not so much for his particular opinions as for his trenchant character portrayals and above all for his devastating wit.

The Scotsman David Hume (1711–1776), on the other hand, was a truly penetrating philosopher. Dedicated like most Enlightenment thinkers to challenging preconceived opinions, Hume pushed skepticism so far in his major work, *An Enquiry Concerning Human Understanding* (1748), that he undermined all assurance that anyone knew anything for certain. Starting with the assumption that human knowledge derives from sense data alone rather than from abstract reason—that "nothing is in intellect which was not first in sense"—Hume proposed that we have no way of ascertaining whether such knowledge really corresponds to objective truths lodged in the real world. Once he arrived at such extreme skepticism, Hume also proposed a philosophy of relativistic ethics: if we know nothing for certain, then there can be no absolute moral laws, and we must decide on proper courses of action from their contexts. Yet, as skeptical as Hume was, he was by no means cynical; rather, he enthusiastically joined in Voltaire's campaign to crush "infamy," or what Hume called "stupidity, Christianity, and ignorance," on the grounds that it is preferable to voyage amidst a sea of uncertainties than to dwell in a forest of supernatural shadows.

David Hume

The most practically oriented of the leading British philosophes was the Scottish economist Adam Smith (1723–1790) whose landmark treatise, *The Wealth of Nations* (1776), is recognized as the classic expression of "laissez-faire" economics. Strongly opposed to mercantilism—that is, any governmental intervention in economic affairs—Smith maintained that the prosperity of all could best be obtained by allowing individuals to pursue their own interests without competition from state-owned enterprises or legal restraints. The term *laissez-faire* comes from the French expression *laissez faire la nature* (let nature take its course), and Smith's advocacy of laissez-faire economic doctrine reveals how deeply indebted he was to the Enlightenment's idealization of both nature and human nature. In other words, espousing "the obvious and simple system of natural liberty," Smith believed that just as the planets revolve harmoniously in their orbits and are prevented from bumping into each other by the invisible force of gravity, so humans can act harmoniously even while pursuing their selfish economic interests if only "the invisible hand" of competitive, free-market forces is allowed to balance equitably the distribution of wealth. Ironically, although Smith thought of himself as the champion of the poor against the economic injustices inherent in state-supported mercantile privileges, his laissez-faire doctrine later became the favored theory of private industrial entrepreneurs who exploited the poor as much if not more than mercantilistic governments ever did. Nevertheless, Smith's free-market economics, as will be seen in subsequent chapters, certainly represented the wave of the future.

Adam Smith

Elsewhere in Europe the circulation of Enlightenment ideas was by no means as widespread as in France and Britain, owing either to stiffer resistance from religious authorities, greater vigilance of state censors, or the

Instruments of Torture. The rack
and the thumbscrew, from an
official Austrian governmental
handbook. Beccaria's influence
helped phase out the use of such
instruments by around 1800.

lack of sufficient numbers of prosperous educated people to discuss
and support progressive thought. Yet, aside from the Papal States, at least
a few prominent philosophes flourished in virtually every country in
Western Europe. In Italy, for example, the Milanese jurist Cesare Beccaria
(1738–1794), argued against arbitrary powers that oppressed humanity in
the same spirit as the French philosophes. In his most influential writing,
On Crimes and Punishments (1764), Beccaria attacked the prevalent view
that judicial punishments should represent society's vengeance on the male-
factor, asserting instead that no person has the right to punish another unless some useful purpose is served. For Beccaria, the only legitimate purpose for punishing crimes was the deterrence of other crimes. This granted,
he argued for the greatest possible leniency compatible with deterrence,
because enlightened humanitarianism dictated that humans should not
punish other humans any more than is absolutely necessary. Above all,
Beccaria eloquently opposed the death penalty, then widely inflicted
throughout Europe for the most trivial offenses, on the grounds that it was
no deterrent and set the bad example of public officials presiding over murder rather than striving to deter it. *On Crimes and Punishments* was so favorably received that it was quickly translated into a dozen languages. Owing
primarily to its influence, most European countries by around 1800 abolished torture, reserved the death penalty for capital crimes, and made imprisonment rather than any form of maiming the main form of judicial
punishment.

The most representative German philosophe was the literary critic and
dramatist Gotthold Lessing (1729–1781), who wrote with great eloquence
of the need for tolerance. In his play *Nathan the Wise* (1779) Lessing led the
audience to see that nobility of character has no relation to religious affiliations, and in his *Education of the Human Race* (1780) he maintained that the
development of each of the world's great religions, Christianity included,
was simply a step in the spiritual evolution of humanity, which would soon
move beyond religion entirely toward pure rationality. The living model
for Lessing's dramatic hero "Nathan the Wise" was his friend, the German
Jewish sage Moses Mendelssohn (1729–1786), another philosophe who
urged tolerance—in his case by writing a history of Judaism—but who also
argued in favor of the immortality of the soul.

Far more difficult to classify is the greatest German philosopher of the
eighteenth century—indeed one of the greatest philosophers of any nation
of any time—Immanuel Kant (1724–1804). An unworldly intellectual who
lived out his life far from the Enlightenment's French center of gravity in
the Prussian city of Königsberg (located so far to the east that today it is
part of Russia), Kant addressed his two masterworks, *The Critique of Pure
Reason* (1781) and The *Critique of Practical Reason* (1788), to criticizing fashionable Enlightenment skepticism as represented most persuasively by
David Hume. One of Kant's positions concerning reality and knowledge
went so far against the grain of standard Enlightenment assumptions that it
can hardly be called "Enlightened" at all. Namely, he maintained, in the
spirit of Platonism, that the existence of a realm of absolute reality consist-

ing of what he termed "things in themselves" cannot be doubted even though this realm remains unknowable to humans. Kant's assumption of absolute but unknowable truth, which implicitly opened philosophy to mystery, was to prove extremely attractive to his German philosophical successors in the nineteenth century, collectively known as "Idealists," but it ill accorded with his own age's stress on scientific verifiability.

In fact, however, Kant did not propose to build an action-oriented system on the basis of his assumed world of "things in themselves"; to the contrary, the bulk of his practical philosophy was more typically Enlightened. Aiming to counteract Hume's skepticism in a second way, he proposed that even though everyday knowledge begins in sense experience, the data of our senses is ordered by our rational minds in the here-and-now world of space and time in such a way as to provide us with reliable knowledge of appearances, or of what Kant called "phenomena." In other words, Kant believed that humans could gain sufficient truth on a daily basis by a combination of sense and reason. Hence he insisted, much like Voltaire, that humans should use their learning faculties to inquire about nature, and, having done so, to improve upon it. Regarding ethics, Kant avoided the extremes of fixing upon conduct arbitrarily according to supernatural divine commandments or relativistically according to changing circumstances. Instead he maintained that if pure reason could neither prove nor disprove the existence of God, practical reason tells us that in the idea of God there exists a notion of moral perfection toward which all must strive. Thus we should always endeavor to act consistently with what Kant called the "categorical imperative": to act as if one's actions were to become a universal law of nature. Kant's principle of the categorical imperative proposed greater moral inflexibility than most philosophes thought realistic in view of the realities of everyday existence, yet it remained reconcilable with the basic Enlightenment worldview inasmuch as it rested on human rather than supernatural determinations.

In taking final stock of the Enlightenment movement, historians customarily raise two major questions. One is whether the philosophes were mere elitists who had no influence on the masses. Certainly, if one studies the sales figures of the philosophes' books or membership lists of eighteenth-century learned societies one finds that the philosophes' immediate audience consisted of aristocrats, government officials, prosperous merchants, and a scattering of members of the higher clergy. To some degree this class bias lay beyond the philosophes' control, for many of the poorer people throughout eighteenth-century Europe remained illiterate, and most of the masses in southern and southeastern Europe—literate and illiterate alike—lived under the sway of an extremely conservative Roman Catholic hierarchy that was determined to keep them ignorant of the philosophes' ideas by means of the strictest censorship. Yet it is also true that many of the philosophes, despite their avowed commitment to clarity, wrote over the heads of most laboring people, and many did not even seek a lower-class audience because they feared that, if taken too far by the "uncouth" masses, their ideas might provoke open revolution. Typical philosophe

Immanuel Kant

Kant's practical philosophy

The audience of the philosophes

elitism is well expressed in Gibbon's praise of imperial Roman religious policy whereby "the various modes of worship . . . were all considered by the people as equally true, by the philosopher as equally false, and by the magistrate as equally useful." Tradition also relates that whenever Voltaire discussed religion with his philosophe friends, he dismissed the servants so that they would not overhear any subversive remarks. Given this prevalent attitude, it is less surprising that Enlightenment ideas hardly percolated down to the masses than that they did have some effect on popular beliefs in France and England. For example, research on religious practices in southern France demonstrates that from 1760 to 1790 fewer and fewer people of all classes requested that masses be said for their souls after death. Apparently, then, some servants were overhearing the philosophes' drawing-room conversations after all.

The philosophes' commitment to social reform

The other major question often asked about the Enlightenment is whether the philosophes were not hopelessly impractical "dreamers rather than doers." Without ignoring the clear vein of utopianism in Enlightenment thought, the answer to this must surely be no. Admittedly, most philosophes were far more optimistic about the chances of human perfectibility than most people are today, after the total wars and gas ovens of the twentieth century. Yet even the most optimistic did not expect utopian miracles to occur overnight. Rather, almost all the philosophes were committed to agitating for piecemeal social reforms that they believed would culminate, step by inevitable step, in a new world of enlightenment and virtue. Often such agitation did lead to significant changes in the conduct of practical affairs, and in at least one case, that of the American Revolution, Enlightenment ideas were the main source of inspiration for constructing a fully new political system. Moreover, sometimes even when Enlightenment propagandizing did not have any immediate practical impact, it did help to accomplish change in the future. For example, many philosophes condemned slavery on humanitarian or utilitarian grounds, thereby initiating a process of discussion that led cumulatively to the triumph of abolitionism throughout the West in the nineteenth century. In short, then, it is impossible to deny that the philosophes as a class were among the most practical-minded and influential intellectuals who ever lived.

4. THE ONWARD MARCH OF SCIENCE

Biology

Although several of the philosophes were natural scientists as well as publicists, it is preferable to treat the progress of eighteenth-century science separately because science, being highly international, is best broached by means of a topical rather than geographical method of review. The three scientific areas that witnessed the greatest progress from around the time of Newton to the end of the eighteenth century were descriptive biology, electricity, and chemistry. Regarding the first, four great pioneers in the use of newly invented high-power microscopes made enormous advances in observing small creatures and plant and cell structures during the last decades of the seventeenth century—the Italian Marcello Malpighi (1628–1694), the Englishman Robert Hooke, and two Dutchmen, Jan Swammerdam (1637–1680) and Antony van Leeuwenhoek (1632–1723). Perhaps most fundamental was the work of the last, a self-taught scientist who discovered bacteria and wrote the first description of human sperm. Building on such accomplishments as well as on numerous observations of his own, the Swedish botanist Karl von Linné (1707–1778)—commonly known by his Latinized name of Linnaeus—formulated the basic system of plant and animal classification that remains in use today. In the "Linnaean Order" there are three realms—animal, vegetable, and mineral—and within the first two there are classes, "genera" and species. Furthermore, in Linnaeus's system every plant and animal is given two scientific Latin names—the first denoting the genus and the second the species. For example, robins are called *Planesticus migratorius:* the migrating species of the genus *Planesticus.*

Rivaling Linnaeus in eighteenth-century biology was the French naturalist Georges Buffon (1707–1788), whose massive *Natural History,* appearing in forty-four volumes from 1749 to 1778, was most advanced in its recognition of the close relationship between humans and other primates. Completely ignoring the biblical version of creation, yet never quite bringing himself to accept the full implications of a theory that located human origins in some form of evolution, Buffon admitted the possibility that the entire range of organic forms had descended from a single species and thus was a precursor of the evolutionism of Charles Darwin.

Georges Buffon

As opposed to developments in descriptive biology, where basic work hardly began before 1660, the "founding father" in the field of electricity was active well before the period under discussion. Around 1600 the Englishman William Gilbert discovered the magnetic properties of lodestones and introduced the word *electricity* into the language (*elektron* is the Greek word for amber, and Gilbert had observed that amber rubbed on fur will attract paper or straw). Yet because Gilbert worked before the triumph of mechanistic thought, he believed magnetism to be a purely occult force and therefore did not even dream of machines that could generate or harness electricity. Starting in the late seventeenth century, on the other hand, scientists from many different countries progressively began to master the science of electricity as we now know it. In 1672 the German Otto von Guericke published results of experiments wherein he generated electricity; in 1729 the Englishman Stephen Gray demonstrated that electricity could be conducted by means of threads and that certain other substances resisted conducting; and in 1745 a team of scientists at the Dutch University of Leyden invented a method for storing electricity in the "Leyden jar." In 1749 by using a kite-string to conduct lightning the American Benjamin Franklin charged a Leyden jar from a thunderstorm and thus was able to conclude that lightning and electricity are identical. This recognition al-

Benjamin Franklin as the God of Electricity by Benjamin West

Chemistry

lowed Franklin to invent the lightning rod, which saves houses from being destroyed by lightning during storms and is one of the best examples of the link between scientific theory and life-enhancing practice.

Probably the greatest theoretical breakthrough made in the second half of the eighteenth century lay in the field of chemistry, which had been languishing for about a century after the work of Robert Boyle. The reason for this delay lay mostly in the wide acceptance of errors concerning such matters as heat, flame, air, and the phenomenon of combustion. The most misleading error was the so-called phlogiston theory, based on the idea that "phlogiston" was the substance of fire. When an object burned, phlogiston was supposed to be given off and the remaining ash was said to be the "true" material. In the second half of the eighteenth century important discoveries were made that discredited this theory and cleared the way for a real understanding of basic chemical reactions. In 1766 the Englishman Henry Cavendish reported the discovery of a new kind of gas obtained by treating certain metals with sulfuric acid. He showed that this gas, now known as hydrogen, would not of itself support combustion and yet would be rapidly consumed by a fire with access to the air. In 1774 oxygen was discovered by another Englishman, the Unitarian minister Joseph Priestley. He found that a candle would burn with extraordinary vigor when placed in the new gas—a fact that indicated clearly that combustion was not caused by any mysterious principle or substance in the flame itself. A few years after this discovery, Cavendish demonstrated that air and water, long supposed to be elements, are respectively a mixture and a compound, the first being composed principally of oxygen and nitrogen, and the second of oxygen and hydrogen.

Antoine Lavoisier

The final blow to the phlogiston theory was administered by the Frenchman Antoine Lavoisier (1743–1794), widely regarded as the greatest scientist of the eighteenth century, who lost his life in the French Revolution. Lavoisier proved that both combustion and respiration involve oxidation, the one being rapid and the other slow. He provided the names for oxygen and hydrogen and demonstrated that the diamond is a form of carbon. But undoubtedly his greatest accomplishment was his discovery of the law of the conservation of mass. He found evidence that "although matter may alter its state in a series of chemical actions, it does not change in amount; the quantity of matter is the same at the end as at the beginning of every operation, and can be traced by its weight." This "law" has, of course, been modified by later discoveries regarding the structure of the atom, and the conversion of some forms of matter into energy. It is hardly too much to say, however, that as a result of Lavoisier's genius chemistry became a true science.

Lavoisier's Apparatus for the Decomposition of Air

Comparative slowness of medical progress

Despite the notable scientific advances of the seventeenth and eighteenth centuries, the development of physiology and medicine progressed rather slowly during the same period for several reasons. One was the inadequate preparation of physicians, many of whom had begun their professional careers with little more training than apprenticeship under an older practitioner. Another was the common disrepute in which surgery was held as a mere trade, like that of a barber or blacksmith. Perhaps the most serious of all was the prejudice against dissection of human bodies for use in anatomical study. As late as 1750 medical schools that engaged in this practice were in danger of destruction by irate mobs. Despite these obstacles some progress was still possible. About 1670 Malpighi and Leeuwenhoek confirmed William Harvey's discovery of the circulation of the blood by observing the actual flow of blood through the network of capillaries connecting the arteries and veins. At approximately the same time an eminent physician of London, Thomas Sydenham, proposed a new theory of fever as a natural process by which diseased material is expelled from the system.

Medical progress during the eighteenth century was somewhat more rapid. Among the noteworthy achievements were the discovery of blood pressure, the founding of histology or microscopic anatomy, and the development of the autopsy as an aid to the study of disease. But the chief milestones of medical advancement in this period were the adoption of inoculation and the development of vaccination for smallpox. Knowledge of inoculation came originally from the Near East, where it had long been employed by the Muslims. Information concerning its use was relayed to England in 1717 through the letters of Lady Mary Wortley Montagu, wife of the British ambassador to Turkey. The first systematic application of the practice in the Western world, however, was due to the efforts of the American Puritan minister Cotton Mather, who implored the physicians of Boston to inoculate their patients in the hope of curbing an epidemic of smallpox that had broken out in 1721. Thereafter inoculation had some success in saving lives, but the practice understandably was widely resisted because smallpox inoculation guaranteed the patient one bout with the disfiguring disease before inducing further immunity to it. Only in 1796 did the Englishman Edward Jenner, noticing that milkmaids always seemed to have clear complexions, conclude that in contracting the virus of cowpox from their daily occupation, milkmaids gained immunity to smallpox. Hence inoculation of humans with the deadly smallpox virus appeared unnecessary, and Jenner introduced *vaccination* (from *vacca*—Latin for cow), employing the mild cowpox virus instead. Once vaccination proved both harmless and marvelously effective, the vast possibilities opened up for the elimination of contagious diseases appeared to confirm the Enlightenment belief in the ability of science to make nature's laws work for the betterment of the human condition.

Inoculation and vaccination

5. CLASSICISM AND INNOVATION IN ART AND LITERATURE

Although the spirit of the scientific revolution and the Enlightenment was reflected in certain great artistic monuments, there were no simple, one-to-one correspondences between intellectual and artistic trends in the late seventeenth and eighteenth centuries. Artists and writers responded to a great variety of influences in addition to the new scientific view of the universe:

*Manifold influences on
artistic trends*

The Finding of Moses by Poussin. The artist has included a pyramid in the background (right) as a token of verisimilitude, but otherwise his scene appears to be set in ancient Rome. Note the stress on monumentality and perpendicular lines.

national stylistic traditions, religious demands, differing political and sociological contexts, and, not least, the internal dynamics of artistic evolution within any given creative field. It is best, then, to look at certain major trends without forcing the explanations for them all to fit the same mold.

As we have seen earlier, the dominant style in European art between about 1600 and the early 1700s was the Baroque. But a few countries resisted the dominance of Baroque influences—particularly France, Holland, and England. The French resistance was primarily nationalistic in inspiration. Since Baroque style was closely associated with the tastes of the Spanish and Austrian Habsburgs, against whom the French were fighting throughout most of the seventeenth and early eighteenth centuries, it seemed inappropriate for France to admit cultural inferiority by imitating the style of its political rivals. In opposition to the exuberant Baroque, then, French artists and architects cultivated restrained classicism. Some of the best earlier examples of this are the canvases of seventeenth-century France's greatest painter, Nicolas Poussin (1594–1665), whose reposeful scenes from classical mythology, governed by the artist's programmatic commitment to "things well ordered," stand in the sharpest contrast to the swirling contortions of Poussin's Baroque contemporary, Rubens.

"Well-ordered" classicism continued to be the preferred style in France during the reign of Louis XIV (1651–1715) for three reasons. First of all, Louis in particular was determined to make sure that France cultivated its own characteristic national style for reasons of state. Second, Louis's own stylistic preferences tended toward the grand and sober. And third, the symmetrical qualities of classicism seemed to complement best the highly

French classicism

See color plates facing page 620 for *Landscape with the Burial of Phocion* by Poussin

Classicism of the Louvre

symmetrical natural order then being posited in France by Cartesian philosophers and scientists. Thus when Louis XIV decided to renovate his palace of the Louvre, the leading Baroque architect of the day, Bernini, submitted plans, but these were rejected in favor of those of a native Frenchman who emphasized severe classical monumentality. Later, when Louis erected his splendid new palace at Versailles, Baroque architectural features were introduced. Yet the Baroque of Versailles was a very restrained Baroque that emphasized massive symmetry rather than the jutting angles and startling curves favored by Bernini.

In the other leading countries that resisted the Baroque, Holland and England, there can be little doubt that artistic preferences had religious as well as nationalistic causes. Since Holland and England were Protestant, they naturally preferred to limit Baroque influences emanating from Rome and the Catholic Spanish Netherlands. We have seen that the greatest seventeenth-century Dutch painter, Rembrandt, developed his own highly personal style, which employed Baroque elements whenever he deemed them appropriate. Rembrandt's slightly later Dutch contemporary, Jan Vermeer (1632–1675), however, eliminated the Baroque entirely in painting the serenest realistic indoor genre scenes, as did most other seventeenth-century Dutch genre, landscape, and portrait painters. Similarly, the dominant stylistic commitment in England, after a brief flirtation with the Baroque during the reign of the Catholic-leaning Charles II, was to a classicizing restraint. Thus the most prominent of all English architects, Christopher Wren (1632–1723), did not hesitate to borrow Baroque ele-

East Entrance of the Louvre, Paris. Built by the French architect Claude Perrault between 1667 and 1670, this facade is an excellent example of the rigorously classical style patronized by Louis XIV.

The Painter in his Studio by Vermeer. The model is posing as Clio, the muse of history, and thus stands for the timeless fame of painting. The fact that the source of light is concealed by the curtain may perhaps be understood to mean that the artist works essentially by the interior illumination of his mind.

Left: *St. Peter's Basilica with Colonnade, Rome.* Right: *St. Paul's Cathedral, London.* The sweeping colonnade in front of St. Peter's was designed by the Baroque architectural master Bernini in 1656. Such showy effects were not to the taste of the English architect Christopher Wren, who in designing St. Paul's hewed more closely to the classicism implicit in the Renaissance style of the Vatican Basilica itself. Wren's "English answer to St. Peter's," however, makes classical columns even more prominent than they were in the Vatican. Note how Wren drew inspiration from Perrault's classical Louvre facade (above, p. 633) in designing St. Paul's second-level elevation.

English architecture

ments when fitting, but emphasized classicism in his columns and domes, most notably in his masterwork, St. Paul's Cathedral (built from 1675 to 1710). More classical still was the "Palladian revival," which dominated English architecture in the first half of the eighteenth century. In this period numerous country houses commissioned by the landed gentry imitated the Renaissance master Palladio's serenely classical and highly symmetrical Villa Rotonda, just as that building had imitated the Roman Pantheon. Indeed, so many English town houses built in the fashionable resort spa of Bath around 1740 imitated Palladian models that Bath was soon called, after Palladio's main area of activity, "the English Vicenza."

Classicism in French literature

As classicism was the prevalent style in seventeenth-century French art, so too did it prevail in literature. This can be seen most clearly in the tragedies of Pierre Corneille (1606–1684) and Jean Racine (1639–1699). Both of these playwrights took as their subjects the heroes and heroines of classical mythology and history such as Medea, Pompey, Andromache, and Phaedra, and both strove as well to imitate the theoretical and structural principles of the classical Greek tragedians. Similarly, the great French writer of comedies, Jean Baptiste Molière (1622–1673), was so committed to symmetrical formalism as to have his characters speak in rhyming couplets. Yet, unlike Corneille and Racine, Molière did set the action of his plays in the present because he believed that "the business of comedy is to represent in general all the defects of men and especially of the men of our time." Accordingly, his work was also highly satirical. In *Tartuffe,* for example, he pilloried religious hypocrisy, and in *The Bourgeois Gentleman* he mocked the vulgar pretentiousness of the social climber. Yet for all his satire, Molière had a measure of sympathy for the trials of human existence, rising to his greatest profundity in *The Misanthrope,* a play that pokes fun at a person who hates society but that also shows that the character has excellent reasons for his alienation. Thus mixing sympathy and occasional melancholy with wit and searing scorn, Molière was perhaps the most gifted European dramatist after Shakespeare.

As in France, in England artistic classicism was paralleled by literary classicism, which flourished in England from about 1660 to 1760. In fact, the English writers of this period expressly called themselves "Augustans." This they did for two reasons: first, the restoration of royalty in 1660 after the English Civil War seemed to presage an age of peace and civility similar to the one installed by Augustus after civil war in ancient Rome; and second, the favored poetic models of the English Augustans were the Augustan Romans—Virgil, Horace, and Ovid. Still another reason why English literary taste became resolutely classical in the later seventeenth century was that the France of Louis XIV had enormous influence in setting fashions throughout Europe, and the English did not wish to be the slightest bit out of date in following the French lead. Finally, as in France, classicism appeared to be the one available style that came closest to being dispassionately "scientific." In other words, just when the English leisured classes were celebrating the triumphs of Newtonianism and endeavoring to make their own contribution to scientific advance by collecting natural specimens or gazing through telescopes, they patronized a form of writing that seemed to resemble Newtonian methods and laws in stressing simplicity, clarity, and symmetry.

The English Augustans

Chiswick House. Built near London around 1725, this country house initiated an English Palladian fad that had its echoes in Thomas Jefferson's Monticello, and later still in the Jefferson Memorial. Note how the design imitates Palladio's Villa Rotonda (above p. 420), just as that building itself was modeled on the Roman Pantheon (above, p. 183).

The Embarkation for Cythera by Watteau. This epoch-making painting broke with the severity of Poussin in favor of a greater stress on motion and lushness. No two art historians agree upon exactly what it means, but the evocation of dreamy pleasure is unmistakable.

Jonathan Swift and Alexander Pope

Of the numerous members of the English Augustan school, the most outstanding were the prose writer Jonathan Swift (1667–1745) and the poet Alexander Pope (1688–1744). The former, a scathing satirist, was atypical of Augustan thinking in his pessimism concerning the potentialities of human nature: in Swift's masterpiece, *Gulliver's Travels,* humans at one point are dismissed as "the most pernicious race of little odious vermin that nature ever suffered to crawl upon the surface of the earth." Yet Swift's prose is fully Augustan in its economy and clarity; as opposed to earlier flowery stylists, Swift insisted on locating, as he said, "proper words in proper places." As for Pope, he was thoroughly Augustan in both style and thought—almost to a fault. A consistent exponent in highly regular rhyming verse of the naturalistic doctrines of the Enlightenment, Pope in such didactic poems as his *Essay on Man* and his *Essay on Criticism* held that humans must study and imitate nature if they were to bring any semblance of order into their affairs. Most necessary for mankind, in Pope's view, was unblinking self-knowledge, which the poet believed could be obtained apart from theology or metaphysics. Summing up the secularistic spirit of his age, Pope responded to Milton's earlier poetic resolve to "justify the ways of God to man" in his most famous couplet: "Know then thyself, presume not God to scan;/the proper study of Mankind is Man."

Rococo painting

As impressive as numerous artistic and literary productions of French and English classicism may have been, the classical movement self-evidently was not highly innovative. Two entirely separate developments of the eighteenth century, on the other hand, emphasized greater originality— namely, the emergence of the Continental Rococo style in art, and the rise of the English novel. Regarding the former, the basic explanation for the emergence of Rococo art and architecture was the sense of relaxation experienced in France at the coming of peace and at the death of Louis XIV in 1715. Whereas the prolonged War of the Spanish Succession had begun to exhaust the country, and whereas Louis in his declining years had become ever more puritanical and ever more determined to enforce his own severe tastes and standards on everyone else, around 1715 the leisured classes of the nation breathed a deep sigh of relief. This reaction, not surprisingly, resulted in an artistic pendulum swing from classical severity to a cheerful abandonment that goes by the name of Rococo style. In painting, the earliest and most gifted Rococo artist was Antoine Watteau (1684–1721), who was influenced more by the Baroque artist Rubens than by any other single source, but who replaced Rubens's massiveness with airy French elegance and grace. Watteau was admitted into the French Academy of Fine Arts in 1717 for his masterpiece, *The Embarkation for Cythera,* even though none of the members would have dreamed of admitting him two years earlier. Moreover, since the Academy had no formal classification for the *Embarkation*—which merely showed graceful people having a dreamily good time—it invented one for the purpose: *fêtes galantes,* best translated as stylish revels. At least Watteau's revellers were clothed, but the figures in the paintings of his Rococo successors François Boucher (1703–1770) and Jean-Honoré Fragonard (1732–1806) were usually half naked and displayed in postures that went well beyond sensuality in the direction of frank eroticism.

See color plates following page 620 for *Le Mezzetin* by Watteau and *Madame de Pompadour* by Boucher

Most of the rest of Europe was too strait-laced to imitate the lasciviousness of French Rococo painting, but French Rococo architecture soon became the dominant style throughout the Continent and remained such for most of the eighteenth century. The reasons for this were, first, that the French architects who pioneered in Rococo building in the years shortly after 1715 took Baroque principles for their standards in replacing classical ones, thereby setting themselves in tune with the rest of their Continental contemporaries, and second, that Rococo building design featured curva-

French Rococo architecture

A Reclining Nude by Boucher. The viewer is left to ponder the significance of the fallen flower.

Rococo and Baroque compared

ceous elegance and thus appealed greatly to the vain European aristocrats who commissioned the major architectural projects of the day.

Perhaps the easiest way to characterize the Rococo building style is to call it the "champagne of Baroque" or "Baroque with a French accent." Both Baroque and Rococo buildings emphasize dynamic movement, but whereas Baroque style exudes force and passion, the Rococo communicates a sense of delicacy and playfulness. Most amazing to initial viewers of Rococo interiors is how light and airy they are: as opposed to Baroque interiors, which are generally sombre, Rococo interiors have walls and ceilings painted in white, gold, and pink. Among the leading European Rococo buildings are the Hôtel de Soubise in Paris, the pavilion known as the Zwinger in Dresden, the jewel-box Vierzehnheiligen church near Bamberg, and the Cuvilliès theater in Munich, which is still used for performances of eighteenth-century operas and plays. Although Rococo art and architecture unquestionably allowed great play for the imagination, from the long-term perspective of art history the Rococo style was an end rather than a beginning inasmuch as it represented the final phase of the Baroque.

Uniqueness of the novel

In contrast, the only really new development in the artistic and literary history of the Enlightenment period that had a promising future was the emergence of the novel. In treating the rise of the novel in eighteenth-century England it must be stressed that the English novel was not invented out of nothing. To the contrary, works of prose fiction known as romances

Two German Rococo Interiors. The Vierzehnheiligen Church near Bamberg (left) and the Wieskirche near Munich (right) are the two foremost works of German Rococo interior decoration.

had been composed in classical antiquity and throughout Western Europe from the twelfth century onward. Indeed, one European romance—Cervantes's *Don Quixote*—atypically had many of the characteristics of the modern novel. Moreover, in France, where the word *roman* means both romance and novel, prose fictions were written without interruption from the Middle Ages to the recognizably modern novels of the nineteenth-century writers Balzac and Flaubert. Nevertheless, there were such major differences between the best English prose fictions of the eighteenth century and all that came before (other than *Don Quixote*) as to make it possible to say that the modern novel was invented in eighteenth-century England.

Novelistic realism

The best way of characterizing the difference between the romance and the novel is that the former is patently a fabrication, whereas the latter (allowing a few inevitable exceptions) purports to be a reliable account of how humans behave. Assuming that a judge in a court of law were asked to accept the testimony of a romance as evidence for trying a case, he would have to throw it out and declare a mistrial because romances generally have little sense of verisimilitude, being written in an ornate style and recounting the adventures of clearly imaginary characters—usually from the mythical or semi-mythical past—who find themselves in preposterous situations. But the testimony of a novel might stand up as excellent legal evidence, for in the novel, from the eighteenth-century English examples onward, experiences seem unique, plots and settings fully believable, and the manner of presentation dispassionately straightforward.

*Reasons for the rise of the
novel*

Two explanations may be offered for the emergence of the novel in eighteenth-century England. One is that the ideals of the Enlightenment unquestionably created the most conducive atmosphere for novel writing insofar as the "scientific," methodical study of human experience was widely regarded as the order of the day. Yet, because Enlightenment thinking predominated in France even more than in England, it remains to be asked why England in particular was the modern novel's first home. The answer to this appears to relate to the distinctive nature of the English reading public. Specifically, England had a much larger nonaristocratic reading audience than France because of England's greater involvement in trade and industry; this class preferred novels to romances because novels were written in a gripping rather than "elevated" style, and the action of the novel's more prosaic characters seemed more relevant to common, nonaristocratic experience. As will also presently be seen, it was by no means irrelevant to the novelistic form in England that the majority of novel readers were not men but women.

*Defoe, Richardson, and
Fielding*

By common consent the three most influential novelists of eighteenth-century England were Daniel Defoe (1660–1731), Samuel Richardson (1689–1761), and Henry Fielding (1707–1754). All three portrayed recognizable, nonaristocratic characters doing their best to make their way in a perilous world, unaffected by any hint of divine intervention for good or ill. In the novels of Defoe and Richardson the narrator is usually a character who participates in the action and thus knows the "truth" of one side directly but of course cannot be expected to understand every other character's point of view. On the other hand, in Fielding's *Tom Jones* an "omnipotent narrator" stands apart from the action, and accordingly has a fuller view of it, but seems by his obtrusive presence to be creating a rather more artificial fiction.

Tom Jones is the only eighteenth-century English novel universally considered to be an enduring classic of world literature, but at the very beginning of the next century the technical achievements of Defoe, Richardson, and Fielding were refined by Jane Austen (1775–1817), whose *Pride and Prejudice* and *Emma* represent for many readers the height of novelistic perfection. That a woman should emerge around 1800 as a greater writer of novels than most men was almost inevitable, above all because early-modern European fiction writing was one of the very few areas of creative expression wherein society easily tolerated female contributions. Indeed, in seventeenth-century France the most widely read authors of romances— Madeleine de Scudéry and the countess de La Fayette—were women, and later in England Fanny Burney (1752–1840), Ann Radcliffe (1764–1823), and Maria Edgeworth (1767–1849) all wrote novels of great popularity and considerable distinction before Jane Austen went to work. Moreover, since the English novel-reading public was predominantly female, women readers understandably were particularly interested in characteristically female problems as seen from a feminine angle, a subject matter and perspective that Jane Austen bountifully provided. But of course Austen would not rank, as she does, among the handful of greatest novelists who ever lived had she been narrowly parochial in her views and lacking in extraordinary artistic skill. Rather, men as well as women can delight in her dry, ironic wit and admire her insight into human nature. Moreover, Jane Austen's technical accomplishments may well represent novelistic skills at their pinnacle. In particular, in compromising between Defoe's and Richardson's first-person narrator and Fielding's omnipotent third-person one by the use of a third-person narrator who remains unobtrusive and pursues events primarily from the point of view of a central character, Jane Austen created a delicate balance between subjectivity and objectivity that may well never have been surpassed.

6. BAROQUE AND CLASSICAL MUSIC

The title of one of the most genial of eighteenth-century symphonic compositions, Haydn's *Surprise* Symphony, can be applied to the music of the entire age, for eighteenth-century music is continually full of surprises. Indeed, in contrast to developments in contemporary art and literature, where innovation was comparatively rare, the eighteenth century was the most fertile period of invention in all of Western European musical history. Probably the major explanation for this is that early-modern composers, unlike artists and writers, did not have to concern themselves about how much they would borrow from the music of classical antiquity because the principles of ancient musical composition were virtually unknown. More free than painters and poets to strike out on their own, early-modern composers invented form after form in two successive major styles, the Baroque and the so-called classical, treating their listeners to surprise after surprise.

Baroque music, like Baroque art and architecture, emerged around 1600 in Italy as an artistic expression of the Counter-Reformation. Yet from the beginning Baroque composers were perforce more inventive than their artistic counterparts, having no equivalent of columns and domes with which to work. The first important figure in the history of Baroque music was the Italian Claudio Monteverdi (1567–1643), who reacted against the highly intricate Renaissance polyphonic style of his major predecessor, Palestrina. Pursuing the Baroque goal of dramatic expressiveness, Monteverdi found that deep human emotions were difficult to convey when members of a chorus were singing against each other as they did in the music of the late Renaissance, and that dramatic intensity becomes greatest when music is combined with theater. Having no classical models to draw upon, Monteverdi thus virtually single-handedly invented a new musical form, that of opera. In addition, to lend his opera singers greater emotional power than they would have had if they had sung alone, Monteverdi wrote instrumental accompaniments so forceful that they have earned him the title of "the father of instrumentation." Since Monteverdi's new form of opera fully suited the spirit of his times, within a generation operas were performed in all the leading cities of Italy. Staged within magnificent settings, and calling upon the talents of singers, musicians, dramatists, and stage designers, opera expressed as clearly as any art form the dedication of Baroque artistic style to grandeur, drama, and display.

With the notable exception of the Englishman Henry Purcell (1659–1695), no enduringly great composers worked in the second half of the seventeenth century. Nonetheless, many imaginative musicians began to create new forms during this period, most notably the instrumental forms of the sonata and the concerto. Moreover, whatever lull there may have been in the composition of masterpieces was more than compensated for in the last phase of the Baroque era by the appearance of Bach and Handel, two of the greatest composers of all time. Born in the same year very near each other in northern Germany, Johann Sebastian Bach (1685–1750) and George Frederick Handel (1685–1759) had very different musical personalities and very different careers. Bach was an intensely pious introvert who remained in the backwaters of provincial Germany all his life and wrote music of the utmost individuality, whereas Handel was a public-pleasing cosmopolitan whose music is more accessible than Bach's in its robust affirmativeness. Despite these differences, however, both Bach and Handel were distinctly late-Baroque stylists in their commitment to writing music of the deepest expressiveness.

Anyone who has any familiarity with classical music can identify in a moment a work of Bach even if he or she has never heard it before because Bach's music is so extraordinarily individualistic. This, however, does not mean that it is in any way predictable, for part of Bach's individuality lay in

Claudio Monteverdi

Later Baroque music

Johann Sebastian Bach

Bach

his very unpredictability. Combining an uncanny imagination and capacious intellect with heroic powers of discipline and an ability to produce music of the greatest genius on demand, Bach was an extremely prolific composer in the entire gamut of contemporary forms (excluding opera), from unaccompanied instrumental pieces to enormous works for vocal soloists, chorus, and orchestra. As a church musician in Leipzig for most of his mature career, Bach's professional duty was to provide new music regularly for Sunday and holiday services. Therefore much of his work consists of religious cantatas (over two hundred surviving), motets, and passions. One might think that the mere requirement to write such music on schedule might have made it routine and lifeless, but Bach, an ardent Protestant who was entirely unaffected by the secularism of the Enlightenment, seems to have written each one of his church pieces with such fervor that the salvation of the world appears to hang on every note. Not content with expressing himself in spiritual music alone, Bach also gloried in creating joyous concertos and suites for orchestra, and succeeded in composing the purest of "pure music"—extraordinarily subtle and complex fugues for keyboard in which the capacity of the human mind for apprehending abstraction appears to approach the celestial.

Handel

Much unlike the provincial, inner-directed Bach, Handel was a man of the world who sought primarily to establish rapport with large, secular audiences. After spending his early creative years in Italy, where he mastered Italian Baroque compositional techniques, Handel established himself in London. There he tried at first to make a living by composing Italian operas, but since the highly florid Baroque operatic style proved too foreign for more staid English tastes, Handel eventually realized that he would never survive unless he turned to some more salable genre. This he found in the oratorio—a variety of music drama intended for performance in concert form. Marking a transition from the spiritual to the secular, Handel's oratorios were usually set to biblical stories but featured very worldly music, replete with ornate instrumentation and frequent flourishes of drums and trumpets. (Some music historians refer to Handel's "big bow-wow" manner.) These highly virile and heroic works succeeded in packing London's halls full of prosperous English people who interpreted the victories of the ancient Hebrews in such oratorios as *Israel in Egypt* and *Judas Maccabaeus* as implicit celebrations of England's own burgeoning national greatness. Of course Handel's music was not for one time but for all, as is demonstrated by the fact that his greatest oratorio, *The Messiah,* is sung widely throughout the English-speaking world every Christmas and its stirring "Hallelujah Chorus" certainly remains the most popular single choral piece in the entire classical repertory.

"The Charming Brute." A contemporary caricature of Handel, engraved by Joseph Groupy, 1754.

The classical style in music

Although only a few decades separated the activity of Bach and Handel from that of their greatest eighteenth-century successors, the Austrians Joseph Haydn (1732–1809) and Wolfgang Amadeus Mozart (1756–1791), the two pairs appear worlds apart because their compositional styles are utterly different. This is to say that whereas Bach and Handel were among the last and certainly the greatest composers of Baroque music, Haydn and Mozart were the leading representatives of the succeeding "classical" style. The latter term is slightly confusing because classicism in music had nothing to do with imitating music written in classical antiquity. Rather, the musical style that prevailed in Europe in the second half of the eighteenth century is called *classical* because it sought to imitate classical principles of order, clarity, and symmetry—in other words, to sound as a Greek temple looked. Moreover, composers of the classical school innovated in creating music that adhered rigorously to certain structural principles. For example, all classical symphonies have four movements, and all open with a first movement in "sonata form," characterized by the successive presentation of themes, development, and recapitulation. Undoubtedly the spread of the ideals of the Enlightenment influenced the development of the classical style, yet there were elements of elegant aristocratic Rococo influence at work as well, for the music of the classical era customarily has a lightness and gaiety about it that is most reminiscent of Rococo pastels.

Certainly the tastes of the same European aristocrats who commissioned Rococo buildings determined the personal fortunes of most composers in the second half of the eighteenth century because these composers no longer had any interest in gaining a livelihood by writing church music as Bach had done, and as yet had no large concert-hall public (Handel's London audience being exceptional). The perils of struggling for a living by composing music in the later eighteenth century can be seen best in the sad career of the sublime genius Mozart. As a phenomenal child prodigy, the young Mozart—who began composing at four, started touring Europe as a keyboard virtuoso at six, and wrote his first symphony at nine—was the darling of the aristocracy. The Austrian empress Maria Theresa embraced him and the pope made him "Knight of the Golden Spur." But as soon as

Three Contemporary Impressions of Mozart. At the left is the child prodigy, aged seven, seated at a keyboard. The first name given as "Theoph." is not a mistake but is Greek for Mozart's real middle name, Amadeus, meaning "who loves God." The drawing of the mature Mozart in the middle is a highly idealized conception; no doubt the painting on the right comes closest to conveying what the composer really looked like.

Top: *Haydn in Livery*. Bottom: *The Composer in London*. While he worked in the pay of the Esterházy family, Haydn was little more than a high-level servant. In London, on the other hand, he was portrayed as an inspired genius with a faraway look in his eye and a sheet of his own music in his hand.

Advance of secular music

Mozart reached puberty he was no longer a curiosity and, owing partly to his rather cantankerous personality, proved unable to gain steady employment in the service of any single wealthy aristocrat. In lieu of that, he strove to support himself as a freelance composer and keyboard performer in Vienna, but could make ends meet only with the greatest difficulty. Although he spent every year of his mature life in bountiful productivity, he had to live from hand to mouth until he died at the age of thirty-five from the effects of an undiagnosed wasting disease. Only a handful of people attended the funeral of one of the greatest creative artists of all time, and he was buried in a pauper's grave. Given these appalling circumstances, it is perfectly amazing that Mozart's music is characteristically sunny and serene. Only rarely did he write in a minor key, and even when he did so, he usually paired a melancholy work with an exuberantly joyful one, as if to demonstrate almost defiantly that the trials of his personal life had no effect on his art.

Haydn's career provides an instructive contrast. Knowing much better how to take care of himself, "Papa Haydn" spent most of his life in the comfortable employment of the Esterházys, an extremely wealthy Austro-Hungarian aristocratic family that maintained its own private orchestra. But this security entailed the indignity of wearing the Esterházy livery, like any common butler. Only toward the end of his life, in 1791, did Haydn, now famous, strike out on his own by traveling to London, where for five years (excluding a brief interval) he supported himself handsomely by writing for a paying public, as Handel once did, rather than for private patrons. The fact that London alone was able to provide opportunities for earning a commercial livelihood to two foreigners is clearly indicative of the city's unusual status in the eighteenth century as one of the few localities where there was a mass market for culture. In this regard London represented the wave of the future, for in the nineteenth century serious music would definitely leave the aristocratic salon for the urban concert hall all over Europe. It may also be noted that whereas in deeply aristocratic Austria Haydn was obliged to wear servants' livery, in London he was greeted as a creative genius—one of the earliest composers to be regarded as such even though poets and painters had been celebrated as geniuses long before. Thus Haydn's *Miracle* Symphony, written for performance in a London concert hall, is so called because during one performance a chandelier came crashing down and many would have been killed had it not been for the fact that the entire audience had moved up as close as possible to get a better view of the "genius" Haydn who was conducting.

Haydn's stay in London foreshadowed the future in still another way, for the music he wrote on that occasion was wholly secular, as opposed to the semi-religious oratorios of Handel. Indeed, the music of the entire classical era was predominantly secular, as most music would remain until the present, and this secular writing advanced primarily on three fronts—opera, chamber music, and orchestral composition. In the field of opera, an important innovator of the classical period was Christoph Willibald von Gluck (1714–1787), who emphasized the necessity for dramatic action at a

Original announcement for Mozart's Don Giovanni. *The advertisement is full of information about the opera, except the name of the person who wrote it. Mozart's name appears once in tiny letters, subordinated even to the name of the librettist, Da Ponte. It is a crowning irony that* Don Giovanni *was probably the greatest opera written by the man who is often considered the greatest operatic composer of all time.*

time when Monteverdi's many successors had made opera much too static. But by far the greatest operatic composer of the era was Mozart, whose *Marriage of Figaro, Don Giovanni,* and *The Magic Flute* remain among the most magnificent and best-loved operas of all time. As for the realm of chamber music (music written for small instrumental ensembles), the classical era was the most fertile age of chamber music, for the genre of the string quartet was invented at the beginning of the period and was soon brought to the fullest fruition in the quartets of both Haydn and Mozart.

Yet probably the most impressive invention of the classical era was the symphony—so to speak the novel of music—for the symphony has since proven to be the most versatile and popular of all classical musical forms. Although not the very first writer of symphonies, Haydn is nonetheless usually termed the "father of the symphony" because in over one hundred works in the symphonic form—and preeminently in his last twelve symphonies, which he composed in London—Haydn formulated the most enduring techniques of symphonic composition and demonstrated to the fullest extent the symphony's creative potential. Yet Mozart's three last symphonies (out of that composer's total of forty-one) are generally regarded as greater even than those of Haydn, for the grace, variety, and utter technical perfection of these works are beyond comparison. Mere words cannot do justice to any of the marvelous musical creations of the eighteenth century, yet it may confidently be stated in conclusion that if just one or two of Mozart's musical compositions had survived instead of literally hundreds, they alone would be enough to place the century among the most inspired ages in the entire history of the human creative imagination.

The symphony

• *Items so designated are available in paperback editions.*

• Baker, Keith, *Condorcet: From Natural Philosophy to Social Mathematics,* Chicago, 1975. Advances the view that Condorcet's greatest significance lies in his attempt to create a quantifiable social science rather than in his theory of historical progress.

Baumer, Franklin L., *Modern European Thought: Continuity and Change in Ideas, 1600–1950,* New York, 1978. An extraordinarily fine intellectual history, organized around major themes rather than the work of individuals.

• Becker, Carl, *The Heavenly City of the Eighteenth-Century Philosophers,* New Haven, 1932. Advances the thesis that the *philosophes* were just as impractical in their commitment to abstract secular rationalism as the medieval Scholastics were in their theological rationalism. Witty and stimulating but widely regarded as out of date in its views.

Briggs, Robin, *The Scientific Revolution of the Seventeenth Century,* New York, 1969. A very brief but extremely valuable survey, with a documentary appendix.

• Bronowski, J., and B. Mazlish, *The Western Intellectual Tradition,* New York, 1960. A superb, old-fashioned intellectual history, which serves as an excellent complement to Baumer for the seventeenth and eighteenth centuries.

Bukofzer, M. F., *Music in the Baroque Era,* New York, 1947.

• Butterfield, H., *The Origins of Modern Science,* London, 1949. As important for its discussion of Newton's breakthrough regarding gravity and the impact of the scientific revolution on the Enlightenment as it is for its discussion of the Renaissance period.

• Chartier, Roger, *The Cultural Origins of the French Revolution,* Durham, N.C., 1991. A cultural history of "de-Christianization."

• Darnton, Robert, *The Business of Enlightenment: A Publishing History of the Encyclopédie, 1775–1800,* Cambridge, Mass., 1979. A masterful and fascinating blend of intellectual, social, and business history.

• Gay, Peter, *The Enlightenment: An Interpretation; Vol. 1, The Rise of Modern Paganism; Vol. 2, The Science of Freedom,* New York, 1966–1969. A cross between an interpretation and a survey. Emphasizes the philosophes' sense of identification with the classical world and takes a generally positive view of their accomplishments. Contains extensive annotated bibliographies.

• Hall, A. Rupert, *The Revolution in Science: 1500–1750,* New York, 1983. The best place to look for clear accounts of specific scientific accomplishments.

• Hampson, Norman, *The Enlightenment,* Baltimore, 1968. Probably the best shorter introduction.

• Hazard, Paul, *The European Mind: The Critical Years (1680–1715),* New Haven, 1953. A basic and indispensable account of the changing climate of opinion that preceded the Enlightenment.

• Hildesheimer, W., *Mozart,* New York, 1982. Widely regarded as the most literate and thought-provoking biography now available of any major musical figure.

• Kimball, F., *The Creation of the Rococo Decorative Style,* Philadelphia, 1943.

Levey, Michael, *Rococo to Revolution: Major Trends in 18th Century Painting,* New York, 1966.

- Manuel, Frank E., *A Portrait of Isaac Newton,* Cambridge, Mass., 1968. A provocative psychobiography.
- Shryock, Richard H., *The Development of Modern Medicine: An Interpretation of the Social and Scientific Factors Involved,* London, 1948. Fascinating reading and still the basic work on the subject.

  Sklar, Judith, *Montesquieu,* Oxford, 1987.
- Summerson, John, *Architecture in Britain, 1530–1830,* 6th ed., Baltimore, 1971. The best introduction to Wren and English Palladianism.
- Wade, Ira O., *The Intellectual Development of Voltaire,* Princeton, 1969. A magnificent synthesis that stresses how Voltaire's "English experience" provided the cornerstone for all his subsequent thought.
- Waterhouse, Ellis K., *Painting in Britain, 1530–1790,* 4th ed., Baltimore, 1979. Very good on eighteenth-century developments.
- Watt, Ian, *The Rise of the Novel,* London, 1957. The basic work on the innovative qualities of the novel in eighteenth-century England.
- Westfall, R. S., *Never at Rest: A Biography of Isaac Newton,* New York, 1980. Illuminates all aspects of Newton's scientific accomplishment.

SOURCE MATERIALS

- Beccaria, Cesare, *An Essay on Crimes and Punishments,* with a Commentary by M. de Voltaire, Stanford, 1953. A reprint of the original English translation of 1767.
- Gibbon, Edward, *The Portable Gibbon: The Decline and Fall of the Roman Empire,* ed. D. A. Saunders, New York, 1952. A convenient abridgment.

  Rousseau, J.–J., *Political Writings,* ed. A. Ritter, New York, 1987.
- Voltaire, *The Portable Voltaire,* ed. Ben Ray Redman, New York, 1949. An excellent anthology including the complete *Candide.*

Part Five

THE FRENCH AND INDUSTRIAL REVOLUTIONS AND THEIR CONSEQUENCES

No two events more profoundly altered the shape of Western civilization than the French and Industrial Revolutions. "Modern" history begins with their occurrence. The major happenings of the nineteenth and early twentieth centuries—the spread of middle-class liberalism and economic success; the decline of the old, landed aristocracies; the growth of class consciousness among urban workers—all had their roots in these two revolutions.

The French and Industrial Revolutions took place at about the same time and affected many of the same people—though in different ways and to varying degrees. Together they resulted in the overthrow of absolutism, mercantilism, and the last vestiges of manorialism. Together they produced the theory and practice of economic individualism and political liberalism. And together they ensured the growth of class consciousness, and the culmination of those tensions between the middle and working classes that imparted new vitality to European history after 1800.

Each revolution, of course, produced results peculiarly its own. The French Revolution encouraged the growth of nationalism and its unattractive stepchild, authoritarianism. The Industrial Revolution compelled the design of a new, urban social order. Yet despite their unique contributions, the two revolutions must be studied together and understood as the joint progenitors of Western history in the nineteenth and early twentieth centuries.

The French and Industrial Revolutions and Their Consequences

POLITICS	SCIENCE & INDUSTRY
	James Watt's steam engine, 1763
American War of Independence, 1775–1783	Spinning jenny patented, 1770
	Beginning of factory system, 1780s
French Revolution begins, 1789	Lavoisier discovers the indestructibility of matter, 1789
France declared a republic, 1792	
Declaration of Pillnitz, 1792	
Reign of Terror, 1793–1794	Cotton gin invented, 1793
Treaty of Campo Formio, 1797	Edward Jenner develops smallpox vaccine, 1796
Napoleon, first consul of France, 1799	
Treaty of Lunéville, 1801	
Napolean declared first consul for life, 1802	
Napoleon crowns himself emperor of the French, 1804	
Continental System established, 1806	
Reforms of Hardenberg and Stein, Prussia, 1808	
Napoleon's invasion of Russia, 1812	
Congress of Vienna, 1814–1815	
Battle of Waterloo, 1815	
"Peterloo Massacre," England, 1819	
Congress of Verona, 1822	Louis Pasteur, 1822–1895
Monroe Doctrine, 1823	
"Decembrist" Revolt, Russia, 1825	First railway, England, 1825
Greek independence, 1829	
Revolution in France, 1830	
"Young Italy," 1831	
Reform Bill of 1832, England	
Slavery abolished, British colonies, 1833	
Poor law reform, England, 1834	
Chartist movement, England, 1838–1848	
Corn Laws repealed, England, 1846	
Revolutions in Europe, 1848	
Karl Marx, *Communist Manifesto,* 1848	
Second Republic, France, 1848	
Frankfurt Assembly, Germany, 1848–1849	
Reign of Louis Napoleon, 1851–1870	Great Exhibition, London, 1851
	Invention of the sewing machine, 1850s
Crimean War, 1854–1856	
Unification of Italy, 1858–1866	Invention of the Bessemer process, 1856
Civil War, United States, 1861–1865	Charles Darwin, *Origin of Species,* 1859
Otto von Bismarck's accession to power, 1862	
First International, 1864	
Parliamentary Reform Bill, England, 1867	
	Suez Canal opened, 1869
	Union Pacific railroad, United States, 1869
Franco-Prussian War, 1870	

1770

1800

1825

1850

ECONOMICS & SOCIETY	ARTS & LETTERS	
		1770
	Ludwig van Beethoven, 1770–1827	
Jeremy Bentham, *The Principles of Morals and Legislation,* 1789		
Utilitarianism, 1790–1870	Johann von Goethe, *Faust,* 1790–1808	
	Romantic movement, 1690–1850	
Tom Paine, *The Rights of Man,* 1791–1792		
Thomas Malthus, *An Essay on the Principle of Population,* 1798	William Wordsworth, *Lyrical Ballads,* 1798	
		1800
	G. W. Hegel, *Phenomenology of the Spirit,* 1807	
	J. G. Fichte, *Addresses to the German Nation,* 1808	
Louis Blanc, 1811–1882		
	Francisco Goya, *The Executions of the Third of May,* 1814	
Founding of Prussian Zollverein, 1818		*1825*
	Honoré de Balzac, *The Human Comedy,* 1829–1841	
	Eugène Delacroix, *Liberty Leading the People,* 1830	
	Realism in literature and art, 1840–1870	
Friedrich Engels, *The Condition of the Working Class,* 1844		
John Stuart Mill, *Principles of Political Economy,* 1848	Pre-Raphaelite Brotherhood formed, 1848	
		1850
	Giuseppe Verdi, *Il Trovatore,* 1853	
	Richard Wagner, *The Ring of the Nibelung,* 1854–1874	
	Charles Dickens, *Hard Times,* 1854	
Emancipation of the serfs, Russia, 1861	Gustave Flaubert, *Madame Bovary,* 1857	
Karl Marx, *Capital,* 1867	Leo Tolstoy, *War and Peace,* 1866–1869	
	Pope Pius IX, *Syllabus of Errors,* 1869	

Chapter 19

THE FRENCH REVOLUTION

Men are born, and always continue, free and equal in respect of their
rights. Civil distinctions, therefore, can be founded only on public utility.
The nation is essentially the source of all sovereignty; nor can any individual, or any body of men, be entitled to any authority which is not expressly derived from it.

—The Declaration of the Rights of Man and of the Citizen, 1789

In 1789, one European out of every five lived in France. And most Europeans, French or not, who thought beyond the boundaries of their
own immediate concerns, perceived of France as the center of European civilization. It followed, therefore, that a revolution in France would
immediately command the attention of Europe, and would from the first
assume far more than mere national significance. Yet the French Revolution attracted and disturbed men and women for reasons other than the fact
that it was French. Both its philosophical ideals and its political realities
mirrored attitudes, concerns, and conflicts that had occupied the minds of
educated Europeans for several decades. When the revolutionaries pronounced in favor of liberty, they spoke not only with the voice of the
eighteenth-century philosophes, but with that of the English aristocracy in
1688 and the American revolutionaries of 1776.

The era of revolution

Absolutism was increasingly the bane of a wide spectrum of thoughtful
opinion and passionate feeling within the societies of continental Europe.
Aristocrats resented monarchical inroads upon their ancient freedoms. Entrepreneurs who had welcomed mercantilist interference on their behalf in
the past now found themselves chafing under absolutist constraints to their
economic independence. Peasants fiercely resented what seemed to them
the never-ceasing demands of central government upon their limited—often impoverished—resources. Nor were resentments focused exclusively
upon absolutist monarchs. They existed as well between country and city
dwellers, between rich and poor, overprivileged and underprivileged. The
tensions that in the end mounted to the point of revolutionary explosion in
France were widespread across the Continent, where elements from top to
bottom of society confronted each other in uneasy hostilities that varied in
intensity but reflected a common mistrust and uncertainty.

Resentments and tension

1. THE COMING OF THE REVOLUTION

Until fairly recently, many historians argued that the French Revolution must be understood in terms of class conflict. Grounding their case on the economic and political theories of the nineteenth-century philosopher Karl Marx (see below, p. 840) these interpreters, strongly influenced by the work of the twentieth-century French scholar Georges Lefebvre, concluded that a rising bourgeoisie, having accumulated wealth and position for several centuries, and inspired by the ideology of Enlightenment philosophers and economists, overthrew the remaining vestiges of an aristocratic order that, despite its declining economic power, nevertheless retained its social and political predominance.

French society

Continuing scholarly investigation has now persuaded most historians to modify, if not entirely discard, this bold thesis. Certainly, to understand the origins of the French Revolution, one must first analyze the nature of the fabric of late eighteenth-century French society. Yet recent studies appear to prove that far from a society in which the bourgeoisie was pitted against the aristocracy, that society was increasingly controlled in all its aspects by an "order" that was an amalgam of aristocratic, professional, and—to a lesser degree—entrepreneurial elements. To comprehend the Revolution, one must thus comprehend the nature of this dominant segment of French society, and of its serious discontents with the government of Louis XVI.

The social borders between noble and non-noble were ill-defined. The French nobility was accessible to those who could pay the price of an en-

A Gentleman of the Third Estate with His Family. A contemporary engraving that illustrates the respectability the third estate wished to see translated into political power.

nobling office. Approximately two-thirds of the eighteenth-century French nobility had acceded to its status since 1600, and close to 50,000 new nobles were created between 1700 and 1789. Here, then, was an order dependent for its vigor upon a constant infusion of talent and economic power from the non-noble yet wealthy "third estate." (The French denominated their society into three estates: the clergy—first estate; the nobility—second estate; and the remainder—third estate.)

The case of the family of that important revolutionary figure Honoré Gabriel Riqueti, the comte de Mirabeau, well illustrates the point. Mirabeau's ancestors had been sixteenth-century merchants. In 1570, however, one of them had purchased the seigneury of Mirabeau. In the following century another bought himself the title of marquis. Despite its commercial origins, the family had acquired positions in the French army. Mirabeau, a lawyer, also held a commission in the cavalry that his grandfather once commanded. Aristocrats spoke of a distinction between the nobility of the sword *(noblesse d'épee)* and of the robe *(noblesse de robe),* the former supposedly of a more ancient and distinguished lineage derived from military service, the latter aristocrats by reason of their purchase of administrative or judicial office (hence the "robe"). Yet the example of the Mirabeau family illustrates how illusory the distinction between robe and sword was in many cases.

Noble families by no means disdained investment in trade and commerce. Most industry was financed by noblemen, who were also heavy investors in banking, and placed their money at risk in such enterprises as ship-owning, the slave trade, mining, and metallurgy. The bulk of their wealth, nevertheless, was what one historian has labeled "proprietary," that is, tied to land, urban properties, purchased offices, and the like. This form of wealth was not the exclusive province of the nobility, however. Proprietary wealth was preferred as a secure investment by rich members of the third estate. Throughout the century, this "bourgeois" wealth was constantly being transformed into "noble" wealth as its owners were transformed into noblemen. Clearly, then, one cannot speak of a separate class consciousness among this economically important bourgeois group. Its members recognized themselves as different from and often opposed to the mass of men and women beneath them who worked with their hands—the populace. But they identified closely with the values of a nobility to which they frequently aspired.

At the same time, however, hostilities and frictions within the middle orders and between bourgeois and noble were both real and important. Less prosperous lawyers—and there were an increasing number of them— were jealous of the privileged position of a favored few in their profession. The escalating price of office, and hence of ennoblement, produced tensions between noncommercial members of the third estate and the very rich in trade and commerce, by and large the only group able to afford the degree of social advancement to which many more aspired. Not surprisingly, down-at-the-heels nobility resented the success of rich, *arriviste* upstarts whose income allowed them the luxury of life in the grand style that was denied to those nobles long on pedigree but short of cash. Yet though these fissures existed, they did not inhibit the members of the dominant order from attacking with mounting vehemence a government and an economy that were not serving its interests.

The dominant order aired its frustrations in public debate among a growing audience of literate men and women. Book production reached a peak in 1788; periodicals and newspapers appeared in greater numbers; the first Paris daily was published in 1777. The *parlements,* France's powerful courts of record, used journals to identify themselves as defenders of a national political community threatened by the attempts of ministers to impose their despotic will. Although ideas may not have "caused" the Revolution, they played a critical role in giving shape and substance to the discontent experienced by so many, particularly among the literate middle orders. The political theories of Locke, Voltaire, Montesquieu, and Condorcet appealed to both discontented nobility and bourgeoisie: Voltaire, because of his general execration of privileged institutions; Condorcet because of his belief in progress; Locke and Montesquieu because of their defense of private property and limited sovereignty. Montesquieu's ideas were especially congenial to the dominant order, which read his doctrine of checks and balances as a defense of *parlements* as the constituted bodies that would provide a check to despotism. The campaign for change was fueled by another group of libertarian thinkers, economic theoreticians called physiocrats in France. Their proposals were grounded in the ideas of the Enlightenment, particularly the notion of a universe governed by mechanistic laws. They argued that production and distribution of wealth were subject to laws as predictable and ultimately salutary as the laws of physics. Those laws would function beneficially, however, only if agriculture and trade were freed from mercantilist regulations. They urged the government to lift its controls on the price of grain, for example, which had been imposed to keep the cost of bread low, but which had not accomplished that goal. By allowing the laws of supply and demand to determine the market price, the government would encourage farmers to grow a crop that was more profitable to them, and an increase in supply would thus eventually reduce the cost to consumers.

Whether or not members of the dominant order were prepared to accept the prescriptions of the physiocrats, they could agree with their diagnosis: that the state of the French economy was seriously ailing. Frenchmen and women were suffering increasingly from severe economic depression. A general price rise during much of the eighteenth century, which permitted the French economy to expand by providing capital for investment, worked hardship on the peasantry and on urban tradesmen and laborers, who found their purchasing power considerably reduced. Their plight deteriorated further at the end of the 1780s, when poor harvests encouraged landlords to extract even larger sums from their dependents in order to compensate for a sharp decline in profits, and when the high price of bread generated desperation among the urban poor. In 1788 families found themselves spending more than 50 percent of their income on bread,

Pre-Revolutionary Propaganda, 1788–1789. These prints support the popular view that the third estate was carrying the burden of national taxation on its shoulders while the privileged orders enjoyed the fruits of the peasant's labors, tax-free.

which comprised the bulk of their diet; the following year the figure rose to as much as 80 percent. Poor harvests contributed to a marked reduction in demand for manufactured goods; families had little money to spend for anything other than food. Peasants could no longer rely on the system of domestic industry to help them make ends meet, since they were receiving so few orders for the textiles and other articles they were accustomed to making at home. Many left the countryside for the cities, hoping to find work there, only to discover that unemployment was far worse than in rural areas. Evidence indicates that between 1787 and 1789 the unemployment rate in many parts of urban France was as high as 50 percent.

Those peasants who remained behind found themselves increasingly embittered by the financial obligations imposed upon them by landlords, church, and state: a tithe and levy on farm produce owed to the Church; fees, called *banalités,* for the use of a landlord's facilities—a mill, a wine press; fees, as well, to the landlord when land changed hands. In addition, peasants were forced to pay a disproportionate share of both direct and indirect taxes—the most onerous of which was the *gabelle,* or salt tax—levied by the government. (For some time the production of salt had been a state monopoly; every individual was required to buy at least seven pounds a year from the government works. The result was a commodity whose cost was often as much as fifty or sixty times its actual value.) Further grievances stemmed from the requirement that peasants work to maintain public roads

Peasant financial obligations

(the corvée) and from the hunting privileges accorded the nobility, which for centuries had regarded the right to indulge in the diversions of the chase, to the exclusion of all others, as a distinctive badge of their order.

The country's financial position was further weakened by an inefficient system of tax collection and disbursal. Not only was taxation tied to differing social status, it varied as well from region to region—some areas, for example, were subject to a much higher *gabelle* than others. The myriad special circumstances and exemptions that prevailed made the task of collectors all the more difficult. Those collectors were in many cases so-called tax farmers, members of a syndicate that loaned the government money in return for the right to collect taxes and to keep for itself the difference between the amounts it took in and the amounts it loaned. The system of disbursal was at least as inefficient as was revenue collection. Instead of one central agency, there were several hundred private accounts, a fact that made it impossible for the government to keep accurate track of its assets and liabilities. The financial system all but broke down completely under the increased expenses brought on by French participation in the American Revolution. The cost of servicing the national debt of approximately 4 billion livres in the 1780s consumed 50 percent of the nation's budget.

Not only were there problems with the economy, there were also weaknesses in France's administrative structure, ultimately the responsibility of the country's absolutist monarch, Louis XVI (1774–1792). Anxious to serve his people in "enlightened" ways, Louis wished to improve the lot of the poor, to remove torture, and to shift the burden of taxation onto the richer classes. Yet he lacked the capacity to manage his own government and thereby to put into effect these reforms. Well-intentioned but ineffectual, his attempts at reform ultimately undermined his own authority. His appointment of outsiders such as Anne Robert Jacques Turgot (1727–1781), a philosopher, physiocrat, and former provincial intendant, and Jacques Necker (1732–1804), a Swiss Protestant banker, as finance ministers aroused opposition among traditionalist factions within the court. He allowed his wife, the young yet strong-willed Marie Antoinette—daughter of Austria's Maria Theresa—a free hand to dispense patronage among her friends. The result was constant intrigue and frequently reshuffled administrative alliances at Versailles. In consequence, although the intendants, administrative representatives of the central government, possessed considerable power, in theory they found that power too often circumscribed by rivalries and indecision among those to whom they reported. Their administrative effectiveness was further undermined by the fact that they shared authority with provincial governors, local military authorities, and, in a third of the provinces—the *pays d'états*—with local tax-levying bodies.

Louis XVI

Also weakening the country's administrative structure was the continuing battle waged between the central government and the provincial *parlements*. As we have noted, the *parlements* had reasserted their independence during the early years of the reign of Louis XV. Throughout the century they had grown increasingly insistent upon what they began to call their "constitutional" rights—in reality, their traditional habit of opposing legislation that did not serve the interests of their members. When Louis XVI pressed for new taxes to be levied on the nobility as well as on the rest of the community after the expensive Seven Years' War, the *parlements* successfully blocked the proposal, insisting upon their right to exemption from major national taxes. In the mid-1770s this episode was reenacted when Turgot, at that time Louis XVI's principal financial minister, attempted to combat the government's indebtedness through a series of reforms that included the curtailing of court expenses, the abolition of the *corvée* in favor of a small tax on landowners and the abolition of certain guild restrictions in order to stimulate manufacturing. These innovations were steadfastly opposed by the Paris *parlement,* whose members claimed that Turgot was trampling upon ancient prerogatives and privileges—as indeed he was.

Battle between central government and provincial parlements

FRANCE UNDER THE ANCIEN RÉGIME

In the end, however, it was not this opposition that doomed Turgot's plan, for the king was persuaded to make use of his power to overrule the Paris *parlement*. Rather the plan failed because the King withdrew his support for Turgot, who fell victim to court intrigue and was dismissed. *Parlements,* though jealous of their prerogatives, could not indefinitely inhibit the reforms of a determined monarch. Inhibition occurred because of Louis XVI's indecisiveness as supreme governor of France. And it was this indecisiveness that those within the dominant order found increasingly intolerable. By 1788, a weak monarch, together with a chaotic financial situation and severe social tensions, had brought absolutist France to the edge of political disaster.

2. THE DESTRUCTION OF THE ANCIEN RÉGIME

The inability of the Louis XVI and his government to resolve the country's financial crisis was the immediate cause of the Revolution. In 1787 and 1788 the king's principal ministers, Charles de Calonne and Loménie de Brienne, attempted to institute a series of reforms to stave off bankruptcy. To meet the mounting deficit, they proposed new taxes, notably a stamp duty and a direct tax on the annual produce of the soil.

Hoping to persuade the nobility to agree to these reforms, the king summoned an Assembly of Notables (last called in 1626) from among the aristocracy. Far from acquiescing, however, this group used the financial emergency to attempt to extract major constitutional reforms. Most important, they insisted that any new tax scheme must have the approval of the Estates-General, representative of the three estates of the realm, and that the king had no legal authority to arrest and imprison arbitrarily. The dominant order, its patience with delay and inefficiency at an end, was speaking as English aristocrats had in 1688, and American revolutionaries had in 1775.

Economic hardship *and* financial chaos in the end compelled Louis XVI in the summer of 1788 to summon the Estates-General (which had not met since 1614) to meet in May of the following year. His action appeared to many as the only solution to France's deepening problems. Long-term grievances and short-term hardships had produced bread riots across the country in the spring of 1789. Looting in Brittany, Flanders, Provence, and elsewhere was accompanied by demands for price-fixing that would bring the cost of bread down to a level the populace could afford. Fear that the forces of law and order were collapsing irrevocably and that the populace might take matters into its own hands spurred the delegates to the Estates-General to a sense of their responsibilities and destiny. Each of the three orders elected its own deputies—the third estate indirectly through local assemblies. These assemblies were charged as well with the responsibility of drawing up lists of grievances—*cahiers des doléances*—further contributing to the general determination that the Estates-General must work to perform mighty change.

The delegates of the third estate, though elected by assemblies chosen in turn by artisans and peasants, were representative of the interests and outlook of what we have called the dominant order. Only 13 percent were men of business. About 25 percent were lawyers; 43 percent were government office-holders of some sort. Thus, despite initial disagreements between members of the second and third estates, once the Estates-General convened there remained within that body a strong sense of common grievance and common purpose.

The major area of disagreement between the second and third estates stemmed from the tradition that each estate meet and vote as a body. In the past, this had generally meant that the first and second estates had combined to defeat the third. Now the third estate made it clear it would not tolerate such an arrangement. Its leaders demanded that the three orders should sit together and vote as individuals. More important, it insisted that the representatives of the third estate should be double the number of the first and second.

Doubling of third estate

During the months prior to May 1789, the question of "doubling the third" was fiercely debated. After having opposed the reform initially, in December 1788 the king agreed to it. His unwillingness to take a strong stand from the first, and his continuing vacillation on the matter of voting procedures, cost him support he might otherwise have obtained from the third estate. Shortly after the opening of the Estates-General at Versailles in May 1789, the representatives of the third estate, angered by the king's attitude, took the revolutionary step of leaving the body and declaring themselves the National Assembly. *What Is the Third Estate?* asked the radical clergyman Abbé Emmanuel Sieyès, one of the most articulate spokesmen for a new order, in his famous pamphlet of January 1789. The answer he gave then—"everything"—was the answer the third estate itself gave when it constituted itself the National Assembly of France. Now the middle-class lawyers and businessmen of the third estate acted on that belief. Locked out of their meeting hall on June 20, the commoners and a handful of sympathetic nobles and clergymen moved to a nearby indoor tennis court.

The National Assembly

Abbé Emmanuel Sieyès

Here, under the leadership of the volatile, maverick aristocrat Mirabeau and the clergyman Sieyès, they bound themselves by a solemn oath not to separate until they had drafted a constitution for France. This Oath of the Tennis Court, on June 20, 1789, can be seen as the beginning of the French Revolution. By claiming the authority to remake the government in the name of the people, the Estates-General was not merely protesting against the rule of Louis XVI but asserting its right to act as the highest sovereign power in the nation, a notion increasingly appealing to many of the nobility as well. On June 27 the king virtually conceded this right by ordering the remaining delegates of the privileged classes to meet with the third estate as members of the National Assembly.

The beginning of revolution

The first stage of the French Revolution extended from June 1789 to August 1792. During most of this period the destiny of France was in the hands of the National Assembly. In the main, this stage was moderate, its actions dominated by the leadership of liberal nobles and equally liberal men of the third estate. Yet three events in the summer and fall of 1789 furnished evidence that the Revolution was to penetrate to the very heart of French society, ultimately touching both the urban populace and the rural peasants.

News of the occurrences of late spring 1789 had spread quickly across France. From the very onset of debates on the nature of the political crisis, public attention was high. It was roused not merely by interest in matters of political reform, however, but also by the economic crisis that, as we have seen, brought the price of bread to astronomical heights. Belief was widespread that the aristocracy and king were together conspiring to punish an upstart third estate by encouraging scarcity and high prices. Rumors circulated in Paris during the latter days of June 1789 that the king was about to stage a reactionary coup d'état. The electors of Paris (those who had voted for the third estate) feared not only a counter-revolution but the actions of the Parisian poor, who had been parading through the streets and threatening violence. These electors were workshop masters, craftspeople, shopkeepers, petty tradespeople, the men and women who would soon come to be called *sans-culottes*—so called because the men did not wear upper-class breeches. They formed a provisional municipal government and organized a militia of volunteers to maintain order. Determined to obtain arms, they made their way on July 14 to the Bastille, an ancient fortress where guns and ammunition were stored. Built in the Middle Ages, the Bastille had served as a prison for many years, but was no longer much

The Tennis Court Oath by David. In the hall where royalty played a game known as *jeu de paume* (similar to tennis) leaders of the Revolution swore to draft a constitution. In the center of this painting, with his arm extended, is Jean Bailly, president of the National Assembly. Seated at the table below him is Abbé Sieyès. Somewhat to the right of Sieyès, with both hands on his chest, is Robespierre. Mirabeau, with a hat in his left hand and wearing a black coat, stands somewhat farther to the right.

The Fall of the Bastille, July 14, 1789. A contemporary engraving celebrating the heroic actions of the citizenry of Paris.

used. However, it symbolized hated royal authority. When crowds demanded arms from its governor, he at first procrastinated and then, fearing a frontal assault, opened fire, killing ninety-eight of the attackers. The crowd took revenge, capturing the fortress (which contained only seven prisoners—five common criminals and two lunatics) and decapitating the governor. At the same time the *sans-culottes* were establishing a revolutionary municipal government in Paris, similar groups assumed control in other cities across France. This series of events—dramatized by the fall of the Bastille—was the first to demonstrate the commitment of the common people to revolutionary change.

The second popular revolt occurred in the countryside, where the peasants were suffering the direct effects of economic privation. They too expected a monarchical and aristocratic counter-revolution. Eager for news from Versailles, their anticipation turned to fear when they began to understand that the Revolution might not address itself to their determination to put an end to the burdens of manorial taxation. Frightened and uncertain, peasants began attacking and burning manor houses, occasionally in an attempt to discover grain hoards, but almost always to seek out and destroy records of manorial obligations. News of these attacks instilled in other peasants a terror that rural brigands were loose across the countryside. This "Great Fear," as historians have labeled it, simply compounded the confusion abroad in rural areas throughout the summer, while strengthening the belief of deputies at Versailles that law and order were fast vanishing from the realm.

The third instance of popular uprising, in October 1789, was brought on by economic crisis. This time Parisian women from the market district, angered by the price of bread and fired by rumors of the king's continuing

The "Great Fear"

The Departure of the Women of Paris for Versailles, October 1789. Note that the contemporary caption refers to the "heroines of Paris." An early example of revolutionary propaganda.

Depart des Heroines de Paris pour Versailles le 5 Octobre 1789.

The "October Days"

unwillingness to cooperate with the Assembly, marched to Versailles on October 5 and demanded to be heard. Not satisfied with its reception by the Assembly, the crowd broke through the gates to the palace, calling for the king to return to Paris. On the afternoon of the following day the king yielded. The National Guard, sympathetic to the agitators, led the crowd back to Paris, the procession headed by a soldier holding aloft a loaf of bread on his bayonet.

*Achievements of the first stage:
(1) the destruction of privilege*

In each of the three cases, these popular uprisings produced a decided effect on the course of political events as they were unfolding at Versailles. The storming of the Bastille helped persuade the king and nobles to treat the National Assembly as the legislative body of the nation. The "Great Fear" inspired an equally great consternation among the debaters in the Assembly. On August 4, ecclesiastical tithes and the *corvée* were formally abolished. The hunting privileges of the nobles were ended. Exemption from taxation and monopolies of all kinds were eliminated as contrary to natural equality. The ultimate effect of these reforms was to obliterate the remnants of feudalism. One week later, the Assembly abolished the sale of offices, thereby sweeping away one of the fundamental institutions of the Old Regime.

*(2) the Declaration of
the Rights of Man*

Following the destruction of privilege the Assembly turned its attention to preparing a charter of liberties. The result was the *Declaration of the Rights of Man and of the Citizen,* issued in September 1789. Property was declared to be a natural right as well as liberty, security, and "resistance to oppression." Freedom of speech, religious toleration, and liberty of the press were declared inviolable. All citizens were guaranteed equality of treatment in the courts. No one was to be imprisoned or otherwise punished except in accordance with due process of law. Sovereignty was affirmed to reside in the people, and officers of the government were made subject to deposition if they abused the powers conferred upon them. These were not new ideas. They represented a consensus expressed in the *cahiers des doléances* and in the Enlightenment tracts read and approved by members of the dominant order.

The king's return to Paris during the October Days confirmed the reforms already underway and guaranteed further liberalization along lines decreed by the majority in the Assembly. In November 1789, the National Assembly resolved to confiscate the lands of the Church and to use them as collateral for the issue of *assignats,* or paper money, which, it was hoped, would resolve the country's inflationary economic crisis. In July of the following year the Civil Constitution of the Clergy was enacted, providing that all bishops and priests should be elected by the people and should be subject to the authority of the state. Their salaries were to be paid out of the public treasury, and they were required to swear allegiance to the new legislation. The secularization of the Church also involved a partial separation from Rome. The aim of the Assembly was to make the Catholic Church of France a truly national and civil institution with no more than a nominal subjection to the papacy.

*(3) secularization of the
Church*

An Assignat

Response to this clerical revolution was mixed. Because the Church had enjoyed a privileged position during the Old Regime, it had earned itself the hatred of many who resented its tolerance of clerical abuses and its exploitation of vast monastic land holdings. Bishops and other members of the higher clergy had often held several ecclesiastical appointments at the same time, had paid scant attention to their duties, and had led far from spiritual lives. Exempt from taxes itself, the Church had not hesitated to extract all it could from the peasantry. And its control of the country's educational system made it a target for those men and women who, influenced by Enlightenment thinkers like Voltaire, had turned against the doctrines of Roman Catholicism. On the other hand, the practice of centuries had made the parish church and priest into institutions of great local importance. Peasants found it very difficult to shed habits of deference and respect overnight. The dramatic changes embodied in the Civil Constitution of the Clergy thus encountered considerable resistance in some parts of rural France, and eventually helped to strengthen the forces of counter-revolution.

Response to secularization

Not until 1791 did the National Assembly manage to complete its primary task of drafting a new constitution for the nation. The constitution as it finally emerged gave eloquent testimony to the position now held by the dominant order. The government was converted into a limited monarchy, with the supreme power virtually a monopoly of the well-to-do. Although all citizens possessed the same civil rights, the vote was allowed only to those who paid a certain amount in taxes. About half the adult males in France made up this latter category of "active" citizen. Yet even their political power was curtailed, for they were to vote for electors, whose property ownership qualified them for that position. Those electors, in turn, chose department officials and delegates to the National—or, as it was henceforth to be called, Legislative—Assembly. The king was deprived of the control he had formerly exercised over the army and local governments. His ministers were forbidden to sit in the Assembly, and he was shorn of all powers over the legislative process except a suspensive veto, which in fact could be overridden by the issuance of proclamations.

(4) constitution of 1791

The economic and governmental changes the National Assembly adopted were as much a reflection of the power of the dominant order as were its constitutional reforms. To raise money, it sold off Church lands, but in such large blocks that peasants seldom benefited by the sales as they had expected to. To encourage the growth of unfettered economic enterprise, guilds and trade unions were abolished. To rid the country of authoritarian centralization and of aristocratic domination, local governments were completely restructured. France was divided into eighty-three equal departments. All towns henceforth enjoyed the same form of municipal organization. All local officials were locally elected. This reorganization and decentralization expressed a belief in the necessity of individual liberty and freedom from ancient privilege. As such these measures proclaimed, as did all the work of the Assembly, that the "winners" of this first stage of the Revolution were the men and women of the dominant order.

3. A NEW STAGE: POPULAR REVOLUTION

The second stage:
(1) disappointment
of the common people

Their triumph did not go unchallenged, however. In the summer of 1792, the Revolution entered a second stage, which saw the downfall of moderate leaders from the dominant order and their replacement by radical republicans claiming to rule on behalf of the common people. Three major reasons accounted for this abrupt and drastic alteration in the course of events. First, the politically literate lower classes grew disillusioned as they perceived that the Revolution was not benefiting them. The uncontrolled free-enterprise economy of the government resulted in constantly fluctuating and generally rising prices. These increases particularly exasperated those elements of the Parisian population that had agitated for change in preceding years. Urban rioters demanded cheaper bread, while their advocates called for governmental control of the ever-growing inflation. Their leaders also articulated the frustrations of a mass of men and women who felt cheated by the constitution. Despite their major role in the creation of a new regime, they found themselves deprived of any effective voice in its operation.

A second major reason for the change of course was a lack of effective national leadership during the first two years of the Revolution. Louis XVI remained the weak, vacillating monarch he had been prior to 1789. Though outwardly prepared to collaborate with the leaders of the Assembly, he remained essentially a victim of events. He was compelled to support measures personally distasteful to him, in particular the Civil Constitution of the Clergy. He was thus sympathetic to the plottings of the queen, who was in correspondence with her brother Leopold II of Austria. Urged on by Marie Antoinette, Louis agreed to attempt an escape from France in June 1791, in hopes of rallying foreign support for counter-revolution. The members of the royal family managed to slip past their palace guards in Paris, but they were apprehended near the border at Varennes and brought back to the capital. Though the Constitution of 1791 declared France a monarchy, after Varennes that declaration was more fiction that fact. From that point on, Louis was little more than a prisoner of the Assembly. The leadership of that body remained in the hands of Mirabeau until his death in 1791. Yet he was a less-than-satisfactory leader. An outstanding orator, possessed of the insight of a statesman, he was nevertheless mistrusted by many revolutionaries because of his dissolute, aristocratic youth and his notorious venality. Nor, despite his continued support of a strong constitutional monarchy, did he enjoy the confidence of the king. Even with his shortcomings, Mirabeau was the most effective leader among the moderate constitutionalists, a group that generally failed to capitalize on its opportunities.

The third major reason for the dramatic turn of affairs was the fact that after 1792 France found itself at war with much of the rest of the Continent. From the outset of the Revolution, men and women across Europe had been compelled, by the very intensity of events in France, to take sides in the conflict. In the years immediately after 1789, the Revolution in France won the enthusiastic support of a wide range of politically committed intellectuals, merchants, men of commerce, and artisans. The English poet William Wordsworth, later to become disillusioned by the subsequent course of revolutionary events, recalled the rapture of his initial mood: "Bliss was it in that dawn to be alive. . . ." His sentiments were echoed across the continent by poets and philosophers, among the latter the German Johann Gottfried von Herder, who declared the Revolution the most important historical moment since the Reformation. Political societies in England proclaimed their allegiance to the principles of the new revolution, often quite incorrectly seeing it as nothing more than a French version of the far less momentous events of 1688. In the Low Countries, a "patriot" group organized strikes and plotted a revolution of its own against dominant merchant oligarchies. Political revolutionaries in western Germany and anticlericals in Italy welcomed the possibility of invasion by the French as a means of achieving radical change within their own countries.

(3) the Revolution abroad

Others opposed the course of the Revolution from the start. Exiled nobles, who had fled France for the haven of sympathetic royal courts in Germany and elsewhere, did all they could to stir up counter-revolutionary sentiment. The distressed clamoring of these emigrés, along with the plight of Louis XVI and his family, aroused the sympathy, if not at first the active support of European defenders of absolutism and privilege. In England the cause was strengthened by the publication in 1790 of Edmund Burke's *Reflections on the Revolution in France*. A Whig politician who had sympathized with the American revolutionaries, Burke nevertheless attacked the Revolution in France as a monstrous crime against the social order. He argued that by remodeling their government as they had, the French had turned their backs on both human nature and history. Men and women were not constitutional abstractions, endowed with an objective set of natural rights, as the Declaration of the Rights of Man had insisted. Rights—and duties as

Edmund Burke

Thomas Paine

well—were the consequence of the individual histories of the countries into which men and women were born. Those histories bound people to the past and entailed a commitment to the future, as well as the present. Hence they had no right to remake their country and its institutions without reference to the past or concern for the future, as Burke insisted the French had. Their failure to pay proper respect to tradition and custom had destroyed the precious fabric of French civilization woven by centuries of national history.

Burke's famous pamphlet, in which he painted a romantic and highly inaccurate picture of the French king and queen, helped arouse sympathy for the counter-revolutionary cause. It is questionable, however, whether that sympathy would have turned to active opposition, had not the French soon appeared as a threat to international stability and the individual ambitions of the great powers. It was that threat which led to war in 1792, and which kept the Continent in arms for a generation. This state of war had a most important impact on the formation of political and social attitudes during this period in Europe. Once a country declared war with France, its citizens could no longer espouse sympathy with the Revolution without paying severe consequences. Those who continued to support the Revolution, as did a good many among the artisan and small tradespeople class, were persecuted and punished for their beliefs. To be found in Britain, for example, possessing a copy of Tom Paine's revolutionary tract, *The Rights of Man* (1791–1792), a pro-revolutionary response to Burke's *Reflections,* was enough to warrant imprisonment. As the moderate nature of the early Revolution turned to violent extension, entrepreneurs and men of commerce eagerly sought to live down their radical sentiments of a few years past. The wars against revolutionary France came to be perceived as a matter of national survival; to ensure internal security, it seemed that patriotism demanded not only a condemnation of the French but of French ideas as well.

The first European states to express public concern about events in revolutionary France were Austria and Prussia. They were not anxious to declare war; their interests at the time centered upon the division of Poland between themselves. Nevertheless, they jointly issued the Declaration of Pillnitz in August 1791, in which they avowed that the restoration of order and of the rights of the monarch of France was a matter of "common interest to all sovereigns of Europe." The leaders of the French government at this time were a moderate faction, but they were afraid of losing political support in France. They pronounced the Declaration of Pillnitz a threat to national security, hoping that enthusiasm for a war would unite the French and result also in enthusiasm for their continued rule. They were aided in their scheme by the activities of monarchists, both within and outside France, whose plottings and pronouncements could be made to appear an additional threat, though to a greater extent than they actually were. On April 20, 1792, the Assembly declared war against Austria and Prussia.

Almost all of the various political factions in France welcomed the war. The political leadership expected that its aggressive policy would solidify the loyalty of the people to their regime. Reactionaries hailed the intervention of Austria and Prussia as the first step in the undoing of all that had happened since 1789. Extremists hoped that initially the French would suffer reverses that would discredit the government and the monarchy, and thus hasten the advent of a more radical regime in France, and the triumph of people's armies and revolutionary ideals across Europe. As the radicals hoped, the forces of the French met serious reverses. By August 1792 the allied armies of Austria and Prussia had crossed the frontier and were threatening to capture Paris. A fury of rage and despair seized the capital. Many believed that the military disasters had been the result of treasonable dealings with the enemy by the king and his conservative followers. On August 10 Parisian rioters, organized by their radical leadership, attacked the royal palace, killing the king's guards and driving him to seek refuge in the meeting hall of the Assembly. At the same time, radicals seized the municipal government in Paris, replacing it with a revolutionary Commune under their control. The Commune successfully demanded that the Assembly suspend the king from his duties and hand him and his family over for imprisonment. Here began a second and far more extreme French Revolution.

Response to war

From this point, the country's leadership passed into the hands of an equalitarian-minded segment of the third estate. These new leaders soon came to be known as *Jacobins,* the name of the political club to which they belonged. Although their headquarters was in Paris, their membership extended throughout France. They proclaimed themselves enemies of the country's former political leaders, the *Girondins,* so called after the department of the Gironde, which was centered about the commercial hub of Bordeaux. By so labeling their political foes, the Jacobins hoped to paint them as defenders of the selfish commercial classes, and to proclaim themselves patriotic spokesmen for the populace. Yet recent analysis suggests

Jacobins and Girondins

Jacobins and Girondins. The key of the Jacobin club is carried into the Convention, symbolizing the passing of the leadership from the Girondins to the Jacobins.

Jacobins. Contemporary drawings by Heuriot.

Domestic reforms

that although the Girondins were more generally opposed to Paris and to violence than the Jacobins, there was not that much to distinguish between the two groups. Many so-called Girondins were in fact members of Jacobin clubs. And both groups contained large numbers of professionals—government officeholders and lawyers in the main—though an increasing number of artisans joined Jacobin clubs as the movement grew.

Neither the Girondins nor the Jacobins were a tightly organized party. Among the latter, a group that sat in the upper left-hand seats of the legislative chamber and that therefore adopted "The Mountain" as their political name, came to rule the decisions of the Legislative Assembly and to dominate the politics of France. One of their first actions was to call for an election by universal suffrage of delegates to a national convention, whose task would be to draft and enact a new and republican constitution. The king's flight to Varennes had ensured that the monarchy would cease to bind the nation together; the Convention's work set the seal on the rapid movement toward republicanism that Louis's attempted escape had begun. This Convention became the effective governing body of the country for the next three years. It was elected in September 1792, at a time when disturbances across France reached a new height. The so-called September massacres occurred when patriotic Paris mobs, hearing a rumor that political prisoners were plotting to escape from their prisons, responded by hauling them before hastily convened tribunals and sentencing them to swift execution. Over one thousand supposed enemies of the Revolution were killed in less than a week. Similar riots engulfed Lyons, Orléans, and other French cities.

When the newly elected Convention met in September, its membership was far more radical than that of its predecessor, the Legislative Assembly, and its leadership was determined to demand an end to the monarchy and the death of Louis XVI. On September 21, the Convention declared France a republic. In December it placed the king on trial, and in January he was condemned to death by a narrow margin. The heir to the grand tradition of French absolutism met his end bravely as "Citizen Louis Capet," beheaded by the guillotine, the frightful mechanical headsman that had become the symbol of revolutionary fervor.

Meanwhile, the Convention turned its attention to the enactment of further domestic reforms. Among its most significant accomplishments over the next three years were the abolition of slavery in French colonies; the prohibition of imprisonment for debt; the establishment of the metric system of weights and measures; and the repeal of primogeniture, so that property might not be inherited exclusively by the oldest son but would be divided in substantially equal portions among all immediate heirs. The Convention also supplemented the decrees of the Assembly in abolishing the remnants of manorialism and in providing for greater freedom of economic opportunity for commoners. The property of enemies of the Revolution was confiscated for the benefit of the government and the lower classes. Some great estates were broken up and offered for sale to poorer citizens on relatively easy terms. The indemnities hitherto promised to the nobles for the loss of their privileges were abruptly cancelled. To curb the

The Execution of Louis XVI. A revolutionary displays the king's head moments after it had been severed by the guillotine in January 1793.

rise in the cost of living, maximum prices for grain and other necessities were fixed by law, and merchants who profiteered at the expense of the poor were threatened with the guillotine. Still other measures of reform dealt with religion. An effort was made to abolish Christianity and to substitute the worship of Reason in its place. In accordance with this purpose a new calendar was adopted, dating the year from the birth of the republic (September 22, 1792) and dividing the months in such a way as to eliminate the Christian Sunday. Later, this cult of Reason was replaced by a Deistic religion dedicated to the worship of a Supreme Being and to a belief in the immortality of the soul. Finally, in 1794, the Convention decreed simply that religion was a private matter, that Church and state would therefore be separated, and that all beliefs not actually hostile to the government would be tolerated.

Much of this program, particularly that which involved the managing of the economy—regulating, price-fixing, requisitioning—was by no means representative of Jacobin political conviction. It was the consequence, rather, of desperate political necessity, and of the pressure Jacobin leaders experienced at the hands of the urban *sans-culottes*. More than anything else, the *sans-culottes* demanded cheap food. In three years after 1790, prices had risen in a crippling way: wheat by 27 percent, beef by 136 percent, potatoes by 700 percent. While the government imposed its maximums in Paris, rioters there and elsewhere attacked those they perceived to be hoarders and war profiteers. Left to its own economic inclinations, the Jacobin leadership would have pursued policies in line with liberal, reformist thinking that had challenged absolutist centralization and control. Yet the dire circumstances of Continental warfare and domestic turmoil left the leadership with no choice but to acquiesce to *sans-culottes* demands.

Pressure from urban sans-culottes

While effecting a political revolution in France, the Convention's leadership at the same time accomplished an astonishingly successful reorganization of its armies. By February 1793, Britain, Holland, Spain, and Austria were in the field against the French. Britain's entrance into the war was dictated by both strategic and economic reasons. The English feared French penetration into the Low Countries directly across the Channel; they were also concerned that French expansion might pose a serious threat to Britain's own growing economic hegemony around the globe. The allied coalition, though united only in its desire to contain this puzzling, fearsome revolutionary phenomenon, was nevertheless a formidable force. To counter it, the French organized an army that was able to win engagement after engagement during these years. In August 1793, the revolutionary government imposed a levy on the entire male population capable of bearing arms. Fourteen hastily drafted armies were flung into battle under the leadership of young and inexperienced officers. What they lacked in training and discipline, they made up for in improvised organization, mobility, flexibility, courage, and morale. (In the navy, however, where skill was of paramount importance, the revolutionary French never succeeded in matching the performance of the British.) In 1793–1794, the French armies preserved their homeland. In 1794–1795, they occupied the Low Countries, the Rhineland, parts of Spain, Switzerland, and Savoy. In 1796, they invaded and occupied key parts of Italy and broke the coalition that had arrayed itself against them.

These achievements were not without their price, however. To ensure their accomplishment, the rulers of France resorted to a bloody authoritarianism that has come to be known as the Terror. Although the Convention

Sans-Culottes Feeding Europe with the Bread of Liberty. In this cartoon justifying Europe's declaration of war against revolutionary France, Holland, Germany and Prussia, Britain, Savoy, and the papacy are shown as threatened by the French *sans-culottes.*

The Death of Marat. This painting by the French artist David immortalized Marat. The bloody towel, the box, and the tub were venerated as relics of the Revolution.

succeeded in 1793 in drafting a new democratic constitution, based upon manhood suffrage, it deferred its introduction because of wartime emergency. Instead, the Convention prolonged its own life year by year, and increasingly delegated its responsibilities to a group of twelve leaders known as the Committee of Public Safety. By this time the Girondins had lost all influence within the Convention. Complete power had passed to the Jacobins, who proclaimed themselves disciples of Jean-Jacques Rousseau and champions of the common man, arguing that the sort of "democratic absolutism" they were imposing accorded with Rousseau's notions of the sovereign state and the general will.

Foremost among the political leadership were Jean Paul Marat, Georges Jacques Danton, and Maximilien Robespierre, the latter two members of the Committee of Public Safety. Jean Paul Marat (1743–1793) was educated as a physician, and by 1789 had already earned enough distinction in that profession to be awarded an honorary degree by St. Andrews University in Scotland. Almost from the beginning of the Revolution he stood as a champion of the common people. He opposed nearly all of the assumptions of his more moderate colleagues in the Assembly, including the idea that France should pattern its government after that of Great Britain, which he recognized to be oligarchic in form. Soon made a victim of persecution and forced to take refuge in unsanitary sewers and dungeons, he persevered in his efforts to rouse the people to a defense of their rights. His exposure to infection left him with a chronic skin affliction from which he could find relief only through frequent bathing. In 1793 he was stabbed through the heart during one of these soothing respites by Charlotte Corday, a young fanatic. In contrast with Marat, Georges Jacques Danton

Georges Jacques Danton

Maximilien Robespierre

(1759–1794) did not achieve prominence until the Revolution was three years old; but, like Marat, he directed his activities toward goading the masses into rebellion. Elected a member of the Committee of Public Safety in 1793, he had much to do with organizing the Terror. As time went on, however, he wearied of ruthlessness and displayed a tendency to compromise that gave his opponents in the Convention their opportunity. In April 1794 Danton was sent to the guillotine. Upon mounting the scaffold he is reported to have said: "Show my head to the people; they do not see the like every day."

The most famous and perhaps the greatest of the radical leaders was Maximilien Robespierre (1758–1794). Born of a family reputed to be of Irish descent, Robespierre was trained for the law and speedily achieved a modest success as an advocate. Of a nervous and timid disposition, he was a less-than-able administrator, but made up for this lack of talent by devotion to principle. He adopted the belief that the philosophy of Rousseau held the one great hope of salvation for all mankind. To put this philosophy into practice he was ready to employ any means that would bring results, regardless of the cost to himself or to others. This passionate loyalty to a gospel that exalted the masses eventually won him a following. Indeed, he was so lionized by the public that he was allowed to wear the knee breeches, silk stockings, and powdered hair of the old society until the end of his life. In 1791 he was accepted as the oracle of the Jacobin Club. Later he became president of the National Convention and a member of the Committee of Public Safety. Though he had little or nothing to do with originating the Terror, he was nevertheless responsible for enlarging its scope. He came to justify ruthlessness as a necessary and therefore laudable means to revolutionary progress.

The years of the Terror were years of stern dictatorship in France.

Meeting of a Revolutionary Committee of Surveillance during the Terror

The Guillotine in Paris

Pressed by foreign enemies from without, the committee faced sabotage from both the political Right and Left at home. In June 1793, responding to the need for absolute political control, leaders of the Mountain, allied with Parisian radicals, purged the Convention of moderates, by means of militant and intimidating political rallies. France was now a one-party state. The purge was one important cause of a royalist counter-revolution that same year that broke out in the western area of the Vendée. The peasantry there had remained generally loyal to Church and king. Government attempts to conscript troops into the revolutionary armies fanned long-smoldering resentments into open rebellion. By the summer, the peasant forces there, led by noblemen in the name of a Royal Catholic Grand Army, posed a serious threat to the Convention. Meanwhile, Girondists helped fuel rebellions in the great provincial cities of Lyons, Bordeaux, and Marseilles. This harvest of the policies of the National Assembly was bitter fruit to the Committee. At the same time they met with the scornful criticism of revolutionaries even more radical than themselves. This latter group, known as the *enragés,* was led by the journalist Jacques Hébert, and threatened to topple not only the government but the country itself by its crusades. Determined to stabilize France, whatever the necessary cost, the Committee dispatched commissioners into the countryside to suppress the enemies of the state. During the period of the Terror, from September 1793 to July 1794, the most reliable estimates place the number of executions as high as 25,000 to 30,000 in France as a whole, less than 20,000 of whom were condemned by the courts. In addition, approximately 500,000 were incarcerated between March 1793 and August 1794. The victims were by no means all aristocrats. Anyone who appeared to threaten the re-

The ruthless suppression of enemies of the state

Patriotic Women's Club. The members of this patriotic club wear "constitutional bonnets" to show their support for the Revolution and the reforms of the Convention.

public, no matter what his or her social or economic position, was at risk. Far more peasants and laborers than noblemen and women were killed. Among those executed was Marie Antoinette ("The Widow Capet"). When some time later the Abbé Sieyès was asked what he had done to distinguish himself during the Terror, he responded dryly, "I lived."

Several points need to be made concerning this "second" French Revolution. First, for a time revolutionary fervor affected the everyday life of French men, women, and children in a remarkably direct way. The city-based *sans-culottes* imposed their style of dress on their fellow citizens. Workers' trousers replaced the breeches that until now were a sartorial badge of the middle classes and the nobility. A red cap, said to symbolize freedom from slavery, was all-but-required headgear, wigs having vanished. Men and women addressed each other as "citizen" or citizenness." Bowing, along with the kissing of a woman's hand, were considered reactionary gestures. Public life was marked by ceremonies designed to celebrate the triumph of a new way of living and thinking. Perhaps the most famous was the "Festival of Reason" sponsored by the radical Paris city government in November 1793. An explicit attack upon Catholicism, the ceremony was held inside the venerable cathedral of Notre Dame, where a mountain was constructed, symbolizing the all-powerful ruling party. Atop the mountain a temple, adorned with the motto "to philosophy," housed a troop of maidens, dressed in white and crowned with laurel. At the appropriate moment, they descended the mount while the audience sang a hymn that, in the words of an admiring contemporary commentator, "expressed natural truths and not mystical and chimerical adulations." As a finale a woman dressed as Liberty emerged from the temple to receive the homage of the crowd. The fact that Liberty was a real person and not a statue was an indication of the desire on the part of the festival's organizers to abolish the tradition and habits of Catholic idolatry. Though radicals and *sans-culottes*

The achievements of the Committee: (1) a new popular culture were a minority, and an urban minority as well, they were a remarkably powerful cultural force, whose influence far outweighed their numbers.

A second point worth making concerning the radical revolution of 1792–1793 is that it dramatically reversed the trend toward decentralization that had characterized the reforms of the Assembly. In addition to dispatching its own commissioners from Paris to quell provincial insurrection, the committee published a *Bulletin des loix,* to inform all citizens what laws were to be enforced and obeyed. And it replaced local officials, some of them still royalist in sympathy, with "deputies on mission," whose task was to conscript troops and generate patriotic fervor. When these deputies appeared too eager to act independently, they were in turn replaced by "national agents," with instructions to report directly to the Committee.

(2) centralization

Third, by fostering the interests of the less economically powerful the Committee significantly retarded the pace of industrial transformation in France. Through policies that assisted the peasant, the small craftsman, and the shopkeeper to acquire property, the government during this "second" revolution encouraged the entrenchment of a class at once devoted to the principle of republicanism while unalterably opposed to a large-scale capitalist transformation of the economy of France.

(3) industrial transformation slowed

The ruthless Terror of the Committee undoubtedly achieved its end by saving France from defeat at the hands of the coalition of European states. Whether the human price extracted in return for that salvation was worth the paying is a matter historians—and indeed all thoughtful human beings—may well never finally resolve.

(4) France saved from defeat

The Committee of Public Safety, though able to save France, could not save itself. It failed to put a stop to inflation, thereby losing the support of those commoners whose dissatisfactions had helped bring the Convention to power. The long string of military victories convinced growing numbers that the Committee's demands for continuing self-sacrifice, as well as its insistence upon the necessity of the Terror, were no longer justified. By July 1794, the Committee was virtually without allies. On July 27 (9 Thermidor, according to the new calendar) Robespierre was shouted down by his enemies while attempting to speak on the floor of the Convention. Desperate, he tried to rally loyal Jacobins to his defense and against the Convention. The following day, along with twenty-one fellow conspirators, he met his death as an enemy of the state on the guillotine. Now the only remaining leaders in the Convention were men of moderate sympathies, who, as time went on, inclined toward increasing conservatism. Much of the work of the radicals was undone. The law of maximum prices and the law against "suspects" were both repealed. Political prisoners were freed, the Jacobins driven into hiding, and the Committee of Public Safety shorn of its absolute powers. The new situation made possible the return of priests, royalists, and other emigrés from abroad to add the weight of their influence to the conservative trend.

The third stage: The Thermidorian reaction

In 1795 the National Convention adopted a new constitution, which lent the stamp of official approval to the victory of the prosperous classes. The constitution granted suffrage to all adult male citizens who could read

The War of Appearances. The *nouveaux riches* of the Directory laugh at those who still dress in the old aristocratic style.

and write. They were permitted to vote for electors, who in turn would choose the members of the legislative body. In order to be an elector, one had to be the proprietor of a farm or other establishment with an annual income equivalent to at least one hundred days of labor. The drafters of the constitution thus ensured that the authority of the government would actually be derived from citizens of considerable wealth. Since it was not practicable to restore the monarchy, lest the old aristocracy also come back into power, executive authority was vested in a board of five men known as the Directory, chosen by the legislative body. The new constitution included not only a bill of rights but also a declaration of the *duties* of the citizen. Conspicuous among the latter was the obligation to bear in mind that "it is upon the maintenance of property . . . that the whole social order rests."

The 1795 constitution

The reign of the Directory has not enjoyed a good historical press. The collection of *nouveaux riches* speculators and profiteers who rose to prominence as they labored to make a good thing for themselves out of the war was not a particularly attractive crew. They were lampooned as ostentatious and vulgar *"incroyables"* and *"merveilleuses"*—outrageously overdressed men and underdressed women. But however anxious they were to live down the self-denying excesses of the past several years by self-indulgent excesses of their own, they were in no mood to see the major accomplishments of the Revolution undone. They had no difficulty in disposing of threats from the Left, despite their failure to resolve that bugbear of all revolutionary governments, inflation and rising living costs. When in 1796 the radical "Gracchus" Babeuf* launched a campaign to abolish private property and parliamentary government, his followers were arrested, and either executed or deported.

The reign of the Directory

To dispatch threats from the Right was not so easy. Elections in March 1797–the first free elections held in France as a republic—returned a large

*Called "Gracchus" after the Roman tribune Gaius Gracchus, a hero of the people.

number of constitutional monarchists to the councils of government. Leading politicians, among them some who had voted for the execution of Louis XVI, took alarm. With the support of the army, the Directory in September 1797 annulled most of the election results of the previous spring. Its bold coup did little, however, to end the nation's political irresolution. Two years later, after a series of further abortive uprisings and purges, and with the country still plagued by severe inflation, the Directors were desperate. This time they called their brilliant young general, Napoleon Bonaparte (1769–1821), to their assistance.

The plight of the Directory

Bonaparte's first military victory in 1793, the recapture of Toulon from royalist and British forces, had earned him promotion from captain to brigadier general at the age of twenty-four. Though arrested as a terrorist following the fall of Robespierre, he was subsequently patronized by Viscount Paul Barras, a Directory politician. Bonaparte had gained further public fame and the gratitude of the Directory when on October 4, 1795 (13 Vendémiaire, new calendar), he had delivered what he called a "whiff of grapeshot" that saved the Convention from attack by opponents of the new constitution. Since that time he had registered a remarkable series of victories in Italy, which had resulted in Austria's withdrawal from the war. Most recently, he had attempted to defeat Britain by attacking its colonies in Egypt and the Near East. Despite initial successes on land, Bonaparte eventually found himself trapped by the British, following the defeat of the French fleet by Admiral Horatio Nelson at Abukir Bay in 1798. A year of further fighting had brought Bonaparte no nearer decisive victory in North Africa.

Napoleon Bonaparte's military record

It was at this point that the call came from the Directory. Bonaparte slipped away from Egypt and appeared in Paris, already having agreed to participate in a coup d'état with the leading director, that former revolutionary champion of the third estate, the Abbé Sieyès. On November 9, 1799 (18 Brumaire), Bonaparte was declared a "temporary consul." He was the answer to the prayers of the Directory: a strong, popular leader who was not a king. Sieyès, who had once declared for revolution in the name of the third estate, now declared for counter-revolution in the name of virtual dictatorship: "Confidence from below, authority from above." With those words Sieyès pronounced the end of the revolutionary period.

The Eighteenth Brumaire. A detail from a painting by Bronchet depicting Napoleon as the man of the hour.

4. NAPOLEON AND EUROPE

Few men in Western history have compelled the attention of the world as Napoleon Bonaparte did during the fifteen years of his rule in France. And few men have succeeded as he has in continuing to live on as myth in the consciousness, not just of his own country, but of all Europe. Napoleon's early career illustrates the degree to which the Revolution facilitated the rise of able men. Son of a provincial Corsican nobleman, he attended the *école militaire* in Paris, graduating an officer and a gentleman. Because the

Revolution had abolished the purchase of military office, he rose beyond the rank of major, a position to which in prerevolutionary France he would have been restricted, given his inability to pay the price of a regimental command.

Napoleon's abilities

Napoleon possessed a mind congenial to the ideas of the Enlightenment—creative, imaginative, and ready to perceive things anew. His primary interests were history, law, and mathematics. His particular strengths as a leader lay in his ability to conceive of financial, legal, or military plans and then to master their every detail; his capacity for inspiring others, even those initially opposed to him; and his belief in himself as the destined savior of the French. That last conviction eventually became the obsession that led to Napoleon's undoing. But supreme self-confidence was just what the French government had recently lacked. Napoleon believed both in himself and in France. That latter belief was the tonic France now needed, and Napoleon proceeded to administer it in liberally revivifying doses.

The plebiscite

During the years from 1799 to 1804, Napoleon ruled under the title of first consul, but in reality as a dictator. Once again, France was given a new constitution. Though the document spoke of universal male suffrage, political power was retained, by the now familiar means of indirect election, in the hands of entrepreneurs and professionals. Recognizing, however, that his regime would derive additional substance if it could be made to appear the government of the people of France, Bonaparte instituted what has since become a common authoritarian device: the plebiscite. The voters were asked to approve the new constitution and did so by the dishonestly achieved and loudly proclaimed vote of 3,011,107 in favor, 1,567 opposed.

Napoleonic reforms:
(1) centralization and finance

Although the constitution provided for a legislative body, that body could neither initiate nor discuss legislation. The first consul made use of a Council of State to draft his laws; but in fact the government depended on the authority of one man. Bonaparte had no desire to undo the major egalitarian reforms of the Revolution. He reconfirmed the abolition of estates, privileges, and local liberties, thereby reconfirming as well the notion of a meritocracy, of "careers open to talent." Through centralization of the administrative departments, he achieved what no recent French regime had yet achieved, an orderly and generally fair system of taxation. His plan, by prohibiting the type of exemptions formerly granted the nobility and clergy, and by centralizing collection, enabled him to budget rationally for expenditures and consequent indebtedness. In this way he reduced the inflationary spiral that had entangled so many past governments. Napoleon's willingness to proceed against the decentralizing tendencies of the earlier years of the Revolution marked him as a student of the absolutist policies of the Bourbons as well as an admirer of the egalitarian reforms of his more immediate predecessors. He replaced the elected officials and local self-government instituted in 1789 with centrally appointed "prefects" and "subprefects" whose administrative duties were defined in Paris, where local government policy was made as well.

Napoleon's most significant accomplishment was his completion of the educational and legal reforms begun during the revolutionary period. He

FRANCE: THE REVOLUTIONARY DEPARTMENTS AFTER 1789

Map labels: ENGLAND, ENGLISH CHANNEL, AUSTRIAN NETHERLANDS, HOLY ROMAN EMPIRE, PALATINATE, WÜRTTEMBERG, SWISS CONFEDERATION, DUCHY OF SAVOY, KINGDOM OF SARDINIA, MEDITERRANEAN SEA, SPAIN, ANDORRA, ATLANTIC OCEAN

Rhine R., Rhine R.

Departments: PAS-DE-CALAIS, NORD, SOMME, SEINE INFÉRIEURE, AISNE, ARDENNES, MOSELLE, OISE, MARNE, MEUSE, MEURTHE, BAS RHIN, MANCHE, CALVADOS, EURE, SEINE-ET-OISE, SEINE-ET-MARNE, AUBE, HAUTE MARNE, VOSGES, HAUT RHIN, FINISTÈRE, CÔTES-DU-NORD, ORNE, EURE-ET-LOIRE, HAUTE SAÔNE, ILLE-ET-VILAINE, MAYENNE, SARTHE, LOIRET, YONNE, CÔTE-D'OR, DOUBS, MORBIHAN, MAINE-ET-LOIRE, INDRE-ET-LOIRE, LOIRE-ET-CHER, CHER, NIÈVRE, JURA, LOIRE INFÉRIEURE, VENDÉE, DEUX-SÈVRES, VIENNE, INDRE, SAÔNE-ET-LOIRE, ALLIER, AIN, CHARENTE-INFÉRIEURE, CHARENTE, HAUTE VIENNE, CREUSE, PUY-DE-DÔME, LOIRE, RHÔNE, ISÈRE, CORRÈZE, DORDOGNE, CANTAL, HAUTE LOIRE, ARDÈCHE, DRÔME, HAUTES ALPES, GIRONDE, LOT, LOZÈRE, LOT-ET-GARONNE, TARN-ET-GARONNE, AVEYRON, GARD, VAUCLUSE, BASSES ALPES, LANDES, GERS, TARN, HÉRAULT, BOUCHES-DU-RHÔNE, VAR, BASSES PYRÉNÉES, HAUTE GARONNE, HAUTES PYRÉNÉES, ARRIÈGE, AUDE, PYRÉNÉES ORIENTALES, GOLO, LIAMONE

Cities: Amiens, Rouen, Varennes, Paris, Versailles, Lunéville, Bordeaux, Lyon, Toulouse, Marseilles

Seine R., Loire R., Garonne R., Rhône R.

0 _____ 200 miles

---

ordered the establishment of *lycées* (high schools) in every major town and
a school in Paris for the training of teachers. To supplement these changes,
Napoleon brought the military and technical schools under state control
and founded a national university to exercise supervision over the entire
system. Like almost all his reforms, this one proved of particular benefit to
the middle class; so did the new legal code promulgated in 1804. The
Code Napoleon, as the new body of laws was called, reflected two principles that had threaded their way through all the constitutional changes
since 1789: uniformity and individualism. The code made French law uniform, declaring past customs and privileges forever abolished. By under-
scoring in various ways a private individual's right to property, by authoriz-

(2) education and law

ing new methods for the drafting of contracts, leases, and stock companies, and by once again prohibiting trade unions, the code worked to the benefit of the dominant order, that elite drawn from all three former estates, which, if it included entrepreneurs and men of commerce, was composed primarily of men whose economic base remained the land.

(3) reconciliation

To accomplish these reforms Napoleon called upon the most talented men available to him, regardless of their past political affiliations. He admitted back into the country emigrés of all political stripes. His two fellow consuls—joint executives, but in name only—were a regicide of the Terror and a bureaucrat of the Old Regime. His minister of police had been an extreme radical republican; his minister of foreign affairs was the opportunist aristocrat Talleyrand. The work of political reconciliation was assisted by Napoleon's 1801 concordat with the pope, which reunited Church and state. Though the action disturbed former anti-Church Jacobins, Napoleon, ever the pragmatist, believed the reconciliation of Church and state necessary for reasons both of domestic harmony and of international solidarity. According to the terms of the concordat, the pope received the right to depose French bishops and to discipline the French clergy. At the same time, the Vatican agreed to lay to rest any claims against the expropriation of former Church lands. Hereafter, that property would remain unchallenged in the hands of its new middle-class rural and urban proprietors. In return, the clergy was guaranteed an income from the state. The concordat did nothing to revoke the principle of religious freedom established by the Revolution. Although the Roman Catholic clergy received state money, so did Protestant clergy.

Napoleon crowns himself emperor

Napoleon's agreement won him the support of those conservatives who had feared for France's future as a godless state. To prove to the old Jacobins, in turn, that he remained a child of their revolution, he invaded the independent state of Baden in 1804 to arrest and then execute the duke of Enghien, a relative of the Bourbons, whom Napoleon falsely accused of a plot against his life. (Three years before he had deported over one hundred Jacobins on a similar charge, but with no permanent political repercussions.) The balancing act only served to increase Napoleon's general popularity. By 1802 the people of France had accepted him as "consul for life." In 1804, they rejoiced when, borrowing ceremonial from the absolutist past, he crowned himself Emperor Napoleon I in the cathedral of Notre Dame in Paris.

Anti-French alliances

Across the boundaries of France, the nations of Europe had watched, some in admiration, others in horror, all in astonishment, at the phenomenon that was Napoleon. A coalition of European powers—principally Austria, Prussia, and Britain—had fought France from 1792 until 1795 in hopes of maintaining European stability. In 1795, Prussia retired from the fray, financially exhausted and at odds with Austria. In 1797, the Austrians, defeated by Bonaparte in northern Italy, withdrew as well, signing the Treaty of Campo Formio, which ceded to France territories in Belgium, recognized the Cisalpine Republic, which Bonaparte had established in Italy, and agreed to France's occupation of the left bank of the Rhine.

Left: *Coronation of Napoleon and Josephine* by David. Napoleon crowned himself and his wife and assumed the title of Napoleon I, emperor of the French. Right: *Napoleon I* by Jean A. D. Ingres. This celebratory portrait incorporates stage props that echo the grandeur of imperial Rome, thereby suggesting the extent to which Napoleon wanted Europe to regard him as its supreme ruler.

By the following year, Britain was left to fight the French alone. In 1798 it formed a second coalition, this one with Russia and Austria. The results did not differ significantly from those of the first allied attempt to contain France. Russia and Austria had no success in driving the French from Italy; the French likewise failed to break Britain's advantage at sea. By 1801, the coalition was in tatters, Russia having withdrawn two years previously. The Treaty of Lunéville, signed by France and Austria, confirmed the provisions of Campo Formio; in addition, the so-called Batavian, Helvetian, Cisalpine, and Ligurian republics—established by Napoleon from territories in the Low Countries, Switzerland, Italy, and Piedmont—were legitimized. The Austrians also acquiesced to a general redrawing of the map of Germany, which resulted eventually in an amalgamation of semi-independent states under French domination into the Confederation of the Rhine. The following year Britain, no longer able to fight alone, settled with the French as well, returning all the territories it had captured in overseas colonial engagements except Trinidad and Ceylon.

Treaty of Lunéville

Under Napoleon's reign, the territories of Central Europe underwent a revolution. This revolution was a thorough governmental reorganization, one that imposed the major egalitarian reforms of the French Revolution upon lands outside the borders of France, while building a French empire. Most affected were territories in Italy (the "Kingdom of Italy" as it was now called); Germany (the Confederation of the Rhine, including the newly formed Kingdom of Westphalia); Dalmatia (the Illyrian provinces);

Napoleon's reforms in Europe

See color map facing page 684

and Holland. (Belgium had been integrated directly into the empire.) Into all these territories Napoleon introduced a carefully organized, deliberate system of administration, based upon the notion of careers open to talent, equality before the law, and the abolition of ancient customs and privileges. The Napoleonic program of reform in the empire represented an application of the principles that had already transformed postrevolutionary France. Manorial courts were liquidated, and Church courts abolished. Provinces were joined into an enormous bureaucratic network that reached directly back to Paris. Laws were codified, the tax system modernized, and everywhere individuals were freed to work at whatever trade they chose. The one freedom denied throughout this new grand hegemony was that of self-government: i.e., all governmental direction emanated from Paris, and therefore from Napoleon.

Impact of Napoleon's changes

The impact of these changes upon the men and women who experienced them was clearly enormous. In those principalities previously ruled by petty princelings and minor despots—the patchwork state of Germany, for example, or the repressive Kingdom of Naples—reforms that provided for more efficient, less corrupt administration, a more equitable tax structure, and an end to customary privileges were welcomed by the majority of inhabitants. Business and professional men, who had chafed against economic restrictions, were quick to appreciate the license given them to trade and practice with a new degree of freedom. Yet the Napoleonic presence was by no means an unmixed blessing. Vassal states shared the task of contributing heavily to the maintenance of the emperor's war machine. Levies of taxes and of manpower, and the burden of supporting armies of occupation in their own countries, constantly reminded Germans, Italians, and Dutch that the price of reform was high. Nor were the changes shaped to accommodate local tradition. When Napoleon received complaints that his legal code ran counter to customary practices in Holland, he haughtily retorted: "The Romans gave their laws to their allies; why should not France have hers adopted in Holland?" It was this arrogance, symbolized in the eyes of many by the self-coronation of 1804, that led the German composer Ludwig van Beethoven to revoke the dedication of his *Eroica* Symphony to Napoleon, declaring, "Now he, too, will trample on all the rights of man and indulge only his ambition."

The Continental System

Napoleon's motives in introducing radical political and administrative changes were by no means altruistic. He understood that the defense of his enormous domain depended on efficient government and the rational collection and expenditure of funds for his armies. His boldest attempt at consolidation, however, a policy forbidding the importation into the Continent of British goods, proved a failure. This "Continental System," established in 1806, was designed as a strategic measure in Napoleon's continuing economic war against Britain. Its purpose was to destroy Britain's commerce and credit—to starve it economically into surrender. The system failed for several reasons. Foremost was the fact that throughout the war Britain retained control of the seas. The British naval blockade of the Continent, implemented in 1807, served, therefore, as an effective counter

THE EMPIRE OF NAPOLEON
AT ITS GREATEST EXTENT • 1812

French territory

French dependencies

Allied with Napoleon

Independent states

NORWAY

SWEDEN

DENMARK • Copenhagen

BALTIC SEA

Tilsit •

Friedland •

PRUSSIA

Warsaw •
DUCHY
OF
WARSAW

Berlin •

Leipzig •

Elbe R.

CONFEDERATION

OF THE

RHINE

Austerlitz •

Vienna •

AUSTRIAN
EMPIRE

ILLYRIAN PROVINCES

RUSSIA

NAPOLEON 1812

Borodino • Moscow

BLACK SEA

OTTOMAN EMPIRE

AEGEAN SEA

NORTH
SEA

ENGLAND

London •

English Channel

IRELAND

ATLANTIC
OCEAN

HOLLAND
Amsterdam •

Rhine R.

Brussels •
Waterloo •

★ Paris

FRENCH
EMPIRE

Bordeaux •

HELVETIC
REPUBLIC

KINGDOM

Ulm •

Po R.

OF

ITALY

Marseilles •

CORSICA

KDM.
OF
SARDINIA

PAPAL
STATES

Rome •

ADRIATIC SEA

KINGDOM
OF
NAPLES

Naples •

KDM. OF
SICILY

MEDITERRANEAN SEA

KDM. OF
PORTUGAL

Lisbon •

Madrid •

SPAIN

500 miles

THE INDUSTRIAL REVOLUTION

Percent of population living in cities
of 100,000 or more

5% or less

6–10%

20% or more

Iron ore deposits

Coal and lignite deposits

Centers of industry

Railroads in 1850

0   300 miles

RUSSIAN EMPIRE

Moscow

St. Petersburg

SWEDEN

Uppsala
Stockholm

NORWAY

DENMARK

NORTH SEA

BALTIC SEA

KINGDOM OF GREAT BRITAIN

Glasgow

Dublin

Liverpool
Manchester
Sheffield
Darlington
Leeds
Nottingham
Birmingham
London
Cardiff

ATLANTIC OCEAN

GERMAN EMPIRE

Hamburg
Bremen
Berlin
Posen
SILESIA
Breslau
Dresden
Leipzig
Warsaw
Łódź
Posen
Cracow
Prague
Pilsen
RUHR
Cologne
Essen
Kassel
Eisenach
Zwickau
Chemnitz
Nuremberg
Munich
Karlsruhe
Stuttgart
Frankfurt
SAAR
Strasbourg
Mulhouse
Basel

NETHERLANDS
Amsterdam
Rotterdam
BELGIUM
Brussels
Liège
Lille
Amiens

FRANCE
Paris
Le Havre
Orleans
Nantes
Tours
Limoges
Lyons
Avignon
Marseilles

SWITZERLAND
Zurich

AUSTRIAN EMPIRE

Vienna
Steyr
Budapest
Lemberg

ITALY
Turin
Milan
Florence
Livorno
Rome
Naples

SPAIN
Madrid
Barcelona
Bilbao
Santander
Gijon
Oviedo
Seville
Jerez
Granada

MEDITERRANEAN SEA

OTTOMAN EMPIRE

BLACK SEA

The Handwriting on the Wall. This English cartoon conjures up the biblical Feast of Belshazzar with a vice-ridden Paris, as the new Babylon, doomed to destruction. Headed by a crazed Napoleon and a grotesque Josephine, the banquet table offers a meal including the head of George III, the Tower of London, and the Bank of England.

to Napoleon's system. While the empire labored to transport goods and raw materials overland to avoid the British blockade, the British worked with success to develop a lively trade with South America. Internal tariffs were a second reason for the failure of the system. Europe remained divided into economic camps, fortified against each other by tariffs, and at odds with each other as they attempted to subsist on nothing more than what the Continent could produce and manufacture. The final reason for the system's collapse was the fact that the Continent had more to lose than Britain. Trade-stagnated ports and manufacturing centers grumbled as unemployment rose.

The Continental System was Napoleon's first serious mistake. As such it was one of the causes of his ultimate downfall. A second cause of Napoleon's decline was his constantly growing ambition and increasing sense of self-importance. Napoleon's goal was a Europe modeled after the Roman Empire. The symbols of his empire—reflected in painting, architecture, and the design of furniture and clothing—were deliberately Roman in origin. But Napoleon's Rome was without question imperial, dynastic Rome. The triumphal columns and arches he had erected to commemorate his victories recalled the ostentatious monuments of the Roman emperors. He made his brothers and sisters the monarchs of his newly created kingdoms, which Napoleon controlled from Paris while their mother allegedly sat at court, anxiously wringing her hands and repeating to herself, "If only it lasts!" In 1809 he divorced his first wife, the Empress Josephine, alleging her childlessness, and ensured himself a successor of royal blood by marrying Marie Louise, daughter of Francis I, of the monarchically respectable house of Habsburg. Even his admirers began to question if

The Empress Josephine

Napoleon's empire was not simply a larger, more efficient, and, therefore, ultimately more dangerous absolutism than the monarchies of the eighteenth century.

War had broken out again in 1805, with the Russians, Prussians, and Austrians, and Swedes joining the British in an attempt to contain France. *Early French victories* But to no avail; Napoleon's military superiority led to defeats, in turn, of all three Continental allies. The Battle of Austerlitz, in December 1805, a mighty triumph for the French against the combined forces of Austria and Russia, became a symbol of the emperor's apparent invincibility. Subsequent victories in the following years—against the Prussians at Jena in 1806, the Russians at Friedland in 1807, and the Austrians at Wagram in 1809—increased the conviction on the part of Europe that it had no choice but to acquiesce in Napoleon's grand Continental design. The great British naval victory at Trafalgar in 1805, which broke the maritime power of France, was perceived at the time by Napoleon's friends and foes alike as no more than a temporary check to his ambitions.

In 1808, Napoleon invaded Spain as a first step toward the conquest of Portugal, which had remained a stalwart ally of the British. Napoleon was *Invasion of Spain* determined to bring the Iberian peninsula into the Continental System. Although he at first promised the senile Spanish king Charles IV that he would cede a part of Portugal to Spain, Napoleon proceeded to overthrow Charles and installed his brother Joseph Bonaparte on the throne. Napoleon then imposed a series of reforms upon the Spanish, similar to those he had instituted elsewhere in Europe. But he reckoned without two factors that led to the ultimate failure of his Spanish mission: the presence of British forces under Sir Arthur Wellesley (later the duke of Wellington), and the determined resistance of the Spanish people. They particularly detested Napoleon's interference in the affairs of the Church, actively opposing his ending of the Inquisition and his abolition of a number of monastic establishments. Together with the British, the Spanish maintained a concerted effort to drive Napoleon from their country, often employing guerrilla warfare to do so. Though at one point Napoleon himself took charge of his army, he could not achieve anything more than temporary victory. The Spanish campaign was the first indication that Napoleon could be beaten. As such, it helped to promote a spirit of anti-Napoleonic defiance that encouraged resistance elsewhere.

A second stage in Napoleon's downfall began with the disruption of his alliance with Russia. As an agricultural country, Russia had suffered a se- *The Russian debacle* vere economic crisis when it was no longer able, as a result of the Continental System, to exchange its surplus grain for British manufactures. The consequence was that Tsar Alexander began to wink at trade with Britain and to ignore or evade the protests from Paris. By 1811 Napoleon decided that he could endure this flouting of the Continental System no longer. Accordingly, he collected an army of 600,000 (only a third of whom were native Frenchmen) and set out in the spring of 1812 to punish the tsar. The project ended in disaster. The Russians refused to make a stand, drawing the French farther and farther into the heart of their country. They permit-

The Retreat from Russia. In this painting by Charlet the horrors of the Russian winter can be seen.

ted Napoleon to occupy their ancient capital of Moscow. But on the night of his entry, a fire of suspicious origin broke out in the city, leaving little but the blackened walls of the Kremlin palaces to shelter the invading troops. Hoping that the tsar would eventually surrender, Napoleon lingered amid the ruins for more than a month, finally deciding on October 19 to begin the homeward march. The delay was a fatal blunder. Long before he had reached the border, the terrible Russian winter was upon his troops. Swollen streams, mountainous drifts of snow, and bottomless mud slowed the retreat almost to a halt. To add to the miseries of bitter cold, disease, and starvation, mounted Cossacks rode out of the blizzard to harry the exhausted army. Each morning the miserable remnant that pushed on left behind circles of corpses around the campfires of the night before. On December 13 a few thousand broken soldiers crossed the frontier into Germany—a small fraction of what had once been proudly styled the *Grande Armée.* The lives of nearly 300,000 soldiers on both sides of the conflict had been sacrificed in Napoleon's Russian adventure.

Following the retreat from Russia, the anti-Napoleonic forces took renewed hope. United by a belief that they might at last succeed in defeating the emperor, Prussia, Russia, Austria, Sweden, and Britain renewed their attack. Most of the fighting during this so-called war of liberation took place in Germany. The climax of the campaign occurred in October 1813

Defeat and abdication of Napoleon

Napoleon's Abdication Proclamation, 1814

Napoleon's return and final defeat

Napoleon's legacy

The legacy of the Revolution and the Napoleonic era

when, at what was thereafter known as the Battle of the Nations, fought near Leipzig, the allies handed the French a resounding defeat. Meanwhile, allied armies won significant victories in the Low Countries and Italy. By the beginning of 1814, they had crossed the Rhine into France. Burdened with an inexperienced army of raw youths, Napoleon retreated to Paris, continuing, despite constant setbacks, to urge the French people to further resistance. On March 31, Tsar Alexander I of Russia and King Frederick William III of Prussia made their triumphant entry into Paris. Napoleon was forced to abdicate unconditionally, and was sent into exile on the island of Elba, off the Italian coast.

Less than a year later he once more set foot on French soil. The allies had in the interim restored the Bourbon dynasty to the throne, in the person of Louis XVIII, brother of Louis XVI.* Despite his undoubted administrative abilities, the less-than-charismatic Louis could not fill the void left by Napoleon's abdication. Not surprisingly when the former emperor staged his escape from Elba, his fellow countrymen once more rallied to his side. By the time Napoleon reached Paris, he had generated enough support to cause Louis to flee the country. The allies, meeting in Vienna to conclude peace treaties with the French, were stunned by the news of Napoleon's return. They dispatched a hastily organized army to counter the emperor's typically bold offensive push into the Low Countries. There, at the battle of Waterloo, fought on June 18, 1815, Napoleon suffered defeat for the final time. Shipped off to the bleak island of St. Helena in the South Atlantic, the once-mighty emperor, now the exile Bonaparte, lived out a dreary existence writing self-serving memoirs until his death in 1821.

Napoleon's legacy was an impressive one. His administrative and legal reforms remained in place after his fall. The Napoleonic legal code persisted not only in France but in the Low Countries, Prussia, and various other German states. The institutions introduced during his reign—centralized bureaucracy, police, and educational systems—became part of the machinery of government and society in many parts of nineteenth-century Europe.

To appreciate the larger impact of the Revolution and the Napoleonic era on Western civilization, one must trace the ideas and institutions it fostered as they worked their way into the history of nineteenth- and twentieth-century Europe and America. Liberty—the concept of individual rights and responsibilities as embodied in popular democratic politics—was a notion dear to those who made the French Revolution, and one that remained embodied in the reforms it produced. So was equality—the notion of legal parity, of rational laws applied evenhandedly to all, regardless of birth or position. National pride, the era's third legacy, was bred in the hearts of the French people as they watched their citizen armies repel attacks against their newly won freedoms. It was instilled, as well, into those whose opposition to the French made them more conscious of their own

---

*Louis XVII, the young son of the executed king and queen, had died under mysterious circumstances in the hands of his revolutionary captors in 1795.

national identity. The three concepts—liberty, equality, and nationality—were now no longer merely ideas; as laws and as a new way of addressing life, they rested at the center of European reality.

5. THE VIENNA SETTLEMENT

The European powers that met at the Congress of Vienna in 1814 to draw up a permanent peace settlement for Europe labored to produce an agreement that would as nearly as possible guarantee international tranquility. At the same time, however, they were by no means unwilling to advance the claims of their own countries to new territories, though such claims threatened conflict, or even war. Although the principal decisions of the congress were made by representatives of the major powers, it was attended by an array of dignitaries from almost all the principalities of Europe. No fewer than six monarchs attended: the tsar of Russia, the emperor of Austria, and the kings of Prussia, Denmark, Bavaria, Sweden, and Württemberg. Great Britain was represented by Lord Castlereagh and the duke of Wellington. From France came the subtle intriguer Talleyrand, who had served as a bishop under Louis XVI, as foreign minister at the court of Napoleon, and who now stood ready to espouse the cause of reaction.

The dominant roles at the Congress of Vienna were played by Tsar Alexander I (1801–1825) and by the Austrian diplomat Klemens von Metternich (1773–1859). The dynamic but baffling tsar played a leading role in the negotiations because Napoleon's defeat had left Russia the most powerful Continental state. Reared at the court of Catherine the Great, he had imbibed Jacobin doctrines from his French tutor, along with notions of absolutist authority from his military-minded father, Tsar Paul. In 1801 he succeeded his murdered father and for the next two decades disturbed the dreams of his fellow sovereigns by becoming the most liberal monarch in Europe. After the defeat of Napoleon in the Russian campaign, Alexander's mind turned more and more to mystical channels. He conceived of a mission to convert the rulers of all countries to the Christian ideals of justice and peace. But the chief effect of his voluble expressions of devotion to "liberty" and "enlightenment" was to frighten conservatives into suspecting a plot to extend his power over all of Europe. He was accused of intriguing with Jacobins everywhere to substitute an all-powerful Russia for an all-powerful France.

The most commanding figure at the congress was Metternich, born at Coblenz in the Rhine valley, where his father was Austrian ambassador at the courts of three small German states. As a student at the University of Strassburg the young Metternich witnessed mob violence connected with the outbreak of the French Revolution, and to this he attributed his life-long hatred of political innovation. He had been active in fomenting discord between Napoleon and Tsar Alexander, after the two became allies in 1807, and had played some part in arranging the marriage of Napoleon to

Tsar Alexander I

Tsar Alexander I

Klemens von Metternich

Metternich

Louis XVIII recognized as sovereign of France

Barriers to French expansion

The German settlement

the Austrian archduchess, Marie Louise. Metternich once declared himself an admirer of the spider, "always busy arranging their houses with the greatest of neatness in the world." At the Congress of Vienna, he attempted at every turn to arrange international affairs with equal neatness, to suit his own diplomatic designs. His two great obsessions were hatred of political and social change and fear of Russia. Above all, he feared revolutions inspired by the tsar for the sake of establishing Russian supremacy in Europe. For this reason he favored moderate terms for France in its hour of defeat, and was ready at one time to sponsor the restoration of Napoleon as emperor of the French under the protection and overlordship of the Habsburg monarchy.

The basic idea that guided the work of the Congress of Vienna was the principle of *legitimacy*. This principle was invented by Talleyrand as a device for protecting France against drastic punishment by its conquerors, but it was ultimately adopted by Metternich as a convenient expression of the general policy of reaction. Legitimacy meant that the dynasties of Europe that had reigned in prerevolutionary days should be restored to their thrones, and that each country should regain essentially the same territories it had held in 1789. In accordance with this principle Louis XVIII was recognized as the "legitimate" sovereign of France; the restoration of Bourbon rulers in Spain and the Two Sicilies was also confirmed. France was compelled to pay an indemnity of 700 million francs to the victorious allies, but its boundaries were to remain essentially the same as in 1789.

To ensure that the French would not soon again overrun their boundaries, however, a strong barrier was erected to contain them. The Dutch Republic, conquered by the French in 1795, was restored as the Kingdom of the Netherlands, with the house of Orange as its hereditary monarchy. To its territory was added that of Belgium, formerly the Austrian Netherlands, with the hope that this now substantial power would serve to discourage any future notions of French expansion. For the same reason the German left bank of the Rhine was ceded to Prussia, and Austria was established as a major power in northern Italy.

The principle of legitimacy was not extended to Germany, however. There, despite pleas from rulers of the sovereign bits and pieces that had existed before 1789, the great powers agreed to reduce the number of states and principalities from over 300 to 39, linked together into the loose German Confederation under the honorary presidency of Austria. Fear of an aggressive Russia led the other European nations to support the maintenance—as an anti-Russian bulwark—of the kingdoms of Bavaria, Württemberg, and Saxony. At the same time, however, Tsar Alexander was demanding that Poland, partitioned into virtual extinction by Russia, Austria, and Prussia in the 1790s, be reconstituted a kingdom with himself as its constitutional monarch. Prussia was prepared to agree with this scheme, provided that it be allowed to swallow Saxony. National avarice for territorial expansion rapidly eclipsed legitimacy as a guiding principle in these negotiations. Metternich, horrified at the double threat thus presented to Austria by Prussia and Russia, allied himself with Talleyrand and

EUROPE AFTER THE CONGRESS OF VIENNA · 1815

Castlereagh, both of whom secretly agreed to go to war against Russia and Prussia, if necessary, in order to prevent them from consummating their Polish-Saxon deal. A compromise was eventually reached, giving to Russia the major part of Poland and to Prussia a part of Saxony. Britain, no less anxious than the other victorious powers to gain compensation for its long years at war, received territories principally under French dominion in South Africa and South America and the island of Ceylon, thus adding further to its commercial empire.

Legitimacy, as expressed in the treaties that concluded the Congress of Vienna, emerged as the latter-day expression of the principles of balance and stability that had shaped diplomacy during the eighteenth century. The

Triumph of the state system

age of absolutism had witnessed the emergence of an international state system dedicated to those principles. By enshrining them in their settlement, the diplomats at Vienna ensured that such a state system would be part of the legacy passed to their nineteenth-century successors.

SELECTED READINGS

•*Items so designated are available in paperback editions.*

• Arendt, Hannah, *On Revolution,* New York, 1963. An analysis of the American and French Revolutions and their meaning for modern man.
• Bergeron, Louis, *France under Napoleon,* Princeton, 1981. Concentrates on the era of Napoleon rather than the man.
  Bosher, J. F., *French Finances, 1770–1790: From Business to Bureaucracy,* Cambridge, 1970. An impressive study concerned with the financial apparatus of Old Regime and revolutionary France.
• ———, *The French Revolution,* New York, 1989. A new interpretation that sees the revolutionary struggle driven by socially mixed and transient groupings.
• Breunig, C., *The Age of Revolution and Reaction, 1789–1850,* 2nd ed., New York, 1989. A well-written survey.
• Brinton, Crane, *Anatomy of Revolution,* rev. ed., New York, 1961. Attempts to create a general model of revolutions by comparing the English, American, French, and Russian Revolutions.
• Bruun, Geoffrey, *Europe and the French Imperium, 1799–1814,* New York, 1938. Describes the impact of Napoleon upon Europe.
• Cobb, R. C., *The Police and the People: French Popular Protest, 1789–1820,* New York, 1970. A survey of peasants and *sans-culottes.*
• Cobban, Alfred, *The Social Interpretation of the French Revolution,* Cambridge, 1964. A penetrating critique of the radical interpretation of the Revolution, more important for its questions than its conclusions.
• Doyle, William, *Origins of the French Revolution.* 2nd ed., Oxford, 1988. A revisionist historian surveys recent research on the political and social origins of the Revolution and identifies a new consensus.
  Geyl, Pieter, *Napoleon: For and Against,* rev. ed., New Haven, 1964. The ways in which Napoleon was interpreted by French historians and political figures.
  Goodwin, Albert, *The Friends of Liberty: The English Democratic Movement in the Age of the French Revolution,* Cambridge, Mass., 1979. Detailed, subtle analysis of English reform movements.
  Goubert, Pierre, *The Ancien Régime: French Society, 1600–1750,* vol. 1., New York, 1969. A masterly analysis of French society under the Old Regime.
  Greer, Donald, *The Incidence of the Terror during the French Revolution: A Statistical Interpretation,* Cambridge, Mass., 1935. An important study that reveals that the lower classes suffered most during the Terror, rather than the nobility or the clergy.

- Hampson, Norman, *A Social History of the French Revolution,* London, 1963. Deals with institutional development.
- Herold, J. Christopher, *The Age of Napoleon,* New York, 1968. A well-written popular history.

  Hunt, Lynn M., *Politics, Culture, and Class in the French Revolution,* Berkeley, Calif., 1984. An analysis of the interaction between political events and socio-cultural phenomena out of which grew a new culture of democracy and republicanism.

  ———, *The Family Romance of the French Revolution,* Berkeley, Calif., 1992.
- Kissinger, Henry, *A World Restored: Metternich, Castlereagh, and the Problems of Peace, 1812–1822,* Boston, 1957. By the former U.S. secretary of state, an admirer of Metternich.
- Lefebvre, Georges, *The Coming of the French Revolution,* Princeton, 1947. An excellent study of the causes and early events of the Revolution.
- ———, *The French Revolution,* 2 vols., New York, 1963–1964. An impressive synthesis by the greatest modern scholar of the Revolution.
- ———, *The Great Fear of 1789,* New York, 1973. The best account of the rural disturbances.

  McManners, John, *The French Revolution and the Church,* New York, 1969. Describes the impact of revolutionary anticlericalism upon the French Church.
- Markham, Felix, *Napoleon,* New York, 1966. An excellent study.
- Nicolson, Harold, *The Congress of Vienna: A Study in Allied Unity,* New York, 1946. An excellent and very readable history, written by a British diplomat.
- Palmer, R. R., *The Age of the Democratic Revolution: A Political History of Europe and America, 1760–1800,* 2 vols., Princeton, 1964. Impressive for its scope; places the French Revolution in the larger context of a worldwide revolutionary movement.
- ———, *Twelve Who Ruled,* Princeton, 1958. Excellent biographical studies of the members of the Committee of Public Safety; demonstrates that Robespierre's role has been exaggerated.
- Rudé, George, *The Crowd in the French Revolution,* Oxford, 1959. An important monograph that analyzes the composition of the crowds that participated in the great uprisings of the Revolution.
- Schama, Simon, *Citizens: A Chronicle of the French Revolution,* New York, 1989. An interesting although controversial treatment of the French Revolution.
- Soboul, Albert, *The Sans-Culottes: The Popular Movement and Revolutionary Government, 1793–1794,* Garden City, N.Y., 1972. An outstanding example of "history from below"; analyzes the pressures upon the Convention in the year of the Terror.
- Thompson, J. M., *Napoleon Bonaparte: His Rise and Fall,* Oxford, 1958. The standard work.
- ———, *Robespierre and the French Revolution,* London, 1953. An excellent short biography.
- Tilly, Charles, *The Vendée: A Sociological Analysis of the Counter-Revolution of 1793,* Cambridge, Mass., 1964. An important economic and social analysis of the factors that led to the reaction in the Vendée.
- Tocqueville, Alexis de, *The Old Regime and French Revolution.* Originally written in 1856, this remains a classic analysis of the causes of the French Revolution.
- Williams, Gwyn A., *Artisans and Sans-Culottes,* New York, 1969. Comparative history of English and French popular movements.

SOURCE MATERIALS

• Burke, Edmund, *Reflections on the Revolution in France,* London, 1790. (Many editions). The great conservative statement against the Revolution and its principles.

• Montesquieu, Baron de, *The Spirit of the Laws,* 1748. (Many editions). See especially Books I, II, III, XI.

• Paine, Thomas, *The Rights of Man,* 1791. (Many editions). Paine's eloquent response to Burke's *Reflections* resulted in his conviction for treason and banishment from England.

• Pernoud, G., and S. Flaisser, eds., *The French Revolution,* New York, 1960. Contains eyewitness reports.

Sieyès, Abbé, *What Is the Third Estate?,* 1789. (Many editions). The most important political pamphlet in the decisive year 1789.

Steward, John Hall, *A Documentary Survey of the French Revolution,* New York, 1951.

Thompson, J. M., *French Revolution Documents, 1789–1794,* Oxford, 1948.

• Walzer, Michael, ed., *Regicide and Revolution: Speeches at the Trial of Louis XVI,* 1974. Contains a thoughtful introduction.

• Young, Arthur, *Travels in France during the Years 1787, 1788, 1789,* New York, 1972. France on the eve of revolution, as seen by a perceptive English observer.

Chapter 20

THE INDUSTRIAL REVOLUTION

Providence has assigned to man the glorious function of vastly improving the productions of nature by judicious culture, of working them up into objects of comfort and elegance with the least possible expenditure of human labor—an undeniable position which forms the basis of our Factory System.

—Andrew Ure, *The Philosophy of Manufactures*

There have been many revolutions in industry during the history of Western civilization, and there will undoubtedly be many more. Periods of rapid technological change are often called revolutions, and justifiably so. But, historically, there is one Industrial Revolution. Occurring during the hundred years after 1780, it witnessed the first breakthrough from a largely rural, handicraft economy to one dominated by urban, machine-driven manufacturing. Moreover, technological changes and new production methods triggered social and political upheavals that had revolutionary consequences for human society.

The uniqueness of the revolution

The fact that it was a European revolution was not accidental. Although in the mid-eighteenth century Europe was a continent still predominantly agricultural, although the majority of its people remained illiterate and destined to live out impoverished lives within sight of the place they were born—despite these conditions, which in our eyes might make Europe appear "underdeveloped," it was of course no such thing. European merchants and men of commerce were established as the world's foremost manufacturers and traders. Rulers relied upon this class of men to provide them with the wherewithal to maintain the economy of their states, both in terms of flourishing commercial activity and of victorious armies and navies. Those men, in turn, had for the most part extracted from their rulers the understanding that the property they possessed, whether invested in land or commerce or both, was theirs outright. That understanding, substantiated by the written contracts that were replacing unwritten, long-acknowledged custom, helped persuade merchants, bankers, traders, and entrepreneurs that they lived in a world that was stable, rational, and predictable. Believing the world was so, they moved out into it with self-

Why a European revolution? (1) the commercial class

confidence and in hopes of increasing their own, and their country's, prosperity. Only in Europe does one find these presuppositions and this class of men in the eighteenth century; only through the activities of such people could the Industrial Revolution have taken place.

(2) expanding markets

These capitalists could not have prospered without an expanding market for their goods. The existence of this market explains further why it was in Europe that the Industrial Revolution took place. Ever since the beginning of the seventeenth century, overseas commercial exploration and development had been opening new territories to European trade. India, Africa, North and South America—all had been woven into the pattern of European economic expansion. The colonies and commercial dependencies took economic shape at Europe's behest. Even the new United States had not been able to declare its economic independence. Whatever commercial and industrial design Europe might devise, all would be compelled to accommodate themselves to Europe's demands.

(3) population growth

A third factor helping to ensure that the revolution would occur in Europe was the population growth that occurred throughout Western Europe in the eighteenth century (see above, p. 529). Increasing populations, along with overseas expansion, provided an ever-growing market for manufactured goods. It furnished, as well, an adequate pool—eventually a surplus—of laboring men, women, and children to work in the manufacture of those goods either at home or in factories.

Qualifications to the concept of "revolution"

Two important facts have inclined historians to qualify the concept of "revolutionary" industrial change. First, the existence of a thriving commercial class, expanding markets, and increasing populations prior to the Industrial Revolution suggests that the changes we are about to analyze had important antecedents. We have already noted, for example, the manner in which proto-industrialization was transforming rural areas into sizable manufacturing regions in the seventeenth and eighteenth centuries (see above, p. 534). Second, the Industrial Revolution did not take place everywhere in Europe—or even in any single country—at the same time and at the same pace. Beginning in northern England and western Scotland in the late eighteenth century, it spread gradually region by region, country by country across Europe. Unlike the French Revolution whose history can be measured by a decade, the Industrial Revolution occurred over the span of at least a century.

See color map facing page 685

1. THE INDUSTRIAL REVOLUTION IN ENGLAND

Why in England?
(1) an economy of abundance

It was in England that the Industrial Revolution first took hold. England's economy had progressed further than that of any other country in the direction of abundance. In simplest terms: fewer people had to struggle just to remain alive; more people were in a position to sell a surplus of the goods they produced to an increasingly expanding market; and more people had enough money to purchase the goods that market offered. English

The Corn Exchange, 1842. This London exchange was evidence of the abundance of both food and capital in Britain during the time of the Industrial Revolution.

laborers, though poorly paid, enjoyed a higher standard of living than their Continental counterparts. They ate white bread, not brown, and meat with some regularity. Because a smaller portion of their income was spent on food, they might occasionally have some to spare for articles that were bought rather than homemade.

Further evidence of this increasing abundance was the number of bills for the enclosure of agricultural land passed by an English Parliament sympathetic to capitalism during the last half of the eighteenth century. The enclosure of fields, pasture, and waste lands into large fenced tracts of land under the private ownership and individual management of capitalist landlords meant an increased food supply to feed an increasing and increasingly urban population. Yet another sign of England's abundance was its growing supply of surplus capital, derived from investment in land or commerce, and available to finance new economic enterprises. London, already a leading center for the world's trade, served as a headquarters for the transfer of raw material, capital, and manufactured products. Portugal alone channeled as much as £50,000 in Brazilian gold per week into London. Thus English capitalists had enough money on hand to underwrite and sustain an industrial revolution.

But the revolution required more than money. It required habits of mind that would encourage investments in enterprises that were risky, but that represented an enormous potential for gain. In England, far more than on the Continent, the pursuit of wealth was perceived to be a worthy end in life. The nobility of Europe had, from the period of the Renaissance,

Abundance of food and capital

(2) climate of opinion

cultivated the notion of "gentlemanly" conduct, in part to hold the line against social encroachments from below. The English aristocrats, whose privileges were meager when compared with those of Continental nobles, had never ceased to respect men who made money; nor had they disdained to make whatever they could for themselves. Their scramble to enclose their lands reflected this sympathy with aggressive capitalism. Below the aristocracy, there was even less of a barrier separating the world of urban commerce from that of the rural gentry. Most of the men who pioneered as entrepreneurs in the early years of the Industrial Revolution sprang from the minor gentry or yeoman farmer class. Men from this sort of background felt themselves free to rise as high as their abilities might carry them on the social and economic ladder.

Respect for financial success

Eighteenth-century England was not by any means free of social snobbery: lords looked down upon bankers, as bankers looked down upon artisans. But a lord's disdain might well be tempered by the fact of his own grandfather's origins in the counting house. And the banker would gladly lend money to the artisan if convinced that the artisan's invention might make them both a fortune. The English, as a nation, were not afraid of business. They respected the sensible, the practical, and the financially successful. Robinson Crusoe, that desert island entrepreneur, was one of their models. In the novel (1719) by Daniel Defoe, the hero had used his wits to master nature and become lord of a thriving economy. His triumph was not diminished because it was a worldly triumph; far from it. "It is our vanity which urges us on," declared the economist Adam Smith, whose writings encouraged capitalist investment in manufacturing. And thank God, Smith implied, for our blessed vanity! An individual's desire to show himself a worldly success worked to produce prosperity for the country as a whole.

(3) expanding markets

England's eighteenth-century prosperity was based upon expanding markets both at home and abroad for whatever goods it manufactured. The English were voracious consumers. By the mid-eighteenth century, yearly fashions were setting styles not only for the very rich but for a growing middle-class clientele as well. "Nature may be satisfied with little," one London entrepreneur declared. "But it is the wants of fashion and the desire of novelties that causes trade." The country's small size and the fact that it was an island encouraged the development of a nationwide domestic market that could respond to increasing demand. The absence of a system of internal tolls and tariffs, such as existed on the Continent, meant that goods could be moved freely to the place where they could fetch the best price. This freedom of movement was assisted by a constantly improving transportation system. Parliament in the years just before the Industrial Revolution passed acts to finance turnpike building at the rate of forty per year; the same period saw the construction of canals and the further opening up of harbors and navigable streams. Unlike the government of France, whose cumbrous mercantilist adventures as often as not thwarted economic growth, the English Parliament believed that the most effective way in which it could help businessmen was to assist them in helping themselves.

If domestic markets promised steady growth, foreign markets promised greater returns—along with greater risks. Expansion was assisted by a favorable political climate: some members of Parliament were businessmen themselves; others had invested heavily in commerce; hence their eagerness to encourage by statute the construction of canals, the establishment of banks, and the enclosure of common lands. And hence their insistence, throughout the eighteenth century, that England's foreign policy respond to its commercial needs. At the end of every major eighteenth-century war, England wrested overseas territories from its enemies. At the same time, England was penetrating hitherto unexploited territories, such as India and South America, in search of further potential markets and resources. In 1759, over one-third of all British exports went to the colonies; by 1784, if we include the newly established United States, that figure had increased to one-half. Export production increased by 80 percent between 1750 and 1770, while production for domestic consumption gained just 7 percent over the same period. The English possessed a merchant marine capable of transporting goods across the world, and a navy practiced in the art of protecting its commercial fleets. By 1780 England's markets, together with its fleet and its established position at the center of world trade, combined to produce a potential for expansion so great as to compel the Industrial Revolution.

English entrepreneurs and inventors grasped the opportunity by revolutionizing the production of cotton textile goods. Although fewer cotton goods were made in eighteenth-century England than woolen goods, the extent of cotton manufacture by 1760 was such as to make cotton more than an infant industry. Tariffs prohibiting the importation of East Indian cottons, imposed by Parliament to stimulate the sale of woolen goods, had instead served to spur the manufacture of domestic cottons. Thus the revolution, when it did occur, took place in an already well-established industry. Yet without the invention of some sort of machinery that would improve the quality and at the same time dramatically increase the quantity of spun cotton thread, the necessary breakthrough would not have come. John Kay's 1733 invention of the fly shuttle, which greatly speeded up the process of weaving, only made the bottleneck in the prior process of spinning more apparent. The problem was solved by the invention of a series of comparatively simple mechanical devices, the most important of which was the spinning jenny, invented by James Hargreaves, a carpenter and hand-loom weaver, in 1764 (patented 1770). The spinning jenny, named after the inventor's wife, was a compound spinning wheel, capable of producing sixteen threads at once. The threads it spun were not strong enough, however, to be used for the longitudinal fibers, or warp, of cotton cloth. It was not until the invention of the water frame by Richard Arkwright, a barber, in 1769, that quantity production of both warp and woof (latitudinal fibers) became possible. The water frame, along with the spinning mule, invented by Samuel Crompton in 1779 and combining the features of both the jenny and the frame, solved the problems that had heretofore curtailed the output of cotton textiles. They increased the mechanical

Richard Arkwright

advantage over the spinning wheel enormously. From six to twenty-four times the amount of yarn could be spun on a jenny as on the wheel; by the end of the century two to three hundred times as much as on the mule. Just as important, the quality of the thread improved not only in terms of strength but also of fineness.

Once these machines came into general use, the revolution proceeded apace. Cotton suited the mule and the jenny because it was a tougher thread than wool; as such cotton was a fiber that could withstand the rough treatment it received at the mechanical hands of the crude early machines. In addition, the supply of cotton was expandable in a way that the supply of wool was not. *The cotton gin*, invented by the American Eli Whitney in 1793, separated seeds from fiber mechanically, thereby making cotton available at a lower price. The invention kept America's slave plantations profitable, and meant that supply would meet increased demand.

The cotton gin

The first machinery was cheap enough to allow spinners to continue to work at home. But as it increased in size it was more and more frequently housed not in the cottages of individual spinners, but in workshops or mills located near water that could be used to power the machines. Eventually, with the further development of steamdriven equipment, the mills could be built wherever it might suit the entrepreneur—frequently in towns and cities in the north of England.

Steam-driven equipment

The transition from home to factory industry was of course not accomplished overnight. Cotton yarn continued to be spun at home at the same time that it was being produced in mills. Eventually, however, the low cost of building and operating a large plant, plus the efficiency realized by bringing workers together under one roof, meant that larger mills more and more frequently replaced smaller workshops. By 1851, three-fifths of

Growth of factories

The Spinning Jenny. Invented by James Hargreaves in 1767.

British Cotton Factory, 1842. The women and girls in this factory card and draw cotton thread that will be used to manufacture cotton cloth.

those employed in cotton manufacture worked in medium- to large-size mills. Weaving remained a home industry until the invention of a cheap, practical power loom convinced entrepreneurs that they could save money by moving the process from home to mill. Hand-loom weavers were probably the most obvious victims of the Industrial Revolution in England. Their unwillingness to surrender their livelihood to machinery meant that they continued to work for less and less—by 1830, no more than a pitiful six shillings a week. In 1815 they numbered about 250,000; by 1850, there remained only 40,000; by 1860, only 3,000.

English cotton textiles flooded the world market from the 1780s. Here was a light material, suitable for the climates of Africa, India, and the more temperate zones of North America. Here was a material cheap enough to make it possible for millions who had never before enjoyed the comfort of washable body clothes to do so. And here was material fine enough to tempt the rich to experiment with muslins and calicos in a way they had not done before. Figures speak eloquently of the revolutionary change wrought by the expanding industry. In 1760, England exported less than £250,000 worth of cotton goods; by 1800 it was exporting over £5 million worth. In 1760, England imported 2.5 million pounds of raw cotton; in 1787, 22 million pounds; in 1837, 366 million pounds. By 1800, cotton accounted for about 5 percent of the national income of the country; by 1812, from 7 to 8 percent. By 1815, the export of cotton textiles amounted to 40 percent of the value of all domestic goods exported from Great Britain. Although the price of manufactured cotton goods fell dramatically, the market expanded so rapidly that profits continued to increase.

The extent of the cotton trade

Unlike the changes in the textile industry, those occurring in the manufacture of iron were not great enough to warrant their being labeled revolutionary. Yet they were most significant. Britain's abundant supply of coal,

The Steam Hammer from a painting by James Nasmyth. This steam-powered machine was used to beat out ingots of white hot metal into strips.

The iron industry

combined with its advanced transportation network, allowed the English, from the middle of the eighteenth century, to substitute coal for wood in the heating of molten metal. A series of discoveries made fuel savings possible, along with a higher quality of iron and the manufacture of a greater variety of iron products. Demand rose sharply during the war years at the end of the century. It remained high as a result of calls for plant machinery, agricultural implements, and hardware; it rose dramatically with the coming of railways in the 1830s and 1840s. Britain was exporting 571,000 tons of iron in 1814; in 1852, it exported 1,036,000 tons out of a world total of almost 2,000,000—more iron than was made by all the rest of the world combined.

The steam engine

The need for more coal required the mining of deeper and deeper veins. In 1711, Thomas Newcomen had devised a crude but effective steam engine for pumping water from mines. Though of value to the coal industry, it was of less use in other industries since it wasted both fuel and power. In 1763, James Watt, a maker of scientific instruments at the University of Glasgow, was asked to repair a model of the Newcomen engine. While engaged in this task he conceived the idea that the machine would be greatly improved if a separate chamber were added to condense the steam eliminating the need to cool the cylinder. He patented his first engine incorporating this device in 1769. Watt's genius as an inventor was not matched by his business ability. He admitted that he would "rather face a loaded cannon than settle a disputed account or make a bargain." As a consequence, he fell into debt in attempting to place his machines on the market. He was rescued by Matthew Boulton, a wealthy hardware manufacturer of Birmingham. The two men formed a partnership, with Boulton providing the capital. By 1800 the firm had sold 289 engines for use in factories and mines. The replacement of water by steam power was a slow process: in 1850 more than a third of the power used in woolen manufacture and an eighth of that used in cotton was still produced by water. Nevertheless, there is no question that without the steam engine there could have been no industrial expansion on the scale that we have described.

Other industries experienced profound changes during the hundred years of the Industrial Revolution. Many of those changes came in response to the growth of textile manufacture. The chemical industry, for example, developed new methods of dyeing and bleaching, as well as improved methods of production in the fields of soap and glassmaking. Production of goods increased across the board as profits from the boom in manufacturing increased the demand for new and more sophisticated articles. Such trades as pottery and metalware expanded to meet demands, in the process adopting methods that in most instances reduced cost and speeded manufacture.

Other advances

To understand fully the nature of the Industrial Revolution in England one must not lose sight of two important factors: the first is that dramatic as the revolution was, it happened over a period of two or three generations, at varying paces in different industries in different parts of the country. Some men and women continued to work at home, much as their grandfathers and grandmothers had. Old tools and old methods were not immediately replaced by new ones, any more than populations fled the countryside overnight for the city. Second, the revolution was accomplished from a very limited technological and theoretical base. Except in the chemical industry, change was not the result of scientific research. It was the product of empirical experimentation—in some cases, of little more than creative tinkering. To say this is not to disparage the work of men such as Arkwright, Hargreaves, Watt, and their like. It is to suggest, however, the reason why England, without a national system of education on any level, was nonetheless able to accomplish the revolution it did. Nor are these remarks

The limits of the Industrial Revolution

Aqueduct in Wales. The 124-foot-high span carried water in a 10-foot wide cast iron trough over the River Dee. Designed by Thomas Telford, this "stream in the sky" was one of the most impressive engineering feats of the early Industrial Revolution.

Old Hetton Colliery, Sunderland, England. Designed by the engineer Thomas Hair about 1840, this large mine was typical of those built to meet the increased demand for coal. Note the railways that connected the mines with the sea.

intended to belittle the magnitude of the change. What occurred in England was a revolution because of the way in which it reshaped the lives, not just of the English, but of people across the globe. By responding as it did to the demands of its apparently insatiable markets, England made a revolution every bit as profound and long-lasting as that which occurred simultaneously in France.

2. THE INDUSTRIAL REVOLUTION ON THE CONTINENT

The Industrial Revolution came in time to the Continent, but not to any important degree before about 1830. As we have seen, manufacturing in eighteenth-century France and Germany clustered in regions whose proximity to raw materials, access to markets, and traditional attachment to particular skills had resulted in their development as industrial centers. Flanders and Normandy in France, and Saxony in Germany were centers for the manufacture of woolen cloth; Switzerland, southern Germany, and Normandy, of cottons; Wallonia (the area around Liège in Belgium), the Marne valley, and Silesia in Germany, of iron. Yet for a variety of reasons, these areas failed to experience the late-eighteenth-century breakthrough that occurred in Britain. Nor were they capable at first of imitating Britain's success, once they began to perceive the great economic advantages that Britain's pronounced lead was bringing it. There were a number of reasons for the delay of Continental industrialization. Whereas England's transportation system was highly developed, those of France and Germany were not. France was far larger than England, it rivers were not as easily navigable, its seaports were farther apart. Central Europe was so divided into tiny principalities, each with its own set of tolls and tariffs, as to make the transportation of raw materials or manufactured goods over any consid-

Reasons for delay: (1) lack of transport and raw materials

See color map facing page 685

erable distance impractical. France itself imposed regulations that thwarted easy shipments. In addition, the Continent was not as blessed with an abundance of raw materials as England. France, the Low Countries, and Germany imported wool. Europe lacked an abundant supply of the fuel that was the new source of industrial energy. Few major coal deposits were known to exist, while the ready availability of timber discouraged exploration that might have resulted in its discovery.

After the French Revolution, middle-class Europeans, though free in theory to rise as high on the social and economic ladder as they might aspire, appear largely to have remained content to make only enough money to sustain a modest-size business. The motivation of the middle class was as often social as it was economic: to ensure the continuity of a family rather than to produce increasing quantities of goods. Furthermore, capital was not as readily available on the Continent as in England. In France, again, the retarded development of agricultural capitalism, due to the tenacious economic perseverance of small peasant landholders, limited the supply of savings, both for investment in industry and for expenditure on manufactured goods, as well as limiting the mobility of labor. Nor was the entrepreneurial spirit that compelled Englishmen to drive competitors to the wall as highly developed in France and Germany in the years after 1815. Exhausted by the competitiveness of war, and fearful of the disruptions that war brought in its train, Continental businessmen resisted new methods of manufacturing and selling.

(2) lack of entrepreneurial spirit

The Continent did not simply stand idle, however, as England assumed its industrial lead. The pace of mechanization was increasing in the 1780s. But the French Revolution and the wars that followed disrupted growth that might otherwise have taken place. Battles fought on French, German, and Italian soil destroyed factories and machinery. Although ironmaking increased to meet the demands of the wars, techniques remained what they had been. Commerce was badly hurt both by British destruction of French

(3) effect of wars

A Swedish Mining Town, 1790

merchant shipping and by Napoleon's Continental System. Probably the revolutionary change most beneficial to industrial advance in Europe was the removal of previous restraints on the movement of capital and labor; for example, the abolition of trade guilds, and the reduction of the number of tariff barriers across the Continent. On balance, however, the revolutionary and Napoleonic wars clearly thwarted industrial development on the Continent, while at the same time intensifying it in England.

A number of factors combined to produce a climate more generally conducive to industrialization on the Continent after 1815. Population continued to increase, not only throughout Europe, but in those areas now more and more dependent upon the importation of manufactured goods—Latin America, for example. European increases, which doubled the populations of most countries between 1800 and 1850, meant that the Continent would now have a growing number of producers and consumers. More people did not necessarily mean further industrialization. In Ireland, where other necessary factors were absent, more people meant less food. But in those countries with an already well-established commercial and industrial base—France and Germany, for example—increased population did encourage the adoption of the technologies and methods of production that were transforming England.

Increases after 1815;
(1) population rise

Transportation improved in Western Europe both during and following the Napoleonic wars. The Austrian Empire added over 30,000 miles of roads between 1830 and 1847; Belgium almost doubled its road network in the same period; France built, in addition to roads, 2,000 miles of canals. In the United States, where industrialization was occurring at an increasingly rapid rate after 1830, road mileage jumped from 21,000 miles in 1800 to 170,000 in 1856. When these improvements were combined with the introduction of rail transport in the 1840s, the resulting increase in markets available to all Western countries encouraged them to introduce methods of manufacturing that would help meet new demands.

(2) improved transportation

Governments played a more direct role in the process of industrialization on the Continent than in Britain. Napoleon's rationalization of French and imperial institutions had introduced Europe to the practice of state intervention. His legal code, which guaranteed freedom of contract and facilitated the establishment of joint-stock enterprises, encouraged other rulers to provide a similar framework for commercial expansion. In Prussia, lack of private capital necessitated state operation of a large proportion of that country's mines. In no European country but Britain would railways be built without the financial assistance of the state. In the private sector more attention was given on the Continent than in England to the need for artificial stimulation to produce industrial change. It was in Belgium that the first joint-stock investment bank—the Société Générale—was founded, an institution designed to facilitate the accumulation of ready capital for investment in industry and commerce. Europeans were also willing for the state to establish educational systems whose aim, among others, was to produce a well-trained elite capable of assisting in the development of industrial technology. What Britain had produced almost by chance, the Europeans began to reproduce by design.

(3) centralization

(4) *the lack of technicians*

Until the Continent produced its own technicians it was compelled to rely on British expertise. But the pace of Continental, and also American, industrialization, even after 1815, remained far slower than in Britain because of Britain's natural reluctance to see its methods of production pirated by others. British industrialists believed it their patriotic duty to prevent the exportation of their techniques, although they were more than willing to raid the Continent for technological experts: Matthew Boulton imported skilled workers from Vienna and Sweden. Continental entrepreneurs likewise argued that it was patriotism, not profit, that inspired them to compete with the British. "Our reasons for building our factory were exactly those which made you oppose it," a German firm wrote to Boulton; "that is patriotic zeal." Until 1825, British artisans were forbidden to emigrate; until 1842, much innovative machinery could not be exported. Laws did not, however, prevent the movement of creative technician-entrepreneurs and their particular skills; many Englishmen, during the first part of the nineteenth century, made fortunes as they taught others in Europe and America to do what they had taught themselves. One such man was William Cockerill, who began his career in England as a carpenter. He and his sons built cotton-spinning equipment on the Continent during the revolutionary wars. In 1817, they purchased the palace of the former bishops of Liège, converting it to a factory producing machinery and steam engines. Yet despite the presence of entrepreneurs like the Cockerills, or of Continental counterparts such as the Westphalian Fritz Harkort, who built and sold steam engines across Europe in the 1820s and 1830s, the general lack of large numbers of European technicians, experts,

A German Textile Factory, 1848. This is an unusually large manufacturing facility for this period on the Continent.

and entrepreneurs undoubtedly hampered rapid industrial expansion in France, Germany, and elsewhere.

The growth of the textile industry in Europe was patterned by the circumstances of the Napoleonic wars. The supply of cotton to the Continent had been interrupted, thanks to the British blockade, but the military's greater demand for woolen cloth meant that expansion occurred more rapidly in the woolen than in the cotton industry. By 1820, the spinning of wool by machine was the common practice on the Continent; weaving, however, was still accomplished largely by hand. Regional centers for the production of wool were located around Rheims and in Alsace in France; in what is now Belgium; and in Saxony and Silesia in Germany. All possessed, at least in some measure, the various elements necessary to the successful growth and development of a regional economic system: transportation, resources, markets, technology, and labor supply. Mechanization was retarded because manual labor was cheap, and by the important fact that since Britain's market was so large, Continental profits too often depended upon the manufacture of some particular specialty not made in England, and therefore without broad commercial appeal. Cotton manufacture was curtailed by the same circumstances. In France, as a result, mechanization occurred first in the silk industry and those sections of the cotton industry that produced finer specialty materials—lace, for example. A tradition of prestige associated with the production of luxury goods, dating back to the reign of Louis XIV, encouraged entrepreneurs to invest in this branch of the textile industry. They were willing to forgo mass markets in the hope that their products would not encounter British competition. France nevertheless remained the largest Continental producer of cotton goods, followed by Belgium and the German territories of the Rhine valley—Saxony, Silesia, and Bavaria.

Silk Weavers of Lyons, 1850. The first significant working-class uprisings in nineteenth-century France occurred here in 1831 and 1834. Note the domestic character of the working conditions.

In the area of heavy industry on the Continent, the picture was much the same as in textiles: i.e., gradual advances in the adoption of technological innovation against a background of more general resistance to change. Here, however, because change came later than in Britain, it coincided with an increased demand for various goods that had come into being as a result of industrialization and urbanization: iron pipe, much in use by mid-century in cities for gas, water, and drainage; metal machinery, now replacing earlier wooden prototypes. Consequently, the iron industry took the lead over textiles on the Continent, accompanied by an increase, where possible, in the production of coal. Coal was scarce, however; in the Rhineland, wood was still used to manufacture iron. The result was an unwillingness on the part of entrepreneurs to make as extensive use of the steam engine as they might have otherwise; it used too much fuel. In France, as late as 1844, hydraulic (i.e., water-driven) engines were employed far more often for the manufacture of iron than were steam engines. One further problem hampered the development of Continental heavy industry during the first half of the nineteenth century. British competition forced Continental machine construction firms to scramble for whatever orders they could get. This need to respond to a variety of requests meant that it was difficult for firms to specialize in a single product. The result was a lack of standardization, and continued production to order, when rationalization and specialization would have resulted in an increased volume of production.

Heavy industry

3. THE COMING OF RAILWAYS

By about 1840, then, Continental countries, and to some degree the United States, were moving gradually along the course of industrialization traced by Britain, producing far more than they had, yet nothing like as much as their spectacular pacesetter. Within the next ten years, the coming of the railways was to alter that situation. Though Britain by no means lost its lead, the stimulus generally provided to Western economies by the introduction of railway systems throughout much of the world carried the Continent and America far enough and fast enough to allow them to become genuine competitors with the British.

Railways as a stimulus to the European and American economies

Railways came into being in answer to two needs. The first was the obvious desire on the part of entrepreneurs to transport their goods as quickly and cheaply as possible across long distances. Despite already mentioned improvements in transportation during the years before 1830, the movement of heavy materials, particularly coal, remained a problem. It is significant that the first modern railway was built in England in 1825 from the Durham coal field of Stockton to Darlington, near the coast. "Tramways"—parallel tracks along which coal carts were pulled by horses—had long been in use at pitheads to haul coal short distances. The Stockton to Darlington railway was a logical extension of this device, designed to answer the transportation needs produced by constantly expanding industrial-

Railways as goods carriers

See color map facing page 685

The New Railway Age. Left: Stephenson's *Rocket.* A reconstruction of the railway engine built by George Stephenson in 1829. Right: "The Railway Juggernaut of 1845." A cartoon from the English humor magazine *Punch* satirizing speculation—often financially disastrous—in railway stocks.

Railways as an investment opportunity

Thomas Brassey

ization. The man primarily responsible for the design of the first steam railway was George Stephenson, a self-made engineer who had not learned to read until he was seventeen. He talked a group of northern England investors into the merits of steam traction and was given full liberty to carry out his plans. The locomotives on the Stockton-Darlington line traveled at fifteen miles per hour, the fastest rate at which machines had yet moved people overland.

Railways were also built in response to other than purely industrial needs: specifically, the need for capitalists to invest their money. Englishmen such as those who had made sizable fortunes in textiles, once they had paid out workers' wages and plowed back substantial capital in their factories, retained a surplus profit for which they wanted a decent yet reliable return. Railways provided them with the solution to their problem. Though by no means as reliable as had been hoped, railway investment proved capable of more than satisfying the capitalists' demands. No sooner did the first combined passenger and goods service open in 1830, on the Liverpool to Manchester line, than plans were formulated and money pledged to extend rail systems throughout Europe, the Americas, and beyond. In 1830, there were no more than a few dozen miles of railway in the world. By 1840, there were over 4,500 miles; by 1850, over 23,000. The English contractor, Thomas Brassey, the most famous, but by no means the only one of his kind, built railways in Italy, Canada, Argentina, India, and Australia.

The railway boom accelerated industrialization generally. Not only did it increase enormously the demand for coal and for a variety of heavy manufactured goods—rails, locomotives, carriages, signals, switches; by enabling goods to move faster from factory to salesroom, railways decreased the time it took to sell those goods. Quicker sales meant, in turn, a quicker return on capital investment, money that could then be reinvested in the manufacture of more goods. Finally, by opening up the world market as it had never been before, the railway boom stimulated the production of such a quantity of material goods as to ensure the rapid completion of the West's industrialization.

The effect of railways on regional manufacturing, however, was not always positive. Clearly, they were a means of moving large amounts of manufactured goods economically from a given region to more widely dispersed markets. But they also brought competition in the form of an influx of goods from outside to challenge local industries. The case of the Dijon area southeast of Paris illustrates the problem. With the coming of the railway, brewers and winegrowers there expanded their trade for a time. Eventually, however, they lost business when railways made possible the long-distance transportation of beer and wine from Alsace and the south of France, which undercut locally produced commodities.

The building of a railway line was an undertaking on a scale infinitely greater than the building of a factory. Railway construction required capital investment beyond the capacity of any single individual. In Britain, a factory might be worth anywhere from £20,000 to £200,000. The average cost of twenty-seven of the more important railway lines constructed between 1830 and 1853 was £2 million. The average labor force of a factory ranged from 50 to 300. The average labor force of a railway, after construction, was 2,500. Because a railway crossed the property of a large number of individual landowners, each of whom would naturally demand as much remuneration as he thought he could get, the planning of an efficient and economical route was a tricky and time-consuming business. The entrepreneur and contractor had to concern themselves not only with the purchase of right-of-way. They also contended with problems raised by the destruction of sizable portions of already existing urban areas, to make

An American Proposal for a Steam-Driven Trolley. The application of the steam engine to transportation inspired inventors to devise novel solutions to perceived problems. This particular steam engine was disguised so as not to frighten horses on crowded city streets.

Construction of the London to Birmingham Railway, London, 1838. This drawing of the building of retaining walls in a new railway cut evokes the chaos created by railway construction within urban areas.

room for stations and switching yards. And they had to select a route that would be as free as possible of the hills and valleys that would necessitate the construction of expensive tunnels, cuts, and embankments. Railway-builders ran tremendous risks. Portions of most lines were subcontracted at fixed bids to contractors of limited experience. A spate of bad weather might delay construction to the point where builders would be lucky to bring in the finished job within 25 percent of their original bid. Of the thirty major contractors on the London to Birmingham line, ten failed completely.

The "navvies"

If the business of a contractor was marked by uncertainty, that of the construction worker was characterized by back-breaking labor. The "navvies," who built railways not only throughout Britain but around the world, were a remarkable breed. Their name derived from "navigator," a term applied to the construction workers on England's eighteenth-century canals. The work that they accomplished was prodigious. Because there is little friction between a train's wheels and its tracks, it can transport heavy loads easily. But lack of friction ceases to be an advantage when a train has to climb or descend a grade, thereby running the risk of slippage. Hence the need for comparatively level roadbeds; and hence the need for laborers to construct those tunnels, cuts, and embankments that would keep the roadbeds level. Navvies worked in gangs, whose migrations throughout the countryside traced the course of railway development. They were a rough lot, living in temporary encampments, often with women who were not their wives. The Irish navvies were a particularly tough breed. A sign posted by local residents in Scotland in 1845 warned that if all the Irish navvies were not "off the ground and out of the country" in a week, they would be driven out "by the strength of our armes and a good pick shaft."

Railway Navvies. Without the aid of machinery, the burden of building Britain's railways fell on the backs of men such as these.

The Dresden Railway Station. Railways had the power to alter the architecture of the city, producing new and dramatic urban spaces.

The magnitude of the navvies' accomplishment was extraordinary. In England and in much of the rest of the world, mid–nineteenth-century railways were constructed almost entirely without the aid of machinery. An assistant engineer on the London to Birmingham line, in calculating the magnitude of that particular construction, determined that the labor involved was the equivalent of lifting 25 billion cubic feet of earth and stone one foot high. This he compared with the feat of building the Great Pyramid, a task he estimated had involved the hoisting of some 16 billion tons. But whereas the building of the pyramid had required over 200,000 men and had taken twenty years, the construction of the London to Birmingham railway was accomplished by 20,000 men in less than five years. Translated into individual terms, a navvy was expected to move an average of twenty tons of earth per day. Railways were laid upon an almost infinite base of human muscle and sweat.

The magnitude of the navvies' achievement

4. INDUSTRIALIZATION AFTER 1850

In the years between 1850 and 1870, Britain remained very much the industrial giant of the West. But France, Germany, Belgium, and the United States assumed the position of challengers. In the iron industry, Britain's rate of growth during these years was not as great as that of either France

Britain still the leader

or Germany (5.2 percent for Britain, as against 6.7 percent for France and 10.2 percent for Germany). But in 1870 Britain was still producing half the world's pig iron; 3.5 times as much as the United States, more than 4 times as much as Germany, and more than 5 times as much as France. Although the number of cotton spindles increased from 5.5 to 11.5 million in the United States between 1852 and 1861, and by significant but not as spectacular percentages in European countries, Britain in 1861 had 31 million spindles at work in comparison with France's 5.5 million, Germany's 2 million, Switzerland's 1.3 million, and Austria's 1.8 million.

Continuing European advance

Most of the gains experienced in Europe came as a result of continuing changes in those areas we have come to recognize as important for sustained industrial growth: transport, commerce, and government policy. The improved transportation systems that resulted from the spread of railways helped encourage an increase in the free movement of goods. International monetary unions were established, and restrictions removed on international waterways such as the Danube. The Prussian *Zollverein,* or tariff union, an organization designed to facilitate internal free trade, was established in 1818 and was extended over the next twenty years to include most of the German principalities outside Austria. Free trade went hand in hand with further removal of barriers to the freedom to enter trades and to practice business unhampered by restrictive regulation. Control of guilds and corporations over artisan production was abolished in Austria in 1859 and in most of Germany by the mid-1860s. Laws against usury, most of which had ceased to be enforced, were officially abandoned in Britain, Holland, Belgium, and in many parts of Germany. Governmental regulation of mining was surrendered by the Prussian state in the 1850s, freeing entrepreneurs to develop resources as they saw fit. The formation of investment banks proceeded apace, encouraged by an important increase in the money supply, and therefore an easing of credit, following the opening of the California gold fields in 1849.

Increased trade in raw materials

A further reason for increased European production was the growing trade in raw materials. Wool and hides imported from Australia helped diminish the consequences of the cotton shortage suffered after the outbreak of the United States Civil War and the Union blockade of the American South. Other importations—guano from the Pacific, vegetable oils from Africa, pyrites (sulfides) from Spain—stimulated the scale of food production and both altered and increased the manufacture of soap, candles, and finished textiles. Finally, discoveries of new sources of coal, particularly in the Pas-de-Calais region of France and in the Ruhr valley in Germany, had dramatic repercussions. Production of coal in France rose from 4.4 million to 13.3 million tons between 1850 and 1869; during the same years, German production increased from 4.2 million to 23.7 million tons.

The slower pace of industrialization in Eastern and Southern Europe

Industrialization in Eastern and Southern Europe after mid-century proceeded at a much slower pace than in Western Europe. This was in part a result of the fact that many Eastern regions played an increasingly specialized role in the economy of the Continent, providing food and agricultural materials to the West. The constantly growing demand for agricultural products from the East resulted in the development of agriculture as a major capitalist industry there. As they rationalized their operations for increased efficiency and hence profitability, entrepreneurs recognized the degree to which they were hampered by the outmoded economic practices of serfdom, a system that prevented the mobility of labor and thus the formation of an effective agricultural work force. Serfdom was abolished in most parts of Eastern and Southern Europe by 1850, and in Poland and Russia in the 1860s.

The fact that industry continued to take a back seat to agriculture does not mean, however, that Eastern Europe was without important manufacturing regions. By the 1880s, the number of men and women employed in the cotton industry in the Austrian province of Bohemia exceeded that in Saxony. In the Czechoslovakian region, textile industries, developed in the eighteenth century, continued to thrive. By the 1830s, there were machine-powered Czech cotton mills and iron works. In Russia, a factory industry producing coarse textiles—mostly linens—had grown up around Moscow. At mid-century, Russia was purchasing 24 percent of the total British machinery exports to mechanize its own mills. Many workers in Russian industry remained serfs until the 1860s—about 40 percent, a number of them employed in mines. Of the over 800,000 Russians engaged in manufacturing by 1860, however, most labored not in factories but in very small workshops, where average employment numbered about 40 persons.

Pockets of industrialization in the East

By 1870 Europe was by no means a fully industrialized continent. Fifty percent of France's labor force remained on farms. Agricultural laborers were the single largest occupational category in Britain during the 1860s. Great stretches of the Continent—Spain, southern Italy, Eastern Europe—were almost untouched by the Industrial Revolution. And in the industrialized countries, much work was still accomplished in tiny workshops or at home. Yet if Europe was by no means wholly industrial, it was far and away the most industrially advanced portion of the globe—and not by accident. In order to maintain its position of producer and seller to the world, Europe, and Britain particularly, made certain that no other areas stood a chance to compete. Europe used its economic and, when necessary, its military strength to ensure that the world remained divided between the producers of manufactured goods—Europe itself—and suppliers of the necessary raw materials and buyers of finished goods—everyone else. Often this arrangement suited those in other parts of the world who made their money by providing the raw materials that fueled the European economy. Cotton-growers in the southern United States, sugar-growers in the Caribbean, wheat-growers in the Ukraine—all remained content with arrangements as dictated by the industrialized West. Those countries that expressed their discontent—Egypt, for example, which in the 1830s attempted to establish its own cotton textile industry—were soon put in their place by a show of force. Western Europeans, believing in their right to industrial leadership in the world, saw nothing wrong with employing soldiers, if they had to, to make others understand their destiny.

Europe's economy within the world

SELECTED READINGS

• *Items so designated are available in paperback editions.*

• Ashton, T. S., *The Industrial Revolution, 1760–1830,* London, 1948. A standard short introduction.

Cameron, R. E., *France and the Industrial Development of Europe,* Princeton, 1968. Valuable material on the Industrial Revolution outside Britain.

Checkland, S. G., *The Rise of Industrial Society in England, 1815–1885,* New York, 1965. Emphasizes the economic organization of England.

• Deane, Phyllis, *The First Industrial Revolution,* Cambridge, 1965.

Henderson, W. O., *The Industrialization of Europe, 1780–1914,* New York, 1969.

———, *The State and the Industrial Revolution in Prussia, 1740–1870,* Liverpool, 1958. A biographical approach. Good on technical education.

• Hobsbawn, Eric, *Industry and Empire: 1750 to the Present Day,* New York, 1968. A general survey of industrialization in Britain, written from a Marxist perspective.

• Landes, David S., *Revolution in Time: Clocks and the Making of the Modern World,* Cambridge, Mass., 1983. The social and economic changes wrought by the advent of cheap and accurate time-keeping.

• ———, *The Unbound Prometheus,* London, 1969. An excellent treatment of the technological innovations and economic results of the Industrial Revolution.

McManners, John, *European History: Men, Machines and Freedom,* New York, 1967.

• Mantoux, Paul, *The Industrial Revolution in the Eighteenth Century,* rev. ed., New York, 1961. The beginnings of the modern factory system in England.

• Mathias, Peter, *The First Industrial Revolution: An Economic History of Britain,* 2nd ed., London, 1983. An important general study of the industrialization process.

Schofer, Lawrence, *The Formation of a Modern Labor Force, 1865–1914,* Berkeley, 1975. Analyzes industrialization and its social consequences in Silesia.

• Taylor, George Rogers, *The Transportation Revolution, 1815–1860,* New York, 1968.

SOURCE MATERIALS

Dodd, George, *Days at the Factories; or the Manufacturing Industry of Great Britain Described, and Illustrated by Numerous Engravings of Machines and Processes,* Totawa, N.J., 1978. A reprint of the 1843 edition.

Mitchell, Brian R., and Phyllis Deane, *Abstract of British Historical Statistics,* Cambridge, 1962. The single best source for statistics on population, trade, manufacturing, etc.

• Smith, Adam, *An Inquiry into the Nature and Causes of the Wealth of Nations,* Chicago, 1977. Written in 1776, this revolutionary work called for the end of mercantilism.

Ward, J. T., *The Factory System, 1830–1855,* New York, 1970. Excerpts from contemporary documents describing, defending, and criticizing the factory system and industrialization.

Chapter 21

CONSEQUENCES OF INDUSTRIALIZATION: URBANIZATION AND CLASS CONSCIOUSNESS (1800–1850)

What Art was to the ancient world, Science is to the modern: The distinctive faculty. In the minds of men the useful has succeeded the beautiful. Yet rightly understood, Manchester is as great a human exploit as Athens.

—Benjamin Disraeli, *Coningsby*

The Industrial Revolution was more than an important event in the economic and technological history of the West. It helped to reshape the patterns of life for men and women, first in Britain, then in Europe and America, and eventually throughout much of the world. By increasing the scale of production, the Industrial Revolution brought about the factory system, which in turn compelled the migration of millions from the countryside and small towns into cities. Once in those cities, men and women had to learn a new way of life, and learn it quickly: how to discipline themselves to the factory whistle and survive in a slum, if they were first-generation urban workers; how to manage a work force and achieve respectable prominence for themselves in the community, if they were businessmen and their wives. One particular lesson that industrialization and urbanization taught was that of class consciousness. Men and women, to a far greater degree than heretofore, began to perceive themselves as part of a class with interests of its own, and in opposition to the interests of men and women in other classes.

We shall examine this range of social and cultural changes as they occurred during the first fifty years or so of the nineteenth century, after looking briefly first at the condition of the bulk of the population, which, despite industrialization, remained on the land. Since the Industrial Revo-

Consequences of the Industrial Revolution

lution came first to Britain, our focus will be on that country. Yet the pattern set by the British was one that was repeated to a great extent in other European countries, as industrialization came to them in time.

1. PEOPLE ON THE LAND

Population patterns

The dramatic story of the growth of industrialization and urbanization must not be allowed to obscure the fact that, in 1850, the population of Europe was still overwhelmingly a peasant population. While in England, by 1830, a sizable minority lived in towns and cities, elsewhere society remained predominantly or overwhelmingly rural. In France and Italy, 60 percent lived in the country; in Prussia, over 70 percent; in Spain, over 90 percent; in Russia, over 95 percent. Demographic pressures, which helped produce chaos in the cities, likewise caused severe hardship in the countryside. The populations of the predominantly agricultural nations lept forward with those that were industrializing. The population of Europe as a whole, estimated roughly at 205 million by 1800, had risen to 274 million by 1850, and to 320 million by 1870. In Britain, with its comparatively high standard of living, the numbers increased from 16 million to 27 million. Yet the rural Irish, despite their periodic famines, increased too, from 5.5 to 8 million, and the Russians from 39 to 60 million, in the same period.

Causes of continuing population expansion

The causes of this continuing population explosion remain obscure. The notion that the explanation can be traced to a desire on the part of parents in industrial countries to produce more family wage-earners is now downplayed by scholars, given the fact that increases occurred in rural regions as well. One contributing factor to this continued growth may have been a decline in the virulence of certain fatal diseases as a result of the cyclical potency of microbes. Certainly the curbing of cholera, through the adoption of sanitary reforms, and smallpox, as Edward Jenner's technique of vaccination gained gradual acceptance after 1796, help to explain the population trend. The increasing ability and desire of governments to monitor and improve the lives of their subjects had a direct effect on the decline of the death rate. At the same time the availability of less expensive foods of high nutritional value—most notably the potato—and the ability to transport foodstuffs cheaply by rail meant European populations would not suffer as much from undernourishment as in the past, and that they would thus be less susceptible to debilitating illness. Other plausible explanations suggest that the population increase was the result of rising birth rates caused by earlier marriages. As serfdom declined, peasants tended to set up households at a younger age. The spread of cottage industries also allowed more rural couples to marry and set up households even without the inheritance of land. This "proletarianization" of the countryside contributed not only to lowered age at marriage but also to a higher number of marriages. A relatively small expansion in the population of a region in one generation would result in a far greater one in the next. As the population grew, the

The Home of a Rural Laborer. This etching from *Punch* portrays the hunger that came with a bad harvest, and could lead to rural violence.

number of young and fertile people grew faster, thereby significantly increasing the ratio of births to total population.

Whatever the reasons for the population increase, conditions remained such as to make the life of the poorer rural inhabitants of Europe seldom more than bleak. Overpopulation brought underemployment, and hence poverty, in its train. Millions of tiny holdings produced a bare subsistence living, if that. Farmers still sowed and harvested by hand. Conditions in rural areas deteriorated sharply whenever there was a bad harvest. The average daily diet for an entire family in a "good" year might amount to no more than two or three pounds of bread—a total of about 3,000 calories. Hunger—often near-starvation—as well as epidemic disease were still common occurrences. The result was a standard of living—if one can dignify the condition with that name—that for many rural inhabitants of many areas in Europe actually declined in the first half of the nineteenth century, although not enough to reverse general population growth. Governments in some countries attempted to solve the related problems of population pressure and impoverishment by passing laws raising the age of marriage. In some of the states of southern and western Germany, as well as in Austria, men were forbidden to marry before the age of thirty, and were also required to prove their ability to support a family. Governments did their best to encourage emigration to ease the overcrowding, the majority of emigrants relocating in the Americas. Emigration from England rose from 57,000 in 1830, to 90,000 in 1840, to 280,000 in 1850. Ireland, in the

Wretched rural conditions

early years of the nineteenth century, witnessed the departure of over 1.5 million before the great potato famine of 1846, when approximately three out of every four acres of potatoes were blighted. After the potato famine, the flow of emigrants increased to a flood.

Agricultural capitalism

Even had such policies acted as an effective curb on population growth—which, in the main, they did not—they would nevertheless have failed to prevent the rural stresses that resulted from the continuing spread of agricultural capitalism. The pace of this change varied across Europe; it was furthest advanced in England and Prussia. Wherever landed proprietors determined to meet increased demand for food by farming large areas as a capital investment, they imposed a series of transformations that were bound to affect the lives of agricultural laborers. First, land must be made a negotiable commodity. It must not, therefore, be tied to ancient customs that clouded its title—as was the case, for example, with common land, to which the poor within a community might have some right of access or cultivation. Second, land must be in the hands of those with capital enough to improve it, in order to make of it a profitable investment. It must be en-closed—"regulated" was the term in Prussia—so that, as we have seen, it could be properly fertilized and drained, or, if it was grazing land, so that breeds might be scientifically improved without fear of mongrelization. Fi-nally, a mobile force of agricultural laborers must be available to work at the capitalists' behest. They must not be "tied" to a particular piece of land, either through systems of customary rights or bondage. They must be free to go where they were told to go, to work whatever land would bring most profit to its owners.

Its results

These requirements, as they were imposed, produced dislocation and hardship. In Scotland, workers were cleared from land that they had farmed as tenants, in order to provide pasturage for the more profitable sheep. In Germany, those serfs emancipated by a reform-minded government in 1807 were compelled to forfeit somewhere between a third to a half of their land in return for their freedom; those who were able to retain small holdings were in most cases pressured to sell out to larger landholders. Not all landlords were ruthless. "Model" improvers among the wealthiest of the English landowners adjusted to capitalist competition without entirely for-swearing traditional responsibilities. They built houses for tenants and la-borers, and provided them with schools and churches. In Eastern Europe there were among the Prussian landlords (Junkers) pietists who acknowl-edged obligations to their tenants as well as to the market.

Variations in the pattern of agricultural development

The speed with which agricultural change occurred in various parts of Europe depended upon the nature of particular governments. Those more sympathetic to new capitalist impulses facilitated the transfer and reorgani-zation of land by means of enabling legislation. They encouraged the elimi-nation of small farms and an increase in larger, more efficient units of pro-duction. In England, over half the total area of the country, excluding waste land, was composed of estates of a thousand acres or more. In Spain, the fortunes of agricultural capitalism fluctuated with the political tenor of successive regimes: with the coming of a liberal party to power in 1820

A Mowing Team in England. Roughly twenty men and boys wielding scythes were required for work that a single threshing machine could accomplish in the same time. In 1870, when this photograph was taken, most threshing was done by machine.

came a law encouraging the free transfer of land; with the restoration of absolutism in 1823 came a repeal of the law. Russia was one of the countries least affected by agricultural change in the first half of the nineteenth century. There land was worked in vast blocks; some of the largest landowners possessed over half a million acres. Until the emancipation of the serfs in the 1860s, landowners claimed the labor of dependent peasant populations for as much as several days per week. But the system of serfdom gave neither landowners nor serfs incentive to improve farming or land-management techniques.

European serfdom, which bound hundreds of thousands of men, women, and children to particular estates for generations, prohibited the use of land as a negotiable commodity and therefore prevented the development of agricultural entrepreneurship. In France, despite the fact that manorialism had been abolished by the Revolution, there was no rapid movement toward large-scale capitalist farming. An army of peasant proprietors, direct beneficiaries of the Jacobins' democratic constitution, continued to work the small farms they owned. The fact that France suffered far less agricultural distress, even in the 1840s, than did other European countries, and the fact that there was less migration in France from the country to the city and overseas than there was in Germany and England, are marks of the general success of this rural lower middle class in sustaining itself on the land. Its members were content to farm in the old way, opposed agricultural innovation, and, indeed, innovation generally. Despite their vener-

The legacy of manorialism

ation of the Revolution, they were among the most conservative elements in European society.

Rural societies and industrialization

Rural populations, though isolated from urban centers, found themselves directly affected by the events of the Industrial Revolution. Factories brought about a decline in cottage industry and a consequent loss of vital income, especially during winter months. Improved communication networks not only afforded rural populations a keener sense of events and opportunities elsewhere, but also made it possible for governments to intrude upon the lives of these men and women to a degree previously impossible. Central bureaucracies now found it easier to collect taxes from the peasantry, and to conscript its sons into their armies.

Rural disturbances

Country people responded with sporadic violence against these and other harsh intrusions upon their lives. In southern England in the late 1820s, small farmers joined forces to burn barns and hayricks in protest to the introduction of threshing machines, a symbol of the new agricultural capitalism. They masked and otherwise disguised themselves, riding out at night under the banner of their mythical leader, "Captain Swing." Their raids were preceded by anonymous threats such as the one received by a large-scale farmer in the county of Kent: "Pull down your threshing machine or else [expect] fire without delay. We are five thousand men [a highly inflated figure] and will not be stopped." Other major rural disturbances occurred in Ireland, Silesia, and Galicia in the 1830s and 1840s, and indeed, to a lesser degree, right across Europe. In Russia, serf uprisings were a reaction to continued bad harvests and exploitation rather than to agricultural innovation and displacement. In no country, however, was the agrarian population a united political force. Those who owned land, those who leased it as tenants, and those who worked it as laborers had interests as different from each other as from those of the urban populations.

Agricultural Disturbances. Mob violence erupted in Kent in 1830 in protest against the introduction of threshing machines.

Manchester, England, at Mid-Century. This powerful photograph evokes the dreary, prison-like atmosphere of the new industrial city.

2. URBANIZATION AND THE STANDARD OF LIVING

If the countryside continued to hold the bulk of Europe's population in the years between 1800 and 1850, the growth of cities nevertheless remains one of the most important facts in the social history of that period. Cities grew in size and number once the steam engine made it practical to bring together large concentrations of men, women, and children to work in factories. Steam engines freed entrepreneurs from their dependence on water power and allowed them to consolidate production in large cities. In cities, transportation was more accessible than in the countryside. Hence it was less costly to import raw materials and ship out finished goods. Workers were more readily available in cities, as well, attracted as they were in large numbers in the hope—often false—of finding steady work at higher wages than those paid agricultural laborers. Industrialization was not the only reason for the growth of cities in the early nineteenth century, however. General population increases combined with industrialization, forcing cities to expand at an alarming rate.

Reasons for the growth of cities

In the ten years between 1831 and 1841 London's population grew by 130,000, Manchester's by 70,000. Paris increased by 120,000 between 1841 and 1846. Vienna grew by 125,000 from 1827 to 1847, into a city of 400,000. Berlin had as large a population by 1848, having increased by 180,000 since 1815. The primary result in these and other fast-growing centers was dreadful overcrowding. Construction lagged far behind popula-

Urban population increases

Women and Boys Fetching Water from a Standpipe in Fryingpan Alley, London. Not until the beginning of the twentieth century did major European cities begin to provide poorer residents with an adequate water supply.

tion growth. In Vienna, though population rose 42 percent during the twenty years before 1847, the increase in housing was only 11.5 percent. In many of the larger cities, old and new, working men and women lived in lodging houses, apart from families left behind in the country. The poorest workers in almost all European cities dwelt in wretched basement rooms, often without any light or drainage.

With cities as overcrowded as they were, it is no wonder that they were a menace to the health of those who lived within them. The middle classes moved as far as possible from disease and factory smoke, leaving the poorest members of the community isolated and a prey to the sickness that ravaged working-class sections. Cholera, typhus, and tuberculosis were natural predators in areas without adequate sewerage facilities and fresh water, and over which smoke from factories, railroads, and domestic chimneys hung heavily. A local committee appointed to investigate conditions in the British manufacturing town of Huddersfield—not by any means the worst of that country's urban centers—reported that there were large areas without paving, sewers, or drains, "where garbage and filth of every description are left on the surface to ferment and rot; where pools of stagnant water are almost constant; where dwellings adjoining are thus necessarily caused to be of an inferior and even filthy description; thus where disease is engendered, and the health of the whole town perilled." Measures were gradually adopted by successive governments in an attempt to cure the worst of these ills, if only to prevent the spread of catastrophic epidemics. Legislation was designed to rid cities of their worst slums by tearing them down, and to improve sanitary conditions by supplying both water and drainage.

Cities as a health menace

Yet by 1850, these projects had only just begun. Paris, perhaps better supplied with water than any European city, had enough for no more than two baths per capita per year; in London, human waste remained uncollected in 250,000 domestic cesspools; in Manchester, fewer than a third of the dwellings were equipped with toilets of any sort.

Conditions such as these are important evidence in the debate that has occupied historians for the past several decades. The question is: Did the standard of living rise or fall in Europe during the first half century of the Industrial Revolution? One school, the "optimists," argues that workers shared in the more general increase in living standards which occurred throughout Europe from 1800 onward. A variation on this optimistic theme maintains that whatever the hardships workers were compelled to suffer during the period of intense industrialization after 1800, they represent the necessary and worthwhile price society had to pay before it could "take off" into a period of "sustained economic growth." Sacrifices, in terms of standard of living, were required to permit accumulation of a capital base sufficient to guarantee economic expansion and an eventual level of general prosperity higher than any civilization had hitherto achieved. Other historians insist that such an analysis encourages one to ignore the evidence of physical squalor and psychological disruption that men, women, and children suffered as they provided the statistical "base" for future economic historians' abstract calculations.

The standard of living debate

The debate is hampered by an absence of reliable evidence about wage levels, hours of work, and cost of living. Some skilled workers within the new factories, along with some artisans in older trades as yet unaffected by industrialization, appear to have benefited from a slight rise in wages and a decline in living costs. But regional variables, along with a constantly fluctuating demand for labor in all countries, suggest that the more lowly paid, unskilled worker, whether in England or on the Continent, led a thoroughly precarious existence. Textile workers in England, if guaranteed

Instability and unemployment

Soup Kitchen Run by Quakers, Manchester, England, 1862. Enterprises of this sort, which doled out charity "indiscriminately"—that is, without investigating the recipient' character—were condemned by many members of the middle class as encouraging the "worst" elements—idlers and loafers—among the poor.

something like full employment, could theoretically earn enough to support a family. Such was not the case in Switzerland, however, where similar work paid only half what was necessary, or in Saxony, where a large portion of the population was apparently dependent upon either poor relief or charity. One of the most depressing features of working-class life in these years was its instability. Economic depressions were common occurrences; when they happened, workers were laid off for weeks at a time, with no system of unemployment insurance to sustain them. Half the working population of England's industrial cities was out of work in the early 1840s. In Paris, 85,000 went on relief in 1840. One particularly hard-pressed district of Silesia reported 30,000 out of 40,000 citizens in need of relief in 1844. Nor should one overlook the plight of those whose skills had been replaced by machinery—the hand-loom weavers being the most notable examples. In the English manufacturing town of Bolton, a hand-loom weaver could earn no more than about three shillings per week in 1842, at a time when experts estimated it took at least twenty shillings a week to keep a family of five above the poverty line. On that kind of pay, workers were fortunate if they did not starve to death. Forced to spend something like 65 percent of their income on food, the per capita meat consumption of the average worker declined to about forty pounds per year in the early nineteenth century.

Stress of urban life

Such figures make the optimists' generalizations hard to countenance. Figures of whatever sort fail to take into account the stress that urban factory life imposed upon the workers. Even workers making thirty shillings a week might well wonder if they were "better off," forced as they were to come to terms with the factory disciplines and living conditions imposed upon them. Of the more than 3 million men, women, and children living in England's sixty largest towns and cities in 1850, less than half had been born there. Though most migrated but a short distance from their place of birth, the psychological distance they traveled was tremendous. These qualitative factors, admittedly difficult to assess, must be weighed along with more easily quantifiable evidence before reaching any conclusion as to the increased standard of living in early-nineteenth-century cities. Whether or not life in cities was pleasant or ghastly, however, it was, for rapidly increasing numbers, a fact of life. Once we examine that life we will better understand the full impact of industrialization and urbanization upon those who first experienced it.

3. THE LIFE OF THE URBAN MIDDLE CLASS

Urban middle class

The urban middle class that emerged during this period was by no means one homogeneous unit, in terms of occupation or income. In a general category that includes merchant princes and humble shopkeepers, subdivisions are important. The middle class included families of industrialists, such as the Peels (cotton) in England and, at a later period, the Krupps (iron) in Germany. It included financiers like the internationally famed Rothschilds, and, on a descending scale of wealth and power, bankers and capitalists throughout the major money markets of Europe: London, Brussels, Paris, Berlin. It included entrepreneurs like Thomas Brassey, the British railway magnate, and John Wilkinson, the English ironmaster, who had himself buried in an iron coffin, and technicians, like the engineer Isambard Kingdom Brunel, designer of the steamship *The Great Western*. It included bureaucrats, in growing demand when governments began to regulate the pace and direction of industrialization, and to ameliorate its harshest social and economic results. It included those in the already established professions—in law particularly, as lawyers put their expertise to the service of industrialists. It included the armies of managers and clerks necessary to the continuing momentum of industrial and financial expansion, and the equally large army of merchants and shopkeepers necessary to supply the wants of an increasingly affluent urban middle-class population. Finally, it included the families of all those who lived their lives in the various subcategories we have listed.

Movement within these ranks was often possible, in the course of one or two generations. Movement from the working class into the middle class, however, was far less common. Most middle-class successes originated within the middle class itself—the children of farmers, skilled artisans, or professionals. Upward mobility was almost impossible without education; education was an expensive, if not unattainable luxury for the children of a laborer. Careers open to talents, that goal achieved by the French Revolution, frequently meant middle-class jobs for middle-class young men who could pass exams. The examination system was an important path for ascendancy within governmental bureaucracies.

If passage from working class to middle class was not common, neither was the equally difficult social journey from middle class to aristocratic, landed society. In Britain, mobility of this sort was easier than on the Continent. Children from wealthy upper-middle-class families, if they were sent, as occasionally they were, to elite schools and universities, and if they left the commercial or industrial world for a career in politics, might effect the change. William Gladstone, son of a Liverpool merchant, attended the exclusive educational preserves of Eton, a private boarding school, and Oxford University, married a connection of the aristocratic Grenville family, and became prime minister of England. Yet Gladstone was an exception to the rule in Britain, and Britain was an exception to the Continent. Movement, when it occurred, generally it did so in less spectacular degrees.

Nevertheless, the European middle class helped sustain itself with the belief that it was possible to get ahead by means of intelligence, pluck, and serious devotion to work. The Englishman Samuel Smiles, in his extraordinarily successful how-to-succeed book *Self Help* (1859), preached a gospel dear to the middle class. "The spirit of self-help is the root of all genuine growth in the individual," Smiles wrote. "Exhibited in the lives of many, it constitutes the true source of national vigor and strength." A corollary to Smiles's discussion was the moral obligation to use the fruits of success in

Isambard Kingdom Brunel. Behind him are lengths of anchor chain from the steamship *The Great Western*.

Movement from the middle class to the aristocracy

Self-help

Left: *A Salon in Vienna, 1830s.* A representation of middle-class home life on the Continent. Right: *A Victorian Family at Tea, 1860s*

accordance with middle-class notions of respectability. Although Smiles's gospel declared that anyone willing to exert himself could rise to a position of responsibility and personal profit, however, and although some men actually did so, the notion remained no more than myth for the great majority.

Seriousness of purpose was reflected in the middle-class devotion to the ideal of family and home. A practical importance attached to the institution of the family in those areas in England, France, and Germany where sons, sons-in-law, nephews, and cousins were expected to assume responsibility in family firms when it came their turn. Yet the worship of family more often ignored those practical considerations and assumed the proportions of sacred belief. Away from the business and confusion of the world, sheltered behind solid masonry and amid the solid comfort of their ornate furnishings, middle-class fathers retired each evening to enjoy the fruits of their daily labors. Indeed, this retreat served as a reaffirmation of power and position for men whose success in the business world might be tenuous and insecure. Inside the home, life was enclosed in a hierarchical and ritualistic system under which the husband and father was master. His wife was called his helpmate, and very occasionally within the middle class—especially in France—a wife might serve as shopkeeper or business associate with her husband. Far more frequently, however, a middle-class wife was treated by her spouse as a kind of superior servant. Her task was to keep the houshold functioning smoothly and harmoniously. She maintained the accounts and directed the activities of the servants—usually two or three women. Called

Family and home

in Victorian England the "Angel in the House," the middle-class woman was responsible for the moral education of her children. Yet she probably spent no more than two or three hours a day at most with her offspring. Until sent to school, they were placed in the custody of a nursemaid or governess. Much of a middle-class woman's day was spent in the company of other women from similar households. An elaborate set of social customs involving "calls" and "at homes" was established in European middle-class society. Women were not expected to improve their minds. They were not expected to be the intellectual companions of their husbands. Rather, they were encourged to be dabblers, education for them usually consisting of little more beyond reading and writing, a smattering of arithmetic, geography, history, and a foreign language, embellished with lessons in drawing, painting in watercolors, singing, or piano-playing.

Queen Victoria, who ascended the British throne in 1837, labored to make her solemn—occasionally almost stolid—public image reflect the feminine middle-class virtues of moral probity and dutiful domesticity. Her public reflection of private virtue emphasized the middle-class reliance upon image and appearance as an indicator of an underlying reality. Her court was eminently proper and preeminently bourgeois, a marked contrast to that of her uncle George IV, whose fleshly and unbuttoned ways had set the style for high life a generation before. Though possessing an imperious temper, Victoria trained herself to curb it in deference to her ministers and her public-spirited, ultra-respectable husband, Prince Albert of Saxe-Coburg. She was a successful queen because she embodied the traits dearest to the middle class, whose triumph she seemed to epitomize and whose habits of mind we have come to call Victorian.

Queen Victoria as prototype

Prince Albert and Queen Victoria. In this photograph by Roger Fenton the royal couple is depicted not as monarch and consort but as a conventional upper-middle-class married couple.

Sexuality

Middle-class wives were indoctrinated to believe that they were superior to their husbands in one area only. A wife was "the better half" of a middle-class marriage because she was deemed pure—the untainted Vestal of the hearth, unsullied by cares of the world outside her home, and certainly untouched by those sexual desires that marked her husband, her natural moral inferior. A wife's charge was to encourage her husband's "higher nature." She must never respond to his sexual advances with equal passion; passion was, for her, a presumed impossibility. If she *was* passionate, and private diaries suggest, not surprisingly, that many middle-class women were, she would find it hard not to feel guilty about the pleasures she was presumed too pure to taste. Contraception, other than withdrawal, was not common practice among the middle classes. The result was that for women, sexual intercourse was directly related to the problems of frequent pregnancies. (Victoria, who had nine children, declared that childbirth was "the shadow side" of marriage.)

Prostitution

The middle-class wife was expected to persuade her husband to seek, through love of home and family, a substitute for the baser instincts with which nature had unhappily endowed the male. Should she fail, she must accept the fact of her "failure" as she was bound to accept the rest of her life: uncomplainingly. That she often did fail was evidenced by the brisk trade in prostitution that flourished in nineteenth-century cities. In all European cities, prostitutes solicited openly. At mid-century the number of prostitutes in Vienna was estimated to be 15,000; in Paris, where prostitution was a licensed trade, 50,000; in London, 80,000. London newspaper reports of the 1850s catalogued the vast underworld of prostitutes and their followers: those who operated out of "lodging houses" run by unsavory entrepreneurs whose names—Swindling Sal, Lushing Loo—suggest their general character; the retinue of procurers, pimps, panderers, and "fancy men" who made the lives of common prostitutes little better than slavery; the relatively few "prima donnas" who enjoyed the protection of rich, upper-middle-class lovers, who entertained lavishly and whose wealth allowed them to move on the fringes of more respectable high society. The heroines of Alexandre Dumas's novel *La Dame aux Camilles,* and of Giuseppe Verdi's opera *La Traviata*—"the lost one"—were prototypes of women of this sort.

Prostitution. A contemporary comment bearing the title "That girl seems to know you, George!" intimates that, as the wife surmises, the flower girl has more to sell than her posies.

Infidelity

If a middle-class wife should herself succumb to "unwomanly desires" by taking a lover, and be discovered to have done so, she could expect nothing less than complete social banishment. The law tolerated a husband's infidelity and at all times respected a husband's rights both to his wife's person and to her property. It made quick work of an "unfaithful" wife, granting to her husband whatever he might desire in terms of divorce, property, and custody, to make amends to him for the personal wrongs and embarrassments he had suffered at the hands of his "unnatural" spouse.

Middle-class family rituals helped to sustain this hierarchy. Daily meals, with the father at the head of the table, were cooked and brought to each place by servants, who were a constant reminder of the family's social position. Family vacations were a particularly nineteenth-century middle-class

The Middle Class at Leisure. The "morning lounge" at Biarritz, a French resort on the Atlantic coast.

invention. Thanks to the advent of the railways, excursions of one or two weeks to the mountains or to the seashore were available to families of even moderate means. Entrepreneurs built large, ornate hotels, adorned with imposing names—Palace, Beau Rivage, Excelsior—and attracted middle-class customers by offering them on a grander scale exactly the same sort of comfortable and sheltered existence they enjoyed at home.

Family vacations

The houses and furnishings of the middle class were an expression of the material security the middle class valued. Solidly built, heavily decorated, they proclaimed the financial worth and social respectability of those who dwelt within. In provincial cities they were often freestanding "villas." In London, Paris, Berlin, or Vienna, they might be rows of five- or six-story townhouses, or large apartments. Whatever particular shape they took, they were built to last a long time. The rooms were certain to be crowded with furniture, art objects, carpets, and wall hangings. Chairs, tables, cabinets, and sofas might be of any or all periods; no matter, so long as they were adorned with their proper complement of fringe, gilt, or other ornamentation. The size of the rooms, the elegance of the furniture, the number of servants, all depended, of course, on the extent of one's income. A bank clerk did not live as elegantly as a bank director. Yet in all likelihood both lived in obedience to the same set of standards and aspirations. And that obedience helped bind them, despite the differences in their material way of life, to the same class.

Houses

See color plates following page 780 for *The Movings* by Boilly

The European middle class had no desire to confront the unpleasant urban by-products of its own success. Members of the middle class saw to it that they lived apart from the unpleasant sights and smells of industrialization. Their residential areas, usually built to the west of the cities, out of the path of the prevailing breeze, and therefore of industrial pollution, were havens from the congestion for which they were primarily responsible. When the members of the middle class rode into the urban centers they took care to do so over avenues lined with respectable shops, or across railway embankments that lifted them above monotonous working-class streets en route to their destination. Yet the middle class, though it turned its face from what it did not want to see, did not turn from the city. Middle-class men and women celebrated the city as their particular creation

Apartment Living in Paris. This print shows that on the Continent rich and poor often lived in the same buildings, the rich on the lower floors, the poor at the top. This sort of residential mixing was unknown in Britain.

The Paris Opera. An exterior view of the Opera. Designed by Charles Garnier, it was constructed between 1861 and 1875. This grandiose display of wealth and luxury epitomized the taste of the new industrial middle class.

and the source of their profits. They even praised its smoke—as a sign of prosperity—so long as they did not have to breathe it night and day. For the most part, it was they who managed their city's affairs. And it was they who provided new industrial cities with their proud architectural landmarks: city halls, stock exchanges, opera houses. These were the new cathedrals of the industrial age, proclamations of a triumphant middle class.

4. THE LIFE OF THE URBAN WORKING CLASS

Like the middle class, the working class was divided into various subgroups and categories, determined in this case by skill, wages, and workplace. The working class included skilled workers in crafts that were centuries old— glassblowing and cabinetmaking, for example. It included as well mechanics equally skilled in new industrial technology. It included the men who built textile machinery and the women and children who tended it. It included the men, women, and children who together worked in mines and quarries. And it included the countless millions who labored at unskilled jobs—dock workers, coal porters, cleaning women, and the like. The nature of workers' experiences naturally varied, depending upon where they worked, where they lived, and, above all, how much they earned. A skilled textile worker lived a life far different from that of a ditch digger, the former able to afford the food, shelter, and clothing necessary for a decent existence, the latter so busy trying to keep himself and his family alive that he would have little time to think about anything but the source of their next meal.

Ranks within the working class

Some movement from the ranks of the unskilled to the skilled was possible, if children were provided, or provided themselves, with at least a rudi-

Schools for the Poor. A rudimentary education could be the key to movement from unskilled to skilled worker.

Social mobility

mentary education. Yet education was considered by many parents a luxury, especially since children could be put to work at an early age to supplement a family's meager earnings. There was movement from skilled to unskilled also, as technological change—the introduction of the power loom, for example—drove highly paid workers into the ranks of the unskilled and destitute. Further variations within the working class were the result of the fact that though every year more men, women, and children were working in factories, the majority still labored either in workshops or at home. These variations mean that we cannot speak of a common European working-class experience during the years from 1800 to 1850. The life we shall be describing was most typical of English workers, during the first half century of their exposure to industrialization. Only in the years 1850–1900 did most Continental workers undergo this harsh process of urban acclimatization.

Housing

Life in industrial cities was, for almost all workers, uncomfortable at best and unbearably squalid at worst. Workers and their families lived in housing that failed to answer the needs of its inhabitants. In older cities single-family dwellings were broken up into apartments of often no more than one room per family. In new manufacturing centers, rows of tiny houses, located close by smoking factories, were built back-to-back, thereby eliminating any cross-ventilation or space for gardens. Whether housing was old or new, it was generally poorly built. Old buildings were allowed by landlords to fall into disrepair; new houses, constructed of cheap material, decayed quickly. Water often came from an outdoor tap, shared by several houses and adjacent to an outdoor toilet. Crowding was commonplace.

Families of as many as eight lived in two or, at the most, three rooms. A newspaper account from the 1840s noted that in Leeds, a textile center in northern Britain, an "ordinary" worker's house contained no more than 150 square feet, and that in most cases those houses were "crammed almost to suffocation with human beings both day and night." When, after 1850, governments began to rid cities of some of their worst slums, many working-class men and women discovered that urban "improvement" meant relocation into dreary "model" tenements whose amenities were matched by their barracklike anonymity; or removal from one dilapidated structure to another in the wake of a clearance scheme—the nineteenth century called

Nineteenth-Century Working-Class Housing. Faced with insatiable demands for urban accommodations, developers responded in a variety of ways. In Oldham (top left), a textile manufacturing center in the north of England, the answer was street after street of row houses; in Glasgow, Scotland (top right), it was multistory tenements; and in the suburbs of Paris (lower right), it was shanties. In all three settings, the result was essentially the same: a bleak existence born of overcrowding and squalor.

it "ventilation"—that replaced ancient, overcrowded housing with a more sanitary—and, for the landlord, more profitable—railway switching yard.

The life of women

The life of working-class wives and mothers was hard. Lack of cheap contraceptive devices and a belief that these devices were immoral helped to keep women pregnant through most of their childbearing years, thus endangering their general health and adding to the burden of their lives. Wives were usually handed a portion of the weekly wage packet by their husbands, and were expected to house, feed, and clothe the family on the very little they were given. Their daily life was a constant round of cooking, cleaning, shopping, and washing—in a tiny space and without enough money. Housewives could not rely, as in the country, on their own gardens to help supply them with food. Instead, they went to markets that catered to their needs with cheap goods, often stale or nearly rotten, or dangerously adulterated. Formaldehyde was added to milk to prevent spoilage. Pounded rice was mixed into sugar. Fine brown earth was introduced into cocoa. A woman's problems were compounded, of course, when she had to work, and therefore had far less time to accomplish the household tasks she was still expected to perform.

Women workers

Women were employed in growing numbers—along with children—in factories during the nineteenth century. Yet many more labored at home or in small workshops—"sweatshops," as they came to be called—for wretchedly low wages based not on the hours they worked but on the amount of work they did: so much per shirt stitched or matchbox glued. By far the greatest number of unmarried working-class young women worked as domestic servants, often a lonely occupation and one that occasionally trapped female servants into undesired sexual relationships with their male employers or their sons.

Female sexuality within the working classes of Western Europe was acknowledged in a way that it was not within the middle class. Demographic evidence reveals a sharp rise in illegitimacy between 1750 and 1850. In

A Laundress and Her Children. Note the cramped and cluttered living quarters.

Frankfurt, Germany, for example, where the illegitimacy rate had been a mere 2 percent in the early 1700s, it reached 25 percent in 1850. In Bordeaux, France, in 1840, one-third of the recorded births were illegitimate. Reasons for this increase are difficult to establish. Illegitimacy in Germany may have been the result of laws forbidding the poor to marry. Certainly, increased mobility meant weaker family ties, less parental supervision, and greater opportunity for an unrestricted life. This is not to say that the majority of working-class women were sexually promiscuous. Premarital intercourse was an accepted practice in preindustrial villages, but, because of the social controls that dominated village life, it was almost always a precursor to marriage. In the far more anonymous setting of a factory town, such controls often did not exist. In addition, the economic uncertainties of the early industrial age meant that a young workingman's promise of marriage based on his expectation of a job might frequently be difficult to fulfill. The same economic uncertainty led some young working-class women to a career—usually temporary—as prostitutes. The anonymity of city life encouraged prostitution. Middle-class men, prepared to postpone marriage until they could afford a house and furnishings reflecting the social position to which they aspired, turned to the sexual underworld to satisfy their desires. Class consciousness encouraged them to regard working-class women—prostitutes or not—as easy prey, possessed of coarser natures and therefore a lesser breed of womankind than the middle-class "ladies" they intended eventually to marry.

Sexuality

New cities could be lonely places, particularly for working-class men and women struggling to cope with an alien environment. If possible, they would live near relatives who had already made the transition and who could assist the newcomers in adjusting to their very different existence. In many cities working-class families lived in districts inhabited primarily by others working at the same trade—weavers in one place, miners in another—and in this way achieved some sense of commonality.

Loneliness

Adjustment to the demands of the factory was every bit as difficult for workers as was acceptance of urban living patterns. The factory system, emphasizing as it did standard rather than individual work patterns, denied skilled laborers the pride in craft that had previously been theirs. Many workers found themselves stripped of the reassuring protection of guilds and formal apprenticeships which had bound their predecessors to a particular trade or place, and which were outlawed or sharply curtailed by legislation in France, Germany, and Britain in the first half of the nineteenth century. Factory hours were long; before 1850 usually twelve to fourteen hours a day. Conditions were dirty and dangerous. Textile mills remained unventilated, so that bits of material lodged in workers' lungs. Machines were unfenced and were a particular danger to child workers, often hired, because of their supposed agility, to clean under and around the moving parts. Manufacturing processes were unhealthy. The use of poison lead in the making of glazed pottery, for example, was a constant hazard to men and women workers in that industry. Surveys by British physicians in the 1840s catalogued the toll that long factory hours and harsh working condi-

*Conditions in factories
and mines*

tions were taking, particularly on young workers. Spinal curvature and other bone malformations resulted from standing hour after hour in unnatural positions at machines. Varicose veins and fallen arches were also common. One concerned doctor stated his belief that "from what I saw myself, a large mass of deformity has been produced by the factory system." And what was true of factories was true as well of mines, in which over fifty thousand children and young people were employed in Britain in 1841. Children were used to haul coal to underground tramways or shafts. The youngest were set to work—often for as long as twelve hours at a stretch—operating doors that regulated the ventilation in the mines. When they fell asleep, which, because of long hours, they frequently did, they jeopardized the safety of the entire work force. Women—sometimes pregnant women—were employed to haul coal and perform other strenuous underground tasks. Lung diseases—popularly known as "black spittle"—and eye infections, not to mention the danger of explosions caused by trapped gas, were constant threats to life and limb in the mines.

Daily routine

As upsetting as the physical working conditions was the psychological readjustment demanded of the first-generation workers in the factories. Preindustrial laborers had to work long hours and for very little monetary reward. Yet, at least to some degree, they were free to set their own hours and structure their own activities, to move from their home workshops to

"Capital and Labour." In its earliest years, *Punch,* though primarily a humorous weekly, manifested a strong social conscience. In this 1843 cartoon, the capitalists are seen revelling in the rewards of their investments while the workers—men, women, and children—who toiled in the mines under cruel and dangerous conditions are found crippled and starving.

their small garden plots and back again as they wished. In a factory, all "hands" learned the discipline of the whistle. To function efficiently, a factory demanded that all employees begin and end work at the same time. Most workers could not tell time; fewer possessed clocks. None was accustomed to the relentless pace of the machine. In order to increase production, the factory system encouraged the breaking down of the manufacturing process into specialized steps, each with its own assigned time, an innovation that upset workers accustomed to completing a task at their own pace. The employment of women and children was a further disturbing innovation. In preindustrial communities, women and children had worked, as well as men, but more often than not, all together and at home. In factory towns women and children were frequently hired instead of men: they could be paid less and were declared to be easier to manage. When this happened, the pattern of family life was severely disrupted, and a further break with tradition had to be endured. It is no wonder that workers began to see machinery itself as the tyrant that had changed their lives and bound them to a kind of industrial slavery. A radical working-class song written in Britain in the 1840s expressed the feeling: "There is a king and a ruthless king;/ Not a king of the poet's dream;/ But a tyrant fell, white slaves know well,/ And that ruthless king is steam."

Faced with a drastic reordering of their lives, working-class men and women reacted in various ways. Some sought "the shortest way out of Manchester" by taking to drink (there were 1,200 public houses in that city in 1850). Many more men and women struggled to make some sort of community out of the street where they lived or the factory where they worked. It was a long and discouraging process. Yet by mid-century their experiences were beginning to make them conscious of themselves as different from and in opposition to the middle class that was imposing a new way of life on them.

Escape

5. THE MIDDLE-CLASS WORLDVIEW

The middle class was not unaware of the many social problems it was generating as it created an industrial society. Despite its confidence that the world was progressing—and at its own behest—the middle class was beset by uncertainties. Its belief in its own undoubted abilities was shadowed by concern as to whether its particular talents might ultimately prove irrelevant to the preservation of prosperity. Self-assurance could dissolve in the face of bankruptcy, and prosperity vanish in the abyss of economic catastrophe. Those who had risen by their own exertions might fall victim to someone else's ambitions. Nor was it always a simple matter for the middle class to reconcile its own affluence with the poverty of the thousands of workers exploited under its aegis. The middle class was responsible for having wrenched European society out of old patterns of living and thrust it into new ones. To those willing to acknowledge that responsibility, the re-

Uncertainty and the need for reassurance

alization was enough to temper confidence with apprehension. No one was certain what the factory system and urbanization might eventually produce. Evidence drawn from the reports of various official commissions and from the intentionally lurid writings of sensational journalists suggested that city life was already spawning an underclass of men and women who preferred a life of promiscuity and criminality to one of honest toil. French novelists began to use the sewers as a metaphor to describe the general condition of urban existence for what was assumed to be a vast number of Parisians. Poverty and crime were linked together in the public—middle-class—mind, until poverty itself began to be defined as criminal. All this was part of a middle-class compulsion to rationalize its own prosperity, and to legitimize its ascendancy over the urban working poor.

Classical economics

To assist themselves in constructing this congenial worldview, the members of the new industrial middle class made use of the theories of a number of political economists. It is important to recognize that a factory-owner or a banker was not likely to have read the works of these theorists. He might, however, have encountered popular journalistic condensations of their ideas, or have participated in discussions at which the conclusions, if not the reasoned arguments, of the economists were aired. Because those conclusions supported his own interests, he grew familiar with them, until, in time, he could talk of the ideas of these men as if they were his own. Because this new middle class—itself a loosely united collection of experiences, goals, and beliefs—was sailing uncharted waters, its members not infrequently employed chunks of seemingly contradictory theories to bolster its own often contradictory aims.

We have noted already the manner in which the ideas of the economist Adam Smith sustained middle-class respect for individual enterprise (see Chapter 18). Enlightenment thought in general had extolled the virtues of

The Interior of the Crystal Palace. This building of iron and glass was constructed to house exhibits sent to the Exhibition of the Works of Industry of All Nations, held in London in 1851. The exhibition celebrated the triumph of middle-class industrialization.

individualism. John Locke, for example, celebrated the reason in men and women that allowed them to make intelligent choices based upon their own enlightened self-interest. Arguments such as these were reinforced by a second generation of economists—particularly the Englishmen Thomas Malthus (1766–1834) and David Ricardo (1772–1823)—whose writings embodied principles appealing to businessmen who desired a free hand to remake the economies of their countries. The chief elements in the theories of these economists were:

(1) Economic individualism. Individuals are entitled to use for their own best interests the property they have inherited or acquired by any legitimate method. People must be allowed to do what they like so long as they do not trespass upon the equal right of others to do the same.

(2) Laissez-faire. The functions of the state should be reduced to the lowest minimum consistent with public safety. The government should shrink itself into the role of a modest policeman, preserving order and protecting property, but never interfering with the operation of economic processes.

(3) Obedience to natural law. There are immutable laws operating in the realm of economics as in every sphere of the universe. Examples are the law of supply and demand, the law of diminishing returns, and so on. These laws must be recognized and respected; failure to do so is disastrous.

Thomas Malthus

(4) Freedom of contract. Individuals should be free to negotiate the best kind of contract they can obtain from any other individual. In particular, the liberty of workers and employers to bargain with each other as to wages and hours should not be hampered by laws or by the collective power of labor unions.

(5) Free competition and free trade. Competition serves to keep prices down, to eliminate inefficient producers, and to ensure the maximum production in accordance with public demand. Therefore, no monopolies should be tolerated, nor any price-fixing laws for the benefit of incompetent enterprises. Further, in order to force each country to engage in the production of those things it is best fitted to produce, all protective tariffs should be abolished. Free international trade will also help to keep prices down.

Businessmen naturally warmed to theories so congenial to their own desires and intentions. But Malthus and Ricardo made further contributions to the middle-class worldview, based upon their perceptions of conflicting interests within society. Malthus, in his controversial *Essay on Population,* first published in 1798, argued that nature had set stubborn limits to the progress of mankind. Because of the voracity of the sexual appetite there was a natural tendency for population to increase more rapidly than the supply of food. To be sure, there were powerful checks, such as war, famine, disease, and vice; but these, when they operated effectively, further augmented the burden of human misery. It followed that poverty and pain were inescapable. Even if laws were passed distributing all wealth equally, the condition of the poor would be only temporarily improved; in a very short time they would begin to raise larger families, with the result that the

Malthus on population

eventual state of their class would be as bad as the earlier. In the second edition of his work, Malthus advocated postponement of marriage as a means of relief, but he continued to stress the danger that population would outrun any possible increase in the means of subsistence.

Malthus's arguments, with their emphasis on the inevitability of poverty and misery, allowed the middle class to acquiesce in the destruction of an

older society that had made some attempt to care for its poor. In England, for example, officials in rural parishes had instituted a system of doles and subsidized wages to help sustain laborers and their families when unemployed. The attempt failed to prevent distress and was met with increasing resistance by taxpayers. Now Malthus told taxpayers that schemes designed to help the poor damaged both rich and poor alike. Poor relief took money, and therefore food, from the mouths of the more productive members of society and put it into the mouths of the least productive. Malthus helped shift the responsibility for poverty from society to the individual, a shift appealing to the middle class, which wished to be freed from the burden of supporting the urban unemployed. The private philanthropy that took the place of poor relief and was strongly influenced by an evangelical religious impulse, allowed charity to be dispensed solely to the "deserving" poor, often through the activities of middle-class women.

Malthusian assumptions played a large role in the development of the theories of the English economist Ricardo. According to Ricardo, wages

seek a level that is just sufficient to enable workers "to subsist and perpetuate their race, without either increase or diminution." This Ricardo held to be an inescapable iron law, in much the same way that Malthus had seen the interplay between population growth and the means of subsistence. According to Ricardo, if wages should rise temporarily above the subsistence standard, men and women would be encouraged to marry earlier and produce more children, the population would increase, and the ensuing competition for jobs would quickly force the rate of pay down to its former level. Ricardo devised a law of rent as well as a law of wages. He maintained that rent is determined by the cost of production on the poorest land that must be brought under cultivation, and that, consequently, as a country's population increases and more land is cultivated and higher rents are charged for more productive land, an ever-increasing proportion of the national income is absorbed by landlords.

Here again, a theorist provided arguments useful to the middle class in its attempt to define and defend itself within a new social order. The law of wages gave employers a useful weapon to protect themselves from their workers' petitions for higher pay. The "inevitability" of both population growth beyond the means of subsistence and the negative effects of overpopulation on wages and rent helped neutralize the middle class's sense of personal responsibility for the plight of the urban poor. In addition, Ricardo's law of rent justified middle-class opposition to the continuing power of landed interests: a class that derived its income not from hard work but simply from its role as rent-collector was profiting unfairly at the expense of the rest of society and deserved to have its profit-making curtailed.

As soon as the middle class began to argue in this fashion, however, it betrayed its devotion to the doctrine of laissez-faire. Businessmen and entrepreneurs vehemently opposed to government intervention, which might deny them the chance to make as much money as they could, were nevertheless prepared to see the government step in and prevent profiteering landlords from making what *they* could from their property. How could this apparent inconsistency be justified? The answer lay in the theories of the Englishman Jeremy Bentham (1748–1832), without doubt among the most influential of middle-class apologists. Bentham, whose major work, *The Principles of Morals and Legislation,* was published in 1789, argued against the eighteenth-century notion that a satisfactory theory of social order could be grounded in a belief in the natural harmony of human interests. Men and women were basically selfish beings. To suppose that a stable and beneficent society could emerge unassisted from a company of self-interested egos was, Bentham believed, to suppose the impossible. Society, if it was to function properly, needed an organizing principle that would both acknowledge humanity's basic selfishness and at the same time compel people to sacrifice at least a portion of their own interests for the good of the majority. That principle, called *utilitarianism,* stated that every institution, every law, must be measured according to its social usefulness. And a socially useful law was one that produced the greatest happiness of the greatest number. If a law passed this test, it could remain on the books; if it failed, it should be abandoned forthwith, no matter how venerable. A selfish man would accept this social yardstick, realizing that in the long run he would do himself serious harm by clinging to laws that might benefit him, but produce such general unhappiness as to result in disruptions detrimental to his own interests as well as to those of others.

Jeremy Bentham

Benthamite utilitarianism

In what ways did this philosophy particularly appeal to the industrial middle classes? First, it acknowledged the importance of the individual. The interests of the community were nothing more than the sum of the interests of those selfish egos who lived within it. Each individual best understood his or her own interests, and was therefore best left free, whenever possible, to pursue those interests as he or she saw fit. Only when they conflicted with the interests—the happiness—of the greatest number were they to be curtailed. Entrepreneurs could understand this doctrine as a license to proceed with the business of industrialization, since, they argued, industrialization was so clearly producing happiness for the majority of the world's population. At the same time, Bentham's doctrines could be used to justify those changes necessary to bring an industrial world into being. Was the greatest happiness produced, English factory-owners might ask, by an antiquated electoral system that denied representation to growing industrial cities? Obviously not. Let Parliament reform itself so that the weight of the manufacturing interests could be felt in the drafting of legislation.

Utilitarianism's appeal to the middle class

Utilitarianism was thus a doctrine that could be used to cut two ways— in favor of laissez-faire; in favor of governmental intervention. And the middle class proceeded to cut both ways at once. Benthamite utilitarianism provided the theoretical basis for many of the middle-class interventionist reforms, such as a revised poor law in Britain and an expanded educational

Individualism and intervention

system in France, achieved between 1815 and 1848 (see Chapter 22). At the same time utilitarianism, combined with the theories of Malthus and Ricardo, fortified the position of those businessmen who believed that unfettered individualism had produced the triumphs of the Industrial Revolution. To restrain that individualism was to jeopardize the further progress of industrialization and hence the greatest happiness of the greatest number.

Belief in improvement

In arguing as it did, the middle class relied upon the conviction that industrialization and the factory system were together showering benefits on all—not just themselves. As we shall see, there were those who disagreed, who pressed, for example, for regulation of factory wages and hours. But the capitalists claimed intervention would inhibit the distribution of those benefits, and hence the proliferation of general happiness. In their support they could cite the English economist Nassau Senior, who claimed that the net profit of any industrial enterprise was derived solely from its last hour of daily operation. Reduce working hours, said Senior, and you eliminate profits, thereby compelling factories to close and workers to starve. The members of the middle class believed Senior because it was clearly in their interest to do so. They also believed him because the enterprise upon which they were embarked was so new that it was hard to prove him wrong. Their uncertainty led them to believe those theories that provided them with the most reassurance and encouraged them to think that what they were doing was of benefit to their fellow men and women.

Saint-Simon and industrial entrepreneurship

Political economists and philosophers in France as well as in England helped provide the new middle class with a congenial worldview. Count Claude de Saint-Simon (1760–1825), while a proponent of utopian schemes for social reorganization, nevertheless preached the gospel of "industrialism" and "industrialists" (two words that he coined). Disciples of Saint-Simon were among the leading proponents in France of industrial entrepreneurship and a standardized and centralized financial system.

Far more generally influential was the positivist philosophy of Auguste Comte (1798–1857). Comte's philosophy, like utilitarianism, insisted that all truth is derived from experience or observation of the physical world. Comte rejected metaphysics as utterly futile; no one can discover the hidden essences of things—why events happen as they do, or what is the ultimate meaning and goal of existence. All one can really know is how things happen, the laws that control their occurrence, and the relations existing between them. *Positivism* derived its name from the assertion that the only knowledge of any current value was "positive," or scientific, knowledge. Comte argued that humankind's ability to analyze society scientifically and to predict its future had reached a point that would soon enable Europe to achieve a "positive" society, organized not in terms of belief but in terms of facts. Such an achievement would not be a simple matter, however; "positive" attitudes and institutions could not replace those of the "metaphysical" stage through which Europe had just passed without a struggle. By dividing the history of the world into progressive stages (a "religious" stage had preceded the "metaphysical"), and by declaring that the achievement of the highest stage was not possible without the turmoil of industri-

Auguste Comte

alization, Comte assured the middle class of its leading role in the better world that was to be.

6. EARLY CRITICS OF THE MIDDLE-CLASS WORLDVIEW

The middle-class worldview did not go unchallenged. Many writers deplored the social disintegration they saw as the legacy of the Industrial Revolution. Others criticized the materialism and hypocrisy they saw as the hallmarks of the middle class. The Scot Thomas Carlyle (1795–1881), though a defender of the French Revolution and a believer in the need for a new aristocracy of industrialists ("captains of industry"), had nothing but contempt for the theories of the utilitarians. In Carlyle's view, they did no more than excuse the greed and acquisitiveness of the new middle class. Equally scathing in his attacks on the middle class was the English novelist Charles Dickens (1812–1870). In such novels as *Oliver Twist, Hard Times,* and *Dombey and Son,* he wrote with sympathy of the tyrannization of industrial workers by the new rich. In France, the Abbé Félicité Lamennais (1782–1854), though preaching respect for private property, nevertheless attacked self-interest. He argued, in his *Book of the People,* that the "little people" of the world enjoyed far too small a share in the direction of their lives. Honoré de Balzac (1799–1850) wrote *The Human Comedy* to expose the stupidity, greed, and baseness of the middle class. Gustave Flaubert (1821–1880), in his foremost novel *Madame Bovary,* depicted the banal, and literally fatal, nature of bourgeois existence for women.

John Stuart Mill

Literary challenges to the middle-class worldview

One of the most trenchant critics of early industrialization was the English philosopher and economist John Stuart Mill (1806–1873). Mill's father had been a close disciple of Bentham, and his son began his adult life a convinced utilitarian. A severe psychological crisis in early manhood compelled him to modify his acceptance of classical economic theory. First, he rejected the universality of economic laws. Though he admitted that there are unchangeable laws governing production, he insisted that the distribution of wealth could be regulated by society for the benefit of the majority of its members. Second, he advocated radical departures from the doctrine of laissez-faire. He favored legislation, under certain conditions, for shortening the working day, and he believed that the state might properly take preliminary steps toward the redistribution of wealth by taxing inheritances and by appropriating the unearned increment of land. In the fourth book of his *Principles of Political Economy* he urged the abolition of the wage system and looked forward to a society of producers' cooperatives in which the workers would own the factories and elect the managers to run them. On the other hand, Mill was no socialist. He distrusted the state; his real reason for advocating producers' cooperatives was not to exalt the power of the workers but to give them the fruits of their labor. In 1859 he wrote what many consider the classic defense of individual freedom, *On Liberty,* in which he attacked what he called "the tyranny of the majority." Yet his

John Stuart Mill's criticisms of industrialization

The Greek Slave by Hiram Powers. The art of the bourgeoisie: titillation combined with a moral lesson.

See color plates facing page 781 for *The Gleaners* by Millet and the *Funeral at Ornans* by Courbet

ringing defense of individualism was as much a treatise against middle-class conformism as it was against the threat of state control. "If all mankind were of one opinion," Mill wrote, "and only one person were of the contrary opinion, mankind would be no more justified in silencing that one person than he, if he had the power, would be justified in silencing mankind." Those sentiments were not the sort to appeal to a society determined to define itself in accordance with rigid codes of conduct.

Artists, too, attacked the values of industrial society in their painting and sculpture. The art preferred by the European middle class in the nineteenth century was that which in some way either told a story or, better still, preached a message. Beauty was surface decoration, which could be admired for its intrinsic richness and for what it therefore declared about its owner's wealth. Or beauty was a moralism, easily understood and, if possible, reassuring. When the Great Exhibition of the Works of Industry in All Nations was held at the Crystal Palace in London in 1851 to celebrate the triumph of industrialism, one of the most popular exhibits was *The Greek Slave,* a statue by the American sculptor Hiram Powers. Depicting a young Christian woman stripped bare and standing, according to the catalogue, before the gaze of an Eastern potentate, the work allowed its Victorian male admirers a chance to relish its salaciousness while also profiting from its depiction of the woman's righteous disdain for her captor.

Some of the artists most critical of the middle class, while repudiating the artificial and decorative, nevertheless reflected the middle-class obsession with art as morality. The self-designated Pre-Raphaelite Brotherhood of English painters was a group of men and women, led by the painter-poet Dante Gabriel Rossetti (1828–1882), determined to express its disdain for contemporary values. They called themselves Pre-Raphaelites as a way of announcing their admiration for the techniques of early Renaissance artists, untainted, supposedly, by corrupted artistic taste. Yet the works of the leading members of the Brotherhood exuded a degree of sentimentality that compromised their rebel nature and rendered them conventionally pietistic and ultimately innocuous as social protest. The same can be said, to a lesser degree, of the work of the Frenchman Jean-François Millet (1814–1875). His *Man with the Hoe* is a stark, bitter statement about peasant life; his *The Angelus* softens the statement to sentiment. In both England and France, however, some of the most talented painters seriously questioned many of the values the middle class revered. Gustave Courbet (1819–1877) and Honoré Daumier (1808–1879) both expressed sympathy toward the plight of the French working class, contrasting scenes of rural and urban misfortune with unflattering caricatures of the bourgeoisie. Daumier, in particular, was a powerful satirist of social and political evils, ridiculing the corruption of petty officials and the hypocritical piety of the rich. There was a harsh bite to most of the work of Daumier and Courbet that proscribed sentimentalizing.

These writers and artists, while critical of the Industrial Revolution and middle-class values, proposed nothing very tangible in the way of radical reform. If they opposed the triumph of a materialistic middle class, they

The Angelus by Jean-François Millet. The artist's peasants accept their humble lot in this sentimental portrayal.

opposed, as well, the idea of complete democracy. Carlyle, in particular, criticized the present by comparing it with a rosy past that had never been. In this he was like one of the doughtiest critics of the new middle-class society, the Englishman William Cobbett (1763–1835). Cobbett, in his newspaper the *Political Register,* argued against industrialization itself as well as its effects. His propaganda mirrored the dilemma most critics had to face, in asking the question: Granted industrialization has brought great social and economic hardship in its train, does this mean that we should try to return to the life of preindustrial society, also often harsh, and always confining, though probably more secure?

Past or present?

For some time, a small band of thinkers had been answering that question with a resounding "no." They argued that there could be no return to old times and old ways, but that society could be at the same time both industrial and humane. These radical thinkers were often explicitly utopian. Two of the most persuasive were the Englishman Robert Owen (1771–1858) and the Frenchman Charles Fourier (1772–1837). Owen, himself the proprietor of a large cotton factory at New Lanark in Scotland, argued against the middle-class belief that the profit motive should be allowed to shape social and economic organization. Having reorganized his own mills to provide good housing and sanitation, good working conditions, free schooling, and a system of social security for his workers, he proceeded to advocate a general reorganization of society on the basis of cooperation, with communities rewarding workers solely as a result of their actual labor. Fourier urged an even more far-reaching reconstitution, including the abolition of the wage system, the division of work according to people's natural inclinations, and the complete equality of the sexes. The numerous followers of Owen and Fourier sought escape from the confu-

Utopian thinkers

The Third Class Carriage by Honoré Daumier. Daumier's realism did not mask his sympathy with the condition of the common people of France.

Louis Blanc

sions of the contemporary world in idealist communities founded according to the principles of their leaders. All these attempts failed after a time, victims of faulty leadership and, in the case of Fourierist communities in France, of charges of moral turpitude resulting from Fourier's revolutionary sexual doctrines.

Less utopian radical theories were proposed during the 1840s, years that witnessed recurring economic depressions and their horrifying consequences. The French politician and journalist Louis Blanc (1811–1882), stood, like many contemporary critics, against the competitiveness of the new industrial society and particularly opposed the exploitation of the working class. His solution was to campaign for universal male suffrage, which would give working-class men control of the state. Following their triumph, these workers would make the state the "banker of the poor" and institute "Associations of Production"—actually a system of workshops governed by workers—that would guarantee jobs and security for all. Once these associations became established, private enterprise would wither through competition, and with it the state, for which there would no longer be any need. As we shall see, these workshops were briefly instituted in Paris during the Revolution of 1848. Another Frenchman, Pierre Proudhon (1809–1865), condemned the profits accruing to employers at the expense of their employees. He, too, proposed new institutions, which he argued could be made to produce goods at a price fairer to the worker, a price based solely on the amount of labor devoted to the manufacture of any particular product.

The theories of the writers and thinkers whom we have been considering—both the defenders and the opponents of the middle-class industrial world—are historically important for two reasons. First, their ideas helped men and women better understand the new social order that had sprung up following the French and Industrial Revolutions, and the part they might play, as members of a class, in that new order. Second, the ideas themselves helped inspire the concrete political, social, and economic changes and events that are the subject of the next two chapters.

SELECTED READINGS

- *Items so designated are available in paperback editions.*

Banks, J. A., *Prosperity and Parenthood: A Study of Family Planning among the Victorian Middle Classes,* London, 1954. Relates middle-class financial pressures to family limitation.
- Bridenthal, Renate, and Claudia Koonz, eds., *Becoming Visible: Women in European History,* 2nd ed., Boston, 1987. Essays on the slowly changing role of women in society.

Briggs, Asa, *Victorian Cities,* New York, 1963. A survey of British cities, stressing middle-class attitudes toward the new urban environment.
- Burn, W. L., *The Age of Equipoise,* London, 1964. A charming account of the mid-Victorian years.
- Chevalier, Louis, *Laboring Classes and Dangerous Classes During the First Half of the Nineteenth Century,* New York, 1973. An intriguing though controversial study of the quality of life in Paris between 1815 and 1848, which concludes that social mobility was downward and that fear of crime dominated middle-class social consciousness.

Foster, John, *Class Struggle and the Industrial Revolution: Early Industrial Capitalism in Three English Towns,* London, 1974. Social analysis of industry in urban areas.
- Halévy, Elie, *The Growth of Philosophic Radicalism,* rev. ed., London, 1949. The best introduction to the thought of Malthus, Ricardo, Bentham, and their philosophical heirs.

———, *England in 1815,* London, 1949. The classic work by the greatest historian of nineteenth-century England.
- Hammond, J. L., and Barbara Hammond, *The Town Labourer, 1760–1832,* London, 1917. An impassioned account of the economic changes that affected the quality of life of the English worker.
- Heilbroner, Robert L., *The Worldly Philosophers,* 6th ed., New York, 1987. An introduction to the thought of economic liberals.
- Hobsbawn, Eric, *The Age of Capital, 1848–1875,* London, 1975. A perceptive world survey that traces the global triumph of capitalism and its impact on the working class, written from a Marxist perspective.

———, *Labouring Men: Studies in the History of Labour,* London, 1964. A series of essays on workers and the working class in England.
- Hobsbawn, Eric, and George Rudé, *Captain Swing: A Social History of the Great English Agricultural Uprising of 1830,* New York, 1975. Analyzes the formation of a rural working-class consciousness.
- Houghton, Walter, *The Victorian Frame of Mind, 1830–1870,* New Haven, 1957. An outstanding synthesis of Victorian middle-class mentality.

- Langer, William L., *Political and Social Upheaval, 1832–1852,* New York, 1969. Comprehensive survey of European history, with excellent analytical chapters and thorough bibliographies.

  McLaren, Angus, *Sexuality and Social Order: The Debate over the Fertility of Women and Workers in France, 1770–1920,* New York, 1983. Examines the relationship betwen private and public morality.

  Manuel, Frank E., *The Prophets of Paris,* Cambridge, Mass., 1962. An entertaining introduction to the philosophers of progress, from Turgot to Comte.

- Rostow, W. W., *The Stages of Economic Growth,* rev. ed., Cambridge, 1971. A synthesis by the exponent of the "take-off" theory of economic development.

- Rudé, George, *The Crowd in History, 1730–1848,* New York, 1964. A study of popular disturbances in France and England.

- Sewell, William, *Work and Revolution in France: The Language of Labor from the Old Regime to 1848,* Cambridge, 1980. Examines the mentalities of workers' organizations.

- Taylor, A. J. *The Standard of Living in Britain in the Industrial Revolution,* New York, 1975. A good introduction to the debate on the effects of industrialization.

  Tilly, Charles, and Edward Shorter, *Strikes in France, 1830–1848,* New York, 1974. A valuable study of early Continental class consciousness.

- Tilly, Louise, and Joan W. Scott, *Women, Work and Family,* New York, 1978. Deals with women in nineteenth-century France and England.

- Thompson, E. P., *The Making of the English Working Class,* London, 1963. Argues that the coincidence of the French and Industrial Revolutions fostered the growth of working-class consciousness. A brilliant and important work.

  Walker, Mack, *German Home Towns: Community, State and General Estate, 1648–1871,* Ithaca, N.Y., 1971. Attempts to explain the absence of a strong middle class in Germany.

- Zeldin, Theodore, *France, 1848–1945,* 2 vols., Oxford, 1973–1977. A highly individualistic synthesis of French history, remarkable for its scope and insight.

SOURCE MATERIALS

- Engels, Friedrich, *The Condition of the Working Class in England,* New York, 1958. A much criticized but reliable firsthand account by the later collaborator of Marx, written in 1844. Presents a devastating portrait of living and working conditions, especially in Manchester.

- Malthus, Thomas R., *An Essay on the Principle of Population,* London, 1798 and 1803. Malthus's famous essay relating population growth and food production.

- Mayhew, Henry, *London Labor and the London Poor,* New York, 1968. A reprint of the 1851 edition; provides a fascinating view of the population and trades of London. A good factual companion to Dickens.

- Mill, John Stuart, *Autobiography,* London, 1873. The intellectual coming-of-age of one of England's major nineteenth-century figures.

- ———, *On Liberty,* London, 1859. The classic defense of individual freedom.

- Owen, Robert, *A New View of Society,* London, 1813. A proposed utopian society based on cooperative villages by the founder of British socialism.

Chapter 22

THE RISE OF LIBERALISM (1815–1870)

The general thought, the hope of France, has been order and liberty re-uniting under constitutional monarchy.

—François Guizot, "Speech on the State of the Nation," 1831

Т he history of nineteenth-century Europe was to a great extent shaped by the interplay of the forces of liberalism and nationalism. The middle classes of France and Britain, where liberalism was strongest, espoused a set of doctrines reflecting their concerns and interests. Liberalism to them meant (1) an efficient government prepared to acknowledge the value of unrestrained commercial and industrial development; (2) a government in which their interests would be protected by their direct representation in the legislature—in all probability, a constitutional monarchy, and most certainly not a democracy; (3) a foreign policy of peace and free trade; and (4) a belief in individualism and the doctrines of the classical economists.

The components of liberalism

Many middle-class men and women in other European countries shared these beliefs and assumptions, and worked diligently and with some success to carry through specific liberal reforms. But for them, an equally important and often more immediate objective was the achievement of some form of national unity. The middle classes in Germany, Italy, Poland, and the Austrian Empire, however dedicated they were to liberalism, believed that their chances of achieving liberal goals would be greatly enhanced if they could unify the patchwork of principalities that surrounded them into a vigorous, "modern" nation-state. In this chapter, we shall examine the phenomenon of liberalism, primarily as it affected the fortunes of France

The compulsion of nationalism

and Britain. In the following chapter, we shall describe the way in which liberalism combined with nationalism to reshape the history of Central Europe.

1. CONSERVATIVE REACTION, 1815–1830

The conservative restoration

The growth of liberalism occurred, in part, as a reaction to the conservative policies adopted by frightened aristocratic rulers anxious to restore domestic and international order following the Napoleonic wars. For a period of about fifteen years after 1815 the governments of most European countries did their best to stem the advance of middle-class liberalism. In most instances, however, their repressive policies only made liberals more determined than ever to succeed. The primary concern of governments was to ensure that Europe would never again fall prey to the sort of revolutionary upheavals that it had experienced during the preceding quarter-century.

The system of alliances

Following Napoleon's final defeat at Waterloo in 1815, the major powers reconfirmed the Vienna Settlement in the hope that their efforts might result in a permanently stable "Concert of Europe." To further ensure an end to revolutionary disturbances, they formed the Quadruple Alliance—Britain, Austria, Prussia, and Russia; when France was admitted as a fifth member in 1818 it became the Quintuple Alliance. Its members pledged to cooperate in the suppression of any disturbances that might arise from attempts to overthrow legitimate governments or to alter international boundaries. At the same time, Tsar Alexander, his mystic nature now in the ascendant, persuaded the allies to join him in the declaration of another alliance—a "Holy Alliance"—dedicated to the precepts of justice, Christian charity, and peace. The only result of this second league was to confuse Europe's leaders as to Alexander's intentions. Was he a liberal—a Jacobin even, as Metternich feared—or a reliable conservative? The confusion was cleared away, as in one country after another, liberal uprisings were stifled by stern repressive policies of the allied governments, Alexander's among them.

Suppression of liberal uprisings

Liberal rebellions in Naples and in Spain brought the allies scurrying to a conference at Troppau in Austria in 1820. Secret brotherhoods, many of them composed of young army officers, had spearheaded these revolts. These organizations, which originated in Italy, called themselves *Carbonari*. They were an active counter-reactionary force whose influence spread throughout Europe in the early 1820s. In both Naples and Spain, they succeeded in forcing reactionary kings to take oaths to establish constitutions modeled on the liberal French constitution of 1789–1791. At Troppau, Austria, Prussia, and Russia reacted to these threats to international order and absolutism by pledging to come to each other's aid to suppress revolution. France and Britain declined to endorse the pledge, not so much because they opposed repression, but because they did not wish to curtail their freedom of action by binding themselves to detailed international treaties. Metternich nevertheless proceeded, with Russian and Prussian concurrence, in a repression of the *Carbonari* rebels through imprisonment or exile.

Two years later, in 1822, another congress was convened at Verona, this one to deal with the continuing liberal threat to stability in Spain, with the series of revolutions occurring in Spanish colonies in South America, and with an insurrection in the Near East. To resolve the Spanish problem, the French dispatched an army of 200,000 men to the Iberian peninsula in 1823. Without much difficulty, this force put an end to the Spanish liberals, who opposed King Ferdinand VII's attempt to undermine representative government. The French assisted Ferdinand in restoring his authority to rule as he pleased. Contrary to their experience in Spain, the defenders of the status quo were unable to succeed in stemming the move to independence and liberalism in the colonies of Central and South America. In 1823 President James Monroe of the United States issued the "Monroe Doctrine," which declared that attempts by European powers to intervene in the affairs of the New World would be looked upon as an unfriendly act by his government. Without British maritime support, the doctrine would have remained a dead letter. Britain was ready to recognize the independence of the South American republics, however, since as new countries they were prepared to trade with Britain instead of Spain. The British therefore used their navy to keep Spain from intervening to protect its vanishing empire.

In the Near East, in 1821, a Greek soldier, Alexander Ypsilanti, was attempting to encourage the formation of a Greek "empire," to be constructed on vaguely liberal principles. In doing so, he had engaged his band of armed followers in battles against the Turks who ruled over Greece. Though Ypsilanti was soon defeated, his movement lived on. Five years later its aims had been narrowed to the more accessible goal of an independent Greece. Supported for reasons of Mediterranean naval strategy by a joint Anglo-French-Russian naval intervention, and by a Russian invasion of the Balkans, the rebels this time succeeded. Their success signaled the extent of changes that had occurred since the Congress of Verona. No longer could Metternich and other reactionaries build alliances on the assumption that, for the powers of Europe, preservation of the status quo was the major goal. Britain, in particular, could not be relied upon. There, by the late 1820s, the liberal movement was gaining momentum fast.

2. LIBERAL GAINS IN WESTERN EUROPE, 1815–1832

For a time, the conservative reaction of 1815–1830 threatened the liberal revolutionary and Napoleonic heritage in France. The upper middle class in France had remained generally content with the domestic settlement agreed upon by the major powers in 1814 and confirmed at the Congress of Vienna the following year. Louis XVIII, a clever yet self-indulgent man, had "granted" a "constitutional charter" upon his succession to the French throne. While refusing to deny himself absolute power in theory, in practice Louis XVIII had willingly enough agreed to support those principles most desired by French middle-class liberals: legal equality; careers open to talent; and a two-chamber parliamentary government, with the vote confined to property-holders. Yet by basing the franchise on age and property qualifications, which made it impossible for the vast majority of those born after 1789 to participate directly in the government of their country, Louis's charter divided France in a way that would contribute to eventual instability.

Charles X and the threat to liberalism

In 1824, Louis died and was succeeded by his brother Charles X (1824–1830). Charles was an honest, determined reactionary, who once declared that only he and Lafayette had not changed since 1789—Lafayette was still a liberal, Charles still a zealous monarchist. By his policies Charles immediately declared himself a foe of liberalism, modernization, and the general legacies of the revolutionary and Napoleonic eras. At his direction the French assembly voted indemnities to those aristocratic emigrés whose land had been confiscated by the state. The Church was allowed to reassert its traditionally exclusive right to teach in French classrooms. The upper middle class, strengthened by its role within the country's growing industrial economy, reacted by heading a rebellion against Charles's reactionary policies. In March 1830, members of the Chamber of Deputies, led by bankers, passed a vote of no confidence in the government. Charles dissolved the chamber, as he was constitutionally empowered to do, and called new elections for deputies. When those elections went against his candidates, Charles further retaliated with a series of ordinances, issued on his own authority, which (1) again dissolved the newly elected chamber before it had even met; (2) imposed strict censorship on the press; (3) further restricted suffrage so as to exclude the upper middle class almost completely; and (4) called for new elections.

The Revolution of 1830 in France

What Charles got in return for these measures was revolution. Led by republicans—workers, artisans, students, writers, and the like—Parisians took to the streets. For three days, in intense fighting behind hastily constructed barricades, they defied the army and the police, neither of which was anxious to fire into the crowds. Sensing the futility of further resistance, Charles abdicated. Those who had manned the barricades pressed for a genuine republic. But those with the power—bankers, merchants, and industrialists—wanted none of that. Instead they brought the duke of Orleans to the throne as King Louis Philippe (1830–1848) of *the French*—not of France—after extracting a promise from him to abide by the constitution of 1814, which had so suited their particular liberal needs. The franchise was extended, from about 100,000 to 200,000 males. But the right to vote was still based upon property ownership. The major beneficiaries of the change were members of the middle class, those whose interests the Revolution of 1830 primarily served. Even the monarch was to remain relatively weak. He was in the words of one French politician, "to reign but not to govern."

The July Revolution of 1830 in Paris. Workers construct street barricades to ward off government troops.

Liberal gains in Britain came after an era of reaction that paralleled that which occurred on the Continent. The conservative Tory party enjoyed almost unbroken political supremacy between 1783 and 1832. Though William Pitt the Younger had begun his career as something of a reformer, the French Revolution had turned him, along with his fellow Tories, into a staunch defender of the status quo. The Tories' political opponents, the Whigs, had throughout the long years of the revolutionary and Napoleonic conflicts remained to some degree conciliatory to the French. But Whigs were as unsympathetic as Tories to democratic notions and as defensive of their rights to the full fruits of their property.

Tories and Whigs in Britain

Hence when rioting broke out in England after 1815 as a result of depression and consequent unemployment, there was general support among the ruling class for the repressive measures adopted by the British government. Spies were hired to ferret out evidence against popular agitators and legislation was adopted to stifle workers' protests. In the industrial north, where conditions were particularly severe, radical members of the middle and working classes capitalized on the general unrest to press their demands for increased representation in Parliament. At Manchester in 1819 a crowd of 60,000, demonstrating for political reform in St. Peter's Field, was fired upon by soldiers. Eleven persons were killed and over 400 injured, including 113 women. The massacre was thereafter called "Peterloo" by British radicals: i.e., a domestic Waterloo. It was the first of several repressive measures taken by the government to stifle reform. Another was the legislation known as the Six Acts, which was passed by Parliament in 1819, and outlawed "seditious and blasphemous" literature, increased the stamp tax on

"Peterloo" and the Six Acts

newspapers, allowed the searching of houses for arms, and restricted the rights of public meeting.

Yet within a surprisingly short time British political leaders reversed their unyielding opposition to reform. Instead, they displayed an ability to compromise which kept their country free from revolution. George Canning, the foreign minister, and Robert Peel, the home secretary, son of a rich cotton manufacturer, were both sensitive to the interests of Britain's liberal-minded capitalist entrepreneurs. Under their direction, the government retreated from its commitment to the intransigent Quintuple Alliance; it was Canning who took the lead in recognizing the new South American republics. At home, these same politicians began to make order out of the inefficient tangle of British laws; for example, they abolished capital punishment for about a hundred different offenses. And Canning liberalized, though he did not abolish, the Corn Laws. These laws levied a tariff on the importation of cheap foreign grain. As such, they benefited English landlords, but hurt manufacturers, who had to pay higher wages to enable their workers to purchase more expensive bread. These "liberalizers" among the still essentially conservative Tories went so far as to abolish the laws that had kept both dissenting Protestants (non-Anglican members of Protestant sects—Baptist, Congregationalist, Methodist) and Roman Catholics from full participation in public political life.

What the conservatives would not do was reform the system of representation in the House of Commons, heavily weighted on the side of the landed interests. Here the Tories, the majority party in Parliament, drew the line and showed themselves still basically committed to the status quo. Yet members of the liberal middle class argued that such a reform was absolutely necessary before they could themselves play a constant and active

The liberalizing Tories

Parliamentary reform

role in shaping British policy to comply with their own interests. "Interest" was, indeed, the key word in the debate over parliamentary reform. For centuries Parliament had represented the interests of landowners, the major propertied class in England. About two-thirds of the members of the House of Commons were either directly nominated by or indirectly owed their election to the patronage of the richest landowners in the country. Many of the parliamentary electoral districts, or boroughs, which returned members to the House of Commons, were controlled by landowners who used the pressure of their local economic power—or, in many cases, outright bribery—to return candidates sympathetic to their interests. These were the "rotten" or "pocket" boroughs, so-called because they were said to be in the pockets of those men who controlled them. Those who favored the system as it was argued that it mattered little that electoral politics were corrupt, that electoral districts represented unequal numbers, or that very, very few (about one in a hundred) were enfranchised. What did matter, they claimed, was that the interests of the nation at large, which they perceived to coincide with the interests of landed property, were well looked after by a Parliament elected in this fashion.

Of course the new industrial middle class did not agree with the arguments of the landowners. It is important to note, however, that the liberal middle class was *not* arguing in favor of reform on the basis of a belief in democracy. Some leaders within the emerging working class did make this argument—and, as we shall see, continued to make it after a reform bill was passed in 1832. Most of those who spoke in favor of reform declared that the middle class was capable of representing the interests of the working class, as well as of itself, in Parliament. Reformers took this position either because they believed it, or because they were afraid of working-class representatives, or because they realized that to favor direct representation for the working class would frighten the more timid reformers and hence defeat their whole campaign.

The middle class and reform

Spurred by the example of liberal reformers on the Continent and by the oratory and organizational abilities of middle-class and artisan radicals at home, the movement for reform intensified after 1830. It was strong enough to topple the Tories and to embolden the Whigs, under the leadership of Lord Grey, to make a party issue of reform by introducing a bill to modify the ancient electoral structure of the country. The government was clearly frightened. Revolution, if it were ever to come in England, would come as a result of the alliance now threatening between middle-class industrialists and the artisan/tradesman leadership of the emerging working class. In Birmingham, a middle-class banker, Thomas Attwood, organized a "Political Union of the Lower and Middle Classes of the People." By July 1830, there were similar organizations in Glasgow, Manchester, Liverpool, Sheffield, Newcastle, and Coventry, some willing to engage in bloody clashes with army units and police. Middle-class shopkeepers declared their determination to withhold taxes and, if necessary, to form a national guard. Plagued as well by an outbreak of cholera, the country appeared to be on the verge of serious general disorder, if not outright revolution. The king,

Alliance of middle class
with working class

*Liberalism and modernization
in other parts of the West:
Russia*

William IV, wrote worriedly to Lord Grey that "miners, manufacturers, colliers, and labourers" appeared ready for some sort of open rebellion. Sensing the grave danger of a possible union of the working and middle classes, the governing class once more accommodated to change, as it had in the 1820s.

The Reform Bill of 1832, however, was not a retreat from the notion of representation by interest. No attempt was made to create equal electoral districts. The franchise, though increased, extended the vote to no more than 3 percent of the total population. It was defined in terms of the amount of property owned and the length of time one had owned it. In other words, the vote was granted to the middle class, but to very few of the working class. Probably more significant than its extension of the franchise was the bill's scheme for a redistribution of seats. One hundred forty-three seats were reallocated, most of them from the rural south to the industrial north, thereby increasing the political power of the industrial middle classes. Though the bill was the product of change and itself brought change in its wake, it was understood as a conservative measure. It by no means destroyed the political strength of landed aristocratic interests, though it reduced that strength somewhat. And it preserved the notion of representation by interest. The liberal, industrial middle classes had been admitted into junior partnership with the landed oligarchy that had for centuries ruled Britain and was to rule it for at least one more generation.

Efforts to introduce liberal political reforms were not limited to France and Britain during this period. Across the world, in Russia, a group of army officers revolted, following the death of Tsar Alexander in 1825, in hopes of persuading his liberally minded brother, Constantine, to assume the throne and guarantee a constitution. In this case, however, the attempt at reform failed. Constantine was unwilling to usurp power from the rightful heir, a third brother, Nicholas. The officers, called Decembrists (because of the month of their rebellion) came from noble families and were members of elite regiments. Learned in the ways of the West, they had obtained a taste of life outside Russia during the Napoleonic wars, when they imbibed the ideas of the Enlightenment and the French Revolution. Politically, they ranged from constitutional monarchists to Jacobin republicans. Their failure was the consequence not only of repression by the tsar but also of their inability to attract mass support from rank and file peasant soldiers. Nicholas I (1825–1855) continued to rule in the severely autocratic ways Alexander had adopted toward the end of his life, creating the Third Section, a political police force, to prevent further domestic disorder. Nicholas's proclaimed goal of "Orthodoxy, Autocracy, and Nationality" meant simply that he would serve as god's lieutenant in an army in which the rest of his countrymen would labor as obedient foot soldiers. Yet even under Nicholas, perhaps Europe's most unremitting conservative, Russia showed signs of modernization. Bureaucracy, less dependent than in the past on the aristocracy, grew more centralized and more efficient. Laws were systematically codified in 1832. Stimulated by European demand for Russian grain, estates were reorganized for more effective production, and railways built to transport the grain to Western markets.

Other countries in Europe caught the revolutionary fever in the early 1830s. In Belgium, an insurrection that combined elements of liberal and national sentiment put an end to the union of that country with the Dutch, instituted by the Congress of Vienna. The European powers strengthened Belgium's political structure, and hence its independence, by agreeing in 1831 to the accession as king of Leopold of Saxe-Coburg, uncle of the future Queen Victoria of England. Once again, a middle class had succeeded in establishing a constitutional monarchy to its liking, congenial to its liberal and entrepreneurial goals. No such fate awaited the liberal nationalists in Poland, who in 1830 moved at this time to depose their ruler, the Russian Tsar Nicholas, whose hegemony extended to Poland as a result of the Vienna Settlement of 1815. Western Europe did not intervene; Russian troops crushed the Polish liberal rebels, and Poland was completely merged into the tsarist empire.

Liberal revolts in Belgium and Poland

Liberal forces in Spain enjoyed a greater success. There, middle-class liberalism was linked to the attempts of Queen Maria Christina, widow of King Ferdinand VII, to secure the throne for her daughter, Isabella. Though no liberal herself, the queen was prepared to court the favor of urban middle-class elites to win her struggle against her late husband's brother, the reactionary Don Carlos. During the so-called Carlist Wars, which lasted from 1834 to 1840, liberals extracted from Isabella II (1833–1868) a constitution that ensured them a strong voice in the legislature, while restricting the franchise to keep the more radical lower middle and artisan classes at bay. By mid-century, however, fear of these radicals led the middle class to acquiesce in a government that was nothing more or less than an authoritarian dictatorship, but that did not threaten directly their own economic interests.

Liberalism in Spain

3. LIBERALISM IN FRANCE AND BRITAIN, 1830–1848

The Revolution of 1830 in France and the Parliamentary Reform Bill of 1832 in Britain represented a setback for aristocratic power in both countries. Aristocrats and their supporters did not cease overnight to play an active role in politics, however. Lord Palmerston, for example, was one of Britain's most influential prime ministers at mid-century and one of Europe's most authoritative arbiters. But no longer would it be possible for the legislatures of France and Britain to ignore the particular interests of the middle class. Henceforth representatives would include members from that class in sufficient numbers to press successfully for programs that accorded with liberal beliefs.

Middle-class interests no longer ignored

The pace of liberal reforms in France was slow for a number of reasons. Industrialization was at its early stages and, though the Chamber of Deputies contained representatives from the upper middle class, they tended to be bankers and merchants generally uninterested in free trade. The principal liberal gains in France occurred in the area of education. Under the succession of governments dominated by France's leading politician

The slow pace of reform in France

of the period, François Guizot (1787–1874), the French expanded their educational system, thereby further underwriting their belief in the liberal doctrine of a meritocracy, or careers open to talent. A French law of 1833 provided for the establishment of elementary schools in every village. Children of indigent parents were to receive a free education; all others would pay a modest fee. In addition, larger towns were to provide training schools for trade and industry, and departments were to provide schools for teacher training. As a result, the number of pupils in France increased from about 2 million in 1831, to about 3.25 million in 1846.

Little else of lasting importance was accomplished during the regime of Louis Philippe. Guizot became more and more an apologist for the status quo. Everyone was free, he argued, to rise to the upper middle class and thus to a position of political and economic power. His advice to those who criticized his complacency was: "enrich yourselves." Politicians followed his advice, finding in schemes for the modernization of Paris and the expansion of the railway system ample opportunities for graft. Louis Philippe did little to counteract the lifelessness and corruption that characterized his regime. Although he had played a minor part in the Revolution of 1830, he was no revolutionary. He did not have the dash and glamor of a Napoleon. He was a paunchy, fussy, and undistinguished person, easily caricatured by his enemies. He appeared to most to be nothing more or less than a typically successful plutocrat. He amassed a fortune that, in characteristic bourgeois fashion, he claimed he had accumulated in order to provide for his five sons and three daughters. He enjoyed the company of bankers and businessmen, though he attempted to develop a reputation as the friend of the people. Rumor had it that when he stopped to shake hands with shopkeepers he wore a special pair of dirty gloves, which he would replace with white kid when hobnobbing with the rich. Louis Philippe was unable to rise above his stodgy public image. The German poet Heinrich Heine reported that the young people of France "yearned for great deeds and scorned the stingy small-mindedness and huckstering selfishness" that the king seemed to embody.

Louis Philippe

Liberal reforms in Britain

Liberal reforms made significant headway in Britain during this period. There were several reasons for this. First, the Reform Act of 1832 gave the middle class a share of political power. Second, and in part a consequence of reform, Parliament was generally sensitive to the needs of industrialists, above all their desire for policies of free trade. And third, rapid industrialization compelled legislative intervention on a number of fronts.

Liberal legislation in Britain: The new poor law

The nature of this intervention was mixed. In some cases, as with public health measures, it created government programs designed actively to improve the conditions of life. In others, it applied laissez-faire principles with little concern for human consequences. The principal example of the last type of legislation was the passage of a new law governing the treatment of paupers. In accordance with a law passed in 1598, each parish in England had been declared responsible for the maintenance of its own poor, either through accommodation in poorhouses, or through a system of doles, coupled with local public employment programs. This system, although it by

An English Workhouse for the Able-Bodied Poor. This workhouse in the county of Devon was built in the late 1830s.

no means eliminated the debilitating effects of poverty, did provide a kind of guarantee against actual starvation. But by 1830 the system had broken down. Population growth and economic depressions had produced a far larger number of underemployed men and women in Britain than had ever before existed, placing tremendous strain upon those funds, levied as taxes, which each parish used to provide relief. Industrialization also demanded that families move in search of employment from one part of the country to another; yet the law as it stood provided assistance only to those who applied in the parish of their birth. The old law did not accord with liberal notions of efficiency; the new Parliament set about to amend it. The result, drafted by Jeremy Bentham's former private secretary, Edwin Chadwick, and passed almost without dissent, clearly reflected the liberal, middle-class notion of how to achieve "the greatest happiness of the greatest number." Doles were to cease forthwith. Those who could not support themselves were to be confined in workhouses. Here conditions were to be made so severe as to all but compel inmates to depart and accept either whatever work they might find outside, no matter how poorly paid, or whatever charity their friends and relatives might be able to provide them. Parishes were to be grouped together into more efficient unions; the law was to be administered by a central board of commissioners in London. Inspiring this new legislation were the liberal belief that poverty was a person's own fault and the liberal assumption that capitalism, though unregulated, was capable of providing enough jobs for all who genuinely wanted them. Economic depressions in the early 1840s proved that latter assumption false, and wrecked the tidy schemes of the poor-law administrators. Doles were once more instituted, taxes once more increased. Yet the law's failure did not shake the liberal conviction that poverty was, in the end, an individual and not an institutional problem.

Repeal of the Corn Laws

Robert Peel

Humanitarian reforms

Opposition to educational reform

Even more symbolic of the political power of Britain's middle class than the new poor law was the repeal of the Corn Laws in 1846. These laws, even after their modification in the 1820s, continued to keep the price of bread artificially high, forcing employers, in turn, to pay wages high enough to allow workers to keep food on their tables. More than that, the Corn Laws symbolized to the middle classes the unwarranted privileges of an ancient and, to their minds, generally useless order: the landed aristocracy. The campaign to accomplish repeal was superbly orchestrated and relentless. The Anti-Corn Law League, an organization of middle-class industrialists and their supporters, held large meetings throughout the north of England, lobbied members of Parliament, and, in the end, managed to persuade Sir Robert Peel, now prime minister, of the inevitability of their goal. The widespread suffering caused by the potato famine in Ireland was a further argument for ending restrictions against the importation of cheap foodstuffs. That Peel was willing to split the Tory—or as it was now coming to be called, Conservative—party to introduce repeal suggests the power of the middle class and its belief in the gospel of free trade.

Legislation during this period reflected other middle-class concerns, and in some cases, directly conflicted with the liberal doctrine of non-intervention. Many members of the urban middle class professed devotion to the tenets of Christianity, particularly the doctrine that argued that all human beings have within themselves a soul that they must work to preserve from sin for their eternal salvation. This belief in the ability of an individual to achieve salvation, which contradicted the older Calvinist doctrine of a predestined "elect," accorded well with more general middle-class notions about the importance of individualism and the responsibility of the individual for his or her own well-being. It produced legislation such as the abolition of the slave trade in British colonies (1833), and the series of Factory Acts, which set limits on the working hours for child labor and which, in 1847, culminated in the curtailment of the workday in some trades to ten hours. Evangelicals such as William Wilberforce, who was throughout his life an eloquent spokesman for enslaved blacks, and Lord Shaftesbury, who campaigned to end the employment of women and children in mines, maintained that individual souls could not find God when imprisoned in the overworked bodies of plantation slaves or factory operatives. They were joined by others who argued, simply, that to keep people tied to their work for as long as twelve or fourteen hours a day was both inhuman and unnecessary.

The religious issue affected educational reform as well. England had no comprehensive system of state education before 1870. What state support there was came, after the 1830s, in the form of government grants to schools managed by the Church of England. Any move to increase this support, however, met with the strong opposition of middle-class dissenters, who saw it as no more than an attempt by the religious Establishment to extend its influence over the young. Middle-class liberals thus found arguments for reform confusing. The laws of classical economics clashed with other prejudices and beliefs, pulling men and women in various directions at once. Their uncertainty mirrored the extent to which no one could discern a right course in this world of new difficulties and fresh options.

Meanwhile radical members of the French and British lower middle and working classes who had assisted—if not propelled—the forces of liberalism to victory in 1830 and 1832 grew increasingly dissatisfied with the results of their efforts. In Britain they soon realized that the Reform Bill had done little to increase their chances for political participation. For a time they devoted their energies to the cause of trade unionism, believing that industrial, rather than political, action might bring them relief from the economic hardships they were suffering.

Growing dissatisfaction of radicals

Trade union organization had been a goal of militant workers since the beginning of the century. Among the first workers' campaigns in the nineteenth century were those often-riotous revolts organized both in Britain and, later, on the Continent against the introduction of machinery. In some instances, factories were attacked by workers and machines smashed, in the belief that machines, by replacing skilled workers, were producing widespread unemployment. In England, the rioters were called Luddites, after "Ned Ludd," who was the mythical leader of the movement. In other instances, the hostility of trade unionists was not directed so much toward machinery as toward those workers who refused to join in unions against their masters. Yet nowhere in Europe were trade unions able to organize themselves into effective bargaining agents before 1850. They came closest in Britain. There, artisans and skilled workers had banded together in the mid-1820s to form both Friendly Societies—mutual aid organizations—and cooperatives—communal stores that cut prices by eliminating the middlemen between producer and consumer. By 1831, there were about 500 cooperative societies in England, with a membership of something like 20,000. These organizations encouraged the parallel growth of trade unions, which, in the early 1830s, reached the peak of their early power and effectiveness. The National Association for the Protection of Labour comprised about 150 separate local unions in the textile and mining industries of the north; the Operative Builder's Union, about 30,000 workers throughout the country. In 1834, a new and potentially far more radical organization, the Grand National Consolidated Trades Union of Great Britain and Ireland, was organized by a group of London artisans. Its leadership declared that only by bringing the country to a standstill with a general strike could workers compel the governing class to grant them a decent life. At that point, the government decided to put an end to unions. In 1834, six organizers for the Grand National were convicted of administering secret oaths (unions were not themselves illegal) and sentenced to transportation (forced emigration to penal colonies in Australia). Subsequently employers demanded that their workers sign a document pledging their refusal to join a union, thereby stifling opportunities for further organization.

Trade unionism

After the defeat of the Grand National, the efforts of radical democratic reformers in England turned back from trade union to political activity, centering on attempts to force further political reform upon the uninter-

Chartism

The Great Chartist Rally of April 10, 1848. Undiscovered in the royal archives until the 1970s, this early photograph draws attention to the respectable attire of working-class radicals and to the decidedly male character of mid-century radicalism.

ested government through the device of the "People's Charter." This document, circulated across the country by committees of Chartists, as they were known, and signed by millions, contained six demands: universal manhood suffrage, institution of the secret ballot, abolition of property qualifications for membership in the House of Commons, annual parliamentary elections, payment of salaries to members of the House of Commons, and equal electoral districts.

The fortunes of the Chartist movement waxed and waned. In some areas its strength depended upon economic conditions: Chartism spread with unemployment and depression. There were arguments among its leaders as to both ends and means: Did Chartism imply a reorganization of industry or, instead, a return to preindustrial society? Were its goals to be accomplished by petition only, or by more violent means if necessary? The Chartist William Lovett, a cabinetmaker, for example, was as fervent a believer in self-improvement as any member of the middle class. He advocated a union of educated workers to acquire their fair share of the nation's increasing industrial bounty. The Chartist Feargus O'Connor, on the other hand, appealed to the more impoverished and desperate class of workers. He urged a rejection of industrialization, and the resettlement of the poor on agricultural allotments. These polarities and disagreements regarding the aims of the movement suggest the extent of the confusion within the working class, whose consciousness as a separate political force was only just beginning to develop. Events answered most of the Chartists' questions for them. Massive petitions calling for the Charter were presented to Parliament in 1839 and 1842 while in the north of England Chartists aided trade unionists in attacks on factories engaging in unfair practices. Still reform evaded the Chartists. In 1848, revolutionary outbreaks across the Continent inspired Chartist leaders to plan a major demonstration and show of force in London. A procession of 500,000 workers was called, to bear to Parliament a petition containing 6,000,000 signatures demanding the six points. Confronted, once again, with the spectre of open class conflict, special constables and contingents of the regular army were marshaled under the now-aged duke of Wellington to resist this threat to order. In the end, only a small delegation of leaders presented the petition to Parliament. Rain, poor management, and unwillingness on the part of many to do battle with the well-armed constabulary put an end to the Chartists' campaign. Increased prosperity among skilled workers disarmed the movement after mid-century.

In France, radical agitation produced very different results. There, those who had manned the barricades in 1830 soon grew disgusted with the liberalism for which they had risked their lives. In their minds they carried memories or myths of the years of the first French Republic—its domestic accomplishments, its foreign victories, if not its Reign of Terror. They were opposed to constitutional monarchy, and unenthusiastic about parliamentary government, especially by a *nouveau riche* upper middle class. They were prepared, if necessary, to use force in order to achieve their ends. Centered in an increasingly industrialized Paris, they were for the most part either writers, students, or working-class leaders. They met in secret, studied the works of the radical theorist, Gracchus Babeuf (see above, p. 678), whose socialist *Conspiracy of Equals,* written during the French Revolution, became their Bible, and succeeded in making constant trouble for the liberal, middle-class governments of Louis Philippe. Their leading spokesman

Radical agitation in France

Louis Philippe in Caricature. In contrast to the portrait of Louis Philippe on page 760 as he wanted to appear, these 1833 caricatures by Charles Philipon depict the king as he increasingly appeared to his subjects and suggest the degree to which Louis Philippe failed in his attempt to celebrate the supposed virtues of the bourgeoisie.

Rue Transnomain. A drawing by Daumier to commemorate the victims of government repression in 1834.

A Caricature of Louis Philippe by Daumier. The inscription reads "Louis Philippe, the Last King of the French." It reflects a popular sentiment of the time.

was the socialist Auguste Blanqui (1805–1881). He decried the victimization of the workers by the middle class, and helped organize secret societies that were to become the instruments of eventual insurrection. Radicals waged some of their most successful campaigns in the press. Honoré Daumier's savage caricatures of Louis Philippe landed him in prison more than once. But campaigners took to the streets as well. In retaliation, the government in 1834 declared radical political organizations illegal. Rioting broke out in Lyons and Paris in protest, where for two days government troops massacred hundreds of insurgents, and arrested some 2,000 republican leaders. In 1835, following an attempt to assassinate Louis Philippe, the government passed a censorship law, which forbade the publication of articles attempting to inspire contempt for the king and which prohibited the printing of any drawing or emblem without prior governmental approval.

These repressive measures served only to increase dissatisfaction with the regime. Guizot was advised by more progressive members of the legislature to extend the franchise to professionals whose lack of wealth now denied them the vote, but whose general adherence to the doctrines of liberalism was unquestioned. Guizot unwisely refused, thereby driving these moderates into the camp of the more radical republicans. By 1847, various elements within the opposition were disaffected enough to instigate a general campaign of agitation throughout France. At political banquets, republicans such as the poet Alphonse de Lamartine (1790–1869) and socialist republicans such as Louis Blanc (see above, p. 748) preached drastic reform, though not outright revolution. Contrary to the expressed wishes of the king, a giant protest meeting was announced for February 22, 1848. The day before, the government forbade the meeting. Rioting and barricading during the following two days ended in the abdication of Louis Philippe and increased demands for a republic.

4. THE REVOLUTION OF 1848 IN FRANCE

The February revolution in France was a catalyst which, as we shall see, helped to produce uprisings in the succeeding months throughout much of Europe. Meanwhile, in Paris, a provisional government was established consisting of ten men, seven of whom, including Lamartine, were middle-of-the-road republicans; three of whom, including Blanc, were socialists. The tensions between middle-class republicans and radical socialists, which had been masked by a common disgust with the government of Louis Philippe, now emerged to shape the political events of the ensuing months in several specific ways. Blanc insisted upon the establishment of national workshops, institutions he had championed as a writer, which were to be organized by trades as producers' cooperatives, where men and women workers would be trained if necessary, put to work, and paid two francs a day when employed and a smaller stipend when unemployed. Instead, the government established what it called workshops, but what amounted to nothing more than a program of public works in and around Paris, where economic conditions had resulted in widespread unemployment. Initially, plans had called for the employment of no more than ten or twelve thousand in projects throughout the city. But with unemployment running as high as 65 percent in construction trades and 51 percent in textiles and clothing, workers began to flood into the government's so-called workshops, as many as 66,000 by April, and 120,000 by June.

Republican-socialist split: Blanc's workshops

Paris meanwhile attracted radical writers, organizers, and agitators. The provisional government had removed all restrictions upon the formation of political clubs and the dissemination of political literature. As a result, 170 new journals and more than 200 clubs formed within weeks; the Central Republican Society, the club headed by the socialist Auguste Blanqui, boasted a membership of some 3,000. Delegations claiming to represent the oppressed of all European countries—Chartists, Hungarians, Poles—moved freely about the city, attracting attention, if not devoted followings, and contributing to tension which was convincing more and more mem-

Moderates elected by universal suffrage

A National Workshop. When few could read, newspapers were heard rather than scanned. Under government auspices, these workshops achieved a good deal less than Louis Blanc had envisioned.

bers of the middle class that stern measures were needed to forestall further insurrectionary outbreaks. This sentiment was fortified as a result of elections held at the end of April. The provisional government had been pressured by Parisian radicals into decreeing universal manhood suffrage. But an extended electorate was no guarantee of radical success: the election returned only a small proportion of radical socialists. The largest blocs consisted of "true," or moderate, republicans and monarchists—this latter group divided, however, between supporters of the Bourbon dynasty and the Orleanist Louis Philippe. The generally conservative tenor of the newly elected assembly strengthened the hand of those who pressed for the repression of the socialists. It also, naturally, convinced the socialists that once again, as in the 1790s, a potentially radical revolution had been betrayed by a middle class more interested in its economic well-being than political equality.

The "June Days"

By late spring, a majority of the assembly believed that the workshop system represented both an unbearable financial drain and a serious threat to social order. At the end of May, the workshops were closed to new enrollment as a first step toward barring membership to all who had resided for less than six months in Paris and sending all members between the ages of eighteen and twenty-five to the army. On June 21 thousands of workers lost their state-financed jobs, and with them their best chance for survival. Desperate, they and their supporters once more threw up barricades across Paris. For four days, June 23–26, they defended themselves in an ultimately hopeless military battle against armed forces recruited, in part, from willing provincials eager enough to assist in the repression of the urban working class. Whether or not the Parisian insurrectionists were fighting as members of a beleaguered class, or simply as men and women on the brink of starvation, is a matter that historians continue to debate. That they were taken seriously as a revolutionary threat can be seen by the ferocity with which they were hunted down once the street fighting had ceased. About 3,000

The Revolution of 1848 in France. A contemporary broadside celebrating the triumph of the people.

were killed and 12,000 more arrested, the majority of whom were deported to Algerian labor camps.

In the aftermath of the "June Days," the French government moved quickly to bring order to the country. Assembly members therefore arranged for the immediate election of a president. Their hope was that a strong leader might assist in bringing dissidents to heel. Four candidates stood: Lamartine, the moderate republican; General Louis Eugène Cavaignac, who had commanded the troops in June; Alexandre August Ledru-Rollin, a socialist; and Louis Napoleon Bonaparte, nephew of the emperor, who polled more than twice as many votes as the other three candidates combined.

The imposition of order

The astonishing upstart Louis Napoleon had spent most of his life in exile. Returning to France after the Revolution of 1830, he was imprisoned a few years later for attempting to provoke a local uprising. But in 1846 he escaped to England, where he was supplied with funds by both British and French reactionaries. By the summer of 1848 the situation in France was such that he knew it was safe to return. In fact, he was welcomed by members of all classes. Conservatives were looking for a savior to protect their property against the onslaughts of the radicals. Workers were beguiled by the glittering schemes for prosperity in his book, *The Extinction of Pauperism,* and by the fact that he had corresponded with Louis Blanc and with Pierre Proudhon, the anarchist. In between these two classes was a multitude of patriots and hero-worshipers to whom the name Napoleon was a symbol of glory and greatness. It was chiefly to this multitude that the nephew of the Corsican owed his astounding triumph. As one old peasant expressed it: "How could I help voting for this gentleman—I whose nose was frozen at Moscow?"

The rise of Louis Napoleon

With dreams of emulating his uncle, Louis Napoleon was not long content to remain president of France. Almost from the first he used the power he already had to achieve the further power he desired. He enlisted the support of the Catholics by permitting them to regain control over the schools and by sending an expedition to Rome in 1849 to restore to the pope the temporal power denied him during the revolutionary struggles of 1848. He courted the workers and the middle class by introducing old-age insurance and laws for the encouragement of business. In 1851, alleging the need for extraordinary measures to protect the rights of the masses, he proclaimed a temporary dictatorship and invited the people to grant him the power to draw up a new constitution. In the plebiscite held on December 21, 1851, he was authorized by an overwhelming majority (7,500,000 to 640,000) to proceed as he liked. The new constitution, which he put into effect in January 1852, made the president an actual dictator. After one year Louis Napoleon Bonaparte ordered another plebiscite and, with the approval of over 95 percent of the voters, established the Second Empire and assumed the title of Napoleon III, emperor of the French.[*]

A second emperor

_____
[*] Napoleon I's son, Napoleon II, had died in Vienna in 1832.

AU NOM DU PEUPLE FRANÇAIS.

LE PRÉSIDENT DE LA RÉPUBLIQUE
DÉCRÈTE:

Art. 1.
L'Assemblée nationale est dissoute.
Art. 2.
Le Suffrage universel est rétabli. La loi du 31 mai est abrogée.
Art. 3.
Le Peuple français est convoqué dans ses comices à partir du 14 décembre jusqu'au 21 décembre suivant.
Art. 4.
L'état de siége est décrété dans l'étendue de la 1ʳᵉ division militaire.
Art. 5.
Le Conseil d'État est dissous.
Art. 6.
Le Ministre de l'intérieur est chargé de l'exécution du présent décret.
Fait au Palais de l'Élysée, le 2 décembre 1851.

LOUIS-NAPOLÉON BONAPARTE.
Le Ministre de l'Intérieur,
DE MORNY.

Napoleon III's Decree Dissolving the National Assembly

The implications of the French Revolution of 1848

What is the significance of the French Revolution of 1848 and its political aftermath in the history of middle-class liberalism, which is our subject? Two points need particular emphasis. First, we must recognize the pivotal role of the liberal middle class. Under Louis Philippe, it increasingly perceived itself and its particular interests as neglected. Denied a direct political voice because of a severely limited franchise, it swung to the left, allying itself with radicals who, by themselves, would probably have stood no chance of permanent success. Yet no sooner had Louis Philippe abdicated than the liberal middle class began to wonder if "success" was not about to bring disaster upon its heels. And so it swung again, this time to the right, where it found itself confronting the mysterious and yet not entirely unattractive prospect of Louis Napoleon. He, in turn, was clever enough to understand this first lesson of 1848, that in France no government could survive that did not cater to the interests of the middle class. By assisting it to achieve its liberal economic goals, the emperor helped it forget just how heavily he was trampling on its political liberties.

Working-class demands

Yet 1848 proved that there was now in France another element—class consciousness may, at this point, not yet be the correct term—that governments ignored at their peril. If mid-nineteenth-century Europe saw the middle class closer than ever to the center of power, it saw the workers moving rapidly in from the edge. Their barricades could, if necessary, be destroyed, and their demands ignored, but only at an increasingly grave risk to the fabric of the state. Middle-class liberalism, if it was to thrive, would not only have to pay lip service to working-class demands, but in some measure accommodate to them as well.

5. LIBERALISM IN FRANCE AND BRITAIN AFTER 1850

Napoleon III recognized the vital role that public opinion had now assumed in the management of affairs of state. He labored hard and successfully to sell his empire to the people of France. He argued that legislative assemblies only served to divide a nation along class lines. With power residing in him, he would unite the country as it had not been for generations. The French, who craved order following their recent political misadventures, willingly bought the program he was selling. Napoleon III modeled his constitution upon that of his uncle. An assembly, elected by universal manhood suffrage, in fact possessed almost no power. It could do no more than approve legislation drafted at the emperor's direction by a Council of State. Elections were manipulated by the government to ensure the return of politically docile representatives. Control of finance, the army, and foreign affairs rested exclusively with the emperor. France was a democracy only in the sense that its people were periodically afforded a chance, through elections, to express their approval of Napoleon's regime.

Napoleon III

In return for the gift of almost absolute power, Napoleon III gave the French what they appeared to want. For the middle class, he provided a chance to make a great deal of money. The device of the *Crédit Mobilier,* an investment banking institution, facilitated the expansion of industry by selling its shares to the public and using its income to underwrite various entrepreneurial schemes. In 1863 a limited liability law encouraged further investment by guaranteeing that stockholders could lose no more than the par value of their stock no matter how indebted the company in which they had invested. Railways, owned by the state, spread across the country, and spurred further industrial expansion. So prosperous did the French economy appear that Napoleon was prepared to follow Britain's lead in pressing for tariff-free trade between the two countries. A treaty was signed in 1860. Though funds were set aside to compensate French industries for any loss they might suffer, they were never completely expended, suggesting that French manufacturers were now well enough established to meet the threat of British competition. The apparent satisfaction of the middle class with Napoleon's regime provides a measure with which to assess the state of liberalism in France after 1850. The fact that the country no longer enjoyed a free press, that universities were politically controlled, and that political opposition was repressed seemed to matter very little to most. Liberalism, if it existed at all, existed as the freedom to have one's own economic way.

French economic prosperity

Napoleon III, though he catered to the middle class, did not fail to court the favor of the workers as well. He encouraged the establishment of hospitals and instituted a program of free medical assistance. More important, he permitted, if he did nothing to encourage, the existence of trade unions and in 1864 introduced legislation to legalize strikes. Ultimately, he ap-

*Napoleon III and the
working class*

Paris under the Second Empire. The Avenue de l'Imperatrice was designed for the enjoyment of the middle class.

Empress Eugénie

pealed to the workers much as he appealed to the middle class, as a glamorous, if not heroic symbol of his country's reemergence as a leading world power. The activities of his court, and of his stylish empress, Eugénie, were well publicized. The reconstruction of Paris into a city of broad boulevards and grand open spaces was calculated to provide appropriate scenery for the theater of empire—as well as to lessen the chances for successful proletarian barricade-building across narrow streets.

Grandeur, however, appeared to Napoleon III to demand an aggressive foreign policy. Although early in his regime he declared himself in favor of that central liberal tenet—international peace—he was soon at war: first against Russia in the Crimea; then in Italy; then in Mexico, where he attempted to assist in the establishment of another empire; and finally and disastrously with Prussia. The details of these adventures are part of the subject of the following chapter. It is enough at this point to remark that Napoleon III's foreign policy reflects clearly how far he—and the rest of France with him—had subordinated the liberal heritage of the first French Revolution to that of another of its legacies: national glory.

What, meanwhile, of the liberal tradition in Britain? There the course of liberalism was altered by changes occurring within the working class. Industrialization had, by this time, begun to foster and sustain a growing stratum of labor "aristocrats," men whose particular skills, and the increasing demand for them, allowed them to demand wages high enough to ensure them a fairly comfortable standard of living. These workers—concentrated for the most part within the building, engineering, and textile industries—turned from the tradition of militant radicalism that had characterized the so-called hungry forties. Having succeeded within the liberal economic system imposed upon Britain by the middle class, they were now prepared to adapt many liberal, middle-class principles to their own ends. They believed in collective self-help, achieved by means of cooperative societies or through trade unions, whose major function was the accumulation of funds to be used as insurance against old age and unemployment. They believed in education as a tool for advancement, and patronized the Mechanics Institutes and other similar institutions either founded by them or on their behalf.

Liberalism in Britain: The
"labor aristocracy"

Yet the labor aristocracy, as it came to appreciate its ability to achieve a decent life for itself within the capitalist system, grew all the more dissatisfied with a political system that excluded it from any direct participation in the governmental process. Although some pressed for extension of the franchise as democrats, as many argued for it on the same grounds the middle class had used in 1832. They were responsible workers, whose loyalty to the state could not be questioned. As such, they were a bona fide "interest," as worthy of the vote and of direct representation as the middle class. They were joined in their campaign by many middle-class reformers who continued to chafe at the privileged position of national institutions that they associated with the landed society and the old order. Many middle-class men and women, for example, were dissenters from the Church of England; yet they were forced to pay taxes to support a church that was staffed, in the main, by sons of the gentry. Their sons were denied the facilities of the nation's ancient universities, Oxford and Cambridge, unless those sons subscribed to the articles of faith of the Anglican Church.

Dissatisfaction with the
government

Together with working-class leaders, these middle-class dissidents organized a Reform League to campaign across the country for a new reform bill and a House of Commons responsive to their interests. Though by no means revolutionary, the reformers made it clear by their actions that they were determined to press their case to the utmost. Politicians in Britain in the 1860s were confronted by a situation not unlike that which had faced

Reform Bill of 1867

The Labor Aristocracy. These men were founding members of an early trade union. Having achieved a comfortable standard of living from their skills, they soon came to demand political rights as well.

Guizot in France in 1848: middle class, lower middle class, and skilled workers discontented and demanding reform. Unlike Guizot, however, the leaders of both British political parties, Conservative (formerly Tory) and Liberal (formerly Whig), were prepared to concede what they recognized it would be dangerous to withhold. Once convinced of this need, the Conservative leader of the House of Commons and future prime minister, Benjamin Disraeli, seized upon reform as an issue with which to belabor the Liberals. In 1867 he steered a bill through Parliament more far-reaching than anything proposed by his political opponents. It doubled the franchise by extending the vote to any males who paid poor rates or rent of ten pounds or more a year in urban areas (this would mean, in general, the skilled workers), and to tenants paying rent of twelve pounds or more in the counties. Seats were again redistributed as in 1832, with large northern cities gaining representation at the expense of the rural south. The "responsible" working class had been deemed worthy to participate in the affairs of state. For the next twenty years it showed its appreciation by accepting its apprentice position without demur, and by following the lead prescribed by the middle class.

The triumph of British liberalism

The decade or so following the passage of the Reform Bill of 1867 marked the high point of British liberalism. The labor aristocracy was accommodated with an Education Act, virtually guaranteeing a primary education to all, with legalization of strikes, and with a series of measures designed to improve living conditions in the great cities; yet it was the middle class that set the governmental tone. Under Disraeli and his Liberal counterpart William Gladstone, and with the cooperation of the newly enfranchised skilled workers, Britain celebrated the triumph of the liberal principles of free trade, representative—but not democratic—government, and general prosperity.

SELECTED READINGS

• *Items so designated are available in paperback editions.*

Anderson, R. D., *Education in France, 1848–1870,* New York, 1975. Covers every level of formal education and its practical and theoretical relationship to state and society.
• Artz, Frederick B., *Reaction and Revolution, 1814–1832,* New York, 1834. A European survey, dated but still useful.
• Blake, Robert, *Disraeli,* London, 1966. A masterful biography.
• Briggs, Asa, *The Age of Improvement, 1783 to 1867.* New York, 1959. A survey of England from 1780 to 1870, particularly strong on Victorian attitudes.
• Duveau, Georges, *1848: The Making of a Revolution,* New York, 1967. Focuses on the working class during the revolution in Paris: their unity at the outset, their division in the "June Days."
Finer, Samuel E., *The Life and Times of Edwin Chadwick,* London, 1952. An excellent biography of the great English Benthamite reformer.

Halévy, Elie, *A History of the English People, 1905–1914,* Vols. II–IV, London, 1949–1952. The best survey of nineteenth-century England, comprehensive and analytical.

• Harrison, Royden, *Before the Socialists: Studies in Labour and Politics, 1861–1881,* London, 1965. Examines the social and political background of franchise extension in Britain.

Johnson, Douglas, *Guizot: Aspects of French History, 1787–1874,* London, 1963. Analytical essays about the leading politician of the July monarchy.

• Kissinger, Henry, *A World Restored: Metternich, Castlereagh, and the Problem of Peace, 1812–1822,* Boston, 1957. By an admirer of Metternich.

• Langer, William L., *Political and Social Upheaval, 1832–1852,* New York, 1969. (Several chapters have been published separately under the title *The Revolutions of 1848.*) A thorough general survey.

Magnus, Philip, *Gladstone: A Biography,* London, 1955. A readable and reliable biography.

Merriman, John M., ed., *1830 in France,* New York, 1975. Recent scholarship emphasizing the nature of revolution and examining events outside of Paris.

• Pinkney, David, *Napoleon III and the Rebuilding of Paris,* Princeton, 1972. An interesting account of the creation of Modern Paris during the Second Empire.

———, *The French Revolution of 1830,* Princeton, 1972. A reinterpretation, now the best history of the revolution.

Raeff, Marc, *The Decembrist Movement,* New York, 1966. Examines the uprising; contains documents.

Roberts, David, *Victorian Origins of the British Welfare State,* New Haven, 1960. Examines various nineteenth-century reforms in England.

• Robertson, Priscilla, *Revolutions of 1848: A Social History,* Princeton, 1960. Surveys the revolutions across Europe.

de Sauvigny, G. de Bertier, *The Bourbon Restoration,* New York, 1966. An outstanding work; the best history of a neglected period.

• Stearns, Peter N., *1848: The Revolutionary Tide in Europe,* New York, 1974. Stresses the social background of the revolutions.

• Thompson, J. L. *Louis Napoleon and the Second Empire,* Oxford, 1954. A good biography. Presents Louis Napoleon as a modern Hamlet.

Woodward, E. L., *The Age of Reform,* Oxford, 1962. An excellent survey from the Oxford History of England series.

• Wright, Gordon, *France in Modern Times: 1760 to the Present,* 4th ed., New York, 1987. The best textbook on modern France.

• Zeldin, Theodore, *The Political System of Napoleon III,* New York, 1958. Examines the processes by which Louis Napoleon maintained power as the first modern dictator.

• ———, *France, 1848–1945,* 2 vols., Oxford, 1973–77.

SOURCE MATERIALS

• Flaubert, Gustave, *L'Education Sentimentale,* London, 1961. Contains an unsympathetic but memorable portrait of the Revolution of 1848 and of the bourgeois style of life that contributed to its outbreak.

• Greville, Charles Fulke, *Memoirs,* ed. by Roger Fulford, New York, 1963. Originally published in seven volumes in 1875, these comprise the diaries of the secretary to the Privy Council for the years 1821–1861. An excellent source for the court and politics of the period.

• Price, Roger, ed., *1848 in France,* Ithaca, N.Y., 1975. An excellent collection of eyewitness accounts, annotated.

Stewart, John Hall, *The Restoration Era in France, 1814–1830,* Princeton, 1968. A brief narrative and a good collection of documents.

Chapter 23

NATIONALISM AND NATION-BUILDING (1815–1870)

The present problem, the first task . . . is simply to preserve the existence and continuance of what is German.

— Johann Fichte, *Addresses to the German Nation*

The great questions of the day will not be decided by speeches or by majority decisions—that was the mistake of 1848 and 1849—but by blood and iron.

— Otto von Bismarck, speech, 1862

I f the history of nineteenth-century Britain and France can be studied against a general background of middle-class liberalism, that of much of the rest of Europe during the same period must be understood in terms of a more complex combination of the forces of liberalism, nationalism, and nation-building. We shall define *nationalism* as a sentiment rooted in broad historical, geographical, linguistic, or cultural circumstances. It is characterized by a consciousness of belonging, in a group, to a tradition derived from those circumstances, which differs from the traditions of other groups. *Nation-building* is the political implementation of nationalism, the translation of sentiment into power.

Nationalism and nation-building defined

Men and women in Britain and France during the nineteenth century entertained national as well as liberal sentiments. When Britain's prime minister, Lord Palmerston, declared in 1850 that any British citizen, in any part of the world, had but to proclaim, like a citizen of the Roman Empire, "civis Romanus sum" ("I am a citizen of Rome") to summon up whatever force might be necessary to protect him from foreign depradations, he was echoing his countrymen's pride in the powers of their nationhood. When the French rejoiced in 1840 at the return of the Emperor Napoleon's remains from St. Helena to an elaborate shrine in Paris, they were reliving triumphs that had become part of their nation's heritage. Palmerston's boast and Napoleon's bones were both artifacts of national traditions and sentiments bound up in the life of the English and the French.

Nationalism in Britain and France

Nineteenth-century nationalism in other areas of Europe was to be a more assertive phenomenon than it was in Britain and France, which had for centuries existed as particular geographical, cultural, and political entities. Elsewhere, common traditions and assumptions were less clearly articulated, because the political unity that might have helped define them did not exist. East Prussians or Venetians had no difficulty in perceiving of themselves as such; history had provided them with those identities. But history had not provided them, except in the most general way, with identities as Germans or Italians. They had to make a deliberate effort to think of themselves in those terms before the terms could have any political reality.

Neither nationalism nor nation-building stood in necessary opposition to liberalism. Indeed, to the extent that nationalism celebrated the achievements of a particular common people over those of a cosmopolitan aristocratic elite, it reflected liberalism's abhorrence of traditional privilege. Liberalism recognized as well the extent to which nationalism and nation-building could facilitate the achievement of liberal goals. Yet to liberalism's readiness to welcome the future, nationalism responded with an appreciation, if not veneration, of the past. And to the liberals' insistence upon the value and importance of individualism, nation-builders replied that their vital task might require the sacrifice of some measure of each citizen's freedom. The success of nation-building rested upon the foundation of a general balance of international power, achieved by the European states during the half century after 1815. The emergence of new nations—a unified Italy and Germany—would require readjustments to that balance. But accommodation remained possible, with only minor skirmishes marring the stability of the settlement achieved at the Congress of Vienna.

1. ROMANTICISM AND NATIONALISM

A William Blake Etching for a Children's Book Written by Mary Wollstonecraft

As we noted in a preceding chapter, nationalism was in part a child of the French Revolution. It was closely related, as well, to the intellectual movement that has been called "romanticism." Romanticism was so broad and so varied that it all but defies definition, if not analysis. Perhaps as much as anything, romanticism represented a reaction against the rationalism of the eighteenth-century Enlightenment. Where the eighteenth century relied on reason, the romantics put their faith in emotion. The eighteenth century understood the mind as a blank tablet, which received knowledge from impressions imprinted upon it through the senses by the external world. Romantics supplemented this reliance on sense experience with an insistence on the importance of the "soul"—that innate faculty that ordered sense experience within an emotional framework. One's individual soul mediated the sense experiences available to all, so that each person's response to the world was necessarily highly subjective, unique, and creative. At the same time, each individual was part of an organic whole, a nature that was unified, animate, and filled with "spirit."

One popular strand of romanticism was explicitly universal in its celebration of nature and, above all, of individual creativity. Whether as a single flower or a mountain range, nature was welcomed as it impressed itself directly on the senses. Men and women were declared free to interpret nature—and life as well—in terms of their individual reactions to it, not simply as it might reflect a set of general rational precepts. The English poet Percy Shelley (1792–1822), the German poet Heinrich Heine (1797–1856), the French novelist Victor Hugo (1802–1885), the Spanish painter Francisco Goya (1746–1828)—all characteristic figures of the romantic movement—expressed in their works romanticism's concern for the experiences of human individuals and their relations to transcendent nature. The paintings of the Englishmen William Blake (1757–1827) and J. M. W. Turner (1775–1851), although they often reflect "Englishness," recorded a universal communion with the fundamental elements of nature.

Celebration of nature

George Sand

Another strand of romanticism elevated the importance of individual experience, unconfined by any boundary—metaphysical or political. Romanticism thus encouraged women to make themselves heard. The Englishwoman Mary Wollstonecraft (1759–1797), author of *A Vindication of the Rights of Women;* Madame Germaine de Staël (1766–1817), an emigré from France to Germany during the revolutionary period, whose essay *De l'Allemagne* (On Germany) was steeped in romanticism; George Sand (1804–1876), whose novels and whose life proclaimed allegiance to the standards of radical individualism—these women exemplify romanticism's readiness to break with the past, and its assumptions and stereotypes, if they stood in the path of individual expression.

This exaltation of individuality expressed itself in the celebration of "genius." The genius was possessed of a spirit that could not be analyzed and must be allowed to make its own rules. The human spirit was never to allow itself to be fettered by political prescriptions, any more than by social conventions, in such a way as to prevent enjoyment of its most precious possession, its freedom.

See color plates following page 780 for *Beatrice and Dante* by Blake, *Execution of Rioters* by Goya, and *Valley of Aosta— Snowstorm, Avalanche, and Thunderstorm* by Turner

Freedom and the problem of self-recognition were major themes in the works of two of the giants of the romantic movement, the composer Ludwig van Beethoven (1770–1827) and the writer Johann Wolfgang von Goethe (1749–1832). The most remarkable quality about Beethoven's compositions is their uniqueness and individuality. In the Fifth Symphony Beethoven reaches the summit of symphonic logic, the Sixth is a glorification of nature, the Seventh a Dionysian revelry, the Eighth a genial conjuring up of the spirit of the eighteenth-century symphony. The deafness that afflicted Beethoven in his later years seems to have encouraged him in his determination to speak out through his music as one extraordinarily powerful, and at times distressed, human being. Five piano sonatas, five string quartets, the Ninth Symphony, and the great Mass, *Missa Solemnis,* constitute his final legacy. They fill the listener with awe not so much because of their unusual form or their vast proportions, but because they express boundless individual will and power.

Ludwig van Beethoven

Goethe's dedication to the idea of individual freedom was, in part, the product of his having been born and raised in the free imperial city of

An Illustration from Goethe's Sorrows of Werther

Individual linked to community through history

Johann von Herder

Frankfurt. Frankfurt was an international center, a trading place open to intellectual winds from all quarters. Goethe was, in terms of his environment, free from the particularist, nationalist influences that directed the work of other German romantics. Goethe's own "genius" drove him first to the study of law, then medicine, then the fine arts and natural sciences. In 1775 he took up residence at the court of the young duke of Weimar. Weimar was a tiny German principality with a population of no more than half a million, another cosmopolitan community and in this respect not unlike Frankfurt. Influenced by the German philosopher Johann von Herder (1744–1803), Goethe had already published various romantically inclined works, including the immensely popular *The Sorrows of Young Werther,* a novel expressive of Goethe's early restlessness and emotionalism. The almost excessive sensitivity characteristic of Goethe's earlier writings gave way, in his middle years, to the search for a new spirit, equally free and yet more ordered. This mode derived from his experiences in Italy and from his study of the ancient Romans and Greeks. In 1790 Goethe published the first part of his masterpiece, *Faust,* a drama in verse, which he completed a year before his death in 1832. The play, in its retelling of the German legend of the man who sold his soul to the devil in return for universal knowledge, reflects the romantic unwillingness to restrain the spirit; it also expresses Goethe's own recognition of the magnitude of humanity's daring in its desire for unlimited knowledge and its own fulfillment.

Yet another strand of romanticism joined the individual to his or her community, which was defined through its historical links to the past. This strand of romantic nationalism, especially prevalent in the German states, adapted the Enlightenment emphasis on knowledge as the key to universal human progress. Now, however, "knowledge" was defined as familiarity with one's history; only by knowing one's past could one act properly in the present and chart the future.

One of the earliest and most influential German nationalist romantics was Johann von Herder (1744–1803). A Protestant pastor and theologian, his interest in past cultures led him, in the 1780s, to set out his reflections in a lengthy and detailed treatise, *Ideas for a Philosophy of Human History.* Herder traced what he perceived to be the progressive development of European society from the time of the Greeks through the Renaissance. He believed that civilization was not the product of an artificial, international elite—a criticism of Enlightenment thinking—but of the genuine culture of the common people, the *Volk.* No civilization could be considered sound which did not continue to express its own unique historical character, its *Volksgeist.* It was the particular genius of an entire people that Herder extolled as the *Volksgeist.* Herder did not argue that one *Volksgeist* was either better or worse than any other. He insisted only that each nation must be true to its own particular heritage. He broke dramatically with the Enlightenment idea that all human beings could be expected to respond to human situations in more or less the same universal fashion, and with the assumption that the value of history was simply to teach by example.

Herder's intellectual heirs, men like the conservative German romantics

Apotheosis of Homer, Jean Auguste Ingres (1780–1867). Though he painted during the romantic period, Ingres did not desert the neoclassical themes and style that dominated art during the Revolutionary and Napoleonic eras. (Louvre)

Beatrice and Dante, William Blake (1757–1827). Blake was a mystical romantic whose work possesses a compelling uniqueness that defies exact categorization. This painting is from his series for *The Divine Comedy*. (The Tate Gallery, London)

Execution of the Rioters, Francisco Goya (1746–1828). Unlike most artists of his time, Goya dealt unflinchingly with suffering, violence, fear, and death. Depicted here is the execution of Spanish rebels by Napoleon's soldiers in 1808. This harshness caused the rebellion to spread over the whole peninsula. (Prado)

Liberty Leading the People, Eugène Delacroix (1798–1863). Delacroix was a romantic painter of dramatic and emotional scenes. In this painting he celebrates the triumph of the revolutionary principle of liberty in a tempestuous allegory. (Louvre)

The Massacre of Chios, Eugène Delacroix. Here Delacroix again puts his brush to work for the cause of liberty, eulogizing the more than 20,000 Greeks slain by the Turks during the Greek war of independence in 1822. (Louvre)

The Movings by Louis Léopold Boilly (1761–1845). Dating from 1822, this realist-allegorical painting depicts Parisians of various classes in the process of moving their household goods. By juxtaposing the buildings of contemporary Paris with the Church of Santa Maria de' Miracoli of Rome, the artist appears to suggest that for some, including the peasants in their wagon leaving the city and the corpse in the horse-drawn hearse heading for its grave, the idea of the metropolis as a place of promise and prosperity is an illusion. (Art Institute of Chicago)

The Last of England, Ford Madox Brown (1821–1893). A haunting scene of a couple emigrating from England by one of the most noted pre-Raphaelites. (The City Museum and Art Gallery, Birmingham, England)

Valley of Aosta—Snowstorm, Avalanche, and Thunderstorm, Joseph M. W. Turner (1775–1851). Turner's complete absorption in light, color, and atmosphere helped to prepare the way for the French impressionists. (MMA)

A Woman Reading, Camille Corot (1796–1875). Corot was a naturalist whose interest in the effects of light prefigured to a degree the work of the impressionists. Sentimentality and a preference for scenes of innocence and simplicity distinguished him from the realists. (MMA)

Public Notary Eltz and His Family by Ferdinand Georg Waldmüller (1793–1865). A portrait that celebrates the rise to power and influence of the bourgeois bureaucrat. (Österreichische Galerie, Vienna)

The Gleaners, Jean François Millet (1814–1875). A realist, Millet remained fascinated with color and setting to a degree that often made his paintings something other than a record of social change. (Louvre)

Funeral at Ornans, Gustave Courbet (1819–1877). Though a less strident realist than his contemporary Daumier, Courbet was concerned to express human nature as he found it—neither more handsome nor more ugly. This painting, in which he used men and women from his village as models, reflects his commitment to personal, as opposed to social, realism. (Louvre)

Friedrich Schlegel (1772–1829) and Friedrich von Savigny (1779–1861) condemned the implantation of democratic and liberal ideas—"foreign" to Germany—in German cultural soil. History, they argued, taught that institutions must evolve organically—a favorite word of the political romantics—and that proper laws were the product of historical growth, not simply deductions from universal first principles. Thus the development of future laws and institutions must be predicated upon an understanding of a nation's past experience. This idea was not peculiar to German romantics. The English romantic poet and philosopher Samuel Taylor Coleridge (1772–1834) argued against the utilitarian state and in favor of giving that ancient institution, the national church, a larger role in the shaping of society. The French conservative Chateaubriand (1768–1848) made much the same case in his treatise, *The Genius of Christianity,* published in 1802. The past, and in particular the religious experiences of the past, are woven into the present, he declared. They cannot be unwoven without destroying the fabric of a nation's society.

The role of history and religion

The theory of the organic evolution of society and the state received its fullest exposition in the writings of the German metaphysician Georg Wilhelm Hegel (1770–1831), a professor of philosophy at the University of Berlin. Hegel wrote of history as development. Social and political institutions grew to maturity, achieved their purposes, and then gave way to others. Yet the new never entirely replaced the old, for the pattern of change was a "dialectic." When new institutions challenged established ones, there was a clash between what had been and what was becoming, producing a "synthesis," a reordering of society that retained elements from the past while adapting to the present. Hegel expected, for example, that the present disunity among the German states, which generated the idea of unity, would inevitably result in the creation of a nation-state. Hegel had no use for the theory of a state of nature, so popular with philosophers like Rousseau and Hobbes. Men and women have always lived within some society or other, Hegel argued. The institution of the state was itself a natural historic organism; only within that institution, protected by its laws and customs from personal depradations, could men and women enjoy freedom, which Hegel defined not as the absence of restraint but as the absence of social disorder.

Georg Wilhelm Hegel

These theories of history and of historical development articulated by the romantics relate directly to the idea of nationalism formulated during the same period. The French Revolution provided an example of what a nation could achieve. Nationhood had encouraged the French to raise themselves to the level of citizenship; it had also allowed them to sustain attacks from the rest of Europe. Applying the historical lessons of the French Revolution and the theories of romantics, Germans, in particular, were roused to a sense of their own historical destiny. The works of the philosopher J. G. Fichte (1762–1814) are an example of this reawakening. As a young professor at the University of Jena, Fichte had at first advanced a belief in the importance of an individual's inner spirit, the creator of its own moral universe. Devoid of national feeling, he welcomed the French

Fichte

Grimm's Fairy Tales. This illustration from "The Golden Egg" depicts villagers running through an idyllic German village.

Revolution as an emancipator of the human spirit. Yet when France conquered much of Germany, Fichte's attitude changed dramatically. He adopted Herder's notion of a *Volksgeist;* what mattered was no longer the individual spirit, but the spirit of a whole people, expressed in its customs, traditions, and history. In 1808, Fichte delivered a series of *Addresses to the German Nation,* in which he declared the existence of a German spirit to be, not just one among many such spirits, but superior to the rest. The world had not yet heard from that spirit; he predicted it soon would. Although the French military commander in Berlin, where Fichte spoke, believed the addresses to be too academic to warrant censorship, they expressed a sentiment that aided the Prussians in their conscious attempt to rally themselves and, as a political *Volk,* to drive out the French.

National themes in literature, art, music

Nationalism, derived from romantic notions of historical development and destiny, manifested itself in a variety of ways. The brothers Grimm, editors of *Grimm's Fairy Tales* (1812–1815), traveled across Germany to study native dialects, and collected folktales that were published as part of a national heritage. The poet Friedrich Schiller's (1759–1805) drama of *William Tell* (1804), the Swiss hero, became a rallying cry for German national consciousness. In Britain, Sir Walter Scott (1771–1832) retold in many of his novels the popular history of Scotland, while the poet William Wordsworth (1770–1850) consciously strove to express the simplicity and virtue of the English people in collections such as his *Lyrical Ballads* (1798). Throughout Europe, countries assiduously catalogued the relics of their historical past as in the society for publishing the *Monumenta Germaniae His-*

torica (Monuments of German History), founded in 1819; the French École des Chartes (1821); and the English Public Records Office (1838). In France, the neoclassical style, typified by the paintings of Jacques Louis David (1748–1825), and used by Napoleon to exalt his image, gave way to the turbulent romanticism of painters like Eugène Delacroix (1798–1863), whose *Liberty Leading the People* (1830) was a proclamation, not only of liberty, but of the courage of the French nation. Music, too, reflected national themes, though not until a generation or so after 1815. Many of Giuseppe Verdi's (1813–1901) operas, *Don Carlo,* for example, contained musical declarations of faith in the possibility of an Italian *risorgimento:* a resurrection of the Italian spirit. The operas of Richard Wagner (1813–1883)—in particular, those based on the German epic, *Song of the Nibelungs*—managed to raise veneration for the myths of Nordic gods and goddesses to the level of pious exaltation. Architects, though they found it difficult to escape entirely from the neoclassicism of the eighteenth century, often tried to resurrect a "national" style in their designs. Sir Charles Barry, assigned the task of redesigning the British Houses of Parliament following their destruction by fire in 1836, managed to mask a straightforward and symmetrical classical plan behind a Gothic screen, intended to acknowledge the country's debt to its own past. All this creative activity was the spontaneous result of artists' and writers' enthusiastic response to the romantic movement. Yet politicians soon perceived how historical romanticism might serve their nationalist ends. They understood how an individual work of art, whether a painting, a song, a drama, or a building, could translate into a national symbol. And they did not hesitate to assist in that translation when they deemed it useful.

Romanticism and nationalism bear much the same relationship to each other in the history of nineteenth-century Europe as they do in the

Giuseppe Verdi

See color plates following page 780 for *Liberty Leading the People* and *The Massacre of Chios* by Delacroix

Houses of Parliament, London. Redesigned by Sir Charles Barry with a Gothic facade after the earlier structure was destroyed by fire.

thought of the men and women we have just surveyed. At some points, as in England, they appear to run separate courses. At others they join together, as they did in Germany, whose own history lies at the center of the history of both romanticism and nationalism.

2. NATIONALISM AND NATION-BUILDING, 1800–1848

Nationalism and reform in Prussia, 1806–1815

The humiliating French occupation of Prussia (1806–1815), combined with the growing sense of national destiny exemplified in Fichte's *Addresses* (1808), resulted in a drive on the part of Prussian intellectuals and political reformers to bring their country once more to its former position among European powers. Prussia's crushing defeat by the French in 1806 had been the logical outcome of the inertia that had gripped the country during the half century or so since the aggressive achievements of Frederick the Great. Unlike the rest of the German states, however, allied directly with France in the Confederation of the Rhine, the separate kingdom of Prussia consciously avoided French "contamination," participating unwillingly in the Continental System, and otherwise holding itself aloof.

Military reforms

Its major task was to rebuild its armies, since only by that means could Prussia reassert itself against Napoleon. To that end, two generals, Gerhard von Scharnhorst and August Gneisenau, instituted changes based on an essential lesson in nation-building they had learned from the French Revolution: that men were far more effective fighters if they believed themselves to have some direct stake in the wars they fought. A reconstituted national army, eventually based upon a system of universal military service, involved the country as a whole in its own defense and grew to become a far more consciously "Prussian" force than it had been heretofore. Officers were recruited and promoted on the basis of merit, not birth, although the large majority continued to come from the Junker (aristocratic) class. This breach with tradition encouraged the Prussian middle class to take a more active and enthusiastic interest in its country's affairs. Old or inefficient officers, despite their social standing, were removed from positions of command; training at the royal cadet school in Berlin was modernized.

These reforms, which illustrate the way in which a liberal desire for modernization might combine with nationalism, paralleled similar changes instituted during the same period under the direction of Prussia's principal minister, Baron Heinrich Friedrich Karl vom und zum Stein (1757–1831), and his successor, Prince Karl August von Hardenberg (1750–1822). Stein was not himself a Prussian; he was initially less interested in achieving a Prussian nation-state than in uniting by some means or other all the various principalities of Germany. He had read Hegel and Fichte, and was convinced that a state must somehow make its citizens aware of their obligations to the national interest. A sense of duty to the state could hardly be kindled, however, without first convincing men and women that loyalty meant reward as well as obligation. Stein therefore labored to dismantle the

Baron Heinrich Friedrich Karl vom und zum Stein

caste system that had until that time characterized Prussia, in order to permit individuals to rise within society. The Edict of 1807 abolished serfdom and the estate system, ended the restrictions that kept nobles from selling their land to the middle class, and opened trades and professions to all classes. The Municipal Ordinance of 1808 was a conscious attempt to increase the middle-class Germans' sense of themselves as citizens—again, a goal shared by both liberals and nationalists. Cities and towns were henceforth required to elect their councilmen, while local justice and security continued to be administered by the central government in Berlin; all other matters, including finance, were left to individual communities. Education played a vital role in nation-building. Schools were ideal agencies for the dissemination of the doctrines of national duty. Recognizing this fact, the Prussian reformers expanded facilities for both primary and secondary education. The University of Berlin, founded in 1810, numbered among its faculty such ardent nationalists as Fichte and Savigny, and was the institutional embodiment of the new spirit that contributed to Prussia's eventual victory over the French.

Stein's governmental reforms

The history of Prussia between 1815 and 1850 can most easily be understood in terms of its continuing struggle to establish itself as the leading independent national power among the thirty-nine states that comprised Germany after 1806, and as a successful rival to Austrian domination. The most important Prussian victory in this respect was the establishment of the *Zollverein,* or customs union, which combined free trade within the German states and a uniform tariff against the rest of the world. By the 1840s, the union included almost all of Germany except German Austria, and offered manufacturers a market of almost 34 million people. The spread of the railways after 1835 provided easy access within this internal market. The writings of the economist Friedrich List (1789–1846) justified this nationalist response to the internationalism of the liberal free-trade economists. List wrote that while free trade might suit the British, it did not suit a nation such as Prussia. Economics, he argued, far from being an abstract science equally applicable everywhere, was a discipline that must be grounded in the particular national experience of individual countries. Germany's, and therefore Prussia's, experience demanded not free trade but high tariffs. Only when sheltered behind a protectionist system could Prussia build the factories and manufacture the goods that would guarantee its economic health.

Economic nationalism

The events that had altered the political shape of Britain and France in the early 1830s—revolution in the latter and liberal reforms in both—had their counterparts in Germany. Liberals resented both Prussian dominance within the German Confederation and the conservatism of the ruling Habsburgs in the Austrian Empire. The governments of both Prussia and Austria were grounded in a combination of autocracy and bureaucracy that stifled the social and political goals of the liberals, who hoped for the achievement of both unity and freedom. The creation of a German nation would lead to the realization of liberal goals, while avoiding the particularism that had haunted Germany's political past and the domination by either

German liberalism thwarted

Austria or Prussia that promised to blight its future. Student societies—*Burschenschaften*—had sprung up throughout Germany following the Napoleonic wars. At an assembly in 1817 at Wartburg Castle, where Martin Luther had three hundred years before proclaimed his ninety-five theses, these modern protestants on behalf of "the holy cause of union and freedom" marched to a bonfire upon which they placed the works of reactionary writers. Repressed for a time by Metternich, the *Burschenschaften* reappeared in the late 1820s, and welcomed the 1830 revolution in France. Minor revolts occurred in Brunswick, Saxony, and Hesse-Cassel; unpopular monarchs were replaced by royal relatives more sympathetic to reform. In 1832 at an all-German festival held at Hambach, on the French border, 25,000 men and women toasted Lafayette and denounced the Holy Alliance. Once again, Metternich imposed a series of repressive reforms upon the German Confederation, which effectively stifled protest and thwarted liberal aspirations.

The politics of Frederick William IV

Prussia avoided revolution as a result of the reforms instituted a generation before by Stein and Hardenberg. In 1840 Frederick William IV (1840–1861) succeeded to the Prussian throne. Apparently devoted to liberal principles, he relaxed censorship laws and encouraged participation in the central government by provincial diets. It soon became apparent, however, that the king was no liberal, but some sort of romantic-nationalist, and an authoritarian as well. He crushed the revolt of thousands of Silesian weavers in 1844, when they protested the importation of English yarn and cotton goods and their consequent unemployment and poverty. He further declared himself opposed to constitutionalism, that central doctrine in the liberal canon of beliefs. When Prussian liberals pressed, in 1847, for control over legislative and budgetary matters in the recently convened assembly of diets (the *Landtag*) the king saw to it that their request was denied. Frederick William then turned his attention to a scheme whereby Prussia might play a far larger role in the German Confederation. But before his plan could receive a hearing, it was overtaken by the revolutionary movement of 1848, which, as we shall see, engulfed Central Europe as it had Western Europe, though with different results.

Nationalism in the Austrian Empire

National sentiment, the spirit that served to unite the Prussians against France, was at the same time operating to divide the heterogeneous elements within the Austrian Empire. Its people, who lived within three major geographical areas—Austria, Bohemia, and Hungary—were composed of a considerable number of different ethnic and language groups: Germans, Czechs, Magyars, Poles, Slovaks, Serbs, and Italians, to name the most prominent. In some parts of the empire, these people lived in isolation; elsewhere they dwelt in direct proximity, if not much harmony, with others. The Habsburgs' attempts to unite these groups failed increasingly, as a spirit of cultural, if not political, nationalism grew persistently stronger in the years after 1815. In the Polish territories of the empire, where the gentry had for generations been conscious of themselves as Poles, the imperial government succeeded in stifling the sentiment by playing off the serfs against their masters, encouraging a class war as a means of preventing an ethnic one. Elsewhere within the empire they were less adroit. In Hungary, nationalism expressed itself in both cultural and political forms. In 1827, a Hungarian national theater was established at Budapest. The year before, Magyar was substituted for Latin as the official language of government. A political movement, whose most formidable leader was the radical nationalist Louis Kossuth (1802–1894), was at the same time seeking independence and a parliamentary government for Hungary.

Pan-Slavism

The most widespread of the Eastern European cultural nationalist movements was Pan-Slavism. Slavs included Russians, Poles, Czechs, Slovaks, Slovenes, Croats, Serbs, and Bulgars. Before 1848 Pan-Slavism was an almost exclusively cultural movement, united by a generalized anti-Western sentiment, yet divided by a tendency to quarrel as to the primacy of this or that particular language or tradition. These divisions did not substantially lessen the effect of Pan-Slavism as a further problem of the Austrian Empire. The literature of the movement—for example, the historian Francis Palacky's (1798–1876) *History of the Bohemian People* and the poetry of the revolutionary Pole Adam Mickiewicz (1798–1855)—fed the desires of those who wished to rid themselves of what they considered a foreign yoke. In Russia, slavophilism had been held in check by the Western-looking Alexander I. After his death in 1825, however, the notion that the Russian people possessed its particular *Volksgeist* increased in general popularity. At the same time, the many ethnic minorities within Russia began pressing for their own recognition.

Nationalism in Italy

Two other national movements were growing beyond infancy during the years before 1848: one in Italy, the other in Ireland. Italy, at the beginning of the nineteenth century, was a peninsula divided into a multitude of states, most of them poor and ineffectually governed. The most efficient governments in Italy after 1815 were those imposed by Austria on the northern territories of Lombardy and Venetia (see map, p. 798) and by the introverted, visionary, yet intensely reform-minded king of Sardinia, Charles Albert (1831–1849). At the opposite pole were the Kingdom of the Two Sicilies and the Papal States, governed by equally obscurantist rulers, Francis I (1825–1830), a Bourbon, and thereafter by his son, Ferdinand II (1830–1859), and Pope Gregory XVI (1831–1846). Popular uprisings in Modena, Parma, and Bologna occurred in 1830, but with no lasting consequences, either for the initiation of local liberal reforms or for the cause of unification of the various disparate states into some sort of national whole. Among the pan-Italian organizations formed in the confused period at the end of the Napoleonic wars, none was louder in its nationalist proclamations than the Italian *Carbonari*. One member of that group, Giuseppe Mazzini (1805–1872), founded a society of his own in 1831, Young Italy, which was dedicated to the cause of uniting the peninsula. In 1834, from Switzerland, Mazzini launched a totally unsuccessful verbal assault against the Kingdom of Sardinia, in the hope that the rest of Italy would join him. Mazzini subsequently contented himself with propagandizing for the cause of Italian nationalism and republicanism, attracting a devoted following, particularly among British liberals. Liberals in Italy,

Giuseppe Mazzini

however, mistrusted him. Although they too wished to see a united Italy, they were dismayed, as "good" liberals, and members of the middle class, by Mazzini's insistence upon a republic, hoping instead to merge existing principalities together into some sort of constitutional monarchy.

Nationalism in Ireland   If Italian nationalism was primarily a middle-class liberal phenomenon at this time, the same was not true of the Irish movement to repeal the union with England. Headed by Daniel O'Connell (1775–1847), it derived its strength from the support of Irish peasants. O'Connell's remarkably successful appeal was based on the hatred all Irish felt for the English, because of the centuries of oppression Irish Catholics had suffered under English Protestant rule. Both before and after the official union of 1801, the English had imposed on the Irish a foreign rule that had brought with it little but poverty and persecution. O'Connell's campaign for the repeal of the union was grounded in the hope that he would be able to negotiate some sort of moderate agreement with the English ruling class. The desires of his followers were far more radical. Neither the separatist hopes of O'Connell, called by the Irish the "Liberator," nor the more genuinely nationalist hopes of his followers, however, were to achieve realization. Unlike the nationalist movements of Central Europe, nationalism in Ireland faced a powerful and determined adversary—Britain—which would for a century deny it victory.

3. NATIONALISM, LIBERALISM, AND REVOLUTION, 1848

The history of the revolutions of 1848 in Central Europe can most easily be understood in terms of two major themes: the first, the struggle of various nationalities, particularly within the Austrian Empire, to assert their own autonomy; the second, the changing relationship between the forces of liberalism and nationalism in Germany.

The "March Days" in Austria   News of the February revolution in France traveled quickly eastward. By the end of March the Austrian Empire was split apart. Hungary, with Kossuth in the lead, severed all but the most tenuous of links with the House of Habsburg and prepared to draft its own constitution. In Vienna, workers and students imitated their counterparts in Paris, erecting barricades and invading the imperial palace. A measure of the political chaos was the fact that Metternich, veteran of a score of threats to the precarious stability he had crafted, found the pressure this time too great, and fled in disguise to Britain. The feeble Habsburg emperor, Ferdinand II, once he had been deserted by Metternich, yielded to nationalist demands from Bohemia and granted that kingdom its own constitution as well. To the south, Italians launched attacks against the Austrian-held territories in Milan, Naples, Venetia, and Lombardy, where the forces of the Sardinian ruler, King Charles Albert, routed the Austrians.

Yet the forces of national sentiment that had brought Austria to its knees then succeeded in allowing the empire to recoup its fortunes. The paradox of nationalism in Central Europe was that as soon as a cultural majority had declared itself an independent or semi-independent state, other cultural minorities within that new state complained bitterly about their newly institutionalized inferiority. This is precisely what happened in Bohemia. There the anti-German Czech majority refused to send delegates to an all-German assembly, which was meeting at Frankfurt in May 1848 to draft a German constitution. Instead, they summoned a confederation of Slavs to Prague. The delegates, most of them from within the boundaries of the old Austrian Empire, immediately recognized that the idea of a united Germany represented a far greater threat to their political and cultural autonomy than the fact of the empire ever had. The German minority in Bohemia, however, was naturally anxious to participate in discussions that might result in closer union with their ethnic counterparts. They resented the Bohemian government's refusal to do so. The resulting animosities made it all the easier for the Austrians to take advantage of a May 1848 insurrection in Prague, subdue the city, send the Slav congress packing, and reassert control in Bohemia. Although the Austrian government was at this time a liberal one, the product of the March revolution in Vienna, it was no less determined than its predecessor had been to prevent the total dismemberment of the empire, for economic as well as political reasons. Hence it was quick to restore Lombardy and Venetia to its realm when quarrels among the heretofore united Italian allies had sufficiently weakened their common stand against the Austrians.

Nationalism and counternationalism in Hungary set the stage for the final act of the restoration of Austrian hegemony. Kossuth's radical party was, above all, a Magyar nationalist party. Once in power, in early 1849 it moved the capital from Pressburg, near the Austrian border, to Budapest, and again proclaimed Magyar as the country's official language. These actions offended national minorities within Hungary, particularly the Croats, who prior to the revolution had enjoyed certain liberties under Austrian rule. The Croatians raised an insurgent army and launched a civil war. The Austrians, once more encouraging division along nationalist lines, named the Croatian rebel Josef von Jellachich their military commander against the Magyars. By this time the Viennese liberals began to recognize—too late—that their turn might come next. They were right. Despite a second uprising in Vienna in October, the revolution was spent. Forces loyal to the emperor descended upon Vienna from Bohemia. On October 31, the liberal government capitulated.

Once the imperial government had reasserted itself, it labored to suppress nationalist impulses as thoroughly as possible. Austria's ministers recognized that, though tactically advantageous at times, nationalist movements operated generally to the detriment of the empire's political and economic unity. The emperor's chief minister, Prince Felix von Schwarzenberg, and the minister of the interior, Alexander Bach, both nation-builders, together centralized the state within one united political system. Hungary and Bohemia no longer enjoyed separate rights. Peasants of all ethnic groups, liberated from serfdom as part of the general reform movement, were permitted to retain their freedom, on the grounds of their loyalty to the empire. The law was reformed, again to achieve uniformity, and railways and roads were constructed to link the empire. Economic nationalism was encouraged through tariffs designed to exclude foreign manufactures, while a free trade area within the empire encouraged domestic industries. Having done all it could to eradicate separatist movements, the Austrian government thus moved to secure its advantage by engaging in a vigorous campaign of nation-building.

The failure of revolution in Prussia

In Prussia, revolution ran a similar course. In March, King Frederick William IV found himself compelled to yield to demands for a popularly elected legislative assembly. When it met, the body proved particularly sympathetic to the plight of the Polish minority within Prussia, and antagonistic toward the Russians, whom radical legislators saw as the major threat to the spread of enlightened political ideas in Central Europe. When the assembly's sympathy with Polish nationalism extended to the granting of self-government to Prussian Poland, however, it generated the same feelings among the German minority there that we have seen arousing minorities within the Austrian Empire. In so doing, it precipitated the same eventual results. Germans in Posen, the major city of Prussian Poland, revolted against the newly established Polish government; not surprisingly, Prussian army units on duty sided with the Germans and helped them crush the new government. Power, it now became clear, lay with the army, professionalized since the days of Gneisenau and Scharnhorst, yet still dominated by the Junkers. Against the armed authority of the military, the radical legislators of Berlin were no match; revolution ended in Prussia as quickly as it had begun.

The Frankfurt Assembly

Meanwhile, at Frankfurt, Germans engaged in the debate that provides the history of Central Europe in these revolutionary years with its second theme: the shifting relationship between liberalism and nationalism. Delegates had been chosen from across Germany and Austria to attend the Frankfurt Assembly. They were largely from the professional classes—professors, lawyers, administrators—and generally devoted to the cause of middle-class liberalism. Many had assumed that their task would resemble that of the assembly that had met in 1789 to draft a constitution for the French: i.e., they would draft a constitution for a liberal, unified Germany. That former convocation, however, had been grounded in the simple but all-important fact that a French nation-state already existed. The French assembly had been elected to give the nation a new shape and new direction. But a centralized sovereign power was there to reshape; there was an authority that could be either commandeered or, if necessary, usurped. The Frankfurt Assembly, in contrast, was grounded upon nothing but its own words. It was a collection of thoughtful, well-intentioned middle-class liberals, committed to a belief that a liberal-national German state could somehow be constituted out of abstract principles.

Almost from the start, the assembly found itself tangled in the problems of nationality. Who, they asked, were the Germans? A majority of the delegates argued that they were all those who, by language, culture, or geog-

Procession of the German National Assembly to Its Opening Session at St. Paul's Church, Frankfurt, May 1848

raphy, felt themselves bound to the enterprise now underway at Frankfurt. The German nation that was to be constituted must include as many of those "Germans" as possible—a goal that seemed achievable in view of the disintegrating Habsburg Empire. This point of view came to be known as the "Great German" position. A minority called for a "Little Germany," one that excluded all lands of the Habsburg Empire. While Great Germans were a numerical majority, they found themselves stymied by the unwillingness of other nationalities to be included in their fold. The Czechs in Bohemia, as we have seen, wanted no part of Great Germany. In the end the Great Germans settled that the nation for which they were drafting a constitution should include, among other territories, all Austrian lands except Hungary. This decision meant that the crown of their new country might most logically be offered to the Habsburg emperor. As the Habsburg Empire began reasserting its strength, the Great German solution grew more impractical. At this point the voice of the Little Germans began to be heard, with the argument that Austria should be excluded altogether and the crown instead offered to King Frederick William of Prussia.

Great Germans vs. Little Germans

Fighting in Frankfurt, September 18, 1848. Note the contrast between the disciplined maneuvers of the troops and the guerilla tactics of the rioting populace.

Liberalism vs. nationalism

The liberalism of the assembly was put to the test by events in Austria and Poland in the fall of 1848. When the imperial forces crushed the Czech and Hungarian rebellions, when the Prussian Junkers put an end to Polish self-government, liberals found themselves forced to cheer. They were compelled to support the suppression of minority nationalities; otherwise there would be no new Germany. But their support was for the forces not only of German nationalism but of antiliberal authoritarianism. The assembly's most embarrassing moment occurred when it found itself compelled to take shelter behind the Prussian army. Riots broke out in Frankfurt protesting the assembly's willingness to withdraw from a confrontation with the Danes over the future of Germans in Schleswig, a Danish province. That particular area, which many considered to be part of Germany, had been annexed by the Danes in March 1848. The Frankfurters had been unable to do more than ask the Prussians to win Schleswig back for them; and the Prussians had refused. Hence the riots; hence a second request, this time heeded, for Prussian assistance.

The end of the assembly

Reduced to the status of dependents, the Frankfurt delegates nevertheless, in the spring of 1849, produced a constitution. By this time Austria, fearing its Prussian rival, had decided to have no more to do with Frankfurt. The Little Germans thus won by default and offered their constitutional monarchy to Frederick William of Prussia. Though tempted, he turned them down, arguing that their constitution was too liberal, embodying as it did the revolutionary notion that a crown could be offered to a monarch. Frederick wanted the crown, but on his own terms. The delegates went home, disillusioned by their experience, many of them convinced that their dual goal of liberalism and nationalism was an impossible one. Some, who refused to surrender that goal, emigrated to the United

States, where they believed the goal had already been achieved. Many of those who stayed behind convinced themselves that half the goal was better than none, and sacrificed the immediate achievement of liberal goals to the seemingly realistic goals of nationalism.

4. NATION-BUILDING, 1850–1870

The twenty years between 1850 and 1870 were years of intense nation-building in the Western world. Of the master-builders, none was more accomplished than the man who brought Germany under Prussian rule, Otto von Bismarck (1815–1898). Born into the Junker class, Bismarck had emerged during the revolutionary period of 1848 and 1849 as a defender of the monarchy. Bismarck was neither a liberal nor a nationalist; he was before all else a Prussian. When he instituted domestic reforms, he did so not because he favored the "rights" of this or that particular group but because he thought that his policies would result in a more united, and hence more powerful, Prussia. When he maneuvered to bring other German states under Prussian domination, he did so not in conformity with a grand Germanic design but because he believed that some sort of union was almost inevitable and, if so, that it must come about at Prussia's behest. He prided himself on being a realist; and he became a first-rate practitioner of what has come to be called *Realpolitik*—the politics of what its practitioners claim to be hardheaded reality. Bismarck readily acknowledged his admiration of power. He at one point had considered a career in the military—not at all surprising in view of his Junker origins. He once wrote that he regretted that he was compelled to serve his country from behind a desk rather than at the front. But whatever his post, he intended to command. "I want to play the tune the way it sounds good to me or not at all," he declared. "Pride, the desire to command. . . . I confess I am not free from these passions." Nor did he consider those passions unworthy of the man who was to undertake the task of shaping the fortunes of the German state.

Bismarck

Bismarck came to power as minister-president of Prussia in 1862 at the behest of King William I (1861–1888), who required Bismarck's assistance in bringing a liberal parliament to heel. Its majority had been produced by an electoral system that was part of the constitution granted by Frederick William to Prussia in 1850, following the collapse of the assembly. The parliament was divided into two houses, the lower one elected by universal male suffrage. Votes were apportioned according to one's ability to pay taxes, however; those few who together paid one-third of the country's taxes elected one-third of the legislators. A large landowner or industrialist exercised about a hundred times the voting power of a poor man. Contrary to the king's expectations, however, under this constitution a liberal majority was succeeding in thwarting the plans of the sovereign and his advisors. Specifically, it had opposed since 1859 a proposed increase in military expenditures, despite pressure from the king. The liberals, having consoli-

Bismarck and the liberals

dated economic and political strengths gained during a decade of industrial growth, would not give way. In Bismarck the liberals more than met their match. When they refused to levy taxes, he dissolved the parliament and collected them anyway, claiming that the constitution, whatever its purposes, had not been designed to subvert the state. When liberals argued that Prussia was setting a poor example for the rest of Germany, Bismarck replied that Prussia was admired not for its liberalism but for its power.

The Crimean War

Whether or not the Germans—or the rest of Europe—admired Prussia's power, they soon found themselves confronted by it. Bismarck proceeded to build a nation that in the short space of eight years came into being as the German Empire. Bismarck was assisted in his task by his readiness to take advantage of international situations as they presented themselves, without concerning himself particularly with the ideological or moral implications of his actions. He was aided as well by developments over which he had no initial control but which he was able to turn to his advantage. The first of these, the Crimean War, had occurred in 1854–1856, prior to his taking office. Russia and Turkey, perennial European squabblers, had precipitated the hostilities. Russia invaded the territories of Moldavia and Walachia (later Rumania) in an attempt to take advantage of the continuing political rot that made the Ottoman Empire an easy prey. Austria, in order to protect her border along the Danube, drove Russia out of these territories and garrisoned her own troops there. In 1854 France and then Britain came to the aid of the Turks by invading Russia's Crimean peninsula. These allies were soon joined by Sardinia. The quarrel had by this time enlarged to include the question of who was to protect the Christians in Jerusalem from the Turks; it was fueled from the start as well by Britain's continuing determination to prohibit a strong Russian presence in the Near East. The allies' eventual victory was primarily the result of a British blockade of Russia. The peace settlement was a severe setback for Russia, whose influence in the Balkans was drastically curbed. Moldavia and

British Encampment near Sebastopol, 1854–1855. Photograph taken by Roger Fenton. The Crimean War was the first to be reported to the world by photograph as well as by news dispatch.

TOWARD THE UNIFICATION OF GERMANY · 1740-1871

Legend:
- Boundary of the German Confederation in 1815
- Prussian acquisitions
- From Austria in 1763 — Prussia in 1815
- From partitions of Poland in 1772, 1793, 1795
- States annexed by Prussia in 1866
- States joining Prussia in Confederation of 1867
- Boundary of North German Confederation
- States added in 1871 to form German Empire
- Territories ceded by France in 1871
- ✕ Battle sites
- □ Fortifications

Walachia were united as Rumania, which, along with Serbia, was granted power as a self-governing principality. Austrian military resources had been severely taxed during the invasion and occupation of Moldavia and Walachia. And Austria's refusal to come to the aid of Russia lost her the support of that powerful erstwhile ally. It was the subsequent weakness of both Russia and Austria, the result of the Crimean War, that Bismarck used to his advantage in the 1860s.

In consolidating the German states into a union controlled by Prussia, Bismarck first moved to eliminate Austria from its commanding position in the German Confederation. As a means to this end he inflamed the long-smoldering dispute with Denmark over the possession of Schleswig and Holstein. Inhabited by Germans and Danes, these two provinces had an anomalous status. Since 1815 Holstein had been included in the German Confederation, but both were subject to the personal overlordship of the king of Denmark. When, in 1864, the Danish king attempted to annex them, Bismarck invited Austria to participate in a war against Denmark. A

Steps to German unification:
(1) weakening of Austria

brief struggle followed, at the end of which the Danish ruler was compelled to renounce all his claims to Schleswig and Holstein in favor of Austria and Prussia. Then the sequel for which Bismarck had ardently hoped occurred: a quarrel between the victors over division of the spoils. The conflict that followed in 1866, known as the Seven Weeks' War, ended in an easy triumph for Prussia over war-weakened Austria. Austria was forced to give up all claims to Schleswig and Holstein, to surrender Venetia, and to acquiesce in the dissolution of the German Confederation. Immediately following the war Bismarck proceeded to isolate Austria by uniting all of the German states north of the Main River into the North German Confederation.

(2) courting the masses

Bismarck's adept use of the Prussian military was matched by his manipulation of public support and opinion. Bismarck willingly turned himself into a democrat to achieve the confederation. He saw that if he was to attain his end, which was a strong union with Prussia at its head, he would need to cultivate a constituency hitherto untapped by any German politicians: the masses. He appreciated the manner by which Napoleon III had reinforced his regime through plebiscites. And Bismarck understood that the majority of Germans were not particularly enthusiastic supporters of capitalist liberals, of the bureaucracies of their own small states, or of the Austrian Habsburgs. The constitution he devised for his confederation provided for two chambers: the upper chamber represented the individual states within the union, though not equally; the lower chamber was elected by universal manhood suffrage. The liberal middle class, to say nothing of the Junkers, was astonished and dismayed, as well they might be. Bismarck's intention was to use popular support to strengthen the hand of the conservative central government against the interests of both landlords and capitalists.

(3) the Franco-Prussian War

Bismarck's final step in the completion of German unity was the Franco-Prussian War of 1870–1871. He hoped that a conflict with France would kindle the spirit of German nationalism in Bavaria, Würtemberg, and other southern states still outside the confederation. Taking advantage of a diplomatic tempest concerning the right of the Hohenzollerns (Prussia's ruling family) to occupy the Spanish throne, Bismarck worked hard to force a Franco-German misunderstanding. King William agreed to meet with the French ambassador at the resort spa of Ems in Prussia to discuss the Spanish succession. When William telegraphed Bismarck that the demands of the French for perpetual exclusion of the Hohenzollern family from the Spanish throne had been refused, Bismarck released portions of the message to the press so as to make it appear that King William had insulted the ambassador—which he had not done. Once the garbled report of what happened at Ems was received in France, the nation reacted with a call for war. The call was echoed in Prussia, where Bismarck published evidence that he claimed proved French designs upon the Rhineland. Upon the declaration of war, the south German states rallied to Prussia's side in the belief that it was the victim of aggression. The war was quickly fought. The French were no match for Prussia's professionally trained and superbly equipped forces. Nor did other European powers come to France's assistance. Austria, the most likely candidate, remained weakened by its recent war with Prussia. The Magyars, who at this time had assumed positions of influence within the Austrian government, were quite prepared to welcome a strengthened Prussia; Prussia's growing strength in Germany would further increase Austria's weakness there. And the weaker Austria was as a German power, the stronger would be the claims of the Magyars to predominance. Once more one nationalist consciousness was grinding against another. The war began in July; it ended in September with the defeat of the French and the capture of Napoleon III himself at Sedan in France.

The German Empire

Following the collapse of the French imperial government, insurrectionary forces in Paris continued to hold out against the Germans until the winter of 1871. Bismarck meanwhile proceeded to consummate the German union toward which he had worked so assiduously. On January 18, 1871, in the great Hall of Mirrors at Versailles the German Empire was proclaimed. All those states, except Austria, which had not already been absorbed into Prussia declared their allegiance to William I, henceforth emperor or kaiser. Four months later, at Frankfurt, a treaty between the French and Germans ceded the border region of Alsace to the new empire, condemned the French to an indemnity of five billion francs, and thereby broadcast to the world the remarkable success of Bismarck's nation-building.

Italian unification

Events in Italy ran a course almost parallel to that which had led to the unification of Germany. Italy before 1848, it will be recalled, was a patchwork of petty states. The most important of those possessing independence were the Kingdom of Sardinia in the north, the Papal States in the central region, and the Kingdom of the Two Sicilies in the south. The former republics of Lombardy and Venetia were held by Austria, while Habsburg dependents ruled in Tuscany, Parma, and Modena. As the revolutionary fervor of 1848 swept across the peninsula, one ruler after another granted democratic reforms. Charles Albert of Sardinia outdistanced all the others by guaranteeing civil liberties and granting a parliamentary form of government. It soon became evident, however, that the Italians were as determined nationalists as they were liberals. For some years romantic patriots had been dreaming of a *Risorgimento,* which would restore the nation to the position of glorious leadership it had held in Roman times and during the Renaissance. To achieve this, it was universally agreed that Italy must be welded into a single state. But opinions differed as to the form the new government should take. Young idealists followed the leadership of Mazzini. Religious-minded patriots believed that the most practicable solution would be to federate the state of Italy under the presidency of the pope. The majority of the more moderate nationalists advocated a constitutional monarchy built upon the foundations of the Kingdom of Sardinia. The aims of this third group gradually crystallized under the leadership of a shrewd Sardinian nobleman, Count Camillo di Cavour (1810–1861). In 1850 he was appointed minister of commerce and agriculture of his native state and in 1852 premier.

Camillo di Cavour

THE UNIFICATION OF ITALY

The Kingdom of Sardinia at the time of the Congress of Vienna, 1815

Territories acquired, 1859-1860

Territories acquired, 1860-1870

Italian War of Liberation

The campaign for unification of the Italian peninsula began with efforts to expel the Austrians. In 1848 revolts were organized in the territories under Habsburg domination, and an army of liberation marched from Sardinia to aid the rebels; but the movement ended in failure. It was then that Cavour, as the new leader of the campaign, turned to less heroic but more practical methods. In 1858 he held a secret meeting with Napoleon III and prepared the stage for an Italian War of Liberation. Napoleon agreed to cooperate in driving the Austrians from Italy for the price of the cession of Savoy and Nice by Sardinia to France. A war with Austria was duly provoked in 1859, and for a time all went well for the Franco-Italian allies.

After the conquest of Lombardy, however, Napoleon III suddenly withdrew, fearful of ultimate defeat and afraid of antagonizing the Catholics in his own country by aiding the avowedly anticlerical government of Cavour. Thus deserted by its ally, Sardinia was unable to expel the Austrians from Venetia. Nevertheless, extensive gains were made; Sardinia annexed Lombardy, and acquired by various means the duchies of Tuscany, Parma, and Modena, and the northern portion of the Papal States. Sardinia was now more than twice its original size and by far the most powerful state in Italy.

The second step in consolidating Italy was the conquest of the kingdom of the Two Sicilies. This kingdom was ruled by a Bourbon, Francis II (1859–1860), who was thoroughly hated by his Italian subjects. In May 1860 a romantic adventurer, Giuseppe Garibaldi (1807–1882), set out with a regiment of one thousand "red shirts" to rescue his fellow Italians from oppression. Within three months he had conquered the island of Sicily and had then marched to the deliverance of Naples, where the people were already in revolt. By November the whole kingdom of Francis II had fallen to Garibaldi. He at first intended to convert the territory into an independent republic but was finally persuaded to surrender it to the Kingdom of Sardinia. With most of the peninsula now united under a single rule, Victor Emmanuel II, king of Sardinia, assumed the title of king of Italy (1861–1878). Venetia was still in the hands of the Austrians, but in 1866, following their defeat in the Seven Weeks' War, they were forced by the Prussians to cede it to Italy. All that remained to complete the unification of Italy was the annexation of Rome. The Eternal City had resisted conquest thus far, largely because of the military protection accorded the pope by Napoleon III. But in 1870 the outbreak of the Franco-Prussian War compelled Napoleon to withdraw his troops. In September 1870 Italian soldiers occupied Rome, and in July of the following year it was made the capital of the by now united kingdom.

The occupation of Rome brought the kingdom of Italy into conflict with the papacy. During the first years of his reign, which began in 1846, Pope Pius IX instituted a series of "modern" improvements: gaslight, railways, vaccination. Yet Pius, who, like his reactionary predecessor, Gregory XVI, continued to rule over the Papal States in the manner of a secular prince, was no friend to either liberalism or nationalism. And no wonder: the movement that had brought Italian troops to Rome had from its inception expressed hostility to the Church as an impediment to unification. Following the occupation of Rome in 1870, an attempt was made to solve the problem of relations between the state and the papacy. In 1871 the Italian parliament enacted the Law of Papal Guaranties, purporting to define and limit the status of the pope as a reigning sovereign. At the same time, a Vatican council in 1870 had proclaimed the doctrine of papal infallibility in spiritual matters. The reigning pontiff, Pius IX, promptly denounced the secular law on the grounds that issues affecting the pope could be settled only by an international treaty to which he himself was a party. Whereupon he shut himself up in the Vatican and refused to have anything to do

Giuseppe Garibaldi

Pope Pius IX. This contemporary cartoon lampoons the pope, shown as a conniving, worldly politician hiding behind the mask of Jesus. Pius IX, though in his early years something of a liberal, took an extreme reactionary political position in the wake of the revolutionary upheaval of 1848.

with a government that had so shamefully treated Christ's vicar on earth. His successors continued this practice of voluntary imprisonment until 1929, when a series of agreements between the Italian government and Pius XI effected settlement of the dispute.

The challenges of nationalism and nation-building also occupied the two countries to the east and west of Europe that were built upon systems of unfree labor: Russia and the United States. Serfdom in Russia, extended and formalized by Peter the Great in his dramatic empire building (1689–1725), began to draw significant protest from the intelligentsia under the reign of Catherine the Great (1762–1796). Tied to the issue of serfdom was the question of how best to fulfill Russia's unique destiny, her *Volksgeist.* In the mid-nineteenth century two schools of thought emerged: *slavophiles,* romantic nationalists who idealized traditional Russian culture, including the peasant commune, and rejected Western ideas and innovations; and the *westernizers,* who wished to raise Russia to the level of Europe by adopting the science, technology, and educational innovations they believed had shaped Europe's history. Both groups agreed that serfdom must be abolished. But not until 1861, under Alexander II, was emancipation effected—and then under a settlement that greatly favored landowners.

Emancipation of serfs in Russia

Alexander II (1855–1881) presented his reluctant nobles with emancipation from above as the only alternative to violent and protracted strife. In America, the eventual end of unfree labor came in the midst of a bloody civil war (1861–1865). But the American Civil War was not about the issue of slavery so much as it was about preserving the union of American states and territories. It was a union that had undergone tremendous stress as the original republic of thirteen states had grown into a huge amalgam of territories that stretched to the Pacific coast. Politically, the so-called Jeffersonian Revolution had moved the young country, founded upon the desire to protect the rights of private property against the leveling tendencies of majorities, toward a number of ultimately democratic objectives. Leaders of the movement under the Democratic-Republican president Thomas Jefferson (1743–1826) supported a political system based on an aristocracy of "virtue and talent," in which respect for personal liberty would be the guiding principle. They were vigorous opponents of special privilege, whether of birth or of wealth. They worked for the abolition of established churches. They led the campaign for the addition of a Bill of Rights to the Constitution and were almost exclusively responsible for its success. Although professing devotion to the principle of the separation of powers, they actually believed in the supremacy of the representatives of the people and viewed with abhorrence the attempts of the executive and judicial branches to increase their power.

Jeffersonian principles

Thomas Jefferson by Gilbert Stuart

By 1820, with the growth of new urban centers as well as the "frontier democracy" that characterized life in the territories of the Louisiana Purchase (1803) and the Northwest Territory (western New York State and Ohio), the more circumscribed equality proposed by the Jeffersonians gave way to a new democratic spirit, shaped around the principle of equality and led by Andrew Jackson (1767–1845). The Jacksonian Democrats trans-

Jacksonian democracy

"Meal Time." Between the decks on an immigrant ship to the United States in the mid-nineteenth century.

formed the doctrines of liberalism into a more radical creed. They pronounced all (excluding slaves, American Indians, and women) politically equal, not merely in rights but in privileges. They were devoted adherents to the causes of suffrage for all white males; the election, rather than appointment, of all governmental officeholders; and the frequent rotation of men in positions of political power—a doctrine that served to put more Democratic politicians into federal office. These democratic beliefs helped encourage a spirit of unity within the United States during a period of rapid territorial expansion.

As the United States continued to acquire more territories in the West (the most notable addition resulting from the conquest of lands in the Southwest from Mexico in 1846), it also faced the problem of assimilating the thousands of immigrants who came to America from Europe in the first half of the century. Many were Scottish and English; for them the difficulties of adjusting to a new life in a new country were generally not difficult since they spoke a common language with their fellow-citizens. For others the problems were far greater. For the Irish, who immigrated in great numbers, particularly during the 1840s, there was the fact of their alien religion, Roman Catholicism. For Germans and others from the Continent, there was the language barrier. The United States's policy toward its immigrants was directed against the creation of any foreign nationalist enclaves apart from the main body of its citizenry. Although foreign-language newspapers were tolerated, and immigrants were free to attend churches and social gatherings as they chose, English remained the language of the public

Immigration

Slavery and the South

schools, the police, the law courts, and the government. To hold a job, a person was almost always forced to learn at least some English. In this way, the United States encouraged immigrants to shed their "foreign" ways and to commit themselves to their adopted nation.

If there was resistance to this emphasis on national identification, it could be found in the South, where the institution of slavery and the economic dependence of the planters upon England produced two distinct minorities, neither of which was to be assimilated without resort to war. During the nineteenth century, slavery had been abolished throughout much of the Western world, for both economic and humanitarian reasons. Southern planters, like Russian serf-owners, continued to insist that without the slave system they would go bankrupt. To humanitarians they responded—just as their Russian counterparts had done—with arguments based upon theories of racial inferiority and upon their self-professed reputation as benevolent masters. The position of these Southern spokesmen grew increasingly distasteful and unconvincing to the North. As the country opened to the west, North and South engaged in a protracted tug-of-war as to which new states were to be "free" and which "slave." Northerners were motivated by more than concern for the well-being of blacks. The North was industrializing fast. Capitalists there were demanding protective tariffs to assist them in their enterprises. Southerners favored free trade, since they wished to import British goods in return for the cotton they sold to the manufacturers of Lancashire.

Thus, in 1861, President Abraham Lincoln undertook the war to defend the unity of the United States. European governments, while never recog-

Slavery in the American South. Left: Slave pens at Pine, Birch & Co., a Virginia slave broker. Right: Cotton being prepared by slaves for the gin on a South Carolina plantation.

nizing the Confederacy officially, nevertheless remained sympathetic to its cause. They hoped that the fragmentation of the United States would result in the opening up of markets for their manufactured goods, much as the dissolution of the Spanish Empire had proved a boon to European commercial interests. The victory of the North in 1865, however, ensured the continued growth of the United States as a nation. The Fourteenth Amendment to the Constitution stated specifically that all were citizens of the United States, and not of an individual state or territory. In declaring that no citizen was to be deprived of life, liberty, or property without due process of law, it established that "due process" was to be defined by the national, and not the state or territorial governments.

The Civil War

The years following the American Civil War witnessed the binding together of the nation economically under the direction of Northern private enterprise. The symbol of the North's triumph as a nation-builder came with the driving of the final spike of the transcontinental Union Pacific railroad in 1869. Nation-building in Europe and the United States helped ensure the continuing expansion of capitalism. Liberalism had provided a general climate of opinion and a set of attitudes toward government that encouraged industrialization. Nation-building, in its turn, produced the necessary economic units—large enough to generate the wherewithal to sustain economic growth and confident enough to enter into competition with the British Goliath.

Nation-building in the West

SELECTED READINGS

- *Items so designated are available in paperback editions.*

Artz, Frederick B., *France under the Bourbon Restoration, 1814–1830,* New York, 1963. A basic survey with a good treatment of romanticism.
- Beales, Derek, *The Risorgimento and the Unification of Italy,* New York, 1971. Objective, concise survey of Italian unification.
- Binkley, Robert C., *Realism and Nationalism, 1852–1871,* New York, 1935. An excellent synthesis despite some dated passages.
- Craig, Gordon, *The Politics of the Prussian Army, 1640–1945,* Oxford, 1964. Much more than the title implies. An excellent analysis of Prussian social structure and the role of the army in social reform and unification.
Deak, Istvan, *The Lawful Revolution: Louis Kossuth and the Hungarians, 1848–1849,* New York, 1979.
- Epstein, Klaus, *The Genesis of German Conservatism,* Princeton, 1966. Provides excellent early-nineteenth-century background.
- Eyck, Erich, *Bismarck and the German Empire,* London, 1958. The best one-volume study of Bismarck.
Eyck, Frank, *The Frankfurt Parliament, 1848–49,* New York, 1968. A detailed study of its composition and procedure.
Ford, Guy Stanton, *Stein: The Era of Reform in Prussia, 1807–1815,* New York, 1922. An old but still valuable work on a leading Prussian reformer.

- Hamerow, Theodore, *Restoration, Revolution, Reaction,* Princeton, 1966. An excellent social and economic history of Germany between 1815 and 1871.
- ———, *The Social Foundations of German Unification, 1858–1871,* 2 vols., Princeton, 1972. Concentrates on economic factors that determined the solution to the unification question. An impressive synthesis.

  Hayes, C. J. H., *The Historical Evolution of Modern Nationalism,* rev. ed., New York, 1968. A valuable survey.
- Hobsbawm, Eric J., *The Age of Revolution, 1789–1848,* New York, 1962. An unrigidly Marxist interpretation, good for the entire period it covers.
- Holborn, Hajo, *History of Modern Germany,* Vols. II and III, Princeton, 1964. The best survey of German history in English.
- Howard, Michael, *The Franco-Prussian War,* New York, 1969. The war's effect on society.
- ———, *War in European History,* Oxford, 1976. The best survey of international conflict sparked by European expansionism.
- Kohn, Hans, *The Idea of Nationalism,* New York, 1944. A perceptive analysis.
- Kolchin, Peter, *Unfree Labor: American Slavery and Russian Serfdom,* Cambridge, Mass., 1987. Seminal comparative study.
- Krieger, Leonard, *The German Idea of Freedom,* Boston, 1957. A difficult but rewarding study of German political thought.

  Macartney, C. A., *The Habsburg Empire, 1790–1918,* London, 1968. A worthwhile survey.

  Mack Smith, Denis, *Garibaldi: A Great Life in Brief,* New York, 1956.

  ———, *The Making of Italy, 1796–1870,* New York, 1968. A narrative with documents.
- Mosse, George, *The Culture of Western Europe: The Nineteenth and Twentieth Centuries,* 3rd ed., Chicago, 1988. An overview that successfully combines compression with breadth of analysis.

  Namier, Lewis B., *1848: The Revolution of the Intellectuals,* London, 1964. A controversial analysis, highly critical of the Frankfurt Assembly.

  Noyes, P. H., *Organization and Revolution: Working-Class Associations in the German Revolutions of 1848–49,* Princeton, 1966. An important monograph analyzing the degree of working-class consciousness at the time of the revolution.
- Pflanze, Otto, *Bismarck and the Development of Germany, 1815–1871,* Princeton, 1963. An impressive analysis of Bismarck's aims and policies.

  Rosenberg, Hans, *Bureaucracy, Aristocracy, and Autocracy: The Prussian Experience, 1660–1815,* Cambridge, Mass., 1958. A difficult but valuable book explaining the forces that molded the modern Prussian state.

  Salvemini, Gaetano, *Mazzini,* London, 1956. Biography with excerpts from Mazzini's writings.

  Sheehan, James J., *German Liberalism in the Nineteenth Century,* Chicago, 1978. Solid synthetic account.
- Snyder, Louis L., *Roots of German Nationalism,* Bloomington, Ind., 1978.
- Taylor, A. J. P., *The Habsburg Monarchy, 1809–1918,* rev. ed., London, 1965. An idiosyncratic account by an eminent historian.

SOURCE MATERIALS

Bismarck, Otto von, *Bismarck, the Man and the Statesman, Written and Dictated by Himself,* London, 1899. Bismarck's memoirs, written after his fall from power.

Clausewitz, Karl von, *On War,* London, 1968. Published posthumously, this work, in reality a philosophy of war, was perceived by the Prussian military bureaucracy as a mandate for total war—for the subjugation of all interests of the state to war.

Fichte, Johann Gottlieb, *Addresses to the German Nation,* New York, 1968. Presented in 1808 while French armies occupied Prussia, these lectures helped stir a German nationalist spirit.

Schurz, Carl, *The Reminiscences of Carl Schurz,* 3 vols., New York, 1907–1908. Especially valuable is Vol. I. A young German liberal in 1848 and a delegate to the Frankfurt Assembly, Schurz spent the rest of his life as an exile in the United States.

Part Six

THE WEST AT THE WORLD'S CENTER

The years between 1870 and 1945 found the West at the center of global affairs. The industrial supremacy of Western Europe and the United States gave them a combined power greater than that possessed by any nation or empire in previous times. Yet world domination was by no means accompanied by any sense of general world order. The economic might of the Western nations, while it resulted in their ability to dominate the less developed quarters of the globe, resulted, as well, in their concern lest one of their number overpower the others. The old system of the balance of power, designed to preserve peace by ensuring that no one country achieved overwhelming predominance at the expense of its neighbors, was strained to the breaking point by economic rivalries that stretched around the world. Meanwhile, tensions mounted within each nation, as landed and middle classes, threatened by the possibility of social turmoil, tried to balance the mounting clamor for political concessions against their desire to retain power in their own hands. Twice during the period, in 1914 and 1939, international and domestic pressures exploded into global wars. Those wars and their results, generated by the rivalries and miscalculations of the Western nations, so sapped the strength of those nations as to depose them thereafter as the sole arbiters of the world's destinies.

The West at the World's Center

POLITICS	SCIENCE & INDUSTRY
	First commercially practical electrical generator, 1870
1870	
Paris Commune, 1871	Gilcrist-Thomas steel process, 1870s
Kulturkampf, Germany, 1872	
League of Three Emperors, 1873	
Constitution for Third French Republic, 1875	Germ theory of disease, 1875
End of First International, 1876	Invention of telephone, 1876
Congress of Berlin, 1878	
Triple Alliance, 1882	
Berlin conference on imperialism, 1885	
Second International formed, 1889	
Pan-Slavism, 1890–1914	
Dreyfus affair, 1894–1899	
Spanish-American War, 1898	Discovery of the X ray, 1895
Boer War, 1899–1902	Marie Curie, discovery of radium, 1898
	Invention of wireless telegraph, 1899
1900	
N. Lenin, *What Is to Be Done?,* 1902	First airplane flight, 1903
Russo-Japanese War, 1904–1905	Ivan Pavlov, Nobel Prize for physiology, 1904
Revolution in Russia, 1905	Albert Einstein, development of relativity theory, 1905–1910
Triple Entente, 1907	Model T Ford, 1908
Bosnian Crisis, 1908	
Revolt of the Young Turks, 1908	
Balkan Wars, 1912–1913	
First World War, 1914–1918	
Russian Revolution, 1917	
Treaty of Versailles, 1919	
Socialist revolution, Germany, 1919	
1920	
League of Nations, 1920–1946	
NEP, Russia, 1921	
Mussolini's March on Rome, 1922	
Hitler's beer-hall putsch, 1923	
New constitution, Soviet Union, 1924	
Locarno agreements, 1925	
	Discovery of viruses, sulfa drugs, and penicillin, 1930s
Hitler, chancellor of Germany, 1933	
New Deal, United States, 1933–1940	World economic conference, 1933
Italy conquers Ethiopia, 1935–1936	National rearmament programs, 1935
Rome-Berlin Axis, 1936	
Spanish Civil War, 1936–1939	
Germany annexes Austria, 1938	
Munich conference, 1938	
Nazi-Soviet pact, 1939	Discovery of atomic fission, 1939
1940 Second World War, 1939–1945	
United States enters war, 1941	
Allied invasion of Normandy, 1944	
Bombing of Hiroshima and Nagasaki, 1945	First atomic bomb test, 1945
United Nations founded, 1945	

ECONOMICS & SOCIETY	ARTS & LETTERS	
	Impressionism in art, 1870–1900	*1870*
Growth of finance capitalism, 1880s		
Social welfare legislation, Germany, 1882–1884		
	Émile Zola, *Germinal,* 1885	
Sherman Antitrust Act, United States, 1890	Henrik Ibsen, *Hedda Gabler,* 1890	
	Paul Cézanne, *The Card Players,* 1890–1892	
Méline tariff, 1892		
	George Bernard Shaw, *Plays Pleasant and Unpleasant,* 1898	
Women's suffrage movement, England, 1900–1914	Sigmund Freud, *The Interpretation of Dreams,* 1900	
Social welfare legislation, France, 1904; 1910		*1900*
Social welfare legislation, England, 1906–1912	Cubism in art, 1905–1930	
	Marcel Proust, *Remembrance of Things Past,* 1913–1918	
	Oswald Spengler, *The Decline of the West,* 1918	
German inflation, 1920s	Bauhaus established, 1919	
	Writers of the "Lost Generation," 1920–1930	
	Surrealism and Dadaism, 1920s	*1920*
	Ludwig Wittgenstein, *Tractatus Logico-philosophicus,* 1921	
Great Depression, 1929–1940	T. S. Eliot, *The Waste Land,* 1922	
	James Joyce, *Ulysses,* 1922	
J. M. Keynes, *General Theory of Employment, Interest, and Money,* 1936	Neo-realism in art, 1930s	
		1940
	Jean-Paul Sartre, *Being and Nothingness,* 1943	

Chapter 24

THE PROGRESS OF INTERNATIONAL INDUSTRIALIZATION AND COMPETITION (1870–1914)

We have conquered for ourselves a place in the sun. It will now be my task to see
to it that this place in the sun shall remain our undisputed possession. . . .

—Kaiser William II, speech, 1901

If most historians now speak of a second Industrial Revolution occurring during the years after 1870, they are quick to qualify the term.
Whatever the changes in technique and in scope—and they were significant—they do not compare to those which characterized the first revolution—*the* Industrial Revolution. There is, however, good reason to distinguish a second period of industrial development and advance from the
first. Successful nation-building meant that the years 1870–1914 would be
characterized by sharply increased international political and economic rivalries, culminating in a scramble after imperial territories in Africa and
Asia. Britain, if it did not actually surrender its industrial primacy during
this period, failed to counter with any real success the energetic and determined challenges from Germany and the United States to its constantly de-
creasing lead. New technology, particularly in the fields of metals, chemicals, and electricity, resulted in new products. Larger populations and
improving standards of living produced greater demand, which, in turn, increased the volume of production. And the need for increased production
called forth significant reorganization to provide a freer supply of capital
and to ensure a more efficient labor force. It is these changes that distinguish the second stage of industrialization from the first, and therefore warrant its separate treatment. Yet they must be perceived as stemming not
only from those economic conditions that were the result of the first stage,
but also from the more general political, social, and cultural climate whose
history we have been tracing.

A second industrial revolution

In analyzing the progress of industrialization, we shall deal with changes in three major areas: in technology, in scope and scale of consumption and production, and in the reorganization of the capitalist system. Finally we shall examine the phenomenon of late-nineteenth-century imperialism, and consider the extent to which that phenomenon can be attributed to increasing economic and industrial rivalries.

1. NEW TECHNOLOGIES

Technology in steel

A most important technological change in this period resulted in the mass production of steel. The advantages of steel over iron—a result of steel's lower carbon content—are its hardness, its malleability, and its strength. Steel can keep its cutting edge, where iron cannot; it can be worked more easily than iron, which is brittle and which, if it is to be used industrially, must almost always be cast (that is, poured into molds). And steel, because of its strength in proportion to its weight and volume, makes a particularly adaptable construction material. These advantages had been recognized by craftsmen for centuries. Until steel could be produced both cheaply and in mass, however, the advantages remained more theoretical than real. Two inventions, during the earlier years of the Industrial Revolution, had reduced the price and increased the output of steel to some degree. The crucible technique, discovered in the eighteenth century in England, called for the heating of relatively small amounts of iron ore to a point at which foreign matter could be removed by skimming, the carbon content reduced, and a proper proportion of carbon distributed evenly throughout the finished product. Although individual crucibles were not large, holding on the average no more than forty-five to sixty pounds, they could be poured together to produce steel ingots of several tons. A century later, in the early 1840s, two Germans adapted the puddling process, used in the production of iron, to the manufacture of steel. While it did not produce steel as hard as that made in crucibles, it reduced its price considerably.

Bessemer, Siemens-Martin, and Gilchrist-Thomas systems

Not until the invention of the Bessemer and Siemens-Martin processes, however, could steel begin to compete with iron. In the 1850s, an Englishman, Henry Bessemer, discovered that by blowing air into and through the molten metal he could achieve a more exact degree of decarbonization in much shorter time, and with far larger quantities of ore, than was possible with either the crucible or puddling methods. Bessemer soon found, however, that his "converters" were incapable of burning off sufficient quantities of phosphorous; and phosphorous in anything but the smallest quantities made the metal unworkable. A partial solution was achieved with the introduction of nonphosphoric hematite ores. Yet this was of little long-term use in most European countries, where supplies of hematite ore were not abundant. This same problem plagued the German inventors Frederick and William Siemens, whose furnace made use of waste gases to increase heat. Not until Pierre Martin, a Frenchman, discovered that the introduc-

The Rise of the Steel Industry. Bristling with massive machinery such as this steam-hammer, the Krupp Works in Essen, Germany, was already a major force in steel production by the 1870s.

tion of scrap iron into the mix would induce proper decarbonization, could the Siemens furnace be used to make steel commercially. And not until the late 1870s was the problem of phosphoreting solved for both the Bessemer and the Siemens-Martin processes. The solution was a simple one, discovered by two Englishmen, a clerk and a chemist: Sidney Gilchrist Thomas and his cousin Sidney Gilchrist. They introduced limestone into the molten iron to combine with the phosphorus, which was then siphoned from the mix. And they lined the converter in such a way that the slag was prevented from eating away the walls and releasing phosphorus back into the molten metal.

Together, these three processes revolutionized the production of steel. Although the use of iron did not end overnight, steel soon moved into the lead. In the British shipbuilding industry, for example, steel had overtaken iron by 1890. In part because Siemens-Martin was particularly suited to the manufacture of steel plates used in shipbuilding, that process dominated the manufacture of steel in Britain, where shipbuilding was a major industry. Bessemer steel, which could be manufactured more cheaply and in larger plants, was more commonly produced on the Continent and in America. The result was a major increase in the production of German steel: by 1901, German converters were capable of pouring annually an average of 34,000 tons, compared to Britain's 21,750. By 1914 Germany was produc-

Increased steel production

New Technology: The Telephone. This 1885 photograph of a New York City telephone exchange bears witness to the transformation wrought by the dramatic expansion of the electrical industry. Note also the extent to which the position of operator has become the province of female employees.

ing twice as much steel as Britain, and the United States twice as much as Germany.

A second and equally important technological development resulted in the availability of electric power for industrial, commercial, and domestic use. Electricity's particular advantages result from the facts that it can be easily transmitted as energy over long distances, and that it can be converted into other forms of energy—heat and light, for example. Although electricity had, of course, been discovered prior to the first Industrial Revolution, its advantages could not have been put to general use without a series of inventions that occurred during the nineteenth century. Of these, some of the most important were the invention of the chemical battery by the Italian Alessandro Volta in 1800; of electromagnetic induction in 1831 and the electromagnetic generator in 1866 by the Englishman Michael Faraday; of the first commercially practical generator of direct current in 1870; and of alternators and transformers capable of producing high-voltage alternating current in the 1880s. These inventions meant that by the end of the century it was possible to send electric current from large power stations over comparatively long distances. Electric power could be manufactured by water—hence cheaply—and delivered from its source to the place where it was needed.

Once it had been delivered to its destination, the power was converted and put to use in myriad ways. Households quickly became one of the major users of electrical power. The invention in 1879 by Thomas Edison of the incandescent filament lamp—or light bulb—was crucial in this regard. As individual houses were electrified to receive the power that was to be

Increased availability of electricity

The uses of electricity

transformed into light, consumer demand for electricity resulted in further expansion of the electrical industry. Demand for electrical power was increasing in the industrial sector as well. Electric motors soon began to power subways, tramways, and, eventually, long-distance railways. Electricity made possible the development of new techniques in the chemical and metallurgical industries. Most important, electricity helped to transform the work patterns of the factory. Heavy steam engines had made equipment and machinery stationery; electric motors meant that comparatively lightweight power tools could be moved—often by hand—to the site of a particular piece of work. The result was far greater flexibility in terms of factory organization. Smaller workshop industries benefited as well; they could accommodate themselves to electrically powered motors and tools in a way they could not to steam.

Steel and electricity were only two of the most important areas where technological changes were taking place. The chemical industry was significantly advanced by developments in the manufacture of alkali and organic compounds. Demand for alkali had increased with the demand for soaps and textiles, and with the changes in the manufacturing process of paper, which required large amounts of bleach. An older, more expensive and wasteful technique used extensively by the British was superseded after 1880 by a new process perfected by the Belgian Ernest Solvay. The result was, again, a rapid overtaking of the British by the Germans in the production not only of alkalis but of sulfuric acid, a by-product recoverable in the Solvay process, and used in the manufacture of fertilizers, petroleum refining, iron, steel, and textiles. In the field of organic compounds, the impetus for further discovery came as a result of demand for synthetic dyes. Although the British and French were the first successful pioneers in this area, the Germans once more moved ahead to a commanding lead by 1900. At the turn of the century German firms controlled about 90 percent of the world market.

Advances in chemical industry

New Technology: The Elevated Train. This electric railway was erected in Paris in the 1880s.

The First Successful Airplane Flight

Improved engines

The need for more and more power to meet increasing industrial demands resulted not only in developments in the field of electricity, already noted, but in the improved design and expanded capacity of steam engines. The most noteworthy invention in this area was the steam turbine, which permitted engines to run at speeds heretofore unobtainable. Internal combustion engines made their appearance during this period as well. Their major advantage lay in their efficiency; i.e., they could be powered automatically, and did not need to be stoked by hand like steam engines. Once liquid fuels—petroleum and distilled gasoline—became available, as they did increasingly with the discovery of oil fields in Russia, Borneo, and Texas about 1900, the internal combustion engine took hold as a serious competitor to steam. By 1914 most navies had converted from coal to oil, as had domestic steamship companies. The automobile and the airplane, both still in their infancies, made little impact upon the industrial world, however, before 1914.

2. CHANGES IN SCOPE AND SCALE

Population increases

These technological changes must be understood as occurring against a background of—indeed in part as a result of—a constantly growing population and a generally increased standard of living for the majority of men and women in the Western world. Between 1870 and 1914, Europe's population increased from 295 million to 450 million. This was the case despite a declining birth rate in the more industrially advanced countries of

Western Europe, where more and more middle- and working-class men and women were postponing marriage and limiting the number of their children, confident that those children they did have stood a fairly decent chance of survival. Population growth was primarily the result of a sharp decline in infant mortality, caused by improved sanitation and diet, and by the virtual elimination of diseases such as cholera and typhus. Increases were greatest in the areas of Central and Eastern Europe, where the birth rate did not drop as dramatically as in the West. Britain's population grew from 34.9 to 45.2 million between 1881 and 1911; France's from 37.4 to 39.1. But Germany's advanced during the same period from 45.2 to 64.9 million, and Russia's from 94 to an estimated 129 million.

The problems of public sanitation and health were slowly brought to heel by men and women working in the wake of scientific discoveries such as those by the Frenchman Louis Pasteur (1822–1895). By locating the source of bacteria, Pasteur's work opened the way for major improvements in the areas of public sanitation and health: among others, the process of ridding food of objectionable bacteria by sterilization—pasteurization—that was named for him. Pasteur, along with the German Robert Koch (1843–1910), also proved conclusively that germs were not, as was commonly supposed, the result but rather the cause of disease.

Louis Pasteur

Declining death rates were an indicator of generally increasing material prosperity. There were, of course, still a great many very poor people, both in cities and in the country: casual laborers, the unemployed, those in declining industries and trades. Those skilled workers and their families whose real incomes did rise as a result of deflation and higher wage rates did not experience anything like the rate of increase enjoyed by most of the middle class. Nor could they expect to avoid altogether the stretches of unemployment that made life so chaotic for so many of their unskilled co-workers. Yet despite these qualifications, it is fair to say that more people enjoyed a higher standard of living than ever before. And a higher standard of living produced the demand for an increase in consumer goods.

Higher living standards

Increased consumption of manufactured goods was by no means uniform; it was higher in urban and industrialized areas than in the country. But even in the country, traditional thrift was challenged as farmers and their wives journeyed by train into the cities, saw what they had not imagined they could have, and then decided they must spend their savings to have it. To accommodate the new and largely middle-class consumers, department stores and chain stores designed their products and their advertising to make shopping as easy and inviting as possible. Behind large plate-glass windows, goods were displayed attractively and temptingly; periodic sales encouraged householders to purchase "bargains"; catalogues and charge accounts made it easy for customers to spend money without leaving home. The result was an enormous increase in the volume of manufactured goods produced for this rapidly expanding consumer market. Bicycles, clocks, appliances, furnishings—these and a great many other things were being made in large quantities, and with new materials (cheap steel) and new techniques (electrical power). Many of these products were de-

New consumers

The Triumph of Middle-Class Consumerism. The interior of the Galeries Lafayette department store in Paris, c. 1890.

signed according to the correct assumption that women were more and more responsible for household purchases. Therefore, goods were fashioned to appeal directly to women, or to the children for whom women were responsible. The foot-powered sewing machine was a particular case in point—the first domestic appliance. Isaac Singer (1811–1875), the American responsible for the development of the treadle and straight needle in the 1850s, was as much an entrepreneur as an inventor. He was a pioneer in the field of advertising and promotion, encouraging purchase on the installment plan and providing courses for would-be domestic seamstresses.

Sewing machines changed far more than the sewing habits of housewives, however. They were inexpensive, lightweight tools, easily installed and easily operated. Workshop masters could set up several, employ a handful of young women at very low wages, and make a profit turning out cheap ready-made clothing in response to increasing demand. This was just one of the ways in which the scale of manufacturing was altered during the latter part of the nineteenth century, with both demand and technology conspiring to produce the change. The sewing machine also led to the development of other new tools that helped cut costs in the clothing industry: button-holers, lace-makers, leather-stitchers. Whereas it took one cobbler ten hours to make a pair of shoes in 1850 by hand, by the end of the century it took a team of cobblers but a few hours to produce ten pairs using machinery. In metal-working, hard-edged steel allowed for the rapid cutting of patterns, which reduced price, in turn encouraging the manufacture of a variety of inexpensive metal goods—kitchenware, for example. In textiles, improved engines doubled the pace of mules and looms. In heavy industry, steam hammers performed the work of many men more precisely and with greater speed than before. New equipment of this sort was expensive. As a result, in heavy industry, it was the larger companies that prospered, and in the course of their prosperity, they grew even larger.

In all the countries of Europe, and in the United States, the pattern was one of expansion and consolidation. This was especially the case in Germany, where in the iron and steel industry nearly 75 percent of those employed worked in factories of a thousand or more, and where over 90 percent of the electrical equipment manufactured was made in factories with over fifty employees. Machinery was thus altering the scale of manufacturing in two directions at once. In the clothing industry, entrepreneurs could use inexpensive machines to make small workshops turn a profit. In steel

Left: *Advertisement for a German Sewing Machine*. The company proclaims the machine's versatility: unsurpassed for use in the home as well as in the workshop or factory. Right: *Sweated Industry*. This English family is "manufacturing" cheap toys at home. While the scale of some industrial enterprises increased, others remained profitable through the employment of badly paid home workers.

BE UNITED AND INDUSTRIOUS

AMALGAMATED SOCIETY OF ENGINEERS, MACHINISTS, MILLWRIGHTS, SMITHS, AND PATTERN MAKERS.

Trade Union Certificate of Membership. Trade unions helped workers as they adapted their skills to factory reorganization and modernization. The classical symbolism on the certificate helped ensure the union's respectability in the eyes of both its membership and the public.

foundries, the cost of new equipment forced small competitors to the wall, with the result that the foundries grew very much bigger.

The increase in the scale of manufacturing had important and often disturbing consequences for workers. The most obvious was the need for men and women to relearn their trades. They were compelled to adapt their older skills to the new machines. Very often this adaptation resulted in a loss of either pay or prestige, or both. Most machine work was not skilled work. A trainee could "pick up" a trade in a week or so. Workers who had prided themselves on a particular skill and had been paid according to their ability to perform it, had to face the fact that industrial change was not only forcing them to relearn, but was compelling them to tell themselves that their new "skills"—if they could be called that—did not amount to very much. For example, when the machine itself could cut metal with infinitesimal accuracy, there was far less need than there had been previously for the skills of a human "fitter." Even if workers were not forced to relearn in these ways in order to accommodate to increased scale, they often had at least to accommodate to factory reorganization and rationalization. In workplaces where the hand-carrying of materials had been a major factor in their final cost, mechanization to reduce that cost would produce a

Effects of increase in scale on workers: (1) relearning

bewildering series of changes. Electric cranes, used together with huge magnets in the iron and steel industries, increased the speed with which goods could be moved, and demanded that workers defer to whatever changes their introduction might entail.

A second—and even more important—effect of the change in scale was the constant demand for further efficiency. The greater the scale of the operation, the more important it became to eliminate waste. One minute lost in the production of every ten pairs of shoes might not make much difference if only fifty pairs were produced in a day. But if hundreds were being made, it became crucial, in the eyes of management, to see that those minutes were no longer lost. In factories where capital had been spent on new machinery, the owners, conscious of the cost of their investment, increased output in order to realize a profit on that investment. In factories where older machinery was still in use, owners believed that the only way they could remain competitive with modernized operations was by extracting all they could from their less productive equipment. In both cases, workers were pressed to produce more and more. One result of this drive for efficiency was a restructuring of wage scales. Prior to this period, although there had been serious wage disputes, both management and labor appeared content to bargain from the traditional notion of "a fair day's wage for a fair day's work." Definitions of what was fair naturally varied. But the level of individual performance was generally set by custom. What workers produced in the course of a day continued to determine what they were expected to produce. From about 1870 onward, however, expectations and procedures began to change. Periodic economic depressions in the last quarter of the nineteenth century saw profits fall before wages. This pattern caused employers to insist on greater individual productivity from their employees. It was no longer enough to work at a job with customary

(2) efficiency

Technological Change and Production Speedup. An early assembly line of the Ford Motor Company, United States, 1913. Car bodies slid down the ramp and were attached to the chassis as they passed through the line below. One thousand cars were produced each day.

speed. Workers were now asked to produce as much as the owners thought they were potentially capable of producing.

But who was to determine that potential? That question plagued industrial relations during these years. Employers, who were adopting precision tools in order to increase production, grew more and more convinced that worker output could be gauged with precision as well. The foremost theoretician of worker efficiency and what was called scientific management of labor was the American Frederick W. Taylor (1865–1915). Taylor devised a three-step system whereby a worker's output could be "scientifically" measured, a system that, he argued, would provide a precise method for the determination of wage scales. First, he observed, timed, and analyzed workers' movements on the job, in order to determine how long a particular task should take. Second, he figured the labor costs of these movements. Third, he produced "norms," or general standards that all workers were expected to maintain. These norms were invariably higher than those that had prevailed under traditional conditions.

In order to encourage workers to accept these increased standards, Taylor urged all factory-owners to adopt piece rates (i.e., payment to workers according to the specific amount produced) rather than hourly or daily wages. Payment by piece rate was already a growing practice in many European and American factories. In theory, at least, workers were not opposed to this method of payment; they reasoned that their only hope for a share in increasing output lay in their chance to be paid directly for what they made. But when they were told that their pay would not increase unless they measured up to predetermined—and, to their mind, unrealistic—norms, they objected. They argued that rates were set according to the performance of the speediest workers. Even though workers might earn more money if they agreed to the new rates, they resented the intrusion of management upon their ability to control the pace of work. Despite this opposition, scientific management spread throughout the industrialized West. In England, the United States, and on the Continent, particularly in the engineering trades, factory after factory subscribed to the new gospel. Where it could not entirely succeed in introducing "efficiency" on the shop floor, management proceeded to rationalize its own procedures. Accounting departments were expanded, and encouraged to attend closely to the problem of cost control in all areas of production and distribution. These reforms were no more than a reflection of the general move in the direction of greater efficiency. They were brought on by the vastly increased scale of production, the need to reduce waste wherever possible, and the desire to derive maximum profits from the elimination of unnecessary motions and unproductive habits.

3. THE NEW CAPITALISM

Responding to increasing consumption and production and to the consequent pressures for further efficiency, the institutions of capitalism began to

The New York Stock Exchange, 1893

reorganize toward the end of the nineteenth century. Hitherto, most firms had been small or at most middle-sized; now, as firms grew and their need for capital increased, they began to incorporate. Limited liability laws, enacted by most countries in the course of the century, worked to encourage this incorporation. "Limited liability" meant that an individual owning stock in a particular corporation could be held liable only for the amount of his or her shares, should that corporation bankrupt itself. Once insured in this way, many thousands of middle-class men and women considered corporate investment a safe and financially promising way of making money for themselves. A stockholding, "rentier" class emerged, brought into existence by the willingness of governments to encourage capitalism through friendly legislation, and by the desire of capitalist businessmen to expand their industrial undertakings to meet increased demands.

The growth of incorporation

More and more companies incorporated. In doing so, their management tended to be removed from the direct control of family founders or of company-based boards of directors. The influence of bankers and financiers, often situated in cities far removed from the factories they invested in, grew accordingly. These men were not investing their own money but the money of their clients; their power to stimulate or to discourage the growth of particular industries and enterprises encouraged a kind of impersonal "finance" capital. One consequence was a growing concern with cutting production costs which as we saw above (pp. 821–822), meant stricter control of labor.

Influence of bankers and financiers

Corporate organization on a large scale facilitated the spread of industrial unification. Some industries—steel, for example—combined vertically.

Vertical organization

*Horizontal organization:
Cartels*

Steel companies, to ensure uninterrupted production, acquired their own coal and iron mines. By doing so, they could guarantee themselves a supply of raw materials at attractive prices. Often the same steel companies would obtain control of companies whose products were made of steel: for example, shipyards or railway factories. Now they would not only possess a ready stock of raw materials but an equally ready market for their manufactured products—steel plates, steel rails, whatever they might be. Such vertical integration was only possible as a result of the money available for investment through the institutions of finance capital.

A second form of corporate organization was a horizontal formation: the cartel. These were combinations of individual companies producing the same kind of goods, joined for the purpose of controlling, if not eliminating, competition. Since their products were identical, an identical price could be charged. Companies involved in the production of coal and steel were especially suited to the organization of cartels because of the costs of initial capitalization. It is very expensive to build, equip, and man a steel foundry; thus there were relatively few of them. And because there were few, they were the more easily organized into a combine. Cartels were particularly strong in Germany; less so in France, where there was not as much heavy industry, where the tradition of the small family firm was particularly entrenched, and where there was longstanding opposition to competition in the form of price-cutting and general intra-industrial warfare. In Britain, though some cartels were formed, continuing subscription to the policy of free trade meant that companies would find it difficult to maintain fixed prices. How could they do so if they could not exclude, by means of a tariff, foreign competitors who wanted to undersell them? Germany had abandoned the policy of free trade in 1879; the United States, where cartels were known as trusts, did the same after the Civil War, though not all at once. Britain, because of its industrial lead and its reliance on foreign markets and imported raw materials, clung to free trade until well into the twentieth century.

Defenders of the cartel argued that the elimination of competition brought more stable prices and more continuous employment. They pointed out as well that cartels almost always reduced the cost of production. Opponents questioned, however, whether those reduced costs were reflected in lower prices, or, as they charged, in higher stockholder profits. Critics of cartels were vocal in the United States, where the so-called captains of industry, most prominently the financier J. P. Morgan (1837–1913), were attacked as a new breed of feudal barons. The Sherman Antitrust Act was passed by Congress in 1890 to curb the practice of industrial combination. It had little effect in retarding the process, however, until the trust-busting presidency of Theodore Roosevelt (1901–1909).

Elsewhere in the West at the end of the nineteenth century, governments and big business tended to develop close working relationships contrary to the laissez-faire theories of early industrial entrepreneurs. A significant manifestation of this new partnership was the appearance of businessmen and financiers as officers of state. Joseph Chamberlain, a Birm-

J. P. Morgan

ingham manufacturer, served as Britain's colonial secretary; the German banker Bernhard Dernburg was German secretary of state for colonies; the Frenchman Charles Jonnart, president of the Suez Canal Company and the Saint-Étienne steel works, was later governor-general of Algeria; Guilio Prinetti, a north Italian industrialist, was his country's foreign minister from 1901 to 1903. The interrelationship between government and industry, like the growth of cartels and combines, was seen as a natural development in the capitalist system which, its defenders argued, was showering its benefits on all classes of society.

4. INTERNATIONAL COMPETITION: BRITAIN VS. GERMANY

Throughout the period we have been examining, Britain and Germany were locked in industrial competition. By 1914, both the United States and Germany were outproducing Britain in a number of areas. Yet the German challenge was, for the British, the more significant. Industrial competition with Germany helped reshape international political alliances at the end of the century. Britain became embroiled in a contest of naval superiority with Germany and, determined not to become diplomatically or militarily isolated, moved to align itself with its ancient enemy France against the Germans.

To what degree did the Germans succeed in overtaking the British? By 1914, Britain's industrial-commercial day was by no means over. The volume of German trade at the turn of the century was no more than 60 percent as great. Because Britain was more mature industrially than Germany, the service sector of its economy was now expanding faster than its manufacturing sector. A greater proportion of the work force was involved in the business of distributing and selling goods than of making them. If Britain's output of manufactured goods did no more than double between 1870 and 1913, as compared to Germany's sixfold increase, it was in part for this reason. Nor should one suppose that all areas of German industry were functioning as efficient, modernized, and technologically advanced units. For every up-to-date chemical plant, for every thriving steel mill, there were many smaller workshops where manufacturing took place on little more than a domestic scale. Having said this, however, the fact remains that the Germans *were* a powerful threat to the British. Even before 1870, Germany had ceased to provide a ready market for British manufactures; the Germans were supplying their own needs thanks to rapid industrialization and tariffs. After 1870, Germany began to export to the rest of the world. Moving into markets that the British had considered exclusively their own, German salesmen promoted German goods in Australia, South America, China, and in Britain itself. In fields such as the manufacture of organic chemicals and electrical equipment, Germany outsold Britain across the globe.

How can Germany's success and, perhaps more important, Britain's inability to counter it be explained? To begin with, Britain was handicapped because it had been the first nation to industrialize. With heavy capital investments in older factories and equipment, the British were reluctant to enter new fields or to exploit new methods. For example, because the British had constructed plants to manufacture alkali by an earlier, less efficient process, they found themselves trapped into continuing to produce in that way after the Solvay process had been discovered. Rather than make the expensive switch, British manufacturers attempted to make their alkali more competitive by cutting costs and improving worker efficiency. But when further refinements were introduced in the 1890s, British output not only failed to keep pace with German and also American increases but actually decreased. The same difficulties arose with steel. Here again Britain was hampered by the problem of priority. Because the British were the first to industrialize, their manufacturing centers took shape in accordance with the scale of early- and mid-nineteenth-century production. Now there was need for large tracts of land, close to transportation, to accommodate steel mills. Because of the cramped layout of Britain's industrial cities, it could not build mills as large as those in Germany or the United States. The result was that by 1900 the largest British steel mills were no bigger than the average-sized mills in Germany. Even new plants built for other manufacturing purposes in Britain were only a third as large as those constructed by its major rival. Because German plants were big, and because, therefore, they represented a large investment of capital, those who managed them did all they could to ensure their efficient operation. They rationalized design and standardized parts to an extent the British, with their smaller plants, continued to believe unnecessary. Smaller firms tended to receive smaller and more specialized orders which did not encourage standardization. Although standardization was accomplished by 1914 in Britain in some industries—notably iron and steel—in many others it remained more the exception than the rule.

Britain's industrial lead, which froze its urban areas into obsolete patterns and thus prevented growth, froze British attitudes as well. Because they had come so far so fast, the British had grown complacent. Nowhere is this fact more clearly reflected than in the British attitude toward education. If the achievements of the first Industrial Revolution—for example, the steam engine, the spinning jenny—were the result of what might be called creative tinkering, those of the second revolution were the product of a close and fruitful union of pure science with technology. Achievement now depended on a generally literate work force, a trained body of mechanics, a scientifically grounded body of technicians, and a corps of highly trained, creative scientists. Germany was producing these cadres; Britain was not. Only in 1870 was a system of public elementary education instituted in Britain, and not until ten years later was it made compulsory. In Germany, compulsory education dated from the eighteenth century. The British governing class believed the primary purpose of working-class education was control: teaching a boy or girl not only how to read and write, but to accept his or her particular place within the social structure. Though German elementary education was authoritarian in many respects as well, the fact that it had begun earlier and was directly joined to systems of secondary education encouraged the development of abilities; it was in this respect far less wasteful than that of the British. As Britain lagged in the area of elementary education, it lagged in the development of scientific and technological laboratories and training centers. In Germany, the state established an elaborate network of such technical institutions; in Britain there were almost none before the First World War.

Complacency was the major reason for this lack. The British tended to believe, wrongly, that practical experience and on-the-job training would produce the skills necessary to keep abreast of change. In addition, the British upper middle class convinced itself that the goal of education was not the production of creative technologists but of "gentlemen." Fathers who had made their fortunes as entrepreneurs during the first Industrial Revolution sent their sons to private boarding schools and to the ancient universities of Oxford and Cambridge to receive a "gentleman's" education—training in Greek and Latin, primarily. Those sons, whose creative talents might otherwise have been channeled into science and technology, chose careers in politics, or in the imperial or domestic bureaucracies instead. The result was a severe narrowing of the pool of creative technologists and dynamic entrepreneurs. There were fewer men than in either Germany or the United States interested in organizing the increasingly large amounts of capital necessary to engage in industrial expansion. It was easier to invest money overseas than to undertake the revitalization of various enterprises at home. A suspicion of what was new, encouraged by the British tendency to rely upon practical experience of the past, prevented Britain from rising in more than a fitful way to the German challenge.

Complacency

5. INTERNATIONAL COMPETITION: IMPERIALISM

The rivalry between Britain and Germany was only the most intense aspect of international competitiveness during the last decades of the nineteenth century. As nations proceeded with the business of industrialization, their search for markets brought them into direct opposition with one another. One result was that the dogma of free trade was abandoned by all save Britain. As we have seen, the Germans rejected the policy of low tariffs in 1879. Austria and Russia had already done so. Spain instituted new scales of import duties in 1877 and again in 1891. In France, two decades of gradual abandonment were climaxed by the passage of the Méline Tariff in 1892. Although individual nations attempted to isolate themselves from each other in this way, developments in international economics mandated the continuing growth and development of an interlocking, worldwide system of manufacturing, trade, and finance. The general adoption by Western Europe and the United States of the gold standard meant that the currencies of the so-called civilized world could be readily exchanged with

A global economy

each other against the measure of a common standard—the international price of gold. Hence countries needing to import from the United States, for example, did not have to sell goods directly to that country. They could sell to South America, exchange the money they received for gold, and then buy from America.

Almost all European countries, dependent on vast supplies of raw materials to sustain their rate of industrial production, imported more than they exported. To avoid the mounting deficits that would otherwise have resulted from this practice, they relied upon "invisible" exports: i.e., shipping, insurance, and interest on money lent or invested. The extent of Britain's exports in these areas was far greater than that of any other country. London was the money market of the world, to which would-be borrowers looked for assistance before turning elsewhere. By 1914, Britain had $20 billion invested overseas, compared with the $8.7 of the French and the $6 billion of the Germans. The insurance firm of Lloyds of London served clients around the world. The British merchant fleet transported the manufactured goods and raw materials of every trading nation. It was the volume of its "invisible" exports that permitted Britain to remain faithful to the doctrine of free trade while other European nations were forced to institute tariffs.

The competition between the principal economic powers of this worldwide marketplace affected not only their relationships with each other but also with those less developed areas upon which they were increasingly dependent for both raw materials and markets. Some of those areas, such as India and China, were the seats of ancient empires. Others, such as Central Africa, sheltered equally complex though less geographically expansive cultures. No matter what the nature of the indigenous civilization, the intrusion upon it of modern science and technology, systematic wage labor, financial and legal institutions caused enormous disruption. Though drawn into the world economy, these areas did not draw from it the benefits that the West did. Native industries such as Indian textile spinning and weaving stood no chance in competition with the factory-made products of Manchester. African herdsmen and hunters endured the disruption of their living habits by the activities of European ranchers and miners. Men who had made their living as boatmen and carters lost their livelihood to the railways constructed by Western nations. New jobs there might be; but they were jobs worked according to a Western style, dictated by Western economic demands, and threatened by Western economic disorders. In great measure the workers of this emerging world were assuming the role of a global unskilled working class under the hegemony of Western capitalism.

With this global background in mind, we can better understand the history of late-nineteenth-century imperialism—the subjugation by the European powers of vast tracts of land and indigenous populations, primarily on the continents of Africa and Asia. Imperialism was by no means a new phenomenon. During the eighteenth century, the French had penetrated Algeria and the British, India. In other parts of the world, where Western powers did not govern directly, they often exercised an indirect influence so

Technology and Empire. A traction engine hauling an army road train in South Africa during the Boer War.

powerful as to shape the policies and dictate the activities of indigenous authorities. When the West "opened" China beginning in 1834, it left the Chinese in nominal charge of their state. But it ensured that affairs would be conducted to its advantage and within its "sphere of influence." Britain added in this way to its "informal" empire, expanding into South America, Africa, and South and East Asia.

As international rivalries increased, European powers moved with greater frequency and determination to control both the government and economy of underdeveloped nations and territories. French politicians supported imperialism as a means of restoring national prestige and honor, lost in the humiliating defeat by the Germans in the Franco-Prussian War of 1870–1871. The British, on the other hand, looked with alarm at the accelerating pace of industrialization in Germany and France and feared losing their existing and potential world markets. The Germans, recently unified in a modern nation, viewed overseas empire as a "national" possession and as a way of entering the "club" of great powers.

European views of overseas empire

The West's inventions of the late eighteenth and nineteenth centuries provided the tools of imperialism. Metal-hulled steamships, widely used for trade with Africa from the 1850s, provided faster, cheaper transportation and allowed for the shipment of bulk cargoes such as unprocessed crops and heavy ores. Travel time between Liverpool and Cape Town was reduced from an average of three months to three weeks. Sail power quickly lost out to steam. By the same token, river and lake steamers overcame the problem of transportation in the African interior. Submarine telegraph cables also brought Africa closer to Europe. By 1885, West and South Africa were linked to London and Paris. With the use of quinine, malaria became

Technology as a tool of imperialism

less threatening and Europeans were emboldened to penetrate the tropical rain forests. In military technology, the shift in Africa from muzzle-loading rifles to fast-firing breechloaders was completed by 1878. European armies gained an even greater advantage with the introduction in 1884 of the Maxim gun, a prototype of the modern machine gun, capable of firing eleven bullets a second. These and other inventions and scientific breakthroughs made imperialist conquest and resource exploitation vastly cheaper and eminently more viable.

Imperialism as economics: Hobson

The scope, intensity, and long-range consequences of this so-called new imperialism of the late nineteenth century have generated a heated debate about its causes. One influential group of social critics and historians has argued that the causes were predominantly, if not exclusively, economic. As early as 1902, the English social reformer and theorist, J. A. Hobson (1858–1940), charged that what he called "the scramble for Africa" had occurred as a result of the economic interests of a small group of extremely rich and influential financiers throughout Western Europe. Hobson declared that the colonization of Africa had produced little economic gain for the taxpayers whose countries had dispatched armies of conquest and occupation at the behest of international capitalists. Profits went only to the rich, who ventured beyond the bounds of economically stagnant Western Europe in search of a higher return on their investments than could be realized at home. Hobson concluded that late-nineteenth-century imperialism was "a depraved choice of national life," appealing primarily to "the lusts of self-seeking acquisitiveness and forceful domination."

Lenin

Hobson's analysis inspired a more influential critique of imperialism by the Russian communist and future revolutionary leader, N. Lenin (1870–1924). Lenin agreed with Hobson that imperialism was an economic phenomenon. But, unlike Hobson, he saw it as an integral and inevitable phase of the capitalist system, as the title of his 1916 treatise, *Imperialism: The Last Stage of Capitalism,* explicitly declared. Capitalist competition, Lenin argued, and the consequent monopolies that it had produced, had lowered domestic profits, and thus compelled the owners of surplus capital to invest it overseas. The alternative, enlarging home markets by raising wages, would serve only further to decrease profits. Imperialism was thus the creature of the internal contradictions of industrial capitalism.

Limits to the economic argument

While most historians would agree that economic pressures were one important cause of imperialism, they have remained uncomfortable with analyses that ignore other factors they consider equally important. They remain prepared to acknowledge the role of economics when it seems to make sense to do so: in the case of Great Britain, for example, where about half its total of £4 billion in foreign investments was at work within its empire. In all Western European countries, demand for raw materials made colonies a necessary investment and helped persuade governments that imperialism was a worthwhile policy. Yet the economic explanation begins to break down when one considers facts like the following: that colonial markets were generally too poor to answer the needs of European manufacturers; that Africa, the continent over which there was the greatest "scramble," was also the poorest and least profitable to investors; that only a very small portion of German capital was invested in German colonies before 1914; that only one-fifth of French capital was so invested; that, indeed, the French had more capital invested in Russia, hoping to stabilize that ally against the Germans, than in all their colonial possessions.

Imperial policy-making was both a response to political and economic considerations, and a corollary to the process of nation-building. National security and the preservation of a general balance of power were issues never far from the forefront of politicians' thinking and planning. Great-power interest in the eastern Mediterranean grew with the demise of the Ottoman Empire. At the Berlin Conference of 1878, France secured from Great Britain and Germany the assurance of a free hand in Tunisia as compensation for its acquiescence in British annexation of Cyprus. This understanding breathed new life into the principle that remuneration of territorial claims in one region must be compensated for by concessions elsewhere.

*Imperialism and
international politics*

Britain's domination of Egypt in the 1880s was the result, in large measure, of its fear of what might occur in the Near East should large portions of the decaying Ottoman Empire fall into Russian hands. Britain had purchased 44 percent of the shares in the Suez Canal Company in 1875, and considered the waterway a strategic lifeline to the East. The canal had been built by the French under the direction of the engineer Ferdinand de Lesseps. Begun in 1859 and completed in 1869, it was expected to assist France in its bid for commercial expansion to the East. Britain obtained its shares in 1875 from the spendthrift khedive (viceroy) of Egypt at a time when he was threatened with bankruptcy. When, in 1882, nationalist rebels protested continuing British intervention in the internal affairs of Egypt, the British claimed they had no choice but to bombard the port of Alexandria and place the Egyptian ruler under their protection. A continuing British presence in Egypt, and the willingness of the British government to support Egyptian claims to the Upper Nile, worried the French, who were growing to fear Britain's political domination of the entire

British domination of Egypt

Dredges and Elevators at Work on the Construction of the Suez Canal, 1869

African continent. Moving to correct what they perceived as a severe political imbalance, the French challenged the British and at Fashoda, in the Sudan, came close to war in 1898. The British called the French bluff, however, and war was averted.

Imperial policy-making

The power struggle over Suez, Egypt, and the Sudan provides an excellent example of the manner in which international politics was directly related to imperial advance. It suggests, as well, that what passed for "imperial policy" was less a matter of long-range planning than of a series of pragmatic and often spontaneous responses to particular colonial political and economic situations. Often those in charge of policy-making found themselves led beyond their original ambitions, not only by the demands of international rivalries, but by the actions of individual explorers and entrepreneurs who established claims to hitherto unknown territories that home governments then felt compelled to recognize and defend.

"The white man's burden"

Imperialism must also be understood as something more than official policy, whether carefully conceived or accidental. A French diplomat once described the dynamic English imperial adventurer Cecil Rhodes as "a force cast in an idea"; the same might be said of imperialism itself. Imperialism as an idea excited the minds of explorers like the English missionary David Livingstone, who believed that his country's conquest of Africa would put an end to the East African slave trade, and "introduce the Negro family into the body of corporate nations." Rudyard Kipling (1865–1936), the English poet and novelist, wrote of "the white man's burden," of his mission to civilize the "half devil, half child" races that inhabited what most Europeans considered the "barbaric" and "heathen" quarters of the globe. To combat slave-trading, famine, filth, and illiteracy seemed to many a legitimate reason for invading the jungles of Africa and Asia.

Imperial propaganda

Imperialism as an idea was also of use to European governments at home. A populace could be encouraged to forget domestic hardships as it celebrated its country's triumphs overseas. Patriotism—a not always attractive corollary to nation-building—was stimulated by arguments such as that expressed by the German historian Heinrich von Treitschke in 1887: that "the colonizing impulse has become a vital question for a great nation"— the implication clearly being that a nation was not great unless it possessed colonies. Associations with a semi-official standing—the Deutsche Kolonialgesellschaft, the Comité de l'Afrique Française, the Royal Colonial Institute—propagandized on behalf of empire, as did newspapers, which recognized in sensational stories of overseas conquest a means of attracting a newly literate clientele.

The colonization of Africa

Imperial competition centered in Africa. In 1875, 11 percent of the continent was in European hands; by 1902, 90 percent. Germans pressed inward from the east; Frenchmen from the west. The Portuguese schemed to connect the ancient colonies of Angola, on the west, with Mozambique, on the east. Most active among the European powers during this initial period of late-nineteenth-century colonization was a privately financed group of Belgians under the leadership of that country's king, Leopold II (1865–1909). In association with H. M. Stanley, an American newspaper-

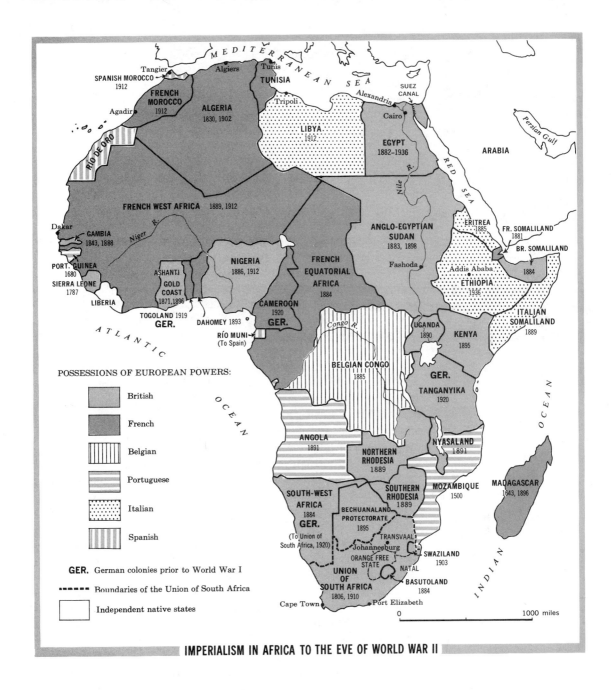

POSSESSIONS OF EUROPEAN POWERS:

- British
- French
- Belgian
- Portuguese
- Italian
- Spanish

GER. German colonies prior to World War I

- - - - Boundaries of the Union of South Africa

Independent native states

IMPERIALISM IN AFRICA TO THE EVE OF WORLD WAR II

0   1000 miles

man and explorer, Leopold and a group of financiers founded the International Association for the Exploration and Civilization of the Congo in 1876, which negotiated treaties with chieftains that opened the Congo River basin to commercial exploitation. A conference, called in Berlin in 1884 was attended by most European nations and the United States and attempted to establish certain ground rules for the game of imperial acquisition. The Congo was declared a Free State, under the trusteeship of

Slaves in Chains, 1896. In Africa, native labor was exploited, sometimes by Europeans and often by other natives, as here.

Leopold (the first example of this later familiar device of protecting "backward" peoples). A European nation with holdings on the African coast was declared to have first rights to territory in the interior behind those coastal regions. Those rights, however, could be sustained only by what was termed "real" occupation—that is, the presence of either administrators or troops. The scramble was on! Occupation was accompanied by the exploitation of native labor. Agreements reached with local chieftains, whom the Europeans courted, authorized the employment of men and women as laborers under conditions little better than slavery. Often compelled to live in compounds apart from their families, Africans were victimized by a system that rooted out prevailing custom without attempting to establish anything like a new civilization in its place. In the Congo, the Arab slave trade was suppressed, replaced by a system of forced labor. Tribal lands were confiscated and rebellions brutally crushed.

The division of the geographical spoils accelerated after 1885. The Portuguese increased their hold in Angola and Mozambique. The Italians invaded Somaliland and Eritrea. They attempted to extend their controls to Ethiopia, but were repulsed in 1896 by an army of 80,000 Ethiopians, the first instance of a major victory by native Africans over whites. Germany came relatively late to the game. Bismarck was reluctant to engage in an enterprise that, he believed, would do little to profit the empire either politically or economically. Eventually concluding, however, that they could not afford to let other powers divide the continent among them, the Germans established colonies in German East Africa, in the Cameroons and Togo on the west coast, and in the desertlike territory of South-West Africa. The French controlled large areas in West Africa and, in the Red Sea, the port of Djibouti. It was to further their plan for an east-west link that the French risked challenging the British at Fashoda. That scheme,

The scramble for territory

however, fell afoul of Britain's need to dominate Egypt, and of its plans for a north-south connection through the African continent.

Cecil Rhodes (1853–1902), the English entrepreneur and imperial visionary, promoted the notion of a Capetown to Cairo railway both before and after his assumption of the prime-ministership of the Cape Colony in 1890. His plans were thwarted in the south, however, by the presence of two independent neighboring republics, the Transvaal and the Orange Free State, both inhabited by descendants of the original Dutch settlers in South Africa. These Boers—the Dutch word for "farmers"—had fled from the British in the Cape Colony and established themselves in their agricultural states in defiant opposition to the freebooting and exploitationist spirit of the British economic adventurers who had driven them from their original settlements. When diamonds and gold were discovered in the Transvaal in 1886, the tension between the British and the Boers grew. As British prospectors and entrepreneurs moved in, the Boers refused to pass laws permitting the exploitation of their resources by foreign firms. They also taxed the interlopers heavily. Rhodes retaliated by attempting to force a war with the republics. His first try, the dispatching of a force of irregular volunteers under the command of Dr. Leander Starr Jameson in 1895, failed to provoke a conflict, but precipitated general censure on the British for harassing a peaceful neighbor. Rhodes was forced to resign as prime minister of the Cape Colony in 1896. War broke out in 1899. Its course,

Left: *"The Rhodes Colossus."* The ambitions of Cecil Rhodes, the driving force behind British imperialism in South Africa, are satirized in this cartoon, which appeared in *Punch.* Right: *"Now We Shant Be Long to Cairo."* So read the banner across Engine No. 1 taking the first train from Umtali to Salisbury, Rhodesia, reflecting Cecil Rhodes's vision of a Capetown to Cairo railway as a symbol of British domination of the African continent.

Boer Commandos under Louis Botha. Botha became the first prime minister of the Union of South Africa following the Boer War.

however, did not run according to British plans. The Boers proved tough fighters. It took three years to secure an armistice; it took further long months and resort to brutal policies such as detention camps and farm-burning to bring the resilient republicans to heel. The war's consequences were British loss of international prestige, and a heightening of the Anglo-German rivalry, the kaiser having publicly pronounced his sympathy with the Boer cause.

Britain managed to increase its hold on its prize imperial possession—India—throughout the nineteenth century. The "informal" rule of the commercially motivated East India Company had proved ineffective in 1857, when native Indian troops and a large number of other disaffected elements within the subcontinent rebelled in what the British chose to call "The Indian Mutiny," but which was in fact a far more serious and deep-seated challenge to foreign control. Henceforth the British government directly administered the subcontinent. But at the same time, they decided to rule through the Indian upper classes, and not, as in the past, in opposition to them. Although instruction in British-sponsored schools continued in English, Indian customs were tolerated as they had not been before, and princes and their bureaucracies were incorporated as protectorates into the general scheme of government. A class of westernized, and yet devotedly Indian civil servants and businessmen thus emerged by the end of the nineteenth century, trained by the British yet burdened by no sense of obligation to their tutors. This group provided the leadership for the nationalist movement that was to challenge British rule in India during the mid-twentieth century. Britain's aim in India was to promote order and stability. Civil servants administered justice even-handedly; they promoted improved sanitation, which, ironically, helped to increase the country's population beyond the point where it could sustain itself. The vast majority of

"The Execution of 'John Company.'" This 1857 *Punch* cartoon graphically depicts the abolition of the East India Company in the wake of the "Indian Mutiny."

THE GREAT POWERS AND IMPERIALISM IN ASIA TO SEPT. 1, 1940

Legend:
- British
- French
- Dutch
- U.S.
- U.S.S.R.
- Controlled by the U.S.S.R.
- Japan
- Controlled by Japan

SEA OF OKHOTSK

UNION OF SOVIET SOCIALIST REPUBLICS

SIBERIA

EUROPE
ASIA

JAPAN
Tokyo
Yokohama
Osaka

Vladivostok

MANCHUKUO
Harbin

SEA OF JAPAN

CHOSEN (KOREA)

MONGOLIA
Peiping
Tientsin

INNER MONGOLIA

OUTER MONGOLIA

Shanghai
Nanking
Yangtze
Wenchow
Foochow
Amoy
Swatow
Canton
Hong Kong (Br.)
HAINAN

E. CHINA SEA

TAIWAN (FORMOSA)

PHILIPPINE ISLANDS

Manila

S. CHINA SEA

PACIFIC OCEAN

CHINESE REPUBLIC

SINKIANG

TIBET

BHUTAN
NEPAL

Chungking

FR. INDO-CHINA
Bangkok
THAI-LAND

SARAWAK
BORNEO

MALAYA
Singapore
SUMATRA
JAVA

CELEBES

MOLUCCAS (SPICE ISLANDS)

NEW GUINEA

Equator

KIRGHIZ S.S.R.
TADZHIK S.S.R.
UZBEK S.S.R.
TURKMEN S.S.R.

AFGHANISTAN
BALUCHISTAN

Indus R.
Delhi
Ganges R.
Calcutta

INDIA
Bombay
Madras

BURMA
Mandalay
Rangoon

BAY OF BENGAL

ANDAMAN ISLANDS

CEYLON

INDIAN OCEAN

ARABIAN SEA

CASPIAN SEA

Moscow

IRAN (PERSIA)
Teheran

OMAN

BRITISH HINTERLAND OF ADEN

HADRAMAUT

YEMEN
Aden

SAUDI ARABIA

KUWAIT
Basra
Baghdad
IRAQ
JORDAN
TRANS-JORDAN
SYRIA
LEBANON
PALESTINE

RED SEA

Nile R.

AFRICA

TURKEY
Ankara
Istanbul

BLACK SEA

MEDITERRANEAN SEA

EUROPE
ASIA

0   1000
miles along the equator

Imperialism. Left: Germans traveling in East Africa, 1907. Right: A British officer in India, c. 1900.

Indians remained desperately poor, victims in many cases of the importation of cheap manufactured goods that threatened indigenous industries and testified to Britain's willingness to subordinate its colonies' economic well-being to its own.

British colonial rule

The pattern of British imperialism differed throughout the world. In areas dominated by white settlers, home rule was introduced in hopes of preventing the sort of disaffection that had produced the American Revolution. Australia was granted self-government in the 1850s, New Zealand in 1852. In 1867, a united Dominion of Canada, with its own federal governments and legislatures, was established.

Imperialism elsewhere

Elsewhere in the world, Western nations hastened to plant their colors upon those territories that promised rewards, either economic or strategic. Britain, France, Germany, and the Netherlands all staked claims in the East Indies, the Dutch achieving an overall hegemony there by 1900. China allowed itself to be victimized by a series of commercial treaties; among the predators was China's neighbor Japan, the only non-Western nation able to modernize in the nineteenth century. The United States played a double game. It acted as champion of the underdeveloped countries in the Western Hemisphere when they were threatened from Europe. Yet the Americans were willing, whenever it suited them, to prey on their neighbors, either "informally" or formally. When, at the end of the century, Spain's feeble hold on its Caribbean and Pacific colonies encouraged talk of rebellion, the United States stepped in to protect its investments and guarantee its maritime security. It declared and won the Spanish-American War in 1898 on trumped-up grounds. In the same year, the United States annexed Puerto Rico and the Philippines, and established a "protectorate" over Cuba. When Colombia's colony, Panama, threatened to rebel in 1903, the Americans quickly backed the rebels, recognized Panama as a republic, and then proceeded to grant it protection while Americans built the Panama Canal on land leased from the new government. Intervention in Santo Domingo and in Hawaii proved that the United States was no less an imperial power than the nations of Western Europe. Together, by the end of the century, those countries had succeeded in binding the world together as it had never been before. The military and economic power with which they had accomplished that achievement meant that, for the time being at any rate, they would be the world's masters.

SELECTED READINGS

- *Items so designated are available in paperback editions.*

- Ashworth, W., *A Short History of the International Economy since 1850,* rev. ed., London, 1975. A good introduction.
- Barkin, Kenneth D., *The Controversy over German Industrialization, 1890–1902,* Chicago, 1970. The political and social struggles between agricultural and industrial interests.
  Cameron, Rondo E., *France and the Economic Development of Europe, 1800–1914,* Princeton, 1961. Emphasizes the export of French capital and skill in the economic growth of Europe.
- Fieldhouse, D. K., *The Colonial Experience: A Comparative Study from the Eighteenth Century,* London, 1966. A general survey from the eighteenth to the twentieth centuries.
  ———, *Economics and Empire, 1830–1914,* London, 1973. Argues against the primacy of economic factors in the spread of imperialism.
- Gollwitzer, Heinz, *Europe in the Age of Imperialism, 1880–1914,* London, 1969. A brief survey with excellent illustrations.
- Headrick, Daniel R., *The Tools of Empire: Technology and European Imperialism in the Nineteenth Century,* Oxford, 1981. A study of the relationship between technological innovation and imperialism.
- Hobsbawm, Eric, *Industry and Empire: The Making of Modern English Society, 1750 to the Present Day,* New York, 1968. Emphasizes the economic background of imperialism.
- ———, *The Age of Empire, 1875–1914,* New York, 1987. Surveys the European scene at a time of apparent stability and real decline.
  Kieran, V. G., *Marxism and Imperialism,* New York, 1975. Argues the Marxist position effectively.
- Kindleberger, C. P., *Economic Growth in France and Britain, 1851–1950,* Cambridge, Mass., 1963. A technical account.
- Landes, David S., *The Unbound Prometheus,* London, 1969. Particularly good on the Anglo-German rivalry.
  Langer, William L., *The Diplomacy of Imperialism, 1890–1902,* New York, 1960. A thorough, standard work, useful for its analysis of the intellectual as well as political origins of imperialism.
  Louis, William Roger, ed., *Imperialism: The Robinson and Gallagher Controversy,* New York, 1976. The best introduction to recent debate over the nature and causes of imperialism.

- Miller, Michael B., *The Bon Marché: Bourgeois Culture and the Department Store, 1869–1920,* Princeton, 1981. Explores the revolution in merchandising of the late nineteenth century.

  Milward, Alan S., and S. B. Saul, *The Development of the Economies of Continental Europe, 1850–1914,* Cambridge, Mass., 1977. An excellent, comprehensive text, particularly good on the smaller European nations.

- Moorehead, Alan, *The White Nile,* London, 1971. Captures much of the excitement of imperial exploration.

  Price, Roger, *The Economic Modernization of France, 1730–1880,* New York, 1975. Rejects conventional periodizations; stresses the advent of railroads, which transformed the market structure of France.

  Robinson, Ronald, and J. Gallagher, *Africa and the Victorians: The Official Mind of Imperialism,* London, 1961. Contains their famous thesis that imperialism was not deliberately pursued as a policy of state, but rather was a response to events in colonial areas. The modern debate over imperialism begins with this work.

- Shannon, Richard, *The Crisis of Imperialism, 1865–1915,* St. Albans, England, 1976. An excellent survey of the transformation of British society in the wake of modern industrialization.

  Stolper, Gustav, et al., *The German Economy, 1870 to 1940,* New York, 1967. A good introduction.

SOURCE MATERIALS

- Court, W. H. B., *British Economic History, 1870–1914; Commentary and Documents,* Cambridge, 1965. An excellent collection of documents.
- Hobson, J. A., *Imperialism: A Study,* London, 1902.
- Lenin, Vladimir, *Imperialism: The Highest Stage of Capitalism,* 1916. (Many English editions.) Lenin's most significant contribution to Marxist ideology. He saw the essence of imperialism as the export of capital rather than goods, which led to worldwide competition, of which World War I was an inevitable result.
- Reitz, Deneys, *Commando: A Boer Journal of the Boer War,* London, 1929. A superb memoir of the Boer War.

Chapter 25

THE MIDDLE CLASS CHALLENGED

The time of surprise attacks, of revolutions carried through by small conscious minorities at the head of unconscious masses, is past. Where it is a question of a complete transformation of the social organization, the masses themselves must also be in it, must themselves already have grasped what is at stake, what they are going in for, with body and soul.

—Friedrich Engels, Introduction to Karl Marx, *The Class Struggles in France, 1848–50*

Capitalism's continuing expansion encouraged middle-class men and women at the end of the nineteenth century to consider themselves the necessary key to the progress of the human race. They believed that society would most successfully advance under their auspices and in accordance with their moral and economic precepts, grounded in a belief in the importance and inevitability of continued material progress. At the same time, however, that belief was being challenged from several directions. In each case, the challenges called into question assumptions close to the core of middle-class consciousness. Socialist doctrine, which was for the first time receiving a widespread hearing, pronounced capitalism a threat, rather than a boon, to society. New scientific theories—particularly the theory of evolution—declared that the key to progress was not the well-laid schemes of humanity, but chance. Psychologists discovered the irrationality of human beings and philosophers their ultimate helplessness. Paintings, poetry, and music proclaimed an artists' revolution on behalf of the idea of art for its own sake, not for the edification of a middle-class public. Together, these various intellectual and cultural currents threatened notions of middle-class superiority.

The dimensions of the challenge

1. THE CHALLENGE OF SOCIALISM

The history of socialism in the latter half of the nineteenth century is, to a great degree, the biography of its most famous propagandist and theoreti-

Karl Marx

The Communist Manifesto

Capital

cian, the German Karl Marx (1818–1883). Marx was both a social thinker and a political leader. At certain times theory dictated his actions; at others, political events led him to alter doctrine. But always he was at the center of the socialist movement, his moral passion, as much as his scholarly research, shaping the course of its events. The fact of his widespread influence is particularly remarkable in light of his exile from the mainstream of Continental socialism. He lived from 1849 until his death in London, in a country whose toleration of socialists was a mark of its comparative immunity from their doctrines.

Like his friend and collaborator Friedrich Engels (1820–1895), Marx was the son of middle-class parents. After study at the university of Berlin, in 1842 he took a job as editor of the *Rhineland Gazette,* hoping to use that position to argue for the transformation of a society he was growing to despise. His radical policies soon put him at odds with his publishers, however. He moved first to Paris and then to Brussels, where he helped found the Communist League, a body whose declared aim was the overthrow of the middle class. While in Paris, Marx had renewed a former friendship with Engels. Engels, who lived in Manchester from 1842–1844 as part of his training for a position in the family firm, had just written *The Condition of the Working Class in England* (1845), in which he portrayed the misery of the recently industrialized urban masses. Together, during the late 1840s, the two men produced a theory of revolutionary change that was published by Marx at the request of the League in 1848, at the height of the struggles on the Continent, as *The Communist Manifesto.*

In the *Manifesto* Marx outlined a theory of history that owed a good deal to the German philosopher Hegel (see above, p. 781). Hegel, it will be recalled, had argued that ideas, the motive force of history, were in constant conflict with each other, and that this clash between ideas in turn would produce an eventual synthesis, representing an advance in the history of the human race. Marx adapted this particular progressive notion of history to his own uses. Whereas Hegel perceived conflict and resolution (a dialectic) in terms of ideas, Marx saw them in terms of economic forces. Society, he argued, was at any time no more than the reflection of a hierarchy of classes dictated by those who own the means of production and control the distribution of its material goods. As history had progressed, so had the means changed. Feudalism and manorialism were vanquished by capitalism. And capitalism, Marx declared, would be vanquished in turn by communism.

During the 1850s and 1860s Marx labored to produce his definitive analysis of capitalist economics. The first volume of *Capital* was published in 1867. The argument of *Capital* owed a great deal to that dialectical idealism and economic materialism that, as we have seen, shaped Marx's earlier thinking and writing. In *Capital* he synthesized ideas he and Engels had enunciated in their previous tracts. He described in detail the processes of production, exchange, and distribution as they operated within the capitalist system. He argued that under capitalism, workers were denied their rightful share of profits. The value of any manufactured item, Marx claimed, was determined by the amount of labor necessary to produce it. Yet workers were hired at wages whose value was far less than the value of the goods they produced. The difference between the value of workers' wages and the value of their work as sold was pocketed by members of the capitalist class, who, according to Marx, made off with far more than a justifiable portion of the sale price. This so-called labor theory of value, borrowed from a somewhat similar doctrine held by David Ricardo and other classical economists, was the basis for Marx's claim that the working class was compelled to suffer under the capitalist system. Because workers were forced to sell their labor they became nothing more than commodities in the economic market.

So long as capitalists refused to pay wages more nearly equal to the labor value of their employees' work, those employees would remain exploited. Marx preached that the only class that, under capitalism, produced more wealth than it enjoyed was the working class, the proletariat. The bourgeoisie, which owned the means of production and was therefore able to appropriate that which was rightfully the workers', had a vested interest in maintaining the status quo; hence its willingness to make use of political, social, religious, and legal institutions to keep the proletariat in its place.

Exploitation of the proletariat

Marx predicted that capitalism would eventually do itself in. He argued that as time passed, market competition would compel the formation of ever-larger industrial and financial combinations. As the smaller entrepreneurial class—the petty bourgeoisie—was squeezed out by more powerful combines, its members would join with the proletariat, until society resembled a vast pyramid, with a much-enlarged proletariat at its base and an opposing force of a few powerful capitalists at its tip. At this point, Marx declared, the proletariat would rise in revolution against what was left of the bourgeoisie.

Marx as prophet

After capitalism had received its death blow at the hands of the workers, it would be followed by a socialist stage, characterized by the dictatorship of the proletariat; payment in accordance with work performed; and ownership and operation by the state of all means of production, distribution, and exchange. In time socialism would be succeeded by communism, the goal of historical evolution. The elimination of private property would also mean the elimination of the proletariat, which existed only in opposition to the property-owning class. Thus communism would bring with it a classless society. The essence of communism was payment in accordance with needs. The wage system would be abolished, and citizens would be expected to work in accordance with their abilities, entitled to receive from the total fund of wealth produced an amount in proportion to their needs. The state would now disappear, relegated to the museum of antiquities, "along with the bronze ax and the spinning wheel." Nothing would replace it except voluntary associations to operate the means of production and provide for social necessities.

The advent of communism

In the ten years after its publication, *Capital* was translated into English (Marx had written it in German), French, Russian, and Italian. The book's widespread appeal was the result of its compelling deterministic certainty

Ferdinand Lassalle

Mikhail Bakunin

and of its vigorous crusading temper. Though most of what *Capital* predicted has failed to occur, middle- and working-class socialists reading it soon after its publication and measuring its pronouncements against the capitalistic world they knew had little difficulty in accepting Marx's reasoning. It seemed to them that he had constructed an objective science of society out of their own experiences. The book became the theoretical rallying point for a growing band of socialists who stood opposed to the world the middle class had made. For a time it breathed life into an organization of Continental and British workers that had been founded in London in 1864: the International Workingmen's Association, usually referred to as the International. This body had been formed with the declared purpose of forging an international working-class alliance to overthrow capitalism and abolish private property. Marx delivered its inaugural address, in which he preached that workers must win political power for themselves if they were ever to escape their industrial bondage. Various difficulties had prevented the formation of a radically oriented workers' organization prior to this time. There was, first of all, fear of official reprisal. Second, the irregular pace of industrialization across Europe meant that workers in one country could have little understanding of the particular plight of their fellow workers elsewhere. Finally, the period after 1850 had witnessed an increase in general prosperity which encouraged the more highly skilled—and more politically conscious—workers to forsake revolutionary goals and to pursue the more immediate end of accommodation with middle-class politicians. The German socialists' dealings with Bismarck (see below, p. 872), were a case in point. Meanwhile, however, the determination of a small band of dedicated radical socialists temporarily surmounted these problems to permit the formation of the first international workers' association.

Marx immediately assumed the direction of the International and labored to exclude both moderates and extreme radicals from its councils. He denounced the German socialists and their leader Ferdinand Lassalle (1825–1864) for their failure to oppose Bismarck. Lassalle, a strong German nationalist, advocated democratic reform within a parliamentary framework. Marx, on the other hand, argued that the duty of socialists was not partnership with the state, but rather its overthrow. At the same time, Marx battled the doctrines of the Russian anarchist Mikhail Bakunin (1814–1876), who challenged the socialist notion that social evil was the product of capitalism. Bakunin argued that the state was the ultimate villain, and preached its immediate destruction through isolated acts of terrorism. He also opposed centralization within the International, urging instead a kind of federal autonomy for each national workers' group. To Marx, these individualist notions represented nothing more than reversion to a kind of primitive rebellion, heroic but ultimately fruitless. After years of conflict, he succeeded in having Bakunin banished from the International in 1872.

The International's successes were largely limited to the 1860s. Individual trade unions in various countries were persuaded to join in its united campaign, which preached revolution and, through the application of pres-

Above: *The Birth of Venus,*
Alexandre Cabanel (1823–
1889). Below: *Luncheon on the
Grass,* Edouard Manet (1823–
1883). Cabanel's painting is a
typical product of the fashionable French Salon, and was at
one time owned by Napoleon
III. It won the Salon prize in
1863 and was copied several
times by the artist (as were
other Salon paintings), emphasizing the fact that it was considered as much a piece of
"decoration" as a piece of art.
This sort of "bestseller" was exceedingly popular with upper-
middle-class collectors, who felt
no need to apologize for its
semi-pornographic nature because of its classical subject
matter. Manet's painting, done
in the same year, created an
enormous furor. Its style broke
with the soft, painterly techniques of the Salon school; instead it was painted with broad,
flat strokes that presaged the
coming of impressionism. Its
subject matter caused a sensation as well. Whereas volup-
tuous classical nudes were respectable art, a painting of a
young woman seated without
her clothing at a picnic with
fully clothed gentlemen friends
conveyed a sense of serious social impropriety to bourgeois
viewers. (Louvre)

Iris beside a Pond, Claude Monet (1840–1926). Monet called some of his paintings impressions, and the name soon came to designate a school. (Art Institute of Chicago)

Pink and Green, Edgar Degas (1834–1917). Degas was an impressionist to the extent of his interest in fleeting motion. But as an admirer of the classicist Ingres, he emphasized line and careful composition. (Metropolitan Museum of Art)

A Woman with Chrysanthemums, Degas. In his portraits, Degas sought to capture his subjects in familiar, informal positions. Avoiding traditional formal sittings, he frequently brought together an assortment of discrete observations first in his imagination, and then on canvas. When this painting was completed in 1858 it was a still life of flowers bearing the imprint of Delacroix; the woman was added in 1865. (Metropolitan Museum of Art)

Luncheon of the Boating Party, Auguste Renoir (1841–1919). The impressionists enjoyed employing their revolutionary artistic techniques to portray the commonplace occasions of everyday life. (Phillips Memorial Gallery)

Montagne Sainte-Victoire with Aqueduct, Paul Cézanne (1839–1906). Cézanne's insistence upon the reduction of the landscape to patterns of form and planes of color illustrates the manner in which his genius created the vital link between impressionism and cubism. (Metropolitan Museum of Art. The H. O. Havemeyer Collection. Bequest of Mrs. H. O. Havemeyer 1929)

The Card Players, Cézanne. Here are exemplified Cézanne's skill in composition, his discriminating sense of color, and the sculptured qualities of solidity and depth he gave to his figures. (Stephen C. Clark)

Above: *Sunflowers in a Vase* (V. W. van Gogh); Below: *The Starry Night* (1889), Vincent van Gogh (1853–1890). Van Gogh's compulsive style and bold technique endow his compositions with a feverish rhythm that is both compelling and disturbing. (Oil on canvas, 29 x 36¼." Collection, The Museum of Modern Art, New York. Acquired through the Lillie P. Bliss Bequest.)

Ia Orana Maria, Paul Gauguin (1848–1903). Gauguin's dissatisfaction with European life compelled his escape to Tahiti, where striking colors, bold patterns of light and shade, and local artistic tradition affected his "fauvist" style of painting. (Metropolitan Museum of Art. Bequest of Sam A. Lewisohn)

The Piano Lesson (late summer 1916), Henri Matisse (1869–1954). Matisse conveyed a freshness of approach and a vitality of line and color. (Oil on canvas, 8' ½" x 6' 11¾." Collection, The Museum of Modern Art, New York. Mrs. Simon Guggenheim Fund)

Portrait of Gertrude Stein, Pablo Picasso (1881–1973). Picasso seems to have given this portrait of the great experimenter in poetry some elements of the distortion of form characteristic of the work of both. (Metropolitan Museum of Art)

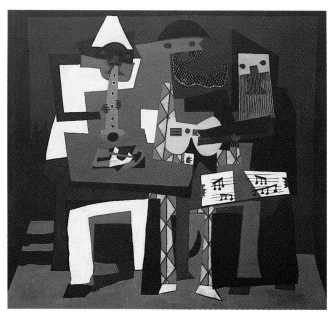

Three Musicians (1921), Pablo Picasso. This painting, regarded by many as the masterpiece of cubism, sums up the final stage of the movement (Oil on canvas, 6' 7" x 7' 3¾." Collection, The Museum of Modern Art, New York. Mrs. Simon Guggenheim Fund)

sure both at the ballot box and in the factory, seemed to promise at least higher wages and shorter hours. Under Marx's direction the International was a highly organized and tightly controlled body, far more effective in this respect than any previous socialist organization.

Yet despite Marx's abilities as an authoritarian chief of staff, the International throughout its existence had to battle those same circumstances that had delayed its foundation. In addition, Marx's insistence upon control from the center thwarted a growing desire on the part of individual socialist organizations to pursue programs of immediate benefit to themselves. These factors weakened the International. What probably brought about its demise was its association with events occurring in Paris after the defeat of France by Germany in 1870 in the Franco-Prussian War.

The troubled International

Following the collapse of Napoleon III, a new republic, generally conservative in tone, had been established by the French. In March 1871, the government attempted to disarm the Paris National Guard, a volunteer citizen army with radical political sympathies. The guard refused to surrender, declared its autonomy, deposed officials of the new government, and proclaimed a revolutionary committee—the Commune—as the true government of France. Though this movement is commonly described as a rebellion of dangerous radicals intent upon the destruction of law and order, most of its members resembled the Jacobins of the first French Revolution and belonged largely to the lower middle class. They did not advocate the abolition of private property but rather its wider distribution. Their respect for the deposits in the Bank of France was as scrupulous as any bourgeois financier might have wished. Their most radical political action was a symbolic one: the toppling of a statue of Napoleon I in the Place Vendôme. The movement was precipitated by bitterness over the defeat of Napoleon III and exhaustion by the long siege of Paris that followed. There were fears as well that the central government would be dominated by the rural population to the disadvantage of the urban masses in the capital. After sev-

The Paris Commune

A Symbol of the Paris Commune. The statue of Napoleon I in Roman garb, a symbol of imperial absolutism, is toppled from its base by the Communards.

Propaganda and the Paris Commune. This photograph, purporting to record the assassination of hostages by the radical Communards, was actually faked by their enemies in an effort to arouse anti-Communard sympathies.

eral weeks of frustrating disputation, the conflict turned into a bloody civil war. The Communards killed about sixty hostages, including the archbishop of Paris. The government numbered its victims by the thousands. The courts-martial which were set up executed twenty-six. Thousands of others were sentenced to imprisonment or banishment in New Caledonia, in the South Pacific.

The Commune and the
International

While middle-class Europe reacted in horror at what it mistakenly perceived as a second Reign of Terror, Marx, in the name of the International, extolled the courage of the Communards, who, he wrote, had fought the first pitched battle in the class war he had predicted. In a pamphlet entitled *The Civil War in France* (1871), Marx claimed that the Commune was an example of the transitional form of government through which the working class would have to pass on its way to emancipation. Yet many of the less radical members of the International were frightened and disturbed, not only by the events of the Commune itself, but by the possibility of reprisals against members of an organization that openly praised men and women who were considered by the middle class to be little more than murderers. In 1872 Marx acknowledged defeat by moving the seat of the International's council to the United States, a country far removed from the organization's affairs and from the criticisms that had begun to be heaped upon Marx for his misdirection. In 1876, the First International expired.

Although the International collapsed, socialism continued to gain ground as both a theory and a program—or rather, as several programs. As indicated by Marx's clashes with Lassalle and Bakunin, different Socialist parties could employ widely differing means toward similar ends, and as a result met with varied successes throughout Europe. The German Social Democratic party was founded in 1875; a Belgian Socialist party in 1879; and in France, despite the disasters of the Commune, a Socialist party was established in 1905. In England, although socialism was much debated and discussed, no party proclaiming itself socialist emerged. When the Labour party came into being in 1901, however, various socialist societies were represented on its executive council, along with less radical, nonsocialist trade union groups.

The spread of socialism

On the periphery of Europe—in Spain, Italy, and Russia—socialism made less headway. There the absence of widespread industrialization and the educational backwardness of large elements within the population retarded the development of a working-class consciousness, and of socialism as its political expression. Russian socialist thought was always the purview of a very small intelligentsia, and until 1905 was confined to expression through underground propagandizing and terrorist activity. Its strong flavor of agrarian idealism, based on the notion of the peasant commune as a rudimentary socialist institution that would allow Russia to bypass industrial capitalism on its way to socialism, differentiated Russian socialist thought from its Western counterparts. The Socialist Revolutionary party, formed clandestinely in 1901, continued to urge peasant socialism, while a more orthodox urban-based Marxism was advocated by the Social Democrat party after 1898.

Russian socialism

During the years before the First World War, socialists continuously and often bitterly debated the course they should follow as they attempted to achieve their goal of radical change. One group, led by Marx himself until his death, urged socialists to avoid collaboration with other parties to achieve such immediate ends as higher wages, shorter working hours, and unemployment insurance. These reforms, the "purists" declared, were the means by which the bourgeoisie could buy off the proletariat and hence indefinitely postpone revolution. On the other hand, "revisionists" urged their followers to take advantage of the fact that many of them now could vote for socialist candidates in elections. They argued that those candidates, if elected, could help them obtain a better life in the immediate future. Socialist theory might proclaim a worldwide struggle of the proletariat against the bourgeoisie, but was this any reason to turn one's back on a chance to make real headway through the ballot box in achieving reforms that would put a better life within reach of workers and their families?

"Purists" vs. "revisionists"

Another important point of disagreement centered on the relative importance of class versus gender. "Pure" socialist theory subsumed the special problems of working-class women under the more general problems of the class as a whole. Some "revisionists," on the other hand, argued that addressing problems specific to women would not dilute the socialist program as a whole and would in fact broaden its appeal. Finally, the problems of agricultural labor posed special challenges to socialists, as the example of Russia indicates. Because Marxism postulated an urban proletariat, many

Class versus gender

socialists split over the merits of incorporating large rural populations into a class struggle.

Revisionism spread despite efforts of the "purists" to put a stop to it. In Germany its most eloquent spokesman was Eduard Bernstein (1850–1932), a Social Democrat and a member of the German parliament, the Reichstag. Bernstein was among the first to question the predictions Marx had made in *Capital*. In his appropriately titled book, *Evolutionary Socialism,* published in 1899, Bernstein pointed out that for most European workers the standard of living had risen since 1850, and that the lower middle class showed no evidence that it wished to identify its interests with those of the proletariat. At the same time, increasingly wider franchises meant that workers had an excellent chance of achieving reform by means of the ballot box. The program of the future was not revolution, but democratic social reform. Bernstein's most outspoken opponent in Germany was his fellow socialist Karl Kautsky (1854–1938), an orthodox Marxist who warned that collaboration would end in the total corruption and demoralization of the proletariat. In France, the same battle was waged by the "purist" Jules Guesde (1845–1922), who preached that the Socialist party's primary goal should be the development of proletarian class consciousness, and Jean Jaurès (1859–1914), socialist leader in the Chamber of Deputies, who advocated a revisionist course. In both Germany and France, revisionists outnumbered purists by a wide margin. This was, to an even greater degree, the case in Britain. There, Fabian socialists—so named from their policy of delay, in imitation of the tactics of Fabius, a Roman general—preached what they called "the inevitability of gradualism." They believed their country would evolve toward socialism by means of parliamentary democracy. Prominent among the Fabians were the social investigators Sidney Webb (1859–1947) and Beatrice Webb (1858–1943), the novelist H. G. Wells (1866–1946), and the playwright George Bernard Shaw (1856–1950).

The continued success of revisionism during the prewar years led its opponents to sharpen their attack and to advocate increasingly violent means to achieve their ends. Their campaigns, though they never managed to convince a majority of the working class, nevertheless attracted an increasing number of adherents. Some who had originally supported the revisionists grew disappointed when reforms did not come as quickly as expected. At the same time, in much of Europe, the cost of living began to rise for many workers. The comparative prosperity that some members of the working class had experienced vanished in the face of price rises that were not matched by wage increases. The result was a frustration that encouraged the adoption of a more militant stance. Germans rallied to the side of the radical socialists Rosa Luxemburg (1871–1919) and Karl Liebknecht (1871–1919), while in France a new revolutionary Socialist party disowned the reformist leader Alexandre Millerand (1859–1943) after he agreed to serve as cabinet member in a nonsocialist government. The Second International, which had been founded in 1889, demanded at a conference in 1906 that affiliated parties declare their goal to be the destruction of the bourgeois order and the state that served its interests.

Jean Jaurès

This militant mood encouraged acceptance of the doctrines of anarchists and syndicalists. *Anarchists* preached the overthrow of capitalism by violence. They differed from socialists, however, in their hatred of the machinery of the state or any government based upon coercion. Socialists argued that until the communist millennium promised by Marx, the state would remain a necessary means to the achievement of that eventual end. Anarchists worked to see the immediate abolition of a state bureaucracy that, no matter who controlled it, they believed would result in tyranny. Bakunin, whom Marx had succeeded in expelling from the First International, was anarchism's most popular propagandist. *Syndicalism,* like anarchism, demanded the abolition of both capitalism and the state. It resembled socialism in its demand that workers share in the ownership of the means of production. Instead of making the state the owner and operator of the means of production, however, the syndicalist would delegate these functions to syndicates of producers. The steel mills would be owned and operated by the workers in the steel industry, the coal mines by the workers in the coal industry, and so on. These associations would take the place of the state, each one governing its own members in their activities as producers.

Syndicalism received its most sympathetic hearing in France, where a General Confederation of Labour, after 1902, resolved to seek solutions to economic problems outside the legally constituted framework of French politics. The most effective spokesman for syndicalism was the Frenchman Georges Sorel (1847–1922). Sorel, in his *Reflections on Violence,* published in 1908, argued that workers should be made to believe in the possibility of a general strike by the proletariat that would result in the end of bourgeois civilization. The general strike might be nothing more than myth, Sorel acknowledged. Yet, as myth, it remained a powerful weapon in the hands of those whose goal was the destruction of society and who must not shy from the employment of violent means to achieve that end.

Socialism before the First World War, then, was not a unified force. It was divided by quarrels between purists and revisionists, and challenged by the even more radical proposals of anarchists and syndicalists. Socialists, intent on their goal of international solidarity among working classes, ignored the appeal that nationalism and imperialism might make to workers in France, Germany, and Britain. Yet despite its divisions and weaknesses, socialism appeared to the middle classes of Europe as a real threat to their continued prosperity. Capitalism had provided the machinery by which the bourgeoisie had achieved power. Socialism attacked capitalism and hence those who were its direct beneficiaries. Although most socialists disapproved of violence, violent acts were attributed by middle-class men and women to an amorphous, anticapitalist body easily labeled "socialist." Riots by trade unionists in Chicago's Haymarket Square in 1886 and in London's Trafalgar Square in 1887; the assassinations of President Sadi Carnot of France in 1894, of King Humbert of Italy in 1900, and of President William McKinley of the United States in 1901; strikes which grew in number and violence throughout Europe and America after 1900—all these events were perceived by members of the middle class as part of a

Georges Sorel

The Haymarket Riots, Chicago, 1886. A contemporary illustration depicting the results of attempts to unionize workers at the McCormick Harvester works.

larger movement whose professed goal was to tear from them their economic, political, and social security.

2. THE CHALLENGE OF SCIENCE AND PHILOSOPHY

Science challenges notions of progress

While socialism grafted the middle-class belief in progress onto an apparently inevitable proletarian revolution, other forces were challenging the notion of "progress" altogether. Science, which had for decades appeared to bolster middle-class notions of progress, gradually undermined deeply held beliefs about man's place in the universe.

Lamarck and inheritance of acquired characteristics

Against the psychologically reassuring fortress of a harmonious universe, biological scientists hurled the bomb of evolutionary theory. We have seen that this theory was at least as old as Anaximander in the sixth century B.C., and that it was accepted by many of the great minds of antiquity. We have learned also that it was revived in the eighteenth century by the scientists Buffon and Linnaeus (see Chapter 18). But neither of these men offered much proof or explained how the process of evolution might work. The first to develop a systematic hypothesis of evolution was the French biologist, Jean Lamarck (1744–1829). The essential principle in Lamarck's hypothesis, published in 1809, was the inheritance of acquired characteristics. He maintained that an animal, subjected to a change in environment, acquired new habits, which in turn were reflected in structural changes. These acquired characteristics of body structure, he believed, were transmissible to the offspring, with the result that after a series of generations a new species of animal was eventually produced. Lamarck's hypothesis was widely attacked, raising as it did serious problems with the idea of nature as the unfolding of a divine plan.

A much more convincing hypothesis of organic evolution was that of the English naturalist Charles Darwin (1809–1882), published in 1859. The son of a small-town physician, Darwin began the study of medicine at the University of Edinburgh, but soon withdrew and entered Cambridge to prepare for the ministry. Here he instead devoted most of his time to natural history. In 1831 Darwin obtained an appointment as naturalist without pay with a government-sponsored expedition aboard H.M.S. *Beagle*, which had been chartered for scientific exploration on a trip around the world. The voyage lasted nearly five years and gave Darwin an unparalleled opportunity to become acquainted at first hand with the manifold variations of animal life. He noted the differences between animals inhabiting islands and related species on nearby continents, and observed the resemblances between living animals and the fossilized remains of extinct species in the same locality. His knowledge of the popular hobby of pigeon-breeding, and the unique characteristics that breeders could select through controlled mating, prompted him to seek a "natural" mechanism for the selection of characteristics. After reading Malthus's essay on population upon his return to London, he was convinced he had found the mechanism he was seeking. Malthus argued that throughout the world of nature many more individuals are born than can survive, and that consequently the weaker ones must perish in the struggle for food. Competition for the means of survival was the "no miracles" mechanism Darwin sought. The fruits of his observations, research, and hypothesizing were eventually published in 1859, in the *Origin of Species*.

Darwin's hypothesis was that of natural selection. He argued that it is nature, or the environment, which selects those variants among offspring that are to survive and reproduce. Because no two offspring are exactly alike, some will have variations such as longer horns or sharper claws or body coloration that will enable them to win out in the struggle for existence and survive as the "fittest" of their generation; the others are eliminated generally before they have lived long enough to reproduce. Darwin regarded variation and natural selection as the primary factors in the origin of new species. In other words, he taught that individual plants and animals with favorable characteristics would transmit their inherited qualities to their descendants through countless generations, and that successive eliminations of the least fit would eventually produce a new species. Darwin applied his concept of evolution not only to plant and animal species but also to humans. In his second great work, *The Descent of Man* (1871), he attempted to show that the human race originally sprang from some apelike ancestor, long since extinct, but probably a common forebear of the existing anthropoid apes and humans.

The two major scientific objections to the Darwinian hypothesis were the exact mechanism for the passing on of variations and the extremely

Charles Darwin

Illustrations from Darwin's First Edition of The Descent of Man. The drawings were used to point up the similarities between a human embryo (top) and that of a dog (bottom).

long timespan needed for the evolution of actual new species through this incremental change. The German August Weismann (1834–1914) flatly rejected the idea that acquired characteristics could be inherited. He conducted experiments to show that body cells and reproductive cells are entirely distinct, and that there is no way in which changes in the former can affect the latter. He concluded, therefore, that the only qualities transmissible to the offspring are those that have always been present in the reproductive cells of the parents. This seemed to deny any possibility of evolution from species to species, until in 1900 the Dutch botanist Hugo De Vries (1848–1935) published his celebrated mutation hypothesis, based upon Darwin's original hypothesis and, in large part, upon laws of heredity discovered by the Austrian monk Gregor Mendel (1822–1884). De Vries asserted that evolution results not from minor variations, as Darwin had assumed, but from radical differences or mutations, which appear in more or less definite ratio among the offspring. When any of these mutations are favorable to survival in a given environment, the individuals possessing them naturally emerge triumphant in the struggle for existence. Not only do their descendants inherit these qualities, but from time to time new mutants appear, some of which are even better adapted for survival than their parents. Thus in a limited number of generations a new species may be brought into existence. The mutation theory of De Vries also solved the problem of the amount of time needed for evolutionary change, a problem that had become more acute after 1860 when physicists like Fleming Jenkin (1833–1885) and William Thomson, Lord Kelvin (1824–1907) showed that the earth was significantly younger than had been assumed. De Vries made it possible to conceive of evolution as proceeding by sudden leaps in a relatively short time.

The theory of evolution by natural selection clearly undermined a belief in an ordered, purposeful universe where progress through time was linear and goal-oriented, whether or not this belief was grounded in a literal interpretation of the Bible. A growing number of people regarded the Bible as containing a combination of myths, legends, history, and profoundly important moral truths. The work of the German theologian David Friedrich Strauss (1808–1874) and of the French historian Ernest Renan (1832–1892) had cast doubt on its historical accuracy, and dealt with its inconsistencies. These writers defended the intentions of the Bible's various authors, while firmly insisting upon their human fallibilities. Their searching yet nevertheless sensitive critiques helped people understand that they need not abandon their Christian faith simply because Darwin insisted that the world and all that lived within it had been created over millions of years and not in six days. Far more difficult to deal with was the notion, explicit in Darwin, that nature was not a changeless harmony, but instead a constant and apparently undirected struggle. Chance, and not order, ruled the universe. Nothing was fixed, nothing perfect; all was in a state of flux. Good and bad were defined only in terms of an ability to survive. The "best" of a species were those that triumphed over their weaker rivals. All of a sudden, the universe had become a harsh and uncompromising place, deprived of pre-

Darwinian certainties; belief in a benevolent God was now much harder to sustain.

Darwin's most vigorous defender, the philosopher Thomas Henry Huxley (1825–1895), was one of those who could no longer reconcile science with a belief in God. Huxley earned himself the nickname of "Darwin's bulldog" because of his stout attacks upon orthodox Christians who refused to accept the implications of Darwinian theory. While he did not reject the possibility of a supernatural power, Huxley averred that "there is no evidence of the existence of such a being as the God of the theologians." He pronounced Christianity to be "a compound of some of the best and some of the worst elements of Paganism and Judaism, moulded in practice by the innate character of certain people of the Western World." Huxley coined the word *agnosticism* to express his contempt for the attitude of dogmatic certainty symbolized by the beliefs of the ancient Gnostics. As propounded by Huxley, agnosticism was the doctrine that neither the existence nor the nature of God nor the ultimate character of the universe is knowable. In a famous debate between Huxley and Samuel Wilberforce, the bishop of Oxford, in 1860, the bishop made the mistake of trying to turn Darwin into a joke, inquiring of the audience if anyone were willing to trace his descent from an ape, whether it was through his grandmother or grandfather. Huxley rejoined that the only ancestor of which he would feel ashamed was a man like the bishop, who so misused his talents to make light of such a serious issue. The sustained applause with which his remarks were greeted suggest the degree to which religious orthodoxy could now be safely challenged in public discussion.

Thomas Henry Huxley

For those who could not sustain orthodox religious belief in light of these scientific and philosophical developments, the search for an ordering principle of human behavior took a number of forms. The so-called Social Darwinists, whose most famous proponent was the English philosopher Herbert Spencer (1820–1903), adapted Darwinian thought to the "science" of human society in a way that would have shocked Darwin himself. Spencer, who coined the phrase "survival of the fittest," grounded his defense of the virtues of competition in evolutionary theory. He insisted upon the idea of evolution as a universal law. Spencer contended that not only species and individuals are subject to evolutionary change, but also planets, solar systems, customs, institutions, and religious and ethical ideas. Everything in the universe completes a cycle of origin, development, decay, and extinction. When the end of the cycle has been reached, the process begins once more and is repeated eternally. As a political philosopher, Spencer was a vigorous champion of individualism. He condemned collectivism as a relic of primitive society, as a feature of the earliest stage of social evolution. Any so-called assistance individuals might receive from the state, Spencer argued, would result not only in their own degeneration, but in that of society as well.

The Social Darwinists

Herbert Spencer

Spencer's followers, less subtly, argued that the apparent "success" of Western civilization was the result of its special fitness. The white race, they boasted, had proved itself superior to the black; non-Jews superior to

Jews; rich superior to poor; the British Empire superior to the subject territories it controlled. If nature was a matter of competition, so was society, with the victory going to that race or nation that could demonstrate its fitness to survive by subduing others.

If Social Darwinists could reassure some by implying the biological right of Western civilization to survive as the "fittest" within the contemporary world, anthropologists—pioneers in what was essentially a new scientific discipline—argued, on the contrary, that no culture could be perceived as "better" than any other. All societies were adaptations to a particular environment. Each society produced its own customs, which could not be declared "good" or "bad," but only successful or unsuccessful, according to the degree to which they helped that society survive. This notion of cultural "relativism" was a theme in the influential work of the Scottish anthropologist Sir James Frazer (1854–1941), whose masterpiece, *The Golden Bough,* demonstrated the relationship of Christianity to primitive practices and magical rites. Similarly, other anthropologists showed that the notions of patriarchy and monogamy were culturally specific, not universal.

Anthropology and cultural relativism

Other attempts to explore the various and sometimes contradictory implications of evolutionary theory helped to undermine the comforting notion of humankind's essential superiority to the rest of the animal kingdom. The work of the Russian psychologist Ivan Pavlov (1849–1936) resulted in the discovery of the conditioned reflex, a form of behavior in which natural reactions are produced by an artificial stimulus. Pavlov showed that if dogs were fed immediately following the ringing of a bell, they would eventually respond to the sound of the bell alone and secrete saliva exactly as if confronted by the sight and smell of the food. Because he insisted that his conclusions applied equally to human beings, Pavlov's discovery suggested the conclusion that the conditioned reflex is an important element in human behavior and encouraged psychologists to center their attention upon physiological experiment as a key to understanding the mind.

Pavlov and the conditioned reflex

Pavlovians inaugurated a type of physiological psychology known as behaviorism. *Behaviorism* is an attempt to study the human being as a purely physiological organism—to reduce all human behavior to a series of physical responses. Such concepts as *mind* and *consciousness* are dismissed as vague and meaningless terms. For the behaviorist nothing is important except the reactions of muscles, nerves, glands, and visceral organs. There is no such thing as an independent psychic behavior; all that humans do is physical. Thinking is essentially a form of talking to oneself. Every complex emotion and idea is simply a group of physiological responses produced by some stimulus in the environment. Such was the mechanistic interpretation of human actions offered by followers of Pavlov.

Behaviorism

In contradiction to this way of understanding human nature stood *psychoanalysis,* the other important school of psychology to make its appearance after the turn of the century. Founded by Sigmund Freud (1856–1939), an Austrian physician, psychoanalysis interprets human behavior mainly in terms of the unconscious mind. Freud admitted the existence of the conscious mind (the ego), but he avowed that the unconscious

Freud and psychoanalysis

(the id) is much more important in determining the actions of the individual. He considered humans as egoistic creatures propelled by basic urges of power, self-preservation, and sex. These urges are much too strong to be overcome; but inasmuch as society (the superego) has branded their unrestrained fulfillment as sinful, they are commonly driven into the unconscious, where they linger indefinitely as suppressed desires. Yet they are seldom completely submerged; they rise to the surface in dreams, or they manifest themselves in lapses of memory, in fears and obsessions, and in various forms of abnormal behavior. Freud believed that most cases of mental and nervous disorder result from violent conflicts between natural instincts and the restraints imposed by an unfortunate environment. His dream theory for the first time grounded dreams in a "scientific" basis, ascribing them to the unconscious mind working through specific experiences of the conscious. Freud hoped that by elucidating his theory of the unconscious he could impose predictable patterns upon the irrationality that seemed to characterize so much human activity. His search for order, however, resembled that of the behaviorists by continuing to stress the extent to which men and women, like animals, were prey to drives, impulses, and reflexes over which they could exercise at best only minimal control.

While Freud minimized the extent to which humans could gain control over their lives, the German philosopher Friedrich Nietzsche (1844–1900) offered a way to increase that control—but only at the expense of characteristics traditionally exalted by Judaism and Christianity. For Nietzsche, accepted notions of good and evil merely trapped men and women in a fruitless search for security and "truth," which he denied existed. Instead, said Nietzsche, they must abandon the idea of service to society, which Nietzsche labeled the "slave morality" of Christianity, and instead master the world through the "will to power" that elevated individuals and their struggle against the chaos of the universe. The individual who abandoned the burden of convention and entered the battle against the maelstrom was, for Nietzsche, a "dionysian man," a barbarian "superman," who creates his own values based on moral courage and strength of character. Nietzsche here adapted the Darwinian notion of natural selection, with the "supermen" triumphing over the moral weaklings who lacked the strength and courage to face the chaos of the universe and overcome it. Before any such process of natural selection could operate, however, religious obstacles would have to be removed. Nietzsche therefore demanded that the moral supremacy of Christianity and Judaism be overthrown. Both of these religions, he alleged, glorified the virtues of the downtrodden. They exalted into virtues qualities that ought to be considered vices—humility, nonresistance, mortification of the flesh, and pity for the weak and incompetent. The enthronement of these qualities prevented the elimination of the unfit and preserved them to pour their degenerate blood into the veins of the race.

Nietzsche, whose philosophy is contained in such works as *Thus Spake Zarathustra* (1883), *Beyond Good and Evil* (1886), and *On the Genealogy of Morals* (1887), lapsed into permanent insanity in 1888 after a decade of ago-

Sigmund Freud

Nietzsche's philosophy

Friedrich Nietzsche

Pope Pius IX

Pope Leo XIII

nizing ill-health. His broad-ranging critiques—of morals, music, academia, and democracy, to name but a few—were later adapted piecemeal by artists, students, and others who selected only those parts of Nietzsche's works that supported their own thought. Perhaps the most extreme example of this tendency was the use of Nietzschean philosophy to justify the politics of racism and virulent German nationalism advocated by Hitler and the National Socialist party in the 1930s.

Under the impact of these various scientific and philosophical challenges, the institutions responsible for the maintenance of traditional faith found themselves hard pressed. Protestantism had based its revolt against Roman Catholic orthodoxy upon the belief that men and women should seek to understand God with the aid of not much more than the Bible and a willing conscience. In consequence, Protestants had little in the way of authoritarian doctrine to support them when their faith was challenged. Some—the fundamentalists—chose to ignore the implications of scientific and philosophical inquiry altogether, and continued to believe in the literal truth of the Bible. Some were willing to agree with the school of American philosophers known as Pragmatists (Charles Peirce, William James), that if belief in a personal God produced mental peace or spiritual satisfaction, that belief must therefore be true. Truth, for the Pragmatists, was whatever provided useful, practical results. Other Protestants sought solace from religious doubt in religious activity, founding missions, and laboring among the poor. Many adherents to this "Social Gospel" were also "Modernists," determined to accept the ethical teachings of Christianity while discarding belief in miracles and the doctrines of original sin and the Incarnation.

The Roman Catholic Church was compelled by its tradition of dogmatic assertion to assist its followers in their response to the modern world. In 1864 Pope Pius IX issued a *Syllabus of Errors* condemning what he regarded as the principal religious and philosophical "errors" of the time. Among them were materialism, free thought, and "indifferentism," or the idea that one religion is as good as another. In 1869 he convoked a Church council, the first to be summoned since the Catholic Reformation. The most notable pronouncement of the Vatican Council was the dogma of papal infallibility. In the language of this dogma the pope, when he speaks *ex cathedra*—that is, in his capacity "as pastor and doctor of all Christians"—is infallible in regard to all matters of faith and morals. Though generally accepted by pious Catholics, the dogma of papal infallibility evoked a storm of protest in many circles. Governments of several Catholic countries denounced it, including France, Spain, and Italy. The death of Pius IX in 1878 and the accession of Pope Leo XIII brought a more accommodating climate to the Church. The new pope was ready to concede that there was "good" as well as "evil" in modern civilization. He added a scientific staff to the Vatican and opened archives and observatories. However, he made no concessions to "liberalism" or "anticlericalism" in the political sphere. He would go no farther than to urge capitalists and employers to be more generous in recognizing the rights of organized labor.

The effect of various scientific and philosophical challenges upon the men and women who lived at the end of the nineteenth century cannot be measured in any exact way. Millions undoubtedly went about the business of life untroubled by the implications of evolutionary theory, content to believe as they had believed. Certainly, for most members of the middle class, the challenge of socialism was understood as "real" in a way that the challenge of science and philosophy probably was not. Socialism was a threat to livelihood. Darwinism, relativism, materialism, and behaviorism, though "in the air" and troublesome to those who breathed that air, did not impinge upon consciousness to the same degree. Men and women can postpone thoughts about their origins and ultimate destiny in a way that they cannot postpone thoughts about their daily bread. And yet the impact of the changes we have been discussing was eventually profound. Darwin's theory was not so complicated as to prevent its popularization. If educated men and women had neither the time nor inclination to read the *Origin of Species,* they read magazines and newspapers which spelled out for them its implications. Those implications augmented an uncertainty that already tempered the optimism of capitalist expansion.

Men and women who had never read the German philosopher Arthur Schopenhauer (1788–1860) might well have agreed with his assessment of this world as one condemned to witness the devouring of the weak by the strong. Yet their commitment to the ways of the world prevented their acceptance of Schopenhauer's particular remedy: an escape into a life of personal asceticism and self-denial. Like the English poet and essayist Matthew Arnold, sensitive men and women might feel themselves trapped in a world resembling no more than "a darkling plain," where there was "neither joy, nor love, nor light, nor certitude, nor peace, nor help for pain."

3. THE CHALLENGE OF LITERATURE AND THE ARTS

After 1850 a handful of artists and a greater number of writers continued to challenge the middle-class worldview, as had their predecessors, by drawing attention to the shortcomings of industrial society. As the century drew to a close, however, one of the major problems these critics now faced was the question of audience: not merely what to say, but whom to say it to. Before the middle of the eighteenth century, that audience had been primarily aristocratic. Between 1750 and 1870 it was both aristocratic and upper middle class. Now, thanks to the fact of an increasingly literate general population, the potential audience appeared to have increased enormously. In 1850 approximately half the population of Europe had been illiterate. In subsequent decades, country after country introduced state-financed elementary and secondary education—in part as an attempt to provide citizens with an opportunity for social mobility, in part as a means of control and as a preventive to the establishment of schools run by workers for workers, and in part as a measure to keep pace with changing technological knowl-

The New Power of the Press. With the spread of literacy, newspapers adapted to the needs and desires of the new mass audience. Here English railway passengers scramble for the latest edition.

edge. Britain instituted elementary education in 1870, Switzerland in 1874, Italy in 1877. France expanded its existing system between 1878 and 1881. After 1871 Germany instituted a state system modeled on Prussia's. By 1900, approximately 85 percent of the population in Britain, France, Belgium, the Netherlands, Scandinavia, and Germany could read. Elsewhere, however, the percentages were far lower, ranging between 30 and 60 percent.

A new journalism

In those countries where literacy rates were highest, capitalist publishers such as Alfred Harmsworth in Britain and William Randolph Hearst in the United States hastened to serve the new reading public. Middle-class readers had for some time been well supplied by newspapers catering to their interests and point of view. *The Times* of London had a readership of well over 50,000 by 1850; the *Presse* and *Siècle* in France, a circulation of 70,000. By 1900, however, other newspapers were appealing to a different mass market—the newly literate—and doing so by means of sensational journalism and spicy, easy-to-read serials.

The distancing of art and literature from the public

These new developments encouraged writers and artists to distance themselves more and more from what seemed to them a vulgar, materialistic culture. They agreed with writers of the mid-century who had insisted that the purpose of art and literature was not to pander or sentimentalize. They went further, however, by declaring that art had no business preaching morality to a public that, in any event, had proved itself unwilling to heed the sermon. This generation of artists and writers argued that one did not look at a painting or read a poem to be instructed in the difference between good and evil, but to understand what was eternally true and beautiful—to appreciate art for its own sake. They were not so much interested in reaching a wider audience, whose standards of taste they generally deplored, as they were in addressing each other. This self-conscious desire not only to live apart but to think apart from society was reflected in their work. In 1850, educated men and women could read a Dickens novel or examine a Daumier print and understand it, even if they did not admire it or agree with its message. In 1900, men and women found it much harder to understand, let alone admire, a painting by Paul Cézanne or a poem by Paul Valéry. Artists and public were ceasing to speak the same language, a fact that contributed, as did the ideas of Darwin and Nietzsche, Pavlov and Freud, to the further confusion and fragmentation of Western culture.

These new perceptions of the artist's relationship to society did not surface to any measurable degree before the very end of the century. Until that time, the arts were dominated by what has come to be called *realism*. Realists were predominantly critics of contemporary society. Swayed by a fervor for social reform, they depicted the inequities of the human condition against the sordid background of industrial society. Like the romantics, the realists affirmed the possibility of human freedom, although realists emphasized more than romantics the obstacles that prevented its achievement. Realists differed most markedly from romantics in their disdain of sentiment and emotional extravagance. Adopting from natural science the idea of life as a struggle for survival, they tried to portray human existence in accordance with hard facts, often insisting that their characters were the irresponsible victims of heredity, environment, or their own animal passions.

Realism

Realism as a literary movement made its initial appearance in France. Its leading exponents included the novelists Honoré de Balzac (1799–1850) and Gustave Flaubert (1821–1880), whose work, as we have already noted (see p. 745), contained a stinging assessment of the dullness and greed of modern life. Indeed, Balzac's portrayal of the effects of social conditions upon the individual earned him a place as Marx's favorite novelist. Émile Zola (1840–1902), another Frenchman, is often called a naturalist rather than a realist, to convey the idea that he was interested in an exact, scien-

Literary realism in France

Balzac's Social Realism. In this illustration from Balzac's *Le Père Goriot,* no attempt is made to idealize the struggle for survival.

tific presentation of the facts of nature without the intrusion of personal philosophy. Naturalism was expected to dismiss moral values in a way that realism was not. Zola did have a definite moral viewpoint, however. His early years of wretched poverty imbued him with a deep sympathy for the common people and with a passion for social justice. Though in novels such as *Nana* (1880) and *Germinal* (1885) he portrayed human nature as weak and prone to vice and crime, he was not without hope that a decided improvement might come from the creation of a better society. Many of his novels dealt with such social problems as alcoholism, poverty, and disease.

Literary realism in Britain

Realism in the writings of the Englishman Charles Dickens (1812–1870) was overlaid with layers of sentimentality. Dickens was a master at depicting the evils of industrial society, but the invariably happy endings of his novels testify to his determined—and unrealistic—unwillingness to allow wrong to triumph over right. No such ambivalence marked the works of the later English novelist Thomas Hardy (1840–1928), however. In such well-known novels as *The Return of the Native* (1878), *Tess of the D'Urbervilles* (1891), and *Jude the Obscure* (1896), he expressed his conception that humans are the playthings of an inexorable fate. The universe, though beautiful, was depicted as in no sense friendly, and the struggle of individuals with nature was a pitiable battle against almost impossible odds. If God existed, he watched with indifference while the helpless denizens of the human ant-heap crawled toward suffering and death. Yet Hardy pitied his fellow creatures, regarding them not as depraved animals but as the victims of cosmic forces beyond their control. Hardy's experiences with a public that met his pessimism with moral outrage led him to give up novel-writing after 1900, to devote himself wholly to poetry, whose publication did not depend on the approval of a prudish middle-class readership.

Henrik Ibsen

Realism in Germany and Scandinavia

Pity for humanity was also a central theme in the work of the German dramatist Gerhart Hauptmann (1862–1946). Calling himself a naturalist, Hauptmann nevertheless reflected the realists' concern for suffering. His plays show the influence of Darwin in their emphasis upon determinism and environment. *The Weavers* (1892), which depicts the suffering of Silesian weavers in the 1840s, is probably his most outstanding work. Doubtless the most eminent playwright among realists and naturalists was the Norwegian Henrik Ibsen (1828–1906). The stark message of Ibsen's early dramas was not favorably received, and while still a young man he decided to abandon his native country. Residing first in Italy and then in Germany, he did not return permanently to Norway until 1891. His writings were characterized most of all by bitter rebellion against the tyranny and ignorance of society. In such plays as *A Doll's House* (1879), *An Enemy of the People* (1882), *The Wild Duck* (1884), and *Hedda Gabler* (1890), he satirized the conventions and institutions of respectable life, and showed, with great insight, how these oppressed women in particular. Along with his scorn for hypocrisy and social tyranny went a profound distrust of majority rule. Ibsen despised democracy as the enthronement of unprincipled leaders who would do anything for the sake of votes to perpetuate themselves in power.

As one of his characters in *An Enemy of the People* says: "A minority may be right—a majority is always wrong."

The literature of the Russians, which flourished during the period of realism, includes within it themes that are both romantic and idealist as well. Russia's three outstanding novelists of the late nineteenth century were Ivan Turgenev (1818–1883), Feodor Dostoevsky (1821–1881), and Leo Tolstoy (1828–1910). They were preceded by the equally talented Alexander Pushkin (1799–1837) who, between 1820 and his death in a duel seventeen years later, established himself as one of Russia's greatest writers. Though his early work was romantic in tone, his epic verse *Eugene Onegin* (1825–1831) demonstrated his sympathy with realistic themes.

Nineteenth-century Russian literature

Turgenev, who spent much of his life in France, was the first of the Russian novelists to become known to Western Europe. His chief work, *Fathers and Sons* (1861), describes in brooding terms the struggle between the older and younger generations. The hero is a nihilist (a term first used by Turgenev), who is convinced that the whole social order has nothing in it worth preserving. The novel inspired a group of young Russian intellectuals, who sought to reform society by abandoning their parents' emphasis on status, wealth, and leisure and turning instead to service to "the people."

Turgenev

Dostoevsky was almost as tragic a figure as any he projected in his novels. Condemned at the age of twenty-eight on a charge of revolutionary activity, he was exiled to Siberia, where he endured four horrible years of imprisonment. His later life was harrowed by poverty, family troubles, and epileptic fits. As a novelist, he chose to explore the anguish of people driven to shameful deeds by their raw emotions and by the intolerable meanness of their lives. He was a master of psychological analysis, probing into the motives of distorted minds with an intensity that was almost morbid. At the same time he filled his novels with a broad sympathy and with a mystic conviction that humanity can be purified only through suffering. His best-known works are *Crime and Punishment* (1866) and *The Brothers Karamazov* (1879–1880).

Dostoevsky

As an earnest champion of the simple life of the peasant, Tolstoy was somewhat less deterministic than Dostoevsky. Yet in *War and Peace* (1862–1869), a majestic epic of Russian conditions during the period of the Napoleonic invasion, he expounds the theme that individuals are at the mercy of fate when powerful elemental forces are unleashed. His *Anna Karenina* (1873–1876) is a study of the tragedy that lurks in the pursuit of individual desire. As Tolstoy grew older he became more and more an evangelist preaching a social gospel. In such novels as *The Kreutzer Sonata* (1889) and *Resurrection* (1899–1900) he condemned most of the institutions of civilized society and called upon men and women to renounce selfishness and greed, to earn their living by manual toil, and to cultivate the virtues of poverty, meekness, and nonresistance. His last years were devoted to attacks upon such evils as war and capital punishment and to the defense of victims of political persecution.

Tolstoy

The works of all these realists and naturalists, whatever their individual

Leo Tolstoy in His Study Dictating to His Secretary

Victor Hugo by Auguste Rodin. The artist's realism enhances his ability to impart human character to his work.

Impressionist technique

differences, shared two things in common: they contained vigorous moral criticism of present-day middle-class society, and they were written in direct and forceful language that the middle class could understand, if it chose to read or listen. The same can be said of realist painters such as Courbet and Daumier, discussed previously, and of the sculptor Auguste Rodin (1840–1917), whose style and message were neither difficult to comprehend nor easy to ignore. Realist artists were still anxious to address the public, if only to attack its members for their shallowness and insensitivity. The advent of the impressionist movement in painting in the 1870s marks the first significant break in this tradition. At this point artists began to turn away from the public and toward each other. The movement started in France, among a group of young artists whose work had been refused a place in the annual exhibitions of the traditionally minded French Royal Academy. They had been labeled "impressionists" in derision by critics who took them to task for painting not an object itself, but only their impression of that object. The name in fact suited the personal, private nature of their work. They were painting to please themselves, to realize their own potential as artists.

In a sense, impressionists were realists, for they were determined to paint only what they saw, and they were vitally interested in the scientific interpretation of nature. But impressionist technique was different from that of the older realist painters. Scenes from the world around them were not depicted as if the result of careful study. On the contrary, the works of impressionists sought to reveal immediate sense impressions, leaving it to the mind of the observer to fill in additional details. This often resulted in a type of work appearing at first glance to be nonnaturalistic. Figures were commonly distorted; a few significant details were made to represent an entire object; and dabs of primary color were placed side by side without a trace of blending. For example, the effect of the green in nature was achieved by placing daubs of pure blue and yellow side by side, allowing the eye to mix them.

Impressionism differed from realism in one other important respect. In these new paintings artists remained detached from their subject. They did not paint to evoke pity, or to teach a lesson. They painted to proclaim the value and importance of painting *as painting*. In doing so, the artist was not deliberately setting out to exclude the viewers. It was clear, however, that the viewer must not expect to understand a painting except on the artist's terms. Probably the greatest of the impressionists were the Frenchmen Claude Monet (1840–1926) and Auguste Renoir (1841–1919). Monet was perhaps the leading exponent of the new mode of interpreting landscapes. His paintings have little structure or design in the conventional sense; they suggest, rather than depict, the outlines of cliffs, trees, mountains, and fields. Intensely interested in the problem of light, Monet would go out at sunrise with an armful of canvases in order to paint the same subject in a dozen momentary appearances. It has been said of one of his masterpieces that "light is the only important person in the picture." Renoir's subjects include not only landscapes but portraits and scenes from contemporary life. He is famous for his pink and ivory nudes, which, as expressions of frank sexuality, represented an additional threat to middle-class sensibilities.

The freedom explicit in the work of the impressionists encouraged other painters to pursue fresh techniques and to define different goals. The expressionists turned upon the impressionists, objecting to their preoccupation with the momentary aspects of nature and their indifference to meaning. Expressionists were not arguing for a return to meaning in the sense of "message." They were instead insisting that a painting must represent the artist's particular intellect. Here again, they were making art a private matter, removing it yet another step from the public. The artist who laid the foundations of expressionism was the Frenchman Paul Cézanne (1839–1906), who labored to express a sense of order in nature that he be-

Monet and Renoir

See color plates following page 844 for *Iris Beside a Pond* by Monet and *Luncheon of the Boating Party* by Renoir

Expressionism: Cézanne

See color plates following page 844 for *Montagne Sainte-Victoire with Aqueduct* and *The Card Players* by Cézanne

The Monarch of the Glen by Sir Edwin Landseer. This was the sort of conventional, easy to comprehend art that appealed to the middle class and that brought forth the revolutionary impressionist movement.

Self-Portrait by Paul Gauguin

See color plates
following page 844 for
representative works by
Gauguin, Matisse, Picasso,
and van Gogh

lieved the impressionists had ignored. To achieve this end, he painted objects as a series of planes, each plane expressed in terms of a color change. While Cézanne was in this way equating form with color, he also began to reduce natural forms to their geometrical equivalents, hoping thereby to express the basic shapes of existence itself. He distorted form into geometrical regularity until abstraction became reality. In all this Cézanne was declaring the painter's right to recreate nature in such a way as to express an intensely personal vision.

Art as personal expression was the hallmark of two other painters in the so-called post-impressionist period, the Frenchman Paul Gauguin (1848–1903) and the Dutchman Vincent Van Gogh (1853–1890). Both, by their life as well as their art, declared war on traditional nineteenth-century values. Dismayed by the artificiality and complexity of civilization, Gauguin fled to the South Sea Islands and spent the last decade of his life painting the hot and luscious colors of an unspoiled, primitive society. Van Gogh, whose passionate sympathy for the sufferings of his fellow humans led him to attempt the life of a minister to poor mining families and undoubtedly contributed to his eventual insanity and ultimate suicide, poured out the full intensity of his feelings in paintings such as *The Starry Night* (1889), which seem to swirl off the canvas.

In the years between 1900 and the First World War, art underwent still further revolutionary development. Henri Matisse (1869–1954) greatly extended Cézanne's use of distortion, thereby declaring once again the painter's right to create according to an individual definition of aesthetic merit. This declaration was given its most ringing prewar endorsement by Pablo Picasso (1881–1973). Picasso, a Catalan Spaniard who came to Paris in 1903, developed a style, cubism, that takes its name from an attempt to carry Cézanne's fascination with geometrical form to its logical conclusion. Influenced both by the work of Cézanne and by African sculpture, cubism

The Joy of Life, by Henri Matisse. The sensuous use of line and boldness of composition celebrate not only life but the artist's freedom to break from past convention.

Girl Before a Mirror by Pablo Picasso

results not only in distortion but in some cases in actual dismemberment. The artist may separate the various parts of a figure and rearrange them in other than their natural pattern. The purpose is to express defiance of traditional notions of form—to repudiate once and for all the conception of art as representational prettiness.

The artistic declaration of independence from middle-class society was enunciated most dramatically by painters, but was heard also in the realms of literature, music and drama. In France, the work of a group calling itself the symbolists, and centered upon the poetry of Paul Verlaine (1844–1896) Arthur Rimbaud (1854–1891) Stéphane Mallarmé (1842–1898) and Paul Valéry (1871–1945) attempted to intensify the personal while transcending reality in a way reminiscent of the impressionists, expressionists, and cubists. In music, as well, there was a break from the romantic tradition that had dominated the nineteenth century and that had been expressed in the works of composers such as Robert Schumann (1810–1856), Felix Mendelssohn (1809–1847), and Franz Liszt (1811–1886). Already the late romantic operas of Richard Wagner (1813–1883) had taken vast liberties with harmony and departed from stereotypical melodic patterns, producing music that was not subject to the tyranny of form but was sensitive to personal expression. Now in the works of composers such as the Austrian Richard Strauss (1864–1949) and the Frenchman Claude Debussy (1862–1918) music moved even further in the direction of the intensely personal. Strauss's opera *Der Rosenkavalier* (1911), although based externally on the conventions of late-eighteenth-century plot, is nevertheless a musical expression of the inner realities of its characters, written to express those realities more directly than heretofore. Both Strauss and Debussy were, like the impressionists, determined to convey atmosphere; Debussy's piano compositions, and his symphonic sketch, *La Mer* (1905), are musical manifestations of the impressionists' regard for association rather than formal structure.

In drama, men and women combined expressionist literary techniques and the theatrical conventions of such popular forms as the cabaret, the melodrama, and the macabre *guignol* to produce avant garde theater that blurred the boundaries between audience and performer. Often collapsing traditional notions of time and space, the new forms also experimented with character and dialogue in ways that challenged—and frequently alienated—the middle-class public. Expressionist drama flourished in France and Germany in the years before World War I, in the works of people such as the Frenchman Alfred Jarry (1873–1907) and the Austrian Oskar Kokoschka (1886–1980).

Whether in painting, in literature, in music, or in drama, artists sought to escape to a position from which they could learn and then express what was closest to their own consciousness. Their direct, calculated dismissal of conventional form and content declared their fundamental disdain for—more important, their complete lack of interest in—the problems of the world at large. Their self-imposed isolation served only to increase the general sense of a fragmented world that, despite its material prosperity, was at war with itself.

SELECTED READINGS

- *Items so designated are available in paperback editions.*

SOCIALISM

- Avineri, S., *The Social and Political Thought of Karl Marx,* London, 1968.
  Berlin, Isaiah, *Karl Marx: His Life and Environment,* New York, 1948. The best short account.
- Cole, G. D. H., *A History of Socialist Thought,* Vols. I–III, London, 1953–1956. A comprehensive treatment of the period 1789–1914.
- Derfler, Leslie, *Socialism since Marx: A Century of the European Left,* New York, 1973. Survey and analysis of Continental socialist movements.
  Edwards, Stewart, *The Paris Commune of 1871,* London, 1971. Straightforward analysis.
  Gay, Peter, *The Dilemma of Democratic Socialism: Eduard Bernstein's Challenge to Marx,* New York, 1952. A good study of German revisionism.
  Goldberg, Harvey, *A Life of Jean Jaurès,* Madison, Wisc., 1962. A fine biography of the eminent French socialist.
- Joll, James, *The Anarchists,* London, 1964. Survey of various radical European groups.

Lichtheim, George, *A Short History of Socialism,* New York, 1970. Provides a useful overview.

Lidtke, Vernon, *The Outlawed Party, Social Democracy in Germany,* Charlotte, N.C. 1966. Deals with German socialists from 1878 to 1890.

• McBriar, A. M., *Fabian Socialism and English Politics, 1884–1918,* Cambridge, 1966. An extensive study of this important circle: their composition, their ideology, their methods.

• Mehring, Franz, *Karl Marx: The Story of His Life,* New York, 1976. A well-done recounting of Marx's life.

Noland, Aaron, *The Founding of the French Socialist Party, 1893–1905,* Cambridge, Mass., 1956. Primarily a narrative account of the translation of ideology into political reality.

• Schorske, Carl E., *German Social Democracy, 1905–1918,* Cambridge, Mass., 1955. A magnificent study of the problems of the Social Democrats in a time of imperialism and war.

SCIENTIFIC THOUGHT

• Butterfield, Herbert B., *The Origins of Modern Science,* rev. ed., New York, 1957. A standard survey.

• Eiseley, Loren C., *Darwin's Century: Evolution and the Men Who Discovered It,* New York, 1961. The history of evolution after Darwin.

• Gay, Peter, *Freud, Jews, and Other Germans: Masters and Victims in Modernist Culture,* New York, 1978. Essays on end-of-the-century German culture.

• Gillespie, C. C., *The Edge of Objectivity,* Princeton, 1960. A history of scientific ideas.

• Hughes, H. Stuart, *Consciousness and Society,* New York, 1958. Examines the reaction to Positivism and the growing interest in the irrational by considering the work of Freud, Max Weber, and others.

• Jones, Ernest, *The Life and Work of Sigmund Freud,* 3 vols., New York, 1953–1957. The official biography, by a close collaborator and eminent psychoanalyst.

• Rieff, P., *Freud: The Mind of the Moralist,* New York, 1959. A useful, one-volume discussion.

Stocking, George, W., Jr., *Victorian Anthropology,* London, 1975. Ties together science and culture.

THE ARTS AND PHILOSOPHY

• Barzun, Jacques, *Darwin, Marx, and Wagner,* Boston, 1941. Argues that these men were not so much originators of new ideas as founders of systems that are mechanistic and pseudoscientific, and therefore threatening to the human cultural heritage.

• Clark, T. J., *The Painting of Modern Life: Paris in the Art of Manet and His Followers,* New York, 1985. Argues for seeing impressionism as a critique of French society.

Evenson, Norma, *Paris: A Century of Change, 1878–1978,* New Haven, Conn., 1979.

• Kaufmann, Walter A., *Nietzsche: Philosopher, Psychologist, Anti-Christ,* 4th ed., Princeton, 1975. A superb intellectual biography.

Lang, Paul, *Music in Western Civilization,* New York, 1940. Useful survey and reference.

• Masur, Gerhard, *Prophets of Yesterday,* New York, 1961. A broad survey of nineteenth-century European thinkers.

Mosse, George L., *The Culture of Western Europe: The Nineteenth and Twentieth Centuries,* 3rd ed., Chicago, 1988. Thoughtful analysis and overview.

• Schorske, Carl, *Fin-de-Siecle Vienna: Politics and Culture,* New York, 1980. Essays on Vienna's cultural impact on the West.

• Shattuck, Roger, *The Banquet Years: The Arts in France, 1885–1918,* New York, 1958. The emergence of modernism in French art, literature, and music.

SOURCE MATERIALS

• Arnold, Matthew, *Culture and Anarchy,* New York, 1971. Originally published in 1867. A perceptive criticism of English society and a call for an authoritarian principle in an increasingly democratic society.

• Darwin, Charles, *The Descent of Man,* Cambridge, Mass., 1964. See especially Chapter XXI.

• ———, *Origin of Species,* Cambridge, Mass., 1964. See especially Chapters IX, XV.

• Edwards, Stewart, ed., *The Communards of Paris, 1871,* New York, 1976. Annotated eyewitness reports, documents, and accounts of the Paris Commune.

• Gosse, Edmund, *Father and Son,* New York, 1963. A moving autobiography by a distinguished Victorian literary critic, this work reveals the conflict between the religious fundamentalism of the father and the skepticism of the son in the wake of Darwinian theory.

Kohn, Hans, *The Mind of Russia,* New Brunswick, N.J., 1955. An edited collection of historical, literary, and philosophical works of nineteenth- and twentieth-century Russian authors, designed to reveal the conflict between traditional and Western thought in Russia.

• Marx, Karl, *Capital,* intro. by G. D. H. Cole, New York, 1974. A good edition of the classic.

• Marx, Karl, and Friedrich Engels, *The Marx-Engels Reader,* 2nd ed., by R. C. Tucker, New York, 1978. Reprints the basic texts.

Thompson, D. M., ed., *Nonconformity in the Nineteenth Century,* London, 1972. Superb collection of documents.

• Webb, Beatrice, *My Apprenticeship,* London, 1926. Beatrice Webb was one of the leading Fabian socialists, and in this first volume of her autobiography she explains how she, as a member of one of England's wealthier families, was converted to a socialist creed.

• Zola, Émile, *L'Assommoir,* London, 1970. Written in 1877 and set in the Paris of the 1860s, this bitterly realistic novel portrays the brutalization of the French working class by the forces of industrial change, poverty, and alcohol.

Chapter 26

A DELICATE EQUILIBRIUM
(1870–1914)

Ah! What a seething there has been, . . . customs worthy of the inquisition and despotism, the pleasure of a few gold-braided individuals setting their heels on the nation, and stifling its cry for truth and justice, under the mendacious and sacrilegious pretext of the interest of the State!

—Émile Zola, "J'accuse"

etween 1870 and 1914, the major powers of Europe balanced between stability and strife. Domestic and international uncertainty was caused by continuing industrialization. Periodic trade depressions tempered the optimism accompanying general prosperity. Almost all classes of society shared in the expansion of material production at least until 1900. Prosperity helped to produce stability, allowing for the establishment in many countries of social welfare systems designed to benefit workers and their families, and thus to gain their political allegiance.

Continuing prosperty

At the same time, various factors operated to make the achievement of a generally stable Western world difficult, and ultimately impossible. First, the process of nation-building, which had resulted in the dramatic creation of a modern Germany and Italy, left potential conflict in its wake. Second, although the majority of citizens in most Western European countries participated at least indirectly in the governance of their country and enjoyed certain guaranteed rights, heated debate continued as to the political usefulness of such arrangements. In France, monarchists threatened the republic; in Germany, democrats battled imperial and bureaucratic oligarchy; in Russia, liberals rose against tsarist autocracy. And across Europe, socialists contended against the political strength of the middle classes.

The roots of instability

Internal tension was resulting as well from shifts in class structure and class consciousness. One of the most dramatic occupational changes to occur in late-nineteenth-century Europe was the rapid growth of a lower- to middle-level, "white-collar" class of bureaucrats, employed in commerce and industry and in expanding government departments. The post office, the railways, the police, and the bureaus charged with the task of administering various social welfare and insurance programs, all demanded growing numbers of recruits. In Germany, for example, by 1914 there were over two million white-collar employees in private firms and two million lower- or middle-range civil servants. Members of this new class were particularly anxious to give sharp definition to the line separating them from skilled "labor aristocrats," who might earn as much money as they did, but whose blue collars were, in the eyes of the white-collar brigades, a badge of their inferior status. Those same "aristocrats," as we have seen, however, often found their skills made obsolete by technological change, with the result that they showed themselves more willing than in the past to make common cause with their unskilled fellow workers against the middle class.

Shifts in class and class consciousness

One further important source of European instability during this period lay in the international rivalries that grew between nations as they reached out to build empires. Nations grouped into alliances, hoping that a balance between power blocs might continue to provide the international stability that Europe had enjoyed since 1815, and that had prevented general war. Instead, the alliances produced only further tensions, and ultimately general world conflict.

International rivalries

1. GERMANY: THE SEARCH FOR IMPERIAL UNITY

During the years immediately following the foundation of the German Empire, Bismarck was particularly anxious to achieve imperial unity under Prussian domination. In this he was aided by the economic and military predominance of the Prussian state, by his willingness to appropriate imperial prerogatives for his own ends, and by the organizational framework upon which the empire had been constructed. All powers not granted to the central government were reserved to the individual states. Each had control over its own form of government, public education, highways, police, and other local agencies. Even the enforcement of the laws was left primarily in the hands of the state governments, since the empire had no machinery for applying its laws against individuals. Despite their apparent autonomy, however, the states were in fact subordinate to the empire, and to the emperor himself, the Prussian William I. The German imperial units were once described as comprised of "a lion, a half-dozen foxes, and a score of mice." The Prussian "lion" exercised authority through the person of the emperor and his chancellor. The empire was not governed by a cabinet system, in which ministers of state were responsible to a popularly elected legislature. Instead, ministers were responsible to the chancellor, and the chancellor was responsible solely to the emperor. William was no mere figurehead; the emperor was vested with extensive authority over the army and navy, over foreign relations, and over the general enactment and execution of imperial laws. He had the authority to declare war if the

The structure of the German Empire

William I of Germany

coasts or territory of the empire were attacked. And as king of Prussia, he controlled that country's delegation in the generally conservative upper house, or Bundesrat, of the imperial parliament, commanding enough votes to veto any bill submitted. The chairman of the Bundesrat, charged with the control and supervision of the federal administration, was also the Prussian prime minister, appointed by the king of Prussia.

The parliament was no rubber stamp, however. Money for the imperial treasury had to be voted by the lower house, the Reichstag, which was elected by universal manhood suffrage, and whose membership was primarily middle class. Yet the Reichstag's powers were essentially negative. Although the parliament could veto proposals of the kaiser (emperor) and his ministers, it could not initiate legislation on its own. Moreover, the monarchy could bypass the legislature by working with a previous year's budget when no new one was formulated. Hence, although Bismarck often found himself temporarily stymied by the activities of an unsympathetic legislature, he could expect, in the end, to have his way. That way was directed toward the goal of a unified Germany under Prussian domination: essentially conservative; antisocialist, though not necessarily opposed to social welfare schemes; protectionist, and thus sympathetic to the interests of German industrialists; and, in foreign affairs, anti-French, standing firm against any threat from that longtime antagonist.

Bismarck's first campaign on behalf of imperial unity was launched against the Roman Catholic Church. Called the *Kulturkampf,* or "struggle for civilization," the attack was initiated, with some help from intellectual liberals, in 1871. Bismarck's motives were almost exclusively nationalistic. He perceived in some Catholic activities a threat to the power and stability of the empire, particularly the support Catholic priests continued to give to the states'-rights movement in southern Germany and to the grievances of Alsatians and Poles. Bismarck was alarmed also by recent assertions of the authority of the pope to intervene in secular matters and by the promulgation in 1870 of the dogma of papal infallibility. For these reasons he resolved to deal such a blow to Catholic influence in Germany that it would never again be a major factor in national or local politics. His weapons were a series of laws and decrees issued between 1872 and 1875, designed to curb the independent power of the Church. Bismarck's campaign backfired, however. The Catholic Center party appealed to the electorate so effectively on behalf of the persecuted clergy, while adopting an economic policy attractive to the upper middle class, that it won fully one-quarter of the seats in the Reichstag in 1874. Recognizing that he needed Catholic support for other elements of his program, Bismarck took the occasion of the election of the more conciliatory Pope Leo XIII to make his peace with the Vatican and to negotiate an alliance of convenience with the Catholic Center party. By 1886 almost all of his anticlerical legislation either had been permitted to lapse or had been repealed.

Having forged a new political combination in 1878, Bismarck shifted the focus of his attacks to German socialism, now perceived by him as a far more immediate threat to the empire than Catholicism. The Social Demo-

The Reichstag's powers

The Kulturkampf

Bismarck and the socialists

cratic party, under the reformist leadership of the politician Wilhelm Liebknecht (1826–1900), successor to Ferdinand Lassalle, was building a substantial following. Bismarck, his memory of the Paris Commune (see above, pp. 845–846) still fresh, feared socialism as anarchy, and therefore as a direct challenge to the stability and unity he was attempting to achieve within the empire. Forgetting for the moment the manner in which he had courted the socialists when he needed their support in the 1860s, Bismarck now appeared determined to extinguish them. His attack was motivated not only by his personal perception of the socialist threat but also by his continuing need to secure the favor of industrialists whom he had won to his side by his policy of protective tariffs. In 1878, two separate attempts were made by unbalanced zealots on the life of the emperor. Although neither would-be assassin had anything but the most tenuous connection with the socialists, Bismarck used their actions as an excuse to secure legislation abolishing workers' rights to meet and to publish. The legislature also agreed to a law that gave the government the right to expel socialists from major cities, as was later done in Berlin, Breslau, and Leipzig. These laws in effect dissolved the Social Democratic party until after 1890, although individual socialist candidates continued to be elected to the Reichstag.

Social welfare legislation

Bismarck was too clever a politician to suppose that he could abolish socialism solely by means of repression. He was prepared to steal at least a portion of the socialists' thunder by adopting parts of their legislative program as his own. In a speech in the Reichstag he frankly avowed his purpose of insuring the worker against sickness and old age so that "these gentlemen [the Social Democrats] will sound their bird call in vain." In addition, he had military purposes in mind. He hoped to make the German worker an effective potential soldier by safeguarding his health in some measure from the debilitating effects of factory labor. Bismarck's program of social legislation was initiated in 1883–1884 with the adoption of laws insuring workers against sickness and accidents. These acts were followed by others providing for rigid factory inspection, limiting the employment of women and children, fixing maximum hours of labor, establishing public employment agencies, and insuring workers against incapacity on account of old age. By 1890, Germany had adopted nearly all the elements, with the exception of unemployment insurance, in the matrix of social legislation that later became familiar in the majority of Western nations.

William's politics

In that same year the Iron Chancellor was dismissed by the young emperor, William II (1888–1918), following the less-than-year-long reign of his father Frederick III. Bismarck's loss of power was to a degree the result of a personality clash between the two men. William's father had remarked that his son had "a tendency to overestimate himself"; his tutor noted that he "imagined he knew everything—without having learned anything." William's arrogance was encouraged by the cult of imperial family worship that had by this time become part of the patriotic creed that was imposed by the state upon its citizens. Yet the quarrel between the young kaiser and his chancellor was a matter of substance as well as personality, involving policies directed at curbing the activities and popularity of the socialists.

Left: *William II of Germany and Bismarck*. Right: *Dropping the Pilot*. This cartoon appeared in the British magazine *Punch* on March 29, 1890, after the inexperienced but ambitious young emperor dismissed Bismarck as chancellor and personally assumed the helm of the ship of state. Note that Bismarck appears stripped of the insignia of office.

Bismarck's dismissal came in part over William's insistence that the antisocialist legislation of the past decade had achieved very little, and his mistaken belief that socialists would respond positively to his determination to rule in his own right and to create a more unified, stable, and powerful reich. Within a few years, however, William was arguing a line that appealed to the landowners, military leaders, and industrialists, whom he continued to court throughout his reign. He wooed the landowners by embarking on a policy of agricultural protection as a means of recovering from the depression brought on by inexpensive imports. And he wooed the military and the industrialists with a vast program of naval rearmament.

Despite his decision to end the ban against the Social Democrats, William did all he could to undermine their growing political strength. State schools were instructed to teach the dangers of socialism by stressing the virtues of patriotism and piety. Admission to the civil service was almost impossible unless one was an officer in the military reserve; and admission to that very influential body was not open to socialists—or to Jews. Stealing a leaf from Bismarck's text, William authorized the extension of earlier programs of social insurance, hoping to dampen enthusiasm for the Social Democrats by granting some of the reforms for which they continued to campaign. But William steadfastly refused to extend any sort of meaningful political participation beyond the powerful industrial, military,

Combating the socialists

and agricultural classes. The country was administered efficiently, but not democratically. With the exception of Count Leo von Caprivi, a military officer, all his chancellors were civil servants, a fact that underscored his determination to keep the administration of the country as far removed as possible from democratic control.

Social Democrats and the political stalemate

Growing opposition to these policies brought the Social Democrats increasingly impressive electoral victories. In 1912 they polled a third of the votes cast, and elected 110 members—the largest single bloc—to the Reichstag. Yet they were thwarted, not only by William's determination to ignore his parliament, but by their inability to resolve the conflict within their own ranks between purist and revisionist theory (see above, p. 847). The party continued to profess itself devoted to the principles of socialist purity, yet the need to cultivate mass electoral support pushed it in the direction of piecemeal reformist legislation. And even with their large bloc of Reichstag votes, the Social Democrats could not command a majority there unless they formed a coalition with conservative center parties. By 1914, German politics were approaching stalemate. The country was spared a domestic constitutional crisis only by the infinitely more profound international crisis of the First World War.

2. FRANCE: THE EMBATTLED THIRD REPUBLIC

Politically divided France

Although in 1870 France was not a newly constructed nation like the German Empire, it was a nation sorely in need of reunification and dedication to a common set of political purposes. Its history for the past century had left it torn between various factions; the ease with which the German Army had conquered them shook the self-confidence of all French citizens. The conflicts experienced after 1870 tended to be more ideological than social, a reflection not only of France's tumultuous political past, but of its comparatively slow rate of industrialization. Monarchists were divided between supporters of the Bourbon and Orleanist dynasties, their allegiance sustained by loyalties either to the descendants of Louis XVIII or of Louis Philippe. Bonapartists looked for political salvation to Napoleon III's son and heir Louis Napoleon. Republicans recalled the short-lived triumphs of their revolutionary ancestors. Socialists called down plagues on all political houses but their own. The result of this deep division was that not until 1875 did France have a constitution under which it could function.

Following the collapse of Napoleon III's empire a provisional government was organized to rule the country until a new constitution could be drafted. Elections held in 1871 for a national constituent assembly resulted in the choice of some 500 monarchists and only about 200 republicans. Conservative political sentiment was further reinforced by the events of the Paris Commune, which occurred during the period immediately following the elections. But the apparent winners, the monarchists, could not agree among themselves as to whether their king should be a Bourbon or an Orleanist. This stalemate led to the eventual passage in 1875—by one vote—

SOUVENIR DU CENTENAIRE 1789·1889

GLOIRE AUX JEUNES HÉROS
DE LA RÉPUBLIQUE

VIALA AGRICOLA
Mort à l'âge de 11 ans
Martyr de la Liberté

BARRA JOSEPH
Mort à l'âge de 13 ans
en criant vive la République

Commemoration of the Revolution. On the centennial of the French Revolution, the memory of the young heroes of the Republic is invoked to help establish support for the newly formed Third Republic.

of a series of constitutive laws that made France a republic. These laws established a parliament with a lower house elected by universal manhood suffrage (the Chamber of Deputies) and an upper house elected indirectly (the Senate), a cabinet of ministers presided over by a premier, and a president. Although at first the relative powers of president and premier were not clearly established, within two years the nation had declared itself in favor of a premier at the head of a government answerable to the Chamber of Deputies. An early president, Marshal Marie-Edmé MacMahon (1808–1893), attempted in 1877 to dismiss a premier with whom he disagreed but who was supported by a majority in the chamber. When new elections were held, MacMahon's policy was repudiated. Henceforth, premiers of the Third Republic were answerable to the chamber and not to the president, who became a figurehead. Yet the resolution of this constitutional question failed to produce political stability, since the premier had no authority to dissolve the legislature. This meant that members of the chamber could vote a premier and his fellow ministers out of office at will, with no risk of being forced to stand for reelection. If defeated on a vote, the premier and his colleagues had no alternative but to resign. The result

The formation of the Third Republic

was no fewer than fifty ministries in the years between 1870 and 1914. The Third Republic, for all its constitutional shortcomings, nevertheless managed to last until 1940—far longer than any system of French government since 1789. Its longevity was due, as much as anything, to the stability of other French institutions—the family, the law courts, and the police, for example. And its stability was attested to by the willingness of French men and women to invest their savings in state loans, rather than in industrial enterprises that appeared far less secure to them.

Radical reactionaries

In the years after 1875, the republicans, who had been feared at first as dangerous radicals, proved themselves to be generally moderate. It was the discontented monarchists and authoritarian sympathizers within the army, the Roman Catholic Church, and among the families of the aristocracy who took to plotting the overthrow of duly constituted governmental authority. Much of the time of successive republican governments was taken up defending the country from these reactionary radicals. In the late 1880s, a general, Georges Boulanger (1837–1891), gathered about him a following not only of Bonapartists, monarchists, and aristocrats, but of working people who were disgruntled with their lot and who believed, with Boulanger, that a war of revenge against Germany would put an end to all their troubles. Thanks to the general's own indecisiveness, the threatened coup d'état came to nothing. But the attempt was a symptom of deep discontents; Boulanger appealed, like Napoleon III, to disparate groups of disenchanted citizens, promising quick, dramatic solutions to tedious problems.

Left: *The Avenue de l'Opéra, c. 1880.* During the era of the Third Republic official Paris declared itself in favor of architecture that bespoke middle-class opulence and respectability as manifested here by the broad street lined with elegant shops and dominated by the unimpeded view of the facade of the Paris Opéra. Right: *The Rue Mouffeta, 1910.* Conditions in this working-class street remained meanwhile much as they had been throughout most of the preceding century.

Alfred Dreyfus Leaving His Court Martial

One further symptom of the divisions that plagued the republic during the later years of the nineteenth century was the campaign of anti-Semitism that the reactionaries adopted to advance their aims. The fact that certain Jewish bankers were involved in scandalous dealings with politicians lent color to the monarchist insistence that the government was shot through with corruption and that Jews were largely to blame. An anti-Semitic journalist, Édouard Drumont (1844–1917) insisted that "Jews in the army" were subverting the national interest. In 1889 he and others founded the Anti-Semitic League. This ugly and heated campaign furnished the background of the famous Dreyfus affair. In 1894 a Jewish captain in the French general staff, Alfred Dreyfus (1859–1935), was accused by a clique of monarchist officers of selling military secrets to Germany. Tried by court-martial, he was convicted and sentenced for life to Devil's Island, a ghastly prison camp in the Caribbean. At first the verdict was accepted as the merited punishment of a traitor; but in 1896 Colonel Georges Picquart (1854–1914), a new head of the Intelligence Division, announced his conclusion that the documents upon which Dreyfus had been convicted were forgeries. A movement was launched for a new trial, which the War Department promptly refused. Soon the whole nation was divided into friends and opponents of Dreyfus. On his side were the radical republicans, socialists, people of liberal and humanitarian sympathies, and such prominent literary figures as Émile Zola and Anatole France. The anti-Dreyfusards included monarchists, clerics, anti-Semites, militarists, and a considerable number of conservative working people. A Roman Catholic newspaper insisted that the question was not whether Dreyfus was guilty or innocent, but whether Jews and unbelievers were not the secret masters of France. Dreyfus was finally set free by executive order in 1899, and in 1906 was cleared of all guilt by the Supreme Court and restored to the army. He was immediately promoted to the rank of major and decorated with the emblem of the Legion of Honor.

The history of the Dreyfus affair gave the republicans the solid ground they had lacked in order to end the plottings of the radical reactionaries once and for all. The leaders of the republic chose to attack their enemies by effectively destroying the political power of the Roman Catholic Church in France. The anticlericalism expressed in this campaign was probably in part the product of a materialistic age, and of a longstanding mistrust by French republicans of the institution of the Church. Its main source, however, was the nationalism that we have already seen fueling Bismarck's *Kulturkampf*.

Anticlericalism

The great majority of the leaders of the Third Republic were hostile to the Church, and naturally so, for the Catholic hierarchy was aiding the monarchists at every turn. Clerics had conspired with monarchists, militarists, and anti-Semites in attempting to discredit the republic during the Dreyfus affair. But in the end they had overreached themselves. In 1901 the government passed a law prohibiting the existence of religious orders not authorized by the state; in 1904 another law forbade members of religious orders to teach in either public or private schools. Finally, in 1905, the union of Church and state was dissolved, thereby prohibiting payment of the clergy from public funds. For the first time since 1801 the adherents of all creeds were placed on an equal basis.

Legislation to curb the Church

The republic was, during these years, pressed from the Left as well as the Right. Socialism was a political force in France, as it was in Germany. Yet the response of republicans in France to socialist pressure differed markedly from that of Bismarck. There was no antisocialist legislation. Indeed, a law was passed in 1881 abolishing "crimes of opinion," thereby extending the freedom of the press considerably. In the same year, another law authorized public meetings without prior official approval. But if there was no attempt at repression, there was little positive social reform. The largest single party in the republic, the Radicals or Radical Socialists, was really a party representing small shopkeepers and lesser propertied interests. The Radicals were willing to found and maintain a democratic compulsory educational system, but they were reluctant to respond to demands for social legislation such as had been instituted in Germany. Those laws that were passed—establishing a ten-hour workday in 1904 and old-age pensions in 1910—were passed grudgingly and only after socialist pressure. The result was a growing belief among socialists and other workers that parliamentary democracy was worthless, that progress, if it was to be made, would be made only as a result of direct industrial action: the strike.

Pressure from the Left

This attitude was reinforced by the same debate—revisionism vs. purism—that we have seen dividing the Social Democrats in Germany. Purists had called it "opportunism" when the socialist Alexandre Millerand (1859–1943) had joined the nonsocialist cabinet of Prime Minister René Waldeck-Rousseau (1846–1904) in 1899. Millerand had insisted that his cooperation would help heal the wounds inflicted on French politics by the Dreyfus affair. His opponents charged that such collaboration was a

Socialist debate

Conflicts and Contrasts in Working-Class Life. Left: In this cartoon tighter work controls led a working-class French woman to complain to her father that "all day long, it's against the rules to sit down." He responded: "Do as we do! Ditch them." Right: At the same time, as this scene of workers on day-holiday at Yarmouth Sands in England suggests, workers enjoyed greater opportunities for at least some leisure-time than ever before. These contrasts helped to produce the class conflicts that characterized European politics before the First World War.

sellout. Their successors pointed to the lack of anything more than occasional and very mild social legislation in succeeding parliaments to prove their point. In response to this growing sentiment came a wave of strikes, which swept the country for several years before 1914, including one by postal workers in 1909 and by teachers and railwaymen in 1910. The government suppressed these actions by ruthless intervention. Tension increased after 1910 during debates over the extension of military conscription from two to three years, opposed by the socialists, and over the institution of an income tax, favored by the socialists as a way of financing social programs threatened as a result of increased military spending. By 1914, the republic, though hardly on the brink of revolution, remained divided. If the threat from the radical Right had been quelled, the challenge from the Left was only just being faced.

3. BRITAIN: FROM MODERATION TO MILITANCE

During the half-century before 1914, the British prided themselves on what they believed to be a reasonable, orderly, and workable system of government. Following the passage of the Second Reform Bill in 1867, which extended suffrage to over a third of the nation's adult males, the two

Suffrages Femmes. Women were denied the vote under the Third Republic and agitated for reform as did postal workers, teachers, and railwaymen in France.

Reform legislation in Britain

Benjamin Disraeli

Gladstone and Disraeli

major political parties, Liberal and Conservative, vied with each other in adopting legislation designed to provide an increasingly larger proportion of the population the chance to lead fuller and healthier lives. Laws that recognized the legality of trade unions, allowed male religious dissenters to participate fully in the life of the ancient universities of Oxford and Cambridge, provided elementary education for the first time to all children, and facilitated the clearance and rebuilding of large urban areas, were among those placed on the books during this period. In 1884, suffrage was once more widened, to include over three-fourths of the adult males, and to allow rural workingmen the chance to vote for the first time. Coupled with a previous act that instituted the secret ballot, this electoral reform bill brought Britain nearer to representative democracy.

Politics were dominated by two figures, the Conservative Benjamin Disraeli (1804–1881) and the Liberal William Gladstone (1809–1898). Disraeli, a converted Jew and popular novelist, and Gladstone, a devout Anglican and moral reformer, were remarkably different men. Disraeli was a pragmatist who remarked upon becoming prime minister that he had at last climbed to "the top of the greasy pole," while Gladstone devised political programs on the basis of his moral convictions. Despite this personality conflict, however, British political parties adopted a similar overall approach to policy-making. Managed by cabinet ministers drawn from either the upper middle class or landed society, they offered moderate programs that appealed to the widening electorate. Cabinet ministers sought to impose a legislative program on the House of Commons but, acknowledging its ultimate authority as duly elected representative of the people, resigned if their program was rejected. The result was political stability. And if differences of opinion did arise—as they did over imperialism, for example—

William E. Gladstone Campaigning, 1885. Perhaps the first politician to make effective use of the railway in his campaigns, Gladstone took advantage of the mobility it provided to reach out to the electorate.

David Lloyd George and Winston Churchill on Their Way to the House of Commons on Budget Day, 1910

both parties generally agreed upon a course steered by men whose similar backgrounds promised a moderation that suited the electorate.

Not everyone was content, however. Prosperity, though widespread enough, did not extend to the unskilled: dock workers, transport workers, and the like. These groups formed trade unions to press their claims. Their determination encouraged other unions to assume a more militant and demanding stance. In the 1890s this activity produced a reaction in the form of anti-trade union employers' associations and a series of legal decisions limiting the right of unions to strike. Workers, in turn, reacted by associating with middle-class socialist societies to form an independent Labour party, which was born in 1901 and five years later managed to send twenty-nine members to the House of Commons. Sensitive to this pressure from the Left, the Liberals, during a ministry that began in 1906, passed a series of reforms they hoped would ensure a minimum standard of living for those who had heretofore known little security. Sickness, accident, old-age, and unemployment insurance schemes were adopted. A minimum wage was decreed in certain industries. Labor exchanges, designed to help unemployed men and women find new jobs, were established. Restrictions on strikes and on the right of trade unions to raise money for political purposes were relaxed.

Liberal reforms, 1906–1914

Much of this legislation was the work of David Lloyd George (1863–1945), a radical lawyer from Wales, much feared by many within the political establishment. Lloyd George was chancellor of the exchequer (finance minister) in the Liberal cabinet of Prime Minister Herbert Asquith (1852–1928), and together with another young Liberal, Winston Churchill (1874–1965), he hammered together legislation that was both a reflection

London Dock Strike, 1911. Police move to clear demonstrators from shops where they have taken refuge after having been fired upon.

of his own political philosophy and a practical response to the growing political power of the working class. To pay for these programs—and for a larger navy to counter the German buildup—Lloyd George proposed a budget in 1909 that included progressive income and inheritance taxes, designed to make wealthier taxpayers pay at higher rates. His proposals so enraged the aristocratic members of the House of Lords that they declared themselves prepared to throw out the budget, an action contrary to constitutional precedent. Asquith countered with a threat to create enough new peers (titled noblemen) sympathetic to the budget to ensure its passage.[*] The House of Lords eventually surrendered; the result of the crisis was an act of Parliament in 1911 which provided that the House of Lords could not veto legislation passed by the House of Commons.

The rancor aroused by this constitutional conflict was intense. Self-proclaimed defenders of the House of Lords screamed threats in a chamber unused to anything but gentlemanly debate. Angry threats were by no means confined to the Houses of Parliament during these years, however. Throughout Britain, men and women threw moderation to the winds as they disputed issues in an atmosphere little short of anarchic. The reasons for this continued agitation were various. A decline in real wages after 1900 kept the working class in a militant mood despite Liberal reforms and produced an unusually severe series of strikes in 1911 and 1912. A Liberal

---

[*] In Britain the monarch had the authority to elevate an unlimited number of men to the peerage. But since the crown acts only on the advice of the prime minister, it is this official who had the actual power to create new members of the House of Lords. If necessary, he could use this power to pack the upper house with his own followers.

plan to grant Home Rule (self-government) to Ireland produced not only panic in the Protestant minority counties of the north (Ulster) but arming and drilling of private militias with an intensity that seemed to forecast civil war.

Perhaps the most alarming—because the most unexpected—of the militant revolts that seized Britain in the years before 1914 was the campaign for women's suffrage. The middle-class women who engaged in this struggle enjoyed more freedom of opportunity than their mothers had known. Laws had been passed easing the process of divorce and permitting married women control of their own property. Some universities had started to grant degrees to women. Contraceptive devices—and feminist propaganda defending their use—had begun to result in changed attitudes toward sexuality within the middle class. Perhaps because of these gains, many women felt their lack of the vote all the more acutely. Although the movement began among middle-class women, it soon included some female members of the working class and the aristocracy. Agitation reached a peak after 1900, when militant suffragettes—under the leadership of Emmeline Pankhurst (1858–1928), her daughters Christabel (1880–1958), and Sylvia (1882–1960), and others—resorted to violence in order to impress upon the nation the seriousness of their commitment. Women chained themselves to the visitors' gallery in the House of Commons; slashed paintings in museums; invaded that male sanctum, the golf course, and inscribed VOTES FOR WOMEN in acid on the greens; disrupted political meetings; burned politicians' houses; and smashed department store windows. The

Violent Suffragette Protest. Emmeline Pankhurst is arrested during a violent demonstration at Buckingham Palace in 1911.

Militant Actions for Women's Suffrage. Left: Emily Davison threw herself under the king's horse at the Derby in 1913. Right: This suffragette was arrested after having joined an attack on Buckingham Palace in 1914. Women resorted to violence to show the nation the seriousness of their commitment to gaining the vote. But attitudes toward the suffragettes were typified by the comments after the trampling of Emily Davison—the queen inquired about the woman, the king about his horse.

government countered violence with repression. When women, arrested for their disruptive activities, went on hunger strikes in prisons, wardens proceeded to feed them forcibly, tying them down, holding their mouths open with wooden and metal clamps, and running tubes down their throats. When hunger strikes threatened to produce deaths and thus martyrs for the cause, the government passed the constitutionally dubious "Cat and Mouse" Act, which sanctioned the freeing of prisoners to halt their starvation and then, once they had regained their health, authorized their rearrest. The movement was not to see the achievement of its goal until after the First World War, when reform came largely because of women's contributions to the war effort.

Whether Britain's militant mood might have led to some sort of general conflict if the war had not begun in 1914 is a question historians continue to debate. Suffice it to say that national sentiment in the last few years before the outbreak of general hostilities was far different from that of the 1870s. Britain, so confident of itself and of its moderation, was proving no less a prey to instability than other European nations.

4. RUSSIA: THE ROAD TO REVOLUTION

In only one European country, Russia, did conditions pass from instability to active insurrection during these prewar years. The early-twentieth-century Russian revolutionary movement had numerous forerunners. Waves of discontent broke out several times during the nineteenth century.

Threatened uprisings between 1850 and 1860, partly a consequence of Russia's defeat in the Crimean War, persuaded Tsar Alexander II, who came to the throne in 1855, to liberate the serfs, to modernize the military establishment, to reform the judicial system, and to grant local self-government.

The law of 1861 granted legal rights to some 22 million serfs, and authorized their title to at least a portion of the land they had worked. Yet the pattern of rural life in Russia did not change drastically. Large-scale landowners managed to retain the most profitable acreage for themselves, and vastly inflated the prices they charged the state for land surrendered to emancipated serfs. Newly liberated serfs, in turn, faced the need to pay the state for the land they received—which, in addition to being of generally poor quality, was often insufficient to sustain themselves and their families. The overall result of emancipation was to compel peasants to return to work as agricultural laborers for their previous masters.

The military reform of 1874 was designed to broaden the ranks to include all males, not just conscripted peasants serving under an officer elite open only to the nobility. The period of active duty was reduced from twenty-five to six years. Schooling was provided for draftees and corporal punishment was abolished.

Russia's judicial system, heretofore secret, corrupt, and tied to a rigid class system that ensured legal inequality, was reformed so as to make the courts for the first time independent of the central administration. All Russians were declared equal before the law; trial by jury was introduced for most criminal cases, although crimes against the state remained the province of secret courts under the Ministry of the Interior. Whereas formerly evidence could be presented only in written form, oral testimony was now permitted, thereby making trials far more public in character. A tiered system of courts, rising from local justices of the peace, provided the right to appeal.

The structure of local government instituted in 1861 placed responsibility in the hands of the *mir,* or village commune, which had traditionally regulated the lives of peasants and serfs. Its officials assigned land and collected taxes. They were also able to restrict the movement of residents in and out of their community, a regulation used by the state to ensure that peasants could not escape their obligation to pay for the land they now occupied as free men. At a higher level, district councils were authorized to administer their own courts and tax collection. In 1864, indirectly elected provincial councils—*zemstvos*—were empowered to manage local welfare and educational programs.

Though only moderately reformist, these *zemstvos* provided forums for the debate of political issues and, along with the extension of educational opportunities, encouraged middle-class Russians to suppose themselves on the way to some sort of liberalized state. The government, however, grown fearful of the path it was treading, called a halt to reform and substituted repression in its place. By 1875, censorship had been extended not only to the *zemstvos,* which were forbidden to discuss general political issues, but to the press and to schools as well. The result of suppression was, not surprisingly, further discontent and active subversion. Middle-class Russians and disaffected students argued privately the virtues of utopian socialism, liberal parliamentarianism, and Pan-Slavism. A growing number, calling themselves nihilists, espoused the doctrines of the anarchist Bakunin (see above, p. 844). Terrorism became the preferred course of action for the student revolutionaries of the People's Will, which had begun as an agrarian socialist party. Increased government repression and failure of peaceful political activity convinced them that assassination of the tsar was the only solution to oppression. They achieved their goal in 1881, when a bomb killed Alexander II.

The most important radical political element in late-nineteenth-century Russia was a large, loosely knit group of men and women who called themselves populists. They believed that although their country must westernize, it could not expect to do so according to examples set elsewhere. They proclaimed a new Russia, yet one based upon the ancient institution of the village commune, which was to serve as a model for the socialist society they hoped to create. Populism sprang primarily from the middle class; a majority of its adherents were young, many of them students; and about 15 percent were women, a significantly large proportion for the period. They formed secret cadres, plotting the overthrow of tsarism by terror and insurrection. They dedicated their lives to "the people" (hence their name), attempting wherever possible to live among common laborers so as to understand and express the popular will. Populism's historical importance lies not so much in what it accomplished, which was little, but in what it promised for the future. A movement that marked the beginning of organized revolutionary agitation in Russia, it was the seedbed for thought and action that would in time produce general revolution. Populists read Marx's *Capital* before it was translated into Russian; they tested and revised his ideas and those of other major revolutionaries of the nineteenth century so as to produce a doctrine suited to Russia's particular destiny.

Autocracy and Russification

The activities of populists and anarchists, however, triggered a floodtide of reaction against the entire policy of reform. Alexander III (1881–1894) governed under the theory that Russia had nothing in common with Western Europe, that its people had been nurtured on despotism and mystical piety for centuries and would be utterly lost without them. He believed that Western ideals such as rationalism and individualism would undermine the deferential faith of the Russian masses and would plunge the nation into anarchy and crime, and that in like manner, Western institutions could never bear fruit if planted in Russian soil. With these doctrines as his guiding principles, Alexander III enforced a regime of stern repression. He curtailed in every way possible the powers of the local assemblies, increased the authority of the secret police, and subjected villages to government by wealthy nobles selected by the state. These policies were continued, though in somewhat less rigorous form, by his son, Nicholas II (1894–1917), a much less effective ruler. Both tsars were ardent proponents of Russification, a more ruthless counterpart of similar nationalistic movements in various countries. Its purpose was to extend the language, religion, and culture of Great Russia, or Russia proper, over all of the subjects of the tsar and thereby to simplify the problem of governing them. It was aimed primarily at the Poles, Finns, and Jews, since these were the nationalities considered most dangerous to the stability of the state. Russification meant repression. The Finns were deprived of their constitution; the Poles were compelled to study their own literature in Russian translations; and high officials in the tsar's government connived at *pogroms,* i.e., wholesale massacres, against the Jews. Other groups whose repression by the state led to long-lasting undercurrents of non-Russian nationalism included the Georgians, Armenians, and Azerbaijanis of the Caucasus Mountains. Tensions between Christians and Muslims within these groups augmented longstanding inter-ethnic tensions, which even a common hatred of forced Russification could not defuse.

Westernization

Despite these attempts to turn Russia's back to the West, however, the nation was being drawn more closely than it had ever been before into the European orbit. Russia was industrializing, and making use of European capital to do so. Economic policies during the 1890s, when Count Sergei Witte (1849–1915) was the tsar's leading minister, resulted in the adoption of the gold standard, which made Russian currency easily convertible.

Railways and telegraph lines were constructed; exports and imports multiplied by factors of seven and five respectively from 1880 to 1913. In addition, Russian writers and musicians contributed in a major way to the enriching of Western culture. We have already noted the singular contributions of Tolstoy, Turgenev, and Dostoevsky. The musical works of Peter Tchaikovsky (1840–1893) and Nikolai Rimsky-Korsakov (1844–1908), while expressing a peculiarly Russian temperament and tradition, were recognized as important additions to the general body of first-rate contemporary composition.

With westernization came the growth of a new wage-earning class. Most of Russia's workers were recruited from the countryside. We have seen that regulations made migration outside the *mir* difficult if not impossible. To live permanently in cities meant surrendering all claim to one's land. The result was that many peasant factory workers lived away from their villages only temporarily, returning to attend to farming's seasonal demands. Consequently, these workers could not easily master a trade, and were forced to take unskilled jobs at extremely low wages. They lived in large barracks; they were marched to and from factories, where conditions were as unsafe and unhealthy as they had been in British factories in the early years of industrialization. An average working day in a textile mill was from twelve to fourteen hours. This sudden and extremely harsh transition from country to city living instilled deep discontent and divisiveness in Russian workers. Those who renounced their village ties and adopted the life of the city tended to be skilled workers who could command higher wages and better working conditions than the unskilled. Workers thus tended to be divided along lines of skill as well as by trade, defusing the development of a uniform working-class consciousness for many years. The heavy concentration of workers in urban areas, however, introduced many,

A new working class

A Railroad Yard in Eastern Russia, 1896

Worker's Quarters in St. Petersburg, c. 1900. These buildings, in which workers from the country were housed temporarily while they labored in factories, were breeding grounds for class consciousness.

especially the generally better-educated skilled workers, to political organizers seeking reform or revolution.

New political parties

As Russia's economy diversified, new class divisions brought the emergence of new political parties. The famine of 1891 encouraged this, as private relief workers saw that agricultural capitalism had made deep inroads into the traditional structure of the *mir*. For the first time it appeared that the rural commune might not be the uniquely Russian answer to the problems of unequal distribution, leading some to develop urban-based political responses to Russian conditions.

Bolsheviks versus Mensheviks

The heavy involvement of the state in the rapid industrialization of the 1890s in general wedded industrialists and capitalists to the autocracy. Other members of the middle class, however, primarily enterprising landowners, came together in 1905 to form a Constitutional Democratic party, whose program included the creation of a nationally elected parliament or Duma to determine and carry out policies that would further the twin goals of liberalization and westernization. Meanwhile, the Social Revolutionaries and the Social Democrats began to agitate for far more radical solutions to the problems of Russian autocracy. The Social Revolutionaries concerned themselves with the onerous plight of the peasants, burdened with land purchase and high taxes. The Social Revolutionaries wanted to equalize the landholdings of peasants within their *mirs,* and to increase the power of the *mirs* in their continuing competition with large landowners. The Social Democrats, on the other hand, concentrated their efforts on behalf of urban workers. They were Marxists, who saw themselves as westerners and as part of the international working-class movement. In 1903 the leadership of the Social Democratic party split in an important disagreement over revolutionary strategy. One group, which achieved a temporary majority (and thus called itself the Bolsheviks—"Majority Group") favored a strongly centralized party of active revolutionaries, and opposed the notion of a postrevolutionary transitional bourgeois state, insisting instead that revolution be succeeded immediately by a socialist regime. The Mensheviks ("Minority Group"), whose position resembled that of other European revisionist socialists, soon managed to regain control of the party. The Bolshevik splinter party remained in existence, however, under the leadership of the young, dedicated revolutionary Vladimir Ulanov (1870–1924), who wrote under the pseudonym of N. Lenin.

The Young Lenin, 1897

Lenin was a member of the middle class, his father having served as an inspector of schools and minor political functionary. He had been expelled from the University of Kazan for engaging in radical activity, following the execution of his elder brother for his involvement in a plot to assassinate Alexander III. Lenin spent three years as a political prisoner in Siberia; from 1900 until 1917 he lived as an exile in Western Europe. His zeal and abilities as both a theoretician and a political activist are evidenced by the fact that he retained leadership of the Social Democrats even while residing abroad. Lenin continued to preach the gospel of Marxism and of a relentless class struggle, but with a difference. Marx had predicted the emergence of capitalism and liberal democracy out of feudalism, giving way over time to socialism and then communism. Lenin argued, however, that Russia's history gave her the opportunity to "skip capitalism" and move directly to socialism. This special path necessitated a working-class consciousness expressed only through the party—that is, the Bolsheviks—instead of developing spontaneously as in Marx's historical model. Lenin's vision of Russia's special destiny was reflected in his treatise *What Is to Be Done?* (1902), a stinging response to revisionists who were urging collaboration with less radical parties. Revolution was what was to be done, Lenin argued, revolution "made" as soon as possible by an elitist group of agitators working through the agency of a disciplined party. Lenin and his followers, by merging the tradition of Russian revolutionism with Western Marxism, and by endowing the result with a sense of immediate possibility, fused the Russian situation in such a way as to make eventual explosion almost inevitable.

Lenin

The revolution that came in 1905, however, took even the Bolsheviks by surprise. Its unexpected occurrence was the result of a war between Russia and Japan, which broke out in 1904, and in which the Russians were soundly beaten. Both countries had conflicting interests in Manchuria and Korea; this fact was the immediate cause of the conflict. On land and sea the Japanese proved themselves the military superiors of the Russians. As dispatches continued to report the defeats of the tsar's army and navy,

The Russo-Japanese War

Bloody Sunday. Demonstrating workers who sought to bring their grievances to the attention of the tsar were met and gunned down by government troops, January 1905.

the Russian people were presented with dramatic evidence of the inefficiency of autocracy.

The Revolution of 1905

Just as defeat in the Crimean War had spurred the movement for reform, so now members of the middle class who had hitherto refrained from association with the revolutionists joined in the clamor for change. Radical workers organized strikes and held demonstrations in every important city. Led by a priest, Father Gapon, a group of 200,000 workers and their families went to demonstrate their grievances at the tsar's winter palace in St. Petersburg on January 22, 1905—known ever after as Bloody Sunday. The demonstrators were met by guard troops and many of them were shot dead. The massacre removed the last vestiges of "naive monarchism," the belief that the tsar sincerely loved his subjects and was prevented from gratifying their needs only through the machinations of his evil councillors. By the autumn of 1905 nearly the entire urban population had enlisted in a strike of protest. Merchants closed their stores, factory-owners shut down their plants, lawyers refused to plead cases in court, even valets and cooks deserted their wealthy employers. It was soon evident to Tsar Nicholas that the government would have to yield. On October 30, he issued a manifesto, pledging guarantees of individual liberties, promising a moderately liberal franchise for the election of a Duma, and affirming that henceforth no law would be valid unless it had the Duma's approval. This was the high-water mark of the revolutionary movement. During the next two years Nicholas issued a series of sweeping decrees that negated most of the promises made in the October Manifesto. He deprived the Duma of many of its powers, and decreed that it be elected indirectly on a class basis by a number of electoral colleges. Thereafter the legislative body contained a majority of obedient followers of the tsar.

There were several reasons for the setback to this movement for major political reform. In the first place, the army remained loyal to its commander-in-chief. Consequently, after the termination of the war with Japan in 1905, the tsar had a large body of troops that could be counted upon if necessary to decimate the ranks of the revolutionists. An even more important reason was the split in the ranks of the revolutionists themselves. After the issuance of the October Manifesto, large numbers of the bourgeoisie became frightened at threats of the radicals and declared their conviction that the revolution had gone far enough. Withdrawing their support altogether, they became known henceforth as Octobrists. The more radical merchants and professional men, organized into the Constitutional Democratic party, maintained that opposition should continue until the tsar had been forced to establish a government modeled after that of Great Britain. This fatal division rendered the middle class politically impotent. Finally, disaffection appeared within the ranks of the workers. Further attempts to employ the general strike as a weapon against the government ended in disaster.

The reasons for setback

But the Russian revolutionary movement of 1905 was not a total failure. Many retrospectively viewed it as a "dress rehearsal" for the revolution of 1917. The vengeance taken by the tsar convinced many people that their government was not a benevolent autocracy, as they had been led to believe, but a stubborn and brutal tyranny. The uprising revealed the ability of working-class leaders to control the destiny of Russia. The general strike had proved a valuable revolutionary tool, as had workers' councils, elected from the factory floor and briefly operating as the only effective government in some areas. In addition, the revolt of 1905 persuaded some of the more sagacious advisors of the tsar that last-ditch conservatism was none too safe. The result was the enactment of a number of conciliatory reforms. Among the most significant were the agrarian programs sponsored by the government's leading minister, Peter Stolypin (1862–1911), between 1906 and 1911. These included transfer of five million acres of royal land to the peasants for a price; the granting of permission to peasants to withdraw from the *mir* and set up as independent farmers; and cancellation of the remaining installments owed by the peasants for their land. Decrees were issued permitting the formation of labor unions, providing for a reduction of the working day (to not more than ten hours in most cases), and establishing sickness and accident insurance. Yet the hopes of some liberals that Russia was on the way to becoming a progressive nation on the Western model proved illusory. The tsar remained stubbornly autocratic. Few peasants had enough money to buy the lands offered for purchase. In view of the rising cost of living, the factory workers considered their modest gains insufficient. A new revolutionary outbreak merely awaited a convenient spark.

Gains from the revolutionary movement

5. THE SEARCH FOR EQUILIBRIUM ELSEWHERE IN THE WEST

Problems in Italy

Other European countries generally found it just as difficult to attain internal stability between 1870 and 1914, as did those whose history we have surveyed. Italy was burdened with the problems of a rapidly increasing population, the need to industrialize quickly, and a stark disparity between a relatively prosperous industrial north and an impoverished agricultural south. As the population increased, so did the stream of rural migration into cities, where there were few jobs available. In its drive to create jobs and to industrialize, the government intervened directly in the economy by placing large orders for military equipment and by undertaking an ambitious program of railway construction. By the First World War the share of industrial production in the national economy had risen to 25 percent.

Trasformismo

These strides were largely the result of policies instituted by Giovanni Giolitti (1842–1928), who was prime minister for almost the entire period between 1900 and 1914. Yet his efforts to spur industrialization widened the division between north and south. Relying on opportunistic maneuvering, which he called *trasformismo,* and which argued the pointlessness of party politics, Giolitti rewarded the support of southern politicians for his program of industrial expansion by allowing the south to remain under the domination of the great landowners, the Church, and—in Sicily—the Mafia, none of which were interested in furthering the economic well-being or political consciousness of the average citizen. Thus whereas illiteracy was reduced in northern Italy to about 11 percent, in the south it remained at 90 percent. By failing to address the desperate economic conditions in the south, *trasformismo* denied the country an opportunity to develop a much needed internal market for its goods.

Socialist split

Hoping to gain support for his program from the socialists, Giolitti engineered passage of laws legalizing trade unions, improving factory conditions, and extending the suffrage to virtually all males over thirty. But attempts to satisfy the Left did not sit well with more conservative elements in Italian society, who remembered bread riots in Milan in 1896, the assassination of King Humbert by radicals in 1900, and widespread strikes in 1902 and 1904. Meanwhile, socialists in Italy were as divided on the matter of strategy as they were elsewhere in Europe. Reformists competed with radicals, organized into chambers of labor—local trade union councils with a revolutionary outlook—which assisted in the takeover of the Socialist party by a militant left wing in 1912.

Nationalism in Austria-Hungary

Nationalist aspirations continued to be a major problem in Eastern Europe. In 1867 an attempt had been made to resolve national differences in Austria by dividing the empire in two—an Austrian empire west of the Leitha River, and a kingdom of Hungary to its east. Each of the two components in this so-called Dual Monarchy was to be the equal of the other, though the two were joined by the same Habsburg monarch, by several common ministries, and by a kind of superparliament. This solution failed to put an end to nationalist divisions, however.

EUROPE AFTER THE CONGRESS OF BERLIN · 1878

The Austrian portion of the monarchy was comprised not only of a German-speaking majority, but of Czechs, Slovaks, Slovenes, and Ruthenians as well. Without concessions to these nationalities the government could expect little peace. Yet to give in to their aspirations was to antagonize the German majority, a group constantly wary of any move that appeared to threaten its predominance. During the 1890s, an attempt to pacify the Czechs by requiring all officials in areas of mixed German and Czech populations to speak both languages infuriated the Germans, who staged violent demonstrations proclaiming the superiority of their culture and forced the government to back down. Anxious to promote industrial development, the bureaucracy recognized that to introduce the requisite economic and financial measures, a Reichstag more sympathetic to modernization and to the needs of diverse imperial constituencies would be necessary. To that end, the Austrians introduced universal male suffrage in 1907, in the belief that newly enfranchised peasants recognized a primary allegiance to the emperor, rather than to any one particular nationality. Because the new

Nationalist tensions in Austria

electoral laws continued to specify quotas for each ethnic minority in the parliament, however, they strengthened the hand of the various national groups in the legislature, encouraging them to demand still further autonomy.

The major issue in the Hungarian half of the monarchy was a proposal to separate out the Hungarian regiments in the imperial army, allowing them their own insignia and requiring that they be commanded in their native language. The emperor, Francis Joseph, rejected these demands countering with a threat to introduce imperial male suffrage, a move the Magyars correctly saw as a challenge to their supremacy, as it had been to the Germans in Austria. The result was a standoff, part of the continuing desperate attempt on the part of the central government to play one side off against the other in order to maintain a shaky *status quo.*

Nationalist tensions in Hungary

In Southeastern Europe nationalist agitation continued to rend the ever-disintegrating Ottoman Empire. Before 1829 the entire Balkan peninsula—bounded by the Aegean, Black, and Adriatic Seas—was controlled by the Turks. But during the next eighty-five years a gradual dismemberment of the Turkish Empire occurred. In some instances the slicing away of territories had been perpetrated by rival European powers, especially by Russia and Austria; but generally it was the result of nationalist revolts by the sultan's Christian subjects. In 1829, at the conclusion of a war between Russia and Turkey, the Ottoman Empire was compelled to acknowledge the independence of Greece and to grant autonomy to Serbia and to the provinces that later became Rumania. As the years passed, resentment against Ottoman rule spread through other Balkan territories. In

The disintegrating Ottoman Empire

Vienna, 1873. Despite the fact that Vienna was the capital of an empire that straddled Eastern and Western Europe, it was by this date clearly a stylish and westernized metropolis.

THE DISMEMBERMENT OF THE OTTOMAN EMPIRE · 1683-1923

Map labels: GERMANY, RUSSIA, FRANCE, AUSTRIA-HUNGARY, YUGOSLAVIA, RUMANIA, BLACK SEA, CASPIAN SEA, MONTENEGRO, BULGARIA, SPAIN, ITALY, ALBANIA, Constantinople, TURKEY, ★Ankara, GREECE, SYRIA (French Mandate), IRAQ (British Mandate 1920-1932), CYPRUS (To Gt. Britain), MEDITERRANEAN, CRETE (To Greece), DODECANESE IS. (To Italy), LEBANON, PERSIAN GULF, TUNISIA, SEA, KUWAIT, ALGERIA, Tripoli, PALESTINE, TRANSJORDAN, ARABIA, LIBYA, EGYPT (British Protectorate 1914-1922), RED SEA

ACQUIRED BY:
Great Britain · France · Italy
Austria-Hungary · Russia

GAINED INDEPENDENCE:

—— Boundary of the Ottoman Empire at its greatest extent
—·—·— 1923 boundaries

0 ————— 1000 miles

1875–1876 there were uprisings in Bosnia, Herzegovina, and Bulgaria, which the sultan suppressed with effective ferocity. Reports of atrocities against Christians gave Russia an excuse for renewal of its age-long struggle for domination of the Balkans. In this second Russo-Turkish War (1877–1878) the armies of the tsar won a smashing victory. The Treaty of San Stefano, which terminated the conflict, provided that the sultan surrender nearly all of his territory in Europe, except for a remnant around Constantinople. But at this juncture the great powers intervened. Austria and Great Britain, especially, were opposed to granting Russia jurisdiction over so large a portion of the Near East. In 1878 a congress of the great powers, meeting in Berlin, transferred Bessarabia to Russia, Thessaly to Greece, and Bosnia and Herzegovina to the control of Austria. Montenegro, Serbia, and

Rumania were recognized as independent states. Seven years later the Bulgars, who had been granted some degree of autonomy by the Congress of Berlin, seized the province of Eastern Rumelia from Turkey. In 1908 they established the independent Kingdom of Bulgaria.

In the very year when this last dismemberment occurred, Turkey itself was engulfed by a tidal wave of nationalism. For some time the more enlightened Turks had grown increasingly disgusted with the weakness and incompetence of the sultan's government. Those who had been educated in European universities were convinced that their country should be rejuvenated by the introduction of Western ideas of science, patriotism, and democracy. Organizing themselves into a society known as the Young Turks, they forced the sultan in 1908 to establish constitutional government. The following year, in the face of a reactionary movement, they deposed the reigning sultan, Abdul Hamid II (1876–1909), and placed on the throne his brother, Mohammed V (1909–1918), as a titular sovereign. The real powers of government were now entrusted to a grand vizier and ministers responsible to an elected parliament. This revolution did not mean increased liberty for the non-Turkish inhabitants of the empire. Instead, the Young Turks launched a vigorous movement to Ottomanize all of the Christian subjects of the sultan. At the same time the disturbances preceding and accompanying the revolution opened the way for still further dismemberment. In 1908 Austria annexed the provinces of Bosnia and Herzegovina, which the Treaty of Berlin had allowed it merely to administer, and in 1911–1912 Italy entered into war with Turkey for the conquest of Tripoli.

Of all the major nations of the West, the United States probably underwent the least domestic turmoil during the several decades before 1914. The Civil War had exhausted the country; until the end of the century the ever-expanding frontier provided an alternative for those discontented with their present lot. Yet the United States also felt, to some degree, the pressures that made stability so hard to sustain in Europe. Though the Civil War had ended, the complex moral problem of racism remained to block all attempts truly to heal the nation. Severe economic crises, particularly an economic depression in the 1890s, accompanied by the collapse of agricultural prices and the closing of factories, caused great suffering and aroused anger at capitalist adventurers who seemed to be profiting at the expense of the country as a whole. Many grew convinced that a restricted money supply had produced the depression. Demand for the issuance of paper money and the increased coinage of silver were at the heart of the programs of the Greenback and the Populist parties, which attracted large followings, and which campaigned as well for an income tax and government ownership of railways, and telephone and telegraph lines. Socialism of a reformist brand was espoused by Eugene V. Debs (1855–1926), leader of a mildly Marxist Socialist party. It failed to appeal to the generally un-class-conscious American worker, who continued to have faith in the dream of economic mobility. More radical was the membership of the Industrial Workers of the World (also known as the Wobblies), a general union whose goal was to

Eugene Debs

organize the unskilled and immigrant worker. Perceived as a device of foreign agitators, the IWW was repressed both by the government and by industrial management. Characteristic of the generally moderate tone of American reformism, the Progressive movement captured both the imagination and votes of a vocal minority of middle-class Americans whose hostility over the accumulation of private economic power and the political corruption of urban "bosses" was balanced by its belief in the democratic process and in the possibility of continuing progress. The movement, many of whose ideas were embodied in the programs of Presidents Theodore Roosevelt (1858–1919) and Woodrow Wilson (1856–1924), was curtailed by the new realities that emerged with the advent of the First World War.

6. INTERNATIONAL RIVALRIES: THE ROAD TO THE FIRST WORLD WAR

Despite the domestic instabilities and uncertainties that characterized the Western world in the years before 1914, a great many men and women retained a faith in the notion of peaceful progress. There had been an absence of multinational armed conflict—with the exception of the Crimean War—for a century. European countries—even autocratic Russia—had been moving gradually toward what most agreed was the worthy goal of democracy. Indeed, instability could be understood as the result of either an overzealous or an overdelayed movement in that direction. Above all, industrialization seemed to be providing a better standard of living for all— or at least all within the Western world. There is little wonder, therefore, that men and women reacted with disbelief as they saw their world crumbling during the days of frantic diplomatic maneuvering just prior to the outbreak of war in August 1914.

The key to understanding the coming of the First World War lies in an analysis of international diplomacy during the years after 1870. Europe had prided itself on the establishment of a balance of power, which had kept any one nation from assuming so predominating a position as to threaten the general peace. During his years as chancellor, Bismarck played a diplomatic variation upon this general theme, in order to ensure that France would not engage in a war of revenge against the German victors of 1870. There was little prospect that the French would attempt war singlehandedly. Therefore, Bismarck determined to isolate France by attaching all of its potential allies to Germany. In 1872 he managed to form an alliance with both Austria and Russia, the so-called Three Emperors' League, a precarious combination that soon foundered. Bismarck then cemented a new and much stronger alliance with Austria. In 1882 this partnership was expanded into a Triple Alliance with Italy. The Italians joined out of fear of the French. They resented the French occupation of Tunisia (1881), a territory that they regarded as properly theirs. Moreover, Italian politicians, still at odds with the Roman Catholic Church, feared that supporters of the papacy in France might gain the upper hand and send a French army to defend the pope. In the meantime, the Three Emperors' League had been revived. Though it lasted officially for only six years (1881–1887), Germany managed to hold the friendship of Russia until 1890, by means of a Reinsurance Treaty (1887) providing for the neutrality of either power if the other went to war.

Bismarck's diplomatic success

Thus after more than a decade of diplomatic maneuvering, Bismarck had achieved his ambition. By 1882 France was cut off from nearly every possibility of obtaining aid from powerful friends. Austria and Italy were united with Germany in the Triple Alliance, and Russia after a three-year lapse was back once more in the Bismarckian camp. The only conceivable quarter from which help might come to the French was Great Britain; but, with respect to Continental affairs, the British were maintaining a policy of "splendid isolation." Therefore, so far as the danger of a war of revenge was concerned, Germany had little to fear. Bismarck's complicated structure of alliances appeared to answer the purpose for which he claimed it had been built—to keep the peace. But the alliance system was a weapon that could cut two ways. In Bismarck's hands, it kept the peace. In hands less diplomatically capable, it might become less an asset than a liability, as was the case after 1890.

A diplomatic realignment

During the years between 1890 and 1907, European nations, competing across the globe for trade and territory, became more suspicious of each other. This general international insecurity produced a diplomatic realignment that obliterated Bismarck's handiwork and threatened Germany. The Germans retained the support of Austria, but they lost the friendship of both Russia and Italy, while Britain abandoned its isolation to enter into agreements with Russia and France. This shift in the balance of power had fateful results. It helped convince the Germans that they were surrounded by a ring of enemies, and that consequently they must do everything in their power to retain the loyalty of Austria-Hungary.

The Triple Entente

The first of the major results of this diplomatic revolution was the formation of the Triple Entente between Russia, France, and Great Britain. William II of Germany, mistrustful of Russian ambitions in the Balkans, refused to renew the Reinsurance Treaty following Bismarck's dismissal in 1890. A growing coolness between the two countries led to Russia's political flirtation with France. Secret military conventions signed by the two countries in 1894 provided that each would come to the aid of the other in case of an attack by Germany, or by Austria or Italy supported by Germany. This Dual Alliance of Russia and France was followed by an Entente Cordiale between France and Great Britain. During the last two decades of the nineteenth century, the British and the French had been involved in frequent altercations over colonies and trade, as in the Sudan. By 1904, however, France, fearing Germany, had buried its differences with Britain and in that year signed the Entente. This was not a formal alliance but a friendly agreement, covering a variety of subjects. The final step in the formation of the Triple Entente was the conclusion of a mutual understanding between Great Britain and Russia in 1907. Again there was no formal alliance, but the ability of the two powers to reconcile their ambitions in Asia suggested a willingness to ally in case of war.

Thus by 1907 the great powers of Europe were arrayed in two opposing combinations, the Triple Alliance of Germany, Italy, and Austria-Hungary, and the Triple Entente of Britain, France, and Russia. Nevertheless, these new groupings were not without internal strains. Italy and Austria, though allied, were bitterly at odds over the disposition of territory in the Adriatic region—Trieste in particular, which the Austrians held and which the Italians claimed as *Italia Irredenta* (unredeemed Italy). The Italians had designs on portions of Africa as well. In the 1890s, under the premiership of Francesco Crispi (1819–1901), a hero of the *Risorgimento,* they had attempted to establish a protectorate over the Ethiopians, only to suffer a devastating loss at Aduwa in 1896. Now the Italians coveted Tripoli in North Africa, which they believed they might more easily obtain, over the objections of Turkey, if they supported the Moroccan claims of their French adversaries. Strains within the Entente were equally apparent. Britain viewed Russia's growing determination to control the Dardenelles as a threat to its supply routes to the East.

The generally fragile state of international relations was certainly one of the important causes of the First World War. Yet it was by no means the only one. The German historian Fritz Fischer and other scholars ignited a controversy in the 1960s by insisting that the paramount reason was Germany's internally generated drive to power, its compulsion to aggrandize itself at the expense of the rest of Europe—not simply to achieve what the emperor had called its "place in the sun," but to see to it that the sun shone no more than fitfully on anyone else. Scholars of this persuasion, writing against the view that all nations must share the blame, point to Germany's rapid commercial expansion, the growth, in particular, of its coal and steel industries, and its dockyards and overseas shipping as indications of its intentions. German capitalists financed the construction of a Berlin to Baghdad railway, as part of a concerted *drang nach osten* (drive to the East). At the same time, the Germans launched a massive campaign to increase the

The Baghdad Railroad. German and Turkish officials celebrate the launching of the enterprise.

size of their navy, a prospect particularly pleasing to the industrial bourgeoisie, who would profit directly from the new construction, and whose sons, excluded from the aristocratically based army, manned the naval officer corps. The naval buildup was accompanied by a brash and effective propaganda campaign—perhaps the first of its kind—directed by the secretary of the navy, Admiral Alfred von Tirpitz (1849–1930), and concerted through "navy leagues," organizations devoted to trumpeting Germany's intention of matching the strength of the British navy.

Others' responsibility

Others have taken issue with the notion that Germany faced the prospect of a preemptive war with equanimity, as it ignores the fact that many German industrialists did not want war since they had heavy investments in the economies of both Russia and France. They further argue that it is a mistake to view the problem of the war's outbreak through the single lens of Germany. They maintain that Britain's rapprochement with Russia and France, for example, reflected the demands of its own imperial policies and not simply a response to overweening German ambition.

Proliferation of "war machines"

Certainly the spirit of militarism extended beyond the borders of Germany, as all major European countries came to deploy massive "war machines." Serbia and Rumania, two very real threats to Austro-Hungarian security, possessed armies of over 400,000 each. In 1913, Russia embarked on a program of military expansion that bolstered its army by 500,000, to over 2,000,000 men, making it roughly equivalent in size to that of Germany. Nation after nation followed the German example by establishing a general staff, an institution one historian has called "the greatest military innovation of the nineteenth century." Problems of supplying and deploying mass armies had compelled governments to create a cadre of high-level planners, professional military advisors who were increasingly heeded by the civilian politicians to whom they reported. General staffs made it their particular business to deal with conscription, mobilization, the laying out of strategic railway lines—all complex technical issues demanding a high level of expertise.

Social impact of militarism

Reliance upon mass armies fostered a preoccupation with national birth rates, public health, and literacy. France regarded its declining birth rate after 1870 with alarm partly because it foretold a diminishing capacity to field a modern world-class army. If birth rates reflected a nation's long-term prospects for military manpower, the physical well-being of draft-age civilians was of immediate concern and encouraged reforms in health care and housing. A report on "physical deterioration" in Britain after the Boer War profoundly disturbed both military and civilian planners by demonstrating that in industrial cities such as Manchester as many as 8,000 out of 11,000 volunteers had been turned away by the army as unfit for military service. And, of course, with the introduction of increasingly sophisticated weaponry that required mastery of technological detail, noncommissioned officers and enlisted men could not function without the ability to read and to figure. The new armies had to be literate armies.

General European militarism was fed by notions of war as a therapeutic exercise. The French historian Ernest Renan had justified armed conflict as a condition of progress, "the sting which prevents a country from going to sleep." Middle-class citizens, anxious to prove themselves as patriotically aggressive as aristocrats, joined in the clamor to establish that the counting house was as much the seat of national fervor as the country estate. People began to speak increasingly of the "just" war. The British politician David Lloyd George praised the formation of a Balkan Alliance to fight the Turks in 1912 as "enlarging the boundaries of freedom."

*Notions of the therapeutic
value of war*

Nationalism, too, fed the militaristic mood. From the beginning of the twentieth century, Serbia moved to extend its jurisdiction over all those alleged to be similar to its own citizens in race and in culture. Some of these peoples inhabited what were then the two Turkish provinces of Bosnia and Herzegovina. Others included Croatians and Slovenes in the southern provinces of Austria-Hungary. After 1908, when Austria suddenly annexed Bosnia and Herzegovina, Serbian activity was directed exclusively against the Habsburg Empire. It took the form of agitation to provoke discontent among the Slav subjects of Austria, in the hope of drawing them away and uniting the territories they inhabited with Serbia. It resulted in a series of dangerous plots against the peace and integrity of the Dual Monarchy.

Nationalism

In many of their activities the Serbian nationalists were aided and abetted by the Pan-Slavists in Russia. The Pan-Slav movement was founded upon the theory that all of the Slavs of Eastern Europe constituted one cultural nation. Therefore, it was argued that Russia, as the most powerful Slavic state, should act as the protector of the smaller Slavic nations of the Balkans. Pan-Slavism was not merely the wishful sentiment of a few ardent nationalists; it was a part of the official policy of the Russian government, and went far toward explaining Russia's aggressive stand in every quarrel that arose between Serbia and Austria.

All these factors—domestic unrest, diplomatic instability, international militarism, and nationalism—combined to produce a series of crises between 1905 and 1913. They were not so much causes as they were symptoms of international animosity. Yet each left a heritage of suspicion and bitterness that made war all the more probable. In some cases hostilities were averted only because one of the parties was too weak at the time to offer resistance. The result was a sense of humiliation, a smoldering resentment that was almost bound to burst into flame in the future. Two of the crises were generated by disputes over Morocco. Both Germany and France wanted to control Morocco; in 1905 and 1911 the two powers stood on the brink of war. Each time the dispute was smoothed over, but not without the usual legacy of suspicion.

The Iron Fist of the Kaiser Strikes Agadir. This British cartoon depicts the Germans' use of gunboat diplomacy in Morocco in 1911 to secure colonial concessions from the French as an overtly hostile and sinister act. In precipitating this Second Moroccan Crisis the Germans hoped to drive a wedge between Britain and France but succeeded only in driving the Entente powers closer together.

In addition to the clash over Morocco, two flare-ups occurred in the Near East, the first in Bosnia in 1908. At the Congress of Berlin in 1878 the two Turkish provinces of Bosnia and Herzegovina had been placed under the administrative control of Austria, though actual sovereignty was still to be vested in the Ottoman Empire. Serbia also coveted the territories; they would double the size of its kingdom and place it within striking distance of the Adriatic. Suddenly, in October 1908, as we have seen, Austria annexed the two provinces, in flat violation of the Treaty of Berlin. The

Serbs were furious and appealed to Russia. The tsar's government threatened war, until Germany addressed a sharp note to St. Petersburg announcing its firm intention to back Austria. Since Russia had not yet fully recovered from its war with Japan and was plagued by internal troubles, Russian intervention was postponed but not renounced. The tsar's government resolved never to let itself be humiliated again.

Balkan Wars

Still more bad blood between the nations of Eastern Europe was created by the Balkan Wars. In 1912 Serbia, Bulgaria, Montenegro, and Greece, with encouragement from Russia, joined in a Balkan League for the conquest of the Turkish province of Macedonia. The war started in October 1912; in less than two months the resistance of the Turks was shattered. Then came the problem of dividing the spoils. In secret treaties negotiated before hostilities began, Serbia had been promised Albania, in addition to a generous slice of Macedonia. But now Austria, fearful as always of any increase in Serbian power, intervened at the peace conference and obtained the establishment of Albania as an independent state. For the Serbs this was the last straw. It seemed to them that at every turn their path to western expansion was certain to be blocked by the Habsburg government. From this time on, anti-Austrian agitation in Serbia and in the neighboring province of Bosnia became ever more venomous.

A world at war

It was the assassination of the Austrian Archduke Francis Ferdinand by a Serbian sympathizer on June 28, 1914, that ignited the conflict. The four-year war that ensued altered the Western world immeasurably. Yet many changes that came either during or after the First World War were the result, not of the war itself, but of pressures and forces we have seen at work during the prewar years, when European power, at its height, was challenged by forces which that power had unleashed and which it proved unable to contain.

SELECTED READINGS

• *Items so designated are available in paperback editions.*

Barrows, Susanna, *Distorting Mirrors: Visions of the Crowd in Late Nineteenth-Century France,* New Haven, 1981. A study of crowd psychology.
• Berghahn, Victor, *Germany and the Approach of War in 1914,* New York, 1973. Examines the domestic background of German foreign policy, especially the naval program.
• Blum, J., *Lord and Peasant in Russia from the Ninth to the Nineteenth Century,* Princeton, 1961. Contains a thorough discussion of emancipation.
Brogan, D. W., *France under the Republic, 1870–1930,* New York, 1940. An excellent survey, comprehensive and analytical.
• Dangerfield, George, *The Strange Death of Liberal England,* New York, 1961. Examines England's three major crises of the prewar period: women's suffrage, labor unrest, and Irish home rule.
• Emmons, Terence, *The Russian Landed Gentry and the Peasant Emancipation of 1861,* Charlotte, N.C., 1968.

- Fischer, Fritz, *Germany's Aims in the First World War,* New York, 1967. An extremely controversial study that seeks to lay major blame for the coming of the First World War on Germany.
- Haimson, L., *The Russian Marxists and the Origins of Bolshevism,* Cambridge, Mass., 1955. Analyzes the revolutionaries as part of the Russian radical tradition.
- Hale, Oron J., *The Great Illusion, 1900–1914,* New York, 1971. A general synthetic treatment of the period that is particularly concerned with mood and spirit.

  Jenks, William A., *Austria under the Iron Ring, 1879–1893,* Charlottesville, Va., 1965. An examination of Austria's attempts at political and social reform, set in the context of a struggle for autonomy from German domination.

  Johnson, Douglas, *France and the Dreyfus Affair,* London, 1966. A good survey, with breadth.
- Jones, Gareth Stedman, *Outcast London,* Oxford, 1971. A remarkable book that examines the breakdown in the relationship between classes in London during the latter half of the nineteenth century.

  Mack Smith, Denis, *Italy: A Modern History,* rev. ed., Ann Arbor, Mich., 1969. An excellent survey.
- McManners, John, *Church and State in France, 1870–1914,* New York, 1972. Particularly good on the question of education and the final separation of Church and state.
- May, Arthur J., *The Hapsburg Monarchy, 1867–1914,* Cambridge, Mass., 1951. A detailed narrative of the period.
- Mosse, W. E., *Alexander II and the Modernization of Russia,* New York, 1958. Brief but useful biography.
- Pulzer, Peter, *The Rise of Political Anti-Semitism in Germany and Austria,* New York, 1964. An excellent study of the roots of anti-Semitism and the part it played in shaping politics.

  Ralston, David B., *The Army of the Republic: The Place of the Military in the Political Evolution of France, 1871–1914,* Cambridge, Mass., 1967. Useful for background to the Dreyfus affair.

  Rémond, René, *The Right Wing in France: From 1815 to De Gaulle,* rev. ed., Philadelphia, 1969. Traces the survival of royalism and Bonapartism in French thought and politics.
- Seton-Watson, Hugh, *The Russian Empire, 1801–1917,* Oxford, 1967. Standard survey.

  Stavrianos, Leften S., *The Balkans, 1815–1914,* New York, 1963. Surveys domestic and international affairs within the entire troubled region.
- Taylor, A. J. P., *The Struggle for Mastery in Europe, 1848–1918,* Oxford, 1971. An excellent diplomatic history.

  Thayer, John A., *Italy and the Great War: Politics and Culture, 1870–1914,* Madison, Wisc., 1964. Written to explain Italian policy and its origins in the prewar period.

  Ulam, Adam, *Russia's Failed Revolutions: From the Decembrists to the Dissidents,* New York, 1981. Activities of revolutionary societies before 1917.
- Vicinus, Martha, ed., *A Widening Sphere: Changing Roles of Victorian Women,* Bloomington, Ind., 1977. Essays that trace the slow emancipation of Victorian women.
- Weber, Eugen, *Peasants into Frenchmen: The Modernization of Rural France, 1870–1914,* Stanford, 1917. Argues that the great achievement of the Third

Republic was the consolidation of France, accomplished by bringing rural areas into the mainstream of modern life.

- Wehler, Hans-Ulrich, *The German Empire, 1871–1918,* Leamington Spa, 1985. Revisionist study of political policy under Bismarck and William II.
- Williams, Roger L., *The French Revolution of 1870–1871,* New York, 1969. A good narrative account.

  Zelnik, Reginald E., *Labor and Society in Tsarist Russia: The Factory Workers of St. Petersburg, 1855–1870,* Stanford, 1971. The growth of class consciousness in tsarist Russia.

SOURCE MATERIALS

- Childers, Erskine, *The Riddle of the Sands,* New York, 1978. A bestseller in England in 1903, this novel concerns a future war between England and Germany. Its reception gives evidence of the rise of anti-German sentiment prior to the First World War.
- Hamerow, Theodore S., ed., *The Age of Bismarck: Documents and Interpretations,* New York, 1973.
- Lenin, Nikolai, *What Is To Be Done?* London, 1918. Written in 1902, this is Lenin's most famous pamphlet. In it he called for the proletarian revolution to be led by elite cadres of bourgeois intellectuals like himself.
- Mackenzie, Midge, ed., *Shoulder to Shoulder,* New York, 1975. A richly illustrated documentary history of the British movement for women's suffrage.

  Pankhurst, Emmeline, *My Own Story,* New York, 1914. The memoirs of one of the leaders of England's militant suffragettes.
- Turgenev, Ivan, *Fathers and Sons,* New York, 1966. Turgenev's greatest novel is set in Russia in the 1860s and portrays the ideological conflict between generations at the time of the emancipation of the serfs and the rise of nihilism.
- Zola, Émile, *Germinal,* New York, 1964. Zola's realistic novel describes class conflict in France's coal-mining region.

Chapter 27

THE FIRST WORLD WAR

Nevertheless, except you share
With them in hell the sorrowful dark of hell.
Whose world is but the trembling of a flare.
And heaven but as the highway for a shell.
You shall not hear their mirth:
You shall not think them well content
By any jest of mine. These men are worth
Your tears. You are not worth their merriment.

—Wilfred Owen, "Apologia Pro Poemate Meo"

The war that broke out in 1914 was not really the "first world war." The wars against Napoleon at the beginning of the nineteenth century had extended beyond the European continent. Yet the war that took place between 1914 and 1918 had an impact that far exceeded any ever fought before. Colonies supported their imperial centers while trading partners were often forced to side with the Allies (initially the Triple Entente) or the Central Powers (initially the Triple Alliance). The scale of the war was such that it quickly became a "people's war," to which civilians as well as soldiers and sailors were directly and totally committed. War bore fruit in revolution, and sowed the seeds of new and even more deadly conflicts in the future. It set the pattern for an age of violence that has continued through most of the twentieth century.

The world at war

1. PRELUDE TO WAR

The assassination of the Austrian archduke was the immediate cause of the First World War. Francis Ferdinand (1863–1914) was soon to become emperor of Austria-Hungary. The reigning monarch, Francis Joseph (1830–1916; reigned 1848–1916), had reached his eighty-fourth year, and his death was expected momentarily. The murder of the heir to the throne was therefore considered in a very real sense as an attack upon the state.

The assassination of Francis Ferdinand

The Assassination at Sarajevo. Left: The Archduke Francis Ferdinand greets Bosnian notables a few hours before his death. Right: The police seize Princip after he had killed the heir to the Habsburg monarchy.

The actual murderer of Francis Ferdinand was a Bosnian student, Gavrilo Princip, the tool of Serbian nationalists. The murder, though committed in Sarajevo, the capital of Bosnia, was the result of a plot hatched in Belgrade, the Serbian capital. The conspirators were members of a secret society officially known as Union or Death, but commonly called the Black Hand. Their opposition to Francis Ferdinand stemmed from his support for a plan that would have resulted in the reorganization of the Habsburg Empire. This plan, designated as *trialism,* entailed changing the Dual Monarchy into a triple monarchy. In addition to German Austria and Magyar Hungary, already virtually autonomous, there was to be a third semi-independent region to accommodate the Slavs. Serbian national extremists opposed this scheme, fearing that if it were put into effect, their Slovene and Croatian kinsmen would be content to remain under Habsburg rule. They therefore determined to assassinate Francis Ferdinand before he could become emperor and press ahead with his reform.

See color map of Europe on the eve of the first World War following page 940

The Austrians were immediately convinced that the Serbian government was behind this violent act. Austria waited for more than three weeks before acting on its suspicions and seizing the opportunity to extract a high price from Serbia for its transgressions. The delay was due in part to Austria's inability to decide how to proceed and in part to its unwillingness to mobilize its forces until after the harvest. On July 23, 1914, the Austrian government dispatched a severe ultimatum to the Serbians consisting of

Austrian ultimatum to Serbia

eleven demands: among them Serbia was to suppress anti-Austrian newspapers, to crush secret patriotic societies, to eliminate from the government and from the army all persons guilty of anti-Austrian propaganda, and to accept the collaboration of Austrian officials in stamping out the subversive movement against the Habsburg Empire. Two days later the Serbian government transmitted its reply. Of the total of eleven demands, only one was emphatically refused, and five were accepted without reservations. The Austrians, however, pronounced the Serbian reply unsatisfactory, severed diplomatic relations, and mobilized parts of their army. The Serbs themselves had been under no illusions about pleasing Austria, since, three hours before transmitting their reply, they had issued an order to mobilize their troops.

The Austrian intransigence vis-à-vis the Serbian response was actually the culmination of a belligerence that had been growing among European nations prior to the events that followed the assassination. As early as July 18 Sergei Sazonov (1861–1927), the Russian foreign minister, warned Austria that Russia would not tolerate any effort to humiliate Serbia. On July 24 Sazonov informed the German ambassador: "I do not hate Austria; I despise her. Austria is seeking a pretext to gobble up Serbia; but in that case Russia will make war on Austria." Russia had the support of France; on the twentieth of July, Raymond Poincaré (1860–1934), president of France, paid a visit to St. Petersburg to strengthen the Russian resolve to "be firm" and to avoid any compromise that might result in a loss of prestige for the Triple Entente. He warned the Austrian ambassador that "Serbia has very warm friends in the Russian people. And Russia has an ally, France."

The attitude of Germany in these critical days was ambiguous. Although the kaiser was shocked and infuriated by the assassination, his government

Russia and France

Nicholas II and Raymond Poincaré, the President of the French Republic, in St. Petersburg on July 23, 1914

did not make any threats until after the actions of Russia gave cause for alarm. Yet both William II and the chancellor, Theobald von Bethmann-Hollweg (1856–1921), adopted the premise that stern punishment must be meted out to Serbia without delay. They hoped in this way to confront the other powers with an accomplished fact. The kaiser declared on June 30: "Now or never! Matters must be cleared up with the Serbs, *and that soon.*" On July 6 Bethmann-Hollweg gave a commitment to the Austrian foreign minister which was interpreted by the latter as a blank check. The Austrian government was informed that the emperor would "stand true by Austria's side in accordance with his treaty obligations and old friendship." The Germans apparently hoped that by taking quick punitive action against Serbia, the Austrians would be able to counter a very real Serbian threat before Russia and its allies could recover from the shock of the assassination and mobilize either diplomatically or militarily.

Austria declared war against Serbia on July 28, 1914. For a fleeting, anxious moment there was a possibility that the conflict might be contained. But it was quickly transformed into a war of larger scope by the action of Russia. On July 24 the Russian government decided to respond to any Austrian military initiative against Serbia with a partial mobilization. By July 30, however, Sazonov and a prowar military clique persuaded Tsar Nicholas II to issue an order mobilizing all troops, not only against Austria but against Germany as well, on the grounds that such a vast country as Russia would require considerable time to get its military machine into operation.

There was now no drawing back from the abyss. The Germans were alarmed by Russian preparations for war. The latest action by the tsar's government made the situation far more critical, since in German military circles, and also in French and Russian, general mobilization meant war. Upon learning that the tsar's decree had gone into effect, William II's government sent an ultimatum to St. Petersburg demanding that mobilization cease within twelve hours. On the afternoon of August 1, the German ambassador requested an interview with the Russian foreign minister. He appealed to Sazonov for a favorable answer to the German ultimatum. Sazonov replied that mobilization could not be halted, but that Russia was willing to continue negotiations. The ambassador repeated his question a second and a third time, emphasizing the terrible consequences of a negative answer. Sazonov finally replied: "I have no other answer to give you." The ambassador then handed the foreign minister a declaration of war and, bursting into tears, left the room. In the meantime, the kaiser's ministers had also dispatched an ultimatum to France demanding that its leaders make known their intentions. Premier René Viviani (1863–1925) replied on August 1 that France would act "in accordance with her interests," and immediately ordered a general mobilization of the army. On August 3 Germany declared war upon France.

These grim timetables had doomed the efforts of Britain's foreign secretary, Sir Edward Grey (1862–1933) to convene a conference to settle the Austro-Serbian dispute. Perhaps if Britain had declared its readiness to go

August 1, 1914. A German officer reads the declaration of war in the streets of Berlin.

to war on the side of France and Russia earlier, that declaration would have compelled Germany and Austria to draw back. Yet Grey was not certain enough of his country's willingness to fight to make such a commitment. Although military conversations between the British and French had bound the former to an expeditionary force on French soil in case of war, the British public did not know this. Opinion was divided: Conservatives generally favored war; the Liberals, still in power, disagreed among themselves; Labour was opposed.

The British position

Fortunately for Grey and the prime minister, Herbert Asquith (1852–1928), both of whom wanted a British declaration of war, Germany's invasion of neutral Belgium brought together parliamentary and public support for intervention. In 1839, along with the other great powers, Britain had signed a treaty guaranteeing the neutrality of Belgium. Moreover, it had been British policy for a century or more to try to prevent domination of the Low Countries, lying directly across the Channel, by any powerful Continental nation. The Germans planned to attack France through Belgium. Accordingly, they demanded of the Belgian government permission to send troops across its territory, promising to respect the independence of the nation and to pay for any damage to property. When Belgium refused, the kaiser's legions began pouring across the frontier. The British foreign secretary immediately went before Parliament and

Britain enters the war

Allied Propaganda Posters. During the war governments, confronted with the bitter fruit of prewar militarism and nationalist rivalry, resorted to using any image that seemed likely to stir the passions of their populations against their foes. Top: French poster claims that "Force will protect the right." Bottom: British poster depicts the Kaiser as Satan.

urged that his country rally to the defense of international law and to the protection of small nations. The next day, August 4, 1914, the cabinet sent an ultimatum to Berlin demanding that Germany respect Belgian neutrality, and that the Germans give a satisfactory reply by midnight. The kaiser's ministers offered no answer save military necessity, arguing that it was a matter of life and death for Germany that its soldiers reach France by the quickest route. As the clock struck twelve, Great Britain and Germany were at war.

Other nations were quickly drawn into the struggle. On August 7 the Montenegrins joined with their kinsmen, the Serbs, in fighting Austria. Two weeks later the Japanese declared war upon Germany, partly because of their alliance with Great Britain, but mainly for the purpose of conquering German possessions in the Far East. On August 1 Turkey negotiated an alliance with Germany, and in October began the bombardment of Russian ports on the Black Sea. Italy, though still technically a member of the Triple Alliance, proclaimed neutrality. The Italians insisted that the Germans were not fighting a defensive war, and that consequently they were not bound to go to their aid. Italy remained neutral until May 1915, when it entered the war on the side of the Triple Entente.

The diplomatic maneuvers during the five weeks that followed the assassination at Sarajevo have probably best been characterized as "a tragedy of miscalculation." Because the war brought such disaster in its train, debate about immediate responsibility for its outbreak has been continual and often acrimonious. The eventual victors—Britain, France, the United States, and their allies—insisted at the war's end that Germany assume that responsibility, and wrote German war "guilt" into the postwar settlement. Historians during the 1920s and 1930s challenged that harsh assessment, arguing instead that all the major European nations—and the alliance systems they had constructed—had driven the world into conflict in those fatal weeks during the summer of 1914. In the 1960s, the historian Fritz Fischer insisted that William II and Bethmann-Hollweg did everything they could to encourage the Austrians to go to war against Serbia, knowing that such a war would almost certainly engage the Russians on the side of the Serbians and the French on the side of the Russians. There were those in positions of power in Germany arguing that war was inevitable, that to wait until Russia had fully recovered from its war with Japan, and until France's armies had been strengthened by its three-year conscription law, was to invite defeat. Better to do battle now, from a position of strength. Bethmann-Hollweg succumbed to such fatalism by July 1914.

2. THE ORDEAL OF BATTLE

Because the war soon demanded the wholehearted support of entire civilian populations, national leaders felt compelled to depict it as a noble conflict rather than a widespread quarrel between imperialist powers or the un-

German Propaganda Posters. As in the British propaganda poster, the foes of the Germans are shown as evil—e.g., Wilson as a serpent—thereby justifying the death and destruction caused by the fighting.

expected outcome of nationalist jealousies. The socialist Second International had declared that workers should respond to a call to arms with a general strike. Although none of the European Socialist parties heeded that call, governments continued to fear subversion of the war effort from "below," and attempted to head off any such movement by ceaseless appeals to patriotism. Propaganda became as important a weapon as the machine gun. The task of the Allies was at first made easier by Germany's treatment of the neutral Belgians: their execution of civilian hostages, destruction of the ancient library at Louvain, and massacre of over six hundred civilians at Dinant.

A "patriotic" war

On August 6, 1914, Prime Minister Asquith declared that Britain had entered the conflict to vindicate "the principle that smaller nationalities are not to be crushed by the arbitrary will of a strong and overmastering Power." Across the Channel, President Poincaré was assuring his fellow citizens that France had no other purpose than to stand "before the universe for Liberty, Justice and Reason." Later, as a consequence of the writings of individuals such as H. G. Wells and Gilbert Murray, and the pronouncements of the American president, Woodrow Wilson, the crusade of the Allied powers became a war to redeem mankind from the curse of militarism. In the opposing camp, the subordinates of the kaiser were doing all in their power to justify Germany's military efforts. The struggle against the Allied powers was represented to the German people as a crusade on behalf of a superior *Kultur* and as a battle to protect the fatherland against the wicked encirclement policy of the Allied nations. German socialist politicians were persuaded to vote for the war on the grounds that a German

Propaganda efforts

war with Russia would help liberate the Russian people from the tsarist yoke.

The First World War fooled military experts who believed it would end quickly. Open warfare soon disappeared from the Western Front—the battle line that stretched across France from Switzerland to the North Sea, where the fighting was concentrated for four years. Germany's initially successful advance into France followed war plans drawn up by General Alfred von Schlieffen (1833–1913) and adopted in 1905. Schlieffen's strategy called for Austria to hold against the Russians while Germany dealt a quick blow to the French, knocking them out of the war. Germany was then to turn, with Austria, to the major task of defeating the Russians. Contrary to expectation, however, the advance to the west, which brought German troops to within thirty miles of Paris, was halted. A series of flanking maneuvers by both sides ended in the extension of the battle lines in a vast network of trenches.

Stalemate

Attacks to dislodge the enemy from their positions on the line failed to achieve more than very limited gains. Protected by barbed wire and machine guns—both making their first major appearance in a European war—defenders had the advantage. The one weapon with the potential to break the stalemate, the tank, was not introduced into battle until 1916, and then with such reluctance by tradition-bound commanders that its half-hearted employment made almost no difference. Airplanes were used almost exclusively for reconnaissance, though occasional "dog-fights" did occur between German and Allied pilots. The Germans sent Zeppelins to raid London, but they did little significant damage. On more than one occasion those in charge of the war attempted to end the stalemate by opening military fronts in other areas of the world. In 1915, Britain and France attempted a landing at Gallipoli, in Asia Minor, in the hope of driving Turkey from the war. The campaign was a disaster for the Allied powers,

Gallipoli Campaign. Allied troops land at Gallipoli on the Turkish peninsula in the summer of 1915.

Trench Warfare. Left: Trenches were dug for protection against tanks and artillery. Here a tank is shown after having crashed into such a trench. Right: After the first few battles, the war on the Western Front settled into static or position warfare. During the four-year period, veritable cities of mud, stone, and timber sprang up behind the trenches.

however, failing, as did others, to refocus the fighting or to free it from the immobility of the trenches.

Life for the common soldier on the Western Front alternated between the daily boredom and extreme unpleasantness of weeks spent in muddy and vermin-ridden trench communities, and the occasional and horrifying experience of battle, a nightmare not only of artillery, machine guns, and barbed wire, but of exploding bullets, liquid fire, and poison gas. Morale among most troops remained remarkably steady, given the dreadful conditions in the trenches and the endless series of battles fought without significant gain to either side. Mutinies did occur among French troops in 1917, when soldiers moved forward in attack bleating like sheep, their pathetic way of protesting their commanders' continued willingness to lead them like lambs to the slaughter. Meanwhile, conditions within Germany worsened, as an Allied blockade slowly reduced the country's raw materials and food supply.

Life in the trenches

By 1916 the war, which appeared to have settled into an interminable stalemate, had extracted a fearful cost. Commanders on both sides embarked on a war of attrition. Only by battering their enemies first with artillery and then with thousands of men armed with rifles, grenades, and bayonets did they believe they could achieve the always-elusive "breakthrough." These assaults produced high casualties and a few extra yards of mud. Over 600,000 were killed and wounded when the Germans unsuccessfully besieged the French stronghold of Verdun, near France's eastern border, in the spring of that year. The Germans acknowledged that their

The enormous human cost

Supplies for the Troops. To provision the armies of millions in the field, mountains of boxes of rations were shipped to supply depots like this one in Rouen and from there to the Front by railway and motor transport.

aim was not so much to take the fortified city, which they knew the French would defend with desperation, but to "bleed France white of all able-bodied men"; yet the Germans lost as many men as the French. In August 1916 the British launched an enormous attack along the Somme River to ease the pressure on Verdun. Lasting from July to November, the battle cost the Germans 500,000, the British 400,000, and the French 200,000 in return for an Allied advance of seven miles across the front. On the first day of fighting alone, over 57,000 British troops were killed or wounded.

In time such losses fueled an unsuccessful move on the part of a minority on both sides to press for a negotiated peace. But in the minds of those *Changes in leadership* who were making decisions, both military and civilian, the immediate effect of the carnage was to reinforce determination to press ahead for total victory. This intransigence led, in turn, to changes in leadership. In Britain, the ineffectual prime minister Asquith was replaced by David Lloyd George, the buccaneer politician behind many of Britain's prewar social reforms. If Lloyd George had little new to propose, nevertheless he projected a properly fervent public image. In France, the following year, Georges Clemenceau (1841–1929) assumed the premiership, again with a mandate to counter a growing defeatist attitude within the military high command. And in Germany, control continued to pass into the hands of Generals Paul von Hindenburg (1847–1934) and Erich Ludendorff (1865–1937), the men responsible as well for the overall military strategy of the Central Powers.

As the conflict dragged on, other countries were drawn into the war. Italy was bribed by the Allies with a promise of Austrian territories and a *The expansion of the conflict* generous slice of the eastern shore of the Adriatic. Bulgaria joined the Central Powers in October 1915, and Rumania sided with the Allies a year later. It was the intervention of the United States on the Allied side, however, in April 1917, that tipped the balance. The United States entered the war vowing, in the words of its president, Woodrow Wilson, to "make the world safe for democracy," to banish autocracy and militarism, and to establish a league or society of nations in place of the old diplomatic maneuvering. Undoubtedly the primary reason for the American decision to enter the war, though, was the government's concern to maintain the international balance of power. For years it had been a cardinal doctrine in American diplomatic and military circles that the security of the United States depended upon a balance of forces in Europe. So long as Great Britain was strong enough to prevent any one nation from achieving supremacy in Europe, the United States was safe. American officials had grown so accustomed to thinking of the British navy as the shield of American security that they found it difficult to contemplate any different situation. Germany, however, presented not merely a challenge to British naval supremacy; it threatened to starve the British nation into surrender and to establish a hegemony over all of Europe.

Submarine warfare

The direct cause of United States participation in the First World War was the U-boat, or submarine, warfare of the Germans. Once it became clear that the war would be one of attrition, the Germans recognized that unless they could break the Allies' stranglehold on their shipping, they would be defeated. In February 1915, the kaiser's government announced that neutral vessels headed for British ports would be torpedoed without warning. President Wilson replied by declaring that the United States would hold Germany to a "strict accountability" if any harm should come to American lives or property. The warning caused Germany to discontinue the campaign, but only temporarily. The Germans were convinced that the U-boat was one of their most valuable weapons, and they considered themselves justified in using it against the British blockade. They also believed, correctly, that the British were receiving war matériel clandestinely shipped aboard passenger ships from the United States, and continued to sink them, thus appearing to violate United States neutrality. When the kaiser's ministers announced that, on February 1, 1917, they would launch a campaign of unrestricted submarine warfare, Wilson cut off diplo-

The success of the Atlantic convoys

The Lusitania *Leaving New York Harbor.* In February 1915 the *Lusitania* was torpedoed and sunk by a German U-boat. Among the 1,200 people drowned were 119 Americans. The disaster was one step in the chain of events that led to the entry of the United States into the war on the side of Britain and France.

matic relations with the Berlin government. On April 6 he went before Congress and requested and received a declaration of war.

The immediate result of U.S. entry was an increase in the amount of war matériel and food—later, in the number of troops—shipped unmolested in armed convoys across the Atlantic. New ship construction overcame earlier losses; submarine warfare, Germany's most effective weapon against the Allies, had been neutralized.

3. REVOLUTION IN THE MIDST OF WAR

Gregory Rasputin

Tsar Nicholas I loses support

In the midst of world war came revolution. Russia, already severely weakened by internal conflicts before 1914, found itself unable to sustain the additional burden of continuous warfare. In a nation ruled as autocratically as was Russia, a successful war effort depended greatly on the ability of its ruler to command and sustain cooperation across the political and social spectrum. But Tsar Nicholas II had seriously undermined his own limited capabilities to enlist support by his actions after the October Revolution of 1905, especially in his determined efforts to erode the minimal political power he had been forced to grant to the Duma. Further mistrust centered on the irrationality of his wife Alexandra, a religious fanatic, and her spiritual mentor, the monk Rasputin. The latter had gained the tsarina's sympathy by his ability to alleviate the sufferings of her hemophiliac son, and used his influence over her to shape policy to his own self-aggrandizing ends.

Tsar Nicholas II and His Family on the Eve of the Revolution

Scenes from the Russian Revolution. Top left: Mass demonstration sponsored by the First All-Russian Congress of Soviets in which Bolshevik banners far outnumber the rest, spring 1917. Top right: Street fighting in Petrograd, summer 1917. Bottom right: Russian soldiers join the Bolsheviks in front of the Winter Palace, fall 1917.

Although the outbreak of war temporarily united Russia against a common enemy, Russia's armies proved incapable of sustained success in the field. In 1914 they managed to advance against the Austrians into Galicia in the south, but suffered two stunning defeats in the north, at Tannenberg and the Masurian Lakes, losing almost 250,000 men in the process. In some instances soldiers were sent to the front without rifles; clothing supplies were inadequate; medical facilities were scarce; and the railway system broke down, producing a shortage of food not only in the army but in cities as well. A major offensive in the summer of 1916, to coincide with the campaign along the Somme in the west, was initially successful. But it turned into a humiliating retreat thanks to transportation breakdowns and a

Collapse of Russian military power

Kerensky (second from right) *and His Aides in the Winter Palace*. This is the last known photograph of Kerensky in Petrograd.

lack of ammunition. By the end of 1916, Russia's power to resist a foreign invader had all but collapsed.

So also had its power to override domestic resistance and rebellion. The disaster of the Somme campaign touched off waves of increasing unrest at home, where a rebellious urban population grew more and more impatient with inflation and shortages of food and fuel. Demands for a popularly elected, broad-based government were met by the tsar's determination to retain power in his own hands, until bread riots in Petrograd (St. Petersburg, whose "Germanic" name had been changed at the beginning of the war) precipitated his forced abdication in March 1917. The bread riots, led by women workers, were merely the latest in a wave of strikes and demonstrations that had crippled Petrograd for months. This particular demonstration, however, moved spontaneously from a protest by women in bread lines into a mass movement that filled the streets and converged on the city center. Troops summoned to quell the uprising broke ranks and joined the protesters, further evidence of the collapse of both civilian and military order. Nicholas tried to put down the uprising by force and to dissolve the Duma, but the Duma refused to obey and the insurgents took over Petrograd. Within five days armed insurrection had forced the end of the tsarist government.

With the overthrow of the tsar, the authority of the government passed into the hands of a provisional ministry organized by leaders in the Duma in conjunction with representatives of workers in Petrograd, calling themselves a *soviet* or government council. With the exception of Alexander Kerensky (1881–1970), who was a member of the rurally based Socialist Revolutionary party, nearly all of the ministers were middle-of-the-road bourgeois liberals, many of whom had served in the *zemstva* or provincial

The March 1917 revolution

Provisional ministry

governing bodies. The ministry's primary responsibility was to prepare for national elections to a constituent assembly; and it also acted to grant and secure civil liberties, release political prisoners, and redirect power into the hands of local government officials. The Petrograd soviet, on the other hand, consisted largely of moderate socialists. It was responsible for coordinating the other soviets formed thoroughout Russia, and retained most of the real power of the provisional government.

Conflict between the two groups soon arose over control of the army and foreign policy. The increasingly powerful soviets of workers and soldiers pressed for social reform, the redistribution of land, and a negotiated settlement with the Central Powers. Yet ministers of the provisional government insisted that demands for domestic change must be subordinated to the war effort, which they defined in terms of previously declared imperialistic aims. They argued that basic governmental and economic reform should await the convening of the constituent assembly. Because the provisional ministers could not govern without the cooperation of the soviets, Kerensky, vice-chairman of the Petrograd soviet, entered the ministry in March as minister of war, leading the coalition government under Prince Georgi Lvov (1861–1925). In July 1917 Kerensky replaced Lvov as prime minister, and organized a government that managed to retain power for several months.

The Bolsheviks, who had failed to gain leadership positions in the provisional government, emerged as an increasingly formidable opposition party, as conflicts between ministers and soviets increased. On April 16, 1917, they gathered at Petrograd's Finland Station to welcome back Lenin, smuggled into Russia by Germans who welcomed his potential as a troublemaker for Kerensky's government. Throughout the spring and summer of 1917, while Kerensky was struggling to hold his government together, Lenin led the Bolsheviks on a bolder course that shunned all collaboration with the bourgeoisie and condemned their war policies. He soon became the leader of a vast popular uprising of workers, soldiers, and peasants; the Bolsheviks at this time clearly spoke to the people's needs as no other party did.

Meanwhile, opposition to the growing radicalization of the ministry—reflected in Kerensky's elevation to prime minister—encouraged conservatives and liberals to make common cause, and to mount a military action led by General Lavr Kornilov (1870–1918), the commander-in-chief of the army, against the government. The attempted coup in September 1917 was crushed. Yet Kerensky's own position had been undermined, his enemies on the Left arguing that Kornilov's ability to mount a counter-revolutionary effort was a sign of Kerensky's ineffectual leadership and willingness to compromise revolutionary aims. Although Lenin had been forced to seek refuge in Finland in mid-summer to escape prosecution as a German agent, he retained control of his party's activities. After Kornilov's failure, Lenin determined to seize power from Kerensky. In October he moved to Vyborg and concentrated on consolidating the Bolsheviks' agenda and sup-

Strife in Ireland, 1916. British troops raiding the office of a Dublin printer who supported the rebellion.

port base. When the second All-Russian Congress of Soviets convened on November 6, Lenin was ready.

On November 6, a coup d'état centered in Petrograd and directed by Lenin's ally Leon Trotsky (1879–1940) succeeded in overturning the provisional government. Lenin immediately proceeded to issue decrees that would give substance to the Bolsheviks' slogan of "Peace, Bread, and Land." "People's Commissars" (ministers) ordered the partition of land and its distribution to peasants, without compensation to former owners; nationalized banks, confiscating private accounts in the process; handed factory control over to workers; and began to negotiate a treaty with the Germans to end the war. The resulting agreement, signed at Brest-Litovsk in March 1918, surrendered Poland, Finland, and the Ukraine to the Germans. The treaty aroused the fury of Lenin's political enemies, both moderates and reactionaries, who were still a force to be reckoned with and who were prepared to plunge Russia into civil war rather than accept the revolution.

Successful coup and revolutionary changes

Yet another outbreak of revolution in this period was the so-called Easter Rebellion in Ireland. At the beginning of the world war, Irish nationalists, who resented the rule of their country by the British, were ripe for revolt. They had been promised self-rule on the eve of the war, but the British later reneged on the grounds that a national emergency must take preeminence over everything else. This greatly angered the Roman Catholic majority of southern Ireland. They scheduled Easter Sunday, 1916, as a day for revolt. British forces quelled the uprising, but not until a hundred people had been killed. Sporadic outbreaks kept the island in turmoil for years thereafter, but were finally brought to a temporary end by an agreement constituting southern Ireland as a free republic. The northern counties, or the province of Ulster, were to continue subject to the British crown.

The Easter Rebellion in Ireland

4. ARMISTICE AND PEACE

While the fighting raged on for four years, various attempts were made to bring about peace negotiations. In the spring of 1917, Dutch and Scandinavian socialists summoned an international socialist conference to meet at Stockholm to draft plans to end the fighting which would be acceptable to all the belligerents. The Petrograd soviet embraced the idea and on May 15 issued an appeal to socialists of all nations to send delegates to the conference and to induce their governments to agree to a peace "without annexations and indemnities, on the basis of the self-determination of peoples." The socialist parties in all the principal countries on both sides of the war accepted this formula and were eager to send delegates to the conference, but when the British and French governments refused to permit any of their subjects to attend, the project was abandoned. The rulers of the Allied states did not reject these proposals because they emanated from socialists. Indeed, a similar formula suggested by the pope was just as emphatically rejected. Nowhere was there a disposition to take peace proposals seriously. Woodrow Wilson, as spokesman for the Allies, declared that negotiation of peace under any conditions was impossible so long as Germany was ruled by the kaiser. The Central Powers regarded the general import of the papal suggestions with favor, but they refused to commit themselves on indemnities and restorations, especially the restoration of Belgium.

Peace proposals

The best known of all the peace proposals was President Wilson's program of Fourteen Points, which he incorporated in an address to Congress on January 8, 1918. Summarized as briefly as possible, this program included: (1) "open covenants openly arrived at," i.e., the abolition of secret diplomacy; (2) freedom of the seas in peace and war; (3) removal of economic barriers between nations; (4) reduction of national armaments "to the lowest point consistent with safety"; (5) impartial adjustment of colonial claims, with consideration for the interests of the peoples involved; (6) evacuation of Russia by foreign armies and general restoration of conquered territories in Russia; (7) restoration of the independence of Belgium; (8) restoration of Alsace and Lorraine to France; (9) a readjustment of Italian frontiers "along clearly recognizable lines of nationality"; (10) autonomous development for the peoples of Austria-Hungary; (11) restoration of Rumania, Serbia, and Montenegro, with access to the sea for Serbia; (12) autonomous development for the peoples of Turkey, with the straits from the Black Sea to the Mediterranean "permanently opened"; (13) an independent Poland, "inhabited by indisputably Polish populations," and with access to the sea; (14) establishment of a League of Nations. On several other occasions Wilson reiterated in public addresses that his program would be the basis of the peace for which he would work. Thousands of copies of the Fourteen Points were scattered by Allied planes over the German trenches and behind the lines, in an effort to convince both soldiers and civilians that the Allied nations were striving for a just and durable peace.

The Fourteen Points

Domestic conflict in Germany

With Russia now no longer a combatant, Germany appeared to have gained an advantage that would almost guarantee ultimate victory. Yet by the late spring of 1918 the Germans were suffering acutely, not only because of the continued effectiveness of the Allied blockade, but because of a growing domestic conflict over war aims. German socialists attacked expansionist goals—control of the steel- and coal-producing areas of Belgium and of the agricultural regions in Eastern Europe—which conservatives continued to urge and which the government endorsed. Socialists were alarmed as well by the reactionary administration imposed upon the territories taken from Russia at Brest-Litovsk. By the fall of 1918, Germany was a country on the verge of civil war.

The collapse of the Central Powers

Meanwhile, fighting continued as it had for four years on the Western Front. A great offensive launched by the British, French, and United States forces in July dealt one shattering blow after another to the German battalions and forced them back almost to the Belgian frontier. By the end of September the cause of the Central Powers appeared hopeless. Bulgaria withdrew from the war on September 29. Early in October the new chancellor of Germany, the liberal Prince Maximilian of Baden, appealed to President Wilson for a negotiated peace on the basis of the Fourteen Points. But the fighting went on, Wilson now demanding that Germany agree to depose the kaiser. Germany's remaining allies tottered on the verge of collapse. Turkey surrendered at the end of October. The Habsburg Empire was cracked open by rebellions on the part of the empire's subject nationalities. A German-Austrian offensive in Italy in October 1917 had gained them a major victory at Caporetto, where Italian military police were ordered to shoot their own soldiers, if necessary, to stem the retreat. Yet a year later, the Italians responded to a similar attack with a counteroffensive that cost Austria the city of Trieste and 300,000 prisoners. On November 3, 1918, Emperor Charles, who had succeeded Francis Joseph in 1916, signed an armistice that took Austria out of the war.

German Supplies Moving toward the Somme during the Last German Offensive in 1918

Germany was now left with the impossible task of carrying on the struggle alone. The morale of its troops was rapidly breaking. The Allied naval blockade was causing such a shortage of food that there was real danger of starvation. Revolutionary tremors that had been felt for some time swelled into an earthquake. On November 8 a republic was proclaimed in Bavaria. The next day nearly all of Germany was in the throes of revolution. A decree was published in Berlin announcing the kaiser's abdication, and early the next morning he was moved across the frontier into Holland. In the meantime, the government of the nation had passed into the hands of a provisional council headed by Friedrich Ebert (1871–1925), leader of the socialists in the Reichstag. Ebert and his colleagues immediately took steps to conclude negotiations for an armistice. The terms as now laid down by the Allied powers provided for acceptance of the Fourteen Points with three amendments. First, the item on freedom of the seas was to be stricken (in accordance with the request of the British). Second, restoration of invaded areas was to be interpreted in such a way as to include reparations, that is, payment to the victors to compensate them for their losses. Third, the demand for autonomy for the subject peoples of Austria-Hungary was to be changed to a demand for independence. In addition, troops of the Allied nations were to occupy cities in the Rhine valley; the blockade was to be continued in force; and Germany was to hand over 5,000 locomotives, 150,000 railway cars, and 5,000 trucks, all in good condition. The Germans could do nothing but accept these terms. At five o'clock in the morning of November 11, 1918, two delegates of the defeated nation met with the commander of the Allied armies, Marshal Foch, in the dark Compiègne forest and signed the papers officially ending the war. Six hours later the order "cease fire" was given to the troops. That night thousands of people danced through the streets of London, Paris, and Rome in the same delirium of excitement with which they had greeted the declarations of war four years before.

The signing of the armistice

The peace concluded at the various conferences in 1919 and 1920 more closely resembled a sentence from a court than a negotiated settlement. Propaganda had encouraged victorious soldiers and civilians to suppose that their sacrifices to the war effort would be compensated for by payments extracted from the "wicked" Germans. The British prime minister, David Lloyd George, campaigned during the election of 1918 on the slogan "Hang the Kaiser!", while one of his partisans demanded "Squeeze the German lemon until the pips squeak!" In all the Allied countries nationalism and democracy combined to make compromise impossible and to reassert the claim that the war was a crusade of good against evil. The peace settlement drafted by the victors inevitably reflected these feelings.

A harsh peace

The conference convoked in Paris* to draft a peace with Germany was technically in session from January until June of 1919, but only six plenary meetings were held. All of the important business of the conference was transacted by small committees. At first a Council of Ten was made up of

The Paris Conference

---

* The conference did most of its work in Paris. The treaty of peace with Germany, however, takes its name from Versailles, the suburb of Paris in which it was signed.

The Council of Four. Meeting to draft a peace treaty in Paris were Orlando of Italy, Lloyd George of Britain, Clemenceau of France, and Wilson of the United States.

the president and secretary of state of the United States, and the premiers and foreign ministers of Great Britain, France, Italy, and Japan. By the middle of March this body had been found too unwieldy and was reduced to the Council of Four, consisting of the American president and the English, Italian, and French premiers. A month later the Council of Four became the Council of Three when Premier Vittorio Orlando withdrew from the conference in a huff because Wilson refused to give Italy all it demanded.

The final character of the Treaty of Versailles was determined almost entirely by the so-called Big Three—Wilson, Lloyd George, and Clemenceau. These men were as different in personality as any three rulers who have ever come together for a common purpose. Wilson was an inflexible idealist, accustomed to dictating to subordinates and convinced that the hosts of righteousness were on his side. When confronted with unpleasant realities, such as secret treaties among the Allied governments for division of the spoils, he had a habit of dismissing them as unimportant and eventually forgetting that he had ever heard of them. Though he knew little of the devious maneuvers of European diplomacy, his unbending temperament made it difficult for him to take advice or to adjust his views to those of his colleagues. Lloyd George, the canny Welshman, possessed cleverness and Celtic humor that enabled him to succeed, on occasions, where Wilson failed; but he was above all a politician—shifty, and not particularly sympathetic to problems such as nationalism.

The Big Three: Wilson, Clemenceau, and Lloyd George

The third member of the great triumvirate was the aged and cynical French premier, Georges Clemenceau (1841–1929). A journalist in the United States just after the Civil War, Clemenceau later won his nickname of "the Tiger" as a relentless foe of clericals and monarchists. He fought for the republic during the stormy days of the Boulangist episode, the Dreyfus affair, and the struggle for separation of Church and state. Twice in his life-time he had seen France invaded and its existence gravely imperiled. Now the tables were turned, and the French, he believed, should take full advantage of their opportunity. Only by keeping a strict control over a prostrate Germany could the security of France be preserved.

From the beginning a number of embarrassing problems confronted the chief architects of the Versailles treaty. The most important was what to do about the Fourteen Points. There could be no doubt that they had been the basis of the German surrender on November 11. It was beyond question also that Wilson had represented them as the Allied program for a permanent peace. Consequently there was every reason for the peoples of the world to expect that the Fourteen Points would be the model for the Versailles settlement—subject only to the three amendments made before the armistice was signed. In actuality, however, no one among the highest dignitaries at the conference, with the exception of Wilson himself, gave more than lip service to the Fourteen Points. In the end, the American president was able to salvage, in unmodified form, only four parts of his famous program: point seven, requiring the restoration of Belgium; point eight, demanding the return of Alsace and Lorraine to France; point ten, providing for independence for the peoples of Austria-Hungary; and the final provision calling for a League of Nations. The others were ignored or modified to such an extent as to change their original meanings.

*Emasculating the
Fourteen Points*

Crowds Greet President Wilson in Paris after the War. Despite public demonstrations of this sort, Wilson's attempt to shape the peace was a failure.

By the end of April 1919 the terms of the Versailles treaty were ready for submission to the enemy, and Germany was ordered to send delegates to receive them. On April 29, a delegation headed by Count von Brock-dorff-Rantzau, foreign minister of the provisional republic, arrived in Versailles. When Brockdorff-Rantzau protested that the terms were too harsh, he was informed by Clemenceau that Germany would have three weeks to decide whether or not to sign. Eventually the time had to be extended, for the heads of the German government resigned their positions rather than accept the treaty. Their attitude was summed up by Chancellor Philip Scheidemann in the pointed statement: "What hand would not wither that sought to lay itself and us in those chains?" The Big Three now made a few minor adjustments, mainly at the insistence of Lloyd George, and Germany was notified that seven o'clock on the evening of June 23 must bring either acceptance or invasion. Shortly after five a new government of the provisional republic announced that it would yield to "overwhelming force" and accede to the victors' terms. On June 28, 1919, the fifth anniversary of the murder of the Austrian archduke, representatives of the German and Allied governments assembled in the Hall of Mirrors at Versailles and affixed their signatures to the treaty.

The provisions of the Treaty of Versailles can be outlined briefly. Germany was required to surrender Alsace and Lorraine to France, northern Schleswig to Denmark, and most of Posen and West Prussia to Poland. The coal mines of the Saar Basin were to be ceded to France, to be exploited by the French for fifteen years. At the end of this time the German government would be permitted to buy them back. The Saar territory itself was to be administered by the League of Nations until 1935, when a plebiscite would be held to determine whether it should remain under the league, be returned to Germany, or be awarded to France. Germany's province of East Prussia was cut off from the rest of its territory, and the port of Danzig, almost wholly German, was subjected to the political control of the League of Nations and the economic domination of Poland. Germany was disarmed, surrendering all its submarines and navy of surface vessels, with the exception of six small battleships, six light cruisers, six destroyers, and twelve torpedo boats. The Germans were forbidden to possess an air force, and their army was limited to 100,000 officers and men, to be recruited by voluntary enlistment. To make sure that Germany would not launch any new attack upon France or Belgium, it was forbidden to keep soldiers or maintain fortifications in the Rhine valley. Last, Germany and its allies were held responsible for all the loss and damage suffered by the Allied governments and their citizens, "as a consequence of the war imposed upon them by the aggression of Germany and her allies." This was the so-called war-guilt provision of the treaty (Article 231), and also the basis for German reparations. The exact amount that Germany should pay was left to a Reparations Commission. In 1921 the total was set at $33 billion.

For the most part, the Treaty of Versailles applied only to Germany.

Separate pacts were drawn up to settle accounts with Germany's allies—Austria-Hungary, Bulgaria, and Turkey. The final form of these treaties was determined primarily by a Council of Five, composed of Clemenceau as chairman and one delegate each from the United States, Great Britain, France, and Italy. The treaties reflected a desire on the part of their drafters to recognize the principle of national self-determination. The experience of the prewar years convinced diplomats that they must draw national boundaries to conform as closely as possible to the ethnic, linguistic, and historical traditions of the people they were to contain. Yet practical, political difficulties made such divisions impossible.

The goal of self-determination

The settlement with Austria, completed in September 1919, was known as the Treaty of St. Germain. Austria was required to recognize the independence of Hungary, Czechoslovakia, Yugoslavia, and Poland, and to cede to them large portions of its territory. In addition, Austria had to surrender Trieste, the south Tyrol, and the Istrian peninsula to Italy. Altogether the Austrian portion of the Dual Monarchy was deprived of three-fourths of its area and three-fourths of its people. Contrary to the principles of self-determination, in several of the territories surrendered the inhabitants were largely German-speaking—for example, in the Tyrol, and the region of the Sudeten mountains awarded to Czechoslovakia. The Austrian nation itself was reduced to a small, land-locked state, with nearly one-third of its population concentrated in the city of Vienna.

The treaty with Austria: The compromising of national self-determination

The second of the treaties with lesser belligerents was that with Bulgaria, which was signed in November 1919 and called the Treaty of Neuilly. Bulgaria was forced to give up nearly all of the territory it had gained since the First Balkan War. Land was ceded to Rumania, to the new kingdom of Yugoslavia, and to Greece. Here again, self-determination was compromised. All of these regions were inhabited by large Bulgarian minorities. Since Hungary was now an independent state, it was necessary that a separate treaty be imposed upon it. This was the Treaty of the Trianon Palace, signed in June 1920. It required that Slovakia be ceded to Czechoslovakia, Transylvania to Rumania, and Croatia-Slovenia to Yugoslavia. Nowhere was the principle of self-determination of peoples more flagrantly violated. Numerous sections of Transylvania had populations that were more than half Hungarian. Included in the region of Slovakia were not only Slovaks but almost a million Magyars and about 500,000 Ruthenians. As a consequence, a fanatical irredentist movement flourished in Hungary after the war, directed toward the recovery of these lost provinces. The Treaty of the Trianon Palace slashed the area of Hungary from 125,000 square miles to 35,000, and its population from 22 million to 8 million.

The treaties with Bulgaria and Hungary

The settlement with Turkey was a product of unusual circumstances. The secret treaties had contemplated the transfer of Constantinople and Armenia to Russia and the division of most of the remainder of Turkey between Britain and France. But Russia's withdrawal from the war after the Bolshevik Revolution, together with insistence by Italy and Greece upon fulfillment of promises made to them, necessitated considerable revision of

The Treaties of Sèvres and Lausanne with Turkey

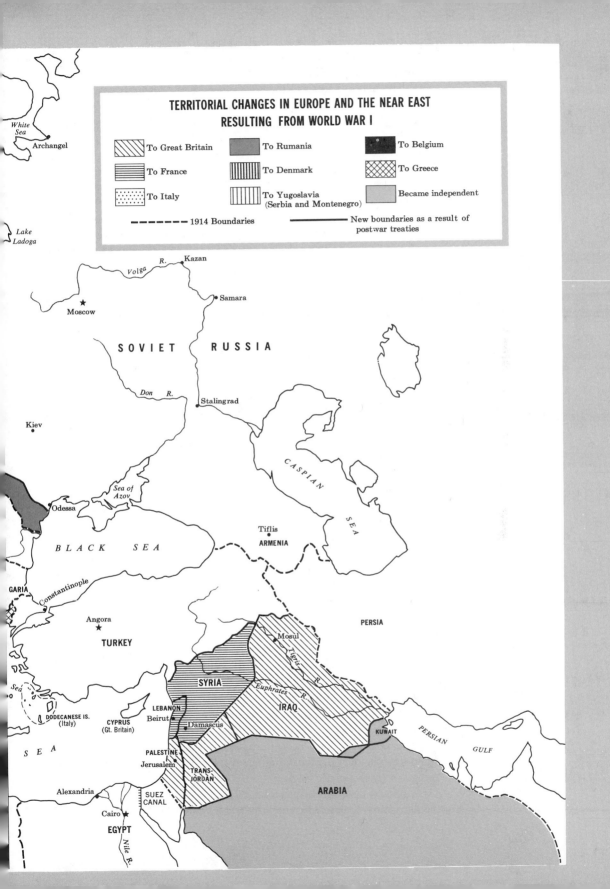

TERRITORIAL CHANGES IN EUROPE AND THE NEAR EAST
RESULTING FROM WORLD WAR I

To Great Britain

To France

To Italy

To Rumania

To Denmark

To Yugoslavia
(Serbia and Montenegro)

To Belgium

To Greece

Became independent

1914 Boundaries

New boundaries as a result of
postwar treaties

Kemal Atatürk

The League of Nations

the original scheme. Finally, in August 1920, a treaty was signed at Sèvres, near Paris, and submitted to the government of the sultan. It provided that Armenia be organized as a Christian republic; that most of Turkey in Europe be given to Greece; that Palestine and Mesopotamia become British "mandates," i.e., to remain under League of Nations control but to be administered by Britain; that Syria become a mandate of France; and that southern Anatolia be set apart as a sphere of influence for Italy. About all that would be left of the Ottoman Empire would be the city of Constantinople and the northern and central portions of Asia Minor. The decrepit government of the sultan, overawed by Allied military forces, agreed to accept this treaty. But a revolutionary government of Turkish nationalists, which had been organized at Ankara under the leadership of Mustapha Kemal (later called Atatürk; 1881–1938), determined to prevent acceptance of the settlement of Sèvres. The forces of Kemal obliterated the republic of Armenia, frightened the Italians into withdrawing from Anatolia, and conquered most of the territory in Europe which had been given to Greece. At last, in November 1922, they occupied Constantinople, deposed the sultan, and proclaimed Turkey a republic. The Allies now consented to a revision of the peace. A new treaty was concluded at Lausanne in Switzerland in 1923, which permitted the Turks to retain practically all of the territory they had conquered. Though much reduced in size compared with the old Ottoman Empire, the Turkish republic still had an area of about 300,000 square miles and a population of 13 million.

Incorporated in each of the five treaties that liquidated the war with the Central Powers was the Covenant of the League of Nations. The establishment of a league in which the states of the world, both great and small, would cooperate for the preservation of peace had long been the cherished dream of President Wilson. Indeed, that had been one of his chief reasons for taking the United States into the war. He believed that the defeat of Germany would mean the deathblow of militarism, and that the road would thenceforth be clear for setting up the control of international relations by a community of nations instead of by the cumbersome and ineffective balance of power. But to get the league accepted he found himself compelled to make numerous compromises. He permitted his original idea of providing for a reduction of armaments "to the lowest point consistent with domestic safety" to be changed into the altogether different phrasing of "consistent with national safety." To induce the Japanese to accept the league he allowed them to keep former German concessions in China. To please the French, he sanctioned the exclusion of both Germany and Russia from his proposed federation, despite his long insistence that it should be a league of *all* nations. These handicaps were serious enough. But the league received an even more deadly blow when it was repudiated by the very nation whose president had proposed it. The United States Congress, citing longstanding national preferences for isolation, refused to ratify American entry into the league.

Established under such unfavorable auspices, the league never achieved the aims of its founder. In only a few cases did it succeed in allaying the threat of war, and in each of these the parties to the dispute were small nations. But in every dispute involving one or more major powers, the league failed. It did nothing about the seizure of Vilna by Poland in 1920, because Lithuania, the victimized nation, was friendless, while Poland had the powerful backing of France. When, in 1923, war threatened between Italy and Greece, the Italians refused to submit to the intervention of the league, and the dispute was settled by direct mediation of Great Britain and France. Thereafter, in every great crisis the league was either defied or ignored. Its authority was flouted by Japan in seizing Manchuria in 1931 and by Italy in conquering Ethiopia in 1936. By September 1938, when the Czechoslovakian crisis arose, the prestige of the league had sunk so low that scarcely anyone thought of appealing to it. Yet the league justified its existence in other, less spectacular, ways. It reduced the international opium traffic and aided poor and backward countries in controlling the spread of disease. Its agencies collected invaluable statistics on labor and business conditions throughout the world. It conducted plebiscites in disputed areas, supervised the administration of internationalized cities, helped find homes for racial and political refugees, and made a notable beginning in codifying international law. Such achievements may well be regarded as providing a substantial groundwork for a later effort at international organization, the United Nations, formed after the Second World War.

*Successes and failures
of the league*

The league, with all its failings, was seen as the one promising result of the war that many soon recognized as a hideously wasteful carnage. The price would have been enormous even if all the results that were supposed to flow from an Allied victory had really been achieved. Altogether 8.5 million men died and more than twice that number were wounded. The total casualties—killed, wounded, and missing—numbered over 37 million. Germany lost 6 million and France almost as many, a larger proportion, indeed, of its total population. But despite these appalling losses, almost nothing was gained. The war that was to "end all wars" sowed the seeds of a new and more terrible conflict in the future. The autocracy of the kaiser was destroyed, but the ground was prepared for new despotisms. The First World War did nothing to abate either militarism or nationalism. Twenty years after the fighting had ended, there were nearly twice as many men under arms as in 1913; and national and ethnic rivalries and hatreds were as deeply ingrained as ever.

A war of waste

If the war failed to make the world less of an armed camp, it nevertheless altered it drastically in other ways. In the first place, it strengthened a belief in the efficacy of central planning and coordination. To sustain the war effort, the governments of all the major belligerents were forced to manage their economies by regulating industrial output, exercising a close control over imports and exports, and making the most effective use of manpower—both civilian and military. Second, the war upset the world trade balance. With few manufactured goods coming from Europe, Japanese, Indian, and South American capitalists were free to develop industries in their own countries. When the war was over, Europe found it had lost many of its previously guaranteed markets, and that it had become a debtor to the

Changes brought by the war

Women at Work. The all-out war effort combined with a manpower shortage at home brought women into factories across Europe in unparalleled numbers. On the left, men and women work side-by-side in a British shell factory. At the right, women toil in a German gun factory.

United States which, throughout the war, had lent large sums to the Allies. Third, while war was altering the patterns of world trade, it was also producing worldwide inflation. To finance their fighting, governments resorted to policies of deficit financing (spending above their income) and increased paper money that, with the shortage of goods, inflated their price. Inflation hit hardest at the middle class, those men and women who had lived on their income from invested money, and now saw that money worth far less than it once had been. Fourth, the war, while it brought hardships to most, brought freedom to many. Women were temporarily emancipated by their governments' need for them in factories and on farms. The contribution of women to the war effort undoubtedly explains the granting of female suffrage in both Great Britain and the United States in 1918 and 1920. Finally, despite this legacy of liberation, the war's most permanent contribution to the spirit of the postwar years was disillusion— particularly within the middle classes. A generation of men had been sacrificed—"lost"—to no apparent end. Many of those left alive were sickened by the useless slaughter, to which they knew they had contributed and for which they believed they must share at least part of the guilt. They were disgusted by the greedy abandonment of principles by the politicians at Versailles. Hatred and mistrust of the "old men" who had dragged the world into an unnecessary conflict, who had then mismanaged its direction with such ghastly results, and who had betrayed the cause of international peace for national gain soured the minds of many younger men and women in the postwar period. The British poet Edmund Blunden expressed this profound disillusionment when he took as the title for a poem, written to celebrate New Year's Day 1921, the biblical verse: "The dog is turned to his own vomit again, and the sow that was washed to her wallowing in the mire."

SELECTED READINGS

- *Items so designated are available in paperback editions.*

THE WORLD WAR AND THE PEACE SETTLEMENT

Albertini, Luigi, *The Origins of the War of 1914,* 3 vols., New York, 1952–1957. An exhaustive, valuable study.

Albrecht-Carré, Rene, ed., *The Meaning of the First World War,* Englewood Cliffs, N.J., 1965. The war's consequences for both soldiers and civilians.

- Balfour, Michael, *The Kaiser and His Times,* London, 1964. An excellent biography of William II.
- Falls, Cyril, *The Great War,* New York, 1961. A military history.

Feldman, Gerald D., *Army, Industry, and Labor in Germany, 1914–1918,* Princeton, 1966. The effect of war on the domestic economy.

- Ferro, Marc, *The Great War, 1914–1918,* London, 1973. Social and economic developments receive particular treatment.

Fischer, Fritz, *War of Illusions,* New York, 1975. Deals with Germany within the context of internal social and economic trends. See also his *Germany's Aims in the First World War,* mentioned in the preceding chapter.

- Fussell, Paul, *The Great War and Modern Memory,* New York, 1975. A brilliant examination of British intellectuals' attitudes toward the war.
- Hardach, Gerd, *The First World War, 1914–1918,* Berkeley, 1977. An excellent economic history of the war.
- Horne, Alistair, *The Price of Glory: Verdun, 1916,* New York, 1963.
- Lafore, Laurence D., *The Long Fuse: An Interpretation of the Origins of World War I,* 2nd ed., Philadelphia, 1971. Argues that the war was the result of obsolete institutions and ideas.

Laqueur, Walter, and G. L. Mosse, eds., *1914: The Coming of the First World War,* New York, 1969. An excellent series of essays by modern scholars.

- Marwick, Arthur, *The Deluge: British Society and the First World War,* Boston, 1965. The war's impact on the home front.

Mayer, Arno, *Politics and Diplomacy of Peacemaking: Containment and Counter-revolution at Versailles, 1918–1919,* New York, 1967. Emphasizes the role of the Russian Revolution in the peacemaking process.

- Moorehead, Alan, *Gallipoli,* London, 1956. A study of the British campaign.

Nicolson, Harold, *Peacemaking, 1919,* Boston, 1933. Written by a participant, provides a good account of the atmosphere of Versailles.

- Steiner, Zara S., *Britain and the Origins of the First World War,* New York, 1977. Argues that external rather than internal strains brought Britain into the war.
- Taylor, A. J. P., *English History, 1914–1945,* New York, 1965. An excellent treatment of the war and its impact on British society.

- Turner, L. C. F., *Origins of the First World War,* New York, 1970. Stresses Russia's role in the prewar diplomatic situation.
- Tuchman, Barbara, *The Guns of August,* New York, 1962. A popular account of the outbreak of war.
- Wheeler-Bennett, J. W., *Brest-Litovsk: The Forgotten Peace, March 1918,* London, 1939. An excellent study of personalities involved in the Russo-German peace treaty.

  Williams, John, *The Home Fronts: Britain, France and Germany, 1914–1918,* London, 1972. A survey of life away from the battlefield and the impact of the war on domestic life.

  Winter, J. M., *The Experience of World War I,* New York, 1989. Comprehensive illustrated history viewing the war from different perspectives.
- Wohl, Robert, *The Generation of 1914,* Cambridge, Mass., 1979. Uses generational analysis to explain attitudes toward the war.

  Zeman, Z. A. B., *The Break-up of the Hapsburg Empire, 1914–1918,* New York, 1961.

THE RUSSIAN REVOLUTION

- Deutscher, Isaac, *The Prophet Armed: Trotsky,* New York, 1954. The first volume of a magnificent biography of Trotsky; covers the years 1879–1921.

  Fischer, Louis, *The Life of Lenin,* New York, 1964. A lengthy, somewhat popularized biography by a journalist who was present during the revolution.

  Keep, John L. H., *The Russian Revolution,* New York, 1977.

  Pares, Bernard, *A History of Russia,* rev. ed., New York, 1953. A useful, straightforward survey.
- Pipes, Richard, *The Formation of the Soviet Union,* New York, 1964. A solid, reliable study.
- Rabinowitch, Alexander, *The Bolsheviks Come to Power,* New York, 1976. A well-researched and carefully documented account.
- Ulam, Adam, *The Bolsheviks,* New York, 1965. Analysis of both ideas and events.
- Wolfe, Bertram D., *Three Who Made a Revolution,* rev. ed., New York, 1964. A study of Lenin, Trotsky, and Stalin.

SOURCE MATERIALS

  Carnegie Foundation, Endowment for International Peace, *The Treaties of Peace, 1919–1923,* 2 vols., New York, 1924.

  Gooch, G. P., and H. Temperley, eds., *British Documents on the Origins of the War, 1898–1914,* London, 1927.
- Keynes, John Maynard, *The Economic Consequences of the Peace,* London, 1919. A contemporary attack upon the peace settlement, particularly the reparations agreements, by the brilliant economist who served on the British delegation to the peace conference.
- Owen, Wilfred, *Collected Poems,* London, 1963. Moving evidence of the horror of life at the front by Britain's most talented war poet.
- Reed, John, *Ten Days That Shook the World,* New York, 1919. (Many editions.) A contemporary account by a sympathetic American journalist of the Bolshevik Revolution.
- Remarque, Erich Maria, *All Quiet on the Western Front,* 1929. (Many editions.) A famous novel describing the war on the Western Front.

Chapter 28

TURMOIL BETWEEN THE WARS

Democracy of the West today is the forerunner of Marxism, which would be inconceivable without it. It is democracy alone which furnishes this universal plague with the soil in which it spreads. In parliamentarianism, its outward form of expression, democracy created a monstrosity of filth and fire. . . .

—Adolf Hitler, *Mein Kampf*

Among the claims made by the Allied Powers during the First World War was that an Allied victory would make the world "safe for democracy." The boast was grounded in a belief in the inevitability of progress, fostered by a century of growing material prosperity and by a habit of mind that found it all but impossible to equate the events of history with something other than the "advance" of civilization. The history of Europe in the 1920s and 1930s, however, would make it increasingly difficult for men and women to believe in progress as they had, or to assume that war might prove of ultimate benefit to mankind. These were decades of disillusionment and desperation, a circumstance brought about not only by the war itself but by the events that followed in the wake of war. Rather than encourage the growth of democracy, those events often caused its decline and fall. A number of Western nations remained democracies—Great Britain, France, and the United States being the most notable cases—yet they nevertheless experienced the same pressures and strains that in other countries resulted in the demise of democracy altogether.

Decline of democracy

Although the reasons for the decline of democracy in the West varied according to particular national circumstances, its failure can be attributed to several major causes. The foremost was a series of continuing disruptions in the world economy. These were brought about by dislocations that followed in the wake of the First World War and the Versailles reparations settlements, and by a worsening agricultural crisis that, in turn, helped precipitate the Great Depression after 1929. A second cause of democracy's

Reasons for the decline

decline was increased class conflict, often rooted in harsh economic realities. A major issue in most parts of continental Europe was whether control of governments and economic systems would remain in the hands of industrialists and financiers, unwilling to surrender more than a fraction of their considerable power to the less-privileged majorities which, at great sacrifice, had made major contributions to the war effort. The common people expected and had been promised that those contributions would be rewarded by greater attention to their political rights and economic needs. When they were ignored, they were naturally embittered, and hence prey to the blandishments of political extremists. Finally, nationalist sentiment encouraged discontent among minorities in the newly established states of Central Europe. Countries weakened by conflicts between national minorities were an unlikely proving ground for democracy, a political system that functions best in an atmosphere of unified national purpose.

Rise of authoritarian dictatorships

The political history of the interwar years must be understood not only in terms of the decline of democracy, however, but also against the background of the rise of authoritarian dictatorships in three major European nations—the Soviet Union, Italy, and Germany. As we shall see, the experiences of those three countries differed significantly, as a result of varying historical circumstances and personalities. Yet in each case, citizens of those countries allowed themselves to be persuaded—or bullied into accepting—that nothing short of radical measures would suffice to bring society to rights. Those measures included the use of violent force, intimidation, and propaganda to divert men and women from the pursuit of their individual interests and to deny them an increasingly large measure of human freedom. Their willingness to accept this sacrifice was a measure of their desperation.

1. THE SOVIET EXPERIENCE AND THE RISE OF STALIN

Lenin

Soon after the 1917 revolution in Russia, the country's desperate plight—a result of wartime devastation and tsarist corruption and mismanagement—compelled the Bolshevik leaders to exercise bold and often ruthless leadership. During this traumatic period, Lenin showed himself as capable a revolutionary administrator and politician as he had been a strategist. He commanded the respect and loyalty of his fellow Bolshevik ministers and won the confidence of the Russian people as well by speaking frankly to them of the dangers and difficulties inherent in a revolution as bold and all-consuming as theirs was. He was what he appeared to be: a selfless man, unwilling to claim special privileges for himself, wholly dedicated to the revolution that he had done so much to bring about. He cared nothing for luxury or personal glory, living an almost monklike existence in two rooms in the Kremlin, and dressing little better than an ordinary worker.

Lenin's ablest and most prominent lieutenant was Leon Trotsky (1879–1940). Originally named Lev Bronstein, Trotsky was born of mid-

Lenin Speaking to Crowds in Moscow. To the right of the platform, in uniform, is Trotsky.

dle-class Jewish parents in the Ukraine. Before the revolution he had refused to identify himself with any particular faction, preferring to remain an independent Marxist. For his part in the revolutionary movement of 1905 he was exiled to Siberia; he escaped, and for some years led a roving existence in various European capitals. He was expelled from Paris in 1916 for pacifist activity and took refuge in the United States. Upon learning of the overthrow of the tsar, he attempted to return to Russia. Captured by British agents at Halifax, Nova Scotia, he was eventually released through the intervention of Alexander Kerensky. He arrived in Russia in April 1917 and immediately began plotting the overthrow of the provisional government and later of Kerensky himself. He became minister of foreign affairs in the government headed by Lenin, and later, commissar for war.

Trotsky

Scarcely had the Bolsheviks concluded the war with the Central Powers than they were confronted with a desperate civil war at home. Landlords and capitalists did not take kindly to the loss of their property. The result was a prolonged and bloody combat between the Reds, or Bolsheviks, and the Whites, including not only reactionary tsarists but also disaffected liberals, Social Revolutionaries, Mensheviks, and peasants. The Whites were assisted for a time by expeditionary forces of British, French, American, and Japanese troops—hoping to defeat the Bolsheviks in order to bring Russia back into the war against Germany—and later by the armies of the newly created republic of Poland. Under the direction of Trotsky, who appealed to the Russian people both in the name of revolution and the fatherland, the Red army was mobilized to a degree that allowed it to withstand both the foreign invaders and the Russian insurgents. By 1922, the Bolsheviks had managed to stabilize their boundaries, although to do so they were forced to cede former Russian territory to the Finns, to the Baltic states of Latvia and Estonia, to Poland, and to Rumania. Internally, the Bolsheviks

The civil war

See color map of the Soviet Union following page 940

The Red Army, 1919. This scene near the southern front shows the celebration of victory over counter-revolutionary forces.

responded to the White counter-revolution by instituting a "terror" far more extensive than the repression that had earned that name during the French Revolution. A secret police force shot thousands of suspects and hostages. The tsar and tsarina and their children were executed by local Bolsheviks in July 1918 as White forces advanced on the town of Ekaterinburg, where the family was held prisoner. That same year "enemies of the state" were hunted down in large numbers following the attempted assassination of Lenin. The terror abated when the regime had satisfied itself that it had destroyed its internal opposition.

Economic and constitutional changes

The civil war was accompanied by an appalling economic breakdown. In 1920 total industrial production was only 13 percent of what it had been in 1913. To alleviate the shortage of goods, the government abolished the payment of wages and distributed supplies among urban workers in proportion to their need. All private trade was prohibited; everything produced by the peasants above what they required to subsist was requisitioned by the state. This system was an expedient to crush bourgeois opposition to the revolutionary regime and to obtain as much food as possible for the army in the field. In 1921 it was superseded by the New Economic Policy (NEP), which Lenin described as "one step backward in order to take two steps forward." The NEP authorized private manufacturing and private trade on a small scale, reintroduced the payment of wages, and permitted peasants to sell their grain in the open market. In 1924 a constitution was adopted, replacing imperial Russia with the Union of Soviet Socialist Republics. The union represented an attempt to unite the various nationalities and territories that had constituted the old empire. Each separate republic was, in theory, granted certain autonomous rights. In fact, government remained centralized in the hands of a few leaders. Further, central authority was maintained by means of the one legal political party—the Communist party—whose Central Committee was the directing force behind both politics and government, and whose organizational apparatus reached out into all areas of the vast country.

The philosophy of Bolshevism, now known as communism, was developed primarily by Lenin during these years. It was proclaimed not as a new body of thought, but as a strict interpretation of Marx's writings. Nevertheless, from the beginning it departed at several important points from Marx's teachings. These changes were the necessary result of the fact that Marx had expected revolution to occur first in highly industrialized countries, whereas it had in fact broken out and succeeded in one of the least industrialized nations in Europe. Marx had assumed that a capitalist stage must prepare the way for socialism; Lenin denied that this was necessary, insisting rather that Russia could leap directly from a feudal to a socialist economy. In the second place, Lenin emphasized the revolutionary character of socialism much more than did its original founder. Marx did believe that in most cases revolution would be necessary, but he was inclined to deplore the fact rather than to welcome it. Finally, communism differed from Marxism in its conception of proletarian rule. When Marx spoke of the "dictatorship of the proletariat," he meant by this a dictatorship of the whole working class over the remnants of the bourgeoisie. Within the ranks of this class, democratic forms would prevail. Lenin, however, was persuaded by the desperate circumstances attendant upon the birth of the Soviet Union to proclaim the need for a dictatorship by the party elite, wielding supremacy not only over the bourgeoisie but over the bulk of the proletariat.

The death of Lenin in January 1924 precipitated a struggle among vari-

Left: *Lenin's Casket Is Carried through the Streets of Moscow*. It was not known with certainty until 1956 that, prior to his death, Lenin had discredited Stalin. Right: *Lenin and Stalin*. Under Stalin this picture was used to show his close relationship with Lenin. In fact, the photograph has been doctored.

ous factions to inherit his mantle of power. Outside of the Soviet Union it was generally assumed that Trotsky would succeed the fallen leader. But the fiery commander of the Red army had a formidable rival in the tough and mysterious Joseph Stalin (1879–1953). The son of a peasant shoemaker in the province of Georgia, Stalin received part of his education in a theological seminary. Expelled at the age of seventeen for "lack of religious vocation," he thereafter dedicated his career to revolutionary activity.

The struggles between Trotsky and Stalin

In 1922 Stalin assumed the secretary-generalship of the Communist party which, in the years that followed, became the heart of the government. Theoretically, the Soviet Union was ruled by a Central Executive Committee, which in turn represented local, provincial, and regional Councils of Workers and Peasants. Because the Central Executive did not remain in continuous session, however, power increasingly fell into the hands of that body responsible for day-to-day operations and decisions: the Council of the People's Commissars—that is, the various departmental ministers. These commissars were nominated by, and were themselves members of, the Communist party. In his position as the party's secretary-general, Stalin was ultimately able to control nominations to the Council of Commissars, and thus to fill the government with party members loyal to him.

Stalin and the party

The battle over Lenin's succession was not simply a struggle for personal power; fundamental issues of political policy were also involved. Trotsky maintained that socialism in the Soviet Union could never be entirely successful until capitalism was overthrown in surrounding countries. Therefore, he insisted upon a continuous crusade for world revolution. Once European governments appeared to stabilize, as they did after 1924, that goal seemed increasingly unrealistic to many. Trotsky's enemies, most notably Nikolai Bukharin (1888–1938), argued in favor of a program that would expand the revolution within the Soviet Union by transferring wealth from the agricultural to the industrial sector of society. Stalin came to accept this view, preaching the goal of "socialism in one country." His advocacy of forced collectivization of peasant farms and of a crash program of industrialization won him further support within the party, since it was clearly the party that would spearhead this drastic change. Stalin's essentially nationalistic strategy had triumphed by the end of the decade. His rivals—most notably Trotsky—were officially disgraced. In 1927 Trotsky was expelled from the Communist party, and two years later he was driven from the country. In 1940 he was murdered in Mexico City by Stalinist agents. Others, including Gregory Zinoviev and Lev Kamenev, were convicted of crimes against the state in public trials and executed in the 1930s.

World revolution

Once Stalin consolidated his power, he reinforced the role of the party as a state within a state, with its own bureaucrats—the *apparatchiki*—assuming ever-increasing influence in the administration of the country and in the determination of its fortunes. He insisted that the Soviet Union's first priority was economic well-being. His major reform was the introduction of the so-called Five-Year Plan, based on the conviction that the Soviet Union had to take drastic steps to industrialize and thereby achieve economic parity among the nations of the world. The plan instituted an elaborate system of priorities. It decreed how much of each major industrial and agricultural

The party and the state: Five-Year Plan

Panel (3) of Painting Number 200 (1914), Wassily Kandinsky (1866–1944). The expressionist painters carried their explorations of the psychological properties of color and line to the point where subject matter was deemed unnecessary and even undesirable. (Oil on canvas, 64 x 31½." Collection, The Museum of Modern Art, New York. Mrs. Simon Guggenheim Fund)

Nude Descending a Staircase, Marcel Duchamp (1887–1968). An example of the impact of film on painting. The effect is that of a series of closely spaced photographs coalescing to create motion. (Philadelphia Museum of Art)

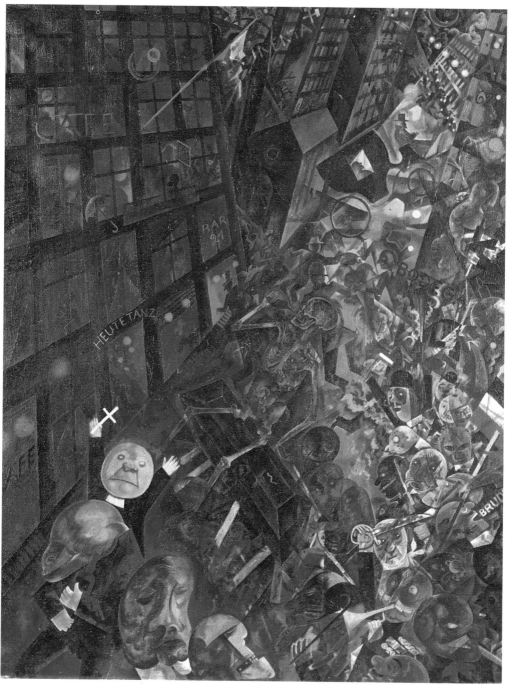

The Funeral Procession, George Grosz (1893–1959). Painted in the late stages of the First World War, this portrayal of a funeral procession gone mad shows death triumphant as humanity is swept into a hell of its own making. The work expressed an anger and a loathing felt by an entire generation. (Reproduced by Permission of the Estate of George Grosz, Princeton, New Jersey)

I and the Village (1911), Marc Chagall (1887–1985). The subject refers to the artist's childhood and youth in Vitebsk, Russia. The profile on the right is probably that of the artist himself. (Oil on canvas, 6' 3⅝" x 59⅝." Collection, The Museum of Modern Art, New York. Mrs. Simon Guggenheim Fund.)

The Table (1928), Georges Braque (1881–1963). An example of later cubism showing the predominance of curvilinear form and line instead of geometric structure. (Oil and sand on canvas, 70¾ x 28¾." Collection, The Museum of Modern Art, New York. Acquired through the Lillie P. Bliss Bequest)

The Persistence of Memory (1931), Salvador Dali (1904–1989). The Spaniard Dali is the outstanding representative of the surrealist school. Many objects in his paintings are Freudian images. (Oil on canvas, 9½ x 13" Collection, The Museum of Modern Art, New York. Purchase)

Barricade (1931), José Clemente Orozco (1883–1949). The Mexican muralist Orozco was one of the most celebrated of contemporary painters with a social message. His themes were revolutionary fervor, satire of aristocracy and the Church, and deification of the common man. (Oil on canvas, 55 x 45." Collection, The Museum of Modern Art, New York. Given anonymously)

Mystery and Melancholy of a Street, Giorgio de Chirico (1888–1978). Employing perspective to fashion familiar components into dreamscapes fraught with anxiety and loneliness, de Chirico had a profound effect on the surrealists. (Lee Boltin)

Around the Fish (1926), Paul Klee (1879–1940). Klee is recognized as the most subtle humorist of twentieth-century art. The central motif of a fish on a platter suggests a banquet, but many of the surrounding objects appear to be products of fantasy. (Oil on canvas, 18⅜ x 25⅛." Collection, The Museum of Modern Art, New York. Abby Aldrich Rockefeller Fund)

Detroit Industry (Detail) by Diego Rivera. Painted between 1931 and 1933, this work aimed to depict the social conditions of the modern world, especially the struggles and triumphs of the working class. (Detroit Institute of Arts)

City Building by Thomas Hart Benton. Painted in 1930 as part of *America Today*, Benton's work also shows the hard labor of the workers. (Collection, The Equitable)

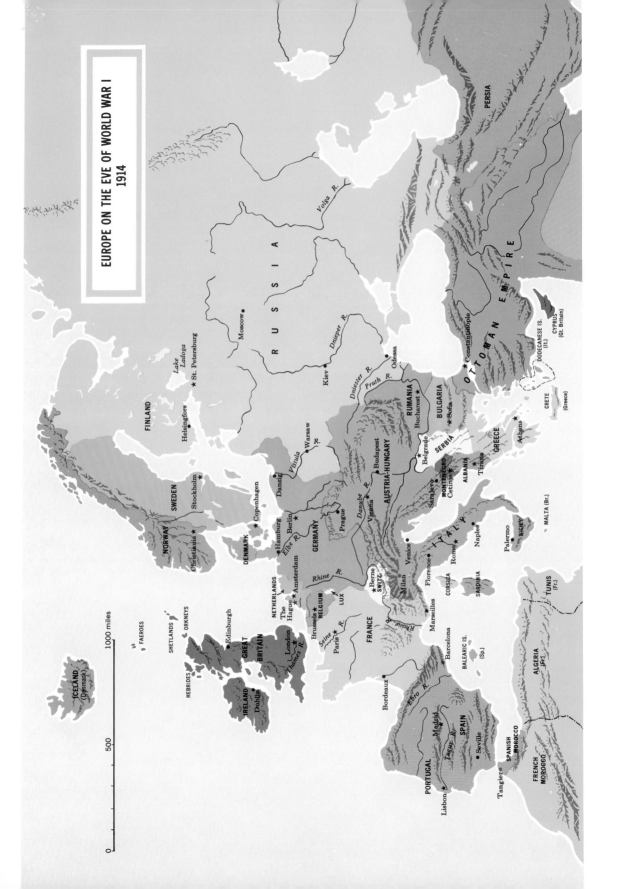

EUROPE ON THE EVE OF WORLD WAR I
1914

THE SOVIET UNION • 1918-1945

The Union of Soviet Socialist
Republics in 1939

Annexed 1940-45

ARCTIC OCEAN

SEA OF OKHOTSK

SEA OF JAPAN

JAPAN

KOREA

Vladivostock

SAKHALIN I.

Khabarovsk

Amur R.

MANCHURIA

Chita

CHINA

Yakutsk

Lena R.

R U S S I A N   S O V I E T   F E D E R A T E D   S O C I A L I S T   R E P U B L I C

Lake Baikal

Irkutsk

Ulan-Bator

MONGOLIA

1000 miles

Krasnoyarsk

Yenisei R.

Novosibirsk

SINKIANG

Omsk

Ob R.

Alma-Ata

KIRGIZ S.S.R.

Frunze

Tashkent

Dushanbe

TADZHIK S.S.R.

KAZAKH S.S.R.

UZBEK S.S.R.

AFGHANISTAN

Ashkabad

TURKMEN S.S.R.

Murmansk

Archangel

URAL MTS.

Perm

Sverdlovsk

Chelyabinsk

Orenburg

Volga R.

Kazan

Kuibyshev

Aral Sea

NORWAY

SWEDEN

Gulf of Bothnia

FINLAND

Helsinki

Kronstadt

Leningrad

Tallinn

Riga

Kalinin

ESTONIAN S.S.R.

LATVIAN S.S.R.

LITHUANIAN S.S.R.

Kaunas

Grodno

WHITE RUSSIAN S.S.R.

Minsk

Bobruisk

Gomel

Danzig

POLAND

Warsaw

Brest-
Litovsk

CZECHOSLOVAKIA

HUNG.

RUMANIA

MOLDAVIAN S.S.R.

Kishinev

Nikolaev

Odessa

Kiev

UKRAINIAN S.S.R.

Kharkov

Orekhovo

Moscow

Yaroslavl

Ivanovo

Gorki

Don R.

Saratov

Stalingrad

Rostov

Krasnodar

Novorossisk

Pyatigorsk

CAUCASUS MTS.

GEORGIAN S.S.R.

Tiflis

ARMENIAN S.S.R.

Erivan

AZERBAIDZHAN S.S.R.

Baku

CASPIAN SEA

BLACK SEA

TURKEY

SYRIA

IRAQ

IRAN

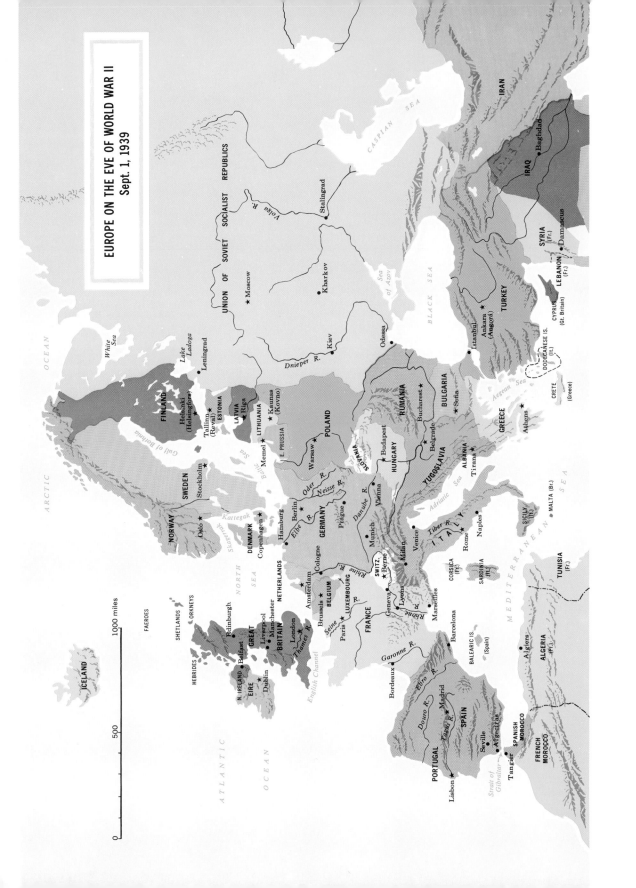

EUROPE ON THE EVE OF WORLD WAR II
Sept. 1, 1939

ICELAND

FAEROES

SHETLANDS

ORKNEYS

HEBRIDES

N. IRELAND
Belfast

EIRE
Dublin

GREAT
BRITAIN

Edinburgh

Liverpool
Manchester

London

Thames R.

English Channel

NORWAY
Oslo

SWEDEN
Stockholm

FINLAND
Helsinki
(Helsingfors)

ESTONIA
Tallinn
(Reval)

LATVIA
Riga

LITHUANIA
Kaunas
(Kovno)

Memel

E. PRUSSIA

DENMARK
Copenhagen

Kattegat

Skagerrak

NORTH
SEA

White
Sea

Lake
Ladoga

Leningrad

Gulf of Bothnia

Baltic Sea

ARCTIC

OCEAN

ATLANTIC
OCEAN

NETHERLANDS
Amsterdam

BELGIUM
Brussels

LUXEMBOURG

FRANCE
Paris

Seine

Hamburg
Berlin

GERMANY

Cologne

Rhine R.

Elbe R.

Oder R.

Neisse R.

POLAND
Warsaw

Prague

Munich

Vienna

Danube R.

SWITZ.
Berne
Geneva

Lyons

Rhône R.

Marseilles

Bordeaux

Garonne R.

SPAIN
Madrid

Tagus R.

PORTUGAL
Lisbon

Douro R.

Seville

Ebro R.

Barcelona

BALEARIC IS.
(Spain)

Algeciras

Tangier

Strait of
Gibraltar

SPANISH
MOROCCO

FRENCH
MOROCCO

ALGERIA
(Fr.)
Algiers

MEDITERRANEAN

TUNISIA
(Fr.)

SEA

SARDINIA
(It.)

CORSICA
(Fr.)

Milan

Venice

Tiber R.

Rome

Naples

ITALY

SICILY
(It.)

MALTA (Br.)

Adriatic Sea

SLOVENIA

HUNGARY
Budapest

YUGOSLAVIA
Belgrade

ALBANIA
Tirana

RUMANIA
Bucharest

BULGARIA
Sofia

GREECE
Athens

Aegean Sea

CRETE
(Greece)

DODECANESE IS.
(It.)

CYPRUS
(Gt. Britain)

TURKEY
Ankara
(Angora)

Istanbul

BLACK SEA

Odessa

Dnieper R.

Kiev

Kharkov

Sea
of Azov

UNION OF SOVIET SOCIALIST REPUBLICS

Moscow

Stalingrad

Volga R.

CASPIAN SEA

IRAN

IRAQ
Baghdad

SYRIA
(Fr.)
Damascus

LEBANON
(Fr.)

1000 miles

500

0

commodity the nation should produce, the wages workers should receive, and the prices that should be charged for goods sold at home and abroad. The first plan, instituted in 1928, was succeeded by others during the 1930s. In some areas goals were met, in a few they were exceeded, in some they fell short. One of the major results of the Five-Year Plans was the creation of an extensive state bureaucracy, charged with the task of organization and supervision at all levels.

Included in the first plan was a program for agricultural collectivization. The scheme was designed to bring rural farms together into larger units of several thousand acres, under the communal proprietorship of peasants. Only with this sort of reorganization, the Soviet Union's rulers declared, could the new and expensive processes of mechanization be introduced, and the country's agricultural yield thereby increased. Not surprisingly, the argument failed to win the support of the more prosperous farmers—the *kulaks*—who had been allowed to retain ownership of their land. Their opposition led to another terror, made all the more deadly by a famine that occurred in southeastern Russia in 1932. The kulaks were liquidated, either killed or transported to distant labor camps; the rural bourgeoisie was eliminated, to be replaced by a rural proletariat. Collectivization was an accomplished fact by 1939. To a vast number of Russians it represented a revolution far more immediate than that of 1917. Twenty million people were moved off the land, which, once it had been reorganized into larger units, and production had been mechanized, required fewer laborers. They were sent to cities, where most went to work in factories. Although agricultural output did not increase during the early years of collectivization, the scheme was nevertheless of benefit to the government. By controlling production, the central bureaucracy was able to regulate the distribution of agricultural products, allocating them for export, where necessary, to pay for the importation of much-needed industrial machinery.

Agricultural collectivization

"The Five-Year Plan in Four Years." Stalin faces down reactionary capitalist enemies in this Soviet propaganda poster of the 1930s.

The Third International

Cooperation with Western European powers

socialism almost gone!

The constitution of 1936

The purge trials

As part of Stalin's campaign to put the interests of the Soviet Union ahead of those of international communism, the Bolshevik regime adopted a new and more conservative foreign policy during the 1930s. Its international goals contradicted the militant socialist internationalism of the 1920s. Lenin had supported revolutionary leftist movements in Europe, sending money and lending moral support to the radical German Marxists Karl Liebknecht and Rosa Luxemburg in 1919 (see below p. 948), and to the short-lived Soviet regime of the Bolshevik Béla Kun in Hungary in the same year. Shortly thereafter, the Third International—later called the Comintern—was formed. It declared its allegiance to international communism; its policy was to oppose cooperation or collaboration with the capitalist governments of the West and to work for their overthrow.

With Stalin's suppression of the internationalism advocated by Lenin and Trotsky, however, came a change in tactics and the revival of an interest in playing the game of power politics. The Soviet army was more than doubled in size and was reorganized in accordance with the Western European model. Patriotism, which strict Marxists despised as a form of capitalist propaganda, was exalted into a Soviet virtue. When Germany once again appeared to threaten Soviet security, as it did in the 1930s, the Soviet leadership looked abroad for allies. Along with their efforts to build up a great army and to make their own country self-sufficient, they adopted a policy of cooperation with the Western European powers. In 1934 they entered the League of Nations, and in 1934 they ratified a military alliance with France.

In June 1936, the Soviets adopted a new constitution, some of whose provisions suggested the possibility of a more liberal regime. Power continued to reside in a governing body (the Presidium) and an administrative agency (the Council of Ministers), both of which were chosen by a two-chamber parliament, the Supreme Soviet, which was elected, in turn, by universal suffrage. This pyramidal structure was not unlike that which it superseded and which, because of the dominant position of the Communist party, had resulted in the concentration of power in the person of Stalin. Now, however, the constitution provided citizens with a bill of rights guaranteeing freedom of speech, of assembly, and of religion. In addition, they were promised the right to employment, the right to leisure, and the right to maintenance at the expense of the state in case of old age or disability.

These guarantees meant very little, however, so long as all aspects of life in the Soviet Union continued to be dominated by the Communist party, whose membership of about 1 million in 1930 was but a small fraction of the total population of 150 million. That the new "bill of rights" was a sham was quickly proved by a series of purges that began shortly after the constitution was adopted. In August 1936, the first of several "show trials" occurred, at which persons alleged to be "Trotskyites" and spies were publicly condemned and either imprisoned, executed, or exiled to Siberia. Although the accused for the most part confessed to their "crimes," those confessions were obtained by physical and psychological torture.

Stalin's victims—almost 9 million imprisoned, banished, or killed—were people at all levels who had opposed his personal rule, men such as Bukharin, now editor of the newspaper *Izvestia,* who had spoken out against the elimination of the kulaks; Karl Radek, a leading political theorist; and a number of "old" Bolsheviks, who had been unwilling to acquiesce in Stalin's refusal to debate policy, who had opposed his increasingly nationalistic foreign policy, or who had hoped that revolution did not mean the complete suppression of personal liberty.

The results of the Soviet revolution were profound. No other regime in the history of Western Europe had ever attempted to reorder completely the politics, economy, and society of a vast nation as the Soviets had in the short space of twenty years. By 1939 private manufacturing and trade had been almost entirely abolished. Factories, mines, railroads, and public utilities were exclusively owned by the state. Stores were either government enterprises or cooperatives in which consumers owned shares. Agriculture had been almost completely socialized. At the same time, the nation had been industrialized. By 1932 over 70 percent of the Soviet Union's national product was industrial in origin. In the area of social reform, illiteracy was reduced from at least 50 percent to about 20 percent, and higher education was made available to increasingly large numbers. Government assistance for working mothers and free hospitalization did a great deal to raise the national standard of health.

But those achievements were purchased at a very high price. In addition to the liquidation of millions of kulaks and political dissidents and the internment of millions of others in slave-labor camps, the Soviet people were subjected to an unrelenting campaign of indoctrination that encompassed every aspect of their lives. Subtle forms of persecution were implemented to discourage religious orthodoxy while the nation's youth were inculcated with the new Soviet ideals of steadfast loyalty to the Soviet state and unquestioning obedience to the Communist party. Over time, experiments in the arts and literature, which had been promoted during the early years of the revolution under Lenin, gave way to the culture of authoritarian bureaucracy. The composers Sergei Prokofiev (1891–1953) and Dmitri Shostakovich (1906–1975), the poet Vladimir Mayakovsky (1893–1930), the writer Maxim Gorky (1868–1936) and his protégé Isaac Babel (1894–1941), the filmmaker Sergei Eisenstein (1898–1948), and other creative men and women flourished in the Soviet Union during the 1920s. Although most of them continued to work through the following decade and after, those who remained in official favor were compelled to compromise their art to conform to the dictates of Stalin's Soviet Union.

Education became a tool of the revolution, much as violence and intimidation had. Control of the minds of the populace was regarded as a prerequisite to building a new society in which individual interests would be sacrificed to those of the state. After two decades of revolutionary change, the Stalinist regime had fastened upon the Soviet people a tyranny as heavy as any imposed by the tsars.

2. THE EMERGENCE OF FASCISM IN ITALY

Italy's long-term problems

That Italy turned its back on democracy may at first seem surprising, in view of the fact that the Italians emerged as victors after the First World War. Yet Italy's difficulties were rooted in longstanding problems that the war had done little to resolve. Italy continued to be divided into two sharply contrasting halves: a relatively prosperous industrialized north, and a wretchedly poor agrarian south. In addition to the problems the country faced as a result of that unhealthy economic split, it was also the victim of an unrequited imperialist impulse that had existed since the 1890s. Its unsuccessful attempts to establish itself as a power in North Africa had left the country with a sense of frustration and humiliation. Before the war, the ruling class was held in public contempt by a younger generation anxious to cleanse the nation of rulers widely perceived to be at once cynical and corrupt, vaccilating and defeatist.

The demoralizing and humiliating effects of the war

Yet the establishment of a dictatorship in Italy would never have been possible without the demoralizing and humiliating effects of the First World War. The chief business of the Italian armies had been to keep the Austrians occupied on the Southern Front while the British, French, and Americans hammered Germany into submission along the battle lines in the west. To accomplish this assignment, Italy had mobilized more than 5,500,000 men; of these nearly 700,000 were killed. The direct financial cost of Italian participation in the struggle was over $15 billion. These sacrifices were no greater than those made by the British and the French; but Italy was a poor country. Moreover, in the division of the spoils after the fighting, the Italians got less than they expected. While Italy did receive most of the Austrian territories promised in the secret treaties, the Italians maintained that these were inadequate rewards for their sacrifices and for their valuable contribution to an Allied victory. At first the nationalists vented their spleen for the "humiliation of Versailles" upon President Wilson, but after a short time they returned to castigating their own rulers. They alleged Premier Orlando had been so cravenly weak and inept that he and those who governed with him had allowed their country to be cheated of its just deserts.

Inflation, radicalism, and economic chaos

The war contributed to the revolutionary mood in a multitude of other ways. It resulted in inflation of the currency, with consequent high prices, speculation, and profiteering. Normally wages would have risen also, but the postwar labor market was glutted by the return to civilian life of millions of soldiers. Furthermore, business was demoralized, owing to extensive and frequent strikes and to the closing of foreign markets. In the minds of the upper and middle classes the most ominous consequence of the war was the growth of socialism. As hardship and chaos increased, the Italian socialists embraced a philosophy akin to Bolshevism. They voted as a party to join the Third International. In the elections of November 1919, they won about a third of the seats in the Chamber of Deputies. During the fol-

Left: *Mussolini Reviews a Fascist Youth Parade*. Totalitarianism demanded the capture of youthful minds. Right: *Mussolini Addressing a Crowd of His Followers from the Balcony of the Palazzo Venezia in Rome.*

lowing winter socialist workers took over about a hundred factories and attempted to run them for the benefit of the workers. Radicalism also spread through rural areas, where so-called Red Leagues organized to break up large estates and to force landlords to reduce their rents. Two large political parties with mass appeal, the Socialists and the Catholic People's party, drained strength from other parties of the Center and moderate Left. Neither preached revolution; yet both urged far-reaching social and economic reforms. Industrialists and landowners were badly frightened and were therefore ready to accept totalitarianism as a less dangerous form of radicalism that might save at least part of their property from confiscation.

How much the Fascist movement depended for its success upon the leadership of Benito Mussolini (1883–1945) is difficult to say. Mussolini was the son of a socialist blacksmith. His mother was a schoolteacher, and in deference to her wishes he eventually became a teacher. But he was restless and dissatisfied, soon leaving Italy for further study in Switzerland. Here he gave part of his time to his books and the rest to writing articles for socialist newspapers. He was eventually expelled from the country for fomenting strikes. Returning to Italy, he became a journalist, and eventually editor of *Avanti,* the leading socialist daily. His ideas in the years before the war were a contradictory mixture of radicalisms. He professed to be a Marxist socialist, but he mingled his socialism with doctrines of corporatism, adapted from the French syndicalists.

The career of Mussolini

Mussolini in fact believed in no particular set of doctrines. No man with a definite philosophy could have reversed himself so often. When war broke out in August 1914, Mussolini insisted that Italy should remain neu-

Mussolini's contradictory ideas

tral. He had scarcely adopted this position when he began urging participation on the Allied side. Deprived of his position as editor of *Avanti,* he founded a new paper, *Il Popolo d'Italia,* and dedicated its columns to arousing enthusiasm for war. He regarded the decision of the government the following spring to go in on the side of the Allies as a personal victory.

The evolution of fascism

The word *fascism* derives from the Latin *fasces,* the ax surrounded by a bundle of sticks representing the authority of the Roman state; the Italian *fascio* means group or band. *Fasci* were organized as early as October 1914, as units of agitation to drive Italy into the war. Their members were young idealists, fanatical nationalists, and frustrated white-collar workers. The original platform of the Fascist party was drafted by Mussolini in 1919. It was a surprisingly radical document, which demanded universal suffrage, abolition of the conservative Senate, the establishment by law of an eight-hour day, a heavy capital levy, a heavy tax on inheritances, confiscation of 85 percent of war profits, acceptance of the League of Nations, and "opposition to all imperialisms." This platform was accepted more or less officially by the movement until May 1920, when it was supplanted by another of a more conservative character. Indeed, the new program omitted all reference to economic reform. On neither of these platforms did the fascists achieve much political success.

The march on Rome

The fascists made up for their initial lack of numbers by disciplined aggressiveness and strong determination. As the old regime crumbled, they prepared to take over the government. In September 1922, Mussolini began to talk openly of revolution. On October 28 an army of about 50,000 fascist militia, in blackshirted uniforms, marched into Rome and occupied the capital. The premier resigned, and the following day the king, Victor Emmanuel III, invited Mussolini to form a cabinet. Without firing a shot the blackshirts had gained control of the Italian government. The explanation of their success is to be found not in the strength of fascism, but in the chaos created by the war and in the weakness and irresolution of the old ruling classes. By the end of the next three years Mussolini's revolution was virtually complete.

Major doctrines of fascism

Italian fascism embodied a variety of doctrines that were an expression of its authoritarian nature:

(1) Statism. The state was declared to incorporate every interest and every loyalty of its members. There was to be "nothing above the state, nothing outside the state, nothing against the state."

(2) Nationalism. Nationhood was the highest form of society. It had a life and a soul of its own apart from the lives and souls of the individuals who composed it. Yet there could be no real harmony of interests between two or more distinct nations. Hence internationalism was a perversion of human progress.

(3) Militarism. Strife was the origin of all things. Nations that did not expand would eventually wither and die. War exalted and ennobled man and regenerated sluggish and decadent peoples.

Declaring his allegiance to these principles, Mussolini began to rebuild Italy in accordance with them. He abolished the cabinet system and all but extinguished the powers of the Parliament. He made the Fascist party an integral part of the Italian constitution. The king was compelled to select a prime minister from a list compiled by the party's Great Council. Voters, as well, were left with no real choice; they were forced to select their candidates from lists prepared by the party. Within a few years, there were no other political parties left in Italy. Mussolini assumed the dual position of prime minister and party leader (*duce*). A potent and effective mechanism of political discipline was the party's militia, which Mussolini used to eliminate his enemies by violent means. Police supervision and censorship of the press and of academic life were soon imposed upon the Italian people by the party.

Mussolini's fascist state

Mussolini reorganized the economy while preaching the end of class conflict as fascist doctrine. He secured worker support by instituting massive public works and building projects, along with state-sponsored programs of library-building, vacations, and social security. He won further popular acclaim when, in 1929, he settled Italy's sixty-year-old conflict with the Roman Catholic Church by a treaty granting independence to the papal residence in the Vatican City and restitution for expropriations that had occurred at the time of Italian unification. The treaty established Roman Catholicism as the official religion of the state, guaranteed religious education in the nation's schools, and made religious marriage ceremonies mandatory.

Mussolini's bid for worker support

At the same time that Mussolini was attempting to pacify the Italian working class, he was pulling the teeth of the country's labor movement. The Italian economy was placed under the management of twenty-two corporations, each responsible for a major industrial enterprise. In each corporation were representatives of trade unions, whose members were organized by the Fascist party, the employers, and the government. Together, the members of these corporations were given the task of determining working conditions, wages, and prices. In fact, however, the decisions of these bodies were closely managed by the government and favored the position of management.

Corporatism

Mussolini's fascism did not truly revolutionize government, economy, and society. Party officers exercised a degree of political supervision over bureaucrats, yet did not infiltrate the bureaucracy in significant numbers. Mussolini remained on friendly terms with the wealthy industrialists and bankers who had assisted his rise to power, insuring that whatever he might proclaim about the distinctions between fascism and capitalism, the economy of Italy would remain dependent upon private enterprise. Further evidence of Mussolini's conservatism was his concordat with the Church—this despite his earlier declarations of allegiance to atheism.

Mussolini's conservatism

The Italian dictator enjoyed boasting that fascism had pulled the country back from economic chaos. The economy did improve somewhat—along with the economies of other European countries—in the late 1920s, yet fascism did little to lessen Italy's plight during the years of worldwide depression which occurred in the 1930s. Although he managed to make his country appear more efficient—his admirers often bragged that he had at

Fascism fails to solve Italy's problems

last "made the trains run on time"—Mussolini failed to solve its major problems, particularly those of the peasantry, whose standard of living remained desperately low. Mussolini's fascism was little more than illusion. It is a measure of the Italians' disgust with their past leaders that they were so ready to be taken in by him.

3. THE RISE OF NAZI GERMANY

Germany: The Spartacists

For a brief period following the First World War, events seemed to be moving Germany significantly to the Left. Most of the leading politicians in the immediate post-armistice government were socialists, members of the Social Democratic party. Their reformist policies, which had seemed radical enough to many prior to the war, now appeared too mild to a group of extreme Marxists who had been encouraged by the revolution in Russia. Calling themselves Spartacists,* and led by Rosa Luxemburg and Karl Liebknecht, they attempted an uprising in 1919 designed to bring the proletarian revolution to Germany. Despite assistance from the Russian Bolsheviks, the rebellion was crushed; Liebknecht and Luxemburg were killed by soldiers while being taken to prison. In engineering the Spartacists' defeat, the German government had recourse to private vigilante groups headed by disillusioned former army officers, men whose true sympathies lay no more with democratic socialism than with Russian communism, and

* After the Roman, Spartacus, who led a slave revolt.

Left: *Karl Liebknecht and Rosa Luxemburg.* Right: *The German Election of 1919.* Here German women line up to vote for the first time.

whose discontent would soon focus on the government they had helped to salvage.

With the Spartacist revolt only just behind them, the leaders of a coalition of socialists, Catholic centrists, and liberal democrats in 1919 drafted a constitution for the new German republic reflecting a generally progressive political and social philosophy. It provided for universal suffrage, for women as well as men; for a cabinet system of government; and for a bill of rights, guaranteeing not only civil liberties but the right of the citizen to employment, to an education, and to protection against the hazards of an industrial society. The republic established under this constitution was beset with troubles from the start. Reactionaries and other extremists plotted against it. Moreover, the German people had had little experience with democratic government. The Weimar Republic (named for the city where its constitution was drafted) did not spring from the desires of a majority of the nation. It was born of change forced upon Germany in its hour of defeat. Its instability made it a likely victim of the forces it was desperately attempting to tame.

Various factors led to the eventual demise of democracy in Germany. First was the sense of humiliation arising from defeat in the war. Between 1871 and 1914, German universities, science, philosophy, and music were known and admired all over the world. The country had likewise attained a remarkable prosperity, by 1914 surpassing Britain and the United States in several fields of industrial production. Then came the defeat of 1918, with Germany left to the mercy of its powerful enemies. It was too much for the German people to understand. They found it difficult to believe that their invincible armies had really been worsted in battle. Quickly the legend grew that the nation had been "stabbed in the back" by socialists and Jews in the government. Though there was no truth in this charge, it helped to salve the wounded pride of German patriots. Those in search of a scapegoat also blamed the laxity and irresponsibility that appeared to distinguish the republican regime. It was alleged that Berlin had displaced Paris as the most frivolous and decadent city of Europe. What the country seemed to need was authoritative leadership to spearhead a campaign to regain the world's respect.

The sense of humiliation was increased by two of the provisions imposed on the Germans in the Versailles treaty. First, Germany was compelled to reduce its army to 100,000 men, a requirement that produced bitter discontent among the politically powerful corps of officers that remained at the head of its ranks. Second, the enormous burden of reparations payments continued to arouse the anger of the Germans. Opponents of the reparations settlement urged an obstructionist policy of nonpayment, arguing that the sum of $33 billion demanded would doom the German economy for the foreseeable future. German politicians of all persuasions agreed that the sum was impossibly large. Yet Weimar's foreign minister in the early 1920s, Walter Rathenau (1867–1922), opposed the obstructionists, and attempted to reach a compromise with the former Allied powers. Rathenau's assassination in 1922, by a secret organization of obstructionist

The Weimar Republic

Defeat in war and demise of democracy

The treaty as humiliation

Rising Unemployment and Despair. In Germany in 1919, there was rising unemployment and out-of-control inflation, leading to demoralization and desperation, and ultimately disillusionment with the republic and democratic government.

Inflation and the German Mark. As German inflation gained momentum and the value of the mark plummeted, various containers were pressed into service to transport money from place to place.

army officers, produced a reaction that led to the German government's refusal to make further payments. The result was French occupation of the Ruhr valley in early 1923, in a fruitless attempt to compel German miners there to produce for France. The ensuing stalemate, which lasted for several months, was ended by the German chancellor, Gustav Stresemann (1878–1929), who recognized the futility of obstructionist tactics. His success in persuading the Germans to accept his point of view was aided by an international agreement to renegotiate reparations under the guidance of a committee of experts headed by the American Charles G. Dawes. Crisis was temporarily averted, but the psychological wounds caused by the reparations controversy did not heal.

Another major reason for democracy's collapse in Germany was the inflation the country suffered in the 1920s. Inflation had plagued the country during the war years. Now the government further increased the supply of money in a desperate effort to finance social welfare programs in the face of rising unemployment and to buy gold with which to make reparations payments. The result was a period of further and more severe inflation, particularly demoralizing to the middle class. Salaries could not keep up with the vast increase in the cost of living. Farmers were angered by the collapse of agricultural prices and by their burden of debts and taxes. University students saw little prospect of gaining a place in already overcrowded professions. Those who existed on fixed incomes—pensioners, stockholders—watched their security vanish. As they lost their faith in the ability of the government to come to their aid, these men and women began, as well, to lose whatever faith they may have had in the republic. The middle class, traumatized by inflation, continued its search for a government that promised attention to its needs and sympathy with its problems. That search intensified with the advent of the Great Depression of 1929. As we shall see, the depression was a major disaster for most of the world. In few countries, however, were its effects more keenly felt than in Germany. Six million workers were unemployed. Once again the middle class saw its savings vanish.

For a brief period in the late 1920s, however, it had appeared that the German economy, and the Weimar Republic with it, might recover. Borrowed money meant that the country was able to make its reparations payments, scaled down in accordance with the Dawes Committee recommendations, and to earn money abroad with cheaply priced exports. Building programs, sponsored by socialist municipal governments in large cities such as Frankfurt, Düsseldorf, and Berlin—schools, hospitals, and low-cost worker housing—suggested that the country was both politically and economically healthier than it actually was. In fact the Dawes Plan, by stressing the need for immediate increases in production, ensured that the economy would remain in the hands of the country's leading industrialists whose tendency to overcapitalize their enterprises impaired their ability to cut costs once the depression struck. These were very conservative men, some of whom sympathized with the restoration of a more authoritarian form of government than Weimar represented. They were allied with equally conservative landowners, bound together by their mutual desire for a protective economic policy that would stimulate the sale of domestically produced goods and foodstuffs. These conservative forces were augmented by the army and civil service, staffed with men opposed to the traditions of parliamentary democracy and international cooperation embodied in the republic.

By the end of the decade, party politics had polarized much as they had in Italy. The moderate parties attracted diminishing support while candidates for the Communist party on the Left and the monarchist German People's party on the Right were enjoying increased success. In 1932 discontent with the republic manifested itself in the national elections, which resulted in the continued presidency of the war hero Marshall von Hindenburg. What was significant, however, was not Hindenburg's return to power, but the fact that the Communists polled about five million votes, and that the candidate of the radical Right, Adolph Hitler, received over eleven million votes, more than one-third of those cast. The Weimar Republic was doomed. And Hitler was its logical nemesis.

Hitler was born in 1889, the son of a petty customs official in the Austrian civil service. Hitler's early life was unhappy and maladjusted. Rebellious and undisciplined from childhood, he seems always to have been burdened with a sense of frustration. He was a failure in school, decided that he would become an artist, and went to Vienna in 1909, where he unsuccessfully attempted to enroll in the Academy. After squandering an inheritance, he eked out a dismal existence as a casual laborer and a painter of watercolors during his last eighteen months in Vienna. Meanwhile he developed violent political prejudices. He became an ardent admirer of certain vociferously anti-Semitic politicians in Vienna; and since he associated Judaism with Marxism, he learned to hate that philosophy as well. When

Weimar's later years

One Step Away from Power. President Hindenburg followed by Hitler.

The early career of Hitler; the early days of the Nazi party

An Anti-Nazi Poster Employed by the Social Democrats in 1932

war broke out, Hitler was living in Munich. Though an Austrian citizen, he immediately enlisted in the German army. Following the war, he joined with other disaffected Germans to denounce the Weimar Republic, choosing as the vehicle to express his alienation the newly formed National Socialist Workers' Party (whose name was soon abbreviated in popular usage to Nazi). Originally a party of the Left, addressing itself primarily to working-class discontents, the Nazis under Hitler's direction in the mid-1920s broadened their appeal to attract disaffected members of the middle class as well. Nazism's doctrines derived in large part from a rambling treatise by Hitler entitled *Mein Kampf* (*My Struggle*), which he wrote while in prison following an attempt by the Nazis' private army to stage a *putsch,* or sudden overthrow of the government, in Munich in 1923. In *Mein Kampf,* Hitler expressed his hatred of Jews and communists, his sense of Germany's betrayal by its enemies, and his belief that only with strong leadership could the country regain its rightful place within the European concert of nations.

Hitler's message appealed to an ever-growing number of his disillusioned and economically threatened countrymen and women. In the election of 1928 the Nazis won 12 seats in the Reichstag. In 1930 they won 107 seats, their popular vote increasing from 800,000 to 6,500,000. During the summer of 1932 the parliamentary system broke down. No chancellor could retain a majority in the Reichstag; the Nazis declined to support any cabinet not headed by Hitler, and the communists refused to collaborate with the socialists. In January 1933, a group of reactionaries prevailed upon President Hindenburg to designate Hitler as chancellor, in the mistaken belief that they could control him. It was arranged that there should be only three Nazis in the cabinet, and that Franz von Papen, a Catholic aristocrat,

Nazis on Parade, 1933.
Politics as theater.

The Nazi Party Congress in Nuremburg, 1934. The Nazis were masters of the use of humanity *en masse* as propaganda. Hitler stands at attention in the center.

should hold the position of vice-chancellor. The sponsors of this plan failed to appreciate the tremendous popularity of the Nazi movement, however. Hitler was not slow to make the most of his new opportunity. He persuaded Hindenburg to dissolve the Reichstag and to order a new election on March 5. When the new Reichstag assembled, it voted to confer upon Hitler practically unlimited powers. Soon afterward the flag of the Weimar Republic was lowered and replaced by the swastika banner of the National Socialists. The new Germany was proclaimed to be the Third Reich, the successor of the Hohenstaufen Empire of the Middle Ages and of the Hohenzollern Empire of the kaisers. *Nazis gain power*

During the next few months, other sweeping changes converted Germany from Bismarck's federalized state into a highly centralized regime. As both chancellor and leader of the Nazi party, Hitler was in a unique position to put the powers of the state to the purposes of the party. To this end, all other political parties were declared illegal. Nazi party luminaries were appointed heads of various government departments, and party *gauleiters,* or regional directors, assumed administrative responsibility throughout the country. Hitler made use of paramilitary Nazi "storm troopers" (the S.A.) to maintain discipline within the party and to impose order on the populace through calculated intimidation and violence. Not even the S.A. itself was immune to the imperatives of terror: when the aspirations of the S.A. leadership to supplant the established army hierarchy threatened to undermine Hitler's support within the military in June 1934, he unleashed a bloody purge in which more than a thousand high-ranking S.A. officials *Nazi rule*

Nazism and the Rural Myth. Left: To stress the rural strength of Aryan Germany, Hitler appeared in lederhosen in the 1920s. Right and center: During the 1930s the Nazi artist W. Willrich painted sober, healthy peasant-types, the ideal Hitler professed to admire and to cultivate.

were summarily executed. Hitler and his associates would brook no interference with their plans to achieve absolute power. During the late 1930s, a second paramilitary organization, the *Schutzstaffel* (bodyguard) or S.S. became the most dreaded arm of Nazi oppression and terror. Headed by the fanatical Heinrich Himmler (1900–1945), who answered to Hitler himself, the S.S. exercised sovereign power over the lives of all Germans, arresting, detaining, imprisoning, and murdering any who appeared to stand in the path of Nazi domination.

Nazi ideology and ruralism

Although Germany was one of the most highly industrialized countries in the world, National Socialist ideology had a peculiarly peasant flavor. The key to Nazi theory was contained in the phrase *Blut und Boden* (blood and soil). The word *soil* reflected not only a deep reverence for the homeland but an abiding affection for the peasants, who were said to embody the finest qualities of the German race. This high regard for country folk came partly, no doubt, from the fact that they had the highest birth rate of the nation's citizens and therefore were most valuable for military reasons. It was explainable also by the reaction of the Nazi leaders against everything that the city stood for—not only intellectualism and radicalism but high finance and the complicated problems of industrial society.

Despite these sentiments, however, the Nazis did little to restructure the economy of Germany. Although they came to power promising to tax department stores heavily so as to benefit the small shopkeeper, they succumbed to pressure from bankers to mitigate those plans. Indeed, they encouraged heavy industry as part of their program of rearmament, forming what amounted to partnerships with such giants as I. G. Farben, the chemical concern, which worked closely with the government on the development of synthetic fuels. Like other Western nations, the Germans battled unemployment with large state-financed construction projects: highways, public housing, and reforestation. Late in the decade, rearmament and a substantial increase in the size of the military establishment all but ended the German unemployment problem—much as the same policies and programs were ending it elsewhere.

Germany's social structure remained relatively untouched by Nazi rule. Government policy encouraged women to withdraw from the labor force, both to ease unemployment and to conform to Nazi notions of a woman's proper role. "Can woman," one propagandist asked, "conceive of anything more beautiful than to sit with her husband in her cozy home and listen inwardly to the loom of time weaving the weft and warp of motherhood . . .?" Like Mussolini, Hitler moved to abolish class conflict by robbing working-class institutions of their power. He outlawed trade unions and strikes, froze wages, and organized workers and employers into a National Labor Front, while at the same time increasing workers' welfare benefits. Class distinctions were to some degree blurred by the regime's insistence on infusing a new national "spirit" into the entire society. Organizations like the Hitler Youth, a sinister variant on the Boy Scout movement, and National Labor Service, which drafted students and others for a term to work on various state-sponsored building and reclamation projects, cut across, but did not abolish, class lines.

For the National Socialists, the great social dividing line was race; its most degrading tenet, anti-Semitism. Anti-Semitism is a centuries-old phenomenon. It had manifested itself in nineteenth-century Europe: in the Russian pogroms; in the Dreyfus affair in France; and in the politics of Germany, where in 1893 sixteen avowed anti-Semites were elected to the Reichstag, and the Conservative party made anti-Semitism part of its official program. Jews were a threat to those who feared urbanization and reform. The majority of Jews lived in cities, where they had advanced themselves in business and finance. They were in the forefront of scientific, cultural, and political innovation. Sigmund Freud was a Jew, as, of course, was Karl Marx. By attacking Jews, anti-Semites could as well attack the modern institutions that they despised and that they associated with a "conspiracy" to deprive civilization of its reassuring base in tradition and authority. They perverted evolutionary theory to suit their arguments. Jews were declared "outsiders," without roots in any particular national culture, and therefore destructive of the racial "purity" necessary for the survival of the race. "The Jews are our national misfortune," the German historian Heinrich von Treitschke wrote in 1879. By that he meant that they were an alien force, subversive to the future of a triumphant German Reich.

Hitler was a fanatical believer in the anti-Semitic dogmas of the Right. The Nazis argued that the so-called Aryan race, which was supposed to include the Nordics as its most perfect specimens, was the only one ever to have made any notable contributions to human progress. They contended further that the accomplishments and mental qualities of a people were determined by blood. Thus the achievements of the Jew forever remained Jewish, no matter how long he or she might live in a Western country. It followed that no Jewish science or Jewish literature or Jewish music could ever truly represent the German nation. A series of laws passed in 1935 deprived Jews and people of Jewish blood of their German citizenship, and prohibited marriage between Jews and other Germans. Eventually, between four and five and a half million Jews were rounded up, tortured, and murdered in concentration camps. Other representatives of "imperfect" racial and social groups—homosexuals, gypsies, and anti-Nazi intellectuals—met a similar fate. The extremism of Hitler's anti-Semitic campaigns underscores the fact that National Socialism was more fanatical than Italian fascism. It was a new religion, not only in its dogmatism and its ritual, but in its fierce intolerance and its zeal for expansion.

The power of Adolf Hitler

If Nazism was a form of perverted religion, Hitler was its high priest. His appeal was based in part on his ability to give the German people what they wanted: jobs for workers, a productive economy for industrialists, a bulwark against communism for the still-influential Junker class. But more important, he preached what the German people wished to hear. His power lay not so much in the programs he championed, many of which were ill-thought-out or contradictory, but in his talent for responding to the sentiments of his fellow-Germans, and for turning those sentiments into holy writ. As one of his early followers remarked: "Hitler responds to the vibrations of the human heart with the delicacy of a seismograph. . . . His words go like an arrow to their target; he touches each private wound on the raw, liberating the mass unconscious, expressing its innermost aspirations, telling it what it most wants to hear." That so many wanted most to listen to the poisonous dogmas of Adolph Hitler is a depressing commentary on the state of the Western world in the 1930s.

The significance of German Nazism and Italian fascism

The significance of German Nazism and Italian fascism remains a subject of controversy among students of modern history. Some argue that they reflected the enthronement of force by capitalists in an effort to save their dying system from destruction. And it is true that the success of both movements in gaining control of the government depended on support from great landowners and captains of industry. Others explain Nazism and fascism as a reaction of debtors against creditors, of farmers against bankers and manufacturers, and of small businessmen against high finance and monopolistic practices. Still others interpret them as a reaction to communist threat, a reversion to primitivism, a result of the despair of the masses, a protest against the weaknesses of democracy, or a supreme manifestation of nationalism. Undoubtedly they were all of these things combined. One further argument holds that fascism and Nazism were extreme expressions of tendencies prevalent in all industrialized countries. If official policies in most Western countries in the 1930s took on more and more of an authoritarian semblance—a tightly controlled economy, limitation of production to maintain prices, and expansion of armaments to promote prosperity—it was because nearly all nations in that period were beset with similar problems and, in varying degrees, frightened of their implications.

4. THE DEMOCRACIES BETWEEN THE WARS

The histories of the three major Western democracies—Great Britain, France, and the United States—run roughly parallel during the years after the First World War. In all three countries there was an attempt by governments to trust to policies and assumptions that had prevailed before the war. The French, not surprisingly, continued to fear Germany and to take whatever steps they could to keep their traditional enemy as weak as possible. Under the leadership of the moderate conservative, Raymond Poincaré (1860–1934), who held office from 1922 to 1924, and again from 1926 to 1929, the French pursued a policy of deflation, which attempted to keep the price of manufactured goods low, by restraining wages. This policy pleased businessmen, but was hard on the working class. Édouard Herriot (1872–1957), a Radical Socialist who served as premier from 1924 to 1926 was, despite his party's name, a spokesman for the small businessman, farmer, and lower middle class. Herriot declared himself in favor of social reform, but refused to raise taxes in order to pay for it. Class conflict lay close to the surface of French national affairs throughout the 1920s. While industries prospered, employers rejected trade unionists' demands to bargain collectively. A period of major strikes immediately after the war was followed by a sharp decline in union activity. Workers remained dissatisfied, even after the government passed a modified social insurance program in 1930, insuring against sickness, old age, and death.

Class conflict in France

Class conflict flared in Britain as well. Anxious to regain its now irretrievably lost position as the major industrial and financial power in the world, Britain, like France, pursued a policy of deflation, designed to lower the price of manufactured goods and thus make them more attractive on the world market. The result was a reduction in wages that undermined the standard of living of many British workers. Their resentment helped to elect a Labour party government in 1924 and 1929. But its minority posi-

Class conflict in Britain

Labor Troubles in Britain. Mounted police escorting delivery wagons through angry strikers during the general strike of 1926.

tion in Parliament left it little chance to accomplish much of consequence, even had its leader, Prime Minister J. Ramsay MacDonald (1866–1937), been a more adventurous socialist than he was. In 1926 British trade unions grew increasingly militant because of the particularly distressing wage levels in the coal mining industry, and because the Conservative government, returned to power under Stanley Baldwin (1867–1947) in 1925, refused to be deflected from its deflationary stance. The unions staged a nationwide general strike which, though it failed as an industrial strategy, turned the middle class more than ever against the workers.

Conservatism in the U.S.

The United States was undoubtedly the most impregnable fortress of conservative power among the democracies. The presidents elected during the 1920s—Warren G. Harding (1865–1923), Calvin Coolidge (1872–1933), and Herbert Hoover (1874–1964)—upheld a social philosophy formulated by the barons of big business in the nineteenth century, while the Supreme Court used its power of judicial review to nullify progressive legislation enacted by state governments and occasionally by Congress.

Roots of the Great Depression

The course of Western history was dramatically altered by the advent of worldwide depression in 1929. We have already seen the way in which depression contributed to the rise of Nazism. But all countries were forced to come to terms with the economic and social devastation it produced. The Great Depression had its roots in a sluggish economic growth rate, which had plagued the West throughout the decade of the 1920s, and which was the result, in part, of competition from the economies of non-European nations. In addition, a significant worldwide drop in agricultural prices meant that the peasant countries of Southern and Eastern Europe, where farm production was geared to small-scale, high-cost agriculture, could not sell their crops profitably on the international market. Their ability to purchase foreign-made manufactured goods thus declined; and that decline seriously affected industrial productivity throughout Europe. Meanwhile, in response to shrinking markets, countries were imposing trade barriers to protect their own domestic manufacturers from foreign competitors, thereby further crippling the economy of the West as a whole.

Crash of New York Stock Exchange

This crisis in production was compounded by the collapse of prices on the New York Stock Exchange in 1929. With a drop in the value of stocks, banks found themselves short of capital and forced to close. International investors called in their debts. Industries, unable to sell their products, stopped manufacturing and started laying off workers. Unemployment further contracted markets—fewer people had money with which to buy goods or services—and that contraction led to more unemployment.

Results of depression: Economic nationalism

The results of the depression took varied forms throughout the West. In 1931 Great Britain abandoned the gold standard; the government of the United States followed suit in 1933. By no longer pegging their currencies to the price of gold, these countries hoped to make money cheaper, and thus more available for programs of public and private economic recovery. This action was the forerunner of a broad program of currency management, which became an important element in a general policy of economic nationalism. As early as 1932 Great Britain abandoned its time-honored

Left: *U.S. Farmers on Their Way West in the 1930s.* Forced from their land by depression debts and by drought, thousands of farmers and their families headed to California, Oregon, and Washington in search of employment. Right: *The Stock Market Crash, October 24, 1929.* Crowds milling outside the New York Stock Exchange on the day of the big crash.

policy of free trade. Protective tariffs were raised in some instances as high as 100 percent.

Domestically, Britain moved cautiously to alleviate the effects of the depression. A national government, which came to power in 1931 with a ministry composed of members from the Conservative, Liberal, and Labour parties, was reluctant to spend beyond its income, as it would have to in order to underwrite effective programs of public assistance. Of the European democracies, France adopted the most advanced set of policies to combat the inequalities and distress that followed in the wake of the depression. In 1936, responding to a threat from ultraconservatives to overthrow the republic, a Popular Front government, under the leadership of the socialist Léon Blum (1872–1950), was formed by the Radical, Radical Socialist, and Communist parties, and lasted for two years. The Popular Front nationalized the munitions industry and reorganized the Bank of France so as to deprive the 200 largest stockholders of their monopolistic control over credit. In addition, it decreed a forty-hour week for all urban workers and initiated a program of public works. For the benefit of the farmers it established a wheat office to fix the price and regulate the distribution of grain. Although the threat from the political Right was for a time quelled by the Popular Front, conservatives were generally uncooperative and unimpressed by its attempts to ameliorate the conditions of the French working class. The anti-Semitism that had appeared at the time of the Dreyfus affair resurfaced; Blum was both a socialist and a Jew. Businessmen saw him as the forerunner of a French Lenin, and were heard to opine, "better Hitler than Blum." They got their wish before the decade was out.

Policies to alleviate effects of depression

Léon Blum

Severity of depression in the U.S.

The most dramatic changes in policy occurred not in Europe.but in the United States. The explanation was twofold. The United States had clung longer to the economic philosophy of the nineteenth century. Prior to the depression the business classes had adhered firmly to the dogma of freedom of contract and insisted upon their right to form monopolies and to use the government as their agent in frustrating the demands of both workers and consumers. The depression in the United States was also more severe than in the European democracies. Industrial production shrank by about two-thirds. The structure of agricultural prices and of common stocks collapsed. Thousands of banks were forced to close their doors. Unemployment rose to one-third of the total labor force. An attempt to alleviate distress was contained in a program of reform and reconstruction known as the New Deal. The chief architect and motivator of this program was Franklin D. Roosevelt (1882–1945), who succeeded Herbert Hoover in the presidency on March 4, 1933.

Achievements of New Deal

The aim of the New Deal was to preserve the capitalist system, by managing the economy and undertaking programs of relief and public works to increase mass purchasing power. Although the New Deal did assist in the recovery both of individual citizens and of the country, through programs of currency management and social security, it left the crucial problem of unemployment unsolved. In 1939, after six years of the New Deal, the United States still had more than 9 million jobless workers—a figure that exceeded the combined unemployment of the rest of the world. Ironically, only the outbreak of a new world war could provide the full recovery that the New Deal had failed to assure, by directing millions from the labor market into the army and by creating jobs in the countless factories that turned to the manufacture of war matériel.

WPA Workers. After 1935 the Works Progress Administration (WPA) put to work unemployed workers who erected and repaired buildings, roads, and bridges throughout the United States.

5. INTELLECTUAL AND CULTURAL TRENDS IN THE INTERWAR YEARS

The First World War, which proved so disillusioning to so many, and the generally dispiriting political events that followed in its train, made it difficult to hold fast to any notion of a purposeful universe. Philosophers, to a greater degree than their predecessors, declared that there was little point in attempting to discover answers to questions about the nature of ultimate reality. These antimetaphysicians broke dramatically with the philosophers of the past century, who had grounded their speculations in a belief in progress and in a search for all-encompassing explanations of human behavior. Probably the most influential of these new thinkers was the Viennese Ludwig Wittgenstein (1889–1951), founder, with the Englishman Bertrand Russell (1872–1970), of the school of Logical Positivism. Developed further by the so-called Vienna Circle, whose leader was Rudolf Carnap (1891–1970), Logical Positivism emerged as an uncompromisingly scientific philosophy. It is not concerned with values or ideals except to the extent that they may be demonstrable by mathematics or physics. In general, the Logical Positivists reject as "meaningless" everything that cannot be reduced to a "one-to-one correspondence" with something in the physical universe. They reduce philosophy to a mere instrument for the discovery of truth in harmony with the facts of the physical environment. They divest it almost entirely of its traditional content and use it as a medium for answering questions and solving problems. They are concerned especially to attack political theory, regarding that subject as particularly burdened with unproved assumptions and questionable dogmas.

Logical Positivism

Bertrand Russell

Sociologists reinforced philosophers in denying the value of metaphysics. One of the most important was the German Max Weber (1864–1920), who, in his book *The Protestant Ethic and the Spirit of Capitalism* (1905), argued that religion must be understood as a cultural force, in this case assisting directly in the spread of capitalism. By making work a cardinal virtue and idleness a supreme vice, Protestantism had encouraged the work ethic, which, in turn, had fueled the energies of early capitalist entrepreneurs. When he turned to a study of the contemporary world, Weber concluded that societies would inevitably fall more and more under the sway of ever-expanding and potentially authoritarian bureaucracies. Recognizing the extent to which such a development might threaten human freedom, Weber posited the notion of "charismatic" leadership as a means of escaping the deadening tyranny of state control. A term derived from the Greek word for gift, "charisma" was, according to Weber, an almost magic quality that could induce hero worship and that, if properly directed by its possessor, might produce an authority to challenge bureaucracy. Weber himself recognized the dangers as well as the attractions of charismatic authority, dangers that the careers of Stalin, Hitler, and Mussolini soon made all too apparent. Another thinker who treated religion as a powerful social and

Religion as a cultural force

psychological force, rather than as a branch of metaphysics, was the Swiss psychologist Carl Jung (1875–1961). Originally a student and disciple of Freud, Jung broke with his intellectual mentor by proclaiming the existence of a force behind individual id, ego, and superego: the "collective unconscious." Jung's literary background and his personal penchant for mysticism helped persuade him of the enduring psychological and therapeutic value of myth and religion, something Freud refused to acknowledge.

The writings of some philosophers during the interwar years not only reflected a sense of crisis and despair but, because of the influence of those works, contributed to it as well. Foremost among these were the Italian Vilfredo Pareto (1848–1923) and the German Oswald Spengler (1880–1936), who agreed in their contempt for the masses, in their belief that democracy was impossible, in their anti-intellectual viewpoint, and in their admiration for strong and aggressive leaders. Spengler was, in many respects, more extreme than Pareto. In his *Decline of the West,* completed in 1918, and even more in his later writings, he gave vent to attitudes that reflect the extent to which authoritarianism might appeal to an "anti-intellectual" intellectual. In his *Hour of Decision,* published in 1933, he fulminated against democracy, pacifism, internationalism, the lower classes, and nonwhite peoples. He sang the praises of those "who feel themselves born and called to be masters," of "healthy instincts, race, the will to possession and power." Spengler despised the analytical reasoning of urban intellectuals and called upon men to admire the "deep wisdom of old peasant families." Human beings, he maintained, are "beasts of prey," and those who deny this conclusion are simply "beasts of prey with broken teeth."

Further confusion and uncertainty were encouraged by the pioneering work of the German physicist Albert Einstein (1879–1955), whose theorizing and experiments were revolutionizing the way in which men and women perceived the universe. In 1905 Einstein began to challenge not merely the older conceptions of matter but practically the entire structure of traditional physics. The doctrine for which he is most noted is his principle of relativity. During the greater part of the nineteenth century, physicists had assumed that space and motion were absolute. Space was supposed to be filled with an intangible substance known as *ether,* which provided the medium for the undulations of light. But experiments performed by English and American physicists near the end of the century exploded the ether hypothesis. Einstein then set to work to reconstruct the scheme of the universe in accordance with a different pattern. He maintained that space and motion, instead of being absolute, are relative to each other. Objects have not merely three dimensions but four. To the familiar length, breadth, and thickness, Einstein added a new dimension of *time* and represented all four as fused in a synthesis that he called the *space-time continuum.* In this way he sought to explain the idea that mass is dependent upon motion. Bodies traveling at high velocity have proportions of extension and mass different from those they would have at rest. Einstein also posited the conception of a finite universe—that is, finite in space. The region of matter

Albert Einstein

does not extend into infinity; the universe has limits. While these are by no means definite boundaries, there is at least a region beyond which nothing exists. Space curves back upon itself so as to make of the universe a gigantic sphere within which are contained galaxies, solar systems, stars, and planets.

The Einstein theories had a major influence in precipitating another revolutionary development in physics: the splitting of the atom to release the energy contained within it. As early as 1905 Einstein became convinced of the equivalence of mass and energy and worked out a formula for the conversion of one into the other, which he expressed as $E = mc^2$. E represents the energy in ergs, m the mass in grams, and c the velocity of light in centimeters per second. In other words, the amount of energy locked within the atom is equal to the mass multiplied by the square of the velocity of light. But no practical application of this formula was possible until after the discovery of the neutron by the Englishman Sir James Chadwick (1891–1974) in 1932. Since the neutron carries no charge of electricity, it is an ideal weapon for bombarding the atom. It is neither repulsed by the positively charged protons nor absorbed by the negatively charged electrons. Moreover, in the process of bombardment it produces more neutrons, which hit other atoms and cause them in turn to split and create neutrons. In this way the original reaction is repeated in an almost unending series.

Releasing the energy within the atom

In 1939 two German physicists, Otto Hahn and Fritz Strassman, succeeded in splitting atoms of uranium by bombarding them with neutrons. The initial reaction produced a chain of reactions, in much the same way that a fire burning at the edge of a piece of paper raises the temperature of adjoining portions of the paper high enough to cause them to ignite. Scientists in Germany, Great Britain, and the United States were spurred on by governments anxious to make use of these discoveries for military purposes during the Second World War. The first use made of the knowledge of atomic fission was in the preparation of an atomic bomb—a device that would further heighten and perpetuate the anxieties of the era.

Laying the groundwork for the atomic bomb

Literary movements during the interwar period showed tendencies similar to those in philosophy. Like the philosophers, the major novelists, poets, and dramatists were disillusioned by the brute facts of world war and by the failure of victory to fulfill its promises. Many were profoundly affected also by revolutionary developments in science, such as the theories of Einstein, and especially by the probings of the new science of psychoanalysis into the hidden secrets of the mind. Much of the literature of the interwar period reflected themes of frustration, cynicism, and disenchantment. The general mood of the era was expressed individually by different writers; for example, by the early novels of the American Ernest Hemingway (1899–1961), by the poetry of the Anglo-American T. S. Eliot (1888–1965), and by the plays of the German Bertolt Brecht (1898–1956). In *The Sun Also Rises* (1926), Hemingway gave the public a powerful description of the essential tragedy of the so-called lost generation and set a pattern that other writers, like the American F. Scott Fitzgerald (1896–1940), were soon to follow. In his poem *The Waste Land* (1922), Eliot presented a philosophy that was

T. S. Eliot

Literary disillusion

close to despair. Life is a living death, to be endured as boredom and frustration. Brecht, in plays written to be performed before the proletarian patrons of cabarets, proclaimed the corruption of the bourgeois state and the pointlessness of war.

The works of many writers in the interwar period reflected to an increasing extent the isolation of self-conscious intellectuals and the constricting of their audience that characterized the years before the First World War. While Brecht carried his revolutionary messages into the streets of Berlin, others wrote primarily for each other or for the small elite group who could understand what they were saying. Eliot crammed his poetry with esoteric allusions. The Irishman James Joyce (1882–1941), whose ability to enter his characters' minds and to reproduce their "stream of consciousness" on paper made him a writer of the very first order, nevertheless wrote with a complexity that relatively few could appreciate. The same was true, though to a lesser extent, of the novels of the Frenchman Marcel Proust (1871–1922) and the Englishwoman Virginia Woolf (1882–1941). In her novels and essays, Woolf was, as well, an eloquent and biting critic of the ruling class of Britain, focusing in part on the enforced oppression of women even in that class.

Virginia Woolf

Politicizing of literature

The depression of the 1930s forced a reexamination of the methods and purposes of literature. In the midst of economic stagnation and threats of totalitarianism and war, literature was politicized. Authors came to believe that their work must indict meanness, cruelty, and barbarism, and point the way to a more just society, that it should also be a literature addressed not to fellow intellectuals, but to common men and women. The American John Steinbeck (1902–1968), in *The Grapes of Wrath* (1939), depicted the sorry plight of impoverished farmers fleeing from the "dust bowl" to California only to find that all the land had been monopolized by companies that exploited their workers. Pervading the novels of the Frenchman André Malraux (1901–1976) was the strong suggestion that the human struggle against tyranny and injustice is that which gives meaning and value to life. Young British writers such as W. H. Auden (1907–1973), Stephen Spender (1909–   ), and Christopher Isherwood (1904–1986) declared, as communist sympathizers, that artists had an obligation to politicize their art for the benefit of the revolution. They rejected the pessimism of their immediate literary forebears for the optimism of political commitment to a common cause.

Jean-Paul Sartre

In this they differed radically from their French contemporary, Jean-Paul Sartre (1905–1980), whose pessimistic philosophy of existentialism was receiving its first hearing at this time. Sartre was a teacher of philosophy in a Paris *lycée* and subsequently a leader of the French Resistance movement against the Germans during the Second World War. His philosophy takes its name from its doctrine that the *existence* of human beings as free individuals is the fundamental fact of life. But this freedom is of no help to humanity; instead it is a source of anguish and terror. Realizing, however vaguely, that they are free agents, morally responsible for all their acts, individuals feel themselves strangers in an alien world. They can have no confidence in a benevolent God or in a universe guided by purpose, for, according to Sartre, all such ideas have been reduced to fictions by modern science. The only way of escape from despair is the path of "involvement," or active participation in human affairs.

Another writer who refused to allow himself the luxury of political optimism was the Englishman George Orwell (1903–1950). Although sympathetic to the cause of international socialism, Orwell continued to insist that all political movements were to some degree corrupted. He urged writers to recognize a duty to write only on the basis of what they had themselves experienced. Above all, writers should never simply parrot party propaganda. Orwell's last two novels, *Animal Farm* (1946) and *Nineteen Eighty-Four* (1949), written during and immediately after the Second World War, are powerful expressions of his mistrust of political regimes—whether of the Left or the Right—that profess democracy but in fact destroy human freedom.

Optimism during the 1930s was generally the property of those writers who were prepared to advocate a violent change in the social order, most notably men and women sympathetic to the doctrines of communism and the achievements of Soviet Russia. An exception to this rule was the British economist John Maynard Keynes (1883–1946), who argued that capitalism could be made to work if governments would play a part in its management, and whose theories helped shape the economic policies of the New Deal. Keynes had served as an economic advisor to the British government during the 1919 treaty-making at Paris. He was disgusted with the harsh terms imposed upon the Germans, recognizing that they would serve only to keep alive the hatreds and uncertainties that breed war. Keynes believed that capitalism with its inner faults corrected could provide a just and efficient economy. First, Keynes abandoned the sacred cow of balanced budgets. He did not advocate continuous deficit financing. He would have the government deliberately operate in the red whenever private investment was too scanty to provide for the economic needs of the country. When depression gave way to recovery, private financing could take the place of deficit spending for most purposes. He favored the accumulation and investment of large amounts of venture capital, which he declared to be the only socially productive form of capital. Finally, Keynes recommended monetary control as a means of promoting prosperity and full employment. He would establish what is commonly called a "managed currency," regulating its value by a process of contraction or expansion in accordance with the needs of the economy. Prosperity would thus be assured in terms of the condition of the home market, and no nation would be tempted to "beggar its neighbor" in the foolish pursuit of a favorable balance of trade.

Trends in art tended to parallel those in literature. For much of the period, visual artists continued to explore aesthetic frontiers far removed from the conventional taste of average men and women. Picasso followed his

George Orwell

John Maynard Keynes

Big Julie by Fernand Léger. Note the artist's fascination with industrial shapes and images.

Trends in art

particular genius as it led him further into cubist variations and inventions. So did others, such as the Frenchman Fernand Léger (1881–1955), who combined devotion to cubist principles and a fascination with the artifacts of industrial civilization. A group more advanced, perhaps, than the cubists, the expressionists argued that since color and line express inherent psychological qualities that can be represented without reference to subject matter, a painting need not have a "subject" at all. The Russian Wassily Kandinsky (1866–1944) carried the logic of this position to its conclusion by calling his untitled paintings "improvisations," and insisting that they meant nothing. A second group of expressionists rejected intellectuality for what they called "objectivity," by which they meant a candid appraisal of the state of the human mind. Their analysis took the form of an attack upon the greed and decadence of postwar Europe. Chief among this group was the German George Grosz (1893–1959), whose cruel, satiric line has been likened to a "razor lancing a carbuncle." Another school expressed its disgust with the world by declaring that there was in fact no such thing as aesthetic principle, since aesthetic principle was based on reason and the world had conclusively proved by fighting itself to death that reason did not exist. Calling themselves *dada-ists* (after a name picked at random, allegedly, from the dictionary) these artists, led by the Frenchman Marcel Duchamp (1887–1968), the German Max Ernst (1891–1976), and the Alsatian Jean Hans Arp (1887–1966), concocted "fabrications" from cutouts and juxtapositions of wood, glass, and metal, and gave them bizarre names: *The Bride stripped bare by her Bachelors, even* (Duchamp), for example. These works were declared by critics, however, to belie their professed meaninglessness,

See color plates following page 940 for representative works by Kandinsky, Grosz, Duchamp, de Chirico, Dali, Orozco, Rivera, and Benton to be, in fact, expressions of the subconscious. Such certainly were the paintings of the surrealists, artists such as the Italian Giorgio de Chirico (1888–1978) and the Spaniard Salvador Dali (1904–1989), whose explorations of the interior of the mind produced irrational, fantastic, and generally melancholy images.

For a time in the 1930s artists, like writers, responded to the sense of international crisis by painting to express their pain and outrage directly to a mass audience. Among the chief representatives of the new movement were the Mexicans Diego Rivera (1886–1957) and José Clemente Orozco (1883–1949), and the Americans Thomas Hart Benton (1889–1975), Reginald Marsh (1898–1954), and Edward Hopper (1882–1967). The fundamental aim of these artists was to depict the social conditions of the modern world and to present in graphic detail the hopes and struggles of peasants and workers. While they scarcely adhered to the conventions of the past, there was nothing unintelligible about their work; it was intended to be art that anyone could understand. Much of it bore the sting or thrust of social satire. Orozco, in particular, delighted in pillorying the hypocrisy of the Church and the greed and cruelty of plutocrats and plunderers.

Art as social commentary

Music, along with the rest of the arts, continued its movement away from nineteenth-century form and intentions. Impressionists, such as Debussy, were succeeded by expressionists, whose work is concerned more

Expressionism in music

Right: *Mural of Kansas City, Missouri* by Thomas Hart Benton. The mural protests the corruption of American politics and the depression misery and degradation of farm workers and industrial laborers. The man in the armchair is the political boss of Kansas City in the 1930s, Tom Pendergast. Left: *"Tie Yourself to the Fatherland, Dear Fatherland"* by George Grosz. Grosz's attacks on unfeeling capitalism during the Weimar years undoubtedly served to weaken the political center during the 1930s.

Igor Stravinsky

*Development of functional
architecture*

with form than with sensuous effects and tends toward abstraction. Expressionism, more radical and more influential than impressionism, comprises two main schools: atonality, founded by the Viennese Arnold Schoenberg (1874–1951), and polytonality, best typified by the Russian Igor Stravinsky (1882–1971). Atonality abolishes key. In this type of music, dissonances are the rule rather than the exception, and the melodic line commonly alternates between chromatic manipulation and strange unsingable leaps. In short, the ordinary principles of composition are reversed. The atonalists attempt, with some success, to let musical sound become a vehicle for expressing the inner meaning and elemental structure of things.

Polytonality is essentially a radical kind of counterpoint, deriving its inspiration partly from baroque practices of counterpoint that were placed in the service of new ideas. However, it does not simply interweave independent melodies, but undertakes to combine separate keys and unrelated harmonic systems, with results that are highly discordant. While the atonalists have retained elements of romanticism, the polytonalists have tried to resurrect the architectural qualities of pure form, movement, and rhythm, stripping away all sentimentality and sensuous connotations.

Architects during this period were also intent upon denying sentimentality. Between 1880 and 1890 designers in Europe and America announced that the prevailing styles of building construction were out of harmony with the facts of modern civilization, and declared as well their intention of restoring that harmony. The chief pioneers of this "functionalism" were Otto Wagner (1841–1918) in Germany, Charles Édouard Jeanneret, known as Le Corbusier (1887–1965) in France, and Louis Sullivan (1856–1924) and Frank Lloyd Wright (1869–1959) in the United States. The basic principle of functionalism is the idea that the appearance of a building should proclaim its actual use and purpose. There must be no addition of friezes, columns, tracery, or battlements merely because some people consider such ornaments beautiful. True beauty consists in an honest adaptation of materials to the purpose they are intended to serve. Func-

Taliesin East by Frank Lloyd Wright. A famous example of the functional style, with the pattern of the house conforming to the natural surroundings.

Contrasting Architectural Styles in Germany between the Wars. Left: The Bauhaus by Walter Gropius. This school in Dessau, Germany, is a starkly functional prototype of the interwar "international style." Right: The Chancellery in Berlin by Albert Speer. Note the massive qualities of the Nazi state style.

tionalism also embodies the notion that architecture should express either directly or symbolically the distinguishing features of contemporary culture. Ornamentation must therefore be restricted to such elements as will reflect an age of science and machines. A leading European practitioner of functionalism was the German, Walter Gropius (1883–1969), who in 1919 established a school— the *Bauhaus*—in Dessau to serve as a center for the theory and practice of modern architecture. Gropius and his followers declared that their style of design, which in time came to be called "international," was the only one that permitted an honest application of new material— chromium, glass, steel, and concrete.

Gropius was one of the multitude of German intellectuals—both Jewish and non-Jewish—to leave their country after Hitler's rise to power. Nazism had its own cultural aesthetic. Functionalism, which celebrated the qualities of material, line, and proportion, had no place in a Nazi regime, where the arts were obliged to advertise the virtues of the state, its tradition, and the aspirations of its people. Instead of Gropius, Hitler had Albert Speer, an architect of unimpressive talents, who produced for him grandiose designs whose vacuous pretentiousness was an unconscious parody of Nazi ideology. Atonality in music was banished along with functionalism in architec-

The arts under Hitler

Propaganda

ture, to be replaced by a state-sponsored revival of the mystical and heroic nationalism of Wagner.

Art was an important part of the new and cultural arm of the regimes of Soviet Russia, Italy, and Germany: propaganda, the practice of indoctrinating populations to believe only what governments wished them to believe. It mattered not at all that belief was based on falsehood, as in the "superiority of the Aryan race," for example. If it served the interest of the state, it was disseminated as truth. Never before had so many of the world's people been able to read. Nineteenth- and twentieth-century governments had encouraged literacy, fearing an ignorant working class as a revolutionary threat. Now authoritarian regimes used education unashamedly as a means of propagating a party line. "All effective propaganda has to limit itself to a very few points and to use them like slogans," Hitler wrote in *Mein Kampf.* "It has to confine itself to little and to repeat this eternally." Books critical of the state were banned, their places on school and library shelves taken by others specifically written to glorify the present leadership. Youth programs instructed children in the virtues of discipline and loyalty to the state. Mass gymnastic displays suggested the ease with which well-trained bodies could be made to respond to the military needs of the nation. Propagandizing was made more effective by the advent of mass-circulation publishing, the radio, and the motion picture. Newspapers, which printed only what the state wanted printed, reached a wider audience than ever before. Party political broadcasts, beamed into homes or blared through loudspeakers in town squares, by their constant repetitiveness made people begin to accept—if not believe—what they knew to be untrue. Films could transform German youths into Aryan gods and goddesses, as they could Russian collective farms into a worker's paradise. Sergei Eisenstein (1898–1948), the Russian director, rewrote Russian history on film to serve the ends of the Soviet state. Hitler commissioned the filmmaker Leni Riefenstahl (1902–) to record a political rally staged by herself and Speer. The film, entitled *Triumph of the Will,* was a visual hymn to the Nordic race and the Nazi regime. And the comedian Charlie Chaplin (1889–1977) riposted in his celebrated lampoon, *The Great Dictator* (1940), an enormously successful parody of Nazi pomposities.

The media in the democracies

In Western democracies, although the media were not manipulated by the state as they were elsewhere, their effectiveness as propagandizers was nevertheless recognized and exploited. Advertising became an industry when manufacturers realized the mass markets that newspapers, magazines, and radio represented. Much that was printed and aired was trivialized by writers and editors who feared that serious or difficult material would antagonize the readers or listeners upon whom they depended for their livelihood. This is not to say that the new media were uniformly banal, or that artists and performers were unable to use them to make thoughtful protests. The film version of Steinbeck's *Grapes of Wrath,* directed by John Ford (1895–1973), though an exception to the normal run of escapist Hollywood comedies and adventures, was perhaps as stinging an indictment of capitalism as the novel, and it reached far more people. During these years popular culture, whatever else it was, remained a powerful and alarming new fact of life: powerful in terms of its vast audience; alarming because of its particular applicability as a means of controlling the minds of men and women.

SELECTED READINGS

- *Items so designated are available in paperback editions.*

GENERAL

- Carsten, F. L., *Revolution in Central Europe, 1918–1919,* London, 1972. A useful treatment of the postwar revolts.
- Collaer, P., *A History of Modern Music,* Cleveland, Ohio, 1961. Useful introduction.
- Galbraith, John Kenneth, *The Great Crash, 1929,* Boston, 1955. An entertaining and informative account by the celebrated economist.
- Gamow, George, *Thirty Years That Shook Physics,* Mineola, N.Y., 1966. An erudite yet readable account.
- Hamilton, George Heard, *Painting and Sculpture in Europe, 1880–1940,* Baltimore, 1967. An excellent survey.
- Hartnack, Justus, *Wittgenstein and Modern Philosophy,* Garden City, N.Y., 1965. Clear introduction to a difficult subject.
- Hitchcock, H. R., *Architecture: 19th and 20th Centuries,* London, 1958. Thorough and well-written survey.
- Kahler, Erich, *The Tower and the Abyss,* New York, 1957. A survey of the arts in the context of contemporary culture.
- Kindleberger, C. P., *The World in Depression, 1929–1939,* Berkeley, 1973. A first-rate study of the worldwide aspects of the slump.
  Laqueur, Walter, and George L. Mosse, eds., *The Left-Wing Intellectuals between the Wars, 1919–1939,* New York, 1966. Essays by modern historians.
  Masur, Gerhard, *Prophets of Yesterday,* New York, 1961. A useful intellectual history of the interwar period.
- Mosse, George L., *The Naturalization of the Masses: Political Symbolism and Mass Movements in Germany from the Napoleonic Wars through the Third Reich,* New York, 1975. Attempts to trace the roots of Nazism in naturalist movements.
- Payne, Stanley G., *Fascism: A Comparative Approach toward a Definition,* Madison, Wisc., 1980. A review of various European fascist movements, written with balance and careful thought.
- Rothschild, Joseph, *East Central Europe between the Two World Wars,* Seattle, 1975. An authoritative survey; does not include Austria.
  Shapiro, Theda, *Painters and Politics: The European Avant-Garde and Society, 1900–1925,* New York, 1976. An analysis of the political and social attitudes of a revolutionary generation in the arts.
- Sontag, Raymond V., *A Broken World, 1919–1939,* New York, 1971. A fine detailed survey of interwar Europe.

THE SOVIET UNION

Carr, E. H., *The Russian Revolution: From Lenin to Stalin,* New York, 1979. A distillation from his ten-volume *History of Soviet Russia.* A fine starting point for the general reader.

- Conquest, Robert, *The Great Terror,* New York, 1968. An analysis of the Stalin purges.
- Daniels, Robert V., *The Conscience of the Revolution,* Cambridge, Mass., 1960. Discusses the opposition to Bolshevism in the 1920s.
- Deutscher, Isaac, *The Prophet Armed,* London, 1954; *The Prophet Unarmed,* London, 1959; *The Prophet Outcast,* London, 1963. A superb, three-volume biography of Leon Trotsky.
- Fitzpatrick, Sheila, ed., *Cultural Revolution in Russia, 1928–1931,* Bloomington, Ind., 1978. A first-rate analysis of the cultural effect of Bolshevik rule.
- Tucker, Robert C., *Stalin as Revolutionary, 1879–1929: A Study in History and Personality,* New York, 1973. An excellent account of Stalin's rise to power, and of the change from revolution to dictatorship in Russia.

GERMANY AND ITALY

- Bracher, Karl Dietrich, *The German Dictatorship: The Origins, Structure, and Effects of National Socialism,* New York, 1970. A penetrating and exhaustive study of the Nazi state by a political scientist.
- Bridenthal, Renate, ed., *When Biology Becomes Destiny: Women in Weimar and Nazi Germany,* New York, 1984. Analysis of the position of women, particularly their progressive subjugation to national ideals.
- Bullock, Alan, *Hitler: A Study in Tyranny,* rev. ed., New York, 1971. The standard biography.
- Eyck, Erich, *History of the Weimar Republic,* 2 vols., Cambridge, Mass., 1962. A sympathetic account by a prominent German liberal.
- Gay, Peter, *Weimar Culture: The Outsider as Insider,* New York, 1970. Examines the failure of commitment to the Weimar Republic by German intellectuals.
- Hale, Oron J., *The Captive Press in the Third Reich,* Princeton, 1964. Examines the manner in which totalitarianism invades journalism.
- Lyttelton, Adrian, *The Seizure of Power: Fascism in Italy, 1919–1929,* 2nd ed., London, 1988. An excellent introduction.
  Mack Smith, Denis, *Mussolini's Roman Empire,* New York, 1976. An able treatment of Italian fascism by the foremost English scholar of Italy.
- Nolte, Ernst, *The Three Faces of Fascism,* New York, 1966. A difficult but rewarding study of Germany, Italy, and France, from a philosophical perspective.
  Rogger, Hans, and Eugen Weber, eds., *The European Right: A Historical Profile,* 1965. A country-by-country survey.
- Schoenbaum, David, *Hitler's Social Revolution: Class and Status in Nazi Germany, 1933–39,* Garden City, N.Y., 1966. Hitler's impact upon the various social and economic classes in Germany.
- Stern, Fritz, *The Politics of Cultural Despair: A Study in the Rise of Germanic Ideology,* Berkeley, 1961. Assesses the way in which cultural beliefs influence politics.
- Zeman, Z. A. B., *Nazi Propaganda,* New York, 1973. Examines an important bulwark of the authoritarian state.

Bullock, Alan, *The Life and Times of Ernest Bevin: Trade Union Leader, 1881–1940,* London, 1960. An excellent study of the British trade unionist and the political and social history of Britain between the wars.

- Burns, James M., *Roosevelt: The Lion and the Fox,* New York, 1956. A readable analysis.

- Colton, Joel, *Léon Blum: Humanist in Politics,* New York, 1966. A first-rate biography that illuminates the history of the Popular Front.

- Graves, Robert, and Alan Hodge, *The Long Weekend: A Social History of Great Britain, 1918–1939,* London, 1940. A striking portrait of England in the interwar years.

- Greene, Nathanael, *From Versailles to Vichy: The Third Republic, 1919–1940,* Arlington Heights, Ill., 1970. Valuable survey.

Harrod, R. F., *The Life of John Maynard Keynes,* 2nd ed., New York, 1952. A solid biography by an admirer of Keynes.

Hughes, H. Stuart, *The Obstructed Path: French Social Thought in the Years of Desperation, 1930–1960,* New York, 1968. Detailed analysis of major French thinkers.

- Leuchtenburg, W. E., *Franklin Roosevelt and the New Deal, 1932–1940,* New York, 1964. A good introduction.

- Mowat, Charles L., *Britain between the Wars, 1918–1940,* Chicago, 1955. A detailed political and social history, especially valuable for its extensive bibliographical footnotes.

- Taylor, A. J. P., *English History, 1914–1945,* New York, 1965. The best survey of the period; witty, provocative, insightful.

Weber, Eugen, *Action Française: Royalism and Reaction in Twentieth Century France,* Stanford, 1962. The best study of this protofascist movement.

SOURCE MATERIALS

Cole, G. D. H., and M. I. Cole, *The Condition of Britain,* London, 1937. A contemporary analysis by English socialists.

- Ehrenburg, Ilya, *Memoirs, 1921–1941,* New York, 1964. The intellectual at work within the Stalinist regime.

- Greene, Nathanael, comp., *European Socialism Since World War I,* Chicago, 1971. A collection of contemporary accounts.

Gruber, H., *International Communism in the Era of Lenin: A Documentary History,* Greenwich, Conn., 1967. A very useful collection of primary materials.

- Hitler, Adolf, *Mein Kampf,* New York, 1962. Hitler's autobiography, written in 1925. Contains his version of history and his vision for the future. Especially important for his insight into the nature of the masses and the use of propaganda.

- Noakes, Jeremy, and Geoffrey Pridham, *Documents on Nazism, 1919–1945,* New York, 1975. An excellent sourcebook; comprehensive and annotated.

- Orwell, George, *The Road to Wigan Pier,* New York, 1972. Vivid description of Britain's interwar poverty and class system by an independently minded socialist.

- Silone, Ignazio, *Bread and Wine,* rev. ed., tr. H. Ferguson, New York, 1965. A moving account of the effects of Italian fascism.
- Speer, Albert, *Inside the Third Reich,* New York, 1964. The self-serving but informative memoirs of one of the leaders of Nazi Germany.

  Tucker, Robert C., ed., *The Great Purge Trial,* New York, 1965. An annotated edition of the transcript of one of the Soviet "show-trials" that so puzzled Western observers.

Chapter 29

THE SECOND WORLD WAR

The President [Roosevelt] and the Prime Minister [Churchill], after a complete survey of the world situation, are more than ever determined that peace can come to the world only by a total elimination of German and Japanese war power. This involves the simple formula of placing the objective of this war in terms of an unconditional surrender by Germany, Italy, and Japan.

—Franklin D. Roosevelt, Casablanca, January 24, 1943

In September 1939, Europe was drawn again into a general war. The peace of 1919–1920 proved to be no more than an armistice; once more millions of people were locked in a conflict whose devastation surpassed any that had occurred heretofore. As had happened in 1914–1918, the new struggle soon became worldwide. Although the Second World War was not merely a continuation of, or a sequel to, the First, the similarity in causes and characteristics was more than superficial. Both were precipitated by threats to the balance of power, and both were conflicts between peoples, entire nations, rather than between governments. On the other hand, there were notable differences between the two conflicts. The methods of warfare in the Second World War had little in common with those of the earlier conflict. Trench warfare was superseded by bombing and by sudden aerial (*blitzkrieg*) attacks, with highly mobile armies, on both civilian populations and military installations. Because whole populations were now vulnerable to the ravages of warfare, the distinction between those on the battlefield and those at home was more completely obliterated in the Second World War than it had been in the First. Finally, this war was not greeted with the almost universal, naïve enthusiasm that had marked the outbreak of the other. Men and women still remembered the horrors of the First World War. They entered the Second with determination, but also with a keener appreciation of the frightful devastation that war could bring than their predecessors had possessed.

A comparison of the two world wars

1. THE CAUSES OF THE WAR

Defects of the peace treaties

The causes of the Second World War related to the failure of the peace terms of 1919–1920. Those terms, while understandable in view of the passions and hatreds engendered by the First World War, created almost as many problems as they solved. By yielding to the demands of the victors for annexation of territory and the creation of satellite states, the peacemakers sowed new seeds of bitterness and conflict. By proclaiming the principle of self-determination while acquiescing in the distribution of national minorities behind alien frontiers, the treaties raised expectations while at the same time frustrating them. Perhaps most important, by imposing harsh terms on Germany and undermining German autonomy, the treaty-makers gave the Germans what seemed to many to be legitimate grievances by depriving them of their rightful share of international power and saddling them with the entire burden of war "guilt."

Power politics

Power politics were a second cause of war. Although Woodrow Wilson and other sponsors of the League of Nations had acclaimed the league as a means of eliminating power struggles, it did nothing of the sort. It merely substituted a new and more precarious balance for the old. The signatures on the peace treaties had scarcely dried when the victors began to construct new alliances to maintain their supremacy. A neutralized zone consisting of the Baltic states, Poland, and Rumania was created as a buffer against the Soviet Union. A "Little Entente" composed of Czechoslovakia, Yugoslavia, and Rumania was established to prevent a revival of Austrian power. These combinations, together with Franco-Belgian and Franco-Polish alliances, isolated Germany. Even the league itself was fundamentally an alliance of the victors against the vanquished. That there would be fears and anxieties over a disturbance of the new power arrangement was natural. The first sign of such a disturbance appeared in 1922 when Germany and the Soviet Union negotiated the Treaty of Rapallo. Though disguised as a trade agreement, it opened the way for political and, according to some accounts, even military collaboration between the two states.

Attempts to preserve international amity

Diplomats made various attempts to preserve or restore international amity during the 1920s and 1930s. Some saw in disarmament the most promising means of achieving their purpose. Accordingly, a succession of conferences was called in the hope of at least limiting a race to rearm. In 1925 representatives of the chief European powers met at Locarno and acted on the suggestion of the German and French foreign ministers, Gustav Stresemann (1878–1929) and Aristide Briand (1862–1932), that Germany and France pledge themselves to respect the Rhine frontiers as established in the Versailles treaty. They agreed also that they would never go to war against each other except in "legitimate defense." More widely celebrated than the Locarno Agreements was the Pact of Paris, or Kellogg-Briand Pact of 1928. Its purpose was to outlaw war as an international crime. Eventually, nearly all the nations of the world signed this agreement renouncing war as "an instrument of national policy" and providing that the settlement of international disputes "of whatever nature or of whatever origin" should never be sought "except by peaceful means." Neither the Locarno Agreements nor the Pact of Paris was much more than a pious gesture. The signatory nations adopted them with so many reservations and exceptions in favor of "vital interests" that they could never be effective instruments for preserving peace. Had the League of Nations been better organized, it might have relieved some of the tensions and prevented clashes between nations still unwilling to relinquish their absolute sovereignty. Yet it was not a league of all nations, since both Germany and the Soviet Union were excluded for much of the interwar period, and the United States was not a member.

Economic conditions were a third important cause of the outbreak of war. The huge reparations imposed upon the Germans, and the French occupation of much of Germany's industrial heartland, helped, as we have seen, to retard Germany's economic recovery and bring on the debilitating inflation of the 1920s. The depression of the 1930s contributed to the coming of the war in several ways. It intensified economic nationalism. Baffled by problems of unemployment and business stagnation, governments resorted to high tariffs in an attempt to preserve the home market for their own producers. The depression was also responsible for a marked increase in armaments production, which was seen as a means of reducing unemployment. Despite the misgivings of some within the governments of Britain and France, Germany was allowed to rearm. Armaments expansion, on a large scale, was first undertaken by Germany about 1935, with the result that unemployment was substantially reduced and business boomed. Other nations followed the German example, not simply as a way of boosting their economies, but in response to Nazi military power. The depression helped as well to produce a new wave of militant expansionism directed toward the conquest of neighboring territories as a means of solving economic problems. Japan took the lead in 1931 with the invasion of Manchuria. The decline of Japanese exports of raw silk and cotton cloth

Economic conditions

The Krupp Shipworks in Germany. Seen here are German submarines in the final stages of assembly.

meant that the nation was unable to pay for needed imports of coal, iron, and other minerals. Japanese militarists were thus furnished with a convenient pretext for seizing Manchuria, where supplies of these commodities could then be purchased for Japanese currency. Mussolini, in part to distract Italians from the domestic problems brought on by economic depression, invaded and annexed Ethiopia in 1936. Finally, the depression was primarily responsible for the triumph of Nazism, whose expansionist policies contributed directly to the outbreak of war.

Nationalism

Nationalism was a further cause of the general discontent that helped increase the chances for world war. In Eastern Europe, national and ethnic minorities remained alienated from the sovereign states into which the treaty-makers had placed them. This was particularly the case of the Sudetenland Germans, who had been included in the newly created state of Czechoslovakia. That country could in fact boast no national majority, including as it did Czechs, Slovaks, Poles, Ruthenians, and Hungarians, as well as Germans. Although it possessed an enlightened policy of minority self-government, the patchwork state of Czechoslovakia remained unstable. And its instability was to prove a key factor as the tensions mounted in the late 1930s.

Appeasement

A final cause of war was the policy of "appeasement" that was pursued by the Western democracies in the face of German, Italian, and Japanese aggression. The appeasers' strategy was grounded in three commonly held assumptions. The first was that the outbreak of another war was unthinkable. With the memory of the slaughter of 1914–1918 fresh in their minds, many in the West embraced pacifism, or at any rate adopted an attitude that kept them from realistically addressing the implications of Nazi and fascist policies and programs. Second, many in Britain and the United States argued that Germany had been mistreated in the Versailles treaty, that the Germans had legitimate grievances that should be acknowledged and resolved. Finally, the appeasers were, for the most part, staunch anti-communists. They believed that by assisting Germany to regain its former military and economic power, they were constructing a bulwark to halt the westward advance of Soviet communism. When Japan invaded Manchuria, the West refused to impose sanctions against the Japanese through the League of Nations, arguing that Japan, too, could serve as a counterweight to the Soviet Union.

Germany invades the Rhineland

Hitler took advantage of this generally tolerant attitude to advance the expansionist ambitions of Germany. As the country rearmed, Hitler played upon his people's sense of shame and betrayal, proclaiming their right to regain their former power within the world. In 1933, he removed Germany from the League of Nations (it had been admitted in 1926) and thus from any obligation to adhere to its declarations. In 1935 Hitler tore up the disarmament provisions of the Treaty of Versailles, announcing the revival of conscription and the return to universal military training. In 1936 he repudiated the Locarno Agreements and invaded the Rhineland. Britain and France did nothing to stop him, as they had done nothing to prevent Mussolini's invasion and conquest of Ethiopia the previous year. Hitler's move

Guernica by Pablo Picasso. This painting, a protest against the bombing of an undefended city during the Spanish Civil War, has come to be recognized as one of the century's most profound antiwar statements.

tipped the balance of power in Germany's favor. While the Rhineland remained demilitarized and German industry in the Ruhr valley unprotected, France had held the upper hand. Now it no longer did so.

In 1936 civil war broke out in Spain; a series of weak republican governments had proved unable to prevent the country's political disintegration. Although they had signed a pact of nonintervention with the other Western powers, Hitler and Mussolini both sent troops and equipment to assist the forces of the rebel fascist commander, Francisco Franco (1892–1975). The Soviet Union countered with aid to the communist troops serving under the banner of the Spanish republic. Again, Britain and France failed to act decisively. The Spanish Civil War lasted three years, with the forces of the fascists finally victorious over those of the republicans. The conflict engaged the commitment of many young European and American leftists and intellectuals, who saw it as a test of the West's determination to resist authoritarian dictatorships. The fighting was brutal; aerial bombardment of civilians and troops was employed for the first time on a large scale. Because of this, the Spanish Civil War has often been seen as a "dress rehearsal" for the much larger struggle that was shortly to follow. The war also served to confirm Hitler's belief that if Britain, France, and the Soviet Union did decide to attempt to contain fascism, they would have a difficult time concerting their policies—another reason, indeed, why Britain and France remained content to do nothing.

The Spanish Civil War

In March of 1938, Hitler annexed Austria, declaring it his intention to bring all Germans into his Reich. Once more, there was no official reaction from the West. Hitler's next target was the Sudetenland in Czechoslovakia, which had a large ethnically German population. With Austria now a part of Germany, Czechoslovakia was almost entirely surrounded by its

Munich and after

The Munich Conference, 1938. Left: Prime Minister Chamberlain of Britain and Hitler during the Munich conference. Right: Chamberlain addressing a crowd on his return from the Munich conference.

hostile expansionist neighbor. Hitler declared that the Sudetenland was a natural part of the Reich and that he intended to occupy it. The British prime minister, Neville Chamberlain (1869–1940), determined to negotiate, but on Hitler's terms. On September 29, Hitler agreed to meet with Chamberlain, Premier Édouard Daladier of France, and Mussolini in a four-power conference in Munich. The result was another capitulation by France and Britain. Ignoring the vital interests of a nation whose territory the Treaty of Versailles had guaranteed, the four negotiators bargained away a major slice of Czechoslovakia, while that country's representatives were left to await their fate outside the conference room. Chamberlain returned to England proclaiming "peace in our time." Hitler soon proved that fatuous boast untrue. In March 1939 he invaded what was left of Czechoslovakia and established a puppet regime in its capital, Prague, the first occupation by Hitler's Germany of a non-German territory. This action convinced British public opinion of the foolhardiness of appeasement. Chamberlain, compelled to shift his policies dramatically, guaranteed the sovereignty of the two states now directly in Hitler's path: Poland and Rumania. France followed suit.

See color map of Europe on the Eve of the Second World War facing page 941

Meanwhile, the appeasement policies of Britain and France had fueled Stalin's fears that the timid Western democracies might strike a bargain with Germany at Soviet expense by diverting Nazi expansion eastward. This, combined with the suspicion that they might make unreliable allies, convinced Stalin that he must look elsewhere for security. Tempted by the traditional Soviet desire for territory in Poland, and promised a share of both Poland and the Baltic states by Hitler, Stalin signed a nonaggression pact with the Nazis in August 1939. In going to Munich, Britain and

Nazi-Soviet pact

See color map of the Soviet Union following page 940

France had put their interests first; the Soviet Union would now look after its own.

2. THE OUTBREAK OF HOSTILITIES

Following the extinction of Czechoslovakia, and despite Chamberlain's guarantee, Hitler demanded the abolition of the Polish Corridor, a narrow strip of previously German territory connecting Poland with the Baltic Sea. The corridor contained a large German population, which Hitler declared must be reunited with the Fatherland. Judging Britain and France by past performance he believed their pledges to Poland worthless. With the Soviets now in his camp, he expected that Poland would quickly capitulate, and that the Western allies would back down once more as they had done at Munich. When Poland stood firm, Hitler attacked. On September 1, 1939, German tanks crossed the Polish border. Britain and France sent a joint warning to Germany to cease its aggression. There was no reply; on September 3, Britain and France declared war against Germany.

Beginning of the war

The conflict with Poland proved to be a brief encounter. In less than three weeks the Polish armies had been routed by combined air and tank attacks, Warsaw had been captured, and the chiefs of the Polish government had fled to Rumania. For some months after that the war resolved itself into a kind of siege, a "phony war" or "sitzkrieg," as it was sometimes called. Such fighting as did occur was largely confined to submarine warfare, aerial raids on naval bases, and occasional battles between naval vessels. In the spring of 1940 the sitzkrieg was suddenly transformed into a blitzkrieg, or "lightning war." The Germans struck blows at Norway, Denmark, Luxembourg, Belgium, the Netherlands, and France, conquering them in short order, and driving the British and French forces back against the English Channel at Dunkirk in Belgium. Despite heavy German air attacks, the British were able to evacuate over 300,000 troops, many of them in commercial and pleasure boats that had been pressed into emergency service. Northern France, including Paris, was occupied by the Germans. In

The blitzkrieg

The Beginning of the Second World War. A long line of German tanks crossing into Poland.

Left: *London during the Blitz*. This picture conveys a vivid impression of the agony that the British capital suffered during the Battle of Britain, which lasted from August 1940 to June 1941. Behind the tumbling ruins brought down by firebombs is St. Paul's Cathedral. Right: *French Refugees Driven from Their Homes during the Early Years of the Nazi Occupation*.

the south, a puppet government loyal to the Germans was established at Vichy under the leadership of the aged First World War hero, Marshal Henri Philippe Pétain (1856–1951).

The Battle of Britain

Before launching an invasion across the Channel, the Nazis decided to reduce Britain's military strength and civilian will by air raids. From August 1940 to June 1941, in the so-called Battle of Britain, thousands of planes dropped millions of tons of bombs on British ports, industrial centers, and air defenses throughout the country. Despite the fact that whole sections of cities were laid in ruins and more than 40,000 civilians killed, the British held firm. Winston Churchill had by this time succeeded Neville Chamberlain as prime minister of Britain. A maverick Conservative, who had served in Britain's First World War government as a Liberal, Churchill was not trusted by his party's leadership, particularly since he had been one of the few who had spoken out in favor of British rearmament during the years of appeasement. Now that his warnings had proved true, he was given direction of the war as head of a national government composed of ministers from the Conservative, Liberal, and Labour parties. Churchill, an exceedingly compelling orator, used the radio to persuade his countrymen and women—and the rest of the free world—that Britain must not, and would not, surrender to the Nazis. His friendship with President Roosevelt, and the latter's conviction that the United States must come to Britain's aid, resulted in the shipment of military equipment and ships to the British under the Lend–Lease Act passed by the U.S. Congress in 1941.

Meanwhile, Germany moved eastward into the Balkans, subduing the Rumanians, Hungarians, Bulgarians, and Yugoslavs. The Italians, less successful in their campaigns in Greece and North Africa, required German assistance to accomplish their missions. Scornful of Mussolini's military inadequacies, Churchill called him Hitler's "jackal." Frustrated in his attempt to subjugate Britain, Hitler broke with his erstwhile ally the Soviet Union, and turned eastward, on June 22, 1941, with a massive invasion. Before the end of the year his armies had smashed their way to the gates of Moscow but never actually succeeded in capturing it. The defense of Moscow by the Soviet armies marked one of the war's important early turning points.

The German invasion of Russia

The war was converted into a global conflict when Japan struck at Pearl Harbor in Hawaii on December 7 of the same year. The Japanese had been involved in a costly war with China since 1937. To wage it successfully they needed the oil, rubber, and extensive food resources of the Netherlands Indies, the Malay Peninsula, and Southeast Asia. They had allied with Germany in 1940. (Germany, Italy, and Japan were together known as the Axis powers, a name derived from the Rome-Berlin diplomatic axis formed in the 1930s.) Now, before attacking south, they considered it necessary to secure their position to the rear by crushing American naval and air power on the base of Pearl Harbor. The next day the United States Congress (as well as Canada and Great Britain) recognized a state of war with Japan, and on December 11 Germany and its allies declared war upon the United States.

Pearl Harbor

This second global war was a total war to an even greater extent than was the case in the First World War. Total populations were mobilized as part of the war effort: governments imposed the rationing of food and clothing and the regulation of manpower and production quotas demanded that factories produce around the clock. In the Soviet Union, all men between the ages of sixteen and fifty-five and all women between the ages of sixteen and forty-five were pressed into service, either in the armed forces or on the home front. The Germans destroyed much of the Soviet Union's industrial plant and existing war matériel in the early months of the war—

Total war

Pearl Harbor, December 7, 1941. This photo shows American battleships sunk at their moorings, following the Japanese raid on what President Franklin D. Roosevelt declared was "the day that will live in infamy."

Aerial Bombardment. Not only the Germans, but also the British and the Americans fire-bombed civilian populations and thereby obliterated large parts of the cities under attack.

over 90 percent of the Soviet Union's tanks, for example. To produce what was necessary, factories were rebuilt in the security of the Ural mountain region, and whole populations moved there to work in them.

The Resistance

In countries conquered and occupied by the Germans and Italians, the Axis powers installed administrations willing to follow their commands without question. (Vidkun Quisling, the Norwegian Nazi leader, made his name synonymous with the word "traitor.") Life for civilians was harsh at best. Rations in occupied France, for example, were less than half the amount considered to be a healthy minimum. Civilians from occupied countries were transported to Germany to work there in factories and labor battalions. In France and elsewhere, Resistance movements emerged, composed of men and women of various political persuasions united in their determination to assist the Allies in driving the Axis powers from their native lands. By transmitting intelligence reports, aiding prisoners to escape, distributing newspapers to counter official propaganda, and undertaking acts of direct sabotage to military and industrial targets, these groups helped the Allied cause immeasurably. The success of the Normandy invasion was in part the result of information concerning German military emplacements sent to Britain by the French Resistance.

Bombing of cities

The war brought devastation in the form of street fighting and air bombardment to most of the major urban centers of Europe. The Allies proved to be fully as ruthless and even more efficient than the Axis powers in this regard. After some debate, British and American strategists abandoned pinpoint bombing in favor of the nighttime aerial bombardment of entire cities. The result was the deliberate fire-bombing of civilian populations, climaxing in Europe in early 1945 with the brutal obliteration of Dresden, a German city without significant industry and filled with refugees. These attacks were equaled by the German bombing of French, Belgian, Dutch, Russian, and British cities and civilian populations.

Ghastly as was the destruction meted out by the armed forces to each other and to civilians, none of it matched in premeditated, obscene horror the systematic persecution by the Nazis of whole Jewish populations, not only in Germany itself but in occupied countries as well. Prisoners who were not killed immediately in the gas chambers of the concentration camps in Germany and elsewhere in German-occupied Europe were starved, diseased, and brutalized. Ultimately six million prisoners lost their lives. Most of the men, women, and children who were imprisoned, tortured, and killed were Jews, although Poles, Russians, Gypsies, homosexuals, and other "traitors" to the Reich were also incarcerated, used for forced labor, and executed.

The concentration camps

After the United States entered the war, events turned slowly but inexorably against the forces of Germany, Italy, and Japan. Churchill and Roosevelt, meeting shortly after the United States's entry into the war, agreed that victory in the West would be their first priority. As an initial step toward that goal, the British succeeded in halting the North African advance of Germany's brilliant tank commander, General Erwin Rommel (1891–1944), who had driven the British back across the Sahara to the Egyptian border. That victory was the prelude to a joint Anglo-American invasion of North Africa in November 1942. The success of this first major combined Allied offensive led in turn to further Mediterranean campaigns in 1943, first in Sicily and then in Italy. Mussolini's government was overthrown, and his successors sued for peace. The Germans, however, sent troops into Italy and resurrected Mussolini as the ruler of a puppet state in the north, where he remained a virtual prisoner of the Nazis until his death at the hands of his countrymen at the time of the general defeat of the Axis powers in Europe. Despite Allied attempts to break the German grip on the peninsula, the Nazi forces continued to hold central and northern Italy until the spring of 1945.

Allied victories in North Africa and Italy

Civilian Losses. This woman on the Russian Front in 1941 watches as her home and village burn to the ground.

The battle of Stalingrad

In Eastern Europe, meanwhile, the Germans had continued to press the war against the Soviets, turning in 1942 to the south and the rich agricultural and industrial areas of the Ukraine, the Donets Basin, and the Caucasus oilfields. The German advance was stopped at Stalingrad, in a military struggle of great strategic and symbolic importance for both sides. The battle saw 300,000 Germans for a time in control of the city, then enclosed by the counterattacking Soviets in a pincers movement, and eventually, by the time of their surrender in February 1943, reduced to fewer than half their original number. The loss of the battle of Stalingrad compelled the Germans to undertake a general retreat. By the spring of 1943, they were no further east than they had been the previous year.

The D-Day invasion

Stalin continued to pressure his allies to open a second front in the west to relieve the concerted Nazi drive against the Soviet Union. The North African and Italian campaigns were a response to that plea. But not until June 1944 did Allied troops invade France. On June 6 (D-Day) a massive invasion force landed on the Normandy coast. Air superiority, plus a tremendous buildup of matériel and manpower, produced a series of successful advances and the liberation of Paris on August 25. Despite a final German assault in December 1944, the Allied armies penetrated deep into Germany itself by the early spring of 1945.

End of the war in Europe

At the same time, Soviet troops were approaching from the east. On April 21, 1945, they hammered their way into the suburbs of Berlin. During the next ten days a savage battle raged amid the ruins and heaps of rubble. Adolf Hitler killed himself in the bomb-proof shelter of the Chancellery on April 30. On May 2 the heart of the city was captured, and the Soviet red banner flew from the Brandenburg Gate. On May 7 representa-

Left: *D-Day*. Cargo ships are seen pouring supplies ashore during the invasion of France on June 6, 1944. Balloon barrages float overhead to protect the ships from low-flying enemy planes. Right: *Signing the German Surrender, May 7, 1945*

German Civilians Compelled to View the Bodies of Concentration Camp Victims at the Landesburg Camp in 1945 as an American Army Officer Lectures Them on the Horrors of the Nazis' "Final Solution"

tives of the German High Command signed a document of unconditional surrender, which was ratified in Berlin the next day.

The war in the Pacific came to an end four months later. Important victories won by the United States Navy against the Japanese at the battles of the Coral Sea and Midway in the spring of 1942 forestalled Japanese attempts to capture Australia and the Hawaiian Islands so as to deprive the United States of advance bases for a counteroffensive against Japan. Final Allied victory followed further naval battles, island assaults, and land battles in Southeast Asia. In June 1945, the Japanese island of Okinawa was taken, after eighty-two days of desperate fighting. The American forces now had a foothold less than 500 miles from the Japanese homeland. The government in Tokyo was anticipating an invasion and calling upon its citizens for supreme endeavors to meet the crisis.

The Pacific war

On July 26 the heads of the United States, British, and Chinese governments issued a joint proclamation calling upon Japan to surrender or be destroyed. In the absence of a reply the United States resolved to make use of a new and revolutionary weapon to end the war quickly. This was the atomic bomb, which could destroy entire cities and their inhabitants, a weapon developed in secrecy in the United States by scientists from Europe and America, some of whom were exiles from Nazi or fascist oppression.

The atomic bomb

Many high military and naval officers contended that use of the bomb was not necessary, on the assumption that Japan was already beaten. Harry Truman (1884–1972), who had succeeded Roosevelt following the latter's death in April 1945, decided otherwise. On August 6, a single atomic bomb was dropped on Hiroshima, completely obliterating about 60 percent of the city. Three days later a second bomb was dropped, this time on Nagasaki. President Truman warned that the United States would continue to

View of Hiroshima after the First Atom Bomb Was Dropped, August 6, 1945. This photo, taken one month later, shows the utter devastation of the city. Only a few steel and concrete buildings remained intact.

use the atom bomb as long as might be necessary to bring Japan to its knees. On August 14, Tokyo transmitted to Washington an unconditional acceptance of Allied demands.

3. THE PEACE SETTLEMENT

During the war the Allied leaders had come together on several occasions to discuss war aims and postwar goals. The public rhetoric of government propaganda spoke of the need for a world without conflict and of the right of all people to political self-determination, objectives expressed in the "Atlantic Charter" issued by Roosevelt and Churchill in August 1941, and in a declaration signed by twenty-six nations, including Britain, the United States, the Soviet Union, and China, the following year. Yet those worthy goals, like Wilson's earlier Fourteen Points, fell victim to the realities of international politics.

A Soldier's View of War. The caption for this cartoon reads "Here you are! Don't lose it again!" In the soldier's hand the tag reads "Victory and peace in Europe."

Stalin, Churchill, and Roosevelt met in two conferences that were of major importance in determining the shape and political complexion of postwar Europe. In both cases, tensions between the three major participants were to some degree glossed over in their desire to present a united front to the world. Yet those tensions were real. The focus of disagreement was Central Europe, and particularly the future of Germany and Poland. Stalin insisted that the Soviet Union retain the Polish territory annexed in 1939 at the time of the Nazi-Soviet pact, an expression of his understandable desire to build a bulwark against any future German aggression, and a reflection of his unwillingness to see postwar Western influence extended too far in the Soviet Union's direction. His memories of Anglo-American participation in the attempt by White Russians to overthrow the newly created communist regime in 1919 were matched by American perceptions of the Soviet Union as an expansionist and politically alien and dangerous regime. All three leaders were also confronted by conflicting plots and aspirations on the part of governments-in-exile from Nazi-occupied countries, and of extra-governmental Resistance groups—often led by communists—whose struggles to retain or to assume leadership in their homelands were exceeded only by their determination to oust the Germans.

Allied conflicts

When the three leaders met in Teheran in December 1943, they managed to put forward a declaration of unified purpose only by postponing the really knotty problems that confronted them. The invasion of France was agreed to for the following year; Stalin undertook to enter the war against Japan following the defeat of Germany. But on the question of Poland, only the most tentative agreement was reached regarding boundary lines, and the nature of the postwar Polish government was left for further negotiation.

The Teheran conference

By the time Stalin, Churchill, and Roosevelt met again, in February 1945 at Yalta, the military situation favored the Soviet Union's position. Soviet troops had occupied Poland the previous spring; they now held part of Czechoslovakia as well, and were poised to invade Germany. Once more the matter of Poland's future arose, as well as that of the composition of postwar regimes. A general declaration outlined plans for Soviet expansion westward into Poland, and the compensation of Poland with territory taken from the Germans. As to Poland's government, though communiqués spoke of the need for free elections there and elsewhere among the occupied countries, the fact remained that the Soviets had already established a communist government in Warsaw, and were unlikely to tolerate its replacement by an anticommunist faction still in London, whatever the results of an election. Yalta produced accord on several important issues: the establishment of a United Nations organization to keep the peace; the terms for Soviet entry into the Japanese war; the positioning of zones of Al-

The Yalta conference

The Yalta Conference. Churchill, Molotov, U.S. Secretary of State Stettinius, at the left, and Stalin, in the center, with glasses raised in a toast. Roosevelt is also to Stalin's left.

lied occupation in Germany and Austria; and agreement in principle to a policy of German reparation payments—though in goods, production, and equipment rather than in gold, as had been the case after the First World War.

The Potsdam conference

Little more than two months after Germany's surrender, the Allies met again, this time at Potsdam, a suburb of Berlin and the former residence of Prussian kings. Roosevelt had died the previous spring, shortly before the German surrender; his place at the conference was taken by his successor, Harry Truman. Churchill represented Britain until replaced, as the result of elections at home, by the new prime minister and Labour party leader, Clement Attlee (1883–1967). Stalin remained to negotiate for the Soviets. As at past conferences, less was settled than was allowed to remain unresolved. Peace treaties were to be prepared with the "recognized democratic governments" of previously occupied lands. Yet the question as to whether those governments set up by the Soviets in Poland and—by this time—elsewhere in Eastern Europe were truly democratic was not settled. Polish boundaries were redrawn to conform to the general agreement reached at Yalta. An inter-Allied war tribunal was established to try major Nazi leaders for "war crimes." In November 1945, the trials began in Nuremberg, Germany. The following September, eighteen of the twenty-two defendants were found guilty and received sentences ranging from ten-years' imprisonment to death.

East-West tensions

The Potsdam conference was shadowed by the East-West conflict that had darkened all the wartime meetings and was to do the same to international politics in the immediate postwar years. The division of Germany into four occupied zones—American, British, French, and Soviet—and the

The Potsdam Conference. Churchill, a cigar in his mouth, is seated in the back to the left; Stalin is at the right; Truman is seated with his back to the camera.

agreement to structure reparations payments on the basis of those zones rather than on a united Germany, forecast the unwillingness of either the Soviet Union or the Western powers to trust each other, or to tolerate the extension of the other's influence in that country which, though devastated, still remained vital to the security and peace of Europe as a whole.

The treaty with Japan, though it too produced disagreement between the Soviet Union and the West, did not reflect conflicts as immediate as those that characterized the European negotiations. The treaty deprived the Japanese of all the territory they had acquired since 1854—their entire overseas empire. They surrendered the southern half of Sakhalin Island and the Kuril Islands to the Soviet Union, and the Bonin and Ryukyu Islands to control by the United States. They also renounced all rights to Formosa, which was left in an undefined status. They yielded as well to the United States the right to continue maintaining military installations in Japan until the latter was able to defend itself. Despite opposition from the Soviets, who feared a U.S. military presence in the Far East, military occupation under the command of U.S. General Douglas MacArthur continued until a peace treaty went into effect in April 1952, restoring full sovereignty to Japan.

The treaty with Japan

As in the case of the Versailles treaty one of the most significant elements in the settlements was their provision for an international organization. The old League of Nations had failed to avert the outbreak of war in 1939, and in April 1946 it was formally dissolved. Yet Allied statesmen continued to recognize the need for some international organization. In February 1945, they agreed at Yalta that a conference to respond to that need should be convoked the following April. Despite the sudden death of Roosevelt two weeks earlier, the conference met in San Francisco as scheduled. A charter was adopted on June 26, providing for a world organization to be known as the United Nations and to be founded upon the principle of "the sovereign equality of all peace-loving states." Its important agencies were to be (1) a General Assembly composed of representatives of all the member states; (2) a Security Council composed of representatives of the United States, Great Britain, the Soviet Union, the Republic of China, and France, with permanent seats, and of ten other states chosen by the General Assembly to fill nonpermanent seats; (3) a Secretariat consisting of a secretary-general and a staff of subordinates; (4) an Economic and Social Council composed of eighteen members chosen by the General Assembly; (5) a Trusteeship Council; and (6) an International Court of Justice.

Establishment of the United Nations

Although the United Nations has failed to live up to the hopes of its founders, it continues to function as the world's longest-lived international assembly of nations. By far the most important functions of the new organization were assigned by the charter to the Security Council. This agency has the "primary responsibility for the maintenance of international peace and security." It has authority to investigate any dispute between nations, to recommend methods for settlement, and, if necessary to preserve the peace, to employ diplomatic or economic measures against an aggressor. If, in its judgment, these have proved, or are likely to prove, inadequate, it may "take such action by air, naval, or land forces" as may be required to

The Security Council

maintain or restore international order. The member states are required by the charter to make available to the Security Council, on its call, armed forces for the maintenance of peace.

The Security Council was so organized as to give almost a monopoly of authority to its permanent members, since no action of any kind could be taken without the unanimous consent of Great Britain, France, the United States, the Republic of China, the Soviet Union, and four other members besides. This absolute veto given to each of the principal states, instead of bolstering the peace of the world, potentially crippled the council and rendered it helpless in the face of many emergencies.

The remaining agencies of the U.N. were given a wide variety of functions. The Secretariat, composed of a secretary-general and a numerous staff, is chiefly an administrative authority. Its duties, though, are by no means routine, for the secretary-general may bring to the attention of the Security Council any matter that, in his opinion, threatens international peace. The functions of the Economic and Social Council are the most varied of all. Composed of eighteen members elected by the General Assembly, it has authority to initiate studies and make recommendations with respect to international social, economic, health, educational, cultural, and related matters, and may perform services within such fields at the request of U.N. members.

During its first three decades the work of various U.N. agencies helped the organization achieve a modestly impressive record of accomplishment. But against its successes must be recorded major failures as well. The United Nations was unable to establish control of nuclear weapons. And it was powerless in the face of any determined effort by a major power to have its own way, as in the case of the Soviet suppression of a revolt in Hungary in 1956; or the massive intervention by the United States in Vietnam in the 1960s and early 1970s. If the United Nations acted upon occasion to defuse potentially explosive world situations, as it did in Korea, it failed to achieve the lofty peacemaking and peacekeeping goals set for it by its founders.

SELECTED READINGS

• *Items so designated are available in paperback editions.*

• Carr, E. H., *The Twenty-Years' Crisis, 1919–1939,* London, 1942. Stimulating, though somewhat dogmatic.
• Carr, Raymond, *The Spanish Tragedy: The Civil War in Perspective,* London, 1977. A thoughtful introduction to the Spanish Civil War and the evolution of Franco's Spain.
• Collins, Larry, *Is Paris Burning?,* New York, 1965. A highly readable account of the liberation of Paris.
• Dawidowicz, Lucy S., *The War Against the Jews, 1933–1945,* New York, 1975. A full account of the Holocaust.
• Divine, Robert A., *Roosevelt and World War II,* Baltimore, 1969. A diplomatic history.

- Feis, Herbert, *Churchill-Roosevelt-Stalin: The War They Waged and the Peace They Sought,* Princeton, 1957. A standard survey.

  Géraud, André, *The Gravediggers of France,* Garden City, N.Y., 1944. A critical and impassioned account of the fall of France.

  Gilbert, Martin, and R. Gott, *The Appeasers,* Boston, 1963. Excellent study of British pro-German sentiment in the 1930s.

  Holborn, Hajo, *The Political Collapse of Europe,* New York, 1951. Examines Europe's position in light of the rise of Russia and the United States as superpowers.

- Jackson, Gabriel, *The Spanish Republic and the Civil War, 1931–1939,* Princeton, 1965. A solid, useful account.

- Koonz, Claudia, *Mothers in the Fatherland,* New York, 1987. Study of women's roles as official nurturers of the next generation in Hitler's Germany.

  Michel, Henri, *The Shadow War: The European Resistance, 1939–1945,* New York, 1972. Thoroughly researched and compelling reading.

- Milward, Alan S., *War, Economy, and Society, 1939–1945,* Berkeley, 1977. Analyzes the impact of the war on the world economy and the ways in which economic resources of the belligerents determined strategies.

  Nash, Gerald D., *World War II and the West: Reshaping the Economy,* Lincoln, Nebr., 1990. Well-argued discussion of the development of an international economy after 1945.

- Paxton, Robert O., *Vichy France: Old Guard and New Order, 1940–1944,* New York, 1972. A bitter account.

- Taylor, A. J. P., *The Origins of the Second World War,* New York, 1962. A controversial but provocative attempt to prove that Hitler did not want a world war.

  Thomas, Hugh, *The Spanish Civil War,* New York, 1961. A thorough and balanced account.

  Wheeler, Bennett, J. W., *Munich: Prologue to Tragedy,* London, 1966. A sensitive treatment of prewar diplomatic negotiations, outdated to some extent, but still evocative.

- Wright, Gordon, *The Ordeal of Total War, 1939–1945,* New York, 1968. Particularly good on the domestic response to war and the mobilization of the resources of the modern state.

SOURCE MATERIALS

- Bloch, Marc, *Strange Defeat: A Statement of Evidence Written in 1940,* London, 1949. An analysis of the fall of France, written by one of France's greatest historians, who later died fighting for the Resistance.

- Churchill, Winston S., *The Second World War,* 6 vols., London, 1948–1954. The war as Churchill saw it and as he wanted history to see it. Especially useful is the first volume on the 1930s, *The Gathering Storm.*

- De Gaulle, Charles, *The Complete War Memoirs,* New York, 1964. De Gaulle's apologia.

- Hershey, John, *Hiroshima,* New York, 1946. A moving account of the aftermath of the U.S. atomic bombing written very soon after the event.

- Noakes, Jeremy, and Geoffrey Pridham, *Documents on Nazism, 1919–1945,* New York, 1975. A helpful collection.

Part Seven

THE EMERGENCE OF WORLD CIVILIZATION

*Western civilization, as we have described and analyzed it, no longer exists today.
Instead, we speak in terms of a world civilization, one that owes much of its
history and many of its most perplexing problems to the West, but one that is
no longer shaped by those few nations that for so many centuries dominated the
globe.*

*The great powers of the nineteenth century—Britain, France, and Germany—
are powers now only insofar as they have agreed to pool their interests in an all-
European Community. The mid-twentieth century powers—the United States
and the Soviet Union—after four decades of confrontation, no longer dominate the
world as they did in the years immediately after the Second World War. The
former Soviet Union is now a collection of weakened, semiautonomous states,
struggling to find enough food to feed their deprived and disgruntled populations,
prey, like much of the rest of Eastern Europe, to serious nationalistic tensions.
The United States, plagued by political disenchantment and an enfeebled
economy, no longer commands the respect and obedience of nations once its
willing allies.*

*Power, and with it the attention of the world, is shifting from the West to the
emerging nations of Africa, the Middle East, Asia, and Latin America. Their vast
natural resources are affording many of them the chance to play the old Western*

game of power politics, and in a world arena wider than ever before. The equally vast dimensions of their internal problems—economic, racial, nutritional, and political—suggest that their solution will have to be worldwide as well. We are all, as the American designer Buckminster Fuller has said, partners for better or worse on "spaceship earth."

The Emergence of World Civilization

POLITICS

SCIENCE & INDUSTRY

Truman Doctrine, 1947
Independence of India, 1947
Communist regimes established in Eastern Europe,
  1947–1948
Marshall Plan, 1948
Division of Germany, 1949
Victory of Chinese communists, 1949
NATO, 1949
Korean War, 1950–1953   Hydrogen bomb, 1952
Death of Stalin, 1953   Discovery of polio vaccine, 1953
                                       Discovery of DNA, 1953

Hungarian revolt, 1956
Suez crisis, 1956

Sputnik launched, 1957

Conflict in the Congo, 1960
Nigerian Civil War, 1960s

Berlin Wall, 1961
Cuban Missile Crisis, 1962
War in Vietnam, 1964–1975
Civil war in Nigeria, 1966–1970
Arab-Israeli war, 1967
Czechoslovakian revolt, 1968

                                   Manned U.S. spacecraft lands on moon, 1969
Civil war in India, 1971   Advent of automation, 1970s

First SALT agreements signed, 1972
Arab-Israeli war, 1973

Egyptian-Israeli peace treaty, 1979
Iranian revolution, 1979
U.S.S.R. invasion of Afghanistan, 1979–1989

Iran-Iraq war, 1980–1988

Assassination of Anwar al-Sadat, 1981
U.S. rejection of SALT II agreement, 1981
Solidarity movement organizes strikes in Poland, 1982

                                   Toxic gas leak at plant in Bhopal, India, 1984
Mikhail Gorbachev assumes power in U.S.S.R., 1985   Two scientific teams report finding AIDS virus, 1986
                                   Nuclear accident at Chernobyl in Soviet Union,
                                      1986

Tiananmen Square, 1989   Exxon *Valdez* oil spill, 1989
Solidarity leaders elected
  to head Polish government, 1989
Fall of Berlin Wall, 1989
Nelson Mandela freed, 1990

Germany reunited, 1990
Persian Gulf War, 1990–1991
Demise of Soviet Union, 1991   Rio summit on environment, 1992

ECONOMICS & SOCIETY	ARTS & LETTERS
	Richard Wright, *Native Son,* 1940
1945	Abstract expressionism in art, mid–1940s
	Albert Camus, *The Plague,* 1947
	Norman Mailer, *The Naked and the Dead,* 1948
Creation of European Coal and	Simone de Beauvoir, *The Second Sex,* 1949–1950
Steel Community, 1951	James Jones, *From Here to Eternity,* 1951
	Samuel Beckett, *Waiting for Godot,* 1952
	Boris Pasternak, *Doctor Zhivago,* 1957
European Common Market established, 1958	
Black civil rights movement, United States,	
1960–1968	"Pop" art, 1960s
Frantz Fanon, *Wretched of the Earth,* 1961	
Youth "revolution," 1960s	François Truffaut, *Jules and Jim,* 1961
Women's liberation movement, 1960s–1970s	James Baldwin, *The Fire Next Time,* 1963
	Arthur Penn, *Bonnie and Clyde* (1967)
1970	Günter Grass, *Local Anaesthetic,* 1970
	Aleksandr Solzhenitsyn, *The Gulag Archipelago,*
	1973
Worldwide inflation and unemployment,	
late 1970s and early 1980s	
1980	
1990 Eastern European countries return to	
market economies, 1990s	

Chapter 30

NEW POWER RELATIONSHIPS
AND THE NEW EUROPE

The end of Communism is, first and foremost, a message to the human
race. It is a message we have not yet fully deciphered and comprehended.
In its deepest sense, the end of Communism has brought a major era in
human history to an end. It has brought an end not just to the 19th and
20th centuries, but to the modern age as a whole.

—Vaclav Havel, president of Czechoslovakia, 1991–1992

In April 1945 European men and women, surveying the devastation that
their countries had brought down upon each other during the past six
years, found it all but impossible to imagine their continent arising from
the ashes of total conflict. As in the First World War, both victors and vanquished had endured punishing destruction. Between 1914 and 1918,
8 million had died. Now the total was four times as great. Although France
and Britain had suffered fewer casualties in the Second than in the First
World War, loss of life elsewhere had been cataclysmic. Poland's population was reduced by 20 percent (in part as a consequence of the Nazis'
ruthless destruction of the Jews); losses in the Soviet Union were close to
15 million; in Germany, they were 5 million.

The costs of war

Across Europe, cities lay in ruins. Hitler had boasted in 1935 that in ten
years Berlin would be transformed so that no one could recognize it. His
prophecy came true, though in a grisly fashion he had not intended. Industrial and commercial centers in France, the Low Countries, Italy, and in the
wasted territories of Central Europe and Russia were largely rubble. Housing was scarce everywhere—in some areas it was practically nonexistent.
Six million houses had been destroyed in German-occupied Soviet Russia;
93 percent of the homes in Dusseldorf, Germany, were deemed uninhabit-
able. Food remained in dangerously short supply, a consequence of the violation of agricultural lands and people, the lack of farm machinery and fertilizer, and a severe drought in the summer of 1945. A year later, about 100
million people in Europe still existed on less than 1,500 calories per day—

The extent of the destruction

Berlin, 1945. The rubble from which the German "miracle" was created.

not enough to sustain working adults in a healthy state. Food rationing remained a dreary fact of life everywhere, for without it a large portion of the
Continent's population would have starved to death. The food shortage
was intensified by a general breakdown of transportation and communication. In the British and American zones of Germany 740 out of 958 major
bridges had been destroyed. France had suffered the loss of about two-
thirds of its railway stock and its merchant fleet. Canals had been bombed;
harbors were choked with scuttled warships. During the winter of
1945–1946, many regions had little or no fuel for heat and what coal there
was (less than half the prewar supply) could not be transported to those
areas most in need of it.

No wonder Europeans were initially dazed by the trauma they had inflicted upon themselves. The wonder, indeed, was that the period of

Ten years later trauma lasted such a relatively short time. Ten years later, Europe had been
transformed—though not restored. Two all-important changes had oc-
curred by then. The first, reflecting an altered balance of international
power, resulted in a divided continent, the East under the control of the
Soviet Union, the West dominated by the military and diplomatic presence
of the United States. The second change, a consequence of human determination and favorable economic trends, produced in the West a buoyant,
lively, and creative civilization, more expansive and up-to-date than even
the most optimistic forecaster might have deemed possible in 1945.

1. A DIVIDED CONTINENT

During the decade after the Second World War the world of nations assumed a bipolar character, in large measure the result of mutual mistrust and increasing hostility between the Soviet Union and the United States. The war had left these two nations the most powerful on earth. Germany, Italy, and Japan were destined for a time to play a subordinate international role as a consequence of their defeat. Britain and France possessed neither populations nor resources great enough to qualify as "superpowers," and the loss of their remaining colonies after the war further sapped their economic potential. China, the other major victor in the conflict, was soon thereafter overwhelmed by a revolution that turned that nation in upon itself. Hence the domination of the United States and the Soviet Union, both vying for world supremacy and both striving to draw the states of Europe into their orbits, efforts they had begun even before the end of the war.

A bipolar world

The Soviet Union had insisted during the negotiations at Teheran and Yalta that it had a legitimate claim to hegemony over Eastern Europe, a claim that Western leaders willingly acknowledged. When visiting Moscow in 1944, Churchill and Stalin had bargained like two Old World power brokers over the fate of several supposedly free nations. Churchill proposed a 90 percent preponderance of Soviet influence in Rumania, countered by 90 percent for the West in Greece; Yugoslavia, 50–50; and so on. Stalin, however, increasingly mistrustful of Western leadership, believed that bargains with the West, no matter how attractive they might appear on paper, were really worth little. "Churchill," he remarked, "is the kind who, if you don't watch him, will slip a kopek out of your pocket. . . . Roosevelt . . . dips in his hands only for bigger coins." Stalin's authoritarian domestic regime was motivated by a siege mentality that saw almost everyone as an enemy or, at best, a threat. Not surprisingly, his foreign policy was dictated by that same state of mind.

Soviet hegemony in the East

Yet Stalin's anti-Western policy was based upon more than personal paranoia. It was a reflection of traditional fears that had characterized Russia's attitudes toward its European neighbors for centuries, of ambivalence toward Western ways that had marked the regimes of Peter the Great, for example, at the beginning of the eighteenth century, and of Alexander III at the end of the nineteenth. Stalin's mistrust of the United States in particular stemmed as well from the prewar years when the Americans had never hesitated to express their antagonism to Stalinist communism. U.S. mistrust was matched by Soviet leaders' escalating fear of American-inspired military and economic encirclement.

From the standpoint of economic power, the United States far outdistanced the other nations of the world. Since 1939 Americans had doubled their national income and quadrupled their savings. The United States had

Winston Churchill Denounces Soviet Tyranny. In a speech at Fulton, Missouri, in March 1946, Churchill coined the phrase "Iron Curtain" to characterize the Soviet's partitioning of Eastern from Western Europe.

been essentially untouched by the war, its industries intact and its financial power seemingly impregnable. Though Americans constituted only 7 percent of the world's population, they enjoyed over 30 percent of the world's estimated income in 1945. For the first time in its history the United States was in a position to be the economic and military arbiter of at least half the earth. The United States controlled both the Atlantic and Pacific Oceans, policed the Mediterranean, and shaped the development of international policy in Western Europe. And until 1949, America had a monopoly of death-dealing atomic weapons.

The Soviet Union emerged from the Second World War as the second-strongest power on earth. Though its navy was small, its land army and possibly its air force by 1948 were the largest in the world. Soviet population was climbing rapidly toward 200 million, and this in spite of the loss of 7 million soldiers and about 8 million civilians during the war. In mineral wealth and petroleum resources the Soviet Union's position compared favorably with that of the richest countries. On the other hand, its industrial machine had been badly crippled by the war. No fewer than 1,700 Soviet cities and towns had been totally destroyed along with 40,000 miles of railway and 31,000 factories. Stalin declared in 1946 that it would probably require at least six years to repair the damage and rebuild the devastated areas.

Because of the need to recoup their enormous industrial losses and their fears of further invasion, the Soviets were determined to maintain political, economic, and military control of those countries in Eastern Europe that they had liberated from Nazi control. They employed diplomatic pressure, political infiltration, and military terrorism to establish "people's republics" in Eastern Europe sympathetic to the Soviet regime. In country after country the process repeated itself: at first, all-party coalition governments from which only fascists were excluded; then further coalitions, in which communists predominated; and finally, one-party states. By 1948, governments that owed allegiance to Moscow were established in Poland, Hungary, Rumania, Bulgaria, and Czechoslovakia. The nations of Eastern Europe did

See color map of Europe facing page 1037

not all succumb without a struggle. Greece, which the Soviets wished to include within their sphere of influence, was torn by civil war until 1949, when with Western aid its monarchy was restored. A direct challenge to the Yalta guarantee of free, democratic elections occurred in Czechoslovakia, where in 1948 the Soviets crushed the coalition government of liberal leaders Eduard Beneš (1884–1948) and Jan Masaryk (1886–1948).

The most important check the Soviets received at this time to their campaign for Eastern European hegemony also occurred in 1948, when the Yugoslavian government of the wartime hero Marshal Tito (1943–1980) declared its independence of Moscow and its determination to steer a course unallied to either East or West. Tito, the only satellite communist leader who had risen to power on his own and not as a Soviet puppet, possessed political authority rooted within his own country, and this secured his position from reprisals once he had established Yugoslavia's freedom from Soviet hegemony. Events in Czechoslovakia and Yugoslavia inspired a series of Soviet-directed purges within the political hierarchies of the various satellite governments, a measure of Stalin's continuing fear of opposition.

The United States countered these moves with massive programs of economic and military aid to Western Europe. In 1947, President Truman proclaimed the Truman Doctrine, which provided assistance programs to prevent further communist infiltration into the governments of Greece and Turkey. The following year, the Marshall Plan, named for Secretary of State George Marshall who first proposed it, provided funds for the reconstruction of Western European industry. The plan was notable in two respects: first, it represented an attempt by the United States to restore the strength of its most serious economic competitors, including its former enemy Germany, in the belief that an economically independent Europe would be less likely to fall prey to Soviet domination. Second, it relied upon a willingness on the part of the Western European nations to coordinate their economic efforts, substituting, at least to some degree, cooperation for competition.

George Marshall

At the same time, the United States moved to shore up the military defenses of the West. In April 1949, a group of representatives of Western European states, together with Canada and the United States, signed an agreement providing for the establishment of the North Atlantic Treaty Organization (NATO). Subsequently Greece, Turkey, and West Germany were added as members. The treaty declared that an armed attack against any one of the signatory parties would be regarded as an attack against all, and that they would combine their armed strength to whatever extent necessary to repel the aggressor. The joint military command, or NATO army, established in 1950, was increased from thirty to fifty divisions in 1953, with a rearmed West Germany contributing twelve of the divisions.

NATO

The Soviets reacted with understandable alarm to the determination of the United States to strengthen Western Europe. In 1947 they organized an international political arm, the Cominform (Communist Information Bureau), responsible for coordinating worldwide communist policy and programs. In addition the Soviets rejected an original offer of Marshall Plan aid, and instead organized an Eastern European counterpart for economic recovery, the Council for Mutual Economic Assistance. They responded to NATO with the establishment of military alliances, confirmed by the Warsaw Pact of 1955. This agreement set up a joint armed forces command among its signatories, and more important, authorized the continued stationing of Soviet troops in Albania, Bulgaria, Czechoslovakia, Hungary, Poland, Rumania, and the eastern portion of Germany, which had remained under Soviet domination since the end of the war.

Cominform and Warsaw Pact

Germany was, in fact, the focal point of East-West tensions during these years. After the war, the Soviets had continued to insist on $10 billion worth of reparations from Germany in the form of industrial production. Although the Soviets' desperate economic condition and fear of a revived Germany played a role in this posture, Britain and the United States read

Focus on Germany

Crises in Berlin. Left: The Berlin Airlift, 1948. For fifteen months the United States, Britain, and France airlifted over two million tons of supplies into West Berlin, around which the Russians had imposed a land blockade. Right: The Berlin Wall, 1961. Thirteen years after the blockade, the East German government constructed a wall between East and West Berlin to stop the flow of escapees to the West. This manifestation of the "Iron Curtain" was dismantled in 1989.

this demand as a reflection of a Soviet desire to keep Germany weak and therefore susceptible to political instability—specifically, to the spread of communism.

By 1946 the joint administration of Germany by the four former Allied powers had collapsed. The Soviet Union remained in control of its satellite, which eventually became the nominally independent German Democratic Republic (East Germany), while the Western powers continued to support the industrial recovery of the area under their control—in its turn to emerge as the Federal Republic of Germany (West Germany). A crisis arose in 1948 when, in retaliation for the reunification of the western zones of control under one authority, the Soviets closed down road, rail, and water access from the west to Berlin. Berlin, though within the territory of East Germany, was administered by all four powers. The Western powers countered with an airlift of food and other necessary supplies, which prevented the collapse of the city into Soviet hands. After almost a year the Soviets lifted the blockade. For many years to come, however, Berlin was to remain one of the hottest spots in the ongoing "cold war," as it came to be called, between the Soviet Union and the West. The city symbolized

The Berlin blockade

the determination of the Western powers to ensure West Germany's economic recovery, as well as their opposition to what they continued to see as communist aggression.

The tensions that produced the cold war were the result of misperceptions on both sides. Americans, who had been persuaded by wartime government propaganda to admire the Soviets as stalwart anti-fascists, were naively disillusioned when they discovered that their erstwhile allies were in fact not democrats. Concerned about the economic weakness throughout postwar Western Europe, U.S. leaders believed that the Soviets were hatching a vast plan to take advantage of that weakness by establishing communist regimes throughout the West, as they had in the East.

The Cold War: U.S. attitudes

Scholars have recently argued convincingly that there was no grand Soviet strategy of this sort. The Soviets were not willing to undertake any such campaign, primarily because they were economically and militarily incapable of doing so. Since the Soviets had long feared encirclement by hostile capitalist powers, however, they saw the Truman and Marshall programs as a direct form of neoimperialism, an American plot to subject Western Europe to the economic hegemony of the United States. Stalin found it useful to orchestrate his propaganda to this theme. As a result of wartime destruction, he needed to convince the Soviet people that they must undergo a further series of rugged Five-Year Plans stressing the production of heavy industrial materials rather than consumer goods. He could demand sacrifices more convincingly if he could point to an international anti-Soviet conspiracy.

Soviet attitudes

Stalin himself remained deeply suspicious, not only of the West, but of any power or personality that he perceived to be a threat to his dictatorial rule. He convened neither Central Committee nor party congress. He relied on a shrinking number of political henchmen to carry out the business of government, among them: Vyacheslav Molotov (1890–1986), the Soviet foreign minister; Lavrenty Beria (1899–1953), head of the powerful secret police; and Andrei Zhdanov (1896–1948), secretary of the party central committee. The latter was charged with the task of devising a new communist gospel, one prescribed by Stalin, which tended to ignore the earlier doctrines of Marx, Engels, and Lenin, and amounted to little more than an apologia for Stalin's repressive personal despotism. Party propaganda preached Soviet superiority to the West. Soviet writers and artists were attacked for imitating their Western counterparts. Economists were taken to task for suggesting that European industry might succeed in recovering from the damages it had sustained. In the realm of science, accepted genetic theory was supplanted by that of the Soviet Trofim Lysenko (1898–1976), whose work implied the inheritance of acquired characteristics; Einstein was vilified; and Freud was pronounced a decadent charlatan.

Stalinism

Only with Stalin's death in 1953 did this relentless barrage of anti-Western propaganda begin to abate somewhat. Although relations between East and West remained wary, tensions eased considerably during the late 1950s and 1960s. The United States, it is true, continued to adhere to a policy of Soviet "containment," seeking as allies those most willing to oppose by

After Stalin

Nikita Khrushchev. Premier (1958–1964) and First Secretary of the Communist Party (1956–1964) of the Soviet Union, Khrushchev visited the U.S. in 1959. Here he is shown joking with an Iowan farmer.

military force, if necessary, the spread of international communism. By the mid-1950s, however, Western European nations had begun to wonder whether U.S. intervention in their affairs might not, in fact, represent as much an American power play as an attempt to protect the West from Soviet aggression. American claims to the role of "protector of the free world" began to sound hollow, particularly after U.S. Secretary of State John Foster Dulles negotiated a diplomatic and military understanding with the aging Spanish dictator Francisco Franco in 1955.

Khrushchev to power

In the Soviet Union, a change of direction was signaled by the accession to power in that same year of Nikita Khrushchev (1894–1971). Khrushchev possessed a kind of earthy directness which, despite his hostility to the West, nevertheless helped for a time to ease tensions. Abandoning the seclusion of the Kremlin, where Stalin had immured himself, he traveled throughout the world. On a visit to the United States in 1959, he traded quips with Iowa farmers and was entertained at Disneyland. Attending a meeting of the United Nations in New York in 1960, he underscored his disagreement with the speaker by banging his desk with his shoe.

Khrushchev's goals and policies

As testimony to his desire to reduce international conflict, Khrushchev soon agreed to the first of a series of summit meetings with the leaders of Britain, France, and the United States. This new Soviet determination to lower international tensions grew out of Khrushchev's need to consolidate his regime at home and to prevent the threatened crumbling of the communist bloc in Eastern Europe. The harsh demands of the Stalin regime had generated discontent among the Soviet people. Dissenters, their voices no longer silenced by the Stalinist police, began to demand a shift from the production of heavy machinery and armaments to the manufacture of consumer goods, and, in the arts, a return to at least a measure of freedom. Their voices were heard in essays and in novels such as Ilya Ehrenburg's *The Thaw* (1954), by which name this period became known. The Soviet leadership followed a tricky and not always successful line, on the one hand denouncing the excesses of the Stalinist regime and the "cult of personality" that Stalin had imposed upon the nation; on the other, as Stalin's heirs, only partially loosening their grip on the lives of their countrymen and women. When, in 1956, Khrushchev delivered a secret speech to the Communist party's twentieth congress on the crimes of the Stalin regime, he did so by describing Stalin himself as a bungler and, ultimately, a madman, but at the same time by defending the system of government that Stalin had created.

Challenges in Eastern Europe: Poland and Hungary

Meanwhile, throughout the other communist states, growing resentment of Soviet demands for rapid industrialization and collectivization generated arguments for easing the restrictions Stalinism had imposed. In response to these pressures the Soviet leaders altered their economic goals and began preaching that there was more than one road to socialism. The Soviet Union's new posture toward its client states in Eastern Europe received its severest test in 1956 when Poland and Hungary demanded greater autonomy in the management of their domestic affairs. In Poland, the government at first responded to major strikes with military repression and then with a promise of liberalization. The anti-Stalinist Polish leader Wladyslaw Gomulka (1905–1982) was able to win Soviet permission for his country to pursue its own "ways of socialist development" by pledging Poland's continued loyalty to the terms of the Warsaw Pact. Events in Hungary produced a different result. There, protests against Stalinist policies developed into a much broader anti-communist struggle and attempted secession from the Warsaw Pact. If the Soviets were prepared to entertain a liberalization of domestic policy, they would not tolerate a repudiation of the Warsaw Pact. On November 4, 1956, Soviet troops reoccupied Budapest; leaders of the Hungarian liberation were taken prisoner and executed.

The limits of coexistence: The Berlin Wall

Despite these events, Khrushchev held to his policy of "peaceful coexistence" with the West. Though he did not renounce his ultimate belief in the triumph of communism, he argued that victory could be achieved by other than military means. Yet Soviet leaders remained unyielding in their determination to reduce any possible German military threat to Eastern Europe. They continued to nurture the fear that Germany might launch a new war, abetted by its capitalist allies. For this reason, they staunchly opposed the reunification of the country. In 1961 the East German government built a high wall separating the two sectors of Berlin in order to cut off the escape of thousands of East Germans to West Berlin and thence to western Germany. For almost thirty years, the wall remained a potent symbol of Soviet determination to prevent the formation of a united Germany—until 1989.

Khrushchev eventually fell prey to political rivals and was deposed in 1964. The reins of Soviet power passed to Alexei Kosygin (1904–1980) as premier and Leonid Brezhnev (1906–1982) as secretary of the Communist

The Occupation of Czechoslovakia. In 1968 the liberalized regime of Alexander Dubcek was suppressed by the Soviets. The violent response by the citizens was put down by military force.

party, with Brezhnev soon emerging as head of state. The Soviets continued to hold the governments of Eastern Europe in check. In 1968 they sent tanks and troops into Czechoslovakia after the Czech leadership under Alexander Dubcek (1921–1992) had attempted to meet criticisms by decentralizing the administration, democratizing the Communist party, pursuing an independent foreign policy, and permitting a brief flowering of intellectual life called the "Prague Spring."

The Czech revolt of 1968

Throughout the 1960s and 1970s, politicians in Western Europe responded in various ways to the fact of their divided continent. Leaders of Communist parties in France, Italy, and elsewhere recognized a need to separate themselves from Moscow's repressive line if they were to retain credibility with their memberships or attain political power. In 1975 the word "Eurocommunism" appeared for the first time in print. Eurocommunists declared their independence of Soviet foreign policy, while proclaiming their continuing adherence to the principles first espoused by Marx and Engels. The practice of yielding to Moscow on matters of foreign policy, so characteristic of Western European Communist parties from the 1920s to the 1950s, was henceforth abandoned. "We, the communists of today," the Spanish leader Santiago Carillo remarked, "have no international discipline imposed upon us. What unites us today are the bonds of affinity, based on the theory of scientific socialism." Eurocommunists showed a new interest in participating as partners in coalition governments with non-communist parties of the Left which they had heretofore shunned. In a joint statement in 1975, the French and Italian communists proclaimed that "socialism is democracy realized in the most complete manner, and the prerequisite in achieving this goal is a continuous democratization of economic, political

Eurocommunism and independence from Soviet policy

and social life." The political division of Europe into Eastern and Western camps over the years weakened the ties of Western communists to the Soviet Union. Moscow had been to them what Rome was to Catholic Christendom, Carillo declared. No longer, however. An international movement had fragmented into a collection of polycentric political entities.

At the same time, Western leaders remained concerned about a divided Europe and sought ways to bring the two halves into closer association with each other. Despite evidence to the contrary in Hungary and Czechoslovakia, Soviet leaders also perceived a need to relax their hold on the satellite nations of the East. Following the Czech invasion in 1968, they proclaimed the so-called Brezhnev Doctrine, which stated that no socialist state should permit itself to adopt policies detrimental to the interests of international socialism and that the Soviet Union could intervene in the domestic affairs of any Soviet-bloc nation if communist rule was threatened. But it also asserted that each state might proceed to determine the most appropriate path for its own development.

The politician most effective in bridging the gap between East and West was the West German Willy Brandt (1913–1992), chancellor of West Germany in the early 1970s. Brandt, in his youth an outspoken enemy of Hitler, had fled Germany in the 1930s to Norway, where he joined the anti-Nazi resistance movement in the Second World War. His wartime record increased his credibility with Eastern Europeans, who, if they were not pleased to be subject to the Soviet Union, had as much historical reason to fear Germany as they did the Soviet Union. Brandt recognized the need to accept the division of Germany into two nations. Accordingly his government initiated a policy to regularize relations with West Germany's eastern neighbors (*Ostpolitic*). A complex series of diplomatic negotiations with the Soviet Union, East Germany, and Poland resulted in treaties that established East and West Germany as separate states within one nation, guaranteed unimpeded Western access to Berlin, and recognized Poland's claim to a western frontier along the Oder and Neisse Rivers as established originally after the Second World War.

Tensions between East and West, which eased during the 1960s and 1970s, arose once more in the next decade, in response to the Soviet Union's meddling in Poland's internal affairs. In 1980, calling their movement "Solidarity," Polish workers had organized strikes that brought the government of the country to a standstill. The strikers were objecting to working conditions imposed by the government to combat a severe economic crisis that had produced high prices. They were led by an electrician from the Gdansk shipyards, Lech Walesa (1943–   ), whose charismatic personality appealed not only to the Polish citizenry but to sympathizers in the West. Again the Soviets assisted a puppet military regime in reimposing authoritarian rule. Though the Soviet Union did not intervene directly, the implied threat that it might do so, reinforced by the presence of increasing numbers of Soviet troops near the Polish border, reemphasized Soviet unwillingness to permit its Eastern European neighbors autonomy over their internal affairs.

West German Chancellor Willy Brandt in Poland, 1970. This widely distributed photograph of Brandt kneeling before a memorial to Jewish victims of the Nazi Holocaust in Warsaw signaled both his determination to make amends for past German war crimes and to ease animosities between East and West.

Solidarity in Poland and Soviet threat

Defiance in Poland. Thousands of striking workers take part in religious services in the Lenin Shipyards in Gdansk on August 24, 1980. This was the scene of the first in a series of strikes that paralyzed an already troubled economic and political system and challenged Soviet domination of Polish governmental policy.

2. ECONOMIC RENAISSANCE

Reasons for postwar boom

In thinking of their successful postwar economic recovery as a "miracle," Western Europeans ignored the degree to which human agencies and predictable economic forces precipitated change. First, the war had encouraged a variety of technological innovations with direct and important peacetime applications: improved communications (the invention of radar, for example), the manufacture of synthetic materials, the increasing use of aluminum and alloy steels, and advances in the techniques of prefabrication. Secondly, through wartime manufacturing, nations had added significantly to the sum of their productive capital during the war. In Britain the total was in excess of one and half billion pounds sterling. Despite the wartime devastation, capital invested in European plants that were easily damaged but difficult to destroy survived to sustain a postwar boom grounded in the recovery initiated by the Marshall Plan. This boom was fueled by a third set of factors: the continued buoyancy of consumer demand and the consequent high level of employment throughout the 1950s and 1960s. These in turn encouraged continued capital investment and technological innovation. Finally, brisk foreign demand for goods convinced Europeans of the need to remove obstacles to international trade and payments. This fortuitous combination of circumstances made possible a remarkable period of dynamic economic growth.

The economic theories of John Maynard Keynes (see above, p. 965), touting the power of governments to maintain high levels of consumption and investment by means of taxation and public spending, had a profound influence on planners throughout the West. As one economic historian has written of the period, "economic growth became a universal creed and a common expectation." The creed was a popular one because it met equally common expectations about rising standards of living that seemed just recompense for the suffering endured during the war and the depression that had preceded it. Europeans were also inspired by the example of the United States. They, too, craved the automobiles, washing machines, radios, and other domestic gadgets that Americans considered necessities but which Europeans had until now perceived as luxuries.

Keynes and the creed of economic growth

Governments resorted to a variety of devices to encourage economic expansion: West Germany provided tax breaks to encourage business investment; Britain and Italy offered investment allowances to their steel and petroleum industries. Virtually all of Western Europe experimented with the nationalization of industry and services in an effort to enhance efficiency and productivity. The result was a series of "mixed" economies combining public and private ownership. France, Britain, Italy, and Austria took the lead in the move toward state-controlled enterprise. In France, where public ownership was already well advanced in the 1930s, railways, electricity and gas, banking, radio and television, and a large segment of the automobile industry were brought under state management. In Britain, the list was equally long: coal and utilities; road, railroad, and air transport; and banking. Though nationalization was less common in West Germany, the railway system—state-owned since the late nineteenth century; some electrical, chemical, and metallurgical concerns; and the Volkswagen company—the remnant of Hitler's attempt to produce a "people's car"—were all in state hands, though the latter was largely returned to the private sector in 1963.

Movement toward "mixed" economies

These government policies and programs contributed to astonishing growth rates. Between 1945 and 1963 the average yearly growth of Gross Domestic Product (Gross National Product minus income received from abroad) in West Germany was 7.6 percent; in Austria, 5.8 percent; in Italy, 6 percent; in Holland, 4.7 percent; and so on. This was a remarkable reversal of the economic patterns of an interwar period that had been beset by slack demand, overproduction, and insufficient investment. In the face of reconstruction and recovery, production facilities were hard pressed to keep up with soaring demand.

Economic growth rates

West Germany's recovery was particularly noteworthy. Production increased sixfold between 1948 and 1964. Unemployment fell to record lows, reaching 0.4 percent in 1965, when there were six jobs for every unemployed person. Though prices rose initially, their subsequent leveling off provided an opportunity for most citizens to participate in a domestic buying spree that caused production to soar. In the 1950s, an average of half a million housing units were constructed annually to accommodate those whose homes had been destroyed, an influx of new resident-refugees from East Germany and Eastern Europe, and transient workers from Italy, Spain,

West German resurgence

Greece, and elsewhere who were attracted by West Germany's demand for labor.

The reasons for West Germany's remarkable economic renaissance were diverse. Certainly the presence of an army of highly skilled workers and a long tradition of industrial know-how counted for much. Other factors included: (1) the split from East Germany, which meant that the powerful and generally reactionary Junker class was no longer able to brake progress as it had since the mid-nineteenth century; (2) the crippling of much of Germany's industrial plant, which provided the opportunity to incorporate up-to-date equipment and techniques into rebuilt factories; and (3) the fact that initially West Germany was expressly forbidden by the occupying powers to spend money on defense.

In France the major economic problem following the war was the need to modernize the nation's industries, many of which remained small family enterprises resistant to technological change. Under the direction of a minister for planning, Jean Monnet, a special office—the General Commissariat for Planning—was established to initiate and execute a program for national economic recovery. Using money provided by the Marshall Plan, the French government played a direct and active role in industrial revival and reform, contributing not only capital but expert advice, and facilitating shifts in the national labor pool to place workers where they were most needed. The plan gave priority to basic industries, with the result that the production of electricity doubled, the steel industry was thoroughly modernized, and the French railway system became the fastest and most efficient on the Continent. Other sectors of the economy tended to stagnate, however, while agriculture remained in the hands of a peasant class loathe to avail itself of government incentives intended to foster productivity

Modernization in France. Technological advancement may be slowed by people reluctant to abandon the old ways of doing things. Modern trains often traverse routes where farms remain small and unmechanized. Left: a modern train traveling over a route in Normandy. Right: Herding livestock in Normandy.

An Italian Washing Machine Factory. Consumer goods once considered luxuries became commonly accepted necessities in postwar Europe.

through mechanization. Nevertheless, the French Gross National Product increased at the creditable rate of about 5 percent per year in the 1950s.

Italy's industrial "miracle" was even more impressive than that of West Germany and France, given the woeful state of the nation's economy immediately following the war. Stimulated by infusions of capital from the government and from the Marshall Plan, Italian companies soon began to compete with other European international giants. The products of Olivetti, Fiat, and Pirelli became familiar in households across the world to an extent that no Italian goods had in the past. Electric power production—particularly important in Italy because of its lack of coal—had by 1953 increased 100 percent over that in 1938. By 1954 real wages were 50 percent higher than they had been in 1938. Yet Italy's success was marred by the enduring poverty of the country's southern regions, where illiteracy remained high and land continued to be held by a few rich families.

Italy's industrial "miracle"

Elsewhere on the Continent, nations with little in common in terms of political traditions or industrial patterns all shared in the general prosperity. Spain's economy changed markedly in the late 1950s, when a combination of rising foreign investment and the lifting of government controls spurred higher levels of production. Tourism was for Spain, as for all European countries, an increasingly important industry. Seventeen million visitors came to Spain in 1966, making it second only to Italy as a tourist attraction. Holland, Belgium, Austria, Greece, and the Scandinavian countries all enjoyed booms in the late 1950s. Though each country succeeded in increasing its GNP significantly, however, there remained marked differences in the levels of prosperity across the Continent. The per capita GNP in Sweden, for example, was almost ten times that of Turkey.

Shared prosperity elsewhere on the Continent

Britain throughout remained a special case. Although it shared in the

Heating Fuel Shortage in Great Britain. This scene of British householders queuing for coal during the severely cold winter of 1948 provides a measure of the degree to which "winners" as well as "losers" suffered in the immediate aftermath of the Second World War.

economic prosperity of the postwar years, it did so to a lesser extent than other European countries. The British rise in GNP averaged 2.5 percent per year between 1948 and 1962—a respectable enough figure when compared with past performance (2.2 percent between 1924 and 1937, for example), but nothing like the spectacular achievements recorded during the same period across the Channel. The Conservative party prime minister Harold Macmillan (1894–1986) campaigned successfully for reelection in 1959 with the slogan "You've never had it so good"—an accurate-enough boast. Yet the British economy remained sluggish. The country was burdened with obsolete factories and techniques, the legacy of its early industralization. It was plagued as well by a series of balance-of-payments crises precipitated by an inability to sell more goods abroad than it imported.

Both trade unions and management shared responsibility for Britain's poor performance. Unions refused to cooperate with management in schemes to increase productivity. A vigorous sense of "us against them," little different from the shop-floor antagonisms of the previous century, continued to prevail. Management remained uninterested in innovation and in devising effective ways to meet rising foreign competition. Industrial leadership suffered from an entrepreneurial failure of nerve. Neither government nor private investors were willing to gamble on the future of British industry in the way their Continental counterparts did. Because shipbuilders refused to invest in new productive capacity, for example, tonnage built fell from 1.2 million in 1949 to 1 million in 1965, while in the same period it increased in Japan from 100,000 to 5 million. Finally, the country's worldwide defense commitments, its unwillingness to surrender its obligations to colonies and former colonies overseas, its position as an island dependent to a great degree upon imports in order to survive—in short its history and its geography—all helped dictate its economic position in the postwar world.

The Western European renaissance was achieved by more than the efforts of individual nations. From the late 1940s on, they took steps to bind themselves together as an effective economic third force between the superpowers. In 1951 the European Coal and Steel Community was created, which placed the management of those industries in France, West Germany, Belgium, Holland, and Luxembourg under a joint High Authority. Consisting of experts from each of the participating countries, the Authority possessed the power to regulate prices, to increase or limit production, and to impose administrative fees. Britain declared itself unwilling to participate, fearing the effects of European economic union on its declining coal industry and on its relationship with longtime trading partners such as Australia, New Zealand, and Canada.

During the mid-1950s, further steps toward transnational economic integration were taken—the establishment of EURATOM, for example, a research organization in the field of nuclear development—culminating in 1958 with the founding of the European Economic Community, or Common Market. The EEC declared its goals to be the abolition of all trade barriers between the initial six members: France, West Germany, Italy, Bel-

Steps toward European economic integration

The Common Market

EEC Headquarters. The central administrative organ of the European Economic Community (EEC), now called the European Community (EC), has its headquarters in Brussels, Belgium.

gium, Holland, and Luxembourg. In addition, the organization pledged itself to common external tariffs, the free movement of labor and capital among the member nations, and the establishment of uniform wage structures and social security systems, so as to foster similar working conditions throughout the EEC. A commission with headquarters in Brussels was charged with the administration of this ambitious program.

Despite inevitable difficulties, particularly in the area of agricultural policy and prices, the European Economic Community was a remarkable success. By 1963, it had become the world's largest importer. Its steel production was second only to that of the United States, and total industrial production was over 70 percent higher than it had been in 1950. Even critics who complained about constant interference of EEC "Eurocrats"—over 3,000 in Brussels by 1962—conceded that centralized European planning and decision-making had brought the Continent extraordinary and unheralded prosperity. The Common Market operated increasingly as a semiautonomous political unit, and in 1972 citizens of member nations voted directly for representatives to an EEC parliament.

Success of the European Economic Community

Although economic development in Eastern Europe was not nearly so dramatic as that of the West, significant advances occurred there as well. National income rose and output increased. Poland and Hungary, in particular, strengthened their economic connections with the West, primarily with France and West Germany. By the 1970s, commerce outside the Soviet bloc accounted for about 30 percent of Eastern Europe's volume of trade. Nevertheless, the Soviet Union required its satellites to design their economic policies to serve more than their own national interests. Regula-

Economic growth in Eastern Europe

tions governing the Eastern European equivalent of the Common Market—the Council of Mutual Economic Assistance, or COMECON—insured that the Soviet Union could sell its exports at prices well above the world level, while other members were compelled to trade with the Soviet Union to their disadvantage. Emphasis initially was on heavy industry and collectivized agriculture, though political tension in countries such as Hungary and Poland compelled the Soviets eventually to moderate their policies so as to permit the manufacture of more consumer goods and the development of a modest trade with the West. As with the Western nations, those in the East demonstrated a continuing determination to free themselves from economic dependence upon a single power.

Expansion of social services in the West

Behind the drive for economic growth in Western Europe lay the determination of individual men and women to improve their standard of living and quality of life. To this end, they demanded more from their governments in the form of social services. Governments, in turn, relied on their generally robust economies to provide for their citizens to a greater degree than ever before. State welfare programs had, of course, existed throughout the twentieth century, their roots extending back to the insurance schemes for old age, sickness, and disability introduced by Bismarck in Germany in the late 1880s. Postwar Western Europe saw the expansion of such programs based on assumptions of state support that were hardly less compelling than the obligation to keep the peace, nowhere stated more clearly than in the preamble of the French constitution: "The nation guarantees the condition necessary for the development of the individual and the family. It guarantees every individual . . . the protection of health, material security, rest and leisure." A survey in 1957 found that public expenditure on health, pensions, family allowances and assistance (excluding housing and education), accounted for 20.8 percent of the national income in West Germany, 18.9 percent in France, and 12.1 percent in Britain. In Sweden, money spent on social services was six times higher in 1957 than in 1930; in Italy, it was fourteen times higher.

3. THE POLITICS OF EUROPEAN RECOVERY

New, moderate leadership: British politics

The governments responsible for these remarkable economic and social changes were ideologically almost uniformly middle-of-the-road. Yet unlike the situation after 1918, when the "old men" resumed power throughout Europe, new men who were unwilling to see Europe return to business as usual moved into positions of authority after 1945. In Britain the Labour party, led by middle-class, mild-mannered socialist Clement Attlee, enacted the social legislation that produced a welfare state. The Labour government gave way in 1951 to the Conservatives who, led most notably by Harold Macmillan from 1957 to 1963, proved more than willing to embrace the promise of economic growth and a continuation of welfare policies. The Labour party returned to power in the mid-1960s, under the prime ministership of Harold Wilson (1916–), who pledged to forge a more prosperous nation in the "white heat" of a new technological revolution. Although Labourites and Conservatives fought partisan campaigns, they appeared to agree upon fundamentals: a mixed economy and an extended program of welfare benefits. Labourites still called themselves socialists, but most defined socialism, as the party's mainstream always had, as centralization, rather than as worker control of the means of production.

Moderates dominated the politics of continental Europe as well. In Germany, France, and Italy, centrist parties affiliated with the Roman Catholic Church held power throughout most of the two decades after 1945: the German Christian Democratic Union; the French *Mouvement Républicain Populaire* (the M.R.P., initially more popular than it would be in the mid-1950s); and the Italian Christian Democrats. The leaders responsible for the direction of European political affairs during the immediate postwar period were no-nonsense men, committed to the achievement of practical economic and social agendas: Robert Schuman (1886–1963), for a time the French premier and the man most responsible for the establishment of the European Coal and Steel Community; Alcide de Gasperi (1881–1954), Italian premier from 1948 to 1953; and Konrad Adenauer (1876–1967), West German chancellor from 1949 to 1963. Adenauer was a former mayor of Cologne, a devout Roman Catholic who, though he despised the traditions of Prussian militarism that had contributed to the rise of Hitler, was apprehensive about the consequences of parliamentary democracy for Germany, and thus tended to govern in a paternalistic if not authoritarian manner. His determination to see an end to the centuries-old hostility between France and Germany contributed significantly to the movement toward economic union. De Gasperi, too, was not particularly enamored of democracy and thwarted attempts by Italian socialists and communists immediately after the war to institute radical reforms.

Yet neither Adenauer nor de Gasperi aroused much real political enmity. Socialists throughout Western Europe, recognizing the political popularity of economic prosperity, toned down their rhetoric and their demands, speaking far less about the inevitability of class war and more often about the contributions workers were making to the European postwar renaissance. The program adopted by the German Socialist party (the Social Democrats) in 1959, for example, abandoned orthodox Marxism by declaring the need to leave economic planning as much as possible to individual enterprise, rather than in the hands of the state.

France's political situation during the early 1950s was tangled in a way that West Germany's and Italy's were not. Party strength was fragmented. Twenty-five percent of the voting population regularly supported the French Communist party, not so much from commitment to its current policies as from a traditional proletarian habit of mind. Several conservative or reactionary parties of the Right existed as well. The political middle, strong in other countries and initially strong in France, gradually eroded after 1945. Matters reached a crisis when successive centrist governments

Alcide de Gasperi of Italy Electioneering during His 1948 Campaign

Charles de Gaulle. With arms upraised, De Gaulle, premier of the République Française (RF), asks the French people to adopt his new constitution.

found it increasingly difficult to resolve a seemingly intactable political problem borne of an independence movement in the French colony of Algeria. In May 1958 a revolt of French nationals in Algeria and disgruntled French army officers, both at home and in the colony, threatened to topple the French government. In desperation, the political leadership stepped down in favor of the Resistance hero, General Charles de Gaulle (1890–1970), who had played a brief role in French politics immediately after the war and then retired.

De Gaulle accepted office on the condition that he be permitted to rule by decree for six months and to draft a new constitution for France. This document, adopted by referendum in September 1958 and ushering in France's Fifth Republic, strengthened the executive branch of the government as a means of avoiding the parliamentary deadlocks that had so weakened France earlier in the decade and, indeed, throughout much of the preceding century. The president was granted power to appoint the premier and dissolve the National Assembly. And the assembly's powers to dismiss a premier were considerably weakened. Thus armed with new authority, de Gaulle set out to restore France to power and prestige. "France is not really herself unless in the front rank," he wrote in his memoirs. "France cannot be France without greatness." De Gaulle assumed that Algeria would have to be granted independence, which in due course it was, in 1963. Concerned about U.S. influence in Europe, he withdrew French troops from NATO in 1966. He cultivated better relations with the Soviet Union and, with Adenauer, he worked toward closer cooperation between France and West Germany. He accelerated the pace of France's economic and industrial expansion by building a modern military establishment, complete with atomic weapons—a nuclear "force de frappe," an independent nuclear strike force whose objectives were primarily political and diplomatic, part of de Gaulle's effort to reclaim France's great power status. De Gaulle's independent stand was largely based upon his belief that invasion of the West was far from the minds of the Soviet leadership.

Like de Gasperi and Adenauer, de Gaulle was not by nature a democrat but was committed to a centrist course. Such a policy entailed avoiding extremism and working hard to produce "practical" solutions to vexing political problems, thereby undermining radical sentiments of the sort that had produced fascism in Italy and Nazism in Germany. Most other Western European nations followed suit. Holland, Belgium, and the Scandinavian countries initiated economic and social policies that echoed those of the British, French, Germans, and Italians. In Spain and Portugal, however, different political, economic, and social agendas were pursued under the dictatorships of General Francisco Franco (1892–1975) and of António Salazar (1889–1970). And in Greece, political instability in the 1950s and early 1960s opened the way for a coup by conservative right-wing generals in 1967. Yet these were exceptions to a two-decade history of domestic tranquility and economic prosperity—a sharp contrast to the tragic failures of the 1920s and 1930s.

4. PATTERNS OF SOCIAL CHANGE

Clearly, economic change of this sort was bound to affect the lives of the men, women, and children who lived in Europe after the Second World War. Prosperity brought with it population shifts. The population of Western Europe in 1940 was 264 million; in 1982 it was 320 million. This increase was the result of an increase in the birthrate. Population growth was sustained by social welfare policies, such as family allowances, which encouraged parents to have children and enabled them to care adequately for them, and by health programs, which extended longevity considerably. As populations increased they also shifted across the Continent. Both West Germany and France found it necessary to import workers in order to sustain their production booms. By the mid-1960s, there were 1.3 million foreign workers in West Germany and 1.8 million in France. Most came from the south, particularly from the agrarian areas of southern Italy, where unemployment remained high, while workers from former colonies emigrated to Britain, often to take low-paid, menial jobs and encounter pervasive discrimination at work and in the community. Migrations of this sort, not to mention the movement of political refugees that occurred during and immediately after the war, contributed to a breaking down of national barriers that was accelerated by the advent of the Common Market.

Economic resurgence also altered patterns and perceptions of class. Commentators were quick to perceive a marked growth in the number of middle-class, white-collar employees, the result, in part, of the bureaucratic expansion of the state. By 1964, the total number of men and women employed in government service in most European states exceeded 40 percent of the labor force, significantly higher than the number in the 1920s and 1930s. In business and industry, the number of "middle-management" employees grew as well. This "managerial class" tended to be more innovative and adventurous than were the owner-managers of business in previous generations. More often than not, these managers possessed university degrees. In the mid-1950s, for example, over 72 percent of a sample of 5,000 French industrialists were university graduates, more than half of them with degrees in engineering. This was in marked contrast to the prewar situation, when managers far more frequently moved directly from secondary education into family-run concerns. What was true of the West was true of the Soviet Union as well where, following educational reforms instituted by Nikita Khrushchev in 1958, programs encouraged bright children to pursue a course of study leading eventually to managerial positions. This new class was not "bourgeois" in the Marxist sense of that term. The technocrats were not "owners of the means of production" or capitalist tycoons. To some degree they saw themselves less as the servants of the company that employed them than of the general public who purchased the goods or services they were providing.

If the nature of the middle class was changing, so was that of the working class. The introduction of complex machinery effectively altered the shape of the factory work force. The proportion of salaried employees—supervisors, inspectors, technicians, and draftsmen—grew significantly. In West Germany, for example, the number of such workers increased between 1950 and 1961 by 95 percent. And manual labor tended to mean something far different from what it had in the nineteenth century. Skills were specialized to a greater degree than ever, based on technological expertise rather than custom and routine. "Skill" meant the ability to monitor automatic controls, to interpret abstract signals, and to make precise, mathematically calculated adjustments.

All of these changes, suggesting a merging of the interests of working class and middle class, led some observers in the mid-1960s to declare class consciousness and its associated fierce antagonisms at an end. In fact, however, events in the late 1960s and 1970s reopened class conflicts, as we shall see. Although men and women earned more money than ever before, performing less physically yet more mentally demanding jobs and living more secure lives, they did not entirely lose their sense of themselves as workers. Trade unions remained powerful institutions: the largest of the French general unions had a membership of 1.5 million; of the Italian, 3.5 million; of the German, 6.5 million. Britain's Trade Union Congress, an affiliation of separate unions, boasted close to 8 million members.

Unquestionably, workers tended to lead lives that more closely resembled those of the prewar middle class than of their own parents and grandparents. They and their children went to school longer. All European countries passed laws providing for the extension of compulsory secondary education—up to the age of sixteen in France, West Germany, and Britain. As a consequence of new legislation and increased birthrates, school populations increased dramatically. Secondary school enrollment in France, Holland, and Belgium doubled between 1950 and 1960. In England and West Germany it grew by more than 50 percent. Higher education was used in the Soviet Union as a means of unifying a nation that remained culturally heterogeneous. Turks and Slavs constituted sizable minorities in the Soviet Union. Concern lest the pull of ethnic "nationality" tear at the none-too-solid fabric of the Soviet "union" increased the government's desire to impose one unifying culture by means of education, not always with success.

Educational reforms were accompanied by a communications revolution. In both Western and Eastern Europe the paperback book, the long-playing record, radio, television, and a variety of computerized information-storing devices brought knowledge—of varying degrees of quality—to millions who heretofore had had neither the time nor the money to acquire it. Workers in the West for the first time found it possible to take inexpensive holidays, often in their own automobiles. Between 1948 and 1965 car ownership increased in Western Europe from 5 million to 44 million. The work week contracted from forty-eight hours to about forty-two. In most countries, workers received over thirty days of paid vacation per year. Britain's prime minister Harold Macmillan was not alone in his belief that "we've never had it so good!"

5. PROTEST AND STAGNATION: THE PRICE OF STABILITY

While 1960 seemed both golden and full of promise, fifteen years later West Europeans were no longer so certain of their prosperity or of their leaders' abilities to provide them with the sort of life they had come to take for granted. From the mid-1960s, social and economic tensions ate away at the consensus that postwar prosperity had created. Societies fragmented in new and confusing ways. Governments were baffled about how to deal with the demands of newly politicized groups. Their problems were compounded after 1975 by a continuing economic crisis that threatened the security a generation had labored so hard to achieve.

Economic uncertainty erodes self-confidence

The years from 1965 to 1972 were marked by widespread protests among young people in Europe and the United States. Young people had, of course, revolted in previous generations—indeed, revolt has always been considered a prerogative of youth. Yet in the past, leadership had come from an older generation. Now it was to come from men and women in their twenties.

Protest and upheaval among the young

Products of the baby boom of the immediate postwar period, young people were jammed into recently expanded universities whose conservative, authoritarian traditions made intellectual reform all but impossible. University enrollment tripled in France, Italy, and Britain between 1938 and 1960; in West Germany, the university population increased from 110,000 in 1950 to 280,000 in 1960. Members of this new generation sought a more permissive society where premarital sex and liberation from traditional patterns of middle-class behavior would become the norm. As students they had little use for the disciplines of the past. Science antagonized them because of its association with warmaking—in particular with the unpopular war the United States was then waging in Southeast Asia (see below, p. 1057). Knowledge that was not perceived as relevant to the world's problems was challenged as worthless.

Universities as breeding grounds of unrest

Vietnam Protest, 1971. Veterans of the U.S. Armed Forces march on the Capitol to protest continued U.S. involvement in the war in Vietnam.

Student Uprising at the University of Paris, May 1968. Following demonstrations calling for sweeping reforms at the university, French students took to the streets to make their case more forcefully and violently at the barricades.

De Gaulle Loses Support. This cartoon from June 1968 says, "Vote always; I'll do the rest." De Gaulle retired from office after losing support in part as a result of the way he handled the student uprisings in Paris.

The women's movement

The most serious outbreak of student unrest in Europe occurred in Paris in the spring of 1968. Inspired in part by the role young people had played in the revolt against Soviet oppression in Czechoslovakia that same year, French students at the University of Paris demanded reforms that would modernize their university. Confrontation with authorities precipitated riots, which in turn brought police interference. Sympathy with the students' cause expanded to encompass opposition to de Gaulle's regime, leading to massive trade union strikes. By mid-May, 10 million French workers had walked off their jobs. The government was able to satisfy the strikers by acquiescing to wage increases, thereby isolating the students, who grudgingly agreed to resume university life. De Gaulle had no sympathy for the students. "Reform, yes—bed messing, no," he is said to have declared at the height of the confrontation. Yet events of May and June 1968 undoubtedly helped weaken de Gaulle's position as president and contributed to his retirement from office in the following year. Young people elsewhere staged protests as well. Students in Berlin rioted at the appearance there of the shah of Iran and against newspapers critical of the revolt of the young. In Italy, undergraduates staged a lengthy series of riots to draw attention to university overcrowding. And in the United States, serious protests against the Vietnam War continued into the early 1970s.

Women, like young people, began to assert themselves during the 1960s and 1970s. As was the case with the youth rebellion, the women's movement first emerged from the middle class and mainly addressed the problems of middle-class women. By the mid-1970s the movement had spread worldwide, including the Third World nations, and was no longer limited to the middle class. Many of the early activists within the movement had been part of the youth rebellion during its most intense phase in the 1960s.

Their activism stemmed, in part, from a realization that even in a radical political atmosphere, women were relegated to second place. Women's position within society had changed dramatically since the nineteenth century. The assumption that the middle-class woman's place was in the home had been challenged by the ever-increasing demand for women workers and by the need experienced by more and more women to hold a job—either for financial reasons or because housework was for a growing number an unfulfilling occupation. The increased availability and social acceptance of birth-control devices meant that women were having fewer children, and that they could begin to exercise more control over the pattern of their lives.

Yet society seemed loath to acknowledge the implication of these changes: that women are equal to men. Women were paid less than men for similar work. Women with qualifications no different from men were turned down because of their gender when they applied for jobs. Women with excellent employment records were forced to rely on their husbands to establish credit. Political action helped alleviate some of these inequities in the late 1960s and the 1970s. The U.S. government instituted programs of "affirmative action" which mandated the hiring of qualified women as well as members of racial minority groups. In Britain an Equal Pay Act, passed in the late 1960s, established that wages for women should be equal to those of men holding the same job. In France, a ministry for the status of women was created in the mid-1970s, and in Germany government agencies were established to deal with family and youth affairs.

Women's political action

The campaign for equality did not meet with universal approval, however. A particularly volatile subject was a woman's right to an abortion. Feminists argued that women must enjoy the freedom to plan for their fu-

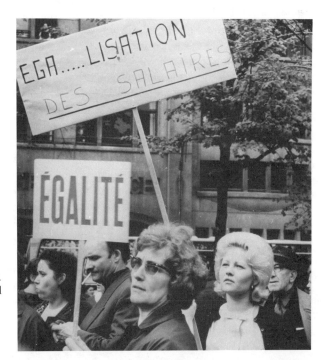

The Women's Movement in France. French women demand equal pay for equal work.

ture unencumbered by the responsibilities of motherhood if they chose, and that their bodies were theirs to govern. Their opponents, who included members of the so-called right-to-life movement, countered with the argument that abortion encouraged sexual irresponsibility; some declared abortion to be the equivalent of murder. By 1990, however, despite the failure in the United States of passage of a constitutional Equal Rights Amendment, the campaigners for women's equality had a good many successes to their credit.

Economic as well as social problems plagued Europe in the 1970s. The stagnation that overtook the Continent was the product of trends that had their roots in the prosperous 1960s. By the middle of that decade, for example, the West German growth rate had slowed. Demand for manufactured goods declined and in 1966 the country suffered its first postwar recession. Volkswagen, that mythic symbol of the German "miracle," introduced a shortened work week; almost 700,000 West Germans were thrown out of work. In France a persisting housing shortage increased the cost of living. While new industries continued to prosper, the basic industries—coal, steel, and railways—began to run up deficits. Unemployment was rising in tandem with prices. Prime Minister Harold Wilson's pledge to revive Britain's economy by introducing new technology foundered on balance-of-payment crises. The Common Market, expanded in 1973 to include Britain, Ireland, and Denmark, and again in the early 1980s to admit Greece, Spain, and Portugal, struggled to overcome problems stemming from the conflict between the domestic economic regulations characteristic of many European states and the free-market policies that prevailed among the EEC countries.

All these difficulties were compounded by the dramatic rise in the price of oil that occurred once the Arab-dominated Organization of Petroleum Exporting Countries (OPEC) instituted an oil embargo against the Western powers for economic and political reasons in 1973. By 1975 the cost per barrel of oil had risen to $10.46, as compared with $1.73 two years before, and continued to rise to over $30 in the early 1980s. This increase produced an inflationary spiral; interest rates rose and with them the price of almost everything else Western consumers were used to buying. Wage demands calculated to meet rising costs produced strikes. The placid industrial relations that had characterized the 1950s and early 1960s were a thing of the past. Meanwhile the U.S. economy was disrupted as a result of its commitment to the war in Southeast Asia. Finally, European manufacturers encountered serious competition, not only from highly developed countries like Japan but also from the increasingly active economies of Asia and Africa, in which the West had invested capital eagerly in the previous decades. By 1980 Japan had captured 10 percent of the automobile market in West Germany and 25 percent in Belgium. By 1984, unemployment in Western Europe had reached about 19 million. The lean years had arrived.

Meanwhile the Soviet Union and its satellites were also experiencing the stagnation that accompanies the maturing of an economy. The Soviet

Communist party proclaimed in 1961 that by 1970 the U.S.S.R. would exceed the United States in per capita production. By the end of the 1970s, however, Soviet per capita production was not much higher than in the less-industrialized countries of Southern Europe. During the same period its rate of economic growth was on a sluggish par with that of other Western nations.

Following an impressive economic performance during the early 1970s, the Eastern European nations encountered serious financial difficulties. Their success had rested in part on capital borrowed not from the Soviet Union but from the West. By 1980 those debts had become serious burdens to their national economies. Poland's hard-currency indebtedness to Western countries, for example, was almost four times as great as its annual exports. The solution to this problem, attempted in Poland and elsewhere, was to cut back on production for domestic consumption in order to increase exports. Yet this policy encountered strong popular opposition. Although there was virtually no unemployment in the East, men and women were by no means happy with their economic situation. Working hours were longer than in the West, and goods and services, even in prosperous times, remained far from abundant.

Western governments also found it difficult to react effectively to the abrupt change in their economic circumstances. Politicians of both the Right and the Left struggled to rediscover the magic that had produced prosperity, but with little success. In Britain, the Labour and Conservative parties alternatively governed through the 1970s, unable to meet the demands of trade unionists, who were angry as they saw their real wages eroded by inflation, or of international bankers, who were impatient with Britain's inability to bring its trade figures into balance. Twenty-four million individual workdays were lost in strikes in 1972, one of the worst years of industrial unrest on record. In the mid-1970s the rate of inflation increased alarmingly, reaching 26 percent in 1976; unemployment rose to 1.4 million that same year; and the value of the pound declined precipitously. The new, radically conservative leader of the Conservative party, Margaret Thatcher (1925–   ), claimed to have the answer, and was elected in 1979—and reelected in 1983 and 1987—on the basis of that claim. Yet despite tax cuts designed to stimulate the economy and the return of many publicly owned enterprises to private hands, the economy remained weak, with close to 15 percent of the work force unemployed by 1986. The standard of living in Britain had sunk below the level of all Western European nations save Greece, Spain, and Portugal. Once the seat of an empire upon which the sun never set, Britain was reduced to the status of a tiny, economically moribund island state.

Margaret Thatcher, Prime Minister of Great Britain, 1979–1990

West Germany, like Britain, veered to the Right in the 1980s. The Social Democratic party, headed in the late 1960s and early 1970s by Willy Brandt, had remained in power after Brandt's resignation as chancellor in 1974 under the leadership of his less charismatic successor, Helmut Schmidt (1918–   ). Schmidt's coalition government attempted in the early 1980s to

Helmut Kohl, Chancellor of the Federal Republic of Germany, 1982–

Newly Elected French President François Mitterand Lays a Symbolic Rose on the Tomb of French Socialist Jean Jaurès in 1981

The European Community

combat economic recession with job-training programs and tax incentives, both financed by higher taxes. These programs did little to assist economic recovery, and Schmidt was replaced in 1982 by the Christian Democrat Helmut Kohl (1930–   ), who, like Margaret Thatcher in Britain, proposed cuts in social programs and unemployment compensation.

France fared little better than its neighbor in the struggle to maintain economic momentum. De Gaulle resigned in 1969, his prestige eroded by the protests and strikes of the previous year. His successors in the 1970s, Georges Pompidou (1911–1974) and Valéry Giscard d'Estaing (1926–   ), pursued a middle course that did no more than keep the country on an even keel. In 1981, Giscard was ousted by a socialist, François Mitterand (1916–   ), whose record as an escaped prisoner of war and Resistance fighter in the Second World War made him a popular figure, and whose public visit to the tomb of the French socialist hero Jean Jaurès was meant to symbolize his intention to govern in accordance with Marxist ideals. Among the array of reforms promptly undertaken by the new government was the further nationalization of major industries and private financial institutions, including the famed 150-year-old Rothschild bank, Pompidou's former employer. Yet these bold moves, bitterly opposed by conservative interests, did not resolve the nation's economic malaise. Inflation and unemployment rose, along with budget and balance-of-trade deficits. Newly nationalized enterprises drained government resources. These difficulties led to a devaluation of the franc, a temporary freeze on wages and prices, and in 1986 to a return to power of more conservative political forces committed to a policy of "privatization" of companies and industries that had been nationalized under the socialists.

Spain and Italy moved Left in the early 1980s. Spain, freed from the rule of General Franco by his death in 1974, and under the nominal rule of his hand-picked successor King Juan Carlos (1938–   ), saw the Socialist Workers party score a major upset in 1982. Intent on modernizing rather than radicalizing Spain, the socialists eschewed widespread government ownership of industry in favor of selective nationalization, which included the nation's electric power grid. Similarly, Italy witnessed increasing victories by parties of the Left at the expense of the previously indomitable Christian Democratic party.

The fact that governments of Right and Left were unable to recreate the sort of economic climate that had characterized Europe's unprecedented postwar prosperity suggests the degree to which economic forces remain outside the control of individual states, prey to the far-from-predictable vagaries of international finance, trade cycles, and human miscalculation.

The economic malaise afflicting Europe led to renewed efforts to address common problems through an organization of European states. By the end of the 1980s, the EEC, now known simply as the European Community (EC), embarked on an ambitious program of integration, planning the elimination of internal borders and restrictive business practices by the end of 1992. Long-term goals, agreed upon in December 1991, include a monetary union, with a central European bank and a single currency, and uni-

The European Community (EC). Left: Jacques Delors, administrative head of the EC. Right: The hard ecu, the proposed single currency of the EC.

fied social policies to reduce poverty and unemployment. Whether the community can overcome the claims of national sovereignty and the logistical problems associated with conducting business in ten official languages remains to be seen.

6. EUROPE RECAST: THE COLLAPSE OF COMMUNISM AND THE END OF THE SOVIET UNION

The major reforms initiated by the European Community during the early 1990s were overshadowed by an extraordinarily rapid and surprising series of events in Eastern Europe: the collapse of communist rule and the introduction of democracy in those countries hitherto dominated by the U.S.S.R., the astonishing disintegration of the Soviet Union itself, and the consequent destabilization of a vast region stretching from the borders of China in the east to the borders of Poland in the west.

The process began with the accession of Mikhail Gorbachev (1931–) to the leadership of the Soviet Communist party in 1985. In his mid-fifties, Gorbachev was significantly younger than his immediate predecessors and less prey to the habits of mind that had shaped Soviet domestic and foreign affairs. He was frankly critical of the repressive aspects of communist society as well as its sluggish economy, and he did not hesitate to voice those criticisms openly. His twin policies of *glasnost* (intellectual openness) and *perestroika* (economic restructuring) held out hope for a freer, more prosperous Soviet Union. Under Gorbachev, a number of imprisoned dissidents were freed, among them Andrei Sakharov, the scientist known as "the father of the Soviet hydrogen bomb," the historian Lev Kopelev, the physicist Yury Orlov, and the poet Irena Ratushinskaya.

Mikhail Gorbachev. General Secretary of the Central Committee of the Communist party of the Soviet Union (1985–1991), Gorbachev instituted policies of reform to revitalize the Soviet Union.

Gorbachev and the Old Guard. Gorbachev is pictured here at the height of his power in 1986, with KGB chief Victor Chebrikov, President Andrei Gromyko, and Premier Nikolai Rzyhkov. *Perestroika* aimed at the privileges of the political elite and would eventually lead to the fall from power of all these men.

Perestroika

The policies of *perestroika* took aim at the privileges of the political elite and the immobility of the state bureaucracy by instituting competitive elections to official positions and limiting terms of office. Economically, Gorbachev's program of *perestroika* called for a shift from the centrally planned economy initiated by Stalin to a mixed economy combining planning with the operation of market forces. In agriculture, *perestroika* accelerated the move away from cooperative production and instituted incentives for the achievement of production tarkets. Gorbachev called for the integration of the Soviet Union into the international economy by participation in organizations such as the International Monetary Fund.

Even these dramatic reforms, however, were proving to be too little too late by the late 1980s. Ethnic unrest threatened to split the Soviet Union apart, while secession movements gathered steam in the Baltic republics and elsewhere. From 1988 onward, fighting between Armenians and Azerbaijanis over an ethnically Azerbaijani region located inside Armenia threatened to escalate into a border dispute with Iran; only the presence of Soviet troops temporarily quelled the conflict.

Old Opponents Meet in Poland, 1989. Lech Walesa, head of Solidarity, and General Wojciech Jaruzelski, who imposed martial law on Poland in 1981, are pictured here after the government agreed to hold open elections.

Spurred on by these events in the Soviet Union, the countries of Eastern Europe began to agitate for independence from Moscow. Gorbachev encouraged open discussion—*glasnost*—not only in his own country but also in the satellite nations. He revoked the Brezhnev Doctrine's insistence on single-party socialist governments and made frequent and inspiring trips to the capitals of neighboring satellites. *Glasnost* rekindled the flame of opposition in Poland, where Solidarity had been defeated but not destroyed by the government in 1981. In 1988 the union launched a new series of strikes. These disturbances culminated in an agreement between the government and Solidarity that legalized the union and promised open elections. The results, in June 1989, astonished the world: virtually all of the government's candidates lost and the Citizen's Committee, affiliated with Solidarity, won a sizeable majority in the Polish parliament.

In Hungary and Czechoslovakia, events followed a similar course during 1988 and 1989. As a result of continuing demonstrations, Janos Kadar (1912–1989), the Hungarian leader since the Soviet crackdown of 1956, resigned in May 1988 and was replaced by the reformist government of the Hungarian Socialist Workers' party. By the spring of 1989 the Hungarian Politburo had been purged of Communist party supporters, and the government had begun to dismantle its security fences along the Austrian border. A year later the Hungarian Democratic Forum, proclaiming its dedication to the reinstatement of full civil rights and to the restructuring of the economy, secured a plurality of seats in the National Assembly.

The Czechs, too, staged demonstrations against Soviet domination in late 1988. Brutal beating of student demonstrators by the police in 1989 led to the radicalization of the nations' workers and to mass demonstrations. Civic Forum, an opposition coalition, called for installation of a coalition government to include non-communists, for free elections, and for the resignation of the country's communist leadership. It reinforced its demands with continuing mass demonstrations and threats of a general strike that resulted in the toppling of the old regime and the election of the playwright and Civic Forum leader, Vaclav Havel (1936–   ), as president.

Undoubtedly the most significant political change in Eastern Europe during the late 1980s was the collapse of communism in East Germany and the reunification of East and West Germany in October 1990. Although long considered the most prosperous of the East-bloc countries, East Germany suffered from severe economic stagnation and environmental degradation. Waves of East Germans registered their discontent with worsening conditions by massive illegal emigration to the West. This movement combined with evidence of widespread official corruption to force the resignation of East Germany's longtime hard-line premier, Erich Honecker (1912–   ). His successor, Egon Krenz, promised reforms, but he was nevertheless faced with continuing protests and continuing mass emigration. On November 4, 1989, the government, in a move that acknowledged its powerlessness to hold its citizens captive, opened its border with

Vaclav Havel. A writer and former dissident, Havel was elected president of Czechoslovakia after the toppling of the communist regime.

Collapse of communism in East Germany

The New Czechoslovakia. Workers remove a Hammer and Sickle from a neon sign that reads, "Glory to Communism"; communist signs were removed from buildings in Czechoslovakia in 1989 for the first time since 1948.

The Fall of the Berlin Wall, 1989. When East German officials announced that citizens could leave the country through any border crossing, rendering the Berlin Wall obsolete, people gathered at the wall to celebrate and to tear it down with picks and axes and small hammers.

Czechoslovakia. This move effectively freed East Germans to travel to the West. In a matter of days, the Berlin Wall, embodiment of the cold war, the Iron Curtain, and the division of East from West, was demolished. Jubilant throngs from both sides walked through the gaping holes that now permitted men, women, and children to take the few steps that symbolized the return to freedom and a chance for national unity.

Free elections were held throughout Germany in March 1990, resulting in a victory for the "Alliance for Germany," a coalition allied with West German Chancellor Helmut Kohl's Christian Democratic Union. With heavy emigration continuing, reunification talks quickly culminated in the formal proclamation of a united Germany on October, 3, 1990.

Reunification of Germany

Throughout the rest of Eastern Europe, single-party governments in the countries behind what was left of the tattered Iron Curtain—Albania, Bulgaria, Rumania, and Yugoslavia—collapsed in the face of democratic pressure for change. Meanwhile, in the Soviet Union itself, inspired by events in Eastern Europe, the Balkan republics of Lithuania and Latvia strained to free themselves from the Soviet yoke. In 1990 they unilaterally proclaimed their independence from the Soviet Union, throwing into sharp relief the tension between "union" and "republics." Gorbachev reacted with an uncertain mixture of armed intervention and promises of greater local autonomy. In the fall of 1991 Lithuania and Latvia, along with the third Baltic state of Estonia, won international recognition as independent republics.

Lithuanian, Latvian, and Estonian independence

The Soviet Union's unproductive economy continued to fuel widespread dissatisfaction. With the failure of *perestroika*—largely the result of a lack of resources and an inability to increase production—came the rise of a powerful political rival to Gorbachev, the latter's erstwhile ally—Boris Yeltsin (1931–). The reforming mayor of Moscow, Yeltsin was elected

Failure of perestroika

president of the Russian Federation—the largest Soviet republic—on an anti-Gorbachev platform in May 1990. Pressure from the Yeltsin camp weakened Gorbachev's ability to maneuver independently of reactionary factions in the Politburo and the military, undermining his reform program and his ability to remain in power.

The Soviet Union's increasingly severe domestic problems led to mounting protests in 1991, when Gorbachev's policies failed to improve—indeed diminished—the living standard of the Soviet people. Demands increased that the bloated government bureaucracy respond with a dramatic cure for the country's continuing economic stagnation. Gorbachev appeared to lose his political nerve, having first ordered and then cancelled a radical "500 day" economic reform plan, while at the same time agreeing to negotiations with the increasingly disaffected republics within the union, now clamoring for independence. Sensing their political lives to be in jeopardy, a group of highly placed hard-line communist functionaries staged an abortive coup in August 1991, incarcerating Gorbachev and his wife and declaring a return to party-line orthodoxy. In response, the Soviet citizenry defied their self-proclaimed saviors. Led by Boris Yeltsin, who at one point mounted a tank in a Moscow street to rally the people, they successfully called the plotters' bluff. Within two weeks, Gorbachev was back in power, and the coup leaders were in prison.

Gorbachev's power was diminished by the August events, however, while Yeltsin's was dramatically increased. Throughout the fall of 1991, as Gorbachev struggled to hold the nation together, Yeltsin capitalized on the discontent throughout the union, which was no longer united by the force of a powerful one-party state. On December 8, 1991, the presidents of the republics of Russia, Ukraine, and Byelorussia (now called Belarus) declared that the Soviet Union was no more. "The U.S.S.R. as a subject of international law and geopolitical reality, is ceasing to exist." Though the prose was flat, the message was momentous. The once mighty Soviet Union, founded seventy-five years before in a burst of revolutionary fervor and vi-

Boris Yeltsin Faces Down the Coup. Russian president Boris Yeltsin stood his ground at the Russian parliament building against the hard-liners who attempted to overthrow Mikhail Gorbachev. Here Yeltsin is encouraging the people to fight the takeover of the central government.

olence, had evaporated overnight, leaving in its wake a collection of eleven far-from-powerful nations loosely joined together as the "Commonwealth of Independent States." On December 25, 1991, Gorbachev resigned the leadership of the now nonexistent union, as the Soviet flag—the hammer and sickle that had symbolized the nation that for fifty years had kept half of Europe in thrall—was lowered for the last time over the Kremlin.

Problems in the former Soviet Union

The mighty fall left mighty problems in its wake. Food shortages worsened during the winter of 1992. The value of the ruble plummeted. The republics could not agree on common military policies, or resolve difficult and dangerous questions concerning the control of nuclear warheads. Ethnic conflicts in Georgia, Armenia, Azerbaijan, and elsewhere flared continuously. Yeltsin's pleas for economic assistance from the West received timid responses. And with freedom have come economic anxiety and political tension as the people of the former union seek to cope with massive and painful change.

Problems in Germany

Despite the high hopes that the upheavals in Eastern Europe have spawned, further change also promises to be far from easy in these countries as well. The achievement of genuine reunification in Germany will take considerable time. Economic development in the East has been slow and uneven, as explicitly racist political movements once again surface, with massive dislocations caused by the shift from central planning to a free market economy. As much of the initial euphoria regarding Germany's future evaporates, it is unclear whether the mild malaise the country continues to suffer will lead to more serious unrest.

Ethnic conflicts in Eastern Europe

Implementing radical economic reorganization in the rest of Eastern Europe has also been difficult. Attempts to create free market economies have brought inflation, unemployment, and—in their wake—anti-capitalist demonstrations. Inefficient industries, work force resistance to change, energy shortages, lack of venture capital, and a severely polluted environment have combined to hinder progress and to sour hopes. In addition, racial and ethnic conflicts have continued to divide newly liberated democracies as

Toppling of Soviet Heroes. Angry Soviet demonstrators pull down the statue of Felix Dzerzhinsky, founder of the KGB security police, in August 1991, after the failure of the hard-line coup.

Fighting in Sarajevo. After the breakup of Yugoslavia into independent states, fighting broke out between Serbs and Moslems for control of the Bosnian capital, the city in which the Archduke Francis Ferdinand was assassinated seventy-eight years before, setting off the First World War.

minorities have waged often violent campaigns for autonomous rights—or outright secession, recalling the divisions that led to the First World War and that have plagued Eastern Europe throughout its history. In Czechoslovakia, the election of deputies calling for Slovakian independence resulted in Havel's resignation and the dissolution of the tight federal union between Czechs and Slovaks. In Yugoslavia, fierce fighting broke out both before and after the interior states of Croatia and Slovenia declared their independence from the Serbian-dominated central government in June 1991. By the spring of 1992, Croatia, Slovenia, Bosnia and Herzegovina, and Macedonia had seceded from Yugoslavia. The violence continued in Bosnia despite the efforts of both the United Nations and the European Community to end the fighting. The conflicts in Yugoslavia and elsewhere have proved that a liberated Eastern Europe poses as much if not more of a threat to international stability as it did under Soviet domination. While the future of the former Soviet Union and the new Eastern European democracies remains uncertain, the only certainty to emerge from the events of 1988–1991 in Eastern Europe has been the wondrous unpredictability of human events.

7. INTELLECTUAL AND CULTURAL PATTERNS

Intellectual life in the West after 1945 was patterned broadly as it had been in the interwar years. The gulf remained wide between the avant-garde and the generally educated public—the latter far larger than ever before thanks

THE POST COLD WAR WEST, 1992

to burgeoning universities. If attendance at museums increased—as it did dramatically—more often than not it was because people were attracted by exhibits of treasures from the distant past—from King Tutankhamen's tomb or from the Renaissance collections of the Vatican Museum. Audiences who welcomed a chance to hear the works of long-dead composers— Mozart and Verdi—sung by internationally acclaimed "stars"—the soprano Maria Callas, the tenor Luciano Pavarotti—rejected as pointless the puzzling works of composers such as John Cage, whose "silent sonata" entitled "4.33" consisted of a pianist seated at the piano for precisely four minutes, thirty-three seconds, but who never once actually struck a note. Intellectuals, on the other hand, railed against the increasing vapidity of mass culture and in particular of television, the "idiot box" that by 1965 had found its way into 62 million homes in the United States, 13 million in Britain, 10 million in West Germany, 5 million each in France and Italy. They also objected to the promotion of art and music as big business, with jampacked "blockbuster" art exhibits attended by tens of thousands and opera tickets sold at prices approaching $100 apiece.

Growing gulf between avant-garde and the educated laymen

Despite this continuing alienation, the work of many of the West's leading writers did reflect the dilemmas of the human condition that prevailed throughout the years after 1945. During the immediate postwar period novelists concerned themselves with the horrors of war and of the totalitarian systems that had spawned the conflict of the 1940s. The Americans James Jones (1921–1977) in *From Here to Eternity* (1951) and Norman Mailer (1923–) in *The Naked and the Dead* (1948) portrayed the coarseness and cruelty of military life with ruthless realism. The German Günter Grass's (1927–) first and probably most important novel, *The Tin Drum*, (1959), depicted the vicious and politically diseased life of Nazi Germany in the 1930s. In France, Jean-Paul Sartre (1905–1980), as a result of his own and his country's wartime experiences, recommitted himself in his novels, plays, and other writings to a life of active political involvement as a Marxist. Whereas he had previously defined hell in terms of individual hostilities, he now defined it in terms of class inequality. Unlike Sartre, his compatriot Albert Camus (1913–1960) was unable to construct a secular faith from his own perceptions of the world and its apparent absurdities. Though idealistic enough to participate in the French resistance movement against the German occupation in the Second World War, and though proclaiming the virtues of rebellion, Camus remained tortured in novels such as *The Stranger* (1942), *The Plague* (1947), and *The Fall* (1956) by the problem of humanity's responsibility for its own miserable dilemma and by the limitations placed upon the ability of men and women to help each other.

Postwar literature

Marxism continued to attract European intellectuals, both as a recipe for changing the world and as a way of explaining it. Historians, economists, and sociologists focused their attention more frequently on the writings of the younger Marx, less on his economic theories, more on his perceptions of alienation and class consciousness. The writings of the Italian Antonio Gramsci (1891–1937) and the Hungarian Georg Lukács (1885–1971), both

Shifting focus on Marx in the West

Roy Medvedev

Simone de Beauvoir

Betty Friedan

concerned with these particular matters, attracted widespread attention. Claude Lévi-Strauss (1908–), a French sociologist who considers himself a Marxist in contemporary matters, nevertheless applied a different model than Marx's essentially idealist and value-laden dialectic to the study of society. A leading exponent of the so-called structuralist school, Lévi-Strauss subjected all elements of the primitive societies he studied—kinship, rituals, and traditions—to analysis in terms of thought structures, which though unconscious, were nevertheless said to possess an objective reality. He argued that his method proved the intrinsic value of every society and that there was rationality where many had previously seen only the irrational or the absurd.

It is worth noting that these reinterpretations of Marx came from outside the Soviet Union. Inside, genuine philosophical debate was repressed by the government until the 1980s, when Gorbachev's political reforms enabled Soviet intellectuals to speak out. Some, like the historian Roy Medvedev (1925–), have been openly critical of certain aspects of the past—above all the Stalinist purges—and even of communism.

The specific issues that drove men and women in Western Europe and America to committed action in the mid-1960s compelled writers to take sides as well. Günter Grass, in *Local Anaesthetic,* published in 1970, was only one of many who wrote of student unrest and political involvement. Women authors described not only the general loneliness of the human condition, but the particular plight of women trapped in a world not of their own making. The Frenchwoman Simone de Beauvoir (1908–1986) in *The Second Sex* (1949), an influential study of the female condition, denounced the male middle class for turning not only workers but also its own women into objects for its own ends. American writers like Germaine Greer (1939–), Betty Friedan (1921–), and the poet Adrienne Rich (1929–) helped define the politics and culture of the women's movement.

The theme of individual alienation and helplessness, a reflection of the problems arising from the growth of state power, was one to which writers addressed themselves with increasing frequency in the 1960s and 1970s. The Russian Boris Pasternak (1890–1960), in his novel *Dr. Zhivago* (1958), indicted the Soviet campaign to shape all its citizens to the same mold. His countryman Aleksandr Solzhenitsyn (1918–) attacked the brutal methods employed by the Soviet Union in its rapid climb to world power. His *Gulag Archipelago,* published in 1974, is a fictionalized account of the fate of those whose willingness to stand in the way of Soviet "progress" sentenced them to life in Siberian labor camps. Although both Pasternak and Solzhenitsyn were awarded the Nobel Prize for literature, the former in 1958 and the latter in 1970, their works were until recently banned by the Soviet government. Solzhenitsyn was deported to West Germany in 1974 and later took up residence in the United States. (Though his Soviet citizenship was restored by Gorbachev in 1990, he has refused to return to his native land on the grounds that his conviction for treason has never been revoked.) Herbert Marcuse (1898–1979), a naturalized American, charged

Four Darks in Red, Mark Rothko (1903–1970). Oil on canvas. Rothko became obsessed with the need to reduce both color and form, achieving thereby a kind of gloomy mysticism. (The Whitney Museum of American Art)

Summer Rental No. 2, Robert Rauschenberg (born 1925). Oil on canvas. Rauschenberg experiments with problems of dimensionality and painterly technique as he strives to achieve a total harmony out of disparate elements. (Collection Whitney Museum of American Art; Gift of the Friends of the Whitney Museum of American Art)

Three Flags, Jasper Johns (born 1930). Encaustic on canvas. Painted with absolute objectivity Johns's objects, in this case three American flags, cease to be mere reproductions and take on distinctive identities of their own. (The Whitney Museum of American Art)

Woman with Dog, Duane Hanson (born 1925). Polyvinyl, polychromed in oil, life size. Hanson recreates the human artifacts of Middle-American culture as symbols of a hollow society. (Collection Whitney Museum of American Art; Gift of Frances and Sydney Lewis)

Grief by Eric Fischl. Fischl takes art in a new direction, beyond abstract expressionism but also beyond the realism depicted in the sculptures of Duane Hanson. (Cincinnati Art Museum)

Gran Cairo, Frank Stella (born 1936). Synthetic polymer paint on canvas. The artist employs absolute symmetry and a rectilinear pattern with compelling effect. (Collection Whitney Museum of American Art; Gift of the Friends of the Whitney Museum of American Art)

EUROPE DURING THE COLD WAR

Members of the North Atlantic Treaty
Organization (NATO)

Members of the Warsaw Pact

Non-aligned States

Other Communist States

miles
0   100   200   300   400   500

that authoritarianism was just as much a fact of life under capitalism as under communism. He argued that industrial capitalism had produced a "one-dimensional" society, in which the interests of individual citizens had been ruthlessly subordinated to those of the powerful corporate interests that were the true governors of the world.

Some authors, although they agreed with indictments of contemporary civilization, believed the human condition too hopeless to warrant direct attack. They expressed their despair by escaping into the absurd and fantastic. In the plays of Samuel Beckett (1906–1986), an Irishman who wrote in French, and of the Englishman Harold Pinter (1930–   ), nothing happens. Characters speak in the banalities that have become the hallmark of modern times. Words that are meaningless when spoken by human beings nevertheless take on a logic of their own; yet they explain nothing. Other authors, less willing, perhaps, to attempt to make a statement out of nothingness, have invaded the realms of hallucination, science fiction, and fantasy. The novels of the Americans William Burroughs (1914–   ) and Kurt Vonnegut (1922–   ) convey their readers from interior fantasizing to outer space. Similarly the writings of the Czech author Milan Kundera (1929–   )—who fled the repressive Czech government to live in Paris—portray the senselessness of resisting the human condition. Significantly one of the most popular books among the young people of the sixties and seventies was *The Lord of the Rings* (1954–1955), a pseudo-saga set in the fantasy world of "Middle Earth," written before the Second World War by the Englishman J. R. R. Tolkien (1892–1973).

Boris Pasternak

The development of new communications and information storage and retrieval systems—above all computers—became the most important precondition for economic growth in the 1970s and 1980s. Two influential French philosophers examined the new technologies and arrived at very different conclusions about their social and cultural impact. Jean Baudrillard analyzed the growth of mass media, particularly television, and argued that far from encouraging communication, they isolated people and hindered meaningful interaction. Jean-François Lyotard, on the other hand, saw in computers a cause for optimism. He asserted that computerized knowledge held out the promise of open access to information, and with it complete freedom of thought and creativity. Lyotard did not overlook the problems of access to information, a subject his fellow countryman Michel Foucault (1926–1984) analyzed in great detail. Foucault wrote extensively on subjects as diverse as contemporary prison reform and the "genealogy" of human society. If there is a central theme in his writings, it is that the ability to control access to information and to define the limits of knowledge is itself power. He showed that without information, physical force is useless in the modern world.

Aleksandr Solzhenitsyn

Analysis of impact of new technologies

In the decades after the Second World War, filmmakers made films that mirrored the problems and concerns of society, with a depth and artistic integrity seldom attempted or achieved previously. The Swede Ingmar Bergman (1918–   ), the Frenchmen Jean-Luc Godard (1930–   ) and François Truffaut (1932–1984), the Italians Frederico Fellini (1920–   ) and

Film

Michelangelo Antonioni (1912–   ), to name but a few of the most gifted directors, dealt in their films with the same themes that marked the literature of the period: loneliness, war, oppression, and corruption. One important factor facilitating the achievement of artistic quality was the general willingness on the part of censors—state or industry sponsored—to reflect public taste by permitting filmmakers great license in the handling of themes such as racism, violence, and sexuality. While there is no question that this relaxation led to exploitation, it cleared the way for extraordinarily powerful film statements, such as the American Arthur Penn's *Bonnie and Clyde* (1967) and the Italian Bernardo Bertolucci's *Last Tango in Paris* (1972), shocking declarations about humanity made possible by explicit depictions of violence and sex. Film, while gaining a general maturity it had heretofore lacked, did not abandon its role as entertainment. The international popularity of the British rock-and-roll group, the Beatles, was translated, for example, into equally successful films—charming, slapstick escapism that nevertheless proclaimed the emancipation of youth from the confining formalities and conventions of their elders.

Fine arts   Unlike writers or filmmakers, the majority of postwar artists did not use their work as a vehicle to express either ideological commitment or a concern for the human situation. Following trends established by the impressionists and cubists, they spoke neither about the world nor to the world, but instead to each other and to the extremely small coterie of initiates who understood their artistic language. Foremost among the postwar schools of art was abstract expressionism, whose chief exponents were the American painters Jackson Pollock (1912–1956), Willem de Kooning (1904–   ), and Franz Kline (1910–1962). Their interests lay in further experimentation with the relationship between color, texture, and surface, to the total ex-

Abstract Expressionism. This untitled painting by Jackson Pollock explores texture and surface to the exclusion of meaning in the traditional sense.

Composition (1955) by Willem de Kooning. A work representative of the abstract expressionists' desire to explore the varieties of light, texture, and surface.

clusion of "meaning" or "message" in the traditional sense. Jasper John's (1930–) painting of the American flag demanded that the viewer see it not as *a* painting—that is, something to be interpreted—but instead as painting, the treatment of canvas with paint. Robert Rauschenberg (1925–) in revolt against the abstract expressionists, exhibited blank white panels, insisting that by so doing he was pressing art to the ultimate question of a choice of medium. Painters fought the notion that their work in some way expressed disgust with an empty civilization. "My paintings are based on the fact that only what can be seen is there," declared the American Frank Stella (1936–), who painted stripes on irregularly shaped canvases. "Pop" art, a phenomenon of the late sixties associated with the work of Andy Warhol (1930–1987), took as its subject everyday objects such as soup cans and comic-strip heroes. According to its practitioners, it was not a protest against the banality of industrialism but another experiment in abstractions.

See color plates following page 1036 for representative works by Rothko, Rauschenberg, Johns, Hanson, Fischl, and Stella

Even the remote and yet extraordinarily compelling abstractions of Mark Rothko (1903–1970), glowing or somber rectangles of color imposed upon other rectangles, were said by the artist himself to represent "nothing but content—no associations, only sensation." Only with the coming, in the 1970s, of the so-called hyper-realists, artists such as the American Duane Hanson (1925–), who recreates his invariably depressing human subjects in plastic down to the last eyelash, can we perhaps say that some artists are making a statement not only about technique but about what they perceive

Divorce of visual arts from social commentary

as the vacuity of life. Increasingly, artists have declared their intent to comment directly upon the elements of alienation, pain, and despair that were a part of Western life in the forty years after the Second World War and upon the generally positive, productive nature of society during that same exciting period.

SELECTED READINGS

• *Items so designated are available in paperback editions.*

Ardagh, John, *The New French Revolution,* New York, 1969. The social impact of economic change.

• Aron, Raymond, *The Imperial Republic: The United States and the World, 1945–1973,* Lanham, Md., 1974. World analysis by a leading French political theorist.

Ash, Timothy, *The Polish Revolution: Solidarity,* New York, 1983. The best account.

• Beer, Samuel, *Britain Against Itself,* New York, 1982. A clear-headed analysis of the reasons for British decline.

Black, C. E., *The Dynamics of Modernization: A Study in Comparative History,* New York, 1966. Includes material on non-Western countries as well.

• Brzezinski, Z., *The Soviet Bloc: Unity and Conflict,* rev. and enl. ed., Cambridge, Mass., 1967. Eastern European politics analyzed by a former U.S. National Security Advisor.

• Crossman, Richard H., ed., *The God That Failed,* New York, 1950. Testimony from former Marxists about their loss of political faith.

• Crouzet, Maurice, *The European Renaissance Since 1945,* New York, 1971. Optimistic appraisal of Europe's postwar recovery.

• Daalder, Hans, and Peter Mair, eds., *Western European Party Systems: Continuity and Change,* London, 1983. Fine overview of political developments at the national level.

• Dahrendorf, Ralf, *Society and Democracy in Germany,* New York, 1971. The extent of the change from fascism to democracy.

• DePorte, A. W., *Europe Between the Superpowers: The Enduring Balance,* New Haven, 1979.

• Ehrmann, Henry W., *Politics in France,* Boston, 1968. Detailed treatment of politics in the decade after 1958.

• Gaddis, John, *The United States and the Origins of the Cold War, 1942–1947,* New York, 1972. Focuses on the United States. A balanced account.

• Gilbert, Felix, with David Clay Large, *The End of the European Era, 1890 to the Present,* 4th ed., New York, 1991. Comprehensive overview of political developments.

Hoffman, Stanley, et al., *In Search of France,* Cambridge, Mass., 1965. Essays providing perceptive analysis of postwar French politics and society.

Hough, Jerry, and Merle Fainsod, *How the Soviet Union Is Governed,* Cambridge, Mass., 1979.

• Kolko, Gabriel, *The Politics of War: The World and United States Foreign Policy,*

1943–1945, New York, 1969. Argues that the blame for the cold war rests with the Western Allies.

- LaFeber, Walter, *America, Russia and the Cold War,* 5th ed., New York, 1985. Another revisionist treatment.
- Laqueur, Walter, *Europe Since Hitler,* rev. ed., New York, 1982. A useful, thorough survey.
- ———, *The Long Road to Freedom: Russia and "Glasnost,"* New York, 1989. Puts recent developments in the Soviet Union in their historical contexts.
- Leslie, R. F., et al., *The History of Poland Since 1863,* New York, 1981. Useful background for current events.

Mayne, Richard, *The Recovery of Europe, 1945–1973,* Garden City, N.Y., 1973. Another reliable account.

Mowat, R. C., *Creating the European Community,* New York, 1973. A diplomatic historian's account of the merging of Europe's economic fortunes.

Parker, Geoffrey, *The Logic of Unity,* 3rd ed., London, 1981. Another study of the forces working for and against European community.

Postan, M. M., *An Economic History of Western Europe, 1945–1964,* London, 1967. A lively account of a lively period.

Sabel, Charles, *Work and Politics: The Division of Labour in Industry,* Cambridge, Eng., 1982. Overview of impact of technological change on twentieth-century society.

- Sampson, Anthony, *The Changing Anatomy of Britain,* New York, 1982. A sharp critical dissection of British society.

Tsoukalis, Loukas, ed., *The European Community: Past, Present, and Future,* Oxford, Eng., 1983. Collection of essays assessing progress toward and chances for European integration.

- Ulam, Adam, *Expansion and Coexistence: Soviet Foreign Policy, 1917–1973,* 2nd ed., New York, 1974.

Wright, Gordon, *Rural Revolution in France: The Peasantry in the Twentieth Century,* Stanford, 1964. The effect of social change on a firmly entrenched peasantry.

SOURCE MATERIALS

Adenauer, Konrad, *Memoirs, 1945–1953,* Chicago, 1966. Adenauer served as chancellor of the Federal Republic of Germany from 1949 to 1963 and sought both American support and the reunification of dismembered Germany.

- Barnes, Thomas G., and Gerald D. Feldman, eds., *Breakdown and Rebirth: 1914 to the Present,* Boston, 1972. An excellent documentary collection of contemporary history, primarily European.
- Baudrillard, Jean, *Selected Writings,* Mark Poster, ed., Stanford, Calif., 1988. Essays and extracts by one of France's leading cultural theorists.

De Gaulle, Charles, *Memoirs of Hope: Renewal and Endeavor,* New York, 1971.

- Foucault, Michel, *Discipline and Punish: The Birth of the Prison,* New York, 1977. Accessible introduction to Foucault's thought.
- Kennan, George F., *Memoirs, 1925–1950,* New York, 1967. Kennan, a career diplomat, was America's leading expert on Russia and instrumental in the formation of the containment policy.

- Lyotard, Jean-François, *The Postmodern Condition: A Report on Knowledge,* Minneapolis, Minn., 1984. Important analysis of social impact of recent developments in communications technology.
- Servan-Schreiber, J. J., *The American Challenge,* New York, 1968. A Frenchman's assessment of the impact of American economy and technology on Europe.

Chapter 31

PROBLEMS OF WORLD CIVILIZATION

Africa, all I ask from you is the courage to know: to look about you and
see what is happening in this old and tired world; to realize the extent and
depth of its rebirth and the promise which glows on your hills.

—W. E. B. Du Bois, *Autobiography*

The nuclear accident at Chernobyl is a tragedy for those killed or injured
by the fire and for the many more who must live with the fear that exposure to radiation may cause cancer and genetic defects in the future. Nevertheless we should remember that the danger from this accident is negli-
gible compared with what would happen in a nuclear war.

—George Rathjens and Jerome Grossman,
Council for a Livable World, 1986

The writing of a final chapter in a textbook of this sort is, for the authors, a difficult task. Not only are they called upon to attempt an
instant analysis of their own society and time; they are expected as
well to discern in present events patterns that will continue to be of some
consequence five to ten years hence. In other words, they are called upon
to pick historical winners, to decide not what *has* mattered, which is difficult enough, but what *will* matter. Historians, whose job it is to acknowledge the way in which human idiosyncrasies make prediction a tricky business, are particularly loath to single out this movement or that trend and to
pronounce it "significant" in terms of the future. We shall therefore merely
content ourselves with a discussion of some of the most serious problems
confronting society in the 1980s and 1990s, calling attention at the outset
to the fact that these problems are rooted in many of the historical developments—industrialization, urbanization, and international competition, for
example—that we have traced in the preceding chapters.

The present as history

1. THE EMERGENCE OF THE THIRD WORLD AND ITS CONSEQUENCES

The emergence of an independent Third World

As significant as any trend in world politics since the end of the Second World War has been the decline of the Western imperial powers, and the concurrent emergence of what has come to be called the Third World— newly independent states in Africa and Asia, along with older nations there as well as in Latin America. Many of these countries have established themselves in territories that were formerly part of European empires. Others— China and the various nations of the Middle East and Latin America, for example—while nominally independent of both the West and the Soviet Union before 1945, nevertheless existed under European hegemony and were forced to acquiesce to European demands. Such is the case no longer. Although many of these so-called emerging nations are poor, and although the people of the Third World are by no means a united bloc, they represent an increasingly independent factor in the world power equation.

Assets and liabilities

Many of these countries are rich in natural resources. Nations in the Middle East, Venezuela in South America, and Nigeria in Africa, possess oil in quantities sufficient to make their every move of vital importance to the West. Other African nations, such as Zaire and Angola, are immensely rich in many mineral resources. Population resources serve as both liability and asset in the Third World. The people of China, by their sheer numbers, constitute an implicit threat to world stability at all times. The people of India, again by dint of their numbers, and lack of food, represent a perpetual threat to the stability of their own country and hence to all Asia. Every area in the Third World is a potential "trouble spot," and the history of the post-1945 Third World is largely a history of often violent internal dissent. This is so, not only because the problems of racism, poverty, hunger, and overpopulation make them particularly vulnerable to violent civil conflicts, but also because the United States, the former Soviet Union, the European nations, and China itself were until recently prepared to engage each other through the medium of Third World adversaries, thus increasing the possibility of conflict by their willingness to encourage it. To protect themselves from direct confrontation with each other, these developed nations interfered in the civil wars of others, on opposite sides and with an intensity that frequently belied their declared interest in avoiding general world war.

A final general observation concerning the Third World: although the governments of most countries have pursued the twin goals of industrialization and urbanization, this policy has not gone unchallenged. In the spring of 1979, for example, the extremely repressive regime of one of the Third World's most devoted "westernizers," the shah of oil-rich Iran, was overthrown by the revolutionary forces of an equally repressive Islamic fundamentalist, the Ayatollah Khomeini, whose explicit policy was to turn his country's back not only on the West but on "progress" as the West had de-

The Ayatollah Ruhollah Khomeini of Iran

Khomeini's Funeral. Hysterical mourners reached out to touch Khomeini's body during funeral ceremonies in Teheran in June 1989.

fined that term for the past two hundred years; internal conflicts over intercourse with the West surfaced again upon Khomeini's death in 1989.

The most radical Third World change resulting from the events of the Second World War was the Chinese revolution. A civil war had raged in China since 1926, when the forces of the nationalists, under Chiang Kai-shek (1887–1975), had engaged in battle first in the south, then in the north, with communist insurgents under the leadership of Mao Zedong (1893–1976), a former teacher and union organizer. A truce in 1937 had allowed both sides to wage common battle against the Japanese. At the end of the war, however, the communists, still led by Mao Zedong, refused to surrender the northern provinces under their control, and civil war broke out again. The United States intervened, first as mediator, then with massive military assistance, as an ally of Chiang—all to no avail. The nationalists, corrupt and unrepresentative of the people, surrendered in 1949 to the communists and decamped to the island of Taiwan. Intensely hostile to the capitalist West, the Chinese communists soon found themselves engaged, as well, in a series of skirmishes, verbal and otherwise, with their erstwhile Marxist co-revolutionaries, the Soviets. The Sino-Soviet rivalry, the willingness of the United States in the 1970s to reach an accommodation with the Chinese in order to capitalize on that rivalry, and the willingness of the Chinese guided by Mao's successor, Deng Xiaoping (1904–   ), to encourage Western capitalist investment in their country, suggest that however much power shifted after the Second World War, power politics remained a game nations believed themselves compelled to play—if necessary, in opposition to their professed ideological commitments. But China's apparent "liberalization" seemed to reverse itself in 1989. Pro-democracy demon-

Mao Zedong. A photograph taken in 1933 when he was the leader of the radical Left opposition to the Kuomintang under Chiang Kai-shek.

Tiananman Square, 1989. Students were crushed to death after government troops and tanks stormed the square, brutally suppressing the peaceful movement for political reform.

strations by students in Beijing's Tiananmen Square were put down by the military, resulting in the deaths of 700 to 800 unarmed civilians, and the

The Chinese Communist Revolution

wounding of thousands. Deng Ziaoping's praise for the military crackdown seemed to indicate a victory for conservative elements within the Chinese Communist party. Foreign reaction to the massacre included the suspension of many diplomatic and economic ties, while Hong Kong—slated for restoration to China in 1997—questioned China's guarantee of the territory's political and civil freedoms. The lifting of martial law early in 1990 was followed by renewed contacts with the West; yet there is little indication that the Chinese leadership is prepared to countenance significant political liberalization.

The Second World War, which had assisted the course of Chinese revolution by dissolving older power structures, served the same purpose within

Indian independence

the colonial empires of the West. The first major British colony to establish self-government after the war was India. Rebel movements had harassed the representatives of Britain in that country throughout the nineteenth century. Flames of revolt burned more fiercely during the First World War and after; another world war added more tinder. By 1945 anti-British resentment had reached such a pitch that the country was ripe for revolution. Resolutions by nationalist bodies such as the Indian National Congress called upon Britain to "quit India." The congress had taken the position that India would fight only as a free nation without limitations imposed by the "mother country." The foremost Indian nationalist leader, Mohandas K. Gandhi (1869–1948) did not approve of armed attacks on rulers and their institutions, however. His methods were noncooperation and civil disobedience. By 1947 he and his comrade and disciple, Jawaharlal Nehru (1889–1964), had gained such widespread support that the British found it

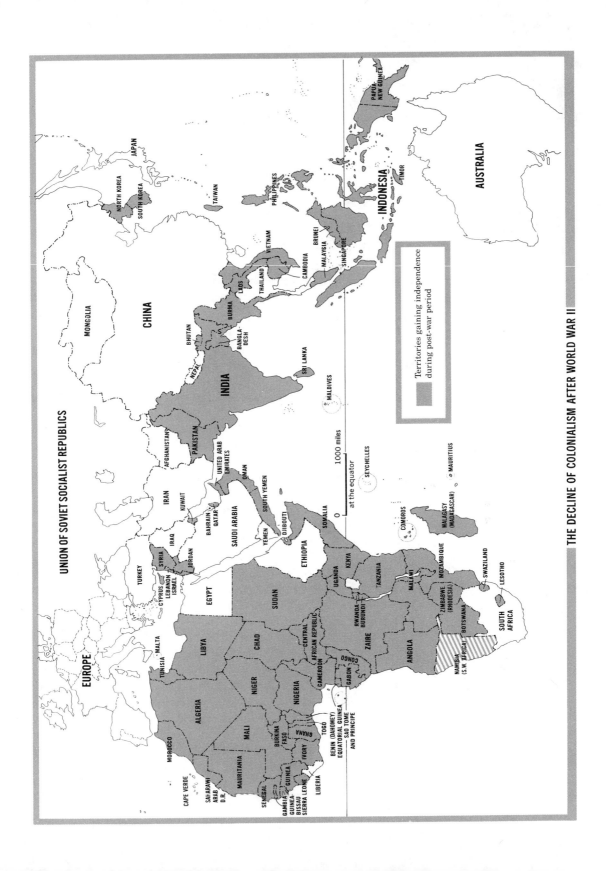

UNION OF SOVIET SOCIALIST REPUBLICS

EUROPE

AUSTRALIA

Territories gaining independence
during post-war period

1000 miles
0   at the equator

THE DECLINE OF COLONIALISM AFTER WORLD WAR II

Gandhi and Nehru at a Meeting of Indian Leaders in 1946

expedient to grant autonomy to India and its neighboring area, Pakistan. In 1950 both countries organized themselves as independent republics. Disorders, stemming largely from religious conflicts between Hindus, Muslims, and Sikhs, continued to plague the two countries, however, finally resulting in a bloody war in 1971. An important outcome of this conflict was the establishment of the independent republic of Bangladesh, formerly East Pakistan.

India's struggle to maintain itself as a democracy

In recent years India has struggled to maintain itself as a democracy in the face of mounting economic and social problems. In the mid-1970s, Prime Minister Indira Gandhi (1917–1984) (the daughter of Nehru) assumed authoritarian powers after declaring a state of emergency. Though defeated in 1977 in free elections that she sanctioned following more than a year of virtual dictatorship, she returned to power in early 1980, only to be felled by an assassin's attack in 1984. Political unrest became more pronounced in the years following the succession of her son, Rajiv Gandhi, who in turn was assassinated in 1991. Continuing instability raises the question of whether a country as dominated by the internal problems of poverty, illiteracy, overpopulation, and near-starvation as India can afford what many Third World leaders claim is the luxury of a slow-moving and comparatively inefficient democracy. Chief among the issues galvanizing the opposition was the government's financial settlement with the U.S. chemical company Union Carbide, compensating the survivors of the 1984 Bhopal toxic gas plant leak, which killed more than 8,000 people and injured about 150,000 more. Another point of strong political disagreement and protest has been the government's attempts since the early 1990s to broaden economic opportunities for traditionally "lower caste" groups.

Indira Gandhi Campaigning on the Eve of Her Return to Power in Early 1980

Important as India was to Great Britain, it was only the first and largest of the colonies surrendered by colonial powers following the war. Vast areas of Africa achieved independence as well after 1945. In 1951 Egyptian nationalists compelled the British to withdraw their troops from Egyptian territory. A year later a group of nationalist army officers seized control of the government. They deposed the playboy king, Farouk, alleged to be subservient to the British, and proclaimed the state a republic. Shortly thereafter an Egyptian colonel, Gamal Abdel Nasser (1918–1970), assumed the presidency of the country. The British misread Nasser's nationalist ambitions. Anthony Eden (1897–1977), prime minister at the time, called Nasser the Middle Eastern equivalent of Adolph Hitler, and accused him, without foundation, of widespread imperial designs. When Nasser nationalized the Suez Canal Company in 1956 in order to finance the construction of a high dam on the Nile at Aswan, the British and French, dependent on the canal as their major trade route to the East, interpreted the Egyptian action as a direct threat to their economic security. Together with the newly created country of Israel—itself a by-product of British decolonization—Britain and France launched an abortive, ill-fated invasion of the canal zone as a way not only of recovering control of the canal but, as Eden put it, of "punishing" Nasser. World opinion—led by the United States—turned against the invaders, who were forced to withdraw.

The British gradually departed from sub-Saharan Africa as well, beginning with Ghana (formerly called the Gold Coast), which was granted self-government in 1954 and independence in 1957. Apologists for British colonial rule claimed that by training indigenous elites and gradually transferring to them responsibility for local administration, British colonies would make the transition to independence more smoothly than would the colonies of other European states where self-government came with less preparation. Despite such protestations, the British colonies' emergence into independence and political and economic stability proved no less difficult than it was for their neighbors. Even in resource-rich Nigeria the euphoria of independence (gained in 1960) fell prey in 1966 to familiar charges of corruption and inefficiency, political assassinations, the overthrow of the government, the secession of the eastern region of the country, and a devastating thirty-one-month civil war in which more than 1 million people perished in battle and of starvation. Kenya, as poor as Nigeria was rich, was beset by the Mau Mau rebellion in 1952, more than a decade before independence. The Mau Mau, an offshoot of the Kikuyu tribe, conducted a four-year reign of terror against white colonists who took their lands, Indian merchants who excluded Africans from their trade, and their kinsmen who were deemed sympathetic to the colonial government. Although driven in part by racial and ethnic antipathies, the Mau Mau uprising was essentially a nationalist movement dedicated to achieving African self-determination over questions of land and governance, a goal realized with independence in 1963 and the election of Kikuyu tribesman and proponent of African socialism Jomo Kenyatta (1893–1978) as the first president of Kenya in 1964. In Rhodesia, however, race was the dominant issue. White Rhodesians had long denied the inevitability of black rule, instituting a system of rigid racial segregation similar to that imposed by whites in South Africa, and in 1965 they unilaterally declared their independence from Great Britain. The white government held firm in its deter-

Jomo Kenyatta Addressing an All-Africa Congress in London

mination to resist black rule until 1977 when the cumulative effect of U.S. and British pressure, economic sanctions, fierce guerilla warfare, and the withdrawal of South African assistance caused the government to open negotiations that eventually led in 1980 to the creation of a state renamed as Zimbabwe, which was dominated by black nationalists and presided over by Robert Mugabe.

The French were perhaps even less successful than the British in surrendering their colonial possessions without conflict. For France, the most *Algeria* painful and protracted withdrawal occurred in its North African colony of Algeria, inhabited by about one million immigrants, mainly French, in a total population of over ten million. The immigrants occupied positions of economic and political power; Arabs and Berbers remained impoverished laborers. In 1954 nationalists' demands for equal status with the immigrants were denied, triggering a seven-year war. During the course of the war, as we have seen (see above p. 1018), Algeria's European settlers grew to fear the French government—and its desire for a resolution of the conflict even at the cost of granting independence to Algeria—almost as much as they feared the Algerian nationalists. Charles de Gaulle's promise of self-determination put an end to the fighting and led to independence in 1962. In the meantime the French extricated themselves from other portions of their North African empire with less difficulty. In 1955 they withdrew from their protectorate over Morocco, and a short time later they renounced their protectorate over Tunisia as well; both countries were granted independence in 1956.

Britain, France, and other European countries that found themselves compelled to liquidate their empires after 1945 attempted to do so in ways that would enhance the prospects for an orderly transition and stable successor governments. Yet in almost no instance—except, perhaps in the is-

Anti-Imperialist Revolt in Algeria, 1960. At Dar-es-Saada, Muslims take furniture from the homes of Europeans and burn it in the streets.

lands of the Caribbean area—was the hope realized. In the wake of independence the unifying symbol of colonial oppression gave way to old ethnic and regional antagonisms dating from the precolonial as well as the colonial eras. These tensions resulted in bitter secessionist movements and devastating civil wars. Belgium's precipitous decision to grant independence to the Congo (later known as Zaire) in 1960 signaled the beginning of a civil war that raged for more than five years between the newly formed central government and the southeastern mineral-rich province of Katanga (later known as Shaba) and continued to smolder into the 1980s with assistance from Angolan-based Katangan refugees.

*The post-independence
resurgence of ethnic and
regional antagonisms*

Conflicts also erupted in the Sudan and Chad between a Muslim north and a Christian/animist south, in Ethiopia between the Marxist central government and the Islamic Eritreans, and in Angola and Zimbabwe between the government and ethnically and regionally based revolutionary movements that had participated in the struggle for independence but not in the subsequent regime. Many of these conflicts were spurred on by support from neighbors or non-African powers. While none of these breakaway resistance movements has yet succeeded, they have left a legacy of suspicion, violence, and instability.

Undoubtedly the most explosive area of conflict on the African continent was South Africa, whose all-white government continued until recently to oppose appeals and pressures from all quarters to relax its racial policy of *apartheid*. This policy enforced a separate and desperately inferior existence for its black and mixed-race population since the Nationalists, an Afrikaner party of the extreme right, began to enact a severe segregationist program affecting every aspect of life in South Africa in the 1950s. Initially, the nonwhite population led by the African National Congress responded to apartheid with campaigns of passive resistance. Government-sponsored repression and violence, however, drove the African National Congress, led by Nelson Mandela (1918–   ) to adopt a more radical and violent strategy after 1960. The government responded by banning the African National Congress as a terrorist organization, hunting down and prosecuting militants, imprisoning Mandela in 1962, and legislating further curbs on the personal liberties of nonwhites. Racial tensions among the nation's 5 million whites, 3 million coloreds (people of mixed race), and over 20 million blacks continued to worsen. South African whites grew even more fearful of the "black menace" when, in 1975, neighboring Angola and Mozambique were granted independence by Portugal and promptly installed Marxist, militantly anti-South African governments that fueled the expectations of black South Africans. Domestic violence erupted again in 1976 in the Johannesburg ghetto of Soweto where police killed more than 1,000 rioting blacks.

Seeking ways to defuse domestic tensions and improve their image abroad, the government of Pieter W. Botha (1916–   ) took steps in the early 1980s to liberalize the country's social and economic policies toward the nonwhite population by authorizing African labor unions to bargain collectively, desegregating some public facilities, and raising wages. But at

F. W. De Klerk and Nelson Mandela. These longtime foes shake hands after jointly receiving the UNESCO Peace Prize in 1992. De Klerk, the president of the Republic of South Africa, and Nelson Mandela, the head of the African National Congress, are negotiating to create a new constitution and government for South Africa that will include people of all races.

the same time nearly 3 million blacks were deprived of citizenship and sent to live in overcrowded "ethnic homelands." A new constitution adopted in 1984 conferred near-dictatorial powers on the president and, while creating a tricameral legislature with separate chambers for whites, coloreds, and Asians, totally excluded blacks from political participation. Angry blacks became more violent still in their opposition to the white regime and Botha declared a state of emergency in mid-1985. By 1986 a wide range of nations, fearing a cataclysmic confrontation between the white minority and the black majority, joined in imposing severe economic sanctions upon South Africa in hopes of persuading the government to come to terms with the black population peacefully. Mandela's release from prison in 1990 (after twenty-seven and a half years of imprisonment) by Botha's successor, F. W. de Klerk (1936–   ), prompted the lifting of some of these sanctions, which in turn led to accusations by black activists that Mandela's freedom was granted primarily to divert attention from the problems attendant upon the promised ending of apartheid. The growth of organizations with widely differing views on how to solve those problems led to dissension and violence—much of it among ethnic groups—within the black community. Despite continuing conflict, the nation's white voters gave overwhelming approval in March 1992 to de Klerk's negotiations for an end to apartheid. The president declared that the referendum "closed the book" on the ideology that had kept the nation bitterly divided. Nonetheless, ongoing violence continues to affect the negotiations to devise a new constitution and a nonracial political system.

The prevailing political turmoil in Africa was compounded by the onset of a massive economic decline in the 1970s after the global escalation of petroleum prices and the attendant inflation in prices for Western technology, seed, and fertilizer. Recurring droughts in the 1980s and 1990s struck nearly every part of the continent, impairing agricultural development and bringing starvation to many areas. African states were compelled to divert currency from development projects to import food for their swelling populations at the very time that falling world prices for agricultural commodities and metals diminished the market value of Africa's major exports and the sources of foreign currency. The severity of the famine exacerbated existing tensions within these drought-stricken areas, and the distribution of famine relief became a frequent arena for political struggle. In addition, in the growing number of African states whose leaders espoused various brands of socialism many government-sponsored corporations were inefficiently managed and became financial liabilities. This made it all the more difficult for these nations to maintain payments to Western financial institutions on debts incurred for development projects during the boom years of the 1960s; and defaulting in turn limited their access to further loans.

Africa's political turmoil compounded by economic decline

The liberation of colonial peoples in the decades following the Second World War heightened racial consciousness and racial conflict, not only in Africa and Asia but in the West as well. Newly independent black nations, on guard against real or perceived threats of neocolonialism, remained understandably sensitive to their economic dependence upon the predominantly white nations of Western Europe and America. Black and Asian immigration into those nations produced tension and frequent violence. And indigenous black populations in the West, particularly in the United States, derived a sense of both their present social and economic inferiority and their potential strength as a political force from the independence movements occurring elsewhere in the world. As a result, the growth of insurgency among American blacks paralleled the rise of black nations in Africa and the Caribbean.

Racial conflict in the West

Through most of the years from the Civil War to 1900, black people were condemned, in the North as well as the South, to a subordinate role within a predominantly white culture. Black political consciousness and black leaders were not unknown before the turn of the century: Harriet Tubman, Sojourner Truth, Frederick Douglass, Nat Turner, and others, were eloquent and powerful spokespeople and activists. But with the twentieth century came a massive emigration of blacks from the South to the North. Although the North shared most of the attitudes of the South, there were more opportunities for blacks in the industrial cities than in the primarily agrarian South. Many thousands of black people emigrated to the North during the years of the First World War, when the lack of white labor created a need for their services.

U.S. blacks after the Civil War

In 1910 the National Association for the Advancement of Colored People was founded and contributed to the growing awareness among black people that they were an oppressed group and that this condition should be changed. The work of the NAACP was supplemented in 1911 with the founding of the National League on Urban Conditions Among Negroes (later known as the National Urban League). The work of black leaders of this time— for example, Ida Wells-Barnett (1862–1931), A. Philip Randolph (1889–1979), W. E. B. Du Bois (1868–1963), Mary McLeod Bethune (1875–1955)—who were visible and vocal opponents of lynching,

Early twentieth-century civil rights movements

Martin Luther King, Jr., American Civil Rights Activist

Black independence: Garvey and Malcolm X

Ethnic and racial tensions

promoters of the organization of blacks into labor unions, of racial equality, and of educational opportunities for blacks, kept the movement for equality alive.

The Second World War saw another influx of blacks into northern cities and intensified their drive for dignity and independence. The Congress of Racial Equality (CORE) was founded by James Farmer in 1942. By 1960 CORE had combined its efforts with those of other political and civil rights organizations seeking the same goals. Together they helped to promote "freedom rides" to desegregate public transportation facilities and boycotts directed at private businesses and public services that discriminated against blacks in the South. The leader of these protests, and the undoubted leader of the black movement in the United States in the 1960s, was Martin Luther King, Jr. (1929–1968), a Baptist minister. Like Farmer, King embraced the Gandhian philosophy of nonviolence. His personal participation in countless demonstrations, his willingness to go to jail for a cause that he believed to be just, and his ability as an orator to arouse both blacks and whites with his message led to his position as the most highly regarded— and widely feared—defender of black rights. His career was ended by assassination in 1968.

The goal of King and of organizations like CORE was a fully integrated society. That of other charismatic black leaders was complete independence from white society. Marcus Garvey (1887–1940), a native of Jamaica who lived in the black ghetto of Harlem in New York City, emphasized the African origins of black Americans. He claimed that his people were the descendants of the "greatest and proudest race who ever peopled the earth." In his campaign for black separatism he generated a movement of black emigration from America to Africa. Another black separatist was Malcolm X (1925–1965), who assumed the "X" after having discarded his "white" surname. For most of his adult life a spokesman for the Black Muslim movement, Malcolm X urged blacks to renew their commitment to their own heritage—the Muslim religion, for example—and to establish black businesses as a way of maintaining economic and psychological distance from white domination. Like King, he was assassinated, in 1965 while addressing a rally in Harlem.

Civil rights laws enacted under the administration of President Lyndon B. Johnson (1908–1973) in the 1960s brought American blacks some measure of equality with regard to voting rights—and, to a much lesser degree, school desegregation. In other areas, such as housing and job opportunities, blacks continue to suffer disadvantage and discrimination. In the early 1990s, debate over social policy centered on continued use of entitlement programs to help narrow the gap between whites and ethnic and racial minorities, especially as the declining economic status of many white Americans led them to perceive such programs as helping minorities directly at their expense. The recessions of the 1980s and 1990s in general heightened ethnic and racial tensions across the United States. Rising numbers of Asian immigrants—many from Vietnam or Cambodia—as well as growing numbers of Hispanic and Latino populations have broadened the scope of con-

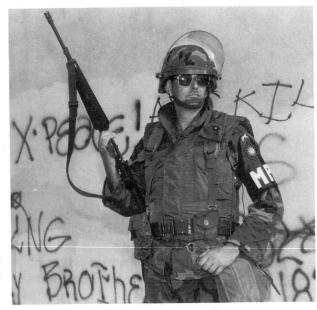

Los Angeles Riots, 1992. After an all-white jury acquitted the white police officers who had beaten black motorist Rodney King, the streets of south-central Los Angeles erupted with violent riots. Left: A black storeowner watches helplessly as his store burns during the riots. Right: National Guardsmen were called in to restore the peace. The graffiti behind him reads, "For Rodney King."

flict rather than diluting the intensity of discrimination against blacks. These problems are not confined to the United States. In Great Britain, for example, where there has been a large immigration of blacks and Asians from former colonies, extreme discrimination in jobs and housing menaces the chances for early or satisfactory integration. Because most black workers are "last hired, first fired," they are particular victims of Britain's rising unemployment. In the summer of 1981 and again in 1985 black frustrations resulted in serious rioting in London and other British cities. Disturbances also broke out again in the United States in 1982 in Miami and in 1992 in Los Angeles and elsewhere across the country. Response to these outbreaks followed the pattern established in the 1960s: immediate concern and investigation, but little else, particularly in terms of solving the problems of economic inequality.

2. WARMAKING AND PEACEKEEPING IN THE NUCLEAR AGE

The violence attendant upon the emergence of new nations was but a part of the pattern of armed confrontations imposed across the globe after 1945 by international rivalries and tensions. The conflicts that have intruded with agonizing consistency upon the world were frequently the result of local circumstance. Yet almost always they produced far more than local consequences. As they unfolded, they proved not only how fragile were the processes of international peacekeeping, but also how vulnerable even the

Frequency of conflicts

The Korean War

mightiest nations were to circumstances that frequently lay beyond their limited control.

The most serious clash between communist and non-communist forces in the first postwar decade occurred not in Europe but in Korea, where armed conflict broke out in 1950. Treaties with Japan at the end of the Second World War had provided that Korea, under Japanese rule since 1910, would become an independent and united country. The United States and the Soviet Union left occupying forces there until 1949, the Americans to the south of the thirty-eighth parallel, the Russians to the north of it. During this period of occupation, the Soviets refused to cooperate with the United Nations-sponsored plan to hold free elections for the entire country. Instead, they established in the north a people's republic similar to those they had erected in Eastern Europe. In June 1950, troops from North Korea crossed the thirty-eighth parallel and invaded the south. Taking advantage of a temporary Russian boycott of the United Nations, the United States was able to avoid a Soviet veto of its plan to counter this invasion by sending a contingent of troops to oppose it. The troops, though nominally under United Nations command, were largely American, directed and supplied by the United States. Initial military gains by this force were countered in November 1950 by the invasion into Korea of troops from the newly established People's Republic of China, sent to aid the North Koreans. A stalemate ensued, President Truman and his advisors being as unwilling to widen the conflict into China—fearing a third world war—as they were to abandon their South Korean allies. After two years of military and diplomatic deadlock, a peace was concluded in July 1953, recognizing the existence of both North and South Korea and abandoning any scheme for their reunion. As in the case of Germany, the limited ability of major powers to achieve their goals completely resulted in a divided settlement—and a divided nation. Recent developments, however, indicate that North and South Korea are themselves now interested in reaching accommodation with each other.

Vietnam also produced the same lesson, in a war far more devastating than that in Korea. After the defeat of Japan in 1945, France had sought to recover its lost empire in the Far East. Vietnam declared its independence from France, and French attempts to reassert control sparked a rebellion of Vietnamese nationalists under the leadership of Ho Chi Minh (1890–1969). The rebels, known as the Viet Minh, resorted to guerilla warfare and inflicted such costly defeats upon the French that the latter decided to abandon the struggle. An agreement was signed at Geneva in 1954 providing for the division of Vietnam into two zones, pending elections to determine the future government of the entire country. Ho Chi Minh became president of North Vietnam and established his capital at Hanoi. Had elections been held as provided by the Geneva Agreement, Ho Chi Minh would probably have been elected president of all of Vietnam. But the government of South Vietnam, backed by the United States, refused to permit elections to be held. As a result, the Viet Cong, communist insurgents aided by Ho Chi Minh, stepped up guerilla warfare against the government and its troops in South Vietnam.

Ho Chi Minh, President of North Vietnam, 1954–1969

From this point on, involvement by the United States in the Vietnamese civil war escalated. President John F. Kennedy (1917–1963) was convinced that a Chinese communist juggernaut would soon roll over all of Southeast Asia: Vietnam, Laos, Cambodia, Malaysia, and Singapore; then Thailand, Burma, and India. As such, in 1961 he sent the first American military advisors to help the South Vietnamese army. How far Kennedy would have gone in his crusade to confront communism had he escaped assassination in 1963 is impossible to say. Kennedy's successor, Lyndon Johnson, hoped that a relatively small force of perhaps 100,000 men would be sufficient to defeat the Viet Cong. Little consideration was given to the fact that the Viet Cong were solidly entrenched in South Vietnam, and that they had been waging a bitter national struggle for upward of eighteen years. They had succeeded in driving out the French in 1954 and were not likely to surrender to a new invader, as they conceived the Americans to be. The Viet Cong and the North Vietnamese regulars, though less well equipped, nevertheless fought the South Vietnamese and their American allies to a standstill on several occasions.

Exasperated by failure to win an easy victory in South Vietnam, the American civilian and military chiefs undertook a campaign of heavy aerial bombardment. A series of incidents in 1964 were contrived so as to provide them with justification. Reports, of doubtful veracity, indicated that North Vietnamese ships had attacked American naval vessels in the Tonkin Gulf. President Johnson pronounced these incidents acts of war and immediately obtained from Congress authorization to use whatever measures might prove necessary to repel communist aggression. Soon afterward the first American air raids began and the first American marines landed. Although evidence accumulated that cast doubt on the efficacy of these raids, they continued. At least as much tonnage in nonnuclear bombs was dropped on tiny Vietnam as was unloaded by the Allied forces on all of Germany in the Second World War. As the struggle entered its fifth year, with no end in

War in Vietnam. Confronted with a new kind of warfare, the American military sought to adapt its methods to the Vietnamese situation.

sight, disillusionment spread throughout the United States. Criticism of President Johnson was so harsh in 1968 that he was forced to abandon his plans to run for a second term.

Johnson's successor, Richard M. Nixon (1913–), elected on the strength of promises to end the war, instead continued its escalation. In May 1970 the United States invaded Cambodia and a few months later the kingdom of Laos. In April 1972, the North Vietnamese, with aid from the Soviet Union and China, launched a powerful counteroffensive with the objective of conquering South Vietnam and driving all foreign armies out of the country. A number of South Vietnamese strongholds were captured. Nixon countered with increased bombing of North Vietnam's factories and railroads and by mining its harbors. Savage raids continued while negotiations were underway in December 1972. A cease-fire, early in 1973, did no more than postpone the inevitable. Two years later, South Vietnam fell to the Viet Cong and the North Vietnamese. The massive intervention had proved a ghastly failure.

The lesson of Vietnam—that in a nuclear age there are limits to national power—was one that the United States, the former Soviet Union, and other countries have continued to find hard to learn. Since the early 1960s, for example, the United States has found it increasingly difficult to maintain its accustomed hegemony over the Caribbean area and Central America. A revolution in Cuba in 1959 brought to power Fidel Castro (1926–), who declared himself a Marxist-Leninist shortly thereafter. His increasingly anti-American regime relied heavily on economic support from the Soviet Union. Castro's insistence on the right to assist revolutionary movements elsewhere in Latin America and in Angola made him, in the minds of U.S. policy-makers, a continuing threat to American interests. In 1979, insurgents in Nicaragua toppled the regime of a pro-American dictator, Anastasio Somoza Debayle (1925–1980). The victorious rebels, calling themselves the Sandinista National Liberation Front (after a guerilla leader treacher-

Fidel Castro of Cuba

U.S. presence in Cuba and Nicaragua

The Nicaraguan Revolution. Sandinista commandos celebrate the fall of the Somoza government by toppling a huge statue of Anastasio Somoza Garcia, the father of the ousted president, in Managua, Nicaragua.

ously slain by Somoza's father), plotted a leftist course for Nicaragua, accepted Cuban and Soviet aid and declared their determination to avoid U.S. domination. Although Sandinist Daniel Ortega (1945–) had been elected president in a national election, the Sandinista regime was perceived by President Ronald Reagan (1911–) as a creation of Soviet ideology and Cuban subversion and as a direct threat to U.S. security. The Reagan administration proceeded to commit the United States to the overthrow of the Sandinistas through a series of increasingly dangerous moves: pressuring financial institutions to withhold loans; supporting and arming a counter-revolutionary force (the Contras); mining Nicaraguan harbors; conducting air and naval maneuvers in nearby waters; building airstrips and camps for joint military exercises in Honduras; and declaring the United States above international law. The posture of the United States hardened the Sandinistas' determination to resist American aggression, inducing a siege mentality and resulting in an increasingly authoritarian regime. Civil war ravaged the country until 1990 when, following agreed-upon elections in which the Contras suffered defeat, they acknowledged the futility of continued warfare and handed their weapons over to a United Nations peacekeeping force.

In El Salvador, a similar coup in 1979 expelled that country's hard-line dictator, General Carlos Humberto Romero. Yet there, in contrast to Nicaragua, the revolutionary government moved to the Right with the support of the United States. State-backed death squads battled an insurgent Democratic Revolutionary Front as the country plunged into civil war. American intervention in both El Salvador and Nicaragua was limited by U.S. unwillingness to engage directly in the conflicts there, and to this extent expressed a realization that even a superpower could not expect to shape the world to its own ends.

Civil war in El Salvador

During the past three decades the former Soviet Union was forced to come to terms with this lesson as well. Having arranged to supply their Cuban ally Fidel Castro with nuclear missiles and other war matériel, the Soviets were confronted by a U.S. naval blockade of the island designed to prevent delivery of the promised equipment in October 1962. The Soviet government, alarmed by the threat of war, agreed to withdraw and to remove the bombers and missiles already on Cuban soil. The incident posed an extremely difficult question for the superpowers: How could one nation convince another of its determination to brook no further interference with its plans, if its adversary could be fairly certain that because of the fear of nuclear war the threat was no more than a bluff?

The Cuban Missile Crisis

In deciding to invade Afghanistan in 1979 in support of a recently installed pro-Soviet regime, however, the U.S.S.R. seemed to repeat the experience of the French and the Americans in Vietnam. Ten years later, a force of 100,000 Soviet troops had been unable to quell Afghani guerrilla resistance, and Soviet troops were recalled. This retreat left the field open for continuing internal warfare fueled by religious conflict.

The Soviet involvement in Afghanistan

To achieve regional order was an almost impossible task in the most persistent trouble spot in the post-Second World War era: the Middle East.

Immigration to Palestine. Left: British soldiers guard the shore as a ship loaded with unauthorized refugees attempts to land in 1947. Right: A view of the unbearably crowded conditions aboard ships bringing refugees to Palestine.

Palestine under British mandate

Here the conflict centered on the presence of the Jewish state of Israel. At the end of the First World War, the country now known as Israel, then called Palestine, was a province of Turkey. Its population was about 70 percent Arab and 30 percent Jewish and Christian. Following Turkey's defeat, Palestine was mandated by the League of Nations in 1922 as a protectorate of Britain. Meanwhile, Zionist organizations in Europe and America worked to convert Palestine into a national home for the Jewish people.

Growing Arab-Jewish tensions

For a time Palestine flourished under the British mandate. By 1929, however, tension between Arabs and Jews had become severe. The paramount cause of Arab concern was the increasing flow of Jews into Palestine. Arabs feared a relentless immigrant wave, backed by foreign capital and bearing a culture alien to the ways of the Muslim majority. This anxiety manifested itself in a series of armed attacks and terrorist raids by Arabs against the Jews in the late 1920s and early 1930s. As news spread of the Nazi persecution of the Jews, pressure increased on the British to allow more and more Jewish immigrants into Palestine. During the period from 1930 to 1933 more than 130,000 European Jews were admitted; uncounted thousands more entered the country illegally. The Arabs rose in open rebellion. Guerilla attacks in rural areas and looting, burning, and sabotage in towns and cities kept the population in turmoil. By 1939, though the British had 20,000 troops in Palestine, they were unable to maintain order.

Little progress toward a lasting settlement had been achieved when, in April 1947, the British government referred the Palestine problem to the United Nations and announced that a year later it would terminate its mandate and withdraw all its troops from the country. On May 14, 1948, the

British mandate came to an end; on the same day a Jewish provisional government proclaimed the establishment of an independent state of Israel. From the day of proclaimed independence until the spring of 1949, Israel and its Arab neighbor countries were at war. United Nations' efforts brought about temporary truces, but nothing lasting was achieved until Israel, Egypt, Jordan, and Syria signed general armistice agreements in early February 1949. The status of the cease-fire was regarded as a victory for Israel and a defeat for the Arab powers. Neither, however, accepted it as final. Violent incidents continued to occur, including retaliatory massacres.

Despite wars with the Arabs, Israel embarked on a concerted program of industrialization to strengthen the economy. Large sums of money flowed into the country, mainly from the United States, Britain, and West Germany, as restitution for the outrages of Nazi persecution. Yet Israel's conflict with its Arab neighbors continued unabated, fueled by Israel's inability to resolve the question of the rights of Palestinian Arabs who still claim the state of Israel as their home and by the Arabs' refusal to recognize Israel as a legitimate state. These tensions were exacerbated by Israeli participation in a poorly conceived action against Egypt in 1956. In 1967 President Nasser of Egypt, in alliance with Jordan and Syria, blockaded the port of Elat on the Gulf of Aqaba, Israel's only direct outlet to the Red Sea. The Israelis responded with a lightning war against Egypt and its allies, whose forces were routed in six days. At the end of the fighting, Israel held the Golan Heights, the West Bank of the Jordan River, the Old City in Jerusalem, all of the Sinai, and the east bank of the Suez Canal. The eventual cease-fire did nothing to ease regional animosities. New outbreaks flared sporadically for more than two years. The Arabs were tormented by loss of confidence and fearful of their own future as a result of their defeat. The Israelis were obsessed with security and determined to preserve it regardless of cost.

Another war in 1973, called the Yom Kippur War, once again failed to resolve the impasse. In that conflict, the Arabs threatened to withhold their immense oil reserves from the West, in hopes that the West would in turn put pressure on the Israelis to negotiate. This tactic succeeded only to the

On the Path to Peace in the Middle East. From left to right, Egyptian President Anwar el-Sadat, U.S. President Jimmy Carter, and Israeli Prime Minister Menachem Begin shake hands at the announcement of the Camp David accord that laid the groundwork for a peace treaty between Egypt and Israel.

Yitzhak Rabin. Rabin is pictured with his supporters after the Labour party's victory in the Israeli general election in June 1992. The hope is that peace negotiations will proceed more smoothly with Rabin as prime minister.

Kurdish Refugees. During the Persian Gulf War in 1991, Saddam Hussein's forces destroyed thousands of Kurdish villages, leaving a multitude of Kurds homeless, hungry, and in fear for their lives.

extent of convincing Europe and America of their dependence on Arab oil, and of their need to escape from that dependence. Since that time, prospects for peace have waxed and waned. In 1977, President Anwar al-Sadat (1918–1981), Nasser's successor, traveled to Jerusalem in a dramatic bid to break the deadlock. And in the fall of 1978 U.S. President Jimmy Carter (1924–   ), having persuaded Sadat and Israeli Prime Minister Menachem Begin (1913–1991) to meet with him at Camp David outside Washington, engineered their agreement to a treaty draft, which was signed in final form by Israel and Egypt in Washington in 1979. Yet factors such as Israel's reluctance to surrender Arab territory on the West Bank and the continuing terrorist campaigns of non-Jewish Palestinians guaranteed that peace would not come easily or soon to the Middle East. Proof of that unhappy truth came yet again in 1982, when Israel launched a ferocious attack against Palestinian forces based in Lebanon. During the conflict the Israelis bombed suspected strongholds of the Palestine Liberation Organization (PLO) in the cities of Tyre, Sidon, and Beirut, whose civilian populations were used by the PLO as human shields for its military activities. The PLO and Israel continued to clash, often violently, during the 1980s and into the 1990s in what became known as the *intifada,* especially over Israeli occupation of the West Bank and Gaza Strip. In 1991, peace talks sponsored by the United States and the Soviet Union brought all the major dissident Middle Eastern factions to the conference table. In July 1992 Yitzhak Rabin, Israel's new prime minister, promised to limit settlements in the occupied West Bank and Gaza Strip and to shift spending away from these territories, a step in the direction of peace. But there was still little indication of an easy or early settlement.

The issue of Israel's place among the nations of the Middle East was by no means the sole cause of that area's political volatility. The revolutionary government of Iran, following the overthrow of the shah in 1979, charted an erratic course that further jeopardized the stability of the region. In 1980 war broke out between Iran and Iraq, ultimately spilling into the Persian Gulf, where it threatened to disrupt vital oil shipping lanes in international waters. In the face of this danger the United States government in 1987 placed American flags on select foreign oil tankers, hoping by this gesture to discourage attack on those ships by the Iranians. The immediate result, however, was an increased number of Iranian mines in the Persian Gulf and an increased threat of general war.

A cease-fire declaration in 1988 formally ended overt hostilities between Iran and Iraq, although peace talks continued for well over a year. The tenuous peace was broken in August 1990 when the Iraqi dictator, Saddam Hussein, ordered an invasion of oil-rich Kuwait, claiming the principality as part of "Greater Iraq" in an effort to bolster Iraq's economy, weakened by the war with Iran. A coalition of twenty-nine countries led by the United States declared war on Iraq. The brief, intense war that followed decimated Iraqi forces. It ended with Iraq's withdrawal from Kuwait and severe internal disorder, especially regarding the fate of the ethnic Kurds in Iraq.

The 1991 Persian Gulf War heightened the theme that has characterized relationships between Middle Eastern and other countries since the 1960s: Western dependence on Arab oil. The Organization of Petroleum Exporting Countries (OPEC), formed in 1960 to regulate the production and pricing of crude oil, assumed an increasingly militant posture in the 1970s under the leadership of its Middle Eastern Arab members. For a time a majority appeared willing to follow the lead of militant Middle Eastern nationalists such as Muammar el-Qaddafi, Libyan chief of state, in attempting to extract a high price—both economic and political—from the West. Western powers tempered their support of Israel and designed their policies toward the PLO at least in part on the basis of their continuing need for oil. In the mid-1980s overproduction and a decrease in the demand for oil brought about by economic recession in Western Europe and the United States made it far more difficult for the OPEC countries to keep the price of oil uniformly high. Yet the resulting price reductions were not an unalloyed boon to Western economies. Many oil-producing nations in the Third World had borrowed large sums of money from Western financial institutions in the 1970s using their "black gold" as collateral. When reduced oil prices resulted in financial crisis for some of those nations—as in Mexico, for example—Western lenders were threatened with default. The problems of oil production and pricing illustrate convincingly the way in which the problems of the world economy and of international peacekeeping are locked together.

The oil crisis

Even without the dangerous conflicts that have scarred global trouble spots since 1945, the world would not be at peace. Terrorism, a plague of apparently senseless acts of human destruction, though often related to larger events and causes, has over the past decade emerged as a frightening and thus far insoluble threat to world stability. Terrorism has been employed by separatist or nationalist movements, the Palestinians (the PLO) in the Middle East, for example, the Basques in northern Spain, or the Catholic (Irish Republican Army, or IRA) and Protestant extremists in Northern Ireland. It has also been the tactic of radical national leaders such

Terrorism

A Meeting of the Organization of Petroleum-Exporting Countries (OPEC) in Qatar, 1976

Former Italian Prime Minister Aldo Moro, victim of the terrorist Red Brigade, May 9, 1978

as the Ayatollah Khomeini of Iran or Muammar el-Qaddafi of Libya. Terrorist outrages in the 1970s and 1980s were frequently the work of radicals: the incendiary attacks and bank robberies of the so-called "Red Army Faction" in Germany in the early 1970s, which were launched to arouse revolutionary sentiment among frustrated youth; the PLO attack against the quarters of Israeli athletes at the 1972 Olympics in Munich; the kidnapping and murder of the Italian politician Aldo Moro by the Italian "Red Brigade" in 1978; the murder of Israel-bound passengers in the Rome airport in 1985; the repeated hijacking of passenger planes, and indeed, on one occasion in 1985 of a Mediterranean cruise ship, the *Achille Lauro;* and the bombing of a Pan American Airlines jet over Lockerbie, Scotland, in 1988. In recent years, however, terrorist incidents have declined in number, perhaps as a result of the achievement of a tentative peace in Lebanon and the waning of extremist sentiment in Iran following the death of Khomeini. An exception to this decline can be seen in Ireland and Great Britain, where attacks have continued, instigated by opposing factions in the unceasing battles between militant Protestants and Catholics.

Looming above all the other issues and circumstances we have surveyed has been the continuing threat of nuclear destruction. During the 1960s and 1970s, both the United States and the Soviet Union vacillated in their willingness to discuss arms control, let alone to move toward actual reduction. Henry Kissinger, U.S. secretary of state under Presidents Richard Nixon and Gerald Ford in the 1970s, proclaimed détente with the Russians as his goal, and devoted much time to negotiations aimed at defusing potentially explosive areas of conflict between the two nations. Both countries were concerned to curb the spread of nuclear weapons and to limit, if possible, the apparently endless expansion of their own arsenals. The Strategic Arms Limitation Treaty (SALT) talks, in which the Russians and Ameri-

Arms control

Antiwar Protest in London, 1983. Demonstrations such as this one directed against the installation of U.S. missiles with nuclear warheads in Europe were a factor influencing the superpowers to negotiate arms reductions.

cans engaged during the 1970s and early 1980s, were an indication of mutual willingness to recognize and tackle a problem of awesome dimensions. Yet the talks produced little in the way of concrete agreement. President Ronald Reagan, who took office in 1981, denounced a second stage of the SALT negotiations during his campaign and subsequently continued to press for dramatic increases in his military budgets for sophisticated armaments, even as he proclaimed his devotion to the cause of disarmament.

Changing leadership within the Soviet Union did not allow for new initiatives from that quarter until 1986, when Mikhail Gorbachev floated a series of proposals that met with mixed response from the Reagan administration, still publicly committed to increased missile deployment and to an elaborate and astronomically expensive space-based "defensive" system. In December 1987, however, despite continuing disagreement on other issues, Gorbachev and Reagan signed a treaty in Washington eliminating all short- and medium-range nuclear missiles from the European arsenals of both East and West. The nuclear threat did not disappear with the breakup of the Soviet Union, although both the U.S. and the former U.S.S.R. began to reduce significantly their nuclear arms stocks as a result of arms agreements negotiated in 1991 and 1992. Yet, countries as diverse as Iraq, Pakistan, and China were in the process of developing nuclear technology that further threatened stability across the globe.

*Nuclear arms
agreements*

3. THE PROBLEMS OF ECOLOGY AND POPULATION

Pessimism about the human condition in the 1980s and 1990s stems from more than the problems of the present. It derives as well from a fear about the future, the future of the earth's human beings, of the earth itself, and of what is termed its ecology. The word *ecology* is often used to refer to human beings and their environment, but it is much broader than that. Ecologists think of humans as related to a vast chain of life that extends through mammals, amphibians, invertebrates, and the simplest microorganisms, either plants or animals. In popular usage ecology may be synonymous with pollution problems. Again this is an oversimplification. The causes and prevention of pollution make up important elements in the study of ecology, but they are not its whole subject. Equally important is the use of our environment in ways that will safeguard the heritage of fertile soil, pure air, fresh water, and forests for those who come after us.

The meaning of ecology

Ecological violations consist not merely of poisoning the atmosphere and contaminating oceans, rivers, and lakes by dumping wastes into them, but of any assault upon them that makes them less valuable for human survival. The excessive construction of dams, for example, causes the silting of rivers and the accumulating of nitrates at a faster rate than the surrounding soil can absorb. The use of insecticides, especially those containing DDT, may result in upsetting the balance of nature. An example in the recent history of Malaysia illustrates such an occurrence. The Malaysian government re-

Assaults upon nature

sorted to extensive spraying of remote areas with DDT in the hope of stamping out malaria-carrying mosquitoes. The DDT killed the mosquitoes but also poisoned the flourishing cockroaches. The cockroaches in turn were eaten by the village cats. The cats died of the DDT poison. The net result was a multiplication of rats formerly kept from a population explosion by their natural enemies, the cats. So badly disturbed was the balance of nature that a fresh supply of cats had to be airlifted from other regions. Other assaults upon the balance of nature have been even more serious. The Aswan High Dam of Egypt, undoubtedly valuable for increasing the water supply of that country, has at the same time cut down the flow of algal nutrients to the Mediterranean, with damaging effects on the fishing industry of various countries. From the ecological standpoint the rapid development of industry in modern times is an almost unmitigated disaster. For thousands of years the human race introduced into the environment no more waste substances than could easily be absorbed by the environment. But modern technology has introduced a variety of wastes never abundant before. Among them are carbon monoxide, sulfur dioxide, and nitrogen oxide. And this is to say nothing of the discharge into nature of pesticides, the great host of synthetic products that are not biologically degradable, and the fallout of nuclear weapons testing. As the nature and gravity of these problems have become apparent, governments have been pressured to take preventive and remedial action. In late 1982 the United States government was actually compelled to purchase the entire town of Times Beach, Missouri, where a pesticide had been sprayed (with permanently damaging effects to the health of its citizens), before it could proceed with a detoxification program. In 1986, a nuclear power station at Chernobyl, near Kiev in the Soviet Union, exploded, producing highly dangerous radioactive fallout

Disaster at the Chernobyl Nuclear Power Station, May 1986. The explosion at this Soviet nuclear power facility (the white arrow indicates the damaged unit surrounded by debris) near Kiev produced radioactive fallout that killed and injured numerous people close to the site, and threatened the health of thousands more as it spread across Europe. This accident fueled the continuing debate on the safety of nuclear power plants not only in the Soviet Union but around the earth.

Environmental Damage. Oil spills or burning oil wells created in peace or war are equally damaging to the environment. Left: Workers are cleaning up oil spilled by the Exxon *Valdez* in 1989 in Prince William Sound in Alaska. Right: Kuwaiti oil wells are burning as a result of fires caused by Iraqi sabotage or Allied bombing during the Persian Gulf War in 1991. Such fires have damaged both the land and air in Kuwait.

not only in the vicinity of the accident but, because of prevailing winds, across the continent of Europe. Affected countries protested, while citizens increased the pressure on their governments to curtail the manufacture of such lethal industrial and military by-products.

The political abuses of ecological resources received renewed attention in the 1991 Iraqi conflict, when between 5 million and 10 million barrels of oil were spilled into the Persian Gulf. Both Iraqi and coalition forces accused the other of causing the spill. The devastation it wrought rivaled that resulting from the 1989 grounding of the Exxon company's *Valdez* oil tanker, in which 11 million gallons of crude oil were spilled into Alaskan waters. Other environmental issues commanding attention in the 1990s include the continued destruction of global rain forests, with the threatened extinction of plant and animal species, and the problem of global warming due to depletion of the ozone layer. Despite an international conference on such issues in June 1992 in Rio de Janeiro, international response to these problems continues to be tentative and conservative.

Oil spills, destruction of rain forests, global warming

A close link exists between the problems of ecology and the population explosion that is occurring throughout the world. Indeed, if population had not increased alarmingly in recent years, the problems of ecology might well have passed unnoticed. For example, New York City on the eve of the Civil War had a total population of 730,000. The area was not essentially smaller than it is now. Yet the inhabitants of the five boroughs constituting the city have multiplied ten times over. The example of New York City can be duplicated in many other overcrowded areas, not only in

Ecology and the population explosion

America but especially in Asia. Calcutta now has a population of 11.6 million, compared with 3 million in 1961. Tokyo has grown from 5 million to over 26 million in little more than twenty years. The total population of the earth at the beginning of the Christian era was about 250 million. More than sixteen centuries passed before another quarter-billion had been added to the total. Not until 1860 did the population of the globe approximate 1 billion. From then on the increase was vastly more rapid. The sixth half-billion, added about 1960, required scarcely more than ten years. By 1979 the earth's population had reached 5.3 billion.

Causes of the demographic revolution

What have been the causes of this demographic revolution overturning the ancient balance between births and deaths which had long kept the population on a stationary or slowly rising level? Fundamentally, what has happened has been the achievement of a twentieth-century death rate alongside a medieval birthrate. Infant mortality rates have markedly declined. Deaths of mothers in childbirth have also diminished. The great plagues, such as cholera, typhus, and tuberculosis, take a much smaller toll than they did in earlier centuries. Wars and famines still number their victims by the millions, yet such factors are insufficient to counteract an uncurbed rate of reproduction. Though the practice of contraception has been approved by the governments of such nations as India, China, and Japan, only in the last decade have the effects of that policy been noticeable. In some countries poverty, ignorance, and the implacable opposition of the Roman Catholic hierarchy have made the widespread use of contraceptives difficult. Leaders in Third World countries charge that attempts by Western powers to encourage them to limit population growth, either by contraceptive devices or by sterilization, is a not-so-subtle form of genocide.

Its uneven effects

The demographic revolution has not affected all countries uniformly. Its incidence has been most conspicuous in the underdeveloped nations of Central and South America, Africa, and Asia. Whereas the population of the world as a whole will double, at present rates of increase, in thirty-five years, that of Central and South America will multiply twofold in only twenty-six years. An outstanding example is that of Brazil. In 1900 its population was estimated to be 17 million. By 1975 this total had grown to 98 million, and by 1986 to 143 million, a more than eightfold increase in less than one hundred years. The population of Asia (excluding the U.S.S.R.) grew from 813 million in 1900 to approximately 2.9 billion in 1986—approximately 60 percent of the world's population. A situation in which the poorest nations are also the most overpopulated does not augur well for the future of world stability.

4. THE ACHIEVEMENTS AND LIMITATIONS OF SCIENCE AND TECHNOLOGY

For solutions to many of these problems, men and women have, paradoxically, turned to those agencies responsible, in many cases, for the creation of the problems: science and technology. Scientists and technicians invented and perfected the internal combustion engine and the chemical DDT. Now other scientists and technicians are seeking ways to combat their deleterious effects. Scientific research has been responsible for the medical advances that have helped to produce worldwide population increase. No one would argue, of course, that the research should not have taken place, or that the continuing battle against disease is not one of humanity's most worthwhile engagements. Most would agree, however, that science must move as quickly as possible to come up with a safe and simple method of controlling birth, as it continues to fight to prolong life.

The achievements of science in the field of health during the past half-century have been truly remarkable. Two discoveries of great importance have enabled scientists to understand more clearly the ways in which the human body receives and transmits disease. The discovery of viruses was the result of experimentation conducted chiefly by the American biochemist Wendell Stanley (1904–1971) in the 1930s. Viruses are microscopic organisms that show signs of life—including the ability to reproduce—only when existing inside living cells. They are the cause of many human diseases, including measles, poliomyelitis (infantile paralysis), and rabies. Not until the nature of viruses was understood could scientists begin to develop means of treating and preventing the virus-produced illnesses in human beings. The second most important discovery increasing our understanding of human life occurred in 1953, when the Englishman F. H. C. Crick (1916–) and the American James D. Watson (1928–) further unlocked the mysteries of genetic inheritance that had been explored by Gregor Mendel at the end of the nineteenth century. Crick and Watson successfully analyzed deoxyribonucleic acid, or DNA, the chemical molecular structure that occurs in the nuclei of gene cells. They discovered that DNA

Science and technology: Cause and cure of the world's problems

The discovery of viruses; DNA

The Decoding of DNA. Left: F. H. C. Crick and James D. Watson discuss their efforts to analyze the molecular structure of DNA. Right: A model of the molecular structure of DNA. The dual spiral chains are called a double helix.

is composed of smaller molecules of four different kinds, linked together in spiral chains. The arrangement of these molecules in each cell forms a distinct chemical message that determines the character of the genes and therefore of the human organism of which they are a part. The knowledge gained through analysis of DNA has enabled scientists and doctors to understand the causes of hereditary disease and also, by altering a patient's body chemistry, to prevent it. Despite the great benefits that have resulted from this recent discovery, scientists and others have warned that an understanding of the workings of DNA could lead to dangerous tampering with the genetic processes, as, for example, in attempts to produce artificially a breed of more "perfect" human beings.

Medical advances: Sulfa drugs, antibiotics, tranquilizers

Experimentation based upon a fuller understanding of the causes of disease has led to the discovery of new medicines to treat it. In 1935 the German Gerhard Domagk (1895–1964) discovered the first of the sulfa drugs, which he called sulfanilamide. Soon others were added to the list. Each was found to be marvelously effective in curing or checking such diseases as rheumatic fever, gonorrhea, scarlet fever, and meningitis. About 1930, the Englishman Sir Alexander Fleming (1881–1955) discovered the first of the antibiotics, penicillin. Antibiotics are chemical agents produced by living organisms and possessing the power to check or kill bacteria. Many have their origin in molds, fungi, algae, and in simple organisms living in the soil. Penicillin was eventually found to be a drug that could produce spectacular results in the treatment of pneumonia, syphilis, peritonitis, tetanus, and numerous other maladies hitherto frequently fatal. Scientists used knowledge obtained through the analysis of DNA to strengthen the cultures used to develop penicillin. In the 1940s the second most famous of the antibiotics—streptomycin—was discovered by the American Dr. Selman W. Waksman (1888–1973). Streptomycin seems to hold its greatest promise in the treatment of tuberculosis, though it has been used for numerous other infections that do not yield to penicillin.

As important as the discovery of new drugs to treat disease has been the development of new means of preventing it. Sir Edward Jenner discovered the first successful vaccine, used to prevent smallpox, in 1796. But not until the 1950s were vaccines found that could protect people from diseases such as mumps, measles, and cholera. One of the most exciting breakthroughs occurred with the development of an inoculation against poliomyelitis by the American Dr. Jonas Salk (1914–   ), in 1953. Still to be discovered are effective agents for the successful treatment of two of the world's most deadly killers, heart disease and cancer, and of a recent and potentially more dangerous worldwide plague Anti-Immune Deficiency Syndrome (AIDS), a virus that attacks the body's immune system, thus making it prey to any number of deadly diseases and infections. Unlike the victims of heart disease and cancer, no AIDS patient has ever been cured.

Dr. Jonas Salk in His Laboratory

Few would today oppose continued campaigns by scientists intent upon eradicating disease. Governments have found it increasingly difficult, however, to justify the spending of vast sums of public money on programs designed to facilitate the exploration of outer space. From their inception, these "experiments" have resembled international competitions between the United States and the Soviet Union as much as they have scientific and technological investigations. On October 4, 1957, the government of the Soviet Union rocketed the first artificial satellite into space at a speed of about 18,000 miles an hour. Though it weighed nearly 200 pounds, it was propelled upward higher than 500 miles. This Russian achievement gave the English language a new word—*Sputnik,* the Russian for satellite or fellow traveler. In April 1961, the Russians succeeded in sending the first man, Yuri Gagarin, into orbit around the earth. Meanwhile, scientists and military specialists in the United States had been competing to match the Soviets' achievements. After a number of successes with animals and "uninhabited" capsules, and the suborbital journey of a manned capsule, they launched the first American manned spaceship into orbit around the earth on February 20, 1962, with John Glenn circling the earth three times. Their successes were climaxed in July 1969 when Neil Armstrong, a civilian astronaut, left his lunar landing module and became the first man on the moon's surface. These voyages and those that followed were hailed as events of capital importance. They promised an extension of our knowledge of outer space and could doubtless prepare the way for exploration of the moon and eventually of distant planets. But by the mid-1970s, both the United States and the Soviet Union had drastically cut back their space programs in response to demands on their economies from other quarters. A space "shuttle" and laboratory, plus continuing experiments of a minor nature, kept the programs alive, despite an accident in 1986 that killed all the crew members of a U.S. space shuttle. But the value of these devices was being questioned, in view of the billions required to keep them operational.

Undoubtedly it was in the area of nuclear science that the largest and most troubling questions arose as to the capabilities, limitations, and implications of science and technology. Even more powerful than the nuclear bombs dropped on Japan at the end of the Second World War was the hydrogen bomb, first tested by the U.S. Atomic Energy commission in November 1952. The tests were conducted at Eniwetok Atoll in the South Pacific; an entire island disappeared after burning brightly for several hours. The hydrogen bomb, or H-bomb, is based upon fusion of hydrogen atoms, a process that requires the enormous heat generated by the splitting of uranium atoms to start the reaction. The fusion results in the creation of a new element, helium, which actually weighs less than the sum of the hydrogen atoms. The "free" energy left over provides the tremendous explosive power of the H-bomb. The force of hydrogen bombs is measured in *megatons,* each of which represents 1,000,000 tons of TNT. Thus a 5-megaton H-bomb would equal 250 times the power of the A-bombs dropped on Hiroshima and Nagasaki.

Governments experimented with schemes to harness nuclear energy for peaceful purposes. Some progress has been made in the development of atomic power as an alternative source of domestic and industrial fuel. But the dangers of radiation as a by-product suggest that this scheme may prove of limited value. During the late 1970s, when the West's supplies of oil were threatened, heated debate continued between advocates of further

The First Lunar Landing. Astronaut Edwin E. Aldrin, Jr., is photographed walking near the lunar module of Apollo 11. Astronaut Neil Armstrong, who took the picture, and part of the lunar module are reflected in Aldrin's face plate.

The H-bomb

The uses of atomic energy; electronics

construction of atomic power plants and those who argued in favor of other energy forms—among them solar—as safer and cheaper alternatives. Meanwhile, technologists working for private industry made use of discoveries in atomic physics to pioneer the field of electronics. Electronics derives from that branch of physics that deals with the behavior and effects of electrons, or negatively charged constituents within the atom. Electronic devices have multiplied in staggering profusion since the Second World War. Among them are devices to measure the trajectory of missiles, to give warnings of approaching missiles or aircraft, to make possible "blind" landings of airplanes, to store and release electrical signals, to amplify and regulate the transmission of light and sound images, and to provide the power for photoelectric cells that open doors, and operate various automatic machines. The spacecraft industry, which has made possible the exploration of outer space, is closely dependent upon electronics. In addition, through automation, expensive and complicated machines are constantly taking the place of much human labor. Data-processing machines and electronic computers are employed to control switching operations in railroad yards, to operate assembly lines, to operate machines that control other machines, and even to maintain blood pressure during critical operations in hospitals.

Technological unemployment

Electronic inventions have proved no more an unmixed blessing than have the other discoveries and developments of scientists and technicians. One obvious problem generated by devices that can do the work of humans is that they put humans out of work. Technological unemployment has become an important problem for the modern world. Though new industries absorbed many workers, others were bound to be displaced by automation. While the demand for skilled labor remained high, the so-called entry jobs performed by the unskilled were fast disappearing. They were being eliminated not by computers so much as by fork-lift trucks and motorized conveyors and sweepers. Mechanization of agriculture also eliminated thousands of jobs for unskilled and uneducated workers.

Science, technology, and an understanding of human nature

Science and technology provide no panaceas for the problems of the world. If those problems are to be solved, men and women, not machines, will have to do the work. They will be better equipped to do so if they possess some sense of their own past. The lesson of history is not that it repeats itself. The lesson is, rather, that the present can be clearly perceived, and the future intelligently planned for, only when those responsible for the world's destiny understand the workings of human nature. And for knowledge of that extraordinarily complicated and fascinating mechanism, there is no better source than history.

SELECTED READINGS

- *Items so designated are available in paperback editions.*

- American Friends Service Committee, *A Compassionate Peace: A Future for the Middle East,* New York, 1981. An examination of the problems and proposals for their solution.

- Barnett, A. Doak, *China and the Major Powers in East Asia,* Washington, D.C., 1977. A careful study of recent international relations.
- Bates, Robert H., *Essays on the Political Economy of Rural Africa,* Cambridge, 1983. An excellent study of the problems of food production in contemporary Africa.

  Bhatia, Krishan, *The Ordeal of Nationhood: A Social Study of India since Independence, 1947–1970,* New York, 1971. Informed and objective account of India's problems.
- Bianco, Lucien, *Origins of the Chinese Revolution, 1915–1949,* tr. Muriel Bell. Stanford, 1971. A brilliant interpretive summary.

  Brain, Robert, *Art and Society in Africa,* London, 1981.
- Butterfield, Fox, *China Alive in the Bitter Sea,* New York, 1982. Poignant and critical.
- Caputo, Philip, *A Rumor of War,* New York, 1977. The best memoir of the American experience in the Vietnam War.
- Coetzee, J. M., *Waiting for the Barbarians,* London, 1980. A searing critique of South Africa by a brilliant Afrikaner novelist.
- Cornish, Edward, *The Study of the Future: An Introduction to the Art and Science of Understanding and Shaping Tomorrow's World,* Washington, D.C., 1977. An introduction to the world of the "futurists."
- Erlich, Paul, *The Population Bomb,* New York, 1968. Discusses the threat of over-population.
- Fall, Bernard B., *The Two Vietnams: A Political and Military Analysis,* rev. ed., New York, 1967.
- Fanon, Frantz, *The Wretched of the Earth,* New York, 1968. The extraordinary and brilliant delineation of the oppression of Third World peoples.
- Fitzgerald, Frances, *Fire in the Lake: The Vietnamese and the Americans in Vietnam,* Boston, 1972. A detailed and moving account.
- Gamow, George, *Thirty Years That Shook Physics,* New York, 1966. A lucid account by a physicist.
- Heilbroner, Robert L., *An Inquiry into the Human Prospect,* New York, 1974, 1980. Optimistic assessment of the durability of Western cultural values.
- Hitching, Francis, *The Neck of the Giraffe: Darwin, Evolution, and the New Biology,* New York, 1982. A good survey of the problems remaining in evolutionary theory in the twentieth century.

  Issawi, Charles, *Egypt in Revolution: An Economic Analysis,* New York, 1963.
- Khouri, Fred J., *The Arab-Israeli Dilemma,* Syracuse, N.Y., 1968.
- Myrdal, Alva, *The Game of Disarmament: How the United States and Russia Run the Arms Race,* New York, 1976.

  Myrdal, Gunnar, *Against the Stream: Critical Essays on Economics,* New York, 1972. Offers pertinent comments on problems of the Third World.

  Nattrass, Jill, *The South African Economy: Its Growth and Change,* Cape Town, 1981.
- Nelson, Nici, ed., *African Women in the Development Process,* London, 1981.

  Ngugi wa Thiong'o, *Petals of Blood,* New York, 1977. A scathing critique of neo-colonialism in Kenya by Africa's best-known novelist.

  O'Connor, Anthony, *The African City,* London, 1983. Explores the various characteristics of tropical African cities in the postcolonial era.
- Rubin, Barry, *Paved with Good Intentions: The American Experience and Iran,* New York, 1980. Reliable account of U.S.-Iranian diplomacy.

  Servan-Schreiber, J. J., *The World Challenge,* New York, 1981. Analyzes problems of distribution of world resources.

- Spence, Jonathan, *The Gate of Heavenly Peace: The Chinese and Their Revolution, 1895–1980,* New York, 1981. A penetrating account of the contributions and frustrations of China's intellectuals.
- ———, *The Search for Modern China,* New York, 1990.
- Thompson, Leonard, and Andrew Prior, *South African Politics,* London, 1982. An excellent, well-balanced survey of contemporary South Africa.
- Toffler, Alvin, *Future Shock,* New York, 1971. An extended essay on the consequences of rapid change in modern industrial society.
- Tordoff, William, *Government and Politics in Africa,* Bloomington, 1984. Highly readable, wide-ranging, and up-to-date.
- Watson, James D., *The Double Helix: A Personal Account of the Discovery of the Structure of DNA,* New York, 1968. Punctures the traditional picture of the scientist as hero.
- Worsley, Peter, *The Third World,* 2d ed., Chicago, 1970.

RULERS OF PRINCIPAL EUROPEAN STATES SINCE 700 C.E.

The Carolingian Dynasty

Pepin, Mayor of the Palace, 714
Charles Martel, Mayor of the Palace, 715–741
Pepin I, Mayor of the Palace, 741; King, 751–768
Charlemagne, King, 768–814; Emperor, 800–814
Louis the Pious, Emperor, 814–840

West Francia

Charles the Bald, King, 840–877; Emperor, 875
Louis II, King, 877–879
Louis III, King, 879–882
Carloman, King, 879–884

Middle Kingdoms

Lothair, Emperor, 840–855
Louis (Italy), Emperor, 855–875
Charles (Provence), King, 855–863
Lothair II (Lorraine), King, 855–869

East Francia

Ludwig, King, 840–876
Carloman, King, 876–880
Ludwig, King, 876–882
Charles the Fat, Emperor, 876–887

Holy Roman Emperors

Saxon Dynasty

Otto I, 962–973
Otto II, 973–983
Otto III, 983–1002
Henry II, 1002–1024

Franconian Dynasty

Conrad II, 1024–1039
Henry III, 1039–1056
Henry IV, 1056–1106
Henry V, 1106–1125
Lothair II (of Saxony), King, 1125–1133; Emperor,
    1133–1137

Hohenstaufen Dynasty

Conrad III, 1138–1152
Frederick I (Barbarossa), 1152–1190
Henry VI, 1190–1197
Philip of Swabia, 1198–1208 ⎫ Rivals
Otto IV (Welf), 1198–1215 ⎭
Frederick II, 1220–1250
Conrad IV, 1250–1254

Interregnum, 1254–1273

Emperors from Various Dynasties
Rudolf I (Habsburg), 1273–1291

Adolf (Nassau), 1292–1298
Albert I (Habsburg), 1298–1308
Henry VII (Luxemburg), 1308–1313
Ludwig IV (Wittelsbach), 1314–1347
Charles IV (Luxemburg), 1347–1378
Wenceslas (Luxemburg), 1378–1400
Rupert (Wittelsbach), 1400–1410
Sigismund (Luxemburg), 1410–1437

Habsburg Dynasty

Albert II, 1438–1439
Frederick III, 1440–1493
Maximilian I, 1493–1519
Charles V, 1519–1556
Ferdinand I, 1556–1564
Maximilian II, 1564–1576
Rudolf II, 1576–1612
Matthias, 1612–1619
Ferdinand II, 1619–1637
Ferdinand III, 1637–1657
Leopold I, 1658–1705
Joseph I, 1705–1711
Charles VI, 1711–1740
Charles VII (not a Habsburg), 1742–1745
Francis I, 1745–1765
Joseph II, 1765–1790
Leopold II, 1790–1792
Francis II, 1792–1806

Rulers of France from Hugh Capet

CAPETIAN KINGS

Hugh Capet, 987–996
Robert II, 996–1031
Henry I, 1031–1060
Philip I, 1060–1108
Louis VI, 1108–1137
Louis VII, 1137–1180
Philip II (Augustus), 1180–1223
Louis VIII, 1223–1226
Louis IX, 1226–1270
Philip III, 1270–1285
Philip IV, 1285–1314
Louis X, 1314–1316
Philip V, 1316–1322
Charles IV, 1322–1328

HOUSE OF VALOIS

Philip VI, 1328–1350
John, 1350–1364
Charles V, 1364–1380
Charles VI, 1380–1422
Charles VII, 1422–1461
Louis XI, 1461–1483
Charles VIII, 1483–1498
Louis XII, 1498–1515
Francis I, 1515–1547

Henry II, 1547–1559
Francis II, 1559–1560
Charles IX, 1560–1574
Henry III, 1574–1589

BOURBON DYNASTY

Henry IV, 1589–1610
Louis XIII, 1610–1643
Louis XIV, 1643–1715
Louis XV, 1715–1774
Louis XVI, 1774–1792

AFTER 1792

First Republic, 1792–1799
Napoleon Bonaparte, First Consul, 1799–1804
Napoleon I, Emperor, 1804–1814
Louis XVIII (Bourbon dynasty), 1814–1824
Charles X (Bourbon dynasty), 1824–1830
Louis Philippe, 1830–1848
Second Republic, 1848–1852
Napoleon III, Emperor, 1852–1870
Third Republic, 1870–1940
Pétain regime, 1940–1944
Provisional government, 1944–1946
Fourth Republic, 1946–1958
Fifth Republic, 1958–

Rulers of England

ANGLO-SAXON KINGS

Egbert, 802–839
Ethelwulf, 839–858
Ethelbald, 858–860
Ethelbert, 860–866
Ethelred, 866–871
Alfred the Great, 871–900
Edward the Elder, 900–924
Ethelstan, 924–940
Edmund I, 940–946
Edred, 946–955
Edwy, 955–959
Edgar, 959–975

Edward the Martyr, 975–978
Ethelred the Unready, 978–1016
Canute, 1016–1035 (Danish Nationality)
Harold I, 1035–1040
Hardicanute, 1040–1042
Edward the Confessor, 1042–1066
Harold II, 1066

HOUSE OF NORMANDY

William I (the Conqueror), 1066–1087
William II, 1087–1100
Henry I, 1100–1135
Stephen, 1135–1154

HOUSE OF PLANTAGENET

Henry II, 1154–1189
Richard I, 1189–1199
John, 1199–1216
Henry III, 1216–1272
Edward I, 1272–1307
Edward II, 1307–1327
Edward III, 1327–1377
Richard II, 1377–1399

HOUSE OF LANCASTER

Henry IV, 1399–1413
Henry V, 1413–1422
Henry VI, 1422–1461

HOUSE OF YORK

Edward IV, 1461–1483
Edward V, 1483
Richard III, 1483–1485

HOUSE OF TUDOR

Henry VII, 1485–1509
Henry VIII, 1509–1547
Edward VI, 1547–1553
Mary, 1553–1558
Elizabeth I, 1558–1603

HOUSE OF STUART

James I, 1603–1625
Charles I, 1625–1649

COMMONWEALTH AND PROTECTORATE, 1649–1659

HOUSE OF STUART RESTORED

Charles II, 1660–1685
James II, 1685–1688
William III and Mary II, 1689–1694
William III alone, 1694–1702
Anne, 1702–1714

HOUSE OF HANOVER

George I, 1714–1727
George II, 1727–1760
George III, 1760–1820
George IV, 1820–1830
William IV, 1830–1837
Victoria, 1837–1901

HOUSE OF SAXE-COBURG-GOTHA

Edward VII, 1901–1910
George V, 1910–1917

HOUSE OF WINDSOR

George V, 1917–1936
Edward VIII, 1936
George VI, 1936–1952
Elizabeth II, 1952–

Prominent Popes

Silvester I, 314–335
Leo I, 440–461
Gelasius I, 492–496
Gregory I, 590–604
Nicholas I, 858–867
Silvester II, 999–1003
Leo IX, 1049–1054
Nicholas II, 1058–1061
Gregory VII, 1073–1085
Urban II, 1088–1099
Paschal II, 1099–1118
Alexander III, 1159–1181

Innocent III, 1198–1216
Gregory IX, 1227–1241
Boniface VIII, 1294–1303
John XXII, 1316–1334
Nicholas V, 1447–1455
Pius II, 1458–1464
Alexander VI, 1492–1503
Julius II, 1503–1513
Leo X, 1513–1521
Adrian VI, 1522–1523
Clement VII, 1523–1534
Paul III, 1534–1549

Paul IV, 1555–1559
Gregory XIII, 1572–1585
Gregory XVI, 1831–1846
Pius IX, 1846–1878
Leo XIII, 1878–1903
Pius X, 1903–1914
Benedict XV, 1914–1922

Pius XI, 1922–1939
Pius XII, 1939–1958
John XXIII, 1958–1963
Paul VI, 1963–1978
John Paul I, 1978
John Paul II, 1978–

Rulers of Austria and Austria-Hungary

*Maximilian I (Archduke), 1493–1519
*Charles I (Charles V in the Holy Roman Empire),
   1519–1556
*Ferdinand I, 1556–1564
*Maximilian II, 1564–1576
*Rudolph II, 1576–1612
*Matthias, 1612–1619
*Ferdinand II, 1619–1637
*Ferdinand III, 1637–1657
*Leopold I, 1658–1705
*Joseph I, 1705–1711
*Charles VI, 1711–1740
Maria Theresa, 1740–1780

*Joseph II, 1780–1790
*Leopold II, 1790–1792
*Francis II, 1792–1835 (Emperor of Austria as Francis I
   after 1804)
Ferdinand I, 1835–1848
Francis Joseph, 1848–1916 (after 1867 Emperor of
   Austria and King of Hungary)
Charles I, 1916–1918 (Emperor of Austria and King of
   Hungary)
Republic of Austria, 1918–1938 (dictatorship after 1934)
Republic restored, under Allied occupation, 1945–1956
Free Republic, 1956–

* Also bore title of Holy Roman Emperor.

Rulers of Prussia and Germany

*Frederick I, 1701–1713
*Frederick William I, 1713–1740
*Frederick II (the Great), 1740–1786
*Frederick William II, 1786–1797
*Frederick William III, 1797–1840
*Frederick William IV, 1840–1861
*William I, 1861–1888 (German Emperor after 1871)

* Kings of Prussia.

Frederick III, 1888
William II, 1888–1918
Weimar Republic, 1918–1933
Third Reich (Nazi Dictatorship), 1933–1945
Allied occupation, 1945–1952
Division into Federal Republic of Germany in west and
   German Democratic Republic in east, 1949–1990
Federal Republic of Germany (united), 1990–

Rulers of Russia

Ivan III, 1462–1505
Vasily III, 1505–1533
Ivan IV, 1533–1584
Theodore I, 1584–1598
Boris Godunov, 1598–1605

Theodore II, 1605
Vasily IV, 1606–1610
Michael, 1613–1645
Alexius, 1645–1676
Theodore III, 1676–1682

Ivan V and Peter I, 1682–1689
Peter I (the Great), 1689–1725
Catherine I, 1725–1727
Peter II, 1727–1730
Anna, 1730–1740
Ivan VI, 1740–1741
Elizabeth, 1741–1762
Peter III, 1762

Catherine II (the Great), 1762–1796
Paul, 1796–1801
Alexander I, 1801–1825
Nicholas I, 1825–1855
Alexander II, 1855–1881
Alexander III, 1881–1894
Nicholas II, 1894–1917
Soviet Republic, 1917–1991
Russian Federation, 1991–

Rulers of Italy

Victor Emmanuel II, 1861–1878
Humbert I, 1878–1900
Victor Emmanuel III, 1900–1946
Fascist Dictatorship, 1922–1943 (maintained in northern
   Italy until 1945)

Humbert II, May 9–June 13, 1946
Republic, 1946–

Rulers of Spain

Ferdinand { and Isabella, 1479–1504
           { and Philip I, 1504–1506
           { and Charles I, 1506–1516
Charles I (Holy Roman Emperor Charles V),
   1516–1556
Philip II, 1556–1598
Philip III, 1598–1621
Philip IV, 1621–1665
Charles II, 1665–1700
Philip V, 1700–1746
Ferdinand VI, 1746–1759
Charles III, 1759–1788
Charles IV, 1788–1808

Ferdinand VII, 1808
Joseph Bonaparte, 1808–1813
Ferdinand VII (restored), 1814–1833
Isabella II, 1833–1868
Republic, 1868–1870
Amadeo, 1870–1873
Republic, 1873–1874
Alfonso XII, 1874–1885
Alfonso XIII, 1886–1931
Republic, 1931–1939
Fascist Dictatorship, 1939–1975
Juan Carlos I, 1975–

ILLUSTRATIONS IN COLOR

(Illustrations appear facing or following the pages indicated)

ILLUSTRATIONS IN THE TEXT

INDEX

Guide to Pronunciation

The sounds represented by the diacritical marks used in this Index are illustrated by the following common words:

āle	ēve	īce	ōld	ūse	bo͞ot
ăt	ĕnd	ĭll	ŏf	ŭs	fo͝ot
fătality	ēvent		ōbey	ūite	
câre			fôrm	ûrn	
ärm					
àsk					

Vowels that have no diacritical marks are to be pronounced "neutral," for example: Aegean = ē-je′an, Basel = bäz′el, Basil = bă′zil, common =kŏm′on, Alcaeus = ăl-sē′us. The combinations ou and oi are pronounced as in "out" and "oil."